SOMETHING ABOUT THE AUTHOR®

Something about
the Author *was named
an "Outstanding
Reference Source,"
the highest honor given
by the American
Library Association
Reference and Adult
Services Division.*

ISSN 0276-816X

someтнing about тнe аuтнor®

Facts and Pictures about Authors
and Illustrators of Books for Young People

volume 169

THOMSON

™

GALE

Detroit • New York • San Francisco • New Haven, Conn. • Waterville, Maine • London • Munich

THOMSON
GALE

Something About the Author, Volume 169

Project Editor
Lisa Kumar

Editorial
Amy Elisabeth Fuller, Michelle Kazensky, Joshua Kondek, Julie Mellors, Mary Ruby, Stephanie Taylor

Permissions
Lisa Kincade, Shalice Shah-Caldwell, Kim Smilay

Imaging and Multimedia
Leitha Etheridge-Sims, Lezlie Light

Composition and Electronic Capture
Tracey L. Matthews

Manufacturing
Drew Kalasky

Product Manager
Leigh Ann Deremer

LIBRARY OF CONGRESS CATALOG CARD NUMBER 62-52046

ISBN 0-7876-8793-6
ISSN 0276-816X

This title is also available as an e-book.
ISBN 1-4144-1070-0
Contact your Thomson Gale sales representative for ordering information.

Printed in the United States of America
10 9 8 7 6 5 4 3 2 1

Contents

Authors in Forthcoming Volumes vii

Introduction ix

SATA Product Advisory Board xi

Acknowledgments xiii

Illustrations Index 185

Author Index 213

A

Alley, Robert W.
   See Alley, R.W. 1

Alley, R.W. 1

Alton, Steve 7

Anderson, Derek 1969- 8

B

Barnard, Bryn 1956- 11

Berenstain, Stan 1923-2005
   Obituary Notice 13

Berenstain, Stanley
   See Berenstain, Stan 13

Birney, Betty G. 1947- 14

Blackwood, Gary L. 1945- 18

Bonning, Tony 1948- 21

Brodeur, Ruth Wallace
   See Wallace-Brodeur, Ruth 173

C

Cooling, Wendy 24

Cooper, Helen 1963- 27

Cosentino, Ralph 31

Crebbin, June 1938- 33

D

Darling, Sandra Louise Woodward
   See Day, Alexandra 38

Davis, Donald 1944- 36

Davis, Donald D.
   See Davis, Donald 36

Day, Alexandra 1941- 38

De la Garza, Phyllis 1942- 48

deGroat, Diane 1947- 43

Doherty, Craig A. 1951- 49

E

Engelbreit, Mary 1952- 52

F

Fensham, Elizabeth 56

Findlay, Jamieson 1958- 56

Fine, Edith Hope 58

G

Gaber, Susan 1956- 60

Gantos, Jack 1951- 64

Gantos, John Bryan, Jr.
   See Gantos, Jack 64

Grooms, Duffy 71

H

Haab, Sherri 1964- 73

Hall, Melanie W. 1949- 75

Harper, Jo 1932- 79

Harris, Jesse
   See Standiford, Natalie 158

Horne, Richard George Anthony
   See Horse, Harry 83

Horrocks, Anita 1958- 81

Horse, Harry 1960- 83

J

James, Emily
   See Standiford, Natalie 158

Jurmain, Suzanne 1945- 87

Jurmain, Suzanne Tripp
 See Jurmain, Suzanne 87

K

Kelly, Katy 1955- 90

Kompaneyets, Marc 1974- 91

Koppes, Steven N. 1957- 92

Koppes, Steven Nelson
 See Koppes, Steven N. 92

Kushner, Lawrence 1943- 94

L

Laliberté, Louise-Andrée 1958- 97

Lang, Aubrey 99

Levy, Elizabeth 1942- 101

Lewin, Betsy 1937- 107

Logan, Rochelle 1954- 112

M

Markel, Michelle 113

McAllister, Margaret I. 1956- 115

McAllister, M.I.
 See McAllister, Margaret I. 115

McDonald, Mercedes 117

McGrath, Barbara Barbieri 1953- 119

Moed-Kass, Pnina 120

Monaco, Octavia 1963- 122

Morreale-de la Garza, Phyllis
 See De la Garza, Phyllis 48

P

Parker, Toni Trent 1947-2005
 Obituary Notice 124

Parks, Rosa 1913-2005
 Obituary Notice 124

Parks, Rosa Louise Lee
 See Parks, Rosa 124

Penner, Fred 1946- 125

Penner, Frederick Ralph Cornelius
 See Penner, Fred 125

Peters, Andrew
 See Peters, Andrew Fusek 129

Peters, Andrew Fusek 1965- 129

R

Rees, Douglas 1947- 133

Richards, Justin 136

Ross, Katharine Reynolds
 See Ross, Kathy 138

Ross, Kathy 1948- 138

Rotner, Shelley 1951- 142

Royston, Angela 1945- 144

S

Saunders-Smith, Gail 1952- 154

Selway, Martina 1940- 155

Standiford, Natalie 1961- 158

T

Taylor, Debbie A. 1955- 161

Tetzner, Lisa 1894-1963 162

Tulloch, Shirley 164

U

Uslan, Michael E. 1951- 165

W

Wallace, Bill 1947- 167

Wallace, William Keith
 See Wallace, Bill 167

Wallace-Brodeur, Ruth 1941- 173

Waugh, Sylvia 1935- 176

Wickstrom, Sylvie 1960- 179

Wilson, Troy 1970- 181

Woolfe, Angela 1976- 182

Z

Zimmer, Tracie Vaughn 183

Authors in Forthcoming Volumes

Below are some of the authors and illustrators that will be featured in upcoming volumes of *SATA*. These include new entries on the swiftly rising stars of the field, as well as completely revised and updated entries (indicated with *) on some of the most notable and best-loved creators of books for children.

*Amelia Atwater-Rhodes ▮ In 1999, at age fifteen, Atwater-Rhodes found herself in the literary limelight when she published her vampire novel *In the Forests of the Night* to a positive critical reception. In the years since, she has expanded her growing list of imaginative novels with works such as the "Kiesha'ra" fantasy series. The "Kiesha'ra" saga includes the novels *Heartsong, Snakecharm, Falcondance,* and *Wolfcry,* and follows the fragile alliance between avian and serpiente shapeshifters.

Jeanne Birdsall ▮ Inspired by the classic fantasy novels she loved as a child, Massachusetts-based writer and fine-art photographer Birdsall produced *The Penderwicks: A Summer Tale of Four Sisters, Two Rabbits, and a Very Interesting Boy* in 2005. Winner of the National Book Award for Young People's Literature, this humorous debut novel is narrated by four sisters who, while spending their summer at a cottage in the Berkshire mountains, encounter adventure while trying to help their new friend, a shy boy named Jeffrey, avoid being shipped off to military school.

Carmela D'Amico ▮ After creating the character Ella the elephant, D'Amico issued her first story featuring the engaging animal online, where it quickly attracted the interest of a mainstream publisher. Now found in books that include *Ella the Elegant Elephant, Ella Sets the Stage,* and *Ella Takes the Cake,* the spunky Ella engages in typical toddler behavior in and around her home on Elephant Island. Ella's adventures are brought to life through drawings created by D'Amico's husband and creative collaborator, artist Steve D'Amico.

*Jean Craighead George ▮ Nature is the focus of the many novels, picture books, and nonfiction titles produced by Newbery Medal-winning author George during her long career. In titles such as *Julie and the Wolves* and *My Side of the Mountain,* George treats readers to fascinating glimpses of the natural world in stories that often find young people learning to survive in nature. Each of the author/illustrator's books are distinguished by George's inclusion of authentic details as well as her curiosity, wonder, and concern for the environment.

Rick Jacobson ▮ A Canadian author and artist with a background in advertising, Jacobson collaborates with his wife, musician and artist Laura Fernandez, on picture-book art, such as their highly acclaimed illustrations for an updated edition of L.M. Montgomery's *Anne of Green Gables.* An author as well as an illustrator, Jacobson has written *Picasso: Soul on Fire,* a biography of famous painter Pablo Picasso, and *The Mona Lisa Caper,* which describes an unusual art theft. The couple's portraits of such notable people as Bill Gates, Sr., and Sir Richard Francis Burton hang in the permanent collection of London's Royal Geographical Society.

Melina Marchetta ▮ Australian writer and educator Marchetta is the author of the young-adult novels *Looking for Alibrandi* and *Saving Francesca.* These books, which draw on their author's own experiences coming of age in Catholic schools, span several generations and focus on the lives of Italian-Australian teens. Having survived the rigors of Catholic secondary school, Marchetta now works as a teacher at an all-boys school in Sydney, New South Wales.

Philip Reeve ▮ A highly popular cartoonist and illustrator of children's books in his native England, Reeve earned fame as a writer on the strength of his "Hungry City Chronicles," futuristic novels in which human cities have become organic and now migrate, mutate, and even gobble each other up. Including the books *Mortal Engines, Predator's Gold, Infernal Devices,* and *A Darkling Plain,* these imaginative novels have drawn comparison to Philip Pullman's popular "His Dark Materials" trilogy, and have also earned Reeve a large and loyal readership. In addition to these novels, he is the author and illustrator of the humorous "Buster Bayliss" series for younger readers.

*Michael Elsohn Ross ▮ A naturalist and writer, Ross brings an engaging prose style and an infectious enthusiasm to his many books for younger readers. In addition to authoring titles such as *Caterpillarology* and *What's the Matter in Mr. Whisker's Room?,* he has contributed volumes to the nonfiction series "You're the Scientist," which provides a creative outlet for budding experimenters. In addition, Ross's contributions to the "Naturalist's Apprentice" series include biographies about noted naturalists paired with factual information about each person's field of study, whether bird, beast, bug, or plant.

*Robert Sabuda ▮ Considered a master of the pop-up book, Sabuda is an author and illustrator whose interactive books incorporate bright colors, stand-out graphics, and cutting-edge examples of paper engineering. Sabuda has created traditional illustrations for classic works such as *Walden* by Henry David Thoreau and has adapted *Alice's Adventures in Wonderland, The Night before Christmas,* and *America the Beautiful* into intricate three-dimensional volumes. In addition to his work as an illustrator, he has also written several original stories, including *Saint Valentine, Tutankhamen's Gift,* and *The Blizzard's Robe,* each of which features his unique artwork.

Belle Yang ▮ Trained at schools in Scotland and Beijing as well as in her native California, Taiwanese-American author and painter Belle Yang creates self-illustrated books that relate stories drawn from her family's immigrant history. In *Baba: A Return to China upon My Father's Shoulders* she retells the tales her father, Baba, told her about his life in Manchuria, China in the early twentieth century, while Yang's own story is the focus of *Hannah Is My Name.* A more fanciful work, her picture book *Chili-Chili-Chin-Chin* focuses on a determined little donkey and the boy who named it.

Introduction

Something about the Author (*SATA*) is an ongoing reference series that examines the lives and works of authors and illustrators of books for children. *SATA* includes not only well-known writers and artists but also less prominent individuals whose works are just coming to be recognized. This series is often the only readily available information source on emerging authors and illustrators. You'll find *SATA* informative and entertaining, whether you are a student, a librarian, an English teacher, a parent, or simply an adult who enjoys children's literature.

What's Inside *SATA*

SATA provides detailed information about authors and illustrators who span the full time range of children's literature, from early figures like John Newbery and L. Frank Baum to contemporary figures like Judy Blume and Richard Peck. Authors in the series represent primarily English-speaking countries, particularly the United States, Canada, and the United Kingdom. Also included, however, are authors from around the world whose works are available in English translation. The writings represented in *SATA* include those created intentionally for children and young adults as well as those written for a general audience and known to interest younger readers. These writings cover the entire spectrum of children's literature, including picture books, humor, folk and fairy tales, animal stories, mystery and adventure, science fiction and fantasy, historical fiction, poetry and nonsense verse, drama, biography, and nonfiction. Obituaries are also included in *SATA* and are intended not only as death notices but also as concise overviews of people's lives and work. Additionally, each edition features newly revised and updated entries for a selection of *SATA* listees who remain of interest to today's readers and who have been active enough to require extensive revisions of their earlier biographies.

Autobiography Feature

Beginning with Volume 103, many volumes of *SATA* feature one or more specially commissioned autobiographical essays. These unique essays, averaging about ten thousand words in length and illustrated with an abundance of personal photos, present an entertaining and informative first-person perspective on the lives and careers of prominent authors and illustrators profiled in *SATA*.

Two Convenient Indexes

In response to suggestions from librarians, *SATA* indexes no longer appear in every volume but are included in alternate (odd-numbered) volumes of the series, beginning with Volume 57.

SATA continues to include two indexes that cumulate with each alternate volume: the Illustrations Index, arranged by the name of the illustrator, gives the number of the volume and page where the illustrator's work appears in the current volume as well as all preceding volumes in the series; the Author Index gives the number of the volume in which a person's biographical sketch, autobiographical essay, or obituary appears in the current volume as well as all preceding volumes in the series.

These indexes also include references to authors and illustrators who appear in *Gale's Yesterday's Authors of Books for Children, Children's Literature Review,* and *Something about the Author Autobiography Series.*

Easy-to-Use Entry Format

Whether you're already familiar with the *SATA* series or just getting acquainted, you will want to be aware of the kind of information that an entry provides. In every *SATA* entry the editors attempt to give as complete a picture of the person's life and work as possible. A typical entry in *SATA* includes the following clearly labeled information sections:

PERSONAL: date and place of birth and death, parents' names and occupations, name of spouse, date of marriage, names of children, educational institutions attended, degrees received, religious and political affiliations, hobbies and other interests.

ADDRESSES: complete home, office, electronic mail, and agent addresses, whenever available.

CAREER: name of employer, position, and dates for each career post; art exhibitions; military service; memberships and offices held in professional and civic organizations.

MEMBER: professional, civic, and other association memberships and any official posts held.

AWARDS, HONORS: literary and professional awards received.

WRITINGS: title-by-title chronological bibliography of books written and/or illustrated, listed by genre when known; lists of other notable publications, such as plays, screenplays, and periodical contributions.

ADAPTATIONS: a list of films, television programs, plays, CD-ROMs, recordings, and other media presentations that have been adapted from the author's work.

WORK IN PROGRESS: description of projects in progress.

SIDELIGHTS: a biographical portrait of the author or illustrator's development, either directly from the biographee—and often written specifically for the *SATA* entry—or gathered from diaries, letters, interviews, or other published sources.

BIOGRAPHICAL AND CRITICAL SOURCES: cites sources quoted in "Sidelights" along with references for further reading.

EXTENSIVE ILLUSTRATIONS: photographs, movie stills, book illustrations, and other interesting visual materials supplement the text.

How a *SATA* Entry Is Compiled

A *SATA* entry progresses through a series of steps. If the biographee is living, the *SATA* editors try to secure information directly from him or her through a questionnaire. From the information that the biographee supplies, the editors prepare an entry, filling in any essential missing details with research and/or telephone interviews. If possible, the author or illustrator is sent a copy of the entry to check for accuracy and completeness.

If the biographee is deceased or cannot be reached by questionnaire, the *SATA* editors examine a wide variety of published sources to gather information for an entry. Biographical and bibliographic sources are consulted, as are book reviews, feature articles, published interviews, and material sometimes obtained from the biographee's family, publishers, agent, or other associates.

Entries that have not been verified by the biographees or their representatives are marked with an asterisk (*).

Contact the Editor

We encourage our readers to examine the entire *SATA* series. Please write and tell us if we can make *SATA* even more helpful to you. Give your comments and suggestions to the editor:

Editor
Something about the Author
Thomson Gale
27500 Drake Rd.
Farmington Hills MI 48331-3535

Toll-free: 800-877-GALE
Fax: 248-699-8070

Something about the Author Product Advisory Board

The editors of *Something about the Author* are dedicated to maintaining a high standard of excellence by publishing comprehensive, accurate, and highly readable entries on a wide array of writers for children and young adults. In addition to the quality of the content, the editors take pride in the graphic design of the series, which is intended to be orderly yet inviting, allowing readers to utilize the pages of *SATA* easily and with efficiency. Despite the longevity of the *SATA* print series, and the success of its format, we are mindful that the vitality of a literary reference product is dependent on its ability to serve its users over time. As literature, and attitudes about literature, constantly evolve, so do the reference needs of students, teachers, scholars, journalists, researchers, and book club members. To be certain that we continue to keep pace with the expectations of our customers, the editors of *SATA* listen carefully to their comments regarding the value, utility, and quality of the series. Librarians, who have firsthand knowledge of the needs of library users, are a valuable resource for us. The *Something about the Author* Product Advisory Board, made up of school, public, and academic librarians, is a forum to promote focused feedback about *SATA* on a regular basis. The nine-member advisory board includes the following individuals, whom the editors wish to thank for sharing their expertise:

Acknowledgments

Grateful acknowledgment is made to the following publishers, authors, and artists whose works appear in this volume.

ALLEY, R.W ∎ Alley, R.W., illustrator. From an illustration in *The Great Googlestein Museum Mystery* by Jean Van Leeuwen. Dial Books for Young Readers 2003. Pictures copyright © 2003 by R. W. Alley. Used by permission of Phyllis Fogelman Books, A Division of Penguin Young Readers, A Member of Penguin Group (USA) Inc., 345 Hudson Street, New York, NY 10014. All rights reserved. / Alley, R.W., illustrator. From an illustration in *Paddington Bear,* by Michael Bond. HarperCollins Publishers 1998. Illustrations copyright © 1998 by HarperCollins Publishers. Used by permission HarperCollins Children's Books, a division of HarperCollins. / Photo courtesy of RW Alley.

ALTON, STEVE ∎ Alton, Steve. From a jacket of *The Malifex* by Steve Alton. Carolrhoda Books, Inc. 2001. Reproduced by permission of Floris Books.

ANDERSON, DEREK ∎ Anderson, Derek, illustrator. From an illustration in *Little Quack,* by Lauren Thomson. Simon & Schuster Books for Young Readers, 2003. Illustrations copyright © 2003 Derek Anderson. Reprinted with the permission of Simon & Schuster Books for Young Readers, an imprint of Simon & Schuster Children's Publishing Division. / Anderson, Derek, photograph. Photo courtesy of Derek Anderson.

BARNARD, BRYN ∎ Barnard, Bryn, photograph. Photo courtesy of Bryn Barnard / Barnard, Bryn, illustrator. From a jacket of *The Well of Sacrifice,* by Chris Eboch. Clarion Books, 1999. Jacket illustration copyright © 1999 by Bryn Barnard. Reproduced by permission of Clarion Books, an imprint of Houghton Mifflin Company.

BIRNEY, BETTY G. ∎ Birney, Betty G., photograph. Reproduced by permission of Betty G. Birney. / Skogstad, Karin, photographer. From a jacket of *Friendship According to Humphrey,* by Betty G. Birney. G.P. Putnam's Sons 2005. Jacket photograph © by Karin Skogstad. Used by permission of G.P. Putnam's Sons, A Division of Penguin Young Readers Group, A Member of Penguin Group (USA) Inc., 345 Hudson Street, New York, NY 10014. / O'Brien, John, illustrator. From an illustration in *Tyrannosaurus Tex,* by Betty G. Birney. Houghton Mifflin, 1994. Illustrations copyright © 1994 by John O'Brien. All rights reserved. Reproduced by permission of John O'Brien. In the U. S. and Canada by permission of Houghton Mifflin Company.

BLACKWOOD, GARY L. ∎ Blackwood, Gary L., photograph. Reproduced by permission. / Blackwood, Gary, illustrator. From a cover of *The Year of the Hangman* by Tristan Elwell. Used by permission of Dutton Children's Books, A Division of Penguin Young Readers Group, A Member of Penguin Group (USA) Inc., 345 Hidson Street, New York, NY 10014. All rights reserved.

BONNING, TONY ∎ Beardshaw, Rosalind, illustrator. From an illustration in *Snog the Frog.* Barrons 2004. Illustrations © Rosalind Beardshaw 2004. Reproduced by permission.

COOLING, WENDY ∎ Moxley, Sheila, illustrator. From an illustration in *Come to the Great World: Poems from around the Globe* by Wendy Cooling. Holiday House 2004. Illustrations copyright © Sheila Moxley 2002. Reproduced by permission of Holiday House, Inc.

COOPER, HELEN ∎ Cooper, Helen, photograph. Reproduced by permission.

COSENTINO, RALPH ∎ Cosentino, Ralph, illustrator. From an illustration in *Honk-Honk-Ashoo and Swella-Bow-Wow,* by Ralph Cosentino. Viking 2005. Used by permission of Viking Children's Books, A Division of Penguin Young Readers Group, A Member of Penguin Group (USA) Inc., 345 Hudson Street, New York, NY 10014. All rights reserved.

CREBBIN, JUNE ∎ McEwen, Katharine, illustrator. From an illustration in *Cows in the Kitchen,* by June Crebbin. Candlewick Press 1999. Illustrations copyright © 1998 by Katharine McEwen. Reproduced by permission of Candlewick Press, Inc., Cambridge, MA, on behalf of Walker Books Ltd., London.

DAY, ALEXANDRA ∎ From an illustration in *Good Dog, Carl,* by Alexandra Day. Simon & Schuster Books for Young Readers, 1985. Copyright © 1985 Alexandra Day. Reprinted with the permission of Simon & Schuster Books for Young Readers, an imprint of Simon & Schuster Children's Publishing Division. / Day, Alexandra Alexandra Day, photograph. Photo courtesy of Alexandra Day.

deGROAT, DIANE ∎ deGroat, Diane, illustrator. From an illustration in *Anna on the Farm,* by Mary Downing Hahn. Clarion Books, 2001. Illustrations © 2001 by Mary Downing Hahn. Reproduced by permission of Clarion Books/Houghton Mifflin Company. All rights reserved./ deGroat, Diane. From an illustration in *Liar, Liar, Pants on Fire,* by Diane deGroat. SeaStar Books 2003. © 1995 by Diane deGroat. Used with permission of Chronicle Books, LLC, San Francisco. Visit ChronicleBooks.com. / deGroat, Diane, photograph. Photo by Amanda Lattrell.

De la GARZA, PHYLLIS ∎ De la Garza, Phyllis, photograph. Courtesy of Phyllis De la Garza. Reproduced by permission.

DOHERTY, CRAIG A. ∎ Doherty, Craig A. From an illustration in *Mount Rushmore,* by Craig A. Doherty. Blackbirch Press Book 1995. Republished by permission of Mount Rushmore National Memorial/National Park Service, U.S. Department of the Interior.

FINDLAY, JAMIESON. ∎ O'Brien, Tim, illustrator. From a cover of *The Blue Roan Child,* by Jamieson Findlay. Scholastic Inc., 2002. Cover illustration copyright © 2004 by Tim O'Brien. Reprinted by permission of Scholastic Inc.

FINE, EDITH HOPE ❚ Moreno, Rene King, illustrator. From an illustration in *Under the Lemon Moon,* by Edith Hope Fine. Lee & Low Books 1999. Illustrations copyright © 1999 by Rene King Moreno. Reproduced by permission of Lee & Low Books, Inc. / Fine, Edith Hope, photograph. Photo courtesy of Edith Hope Fine.

GABER, SUSAN ❚ Gaber, Susan, illustrator. From an illustration in *Angel Coming,* by Heather Henson. Atheneum Books for Young Readers, 2005. Illustrations copyright © 2005 Susan Gaber. Reprinted with the permission of Atheneum Books for Young Readers, an imprint of Simon & Schuster Children's Publishing Division. / Gaber, Susan, illustrator. From an illustration in *The Language of Birds,* by Rafe Martin. G.P. Putnam's Sons 2000. Illustrations copyright © 2000 by Susan Gaber. Used by permission of G.P. Putnam's Sons, A Division of Penguin Young Readers Group, A member of Penguin Group (USA) inc., 345 Hudson Street, New York, NY 10014. All rights reserved. / Gaber, Susan, illustrator. From an illustration in *The Princess and the Lord of Night,* by Emma Bull. Harcourt Brace & Company, 1994. Illustrations copyright © 1994 by Susan Gaber. Reprinted by permission of Harcourt, Inc.

GANTOS, JACK ❚ Rubel, Nicole, illustrator. From an illustration in *Rotten Ralph's Rotten Romance,* by Jack Gantos. Houghton Mifflin Company 1997. Illustrations copyright © 1997 by Nicole Rubel. Reproduced by permission of Houghton Mifflin Company./ Gantos, Jack, photograph by Merry Scully. Reproduced by permission of Farrar, Straus & Giroux, Inc. / Selznick, Brian, illustrator. From a cover of *What Would Joey Do?* by Jack Gantos. HarperTrophy 2003. Cover art © 2004 Brian Selznick. Reproduced by permission HarperCollins Children's Books, a division of HarperCollins.

HAAB, SHERRI ❚ Haab, Sherri, photograph by Pete Fox. Reproduced by permission.

HALL, MELANIE W. ❚ Hall, Melanie, illustration. From an illustration in *I Asked a Tiger to Tea, and Other Poems,* by Ivy O. Eastwick, compiled by Walter B. Barbe, Ph.D.illustrated by Melanie Hall (Wordsong, an imprint of Boyds Mill Press, 2002). Reprinted with the permission of Boyds Mills Press, Inc. Illustrations copyright © 2002 by Melanie Hall. Reproduced by permission. / Hall, Melanie, illustrator. From an illustration in *Weather,* by Lee Bennett Hopkins. HarperCollins Publishers 1994. Illustrations copyright © 1994 by Melanie Hall. Reproduced by permission HarperCollins Children's Books, a division of HarperCollins. / Hall, Melanie, photograph. Reproduced by permission of Melanie Hall.

HARPER, JO ❚ Harper, Jo, photograph by Loma Walker. Reproduced by permission of Jo Harper. / Henderson, Meryl, illustrator. From an illustration in *Wilma Rudolph, Olympic Runner,* by Jo Harper. Aladdin Paperbacks, 2004. Illustrations copyright © 2004 Meryl Henderson. Reprinted with the permission of Aladdin Paperbacks, an imprint of Simon & Schuster Children's Publishing Division.

HORROCKS, ANITA ❚ Horrocks, Anita, photograph. Courtesy of Lorne Kemmet Photography. / Tarabay, Sharif, illustrator. From a cover of *Topher,* by Anita Harrocks. Stoddart Kids 2000. Reproduced by permission.

HORSE, HARRY ❚ Horse, Harry, Illustrator. From an illustration in *Little Rabbit Runaway,* by Harry Horse. Peachtree 2005. Illustrations © 2005 by Harry Horse. Reproduced by permission.

JURMAIN, SUZANNE ❚ Day, Larry, illustrator. From an illustration in *George Did It,* by Suzanne Jurmain. Dutton Children's Books 2006. Illustrations copyright © 2005 by Larry Day. Used by permission of Viking Children's Books, A Division of Penguin Young Readers Group, A Member of Penguin Group (USA) Inc., 345 Hudson Street, New York, NY 10014. All rights reserved.

KELLY, KATY ❚ Rex, Adam, illustrator. From an illustration in *Lucy Rose, Big on Plans,* by Katy Kelly. Delacorte Press, 2005. Jacket illustration copyright © 2005 Adam Rex. All rights reserved. Used by permission of Random House Children's Books, a division of Random House, Inc.

KOMPANEYETS, MARC ❚ Kompaneyets, Marc, illustrator. From a jacket of *The Squishiness of Things,* by Marc Kompaneyets. Alfred A. Knopf 2005. Copyright © 2005 by Marc Kompaneyets. Used by permission of Alfred A. Knopf, an imprint of Random House Children's Books, a division of Random House, Inc.

KOPPES, STEVEN N. ❚ Koppes, Steven N. For an illustration in *Killer Rocks from Outer Space,* by Steven N. Koppes. NASA Public Services Division.

KUSHNER, LAWRENCE ❚ Majewski, Dawn W., illustrator. From an illustration in *Because Nothing Looks Like God,* by Lawrence Kushner. Jewish Lights Publishing, 2000. Illustrations copyright © 2000 by Jewish Lights Publishing. Reproduced by permission./ Baek, Matthew J., illustrator. From an illustration in *In God's Hands,* by Lawrence Kushner. Jewish Lights Publishing, 2005. Illustrations © 2005 by Matthew J. Baek. Reproduced by permission.

LALIBERTÉ, LOUISE-ANDRÉE ❚ Laliberté, Louise-Andrée., illustrator. From a book cover in *Mormor Moves In,* written by Susan Nielsen-Fernlund and illustrated by Laliberté, Louise-Andrée. Orca Book Publishers.

LANG, AUBREY ❚ Lynch, Wayne, photographer. From a photograph in *The Adventures of Baby Black Bear,* by Aubrey Lang. Fitzhenry & Whiteside, 2001. Photographs copyright © 2001 Aubrey Lang. Reproduced by permission.

LEVY, ELIZABETH ❚ Gerstein, Mordicai, illustrator. From an illustration in *A Hare-Raising Tale,* by Elizabeth Levy. Aladdin Paperbacks, 2002. Illustrations copyright © 2002 Mordicai Gerstein. Reprinted with the permission of Aladdin Paperbacks, an imprint of Simon & Schuster Children's Publishing Division. / Comport, Sally Wern, illustrator. From an illustration in *Vampire State Building,* by Elizabeth Levy. HarperTrophy 2002. Illustrations copyright © 2002 by Sally Wern Comport. Reproduced by permission HarperCollins Children's Books, a division of Harper. / Photo by Barbara Bordnick. Courtesy of Elizabeth Levy.

LEWIN, BETSY ❚ Lewin, Betsy, India, 1996, photograph. Reproduced by permission. / Lewin, Betsy, illustrator. From an illustration in *Cat Count,* by Betsy Lewin. Henry Holt & Company 1981. Illustrations copyright © 2003 by Betsy Lewin. Reprinted by permission of Henry Holt & Company, LLC. / Lewin, Betsy, illustrator. From an illustration in *Animal Snackers,* by Betsy Lewin. Henry Holt & Company 2004. Illustrations copyright © 2004 by Betsy Lewin. Reprinted by permission of Henry Holt & Company, LLC.

MARKEL, MICHELL ❚ Lisker, Emily, illustrator. From an illustration of a man in a blue smock and red hat from *Dreamer from the Village,* written by Michelle Markel. Henry Holt & Company 2004. Illustrations copyright © 2005 by Emily Lisker. Reproduced by permission of Henry Holt & Company, LLC.

McALLISTER, MARGARET, I. ❚ Morgan, Barbara, illustrator. From a jacket of *Ghost at the Window,* by Margaret McAllister. Dutton Children's Books 2002. Jacket illustration © 2002 by Barbara Morgan. Used by permission of Dutton Children's Books, A Division of Penguin Young Readers Group, A Member of Penguin Group (USA) Inc., 345 Hudson Street, New York, NY 10014. All rights reserved./ McAllister, Margaret, photograph. Reproduced by permission.

McDONALD, MERCEDES ❚ McDonald, Mercedes, photograph. Reproduced by permission of Mercedes McDonald. / McDonald, Mercedes, illustrator. From an illustration in *Fairy Trails: A Story*

Told in English and Spanish, by Susan Middleton Elya. Bloomsbury Children's Books, 2005. Illustrations copyright © 2005 by Mercedes McDonald. Reproduced by permission.

McGRATH, BARBARA BARBIERI ▌ Alexander, Martha, illustrator. From an illustration in *The Little Green Witch,* by Barbara Barbieri McGrath. Charlesbridge Publishing, Inc., 2005. Text copyright © 2005 by Barbara Barbieri McGrath. Illustrations copyright © 2005 by Martha Alexander. All rights reserved. Used with permission by Charlesbridge Publishing, Inc.

MOED-KASS, PNINA ▌ Stockbytel/Picture Quest. From a jacket of *Real Time,* by Pnina Moed Kass. Clarion Books 2004. Front jacket photo: copyright © 2004 Stockbyte/Picture Quest. Reproduced by permission.

PENNER, FRED ▌ Reichert, Renee, illustrator. From a jacket of *The Cat Came Back,* by Fred Penner. Roaring Brook Press 2005. Illustrations copyright © 2005 by Renee Reichert. Reprinted by permission of the illustrator.

PETERS, ANDREW FUSEK ▌ Peters, Andrew Fusek, photograph. Reproduced by permission. / Higham, Amanda Montgomery, illustrator. From an illustration in *Monkey's Clever Tale,* by Andrew Fusek Peters. Child's Play International Ltd., 2003. Illustrations © 2003 A. Twinn. Reproduced by permission.

REES, DOUGLAS ▌ Clarke, Greg, illustrator. From a cover of *Vampire High,* by Douglas Rees. Dell Laurel-Leaf, 2003. Used by permission of Random House Children's Books, a division of Random House, Inc. / S.D. Schindler, illustrator. From an illustration in *Grandy Thaxter's Helper,* by Douglas Rees. Antheneum Books for Young Readers, 2004. Illustrations copyright © 2004 S.D. Schindler. Reprinted with the permission of Antheneum Books for Young Readers, an imprint of Simon & Schuster Children's Publishing Division. / Rees, Douglas, photograph. Photo by Glen Kaltenbrun Courtesy of Douglas Rees.

RICHARDS, JUSTIN ▌ Frankland, David, illustrator. From a jacket of *The Invisible Detectiv: Double Life,* by Justin Richards. G. P. Putnam's Sons. Jacket art © 2005 by David Frankland. Used by permission of G.P. Putnam's Sons, A Division of Penguin Young Readers Group, A Member of Penguin Group (USA) Inc., 345 Hudson Street, New York, NY 10014. All rights reserved.

ROSS, KATHY ▌ Stone, Parker II. Ross, Kathy, photograph. Reproduced by permission.

ROYSTON, ANGELA ▌ From a photograph in *How Is Chocolate Made?* photograph. Angela Royston. Corbis.

SELWAY, MARTINA ▌ Selway, Martina. From an illustration in *So Many Babies,* by Martina Selway. Hutchinson 2001. Reproduced by permission of The Random House Group Ltd.

STANDIFORD, NATALIE ▌ Doucent, Bob, illustrator. From an illustration in *The Stone Giant,* by Natalie Standiford. Golden Book, 2001. Illustrations © 2001 Bob Doucent. Used by permission of Random House Children's Books, a division of Random House, Inc.

TAYLOR, DEBBIE A. ▌ Morrison, Frank, illustrator. From an illustration in *Sweet Music in Harlem,* by Debbie A. Taylor. Lee & Low Books, Inc. 2004. Illustrations copyright © 2004 by Frank Morrison. Reproduced by permission of Lee & Low Books, Inc. / Taylor, Debbie A, photograph. Photo by Charles Taylor III Courtesy of photographer

TETZNER, LISA ▌ Binder, Hannes, illustrator. From an illustration in *The Black Brothers,* by Lisa Tetzner, translated by Peter F. Neumeyer. Front Street, 2002. Reprinted with the permission of Boyds Mills Press, Inc.

WALLACE, BILL ▌ Gurney, John Steven, illustrator. From an illustration in *The Meanest Hound Around,* by Carol Wallace and Bill Wallace. Aladdin Paperbacks, 2003. Illustrations copyright © 2003 John Steven Gurney. Reprinted with the permission of Simon & Schuster Books for Young Readers, an imprint of Simon & Schuster Children's Publishing Division. / Cowdrey, Richard, illustrator. From an illustration in *Coyote Autumn,* by Bill Wallace. Aladdin Paperbacks, 2000. Reproduced with the permission of Aladdin Paperbacks, an imprint of Simon & Schuster Children's Publishing Division and Richard Cowdrey. / Torline, Kevin, illustrator. From a cover of *No Dogs Allowed!* by Bill Wallace. Cover design by Lisa Vega. Aladdin Paperbacks 2004. Cover illustration copyright © 2004 by Kevin Torline. Reproduced by permission of Aladin Paperbacks, an imprint of Simon & Schuster Children's Publishing Division and Kevin Torline. / Torline, Kevin, illustrator. From a jacket of *Pick of the Litter,* by Bill Wallace. Holiday House 2005. Jacket art copyright © 2005 by Kevin Torline. Reproduced by permission of Holiday House, Inc.

WALLACE-BRODEUR, RUTH ▌ Wallace-Brodeur, Ruth, photograph by Jeb Wallace-Brodeur. Reproduced by permission. / Steele, Robert Gantt, illustrator. From a jacket of *Heron Cove,* by Ruth Wallace-Broduer. Dutton Children's Books 2005. Jacket art copyright © 2005 by Robert Gantt Steele. Used by permission of Dutton Children's Books, A Division of Penguin Young Readers Group, A Member of Penguin Group (USA) Inc., 345 Hudson Street, New York, NY 10014. All rights reserved. / Low, William, illustrator. From a cover of *Blue Eyes Better,* by Ruth Wallace-Brodeur. Puffin Books 2002. Cover illustration copyright © William Low, 2002. Used by permission of Dutton Children's Books, A Division of Penguin Young Readers Group, A member of Penguin Group (USA) inc., 345 Hudson Street, New York, NY 10014. All rights reserved.

WAUGH, SYLVIA ▌ Matje, Martin, illustrator. From a jacket of *Earthborn,* by Sylvia Waugh. Dell Yearling, 2002. Copyright © 2002 by Sylvia Waug. Used by permission of Random House Children's Books, a division of Random House, Inc. / Matje, Martin, illustrator. From a jacket of *Who Goes Home?* by Sylvia Waugh. The Bodley Head, 2003. Jacket illustration copyright © by Martin Matje. Used by permission of Random House Children's Books, a division of Random House, Inc.

WICKSTROM, SYLVIE ▌ Wickstrom, Sylvie, photograph. Courtesy of Sylvie Wickstrom. / Wickstrom, Sylvie. From an illustration in *I Love You, Mister Bear,* by Sylvie Wickstrom. HarperCollins Publishers 2003. Reproduced by permission HarperCollins Children's Books, a division of HarperCollins.

WILSON, TROY ▌ Wilson, Troy, photograph by Lawrence Ormerod. Courtesy of Troy Wilson. Reproduced by permission. / Dean Griffiths, illustrator. From an illustration in *Perfect Man,* by Troy Wilson. Orca 2004. Illustrations copyright © 2004 Dean Griffiths. Reproduced by permission of Orca Book Publishers.

ZIMMER, TRACIE VAUGHN ▌ Glass, Andrew, illustrator. From an illustration of *Sketches from a Spy Tree,* by Tracie Vaughn Zimmer. Clarion Books 2005. Illustrations copyright (c) 2005 by Andrew Glass. Reproduced by permission of Houghton Mifflin Company.

something ABOUT the AUThOR

ALLEY, Robert W.
   See ALLEY, R.W.

*   *   *

ALLEY, R.W.
   (Robert W. Alley)

Personal

Born in Lexington, VA; married; wife's name Zoë; children: Cassie, Max. *Education:* Graduated from Haverford College.

Addresses

Home—Barrington, RI. *Agent*—Jane Feder, 305 E. 24th St., New York, NY 10010. *E-mail*—rwalleymail@aol.com.

Career

Illustrator and graphic artist.

Writings

SELF-ILLUSTRATED

The Ghost in Dobb's Diner, Parents Magazine Press (New York, NY), 1981.
The Silly Riddle Book, Golden (New York, NY), 1981.

R.W. Alley

Busy Farm Trucks, Grosset & Dunlap (New York, NY), 1986.
(Reteller) *Seven Fables from Aesop,* Dodd, Mead (New York, NY), 1986.

Busy People All around Town, Western Publishing (New York, NY), 1988.

Busy Things That Go, Western Publishing (New York, NY), 1988.

The Clever Carpenter, Random House (New York, NY), 1988.

Watch out, Cyrus!: A Wacky Adventure on Land, on Sea, and in the Air; or, How to Get from Here to There, Grosset & Dunlap (New York, NY), 1990.

Wee Wheels, Grosset & Dunlap (New York, NY), 1990.

The Wheels on the Bus, Western Publishing (Racine, WI), 1992.

One Little Duck, HarperFestival (New York, NY), 1995.

There Once Was a Witch, HarperFestival (New York, NY), 2003.

Author and illustrator of *Making a Boring Day Better: A Kid's Guide to Battling the Blahs* ("Elf-Help" series), Abbey Press (St. Meinrad, IN).

Some of Alley's titles have been translated into French.

ILLUSTRATOR

David Lyon, *The Brave Little Computer,* Simon & Schuster (New York, NY), 1984.

Ross Robert Olney and Patricia Olney, *How Long?: To Go, to Grow, to Know,* Morrow (New York, NY), 1984.

Jane O'Connor, *The Teeny Tiny Woman,* Random House (New York, NY), 1986.

Amy Ehrlich, *Buck-buck the Chicken,* Random House (New York, NY), 1987.

Charlotte Pomerantz, *How Many Trucks Can a Tow Truck Tow?,* Random House (New York, NY), 1987.

Dinah L. Moché, *Amazing Space Facts,* Western Publishing (Racine, WI), 1988.

ABC Rhymes, D.C. Heath (Lexington, MA), 1989.

Patricia Baehr, *School Isn't Fair!,* Four Winds (New York, NY), 1989.

Stephanie Calmenson, *The Little Witch Sisters,* Parents Magazine Press (New York, NY), 1989.

Joanna Cole, *Who Put the Pepper in the Pot?,* Parents Magazine Press (New York, NY), 1989.

Harriet Ziefert, *The Prince Has a Boo-boo!,* Random House (New York, NY), 1989.

Gail Herman, *Ice Cream Soup* (based on a story by Jack Kent), Random House (New York, NY), 1990.

Robin Pulver, *Mrs. Toggle's Zipper,* Four Winds (New York, NY), 1990.

Harriet Ziefert, *The Prince's Tooth Is Loose,* Random House (New York, NY), 1990, reprinted, Sterling (New York, NY), 2005.

Old MacDonald Had a Farm, Grosset & Dunlap (New York, NY), 1991.

William H. Hooks, *Where's Lulu?,* Bantam (New York, NY), 1991.

Brian Mangas, *Follow That Puppy!,* Simon & Schuster (New York, NY), 1991.

Robin Pulver, *Mrs. Toggle and the Dinosaur,* Four Winds (New York, NY), 1991.

Teddy Slater, *Listening with Zachary,* Silver Press (Englewood Cliffs, NJ), 1991.

Teddy Slater, *Looking for Lewis,* Silver Press (Englewood Cliffs, NJ), 1991.

Sue Brownlee, *Best Kids Cookbook,* photographs by Tom Wyatt, Sunset (Menlo Park, CA), 1992.

Steven Krensky, *The Pizza Book,* Scholastic (New York, NY), 1992.

Charlotte Pomerantz, *Serena Katz,* Macmillan (New York, NY), 1992.

Victoria Hartman, *The Silliest Joke Book Ever,* Lothrop, Lee & Shepard (New York, NY), 1993.

Fran Manushkin, *My Christmas Safari,* Dial (New York, NY), 1993.

David Packard, *The Ball Game,* Scholastic (New York, NY), 1993.

Molly Kates, *The Little Firehouse,* Random House (New York, NY), 1994.

Marcia Leonard, *When the Giants Came to Town,* Scholastic (New York, NY), 1994.

Robin Pulver, *Mrs. Toggle's Beautiful Blue Shoe,* Four Winds (New York, NY), 1994.

Richard Schotter, *There's a Dragon About: A Winter's Revel,* Orchard (New York, NY), 1994.

Alan Sincic, *Edward Is Only a Fish,* Holt (New York, NY), 1994.

Marilyn Singer, *Family Reunion,* Macmillan (New York, NY), 1994.

Nancy White Carlstrom, *Who Said Boo?: Halloween Poems for the Very Young,* Simon & Schuster (New York, NY), 1995.

Michele Sobel Spirn, *The Know-Nothings,* HarperCollins (New York, NY), 1995.

Robin Dexter, *Young Arthur Ashe,* Troll (Mahwah, NJ), 1996.

Katy Hall and Lisa Eisenberg, *Sheepish Riddles,* Dial (New York, NY), 1996.

Katy Hall and Lisa Eisenberg, *Trick or Eeek!: And Other Ha Ha Halloween Riddles,* HarperFestival (New York, NY), 1996.

Tony Johnston, *The Bull and the Fire Truck,* Scholastic (New York, NY), 1996.

Elizabeth Koehler-Pentacoff, *Louise the One and Only,* Troll (Mahwah, NJ), 1996.

Judith Benét Richardson, *Old Winter,* Orchard (New York, NY), 1996.

James Skofield, *Detective Dinosaur,* HarperCollins (New York, NY), 1996.

Cindy Wheeler, *The Emperor's Birthday Suit,* Random House (New York, NY), 1996.

Katy Hall and Lisa Eisenberg, *Easter Yolks: Egg-cellent Riddles to Crack You Up,* HarperFestival (New York, NY), 1997.

Katy Hall and Lisa Eisenberg, *Hearty Har Har: Valentine Riddles You'll Love,* HarperFestival (New York, NY), 1997.

Barbara Shook Hazen, *The New Dog,* Dial (New York, NY), 1997.

Michele Sobel Spirn, *A Know-Nothing Birthday,* Harper-Collins (New York, NY), 1997.

Stuart J. Murphy, *Animals on Board,* HarperCollins (New York, NY), 1998.

James Preller, *The Case of the Missing Hamster* ("Jigsaw Jones" series), Scholastic (New York, NY), 1998.

James Preller, *The Case of the Christmas Snowman* ("Jigsaw Jones" series), Scholastic (New York, NY), 1998.

James Skofield, *Detective Dinosaur: Lost and Found*, HarperCollins (New York, NY), 1998.

Nola Buck, *Hey, Little Baby!*, HarperFestival (New York, NY), 1999.

Nancy White Carlstrom, *Thanksgiving Day at Our House: Thanksgiving Poems for the Very Young*, Simon & Schuster (New York, NY), 1999.

Katy Hall and Lisa Eisenberg, *Kitty Riddles*, Dial (New York, NY), 2000.

Robin Pulver, *Mrs. Toggle's Class Picture Day*, Scholastic (New York, NY), 2000.

Michele Sobel Spirn, *A Know-Nothing Halloween*, HarperCollins (New York, NY), 2000.

Michele Sobel Spirn, *The Know-Nothings Talk Turkey*, HarperCollins (New York, NY), 2000.

Cynthia C. DeFelice, *The Real True Dulcie Campbell*, Farrar, Straus (New York, NY), 2002.

Susan Katz, *Mrs. Brown on Exhibit, And Other Museum Poems*, Simon & Schuster (New York, NY), 2002.

Dandi Daley Mackall, *Off to Bethlehem!*, HarperFestival (New York, NY), 2002.

Gloria Rand, *Little Flower*, Holt (New York, NY), 2002.

Kate Laing, *Best Kind of Baby*, Dial (New York, NY), 2003.

Kate McMullan, *Pearl and Wagner: Two Good Friends*, Dial (New York, NY), 2003.

Jane O'Connor, *The Teeny Tiny Woman*, Random House (New York, NY), 2003.

Jean Van Leeuwen, *The Great Googlestein Museum Mystery*, Phyllis Fogelman (New York, NY), 2003.

Bethany Roberts, *Cat Skidoo*, Holt (New York, NY), 2004.

Susan Katz, *A Revolutionary Field Trip: Poems of Colonial America*, Simon & Schuster (New York, NY), 2004.

Kate McMullan, *Pearl and Wagner: Three Secrets*, Dial (New York, NY), 2004.

Teri Sloat, *This Is the House That Was Tidy and Neat*, Holt (New York, NY), 2005.

Claudia Mills, *Ziggy's Blue-Ribbon Day*, Farrar, Straus (New York, NY), 2005.

Richard Krieb, *We're off to Find the Witch's House*, Dutton (New York, NY), 2005.

Bill Harley, *Dear Santa: The Letters of James B. Dobbins*, HarperCollins (New York, NY), 2005.

Andrew Clements, *Because Your Daddy Loves You*, Clarion (New York, NY), 2005.

Larry Dane Brimner, *Spring Sail*, Child's World (Chanhassen, MN), 2005.

Harriet Ziefert, *A Bowlful of Rain*, Sterling (New York, NY), 2006.

Ann Heinrichs, *Mother's Day*, Child's World (Chanhassen, MN), 2006.

Ann Heinrichs, *Father's Day*, Child's World (Chanhassen, MN), 2006.

S.J. Fore, *Tiger Can't Sleep*, Viking (New York, NY), 2006.

Larry Dane Brimner, *Winter Blanket*, Child's World (Chanhassen, MN), 2006.

Larry Dane Brimner, *One Summery Day*, Child's World (Chanhassen, MN), 2006.

Larry Dane Brimner, *In the Fall*, Child's World (Chanhassen, MN), 2006.

Kimberly Brubaker Bradley, *Ballerino Nate*, Dial (New York, NY), 2006.

ILLUSTRATOR; "ELF HELP" SERIES; FOR ADULTS

Cherry Hartman, *Be-Good-to-Yourself Therapy*, Abbey Press (St. Meinrad, IN), 1987.

Michael Joseph, *Play Therapy*, Abbey Press (St. Meinrad, IN), 1990.

Lisa Engelhardt, *Happy Birthday Therapy*, Abbey Press (St. Meinrad, IN), 1993.

Karen Katafiasz, *Christmas Therapy*, Abbey Press (St. Meinrad, IN), 1994.

Daniel Grippo, *Work Therapy*, Abbey Press (St. Meinrad, IN), 1995.

Linus Mundy, *Everyday-Courage Therapy*, Abbey Press (St. Meinrad, IN), 1995.

Clair Bradshaw, *Get-Well Therapy*, One Caring Place (St. Meinrad, IN), 1996.

Karen Katafiasz, *Living from Your Soul*, Abbey Press (St. Meinrad, IN), 1997.

Kass P. Dotterweich, *Be-Good-to-Your-Family Therapy*, One Caring Place (St. Meinrad, IN), 1997.

Karen Katafiasz, *Teacher Therapy*, One Caring Place (St. Meinrad, IN), 1997.

Carol Ann Morrow, *Trust-in-God Therapy*, One Caring Place (St. Meinrad, IN), 1998.

Linus Mundy, *Elf-Help for Overcoming Depression*, One Caring Place (St. Meinrad, IN), 1998.

Jim Auer, *Elf-Help for Raising a Teen*, Abbey Press (St. Meinrad, IN), 2000.

Janet Getsz, *Elf-Gelp for Being a Good Parent*, Abbey Press (St. Meinrad, IN), 2000.

Daniel Grippo, *Worry Therapy*, Abbey Press (St. Meinrad, IN), 2000.

Rosemary Purdy, *'Tis a Blessing to Be Irish*, Abbey Press (St. Meinrad, IN), 2001.

Also illustrator of *Believe-in-Yourself Therapy, Healing Thoughts for Troubled Times*, and *Loneliness Therapy*, all by Daniel Grippo; *Grieving at Christmastime*, by Dwight Daniels; *Elf-Help for Giving the Gift of You!* and *Elf-Help for Coping with Pain*, both by Anne Calodich Fone; *Take Charge of Your Eating*, by Laura Pirott; *Elf-Help for Dealing with Difficult People, New Baby Therapy*, and *Acceptance Therapy*, all by Lisa Engelhardt; *Nature Therapy* and *Elf-Help for a Happy Retirement*, both by Ted O'Neal; *Gratitude Therapy*, by Christine A. Adams; *Elf-Help for Busy Moms*, by Molly Wigand; *Stress Therapy*, by Tom McGrath; *Making-Sense-out-of-Suffering Therapy*, by Jack Wintz; *Anger Therapy*, by Engelhardt and Karen Katafiasz; *Caregiver Therapy*, by Julie Kuebelbeck and Victoria O'Connor; *Self Esteem Therapy, Grief Therapy*, and *Celebrate-Your-Womanhood Therapy*, all by Katafiasz; *Peace Therapy*, by Carol Ann Morrow; *Take-Charge-of-Your-Life Therapy; Friendship Therapy*, by Kass P. Dotter-

Alley's whimsical pen-and-ink art captures the humor in Jean Van Leeuwen's fun-filled adventure starring Marvin the Magnificent Mouse and friends in **The Great Googlestein Museum Mystery.**

weich and John D. Perry; *Forgiveness Therapy,* by David Schell; *Keep-Life-Simple Therapy* and *Slow-down Therapy,* both by Linus Mundy; *Be-Good-to-Your-Body Therapy,* by Steve Ilg; *Keeping-up-Your-Spirits Therapy,* by Linda Allison-Lewis; *One-Day-at-a-Time Therapy,* by Adams; *Prayer Therapy,* by Keith McClellan; *Be-Good-to-Your-Marriage Therapy,* by Dotterweich; and *More Be-Good-to-Yourself Therapy,* by Cherry Hartman; all for Abbey Press (St. Meinrad, IN).

ILLUSTRATOR; "ELF HELP" SERIES; FOR CHILDREN

Michaelene Mundy, *Sad Isn't Bad: A Good-Grief Guidebook for Kids Dealing with Loss,* One Caring Place (St. Meinrad, IN), 1998.

Emily Menendez-Aponte, *When Mom and Dad Divorce: A Kid's Resource,* Abbey Press (St. Meinrad, IN), 1999.

Michaelene Mundy, *Mad Isn't Bad: A Child's Book about Anger,* One Caring Place (St. Meinrad, IN), 1999.

Molly Wigand, *Help Is Here for Facing Fear,* One Caring Place (St. Meinrad, IN), 2000.

Michaelene Mundy, *Getting out of a Stress Mess!: A Guide for Kids,* One Caring Place (St. Meinrad, IN), 2000.

Tom McGrath, *When You're Sick or in the Hospital: Healing Help for Kids,* Abbey Press (St. Meinrad, IN), 2002.

Michaelene Mundy, *Keeping School Cool!: A Kid's Guide to Handling School Problems,* Abbey Press (St. Meinrad, IN), 2002.

Victoria Ryan, *When Your Grandparent Dies: A Child's Guide to Good Grief,* One Caring Place (St. Meinrad, IN), 2002.

Jim Auer, *Standing up to Peer Pressure: A Guide to Being True to You,* Abbey Press (St. Meinrad, IN), 2003.

J.S. Jackson, *Bye-bye, Bully!: A Kid's Guide for Dealing with Bullies,* Abbey Press (St. Meinrad, IN), 2003.

Carol Ann Morrow, *Forgiving Is Smart for Your Heart,* One Caring Place (St. Meinrad, IN), 2003.

Ted O'Neal, *When Bad Things Happen: A Guide to Help Kids Cope,* One Caring Place (St. Meinrad, IN), 2003.

Victoria Ryan, *When Your Pet Dies: A Healing Handbook for Kids,* One Caring Place (St. Meinrad, IN), 2003.

Susan Heyboer O'Keefe, *Be the Star That You Are!: A Book for Kids Who Feel Different,* One Caring Press (St. Meinrad, IN), 2005.

Michaelene Mundy, *Saying Good-bye, Saying Hello: When Your Family Is Moving,* One Caring Place (St. Meinrad, IN), 2005.

Also illustrator of *A New Baby Is Coming!: A Guide for a Big Brother or Sister,* by Emily Menendez Aponte; *When Someone You Love Has Cancer: A Guide to Help Kids Cope,* by Alaric Lewis; *A Kid's Guide to Keeping Family First,* by J.S. Jackson; *Learning to Be a Good Friend: A Guidebook for Kids,* by Christine A. Adams; *Playing Fair, Having Fun: A Kid's Guide to Sports and Games,* by Daniel Grippo; and *A Book of Prayers for All Your Cares,* by Michalene Mundy, all for Abbey Press (St. Meinrad, IN).

ILLUSTRATOR; "PADDINGTON BEAR" SERIES

Michael Bond, *Paddington Bear and the Christmas Surprise,* HarperCollins (New York, NY), 1997.

Michael Bond, *Paddington Bear All Day,* HarperFestival (New York, NY), 1998.

Michael Bond, *Paddington the Artist,* Collins (London, England), 1998.

Michael Bond, *Paddington at the Fair,* Collins (London, England), 1998.

Michael Bond, *Paddington and the Tutti Frutti Rainbow,* Collins (London, England), 1998.

Michael Bond, *Paddington at the Zoo,* Collins (London, England), 1998.

Michael Bond, *Paddington Bear and the Busy Bee Carnival,* HarperCollins (New York, NY), 1998.

Michael Bond, *Paddington Bear Goes to Market,* HarperFestival (New York, NY), 1998.

Michael Bond, *Paddington Bear,* new edition, HarperCollins (New York, NY), 1998.

Michael Bond, *Paddington at the Palace,* Collins (London, England), 1999.

Michael Bond, *Paddington and the Marmalade Maze,* Collins (London, England), 1999.

Michael Bond, *Paddington Minds the House,* Collins (London, England), 1999.

Michael Bond, *Paddington's Busy Day,* Collins (London, England), 1999.

Michael Bond, *Paddington's Party Tricks,* Collins (London, England), 2000.

Michael Bond, *Paddington in Hot Water,* Collins (London, England), 2000.

Michael Bond, *Paddington Bear at the Circus,* HarperCollins (New York, NY), 2000.

Michael Bond, *Paddington Bear Goes to the Hospital,* HarperCollins (New York, NY), 2001.

Michael Bond, *Paddington Bear in the Garden,* HarperCollins (New York, NY), 2002.

Illustrator of new editions of earlier "Paddington Bear" picture books.

Sidelights

Author and illustrator R.W. Alley had intended to be a serious scholar of the history of art, but during college he found himself "doodling in the margins and dreaming up stories," as he explained on his home page. Just after he graduated from college, Alley sold his first book, *The Ghost in Dobb's Diner,* and he has been writing and illustrating picture books, chapter books, and easy readers for children ever since. After a brief, four-year career as an in-house greeting card artist and writer and editor, first with Hallmark Cards in Kansas City,Missouri and then with Paramount Cards in Pawtucket, Rhode Island, he has been making his pictures from his home studio while wearing his slippers. Working with Abbey Press, Alley has illustrated the multi-volume "Elf Help" series for children and adults that walks readers through ways to deal with troubles in their lives. In 1997 he was given the opportunity to illustrate Michael Bond's new "Paddington Bear" picture-book stories, based on the author's classic 1958 children's novel *A Bear Called Paddington.* "Alley may be best known for the 'Paddington Bear' books he illustrates with tiny, tumbling scenes of ursine life," wrote Amy Myrick in *East Bay Newspapers,* adding that "the books, translated into many foreign languages, have earned him international recognition."

Though Alley has written several self-illustrated titles, he is better known for the illustrations he creates for

Forty years after his first appearance, the little lost bear created by Michael Bond returns to entertain a new generation via Alley's charming line-and-watercolor art. (From Paddington Bear.)

other writers. Of his work on Richard and Roni Schotter's picture book *There's a Dragon About: A Winter's Revel,* Linda Callaghan wrote in *Booklist* that "Alley's pen-and-ink drawings with bright watercolors capture the enthusiasm" of the tale. Reviewing *Old Winter,* written by Judith Benét Richardson, Carolyn Phelan commented in *Booklist* that "children will delight in the details of Alley's lively ink-and-watercolor illustrations." Tony Johnston's *The Bull and the Fire Truck* caused Phelan to write in a subsequent *Booklist* review that "Alley's line-and-watercolor artwork brims with action and humorous details." A *Publishers Weekly* critic commented on Alley's illustrations for *Little Flower,* written by Gloria Rand: "Alley's kicky ink-and-watercolor artwork captures the warmth of the bond" displayed between the young pet owner heroine and her pet pig. In a review of the same title for *School Library Journal,* Jody McCoy wrote that "Alley's colorful cartoon illustrations . . . suit the text delightfully" and "flow from page to page with variety and verve." The story of a farm girl who longs to be a princess, is told in *The Real, True Dulcie Campbell,* written by Cynthia C. DeFelice. Phelan, in her *Booklist* review, considered Alley's work for DeFelice's book "lively" and "appealing," while Ruth Semrau noted in *School Library Journal* that the illustrator's "pastel watercolors are light and cheerful, never too scary, even in the creepy parts." About Kate Laing's *Best Kind of Baby,* in which Sophie does not want to acknowledge that she is going to be a big sister, Connie Fletcher wrote in *Booklist:* "Alley's warmly humorous watercolors underscore Sophie's troubled state." Alley's illustrations tackle such subjects as fear of the dark in S.J. Fore's *Tiger Can't Sleep* and feeling out of place in both *Ballerino Nate* by Claudia Mills and *Ziggy's Blue Ribbon Day* by Kimberly Brubaker Bradley.

In his work as illustrator, Alley divides his time between picture books and chapter books. In *The Great Googlestein Museum Mystery,* a chapter book featuring adventurous mice written by Jean VanLeeuwen, "Alley's black-and-white sketches add to the fun and help to clarify some of the story's details," according to Kay Weisman in *Booklist.* Shara Alpern, reviewing the same title for *School Library Journal,* wrote that "the small, amusing black-and-white drawings scattered throughout further enhance the reading experience." The "Pearl and Wagner" stories, written by Kate McMullan, are easy-to-read chapter books about a rabbit and a mouse who are the closest of friends. "Alley's expressive art captures the emotions and high jinks with winsome detail," wrote Gillian Engberg in a *Booklist* review of *Pearl and Wagner: Two Good Friends.* Laura Scott, reviewing the same title in *School Library Journal,* commented that the "cheerful illustrations enhance the text with appealing animal characters rendered with extraordinary expression." Commenting that readers will feel as though they, along with Pearl and Wagner, are members of Ms. Star's class, a *Publishers Weekly* critic wrote that "Alley's illustrations enhance this effect with their knee-level or just-at-the-next-desk perspective."

Along with his work on picture books and chapter books, Alley has also illustrated poetry collections. *Mrs. Brown on Exhibit, and Other Museum Poems* features twenty-one poems by Susan Katz about students and their eccentric teacher as they travel through a museum on a field trip. "Full of intriguing details and humorous touches, Alley's cheerful watercolor illustrations give young children plenty to look at," Phelan wrote in *Booklist.* Commenting on the same title for *Publishers Weekly,* a critic cited Alley's "sprightly, realistic" art. "Alley's delightful cartoon-like illustrations emphasize the fun and the action" in the poetry, according to a *Kirkus Reviews* contributor.

When HarperCollins began publishing more of Bond's "Paddington Bear" picture-book stories in 1997, they asked Alley to create the new illustrations. They were so impressed with his work that they also hired him to re-illustrate the earlier "Paddington" picture books, and Alley's illustrations are now featured in both older and newer "Paddington Bear" stories around the world. *Paddington Bear,* a picture book in which Bond retells his original story of how the Brown family first met the traveling bear at Paddington Station in London, was released to celebrate Paddington's fortieth anniversary. "Alley's lively ink-and-watercolor-wash illustrations capture the winsome charm and gentle humor of this unassuming bear," wrote Phelan in her *Booklist* review of the book. Discussing Alley's more recent work, *Paddington Bear in the Garden,* Phelan wrote that "Alley's endearing ink-and-watercolor illustrations offer expressive drawings in pleasing colors" and added that the title would be well liked by Paddington fans.

Alley wrote on his home page: "I have been making up stories and drawing pictures to illustrate them for about as long as I can remember. In many ways, I still spend my days the same way I did when I was ten. This is somewhat confusing to my wife and children, but I don't seem to be able to help myself."

"I have never wanted to be the sort of visual artist who creates images to hang on the wall or set on a pedestal," Alley told *SATA:* "I've always enjoyed looking at these things, thinking about them, visiting galleries and museums full of them and, of course, studying their history. But, making them . . . no, that wasn't me. Making art for me has always been about telling stories and sharing those stories with as many people as possible. I figured out early on that books were the way to do this. I like writing my own stories because I have complete control over what part of the story is told with words and what is told with pictures. In illustrating another author's words, my focus changes; I have to find ways into the story that will allow me to add to the words, without changing their tone and meaning. In both cases, the key to being a good illustrator is, I think, to be able to first present the narrative of the story in a clear and inviting format and then to enlarge the narrative with strong character drawing and scene-setting. I know I've been successful when I go to a library and find copies

of my books that have been truly worn and torn." Though he enjoys what he does, as he explained to Amy Myrick for *East Bay Newspapers,* "It's work, it's definitely work. . . . It's work because it doesn't get done unless you make yourself do it."

Biographical and Critical Sources

PERIODICALS

Booklist, November 1, 1994, Linda Callaghan, review of *There's a Dragon About: A Winter's Revel,* p. 509; July, 1995, Stephanie Zvirin, review of *The Know-Nothings,* p. 1885; September 15, 1995, Hazel Rochman, review of *Who Said Boo?: Halloween Poems for the Very Young,* p. 168; February 15, 1996, Carolyn Phelan, review of *Young Arthur Ashe: Brave Champion,* p. 1011; October 1, 1996, Carolyn Phelan, review of *Old Winter,* p. 359; February 1, 1997, Carolyn Phelan, review of *The Bull and the Fire Truck,* p. 949; August, 1997, Stephanie Zvirin, review of *The New Dog,* p. 1906; February 1, 1998, Ilene Cooper, review of *Detective Dinosaur: Lost and Found,* p. 928; April, 1998, Carolyn Phelan, review of *Paddington Bear All Day,* p. 1329; November 1, 1998, Kathy Broderick, review of *Animals on Board,* p. 504; January 1, 1999, Carolyn Phelan, review of *Paddington Bear,* p. 886; February 1, 1999, Hazel Rochman, review of *Hey, Little Baby!,* p. 978; February 15, 2000, Hazel Rochman, review of *Kitty Riddles,* p. 1123; April 15, 2002, Carolyn Phelan, review of *Paddington Bear in the Garden,* p. 1405; June 1, 2002, Carolyn Phelan, review of *Mrs. Brown on Exhibit, and Other Museum Poems,* p. 1714; August, 2002, Carolyn Phelan, review of *The Real, True Dulcie Campbell,* p. 1969; February 1, 2003, Kay Weisman, review of *The Great Googlestein Museum Mystery,* p. 996; July, 2003, Gillian Engberg, review of *Pearl and Wagner: Two Good Friends,* p. 1899; August, 2003, Connie Fletcher, review of *Best Kind of Baby,* p. 1989.

East Bay Newspapers, October 28, 2003, Amy Myrick, "Drawing Flights of Fancy in Barrington."

Kirkus Reviews, March 1, 2002, review of *Little Flower,* p. 344; June 15, 2002, review of *Mrs. Brown on Exhibit, and Other Museum Poems,* p. 883; March 15, 2003, review of *The Great Googlestein Museum Mystery,* p. 480.

People, November 4, 1996, Kristin McMurran, review of *Trick or Eeek!,* p. 43.

Publishers Weekly, February 18, 2002, review of *Little Flower,* p. 95; June 3, 2002, review of *Mrs. Brown on Exhibit, and Other Museum Poems,* p. 88; July 15, 2002, review of *The Real, True Dulcie Campbell,* p. 73; May 26, 2003, review of *Best Kind of Baby,* p. 70.

School Library Journal, August, 2002, Susan Scheps, review of *Mrs. Brown on Exhibit, and Other Museum Poems,* p. 177; August, 2002, Jody McCoy, review of *Little Flower,* p. 165; September, 2002, Ruth Semrau,

review of *The Real, True Dulcie Campbell,* p. 183; May, 2003, Shara Alpern, review of *The Great Googlestein Museum Mystery,* p. 131; July, 2003, Martha Topol, review of *Best Kind of Baby,* p. 100; September, 2003, review of *Pearl and Wagner,* p. 184.

ONLINE

R.W. Alley Home Page, http://www.rwalley.com (March 31, 2006).

*   *   *

ALTON, Steve

Personal

Born in Yorkshire, England; married. *Education:* University of York, degree (biology). *Hobbies and other interests:* Cooking, gardening, painting, playing computer games, listening to music, growing carnivorous plants.

Addresses

Home—England. *Agent*—c/o Author Mail, Carolrhoda Books/Lerner Publishing Group, 1251 Washington Ave. N, Minneapolis, MN 55401. *E-mail*—steve.alton@tiscali.co.uk.

Career

Writer. Worked as a river surveyor; conservation officer in Nottinghamshire, England, for seven years; Royal Botanic Gardens, Kew, England, currently plant collector.

Writings

The Malifex, Flyways (Edinburgh, Scotland), 2001, Carolrhoda Books (Minneapolis, MN), 2002.
The Firehills, Carolrhoda Books (Minneapolis, MN), 2005.

Sidelights

British writer Steve Alton is the author of *The Malifex,* a fantasy novel that reflects its author's love of the English landscape, particularly of Dorsetshire, where Alton's story is set. The story introduces Sam, who hopes to avoid the rural surroundings his parents have chosen to summer in by befriending a local girl named Charly. While normally interested more in video games than in other people, Sam is inspired by the adventurous Charly to explore the wild areas near their Dorset town. When the two teens stumble on an ancient grave and accidentally release Amergin, the spirit of the powerful apprentice of Merlin the magician, their summer becomes more exciting than any of Sam's video games. Amergin

Combining Celtic myth and Wiccan magic, Alton's novel finds two teens forced into an ancient battle between good and evil after they inadvertently unleash an apprentice of Merlin the magician.

explains that the children are being pursued by shape-shifting underlings loyal to the evil Malifex, and outlines their role in preserving the delicate balance between good and evil that the Malifex seeks to disrupt. Alton's novel "is plot driven, and has plenty of action," commented *School Library Journal* critic Michele Capozzella, while John Peters wrote in *Booklist* that *The Malifex* "takes readers down a well-traveled road, but it's a smooth ride, with lighter moments and drama in generous measure." A *Kirkus Reviews* critic went so far as to state that the novel presents "an interesting counterpoint to the many fantasies with a more Judeo-Christian take on the battle between good and evil."

Alton continues the adventures of Sam, Charly, and Amergin in *The Firehills,* as the aftershocks of the battle against the region's evil forces begin to be felt. Each of the familiar characters has been somewhat changed by their ordeal: Sam now possesses startling new powers; Charly, whose mother practices white magic, has been initiated into the world of wizard craft; and Amergin has lost his energy and digressed into an otherworldly couch potato. The three must unite however, against the

threat of a group of vicious fairies called the Sidhe, who are intent upon channeling the powers of a local Celtic harvest god for their evil purposes. Krista Hutley, reviewing the novel for *Booklist,* stated that, "a quickly wrapped-up ending notwithstanding," *The Firehills* "won't disappoint fans of the first book." Noting that "large dollops of occult ritual and philosophy" mix with Celtic folklore in the book, a *Kirkus Reviews* writer added that readers will eagerly turn pages as Alton's "fast-paced plot gallops to the dramatic climax."

Trained as a biologist, Alton now works as a conservationist and helps manage and maintain a property for the Royal Botanic Gardens. Discussing the basis for his fantasy fiction, Alton noted on his home page that he was inspired by reading Susan Cooper's fantasy series "The Dark Is Rising" as a child. Cooper's book "is firmly rooted in places I had visited on holiday, places like Cornwall and Wales, and really brings those places to life. . . . I wanted to do something similar for Dorset."

Biographical and Critical Sources

PERIODICALS

Booklist, September 1, 2002, John Peters, review of *The Malifex,* p. 122; October 1, 2005, Krista Hutley, review of *The Firehills,* p. 47.
Kirkus Reviews, July 15, 2002, review of *The Malifex,* p. 1026; September 1, 2005, review of *The Firehills,* p. 968.
School Library Journal, November, 2002, Michele Capozzella, review of *The Malifex,* p. 154.
Voice of Youth Advocates, October, 2002, review of *The Malifex,* p. 290.

ONLINE

Steve Alton Home Page, http://steve-alton.com (February 24, 2006).

* * *

ANDERSON, Derek 1969-

Personal

Born March 21, 1969; son of Marvin (a physicist) and Carol (a grade school teacher) Anderson. *Education:* Iowa State University, B.A. (drawing and painting).

Addresses

Home—Minneapolis, MN. *Agent*—c/o Author Mail, Simon & Schuster, 1230 Avenue of the Americas, New York, NY 10020.

Derek Anderson

Career

Children's book writer and illustrator. Also worked as a designer and sculptor of Warner Brothers and Disney figurines.

Awards, Honors

American Library Association/Children's Book Council Children's Choice Award, and National Parenting Publication Gold Award, both for *Little Quack* by Lauren Thompson; National Parenting Publication Gold Award, 2005, for *Little Quack's Bedtime,* by Thompson.

Writings

SELF-ILLUSTRATED

Gladys Goes out to Lunch, Simon & Schuster Books for Young Readers (New York, NY), 2005.

Over the River: A Turkey's Tale, Simon & Schuster Books for Young Readers (New York, NY), 2005.

Blue Burt's Bluff, Simon & Schuster Books for Young Readers (New York, NY), 2006.

How the Easter Bunny Saved Christmas, Simon & Schuster Books for Young Readers (New York, NY), 2006.

Blue Burt and Wiggles, Simon & Schuster Books for Young Readers (New York, NY), 2006.

ILLUSTRATOR

Vaunda Micheaux Nelson, *Ready? Set. Raymond!,* Random House (New York, NY), 2002.

Lauren Thompson, *Little Quack,* Simon & Schuster Books for Young Readers (New York, NY), 2003.

Lauren Thompson, *Little Quack's Hide and Seek,* Simon & Schuster Books for Young Readers (New York, NY), 2004.

Lauren Thompson, *Little Quack's Bedtime,* Simon & Schuster Books for Young Readers (New York, NY), 2005.

Lauren Thompson, *Little Quack's New Friend,* Simon & Schuster Books for Young Readers (New York, NY), 2006.

Sidelights

Author and illustrator Derek Anderson recognized that he had a passion for drawing when he was in kindergarten; as he told *SATA* about his career decision, "Somehow I don't think I ever really had a choice. Writing and painting chose me." Anderson's illustrations for Lauren Thompson's picture book about a duck titled *Little Quack* helped the book become a best seller and also led to several awards. With this success, and several more "Little Quack" books to his credit, Anderson has since added writing to his list of talents. His original self-illustrated stories include *Over the River: A Turkey's Tale* and *Gladys Goes out to Lunch.*

In *Over the River* "Anderson's amusing acrylic artwork provides a new twist on a favorite holiday song," according to *School Library Journal* reviewer Roxanne

Anderson's illustrations for Lauren Thompson's **Little Quack** *bring to life the story of a little duckling as he is encouraged to leave the safety of his nest for adventures in the vast outside world.*

Burg. As a family of turkeys make their way through the woods on their way to grandma's house, they encounter a wide array of characters, some comical and some more mischievous. "Children will enjoy looking at the entertaining illustrations and comparing the chaos pictured there to the words of the old song," commented Burg. A *Kirkus Reviews* critic stated that "young readers will be . . . captivated by the fracas in Anderson's big, exuberant cartoons."

In *Gladys Goes out to Lunch* Anderson once again captivates the storyhour set with his bright, vibrantly colored illustrations. One day Gladys, an oddly colored purple and blue gorilla with a passion for bananas, catches a whiff of something desirable in the air and goes on a quest to find out what it is. Readers follow as she visits a variety of restaurants, none of which proves to be the source of the intriguing and appetizing smell. As Gladys meanders back to the zoo, the answer is revealed: a vendor's cart parked near Gladys's home is filled to the brim with banana bread! "This humorous book will tickle children and could also fit well into a unit of the five senses," stated Judith Constantinides in *School Library Journal.* A *Kirkus Reviews* critic commented that, "Like Gladys's bananas, Anderson's story is simple comfort food, with eye-candy artwork providing a welcome dash of spice."

Biographical and Critical Sources

PERIODICALS

Booklist, February 1, 2003, Connie Fletcher, review of *Little Quack,* p. 1002.

Kirkus Reviews, June 1, 2005, review of *Gladys Goes out to Lunch,* p. 632; September 15, 2005, review of *Over the River: A Turkey's Tale,* p. 1019.

Publishers Weekly, November 11, 2002, review of *Little Quack,* p. 62; June 30, 2003 "Flying Starts," p. 18; February 9, 2004, "More Duck and Bunny Tales," p. 83.

School Library Journal, December, 2002, Kay Bowes, review of *Ready? Set. Raymond!,* p. 104; August, 2005, Judith Constantinides, review of *Gladys Goes out to Lunch,* p. 84; October, 2005, Roxanne Burg, review of *Over the River,* p. 102.

ONLINE

Derek Anderson Home Page, http://www.derekanderson. net (February 24, 2006).

B

BARNARD, Bryn 1956-

Personal

Born February 2, 1956, in Los Angeles, CA; son of Ernest Raymond (an electrical engineer) and Elaine (an actress and playwright; maiden name, Elliott) Barnard; married Rebecca Parks (a writer, designer, and color consultant), June 8, 1985; children: Wynn Adele, Parks Elliott. *Education:* Attended University of California, Irvine, 1974-75; attended Universiti Sains Malaysia, Penang, 1977; University of California, Berkeley, B.A. (studio art and Asian studies; magna cum laude), 1979; attended Art Center College of Design, 1979-81.

Addresses

Home and office—417 Point Caution Drive, Friday Harbor, WA 98250-9222. *Agent*—c/o Author Mail, Crown, Random House, 1745 Broadway, New York, NY 10019. *E-mail*—bryn@brynbarnard.com.

Career

Children's book illustrator and author, and graphic and fine artist. University of Delaware, Newark, assistant professor of art, 1991-95; University of the Arts, Philadelphia, PA, adjunct professor of illustration, 1994-96. Creative consultant for companies in Malaysia; consulting associate for Universities Field Staff International. *Exhibitions:* Work exhibited in solo and group shows in the United States, Europe, and Asia. Paintings included in permanent collections at National Air and Space Museum, Washington, DC; Kennedy Space Center, FL; Stennis Space Center, MS; Jet Propulsion Laboratories, Pasadena, CA; and other private and corporate collections. Murals installed in Jenet Sinegal Patient Care Building and Melinda French Gates Ambulatory Care Building, both at Children's Hospital Seattle.

Member

Society of Illustrators, Institute of Current World Affairs, Phi Beta Kappa.

Bryn Barnard

Awards, Honors

Crane-Rogers Foundation fellowship, 1981-83; New Jersey State Arts Council fellowship, 1992; Society of Illustrators, Los Angeles, Silver Medal, 1994; Society of Illustrators, New York, award of merit, 1994, 1997, 2000, 2005; Fulbright fellowship, 1999-2000.

Writings

SELF-ILLUSTRATED

Dangerous Planet: Natural Disasters That Changed History, Crown (New York, NY), 2003.

11

Outbreak: Plagues That Changed History, Crown (New York, NY), 2006.

Contributor to *International Studio* and *New York Times Book Review.*

ILLUSTRATOR

Harry Harrison, *Galactic Dreams* (short stories), Tor (New York, NY), 1994.

Victoria Crenson, *Bay Shore Park: The Death and Life of an Amusement Park,* W.H. Freeman (New York, NY), 1995.

Mary Quattlebaum, reteller, *In the Beginning,* Time-Life for Children (Alexandria, VA), 1995.

Herman J. Viola, *North American Indians,* Crown (New York, NY), 1996.

Mary Martin, reteller, *Adam and Eve,* Time-Life Kids (Alexandria, VA), 1996.

Lucille Recht Penner, *Westward Ho!: The Story of the Pioneers,* Random House (New York, NY), 1997.

Joyce Milton, *Gorillas: Gentle Giants of the Forest,* Random House (New York, NY), 1997.

Melvin Berger, *Don't Believe It!: Fibs and Facts about Animals,* Scholastic (New York, NY), 1997.

Marjorie Cowley, *Anooka's Answer,* Clarion (New York, NY), 1998.

Chris Eboch, *The Well of Sacrifice,* Clarion (New York, NY), 1999.

Lucille Recht Penner, *Big Birds,* Random House (New York, NY), 1999.

Nathan Zimelman, *Sold!: A Mothematics Adventure,* Charlesbridge (Watertown, MA), 2000.

Michelle Knudsen, *Colorful Chameleons!,* Random House (New York, NY), 2001.

Joyce Milton, *Gorillas: Gentle Giants of the Forest,* Random House (New York, NY), 2003.

Shirley-Rae Redmond, *Tentacles!: Tales of the Giant Squid,* Random House (New York, NY), 2003.

Sidelights

Beginning his illustration career in the mid-1980s, Bryn Barnard creates artwork for both fantasy-based children's novels and fact-based nonfiction for younger readers. In addition, in 2003 Barnard also took on the role of author with *Dangerous Planet: Natural Disasters That Changed History,* which profiles nine of the most prominent natural disasters ever recorded in world history. With profiles ranging from the asteroid that hit Earth and killed off the dinosaurs over sixty-five million years ago to the tidal wave that swept away Minoan civilization and the deadly storms that ravaged the armies of England's King Edward III in 1360, the book was praised by *Booklist* contributor Ilene Cooper as a "fascinating offering" in which "Barnard describes . . . events and more in an absorbing narrative that includes touches of humor."

Similar in format to *Dangerous Planet,* Barnard's *Outbreak: Plagues That Changed History* starts with the microscopic: the microorganisms that periodically cause

massive outbreaks of disease among the human populations of the world. Barnard includes discussions of the Black Death, which decimated European and Asian populations during the fourteenth century, as well as of smallpox, cholera, tuberculosis, and influenza, among others. In *School Library Journal* Deanna Romriell praised the book as "fascinating and informative," noting Barnard's focus on how these waves of disease have altered human history. In the *New York Times Book Review,* Julie Just dubbed the work "timely" due to its publication in the midst of news warnings of a coming "bird flu" pandemic, while a *Denver Post* writer noted that the author/illustrator's "chatty, lucid explanations of the microbes responsible for death on a wide scale" would find fans among followers of the popular *CSI* television series.

As an illustrator, Barnard's work has been cited for its ability to expand and enhance the texts it accompanies. Discussing Joyce Milton's *Gorillas: Gentle Giants of the Forest,* which discusses the gorilla life cycle, habitat, and way of life, Hazel Rochman wrote in *Booklist* that Barnard's illustrations are "dramatic and colorful." *Westward Ho!: The Story of the Pioneers,* a nonfiction treatment of the types of journeys made by early American settlers, written by Lucille Recht Penner, contains "plentiful illustrations" by Barnard that "lend an inviting air to the large pages," according to Steven Engelfried in *School Library Journal.* For *Bay Shore Park: The Death and Life of an Amusement Park,* written by Victoria Crenson, Barnard's illustrations record the changes in the land over the period of nearly fifty years after an amusement park in Maryland was demolished and the land left to nature. *School Library Journal* reviewer Eva Elisabeth Von Ancken remarked that the book's "lush illustrations and text record the changes [to the land] over time," reminding readers of "the indomitable forces of nature."

Barnard's artistic contributions to children's fiction include his work for Marjorie Cowley's *Anooka's Answer,* which is set in southern France during the Paleolithic era, some twelve thousand years ago, and focuses on twelve-year-old Anooka. "The addition of illustrations . . . will help youngsters understand a time period with which they have little familiarity," attested Jeanette Larson in *School Library Journal.* In Chris Eboch's *The Well of Sacrifice* Barnard's artwork brings to life the coming-of-age crisis experienced by a young girl on the verge of womanhood. Barnard has also contributed the illustrations to *Galactic Dreams,* a collection of short stories by the popular humor writer for children Harry Harrison.

Barnard once told *SATA:* "Not many American illustrators start their art careers in Malaysia. Mine began there in 1973, when my polychrome dervish-as-spin-art act won the Johor Baru Mad Artist competition. Though I now live on an island in Puget Sound and have traded performance art antics for the illustrator's brush and mouse, my affection for Malaysia and the influence of

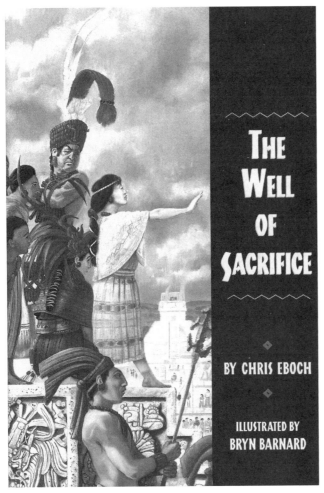

Beginning his career as an illustrator before adding on the role of writer, Barnard creates detailed paintings for books such as this 1999 novel, set in the ninth century amid a sometimes brutal Mayan culture.

that culture on my work remains undiminished. I have returned to the country again and again: in 1977-78 to study batik and perform with a shadow puppet theater troupe, in 1981-84 to investigate the art and ethos of intercultural advertising, and from November 1999 to February 2000, as a Fulbright fellow, to paint, draw, and lecture on illustration and design at the Universiti Sains Malaysia on the island of Penang.

"My mixed-media art incorporates acrylic, oil, transfer, and digital imagery and spans the range from magic realist landscapes, to scientific and historical tableaux, to children's book illustration. In my work for kids, my own children are my inspiration, models, and severest critics. If it passes muster with them, I know my work may have a chance in the wider world.

"Always based on observation, my style harkens to the work of the European academics. I worship at the shrines of the French painters Jean Leon Gerome and Alexandre Cabanel, the English neo-classicists Lawrence Alma-Tadema and J.W. Waterhouse, and the great Russian itinerants Vasily Vereshchagin, Ilya Repin, and Iwan Schischkin. One day, perhaps, I will be able to walk in their shadows."

Biographical and Critical Sources

PERIODICALS

Booklist, May 1, 1997, Hazel Rochman, review of *Gorillas: Gentle Giants of the Forest,* p. 1504; July, 2003, Gillian Engberg, review of *Tentacles! Tales of the Giant Squid,* p. 1900; December 1, 2003, Ilene Cooper, review of *Dangerous Planet: Natural Disasters That Changed History,* p. 674.
Bulletin of the Center for Children's Books, November, 2003, Deborah Stevenson, review of *Dangerous Planet,* p. 93; February, 2006, Deborah Stevenson, review of *Outbreak: Plagues That Changed History,* p. 259.
Children's Digest, March-April, 2006, Emily Johnson, review of *Outbreak,* p. 19.
Denver Post, April 30, 2006, review of *Outbreak.*
New York Times Book Review, November 16, 2003, Natalie Angier, review of *Dangerous Planet;* March 12, 2006, review of *Outbreak.*
Publishers Weekly, February 28, 1994, p. 76; March 29, 1999, p. 105.
School Library Journal, August, 1995, Eva Elisabeth Von Ancken, review of *Bay Shore Park,* p. 133; March, 1998, Steven Engelfried, review of *Westward Ho!,* p. 200; December, 1998, Jeanette Larson, review of *Anooka's Answer,* p. 121; May, 1999, Cynthia M. Sturgis, review of *The Well of Sacrifice,* p. 122; November, 2003, Patricia Manning, review of *Dangerous Planet,* p. 153; February, 2006, Deanna Romriell, review of *Outbreak,* p. 140.

ONLINE

Bryn Barnard Home Page, http://www.brynbarnard.com (April 12, 2006).

*   *   *

BERENSTAIN, Stan 1923-2005
(Stanley Berenstain)

OBITUARY NOTICE— See index for *SATA* sketch: Born September 29, 1923, in Philadelphia, PA; died of lymphoma, November 26, 2005, in Doylestown, PA. Illustrator and author. Along with his wife, Jan, Berenstain was the creator of the popular "Berenstain Bears" series of children's picture books. The Berenstains first met while attending classes in 1941 at what was then the Philadelphia Museum School of Industrial Art. America entered World War II the next year, and Berenstain enlisted in the U.S. Army, where he worked as an illustrator. After the war, he married Jan and studied for three more years at the Pennsylvania Academy of Fine Arts. The young couple then aspired to become cartoonists. After a rocky first year, they found their first success selling their work to the *Saturday Evening Post.* They

learned that they could get laughs by spoofing everyday American family life, notably with their "It's All in the Family" cartoon, which appeared in *McCall's* and then *Good Housekeeping.* It was Theodore Seuss Geisel—better known as Dr. Seuss—who suggested the couple write children's books. At the time, Geisel was an editor at Random House, and he liked the sample cartoon the Berenstains provided featuring a family of bears. The series premiered in 1962 with *The Big Honey Hunt,* with the couple serving as both authors and illustrators. The goal of the "Berenstain Bears" series is to encourage children ages four to eight years old to read while offering everyday lessons in life, such as the value of sharing and the importance of going to the dentist. Sometimes, the couple addressed more weighty subjects, such as pregnancy and the environment, but usually the topics are more benign. Critics praised the books, for their well-developed characters and plots, and the series earned the Berenstains numerous awards. Over a period that spanned five decades, the Berenstains produced over two hundred books in their series, which they also adapted to television, CD-ROM, coloring books, and even a Christmas musical. Later in their career, sons Leo and Michael Berenstain joined the team to continue the pace of the series, which often produced ten new books a year.

OBITUARIES AND OTHER SOURCES:

PERIODICALS

Chicago Tribune, November 30, 2005, section 3, p. 9.
Los Angeles Times, November 30, 2005, p. B10.
New York Times, November 30, 2005, p. C19.
Times (London, England), December 7, 2005, p. 56.
Washington Post, November 30, 2005, p. B5.

*   *   *

BERENSTAIN, Stanley
See BERENSTAIN, Stan

*   *   *

BIRNEY, Betty G. 1947-

Personal

Born April 26, 1947, in St. Louis, MO; daughter of Edgar J. (in business) and Ella (a homemaker; maiden name, Mohrmann) Griesbaum; married (marriage dissolved); married Frank W. Birney (an actor), November 26, 1982; children: Walshe; (stepchildren) Rebecca, Anna. *Education:* Webster College (now Webster University), B.A. (cum laude), 1969; attended University of Missouri-Columbia, 1970-71. *Politics:* "Independent." *Religion:* Presbyterian. *Hobbies and other interests:* "Reading (of course!), playing piano, computer stuff."

Betty G. Birney

Addresses

Home—Sherman Oaks, CA. *Agent*—c/o Author Mail, Atheneum, 1230 Avenue of the Americas, New York, NY 10020. *E-mail*—bettybirney@bettybirney.com.

Career

Children's book author, scriptwriter, and author of educational software. Advertising copywriter for agencies in St. Louis, MO, and Chicago, IL; Disneyland, Anaheim, CA, advertising copywriter, 1977-79; Walt Disney Co., Burbank, CA, publicist, 1979-81; freelance television writer, 1982—. Trustee, Humanitas Prize.

Member

Society of Children's Book Writers and Illustrators, Authors Guild, PEN Center USA, Writers Guild of America—West.

Awards, Honors

ANDY Award, New York Ad Club; Flair Award, St. Louis Ad Club; Writers' Guild of America Award, 1991, and Pappenheim Award, Jewish Family Services, both for "But He Loves Me"; Humanitas Prize, Human Family Educational and Cultural Institute, 1991, for "Wish upon a Fish" (*Camp Candy* episode), 1993, for "Big Boys Don't Cry," 1996, for "Fast Forward"; Emmy Award nomination, Academy of Television Arts and Sciences, 1994, for "Big Boys Don't Cry," and 2001, for *Madeline*; Cybermania '94 award, Academy of In-

teractive Arts and Sciences, 1994, for "Berenstain Bears on Their Own"; Gold Apple honor, National Educational Media Network, 1996; Humanitas Prize finalist, 1996, for "Madeline and the Treasure Hunt," 2001, for "Madeline and the Giants"; Daytime Emmy Award, Academy of Television Arts and Sciences, 2002, for *Madeline*; Beehive Award nomination, Children's Literature Association of Utah, 2005-06, for *The World according to Humphrey*; ACE award nomination, for *Welcome to Pooh Corner* and *Too Smart for Strangers*; Cine Golden Eagle award, for "It Happened to Me," "But He Loves Me," and "Big Boys Don't Cry"; Golden Cindy award, for "Berenstain Bears on Their Own" and *Richard Scarry's Busiest Disc Ever.*

Writings

PICTURE BOOKS

What's My Job?: A Riddle Flap Book, illustrated by Lisa Berrett, Simon & Schuster (New York, NY), 1992.

Who Am I?: A Riddle Flap Book, illustrated by Lisa Berrett, Simon & Schuster (New York, NY), 1992.

Raja's Story, St. Louis Zoo (St. Louis, MO), 1993.

Tyrannosaurus Tex, illustrated by John O'Brien, Houghton (Boston, MA), 1994.

(Adaptor) Anna Sewell, *Black Beauty,* Western Publishing (Racine, WI), 1994.

Meltdown at the Wax Museum (based on *Animaniacs* cartoon series), Western Publishing (Racine, WI), 1995.

Pie's in the Oven, illustrated by Holly Meade, Houghton (Boston, MA), 1996.

Let's Play Hide and Seek, illustrated by Dara Goldman, Scholastic (New York, NY), 1997.

MIDDLE-GRADE NOVELS

The World according to Humphrey, Putnam (New York, NY), 2004.

Friendship according to Humphrey, Putnam (New York, NY), 2005.

Seven Wonders of Sassafras Springs, illustrated by Matt Phelan, Atheneum (New York, NY), 2005.

"DISNEY" SERIES; FOR CHILDREN

(Coauthor) *Disney Babies Bedtime Stories,* Mallard, 1990.

Disney's Chip 'n' Dale Rescue Rangers: The Rescue Rangers Save Little Red, illustrated by Don Williams, Western Publishing (Racine, WI), 1991.

(Adaptor) *Disney's The Little Mermaid,* illustrated by Kerry Martin and Fred Marvin, Western Publishing (Racine, WI), 1992.

Disney's Beauty and the Beast: The Tale of Chip the Teacup, illustrated by Edward R. Gutierrez and Mones, Western Publishing (Racine, WI), 1992.

Bambi's Snowy Day, illustrated by David Pacheco and Diana Wakeman, Western Publishing (Racine, WI), 1992.

Walt Disney's Sleeping Beauty, illustrated by Mones, Western Publishing (Racine, WI), 1993.

(Adaptor) *Disney's Toy Story,* Western Publishing (Racine, WI), 1995.

Walt Disney's Bambi: A Snowy Day, Golden Books (New York, NY), 1998.

"WINNIE-THE-POOH" SERIES; BASED ON CHARACTERS CREATED BY A.A. MILNE

Oh Bother, Somebody's Not Listening, illustrated by Darrell Baker, Western Publishing (Racine, WI), 1991.

Oh Bother, Somebody's Fibbing, illustrated by Sue DiCicco, Western Publishing (Racine, WI),1991.

Oh Bother, Somebody's Grumpy, illustrated by Sue DiCicco, Western Publishing (Racine, WI), 1992.

Walt Disney's Winnie the Pooh: Half a Haycorn Pie, illustrated by Darrell Baker, Western Publishing (Racine, WI), 1992.

Walt Disney's Winnie the Pooh and the Missing Pots, illustrated by Russell Hicks, Western Publishing (Racine, WI), 1992.

Oh Bother, Somebody's Messy, illustrated by Nancy Stevenson, Western Publishing (Racine, WI), 1992.

Walt Disney's Winnie the Pooh and the Little Lost Bird, illustrated by Russell Hicks, Western Publishing (Racine, WI), 1993.

(Adaptor) *Disney's Beauty and the Beast,* illustrated by Mones, Western Publishing (Racine, WI), 1993.

Oh Bother, Somebody Won't Share, illustrated by Nancy Stevenson, Western Publishing (Racine, WI), 1993.

Walt Disney's Winnie the Pooh: The Merry Christmas Mystery, illustrated by Nancy Stevenson, Western Publishing (Racine, WI), 1993.

Oh Bother, Somebody's Jealous, illustrated by Nancy Stevenson, Western Publishing (Racine, WI), 1993.

Oh Bother, Somebody's Afraid of the Dark, illustrated by Darrell Baker, Western Publishing (Racine, WI), 1993.

Walt Disney's I Am Winnie the Pooh, illustrated by Darrell Baker, Western Publishing (Racine, WI), 1993.

Oh Bother, Somebody's Jealous, illustrated by Nancy Stevenson, Golden Books (Racine, WI), 1997.

Oh Bother, Somebody's Messy, illustrated by Nancy Stevenson, Golden Books (Racine, WI), 1997.

SCRIPTS AND ELECTRONIC MEDIA

Divorce Court (television series), 1986.

Zoobilee Zoo (television series), DIC/PBS, 1986.

Maxie's World (animated television series), DIC, 1987.

(Story editor) *Camp Candy* (television series), DIC/Saban/ NBC/World Vision, 1989.

"But He Loves Me," *CBS Schoolbreak Special,* Churchill Pictures, 1991.

"Big Boys Don't Cry," *CBS Schoolbreak Special,* Churchill Pictures, 1993.

The New Adventures of Madeline (animated television series), DIC/ABC/Family Channel, 1995.

(And supervising producer) "Fast Forward," *ABC Afterschool Special,* Wild Films, 1995.

(With Valerie Red Horse) "My Indian Summer," *CBS Schoolbreak Special,* Big Daddy Productions, 1995.

Brand Spanking New! Doug (animated television series), Jumbo Pictures/Nickelodeon, 1996.

Mama, Do You Love Me? (video), 1999.

Mary Christmas (made-for-television movie), 2002.

Also author of scripts for live-action television series and special programs, including *The Puzzle Place,* PBS; *Talking with TJ,* Hallmark/UBU; *It Happened to Me,* Boy Scouts of America; *Too Smart for Strangers,* Disney Channel; *Dumbo's Circus,* Disney Channel; and *Secret Lives,* Barry Enright Productions/Syndication. Writer and story editor for *Welcome to Pooh Corner,* Disney Channel. Author of scripts for animated television programs, including *Madeline,* Disney Channel/DIC; *Book of Virtues,* Porchlight/PBS; *The Good Samaritan,* Sony Wonder; *Little Mouse on the Prairie,* syndicated; *Where's Waldo,* Where's Waldo Productions/Goodtimes; *Prince Valiant,* Hearst/Family Channel; *Bobby's World,* Film Roman/Fox; *Once upon a Forest,* Hanna-Barbera; *The Chipmunks,* Bagdasarian/NBC; *Fraggle Rock,* Marvel/Henson/NBC; *The Moondreamers,* Marvel; *The Snorks,* Hanna-Barbera/NBC; *Winnie the Pooh and You,* Curious Pictures/Disney Channel; *Clifford,* Fox/Scholastic; *The Little Drummer Boy,* Fox; and *Inspector Badger,* Disney Channel. Author of interactive software for Electronic Arts, Philips, and Sega, including *Ethan's Parables, The Crayon Factory, Ber-*

enstain Bears on Their Own, Wacky Tales, Richard Scarry's Busiest Disc Ever, and *The Dark Fables of Aesop.*

Sidelights

Betty G. Birney is the author of numerous works for children appearing in a variety of formats, including conventional picture books and lift-the-flap books as well as live-action and animated television programs and interactive software. With the launch of cable television's Disney Channel, she also began writing for cartoon and live-action children's television, and has worked on such familiar programs as *Fraggle Rock, Zoobilee Zoo,* and *Brand Spanking New! Doug.* Her work on after-school specials and other live-action television programs includes *Mary Christmas,* which has aired on the PAX network every holiday season since 2002.

Among Birney's books for children is *Tyrannosaurus Tex,* a humorous story that plays upon the enduring popularity of dinosaurs among young audiences. Called a "modern tall tale" by Elizabeth S. Watson in *Horn Book,* the story, which features a huge cowboy dinosaur, also relies upon Texas mythology, in which everyone is a cowboy and everything is supersized. Thus Tyrannosaurus Tex shows up one night on the range, and after eating a pot of beans, pot and all, joins the other cowboys around the fire to tell tall tales. That night he saves the others by putting out a fire with his ten-thousand-gallon hat. Birney's alliterative text delighted several reviewers, Claudia Cooper recommending the book as "a tumbleweed-tumbling, rip-roaring good tale" in *School Library Journal. Booklist* contributor Hazel Rochman cited *Tyrannosaurus Tex* as "great for reading aloud with the appropriate drawl."

Less a knee-slapping tall tale than a charming feel-good story, Birney's *Pie's in the Oven* was equally warmly received by critics. When a boy and his grandfather arrive home with a basket full of freshly picked apples, the boy joins his grandmother in spending the day making apple pie. The smell of the pie as it bakes fills not only the boy with delightful anticipation, but draws in aunts, uncles, friends, and even the mail carrier, each of whom is invited to join in the feast. "The narration offers the exuberant youngster's perspective on the events," noted Kathy Piehl in *School Library Journal.* The simplicity of the story, coupled with Birney's gently rhythmical prose, adds up to a "sweet celebration of family and friends," according to a critic in *Kirkus Reviews.*

Along with her picture books for young readers, Birney has also written several middle-grade novels. Two of these books feature Humphrey, a very intuitive hamster, as he does his best to solve problems for the humans he cares about. In *The World according to Humphrey* the savvy rodent is brought by a substitute teacher to Room 26 to become class pet. Unfortunately, the regular

John O'Brien's watercolor-and-ink illustrations bring to life **Tyrannosaurus Tex,** *Birney's taller-than-tall tale about a T-rex who comes to the rescue of some Texas cattle ranchers.*

teacher, Mrs. Brisbane, wants nothing to do with a rodent; fortunately, class members devise a solution: they decide to take turns keeping Humphrey at home. Humphrey's travels to the homes of the different students of Room 26 reveal interesting facts about their lives, and provide the kind-hearted Humphrey the chance to return their kindness by helping a shy girl speak up, helping the lonely janitor of the school find the possibility of love, and even helping the rodent-averse Mrs. Brisbane come to terms with harboring a class pet. "The story deftly avoids triteness while still feeling breezy and acknowledging deeply felt troubles," wrote a *Kirkus Reviews* contributor, while in *Publishers Weekly* a critic commented: "Given the perky protagonist['s] mad chipper delivery, middle-grade readers are sure to savor this classroom caper." Of the hamster himself, *Booklist* critic Shelle Rosenfeld wrote: "Humphrey, a delightful, irresistible character, is big hearted, observant, and creative."

The likeable hamster returns in *Friendship according to Humphrey,* in which the class mascot has to deal with his jealousy over a new class pet, Og the Frog. The children seem more interested in Og than in Humphrey, and even though the hamster tries to make friends with his reptilian rival, Og seems uninterested. Despite these worries, Humphrey still manages to help out in the lives of the students, coming to terms with Og in the process. "Readers will find that seeing the world from Humphrey's standpoint is mighty satisfying," wrote a contributor to *Kirkus Reviews,* while Debbie Whitbeck noted in *School Library Journal* that "the theme of friendship is as pervasive as the title implies, making this chapter book a charming read-aloud."

In Birney's *The Seven Wonders of Sassafras Springs,* set in 1923, eleven-year-old Eben McAllister longs to go out and explore the world beyond his home in Sassafras Springs, Missouri. His father promises him that he can venture out and explore the world if he can first locate seven wonders right in his own backyard. By talking to neighbors and friends, Eben begins to realize that there is plenty to explore right in his own home town. A *Publishers Weekly* critic considered the tale a "tender and captivating gem of a novel," while Connie Tyrrell Burns in *School Library Journal* called it "a literary folk story blending down-home narrative and characters with a sprinkling of magical realism." Cindy Dobrez, reviewing the book for *Booklist,* criticized Birney's "tall tale" as being "a bit heavy on the message and cliche," but felt that "the magic realism of the episodic wonders . . . provide grist for a solid read-aloud." A *Kirkus Reviews* contributor noted that, of the wonders Eben finds in *The Seven Wonders of Sassafras Springs,* "It's not the objects themselves that are so extraordinary . . . as much as his neighbors' magical stories that accompany them."

Birney once told *SATA:* "Some people find it strange that I've worked in so many mediums, from books to TV movies to animation to CD-ROM software. What

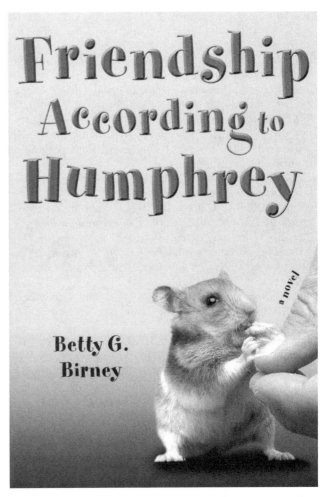

In Birney's whimsical tale, when the classroom hamster returns from vacation to find himself upstaged by a lowly frog, he learns that a new friendship is the best cure for hurt feelings. (Cover designed by Gina DiMassi.)

links these different kinds of projects—and makes my career very interesting to me—is the fact that a story is a story and I am a storyteller. Some stories are better told in a small flap book. Others belong on the big screen. Once I get 'inside the story,' it doesn't matter whether I'm telling the story of a honey-loving bear or an abused teenager; the process of creating characters and plots is really the same and never, ever boring."

Biographical and Critical Sources

PERIODICALS

Booklist, June 1, 1994, Hazel Rochman, review of *Tyrannosaurus Tex,* p. 1835; July, 1996, p. 1828; March 1, 2004, Shelle Rosenfeld, review of *The World according to Humphrey,* p. 1188; September 1, 2005, Cindy Dobrez, review of *The Seven Wonders of Sassafras Springs,* p. 130.

Bulletin of the Center for Children's Books, April, 2004, Janice Del Negro, review of *The World according to Humphrey,* p. 316.

Children's Bookwatch, April, 2004, James A. Cox and Diane C. Donovan, review of *The World according to Humphrey,* p. 1.

Horn Book, May-June, 1994, Elizabeth S. Watson, review of *Tyrannosaurus Tex,* p. 306.

Kirkus Reviews, August 1, 1996, review of *Pie's in the Oven,* p. 1147; January 1, 2004, review of *The World according to Humphrey,* p. 33; January 1, 2005, review of *Friendship according to Humphrey,* p. 48; June 15, 2005, review of *The Seven Wonders of Sassafras Springs,* p. 678.

MBR Bookwatch, May, 2005, Vicki Arkoff, review of *Friendship according to Humphrey.*

Publishers Weekly, January 24, 1994, review of *Tyrannosaurus Tex,* pp. 54-55; April 28, 1997, review of *Pie's in the Oven,* p. 77; January 19, 2004, review of *The World according to Humphrey,* p. 76; August 8, 2005, review of *The Seven Wonders of Sassafras Springs,* p. 234.

School Library Journal, May, 1994, p. 84; September, 1996, review of *Pie's in the Oven,* p. 170; April, 2004, Pat Leach, review of *The World according to Humphrey,* p. 102; Feburary, 2005, Debbie Whitbeck, review of *Friendship according to Humphrey,* p. 94; August, 2005, Connie Tyrrell Burns, review of *The Seven Wonders of Sassafras Springs,* p. 121.

ONLINE

Betty G. Birney Home Page, http://www.bettybirney.com (March 30, 2006).*

*   *   *

BLACKWOOD, Gary L. 1945-

Personal

Born October 23, 1945, in Meadville, PA; son of Roy W. and Susie (Stallsmith) Blackwood; married Jean Lantzy, October 3, 1977; children: Gareth, Giles, Tegan. *Education:* Grove City College, B.A., 1967. *Hobbies and other interests:* Music, outdoor pursuits.

Addresses

Home—206 Loop 6, Tatamagouche, Nova Scotia B0K 1V0, Canada. *E-mail*—gblackwood@hotmail.com.

Career

Writer of fiction and nonfiction books, playwright, and writing teacher. Missouri Southern State College, teacher of playwriting, 1989-93, 1997—; Trinidad State Junior College, teacher of writing-for-publication course, 1995. *Military service:* U.S. Army, sergeant class E-5, 1968-70.

Awards, Honors

Friends of American Writers Best YA Novel, 1989, for *The Dying Sun;* Best Book for Young Adults citation, American Library Association (ALA), 1998, for *The*

Gary L. Blackwood

Shakespeare Stealer, Shakespeare's Scribe and *The Year of the Hangman;* ALA Notable Book designation, for *The Shakespeare Stealer;* Best Book designation, *School Library Journal,* for *The Shakespeare Stealer* and *The Year of the Hangman;* Notable Book designation, *Smithsonian,* for *The Shakespeare Stealer* and *Moonshine.*

Writings

NOVELS

The Lion and the Unicorn, Eagle Books, 1983.

Wild Timothy, Atheneum (New York, NY), 1987.

The Dying Sun, Atheneum (New York, NY), 1989.

Beyond the Door, Atheneum (New York, NY), 1991.

Time Masters, EPB Publishers, 1995.

The Shakespeare Stealer, Dutton (New York, NY), 1998.

Moonshine, Marshall Cavendish (Tarrytown, NY), 1999.

Shakespeare's Scribe, Dutton (New York, NY), 2000.

The Year of the Hangman, Dutton (New York, NY), 2002.

Wild Timothy, Puffin (New York, NY), 2002.

Shakespeare's Spy, Dutton (New York, NY), 2003.

Alien Creatures, Players Press (Studio City, CA), 2004.

Second Sight, Dutton (New York, NY), 2005.

The Just-So Woman, illustrated by Jane Manning, HarperCollins (New York, NY), 2006.

NONFICTION

Rough Riding Reformer: Theodore Roosevelt, Benchmark (New York, NY), 1998.
Life on the Oregon Trail, Lucent (San Diego, CA), 1999.
Life in a Medieval Castle, Lucent (San Diego, CA), 1999.

"UNSOLVED HISTORY" SERIES

Debatable Deaths, Marshall Cavendish (Tarrytown, NY), 2005.
Enigmatic Events, Marshall Cavendish (Tarrytown, NY), 2005.
Perplexing People, Marshall Cavendish (Tarrytown, NY), 2005.
Legends or Lies?, Marshall Cavendish (Tarrytown, NY), 2005.

"SECRETS OF THE UNEXPLAINED" SERIES

Alien Astronauts, Benchmark (New York, NY), 1999.
Extraordinary Events and Oddball Occurrences, Benchmark (New York, NY), 1999.
Fateful Forebodings, Benchmark (New York, NY), 1999.
Long-Ago Lives, Benchmark (New York, NY), 1999.
Paranormal Powers, Benchmark (New York, NY), 1999.
Spooky Spectres, Benchmark (New York, NY), 1999.

"BAD GUYS" SERIES; NONFICTION

Pirates, Benchmark (New York, NY), 2001.
Highwaymen, Benchmark (New York, NY), 2001.
Outlaws, Benchmark (New York, NY), 2001.
Swindlers, Benchmark (New York, NY), 2001.
Gangsters, Benchmark (New York, NY), 2001.

OTHER

Futures: A Dining-Room Comedy-Drama in Three Acts, Players Press, 1996.

Also author of other short plays.

Sidelights

Gary L. Blackwood started his writing career as a teen, and has since become a prolific author of novels for both young adults and middle-grade readers, in addition to penning plays and nonfiction. Popular particularly with boys due to their western and history themes, Blackwood's books include the alternate Revolutionary War history *The Year of the Hangman,* the nonfiction "Bad Guys" series, and his series of adventure novels centering around Elizabethan playwright William Shakespeare and featuring an orphaned teen named Widge. Praising series installment *The Shakespeare Stealer,* Nancy Menaldi-Scanlan wrote in *School Library Journal* that the book features "topnotch writing with a touch of humor." Reviewing Blackwood's non-fiction series, which features such titles as *Highwaymen, Gangsters, Swindlers,* and *Outlaws, Booklist* contributor Carolyn Phelan deemed the titles "well written and well designed," citing the author's focus on fascinating ne'erdowells from history. Laura Glaser wrote in *School Library Journal* that, rather than trying to excuse or explain the moral and ethical choices of past criminals, Blackwood "sticks to the facts and colorful details," making the "Bad Guys" books "simultaneously entertaining and informative reading."

Growing up in rural Cochranton, Pennsylvania, Blackwood became a book lover. "While I was still young enough to be sleeping in a crib," he once commented. "I struck a deal with my mother: I'd give up sucking my thumb if she bought me a series of Gene Autry comics I'd seen advertised on the back of a cereal box." As a child, Blackwood attended one of the last remaining one-room schoolhouses in his state, and recalled that the school library "consisted only of a single set of bookshelves, but it did contain a full set of the Dr. Doolittle books. I had a competition going with one of my classmates to see who could read the entire series first."

One of Blackwood's most popular books, *The Shakespeare Stealer,* was inspired by a newspaper article he first read in the mid-1960s. "It informed me that, in the sixteenth century, an English doctor named Timothy Bright had invented an early system of shorthand," he once explained. "I knew something of that time period already, from studying Shakespeare in college. The elements of shorthand and Shakespeare melded in my mind, and expanded to become my first novel, which I called *An Art of Short, Swift, and Secret Stealing.*"

Blackwood never found a publisher for the book, so he put it aside for a number of years, then decided to rewrite it "as a book for kids." "For a long time," Blackwood explained, "it looked as if the new improved version of the book, now called *The Shakespeare Stealer,* would be consigned to oblivion like its predecessor. Most of the editors who saw it liked it a lot, but didn't feel it would sell well. . . . After being turned down sixteen times over a period of seven years, the book finally found a home at Dutton." The work has since gone on to receive substantial critical recognition.

The Shakespeare Stealer concerns Widge, a fourteen year old who has been raised in a Yorkshire orphanage. Widge is apprenticed to Dr. Bright, a minister who teaches the teen his system of "charactery" (or shorthand) for the purpose of gaining the boy's help in stealing other ministers' sermons. Before long, Bright sells his young apprentice for the sum of ten pounds to Simon Bass, a London theatrical manager. Bass plans to use the boy's shorthand skills to have him steal William Shakespeare's new play, *The Tragedy of Hamlet, Prince of Denmark,* so that Bass's own theater can produce it without having to pay royalties.

Widge is not far along with his transcript when he is discovered hiding in a balcony by the actors of the Globe Theatre; thinking fast, the teen pretends to be stage struck and is ultimately hired as an acting apprentice for Shakespeare's acting troupe, the Lord Chamberlain's Men. At first Widge sticks to Bass's plan and tries to use his new position to steal the Globe's own copy of the play, but the "brave new world of friendship, fun, and backstage intrigue," in the words of a *Kirkus Reviews* critic, make him question the ethics of his efforts. Instead, Widge practices lines, learns the arts of stagecraft and sword fighting, and works to evade Bass's brutal henchmen. Jennifer M. Brabander, writing in *Horn Book,* pointed out that, "like *Hamlet,* Blackwood's story focuses on its protagonist's doubt and deliberation about his interrupted quest." By the end of the story, Widge plays the role of Ophelia in a command performance before Queen Elizabeth I.

Appraising *The Shakespeare Stealer,* Deborah Stevens noted in her review for the *Bulletin of the Center for Children's Books* that the "pleasing air of high adventure to Widge's escapades . . . is enhanced by Blackwood's careful but never dry use of period and theatrical detail." Brabander, writing in *Horn Book,* credited Blackwood with "set[ting] the stage for future reading and play-going" for his young fans, and a *Kirkus Reviews* critic called the book a "delightful and heartwarming romp through Elizabethan England." A *Publishers Weekly* reviewer remarked on the author's inclusion of colorful historical details—such as Widge having his supper warmed on a stove, and to the recovery of an injured man in a hospital—and cited in particular the book's "lively depictions of Elizabethan stagecraft and street life." Sally Margolis, who reviewed the book for the *School Library Journal,* wrote that "Blackwood puts a young boy in a sink-or-swim predicament in alien territory where he discovers his own strength. It's a formula with endless appeal." Carolyn Phelan, writing in *Booklist,* commented that "this historical novel makes an exciting introduction to the period and to Shakespearean theater."

Sequels to *The Shakespeare Stealer* include *Shakespeare's Scribe* and *Shakespeare's Spy. Shakespeare's Scribe* finds Widge and the acting troupe traveling to different towns to perform, even as rumors of the growing spread of the plague reveal the threat to London. As Widge helps transcribe a play for the injured Shakespeare, he meets a man who claims to be his father and learns a great deal about himself in the process. As stage props and costumes start to go missing and threaten the troupe's stage success with plays such as *Hamlet* and *Measure for Measure,* Widge—now an actor—must become an undercover investigator in *Shakespeare's Spy,* while a subplot finds him falling in love with the popular playwright's daughter, Judith. In a *Horn Book* review Brabander called *Shakespeare's Scribe* an "engaging portrayal of a young boy's coming of age in Elizabethan England," while *School Library*

Taking place in 1777, Blackwood's novel finds a young British aristocrat forced to rethink his loyalties after a job working for Ben Franklin's newspaper introduces him to the rebel cause. *(Cover illustration by Tristan Elwell.)*

Journal contributor Nancy Menaldi-Scanlan lauded Blackwood's book as "extremely well structured, with . . . interesting subplots" and "realistic" dialogue. Carolyn Phelan stated in *Booklist* that "Widge and many of the other characters emerge as memorable, complex individuals that children will want to meet again." In *Horn Book,* Jeannine M. Chapman wrote that, despite the many plot lines, *Shakespeare's Spy,* "with its intrigues, romances, and plagues, is an enjoyable read," and a *Kirkus Reviews* writer deemed it "peppered like its predecessors with hilarious wordplay and real stagecraft."

Blackwood also appeals to readers looking for fast-moving, action-filled plots and likeable characters in novels such as *The Year of the Hangman* and *Second Sight.* In the former, he plays out an alternate history in which the British vanquished North American colonials during the American Revolution, leaving General George Washington captive and Benjamin Franklin hid-

ing in a New Orleans safe house. In the novel fifteen-year-old juvenile delinquent Brit Creighton Brown is sent to the colonies to build character, and winds up in the hands of the colonial underground. Joining with rebel leader Benedict Arnold, he attempts to rescue Washington and learns a lot about honor and loyalty in the process. A *Publishers Weekly* reviewer found the novel "adventurous, if somewhat unrealistic," but also praised the book's "clever dialogue" and "compelling questions," while in *School Library Journal* Starr E. Smith wrote: "Packed with action . . . and compelling portrayals of real-life and fictional characters," *The Year of the Hangman* "will appeal to fans of both history and fantasy."

Moving closer to the historical record, *Second Sight* focuses on a presidential assassination: the murder of Abraham Lincoln during the U.S. Civil War. The main character and narrator, teenager Joseph Ehrlich, is a struggling actor who performs a stage act with his father, Nicholas, during which he feigns clairvoyance. Then he meets Cassandra Quinn, a girl living in his family's boarding house who demonstrates a real ability to foresee the future. When Cassandra predicts Lincoln's death, and states that politically radical actor John Wilkes Booth will be the killer, Joseph realizes that he must attempt to derail this tragedy. Noting that Blackwood "twist[s] history with some surprising results," Renee Steinberg praised the novel in *School Library Journal* as useful as a "springboard for some interesting class discussions." Introducing the novel as "brilliantly re-envisioned history," a *Kirkus Reviews* writer concluded that Blackwood casts his dramatic novel with "historical people and events, sets them in the most vivid evocation" of the mid-1800s, and then "caps his mesmerizing thriller with a stunning twist."

Biographical and Critical Sources

PERIODICALS

Booklist, June 1, 1998, Carolyn Phelan, review of *The Shakespeare Stealer,* p. 1763; September 1, 1999, p. 131; September 1, 2000, Carolyn Phelan, review of *Shakespeare's Scribe,* p. 112; January 1, 2002, Carolyn Phelan, review of *Highwaymen* and *Swindlers,* p. 850; March 15, 2003, review of *Year of the Hangman,* p. 1290; September 1, 2003, Carolyn Phelan, review of *Shakespeare's Spy,* p. 119; October 1, 2005, Carolyn Phelan, review of *Second Sight,* p. 48.

Bulletin of the Center for Children's Books, July-August, 1998, Deborah Stevens, review of *The Shakespeare Stealer,* p. 483; December, 2002, review of *The Year of the Hangman,* p. 144.

English Journal, December, 1989, p. 77.

Horn Book, July-August, 1989, p. 485; June, 1998, Jennifer M. Brabander, review of *The Shakespeare Stealer,* p. 353; November, 2000, Jennifer M. Brabander, re-

view of *Shakespeare's Scribe,* p. 752; November-December, 2003, Jeannine M. Chapman, review of *Shakespeare's Spy,* p. 739.

Kirkus Reviews, April 15, 1998, review of *The Shakespeare Stealer,* p. 576; October 15, 2003, review of *Shakespeare's Spy,* p. 1269; August 1, 2005, review of *Second Sight,* p. 844.

Kliatt, September, 2002, Claire Rosser, review of *The Year of the Hangman,* p. 6, and Sally M. Tibbetts, review of *Shakespeare's Scribe,* p. 15; March, 2004, Janet Julian, review of *The Year of the Hangman,* p. 59.

Publishers Weekly, June 1, 1998, review of *The Shakespeare Stealer,* p. 63; September 16, 2002, review of *The Year of the Hangman,* p. 70.

School Library Journal, October, 1987, p. 137; May, 1989, p. 124; March, 1991, p. 192; June, 1998, Sally Margolis, review of *The Shakespeare Stealer,* p. 140; March, 1999, pp. 216-217; August, 1999, p. 166; October, 1999, p. 144; September, 2000, Nancy Menaldi-Scanlan, review of *Shakespeare's Scribe,* p. 225; January, 2002, Laura Glaser, reviews of *Highwaymen, Gangsters,* and *Outlaws,* p. 146; September, 2002, Starr E. Smith, review of *The Year of the Hangman,* p. 219; December, 2002, review of *The Year of the Hangman,* p. 41; September 1, 2003, Carolyn Phelan, review of *Shakespeare's Spy,* p. 119; October, 2003, Susan Colley, review of *Shakespeare's Spy,* p. 158; February, 2004, Nancy Menaldi-Scanlan, review of *The Shakespeare Stealer,* p. 82; September, 2005, Renee Steinberg, review of *Second Sight,* p. 198.

Voice of Youth Advocates, October, 2002, review of *The Year of the Hangman,* p. 269.

Wilson Library Bulletin, January, 1990, p. 99; March, 1990.

ONLINE

Gary Blackwood Home Page, http://mowrites4kids.drury.edu/authors/blackwood (April 12, 2006).

Edgar Wolfe Literary Award Web site, http://www.kckpl.lib.ks.us/FOL/ (February 21, 2003), "Gary L. Blackwood."

*   *   *

BONNING, Tony 1948-

Personal

Born 1948, in Crosshill, Carrick, Scotland. *Education:* Studied engineering.

Addresses

Home—Scotland. *Agent*—c/o Croig Police Close, 82 High St., Kirkudbright DG6 4JL, Scotland. *E-mail*—tony.bonning@virgin.net.

Career

Journalist and author. Freelance writer, 1994—. Children's poet-in-residence, Taigh Chearsabhagh on North

Uist March, 2001. *Markings* (poetry magazine, co-publisher; Galloway Children's Festival, founder and director.

Member

Scottish Storytelling Centre.

Writings

FOR CHILDREN

Another Fine Mess, illustrated by Sally Hobson, Little Tiger Press (Waukesha, WI), 1998.
The Great Goat Cheese, Little Tiger Press (London, England), 1999.
Stone Soup, illustrated by Sally Hobson, David & Charles Children's (London, England), 2001, published as *Fox Tale Soup,* Simon & Schuster Books for Young Readers (New York, NY), 2002.
Snog the Frog, illustrated by Rosalind Beardshaw, Barron's (Hauppauge, NY), 2005.

OTHER

Galloway, photographs by Allan Wright, Cauldron Press (Castle Douglas, Scotland), 1999.
Arran, photographs by Allan Wright, Cauldron Press (Castle Douglas, Scotland), 2002.

Sidelights

Scottish author and journalist Tony Bonning studied engineering before turning to writing full-time in 1994. In addition to his work penning children's books, he is also co-publisher of the poetry magazine *Markings,* and founded and directs the annual Galloway Children's Festival. Bonning's books for children include *Another Fine Mess, Fox Tale Soup* (published in Great Britain as *Stone Soup*), and *Snog the Frog,* the last a clever variation on the classic folk tale "The Frog Prince." Reviewing *Fox Tale Soup,* another folk-tale adaptation that finds a clever fox outwitting his silly dinner guests, *Booklist* contributor Gillian Engberg noted that Bonning incorporates "a refreshing twist in[to] an old favorite."

In *Snog the Frog* Bonning introduces his title character on the morning of his birthday. Well versed in fairy-tale lore, Snog—his name a play on British slang for "kiss"—is determined to achieve his rightful destiny and feel like a handsome prince on his special day. Snog asks everyone he meets for a kiss. After getting rejected from a cow, a sheep, and even a pig, Snog finally happens upon a beautiful princess who grants his request because she also has the expectation that kissed frogs turn into handsome princes. After several smooches, the princess realizes that Snog the Frog is

A frog well schooled in fairy tales decides that his birthday is the perfect time to see whether a kiss from the right girl will transform him into a human prince in Bonning's Snog the Frog. *(Illustration by Rosalind Beardshaw.)*

not to be her Prince Charming; he is just an ordinary frog. Snog is quite pleased, however; being kissed by a princess has left him feeling like a prince! Be Astengo, writing in *School Library Journal,* stated that "readers and listeners need to be familiar with the original tale to get the punch line, but the story is engaging enough to work well without it." A *Kirkus Reviews* critic commented that "younger readers on this side of the pond may not get the title's pun at first, but by the end will be lining up for snogs of their own."

Biographical and Critical Sources

PERIODICALS

Booklist, November 15, 1998, Lauren Peterson, review of *Another Fine Mess,* p. 594; February 1, 2002, Gillian Engberg, review of *Fox Tale Soup,* p. 942.
Bulletin of the Center for Children's Books, March, 2002, review of *Fox Tale Soup,* p. 235.
Kirkus Reviews, December 15, 2001, review of *Fox Tale Soup,* p. 1754; January 1, 2005, review of *Snog the Frog,* p. 48.
Publishers Weekly, December 17, 2001, review of *Fox Tale Soup,* p. 90.
School Librarian, summer, 1999, review of *Another Fine Mess,* p. 73; spring, 2002, review of *Stone Soup,* p. 17.
School Library Journal, February, 1999, JoAnn Jonas, review of *Another Fine Mess,* p. 77; March, 2002, Lisa

Gangemi Krapp, review of *Fox Tale Soup,* p. 172; August, 2005, Be Astengo, review of *Snog the Frog,* p. 85.

ONLINE

Children's Book Page Web site, http://www.bookpage. com/ (February 24, 2006), Karen Trotter Elley, review of *Fox Tale Soup.*

Scottish Storytelling Centre Web site, http://www. scottishstorytellingcentre.co.uk/ (December 14, 2005), "Tony Bonning."*

*   *   *

BRODEUR, Ruth Wallace
See WALLACE-BRODEUR, Ruth

C

COOLING, Wendy

Personal
Born in England. *Education:* London University, M.A. (education).

Addresses
Home—11 Kingsmead, Barnet, Hertfordshire EN5 5AX, England. *E-mail*—WendyCooling@Bookconsult. freeserve.co.uk.

Career
United Kingdom Year of Literature festival, Swansea, Wales, coordinator, 1995; WORDPLAY children's festival, organizer, 1995—; Book House Training Centre, director of course on children's publishing, 1995—; Disney Consumer Products, director of course on children's publishing, 1997; National Literacy Strategy and National Year of Reading, contact person, 1999. Former member of civil service; former secondary-school English teacher in London, England. Worked variously as library director, bookstore manager, and book promoter; advisory teacher with ILEA Resources Support Group. Director of Farms for City Children and Children's Book Foundation. Judge of children's literature awards, including March Award, Mother Goose Award, and National Association for Special Education Needs Book Award. Polka Children's Theatre, member of board. Book consultant and advisor to schools, libraries, and parents; researcher; has appeared on *Treasure Islands,* BBC Radio 4.

Member
International Board on Books for Young People (chair of British section for three years), National Literacy Association (executive member), Children's Literature Research Centre (member of advisory panel), Poetry Society (member of advisory panel), LISC (member of working party).

Writings
Finding out . . . How to Find Out, Penguin (Harmondsworth, England), 1989.
Fame!: Who's Who in History at Madame Tussaud's, illustrated by Nick Duffy, Puffin (London, England), 1992.
Sandy the Seal, Trafalgar Square (North Pomfret, VT), 1994.
(With Paul Kropp) *The Reading Solution,* Penguin (Harmondsworth, England), 1995.
Books to Enjoy, 12-16 (guide), School Library Association (Swindon, England), 1996.
(Reteller) *Farmyard Tales from Far and Wide* (companion to *Forest Tales from Far and Wide,* edited by Marleen Vermeulen), illustrated by Rosslyn Moran, Barefoot Books (Bath, Somerset, England), 1998.
An Interview with Jenny Nimmo, Mammoth (London, England), 1999.
Books to Enjoy: With Boys in Mind, School Library Association (Swindon, England), 1999.
More Books to Enjoy, 12-16 (guide), School Library Association (Swindon, England), 2000.
D Is for Dahl: A Gloriumptious A-Z Guide to the World of Roald Dahl, illustrated by Quentin Blake, Penguin (New York, NY), 2005.

Also author of children's guides for British National Trust. Contributor to periodicals, including *Books for Keeps, Junior Education,* London *Guardian,* and *Times Educational Supplement.*

EDITOR

Paul Jennings, *Thirteen! Unpredictable Tales,* Viking (London, England), 1995.
Roald Dahl, *The Great Automatic Grammatizator, and Other Stories,* Viking (London, England), 1996.
The Puffin Book of Stories for Five Year Olds, Puffin (London, England), 1996.
The Puffin Book of Stories for Six Year Olds, Puffin (London, England), 1996.

The Puffin Book of Stories for Seven Year Olds, Puffin (London, England), 1996.

The Puffin Book of Stories for Eight Year Olds, Puffin (London, England), 1996.

Read Me a Story Please, Orion (London, England), 1998.

Roald Dahl, *Skin, and Other Stories,* Puffin (London, England), 1999.

Football Shorts, Dolphin (London, England), 1999.

Centuries of Stories: New Stories for a New Millennium, HarperCollins (London, England), 1999.

What Fun to Be a Hippo, illustrated by Anthony Lewis, F. Watts (London, England), 2000.

Who Has Seen the Wind?: Poems about the Weather, F. Watts (London, England), 2000.

The Animals' Bedtime Storybook, illustrated by Penny Dann, Orion (London, England), 2000.

Listen to Me!: Winning Short Stories Written by Teenagers, Collins (London, England), 2000.

Mud between the Toes: Poems about Feelings, illustrated by Anthony Lewis, Watts (New York, NY), 2000.

Me!: Poems about Being Born and Growing Older, illustrated by Rowan Barnes-Murphy, Watts (New York, NY), 2000.

Nearly Best Friends: Poems about Relationships, illustrated by Rowan Barnes-Murphy, Watts (London, England), 2000.

Earth-wise Poems about Our World, illustrated by Rowan Barnes-Murphy, Watts (London, England), 2000.

Mirrors: Sparkling New Stories from Prize-Winning Authors, illustrated by Sarah Young and Tim Stevens, Collins (London, England), 2001.

The Kingfisher Book of Stories for Beginning Readers, Kingfisher (London, England), 2001.

The Puffin Book of Stories for Nine Year Olds, illustrated by Steve Cox, Puffin (London, England), 2001.

The Puffin Book of Stories for Ten Year Olds, illustrated by Steve Cox, Puffin (London, England), 2001.

The Puffin Book of Christmas Stories, illustrated by Nick Ward, Puffin (London, England), 2001.

(Author of introduction) *The Children's Book of Alphabets,* Chicken House (Frome, Somerset, England), 2002.

Ten of the Best: School Stories with a Difference, Collins (London, England), 2002.

With Love: A Celebration of Words and Pictures for the Very Young, Orchard (London, England), 2004, published as *Come to the Great World: Poems from around the Globe,* Holiday House (New York, NY), 2004.

All the Colours of the Earth: Poems from around the World, Frances Lincoln (London, England), 2004, published as *Come to the Great World: Poems from around the Globe,* Holiday House (New York, NY), 2004.

Editor of *It's Christmas, Simply Spooky,* and *Surprise Surprise,* all for Dolphin. Consultant on books, including *The Caterpillar That Roared?* by Michael Lawrence, Dorling Kindersley (London, England), 2000; series consultant for "NSPCC Happy Kids" series, published by Egmont World (Handforth, England).

EDITOR; "QUIDS FOR KIDS" SERIES

Aliens to Earth, Orion (London, England), 1997.

Animal Stories, Orion (London, England), 1997.

Bad Dreams, Orion (London, England), 1997.

Ghost Stories, Orion (London, England), 1997.

Go for Goal, Orion (London, England), 1997.

Horror Stories, Orion (London, England), 1997.

On the Run, Orion (London, England), 1997.

Soccer Stories, Orion (London, England), 1997.

Spine Chillers, Orion (London, England), 1997.

Stars in Your Eyes, Orion (London, England), 1997.

Stories of Growing Up, Orion (London, England), 1997.

Stories of Hopes and Dreams, Orion (London, England), 1997.

Stories of Past and Future, Orion (London, England), 1997.

Stories of Strange Visitors, Orion (London, England), 1997.

Stories of the Unexpected, Orion (London, England), 1997.

Stories to Keep You Guessing, Orion (London, England), 1997.

Time Watch, Orion (London, England), 1997.

Top Secret, Orion (London, England), 1997.

Weird and Wonderful, Orion (London, England), 1997.

Wild and Free, Orion (London, England), 1997.

Sidelights

In addition to being a children's book author, editor, and reviewer, Wendy Cooling is a well-known consultant in the field of children's literacy, and she often appears as a guest on radio and television programs in her native England to discuss children's literature. Beginning her career in education as a secondary-school English teacher, Cooling left teaching in 1990 to run the Children's Book Foundation, a group that organizes Britain's National Children's Book Week and promotes childhood literacy. After leaving the Children's Book Foundation, Cooling became a freelance consultant and anthologist, and is one of the founders of Britain's Book Start project.

As an anthologist, Cooling has edited several collections of stories for young readers, including *The Puffin Book of Stories for Five Year Olds, The Puffin Book of Stories for Six Year Olds,* and sequential volumes up to *The Puffin Book of Stories for Ten Year Olds.* Ann G. Hay, in *School Librarian,* called *The Puffin Book of Stories for Five Year Olds* "a delightful collection of old favorites and new." Reviewing the same work, Marcus Crouch observed in *Junior Bookshelf* that the anthology contains "very fine things" that "have the merit of brevity." Another *Junior Bookshelf* contributor wrote that "the range of subjects" in *The Puffin Book of Stories for Seven Year Olds* "is likely to appeal to young juniors," and that *The Puffin Book of Stories for Eight Year Olds* depicts "an interesting range of people, places, and magical possibilities."

Cooling has also edited a number of entries in the "Quids for Kids" collection of books for children. The series takes its name from "quid," the British slang

One of Cooling's many anthologies, Come to the Great World *includes a range of verses, carrying willing readers on a rhyming trip around the globe. (Illustration by Sheila Moxley.)*

term for the British currency measure of one pound. Each of the low-priced books—which cost one pound, or a quid—contains five or six stories centering on a single theme. *School Librarian* contributor Ruth France applauded the objective of making affordable books available to children, and commented that the volumes' brevity could introduce children "to the world of reading."

Read Me a Story Please, edited by Cooling and illustrated by Penny Dann, is a collection of fifty original and retold tales for young readers and listeners to enjoy at bedtime. Divided into "two-minute tales," "five-minute tales," and "ten-minute tales," the collection makes it easy for parents to determine what stories they will have time for before they turn out the lights. Dann and Cooling worked together on *The Animals Bedtime Storybook* as well, assembling forty original stories commissioned by Cooling to describe the tales the animals on Noah's ark told each night to while away the forty rainy days they were seabound.

Cooling has also edited several books of poetry for young readers, including *Who Has Seen the Wind?: Poems about the Weather, Nearly Best Friends: Poems about Relationships,* and *All the Colours of the Earth: Poems from around the World.* The last, published in the United States as *Come to the Great World: Poems from around the Globe,* features selected poetry from classic authors, including Robert Louis Stevenson, and less-familiar children's poets, including Rabindranath Tagore, as well as chants from the Maori and Inuit cultures and a jump-rope rhyme from Guyana. Despite the diversity of settings, according to Margaret R. Tassia, writing for *School Library Journal,* the poems "focus on common issues and concerns of youngsters everywhere." *Booklist* contributor Hazel Rochman enjoyed the "lively anthology," but pointed out one of the book's flaws: though it collects prose from many areas of the globe, the collection contains "not a single poet from an African country."

Though predominantly an editor and consultant, Cooling also has also authored several titles. Her book

Fame!: Who's Who in History at Madame Tussaud's offers biographical sketches on thirty-nine of the well-known people who have been memorialized in wax for the famous London museum. Alasdair Campbell wrote in *School Librarian* that about half of Cooling's choices are individuals who were politically influential in their time and that the rest "are a mixed bag indeed," and include American actress Marilyn Monroe, American singer and actor Elvis Presley, and noted nineteenth-century mass murderer Jack the Ripper. Campbell noted that "there is certainly food for some thought in these chapters" about the nature of fame.

Having edited some work by noted British writer Roald Dahl, it was a natural move for Cooling to create an alphabet and fact book based on books by the famous children's author. Part biography and part picture book, *D Is for Dahl: A Gloriumptious A-Z Guide to the World of Roald Dahl* associates each letter of the alphabet with a fun fact about Dahl's life and works. Though Ilene Cooper, writing in *Booklist,* found the layout to be confusing, she acknowledged that the book contains "interesting, amusing, and, in some cases, surprising nuggets of information." Anne Chapman, writing for *School Library Journal,* noted that Cooling's "dictionary-of-sorts is entertaining, insightful, and of particular interest to Dahl's fans. . . . The writing is clear, wicked, and fun."

Cooling once told *SATA:* "After a varied early career and two years drifting around the world, I settled down to teaching. I worked in Inner London secondary schools as an English teacher, deputy teacher, and acting head teacher for many years, running libraries, bookshops and help sessions for parents in any spare time. In one of the more exciting times, I worked with a librarian and a media-resources officer to run a library resource center in a secondary school, where the development of autonomous learning was seen as a priority—this at a time when money was not in short supply. I worked for two years as an advisory teacher with the ILEA Resources Support Group, advising schools . . . on the setting-up of libraries, the development of independent reading, and resource-based learning. I also studied part-time at London University's Institute of Education for an M.A. and wrote a dissertation on the role of the school library in curriculum development.

"At the end of 1990, I left teaching to run the Children's Book Foundation (CBF): talking and writing about children's books and reading, organizing National Children's Book Week, overseeing the annual production of *Children's Books of the Year,* and working on a range of projects to promote reading.

"One of my most interesting projects with the CBF was Bookstart, which aims to encourage parents to read with their children from a very early age. It is run in cooperation with local health centers and public libraries and involves the gift of a book and a pack about reading to families taking their babies to the clinic for

the nine-month health check. I still act as a consultant to Bookstart, and the project, now operating nationwide, has brought many opportunities to speak on radio and at conferences about the importance of pre-school book-related experiences and choosing books. At the other end of the age range, I have discussed teenage reading on BBC Radio 4's *Treasure Islands* with Michael Rosen, spoken at numerous conferences, run courses on boys and reading and worked with librarians on the selection of teenage fiction.

"I'm now working as a consultant with a range of children's publishers; reviewing books; running in-service training sessions for infant, primary and secondary school teachers and librarians; making presentations at conferences and to parent groups; working with children on special projects having to do with books; writing children's guides for the National Trust and acting as their literary advisor, and editing story collections. In 1995 I was the coordinator of the children's festival for the UK Year of Literature and Writing, held in Swansea—the WORDPLAY children's festival has become an annual event which I continue to organize.

"I have been involved in judging for children's book awards, including the Mother Goose Award (for the most promising new children's picture-book illustrator), the NASEN Special Education Needs Book Award and the Marsh Award for a book in translation. I have [also] been course director of Book House Training Centre's course on children's publishing; this covers all aspects of children's publishing: editorial, rights, design, production, marketing, and bookselling. In 1997 I ran a similar course for Disney Consumer Products; delegates were from all European countries.

"I am, as will be clear from the above, immersed in children's books—producing, reviewing, and promoting them. I am really committed to getting more books and more stories to more children."

Biographical and Critical Sources

PERIODICALS

Booklist, March 15, 2004, Hazel Rochman, review of *Come to the Great World: Poems from around the Globe,* p. 1307; August, 2005, Ilene Cooper, review of *D Is for Dahl: A Gloriumptious A-Z Guide to the World of Roald Dahl,* p. 2020.

Books, April, 1997, p. 24.

Junior Bookshelf, June, 1996, Marcus Crouch, review of *The Puffin Book of Stories for Five Year Olds,* p. 106; December, 1996, review of *The Puffin Book of Stories for Eight Year Olds,* and *The Puffin Book of Stories for Seven Year Olds,* pp. 248-249.

Kirkus Reviews, February 15, 2004, review of *Come to the Great World,* p. 175.

Library Association Record, February, 1997, p. 101.

Magpies, November, 2004, Lyn Linning, review of *With Love: A Celebration of Words and Pictures for the Very Young,* p. 26.

School Librarian, August, 1992, Alasdair Campbell, review of *Fame!: Who's Who in History at Madame Tussaud's,* p. 105; August, 1996, Ann G. Hay, review of *The Puffin Book of Stories for Five Year Olds,* p. 98; August, 1997, Ruth France, review of "Quids for Kids" series, p. 136; summer, 1998, pp. 99-100; autumn, 1998, pp. 129-130; winter, 1999, review of *Centuries of Stories,* p. 209; spring, 2001, review of *Listen to Me!: Winning Short Stories Written by Teenagers,* p. 44; winter, 2001, review of *Mirrors: Sparkling New Stories from Prize-Winning Authors,* p. 210; spring, 2002, review of *The Puffin Book of Stories for Ten Year Olds,* p. 23; autumn, 2004, Vivienne Smith, review of *All the Colours of the Earth,* p. 154; winter, 2004, Chris Brown, review of *With Love,* p. 185.

School Library Journal, April, 2004, Margaret R. Tassia, review of *Come to the Great World,* p. 130; October, 2005, Anne Chapman, review of *D Is for Dahl,* p. 184.

ONLINE

Barefoot Books UK Web site, http://www.barefoot-books.com/ (March 29, 2006), profile of Cooling.

HarperCollins Children's Books Web site, http://www.harpercollinschildrensbooks.co.uk/ (March 29, 2006), profile of Cooling.*

*   *   *

COOPER, Helen 1963-

Personal

Born May 9, 1963, in London, England; daughter of Sean (a teacher) and June (a teacher) Cooper; married Ted Dewan (an author and illustrator), October 20, 1994; children: Pandora. *Education:* Attended Royal Academy of Music. *Politics:* Labor Party. *Religion:* Church of England (Anglican). *Hobbies and other interests:* Playing piano, classical and lounge music; Americana, especially roadside graphics, mini golf, eggs, all things small and beautiful.

Addresses

Home—Oxford, England. *Office*—c/o Transworld Publishers, 61-63 Oxbridge Rd., London W5 5SA, England. *Agent*—Hilary Delemere, The Agency, 24 Pottery La., Holland Park, London W11 4LZ, England. *E-mail*—helen.cooper@wormworks.com.

Career

Author and illustrator.

Member

British Society of Authors.

Helen Cooper

Awards, Honors

Smarties Young Judges Prize shortlist, Kate Greenaway Award, and TSB Children's Book Award, all for *The Bear under the Stairs;* Washington Children's Choice Picture Book Award shortlist, for *The House Cat;* Kate Greenaway Medal, 1997, Gold Award in Best Toy Awards book section, *Right Start* magazine, and *Parents* magazine Play and Learn Award, all for *The Baby Who Wouldn't Go to Bed;* Kate Greenaway Medal, 1998, and Kurt Maschler Award shortlist, both for *Pumpkin Soup*; Kate Greenaway Medal shortlist, and Norfolk Libraries Children's Book Award shortlist, both for *Tatty Ratty.*

Writings

Sandmare, illustrated by husband, Ted Dewan, Young Corgi (London, England), 2001.

SELF-ILLUSTRATED

Kit and the Magic Kite, Hamish Hamilton (London, England), 1987.
(With Moira Miller) *Lucy and the Egg Witch,* Hamish Hamilton (London, England), 1989.
Ella and the Rabbit, Crocodile Books (Northampton, MA), 1990.
Chestnut Grey: A Folktale from Russia, Francis Lincoln (London, England), 1993.
The Bear under the Stairs, Dial (New York, NY), 1993.
The House Cat, Scholastic (New York, NY), 1993.
The Tale of Bear; The Tale of Duck; The Tale of Pig; The Tale of Frog (board books), Doubleday (New York, NY), 1994.
Little Monster Did It!, Dial (New York, NY), 1995.
The Baby Who Wouldn't Go to Bed, Doubleday (London, England), 1996, published as *The Boy Who Wouldn't Go to Bed,* Dial (New York, NY), 1997.
Pumpkin Soup, Doubleday (London, England), 1998, Farrar, Straus (New York, NY), 1999.

Toy Tales, Young Corgi (London, England), 1999, Farrar, Straus (New York, NY), 2000.
Tatty Ratty, Doubleday (London, England), 2001.
A Pipkin of Pepper, Doubleday (London, England), 2004.

Cooper's books have been translated into over twenty languages, including Welsh.

ILLUSTRATOR

Saviour Pirotta, *Solomon's Secret,* Methuen/Dial (New York, NY), 1989.
Sally Grindley, editor, *Christmas Stories for the Very Young,* Kingfisher (London, England), 1990.
Eric Johns, *The Three Bears Lend a Hand,* Young Corgi (London, England), 1990.
Edward Lear, *The Owl and the Pussycat,* Hamish Hamilton (London, England), 1991.

Sidelights

A primarily self-taught artist, Helen Cooper has written and illustrated a number of well-received picture books that have been celebrated as much for their cadenced, flowing text as for Cooper's skilled artwork. Cooper reached the pinnacle of achievement for a British children's book illustrator with *The Baby Who Wouldn't Go to Bed,* which earned her the prestigious Kate Greenaway Medal in 1997. In awarding the medal to the book, which was published in the United States as *The Boy Who Wouldn't Go to Bed,* Lesley Sim, chair of the Youth Libraries Group judging panel, announced: "Cooper has created the ultimate reassuring bedtime picture book. With warm, subtle colors, and lyrical text, she beautifully captures the surreal, twilight world of a sleepy child. In awarding Helen this prize, we are celebrating the talent, determination and sheer hard work which has made her a major figure in the children's book world."

Cooper is unusual among her fellow author-illustrators in having learned most of what she knows by self-study of other artists' works, though she does cite Angela Lee as an influential art teacher from her school days. As an undergraduate majoring in music, Cooper was already showing a marked preference for self-study, choosing to read independently for her degree before traveling to London to take her final exams. After college, she decided to pursue her interest in children's-book illustration. When she could not locate a college that offered a specialized course in children's illustration, "I went to the library and found everything that I needed," she once recalled. She found children's librarians helpful in "talking me through their newest books and explaining why they thought some worked more successfully than others." Interlibrary loans helped Cooper pursue bibliographical references on more specialized topics. "It was all an excellent fast track to knowledge of the children's book market. And it worked. I had my first book, *Kit and the Magic Kite,* accepted for publication in 1986."

Cooper claims that neither the text nor the art generally come easily for her, though a job in a factory painting animals on china, undertaken while she was still an undergraduate, helped her gain facility with paint and brush. "It took me longer to learn how to write," Cooper confessed to Geraldine Brennan in an interview in the *Times Educational Supplement*. "Writing a picture book text feels like writing haiku, having to be so concise. I learned to use rhythm, rhyme, and onomatopoeia partly to draw the child into the text and partly to give me a structure. The hard thing was discovering that any writing I really like was descriptive and it had to go. Now I find color and texture easy, but I still struggle with drawing. I start by drawing very small, to work myself into the idea."

Cooper drew on her love of animals to create *Kit and the Magic Kite*, the tale of a cat that finds an abandoned kite in a tree and uses it to escape into a series of adventures. First Kit tries his paw as a tough alley cat but fails miserably, because his previous soft life has not prepared him for the rigors of street existence. Nor do Kit's pampered ways give him any idea of what to expect when he becomes a ship's mascot or a witch's companion. Kit enjoys boasting of his adventures, however, when he returns home. Evaluating the book in *Growing Point*, Margery Fisher praised the author for her "bright, brisk sequence of pictures," proclaiming the work "as attractive as it is entertaining." Writing in the *Times Educational Supplement*, Jenny Marshal noted the "charming" illustrations.

The year 1993 was a banner one for Cooper: it marked the release of three of her most acclaimed works: *Chestnut Grey: A Folktale from Russia, The House Cat,* and *The Bear under the Stairs. Chestnut Grey* is a retelling of a Russian folktale in which the youngest son outperforms his older brothers by taming and befriending a magic horse that enables him to win the hand of a princess. Writing in *School Librarian*, G.B. Harrison praised the "elegant economy" of the author's story line and the "stylish draftsmanship and composition of the illustrations." Echoing these sentiments, *Junior Bookshelf* critic Marcus Crouch praised *Chestnut Grey* as a "richly satisfying" story offering pictures that are "drawn with great assurance and a strong feeling" for the period.

Returning to a subject that inspired her initial picture book success, Cooper offers another dose of feline humor in *The House Cat*. In this story, Tom Cat belongs to the house, even though the families living there both think of him as their cat. When one family moves and takes Tom Cat along, he escapes and has a series of harrowing adventures before returning to the familiar old homestead. Of course, both old and new tenants continue to think Tom belongs to them. *School Library Journal* contributor Beth Irish praised Cooper's "rich watercolor illustrations and brief text" for capturing "the loneliness and displacement moving can bring about and the comfort of the familiar."

Casting about for a topic for her next book, Cooper took the advice of a friend who told her to try to recall her own early childhood. "I thought back to the hungry lion who lived under my stairs when I was three," Cooper recalled. "Then I sat down and wrote *The Bear under the Stairs.*" In actuality, the process of composition was a bit more complicated than Cooper's brief summary suggests, as Jane Doonan explained in a *Books for Keeps* profile. The lion started out as an imaginary pet for young Cooper, but eventually got so big from being fed Smarties and cabbage leaves that Cooper grew scared of him. When she later decided to record her childhood experience in a book, "she did not intend to have the animal represented at all, in case it frightened children," according to Doonan. "But she also knew that as an idea for a picture book it somehow didn't work, so the manuscript went into a drawer. Then in 1990 she illustrated Stephen Gammell's text, 'Wake up, Bear . . . It's Christmas' in *Christmas Stories for the Very Young*. . . . She enjoyed drawing the bear so much she just had to find a story for it. So, she opened the drawer and there it was."

The Bear under the Stairs, Doonan noted, can be read on two levels. On the literal level it is the humorously absurd story of a bear who invites himself to stay in a family's house. From another point of view, however—that of William, the child who is afraid of bears and the dark cupboard under the stairs—it is a potentially scary tale of a boy who, like the bear, has an active imagination. Doonan maintained that William and the bear are like two sides of the same character. "William and the bear seamlessly exchange roles as hero, villain, perpetrator, and victim, depending on where we do our viewing from—inside or outside the cupboard."

Throughout the book, the art serves to emphasize the mood of the story. Doonan pointed out that readers first see William "on a small scale, from behind, climbing a darkened staircase, which curves from right to left. The banisters throw shadows of bars on his body, as if caging him in fear. His form moves away from us literally, and because of the orientation of the staircase, he appears to be turning in on himself." Doonan commended Cooper for her acute insight into the characteristics of young minds and her sense of how much they can handle. "Just how Helen Cooper manages to find equivalencies for fear and the strategies we devise for handling it, without giving her young viewers a terrible dose of the horrors, is a tribute to her skill with picture book form." The light tone of the text, for example, "plays a key role in counter-balancing the seriousness of the theme."

Other critics echoed Doonan's enthusiasm. "With elegant simplicity Helen Cooper has constructed a text admirably suited to the picture-book genre," asserted Mary M. Burns in *Horn Book*, while a *Junior Bookshelf* reviewer raved: "Cooper's beautifully and evocatively illustrated book is a gem." A *Publishers Weekly* com-

mentator maintained that Cooper's "sunny approach . . . is bolstered by deft use of light and shadow."

In her next two books, Cooper takes on two fairly common subjects in children's literature—favorite stuffed toys, and sibling rivalry—but manages to give each a fresh new twist. In *The Tale of Bear,* one of a series of four board books, Bear goes wherever Tim goes. Bear, a stuffed toy, worries that as he gets scruffier, especially after being put in the washing machine by mistake, Tim may not like him as much. Yet nothing could be farther from the truth. A *Junior Bookshelf* reviewer called *The Tale of Bear* an "enchanting story." In *Little Monster Did It!* the prospective parents of a new baby buy toddler daughter Amy a stuffed monster to care for, in hopes that the toy will alleviate some of the inevitable jealously Amy will feel watching the new baby receive so much attention. "Little Monster," however, is the one that proves to be not at all pleased by the arrival of the baby, and wreaks comic havoc throughout the household to make his feelings known. "Warm watercolors show Amy and Little Monster as irrepressible partners in crime," noted a *Kirkus Reviews* critic, who added that the book "stand[s] out from the pack of sibling rivalry books on the strength of the appealing artwork, Amy's conflicting feelings, and a great twist at the end." Elizabeth Bush, writing in the *Bulletin of the Center for Children's Books,* remarked: "The darkish, densely textured watercolors of the petulant toddler, cheerfully passive baby, and exhausted, befuddled parents have a cozy credibility that makes all this lunacy plausible as well as enjoyable." London *Guardian* reviewer Sarah Harrington deemed Cooper's "stunning picture book" "a delight to read."

The idea for *The Baby Who Wouldn't Go to Bed* "came from watching a friend's daughter playing with a toy pedal car," Cooper once recalled. "It struck me that the image of a baby driving along a wide open road would be a lovely symbol of childhood imagination and adventure." The text took the author only two hours to write down once she had the opening lines: "'Bedtime!' said the Mother. 'No!' said the Baby." Yet it took another year for Cooper to complete her artwork for the story. She was inspired by a trip to Las Vegas, with its surreal architecture and unique imagery, which she found eminently suitable for a child's sleep-time fantasy.

The Baby Who Wouldn't Go to Bed was described as "wonderful. . . . A meaty book, with touches of brilliance," by Stephanie Nettell in *Books for Keeps.* Cooper's pictures "handily move between the pedestrian reality of the boy's home hallway to the fantastical roadway of his bedtime journey," commented Janice M. Del Negro in a review for the *Bulletin of the Center for Children's Books.* Noting the "looming toilet" in the boy's bathroom, a *Publishers Weekly* reviewer observed that Cooper "exhibits a visual wit that keeps her pictures from lapsing into self-conscious prettiness."

Cooper's *Pumpkin Soup* met with similar praise, and was awarded a Kate Greenaway medal. In the story, Cat, Squirrel, and Duck are making soup together, and each has a specific job. When Duck wants to switch tasks, the friends get into a terrible argument and Duck leaves angrily. The other two realize, however, that the soup is just not the same without Duck, and worry about where he might have gone; when Duck eventually comes home they greet him excitedly and give him a big welcome. "Cooper's richly colored illustrations . . . suggest a sense of security," wrote Kay Weisman in *Booklist,* noting that readers will feel confident that everything will turn out right in the end. A *Publishers Weekly* critic commented, "children will be able to laugh at this trio . . . and recognize that true friendship can weather most any storm."

The three friends return in *A Pipkin of Pepper,* in which they realize that they must go into the city to retrieve the appropriate spices for their famous soup. Duck manages to get separated from his friends, and it is only with the help of a kindly mother hen that he can retrace his steps and be reunited with his companions. Jennifer Mattson, in *Booklist,* noted the book's "folksy paintings in spice-cabinet colors and a text that sparkles brightest when read aloud," while a *Kirkus Reviews* contributor commented that *A Pipkin of Pepper* is "at least as charming" as *Pumpkin Soup* and deemed the author's "glowing pictures . . . both gorgeous and delightful." Noting that the message may come across as heavy to some, Julia Eccleshare wrote in the London *Guardian* that "Duck's terrors in a landscape of skyscraping pepperpots is a visual treat that far outweighs any moralising."

Tatty Ratty returns Cooper to her stuffed-animal themes, but this time, the tale is of young Molly who has lost her favorite stuffed rabbit, Tatty Ratty. In order to comfort Molly, her parents make up stories of the adventures Tatty Ratty is having as he tries to get home to Molly. As he meets characters from fairy tales, battles fierce pirates, and makes friends with a dragon, Tatty Ratty also finds himself being restored and made good as new. When Molly's parents take her to the toy shop to "find" her lost companion, the fact that he looks different does not fool Molly—she knows she and her beloved toy have been reunited. "This is a wise and respectful tribute to children's storytelling power," wrote a *Publishers Weekly* critic. According to Joy Fleishhacker in *School Library Journal,* "Cooper presents a common dilemma and then allows her protagonist to confront the problem by using her imagination." A *Kirkus Reviews* contributor commented that "whimsical illustrations depict the dual story of Tatty Ratty's adventures and Molly's life at home," giving young readers both sides of the story. "Cooper creates two wonderful worlds: one where comforting parents take a child's concerns seriously, and a fairy-tale realm" of bunny adventures, noted *Booklist* contributor Ilene Cooper.

Along with her self-illustrated titles, Cooper has also collaborated with her husband, author/illustrator Ted

Dewan, in *Sandmare.* In the book, Polly wishes that the horse she draws with her father in the sand could run free, like a real horse. The horse wishes it as well, and soon, the magical creature rises from the sand and gallops across the dunes. Sandmare knows there is a chance that her image will get washed up as the tide changes, putting an end to her adventures. Reunited with Polly, the two try to solve the dilemma so that Sandmare can always run free. "Young readers will happily curl up to read each chapter in this creative tale," assured a critic for *Kirkus Reviews.* Diane Foote, writing in *Booklist,* noted that "Beach buffs, horse lovers, and fantasy fans will enjoy this light, fantastical story."

On her home page, Cooper commented about the differences she has observed between writing and illustrating children's books. "I write my stories quite quickly, sometimes it takes me a morning and sometimes two weeks. The pictures take a year to draw and paint." When explaining what she likes best about being a children's illustrator, she responded: "That I can explore my own preoccupations within my books and that I can listen to the radio or my favorite music while I work."

"Children's perception of the world fascinates me," Cooper once told *SATA.* "The blurred hinterland where fantasy and reality meet, where bears live under the stairs, and toys have lives of their own. . . . Sibling rivalry, fear of the dark, secret fears that niggle in the back of the brain. . . . Children have these fears a lot, and build them up into huge problems. Books are a way of finding solutions."

Biographical and Critical Sources

PERIODICALS

Booklist, August, 1993, p. 1898; September 1, 1999, Kay Weisman, review of *Pumpkin Soup,* p. 147; February 15, 2002, Ilene Cooper, review of *Tatty Ratty,* p. 1019; May 1, 2003, Diane Foote, review of *Sandmare,* p. 1591; August, 2005, Jennifer Mattson, review of *A Pipkin of Pepper,* p. 2033.

Books for Keeps, May, 1993, p. 35; May, 1994, pp. 4-5, 7; July, 1995, p. 7; September, 1996, Stephanie Nettell, review of *The Baby Who Wouldn't Go to Bed,* p. 32.

Bulletin of the Center for Children's Books, May, 1996, Elizabeth Bush, review of *Little Monster Did It!,* p. 297; September, 1997, Janice M. Del Negro, review of *The Boy Who Wouldn't Go to Bed,* p. 8; April, 2003, review of *Sandmare,* p. 309.

Carousel, winter, 1997, p. 18.

Christian Parenting Today, July, 2001, Carla Barnhill, review of *The Boy Who Wouldn't Go to Bed,* p. 52.

Growing Point, September, 1987, Margery Fisher, review of *Kit and the Magic Kite,* p. 4866.

Guardian (London, England), April 25, 2000, Sarah Harrington, review of *Little Monster Did It!*; October 23, 2004, Julia Eccleshare, review of *A Pipkin of Pepper.*

Horn Book, May-June, 1993, Mary M. Burns, review of *The Bear under the Stairs,* pp. 313-314.

Junior Bookshelf, April, 1993, Marcus Crouch, review of *Chestnut Gray,* p. 57; August, 1993, p. 127; February, 1995, p. 8.

Kirkus Reviews, May 15, 1996, review of *Little Monster Did It!,* p. 743; February 1, 2002, review of *Tatty Ratty,* p. 178; January 1, 2003, review of *Sandmare,* p. 141; September 1, 2005, review of *A Pipkin of Pepper,* p. 970.

Library Media Connection, October, 2003, Kim Sutherland, review of *Sandmare,* p. 56.

Publishers Weekly, June 14, 1993, review of *The Bear under the Stairs,* p. 68; May 12, 1997, review of *The Boy Who Wouldn't Go to Bed,* p. 75; November 1, 1999, review of *Pumpkin Soup,* p. 83; December 24, 2001, review of *Tatty Ratty,* p. 63; January 6, 2003, review of *Sandmare,* p. 60.

Reading Teacher, October, 2003, review of *Tatty Ratty,* p. 167.

School Librarian, February, 1991, p. 18; May, 1993, G.B. Harrison, review of *Chestnut Gray,* p. 54; spring, 2002, review of *Tatty Ratty* and *Sandmare,* p. 17.

School Library Journal, January, 1995, Beth Irish, review of *The House Cat,* p. 83; July, 1996, p. 58; September, 1999, Gay Lynn Van Vleck, review of *Pumpkin Soup,* p. 179; April, 2002, Joy Fleishhacker, review of *Tatty Ratty,* p. 102; July, 2003, Shara Alpern, review of *Sandmare,* p. 89; September, 2005, Rosalyn Pierini, review of *A Pipkin of Pepper,* p. 168.

Times Educational Supplement, June 5, 1987, Jenny Marshal, review of *Kit and the Magic Kite,* p. 62; January 31, 1997, Geraldine Brennan, interview with Cooper, p. R7.

ONLINE

Helen Cooper Home Page, http://www.wormworks.com/helenpages (March 29, 2006).

*   *   *

COSENTINO, Ralph

Personal

Born in New York, NY; son of flamenco dancers; married; wife's name Lisa; children: three. *Ethnicity:* "Argentine."

Addresses

Home—OH. *Agent*—c/o Author Mail, Viking, Penguin Putnam, 375 Hudson St., New York, NY 10014. *E-mail*—Ralph@ralphcosentino.com.

Career

Comic-book writer and illustrator, author, and toymaker. U.F.O. (Unidentified Fun Object) Toys, founder and designer; creator figurines, including Black Terror, Kaiju Kids, Honk-Honk-Ashoo, and Funboy.

The Story of Honk-Honk-Ashoo and Swella-Bow-Wow *introduces Ralph Cosentino's whimsical characters to the toddler set.*

Writings

SELF-ILLUSTRATED

The Story of Honk-Honk-Ashoo and Swella-Bow-Wow, Viking (New York, NY), 2005.
The Marvelous Misadventures of Fun-Boy, Viking (New York, NY), 2006.

Work in Progress

A comic-book series called *The Black Terror,* based on the character created by Richard E. Hughes and Don Gabrielson and featured in *Exciting Comics* issue 9, 1942.

Sidelights

While growing up in New York City, Ralph Cosentino became a huge fan of superhero comics. As a writer, illustrator, and toy designer, his passion for the amuse-ments of childhood have not waned; Cosentino is the founder of U.F.O Toys, has designed a number of Japanese-inspired figurines, and has published two children's books based on his creations: the picture book *The Story of Honk-Honk-Ashoo and Swella-Bow-Wow* and the wordless *The Marvelous Misadventures of Fun-Boy.*

In *The Story of Honk-Honk-Ashoo and Swella-Bow-Wow,* Honk-Honk-Ashoo—who has a pillow for a head—finds a little lost dog sitting on his doorstep one day. After calling the dogcatcher to come take the pup away, Honk-Honk-Ashoo cannot get the lost puppy out of his thoughts. Honk-Honk-Ashoo finally decides to take action, and he adopts the dog himself. Upon returning at home with his newfound friend he decides to name the little pup Swella-Bow-Wow after a friend calls the pooch marvelous. Marge Loch-Wouters, writing in *School Library Journal,* stated that Cosentino's book presents readers with "a fine story about friendship and finding the place where you belong," while a

Kirkus Reviews critic deemed *The Story of Honk-Honk-Ashoo and Swella-Bow-Wow* "a tender tale of togetherness."

Biographical and Critical Sources

PERIODICALS

Kirkus Reviews, December 15, 2004, *The Story of Honk-Honk-Ashoo and Swella-Bow-Wow*, p. 1199.
Publishers Weekly, January 31, 2005, review of *The Story of Honk-Honk-Ashoo and Swella-Bow-Wow*, p. 66.
School Library Journal, February, 2005, Marge Loch-Wouters, review of *The Story of Honk-Honk-Ashoo and Swella-Bow-Wow*, p. 96.

ONLINE

Toi Protocol Web site, http://www.toiprotocol.com/ (February 24, 2006).
Toy Toons Web site, http://www.figures.com/ (February 24, 2006), interview with Cosentino.
Honk-Honk-Ashoo Web site, http://www.honkhonkashoo.com/ (February 24, 2006).*

*   *   *

CREBBIN, June 1938-

Personal

Born May 26, 1938, in Birstall, Leicestershire, England; married; husband's name John (a teacher); children: Peter, Philip. *Education:* Attended Dudley Training College. *Hobbies and other interests:* Walking, reading, horseback riding, theater-going, "looking after my rabbit."

Addresses

Home—Ivy Cottage, 13 Perseverance Rd., Birstall, Leicestershire LE4 4AU, England. *Agent*—c/o Author Mail, Walker Books, 87 Vauxhall Walk, London SE11 5HJ, England.

Career

Worked as a teacher in Leicestershire, England, 1960-90, Yorkshire, England, 1962-64, and Kalamazoo, MI, 1965-66. Has also worked as a supply teacher for primary grades, and lecturer and workshop leader for both primary and adult students.

Member

Society of Authors (committee member), Poetry Society.

Awards, Honors

Book of the Year citation, 1989, and 1993, both for *Fly-by-Night* and *Carrie Climbs a Mountain*.

Writings

The Jungle Sale (poems), illustrated by Thelma Lambert, Viking Kestrel (London, England), 1988.
Finders Keepers, Viking Kestrel (London, England), 1989.
Ride to the Rescue, illustrated by Catherine Bradbury, Viking Kestrel (London, England), 1989.
(Editor) *Best Friends* (stories and poems), illustrated by Julie Park, Dent (London, England), 1990.
Toby's Bark, illustrated by Teresa O'Brien, Dent (London, England), 1991.
The Dinosaur's Dinner (poems), illustrated by Thelma Lambert, Viking (London, England), 1992.
Fly-by-Night, illustrated by Stephen Lambert, Walker (London, England), 1993.
Carrie Climbs a Mountain, illustrated by Thelma Lambert, Walker (London, England), 1993.
Cows Moo, Cars Toot: Poems about Town and Country, illustrated by Anthony Lewis, Viking (London, England), 1995.
Danny's Duck, illustrated by Clara Vulliamy, Candlewick Press (Cambridge, MA), 1995.
The Train Ride, illustrated by Stephen Lambert, Candlewick Press (Cambridge, MA), 1995.
Into the Castle, illustrated by John Bendall-Brunello, Candlewick Press (Cambridge, MA), 1996.
Don't Be Late!, illustrated by Peter Kavanagh, Cambridge University Press (Cambridge, England), 1996.
The Dog Show, illustrated by Peter Kavanagh, Cambridge University Press (Cambridge, England), 1996.
The Pyjama Party, illustrated by Peter Kavanagh, Cambridge University Press (Cambridge, England), 1996.
Spike and the Concert, illustrated by Peter Kavanagh, Cambridge University Press (Cambridge, England), 1996.
Cutting and Sticking, illustrated by Peter Kavanagh, Cambridge University Press (Cambridge, England), 1996.
The Flying Football, illustrated by Susan Hellard, Cambridge University Press (Cambridge, England), 1997, Candlewick Press (Cambridge, MA), 2004.
Apples!, illustrated by Susan Hellard, Cambridge University Press (Cambridge, England), 1997.
Granny's Teeth, illustrated by Susan Hellard, Cambridge University Press (Cambridge, England), 1997.
Wrigglebottom, illustrated by Susan Hellard, Cambridge University Press (Cambridge, England), 1997.
Nibbles, illustrated by Susan Hellard, Cambridge University Press (Cambridge, England), 1997.
The Puppy Chase, illustrated by Susan Hellard, Cambridge University Press (Cambridge, England), 1997.
Cows in the Kitchen, illustrated by Katharine McEwen, Candlewick Press (Cambridge, MA), 1998.
Emmelina and the Monster, illustrated by Tony Ross, Walker (London, England), 1998.
Snap-Happy Annie, illustrated by Emily Bolam, Viking (London, England), 1999.
(Editor) *The Puffin Book of Fantastic First Poems*, Puffin (London, England), 1999.
Tarquin the Wonder Horse, illustrated by Tony Ross, Walker (London, England), 2000.
Dinnertime Rhyme, illustrated by Ana Martin Larranaga, Walker (London, England), 2001.

My Dog, illustrated by Russell Ayto, Walker (London, England), 2001.

In My Pocket, illustrated by Katharine McEwen, Walker (London, England), 2001.

No Tights for George!, illustrated by Tony Ross, Walker (London, England), 2002.

The Dragon Test, illustrated by Polly Dunbar, Walker (London, England), 2003.

Hal the Highwayman, illustrated by Polly Dunbar, Walker (London, England), 2003.

Hal the Pirate, illustrated by Polly Dunbar, Walker (London, England), 2004.

Lucy and the Firestone, illustrated by Polly Dunbar, Walker (London, England), 2004.

Jumping Beany, Walker (London, England), 2004.

(Editor) *Horse Tales,* illustrated by Inga Moore, Candlewick Press (Cambridge, MA), 2005.

The Crocodile Is Coming!, illustrated by Mini Grey, Walker (London, England), 2005.

The King's Shopping, illustrated by Warwick Johnson Cadwell, Walker (London, England), 2005.

Dinnertime Rhyme Jigsaw Book, illustrated by Ana Martin Larranaga, Walker (London, England), 2006.

Editor of anthologies, including *Walker Book of School Stories, Walker Book of Stunning Stories,* and *Walker Book of Adventure Stories.* Contributor of poems to *New Poetry, Poetry Nottingham, Charnwood Writers,* and *The North,* some of which have been broadcast on radio program *Pen to Paper,* BBC Radio North West; contributor of articles to *Junior Education.*

Author's books have been translated into Spanish.

Sidelights

June Crebbin worked as a teacher in both her native England and in Kalamazoo, Michigan, for three decades before retiring to begin her second career as a children's writer in 1990. As she once told *SATA,* in 1986, while still teaching full time, she began work on her first book, the poetry collection *The Jungle Sale,* using her eight-and nine-year-old students as a sounding board before sending her manuscript to London-based publisher Viking. *The Jungle Sale* was published in 1988, and Crebbin has gone on to amass a long list of other published books, among them *The Train Ride, Cows in the Kitchen,* and several fiction anthologies. Containing fourteen tales that focus on one of the author's long-time loves—horses—*Horse Tales* introduces notable steeds from myth, folklore, and literature. Featuring stories by writers such as Marguerite Henry, Michael Morpurgo, and Anna Sewell, *Horse Tales* introduces readers to the fantastical unicorn; Bucephalus, the powerful steed Alexander the Great rode into battle; the beloved Black Beauty of Sewell's classic novel; and the pony protagonist of Henry's *Misty of Chincoteague,* among others. A *Kirkus Reviews* contributor dubbed the collection "a blue-ribbon winner," while in *School Library Journal* Carol Schene called Crebbin's collection an "excellently conceived" anthology that "captures all of the romance and majesty of horses and their riders."

Based on the song "Skip to My Lou," Crebbin's rollicking Cows in the Kitchen *finds the livestock taking over the house of Farmer Tom. (Illustration by Katharine McEwen.)*

Crebbin's original stories have been as popular with younger readers as have her anthologies. Featuring illustrations by Stephen Lambert, *Fly by Night* focuses on a fidgety owlet named Blink who awaits his first chance to stretch his wings and fly. A young girl shares a similar anticipation in *The Train Ride,* as she and her mother make their first trip to Grandmother's house. In *Booklist* Lauren Peterson noted that Crebbin's text in *The Train Ride* "simulates the gentle motion of the train," while a *Publishers Weekly* writer deemed the book a "sweet" story that "offers youngsters a nostalgic look at a favorite mode of transportation."

Featuring a rollicking text and animal sounds guaranteed to animate young listeners, Crebbin's *Cows in the Kitchen* finds a host of barnyard animals—from ducks and sheep to cows and horses—quietly invading Farmer Tom's home while the unsuspecting man naps in the barn's haystack. "The merriment of this mischievous book is contagious," noted a *Publishers Weekly* reviewer, the critic praising Crebbin's "clever pacing" and illustrator Katherine McEwen's "highly animated . . . cartoon drawings." In *Booklist,* Hazel Rochman predicted that the book's "bouncing repetitive chant" will captivate preschool listeners, while the storyline's focus on "domestic chaos"—sheep bounce on the sofa while ducks roost in the kitchen cupboards—guarantee the book a favored place in storyhour circles.

Discussing her work writing for children, Crebbin once explained to *SATA:* "Most of my stories and poems start with something I have seen or heard; sometimes in the classes I . . . [taught]; sometimes a memory of my own or my children's; sometimes, as in *Fly-by-Night,*

when I found a baby owl which had fallen out of its tree, an incident involving an animal. Then I build on that idea. It's very exciting. I like to get the shape of the writing exactly right.

"I write at home, which is a Victorian villa built in 1884, not in my study but usually wrapped in a blanket on the bed in the spare room. In summer I *always* write in the garden whenever the weather allows me. I need a walk at some point during the day. Sometimes I visit a nearby steam train station; sometimes the river; sometimes I walk across the fields to the shops. Then there is always the eternal problem of what to have for tea!

"I enjoy writing stories, poems, and picture books for children from ages three to eleven. I find the picture-book medium particularly challenging, combining, as it seems to me, the complexity of a story with the economy of a poem. The work of Philippa Pearce has influenced me greatly. Her book, *Tom's Midnight Garden,* is a classic.

"To aspiring writers I would say, 'Never give up'—the best advice I was ever given."

Biographical and Critical Sources

PERIODICALS

Booklist, May 15, 1995, Lauren Peterson, review of *The Train Ride,* p. 1651; June 1, 1995, Leone McDermott, review of *Danny's Duck,* p. 1783; August, 1996, Annie Ayres, review of *Into the Castle,* p. 1906; September 1, 2005, Carolyn Phelan, review of *Horse Tales,* p. 133.

Junior Bookshelf, August, 1989, p. 169; October, 1990, p. 228.

Kirkus Reviews, July 15, 2005, review of *Horse Tales,* p. 787.

Magpies, July, 1995, review of *The Train Ride,* p. 20; September, 1998, review of *Cows in the Kitchen,* p. 27, and *Emmelina and the Monster,* p. 33.

Publishers Weekly, May 24, 1993, review of *Fly by Night,* p. 84; May 29, 1995, review of *The Train Ride,* p. 83; July 13, 1998, review of *Cows in the Kitchen,* p. 76.

School Librarian, spring, 2000, review of *Snap-Happy Annie,* p. 18; summer, 2000, review of *The Puffin Book of Fantastic First Poems,* p. 95; summer, 2001, review of *Tarquin the Wonder Horse,* p. 80; winter, 2004, Sarah Jupe, review of *Hal the Pirate,* p. 186.

School Library Journal, November, 1989, p. 150; April, 1993, p. 94; May, 1995, Ruth Semrau, review of *Danny's Duck,* p. 83; October, 1995, Carole D. Fiore, review of *The Train Ride,* p. 97; April, 1996, Helen Rosenberg, review of *Into the Castle,* p. 106; August, 2005, Carol Schene, review of *Horse Tales,* p. 126.

Times Educational Supplement, December 16, 1988, p. 20.

ONLINE

Walker Books Web site, http://www.walkerbooks.co.uk/ (March 27, 2006), "June Crebbin."

D-E

DARLING, Sandra Louise Woodward
See DAY, Alexandra

*   *   *

DAVIS, Donald 1944-
(Donald D. Davis)

Personal
Born June 1, 1944, in Waynesville, NC; son of Joseph (a banker) and Lucille (a teacher; maiden name, Walker) Davis; married Merle Smith (a teacher), April 16, 1992; children: Douglas, Patrick, Kelly, Jonathan. *Ethnicity:* "Caucasian" *Education:* Davidson College, B.A., 1966; Duke University, M.Div., 1969.

Addresses
Home and office—Storyteller, Inc., P.O. Box 397, Ocracoke Island, NC 27960. *E-mail*—donald@ddavisstoryteller.com.

Career
Christ United Methodist Church, High Point, NC, minister, 1967-89; storyteller, lecturer, and writer, 1967—. Has appeared at numerous storytelling festivals, conferences, and teachers' workshops in United States and abroad, including National Storytelling Festival, Sierra Storytelling Festival, and Three Apples Storytelling Festival.

Member
National Association for the Preservation and Perpetuation of Storytelling (member of board of directors, 1982-89; board chair, 1983-89).

Awards, Honors
Anne Izard Storyteller's Choice Award, 1992, for *Listening for the Crack of Dawn,* and 1994, for *Jack Always Seeks His Fortune;* D.H.L., La Grange College, 1994; selected for "Circle of Excellence" by National Storytelling Association, 1996; South Carolina Middle-School Young Reader's Award, for *Listening for the Crack of Dawn;* Storytelling World awards, for *Big-Screen Drive-In Theater, Father Was a Wise Old Man,* and *Grand Canyon.*

Writings

RECORDED STORIES

Storytelling Festival, two volumes, National Association for the Preservation and Perpetuation of Storytelling, 1983.
(With Pat Floyd) *Old Testament Stories to Hear and Tell,* Graded Press (Nashville, TN), 1983.
Live and Learn, Weston Woods (New York, NY), 1984.
Jack Tales: More than a Beanstalk, Weston Woods (New York, NY), 1985.
Listening for the Crack of Dawn, August House (Little Rock, AR), 1991.
Rainy Weather, August House (Little Rock, AR), 1992.
Jack's First Job, August House (Little Rock, AR), 1992.
Uncle Frank Invents the Electron Microphone, August House (Little Rock, AR), 1992.
Party People, August House (Little Rock, AR), 1993.
Miss Daisy, August House (Little Rock, AR), 1993.
Christmas at Grandma's, August House (Little Rock, AR), 1994.
The Southern Bells, August House (Little Rock, AR), 1994.
Jack's First Job, August House Audio (Little Rock, IL), 1994.
Walking through Sulphur Springs, August House (Little Rock, AR), 1995.
Jack and the Animals: An Appalachian Folktale, August House (Little Rock, AR), 1995.
Grandma's Lap Stories, August House (Little Rock, AR), 1995.
Mrs. Rosemary's Kindergarten, August House (Little Rock, AR), 1995.

See Rock City, August House (Little Rock, AR), 1996.

Big-Screen Drive-In Theater, August House (Little Rock, AR), 1996.

Stanley Easter, August House (Little Rock, AR), 1997.

Jack and Granny Ugly, August House (Little Rock, AR), 1997.

Dr. York, Miss Winnie, and the Typhoid Shot, August House (Little Rock, AR), 1997.

Grand Canyon, August House Audio (Little Rock, IL), 1998.

Braces, August House Audio (Little Rock, AR), 1999.

Grandma's Boy, August House Audio (Little Rock, IL), 1999.

Ride the Butterflies, August House Audio (Little Rock, IL), 2000.

Father Was a Wise Old Man, August House Audio (Little Rock, IL), 2001.

Room of My Own, August House Audio (Little Rock, IL), 2002.

Mama Learns to Drive, August House (Little Rock, AR), 2005.

FOR CHILDREN; BASED ON RECORDED STORIES

Listening for the Crack of Dawn, August House (Little Rock, AR), 1990.

Barking at a Fox-Fur Coat, August House (Little Rock, AR), 1991.

Jack Always Seeks His Fortune: Authentic Appalachian Jack Tales, August House (Little Rock, AR), 1992, published as *Southern Jack Tales,* 1997.

Jack and the Animals: An Appalachian Folktale, illustrated by Kitty Harvill, August House (Little Rock, AR), 1995.

The Pig Who Went Home on Sunday: An Appalachian Folktale, illustrated by Jennifer Mazzucco, August House (Little Rock, AR), 2001.

Mama Learns to Drive, and Other Stories: Stories of Love, Humor, and Wisdom, August House (Little Rock, AR), 2005.

Christmas at Grandma's, August House (Little Rock, AR), 2005.

OTHER

My Lucky Day: Stories of a Southern Appalachian Storyteller (memoir), Johnson Publishing (Chicago, IL), 1984.

Telling Your Own Stories: A Guide to Family, Classroom, and Personal Storytelling, August House (Little Rock, AR), 1993, revised as *Telling Your Arkansas Stories,* 2002.

Thirteen Miles from Suncrest (novel), August House (Little Rock, AR), 1994.

See Rock City: A Story Journey through Appalachia, August House (Little Rock, AR), 1996.

Writing as a Second Language, August House (Little Rock, AR), 2002.

Also author of *My Uncle Frank Used to Say.* Contributor to books, including *Jack in Two Worlds,* edited by William Bernard McCarthy, University of North Caro-

lina Press (Chapel Hill, NC), 1994. Contributor to periodicals, including *Utne Reader, Teacher, Parenting, Time,* and *Mother Earth News.*

Sidelights

Although he has published books for adults and children, Donald Davis considers himself foremost a storyteller. Born in the mountainous region of western North Carolina in 1944, Davis told Robert Jordan of the *Winston-Salem Journal* that storytelling was an element of his daily life while growing up, particularly as part of his relationship with his Grandma Walker. "My grandmother did lots of telling," Davis recalled. "I remember hearing those stories, and I remember by the time I was in the second grade telling other kids in school stories I'd heard my grandmother tell." Among those stories are those he retells in such works as *The Pig Who Went Home on Sunday: An Appalachian Folktale,* a home-grown version of "The Three Little Pigs" that *School Library Journal* contributor Linda M. Kenton praised as "a readable story with just the right amount of repetition for sharing aloud."

Davis's storytelling has led to several successful publishing outlets, including CDs, tapes, and videos. Among the dozens of recorded works Davis has created are several that feature the ubiquitous fairy-tale figure of Jack. Well-known from such stories and nursery rhymes as "Jack and the Beanstalk" and "Jack and Jill," this teenaged hero stars in *Jack's First Job* and *Jack and Granny Ugly.* Retold as part of the Appalachian oral tradition, Davis's rich versions of various classic tales incorporating this Everyman figure, the "Jack" stories demonstrate the importance of humor and the endearing, universal qualities of an adolescent character.

Jack also appears in the stories Davis has collected in book form. In *Jack and the Animals* Davis sets his version of the Grimm Brothers' tale "The Bremen Town Musicians" in the Appalachian Mountains. Using simple, direct language, he recounts how the kindhearted Jack adopts five animals, all of whom seem to have outgrown their usefulness. He happens upon an aging cow, for example, and learns that she can no longer produce milk. She and the other animals join Jack on his travels in search of fortune. When the group happens upon a band of robbers, Jack and these formerly valueless creatures foil the evildoer's lawless plot and save the day.

Several of Davis's writings are based on personal sources. In his novel *Thirteen Miles from Suncrest,* he presents a slice-of-life story set in the mountains of North Carolina early in the twentieth century. The story's narrator, Medford Henry McGee, was born in the year 1900, and in a journal given him on his tenth birthday, he chronicles his experiences between the years 1910 and 1913, recording the gradual encroachment of the "modern world" into the western regions of North Carolina. Judy Sokoll, writing in *School Library Jour-*

nal, observed that "Medford is a captivating narrator—sensitive, trusting, loving, natural, and filled with wide-eyed curiosity about the world. All of the characters are wonderfully created and the sense of a simpler time is masterfully crafted." A *Publishers Weekly* critic likewise praised the work, noting that "the novel's themes—hardship and tragedy set against the strength and beauty of family love—prove affecting and timeless."

See Rock City: A Story Journey through Appalachia represents another of Davis's forays into the history of his native North Carolina. Transporting readers back to 1948, the year Davis entered kindergarten, the book follows the author's life and the tales of his family through his second year of college. Audiobooks such as *Braces* and *Grandma's Boy* also draw from the narrator's youth, telling coming-of-age stories that focus on a boy growing up in a close-knit, multigenerational family. *Mama Learns to Drive*—which like many of Davis's works was produced both in an audio and print version—returns readers to the 1950s, as Davis introduces his Appalachian-born mother and contrasts her willingness to embrace life's challenges as a young woman with his more recent recollections of her elder years. Discussing the eight vignettes recorded in the book version, published as *Mama Learns to Drive, and Other Stories: Stories of Love, Humor, and Wisdom,* Susan Hepler wrote in *School Library Journal* that readers will "envy" Davis's "freedom and the coziness of his family life, school and community," and a *Publishers Weekly* contributor praised *Grandma's Boy,* noting that "consummate story teller Davis" uses "plenty of down-home warmth and humor" to recount his visits, as a boy, to his grandmother's rural home in the hills of North Carolina.

As Davis mines the tales of his life, retells the classic stories of the past, and creates his own legends, his activities as a writer and traveling storyteller show no sign of slowing. In fact, he believes that both of these occupations are common aspects of life for everyone. As he told Jordan in the *Winston-Salem Journal,* "Any time you tell somebody about a place you've been that you wish they could go, you're telling a story. A lot of it is just realizing that it is a very natural process."

Biographical and Critical Sources

PERIODICALS

Booklist, September 15, 1994, p. 111; October 1, 1995, p. 322; April 15, 2000, Lolly Gepson, reviews of *Grandma's Boy* and *Braces,* p. 1560; August, 2005, Gillian Engberg, review of *Mama Learns to Drive, and Other Stories: Stories of Love, Humor, and Wisdom,* p. 2026.

Kirkus Reviews, July 1, 1994, p. 864; April 15, 1999, Lolly Gepson, review of *Braces* and *Grandma's Boy,* p. 1560; July 1, 2004, review of *The Pig Who Went Home on Sunday: An Appalachian Folk Tale,* p. 626.

Publishers Weekly, August 8, 1994, review of *Thirteen Miles from Suncrest,* p. 380; October 11, 1999, review of *Grandma's Boy,* p. 30; July 12, 2004, review of *The Pig Who Went Home on Sunday,* p. 62.

School Library Journal, January, 1995, Judy Sokoll, review of *Thirteen Miles from Suncrest,* p. 183; January, 1996, p. 100; September, 1996, p. 240; August, 2004, Lina M. Kenton, review of *The Pig Who Went Home on Sunday,* p. 106.

Winston-Salem Journal, November 24, 1995, article by Robert Jordan, pp. C9-C10.

ONLINE

Call of Story Web site, http://www.callofstory.org/ (April 27, 2006), "Donald Davis."

Donald Davis Home Page, http://www.ddavisstoryteller.com (April 15, 2006).*

*   *   *

DAVIS, Donald D.
See DAVIS, Donald

*   *   *

DAY, Alexandra 1941-
(Sandra Louise Woodward Darling)

Personal

Born September 7, 1941, in Cincinnati, OH; daughter of Charles Lawson (an artist) and Esther Grace (a homemaker; maiden name, Claflin) Woodward; married Harold Darling (a cinema/bookstore owner and publisher), 1967; children: Sacheverell Austen, Rabindranath Tagore, Lafcadio Hearn, Christina Rossetti. *Education:* Swarthmore College, B.A., 1963; trained as an artist at Art Students' League (New York, NY), 1963-64. *Religion:* Episcopalian. *Hobbies and other interests:* Fashion design and dressmaking.

Addresses

Home—3698 E. High La., Seattle, WA 98112. *Office*—Blue Lantern Studio, 4649 Sunnyside Ave. N., Seattle, WA 98103-6900. *E-mail*—aday@gooddogcarl.com.

Career

Fine artist, writer, illustrator, and book publisher. Freelance artist, 1965—; Green Tiger Press, San Diego, CA, founder and owner with husband, Harold Darling, and note cards and stationery designer, 1969-86; children's author and illustrator, 1983—; Blue Lantern Studio, San Diego, CA (after 1993 Seattle, WA), owner with H. Darling, 1986—, Laughing Elephant Publishing (gift-book and paper goods manufacturer), Seattle, co-founder, 1992—, creator of Darling & Co. imprint,

Alexandra Day

1999, reacquisition of Green Tiger Press from Simon & Schuster, 2004—. Young Men's Hebrew Association, New York, NY, former crafts teacher. *Exhibitions:* Work exhibited at Every Picture Tells a Story, Los Angeles, and Art of Illustration, Seattle.

Awards, Honors

Special mention, Children's Jury, Bologna Book Fair, and Children's Choice Award, International Reading Association/Children's Book Council, 1984, both for *The Teddy Bears' Picnic;* Parents' Choice Award for Illustration, 1984, for *The Blue Faience Hippopotamus.*

Writings

SELF-ILLUSTRATED; "CARL" SERIES

Good Dog, Carl, Green Tiger Press (San Diego, CA), 1985.
Carl Goes Shopping, Farrar, Straus (New York, NY), 1989.
Carl's Christmas, Farrar, Straus (New York, NY), 1990.
Carl's Afternoon in the Park, Farrar, Straus (New York, NY), 1991.
Carl's Masquerade, Farrar, Straus (New York, NY), 1992.
Carl Goes to Daycare, Farrar, Straus (New York, NY), 1993.
Carl Makes a Scrapbook, Farrar, Straus (New York, NY), 1994.
Carl Pops Up, includes illustrations by Vicki Teague Cooper, Simon & Schuster (New York, NY), 1994.
Carl's Birthday, Farrar, Straus (New York, NY), 1995.
Carl's Baby Journal, Farrar, Straus (New York, NY), 1996.
Follow Carl!, Farrar, Straus (New York, NY), 1998.
Carl's Sleepy Afternoon, Farrar, Straus (New York, NY), 2005.

Several "Carl" books have been translated into Spanish, Japanese, and French.

SELF-ILLUSTRATED

Frank and Ernest, Scholastic (New York, NY), 1988.
Paddy's Pay-Day, Viking (New York, NY), 1989.
Frank and Ernest Play Ball, Scholastic (New York, NY), 1990.
River Parade, Viking (New York, NY), 1990.
Frank and Ernest on the Road, Scholastic (New York, NY), 1994.
A Bouquet, Blue Lantern Studio (San Diego, CA), 1996.
(With Cooper Edens) *The Christmas We Moved to the Barn,* HarperCollins (New York, NY), 1997.
Boswell Wide Awake, Farrar, Straus (New York, NY), 1999.
(With Cooper Edens) *Darby, the Special Order Pup,* Penguin Putnam (New York, NY), 2000.
(With Cooper Edens) *Special Deliveries,* HarperCollins Children's Books (New York, NY), 2001.
Puppy Trouble (pop-up book), Farrar, Straus (New York, NY), 2002.
The Flight of a Dove, Farrar, Straus (New York, NY), 2004.
Not Forgotten: A Consolation for the Loss of an Animal Friend, Laughing Elephant (Seattle, WA), 2004.

Also author and illustrator of *My Puppy's Record Book,* Farrar, Straus (New York, NY).

ILLUSTRATOR

Jimmy Kennedy, *The Teddy Bears' Picnic* (book and record set), Green Tiger Press (San Diego, CA), 1983.
Joan Marshall Grant, *The Blue Faience Hippopotamus,* Green Tiger Press (San Diego, CA), 1984.
Cooper Edens, *Children of Wonder,* Volume 1: *Helping the Sun,* Volume 2: *Helping the Animals,* Volume 3: *Helping the Flowers & Trees,* Volume 4: *Helping the Night,* Green Tiger Press (San Diego, CA), 1987.
Ned Washington, *When You Wish upon a Star,* Green Tiger Press (San Diego, CA), 1987.
Abigail Darling, *Teddy Bears' Picnic Cookbook,* Puffin Books (New York, NY), 1993.
Christina Darling, *Mirror,* Farrar, Straus (New York, NY), 1997.

OTHER

(Editor with Cooper Edens and Welleran Poltarnees) *Children from the Golden Age, 1880-1930,* Green Tiger Press (San Diego, CA), 1987.
(Editor with Welleran Poltarnees) *A.B.C. of Fashionable Animals,* Green Tiger Press (San Diego, CA), 1989.

Sidelights

Best known for introducing readers to a lovable rottweiler named Carl, the author and artist Alexandra Day is the pen name of Sandra Darling. As Day, she is the creator of the picture-book classic *Good Dog, Carl* and its many sequels, as well as the author and/or illustrator of several other books. As Darling, she had become well-known in publishing circles, founding the historic

Green Tiger Press in 1969 and reissuing—through imaginative marketing and publishing efforts that have also drawn on the talents of her husband, Harold Darling, as well as other family members—the illustrations and philosophy of the Golden Age of illustration. Green Tiger Press, which was sold to New York publisher Simon & Schuster in the mid-1980s, has since been reacquired by the Darlings under their more-recently established Seattle, Washington-based Laughing Elephant Publishing.

As the granddaughter of an architect and the daughter of a painter, Day grew up in a family where art was viewed as important. As she recalled in *SAAS*, "my home was always well supplied with those things necessary for creation, repair, and transformation—pencils, chalk, paint, brushes, paper, tools, wire, nails, glue, and so on. My sisters and I were always made to feel that these materials were there to be freely used. Even more significant was the assumption in our family that if you wanted something, whether it was a kite, a strawberry pie, a prom dress, or a tree house, with a little ingenuity and application (and help, if necessary) you could make it."

In this creative environment, Day also gained an early love of reading, telling *SAAS* that she read "Nancy Drew, the Black Stallion books, Laura Ingalls Wilder, E. Nesbit, and wept with *Black Beauty* and *Little Women*." Her favorite authors included George Macdonald, C.S. Lewis, G.K. Chesterton, J.R.R. Tolkien,

Inspired by her own family's beloved pet, Day's Good Dog Carl *has become a picture-book classic and sparked a series of books featuring the gentle rottweiler.*

and Charles Williams. The works of the authors, who posed fantastic stories, would greatly influence Day's later work.

After attending Swarthmore College, where she majored in English literature, Day moved to New York City and worked at the Young Men's Hebrew Association as a crafts teacher. She also took classes in figure drawing and painting at the Art Students' League and from Will Barnet. On a trip to California, she met Harold Darling, who owned a cinema and book store (housed in the same building), and they were married in 1967. Harold had three children from a previous marriage, and during the next seven years the couple had four more children, each named after lesser-known authors the bookish couple admired.

Drawing on the vast collection of antique children's books Day and Darling collected, in 1969, the couple founded Green Tiger Press. The business, located in San Diego, California, originally published postcards, notecards and bookmarks featuring artwork from such talents as Arthur Rackham, L. Frank Baum, and others. Three years later they published their first book, *All Mirrors Are Magic Mirrors,* written by Harold Darling, and sold 50,000 copies by mail order. As Day recalled, the company grew, hired staff, and expanded its publications; then, after a dozen years a quandary pushed her into a new phase of her career. Needing an illustration for an old song, "The Teddy Bears' Picnic," and not having an appropriate image, she decided to create the art herself. The book was a success, and Day soon found herself illustrating other books published by Green Tiger Press.

On a trip in Zurich, Switzerland, the Darlings discovered an antique German broadsheet titled *Der brave Karo,* about a poodle and a baby who played together while the baby should have been napping. Charmed by the story, the Darlings decided to create a similar work, casting the family rottweiler Toby in the poodle's role and Day's granddaughter Madeleine as the baby. *Good Dog, Carl,* published in 1985, proved to be "an even larger success than *The Teddy Bears' Picnic,*" according to Day in *SAAS*. "It, and its sequels, continue to sell enormously, and I have to fight off the pressure to make a career of babies and dogs." Since 1989, when the loveable Carl made his second picture-book appearance in *Carl Goes Shopping,* she has published several more "Carl" books, each characterized by a brief text and Day's engaging paintings.

In *Good Dog, Carl,* a child's mother tells the family dog to watch the baby while she leaves the room; her words of praise upon her return are "Good dog, Carl!" Because the text is so brief, Day's illustrations, tell the story; rendered in what a *People* contributor described as "lustrous oils," Day's art is "a handsome counterpoint to the whimsy of the narrative." One of the last books to be published by Green Tiger Press prior to its sale to Simon & Schuster, the book sold over a half-

million copies during its first five years. In addition to sparking a publishing phenomenon due to its small-press origins, the book also had another surprising effect. As Kelli Pryor explained in *Entertainment Weekly* as the "Carl" series took shape: "The warmth Day put into her realistically rendered oil paintings has earned the books so much adoration that it's not farfetched to speculate that Carl is partly responsible for boosting rottweilers . . . into the top five of the American Kennel Club's most-popular breeds list." While, over time, the models for Carl have changed as the Darlings' beloved family dogs have successively passed on, the personality of the original Toby shines through in all the "Carl" books.

In *Carl Goes Shopping* Carl watches over a toddler and carries her into various departments in the store. Calling the book a "thoroughly enjoyable adventure," a reviewer in *Horn Book* suggested that Day offers "the most pinchable baby and pettable dog of the season." After wreaking havoc everywhere they go, they return before the mother does. The third book in the series, *Carl's Christmas,* in the words of a *Publishers Weekly* critic, is "imbued with enough 'good will towards man' to warm a whole town." Carl takes care of a puppy and a baby in *Carl's Afternoon in the Park,* published in 1991. In this book "the dogs are as charmingly true to life as ever," according to a *Kirkus Reviews* critic.

Carl and his toddler charge continue to charm young readers in *Carl's Masquerade, Carl Goes to Daycare,* and *Carl's Sleepy Afternoon,* among others. When toddler Madeleine follows her parents to a costume party, the loyal rottweiler comes to her rescue in *Carl's Masquerade.* According to Roger Sutton, writing in the *Bulletin of the Center for Children's Books,* the picture book's setting "allows Day free rein for her deliberately *outré,* painterly style and whimsical turn of imagination." In *Carl Goes to Daycare* the resourceful pup takes charge of Madeleine's preschool class when the teacher is accidentally locked outside. Ellen Mandel asserted in *Booklist* that this book "is sure to be a favorite in a deservedly popular series."

A *Publishers Weekly* critic wrote that "everyone's favorite rottweiler is back in top form" in *Carl's Birthday,* in which Carl and Madeleine secretly aid her mother's party preparations, while in *Follow Carl!* Carl leads the neighborhood children in a game of Follow the Leader. As a reviewer in *Publishers Weekly* noted of the latter, "The combination of grassy settings, friendly village shops and, of course, tender companionship adds up to an excursion virtually any reader would enjoy." In *Carl's Sleepy Afternoon* the pup decides that an afternoon on his own would be better spent out and about than sleeping at home in the sun. When Madeleine and Mother go to town on errands, Carl is not far behind, catching a ride on a passing van. Spotting Madeleine in a bakery, the pup sneaks in and is given a cookie; helpful visits to a nearby druggist and a burning garage where he rescues a litter of stranded puppies round out

Carl's day, and the two unsuspecting shoppers find him sleeping in the sun upon their return home. Noting that *Carl's Sleepy Afternoon* marks more than two decades of "Carl" books, a *Publishers Weekly* writer noted that the rottweiler "has lost none of his appeal—or his spunk," and added that "Day's stunningly realistic, brightly hued illustrations are as timeless and endearing as the plot." In *Booklist* John Peters deemed the book "another fan-pleasing, tongue-in-cheek outing" for Carl, while Lynn K. Vanca wrote in *School Library Journal* that *Carl's Sleepy Afternoon* "is a must-read for fans, and it stands well on its own."

In addition to the "Carl" books, Day has also written and illustrated a number of other highly praised children's books, including a short series featuring a bear named Frank and an elephant named Ernest. In the first book, *Frank and Ernest,* the watercolor-illustrated pair runs a '50s-style diner, using amusing diner dialogue which is explained in a glossary. Trev Jones, writing in *School Library Journal,* concluded that the book is "bound to become standard fare for story hour specials." *Frank and Ernest Play Ball* finds the pair managing a baseball team and using a dictionary to understand their job, while *Frank and Ernest on the Road* follows the duo as they find work as truckers, mastering Citizen's Band (CB) radio jargon along with readers. "Fans of the dynamic duo's previous adventures will appreciate this exploration of a new linguistic frontier," wrote Zena Sutherland in the *Bulletin of the Center for Children's Books,* referencing Day's inclusion of a glossary of CB terms.

In the picture book *Boswell Wide Awake* Day tells the story of a little bear who gets up in the middle of the night and does work around the house that was left undone at bedtime. "Day turns the plot into something of a tour de force," noted a reviewer in *Publishers Weekly,* "bringing to her visual storytelling the same extraordinary tenderness and seamless blend of fantasy and realism that characterize her Carl books." Other picture books by Day include *Puppy Trouble,* a pop-up book in which a young, rambunctious pup gets into a series of small, harmless scrapes with trouble, and *The Flight of a Dove.* In the latter book, based on a true story, Day focuses on a preschooler named Betsy who has autism and lives in a very lonely world due to her condition. Betsy's first experience at a new school is a frightening one, until an interaction with the class dog, and her experience watching a beautiful dove flutter around the room makes Betsy feel more comfortable with her surroundings and results in her first spoken word. While noting the story's somber theme, *School Library Journal* contributor Linda Beck praised Day's illustrations, writing that "the beautiful artwork effectively highlights [Betsy's] . . . sense of isolation and [ultimate] happiness," while in *Booklist* Linda Perkins explained that "the lush watercolor art . . . brings the story to life" and "demonstrates the miraculous therapeutic power of animals."

Day has also worked with fellow illustration aficionado and artist Cooper Edens on several picture books, among them *The Christmas We Moved the Barn, Darby, the Special0Order Pup,* and *Special Deliveries.* Of *Darby, the Special-Order Pup,* Lucinda Snyder Whitehurst in the *School Library Journal* wrote that Day has "created another canine that children will love" as much as they have her famous Carl the rottweiler. Peter F. Neumeyer, in a review for the *Boston Sunday Globe,* called *Darby, the Special-Order Pup* "that rare, sophisticated specimen—a picture storybook in which the illustrations tell their own story and play off their own jokes in counterpoint to the written text." *Special Deliveries* was called an "imaginative, funny book" that "is alive with great pictures" by reviewer Ellen Mandel in *Booklist.*

Continuing their publishing efforts as Laughing Elephant Publishing, Day and her family now make their home in Seattle, Washington, where they run Blue Lantern Studio and publish gift books and other paper products under the Green Tiger Press and Darling & Company imprints. While Day and Darling continue to oversee the company's direction, the business is also a family affair; in addition to family members serving in various production and business capacities, Day's creativity has also been inherited. She has illustrated the *Teddy Bears' Picnic Cookbook,* a cookery book written by her stepdaughter, Abigail Darling, and *Mirror,* illustrated by Day, was written by her youngest daughter, Christina Darling. In a *Publishers Weekly* review, a critic wrote that this fantasy storybook is a "good reflection on this mother/daughter team." Discussing their publishing philosophy on the *Laughing Elephant Web site,* the Darlings explain: "All of our imprints reflect our belief that values and ideals are enduring, and that the insights of past times are still valuable."

"The visual beauty of the physical world has always been of great importance to me, and the source of my lifelong impulse to be a visual artist," Day once noted of her work. "I became an illustrator because we had a publishing company, but I had already trained myself as a 'fine art' painter, and have continued this pursuit along with the book illustration. I think this accounts largely for both my style and my tendency to prefer books with very few words—that is, books in which the pictures, by their style, execution and content (all the things a good painting has) do the primary work of the book.

"My feelings of kinship with all creation and my conviction of the reality of a spiritual dimension to the universe are naturally very important in my choice of subject matter and in my attempt to convey what I believe we should strive for in our relations with our world."

Biographical and Critical Sources

BOOKS

Children's Literature Review, Volume 22, Thomson Gale (Detroit, MI), 1991.

Silvey, Anita, editor, *Children's Books and Their Creators,* Houghton (Boston, MA), 1995.
Something about the Author Autobiography Series, Thomson Gale (Detroit, MI), Volume 19, 1995.

PERIODICALS

Booklist, December 15, 1993, Ellen Mandel, review of *Carl Goes to Daycare,* p. 763; November 15, 1994, p. 610; January 1, 1996, p. 843; March 1, 1997, p. 1170; May 1, 2001, Ellen Mandel, review of *Special Deliveries,* p. 1688; May 1, 2001, Ellen Mandel, review of *Special Deliveries,* p. 1688; November 15, 2004, Linda Perkins, review of *The Flight of a Dove,* p. 580; September 1, 2005, John Peters, review of *Carl's Sleepy Afternoon,* p. 143.
Boston Sunday Globe, September 3, 2000, Peter F. Neumeyer, "Strong Animal Tales, from Then and Now," p. M3.
Bulletin of the Center for Children's Books, January, 1990, p. 108; December, 1992, Roger Sutton, review of *Carl's Masquerade,* p. 109; March, 1994, Zena Sutherland, review of *Frank and Ernest on the Road,* p. 219.
Horn Book, January-February, 1990, review of *Carl Goes Shopping,* p. 50.
Entertainment Weekly, September 27, 1991, Kelli Pryor, "Day's Dog."
Kirkus Reviews, September 15, 1991, review of *Carl's Afternoon in the Park,* p. 1230; October 15, 1994, p. 1406.
People, September 23, 1991, "Top Dog," p. 83.
Publishers Weekly, September 14, 1990, review of *Carl's Christmas,* p. 123; November 22, 1993, p. 63; August 22, 1994, p. 54; October 23, 1995, review of *Carl's Birthday,* p. 67; January 13, 1997, review of *Mirror,* p. 75; June 29, 1998, review of *Follow Carl!,* p. 57; November 8, 1999, review of *Boswell Wide Awake,* p. 66; June 4, 2001, review of *Special Deliveries,* p. 79; October 28, 2002, review of *Puppy Trouble,* p. 74; September 13, 2004, review of *The Flight of a Dove,* p. 78; August 22, 2005, review of *Carl's Sleepy Afternoon,* p. 62.
School Library Journal, August, 1988, Trev Jones, review of *Frank and Ernest,* p. 80; February, 1994, p. 83; November, 1994, p. 74; December, 1995, p. 79; October, 2000, Lucinda Snyder Whitehurst, review of *Darby, the Special-Order Pup,* p. 120; May, 2001, Holly Belli, review of *Special Deliveries,* p. 114; September, 2004, Linda Beck, review of *The Flight of a Dove,* p. 157; October, 2005, Lynn K. Vanca, review of *Carl's Sleepy Afternoon,* p. 110.

ONLINE

Farrar, Straus & Giroux Kids Web site, http://www.fsgkidsbooks.com/ (December 1, 2005), "Alexandra Day."
Good Dog Carl Web site, http://www.gooddogcarl.com (April 12, 2006).

Laughing Elephant Web site, http://www.laughingelephant. com/ (December 3, 2005), "A Little History of the Laughing Elephant."

*   *   *

deGROAT, Diane 1947-

Personal
Born May 24, 1947, in Newton, NJ; married Daniel Markham, 1975; children: Amanda Lee. *Education:* Attended Phoenix School of Design, 1964; Pratt Institute, B.F.A., 1969.

Addresses
Home—Amherst, MA. *Agent*—c/o Author Mail, Harper-Collins, 1350 Avenue of the Americas, New York, NY 10019-4703. *E-mail*—dianedegroat@comcast.net.

Career
Illustrator and author of books for children, 1971—. Holt, Rinehart & Winston (book publishers), New York, NY, book designer, then art director of Basic Reading Program, 1969-72. *Exhibitions:* Work has appeared in shows, including Society of Illustrators Annual National Exhibition, New York, NY, 1973, 1975; Art Directors Club, New York, 1974; and American Institute of Graphic Arts Annual Book Show, New York, 1978. Work exhibited at R. Michelson Gallery, Amherst, MA.

Awards, Honors
California Young Readers Award, 1975, for *Little Rabbit's Loose Tooth,* by Lucy Bate; Arkansas State Children's Book Award, North Carolina State Children's Book Award, and Children's Choice, International Reading Association/Children's Book Council, all for *Roses Are Pink, Your Feet Really Stink.*

Writings

SELF-ILLUSTRATED

Alligator's Toothache, Crown (New York, NY), 1977.
Annie Pitts, Artichoke, Chronicle (New York, NY), 1992.
Annie Pitts, Swamp Monster, Chronicle (New York, NY), 1993.
Roses Are Pink, Your Feet Really Stink, Morrow (New York, NY), 1995.
Trick or Treat, Smell My Feet, Morrow (New York, NY), 1998.
Happy Birthday to You, You Belong in a Zoo, Morrow (New York, NY), 1999.
Jingle Bells, Homework Smells, HarperCollins (New York, NY), 2000.
Annie Pitts, Burger Kid, SeaStar (New York, NY), 2000.

Diane deGroat

We Gather Together—Now Please Get Lost!, Chronicle (New York, NY), 2001.
Lola the Elf, Night Sky Books (New York, NY), 2002.
Love, Lola, Night Sky Books (New York, NY), 2002.
Good Night, Sleep Tight, Don't Let the Bedbugs Bite, Chronicle (New York, NY), 2002.
Liar, Liar, Pants on Fire, Chronicle (New York, NY), 2003.
Lola's Costume, HarperFestival (New York, NY), 2004.
Lola Hides the Eggs, HarperFestival (New York, NY), 2004.
Brand-New Pencils, Brand-New Books, HarperCollins (New York, NY), 2005.
No More Pencils, No More Books, No More Teacher's Dirty Looks!, HarperCollins (New York, NY), 2006.
Last One in Is a Rotten Egg, HarperCollins (New York, NY), 2007.

ILLUSTRATOR

Eleanor L. Clymer, *Luke Was There,* Holt (New York, NY), 1973.
Elinor Parker, *Four Seasons, Five Senses,* Scribner (New York, NY), 1974.
Marcia Newfield, *A Book for Jodan,* Atheneum (New York, NY), 1975.
Lucy Bate, *Little Rabbit's Loose Tooth,* Crown (New York, NY), 1975.
Mamie Hegwood, *My Friend Fish,* Holt (New York, NY), 1975.
Anne Snyder, *Nobody's Family,* Holt (New York, NY), 1975.

Miriam B. Young, *Truth and Consequences,* Four Winds (New York, NY), 1975.

Sylvia Sunderlin, *Antrim's Orange,* Scribner (New York, NY), 1976.

Maria Polushkin, *Bubba and Babba: Based on a Russian Folktale,* Crown (New York, NY), 1976.

Harriett M. Luger, *Chasing Trouble,* Viking (New York, NY), 1976.

Kathryn F. Ernst, *Mr. Tamarin's Trees,* Crown (New York, NY), 1976.

Eve Bunting, *One More Flight,* Warne (New York, NY), 1976.

Kathryn F. Ernst, *Owl's New Cards,* Crown (New York, NY), 1977.

Ann Tompert, *Badger on His Own,* Crown (New York, NY), 1978.

Tobi Tobias, *How Your Mother and Father Met, and What Happened After,* McGraw Hill (New York, NY), 1978.

Lois Lowry, *Anastasia Krupnik,* Houghton (Boston, MA), 1979.

Seymour Simon, *Animal Fact/Animal Fable,* Crown (New York, NY), 1979.

Elizabeth T. Billington, *Part-Time Boy,* Warne (New York, NY), 1980.

Valerie Flournoy, *The Twins Strike Back,* Dial (New York, NY), 1980.

Lois Lowry, *Anastasia Again!,* Houghton (Boston, MA), 1981.

Christine McDonnell, *Don't Be Mad, Ivy,* Dial (New York, NY), 1981.

Barbara Dillon, *Who Needs a Bear?,* Morrow (New York, NY), 1981.

Lynn Luderer, *The Toad Intruder,* Houghton (Boston, MA), 1982.

Christine McDonnell, *Toad Food and Measle Soup,* Dial (New York, NY), 1982.

Johanna Hurwitz, *Tough Luck Karen,* Morrow (New York, NY), 1982.

Susan Shreve, *Bad Dreams of a Good Girl,* Knopf (New York, NY), 1982.

Lois Lowry, *Anastasia at Your Service,* Houghton (Boston, MA), 1982.

Johanna Hurwitz, *DeDe Takes Charge!,* Morrow (New York, NY), 1984.

Susan Shreve, *The Flunking of Joshua T. Bates,* Knopf (New York, NY), 1984.

Bonnie Pryor, *Amanda and April,* Morrow (New York, NY), 1986.

Steven L. Nickman, *When Mom and Dad Divorce,* Messner (New York, NY), 1986.

Johanna Hurwitz, *Hurricane Elaine,* Morrow (New York, NY), 1986.

Niki Yektai, *Bears in Pairs,* Simon & Schuster (New York, NY), 1987.

Barbara Cohen, *The Christmas Revolution,* Lothrop (New York, NY), 1987.

Robin A. Thrush, *The Gray Whales Are Missing,* Harcourt (San Diego, CA), 1987.

Christine McDonnell, *Just for the Summer,* Viking (New York, NY), 1987.

Barbara Isenberg, *Albert the Running Bear Gets the Jitters,* Houghton (Boston, MA), 1988.

Lois Lowry, *All about Sam,* Houghton (Boston, MA), 1988.

Barbara Cohen, *The Orphan Game,* Lothrop (New York, NY), 1988.

Kate McMullan, *Great Advice from Lila Fenwick,* Puffin (New York, NY), 1989.

Johanna Hurwitz, *Aldo Peanut Butter,* Morrow (New York, NY), 1990.

Joanne Rocklin, *Jace the Ace,* Simon & Schuster (New York, NY), 1990.

Bonnie Pryor, *Merry Christmas, Amanda and April,* Morrow (New York, NY), 1990.

Barbara Cohen, *The Long Way Home,* Lothrop (New York, NY), 1990.

Kate McMullan, *The Great Eggspectations of Lila Fenwick,* Farrar, Straus (New York, NY), 1991.

Jamie Gilson, *Itchy Richard,* Houghton (Boston, MA), 1991.

Eve Bunting, *A Turkey for Thanksgiving,* Houghton (Boston, MA), 1991.

Lois Lowry, *Attaboy, Sam!,* Houghton (Boston, MA), 1992.

Lisa G. Evans, *An Elephant Never Forgets Its Snorkel: How Animals Survive without Tools and Gadgets,* Crown (New York, NY), 1992.

Jean Van Leeuwen, *The Great Summer Camp Catastrophe,* Dial (New York, NY), 1992.

Kevin Roth, *Lullabies for Little Dreamers,* Random House (New York, NY), 1992.

Carol P. Saul, *Peter's Song,* Simon & Schuster (New York, NY), 1992.

Eve Bunting, *Our Teacher's Having a Baby,* Clarion (New York, NY), 1992.

Susan Shreve, *Wait for Me,* Morrow (New York, NY), 1992.

Eve Merriam, *Where Is Everybody?: An Animal Alphabet,* Simon & Schuster (New York, NY), 1992.

Susan Shreve, *Amy Dunn Quits School,* Morrow (New York, NY), 1993.

Ruth Westheimer, *Dr. Ruth Talks to Kids: Where You Came From, How Your Body Changes, and What Sex Is All About,* Simon & Schuster (New York, NY), 1993.

Teddy Slater, *The Wrong-Way Rabbit,* Scholastic (New York, NY), 1993.

A.C. LeMieux, *Fruit Flies, Fish, and Fortune Cookies,* Morrow (New York, NY), 1994.

Jamie Gilson, *It Goes Eeeeeeeeeeee,* Houghton (Boston, MA), 1994.

Stephanie Calmenson, *Kinderkittens: Show and Tell,* Scholastic (New York, NY), 1994.

P.J. Petersen, *Some Days, Other Days,* Scribner (New York, NY), 1994.

Eve Bunting, *Sunshine Home,* Houghton (Boston, MA), 1994.

Jamie Gilson, *You Don't Know Beans about Bats,* Houghton (Boston, MA), 1994.

John Dennis Fitzgerald, *The Great Brain Is Back,* Dial (New York, NY), 1995.

Stephanie Calmenson, *Kinderkittens: Who Took the Cookie from the Cookie Jar?,* Scholastic (New York, NY), 1995.

Lois Lowry, *See You Around, Sam!,* Houghton (Boston, MA), 1996.

Pam Muñoz Ryan, *A Pinky Is a Baby Mouse, and Other Baby Animal Names,* Hyperion (New York, NY), 1997.

Pam Muñoz Ryan, *Armadillos Sleep in Dugouts, and Other Places Animals Live,* Hyperion (New York, NY), 1997.

Amy Goldman Koss, *How I Saved Hanukkah,* Dial (New York, NY), 1998.

Patricia Hubbell, *Pots and Pans,* HarperFestival (New York, NY), 1998.

Jamie Gilson, *Bug in a Rug,* Clarion (New York, NY), 1998.

Kimberley Weinberger, *Our Thanksgiving,* Scholastic (New York, NY), 1999.

Lois Lowry, *Zooman Sam,* Houghton Mifflin (Boston, MA), 1999.

Mary Downing Hahn, *Anna All Year Round,* Clarion (New York, NY), 1999.

Joan Lowrey Nixon, *Gus & Gertie and the Missing Pearl,* SeaStar (New York, NY), 2000.

Joanna Hurwitz, *One Small Dog,* HarperCollins (New York, NY), 2000.

Joan Lowrey Nixon, *Gus & Gertie and the Lucky Charms,* SeaStar (New York, NY), 2001.

Mary Downing Hahn, *Anna on the Farm,* Clarion (New York, NY), 2001.

Sidelights

In addition to writing her own books, Diane deGroat has illustrated numerous books by some of the most prominent authors in children's literature, including Lois Lowry, Eve Bunting, and Joan Lowrey Nixon. De-Groat's interest in art began during her childhood, growing up in Belleville, New Jersey. She took her first painting lessons at the age of seven, and by the time she reached her junior year of high school she had won a scholarship to study at the Phoenix School of Design in New York City for a summer. She attended college at the highly regarded Pratt Institute.

After graduating from Pratt, deGroat worked as a book designer for New York publisher Holt, Rinehart & Winston, designing their first basic reading program. There she learned about book production and developed an interest in children's books. In 1972 she left Holt to become a freelance illustrator.

After twenty years of illustrating for other authors, de-Groat was inspired to write and illustrate the first of her amusing stories about third-grader Annie Pitts, who wants nothing in the world more than to be a famous actress. She thinks that her big break to stardom is waiting around every corner, which leads her into many funny situations. In *Annie Pitts, Artichoke,* Annie accompanies her class on a field trip to the supermarket. While there, she hopes that the store manager will notice her and ask her to appear in his next television commercial. When Annie winds up hitting her classmate Matthew in the head with a dead fish, however, the class is asked to leave the store. As punishment, the teacher makes Annie play the undesirable role of an artichoke in the school play. In a *Booklist* review, Ellen Mandel called *Annie Pitts, Artichoke* "amusing and highly palatable reading fare, with sprightly, realistically drawn illustrations that enhance the book's energy and fun."

In 1993's *Annie Pitts, Swamp Monster,* Annie jumps at the chance to star in a low-budget horror movie being produced by a high-school student as a class project. She takes her role as the swamp monster very seriously, hoping it could be the opportunity she has been waiting for to get into show business. The filming turns into one hilarious disaster after another, however, and Annie is embarrassed when the video is shown to her grade-school class. Lucinda Snyder Whitehurst, writing in *School Library Journal,* called the book "breezy and lighthearted" and noted that "the slapstick humor will have young readers giggling." *Booklist* reviewer Chris Sherman added that "the black-and-white illustrations are delightful" and claimed that the book was "sure to win new fans for author-illustrator deGroat."

Annie Pitts returns for a new adventure in *Annie Pitts, Burger Kid.* Annie is determined to become the next poster model for Burger Barn. But before her audition, she must catch up with a heavy dose of homework and deal with an awkward Thanksgiving dinner with too many guests. "Readers will admire the redhead's spunk," wrote Gay Lynn Van Vleck in *School Library Journal,* while Ellen Mandel wrote in *Booklist* that "fans of . . . Annie's other adventures won't be disappointed."

With *Roses Are Pink, Your Feet Really Stink* deGroat introduces readers to Gilbert, a woodland creature who is attending elementary school. When his class assignment is to write a Valentine card for every person in the class, Gilbert cannot think of anything nice to say about class bully Lewis or mean Margaret. Instead, he writes clever insults about both of them, signing the other's name to the card. It does not take long to figure out the culprit, and after Gilbert gets in trouble, both Lewis and Margaret apologize for hurting his feelings. "The winning touch here is deGroat's characteristically buoyant watercolor art," commented a critic for *Publishers Weekly.* "Kids will enjoy all the rhymes, and they'll want to make up their own playful parodies," added *Booklist* reviewer Hazel Rochman.

Gilbert and friends return in *Trick or Treat, Smell My Feet.* Here Gilbert is excited to be a space pilot for Halloween, but when he opens the bag containing his costume, he realizes that he and his sister Lola accidentally switched the bags containing their Halloween costumes. At first mortified by the though of dressing up as a ballerina, when Gilbert ends up as the only ballerina in a class of space pilots, he decides it is fun to be unique and has fun posing as a ballerina until his sister demands her costume back. "Gilbert's good-natured blunderings make for a kid-appealing Halloween treat,"

When Gilbert makes a misstep while cast in the role of George Washington in the school play, he realizes that admitting to an untruth is easier on stage than in person in deGroat's Liar, Liar, Pants on Fire.

wrote *Horn Book* reviewer Marilyn Bousquin, while Hazel Rochman wrote in *Booklist* that deGroat's "funny watercolor pictures capture the various animal creatures' very human expressions."

Gilbert and company star in several other adventures, including *Happy Birthday to You, You Belong in a Zoo,* in which Gilbert is invited to bully Lewis's birthday party. Not wanting to get Lewis anything good, Gilbert suggests to his Mom that buying him a frying pan would be a good idea; when he enjoys himself at the party, he begins to feel guilty about the gift, only to realize as Lewis opens the present from Gilbert that his mother bought a good gift instead. "DeGroat's watercolors capture Gilbert's changing moods perfectly," complimented a critic for *Publishers Weekly,* while Kathy Broderick

noted in *Booklist* that "both story and watercolor pictures excel at capturing the anguish children often feel" in awkward social situations. In *Jingle Bells, Homework Smells* Gilbert puts off doing his homework over a weekend while preparing for Christmas, and by Monday morning, he has completely forgotten about it. "Gilbert's dilemma is a common one and most readers will appreciate his last-minute attempt to appease his teacher," wrote a *School Library Journal* reviewer.

Camp Hi-Dee-Ho is the setting for Gilbert's first overnight camping experience in *Good Night, Sleep Tight, Don't Let the Bedbugs Bite!* Here Gilbert is scared when other campers tell ghost stories, but a midnight trek to the bathroom reveals that he is not the only one frightened. "Those anticipating . . . an inaugural camp expe-

rience especially will revel in this realistic yet reassuring visit," wrote a *Publishers Weekly* critic. According to Kitty Flynn in *Horn Book,* deGroat "gets the thrills and (slight) chills of a first overnight camping experience just right." Gilbert is given the role of George Washington in a class skit in *Liar, Liar, Pants on Fire.* Though his line is "I cannot tell a lie," when faced with a tough situation, Gilbert realizes that telling the truth is often much harder than lying. Ilene Cooper, writing in *Booklist,* commented on the "humorous text, the sprightly art with its all-animal cast, and the message that peeks through the fun." According to Anne Knickerbocker in *School Library Journal,* "this entertaining tale provides good discussion material and should be a winner at storytime."

With *Brand-New Pencils, Brand-New Books,* deGroat tells the story of Gilbert's very first day of school. While some things go wrong on his first day, he realizes that he has strengths his classmates do not, while some of them excel at things that he is not good at. *Booklist* critic Gillian Engberg felt that "deGroat skillfully shows a child's common anxieties throughout a school day." The "Gilbert" books continue on with *No More Pencils, No More Books, No More Teacher's Dirty Looks!* as well as a spin-off series features stories about Lola, Gilbert's little sister.

Among the many books deGroat has illustrated for other authors is Eve Bunting's *Sunshine Home.* The story centers around seven-year-old Timmy, whose grandmother has been placed in a nursing home after injuring herself in a fall. On his first visit to Sunshine Home, Timmy is nervous about what he will find there. Although he does not like the "barf green" walls or the way the place smells, the boy is relieved that his grandmother seems the same and their visit goes well. After his family leaves, however, Timmy's mother begins to cry. Discovering that he has forgotten to give his grandmother a copy of his school picture, Timmy runs back into the nursing home and finds his grandmother crying too. When he brings his parents back inside to talk to his grandmother again, everyone in the family is able to confront their true feelings about the situation. In *Booklist,* Ellen Mandel wrote that, "in her realistic watercolors, deGroat defines the images of Bunting's tender, true-to-life story," and Jody McCoy added in *School Library Journal* that the book's illustrations "are appropriately heavy on institutional green and poignantly support the text."

DeGroat has worked on titles for many other prominent authors, including Lois Lowry, for whom she illustrates both the "Anastasia Krupnik" and "Sam" series. For Patricia Hubbell, deGroat illustrated *Pots and Pans,* a noisy tale about a young child who loves banging wooden spoons against pots, pans, and boxes. "The watercolor illustrations capture the curious wonder, adventurous spirit, and total joy" of the child musician, according to Linda Perkins in *Booklist.* For texts by writer Mary Downing Hahn, deGroat has created artwork

A nine year old's experiences while away from her home in early-twentieth-century Baltimore and visiting rural relatives are brought to life in deGroat's detailed artwork for Mary Downing Hahn's **Anna on the Farm.**

bringing to life the stories about a young girl named Anna, who is growing up in the early 1900s. In *Anna on the Farm,* Anna visits her uncle's farm and tries to convince her annoying cousin that she is not just a city slicker. DeGroat's illustrations were praised as "perfectly in tune with the mood of the story," according to Debbie Whitbeck in *School Library Journal.*

DeGroat has enjoyed the varied demands of her multifaceted career as an illustrator, author, and artist. "My picture books enable me to explore the world of fantasy, while the novels I've illustrated are very realistic in style," she explained in *Illustrators of Children's Books 1967-76.* "My work in fine art is an infusion of these two styles."

Biographical and Critical Sources

BOOKS

Lee Kingman and others, *Illustrators of Children's Books, 1967-1976,* Horn Book (Boston, MA), 1978.

PERIODICALS

Booklist, October 15, 1992, Ellen Mandel, review of *Annie Pitts, Artichoke,* p. 428; March 15, 1994, Ellen Man-

del, review of *Sunshine Home,* p. 1371; June 1, 1994, Chris Sherman, review of *Annie Pitts, Swamp Monster,* p. 1815; March 1, 1996, Hazel Rochman, review of *Roses Are Pink, Your Feet Really Stink,* p. 1187; October 1, 1996, Hazel Rochman, review of *See You Around, Sam!,* p. 349; August, 1998, review of *Pots and Pans,* p. 2015; September 1, 1998, Hazel Rochman, review of *Trick or Treat, Smell My Feet,* p. 132; August, 1999, Kathy Broderick, review of *Happy Birthday to You, You Belong in a Zoo,* p. 2063; September 1, 2000, Carolyn Phelan, review of *Jingle Bells, Homework Smells,* p. 69; October 1, 2000, Ellen Mandel, review of *Annie Pitts, Burger Kid,* p. 339; February 15, 2001, Kay Weisman, review of *Anna on the Farm,* p. 1136; September 1, 2001, review of *We Gather Together—Now Please Get Lost!,* p. 120; July, 2002, Ellen Mandel, review of *Good Night, Sleep Tight, Don't Let the Bedbugs Bite!,* p. 1856; February 15, 2003, Ilene Cooper, review of *Liar, Liar, Pants on Fire,* p. 1072; August, 2005, Gillian Engberg, review of *Brand-New Pencils, Brand-New Books,* p. 2038.

Bulletin of the Center for Children's Books, May, 1977, p. 140; January, 2001, review of *Annie Pitts, Burger Kid,* p. 179.

Horn Book, July-August, 1989, p. 476; September-October, 1996, Roger Sutton, review of *See You Around, Sam!,* p. 597; September-October, 1998, Marilyn Bosquin, review of *Trick or Treat, Smell My Feet,* p. 597; September, 1999, Roger Sutton, review of *Zooman Sam,* p. 613; July-August, 2002, Kitty Flynn, review of *Good Night, Sleep Tight, Don't Let the Bedbugs Bite!,* p. 444.

Kirkus Reviews, January 1, 1977, review of *Alligator's Toothache,* p. 1; September 15, 1992, p. 1185; June 15, 1994, p. 843; February 1, 2003, review of *Liar, Liar, Pants on Fire,* p. 228.

Publishers Weekly, January 24, 1977, review of *Alligator's Toothache,* p. 333; May 19, 1989, p. 81; February 5, 1996, review of *Roses Are Pink, Your Feet Really Stink,* p. 89; September 28, 1998, review of *Trick or Treat, Smell My Feet,* p. 94; July 5, 1999, review of *Happy Birthday to You, You Belong in a Zoo,* p. 70; September 27, 1999, review of *Trick or Treat, Smell My Feet,* p. 50; September 25, 2000, review of *Jingle Bells, Homework Smells,* p. 69; May 7, 2001, review of *Annie Pitts, Artichoke* and *Annie Pitts, Swamp Monster,* p. 249; April 8, 2002, review of *Good Night, Sleep Tight, Don't Let the Bedbugs Bite!,* p. 227; December 2, 2002, review of *Love, Lola,* p. 54; January 13, 2003, review of *Liar, Liar, Pants on Fire,* p. 59; September 22, 2003, review of *Jingle Bells, Homework Smells,* p. 107.

School Library Journal, July, 1989, p. 73; September, 1992, p. 202; April, 1994, Jody McCoy, review of *Sunshine Home,* p. 100; July, 1994, Lucinda Snyder Whitehurst, review of *Annie Pitts, Swamp Monster,* p. 102; April, 1996, Claudia Cooper, review of *Roses Are Pink, Your Feet Really Stink,* p. 106; October, 1996, Starr LaTronica, review of *See You Around, Sam!,* p. 102; June, 1998, Anne Knickerbocker, review of *Bug in a Rug,* p. 103; October, 1998, John Peters, review of *Trick or Treat, Smell My Feet,* p. 94;

September, 1999, Marlene Gawron, review of *Zooman Sam,* p. 193; October, 1999, Alicia Eames, review of *Happy Birthday to You, You Belong in a Zoo,* p. 112; October, 2000, review of *Jingle Bells, Homework Smells,* p. 58, and Gay Lynn Van Vleck, review of *Annie Pitts, Burger Kid,* p. 120; March, 2001, Debbie Whitbeck, review of *Anna on the Farm,* p. 209; August, 2001, review of *We Gather Together—Now Please Get Lost!,* p. 146; August, 2002, Lisa Dennis, review of *Good Night, Sleep Tight, Don't Let the Bedbugs Bite!,* p. 149; May, 2003, Anne Knickerbocker, review of *Liar, Liar, Pants on Fire,* p. 112.

ONLINE

Diane deGroat Home Page, http://www.author-illustrsource.com/dianedegroat.htm (March 28, 2006).

* * *

De la GARZA, Phyllis 1942-
(Phyllis Morreale-de la Garza)

Personal

Born January 28, 1942, in Woodstock, IL; daughter of Joseph (in real estate) and Marie (in real estate) Morreale; married Luis De la Garza (a riding instructor), June 6, 1967. *Ethnicity:* "Italian/German." *Politics:* "Independent." *Hobbies and other interests:* Handweaving, vintage clothing.

Addresses

Office—5311 E. Arzberger Rd., Willcox, AZ 85643.

Career

Writer and weaver. Former owner, with husband Luis De la Garza, of equestrian school in San Miguel Allende, Mexico, c. 1970s.

Awards, Honors

Spur Award finalist for short nonfiction, Western Writers of America, 1995, for "Apache Kid."

Writings

Chacho, New Readers Press (Syracuse, NY), 1990.
The Story of Dos Cabezas, Westernlore Press (Tucson, AZ), 1995.
The Apache Kid, Westernlore Press (Tucson, AZ), 1995.
Charissa of the Overland, Royal Fireworks Press (Unionville, NY), 1998.
Bounty Hunter's Daughter: A Western Story, Five Star (Unity, ME), 1998.
Camels West, Royal Fireworks Press (Unionville, NY), 2000.

Phyllis De la Garza

The Iron Horse, Silk Label Books (Unionville, NY), 2002.
Death for Dinner: The Benders of (Old) Kansas, Talei Publishers (Honolulu, HI), 2003.
Silk and Sagebrush: Women of the Old West, Silk Label Books (Unionville, NY), 2004.
Gun Barrels: A Steed Wilson Mystery, Silk Label Books (Unionville, NY), 2005.

Short fiction included in anthology *No Place for a Lady,* Thorndike Press. Contributor of articles and reviews to periodicals, including *Handwoven, Seasons, Chronicle of the Old West, Spin-Off, Sombrero, Tombstone Epitaph, Cochise Quarterly, Sunsitter, True West, Old West, Wild West, Roundup,* and *Seasons.*

Work in Progress

More books in the "Steed Wilson Mystery" series, for Silk Label Books.

Sidelights

A resident of Arizona for over a decade, Western writer Phyllis De la Garza has made a name for herself in a field dominated by male writers. Her books include the young-adult novels *Charissa of the Overland* and *Camels West,* the latter an historical novel about a young woman named Graciela who, in the 1850s, becomes involved with an attempt to introduce camels into the

American Southwest at Camp Verde, Texas. Orphaned as a newborn when her parents were killed at the siege of the Alamo in San Antonio, the Mexican teen was raised by a healer and has learned the healing trade. Unable to speak, Graciela communicates to those she heals through sign language; when a wounded camel is brought to her for care, the teen joins the group endeavoring to herd a group of the unusual creatures west to Los Angeles.

Other works by De la Garza include the 1995 biography *The Apache Kid,* the nonfiction title *Silk and Sagebrush: Women of the Old West,* and *Gun Barrels,* the last a novel beginning the author's "Steed Wilson Mystery" series. A talented weaver who has studied at the Instituto Allende in Guanajuato, Mexico, De la Garza also enjoys horseback riding, and in the 1970s helped her husband, former Mexican cavalry officer Luis De la Garza, in operating an equestrian school in Mexico. She explained of her craft to Jane Eppinga for *Arizona Senior World:* "I tell those who have yet to be published to have patience, keep writing and don't give up. In the long run the only real proof of your talent is your perseverance."

Biographical and Critical Sources

PERIODICALS

Arizona Daily Star, July 2, 1999, J.C. Martin, "Patience Pays for Willcox Author."
Arizona Senior World, January, 2001, Jane Eppinga, "A Busy, Successful Western Writer Has This Advice."
Roundup, December, 1995, review of *The Story of Dos Cabezas,* p. 20; June, 1996, review of *The Apache Kid,* p. 21; August, 1998, review of *Bounty Hunter's Daughter: A Western Story,* p. 29; August, 1999, review of *Charissa of the Overland,* p. 28; December, 1999, review of *Camels West,* p. 29; February, 2003, review of *The Iron Horse,* p. 29; October, 2004, Jane Eppinga, review of *Death for Dinner: The Benders of (Old) Kansas,* p. 23; February, 2005, review of *Silk and Sagebrush: Women of the Old West,* p. 27.
School Library Journal, March, 2000, Ellen A. Greever, review of *Camels West,* p. 237.

*   *   *

DOHERTY, Craig A. 1951-

Personal

Born March 23, 1951, in Boston, MA; son of Kenneth A. (an airline pilot) and Dorothy A. (a homemaker) Doherty; married Katherine Mann (a librarian and writer), June 16, 1973; children: Meghan C. *Education:* Attended University of New Mexico, 1970-73; University of Massachusetts, B.A., 1979.

Addresses

Home—RFD-1, Box 572, Milan, NH 03588. *Agent*—c/o Author Mail, Facts on File, Inc., 123 W. 31st St., New York, NY 10001.

Career

Berlin High School, Berlin, NH, English teacher, 1987—. Writer.

Writings

COAUTHOR; WITH WIFE, KATHERINE M. DOHERTY

The Apaches and Navajos, F. Watts (New York, NY), 1989.
The Iroquois, F. Watts (New York, NY), 1989.
Benazir Bhutto, F. Watts (New York, NY), 1990.
Arnold Schwarzenegger: Larger than Life, Walker (New York, NY),1993.
The Zunis, F. Watts (New York, NY), 1993.
King Richard the Lionhearted and the Crusades in World History ("World History" series), Enslow (Berkeley Heights, NJ), 2002.
Northeast Indians, Facts on File (New York, NY), 2006.

"NATIVE AMERICAN PEOPLE" SERIES; WITH KATHERINE M. DOHERTY

The Cahuilla, Rourke (Vero Beach, FL), 1994.
The Chickasaw, Rourke (Vero Beach, FL), 1994.
The Crow, Rourke (Vero Beach, FL), 1994.
The Huron, Rourke (Vero Beach, FL), 1994.
The Narragansett, Rourke (Vero Beach, FL), 1994.
The Ute, Rourke (Vero Beach, FL), 1994.

"BUILDING AMERICA" SERIES; WITH KATHERINE M. DOHERTY

The Gateway Arch, Blackbirch Press (Woodbridge, CT), 1995.
The Golden Gate Bridge, Blackbirch Press (Woodbridge, CT), 1995.
The Hoover Dam, Blackbirch Press (Woodbridge, CT), 1995.
Mount Rushmore, Blackbirch Press (Woodbridge, CT), 1995.
The Sears Tower, Blackbirch Press (Woodbridge, CT), 1995.
The Washington Monument, Blackbirch Press (Woodbridge, CT), 1995.
The Statue of Liberty, Blackbirch Press (Woodbridge, CT), 1996.
The Seattle Space Needle, Blackbirch Press (Woodbridge, CT), 1997.
The Houston Astrodome, Blackbirch Press (Woodbridge, CT), 1997.
The Erie Canal, Blackbirch Press (Woodbridge, CT), 1997.

The Empire State Building, Blackbirch Press (Woodbridge, CT), 1997.
The Alaska Pipeline, Blackbirch Press (Woodbridge, CT), 1998.

"THIRTEEN COLONIES" SERIES; WITH KATHERINE M. DOHERTY

Virginia, Facts on File (New York, NY), 2005.
Rhode Island, Facts on File (New York, NY), 2005.
Pennsylvania, Facts on File (New York, NY), 2005.
North Carolina, Facts on File (New York, NY), 2005.
New York, Facts on File (New York, NY), 2005.
Delaware, Facts on File (New York, NY), 2005.
New Jersey, Facts on File (New York, NY), 2005.
New Hampshire, Facts on File (New York, NY), 2005.
Maryland, Facts on File (New York, NY), 2005.
South Carolina, Facts on File (New York, NY), 2005.
Massachusetts, Facts on File (New York, NY), 2006.
Connecticut, Facts on File (New York, NY), 2006.
Georgia, Facts on File (New York, NY), 2006.

Sidelights

Craig A. Doherty has joined with his wife, Katherine M. Doherty, to co-author numerous nonfiction books for young students, their topics ranging from Native American cultures to U.S. history to the construction of America's architectural landmarks. Most of the Dohertys' books, which include volumes in the "Thirteen Colonies," "Building America," and "Native American People" series, assemble information for school report writers and others interested in the topics covered. Praising their contributions to the "Thirteen Colonies" series published by Facts on File, Linda Beck noted in *School Library Journal* that the Dohertys have created thorough, excellent-quality titles" that clearly present the history of the original colonies from the American Revolution through the Constitutional Convention held in 1787.

The Dohertys—Craig worked as an English teacher and Katherine worked as a librarian—began their writing career in 1989 with two books that profile Native American groups: *The Apaches and Navajos* and *The Iroquois*. Each book includes information about the tribes' history, religion, social organizations, crafts, daily life, and interaction with European colonists. Ilene Cooper, writing in *Booklist*, found the books "well-written with attractive visuals," although a *Kirkus Reviews* contributor wrote that the reading level is "relatively difficult" and requires readers to have some background in the subject matter.

The Dohertys have also collaborated on biographies of contemporary and historic figures. *Benazir Bhutto,* published in 1990, profiles the first woman to be elected prime minister of a Muslim nation; she was sworn in as the leader of Pakistan in 1988 and ruled the country in-

Written with wife, Katherine M. Doherty, Mount Rushmore *describes the creation of one of the most monumental memorial landmarks in the United States.*

termittently until 1999. The book includes background on the history of Pakistan, and then follows Bhutto through her education at Harvard and Oxford universities, her imprisonment and exile for her political views, and her first years as prime minister. In a review for *School Library Journal,* Ellen D. Warwick stated that the authors "manage to make sense of a welter of political events" and provide a "clear, nuanced, highly readable study of an appealing subject."

In *Arnold Schwarzenegger: Larger than Life* the Dohertys profile the Austrian-born bodybuilder and future "governator" through his successful career as the star of Hollywood action films. Published in 1993, the book begins with Schwarzenegger's strict upbringing in Austria, then examines his successful bodybuilding and film careers in detail. It also covers his marriage to journalist Maria Shriver and his work on behalf of Special Olympics and children's fitness. A writer for *Kirkus Reviews* called the book "a portrait of a giant with a sense of purpose, a heart of gold, and an impish sense of humor." A giant from another time is the subject of *King Richard the Lionhearted and the Crusades in World History,* which profiles the king who ruled Britain from 1189 to 1199 and led the successful yet brutal Third Crusade to the Holy Land. Praising the Dohertys' abil-

ity to "compress . . . a large portion of history into a brief, accessible work," *School Library Journal* contributor Laura Reed also cited the book for revealing Richard's charisma as well as his harsh determination.

In addition, the Dohertys have produced six books describing the history, social structure, and customs of various groups for the "Native American People" series; a series profiling each of the original thirteen American colonies; and a dozen books devoted to the construction of well-known U.S. historic and tourist sites, collected as the "Building America" series. With subjects ranging from the Erie Canal and Mount Rushmore to the Houston Astrodome and the Seattle Space Needle, the "Building America" books reveal the planning, funding, engineering, and history of America's most beloved landmarks. From the controversy surrounding the acquisition of land for Mount Rushmore from the Sioux people to the challenges of maintaining a turf environment inside the Houston Astrodome and keeping windows clean in the Sears Tower, the books were praised as "useful for school reports" by *Booklist* contributor Carolyn Phelan, while Susan Dove Lempke noted in the same periodical that series installment *The Houston Astrodome* "will attract architecture and sports fans alike."

Biographical and Critical Sources

PERIODICALS

Booklist, October 1, 1989, Ilene Cooper, review of *The Apaches and Navajos,* p. 344; December 1, 1993, p. 682; September 15, 1995, Carolyn Phelan, review of *Mount Rushmore,* p. 155; February 15, 1997, Susan Dove Lempke, review of *The Houston Astrodome* and *The Erie Canal,* p. 1018.

Kirkus Reviews, September 15, 1989, review of *The Iroquois,* p. 1402; December 15, 1993, review of *Arnold Schwarzenegger: Larger than Life,* p. 1589.

School Library Journal, February, 1991, Ellen D. Warwick, review of *Benazir Bhutto,* pp. 86-87; February, 1994, pp. 108, 123; July, 1995, pp. 84-85; January, 1997, Pamela K. Bomboy, review of *The Statue of Liberty,* p. 99; February, 1997, Katherine Borchert, review of *The Erie Canal,* p. 89, and *The Houston Astrodome* p. 113; April, 1998, Mollie Bynum, review of *The Alaska Pipeline,* p. 144; June, 2002, Laura Reed, review of *King Richard the Lionhearted and the Crusades in World History,* p. 156; August, 2005, Linda Beck, review of *North Carolina, Pennsylvania,* and *Rhode Island,* p. 144.

Voice of Youth Advocates, February, 1991, p. 374; April, 1994, p. 45.*

* * *

ENGELBREIT, Mary 1952-

Personal

Born 1952 in St. Louis, MO; married Phil Delano (a social worker), 1977; children: Evan, Will.

Addresses

Office—Mary Engelbreit Studios, 1001 Highlands Plaza Drive W., Ste. 450, St. Louis, MO 63110.

Career

Artist, entrepreneur, and author. Designer for advertising agency, c. 1972-73; staff artist for newspaper; freelance illustrator, mostly for greeting cards; Mary Engelbreit Card Company (now Mary Engelbreit Studios), St. Louis, MO, founder, c. 1983, publisher of *Mary Engelbreit's Home Companion,* 1996; licensor with Sunrise Publications, 1986.

Awards, Honors

Given Star on St. Louis Walk of Fame, 2001; Best Art License of the Year, International Licensing Industry Merchandisers' Association, 2002, for Mary Engelbreit Studios.

Writings

SELF-ILLUSTRATED; FOR CHILDREN

Hey Kids! Come Craft with Me, edited by Carol Field Dahlstrom, Meredith Press (Des Moines, IA), 1999.

Booky, HarperFestival (New York, NY), 2003.
Lovey Dovey, HarperFestival (New York, NY), 2003.
Queen of Christmas, HarperCollins (New York, NY), 2003.
Honey Bunny, HarperFestival (New York, NY), 2004.
One, Two, Peek-a-Boo!, HarperFestival (New York, NY), 2004.
Queen of the Class (with paper doll), HarperCollins (New York, NY), 2004.
Baby Booky: Sweet Heart, HarperFestival (New York, NY), 2005.
Queen of Hearts, HarperCollins (New York, NY), 2005.
Queen of Easter, HarperCollins (New York, NY), 2006.

SELF-ILLUSTRATED

(With Patrick Regan) *Mary Engelbreit: The Art and the Artist,* Andrews McMeel (Kansas City, MO), 1996.
Crafts to Decorate Your Home, edited by Carol Field Dahlstrom, Meredith Press (Des Moines, IA), 1999.
Crafts to Celebrate the Seasons, Meredith Press (Des Moines, IA), 1999.
Wrap It Up!: Gifts to Make, Wrap, and Give, Meredith Press (Des Moines, IA), 1999.
Decorating Ideas: Projects to Make for Indoors and Out, edited by Carol Field Dahlstrom, Meredith Press (Des Moines, IA), 2001.
Mary Engelbreit Christmas Ideas: Make Good Cheer!, Meredith Press (Des Moines, IA), 2001.
(With Patrick Regan) *Tiny Teeny Halloweeny Treasury,* Andrews McMeel (Kansas City, MO), 2001.
(Compiler) *The Blessings of Friendship: A Friendship Treasury,* Andrews McMeel (Kansas City, MO), 2002.
Marh Engelbreit's Home Sweet Home: A Journey through Mary's Dream Home, Andrews McMeel (Kansas City, MO), 2004.
Mary Engelbreit's A Merry Little Christmas, HarperCollins (New York, NY), 2006.

ILLUSTRATOR; FOR CHILDREN

Hans Christian Andersen, *The Snow Queen,* Workman Publishing, 1993.
Vitta Poplar, *Christmas with Mary Engelbreit: Here Comes Santa Claus,* Andrews McMeel (Kansas City, MO), 2002.
Clement C. Moore, *The Night before Christmas,* HarperCollins (New York, NY), 2002.
What Kids Do, Andrews McMeel (Kansas City, MO), 2003.
Mary Engelbreit's Mother Goose, HarperCollins (New York, NY), 2004.

ILLUSTRATOR

The Baby Book, Andrews McMeel (Kansas City, MO), 1992.
A Good Marriage, Andrews McMeel (Kansas City, MO), 1992.
Life Is Just a Chair of Bowlies, Andrews McMeel (Kansas City, MO), 1992.

Pals, Andrews McMeel (Kansas City, MO), 1992.

There Is No Friend like a Sister, Andrews McMeel (Kansas City, MO), 1993.

Mother o' Mine, Andrews McMeel (Kansas City, MO), 1993.

Don't Waste the Miracle, Andrews McMeel (Kansas City, MO), 1993.

Have Your Cake and Eat It Too!, Andrews McMeel (Kansas City, MO), 1993.

She Who Loves a Garden, Andrews McMeel (Kansas City, MO), 1993.

Take Good Care, Andrews McMeel (Kansas City, MO), 1993.

Thank You, Andrews McMeel (Kansas City, MO), 1993.

Don't Look Back, Andrews McMeel (Kansas City, MO), 1993.

Growing Up, Andrews McMeel (Kansas City, MO), 1993.

Mary Engelbreit's Sweetie Pie, edited by Jill Wolf, Antioch (Wellow Springs, OH), 1993.

Mary Engelbreit's Bountiful Harvest, edited by Jill Wolf, Antioch (Yellow Springs, OH), 1994.

Over the River and through the Woods, Andrews McMeel (Kansas City, MO), 1994.

'Tis the Season, Andrews McMeel (Kansas City, MO), 1994.

Mary Engelbreit's Home Companion: The Mary Engelbreit Look and How to Get It, text by Charlotte Lyons, Andrews McMeel (Kansas City, MO), 1995.

Home Sweet Home: A Homeowner's Journal and Project Planner, Andrews McMeel (Kansas City, MO), 1995.

All You Need Is a Friend, Andrews McMeel (Kansas City, MO), 1995.

Everyone Needs Their Own Spot: A Changing Picture Book, Andrews McMeel (Kansas City, MO), 1995.

It Never Hurts to Ask: A Changing Picture Book, Andrews McMeel (Kansas City, MO), 1995.

Christmas Companion: The Mary Engelbreit Look and How to Get It, text by Charlotte Lyons, Andrews McMeel (Kansas City, MO), 1995.

Something Tells Me It's Your Birthday . . . . : A Changing Picture Book, Andrews McMeel (Kansas City, MO), 1996.

Jan Miller Girando, *Home Is Where the Heart Is,* Andrews McMeel (Kansas City, MO), 1996.

Charlotte Lyons, *Mary Engelbreit's Autumn Craft Book,* Andrews McMeel (Kansas City, MO), 1996.

Charlotte Lyons, *Mary Engelbreit's Outdoor Companion: The Mary Engelbreit Look and How to Get It,* Andrews McMeel (Kansas City, MO), 1996.

Charlotte Lyons, *Mary Engelbreit's Winter Craft Book,* Andrews McMeel (Kansas City, MO), 1996.

Teaching Is Touching Tomorrow: A Changing Picture Book, Andrews McMeel (Kansas City, MO), 1996.

Jan Miller Girando, *Lives . . . Get One,* Andrews McMeel (Kansas City, MO), 1997.

Charlotte Lyons, *Mary Engelbreit's Children's Companion: The Mary Engelbreit Look and How to Get It,* Andrews McMeel (Kansas City, MO), 1997.

Charlotte Lyons, *Mary Engelbreit's Spring Craft Book,* Andrews McMeel (Kansas City, MO), 1997.

Charlotte Lyons, *Mary Engelbreit's Summer Craft Book,* Andrews McMeel (Kansas City, MO), 1997.

Time for Tea with Mary Engelbreit!, Andrews McMeel (Kansas City, MO), 1997.

The Wit of Whimsy of Mary Engelbreit, Andrews McMeel (Kansas City, MO), 1997.

William Henry Channing, *My Symphony,* Andrews McMeel (Kansas City, MO), 1997.

Mary Engelbreit's Cookies Cookbook, Andrews McMeel (Kansas City, MO), 1998.

Mary Engelbreit's Queen of the Kitchen Cookbook, Andrews McMeel (Kansas City, MO), 1998.

Terry Lee Bilsky, *This Woman Deserves a Party,* Andrews McMeel (Kansas City, MO), 1998.

Believe: A Christmas Treasury, Andrews McMeel (Kansas City, MO), 1998.

Crafts to Decorate Your Home, Better Homes & Gardens, 1999.

Words to Live By, Andrews McMeel (Kansas City, MO), 1999.

Mary Engelbreit's Sweet Treats: Dessert Cookbook, Andrews McMeel (Kansas City, MO), 1999.

A Very Mary Christmas: A Collection of Holiday Art, Andrews McMeel (Kansas City, MO), 1999.

Jan Miller Girando, *When a Child Is Born, So Is a Grandmother,* Andrews McMeel (Kansas City, MO), 1999.

Words for Mothers to Live By, Andrews McMeel (Kansas City, MO), 2000.

Mary Engelbreit's 'Tis the Season Holiday Cookbook, Andrews McMeel (Kansas City, MO), 2000.

Terry Lee Bilsky, *Sweetest Heart: A Book about Love,* Andrews McMeel (Kansas City, MO), 2000.

Words for Friends to Live By, Andrews McMeel (Kansas City, MO), 2001.

Virginia Carey, *Christmas with Mary Engelbreit: Let the Merrymaking Begin,* Andrews McMeel (Kansas City, MO), 2001.

Patrick Regan, *Happy to You: It's Your Birthday!,* Andrews McMeel (Kansas City, MO), 2001.

Mary Engelbreit Poster Book: Classic Collection, Andrews McMeel (Kansas City, MO), 2001.

Mary Engelbreit's Dining out Cookbook, Andrews McMeel (Kansas City, MO), 2001.

Mary Engelbreit's Let's Party Cookbook, Andrews McMeel (Kansas City, MO), 2001.

Words for Teachers to Live By, Andrews McMeel (Kansas City, MO), 2002.

Patrick Regan, *All Hail the Birthday Queen,* Andrews McMeel (Kansas City, MO), 2002.

Be It Ever So Humble, Andrews McMeel (Kansas City, MO), 2002.

Patrick Regan, *A Friend Indeed,* Andrews McMeel (Kansas City, MO), 2002.

The Best Christmas Ever with Mary Engelbreit, Andrews McMeel (Kansas City, MO), 2003.

Mary Engelbreit's You're Invited: A Cookbook for Special Occasions, Andrews McMeel (Kansas City, MO), 2003.

Words for Gardeners, Andrews McMeel (Kansas City, MO), 2003.

Such Devoted Sisters: A Sister's Treasury, Andrew McMeel (Kansas City, MO), 2005.

Adaptations

Artwork has been adapted as cross-stitch and other craft patterns. *Mary Engelbreit's Mother Goose* was adapted as an audiobook, read by Lynn Redgrave, HarperChildren's Audio, 2005.

Sidelights

Known for creating brightly colored artwork that combines gingham borders, cozy cottage interiors, Scotty dogs, and round-faced children with a nostalgic air, Mary Engelbreit is also a book illustrator and author who has produced everything from inspirational gift books and home-decorating guides to children's picture books. Inspired by the storybook illustrations recalled from childhood and favoring holidays and seasonal traditions, she is particularly notable for her holiday books such as *Believe: A Christmas Treasury,* a 1998 anthology of poems, carols, and holiday lore that Toni Hyde described in *Booklist* as an "imaginative and utterly enthralling collection" that is "literally overflowing with vibrant illustrations." A prolific artist who has created thousands of designs, she has also adapted one of her most popular characters, a blonde, bobbed-haired girl with large glasses named Ann Estelle, as the main character in a series of picture books that include *Queen of the Class, Queen of Christmas,* and *Queen of Hearts.*

Engelbreit's success has caused her to be compared with such creative talents as American painter Norman Rockwell, while her savvy as a businesswoman has made her as well known to home-style-watchers as Martha Stewart and Laura Ashley. *People* contributor Paula Chin described the artist's trademark style as "a cute and cluttered version of American homeyness"; Engelbreit's many greeting cards, mugs, posters, textiles, clothing, wallpapers, and other decorative creations feature "round-faced, impish kids, benign animals, flowered and checkered borders," according to Chin. Appraising *Mary Engelbreit: The Art and the Artist,* which profiles the artist's career and philosophy, a *Publishers Weekly* contributor described Engelbreit's art as "whimsical, nostalgic, and often veering to the cute or sentimental," yet also reflecting the artist's "celebration of love, faith, decency and the vicissitudes of everyday life."

Born in St. Louis, Missouri, in 1952, Engelbreit demonstrated enough enthusiasm and talent for drawing that her parents allowed her the use of an empty linen closet as a "studio" when she was age eleven. In addition to art, she exhibited an early talent for commerce, and with the encouragement of friends, was selling her original artwork while still in high school. Rather than go to college, she found a job at a St. Louis art-supply store, then moved to a local advertising agency. Meanwhile, in 1977 she married Phil Delano, with whom she would have two sons. Hoping to work from her own imagination, she took a portfolio of her works to New York City, but found that her dream of illustrating children's books was not a possibility. Undaunted by her rejec-

tions from book publishers, Engelbreit decided to pursue greeting-card sales, and by the mid-1980s was successfully licensing several of her designs. "I have always appreciated the little things that happen every day: laughing with friends, a hug, a beautiful sunset," she explained to *Hopscotch* interviewer Patricia Nikolina Clark. "From the time I was little, I collected those little moments in my head. That's what I illustrate . . . [on my cards]—those little moments."

Encouraged by her husband, Engelbreit decided to follow her dream to establish her own company. From its base of operations in the couple's basement, in 1983 the Mary Engelbreit Greeting Card Company marketed twelve of Engelbreit's designs at the annual National Stationery Show in New York City. On the back of each of her cards, she printed "This illustration is by Mary Engelbreit, who thanks you from the bottom of her heart for buying this card," a sentiment that has become something of a trademark. Within two years the company was producing a hundred designs and was licensing art for use in cards, calendars, and other objects. Delano left his job as a social worker to become Engelbreit's business manager, and the business prospered further as a result.

By the mid-1986 the Mary Engelbreit Card Company was involved in the design of thousands of cards and other objects, and the artist had begun cultivating a talented and creative staff to help her. More recently, the company has expanded into the Mary Engelbreit Studios, located in the author/artist's hometown of St. Louis. In addition to illustrations and licensed designs, Engelbreit has also established the Mary Engelbreit Store to retail her many products, and her company publishes *Mary Engelbreit's Home Companion,* a lifestyle magazine that provides readers with creative ways to bring the Engelbreit style home in each bi-monthly issue.

In 1992 Engelbreit's success in business was such that she was able to take some time to revisit her first love: children's book illustration. For three months she created illustrations for *The Snow Queen,* a version of Hans Christian Andersen's classic tale that became a bestseller. "I picked this story because it's one of the only fairy tales in which a little girl is the hero," Engelbreit explained on her company's Web site. After illustrating another classic work, William Henry Channing's poem "My Symphony," in 1998, she began a relationship with HarperCollins publisher and produced an illustrated version of *The Night before Christmas* which stayed on the *New York Times* bestseller list for over ten weeks in 2002.

Engelbreit has continued her relationship with Harper-Collins with her "Ann Estelle" books, beginning with 2003's *Queen of Christmas.* In this story, the young overachiever creates a comprehensive list for Santa that includes absolutely everything she has ever desired. As the holidays unfold, the girl becomes involved in fam-

ily activities such as cookie-baking, holiday decorating, and ice-skating and sledding, and the objects on the list fade in importance. The role of the queen in the school play is the subject of *Queen of the Class,* as Ann Estelle is appointed as stage manager rather than star and learns that the most important roles are not always the ones performed on stage. In *Publishers Weekly* a reviewer noted that Engelbreit's story in *Queen of Christmas* "authentically captures a child's anticipation" and contains "lots of heart," while in *Queen of the Class* "disappointment is majestically turned into exuberance," according to a *Kirkus Reviews* writer. Praising the "nostalgic artwork" created for *Queen of Hearts,* a *Kirkus Reviews* writer also noted that Engelbreit's Valentine's Day story presents young fans of Ann Estelle with "a sincere message amid the furbelows and frivolity" of the holiday's tradition.

"I have always believed that, if you chose a job you love, you'll never work a day in your life," Engelbreit noted on her company Web site. Describing her busy life as "a day-to-day adventure," she added: "I always adhere to this advice: Remain true to what you love doing most and believe in yourself."

Biographical and Critical Sources

BOOKS

Engelbreit, Mary, and Patrick Regan, *Mary Engelbreit: The Art and the Artist,* Andrews McMeel (Kansas City, MO), 1996.

Newsmakers 1994, issue 4, Thomson Gale (Detroit, MI), 1994.

PERIODICALS

Booklist, November 1, 1996, Ilene Cooper, review of *Mary Engelbreit,* p. 472; October 15, 1998, Toni Hyde, review of *Believe: A Christmas Treasury,* p. 374.

Hopscotch, April-May, 2005, Patricia Nikolina Clark, "The Queen of Everything" (interview), p. 10.

Kirkus Reviews, November 1, 2002, review of *The Night before Christmas,* p. 1623; June 1, 2004, review of *Queen of the Class,* p. 536; December 15, 2004, review of *Queen of Hearts,* p. 1201.

People, January 10, 1994, Paula Chin, interview with Engelbreit.

Publishers Weekly, September 11, 1995, review of *Christmas Companion: The Mary Engelbreit Look and How to Get It,* p. 82; August 26, 1996, review of *Mary Engelbreit,* p. 87; September 22, 2003, review of *Queen of Christmas,* p. 69; November 14, 2005, review of *Mary Engelbreit's Mother Goose,* p. 72.

School Library Journal, March, 1994, Karen K. Radkte, review of *The Show Queen,* p. 220; October, 2003, Eva Mitnick, review of *Queen of Christmas,* p. 62; July, 2004, Grace Oliff, review of *Queen of the Class,* p. 69; December, 2004, Julie Roach, review of *Queen of Hearts,* p. 106.

ONLINE

Mary Engelbreit Studios Web site, http://www.maryengelbreit.com (March 27, 2006).*

F

FENSHAM, Elizabeth

Personal
Born in Sydney, New South Wales, Australia; father a headmaster; married; husband an artist; children: two sons. *Education:* Sydney University, graduated.

Addresses
Home—Dandenong Ranges, Victoria, Australia. *Agent*—c/o Author Mail, Bloomsbury Publishing, 38 Soho Sq., London W1D 3HB, England.

Career
Writer. Worked variously as an assembly-line worker in a meat cannery, a nurse's aide, a house assistant in an orphanage, and a care-giver for intellectually disabled adults. Teacher in Dandenong Ranges, Victoria, Australia, beginning c. 1991, and head of English department.

Writings

Helicopter Man, Bloomsbury (New York, NY), 2005.

Biographical and Critical Sources

PERIODICALS

Booklist, August, 2005, Debbie Carton, review of *Helicopter Man,* p. 2015.
Kirkus Reviews, May 15, 2005, review of *Helicopter Man,* p. 587.
Magpies, September, 2005, Anne Briggs, review of *Helicopter Man,* p. 34.
School Librarian, autumn, 2005, Sophie Smiley, review of *Helicopter Man,* p. 154.

School Library Journal, June, 2005, Cooper Renner, review of *Helicopter Man,* p. 159.
Voice of Youth Advocates, June, 2005, Amanda Soliman, review of *Helicopter Man,* p. 128.

ONLINE

Bloomsbury Press Web site, http://www.bloomsbury.com/ (February 24, 2006), "Elizabeth Fensham."

*   *   *

FINDLAY, Jamieson 1958-

Personal
Born 1958, in Canada. *Education:* Queen's University (Toronto, Ontario, Canada), graduated; studied in Paris.

Addresses
Home—Ottawa, Ontario, Canada. *Agent*—c/o Author Mail, Random House of Canada, Toronto St., Unit 300, Toronto, Ontario M5C 2V6, Canada.

Career
Freelance writer, teacher, and science journalist.

Awards, Honors
Silver Medal, National Magazine Awards, 2001, for article in *Canadian Geographic.*

Writings

The Blue Roan Child, Doubleday (Toronto, Ontario, Canada), 2002, Scholastic (New York, NY), 2004.

Contributor of articles to periodicals, including *Canadian Geographic.*

When the colts of a beautiful mare are stolen, Syeira and the mare undertake a daunting quest: to locate the colts and free them from the evil lord who holds them captive. (Cover illustration by Tim O'Brien.)

Work in Progress

Another novel.

Sidelights

Award-winning Canadian science journalist and teacher Jamieson Findlay made his publishing debut in 2002 with the fantasy novel *The Blue Roan Child.* Taking place in an ancient time, the novel tells the story of a twelve-year-old orphan girl named Syeira who has a gift for working with horses. While employed in the royal stables in the kingdom of Hayselean, Syeira is especially drawn to Arwin, a blue roan mare of special intelligence who can communicate feelings and images through scent pictures. Of the highly prized Arva breed, Arwin has been recently captured in the wild along with her two foals. When the foals are stolen by Ran, the evil leader of the rival kingdom of Stormsythe, Syeira frees Arwin and joins the mare on a dangerous journey to Stormsythe to recover the lost foals, helped in her quest by a hermit knight and a lame sea captain named Grulla. Noting that "lots of olfactory details enrich the [novel's] well-realized, preindustrial setting," *School Library Journal* reviewer Beth Wright deemed

the book "an enjoyable fantasy from a new writer to be watched" Jennifer Mattson, reviewing the novel for *Booklist,* also enjoyed Findlay's debut, commenting that, despite the author's "lingering affection for dense description, symbolism, and stories within stories, . . . many fantasy devotees will relish his richly embroidered imaginings." In *Publishers Weekly* a critic deemed *The Blue Roan Child* "elegantly written," while in *Resource Links* K.V. Johansen cited Syeira as a "convincing and realistic" heroine whose "moral struggle and growth" add an ethical element to Findlay's "complex, suspenseful, and well-contrived" story.

In an interview for the Chicken House Publishers Web site, Findlay had some advice for aspiring writers: "The novelist Doris Lessing said that the most important part of writing is living. I would recommend going as deeply into life as you can, exploring it to the utmost, experiencing it fully—because you only get one chance. As a start, you might want to unplug your television." Findlay, who makes his home in Ottawa, has been inspired by his memories of growing up in Canada's remote Yukon Territory, but admits to getting many of his story ideas from dreams, from asking questions, and from "generally being as unproductive as possible."

Biographical and Critical Sources

PERIODICALS

Books in Canada, September, 2002, Karen Krossing, review of *The Blue Roan Child,* p. 44.
Booklist, June 1, 2004, Jennifer Mattson, review of *The Blue Roan Child,* p. 1726.
Bulletin of the Center for Children's Books, September, 2004, Krista Hutley, review of *The Blue Roan Child,* p. 15.
Canadian Book Review Annual, 2002, review of *The Blue Roan Child,* p. 490.
Kirkus Reviews, June 1, 2004, review of *The Blue Roan Child,* p. 536.
Publishers Weekly, August 2, 2004, review of *The Blue Roan Child,* p. 71.
Resource Links, October, 2002, K.V. Johansen, review of *The Blue Roan Child,* p. 13.
School Librarian, winter, 2004, Tricia Adams, review of *The Blue Roan Child,* p. 201.
School Library Journal, July, 2004, Beth Wright, review of *The Blue Roan Child,* p. 105.
Teacher Librarian, April, 2004, Helen Moore, review of *The Blue Roan Child,* p. 10.
Voice of Youth Advocates, October, 2004, Vivian Howard, review of *The Blue Roan Child,* p. 313.

ONLINE

Chicken House Web site, http://www.doublecluck.com/ (December 14, 2005), interview with Findlay.*

FINE, Edith Hope

Personal

Born in MI; daughter of Lawrence F. (a mechanical engineer) and Gertrude W. (a librarian, community volunteer) Hope; children: Michael S., Gregory S. *Education:* Ohio Wesleyan University, B.A., 1965. *Hobbies and other interests:* Recycling, composting, reading, politics and international relations, swimming.

Addresses

Agent—c/o Author Mail, Enslow Publishers, Box 398, 40 Industrial Rd., Berkeley Heights, NJ 07922-0398.

Career

Teacher, 1965-95; writer, beginning 1980; San Diego State University, San Diego, CA, teacher, 1985-2003.

Member

California Reading Association, California Association of Teachers of English, Society of Children's Book Writers and Illustrators (San Diego chapter), American Association of University Women, Voices of Women.

Awards, Honors

EDPress Award for Excellence for Juvenile Feature; *Smithsonian* Notable Children's Book designation; Parents' Choice Silver Honor; Notable Social Studies Trade Books for Young People.

Edith Hope Fine

Writings

The Python and Anaconda, edited by Judy Lockwood, Crestwood House (Mankato, MN), 1988.

The Turtle and Tortoise, edited by Judy Lockwood, Crestwood House (Mankato, MN), 1988.

(With Pat Dorff and Judith A. Josephson) *File—Don't Pile!: For People Who Write: Handling the Paper Flow in the Workplace or Home Office,* St. Martin's Press (New York, NY), 1994.

Barbara McClintock: Nobel Prize Geneticist, Enslow Publishers (Springfield, NJ), 1998.

(With Judith P. Josephson) *Nitty-Gritty Grammar: A Not So-Serious Guide to Clear Communication,* Ten Speed Press (Berkeley, CA), 1998.

Under the Lemon Moon, illustrated by Renée King Moreno, Lee & Low Books (New York, NY), 1999.

Gary Paulsen: Author and Wilderness Adventurer, Enslow Publishers (Berkeley Heights, NJ), 2000.

Snapshots, Bebop Books (New York, NY), 2001.

(With Judith P. Josephson) *More Nitty-Gritty Grammar: Another Not-So-Serious Guide to Clear Communication,* Ten Speed Press (Berkeley, CA), 2001.

CryptoMania!: Teleporting into Greek and Latin with the CryptoKids, illustrated by Kim Doner, Tricycle Press (Berkeley, CA), 2004.

Rosa Parks: Meet a Civil-Rights Hero, Enslow (Berkeley Heights, NJ), 2004.

Cricket at the Manger, illustrated by Winslow Pels, Boyds Mills Press (Honesdale, PA), 2005.

Martin Luther King, Jr.: Champion of Civil Rights, Enslow (Berkeley Heights, NJ), 2006.

Work in Progress

"Three books, one set in Mexico, written with Judith P. Josephson, for Lee & Low, 2007; one set during the Yukon gold rush; and one about early automotive history, plus hundreds others waiting backstage."

Sidelights

Edith Hope Fine told *SATA:* "I'm crazy about books! I grew up reading, starting with comic books like Little Lulu and Scrooge McDuck. I wrote a zany dictionary with I was twelve—inventing words and making up definitions. My mother, who also loved words, typed it for me. She put the pages into a small notebook, which showed me that words are cool and that she valued my ideas. Today I still read everything I can get my hands on: kids' books, young-adult books, novels, mysteries, newspapers, billboards, cereal boxes. . . .

"Some books are meant to be savored. I read them slowly. Their rhythmic, wondrous sentences beg to be

read over and over. Out loud. And sometimes a book is so funny or poignant or moving or ethical that the minute I finish, I'll go right back to the beginning and start again, this time watching for clues as to how the writer swept me into the story.

"After years of teaching, I started writing seriously in 1980—for newspapers and magazines (both for adults and children). I wrote a weekly newspaper column for thirteen years—that cured me of writer's block, for sure. Since 1989, I've written thirteen books, three of them with colleague Judith P. Josephson. My book club meets monthly and my writing group has met every other Wednesday since 1989. My *CryptoMania!: Teleporting into Greek and Latin with the CryptoKids* has evolved into the CryptoKids Decoder Program, now in use across the country, helping young readers teleport into Greek and Latin roots.

"I speak often at conferences and do author visits and schools and libraries. I salute teachers and librarians: they forge on, never knowing the full impact of their important work.

"When I'm not writing or reading, you'll find me at the swimming pool or walking, making soup (I love soup) or baking, watching old-time movies, doing Sukokus or jigsaw puzzles, knitting, having fun with friends, family, and four grands, e-mailing pals around the country, and composting and recycling (I've been dubbed 'the Recycling Queen'). I pay attention to what's going on in the world, believe we can all work together for fairness and justice on this small blue marble we call home.

"My advice to new writers? Start now—today! This minute! And persist. Be original. Believe in yourself."

Biographical and Critical Sources

PERIODICALS

Booklist, January 1, 1999, Carolyn Phelan, review of *Barbara McClintock: Nobel Prize Geneticist,* p. 848; Mary 15, 1999, Susan Dove Lempke, review of *Under the Lemon Moon,* p. 1702; February 15, 2004, Hazel Rochman, review of *Rosa Parks: Meet a Civil-Rights Hero,* p. 1073; September 1, 2005, Julie Cummins, review of *Cricket at the Manger,* p. 144.

Instructor, October, 2001, review of *Under the Lemon Moon,* p. 18.

Kirkus Reviews, November 1, 2005, review of *Cricket at the Manger,* p. 1193.

Library Journal, June 1, 1998, Lisa J. Cihlar, review of *Nitty-Gritty Grammar: A Not-So-Serious Guide to Clear Communication,* p. 108.

Parents, June, 2002, review of *Under the Lemon Moon,* p. 126.

After the fruit from her tree is stolen, Rosalinda enlists the help of la Anciana, an aged woman who travels Mexico and helps plants to grow, in **Under the Lemon Moon.** *(Illustration by René King Moreno.)*

Plays, October, 1999, review of *Nitty-Gritty Grammar,* p. 64.

Publishers Weekly, Mary 4, 1998, review of *Nitty-Gritty Grammar,* p. 200; April 19, 1999, review of *Under the Lemon Moon,* p. 72.

School Education, May, 2000, review of *Under the Lemon Moon,* p. 14.

School Library Journal, March, 1989, Karey Wehner, review of *The Python and Anaconda,* p. 190; March, 1999, Ann G. Brouse, review of *Barbara McClintock,* p. 220; April, 1999, Ann Welton, review of *Under the Lemon Moon,* p. 94; September, 2000, Carol Faziolo, review of *Gary Paulsen: Author and Wilderness Adventurer,* p. 244; November, 2004, Lynda Ritterman, review of *Teleporting into Greek and Latin with the Crypto Kids,* p. 143.

Writer, August, 1999, review of *Nitty-Gritty Grammar,* p. 47.

ONLINE

Edith Fine Web site, http://www.grammarpatrol.com (February 24, 2006).

G

GABER, Susan 1956-

Personal

Born June 23, 1956, in Brooklyn, NY; married Richard Barkey, 1988; children: Elias. *Education:* C.W. Post College/Long Island University, B.F.A., 1978. *Hobbies and other interests:* Gardening, herbology.

Addresses

Home—44 Dunlop Rd., Huntington, NY 11743. *E-mail*—info@susangaber.com.

Career

Illustrator and graphic artist.

Member

Graphic Artists' Guild.

Illustrator

Alvin Silverstein, *The Story of Your Ear,* Coward, McCann & Geoghegan (New York, NY), 1981.

Jay H. Heyman, *The Gourmet Guide to Water Cookery,* Avon (New York, NY), 1983.

Heather Forest, *The Baker's Dozen,* Harcourt (New York, NY), 1988.

Heather Forest, *The Woman Who Flummoxed the Fairies,* Harcourt (New York, NY), 1990.

Jacqueline Briggs Martin, *The Finest Horse in Town,* HarperCollins (New York, NY), 1992.

Jacqueline Briggs Martin, *Good Times on Grandfather Mountain,* Orchard Books (New York, NY), 1992.

Elizabeth Enright, *Zeee,* Harcourt (New York, NY), 1993.

Emma Bull, *The Princess and the Lord of Night,* Harcourt (New York, NY), 1994.

Lee Bennett Hopkins, *Small Talk,* Harcourt (New York, NY), 1995.

Steve Sanfield, *Bit by Bit,* Philomel (New York, NY), 1995.

Alma Flor Ada, *Jordi's Star,* Putnam (New York, NY), 1996.

Liz Rosenberg, *Eli and Uncle Dawn,* Harcourt (New York, NY), 1997.

Rafe Martin, *The Brave Little Parrot,* Putnam (New York, NY), 1997.

Heather Forest, *Stone Soup,* August House, 1998.

Erica Silverman, *Raisel's Riddle,* Farrar, Straus (New York, NY), 1998.

Rhonda Growler Greene, *The Stable Where Jesus Was Born,* Atheneum (New York, NY), 1999.

Jennifer Armstrong, *Pierre's Dream,* Dial (New York, NY), 1999.

Rafe Martin, *The Language of Birds,* Putnam (New York, NY), 2000.

Nancy Van Laan, *When Winter Comes,* Atheneum (New York, NY), 2000.

Phyllis Root, *Ten Sleepy Sheep,* Candlewick Press (Cambridge, MA), 2004.

Heather Henson, *Angel Coming,* Atheneum (New York, NY), 2005.

Dianna Hutts Aston, *Mama Outside, Mama Inside,* Henry Holt (New York, NY), 2006.

Illustrations have appeared in *Child, Spider, Home, Fifty Plus,* and *House Beautiful.*

Sidelights

Whether working in muted impressionistic tones, in more vibrant colors, or in a folksy, homespun medium, Susan Gaber has built an impressive list of illustration credits, and has garnered much critical acclaim for her work. Worked in watercolors, acrylics, or colored pencils, Gaber's illustrations "captivate the eye," as Barbara Elleman noted in *School Library Journal.* At times her artistic contributions imbue stories with a folksy feel, while others impart a lushness and vividness of tone, sometimes gaining the feel of elegant fine-art reproductions. Her versatility is particularly well suited to mythic stories and folk tales such as *The Baker's Dozen* by Heather Forest and Rafe Martin's *The Language of Birds,* as well as to fanciful stories such as Phyllis Root's *Ten Sleepy Sheep.*

With all the beauty of a Renaissance tapestry, Susan Gaber's illustrations for **The Princess and the Lord of Night** *enhance Emma Bull's fairy tale about a girl determined to end a curse put on her at birth.*

Born in Brooklyn, New York, Gaber grew up in Wantagh, Long Island. Graduating from high school in 1974, she attended Long Island University where she earned a bachelor of fine arts degree with honors in 1978. That same year she began her freelancing career, working as an illustrator for card companies as well as newspapers and magazines. By 1988 she had enlarged her repertoire to included illustrations for children's books.

Gaber's first children's title was 1988's *The Baker's Dozen,* published the same year she married. The artist teamed up with Forest again in 1990 for *The Woman Who Flummoxed the Fairies,* and again in 1998 for *Stone Soup,* another traditional tale about two hungry travelers who declare they can make soup from a stone when they are denied food at a mountain village. But they explain they just need a carrot for taste, and then perhaps a little potato would also help. In this way the duo manage to outwit the villagers and create a pot of steaming soup. "Gaber's bold acrylic paintings emphasize the black soup tureen and the brightly colored vegetable ingredients," noted a reviewer for *Publishers Weekly,* while Kathleen Whalin commented in *School Library Journal* that "Gaber's brilliantly colored paintings illuminate a mountain village with a multicultural population."

Gaber teamed up with writer Jacqueline Briggs Martin for *The Finest Horse in Town* and *Good Times on Grandfather Mountain.* The first book, a fictionalized memoir of Martin's two great-aunts, introduces readers to sisters who run a dry goods store in nineteenth-century Maine and to their carriage horse, Prince. A contributor to *Publishers Weekly* felt that "Gaber's exquisite watercolors have the naive beauty of early American folk paintings," and Charlene Strickland noted in *School Library Journal* that the book's "full-color paintings illustrate the mild humor of the incidents and capture the essence of small-town concerns." *Good Times on Grandfather Mountain* tells of Old Washburn who always looks on the bright side of things: when the cow runs off he has a drum instead of milk bucket; when the pig follows suit, the former fence posts become drum sticks. Told in the cadences of a folk tale, the book is a "rustic narrative," according to *Publishers Weekly,* and "Gaber's watercolors imbue this cautionary tale with a folksy flavor that suggest good times indeed." As *Horn Book* contributor Nancy Vasilakis noted, "The imagery of humans in communal harmony with nature is carried through in illustrations."

Gaber turns from rustic to fanciful with illustrations for Elizabeth Enright's *Zeee.* The book introduces an ancient, misanthropic fairy whose hatred for humankind changes when he is befriended by young Pandora, a girl who offers Zeee the comfort of her dollhouse. Writing of Gaber's illustrations in *School Library Journal,* Valerie F. Patterson noted that they are "colorful and attractive," and "feature colored shadings of brown and green with occasional flashes of red." *Booklist* critic Ellen Mandel commented that "Gaber's lush watercolors delight in their conjuring of Zeee's first tidy home, with its milkweed pod bed, clamshell bathtub, and chrysalis lantern."

Gaber's illustrations for Emma Bull's *The Princess and the Lord of Night* bring to life the story about a lord who puts a curse on the infant princess so that if she ever wishes for something she cannot have, the kingdom will fall and her parents will die. Reviewing the book in *School Library Journal,* Lauralyn Persson wrote that Gaber's "romantic watercolor-and-colored pencil illustrations are lush yet delicate, with clear, rich colors and lovely, flowing lines," while a *Publishers Weekly* reviewer deemed them "elegant illustrations" containing "a Renaissance luminosity and precision."

Thirty-three short poems are collected by Lee Bennett Hopkins in *Small Talk,* a celebration of simple moments in life for which Gaber contributed the illustrations. The verses deal with the seasons, growing up, the process of a day to night, the birth of a kitten, and dozens of other domestic joys from the pens of poets such as Langston Hughes, Sara Teasdale, and Carl Sandburg, among others. Dot Minzer, reviewing the picture book in *School Library Journal,* felt "Gaber's watercolor and colored-pencil illustrations appear as little gems at the top of many of the poems and as double-page backgrounds for

others." Minzer concluded that Gaber and Hopkins's collaboration results in a "stunning little book." In *Horn Book* Nancy Vasilakis commented that "this small, well-designed book with its lovely watercolor spots and double-page-spread illustrations has copious depths to be mined."

Based on a Yiddish folk song, Steven Sanfield's *Bit by Bit* tells the story of Zundel, a tailor who wears out his favorite coat and then turns the scraps into further favorite garments which he proceeds to wear out bit by bit. "Imaginative pictures embroider the story line in this suitably homespun adaptation," noted a reviewer for *Publishers Weekly*. Barbara Kiefer, writing in *School Library Journal*, commented that "Gaber's folk-like paintings, done in strong, clear colors, echo the brightly painted threads that are central to the tale." As Kiefer added, "Gaber shows us what the words don't tell us, that as Zundel's garments become smaller and smaller, his life becomes richer and fuller." *Booklist* critic Hazel Rochman echoed this sentiment, noting that the "pictures extend the song, showing the tailor with his loving family through the years, as each piece of clothing wears out."

The traditional Cinderella tale gets a revamping in Silverman's *Raisel's Tale,* inspired by another Yiddish tale. Finding work in the kitchen of a famed rabbi, Raisel,

Gaber's illustrations for Rafe Martin's The Language of Birds, *a tale about two brothers whose values are tested by adversity, reflect the story's Russian folktale origins.*

the orphan of a scholar, is mistreated by the cook and kept from the Purim party. However, Raisel disguises herself as Queen Esther, attends the party, and there charms the rabbi's son. *Booklist* contributor GraceAnne A. DeCandido commented that "the illustrations in velvety, muted colors make use of strong geometric shapes and varying perspectives," and concluded: "This universal story fits into its Jewish milieu as neatly as a key in a lock." Susan P. Bloom, reviewing the title in *Horn Book,* cited the work for conveying "a folkish simplicity with a sophisticated line."

A traditional jataka tale from India is the core of *The Brave Little Parrot,* one of several collaborations between Gaber and writer Rafe Martin. In this story, a small gray parrot takes on a raging forest fire. "Gaber's paintings are rich with lush greens and flaming oranges," remarked Judith Gloyer in *School Library Journal,* describing the illustrator's contribution to Martin's work. "Gaber's moving, full-page, color illustrations increase the drama of the fire," commented *Booklist* reviewer Karen Morgan, adding that the artwork reflect "the precious beauty of water and its relationship to continued life." Gaber has also teamed up with Martin on *The Language of Birds,* based on a Russian folktale about a young man able to understand the birds of the air. Describing Gaber's art for this book as including "lush, stylized scenes . . . rendered in a richly saturated palette whose subtle gradations recall old oriental rugs," a *Horn Book* contributor cited the overall effect as "dramatic and expressive." Praising in particular Gaber's border art, which features "stylized bird tracks, profiles of birds, and feathers," Denise Anton Wright noted in *School Library Journal* that Gaber's "pictures are often quite powerful." Citing the artist's "stunning" illustrations as "the high point of this Russian fairytale," a *Publishers Weekly* critic deemed *The Language of Birds* "a memorable presentation."

Fantasy takes over in Liz Rosenberg's *Eli and Uncle Dawn* in which young Eli learns that his uncle's magic is for real. Forgetting his stuffed elephant at a picnic, the boy is able to float through the night to retrieve it, thanks to Uncle Dawn. A contributor to *Publishers Weekly* commented that Gaber "crafts a stimulating backdrop to this imaginative tale" by using "a color-saturated blend of watercolor, acrylic and colored pencil, and setting a lively visual pace that skips from full-page illustrations to small insets." In *Pierre's Dream,* by Jennifer Armstrong, another night-time, dream-like pursuit results in a rescued animal—this time real—when lazy Pierre recaptures a lion from the circus. Reviewing the 1999 work, a *Publishers Weekly* reviewer noted that "Gaber fills in any gaps in narrative logic with a soft impressionistic touch that gracefully moves between the real and imagined."

In addition to exploring the folk and fantasy tales of other lands, Gaber has also worked on books that bring to life the unique aspects of American culture and history. In her work for *The Very First Thanksgiving Day,*

In Heather Henson's Angel Coming *the author and illustrator Gaber collaborate on a picture-book tribute to the Frontier Nursing Service that worked throughout the rural United States during the early twentieth century.*

which features a rhyming text by Rhonda Gowler Greene, she contributes "pleasing acrylic paintings" that move the text from "adequate to engaging," according to *School Library Journal* contributor Jody McCoy. Moving to the twentieth century, her paintings for Heather Henson's *Angel Coming* evokes the quiet world of rural Appalachia during the 1920s. In Henson's story, a girl waits excitedly for a new sibling to be born into the world, and Gaber's "attractive, realistic acrylic paintings show the family's preparations" for the baby's coming, according to *School Library Journal* reviewer Maryann H. Owen. Noting the story's basis in the history of the Frontier Nursing Service, a *Kirkus Reviews* writer noted that Gaber's sunlit landscapes and rendering of the story's characters "seem lit from within." Another farm family is brought to life in the artist's work for *Mama Outside, Mama Inside,* a bedtime storybook that finds a pregnant mother awaiting her first baby inside her home while a bluebird feathers her nest and lays her eggs outside. In *Booklist,* Gaber's art was praised by Jennifer Mattson as "outstanding,

rich in color and texture and filled with details to enhance side-by-side sharing." "Warm, expressive paintings make this picture book a joyful experience," wrote Andrea Tarr in *School Library Journal,* while a *Kirkus Reviews* writer cited *Mama Outside, Mama Inside* as "a gentle reminder of nature's parallels."

Biographical and Critical Sources

PERIODICALS

Booklist, June 1 & 15, 1993, Ellen Mandel, review of *Zeee,* pp. 1830-1831; March 15, 1995, Hazel Rochman, review of *Bit by Bit,* p. 1336; December 1, 1996, Susan Dove Lempke, review of *Jordi's Star,* p. 652; February 15, 1998, Karen Morgan, review of *The Brave Little Parrot,* pp. 1014, 1016; May 1, 1999, GraceAnne A. DeCandido, review of *Raisel's Riddle,* p. 1590; July, 2001, Stephanie Zvirin, review of *The*

Language of Birds, p. 2011; April 1, 2004, Jennifer Mattson, review of *Ten Sleepy Sheep,* p. 1370; July, 2005, Carolyn Phelan, review of *Antel Coming,* p. 1922.

Horn Book, May-June, 1992, Nancy Vasilakis, review of *Good Times on Grandfather Mountain,* pp. 332-333; May-June, 1995, Nancy Vasilakis, review of *Small Talk,* pp. 338-339; March-April, 1999, Susan P. Bloom, review of *Raisel's Riddle,* p. 215; July, 2000, review of *The Language of Birds,* p. 470; May-June, 2005, Lauren Adams, review of *Ten Sleepy Sheep,* p. 319.

Kirkus Reviews, May 15, 2005, review of *Angel Coming,* p. 590; March 1, 2006, review of *Mama Outside, Mama Inside,* p. 226.

Publishers Weekly, February 3, 1992, review of *Good Times on Grandfather Mountain,* p. 80; June 22, 1992, review of *The Finest Horse in Town,* p. 61; February 28, 1994, review of *The Princess and the Lord of Night,* p. 87; March 20, 1995, review of *Bit by Bit,* p. 59; November 4, 1996, review of *Jordi's Star,* p. 75; February 3, 1997, review of *Eli and Uncle Dawn,* p. 105; May 25, 1998, review of *Stone Soup,* p. 89; May 31, 1999, review of *Pierre's Dream,* p. 92; June 19, 2000, review of *The Language of Birds,* p. 79; February 9, 2004, review of *Ten Sleepy Sheep,* p. 79; May 2, 2005, review of *Angel Coming,* p. 198.

School Library Journal, August, 1992, Kate McClelland, review of *Good Times on Grandfather Mountain,* p. 144; August, 1992, Charlene Strickland, review of *The Finest Horse in Town,* p. 144; June, 1993, Valerie F. Patterson, review of *Zeee,* pp. 74-75; May, 1994, Lauralyn Persson, review of *The Princess and the Lord of Night,* p. 89; May, 1995, Dot Minzer, review of *Small Talk,* p. 99; August, 1995, Barbara Kiefer, review of *Bit by Bit,* p. 128; May, 1998, Judith Gloyer, review of *The Brave Little Parrot,* p. 135; May, 1998, Kathleen Whalin, review of *Stone Soup,* pp. 131-132; June, 1999, Barbara Elleman, review of *Pierre's Dream,* p. 85; July, 2000, Denise Anton Wright, review of *The Language of Birds,* p. 96; October, 2002, Jody McCoy, review of *The Very First Thanksgiving Day,* p. 111; July, 2005, Maryann H. Owen, review of *Angel Coming,* p. 75; March, 2006, Andrea Tarr, review of *Mama Outside, Mama Inside,* p. 174.*

*   *   *

GANTOS, Jack 1951-
(John Bryan Gantos, Jr.)

Personal

Born July 2, 1951, in Mount Pleasant, PA; son of John (a construction superintendent) and Elizabeth (Weaver) Gantos (a banker); married Anne A. Lower (an art dealer), November 11, 1989; children: Mabel Grace. *Education:* Emerson College, B.F.A., 1976, M.A., 1984. *Politics:* "Liberal Democrat." *Religion:* Roman Catholic.

Jack Gantos

Addresses

Home—38 W. Newton St., Boston, MA 02118.

Career

Author and educator. Emerson College, Boston, MA, professor of creative writing and literature, 1978-95. Visiting professor at Brown University, 1986, University of New Mexico, 1993, and Vermont College, 1996. Frequent speaker at schools, libraries, and educational conferences; facilitator of writing workshops.

Member

Pen International, American Association of University Professors, National Council of Teachers of English, Society of Children's Book Writers and Illustrators, Writer's Guild, Amnesty International.

Awards, Honors

Best Books for Young Readers citation, American Library Association (ALA), 1976-93, for "Rotten Ralph Readers" series; Children's Book Showcase Award, 1977, for *Rotten Ralph;* Emerson College Alumni Award, 1979, for outstanding Achievement in Creative Writing; Massachusetts Council for the Arts Awards finalist, 1983, 1988; Gold Key Honor Society Award for Creative Excellence, 1985; National Endowment for the Arts grant, 1987, and fellowship; Quarterly West Novella Award, 1989, for *X-Rays;* Children's Choice cita-

tion, International Reading Association (IRA), 1990, for *Rotten Ralph's Show and Tell;* Batavia Educational Foundation grant, 1991; West Springfield Arts Council grant, 1991; Parents' Choice citation, 1994, for *Not So Rotten Ralph;* New York Public Library Books for the Teen Age designation, 1997, for *Jack's Black Book,* and 2002, for *Hole in My Life;* Silver Award, 1999, for *Jack on the Tracks;* Great Stone Face Award, Children's Librarians of New Hampshire, National Book Award finalist for Young People's Literature, ALA Notable Children's Book, National Council of the Social Studies/Children's Book Council Notable Children's Trade Book designation in the field of social studies, *School Library Journal* Best Book of the Year designation, named *Riverbank Review* Children's Book of Distinction, and New York Public Library One Hundred Titles for Reading and Sharing listee; all 1999, Iowa Teen Award, Iowa Educational Media Association, Flicker Tale Children's Book Award nomination, North Dakota Library Association, and Sasquatch Award nomination, all 2000, all for *Joey Pigza Swallowed the Key;* Newbery Honor, ALA, 2001, for *Joey Pigza Loses Control;* Michael L. Printz Honor, ALA Best Book for Young Adults designation, Massachusetts Children's Book Award, Parents' Choice Award, and Robert F. Sibert honor, all c. 2002, all for *Hole in My Life;* other regional and child-selected awards.

Writings

"ROTTEN RALPH READERS" PICTURE-BOOK SERIES

Rotten Ralph, illustrated by Nicole Rubel, Houghton Mifflin (Boston, MA), 1976.
Worse than Rotten, Ralph, illustrated by Nicole Rubel, Houghton Mifflin (Boston, MA), 1978.
Rotten Ralph's Rotten Christmas, illustrated by Nicole Rubel, Houghton Mifflin (Boston, MA), 1984.
Rotten Ralph's Trick or Treat!, illustrated by Nicole Rubel, Houghton Mifflin (Boston, MA), 1986, reprinted, 2004.
Rotten Ralph's Show and Tell, illustrated by Nicole Rubel, Houghton Mifflin (Boston, MA), 1989.
Happy Birthday Rotten Ralph, illustrated by Nicole Rubel, Houghton Mifflin (Boston, MA), 1990.
Not So Rotten Ralph, illustrated by Nicole Rubel, Houghton Mifflin (Boston, MA), 1994.
Rotten Ralph's Rotten Romance, illustrated by Nicole Rubel, Houghton Mifflin (Boston, MA), 1997.
The Christmas Spirit Attacks Rotten Ralph, illustrated by Nicole Rubel, HarperCollins (New York, NY), 1998.
Rotten Ralph's Halloween Howl, illustrated by Nicole Rubel, HarperCollins (New York, NY), 1998.
Back to School for Rotten Ralph, illustrated by Nicole Rubel, HarperCollins (New York, NY), 1998.
Wedding Bells for Rotten Ralph, illustrated by Nicole Rubel, HarperCollins (New York, NY), 1999.
Rotten Ralph's Thanksgiving Wish, illustrated by Nicole Rubel, Farrar, Strauss (New York, NY), 1999.

Rotten Ralph Helps Out, illustrated by Nicole Rubel, Farrar, Strauss (New York, NY), 2001.
Rotten Ralph Plays Fair, illustrated by Nicole Rubel, Farrar, Strauss (New York, NY), 2002.
Practice Makes Perfect for Rotten Ralph, illustrated by Nicole Rubel, Farrar, Strauss (New York, NY), 2002.
Rotten Ralph Feels Rotten, illustrated by Nicole Rubel, Farrar, Strauss (New York, NY), 2004.
Best in Show for Rotten Ralph, illustrated by Nicole Rubel, Farrar, Strauss (New York, NY), 2005.

The "Rotten Ralph" books have been translated into other languages, including Hebrew and Japanese.

PICTURE BOOKS

Sleepy Ronald, illustrated by Nicole Rubel, Houghton Mifflin (Boston, MA), 1976.
Fair-Weather Friends, illustrated by Nicole Rubel, Houghton Mifflin (Boston, MA), 1977.
Aunt Bernice, illustrated by Nicole Rubel, Houghton Mifflin (Boston, MA), 1978.
The Perfect Pal, illustrated by Nicole Rubel, Houghton Mifflin (Boston, MA), 1979.
(With Nicole Rubel) *Greedy Greeny,* illustrated by Nicole Rubel, Doubleday (New York), 1979.
Swampy Alligator, illustrated by Nicole Rubel, Simon & Schuster (New York, NY), 1980.
The Werewolf Family, illustrated by Nicole Rubel, Houghton Mifflin (Boston, MA), 1980.
Willy's Raiders, illustrated by Nicole Rubel, Parents Magazine Press (New York, NY), 1981.

"JACK HENRY" SERIES; AUTOBIOGRAPHICAL FICTION FOR MIDDLE-GRADE READERS

Heads or Tails: Stories from the Sixth Grade, Farrar, Straus (New York, NY), 1994.
Jack's New Power: Stories from a Caribbean Year, Farrar, Straus (New York, NY), 1995.
Jack's Black Book, Farrar, Straus (New York, NY), 1997.
Jack on the Tracks: Four Seasons of Fifth Grade, Farrar, Straus (New York, NY), 1999.
Jack Adrift: Fourth Grade without a Clue, Farrar, Straus (New York, NY), 2003.

"JOEY PIGZA" MIDDLE-GRADE NOVEL SERIES

Joey Pigza Swallowed the Key, Farrar, Straus (New York, NY), 1998.
Joey Pigza Loses Control, Farrar, Straus (New York, NY), 2000.
What Would Joey Do?, Farrar, Strauss (New York, NY), 2002.
I Am Not Joey Pigza, Farrar, Strauss (New York, NY), 2007.

OTHER

Zip Six (adult novel), Bridge Works (Bridgehampton, NY), 1996.

Desire Lines (young-adult novel), Farrar, Straus (New York, NY), 1997.

Hole in My Life (young-adult autobiography), Farrar, Strauss (New York, NY), 2001.

(Author of introduction) Edward Eager, *Half Magic* (50th anniversary edition), illustrated by N.M. Bodecker, Harcourt (Orlando, FL), 2004.

The Love Curse of the Rumbaughs (young-adult novel), Farrar, Straus (New York, NY), 2006.

Also author of novella *X-Rays*. Contributor of short fiction to anthologies, including *No Easy Answers: Short Stories about Teenagers Making Tough Choices*, edited by Donald R. Gallo, Delacorte, 1997; and *On the Fringe*, edited by Gallo, 2001. Contributor to magazines, including *Storyworks*.

Adaptations

Joey Pigza Swallowed the Key, read by the author, was released on audio cassette by Listening Library in 1999; *Heads or Tails: Stories from the Sixth Grade* was released on audio cassette; *What Would Joey Do?* was adapted for audiobook by Listening Library, 2002. The "Rotten Ralph" books have been adapted for television. Two Rotten Ralph animated specials were produced and broadcast on the Disney Channel; in addition, the BBC produced individual programs based on the character for broadcast in the English-speaking European and Asian markets.

Work in Progress

A four-book series for upper elementary readers.

Sidelights

A popular and prolific author of books for readers ranging from the early primary grades through adults, Jack Gantos is considered both a gifted humorist and an insightful observer of childhood feelings and behavior. His middle-grade fiction presents bittersweet reflections on the pains and pleasures of growing up, while his novels for young adults deal frankly with serious themes. Gantos is perhaps best known as the creator of Rotten Ralph, a large, red, anthropomorphic cat whose devilish and unrepentant behavior is always forgiven by his patient young owner, Sarah. Gantos has collaborated on a series of picture books featuring the rascally feline with illustrator Nicole Rubel, whose bright colors and bold designs complement the author's brisk, droll prose.

Gantos's "Jack Henry" books describe the experiences of the author's alter ego during his fifth-, sixth-, and seventh-grade years. *Joey Pigza Swallowed the Key*, a story about a boy with Attention Deficit Hyperactive Disorder (ADHD), introduces another of Gantos's popular series characters, while in the YA novel *Desire Lines* a teen outs two lesbian classmates in order to save his own reputation. Other works address issues important to teens, such as the nature of friendship, dealing with jealousy and loneliness, being forgiven and accepted,

the importance of playing fair and doing the right thing, and learning how to fit into the often baffling world of adults. Although some of the award-winning author's books have been labeled as exaggerated, irreverent, or unsubtle, and include elements that are considered gross or unsettling, many critics have cited the positive values in Gantos's books, as well as his stories' outrageous humor and underlying poignancy. His memoir *Hole in My Life* has received many awards.

Born in Mount Pleasant, Pennsylvania, Gantos was the first son born to John Gantos, Sr., a construction superintendent and salesman of Lebanese descent, and Elizabeth Weaver Gantos. He began expressing his creativity at an early age, and when he was in the second grade, he received a diary, which he had coveted because his older sister had one. "I wrote the date, the weather, and what I ate for breakfast, lunch, and dinner," Gantos later recalled of his daily diary entries. "Food was the most important thing in the world to me and so I wrote about it all the time." As a child Gantos also collected what he would later call "a lot of junk": shells, rocks, stamps, pennies, bottle caps, baseball cards, butterflies, and "lots more good stuff."

In second grade Gantos moved with his family from Pennsylvania to Barbados, where his father hoped to find work. Jack moved his collections by incorporating them into his diaries, gluing, pasting, and even drilling holes in the books. The move to Barbados prompted a change in Jack's journal entries. "I began to write about all the stuff that was in my diary. I wrote about where I caught my bugs. I wrote about the stamps I collected. I wrote stories about the photographs I had saved. And I became a lot more excited about keeping a diary because so much of what I wrote about had personal meaning to me. To this day I still put lots of junk in my notebooks and write about it. The junk and stuff has become the details in much of my writing."

While in Barbados, Gantos attended British schools that emphasized the importance of reading and writing; he later claimed that by fifth grade he had managed to learn ninety percent of what he knows as an adult. When the family relocated to south Florida, Gantos's new classmates were disinterested in their studies, and teachers generally acted more like disciplinarians than instructors. In addition to spending more of his time reading, in the sixth grade he began collecting anecdotes and writing down his own thoughts and feelings. "Most of the stories were from real life," he recalled. "I saw a plane crash and wrote about it. My father rescued a drowning husband and wife in the ocean. He was heroic, and I wrote about it. Once my sister accidentally started a grease fire in the kitchen. The whole house almost burned down but my mom was only thankful that we were safe. She wasn't even angry, and I wrote about how she loved us. I wrote many more stories from my life." Many of these stories would provide the inspiration for the author's "Jack Henry" series.

In junior high, Gantos attended a school that had once been a state prison. In this inspiring setting, he once again spent most of his time reading outside of the classroom. By high school, writing professionally was his career goal; as he told an interviewer for *Amazon. com,* his "diary and journal writing background gave me a lot of confidence that writing was something I had loved all my life." After graduating from high school, Gantos attended Boston's Emerson College, where he met art student Nicole Rubel; the pair became friends and decided to work together on picture books for children. "I made a lot of mistakes," he recalled of his early efforts. "I thought children's books had to be sweet, warm, and gentle." After the rejection letters began to arrive, he grew frustrated. "Then," he recalled, "I remembered what one of my teachers had told me. She said, 'Write about what you know.' I was sitting at my desk and I looked down at the floor and saw my lousy, grumpy, hissing creep of a cat that loved to scratch my ankles, throw fur around the house, and shred the clothes in my closet." This cat became Rotten Ralph, and a new antihero was born. Gantos's first book, *Rotten Ralph,* was published in 1976, the year he earned his B.F.A. in creative writing from Emerson College. He went on to earn his M.F.A. and established a career as an educator in addition to developing his work in children's literature. He married art dealer Anne A. Lower in 1989; the couple have a daughter, Mabel Grace.

In *Rotten Ralph* the title character indulges in bad behavior at home, such as crashing his bike into the dining room table; sawing the tree limb that supports the swing of his owner, Sarah; and wearing Father's slippers. Sarah's family takes Ralph to the circus, but he misbehaves so badly that he is left there as punishment. Unhappy as a circus performer, Ralph runs away and is found, ill and underfed, by Sarah, who welcomes him back home. While it first appears that Ralph has learned his lesson and will become less rotten, the cat ultimately reverts to his impish self. Writing in *Language Arts,* Ruth M. Stein called *Rotten Ralph* a "successful first book by both author and illustrator." Although Zena Sutherland noted in the *Bulletin of the Center for Children's Books* that Gantos's humor "seems overworked," *Washington Post Book World* critic Brigitte Weeks called *Rotten Ralph* "a moral tale" that children will "highly appreciate."

In subsequent volumes of the series, Ralph continues to get away with his naughty behavior, ruining holidays and spoiling Sarah's Show and Tell and birthday parties, and even a wedding. In each installment, the books engage even reluctant readers, adding unusual word combinations and quirky images to budding book-worms' expanding vocabularies. In addition, the cat engages in such activities as tormenting his sweet, well-mannered cousin Percy; leading a gang of neighborhood alley cats on a day-long trouble-making spree; clawing his way into Santa's toy sack on Christmas Eve; attempting to get in top shape to beat Percy at a cat show;

and stealing Aunt Martha's wedding bouquet. In *Not So Rotten, Ralph* mild-mannered Sarah takes her unruly pet to Mr. Fred's Feline Finishing School, where Ralph is hypnotized into good behavior; however, Sarah soon misses his mischievous spirit and lures him back into his natural state. *Rotten Ralph Feels Rotten* finds the feline flat on his back with a tummy ache after a night of foraging in neighborhood garbage cans.

In each of the "Rotten Ralph" books the cat behaves very much like a child, and young readers have been attracted to his gleeful overindulgence and the fact that he ultimately gets away with his crimes and is still accepted by the patient and non-confrontational Sarah. In their review of *Rotten Ralph's Rotten Christmas,* Donnarae MacCann and Olga Richard stated, "Rotten Ralph may be satirizing the arrested development of the spoiled child, but the character of Sarah serves as a wry comment upon overindulgent parents." Writing in *Horn Book* about *Rotten Ralph's Rotten Romance,* Elizabeth S. Watson noted: "It's no wonder kids love Ralph—what a perfect vicarious way to get back at all those well-meaning adults who make you go to parties where everyone else seems to be having a great time." Assessing the same title in *Booklist,* Stephanie Zvirin commented that this work, like all of the books in the series, "allows children the vicarious thrill of being unabashedly naughty. But at the same time it provides assurance that even in the face of bad behavior they'll still be loved—something worth talking about." In his review of *Back to School for Rotten Ralph* in *Booklist,* Michael Cart called Ralph "a cat so rambunctiously rotten that you've just gotta love him," while a reviewer for *Horn Book* added that "Gantos's skillful examination of the child's world is once again evident as the author probes a common negative emotion and suggests, but never preaches, a positive outcome."

In addition to their works about Rotten Ralph, Gantos and Rubel have collaborated on several other picture books. *Sleepy Ronald* focuses on a little rabbit whose constant sleepiness—on roller skates, on the diving board, in the bathroom, and in rehearsals for a Wagnerian opera—brings him trouble until his friend Priscilla realizes that Ronald's ears droop over his eyes and fool him into thinking that it is nighttime. In *Aunt Bernice,* young Ida's parents are going away for the summer, so her Aunt Bernice and her dog, Rex, come to babysit. Aunt Bernice's behavior—such as laughing at a mushy movie, which gets her and Ida kicked out of the theater, and dressing up as a gorilla to scare Ida's friends at a slumber party—embarrasses her niece, and Rex drools and gets his fleas all over everything. Finally, Ida realizes that she is growing fond of Bernice and Rex despite their shortcomings. A reviewer for *Publishers Weekly* commented that "the spiffy nonsense of Gantos is perfectly complemented . . . by Rubel's nutty, brashly colored cartoons," creating "a comic masterpiece." A critic in *Kirkus Reviews* similarly stated that "Gantos's story provides a suitable outlet for Rubel's manic energy."

With illustrations by frequent collaborator Nicole Rubel, Gantos's **Rotten Ralph's Rotten Romance** *finds a crafty cat forced to suffer some misplaced affection on Valentine's Day.*

In 1994 he produced the first of his "Jack Henry" books, *Heads or Tails: Stories from the Sixth Grade.* In this collection of autobiographical and semi-autobiographical vignettes, Jack, who has lived in nine houses and has gone to five schools because of his dad's desire to find a better job by moving from place to place, is living in southern Florida. The text, written in diary form, is accompanied by samples of Jack's hand-writing and photocopied items such as a mouse skin and a squashed bug. Jack gets into situations with family, friends, and neighbors and at school. He fights with his know-it-all sister, attends the funeral of his maternal grandfather, sees his dog eaten by an alligator, and generally tries to do the right thing but lands in trouble. Calling Jack "a survivor, an 'everyboy' whose world

may be wacko but whose heart and spirit are eminently sane and generous," *School Library Journal*'s Cart called *Heads or Tails* a "memorable book" and Gantos a "terrific writer with a wonderfully wry sensibility, a real talent for turning artful phrases, and a gift for creating memorable characters." A *Publishers Weekly* reviewer concluded that a "bittersweet resonance filters the humor in these stories and lingers most welcomely."

In *Jack's New Power: Stories from a Caribbean Year* Jack and his family move to Barbados, where Jack makes new friends, thinks his parents are lost at sea, gets his heart broken, sees his dad rescue a drowning couple who turn out to be English royalty, loses his birthday money to a shady friend of his father's, and

searches for a lost boy who turns up dead. He also thinks that he has gained the power to make things happen and, in the process of trying to be a man, conquers his fear of horses. As in the first volume, Gantos presents readers with both laughable moments and serious thoughts. Writing in _Booklist,_ Susan Dove Lempke wrote that "the eight stories here convey with sharp humor Jack's uncomfortable yet exhilarating early adolescence" and concluded that readers will "anxiously await the next installment of Jack's life." Elizabeth S. Watson added in _Horn Book_ that, as in the first book in the collection, "the first-person narrative authentically reproduces the language and observations of twelve year olds. Quirky and funny with some good advice subtly inserted."

In _Jack's Black Book_ Jack is back in Florida after the end of his seventh-grade year. Deciding that he wants to be a serious writer, he buys a black book in which to write a novel. His junior high, a former detention center, is a magnet school for students training in shop; consequently, the pressure is on him to do well in this subject. Jack makes a dog coffin for his class project, and then has to dig out his dead dog in order to pass the seventh grade. When he tries to make a summer business by writing postcards for hire, Jack loses out when a client, a prisoner out on furlough, does not like his work and tosses the boy's typewriter into the ocean. Hanging out with his next-door neighbor, juvenile delinquent Gary Pagoda, Jack gets a tattoo of his dead dog on his big toe, and ultimately decides to give up his schemes to concentrate on just being himself. While a critic for _Kirkus Reviews_ noted that Gantos "trots out one disgusting and dangerous event after another to give his morose protagonist material for jokes," a _Horn Book_ reviewer wrote: "There's enough descriptive disaster, some good solid writing, and a bizarre plot that even reluctant adults can't help but appreciate."

Jack Adrift: Fourth Grade without a Clue and _Jack on the Tracks: Four Seasons of Fifth Grade_ serve as prequels to the first volume in the "Jack Henry" series. _Jack Adrift_ finds the preteen moving with his family to the coast of North Carolina, where teachers and fellow students present unusual challenges. In _Jack on the Tracks_ Jack bonds with his father when the man eats a fifty-pound steak, accidentally kills his cat, writes a gross story that appalls his teacher, is punished by being locked out of the house naked after putting a live roach in his sister's mouth, and hides from what he thinks are two escaped convicts (actually two of his friends) by lying in a shallow hole along the railroad tracks as a train passes overhead. Jack also wonders why he cries all the time, tries to exercise more self-control, and resolves to do the adult thing rather than the childish one. Writing in _Booklist,_ Susan Dove Lempke stated that Gantos's "books about Jack Henry . . . succeed precisely because they present a hilarious, exquisitely painful, and utterly on-target depiction of the life of an adolescent and preadolescent boy." "Jack's

realistic struggle with the pull between childhood and the world of adults will resonate with the book's audience."

While Gantos draws on the ups and downs of his own childhood in his "Jack" novels, in _Hole in My Life_ he moves to out-and-out autobiography, describing his senior year in high school and recounting the juvenile criminal activity that landed him in jail. More serious in tone than the author's fiction, _Hole in My Life_ finds Gantos leaving his family, which is now living in Puerto Rico, and returning to Florida to complete high school. Living in a run-down motel, he begins dealing drugs, and soon goes through his savings. Offered thousands of dollars to sail a load of hashish into the United States, Gantos is arrested, and readers follow him into the federal prison where he spent the early 1970s. Noting that parts of the novel are "quite raw and harsh," _School Library Journal_ contributor Barbara Scotto called _Hole in My Life_ "compelling," while in _Horn Book_ Christine M. Heppermann described Gantos's tale as "laced with edgy anecdotes, some comic and some not." Noting the author's focus on his growing self-awareness and desire to communicate, Cart wrote in _Booklist_ that the author's "spare narrative" is "more than a harrowing, scared-straight confession: it is a beautifully realized story about the making of a writer."

Taking a break from children's books, in 1996 Gantos produced the adult novel _Zip Six._ In this novel a drug dealer meets an Elvis impersonator in prison, becomes his manager on the prison circuit, and is betrayed by him on the outside. _Desire Lines,_ published the following year, is a young-adult novel about sixteen-year-old Walker, a loner who lives in Fort Lauderdale, Florida, and spends much of his time alone on a golf course. Walker has been spying on two classmates, Karen and Jennifer, who have been making love at a duck pond on the course. When an anonymous teenage preacher comes to the school to enlist students for the hate group headed by his minister father, Walker refuses to participate. The teen preacher then tries to blackmail Walker, accusing the teen of being gay, and in order to prove his masculinity Walker forms an alliance with three tough classmates in a gang they call the Box. When the Box members desecrate the preacher's family church and Walker is caught, the boys in the Box turn on him. Pressured to identify gays at school, Walker outs Karen and Jennifer to save himself, thus propelling the novel's tragic end. A critic noted in _Publishers Weekly_ that "Gantos projects an unsettling image of cowardice and survival of the toughest," and "transmits a one-sided (and pessimistic) view of humanity." A critic in _Kirkus Reviews_ called the author's approach "explicit when demonstrating how a climate of fear and suspicion can be concocted in a community, and how insecure young people—gay, straight—can be tormented by it."

In 1998 Gantos introduced another popular character in the middle-grade novel _Joey Pigza Swallowed the Key._ In this book readers meet elementary schooler Joey, a

boy who has ADHD. Joey inadvertently does things like swallowing his house key, cutting off his fingernail in a pencil sharpener, and slicing off the tip of his classmate's nose while running with a pair of scissors. Sent to a special education center for six weeks, he is given regulated medication and learns how to manage his behavior. Joey feels strong and hopeful when his treatment is completed. At the end of the story, he returns to his old school, where he is allowed to sit and read in the Big Quiet Chair. Throughout the book, which is narrated by Joey with flashes of humor, readers learn that the boy has been emotionally abused by his grandmother, who, like Joey, is hyperactive. *Horn Book* critic Jennifer M. Brabander noted that Joey's "own brand of goodness has an unaffected charm and an uncloying sweetness," while Susan Dove Lempke added in *Booklist* that "most teachers and students know at least one child with attention deficit hyperactivity disorder (ADHD), and this book will surely help them become more understanding, even as they enjoy Gantos's fresh writing style and tart sense of humor." Writing in *School Library Journal*, Shawn Brommer commented that, "from the powerful opening lines and fast-moving plot to the thoughtful inner dialogue and satisfying conclusions, readers will cheer for Joey, and for the champion in each of us."

Joey returns for a third go-round in *What Would Joey Do?* Bolstered by medication to control his ADHD, Joey now takes an altruistic tact in an effort to stabilize his off-kilter world, but his helpfulness soon makes the preteen exhausted and overwhelmed. His parents' relationship continues to erupt in yelling matches, fights, and legal action, while on the education front his homeschooling is taken over by a religious fundamentalist whose daughter Olivia is the study partner from Hell. Meanwhile, Joey's beloved Grandma had emphysema and is entering the last days of life. Noting that Joey "turns out to be terrifically perceptive" in his helper role, Steven Engelfried wrote in *School Library Journal* that the boy's "ability to connect with several diversely troubled personalities sets up many humorous scenes." Noting the humor in Gantos's book, a *Kirkus Reviews* writer deemed *What Would Joey Do?* "a poignant story of family, loss, [and] lessons learned," and in *Horn Book* Jennifer M. Brabander called the young protagonist "a distinctive antihero who makes an . . . entertaining, remarkably lucid narrator." Crafting tidy resolutions "isn't Gantos' style," concluded Susan Dove Lempke in *Booklist,* noting that Joey is given "the perseverance to keep aiming in the right direction—no matter what."

A frequent speaker at schools and other groups, Gantos has facilitated writing workshops on children's literature for both students and teachers. Regarding his literary career, he once noted: "I write for children because they are sincere and authentic in their reactions. I write for adults because I am an adult and I need to write about subjects, dreams, and characters outside the lim-

As everything spirals out of control around him, Joey Pigza is determined to try to make things better in Gantos's award-winning novel for middle-graders. (Cover illustration by Brian Selznick.)

ited scope of the children's genre. I enjoy my work as much as possible. I read good books and I want to write good books."

Biographical and Critical Sources

BOOKS

Children's Literature Review, Volume 18, Thomson Gale (Detroit, MI), 1989, pp. 140-143.

PERIODICALS

Booklist, October 1, 1976, Betsy Hearne, review of *Sleepy Ronald,* p. 251; October 15, 1979, Denise M. Wilms, review of *Greedy Greeny,* p. 351; December 1, 1995, Susan Dove Lempke, review of *Jack's New Power,* p. 616; November 15, 1996, Stephanie Zvirin, review of *Rotten Ralph's Rotten Romance,* p. 593; August, 1998, Michael Cart, review of *Back to School for Rotten Ralph,* p. 201; December 15, 1998, Susan Dove Lempke, review of *Joey Pigza Swallowed the Key,* p.

752; June 1, 1999, Ilene Cooper, review of *Wedding Bells for Rotten Ralph;* September 1, 1999, Susan Dove Lempke, review of *Jack on the Tracks: Four Seasons of Fifth Grade,* p. 132; March 1, 2002, Gillian Engberg, review of *Practice Makes Perfect for Rotten Ralph,* p. 1136; April 1, 2002, Michael Cart, review of *Hole in My Life,* p. 1336; October 1, 2002, Susan Dove Lempke, review of *What Would Joey Do?,* p. 323; April 1, 2003, Lolly Gepson, review of *What Would Joey Do?,* p. 1414; August, 2003, Ilene Cooper, review of *Jack Adrift: Fourth Grade without a Clue,* p. 1983; July, 2004, Jennifer Mattson, review of *Rotten Ralph Feels Rotten,* p. 1850; September 15, 2005, Hazel Rochman, review of *Best in Show for Rotten Ralph,* p. 72.

Bulletin of the Center for Children's Books, July, 1976, Zena Sutherland, review of *Rotten Ralph,* p. 174.

Children's Book Review Service, November, 1978, review of *Worse than Rotten, Ralph,* p. 22; December, 1980, review of *The Werewolf Family,* p. 24.

Emergency Librarian, November 1, 1997.

Horn Book, November-December, 1984, Ann A. Flowers, review of *Rotten Ralph's Rotten Christmas,* p. 740; March-April, 1996, Elizabeth S. Watson, review of *Jack's New Power,* p. 231; November-December, 1996, Elizabeth S. Watson, review of *Rotten Ralph's Rotten Romance,* p. 723; January, 1998, review of *Jack's Black Book,* p. 70; September, 1998, review of *Back to School for Rotten Ralph,* p. 598; November-December, 1998, Jennifer M. Brabander, review of *Joey Pigza Swallowed the Key,* pp. 729-730; May-June, 2002, Betty Carter, review of *Practice Makes Perfect for Rotten Ralph,* p. 330, and Christine M. Heppermann, review of *Hole in My Life,* p. 345; November-December, 2002, Jennifer M. Brabander, review of *What Would Joey Do?,* p. 757; November-December, 2003, Kitty Flynn, review of *Jack Adrift,* p. 745; September-October, 2004, Betty Carter, review of *Rotten Ralph Feels Rotten,* p. 583; September-October, 2005, Betty Carter, review of *Best in Show for Rotten Ralph,* p. 576.

Journal of Adolescent and Adult Literacy, September, 2002, Alleen Pace, review of *Hole in My Life,* p. 82, and James Blasingame, interview with Gantos, p. 85; February, 2003, Elizabeth Inchbald, review of *What Would Joey Do?,* p. 446.

Kirkus Reviews, August 15, 1976, review of *Sleepy Ronald,* p. 903; February 15, 1978, review of *Aunt Bernice,* pp. 173-174; February 1, 1980, review of *Greedy Greeny,* pp. 120-121; October 1, 1980, review of *The Werewolf Family,* p. 1293; February 15, 1997, review of *Desire Lines;* August 1, 1997, review of *Jack's Black Book,* p. 1221; September 15, 2002, review of *What Would Joey Do?,* p. 1390; July 1, 2003, review of *Jack Adrift,* p. 910.

Kliatt, July, 2004, Jennifer Baldwin, review of *What Would Joey Do?,* p. 17.

Language Arts, May, 1977, Ruth M. Stein, review of *Rotten Ralph,* p. 582.

Publishers Weekly, February 6, 1978, review of *Aunt Bernice,* p. 101; August 22, 1988, review of *Rotten Ralph's Trick or Treat,* p. 95; June 6, 1994, review of *Heads or Tails,* p. 66; February 24, 1997, review of *Desire Lines,* p. 92; August 14, 2000, review of *Joey Pigza Loses Control,* p. 356; March 25, 2002, review of *Practice Makes Perfect for Rotten Ralph,* p. 66; January 27, 2003, "News from Philadelphia: Hyperion, Roaring Brook Win Newbery, Caldecott Medals."

School Library Journal, October, 1976, Allene Stuart Phy, review of *Sleepy Ronald,* p. 97; October, 1978, Mary B. Nickerson, review of *Worse than Rotten, Ralph,* p. 132; October, 1980, Patricia Homer, review of *The Werewolf Family,* p. 134; October, 1986, John Peters, review of *Rotten Ralph's Trick or Treat,* p. 160; June, 1994, Michael Cart, review of *Heads or Tails,* p. 128; November, 1995, p. 119; December, 1998, Shawn Brommer, review of *Joey Pigza Swallowed the Key,* p. 124; February, 2000, Jo-Ann Carhart, review of *Joey Pigza Swallowed the Key,* p. 68; May, 2002, Barbara Scotto, review of *Hole in My Life,* p. 170; September, 2002, Steven Engelfried, review of *What Would Joey Do?,* p. 225; May, 2003, B. Allison Gray, review of *What Would Joey Say?,* p. 79; September, 2003, Vicki Reutter, review of *Jack Adrift,* p. 210; September, 2004, Sandra Welzenbach, review of *Rotten Ralph Feels Rotten,* p. 160; November, 2004, Alison Follos, review of *Jack's New Power: Stories from a Caribbean Year,* p. 65; June, 2005, Steven Engelfried, review of *Jack Adrift,* p. 55; August, 2005, Carol L. MacKay, review of *Best in Show for Rotten Ralph,* p. 94.

Teaching Pre-K-8, March, 1996.

Washington Post Book World, June 13, 1976, Brigitte Weeks, review of *Rotten Ralph,* p. 112.

Wilson Library Bulletin, February, 1985, Donnarae MacCann and Olga Richard, review of *Rotten Ralph's Rotten Christmas,* p. 404.

ONLINE

Book Nuts Reading Club, http://www.booknutsreadingclub.com/ (October 1, 2003), "Jack Gantos."

Jack Gantos Home Page, http://www.jackgantos.com (March 28, 2006).

*   *   *

GANTOS, John Bryan, Jr.
See GANTOS, Jack

*   *   *

GROOMS, Duffy

Personal

Female. *Education:* Pacific Lutheran University, B.A. (classics); M.A. (liberal arts).

Addresses

Agent—c/o Author Mail, Tricycle Press, P.O. Box 7123, Berkeley, CA 94707.

Career

Student and writer. Tutor for Kitsap Literacy Council.

Writings

(With Laura J. Henson) *Ten Little Elvi,* illustrated by Dean Gorissen, Tricycle Press (Berkeley, CA), 2004.

Work in Progress

"Always something!"

Sidelights

Duffy Grooms told *SATA:* "With various interests, from good old-fashioned rock 'n' roll to mythology, I always have an idea or two flitting about my head, and some that I am still shopping for a publisher. I have just graduated from Pacific Lutheran University with a bachelor's degree in classic and a minor in English literature and hope to teach at the college level after my master's degree. As a classicist, I have been looking at the great adventure stories from ancient times and am developing several of these tales for young readers."

Biographical and Critical Sources

PERIODICALS

Publishers Weekly, November 29, 2004, review of *Ten Little Elvi,* p. 39.
School Library Journal, February, 2005, Jane Marino, review of *Ten Little Elvi,* p. 97.

ONLINE

Ten Speed Press Web site, http://www.tenspeedpress.com/ (February 24, 2006), "Duffy Grooms."

H

HAAB, Sherri 1964-

Personal
Born November 7, 1964, in Idaho Falls, ID; daughter of James R. (a data technician) and Shirley (a loan officer; maiden name, Gray) Hofmann; married Dan Haab (an electrical engineer), May 1, 1986; children: Rachel, Michelle, David. *Education:* Attending Brigham Young University. *Religion:* Church of Jesus Christ of Latter-Day Saints (Mormon).

Addresses
Home—948 South 2350 E., Springville, UT 84663. *E-mail*—sherri@sherrihaab.com.

Career
Freelance illustrator; jewelry and craft designer.

Awards, Honors
Cuffie Award, *Publishers Weekly;* Oppenheim Toy Portfolio Gold Award; Family Fun Toy Awards; Parents' Choice Award.

Writings

(And illustrator) *The Incredible Clay Book: How to Make and Bake a Million-and-One Clay Creations,* Klutz (Palo Alto, CA), 1994.

Nail Art, Klutz (Palo Alto, CA), 1997.

(With the editors of Klutz) *Shrinky Dinks Book,* Klutz (Palo Alto, CA), 1999.

(With Laura Torres) *Create Anything with Clay,* Klutz (Palo Alto, CA), 1999.

(With Laura Torres) *Wire-o-Mania,* Klutz (Palo Alto, CA), 2000.

Picture Bracelets, Klutz (Palo Alto, CA), 2002.

Sherri Haab

(With the editors of Klutz) *Shrinky Dinks: All the Art, All the Shrink Plastic, Everything You Need,* Klutz (Palo Alto, CA), 2003.

The Art of Metal Clay, Watson-Guptill (New York, NY), 2003.

The Hip Handbag Book: Twenty-five Easy-to-Make Totes, Purses, and Bags, illustrated by Nina Edwards, Watson-Guptill (New York, NY), 2004.

Holiday Picture Bracelets, Klutz (Palo Alto, CA), 2004.

Designer-Style Jewelry Techniques and Projects for Elegant Designs from Classic to Retro, Watson-Guptill (New York, NY), 2004.

Designer-Style Handbags: Techniques and Projects for Unique, Fun, and Elegant Designs from Classic to Retro, Watson-Guptill (New York, NY), 2005.

(With daughter, Michelle Haab) *Dangles and Bangles: Twenty-five Funky Projects to Make and Wear,* illustrated by Barbara Pollack, Watson-Guptill (New York, NY), 2005.

The Art of Resin Jewelry, Watson-Guptill (New York, NY), 2006.

ILLUSTRATOR

(With others) *Kids Travel,* Klutz (Palo Alto, CA), 1994.

(With others) Nancy Cassidy, *Hullabaloo,* Klutz (Palo Alto, CA), 1995.

(With husband, Dan Haab) Laura Torres, *Disney Princess Crafts,* Klutz (Palo Alto, CA), 2001.

Sidelights

Crafter and writer Sherri Haab has published a number of how-to and do-it-yourself craft books for young readers. Several of her books are written as part of a kit, providing young jewelry makers and designers with all the equipment they will need to begin crafting their own projects. Beginning with her first book, *The Incredible Clay Book: How to Make and Bake a Million-and-One Clay Creations,* Haab's books have been popular purchases, many of her titles selling over a million copies each.

Haab has worked with a number of mediums, from clay and metal clay to wire to shrinky dinks. Many of her titles, such as *Nail Art* and *Picture Bracelets,* are specifically designed to appeal to girl crafters. *The Hip Handbag Book: Twenty-five Easy-to-Make Totes, Purses, and Bags* and *Dangles and Bangles: Twenty-five Funky Projects to Make and Wear* are both geared toward slightly older readers, providing plans for twenty-five projects to make and either carry or wear.

The Hip Handbag Book shows crafters how to use household materials and easy-to-find tools do create handbags that are also works of art. "This book shows how to take items . . . and decorate them in your own dynamic fashion," commented *Kliatt* reviewer Sherri Ginsberg, who felt the title is appropriate for middle-grade and senior-high students. Most of the projects involve basic sewing techniques that even crafters unfamiliar with sewing can easily pick up.

With her daughter Michelle Haab, Haab developed *Dangles and Bangles.* From key chains to belts to decorative pins, the book covers a wide array of projects, some on the easy end of the spectrum, while others require more complex tools and equipment. "Funky may be the operative word here," wrote Ilene Cooper in a *Booklist* review; "diverse is another." *Kliatt* contributor

Shirley Reis predicted that "girls will be inspired to create some stylish, yet inexpensive accessories." Augusta R. Malvagno, reviewing the title for *School Library Journal,* wrote: "Packed with wonderful ideas, this irresistible title will be popular with young crafters."

Haab once told *SATA:* "I was raised in Seattle, Washington. My sister and I spent a lot of time making things when we were young. I guess it's because of the rainy days Seattle provides—that and the fact that our mom took us to fabric and craft stores with her. I always found great enjoyment from art; it was my favorite subject in school. I was always the one kid so excited about working on a project that I was standing at my desk working while other kids were sitting. I was interested in anything made of clay: ceramics, bread dough, plasticine, even Play-Doh and homemade clays. I think that 3-D illustrations are one of the most interesting forms of art, especially in children's literature.

"For the first few years of my marriage I worked in a business office to support our family while my husband finished his degree. After he graduated I started my own business making jewelry out of clay. I didn't make very much money and worked very long hours to fill orders. Although it seemed like a failed business at the time, it gave me the experience that I needed to refine my art. My work led to a book that teaches children how to use the same clay I use in my own studio . . . polymer clay. It comes in a wide range of colors and can be cured in a regular oven. It is easily manipulated and holds detail very well. Clay can be made to look like many other materials, depending on the surface treatments used. I find it more versatile than other mediums. You can create any scene with any tone you desire; the sky is the limit!

"When I work it feels like I'm ten years old again; it's like playing on the job. I get a kick out of the creativity of the children around me—they aren't the least bit afraid to try something new. They are the ones who inspire me. My husband and I now live in a small town in Utah, with our three children, a cat named Susie, and a few assorted fish. Most of the day revolves around helping children with school, and getting them to piano lessons, softball, or gymnastics. I always stay up late to have time to work on current projects. I believe it is important to do what you love and find balance in all areas of your life."

Biographical and Critical Sources

PERIODICALS

Booklist, July, 2005, Ilene Cooper, review of *Dangles and Bangles: Twenty-five Funky Projects to Make and Wear,* p. 1914.

Kliatt, March, 2005, Sherri Ginsberg, review of *The Hip Handbag Book: Twenty-five Easy-to-Make Totes, Purses, and Bags,* p. 44; September, 2005, Shirley Reis, review of *Dangles and Bangles,* p. 42.

Publishers Weekly, April 26, 1999, review of *Create Anything with Clay,* p. 85; November 8, 1999, Marilyn Green, "Klutz Cornucopia," and review of *Shrinky Dinks Book,* p. 70; May 15, 2000, "Busy, Busy," p. 119, and review of *Wire-o-Mania,* p. 119; March 31, 2003, review of *Picture Bracelets,* p. 69.

School Arts, October, 2004, Eldon Katter, review of *The Art of Metal Clay,* p. 68.

School Library Journal, October, 2005, Augusta R. Malvagno, review of *Dangles and Bangles,* p. 188.

Threads, June-July, 1996, David Page Coffin, review of *The Incredible Clay Book: How to Make and Bake a Million-and-One Clay Creations,* p. 82.

ONLINE

Sherri Haab Home Page, http://www.sherrihaab.com (March 28, 2006).

*   *   *

HALL, Melanie W. 1949-

Personal

Born November 20, 1949, in Gloucester, MA; daughter of Edward A. (a doctor) and Doris (a homemaker; maiden name, Goldfield) Winsten; married Ronald Hall (an artist and musician), 1982. *Education:* Attended Rhode Island School of Design, 1967-70; Pratt Institute, B.F.A., 1978; Marywood College, M.A., 1993. *Hobbies and other interests:* Archery, reading, meditation.

Addresses

Home and office—Cat's Paw Studio, 22 Krom Rd., Olivebridge, NY 12461. *E-mail*—mhallart@netstep.net.

Career

Worked variously as a painter, museum curator, printer's assistant, editorial illustrator, graphic designer, and fashion illustrator. Freelance illustrator and painter, 1978—; children's book illustrator, 1991—. Lecturer, Pratt Institute and Marywood University.

Member

Society of Children's Book Writers and Illustrators, Graphic Artists Guild.

Awards, Honors

Award for work exhibited at Original Art Show, Society of Illustrators, 1992; Don Freeman grant, Society of Children's Book Writers and Illustrators, 1993; Parents' Choice Award.

Illustrator

Charles Temple, *On the Riverbank,* Houghton (Boston, MA), 1992.

Melanie W. Hall

Washington Irving, *The Legend of Sleepy Hollow,* adapted by Freya Littledale, Scholastic (New York, NY), 1992.

Lee Bennett Hopkins, selector, *Weather,* HarperCollins (New York, NY), 1994.

Patrick Lewis, *July Is a Mad Mosquito,* Atheneum (New York, NY), 1994.

Charles Temple, *Shanty Boat,* Houghton (Boston, MA), 1994.

Cathy Goldberg Fishman, *On Passover,* Atheneum (New York, NY), 1997.

Cathy Goldberg Fishman, *On Rosh Hashanah and Yom Kippur,* Atheneum (New York, NY), 1997.

Cathy Goldberg Fishman, *On Hanukkah,* Atheneum (New York, NY), 1998.

Nancy Sohn Swartz, *In Our Image: God's First Creatures,* Jewish Lights (Woodstock, VT), 1998.

Cathy Goldberg Fishman, *On Purim,* Atheneum (New York, NY), 2000.

Cathy Goldberg Fishman, *On Shabbat,* Atheneum (New York, NY), 2001.

Ivy O. Eastwick, *I Asked a Tiger to Tea, and Other Poems,* compiled by Walter B. Barbe, Wordsong/Boyds Mills Press (Honesdale, PA), 2002.

Melinda Kay Busch, *Born on Christmas Morn: The Story of Jesus' Birth, Luke 2:1-20 for Children,* Concordia (St. Louis, MO), 2003.

Nancy Sohn Swartz, *How Did the Animals Help God?,* SkyLight Paths (Woodstock, VT), 2004.

Rebecca Kai Dotlich, *Over in the Pink House: New Jump Rope Rhymes,* Wordsong/Boyds Mills Press (Honesdale, PA), 2004.

Lee Bennett Hopkins, selector, *Christmas Presents: Holiday Poetry,* HarperCollins (New York, NY), 2004.

Lee Bennett Hopkins, selector, *Hanukkah Lights: Holiday Poetry,* HarperCollins (New York, NY), 2004.

Cathy Goldberg Fishman, *On Sukkot and Simchat Torah,* Kar-Ben (Minneapolis, MN), 2005.

Deborah Bodin Cohen, *The Seventh Day,* Kar-Ben (Minneapolis, MN), 2005.

Work included in *The Very Best of Children's Book Illustration,* Society of Illustrators/Northlight Books, 1993.

Sidelights

Melanie W. Hall is an illustrator of children's books noted for employing a variety of mixed media, from watercolors to crayons. Hall's artwork can be both folksy and vibrant, even flashy, depending on the theme of the material she is illustrating. Working in collaboration with authors such as Charles Temple and Cathy Goldberg Fishman, she has illustrated books dealing with topics from a day on the river to the months of the year and weather to the Jewish holidays.

"Illustrating children's books is a dream come true for me," Hall once told *SATA.* "When I was a little girl I made a series of books called 'The Fun Book,' which came out seasonally and were filled with illustrations, rebuses, puzzles, and stories. I laugh to myself remembering how I sat on the beach with colored pencils and paper finishing up the latest fun book so I wouldn't be late for the deadline. I didn't know that was a taste of what was to come."

After attending the prestigious Rhode Island School of Design from 1967 to 1970, Hall worked in a variety of careers allied to the visual and studio arts. "I've had a checkered career as a painter, museum curator, printer's assistant, editorial illustrator, graphic designer, and fashion illustrator," Hall once recalled to *SATA.* She returned to school to earn her B.F.A. at the Pratt Institute, but still did not discover her niche. "I wasn't very happy. One day, while sitting at my drawing table doing my umpteenth fashion illustration, I wondered, 'Will I be doing this boring stuff when I'm sixty?' I complained to my girlfriend, 'I want to do children's books!' She replied, 'Well, why don't you?' At that moment, lights flashed and bells rang. I said to myself, 'Yeah, why don't I? What's stopping me?' Everything fell into place. I went back to school and learned how to do children's books.

"The day I got my first book contract changed my life forever. After my editor, Matilda Welter of Houghton Mifflin, offered me *On the Riverbank,* I jumped up and down and whooped for joy. I tried to sound calm, cool, and collected but failed miserably. Matilda chuckled appreciatively at my delight. I told her, 'This is the day all my dreams come true,' quoting Bob Dylan's song 'New Morning.' Afterward, I called up every member of my family and every friend to crow about the news."

Hall's first illustrated title, Temple's *On the Riverbank,* is a story of a family of three who are out for a fishing trip on the shores of a river lit by moonlight. Daddy and Mama bring along a picnic basket and all the assorted gear necessary for an evening of catfishing. Together the young narrator and his father bait the lines and eagerly await the first bites. Told in pulsing, rhythmic stanzas, the book details the simple joys of catching fish and swapping tall tales around a campfire. Hall adds to the down-home feel with her debut illustration effort; her "rustic-looking, mixed-media paintings call to mind colored woodblock prints," noted a reviewer for *Publishers Weekly.* The "cool palette of blues, purples and shimmering whites winningly matches the story's setting of a June night steeped in moonglow," the critic added. *Booklist* contributor Denia Hester called attention to Hall's technique, noting that "the several applications of paint give the art a textured look." "This effect sometimes roughens the art, occasionally obscuring a facial detail," Hester added, "but it also gives the book a unique look." Anne Connor, reviewing *On the Riverbank* in *School Library Journal,* felt that the "soft, mixed media illustrations have a verve that echoes the text and adds a romanticized dimension of a fond reminiscence to this story of an African-American family that has spent a winter anticipating such an outing."

Hall again collaborated with Temple on *Shanty Boat,* a 1994 picture book about the life of Uncle Sheb, a boatman who plies his trade on the Mississippi River. Sheb spent his whole life on the river, never settling down or having a family. In fact, Sheb's home WAS the river, and after his death people reported seeing him and his ramshackle little boat when the moon shines brightly. Against this story, Hall paced her paintings to Temple's hard-driving textual rhythms, and her "mixed-media illustrations . . . portray the bucolic existence of this solitary oarsman," according to *Booklist* critic Kay Weisman. A *Publishers Weekly* reviewer called Hall and Temple's picture-book collaboration "part ballad, part ghost story and part tall tale," noting that "Hall's collagraphs bustle with a tone of joyous confusion." Reviewing the same title in *School Library Journal,* Lisa S. Murphy commented: "The art is luminous with light ranging from the warmth of the morning sun to the mysterious glow of the moon."

Hall has also provided artwork for an adaptation of the classic *The Legend of Sleepy Hollow,* and her artwork has appeared in the anthology *The Very Best of Children's Book Illustration,* compiled by the Society of Illustrators. Her inclusion in the latter stands as a compliment to an illustrator with—at the time of that volume's 1993 publication—only two books to her credit. In 1994 Hall teamed up on two poetry book projects: *Weather,* a book of verses edited by Lee Bennett Hopkins, and Patrick Lewis's *July Is a Mad Mosquito.* In the former title, Hall provided artwork to accompany the poems of both famous—such as Carl Sandburg and Ogden Nash—and lesser-known versifiers. "The dominant col-

Hall's pastel and colored-pencil drawings reflect the magic in the many verses collected by well-known anthologist Lee Bennett Hopkins in his simply titled poetry collection Weather.

ors are pink and orange—more sunny than rainy," noted Ruth K. MacDonald in *School Library Journal*. MacDonald went on to observe in her review that "the overall impression is of brightness, lightheartedness, and fun." *Horn Book* critic Margaret A. Bush noted that Hall's work for the book includes "pastel sketches, warmly energetic views of children and simple nature scenes."

To accompany Lewis's twelve poems about the months of the year, collected as *July Is a Mad Mosquito,* Hall produced "zippy collagraphs," according to a critic for *Publishers Weekly*. If the text falters, "Hall's literal interpretations should clear up any confusion," the same reviewer decided. Judy Greenfield, writing in *School Library Journal*, called attention to the "full-color, double-spread impressionistic painting" designed to interpret the central motif of each poem, while *Booklist* contributor Carolyn Phelan cited "Hall's lively illustrations, fanciful scenes in popsicle-bright pastels and muted blues and browns."

Hall has worked with author Cathy Goldberg Fishman on several books dealing with Jewish holidays. Passover is the subject of their first collaborative effort, *On Passover,* which *Booklist* critic Ilene Cooper called "more attractive and lyrical than many other Passover

books." Here the story is told by a young girl who asks a series of questions of her family as they prepare for the traditional Jewish holiday. There is the ritual dinner, the Seder plate, and the Passover service, among other parts of the ceremonial aspects of the holiday. A *Publishers Weekly* reviewer concluded that "Hall's rich mixed-media creations bustle with energy." Further collaborative efforts have produced *On Rosh Hashanah and Yom Kippur, On Hanukkah, On Purim,* and *On Shabbat*. In the first-named book, the High Holidays are explored, with particular focus on Rosh Hashanah, again employing a little girl's voice to get to the heart of the celebration. Once more, Fishman's text explores both the meaning of the holiday as well as the common holiday practices and food. "Hall's beautiful, rosy, expressionistic pictures are a fine complement to Fishman's text," according to Stephanie Zvirin in *Booklist*. Reviewing *On Hanukkah* in *Booklist*, Julie Corsaro felt that Hall's "fanciful, mixed-media paintings feature strong texturing and glowing, gilt-edged colors." *On Shabbat* explains the weekly celebration of the Sabbath. "Hall's marbled, multilayered collagraphs are alive with intriguingly textured images," wrote Ellen Mandel of *Booklist,* adding that "they radiate the warmth, comfort, and refreshing strength" symbolized by Shabbat. According to *School Library Journal* contributor Martha Link, "the illustrations are the highlight of this book."

Hall turned to biblical stories for her illustrations of Nancy Sohn Swartz's picture book *In Our Image: God's First Creatures*. This "nondenominational, nonsectarian retelling of the creation story . . . focuses on the period before man and woman were created," as Yapha Nussbaum Mason described the book in a *School Library Journal* review. In Swartz's tale, a group of animals informs God of the gifts they would like to present to humans, including the chimps who think curiosity would be a fine thing, and the ostriches who opt for humans minding their own business. Worried when God tells them that humans will have dominion over them, the animals are finally reassured when God further informs them that the humans will not abuse this sacred trust. "The vibrantly colored illustrations nearly leap off the page in this delightful interpretation," concluded Mason. *Booklist* critic Ilene Cooper deemed Hall's artwork "particularly nice," noting that her illustrations both extend and elaborate Swartz's text, and "capture the feeling of life that is the essence of the story." A reviewer for *Publishers Weekly* concluded of the combination of soft watercolor with sharper, black and neon images, "the effect is both complex and magical."

Ivy O. Eastwick's poems, collected in *I Asked a Tiger to Tea, and Other Poems* and jump rope rhymes collected by Rebecca Kai Dotlich in *Over in the Pink House: New Jump Rope Rhymes,* have both provided Hall with new subjects for her illustrations. The poetry in Eastwick's compilation are based on the poet's childhood in early 1900's England. The poems "are in concert with Hall's richly textured, lushly colored art," according to Ellen Mandel in *Booklist*. Kathleen Whalin,

writing in *School Library Journal,* felt while that the poems have been better collected in other compilations, "Hall's bright, impressionistic paintings do much to enliven the book." The traditional rhymes of *Over in the Pink House* contain elements of folklore and fantasy, as well as realistic images accompanied by a steady jumping beat. "The style of each picture perfectly captures the tone of the accompanying poem," wrote Sally R. Dow in her *School Library Journal* review. Hazel Rochman noted in *Booklist* that "Hall's clear, colorful illustrations . . . keep the scenarios open, whether realistic or magical."

In 2004, Hall again provided illustrations for collections of poetry selected by Lee Bennett Hopkins. Focusing on the winter holidays, *Christmas Presents: Holiday Poetry* and *Hanukkah Lights: Holiday Poetry* both feature poetry and illustrations to tie in with the season. Of both books, a *Horn Book* reviewer noted that Hall's paintings "accent the verses without overwhelming them." A *Kirkus Reviews* contributor wrote of *Christmas Presents* that "Hall's attractive illustrations eschew traditional Christmas colors" and give the collection "a lively flair." In the same periodical, a reviewer noted of

Hanukkah Lights: "Whimsical paintings full of swirls and curves . . . complete the Judaic settings for each poem." A *Publishers Weekly* critic found that Hall's paintings in the same book "combine visual flights of fancy with cozy scenes of Jewish domesticity."

A traditional Jewish tale is the focus of *The Seventh Day,* written by Rabbi Deborah Bodin Cohen. The author combines the creation story with a prayer that names God an artist, a potter, and a musician. "The mixed-media illustrations are quite lovely, with a Chagall-like feel," complimented Amy Lilien-Harper in a review for *School Library Journal.* A *Publishers Weekly* critic felt that Hall's illustrations "swirl with color and energy. Her palette balances purple sunsets, fluffy white clouds and verdant fields and mountains all in a vibrant, appealing rainbow of life."

Both magical and earthy, Hall's illustrations assure her a continued place in children's-book illustration. Having come a long way from her fashion-designing days, she doubts she will seek another career change. As she once concluded to *SATA:* "I am completely happy now and love what I do!"

Biographical and Critical Sources

PERIODICALS

Artist's, May, 1992; January, 1994.
Booklist, November 15, 1992, Denia Hester, review of *On the Riverbank,* p. 64; June 1, 1994, Kay Weisman, review of *Shanty Boat,* p. 1846; July, 1994, Carolyn Phelan, review of *July Is a Mad Mosquito,* p. 1950; March 1, 1997, Ilene Cooper, review of *On Passover,* p. 1165; October 1, 1997, Stephanie Zvirin, review of *On Rosh Hashanah and Yom Kippur,* p. 322; September 1, 1998, Julie Corsaro, review of *On Hanukkah,* p. 132; October 1, 1998, Ilene Cooper, review of *In Our Image: God's First Creatures,* p. 345; April, 1, 2001, Ellen Mandel, review of *On Shabbat,* p. 1474; December 15, 2002, Ellen Mandel, review of *I Asked a Tiger to Tea,* p. 756; May 1, 2004, Hazel Rochman, review of *Over in the Pink House: New Jump Rope Rhymes,* p. 1560; August, 2004, Jennifer Mattson, review of *Christmas Presents: Holiday Poetry,* p. 1938.
Children's Bookwatch, May, 2005, review of *Over in the Pink House.*
Horn Book, July-August, 1994, Margaret A. Bush, review of *Weather,* p. 468; November-December, 2004, review of *Christmas Presents* and *Hanukkah Lights: Holiday Poetry,* p. 661.
Kirkus Reviews, March 15, 2004, review of *Over in the Pink House,* p. 267; November 1, 2004, review of *Christmas Presents,* p. 1050, review of *Hanukkah Lights,* p. 1050.
Publishers Weekly, October 5, 1992, review of *On the Riverbank,* p. 70; February 14, 1994, review of *Shanty Boat,* p. 87, and review of *July Is a Mad Mosquito,* p.

Hall's whimsical art is a perfect match for the quirky poems created by well-known writer Ivy O. Eastwick and collected in I Asked a Tiger to Tea, and Other Poems.

89; February 24, 1997, review of *On Passover,* p. 83; September 28, 1998, review of *In Our Image,* p. 95; September 27, 2004, "Hanukkah Notes," p. 60; February 14, 2005, review of *The Seventh Day,* p. 78.

School Library Journal, November, 1992, Anne Connor, review of *On the Riverbank,* p. 79; March, 1994, Ruth K. MacDonald, review of *Weather,* p. 216; April 1994, Judy Greenfield, review of *July Is a Mad Mosquito,* p. 120; July, 1994, Lisa S. Murphy, review of *Shanty Boat,* p. 98; March, 1999, Yapha Nussbaum Mason, review of *In Our Image,* p. 202; February, 2000, Amy Lilien-Harper, review of *On Purim,* p. 110; August, 2001, Martha Link, review of *On Shabbat,* p. 168; November, 2002, Kathleen Whalin, review of *I Asked a Tiger to Tea,* p. 142; April, 2004, Sally R. Dow, review of *Over in the Pink House,* p. 130; October, 2004, review of *Over in the Pink House,* p. S26; August, 2005, Amy Lilien Harper, review of *The Seventh Day,* p. 86.

ONLINE

Melanie Hall Home Page, http://www.mhallillustration. com (March 28, 2006).*

*   *   *

HARPER, Jo 1932-

Personal

Born January 12, 1932, in Lockney, TX; daughter of J.B. (a farmer and investor) and Melba (Floyd) Harper; married James Lowell Hoggins (marriage ended); children: Josephine M. Harper, James Francis Lowell, De Agon Higgins. *Education:* Texas Tech University, B.A., 1951, M.A., 1964; Pennsylvania State University, doctoral study, 1970-71; also attended Columbia University, 1977, Escuela Internacional Sampere (Madrid, Spain), 1974, Inter-American University (Saltillo, Mexico), 1978, Cuernavaca Language School (Cuernavaca, Mexico), 1979, and University of Texas at Austin.

Addresses

Home—1605 Huge Oaks, Houston, TX 77055. *Agent*—Erin Murphy, 2700 Woodlands Village, No. 300-458, Flagstaff, AZ 86001-7127. *E-mail*—joharper@juno.com.

Career

Plainview, TX, Public Schools, junior-high-school librarian, 1951-52, first-grade teacher for Spanish-speaking children, 1959-60, high school teacher of English, Spanish, and humanities, 1964-68; Texas A & I University, Kingsville, instructor in English, 1968-70; Rockingham Community College, Wentworth, NC, instructor in English and Spanish, 1971-77; Armstrong State College, Savannah, GA, assistant professor of English and Spanish, and foreign student adviser, 1977-80; Texas Southern University, Houston, director of inten-

Jo Harper

sive English for foreign students, 1980-84; University of Houston, Houston, lecturer in English, 1984-96; Spring Branch Education Center, Houston, teacher of English to at-risk high school students, 1996—; Houston Community College, adjunct instructor in English, 1999—. Museum of Fine Arts, senior docent; Houston Arboretum, volunteer; storyteller at local elementary schools.

Awards, Honors

Willa Cather Award, 1999, for *Prairie Dog Pioneers;* Western Heritage Award, 2001, for *Delfino's Journey.*

Writings

The Harpers' Voices—Caves and Cowboys: Family Song Book, illustrated by Robert Boustany, photographs by George R. Jefferson, JCH Press, 1988.

Pals, Potions, and Pixies: Family Songbook, illustrated by Robert Boustany, photographs by George R. Jefferson, JCH Press, 1988.

Jalapeño Hal, illustrated by Jennifer Beck Harris, Simon & Schuster (New York, NY), 1993.

Outrageous, Bodacious Boliver Boggs!, illustrated by JoAnn Adinolfi, Simon & Schuster (New York, NY), 1996.

Deaf Smith: Scout, Spy, Texas Hero, illustrated by Virginia Rhoeder, Eakin Publications (Austin, TX), 1996.

Bigfoot Wallace: Texas Ranger and Mier Survivor, Eakin Publications (Austin, TX), 1997.

The Legend of Mexicatl, Turtle Press (New York, NY), 1998.

(With daughter, Josephine Harper) *Prairie Dog Pioneers,* Turtle Press (New York, NY), 1998.

Delfino's Journey, Texas Tech University Press (Lubbock, TX), 2001.

Ollie Jolly, Rodeo Clown, illustrated by Amy Meissner, WestWinds Press (Portland, OR), 2002.

Mayor Jalapeño Hal, illustrated by Joel Cook and Vuthy Kuon, Eakin Publications (Austin, TX), 2003.

(With others) *Wilma Rudolph: Olympic Runner,* Aladdin (New York, NY), 2004.

(With Josephine Harper) *Finding Daddy: A Story of the Great Depression,* illustrated by Ron Mazellan, Turtle Books (New York, NY), 2005.

(With Josephine Harper) *Teresa's Journey* (sequel to *Delfino's Journey*), Texas Tech University Press (Lubbock, TX), 2006.

(With Josephine Harper) *Mier Men,* Eakin Press (Austin, TX), 2006.

I Could Eat You Up!, illustrated by Kay Chorao, Holiday House (New York, NY), 2007.

Contributor to magazines and newspapers.

Harper's books have been translated into Spanish.

Work in Progress

Choosing Comanche (working title), for Turtle Books; *White Indian* (working title).

Sidelights

Jo Harper, a professional storyteller and award-winning children's author, has always enjoyed spinning tales. Along with writing picture books, Harper has also written novels for slightly older readers, including *Delfino's Journey,* which won the Western Heritage award for best juvenile book in 2001. She has also collaborated on several original titles with her daughter, writer Josephine Harper. Their work together includes the Willa Cather Award-winning picture book *Prairie Dog Pioneers.*

Harper started her career in children's books with two collections of songs designed for family sing alongs. Her first picture book, *Jalapeño Hal,* tells the story of a cowboy with such "mean breath" that he can cause steam to rise from his mouth. This talent comes in handy when a town is in need of rain; by convincing everyone to munch on jalapeños, Hal manages to get everyone's breath to rise, eventually putting enough moisture into the air that it begins to rain. The story is told, in true Texas style, by Hal's sidekick, a young boy named Kit, and "will satisfy latter-day Davy Crocketts and encourage a craving for the piquant," according to a *Publishers Weekly* contributor.

Moving from tall tale to more traditional folk tale, Harper is also the author of *The Legend of Mexicatl.* Based on Mexican folklore, the story focuses on a boy named Mexicatl, whose destiny is to lead his people to a place where they can find both water and peace. "Harper's telling will hold children's interest," assured Ilene Cooper in a review for *Booklist.*

With daughter Josephine Harper, Harper retells a chapter from her own family history in *Prairie Dog Pioneers.* Young Mae Dean, an ancestor of Harper's, does not understand why her family had to move to Texas, and she is even more confused when, on the long trip south, her father seems more concerned about their possessions than the family members themselves. When Papa finally explains the dangers and the benefits of the new place they will call home, Mae Dean begins to understand the reason for the family's sacrifices. Calling the tale a "quiet story," Kay Weisman wrote in *Booklist* that *Prairie Dog Pioneers* "is a good choice for primary story hours."

Mother and daughter team up again on *Finding Daddy: A Story of the Great Depression,* the story of young Bonnie whose despairing father leaves the family during the economic depression of the 1930s. Determined to get her father back home, Bonnie goes out searching for him, in an effort to give the man back his faith in himself and his belief that he can support his family. The Harpers weave period music into the telling of the tale reflecting Bonnie's use of music to reach her father. "Adults will want to share this with children and sing the old songs," wrote Hazel Rochman in *Booklist,* while Suzanne Myers Harold noted in *School Library Journal* that *Finding Daddy* "offers a way to make history more personal."

Delfino's Journey, one of Harper's few novels for middle-grade readers, is a timely novel that tells the story of sixteen-year-old Delfino. Feeling the responsibility of being the man in the family, he feels that the best way to help his pregnant sister to give birth to her child safely is to move her from Mexico north into Texas. She has already lost one child, and Delfino is determined to help her make sure she does not lose another. With his cousin Salvador, the teen works out a plan to cross the Rio Grande into the land of promise. The book features Aztec legends and culture and the Nahuatl language, Delfino's native tongue. Roger Leslie, writing in *Booklist* considered the novel "an exciting and emotionally satisfying read."

Though most of Harper's books draw on her background growing up in Texas or are based on Mexican legends and current issues, she is also the author of a fictional biography of Wilma Rudolph, an Olympic track star who grew up in the 1940s. In *Wilma Rudolph: Olympic Runner* Harper traces Rudolph's history: stricken by polio, which twisted her leg when she was a

Harper tells the story of the woman who overcame childhood polio to become the first female runner to win three Olympic gold medals in **Wilma Rudolph, Olympic Runner.** *(Illustration by Meryl Henderson.)*

child, she overcame the illness to become a medal-winning athlete. The facts in the book are presented in a fictional manner to draw in young readers, and the technique "works because it never pretends to be documented biography," according to Hazel Rochman in *Booklist.*

Harper once told *SATA:* "I grew up in the Texas Panhandle riding horses, eating jalapeno peppers, and spinning whoppers. I used to go with my grandfather to auctions and bid on cattle as they ran through the ring. When I was seventeen I got my first car and drove to Mexico City. Even though these are miles and years away from me now, the Panhandle and things Mexican still permeate my work. *Jalapeño Hal* and *Outrageous, Bodacious Boliver Boggs!* are Texas tall tales. *Deaf Smith, Bigfoot Wallace,* and *Mier Men* are about Texas heroes. *Caves and Cowboys* and *Pals, Potions, and Pixies* are printed in both English and Spanish, as are several of my other books. *The Legend of Mexicatl* is the story of the legendary founder of the Aztecs, and *Prairie Dog Pioneers* is based on a true story about going up the Cap Rock in a covered wagon and living in a dugout on the prairie."

Biographical and Critical Sources

PERIODICALS

Booklist, October 1, 1993, Sheilamae O'Hara, review of *Jalapeño Hal,* p. 352; April 15, 1998, Ilene Cooper, review of *The Legend of Mexicatl,* p. 1448; September 15, 1998, Kay Weisman, review of *Prairie Dog Pioneers,* p. 237; April 15, 2001, Roger Leslie, review of *Delfino's Journey,* p. 1545; May 15, 2004, Hazel Rochman, review of *Wilma Rudolph: Olympic Runner,* p. 1619; July, 2005, review of *Finding Daddy: A Story of the Great Depression,* p. 1925.
Black Issues Book Review, May-June, 2004, Suzanne Rust, "Learning as We Climb: Stories about the Civil Rights Movement for Young Readers," pp. 58-61.
Canadian Review of Materials, March 14, 2003, review of *Ollie Jolly, Rodeo Clown.*
Children's Book Review Service, spring, 1996, p. 134.
Publishers Weekly, July 26, 1993, review of *Jalapeño Hal,* p. 70; September 21, 1998, review of *Prairie Dog Pioneers,* p. 85.
School Library Journal, March, 1994, Claudie Cooper, review of *Jalapeño Hal,* p. 198; April, 1996, p. 110; October, 2004, review of *The Legend of Mexicatl,* p. S22; September, 2005, Suzanne Myers Harold, review of *Finding Daddy,* p. 171.

ONLINE

Humboldt Children's Author Festival 2005 Web site, http://www.authorfest.org/ (March 28, 2006), profile of Harper.
Jo Harper Home Page, http://home.earthlink.net/~joharper (March 28, 2006).

*   *   *

HARRIS, Jesse
See STANDIFORD, Natalie

*   *   *

HORNE, Richard George Anthony
See HORSE, Harry

*   *   *

HORROCKS, Anita 1958-

Personal

Born May 13, 1958, in the Pas, Manitoba, Canada; daughter of William (in sales) and Bertha (a teacher; maiden name Wiens) Dyck; married Bryan Horrocks (a city manager), September 21, 1984; children: (stepchil-

Anita Horrocks

dren) Wade Horrocks, Lindsay Horrocks. *Education:* Northern Alberta Institute of Technology, diploma (biological sciences; with honors), 1978; Lethbridge Community College, diploma (print journalism; with honors), 1986; University of Lethbridge, marketing certificate, 1992, B.A. (English; with distinction), 1997. *Hobbies and other interests:* Fitness, cycling, golf, swimming, hiking, quilting, reading.

Addresses

Home—428 Canyon Blvd. W., Lethbridge, Alberta T1K 6V2, Canada. *E-mail*—anitahorrocks@shaw.ca.

Career

Banff National Park, Banff, Alberta, Canada, park naturalist, 1979; Helen Schuler Coulee Centre, Lethbridge, Alberta, Canada, park interpreter, 1981-84; City of Lethbridge, parks information project writer, 1986-87; University of Lethbridge, Lethbridge, public-relations assistant, 1987, coordinator of communications and public relations, 1988-94; freelance writer, 1994—. Presenter at schools and writing conferences.

Member

Canadian Society of Children's Authors, Illustrators, and Performers; Canadian Children's Book Centre; Writers' Union of Canada; Young Alberta Book Society; Lethbridge Children's Literature Roundtable.

Awards, Honors

MacDonald Dettwiler Award for Best Science and Technology Article, Western Magazine Awards, 1985; Governor General's Silver Academic Medal, 1996; Alberta Book Award's R. Ross Annett Children's Literature Award shortlist, and New York Public Library Books for the Teen Age selection, both 1997, both for *Breath of a Ghost;* R. Ross Annett Children's Literature Award, 1999, and New York Public Library Books for the Teen Age selection, and Red Maple Award, Ontario Library Association, both 2000, all for *What They Don't Know;* R. Ross Annett Children's Literature Award, 2001, and Golden Eagle Children's Choice Award runner-up, 2003, both for *Topher.*

Writings

Breath of a Ghost, Stoddart Kids (Toronto, Ontario, Canada), 1996.
What They Don't Know, Stoddart Kids (Toronto, Ontario, Canada), 1998.
Topher, Stoddart Kids (Toronto, Ontario, Canada), 2000.
Almost Eden, Tundra Books (Plattsburgh, NY), 2006.

Sidelights

Anita Horrocks grew up in the central Canadian prairie, where sports and reading became two of her favorite pastimes. "I loved the smell of books and the feel of the pages, but mostly, I loved the stories that took me on so many wonderful adventures," the author noted on the Albert Author Connection Web site. Early in her career she combined these two loves by working as an interpreter at various provincial, national, and municipal parks. After juggling a series of jobs while raising her children and completing her education at the University of Lethbridge, where she worked as a public-relations coordinator, Horrocks established a successful career writing for both children and young adults, with several award-winning novels for middle-grade and young-adult readers to her credit.

In *Breath of a Ghost* twelve-year-old Darien mourns the death of his little brother Jeri, who died of leukemia. Although he still senses his brother's supportive presence, Darien is now haunted by nightmares about a sinister coyote that means him harm. As Halloween approaches, the hauntings accelerate, prompting Darien to attempt to end these dreams; with his dog, Ringo, he goes to a remote area near his home, where he confronts both the creature and the great sadness now overwhelming him.

Almost Eden focuses on another twelve year old, Elsie, who must deal with the mental illness of a parent. Like Darien, in *Breath of a Ghost,* Elsie is also isolated with her feelings of guilt and confusion, but this time it is her emotionally distant Mennonite community that leaves her with little guidance. Ultimately, through her

faith and her willing to accept the challenges of her changing family, Elsie is able to confront her feelings and understand where her true responsibilities are.

Also for middle-graders, *Topher* focuses on two children who fall in love with Grandmother McCrae's lakeside cabin in a remote part of Saskatchewan. When their father insists that the family property be quickly fixed up and sold after his mother's death, twelve-year-old Chris and seven-year-old Stacie are brokenhearted. Puzzled by their father's decision, and concerned by the visions now haunting Stacie, the siblings investigate the history of the cabin and learn that a family tragedy occurring thirty years in the past is the source of their father's dislike of the family home place. Praising *Topher* as a "fast-paced adventure full of intrigue," a *Resource Links* contributor added that "children who are fond of science fiction and fantasy are sure to enjoy the supernatural elements" in Horrocks's novel.

Another effort to deal with difficult emotions is the focus of Horrocks's award-winning young-adult novel *What They Don't Know*. In this 1998 work, which is also set in Canada, fourteen-year-old Hannah lashes out

A trip Chris and Stacie take to the family cabin is haunted by a mysterious boy and a secret that threatens to tear their family apart in Horrocks's suspenseful novel. (Cover illustration by Sharif Tarabay.)

at everyone, but mostly at herself. Watching her younger sister spiral downward into a life of alcohol and drugs with the encouragement of some bad-news friends, seventeen-year-old Kelly is determined to discover the reason for Hannah's anger. Realizing that her parents' divorce and her custodial father's current romantic relationship may be part of the problem, Kelly delves into her parents' past and in the process unearths the family secret that has set Hannah on her self-destructive path. Praising the novel as a "realistic family portrait," Debbie Carton wrote in *Booklist* that *What They Don't Know* is a "psychological drama" that is "beautifully portrayed."

Biographical and Critical Sources

PERIODICALS

Booklist, November 1, 1999, Debbie Carton, review of *What They Don't Know,* p. 515.

Books in Canada, November, 1996, review of *Breath of a Ghost,* p. 32; summer, 1999, review of *What They Don't Know,* p. 45.

Canadian Book Review Annual, 1996, review of *Breath of a Ghost,* p. 479; 1998, review of *What They Don't Know,* p. 507; 2000, review of *Topher,* p. 480.

Canadian Children's Literature (annual), 2000, review of *What They Don't Know,* pp. 74-76; summer, 2001, review of *Topher,* p. 90.

Quill & Quire, January, 1999, review of *What They Don't Know,* p. 46; March, 2000, review of *Topher,* p. 65; March, 2006, review of *Almost Eden,* p. 81.

Resource Links, February, 1999, review of *What They Don't Know,* p. 25; October, 2000, review of *Topher,* p. 8.

School Library Journal, August, 1999, Jeanette Larson, review of *What They Don't Know,* p. 158; December, 2000, Heather Deiffenbach, review of *Topher,* p. 145.

Voice of Youth Advocates, April, 2001, review of *Topher,* p. 52.

ONLINE

Alberta Author Connection, http://tlc.epsb.ca/aauthor/ (April 12, 2006), "Anita Horrocks."

Canadian Society of Children's Authors, Illustrators, and Performers Web site, http://www.canscaip.org/ (April 12, 2006), "Anita Horrocks."*

*   *   *

HORSE, Harry 1960-
[A pseudonym]
(Richard George Anthony Horne)

Personal

Born Richard Horne, May 9, 1960, in Earlsdon, Coventry, Warwickshire, England; son of Henry Derek (a chartered surveyor) and Josephine Anne (a homemaker;

maiden name, Moody) Horne; married Amanda Grace Williamson (an artist), March 23, 1990. *Education:* Attended Wrekin College. *Politics:* Liberal. *Religion:* Church of England (Anglican). *Hobbies and other interests:* Playing the banjo.

Addresses

Home—Edinburgh, Scotland. *Agent*—Caroline Sheldon, 71 Hillgate Place, London W8 7SS, England.

Career

Illustrator, writer, cartoonist, and musician. Candlemaker Row, Edinburgh, Scotland, and Silvermills Lane, Edinburgh, Scotland, book illustrator, 1977-80; Symington Mains, Fountainhall, The Borders, Scotland, book illustrator, 1980-83. *Scotland on Sunday,* political cartoonist, 1987-92; freelance writer and illustrator of children's books. Musician in Cajun bands Swamptrash, 1987, and Hexology; also worked as a forger, early 1980s. Creator of video games, including *Drowned God* and *CULT.*

Awards, Honors

Writer of the Year Award, Scottish Arts Council, 1984, and SAC Publishers Award, both for *The Ogopogo;* Smarties Gold Award, British Book Trust, 1998, for *The Last Gold Diggers;* Kinderjury Award, 1998, for *The Last Polar Bears;* Smarties Silver Award for Six-to-Eight Category, 2003, for *The Last Castaways.*

Writings

SELF-ILLUSTRATED

The Ogopogo; or, My Journey with the Loch Ness Monster, MacDonald (Loanhead, Scotland), 1981.
The Last Polar Bears, Viking (London, England), 1993.
A Friend for Little Bear, Candlewick (Cambridge, MA), 1996.
The Last Gold Diggers, Puffin (London, England), 1998.
The Last Cowboys, Puffin (London, England), 1999.
Little Rabbit Lost, Peachtree (Atlanta, GA), 2002.
The Last Castaways: Being, as It Were, an Account of a Small Dog's Adventures at Sea, Puffin (London, England), 2003.
Little Rabbit Goes to School, Peachtree (Atlanta, GA), 2004.
Little Rabbit Runaway, Peachtree (Atlanta, GA), 2005.

Writer and designer of *Drowned God,* a CD-ROM computer game published by Time Warner, 1996.

ILLUSTRATOR

Michael Mullin, *Magus the Lollipopman,* Canongate (Edinburgh, Scotland), 1981.

David Hamilton, *The Good Golf Guide to Scotland,* Canongate (Edinburgh, Scotland), 1982, published as *The Scottish Golf Guide,* 1985.
Robert Louis Stevenson, *The Strange Case of Dr. Jekyll and Mr. Hyde,* Canongate (Edinburgh, Scotland), 1986, Dufour Editions (Chester Springs, PA), 1987.
Stuart McDonald, *The Adventures of Endill Swift,* Canongate (Edinburgh, Scotland), 1990.
Martin C. Strong, *The Great Rock Discography,* Canongate (Edinburgh, Scotland), 1994.
Yefim Druts and Alexei Gessler, *Russian Gypsy Tales,* Trafalgar Square (North Pomfret, VT), 1995.
Susan Price, editor, *Horror Stories,* Larousse Kingfisher Chambers (London, England), 1995, Kingfisher (Boston, MA), 1998.
Martin C. Strong, *The Wee Rock Discography,* Canongate (Edinburgh, Scotland), 1996.
Jim Dodge, *Fup,* Rebel, Inc., 1997.
Dick King-Smith, *Noah's Brother,* Puffin (London, England), 1998.
Dick King-Smith, *Tumbleweed,* Puffin (London, England), 1998.
Dick King-Smith, *Toby Man,* Penguin (London, England), 1998.
Martin C. Strong, *The Great Metal Discography,* Interlink, 1999.
Higglety Pigglety Pop (collected poems), Walker (London, England), 1999.
Margaret Mahy, *A Villain's Night Out,* Puffin (London, England), 1999.
Tony Mitton, *What's the Time Mr Wolf?,* Walker (London, England), 1999.
Dick King-Smith, *Julius Caesar's Goat,* Penguin (London, England), 1999.
Dorothy O. Van Woerkom, reteller, *Abu Ali Counts His Donkeys: A Folktale from the Middle East,* Walker (London, England), 1999, Candlewick Press (Cambridge, MA), 2000.
Michael Rosen, *Centrally Heated Knickers,* Puffin (London, England), 2000.
Helen Armstrong, *The Road to Somewhere,* Orion (London, England), 2000.
Ann Harvey, editor, *The Naughtiest Children I Know,* Red Fox (London, England), 2000.
Dick King-Smith, *Chewing the Cud,* Viking (London, England), 2001.
Vivian French, *Jack and the Beanstalk* (play), Walker (London, England), 2001.
John Wallace, *Anything for You,* Puffin (London, England), 2003, HarperCollins (New York, NY), 2004.

Contributor of cartoons to numerous publications, including London *Guardian,* London *Sunday Telegraph,* and *New Yorker,* and of weekly cartoon "Horsebox" to *Scotsman.*

Adaptations

The Last Polar Bears was adapted for film, Telemagination/ITV, 2000.

Sidelights

Harry Horse is the pen name of British author, cartoonist, and illustrator Richard Horne. Beginning his career writing and illustrating the award-winning 1981 book *The Ogopogo; or, My Journey with the Loch Ness Monster,* Horse worked as an illustrator for several years before penning another story. His next self-illustrated book, 1993's *The Last Polar Bears,* details the story of an adventurous grandfather and his dog, Roo, who are on a journey to seek the last polar bears. The tale is uniquely told through a collection of letters from the grandfather, traveling in the Arctic, to his grandchild back home. This frequently humorous tale also addresses serious issues like the hazards of such a journey, as well as larger issues such as pollution and global warming. *The Last Polar Bears* met with an enthusiastic reception by critics, George Hunt writing in *Books for Keeps* that Horse's line drawings are "sprightly and facetious," and that the work as a whole creates an "original atmosphere." *School Librarian* critic Janet Tayler also praised the artwork, raving: "I love the delightful illustrations . . . that accompany the text as Grandfather's sketches in his letters."

A heartwarming story that focuses on the true meaning of friendship, *A Friend for Little Bear* finds Little Bear stranded, all alone, on a deserted island. Wishing for a playmate, the lonesome bear begins pulling all sorts of things from the sea, including a wooden horse. While wooden horse becomes Little Bear's first playmate, the bear continues to search for a best friend, until an accident helps him realize what a true friend is. Patricia Mahoney Brown, writing in *School Library Journal,* paid tribute to Horse's self-illustrated storybook, terming it an "effective springboard for discussions on friendship, values, materialism, loneliness, and happiness." A critic for *Kirkus Reviews* also deemed the book a worthy effort, remarking that it "has a message, one worth repeating," and noting Horse's "sweet, engaging" drawings." In a *Publishers Weekly* review, although the critic found Horse's story somewhat "contrived," the author's watercolor illustrations were dubbed "a cut above" and "refreshing."

Like *A Friend for Little Bear, Little Rabbit Lost* also finds a young creature all alone and making the best of things. In this case, Little Rabbit has a birthday and knows that with this extra year he is now ready to deal independently with the world. When his family decides to take him to the Rabbit World amusement park, Little Rabbit rushes on ahead, assuring his parents that he knows the way but getting lost instead. Horse's story "perfectly captures the wonder . . . of a child on the cusp between toddler and big kid," wrote a *Publishers Weekly* reviewer, while in *Booklist* Helen Rosenberg predicted that "children will welcome this charming story" and enjoy the illustrations' "clever details." *School Library Journal* Jane Marino praised the book for its "deft and light touch," adding that Horse's gentle watercolor paintings effectively bring to life his "small, but intrepid protagonist." Little Rabbit reappears in several other books, including *Little Rabbit Goes to School,* in which a favorite toy is smuggled into class on the first day of school, and *Little Rabbit Runaway,* in which the author/illustrator "once again demonstrates his intuitive understanding of preschoolers' minds and moods," according to a *Publishers Weekly* critic. Noting the "universal appeal of tales about running away," Suzanne Myers Harold noted in *School Library Journal* that Horse's saga of the little bunny that leaves home to avoid his parents only to find that a new friend is even more bossy is "amusing and realistic."

In addition to picture books, Horse has built a following as a political cartoonist through his "Horsebox" comic strip published in the *Scotsman* and his work in several major publications, and he was cartoonist on staff of the *Scotland on Sunday* from 1987 to 1992. In the 1990s he also illustrated several nonfiction adult titles focusing on contemporary music that were written by Martin C. Strong, among them *The Great Metal Discography, The Great Rock Discography,* and *The Great Psychedelic Discography.* He is also the creator of the *Drowned God* video game, which posits that the world we know may have roots other than those history has revealed. As Horse explained in an interview on *Gamespot.com,* "The idea behind *Drowned God* is that history may have been manipulated to hide certain facts that might drastically change the way we see ourselves as a race. . . . that maybe the evolution of mankind was aided or altered by outside forces."

Horse once told *SATA:* "I wanted to become an illustrator at a ridiculously precocious age. I was seven when I first told my parents that I wanted to illustrate books when I grew up. Their reaction to this news was not what I had anticipated. It was to become a source of conflict for the next ten years, culminating with me running away from home at the age of seventeen to pursue my chosen career.

"I had no formal art training, as I was unable to attend art college without my parents' help. So I began work in Edinburgh as a staff illustrator on a magazine called *City Lynx.* I was nineteen when I illustrated *Magus the Lollipopman,* a delightful story by the Irish writer Michael Mullin. Two years later, I wrote my first book, and it contained many of the threads that I have revisited in my work—namely, an old man's last journey on this earth."

Biographical and Critical Sources

PERIODICALS

Booklist, October 1, 2005, Jennifer Mattson, review of *Little Rabbit Runaway,* p. 63.
Books for Keeps, January, 1997, George Hunt, review of *The Last Polar Bears,* pp. 21-22; December 1, 2002, Helen Rosenberg, review of *Little Rabbit Lost,* p. 674; August, 2004, Stephanie Zvirin, review of *Little Rabbit Goes to School,* p. 1948

A little rabbit leaves home so nobody can tell him what to do, but finds a bossy friend who is more demanding than his parents in **Little Rabbit Runaway.**

Carousel, spring, 1999, p. 30.

Kirkus Reviews, July 15, 1996, review of *A Friend for Little Bear,* p. 1049; August 15, 2004, review of *Little Rabbit Goes to School,* p. 807; September 1, 2005, review of *Little Rabbit Runaway,* p. 974.

Publishers Weekly, August 19, 1996, review of *A Friend for Little Bear,* p. 66; September 2, 2002, review of *Little Rabbit Lost,* p. 74; February 9, 2004, review of *Anything for You,* p. 79; September 6, 2004, review of *Little Rabbit Goes to School,* p. 61; July 25, 2005, review of *Little Rabbit Runway,* p. 74.

School Librarian, autumn, 1999, review of *The Last Cowboys,* pp. 136, 145; spring, 2001, review of *The Last Polar Bears,* p. 18.

School Library Journal, February, 1994, Janet Tayler, review of *The Last Polar Bears,* p. 21; September, 1996, Patricia Mahoney Brown, review of *A Friend for Little Bear,* p. 180; October, 2002, Jane Marino, review of *Little Rabbit Lost,* p. 112; October, 2004, Judith Constantinides, review of *Little Rabbit Goes to School,* p. 118; September, 2005, Suzanne Myers Harold, review of *Little Rabbit Runaway,* p. 173.

ONLINE

Gamespot.com, http://www.gamespot.com/ (March 28, 2006), interview with Horse.

J

JAMES, Emily
See STANDIFORD, Natalie

* * *

JURMAIN, Suzanne 1945-
(Suzanne Tripp Jurmain)

Personal

Born 1945, in New York, NY; daughter of Paul (an actor and writer) and Ruth (an actress; maiden name, Enders) Tripp; married Richard B. Jurmain (a physician), 1966; children: Sara, David. *Education:* University of California, Los Angeles, B.A. (with honors), 1966.

Addresses

Home—Los Angeles, CA. *Agent*—Dorothy Markinko, McIntosh & Otis, Inc., 353 Lexington Ave., New York, NY 10016.

Career

Actress, beginning in 1949; *TV Guide,* Los Angeles, CA, assistant editor, 1966; Legal Directories Publishing Co., Los Angeles, editor, 1967; University of California Museum of Cultural History, Los Angeles, editor and public relations coordinator, 1968-77; freelance writer and editor, 1978—.

Member

Society of Children's Book Writers and Illustrators, Phi Beta Kappa.

Awards, Honors

Golden Kite Honor Book for Nonfiction designation, Society of Children's Book Writers and Illustrators, 2005, and Orbis Pictus Honor Book designation, National Council of Teachers of English, 2006, both for *The Forbidden Schoolhouse.*

Writings

From Trunk to Tail: Elephants Legendary and Real, Harcourt (New York, NY), 1978.

Once upon a Horse: A History of Horses and How They Shaped Our History, Lothrop (New York, NY), 1989.

Freedom's Sons: The True Story of the Amistad Mutiny, Lothrop (New York, NY), 1998.

(As Suzanne Tripp Jurmain) *George Did It,* illustrated by Larry Day, Lothrop (New York, NY), 1998.

The Forbidden Schoolhouse: The True and Dramatic Story of Prudence Crandall and Her Students, Houghton Mifflin (Boston, MA), 2005.

Sidelights

Suzanne Jurmain is the author of several nonfiction works, some focusing on animals and their relationship to humans throughout time and others examining significant episodes in U.S. history. While many of her books, such as *Once upon a Horse: A History of Horses and How They Shaped Our History* and *The Forbidden Schoolhouse: The True and Dramatic Story of Prudence Crandall and Her Students,* present a detailed overview of their subjects, in *George Did It* she focuses on a single episode: George Washington's trip from his home at Mount Vernon to the temporary capital of the fledgling nation in New York to grudgingly take up the role of president of the United States. In *Publishers Weekly* a reviewer praised Jurmain's "snappy tone," while a contributor to *Kirkus Reviews* described the book as an "amusing historical anecdote."

From Trunk to Tail: Elephants Legendary and Real explores symbolic references to elephants in folklore, as well as their real-life roles as domestic servants, circus performers, and prey. In *Once upon a Horse,* which a *Los Angeles Times* reviewer called "the best horse book to come down the pike in some time," Jurmain examines the relationship between horses and humans from prehistoric times through the 1980s.

In **George Did It** *Jurmain shows that the brave General George Washington had more trepidations about becoming president than he did about crossing the Delaware. (Illustration by Larry Day.)*

Once upon a Horse surveys the use of the animal in transportation and sports, and the ways in which horses have aided (or been exploited by) hunters, warriors, miners, farmers, and mail-carriers. The stories and illustrations—including photographs of ancient coins and cave paintings—reflect the representation of horses in literature, archaeology, and art. Reviewers appreciated the format and illustrations, although some found fault with the writing style and factual information. While Charlene Strickland, commenting on *Once upon a Horse* in *School Library Journal,* found the text somewhat "awkward," and lacking in "sufficient lore to satisfy curious equestrians," a *Kirkus Reviews* contributor praised the book's content as "illuminating far beyond its factual level." In *Booklist* contributor Denise Wilms called *Once upon a Horse* "a handsome history."

Other historical works include *Freedom's Sons: The True Story of the Amistad Mutiny* and *The Forbidden Schoolhouse.* Praised for its "meticulous research and . . . storyteller's knack for pace and well-placed detail" by *Booklist* reviewer Randy Meyer, *Freedom's Song* follows the saga of the slave ship *Amistad,* which became embroiled in extensive litigation in 1839, when the ship's Cuban crew mitinied and its human cargo of West Africans were taken in by New England families and communities. The history of the first African-American girl's school in the United States, which was founded by Quaker educator Prudence Crandall in eastern Connecticut in 1883, is taken up by Jurmain in *The Forbidden Schoolhouse,* a "fast-paced read" that draws

on original sources and places Crandall's boarding school within the broader history of school integration, according to a *Kirkus Reviews* writer. In *Booklist* Ilene Cooper deemed the book "compelling" and "highly readable," while praising Jurmain's text as including "a sense of drama that propels readers forward." In *Horn Book* Robin Smith maintained that readers will be inspired by Crandall's "dedication, strength, and moral compass," while Kelly Czarnecki wrote in *School Library Journal* that, with its illustrations, appendix, and wealth of facts, *The Forbidden Schoolhouse* "offers a fresh look" at the educational opportunities for blacks and women during the early nineteenth century.

Jurmain once told *SATA:* "When I was little, my parents' apartment had more books than furniture—so it's not surprising that books are practically the first things I remember. My mother read me nursery rhymes, fairy tales, 'Oz' books, and A.A. Milne. My father told me stories. And what stories they were! Some came straight from his own imagination; some, from mythology; but many of the best were about real-life heroes, heroines, and villains. As we rode across New York on the subway, he told me about the amazing adventures of Cleopatra, Columbus, Richard Lionheart, Pocahontas—and by kindergarten I'd already learned that facts could be as exciting as fiction.

"At age four I saw my mother play Maria in a Broadway production of Shakespeare's *Twelfth Night*—and from that moment on, I wanted to be an actress. After making my debut on my father's television show, *Mr. I. Magination,* I wanted to perform as much as possible. My parents, however, felt school was more important than acting experience, and during my childhood I was only allowed to make occasional television appearances. As a teenager, however, I appeared in several television soap operas and studies acting at New York City's High School of Performing Arts until my parents moved to Los Angeles at the end of my junior year. Still determined to become an actress, I entered the University of California, Los Angeles, as a theatre arts major—and then everything changed.

"In college I met my husband, switched my major to English, lost interest in acting, and discovered that I liked writing and telling stories. I began to think that one day I would enjoy writing for young people, but I wasn't sure whether I wanted to write fiction or nonfiction.

"Today, when I visit classrooms, children—who have grown up thinking that facts are about as appealing as fried grasshoppers in library paste—often ask why on Earth I write nonfiction. The answer is very simple: I enjoy it. I love to do research. I love to tell stories. And I hope that—like my father—I'll be able to show others that facts can be just as fascinating as fiction."

Biographical and Critical Sources

PERIODICALS

Booklist, December 15, 1989, Denise Wilms, review of *Once upon a Horse: A History of Horses and How They Shaped Our History,* p. 832; February 15, 1998, Randy Meyer, review of *Freedom's Sons: The True Story of the Amistad Mutiny,* p. 1003; October 1, 2005, Ilene Cooper, review of *The Forbidden Schoolhouse: The True and Dramatic Story of Prudence Crandall and Her Students,* p. 52.

Bulletin of the Center for Children's Books, May, 1998, review of *Freedom's Sons,* p. 325.

Horn Book, November-December, 2005, Robin Smith, review of *The Forbidden Schoolhouse,* p. 736.

Kirkus Reviews, November 1, 1989, review of *Once upon a Horse;* November 15, 2005, review of *George Did It,* p. 1234; August 1, 2005, review of *The Forbidden Schoolhouse,* p. 851.

Los Angeles Times, November 26, 1989, review of *Once upon a Horse.*

Publishers Weekly, November 14, 2005, review of *George Did It,* p. 68.

School Library Journal, September, 1979, pp. 140-141; January, 1990, Charlene Strickland, review of *Once upon a Horse,* p. 113; April, 1998, Carrie Schadle, review of *Freedom's Sons,* p. 147; November, 2005, Kelly Czarnecki, review of *The Forbidden Schoolhouse,* p. 164.

Voice of Youth Advocates, April, 1990, p. 50; August, 1999, review of *Freedom's Sons,* p. 163.

Washington Post Book World, March 11, 1979, p. F5; November 5, 1989, p. 20.*

*   *   *

JURMAIN, Suzanne Tripp
See JURMAIN, Suzanne

K

KELLY, Katy 1955-

Personal

Born 1955; daughter of Tom (a journalist) and Marguerite (a columnist and writer) Kelly; married; husband an art director for television; children: Emily, Marguerite.

Addresses

Home—Chevy Chase, MD. *Agent*—c/o Author Mail, Delacorte Press, Bantam Dell, 1745 Broadway, New York, NY 10019.

Career

Journalist. *People* magazine, reporter; *USA Today,* feature writer for Life section; *U.S. News & World Report,* currently senior editor.

Writings

Lucy Rose: Here's the Thing about Me, illustrated by Adam Rex, Delacorte Press (New York, NY), 2004.
Lucy Rose: Big on Plans, illustrated by Adam Rex, Delacorte Press (New York, NY), 2005.
Lucy Rose: Busy like You Can't Believe, illustrated by Adam Rex, Delacorte Press (New York, NY), 2006.

Adaptations

The "Lucy Rose" novels have been adapted as audiobooks, Listening Library, 2005.

Sidelights

Growing up in Washington, DC, as the daughter of two journalists, Katy Kelly knew what would be involved in pursuing a career as a reporter and writer. In addition to a successful journalism career that has included stints at *People, USA Today,* and *U.S. News & World Report,* where she now works as a senior editor, Kelly was inspired to begin a series of books for younger readers that feature the vivacious eight-year-old Lucy Rose. Including the novels *Lucy Rose: Here's the Thing about Me* and *Lucy Rose: Big on Plans,* Kelly's novels have been praised for her engaging fourth-grade heroine and their use of the diary format. "I lifted a lot of Lucy Rose's life from my own," the author told *Publishers Weekly* interviewer Sally Lodge, "and then . . . stirred it around." Commenting on her second job, Kelly added: "It's not work for me, since I have so much fun with Lucy Rose. And writing each book is a very different experience. I learn something new with every go."

Readers meet Lucy Rose in *Lucy Rose: Here's the Thing about Me,* as the girl moves from Michigan to Washington, DC on the heels of her parents' separation. Living with her mother, Lucy Rose also learns a lot from her grandmother, an advice columnist who lives nearby and becomes the young girl's confidante. Dealing with the ups and downs of a new school in fine style, Lucy Rose "narrates in breathless run-on sentences" and "has a truly original perspective," according to a *Publishers Weekly* reviewer. In *School Library Journal* Linda Zeilstra Sawyer noted that Lucy Rose confronts the problems shared by many children dealing with broken homes, and "meets her challenges with humor and honesty," while a *Kirkus Reviews* critic noted that Kelly's text successfully "delivers . . . mature and complex concepts simply enough for her young audience."

A busy summer vacation rolls out in *Lucy Rose: Big on Plans*, as the young diarist expresses her worries about everything from her parent's divorce and her grandparents' problem with hungry squirrels to a bully who seems determined to cause Lucy Rose grief. "The book's language is rich and the characters are likeable," Teresa Bateman noted in *School Library Journal,* while in *Booklist* Cindy Dobrez wrote that "Lucy Rose's exuberance is evident in her long, run-on sentences." "Lucy is energetic and positive, but her life is a realistic blend of fun and challenges," according to a *Kirkus Reviews* contributor.

In **Lucy Rose: Big on Plans** *a nine-year-old diarist finds that her ambitious plans for her all-too-brief summer vacation cause a few sleepless nights. (Illustration by Adam Rex.)*

Biographical and Critical Sources

PERIODICALS

Booklist, November 1, 2004, Ilene Cooper, review of *Lucy Rose: Here's the Thing about Me,* p. 485; April 15, 2005, Patricia Austin, review of *Lucy Rose: Here's the Thing about Me,* p. 1476; August, 2005, Cindy Dobrez, review of *Lucy Rose: Big on Plans,* p. 2028.

Bulletin of the Center for Children's Books, October, 2004, Timnah Card, review of *Lucy Rose: Here's the Thing about Me,* p. 83.

Kirkus Reviews, September 1, 2004, review of *Lucy Rose: Here's the Thing about Me,* p. 868; June 1, 2005, review of *Lucy Rose: Big on Plans,* p. 638.

Library Media Connection, January, 2005, Terry Day, review of *Lucy Rose: Here's the Thing about Me,* p. 75.

Publishers Weekly, September 20, 2004, review of *Lucy Rose: Here's the Thing about Me,* p. 63; December 20, 2004, "Flying Starts," p. 30.

School Library Journal, September, 2004, Linda Zeilstra Sawyer, review of *Lucy Rose: Here's the Thing about Me,* p. 170; June, 2005, Terrie Dorio, review of *Lucy*

Rose: Big on Plans, p. 118; September, 2005, Teresa Bateman, review of *Lucy Rose: Big on Plans,* p. 78.

U.S. News & World Report, October 11, 2004, Vicky Hallett, "Born to Write a Kid's Book," p. 68.

ONLINE

Random House Web site, http://www.randomhouse.com/ (February 24, 2006), "Katy Kelly."*

*   *   *

KOMPANEYETS, Marc 1974-

Personal

Born 1974, in Moscow, USSR (now Russia); immigrated to United States; son of Katya Kompaneyets (an artist). *Education:* Attended School of the Art Institute of Chicago, 1992-93; attended Pennsylvania Academy of the Fine Arts, 1993-96; University of Pennsylvania, B.F.A. (cum laude), 1997.

Addresses

Home—Los Angeles, CA. *Agent*—c/o Author Mail, Knopf Publishing Group, Random House, 1745 Broadway, New York, NY 10019. *E-mail*—mkompaneyets@ yahoo.com.

Career

Artist, illustrator, and author. Muralist and fine artist, 1992—; writer and illustrator, 2000—; Santa Monica College, Santa Monica, CA, adjunct professor of art. *Exhibitions:* Paintings included in private collections. Murals installed in residences, hospitals, and commercial locations.

Writings

The Squishiness of Things, Alfred A. Knopf (New York, NY), 2005.

Sidelights

Russian-born author Marc Kompaneyets made his publishing debut with the children's book *The Squishiness of Things* in which all-knowing Hieronymus sets out with the self-imposed task of documenting and recording everything worth knowing. Ironically, just when he believes he has completed his task, an intriguing hair blows through his study window, its origins tantalizing the know-it-all with a new mystery. Hieronymus, determined to uncover the source of the hair and thus complete his challenge, winds up traveling the world in search of the tiny object's origins. Finally, defeated, he returns home, where a talk with his assistant reveals the answer to his search.

Just when the brilliant Hieronymus thought he had it all figured out, a stray hair blows through his window, sending him on a journey that yields some surprising discoveries in Kompaneyets' unique picture book.

Noting that Kompaneyets' "witty and intelligent narrative includes direct addresses to the audience," Wendy Lukehart wrote in *School Library Journal* that *The Squishiness of Things* is a "thought-provoking study of the agony and ecstasy of the pursuit of knowledge." Reflecting the opinion of *Booklist* contributor Karin Snelson that Kompaneyets plots an "almost Oz-like journey through strange lands," a *Publishers Weekly* critic wrote that the story "takes the form of a classic parable, as the search ends in Hieronymus's own backyard." In *Curled Up with a Good Kids' Book* online, Marie D. Jones concluded that the novel "combines great storytelling, eye-catching illustrations and a theme that hopefully will instill a love for knowledge and the wonder of exploring the world . . . in every child that reads it."

Biographical and Critical Sources

PERIODICALS

Booklist, July, 2005, Karin Snelson, review of *The Squishiness of Things,* p. 1925.
Kirkus Reviews, June 1, 2005, review of *The Squishiness of Things,* p. 639.

Library Media Connection, August-September, 2005, Christine Markley, review of *The Squishiness of Things,* p. 70.
Publishers Weekly, July 18, 2005, review of *The Squishiness of Things,* p. 206.
School Library Journal, August, 2005, Wendy Lukehart, review of *The Squishiness of Things,* p. 99.

ONLINE

Marc Kompaneyets Home Page, http://www.mkompan. com (December 14, 2005).
Curled Up with a Good Kids' Book Web site, http://www. curledupkids.com/ (February 24, 2006), Marie D. Jones, review of *The Squishiness of Things.**

*　　*　　*

KOPPES, Steven N. 1957-
(Steven Nelson Koppes)

Personal

Born August 28, 1957, in Manhattan, KS; son of Ralph (a printer) and Mary (a clerical worker) Koppes; married Susan Keaton (a newspaper editor), May 18, 1984 (divorced). *Education:* Kansas State University, B.S. (anthropology), 1978; University of Kansas, M.S., 1982. *Politics:* "Independent." *Religion:* "Agnostic." *Hobbies and other interests:* Long-distance running, backpacking, reading.

Addresses

Home—1355 Jeffery Dr., Homewood, IL 60430. *Office*—University of Chicago News Office, 5801 S. Ellis Ave. Room 200, Chicago, IL 60637. *E-mail*—steve@ mrmeteor.com.

Career

Science writer. *Morning Sun* (newspaper), Pittsburg, KS, journalist, 1981-83; worked in family restaurant, 1983-85; Arizona State University News Bureau, writer, assistant director, then interim director, 1985-97; University of Georgia, Athens, assistant director of research communications, 1997-98; University of Chicago News Office, Chicago, IL, science writer, 1998—. Publisher of Tempe, AZ, entertainment tabloid, c. mid-1980s.

Member

National Association of Science Writers, Society of Children's Book Writers and Illustrators.

Awards, Honors

Nonfiction Honor List inclusion, *Voice of Youth Advocates,* 2003, and Best Book for Children designation, *Science Books & Films* magazine, named Outstanding

Science Trade Book, National Science Teachers Association/Children's Book Council, and Honor Book for Grades 7-12, Society of School Librarians International, all 2004, all for *Killer Rocks from Outer Space.*

Writings

Killer Rocks from Outer Space: Asteroids, Comets, and Meteorites, Lerner Publications Co. (Minneapolis, MN), 2004.

Work in Progress

A biography of the late Robert S. Diez, a geologist.

Sidelights

Steven N. Koppes also answers to the name "Mr. Meteor." In his book *Killer Rocks from Outer Space: Asteroids, Comets, and Meteorites* Koppes describes the many impacts upon planetary surfaces that have occurred in our solar system, including those by caused by comets, asteroids, and meteorites. Noting that Earth has sometimes been the direct target, Koppes explores the effects of such activity, including the extinction of Earth's dinosaurs and the possibility of future impacts on the planet's surface. Color photos and illustrations accompany Koppes's text, in which "better readers . . . will find lots for reports or for personal interest," according to *Booklist* contributor Jennifer Locke. Jeffrey A. French wrote in *School Library Journal* that Koppes has created "an attractive and readable look at planetary impacts by comets, asteroids, and meteorites," and continued: "While Koppes focuses on the possibility, of future impacts on Earth and the danger they present, his writing is not as sensationalistic as the title" implies.

Koppes told *SATA:* "My parents encouraged me to read and learn and as a result I developed an interest in writing at a fairly young age. I wrote my first 'book,' on human evolution, in grade school. The first article that was published under my byline was a book review that appeared on August 19, 1979, in my hometown newspaper, the *Manhattan [Kansas] Mercury.*

"After completing my master's degree in journalism at the University of Kansas I landed my first full-time writing job as a reporter at the *Morning Sun* in Pittsburg, Kansas, where I worked from 1981 to 1983. From 1983 to 1985 I was in the restaurant business with my brothers. Still I wrote, edited and published an entertainment tabloid newspaper that we distributed in our restaurant in Tempe, Arizona. Then I began my career in higher education, at Arizona State University.

"Geologist Robert S. Dietz inspired me to writer *Killer Rocks from Outer Space.* I met Dr. Dietz at Arizona State University in 1985 and interviewed him regularly for scientific news reports until the latter's death in

Koppes focuses on the asteroids, comets, and meteorites shooting across the galaxy, and discusses what danger they pose to life on Earth, in Killer Rocks from Outer Space.

1995. Dietz made pioneering research contributions to three distinct divisions of the geosciences: sea-floor spreading, the recognition of meteorite and asteroid impact structures on Earth, and the impact origin of the moon's surface. He also conceived and organized Project Nekton, the plan to dive to the deepest spot on the ocean floor. Project Nekton culminated on January 23, 1960, when the Trieste submersible and its two-man crew dived seven miles to the bottom of the Pacific Ocean's Challenger Deep."

Biographical and Critical Sources

PERIODICALS

Booklist, January 1, 2004, Jennifer Locke, review of *Killer Rocks from Outer Space: Asteroids, Comets, and Meteorites,* p. 841.
Library Media Connection, April-May, 2004, review of *Killer Rocks from Outer Space,* p. 78.
School Library Journal, March, 2004, Jeffrey A. French, review of *Killer Rocks from Outer Space,* p. 237.
Science Teacher, February, 2004, Diana Wiig, review of *Killer Rocks from Outer Space,* p. 81.

ONLINE

Steven N. Koppes Home Page, http://mrmeteor.com (February 24, 2006).

*   *   *

**KOPPES, Steven Nelson
See KOPPES, Steven N.**

KUSHNER, Lawrence 1943-

Personal

Born 1943, in Detroit, MI; married; wife's name Karen (a community outreach director); children: three. *Education:* University of Cincinnati, degree, 1965; Hebrew Union College, ordained rabbi, 1969. *Hobbies and other interests:* Graphic design, computers, Mozart, "hanging around sailboats."

Addresses

Office—c/o The Congregation Emanu-El, 2 Lake St., San Francisco, CA 94118.

Career

Rabbi, educator, and writer. Congregation Solel, Highland Park, IL, rabbinic fellow-in-residence, 1969-71; Congregation Beth El, Sudbury, MA, rabbi, 1971-99; Congregation Emanu-El, San Francisco, CA, currently scholar-in-residence. Hebrew Union College-Jewish Institute of Religion, New York, NY, instructor, beginning 1986, and rabbi-in-residence; Graduate Theological University, Berkeley, CA, visiting professor of Jewish spirituality.

Writings

The Book of Letters: A Mystical Hebrew Alef-Bait, Jewish Lights (Woodstock, VT), 1975.
Honey from the Rock: Visions of Jewish Mystical Renewal, Jewish Lights (Woodstock, VT), 1977.
The River of Light: Spirituality, Judaism, and the Evolution of Consciousness, Harper (New York, NY), 1981.
(With Deborah Kerdeman) *The Invisible Chariot: An Introduction to Kabbalah and Spirituality for Young Adults,* A.R.E. Publishing (Denver, CO), 1986.
The Book of Miracles: A Young Person's Guide to Jewish Spiritual Awareness, Union of American Hebrew Congregations (New York, NY), 1987.
God Was in This Place and I, I Did Not Know: Finding Self, Spirituality, and Ultimate Meaning, Jewish Lights (Woodstock, VT), 1991.
(Translator and editor, with Kerry Olitsky) *Sparks beneath the Surface: Selections from Itturay Torah on the Weekly Parasha,* Jason Aronson (Northvale, NJ), 1993.
The Book of Words: Talking Spiritual Life, Living Spiritual Talk, Jewish Lights (Woodstock, VT), 1993.
Invisible Lines of Connection: Sacred Stories of the Ordinary, Jewish Lights (Woodstock, VT), 1996.
Eyes Remade for Wonder: A Lawrence Kushner Reader, Jewish Lights (Woodstock, VT), 1998.
Kabbalah: The Way of Light, illustrated by Jo Gershman, Peter Pauper Press (White Plains, NY), 1999.
Because Nothing Looks like God, Jewish Lights (Woodstock, VT), 2000.
The River of Light: Jewish Mystical Awareness, Jewish Lights (Woodstock, VT), 2000.

(With wife, Karen Kushner) *Where Is God?,* illustrated by Dawn W. Majewski, Skylight Paths (Woodstock, VT), 2000.
Honey from the Rock: An Introduction to Jewish Mysticism, Jewish Lights (Woodstock, VT), 2000.
Jewish Spirituality, Jewish Lights (Woodstock, VT), 2001.
(With Karen Kushner) *What Does God Look Like?,* illustrated by Dawn W. Majewski, Skylight Paths (Woodstock, VT), 2001.
(With Karen Kushner) *How Does God Make Things Happen?,* illustrated by Dawn W. Majewski, Skylight Paths (Woodstock, VT), 2001.
The Way into Jewish Mystical Tradition, Jewish Lights (Woodstock, VT), 2001.
(With Nehemia Polen) *Filling Words with Light: Hasidic and Mystical Reflections on Jewish Prayer,* Jewish Lights (Woodstock, VT), 2004.
(With Gary Schmidt) *In God's Hands,* illustrated by Matthew J. Baek, Jewish Lights (Woodstock, VT), 2005.
Kabbalah: A Love Story, Morgan Road Books (New York, NY), 2006.

Sidelights

Lawrence Kushner, who served as rabbi of his Sudbury, Massachusetts, congregation for twenty-eight years before moving to northern California to teach and write, examines the Jewish faith and ideology in several books. Written primarily for younger readers, works such as *The Book of Miracles: A Young Person's Guide to Jewish Spiritual Awareness* presents a series of chapters that address questions children might have about Judaism and spirituality in general. In contrast, *Invisible Lines of Connection: Sacred Stories of the Ordinary* includes a collection of tales that are culled from Kushner's own experiences with his family, friends, and even strangers, and the author uses these encounters to reveal spiritual insights. Some of Kushner's titles include writings appropriate for both adults and children, among them the anthology *Eyes Remade for Wonder: A Lawrence Kushner Reader,*. A *Booklist* reviewer noted that this 1998 collection will "strike a chord with a wide range of readers." According to a critic for *Publishers Weekly,* "Kushner's blend of scholarship, imagination, psychology, mysticism, and humor will make readers feel that he is speaking personally to them."

Kushner has published several books designed for very young readers, often working with a co-writer. With his wife, Karen Kushner, he wrote *What Does God Look Like?, How Does God Make Things Happen?,* and *Because Nothing Looks like God,* three titles designed to help young children understand difficult concepts about religion and spirituality. Instead of trying to offer philosophical answers, the Kushners describe God as being in worms as they circulate the soil, as well as in the embraces of family and friends, and assure readers that, although God cannot be seen, He can be felt, just like the wind or human emotions. The Kushners' books also encourage children in the belief that God works through them. Reviewing *Because Nothing Looks like God,* a

critic for *Publishers Weekly* noted: "Parents who want help teaching difficult religious concepts will like the Kushners' method of bridging abstract ideas and concrete images," and *Booklist* reviewer Ellen Mandel considered it a "valuable book." Teri Markson, reviewing the same title for *School Library Journal,* felt that "because the Kushners' intent is to explore rather than describe God, there is room for children's own spiritual awareness to grow."

Kushner teamed up with fellow author Gary Schmidt in writing *In God's Hands,* a retelling of a Jewish legend. In the story, David, a poor man, wonders how to feed his family. Jacob, a rich man, typically dozes in synagogue, but wakes just as a passage from the book of Leviticus, commanding Moses to bake challah bread for God, is being read. Jacob feels this scripture is meant to be taken literally; he bakes bread and places the loaves in a holy ark. When David, who works as a janitor for the synagogue, finds the loves, he knows that God has answered his prayers about feeding his family. For years, the two men repeat the ritual, each thinking that God is granting him a miracle. Finally, a rabbi reveals what is actually happening, but shows the men that they have both acted their part in God's ultimate design. The "narrative unwinds with a crisp rhythm," commented a critic for *Publishers Weekly,* while a *Kirkus Reviews* contributor recommended the title as "a worthy choice for all collections." As *Booklist* reviewer Ilene Cooper wrote, "This lovely piece of bookmaking combines a good tale with a strong, easily understood message."

After many years of writing and teaching from his home in Massachusetts, Kushner and his family moved to California. There, he serves as scholar-in-residence for Congregation Emanu-El in San Francisco, and also serves as a visiting professor of Jewish spirituality at the Graduate Theological University in Berkeley. In his

Kushner joins Gary Schmidt in retelling an ancient legend about two men of differing means who find that their worth is measured in something other than money in **In God's Hands.** *(Illustration by Matthew J. Baek.)*

free time, the rabbi and writer enjoys "hanging around sailboats and trying to learn how to play the clarinet," as he noted on his home page.

Biographical and Critical Sources

PERIODICALS

Booklist, June 1, 1996, review of *Invisible Lines of Connection: Sacred Stories of the Ordinary,* p. 1636; January 1, 1999, Ilene Cooper, review of *Eyes Remade for Wonder: A Lawrence Kushner Reader,* p. 800; January 1, 2001, Ellen Mandel, review of *Because Nothing Looks like God,* p. 963; October 1, 2001, Ray Olson, review *Jewish Spirituality: A Brief Introduction for Christians,* p. 284.

Choice, February, 1982, p. 778.

Kirkus Reviews, August 1, 2005, review of *In God's Hands,* p. 852.

Library Journal, September 15, 1981, p. 1742; October 1, 1996, review of *Invisible Lines of Connection,* p. 86; November 15, 2001, Naomi Hafter, *Jewish Spirituality,* p. 72.

Publishers Weekly, December 13, 1993, p. 33; April 8, 1996, review of *Invisible Lines of Connection,* p. 60; January 26, 1998, review of *The Book of Miracles: A Young Person's Guide to Jewish Spiritual Awareness,*

Kushner and his wife, Karen Kushner, address the questions children of all faiths ask about God, creation, and their special place in the world in their highly acclaimed picture book **Because Nothing Looks like God.** *(Illustration by Dawn W. Majewski.)*

p. 87; October 26, 1998, review of *Eyes Remade for Wonder,* p. 61; September 27, 1999, review of *Kabbalah: The Way of Light,* p. 96; September 10, 2001, review of *Jewish Spirituality,* p. 88; July 25, 2005, review of *In God's Hands,* p. 80.

School Library Journal, February, 2001, Teri Markson, review of *Because Nothing Looks like God,* p. 112; October, 2005, Rachel Kamin, review of *In God's Hands,* p. 118.

Stepping Stones, September-October, 1998, review of *The Book of Miracles,* p. 32.

ONLINE

Lawrence Kushner Home Page, http://www.rabbikushner. org (March 27, 2006).

L

LALIBERTÉ, Louise-Andrée 1958-

Personal

Born March 12, 1958, in Québec City, Québec, Canada; daughter of Marcel (an engineer) and Madeleine (a health care worker; maiden name, Monette) Laliberté; married Marc Riverin (a technician), December 29, 1984; children: Simon, François. *Education:* Laval University, B.A. (visual arts), 1982, teaching certificate, 1983. *Hobbies and other interests:* Swimming, skiing, writing, reading, talking, sleeping, non-commercial music, non-commercial movies, "I love wind, sun, rain, snow, heat, freezing cold, storms, ice storms . . . birds, dogs, trees, wild flowers, water, rivers, oceans, friends and people . . . hate stinging insects. November, contempt, injustice . . . Idols: Mahatma Ghandi, Martin Luther King, Don Quixote, and Santa Claus for their integrity, their optimism, and their ingenuousness."

Addresses

Home and office—1111, Gustave-Langelier, Québec, Québec G1Y 2J3, Canada. *E-mail*—la.laliberte@sympatico.ca.

Career

Illustrator and graphic designer, beginning 1980s. College teacher and art specialist in secondary schools. Performer in school and library visits. *Exhibitions:* Has exhibited painting and photography at galleries, including Galerie Magella-Paradis, Québec City.

Member

Association des illustrateurs et illustratrices du Québec, Communication-Jeunesse, Regroupement des artistes en arts visuels du Québec.

Awards, Honors

Salon de l'illustracion québecoise jury selection, 1990, for editorial illustration; Canadian Association of Photographers and Illustrators in Communication Gold Prize for book illustration, 1997; Biennale de l'illustration québecoise jury selection, 2003, for book cover; *Resource Links* Year's Best designation, 2004, Edmonton Public Library Best of the Best Book list inclusion, 2005, and Chocolate Lily Book Award nomination, 2005-06, all for *Mormor Moves In* by Susin Nielsen-Ferlund; Mr. Christie Book Award Silver Seal, and *Resource Links* Year's Best distinction, both 2004, and Blue Spruce Award nominee, Kentucky Bluegrass Award nominee, and Chocolate Lily Book Award nominee, all 2004-05, all for *Hank and Fergus* by Nielsen-Ferlund; Young Readers Choice, Communication-Jeunesse awards, 2004-05, for *Vendredi 13* by Gilles Tibo; Edmonton Public Library Best of the Best Booklist, Shining Willow Award nomination, and Canadian Toy Council Great Book Award, all 2005, all for *A Noodle up Your Nose* by Frieda Wishinsky.

Illustrator

M.C. Hall, *Whitney's New Puppy,* CTW (New York, NY), 1998.

Frieda Wishinsky, *A Noodle up Your Nose,* Orca Book Publishers (Victoria, British Columbia, Canada), 2003.

Susin Nielsen-Fernlund, *Hank and Fergus,* Orca Book Publishers (Victoria, British Columbia, Canada), 2003.

Danielle Simard, *Dans le coeur de mon grand-père,* Éditions du Renouveau pédagogique (Montréal, Québec, Canada), 2003.

Frieda Wishinsky, *A Bee in Your Ear,* Orca Book Publishers (Victoria, British Columbia, Canada), 2004.

Susin Nielsen-Fernlund, *Mormor Moves In,* Orca Book Publishers (Victoria, British Columbia, Canada), 2004.

Frieda Wishinsky, *Dimples Delight,* Orca Book Publishers (Victoria, British Columbia, Canada), 2005.

ILLUSTRATOR; "LA BANDE DES CINQ CONTINENTS" SERIES

Camille Bouchard, *La mèche blanche,* Soulières (Saint-Lambert, Québec, Canada), 2005.

Camille Bouchard, *Le monstre de la Côte-Nord,* Soulières (Saint-Lambert, Québec, Canada), 2006.

Camille Bouchard, *L'etrange M. Singh,* Soulières (Saint-Lambert, Québec, Canada), 2006.

Camille Bouchard, *Les vampires des montagnes,* Soulières (Saint-Lambert, Québec, Canada), 2007.

ILLUSTRATOR; "NOÉMIE" SERIES

Gilles Tibo, *Le secret de Madame Lumbago,* Québec-Amérique (Boucherville, Québec, Canada), 1996, translated as *Naomi and Mrs Lumbago,* Tundra Books (Toronto, Ontario, Canada), 2001.

Gilles Tibo, *L'incroyable journée,* Québec-Amérique (Montréal, Québec, Canada), 1996.

Gilles Tibo, *La clé de l'énigme,* Québec-Amérique (Montréal, Québec, Canada), 1997.

Gilles Tibo, *Les sept vérités,* Québec-Amérique (Montréal, Québec, Canada), 1997.

Gilles Tibo, *Albert aux grandes oreilles,* Québec-Amérique (Montréal, Québec, Canada), 1998.

Gilles Tibo, *Le château de glace,* Québec-Amérique (Montréal, Québec, Canada), 1998.

Gilles Tibo, *La nuit des horreurs,* Québec-Amérique (Montréal, Québec, Canada), 1999.

Gilles Tibo, *Le jardin zoologique,* Québec-Amérique (Montréal, Québec, Canada), 1999.

Gilles Tibo, *Adieu, grand-maman,* Québec-Amérique (Montréal, Québec, Canada), 2000.

Gilles Tibo, *La boîte mystérieuse,* Québec-Amérique (Montréal, Québec, Canada), 2000, translated as *Naomi and the Secret Message,* Tundra Books (Toronto, Ontario, Canada), 2004.

Gilles Tibo, *Les souliers de course,* Québec-Amérique (Montréal, Québec, Canada), 2001.

Gilles Tibo, *La cage perdue,* Québec-Amérique (Montréal, Québec, Canada), 2002.

Gilles Tibo, *Vendredi 13,* Québec-Amérique (Montréal, Québec, Canada), 2003.

Gilles Tibo, *Le voleur de grand-mère,* Québec-Amérique (Montréal, Québec, Canada), 2004.

Gilles Tibo, *Le grand amour,* Québec-Amérique (Montréal, Québec, Canada), 2005.

Gilles Tibo, *Grand-maman fantôme,* Québec-Amérique (Montréal, Québec, Canada), 2006.

Work in Progress

Illustrating more books in the "Noémie" series by Gilles Tibo and the "La bande des cinqu continents" series by Camille Bouchard; preparing photos and text for a book about Québec City churches, titled *L'art dans les églises de Québec,* forthcoming, 2008; a comic-book project with author Denis Côté.

Sidelights

Louise-Andrée Laliberté told *SATA:* "Before learning to read I used to pick up picture books and, inspired by the images I saw, loudly improvise stories of my own, and make everybody laugh.

Laliberté's artwork brings to life Susin Nielsen-Fernlund's **Mormor Moves In,** *a story about a young girl whose anticipation over the arrival of her Swedish grandmother is crushed by the woman's dour mood.*

"I also loved to draw. I drew with everything, everywhere: with all kinds of pencils on the cardboard pieces that came along with my father's cleaned shirts, or on every kind of 'drawable' surfaces my mother gave me; on the basement walls with chalk; on the street with pieces of plasterboard we took from the builder's yards all around; even with markers on my bedroom walls, but this used to put me into trouble.

"In school, I was a kid who didn't like to read. I loved books though, but I only liked to look at the images in them and let my imagination travel. One of my favourite was the real big *Dictionnaire de la langue française au Canada.* About five inches thick, the fabulous book presented numerous glossed colour plates covered with fishes, mushrooms, butterflies, birds, flowers, boats, planes. . . . I never stopped looking at the pictures, but it softly drew me to love reading quite as much.

"I never stopped drawing everywhere either, colouring everything, so now it's me who makes the pictures in the books. Images help words succeed in interesting all those kids for whom reading is hard or boring. With intelligence and versatility, illustrations help words to communicate with everyone: illiterates, kids, teens as well as good readers. Before words get winded, illustrations back, clarify, simplify, describe, intensify, interrogate, and invite readers to enter the beautiful world of

books that inspire curiosity, imagination, and dreams: the fascinating country of 'going ahead.'"

Biographical and Critical Sources

PERIODICALS

Kirkus Reviews, September, 2003, review of *Hank and Fergus;* September, 2004, review of *Mormor Moves In.*

Maclean's, December, 2003, Sue Ferguson, review of *Hank and Fergus,* p. 50.

Publishers Weekly, December, 2003, review of *Hank and Fergus.*

Revue Prestige, December, 2003-January, 2004, Catherine Lemieux, interview with Laliberté, p. 84.

Resource Links, Volume 9, number 3, Linda Berezowski, review of *Hank and Fergus,* p. 4; Volume 9, number 4, review of *Naomi and the Secret Message;* Volume 9, number 5, review of *A Noodle up Your Nose;* October, 2004, Isobel Lang, review of *Mormor Moves In,* p. 8, and Carolyn Cutt, review of *A Bee in Your Ear,* p. 24; Volume 11, number 3, review of *Dimples Delight.*

ONLINE

Canadian Review of Materials, http://www.umanitoba.ca/cm/ (April 12, 2006), Lynne McKechnie, review of *Hank and Fergus;* Dave Jenkinson, review of *A Noodle up Your Nose;* Liz Greenaway, review of *Mormor Moves In;* Denise Weir, review of *A Bee in Your Ear.*

Random House Web site, http://www.randomhouse.com/ (April 12, 2006), "Louise-Andrée Laliberté."

*　　*　　*

LANG, Aubrey

Personal

Married Wayne Lynch (a photographer).

Addresses

Home—Calgary, Alberta, Canada. *Agent*—c/o Author Mail, Fitzhenry & Whiteside, 195 Allstate Pkwy., Markham, Ontario L3R 4T8, Canada.

Career

Writer and photographer.

Writings

Eagles, photographs by husband, Wayne Lynch, Sierra Club Books (San Francisco, CA), 1990.

Rudy Visits the North, illustrated by Muriel Hope, Hyperion Books for Children (New York, NY), 1992.

Bears, illustrated by Ian Stirling, Rodale Press, 1993.

Loons, photographs by Wayne Lynch, Thunder Bay (San Diego, CA), 1996.

Wild Birds across the Prairies, Fitzhenry & Whiteside (Toronto, Ontario, Canada), 1999.

Contributor of photographs to periodicals, including *National Geographic, Owl, Ranger Rick,* and *Canadian Geographic.*

"NATURE BABIES" SERIES

Baby Bear, photographs by Wayne Lynch, Fitzhenry & Whiteside (Toronto, Ontario, Canada), 2002.

Baby Fox, photographs by Wayne Lynch, Fitzhenry & Whiteside (Toronto, Ontario, Canada), 2002.

Baby Elephant, photographs by Wayne Lynch, Fitzhenry & Whiteside (Toronto, Ontario, Canada), 2002.

Baby Penguin, photographs by Wayne Lynch, Fitzhenry & Whiteside (Toronto, Ontario, Canada), 2002.

Baby Koala, photographs by Wayne Lynch, Fitzhenry & Whiteside (Toronto, Ontario, Canada), 2002.

Baby Lion, photographs by Wayne Lynch, Fitzhenry & Whiteside (Toronto, Ontario, Canada), 2002.

Baby Seal, photographs by Wayne Lynch, Fitzhenry & Whiteside (Toronto, Ontario, Canada), 2004.

Baby Owl, photographs by Wayne Lynch, Fitzhenry & Whiteside (Toronto, Ontario, Canada), 2004.

Baby Ground Squirrel, photographs by Wayne Lynch, Fitzhenry & Whiteside (Toronto, Ontario, Canada), 2004.

Baby Sloth, photographs by Wayne Lynch, Fitzhenry & Whiteside (Toronto, Ontario, Canada), 2004.

(With Nancy Hundal) *Baby Sea Turtle,* photographs by Wayne Lynch, Fitzhenry & Whiteside (Toronto, Ontario, Canada), 2006.

Baby Porcupine, photographs by Wayne Lynch, Fitzhenry & Whiteside (Toronto, Ontario, Canada), 2006.

Baby Grizzly, photographs by Wayne Lynch, Fitzhenry & Whiteside (Toronto, Ontario, Canada), 2006.

"OUR WILD WORLD" SERIES

Rocky Mountains, photographs by Wayne Lynch, Northword, 2006.

Prairie Grasslands, photographs by Wayne Lynch, Northword, 2006.

Sidelights

Together with husband and fellow photographer Wayne Lynch, writer and photographer Aubrey Lang has dedicated much of her career to documenting and observing animals. In addition to featuring their photographs in such periodicals as *National Geographic, Canadian Geographic,* and *Ranger Rick,* Lang and Lynch have collaborated on several highly praised nature books, including the "Nature Babies" series. Geared toward the

Part of the "Nature Babies" series, Lang's **Baby Bear** *follows the adventures of a trio of black bear cubs who set out to explore the world on their own. (Photograph by Wayne Lynch.)*

budding naturalist, each book in the series focuses on a different region and baby animal. Through a combination of text and engaging color photographs, young readers are introduced to the daily schedules of some of the world's cutest creatures. Titles in the series include *Baby Bear, Baby Penguin, Baby Seal, Baby Fox,* and *Baby Elephant,* allowing readers to jump continents in their introduction to nature.

In *Canadian Review of Materials* Liz Greenaway praised Lang's text as "straightforward and fact-filled," and cited Lynch's photography as "stunning." A *School Library Journal* critic commented of the series that, "with texts that read like stories, these inviting volumes provide introductions to fascinating animals, emphasizing the bond between mothers and babies and incorporating details about habits." Antonia Gisler, reviewing Lang and Lynch's books for *Resource Links,* stated that "the series is a nice introduction to animals and once read, children will ask for further information about these creatures."

Biographical and Critical Sources

PERIODICALS

Booklist, December 15, 2001, Helen Rosenberg, review of *Baby Bear,* p. 735; February 1, 2005, Hazel Rochman, review of *Baby Koala,* p. 963.

Bulletin of the Center for Children's Books, February, 1991, review of *Eagles,* p. 145; May, 2003, review of *Baby Lion,* p. 366.

Canadian Book Review Annual, 2001, review of *Baby Penguin,* p. 576; 2002, review of *Baby Elephant,* p. 570.

Children's Bookwatch, November, 2004, review of *Baby Seal.*

Horn Book, March-April, 1991, Margaret A. Bush, review of *Eagles,* p. 215.

Kirkus Reviews, January 1, 2005, review of *Baby Koala,* p. 54.

Language Arts, October, 1991, review of *Eagles,* p. 496.

Nature, July 25, 1996, review of *Loons,* p. 311.
Quill & Quire, October, 2001, review of *Baby Penguin,* p. 44.
Reading Teacher, December, 1991, review of *Eagles,* p. 312.
Resource Links, December, 2001, Veronica Allan, review of "Nature Babies" series, p. 27; October, 2002, review of *Baby Seal,* p. 20; June, 2003, review of *Baby Elephant,* p. 21; October, 2004, Antonia Gisler, review of *Baby Ground Squirrel,* p. 24.
School Library Journal, July, 1992, Susan Oliver, review of *Bears,* p. 88; February, 2002, Nancy Call, review of *Baby Penguin,* and Arwen Marshall, review of *Baby Bear,* p. 123; December, 2002, Arwen Marshall, review of *Baby Fox,* p. 126; February, 2005, Nancy Call, review of *Baby Ground Squirrel,* p. 123; April, 2005, Nancy Call, review of *Baby Koala,* p. 124; October, 2005, review of *Baby Ground Squirrel,* p. 31.

ONLINE

Canadian Review of Materials Online, http://www.umanitoba.ca/cm/ (January 18, 2002), review of *Baby Penguin;* (September 6, 2002) Lia Greenaway, reviews of *Baby Fox* and *Baby Seal;* (April 11, 2003) review of *Baby Lion.*
Fitzhenry & Whiteside Web site, http://www.fitzhenry.ca/ (December 14, 2005).

*   *   *

LEVY, Elizabeth 1942-

Personal

Born April 4, 1942, in Buffalo, NY; daughter of Elmer Irving and Mildred (Kirschenbaum) Levy. *Education:* Brown University, B.A. (magna cum laude), 1964; Columbia University, M.A.T., 1968. *Hobbies and other interests:* Marathons, bike tours, baseball.

Addresses

Agent—Amy Berkower, Writers House, 21 W. 26th St., New York, NY 10010. *E-mail*—elizlevy@elizabethlevy.com.

Career

Writer, 1971—. American Broadcasting Co., New York, NY, editor and researcher in news department, 1964-66; Macmillan Publishing Co., Inc., New York, NY, assistant editor, 1967-69; New York Public Library, New York, NY, writer in public relations, 1969; JPM Associates (urban affairs consultants), New York, NY, staff writer, 1970-71.

Member

Authors Guild, Authors League of America, Mystery Writers of America, PEN.

Elizabeth Levy

Awards, Honors

Outstanding Book of the Year, *New York Times,* 1977, for *Struggle and Lose, Struggle and Win: The United Mine Workers;* Outstanding Science Book for Children, National Science Teachers Association, 1977, for *Before You Were Three;* Charlie May Simon Children's Book Award, Arkansas Department of Education, 1995, for *Keep Ms. Sugarman in the Fourth Grade;* named among 100 Best Books of 1997, New York Public Library, and Maryland State Award, and Georgia Children's Book Award, both 2000-01, all for *My Life as a Fifth-Grade Comedian;* American Booksellers Association (ABA) Pick of the Lists, 2000, for *Seventh-Grade Tango.*

Writings

NONFICTION

The People Lobby: The SST Story, Delacorte (New York, NY), 1973.
Lawyers for the People, Knopf (New York, NY), 1974.
By-Lines: Profiles in Investigative Journalism, Four Winds Press (New York, NY), 1975.
(With cousin, Robie H. Harris) *Before You Were Three: How You Began to Walk, Talk, Explore, and Have Feelings,* Delacorte (New York, NY), 1977.
(With Mara Miller) *Doctors for the People: Profiles of Six Who Serve,* Knopf (New York, NY), 1977.
(With Tad Richards) *Struggle and Lose, Struggle and Win: The United Mineworkers Story,* Four Winds Press (New York, NY), 1977.

(With Earl Hammond and Liz Hammond) *Our Animal Kingdom,* Delacorte (New York, NY), 1977.

If You Lived When They Signed the Constitution, Scholastic (New York, NY), 1987.

Are We There Yet?: Europeans Meet the Americans, illustrated by Mike Dietz, Scholastic (New York, NY), 2001.

Awesome Ancient Ancestors, illustrated by Daniel McFeeley, Scholastic (New York, NY), 2001.

Who Are You Calling a Woolly Mammoth?: Prehistoric America, illustrated by Daniel McFeeley, Scholastic (New York, NY), 2001.

Cranky Colonials: Pilgrims, Puritans, Even Pirates, illustrated by Daniel McFeeley, Scholastic (New York, NY), 2002.

Westward, Ha-ha!: 1850-1850, illustrated by Daniel McFeeley, Scholastic (New York, NY), 2003.

Revolting Revolutionaries: 1750s-1790s, illustrated by Daniel McFeeley, Scholastic (New York, NY), 2003.

FICTION; FOR CHILDREN

Nice Little Girls, Delacorte (New York, NY), 1974.

Lizzie Lies a Lot (also see below), Dell (New York, NY), 1976.

The Tryouts, Four Winds Press (New York, NY), 1979.

Running out of Time, Knopf (New York, NY), 1980.

Running out of Magic with Houdini, Knopf (New York, NY), 1981.

The Shadow Nose, Morrow (New York, NY), 1983.

The Computer That Said Steal Me, Four Winds Press (New York, NY), 1983.

Cold as Ice, Morrow (New York, NY), 1988.

Keep Ms. Sugarman in the Fourth Grade, Harper (New York, NY), 1992.

Cleo and the Coyote, illustrated by Diana Bryer, Harper (New York, NY), 1996.

My Life as a Fifth-Grade Comedian, Harper (New York, NY), 1997.

Third-Grade Bullies, illustrated by Tim Barnes, Hyperion (New York, NY), 1998.

Seventh-Grade Tango, Hyperion (New York, NY), 2000.

Big Trouble in Little Twinsville, illustrated by Mark Elliott, Harper (New York, NY), 2001.

Take Two, They're Small (sequel to *Big Trouble in Little Twinsville*), illustrated by Mark Elliott, HarperCollins (New York, NY), 2003.

YOUNG-ADULT FICTION

Come out Smiling, Delacorte (New York, NY), 1981.

Double Standard, Avon (New York, NY), 1984.

The Dani Trap, Morrow (New York, NY), 1984.

Night of Nights, Ballantine (New York, NY), 1984.

All Shook Up, Scholastic (New York, NY) 1986.

Cheater, Cheater, Scholastic (New York, NY), 1993.

The Drowned, Hyperion (New York, NY), 1995.

Tackling Dad, HarperCollins (New York, NY), 2005.

"SOMETHING QUEER" MYSTERY SERIES

Something Queer Is Going On, Delacorte (New York, NY), 1973.

Something Queer at the Ballpark, Delacorte (New York, NY), 1975.

Something Queer at the Library, Delacorte (New York, NY), 1977.

Something Queer on Vacation, Delacorte (New York, NY), 1980.

Something Queer at the Haunted School, Delacorte (New York, NY), 1982.

Something Queer at the Lemonade Stand, Delacorte (New York, NY), 1982.

Something Queer in Rock 'n' Roll, Delacorte (New York, NY), 1987.

Something Queer at the Birthday Party, Delacorte (New York, NY), 1990.

Something Queer in Outer Space, Hyperion (New York, NY), 1993.

Something Queer in the Cafeteria, Hyperion (New York, NY), 1994.

Something Queer at the Scary Movie, Hyperion (New York, NY), 1995.

Something Queer in the Wild West, Hyperion (New York, NY), 1997.

"BAMFORD BROTHERS" HORROR NOVELS; FOR CHILDREN

Frankenstein Moved in on the Fourth Floor, Harper (New York, NY), 1979.

Dracula Is a Pain in the Neck, Harper (New York, NY), 1983.

Gorgonzola Zombies in the Park, illustrated by George Ulrich, Harper (New York, NY), 1993.

Wolfman Sam, illustrated by Bill Basso, Harper (New York, NY), 1996.

Night of the Living Gerbil, illustrated by Bill Basso, Harper (New York, NY), 2001.

Vampire State Building, illustrated by Sally Wern Comport, Harper (New York, NY), 2002.

"JODY AND JAKE MYSTERY" SERIES; FOR CHILDREN

The Case of the Frightened Rock Star, Pocket Books (New York, NY), 1980.

The Case of the Counterfeit Race Horse, Pocket Books (New York, NY), 1980.

The Case of the Fired-up Gang, Pocket Books (New York, NY), 1981.

The Case of the Wild River Ride, Pocket Books (New York, NY), 1981.

"FAT ALBERT AND THE COSBY KIDS" SERIES; FOR CHILDREN

The Shuttered Window, Dell (New York, NY), 1981.

Mister Big Time, Dell (New York, NY), 1981.

Take Two, They're Small, Dell (New York, NY), 1981.

Spare the Rod, Dell (New York, NY), 1981.

Mom or Pop, Dell (New York, NY), 1981.

The Runt, Dell (New York, NY), 1981.

"MAGIC MYSTERIES" SERIES; FOR CHILDREN

The Case of the Gobbling Squash, Simon & Schuster (New York, NY), 1988.

The Case of the Mind-Reading Mommies, Simon & Schuster (New York, NY), 1989.

The Case of the Tattletale Heart, Simon & Schuster (New York, NY), 1990.

The Case of the Dummy with Cold Eyes, Simon & Schuster (New York, NY), 1991.

"GYMNASTS" SERIES; FOR CHILDREN

The Beginners, Scholastic (New York, NY), 1988.

First Meet, Scholastic (New York, NY), 1988.

Nobody's Perfect, Scholastic (New York, NY), 1988.

The Winner, Scholastic (New York, NY), 1989.

The Trouble with Elizabeth, Scholastic (New York, NY), 1989.

Bad Break, Scholastic (New York, NY), 1989.

Tumbling Ghosts, Scholastic (New York, NY), 1989.

Captain of the Team, Scholastic (New York, NY), 1989.

Crush on the Coach, Scholastic (New York, NY), 1990.

Boys in the Gym, Scholastic (New York, NY), 1990.

Mystery at the Meet, Scholastic (New York, NY), 1990.

Out of Control, Scholastic (New York, NY), 1990.

First Date, Scholastic (New York, NY), 1990.

World-Class Gymnast, Scholastic (New York, NY), 1990.

Nasty Competition, Scholastic (New York, NY), 1991.

Fear of Falling, Scholastic (New York, NY), 1991.

The New Coach, Scholastic (New York, NY), 1991.

Tough at the Top, Scholastic (New York, NY), 1991.

The Gymnast Gift, Scholastic (New York, NY), 1991.

Go for the Gold, Scholastic (New York, NY), 1992.

"BRIAN AND PEA BRAIN" MYSTERY SERIES; FOR CHILDREN

School Spirit Sabotage, illustrated by George Ulrich, Harper (New York, NY), 1994.

Rude Rowdy Rumors, illustrated by George Ulrich, Harper (New York, NY), 1994.

A Mammoth Mix-Up, illustrated by George Ulrich, Harper (New York, NY), 1995.

"INVISIBLE INC." MYSTERY SERIES; FOR CHILDREN

The Schoolyard Mystery, illustrated by Denise Brunkus, Scholastic (New York, NY), 1994.

The Mystery of the Missing Dog, illustrated by Denise Brunkus, Scholastic (New York, NY), 1995.

The Snack Attack Mystery, illustrated by Denise Brunkus, Scholastic (New York, NY), 1995.

The Creepy Computer Mystery, illustrated by Denise Brunkus, Scholastic (New York, NY), 1996.

The Karate Class Mystery, illustrated by Denise Brunkus, Scholastic (New York, NY), 1996.

Parents' Night Fright, illustrated by Denise Brunkus, Scholastic (New York, NY), 1998.

"FLETCHER MYSTERIES"; FOR CHILDREN

A Hare-Raising Tail, illustrated by Mordicai Gerstein, Aladdin (New York, NY), 2002.

The Mystery of Too Many Elvises, illustrated by Mordicai Gerstein, Aladdin (New York, NY), 2003.

The Mixed-Up Mask Mystery, illustrated by Mordicai Gerstein, Aladdin (New York, NY), 2003.

The Cool Ghoul Mystery, illustrated by Mordicai Gerstein, Aladdin (New York, NY), 2003.

PLAYS

(Coauthor) *Croon* (one-act), produced in New York, NY, 1976.

(Coauthor) *Never Waste a Virgin* (two-act), produced in New York, NY, 1977.

Lizzie Lies a Lot (based on her novel of the same title), produced by the Cutting Edge, 1978.

OTHER

Marco Polo: The Historic Adventure Based on the Television Spectacular, Random House (New York, NY), 1982.

Father Murphy's First Miracle (based on the television series *Father Murphy*), Random House (New York, NY), 1983.

Return of the Jedi (based on the film of the same title), Random House (New York, NY), 1983.

The Bride (based on the film of the same title), Random House (New York, NY), 1985.

Sidelights

From children's series fiction, chapter books, and picture books to young-adult novels and nonfiction, Elizabeth Levy's works encompass a wide range of reading levels and genres. As Levy once told *SATA,* "As a child I read all the time and omnivorously. My mother recalls coming into my room when I was twelve years old and finding *Winnie-the-Pooh, War and Peace, Peyton Place,* and a "Nancy Drew" mystery scattered on my bed. My eclectic reading habits haven't changed much since then, which accounts in part for the variety of books I write." On her home page, Levy commented: "Friendship and laughing are a big part of my life and they're in all my books, whether they're novels or history."

One of Levy's first works of fiction for younger readers, *Lizzie Lies a Lot,* deals with the issue of honesty as a young girl realizes that her lies threaten a friendship. Lizzie lies to her parents to make them think she is a good dancer, and to her friend Sara to entertain her. Eventually tiring of telling lies, Lizzie realizes that she must change. *Lizzie Lies a Lot* "is the most autobiographical of my books," Levy once admitted to *SATA.*

"I did lie a lot as a child, and I can distinctly remember what it felt like when I knew I was lying and no one else did. Like Lizzie in my novel, I told my mother I had been asked to perform in a school assembly and I kept up that lie for months.

"Oddly enough, my first published work was a lie. When I was in third grade, a newspaper published my poem 'When I Grow up I Want to Be a Nurse All Dressed in White.' I didn't want to be a nurse. If I wanted to be anything, I wanted to be a writer, but the idea of being a writer seemed a fantasy. I grew up without any concrete ambitions, but with an entire card catalog of fantasies."

Although Levy draws upon her childhood for many of her plots, she also bases her books on what interests her today. "When I write for children," she once told *SATA*, "I am really writing about things that seem funny or interesting to me now. I don't think writing a good book for children is very different from writing one for teenagers or adults. The emotions we have as children are in many ways as complex as those we have as adults. The best children's writers know this and are not tempted to oversimplify. . . . I think about my own childhood a lot, and when I write about a certain age I have very vivid memories of what it felt like then. I think that memories from childhood are like dreams. It's not important to remember all of them, but what you do remember is important."

Among Levy's most popular works for children are the adventures of the Bamford brothers, Sam and Robert. The pair's escapades, which begin in *Frankenstein Moved in on the Fourth Floor* and *Dracula Is a Pain in the Neck,* are continued in *Gorgonzola Zombies in the Park.* In this last story, Sam and Robert's eight-year-old cousin, Mabel, has come to New York City for a visit. Annoyed by her constant teasing, the boys convince Mabel that the statues in Central Park were once-living things that were transformed into statues by a zombie with breath that smells as bad as Gorgonzola cheese, one of Mabel's favorite foods. When someone smears the smelly cheese on the statues, the cousins embark on a search for the culprit. Bonnie Siegel praised the book's "strong characters and snappy dialogue" in a *School Library Journal* review, and *Booklist* critic Stephanie Zvirin asserted that the plot "will win over middle-grade readers, especially those who have enjoyed the brothers' previous comic adventures."

In *Wolfman Sam,* another installment in the chronicles of the Bamford boys, Sam is chosen as the school's disc jockey, and adopts the name Wolfman Sam. Robert, jealous of all the attention Sam is getting, finds a list of the identifying characteristics of werewolves, which scares Sam into thinking he might really be one. Robert's scheme sets off a series of humorous episodes in what *School Library Journal* contributor Suzanne Hawley called "a lighthearted and believable story." Stephanie Zvirin, writing for *Booklist,* observed that

In **Vampire State Building,** *when Sam's online junior chess partner comes to New York City from Romania for a tournament, his pointy teeth and secretive behavior give rise to concern. (Illustration by Sally Wern Comport.)*

"the relationship between the brothers is solidly grounded," and this relationship grows stronger in *Vampire State Building.* In this series installment Sam and Robert are involved in a New York City chess tournament, where players are coming from all around the globe. Sam has only met his teammate, Vlad, online, and Robert begins to suspect that Vlad may not be entirely human. "The humorous dialogue rings true," wrote Elaine E. Knight in a review for *School Library Journal.*

Levy's series of easy-to-read chapter books for children, the "Brian and Pea Brain" mysteries, includes *Rude Rowdy Rumors.* In this work, seven-year-old Brian is a star soccer player, and a jealous teammate is stirring up trouble by spreading wild lies about him. Accompanied by his younger sister Penny—affectionately known as Pea Brain—Brian sets out to discover the source of the hurtful rumors. Blair Christolon, in a review for *School Library Journal,* noted that "Levy presents a straightforward tale using basic vocabulary and simple sentence structure," adding that the mystery "ends on a clever, humorous note that will leave readers chuckling." *Booklist* critic Lauren Peterson praised the book's "fast-paced plot" and called Brian an "appealing, likable protagonist."

A departure from Levy's series work is her collaboration with illustrator Diana Bryer on the picture book *Cleo and the Coyote.* Here an abandoned dog named Cleo, who has just found a home with a boy and his mother, finds herself on a plane to Utah to visit the boy's sheep-rancher uncle. Levy's story chronicles Cleo's adventures in her new desert surroundings, including her relationship with a wild coyote. Susan Powers, writing in *School Library Journal,* declared that "everything about this book is warm. . . . Levy departs boldly and successfully from her dog-meets-boy story and extends the breadth of this tale."

The characters in Levy's long-running "Gymnasts" series, which she wrote between the late 1980s and early 1990s, became particularly special to her in the course of dreaming up their adventures. "I've found that writing a series so intensely is a very vivid experience," she explained. "The characters take on their own life, and actually kept me company. I took a lot of comfort and joy from my gymnasts. They were good friends to each other, and good friends to me through some family illnesses. I've spoken to other authors of series and they agree. Writing a series of twenty-two books with the same characters is similar to creating a make-believe group of 'best friends' who move in with you, driving your family nuts, but giving you a lot of comfort."

Many of Levy's other works for children employ the mystery-series format. Her "Invisible, Inc." mysteries chronicle the adventures of three young sleuths: Chip, who is invisible; Justin, who is hearing impaired and a lip reader; and Charlene, the leader of the group. In *Parents' Night Fright,* the prize-winning story Charlene is supposed to read at Parents' Night disappears, and the trio follows a trail of suspects and clues before apprehending the story thief. In a *School Library Journal* review, Pam Hopper Webb maintained that "this fast-paced contemporary story grabs readers' attention much like a prime-time sitcom." *Booklist* contributor Stephanie Zvirin noted that "the interactions between the characters have solid appeal, and the meaty text . . . gives children a good opportunity to practice their reading skills."

Levy's "Something Queer" mystery series for younger readers features girl sleuths Gwen and Jill, who solve puzzling mysteries at school and in their neighborhood. In *Something Queer at the Haunted School* they track down what may be a real ghost, while in *Something Queer on Vacation* they discover who has been knocking down sandcastles at the beach. Among the most engaging aspects of the series, a reviewer for the *Bulletin of the Center for Children's Books* observed, are a "light style, active girl detectives, humor, and a gratifying solution to the mystery."

The "Something Queer" series spun off with "Fletcher's Mysteries," a series where Gwen and Jill's dog, Fletcher, becomes the detective. In this series, designed for younger readers, Fletcher and his flea Jasper track

When the class rabbit goes missing, all fingers point to Fletcher the basset hound until a student magician conjures up the hidden hare in Levy's easy-reading **A Hare-Raising Tale.** *(Illustration by Mordecai Gerdstein.)*

down missing pets, uncovering villains plotting doggy danger and catching wig thieves in the process. "Readers will enjoy the unlikely but likable dog detective," wrote Shelle Rosenfeld in a review of the first book in the series, *A Hare-Raising Tale,* for *Booklist.* Of *The Mixed-Up Mask Mystery,* a *Kirkus Reviews* contributor commented that "the first-canine perspective, complete with rear-end sniffing, will have everyone howling." *The Mystery of Too Many Elvises,* in which Fletcher performs as an Elvis impersonator, was met with enthusiasm by Kristina Aaronson, who wrote in *School Library Journal* that "the idea of a pet talent show, the likable dog detective, and the easy-to-resolve mystery will appeal to young readers." Of *The Cool Ghoul Mystery,* Laura Scott wrote in *School Library Journal:* "Beginning chapter-book readers will feel right at home with Fletcher and his friends."

Levy takes a different approach with each new mystery she writes. "I find writing mysteries very different from writing novels," she once told *SATA.* "The great pleasure of writing a mystery is that I know how the book

will end. Before I begin a mystery, I have to figure out who did it and why. I know that by the end of the book my detectives will expose the character. Usually I do not know the path my detectives will take to make this discovery. I have to go back and on the second and third drafts I must change significant parts of the book to lay clues that develop towards the end of the book.

"However, the end is always in place. I think that is why we like mysteries. People who don't read mysteries can never understand how I can read them at night before I go to sleep. 'Don't they keep you up?,' friends ask. I find mysteries comforting. I read them when I'm tired or upset. Unless the writer is a cheat, I know the book will have a satisfactory ending. The bad will be punished and the characters I like will survive to live in another book. I only like mystery 'series.'

"Novels are completely different. Usually I write a novel about a conflict that I remember from my own childhood or something that I have experienced recently but believe that I also experienced when I was younger. I believe that the gift of a novel is to let others know that they are not alone, and that our secrets are usually far more shameful if kept hidden than if allowed out in the open. In most of my books, friendship is important. My friends are a huge part of my life, without them I would be bereft, and in my books I try to celebrate the healing power of friendship."

Levy's novels for middle graders and young adults deal with a wide variety of themes. *Cheater, Cheater* explores the difficulties of middle-school life. Seventh grader Lucy Lovello cheats at a friend's bowling party in order to impress a boy and, as a result, must deal with the consequences of being labeled a cheater. Jana R. Fine, writing in *School Library Journal,* asserted that in *Cheater, Cheater* "all of [Levy's] characters show realistic idiosyncrasies associated with young teens," and dubbed the book "a well-tempered portrayal of young adolescent life." A *Kirkus Reviews* critic praised the book's "natural, smooth dialogue leading to a thought-provoking resolution."

Geared for teen readers, *The Drowned* incorporates supernatural and horror-story elements. The book's protagonist, Lily, is spending the summer in Atlantic City, where her father drowned a few years earlier, leaving her with a fear of the ocean. Lily and a mysterious friend decide to make some money by leading a tour of spooky Atlantic City sights, including the house of a boy who drowned. Lily becomes ill at the house and is cared for by the boy's mother, at which point the story takes a scary and surprising turn. Deborah Stevenson, in the *Bulletin of the Center for Children's Books,* noted that the story has "an enticing blend of local atmosphere and classic supernatural horror motifs," as well as a "straightforward and accessible style." *Booklist* critic Janice Del Negro asserted that Levy's "supernatural potboiler will be an easy booktalk."

Another young-adult novel, *Tackling Dad,* features thirteen-year-old Cassie who wants to play football like her father. As a child, Cassie was the star of the Peewee League, but now that her middle school is allowing girls to join the football team, her father refuses to support her decision to join. Coach Harris, a family friend of Cassie's who is also the middle-school coach, encourages Cassie to follow her dream of playing on the team. Coach Harris "has an especially endearing relationship to the protagonist," according to Jennifer Cogan in *School Library Journal.* Julie Cummins, writing for *Booklist,* felt that Levy's "realistic story . . . is sure to score big with girls."

My Life as a Fifth-Grade Comedian is the humorous story of class clown Bobby, whose constant shenanigans annoy everyone and soon threaten his relationship with his family and his success in school. Finally Bobby's teacher, Mr. Matous, gives Bobby the job of organizing a school-wide comedy competition, and the boy has a chance to turn his comedic energy into something productive. A *Kirkus Reviews* critic called *My Life as a Fifth-Grade Comedian* "hard to put down," while Darcy Schild praised its "realistic setting" and "believable emotions" in her *School Library Journal* review.

Big Trouble in Little Twinsville and *Take Two, They're Small* introduce fourth-grader Eve, who has two twin sisters entering kindergarten. What makes things worse is that Eve's teacher is the identical twin of the kindergarten teacher. When Eve gets paired up with one of her sisters for a cross-grade project, she wonders if she will ever be able to escape twin-dom. Levy "gets across the rivalry, uproar, and love among siblings in a happy family," wrote Kathy Broderick in *Booklist,* while a *Kirkus Reviews* writer noted that the book's "lively plot and winning characters are just right for each other."

"While her books are characterized by a breezy humor, Levy also displays a sympathetic understanding of the problems faced by children and teens," commented a contributor to the *St. James Guide to Children's Writers.* "One of Levy's greatest strengths as a writer is that she allows her young characters to find their own paths without moralizing lectures by the narrator or adult characters." The books promote "respect and acceptance of others" while also featuring characters who are "funny and sassy," the essayist added. Remarking on the combination of serious and humorous elements in her works, Levy once told *SATA:* "For my characters to triumph they learn a lot about love and being loved. So there's a serious side to my characters and me, but I also love knowing why it's so easy to fool vampires. *Because they're suckers.* That's not a put-down. It's just a joke and it's funny."

Biographical and Critical Sources

BOOKS

St. James Guide to Children's Writers, 5th edition, St. James Press (Detroit, MI), 1999.

PERIODICALS

ALAN Review, November 26, 2005, review of *Tackling Dad.*

Booklist, October 1, 1993, p. 330; December 1, 1993, Stephanie Zvirin, review of *Gorgonzola Zombies in the Park,* p. 691; January 1, 1995, Lauren Peterson, review of *Rude Rowdy Rumors,* pp. 820-821; December 1, 1995, Janice Del Negro, review of *The Drowned,* pp. 620-621; November 15, 1996, Stephanie Zvirin, review of *Wolfman Sam,* p. 588; August, 1997, pp. 1901-1902; April 15, 1998, pp. 1445-1446; July, 1998, Stephanie Zvirin, review of *Parents' Night Fright,* p. 1890; September 1, 2002, Shelle Rosenfeld, review of *A Hare-Raising Tale,* p. 124; April 1, 2003, Kathy Broderick, review of *Take Two, They're Small,* p. 1397; May 1, 2003, Gillian Engberg, review of *The Mystery of Too Many Elvises,* p. 1529; September, 2005, Julie Cummins, review of *Tackling Dad,* p. 118.

Bulletin of the Center for Children's Books, May, 1983; October, 1983; March, 1984; November, 1984; December, 1987, review of *Something Queer in Rock 'n' Roll;* December, 1995, Deborah Stevenson, review of *The Drowned,* p. 131; January, 1998, p. 164.

Horn Book, July 15, 1993, review of *Cheater, Cheater,* p. 936; January 15, 1996, p. 137; June 15, 1997, review of *My Life as a Fifth-Grade Comedian,* p. 952.

Kirkus Reviews, November 15, 2002, review of *Take Two, They're Small,* p. 1697; January 1, 2003, review of *The Mixed-Up Mask Mystery,* p. 62.

Los Angeles Times, May 31, 1981.

New York Times Book Review, April 26, 1981; April 25, 1982.

Publishers Weekly, November 15, 1991, review of *Keep Ms. Sugarman in the Fourth Grade,* p. 73; August 9, 1993, review of *Cheater, Cheater,* p. 479; May 23, 1994, review of *School Spirit Sabotage,* p. 89; June 23, 1997, review of *My Life as a Fifth-Grade Comedian,* p. 92; January 24, 2000, review of *Seventh-Grade Tango,* p. 312.

School Library Journal, October, 1993, Jana R. Fine, review of *Cheater, Cheater,* p. 126; December, 1993, Bonnie Siegel, review of *Gorgonzola Zombies in the Park,* p. 91; January, 1995, Blair Christolon, review of *Rude Rowdy Rumors,* pp. 88-89; December 15, 1995, p. 131; May, 1996, Susan Powers, review of *Cleo and the Coyote,* p. 94; April, 1997, Suzanne Hawley, review of *Wolfman Sam,* p. 113; September, 1997, Darcy Schild, review of *My Life as a Fifth-Grade Comedian,* p. 219; July, 1998, p. 78; September, 1998, Pam Hopper Webb, review of *Parents' Night Fright,* p. 176; November, 2002, Elaine E. Knight, review of *Vampire State Building,* p. 129; January, 2003, review of *A Hare-Raising Tale,* p. 98, and review of *Take Two, They're Small,* p. 105; October, 2003, Kristina Aaronson, review of *The Mystery of Too Many Elvises,* p. 129; August, 2005, Jennifer Cogan, review of *Tackling Dad,* p. 130.

Voice of Youth Advocates, December, 1993, p. 294.

Washington Post Book World, May 9, 1982; November 6, 1983.

ONLINE

Elizabeth Levy Home Page, http://www.elizabethlevy.com (March 24, 2006).

*   *   *

LEWIN, Betsy 1937-

Personal

Born May 12, 1937, in Clearfield, PA; daughter of John K. (in insurance sales) and Winifred (a teacher; maiden name, Dowler) Reilly; married Ted B. Lewin (a writer and illustrator), 1963. *Education:* Pratt Institute of Art, B.F.A., 1959. *Hobbies and other interests:* Traveling to wilderness areas throughout the world, hiking, canoeing, and observing wildlife.

Addresses

Home—152 Willoughby Ave., Brooklyn, NY 11025. *E-mail*—betsyandted@aol.com.

Career

Freelance writer and illustrator. *Exhibitions:* joint exhibition with Ted Lewin at National Center for Children's Illustrated Literature, Abilene, TX, 2002.

Awards, Honors

Pick of the List, American Booksellers, 1990, for *Araminta's Paintbox,* and 1993, for *Ho! Ho! Ho! The Complete Book of Christmas Words,* written by Lynda Graham Barber; Children's Choice, 1994, for *Yo! Hungry Wolf,* written by David Vozar, and *Somebody Catch My Homework,* written by David L. Harrison; Best Books, *School Library Journal,* 1995, for *Booby Hatch;* Notable Book for Children designation, *Smithsonian* magazine, 1999, and Outstanding Science Trade Books for Children designation, National Science Teachers Association (NSTA)/CBC, 2000, both for *Gorilla Walk;* John Burroughs Award, American Museum of Natural History, and Outstanding Trade Books for Children Award designation, NSTA/CBC, both 2000, both for *Elephant Quest.*

Writings

SELF-ILLUSTRATED

Animal Snackers, Dodd (New York, NY), 1980, revised with new illustrations, Henry Holt (New York, NY), 2004.

Cat Count, Dodd (New York, NY), 1981, revised with new illustrations, Henry Holt (New York, NY), 2003.

Hip, Hippo, Hooray, Dodd (New York, NY), 1982.

Betsy Lewin

Booby Hatch, Houghton (Boston, MA), 1995.

Walk a Green Path, Lothrop (New York, NY), 1995.

Chubbo's Pool, Houghton (Boston, MA), 1997.

What's the Matter, Habibi?, Clarion (New York, NY), 1997.

Wiley Learns to Spell, Scholastic (New York, NY), 1998.

(With husband, Ted Lewin) *Gorilla Walk,* Lothrop (New York, NY), 1999.

(With Ted Lewin) *Elephant Quest,* HarperCollins (New York, NY), 2000.

Groundhog Day, Scholastic (New York, NY), 2000.

(With Ted Lewin) *Top to Bottom Down Under,* HarperCollins (New York, NY), 2005.

ILLUSTRATOR

Helen Kronberg Olson, *The Strange Thing That Happened to Oliver Wendell Iscovitch,* Dodd, Mead (New York, NY), 1983.

Berniece Freschet, *Furlie Cat,* Lothrop (New York, NY), 1986.

Beatrice Schenk de Regniers, *Penny,* Lothrop (New York, NY), 1987.

Arnold Adoff, *Greens: Poems,* Lothrop (New York, NY), 1988.

Maria Polushkin, *Kitten in Trouble,* Bradbury Press (New York, NY) 1988.

Maria Polushkin, *Here's That Kitten,* Bradbury Press (New York, NY), 1989.

Peter Limberg, *Weird: The Complete Book of Halloween Words,* Bradbury Press (New York, NY), 1989.

Karen Ackerman, *Araminta's Paintbox,* Atheneum (New York, NY), 1990.

Lynda Graham Barber, *Mushy: The Complete Book of Valentine's Words,* Bradbury Press (New York, NY), 1990.

Winifred Morris, *What If the Shark Wears Tennis Shoes?,* Atheneum (New York, NY), 1990.

Lynda Graham Barber, *Gobble: The Complete Book of Thanksgiving Words,* Bradbury Press (New York, NY), 1991.

Harry Allard, *The Hummingbirds' Day,* Houghton (Boston, MA), 1991.

Patricia Reilly Giff, *The War Began at Supper: Letters to Miss Loria,* Dell (New York, NY), 1991.

Carolyn Haywood, *Eddie and the Fire Engine,* Beach Tree, 1992.

Grace Maccarone, *Itchy, Itchy Chicken Pox,* Scholastic (New York, NY), 1992.

Russell Hoban, *Jim Hedgehog and the Lonesome Tower,* Houghton (Boston, MA), 1992.

Russell Hoban, *Jim Hedgehog's Supernatural Christmas,* Houghton (Boston, MA), 1992.

Lynda Graham Barber, *Doodle Dandy: The Complete Book of Independence Day Words,* Bradbury Press (New York, NY), 1993.

Joanne Ryder, *First Grade Elves,* Troll (Metuchen, NJ), 1993.

Joanne Ryder, *First Grade Ladybugs,* Troll (Metuchen, NJ), 1993.

Joanne Ryder, *First Grade Valentines,* Troll (Metuchen, NJ), 1993.

Stephen Krensky, *Fraidy Cats,* Scholastic (New York, NY), 1993.

Joanne Ryder, *Hello, First Grade,* Troll (Metuchen, NJ), 1993.

Lynda Graham Barber, *Ho! Ho! Ho! The Complete Book of Christmas Words,* Bradbury Press (New York, NY), 1993.

Ida Luttrell, *Mattie's Little Possum Pet,* Atheneum (New York, NY), 1993.

David L. Harrison, *Somebody Catch My Homework: Poems,* Boyds Mills Press (Honesdale, PA), 1993.

David Vozar, *Yo! Hungry Wolf: A Nursery Rap,* Doubleday (New York, NY), 1993.

David L. Harrison, *The Boy Who Counted Stars: Poems,* Boyds Mills Press (Honesdale, PA) 1994.

Caroline A. Levine, *The Detective Stars and the Case of the Super Soccer Team,* Dutton (New York, NY), 1994.

Steven Kroll, *I'm George Washington and You're Not!,* Hyperion (New York, NY), 1994.

Evan Levine, *What's Black and White and Came to Visit?,* Orchard Books (New York, NY), 1994.

Grace Maccarone, *The Classroom Pet,* Scholastic (New York, NY), 1995.

Grace Maccarone, *The Lunch Box Surprise,* Scholastic (New York, NY), 1995.

Grace Maccarone, *My Tooth Is about to Fall Out,* Scholastic (New York, NY), 1995.

David Vozar, *M.C. Turtle and the Hip Hop Hare: A Nursery Rap*, Doubleday (New York, NY), 1995.

Grace Maccarone, *The Gym Day Winner*, Scholastic (New York, NY), 1996.

Grace Maccarone, *The Recess Mess*, Scholastic (New York, NY), 1996.

Grace Maccarone, *Sharing Time Troubles*, Scholastic (New York, NY), 1996.

Jackie French Koller, *No Such Thing*, Boyds Mills Press (Honesdale, PA), 1997.

David Vozar, *RAPunzel: A Happenin' Rap*, Doubleday (New York, NY), 1998.

Carol Sonenklar, *Bug Girl*, Holt (New York, NY), 1998.

Elizabeth Nygaard, *Snake Alley Band*, Doubleday (New York, NY), 1998.

Grace Maccarone, *I Have a Cold*, Scholastic (New York, NY), 1998.

Mary Skillings Prigger, *Aunt Minnie McGranahan*, Clarion (New York, NY), 1999.

Grace Maccarone, *The Class Trip*, Scholastic (New York, NY), 1999.

Elizabeth Winthrop, *Promises*, Clarion (New York, NY), 2000.

Patricia Lauber, *Purrfectly Purrfect: Life at the Acatemy*, HarperCollins (New York, NY), 2000.

Nikki Grimes, *Is It Far to Zanzibar?: Poems about Tanzania*, Lothrop (New York, NY), 2000.

Doreen Cronin, *Click, Clack, Moo: Cows That Type*, Simon & Schuster (New York, NY), 2000.

Elizabeth Winthrop, *Dumpy La Rue*, Henry Holt (New York, NY), 2001.

Grace Maccarone, *First Grade Friends: Softball Practice*, Scholastic (New York, NY), 2001.

Barbara M. Joosse, *A Houseful of Christmas*, Holt (New York, NY), 2001.

Mary Skillings Prigger, *Aunt Minnie and the Twister*, Clarion (New York, NY), 2002.

Laura Krauss Melmed, *A Hug Goes Around*, HarperCollins (New York, NY), 2002.

Doreen Cronin, *Giggle, Giggle, Quack*, Simon & Schuster (New York, NY), 2002.

Sarah Weeks, *Two Eggs, Please*, Atheneum (New York, NY), 2003.

Grace Maccarone, *The Sleep Over*, Scholastic (New York, NY), 2003.

Doreen Cronin, *Duck for President*, Simon & Schuster (New York, NY), 2004.

Erica Silverman, *Cowgirl Kate and Cocoa*, Harcourt (New York, NY), 2005.

Karla Kuskin, *So, What's It Like to Be a Cat?*, Atheneum (New York, NY), 2005.

Doreen Cronin, *Click, Clack, Quackity-Quack: An Alphabetical Adventure*, Atheneum (New York, NY), 2005.

Erica Silverman, *Cowgirl Kate and Cocoa: Partners*, Harcourt (Orlando, FL), 2006.

Doreen Cronin, *Dooby Dooby Moo*, Atheneum (New York, NY), 2006.

Doreen Cronin, *Click, Clack, Splish, Splash: A Counting Adventure*, Atheneum (New York, NY), 2006.

Eileen Spinelli, *Heat Wave*, Harcourt (Orlando, FL), 2007.

Sidelights

The lively and whimsical illustrations of Betsy Lewin grace the pages of dozens of books for children, including both her original stories and the tale of other writers. Growing up in Clearfield, Pennsylvania, Lewin revealed her creativity and imagination early on. "Drawing and painting have always been my main interests," she once told *SATA*, "and there was never a doubt in my mind when I was a child that I would be anything but an artist." Lewin completed her formal training in fine arts at New York City's Pratt Institute, and in 1963, she married fellow author/illustrator Ted Lewin. Though the couple have lived in a brownstone in Brooklyn, New York, for many years, they share a love of the outdoors that has led them to travel all over the world. The adventurous Lewin has observed animals in Africa, Australia, Brazil, and the Galapagos Islands. She has also hiked into a volcanic crater in Hawaii, canoed through the Everglades in Florida, and watched whales off the coast of Baja California in Mexico, and such incidents from her vast travels have found her way into many of her books. "My books combine my love of drawing, the sound of words, and the touching humor in much animal behavior," Lewin explained to *SATA*. "I observe and draw animals and wildlife and paint flowers in watercolors."

In *Walk a Green Path* Lewin introduces young readers to many of the exotic places she has visited. In a series of large watercolor paintings she depicts the plants native to various regions of the world: her detailed art brings to life giant lily pads in the Amazon River; tiny mosses growing on a dead stump in a woodland near a lake in upstate New York; the lush, dense greenery of the Australian rain forest; and potted flowers sunning themselves on an iron staircase in New York City. Each spread is accompanied by a short statement describing the vegetation and a brief poem expressing Lewin's impressions of the scene. "Most of the writing is intensely, compactly personal," stated a writer for *Kirkus Reviews*, "giving readers the impression that they are tagging along Lewin's trail." In a review for *Booklist*, Mary Harris Veeder called the illustrations "the most memorable part of the book, beautifully conveying a sense of Lewin's affection for growing things." Kathy Piehl, writing in *School Library Journal*, added that *Walk a Green Path* should "encourage readers to view their own surroundings with renewed attention."

Lewin goes on many of her travels in the company of her husband, and in several books the Lewins collaborate in relating these shared experiences. A 1997 trip to the mountains of Uganda is the subject of *Gorilla Walk*, a profile of the habitat of the rare mountain gorilla that was praised for its "handsome paintings and carefully focused text" by *Horn Book* contributor Margaret A. Bush. As Bush added, the Lewins share with their readers "intriguing glimpses of both the rarely seen animals and the ambiguities of ecotourism." Another collabora-

One of Lewin's most popular picture books, **Animal Snackers** *is a collection of rhyming poems that describe the meal-time habits of a varied roster of dinner guests.*

tion by the well-traveled couple, *Elephant Quest* opens a window on to the savannahs of Africa as the Lewins' "cheerful, humorous tone combines with reverence for the beauty and variety of nature," according to another *Horn Book* writer. In *Top to Bottom Down Under* armchair travelers can explore the vast continent of Australia, ranging from Kakadu National Park in the north to Kangaroo Island in Australia's cooler southern climes. Illustrated with Ted Lewin's paintings and Betsy Lewin's field sketches, *Top to Bottom Down Under* was praised by *School Library Journal* contributor Patricia Manning as an "eye-catching and informative . . . treat for animal lovers and adventurers alike." Citing the inclusion of animal facts in the book, *Booklist* reviewer Karin Snelson wrote that *Top to Bottom Down Under* allows readers to share the creative couple's "contagiously cheerful Aussie expedition."

Like many of her fictional picture books, *Booby Hatch* grew out of Lewin's travels, in this case to the Galapa-

gos Islands. The picture book tells the story of Pepe, an unusual bird known as a blue-footed booby, that hatches from his egg to live along the islands' rocky shore. As Pepe grows up he learns how to fly, dive into the ocean and catch fish, and avoid being eaten by bigger animals. Before long, he meets a female booby and engages in a mating dance. Lewin's story ends with another egg nestled among the rocks, as the cycle of life begins again. Carolyn Phelan, writing in *Booklist,* praised the book as "a simple, appealing nature study for young children." In *School Library Journal*, Ellen Fader called *Booby Hatch* "a lovely book that succeeds in every way," adding that "Lewin's watercolor landscapes are spare and evocative."

At the start of her career, Lewin published several picture books that have proved so enduring that she has more recently re-illustrated them for new generations of children. *Animal Snackers,* a collection of unrhymed couplets that pair with illustrations to describe the way

different animals deal with dinnertime, was first published in 1980. While the original version featured artwork incorporating bread-dough animals, Lewin reissued the book twenty years later, this time creating the ink-and-watercolor illustrations she has become known for. The new edition of the book, which also includes several new poems, was praised by several reviewers, including Rachel G. Payne, who in *School Library Journal* wrote that Lewin's "new art offers clearer and more naturalistic images of the snacking creatures." A *Kirkus Reviews* writer deemed the book "a light brush" with nature that will "leave young readers . . . rolling in the aisles." Featuring pen-and-ink art in its 1981 edition, *Cat Count* was also reissued with watercolor art, its simple rhyming text recounting a child's ten friends and their cat-filled households, with resident felines ranging in population from one to ten. From partying cats and circus cats to sleeping cats, musical cats, and very, very lazy cats, the book contains fifty-five cats in total, . . . until one particularly fat cat proves to be a mother cat as well. "Cat lovers and children just learning how to count will be entranced by this colorful, energetic book," wrote *Booklist* contributor Diane Foote, while in *School Library Journal* Joy Fleishhacker noted that Lewin's picture-book revival "glows with warmth and visual humor."

In addition to creating art for both her fictional stories and her real-life adventures, Lewin illustrates books for many other writers, most of which feature animals as prominent characters. *Mattie's Little Possum Pet,* written by Ida Luttrell, tells the story of a woman named Mattie who, on her way to pick flowers, finds a possum

When a little girl decides to pick ten people and add up all the cats they collectively own, she realizes that a single set of fingers and toes will not do in Lewin's amusing Cat Count.

lying on its back with its tongue hanging out and its eyes rolled back in its head. Mattie feels sorry for the little creature, which is actually playing dead, and takes it home with her. Her cat and dog do not trust the possum, however, and before long the wild creature proves them right by causing trouble and arranging for the pets to take the blame. Finally, Mattie realizes that the mischievous possum has been fooling her all along and is better off living out in the wild. "Excitement, action, and fun characterize Lewin's lively drawings, which seem to have been effortlessly and spontaneously executed," Anna Biagioni Hart wrote in a review for *School Library Journal.*

Other animal tales enhanced by Lewin's illustrations include *What's Black and White and Came to Visit?,* by Evan Levine, as well as a series of books by Doreen Cronin that include *Click, Clack, Moo: Cows That Type, Duck for President,* and *Giggle, Gaggle, Quack. What's Black and White and Came to Visit?* begins when a young girl named Lily discovers a skunk in the drainpipe of her house. Her parents are not sure how to get the skunk to come out without causing it to create an odor. They call the fire department, but the firemen do not know how to handle the situation either. Before long the police department, the town's expert yodeler, and a variety of other characters have taken over Lily's lawn in a noisy disagreement about how to proceed. Finally, the skunk is forced to abandon its hiding place in the drainpipe and run back into the woods in order to find some much-wanted peace and quiet. In a review for *School Library Journal,* Mary Lou Budd noted that "Lewin's pen-and-ink drawings, colored in with soft, watercolor pastels, deftly express the story's fun, action, and emotion."

Duck for President, like *Click, Clack, Moo* and others in Cronin's humorous series, features a clever barnyard resident with a lazy streak and ambitions that range beyond the quiet of his rural home. Caught up in the excitement surrounding the presidential election, Duck decides that being voted chief of the barnyard will allow him to delegate his chores and be boss instead. Pitted against Farmer Brown, Duck's energetic campaigning wins him the election and causes him to set his sights on the state governorship and, ultimately the presidency of the United States. Noting that the book is entertaining to both youngsters and more history-savvy adults, a *Publishers Weekly* contributor added that "Lewin's chunky-outlined watercolors . . . cater to the younger crowd with her usual dashes of humor and daffy sweetness."

Biographical and Critical Sources

PERIODICALS

Booklist, May 15, 1992, p. 1680; August, 1993, p. 2071; October 15, 1994, p. 436; March 1, 1995, Carolyn

Phelan, review of *Booby Hatch,* p. 1248; June 1, 1995, Mary Harris Veeder, review of *Walk a Green Path,* p. 1778; August 1996, Lauren Peterson, review of *Chubbo's Pool,* p. 1907; August, 1999, Stephanie Zvirin, review of *Gorilla Walk,* p. 2054; April 1, 2003, Diane Foote, review of *Cat Count,* p. 1403; January 1, 2005, Karin Snelson, review of *Top to Bottom Down Under,* p. 866.

Bulletin of the Center for Children's Books, November, 1982, p. 50; October, 1996, review of *Chubbo's Pool,* p. 68; September, 1997, review of *What's the Matter, Habibi?,* p. 17.

Horn Book, June, 1981, p. 294; November, 1999, Margaret A. Bush, review of *Gorilla Walk,* p. 758; January, 2001, review of *Elephant Quest,* p. 111.

Kirkus Reviews, March 15, 1995. review of *Walk a Green Path*; March 1, 2003, review of *Cat Count,* p. 390; August 15, 2004, review of *Animal Snackers,* p. 809; February 15, 2005, review of *Top to Bottom Down Under,* p. 231.

Publishers Weekly, March 16, 1990, p. 68; March 23, 1992, p. 72; July 19, 1993, p. 253; October 11, 1993, p. 88; August 8, 1994, p. 428; June 2, 1997, review of *What's the Matter, Habibi?,* p. 70; August 2, 1999, review of *Gorilla Walk,* p. 84; July 24, 2000, review of *Elephant Quest,* p. 95; February 16, 2004, review of *Duck for President,* p. 170.

School Library Journal, June, 1990, p. 105; June, 1992, p. 95; September, 1993, Anna Biagioni Hart, review of *Mattie's Little Possum Pet,* p. 210; September, 1994, Mary Lou Budd, review of *What's Black and White and Came to Visit,* p. 188; April, 1995, Kathy Piehl, review of *Walk a Green Path,* p. 126; May, 1995, Ellen Fader, review of *Booby Hatch*; September, 1996, Patricia Pearl Dole, review of *Chubbo's Pool,* p. 184; September, 2000, Margaret Bush, review of *Elephant Quest,* p. 251; April, 2003, Joy Fleishhacker, review of *Cat Count,* p. 132; October, 2004, Rachel G. Payne, review of *Animal Snackers,* p. 144; March, 2005, Patricia Manning, review of *Top To Bottom Down Under,* p. 196.

ONLINE

Betsy Lewin Home Page, http://www.betsylewin.com (April 12, 2006).

*   *   *

LOGAN, Rochelle 1954-

Personal

Born December 23, 1954, in San Francisco, CA; daughter of Vernon F. (a small-business owner) and Kathryn B. (a homemaker) Alley; married Thomas E. Logan (an airline pilot) June 19, 1977; children: Andrea, Kathryn. *Education:* Attended Humboldt State University, 1973-76; Texas Tech University, B.S. (business administration), 1978; University of Denver, M.L.I.S., 1999.

Addresses

Home—9588 Cherryvale La., Highlands Ranch, CO 80126. *Office*—Douglas County Libraries, 100 S. Wilcox St., Castle Rock, CO 80103. *E-mail*—rochellelogan@comcast.net.

Career

Colorado State University, Denver, associate director of library research service, 1999-2001; Douglas County Libraries, Castle Rock, CO, associate director, 2001—; writer. Institute of Museum and Library Services National Leadership Grant, member of advisory committee, 1999-2001; Library and Information Technology Association, member of education committee, 1999-2002; chair of Endeavor student writing award committee, 2001-02; Acquisition of Information Resources statewide task force, member, 2001-02; Colorado Council on Library Development, member of advocacy committee, 2001-03; Colorado Library Marketing Council, member, 2001-04; Colorado Library advisory board, member of strategic planning task force, 2004-05; Highlands Ranch Community Association, member of public issues committee, 2005—. Judge, Colorado Center for the Book Colorado Book Awards, 2004-05.

Member

American Library Association, Public Library Association (chair of research and statistics committee, 1999-2003), Council of Library Administration and Management Association Affiliates (secretary, 2003-04), Colorado Association of Libraries (member of intellectual freedom committee, 1999-2004; chair of executive board of management and administration division, 2001-04).

Writings

(With Julie Halverstadt) *100 Most Popular Business Leaders for Young Adults: Biographical Sketches and Professional Paths,* Libraries Unlimited (Greenwood Village, CO), 2002.

Biographical and Critical Sources

PERIODICALS

Booklist, November 1, 2002, "Business Trailblazers," p. 522.
Reference & Research Book News, August, 2002, review of *100 Most Popular Business Leaders for Young Adults: Biographical Sketches and Professional Paths,* p. 75.*

M

MARKEL, Michelle

Personal
Married; husband an anthropologist; children: two daughters. *Education:* University of Southern California, B.A. (French; cum laude); California State University, Northridge, B.A. (journalism); University of California, Los Angeles, M.A. (French literature).

Addresses
Home—West Hills, CA. *Agent*—c/o Author Mail, Heyday Books, P.O. Box 9145, Berkeley, CA 94709. *E-mail*—markelwrites@earthlink.net.

Career
Writer, journalist, teacher, and translator. California State University, Northridge, teacher of creative writing and French; presenter to schools.

Member
CAN!, Society of Children's Book Writers and Illustrators, Children's Book Council of Southern California.

Awards, Honors
California Readers Collection selection, 2005, for *Cornhusk, Silk, and Wishbones.*

Writings

Gracias, Rosa, illustrated by Diane Paterson, Albert Whitman (Morton Grove, IL), 1995.
Cornhusk, Silk, and Wishbones: A Book of Dolls from around the World, Houghton Mifflin (Boston, MA), 2000.
Dreamer from the Village: The Story of Marc Chagall, illustrated by Emily Lisker, Henry Holt (New York, NY), 2004.

Dream Town, illustrated by Rick Reese, Heyday Books (Berkeley, CA), 2006.

Contributor to periodicals, including *Wall Street Journal* and *Los Angeles Times.*

Sidelights
Although her college degrees are in French and journalism, Michelle Markel began a career as a children's book writer with *Gracias, Rosa.* Published in 1995, the book was inspired by Markel's experience observing the Central American women who worked as babysitters in her California neighborhood and the deep and supportive bond she witness between them. Annie Ayres, reviewing the book for *Booklist* commented that *Gracias, Rosa* "tells a contemporary story about the special friendship that develops between a young girl and her Latina babysitter, and the cultural bridge that is built through their relationship."

Other books by Markel include *Cornhusk, Silk, and Wishbones: A Book of Dolls from around the World,* which reflects its author's interest in folk art. An alphabet book, the work features photographs of dolls collected from around the world, some dating back a thousand years, with maps and prose descriptions discussing each image. Deeming the book an imaginative introduction to letters, *School Library Journal* contributor Ann Welton wrote that Markel's "text is lively and engaging and imparts . . . information in a painless manner."

Markel, whose maternal grandparents came from Russia's Pale of Settlement, chose the life of Russian-born artist Marc Chagall as the subject of her 2004 book, titled *Dreamer from the Village: The Story of Marc Chagall.* Featuring illustrations by Emily Lisker, the book was praised by a *Kirkus Reviews* writer as "a worthwhile introduction for younger readers." *Booklist* writer Gillian Engberg called the book "straightforward and whimsical," while Lolly Robinson wrote in *Horn Book* that Markel describes Chagall's career "in an understated but absorbing narrative."

Markel tells the story of Russian-born painter Marc Chagall and his role in twentieth-century art in her picture-book biography **Dreamer** from the **Village.** *(Illustration by Emily Lisker.)*

In Markel's *Dream Town* a grandmother tells her grandson about the urban landscape of Los Angeles in the 1950s and 1960; the years of the author's own childhood. In *Bloomsbury Review,* Sofia Walker wrote of the book that "poetic prose and illustrations . . . join together to create a paean to the wonders that exist in the overlapping worlds of our imagination and reality."

Biographical and Critical Sources

PERIODICALS

Bloomsbury Review, March-April, 2006, Sofia Walker, review of *Dream Town.*

Booklist, June 1, 1995, Annie Ayres, review of *Gracias, Rosa,* p. 1787; October 1, 2000, Carolyn Phelan, review of *Cornhusk, Silk, and Wishbones: A Book of Dolls from around the World,* p. 333; August, 2005, Gillian Engberg, review of *Dreamer from the Village: The Story of Marc Chagall,* p. 2033.

Horn Book, September-October, 2005, Lolly Robinson, review of *Dreamer from the Village,* p. 604.

Kirkus Reviews, July 1, 2005, review of *Dreamer from the Village,* p. 738.

Publishers Weekly, September 11, 2000, review of *All Dolled Up,* p. 93.

School Arts, November, 2005, Ken Marantz, review of *Dreamer from the Village,* p. 53.

School Library Journal, May, 1995, Maria Redburn, review of *Gracias, Rosa,* p. 87; November, 2000, Ann Welton, review of *Cornhust, Silk, and Wishbones,* p. 145.

ONLINE

Children's Authors Network, http://www.childrens-authorsnetwork.com/ (February 24, 2006), "Michelle Markel."

Learning about Michelle Markel, http://www.scils.rutgers.edu/~kvander/markel.html (February 24, 2006).

Michelle Markel Home Page, http://home.earthlink.net/%7Ecohen_markel/1.htm (February 24, 2006).

* * *

McALLISTER, Margaret I. 1956-
(M.I. McAllister)

Personal

Born August, 1956, in Tynemouth, England; daughter of Douglas Hay (a research engineer) and Sheila Elizabeth McAllister; married; husband's name Tony (a Methodist minister), 1978; children: Elinor, Adam, Iain. *Education:* Newcastle Polytechnic, degree (education and English). *Politics:* "Center." *Religion:* Christian. *Hobbies and other interests:* Theater, dance, music, history.

Addresses

Home—Yorkshire, England. *Agent*—Caroline Sheldon Literary Agency, Thorley Manor Farm, Thorley, Yarmouth, Isle of Wight PO41 0SJ, England.

Career

Buddle Arts Centre, Wallsend, England, teacher of dance and drama. Also worked as teacher of creative writing, church cleaner, supply teacher, teacher of excluded children, and dogsbody in a retreat house.

Writings

A Friend for Rachel, Oxford University Press (Oxford, England), 1997, published as *The Secret Mice,* 2002.

Hold My Hand and Run, Oxford University Press (Oxford, England), 1999, Dutton (New York, NY), 2000.

Never Wash Your Hair, illustrated by Tim Archbold, Pacific Learning, 1999.

Ghost at the Window, Oxford University Press (Oxford, England), 2000, published as *Fire Lion,* 2001, published under original title, Dutton (New York, NY), 2002.

The Worst of the Vikings, Pacific Learning, 2000.

The Mean Dream Wonder Machine, Pacific Learning, 2000.

The Doughnut Dilemma, Oxford University Press (Oxford, England), 2000.

(Adapter) Charlotte Brontë, *Jane Eyre,* Pacific Learning, 2000.

Margaret I. McAllister

My Guinea-Pig Is Innocent, Oxford University Press (Oxford, England), 2001.

Wimmer, illustrated by Maureen Bradley, Oxford University Press (Oxford, England), 2001.

(Adapter) Robert Louis Stevenson, *Kidnapped,* Oxford University Press (Oxford, England), 2001.

The Octave of Angels, Oxford University Press (Oxford, England), 2001, Eerdmans (Grand Rapids, MI), 2002.

The Jam Street Puzzle, illustrated by Tony Sumpter, Oxford University Press (Oxford, England), 2002.

The Life Shop, Lion (Oxford, England), 2004.

"MISTMANTLE CHRONICLES" NOVEL SERIES; UNDER NAME M.I. McALLISTER

Urchin of the Riding Stars, Hyperion (New York, NY), 2005.

Urchin and the Heartstone, Bloomsbury (London, England), 2006.

Author's books have been translated into six languages.

"OXFORD READING TREE" SERIES

Threads of Deceit, illustrated by Tim Clarey, Oxford University Press (Oxford, England), 2003.

Black Death, illustrated by Alice Englander, Oxford University Press (Oxford, England), 2003.

Snow Troll, illustrated by Steve Cox, Oxford University Press (Oxford, England), 2003.

The Magic Porridge Pot, illustrated by Peter Utton, Oxford University Press (Oxford, England), 2003.
Emily and the Lamb, illustrated by Dawn Vince, Oxford University Press (Oxford, England), 2005.

Sidelights

When asked in an interview for the *Mistmantle Web site* how long she had been writing books, Margaret I. McAllister responded: "Since I could write. Before that, I made up stories in my head." An imaginative author who includes fantasy elements in much of her fiction, McAllister published her first book, *A Friend for Rachel,* in 1997. *A Friend for Rachel* focuses on a girl who desperately needs a friend after her family moves to a new town. What Rachel finds instead are two talking church mice which she must keep secret from her parents. McAllister's more recent books include her "Mistmantle Chronicles" novels, published under the name M.I. McAllister. Including *Urchin of the Riding Stars* and *Urchin and the Heartstone,* the "Mistmantle Chronicles" have been translated into six languages.

McAllister's novel *Hold My Hand and Run* is set in the 1600s in England and tells the story of Kazy Clare and her efforts to protect her sister Beth from their wicked aunt's abuse. The best course of action seems to be running away, so Kazy and Beth flee, hoping to find safety. While noting that McAllister's characters are not always well rounded, *Booklist* contributor Stephanie Zvirin wrote that "the adventure . . . will hold young readers." Debbie Stewart, writing for *School Library Journal,* cited the book as "a readable historical novel set in a period not frequently explored." *Booklist* contributor GraceAnne A. DeCandido, reviewing another of McAllister's historical novels, commented that the author demonstrates "a flair for historical fiction" in *Hold My Hand and Run.*

Incorporating a mix of fantastic elements, *Ghost at the Window* is a story about Ninian House, a building that seems to move through time. The community accepts this oddity, and young Ewan, who lives in Ninian House, is accustomed to the bizarre change in scenery around his home. However, when a young girl named Elspeth appears to him, asks for help, and then vanishes, he realizes that more than time travel is at work. McAllister's "tightly wound plot speeds along without a wasted word," reported a contributor to *Kirkus Reviews,* while Beth L. Meister noted in *School Library Journal* that the building's "time-shifting, casually accepted by Ewan's parents and other local residents, gives this fast-paced ghost story an unusual twist."

Urchin of the Riding Stars, the first novel in the "Mistmantle Chronicles," is a book McAllister waited for several years to write. "I've had the idea of the misty island for ages, but I don't know where it came from," she explained in an interview on the *Mistmantle Web site.* "A friend suggested I write an animal story so I moved the animals into the island and it worked." The

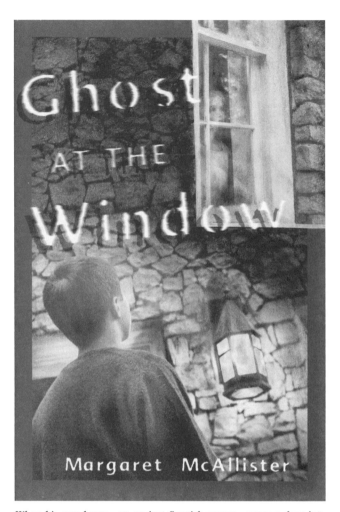

When his new home—an ancient Scottish manor—opens a door into the past, Ewan must find a way to help a young ghost who was trapped by the house over half a century before. (Cover illustration by Barbara Morgan.)

book's setting, the island of Mistmantle, is inhabited by an animal court ruled by a kindly hedgehog king who is manipulated by his trusted advisor, Captain Husk. The valorous Captain Crispin is a threat to Husk's plans, and when Crispin is exiled, his page, Urchin, begins to think it may be up to him to keep all of Mistmantle from falling to Husk's evil. "Urchin is a sweet hero," noted GraceAnne A. DeCandido in a review of the first series installment in *Booklist.* A *Publishers Weekly* critic compared McAllister's "brisk and colorful tale" to Brian Jacques's popular "Redwall" series and Kenneth Graeme's classic novel *Wind in the Willows.*

Though McAllister often writes in the genres of science fiction and fantasy, her novels tackle real-life issues. Both her science-fiction novel *The Life Shop,* and the "Mistmantle Chronicles" ponder the idea of a perfect world created by sacrificing the weak or the infirm. In an interview with *Bookseller,* McAllister explained that this concept is woven into *Urchin of the Riding Stars* through the relationships among animal characters that "have . . . implicit trust in their leaders. Captain Husk culls any young animals born in any way weak or dam-

aged, and the idea is, 'We have to do it. It's necessary and kinder to them really.' So the animals don't like it, but they accept it." In the futuristic *The Life Shop,* heroine Lorna stands against those attempting to weed out weakness in order to create a perfect world by defending her disabled brother.

McAllister once told *SATA:* "Aspiring writers sometimes feel discouraged because they think you have to be brainy to succeed. I'm not! I just like words and stories.

"I suppose I write about the things that make an impression on me—ancient churches with their candlelit festivals, and the history of the north of England, for example. Writing is a way of immersing myself in these things and inviting the reader in, too.

"For me, the mark of a really good children's book is that you can enjoy it at any age. If you can fall in love with a book as a child, and come back to it as an adult without feeling patronized or uneasy, it has strength. I could go on reading C.S. Lewis and Lucy Boston forever."

Biographical and Critical Sources

PERIODICALS

Booklist, April 1, 2000, Stephanie Zvirin, review of *Hold My Hand and Run,* p. 1477; May 1, 2002, review of *Ghost at the Window,* p. 1459; October 1, 2005, GraceAnne A. DeCandido, review of *Urchin of the Riding Stars,* p. 59.
Bookseller, December 10, 2004, "Something Rotten in Mistmantle," p. 28.
Books for Keeps, May, 1997, p. 24; July, 1999.
Bulletin of the Center for Children's Books, June, 2002, review of *Ghost at the Window,* p. 373.
Kirkus Reviews, July 1, 2002, review of *Ghost at the Window,* p. 958; July 1, 2005, review of *Urchin of the Riding Stars,* p. 739.
Magpies, July, 1997, review of *A Friend for Rachel,* p. 34.
Publishers Weekly, September 12, 2005, review of *Urchin of the Riding Stars,* p. 72.
School Librarian, August, 1997, p. 158; spring, 2003, review of *The Secret Mice,* p. 33; spring, 2005, Joan Nellist, review of *The Life Shop,* p. 35.
School Library Journal, July, 2000, Debbie Stewart, review of *Hold My Hand and Run,* p. 107; August, 2002, Beth L. Meister, review of *Ghost at the Window,* p. 194.
Voice of Youth Advocates, August, 2000, review of *Hold My Hand and Run,* p. 190; August, 2002, review of *Ghost at the Window,* p. 204; April, 2003, review of *Ghost at the Window,* p. 13.

ONLINE

Bloomsbury Publishing Web site, http://www.bloomsbury.com/ (March 24, 2006), profile of McAllister.
Lion Publishing Web site, http://www.lion-publishing.co.uk/ (March 24, 2006), profile of McAllister.
Mistmantle Web site, http://www.mistmantle.co.uk/ (March 24, 2006).

*   *   *

McALLISTER, M.I.
See McALLISTER, Margaret I.

*   *   *

McDONALD, Mercedes

Personal

Born in Raleigh, NC; daughter of Robert B. (an artist and landscape architect) and Marjorie M. (a registered nurse and art-gallery owner) McDonald; married Michel Rouhani (an attorney), April 4, 1985. *Education:* Atlanta College of Art, B.F.A., 1980; attended California College of Arts and Crafts, 1982-83; San Francisco Art Institute, M.F.A., 1987. *Hobbies and other interests:* Cats.

Addresses

Agent—c/o Author Mail, Bloomsbury USA, 175 5th Ave., New York, NY 10010. *E-mail*—mercedesmcdonald@aol.com.

Career

Freelance illustrator. California College of Arts and Crafts, San Francisco, adjunct professor of illustration, 1989-95; member of adjunct faculty at College of the Canyons, Valencia, CA, and California State University Fullerton.

Awards, Honors

Award from *Communication Arts,* 1990, for feature article; Maxwell Award, Dog Writer's Association of America, 1998, for *Cooking with Dogs.*

Illustrator

Jennifer Trainer Thompson, *Hot Licks: Great Recipes for Making and Cooking with Hot Sauces,* Chronicle Books (San Francisco, CA), 1994.
Marguerite M. Davol, *How Snake Got His Hiss: An Original Tale,* Orchard Books (New York, NY), 1996.
Anne A. Johnson, *Smoothies: Twenty-two Frosty Fruit Drinks,* Klutz Press, 1997.
Cindy Chang, compiler, *Family,* designed by Kathryn Siegler, Andrews McMeel (Kansas City, MO), 1997.
Heather J. Gondek, *Morning in the Garden/Nightime in the Garden,* Intervisual Books, 2001, published as *Morning in the Garden,* Barron's (Hauppauge, NY), 2002.

Mercedes McDonald

Susan Middleton Elya, *Fairy Trails: A Story Told in English and Spanish,* Bloomsbury (New York, NY), 2005.

Contributor to magazines, including *Communication Arts.* Contributor of artwork to books, including *Cooking with Dogs,* by Karen Dowell, 1998.

Sidelights

Art has been a part of Mercedes McDonald's life since she was a very young girl. Her career began with drawing at the dining-room table as a child, and progressed to studies at the Atlanta College of Art and the San Francisco Art Institute. In 1994, McDonald's illustrations were featured in the cookbook *Hot Licks: Great Recipes for Making and Cooking with Hot Sauces.* Since illustrating that title, McDonald had also established herself as a children's book illustrator, where her art has helped bring to life tales for young readers.

How Snake Got His Hiss: An Original Tale is a folk-style tale told by Marguerite M. Davol and accompanied by McDonald's illustrations. The snake's motions are described in the text and revealed through the art; a *Publishers Weekly* critic commented that the "motion-filled, stylized pastels . . . handily match the tale's exuberance." Janice del Negro, writing in *Booklist,* felt that the illustrator's "use of strong geometric patterns adds energy to an already energetic tale."

In 2005, McDonald's work was featured in the bilingual *Fairy Trails: A Story Told in English and Spanish. Booklist* contributor Stella Clark felt that the text and artwork were "beautifully conceived," while a *Kirkus Reviews* contributor noted that the illustrations feature "luminous colors to convey a dream sense of well-be-

ing." Melissa Christy Buron commented in her *School Library Journal* review that McDonald's "illustrations have an appealing folk-art quality."

McDonald once told *SATA:* "I am a fine artist lucky enough to make a career out of art. I started doing illustration while in graduate school, and I love what I do. Illustration allows me time (not much) to pursue my fine art, and I love having my studio at home. In my spare time, I try to do outdoor activities such as hiking and horseback riding. Also, since I love cats, I try to devote time to animal rescue; my niche is the care and feeding of orphan kittens. I also enjoy finding collectibles and odd junk at flea markets. I try to have fun with my art, and hopefully that shows in the work."

Biographical and Critical Sources

PERIODICALS

Booklist, April 15, 1996, Janice del Negro, review of *How Snake Got His Hiss: An Original Tale,* p. 1445; May 15, 2005, Stella Clark, review of *Fairy Trails: A Story Told in English and Spanish,* p. 1664.

McDonald's illustrations for Susan Middleton Elya's Fairy Trails *add an ethnic flavor to the English/Spanish text about two children's encounter with fairy-tale characters during a walk in the woods.*

Kirkus Reviews, May 1, 2005, review of *Fairy Trails,* p. 537.

Publishers Weekly, January 29, 1996, review of *How Snake Got His Hiss,* p. 100.

School Library Journal, March, 1996, Judith Constantinides, review of *How Snake Got His Hiss,* p. 167; August, 2005, Melissa Christy Buron, review of *Fairy Trails,* p. 93.

ONLINE

College of the Canyons Art Department Web site, http://www.canyons.edu/departments/ART/ (March 24, 2006), profile of McDonald.

Mercedes McDonald Home Page, http://www.mercedesmcdonald.com (March 24, 2006).

*   *   *

McGRATH, Barbara Barbieri 1953-

Personal

Born September 29, 1953, in Wellesley, MA; daughter of Albert and Dorothy Barbieri; married William M. McGrath, April 16, 1978; children: Emily M., William Louis. *Education:* Laseil College, B.A. *Religion:* Roman Catholic. *Hobbies and other interests:* Surfcasting, SCUBA diving, collecting "sea-pottery."

Addresses

Home and office—7 Jennings Pond Rd., Natick, MA 01760. *E-mail*—authorvisits@aol.com.

Career

Writer. Also worked as preschool teacher.

Member

Society of Children's Book Writers and Illustrators.

Awards, Honors

Teachers' Choice Award, 1994, and Pick of the List citation, American Bookseller's Association, both for *The M&M's Brand Chocolate Candies Counting Book.*

Writings

The M&M's Brand Chocolate Candies Counting Book, Charlesbridge (Watertown, MA), 1994.

More M&M Math, Scholastic (New York, NY), 1998.

The Cheerios Counting Book, Scholastic (New York, NY), 1998.

Pepperidge Farm Goldfish Counting Board Book, Scholastic (New York, NY), 1998.

Hershey's Kisses: Counting Board Book, Corp Board Books, 1998.

The Baseball Counting Book, Scholastic (New York, NY), 1999.

The Cheerios Counting Book: 1, 2, 3 (board book), illustrated by Frank Mazolla, Cartwheel Books, 2000.

Skittles Riddles Math, Charlesbridge (Watertown, MA), 2000.

The M&M's Brand Valentine Book, Charlesbridge (Watertown, MA), 2000.

Necco Sweethearts Be My Valentine Book, HarperFestival (New York, NY), 2000.

Kellogg's Froot Loops! Counting Fun Book, Mariposa, 2000.

Pepperidge Farm Goldfish Counting Fun Book, HarperFestival (New York, NY), 2000.

The M&M's Brand Halloween Treat Book, Charlesbridge (Watertown, MA), 2000.

The M&M's Brand Christmas Gift Book, Charlesbridge (Watertown, MA), 2000.

Kellogg's Froot Loops Color Fun Book, HarperFestival (New York, NY), 2001.

The M&M's Brand Birthday Book, Charlesbridge (Watertown, MA), 2001.

The M&M's Brand Easter Egg Hunt, Charlesbridge (Watertown, MA), 2001

The M&M's Brand Color Pattern Book, illustrated by Roger Glass, Charlesbridge (Watertown, MA), 2002.

The M&M's Brand All-American Parade Book, illustrated by Peggy Tagel, Charlesbridge (Watertown, MA), 2003.

I Love Words, Charlesbridge (Watertown, MA), 2003.

The M&M's Count-to-One Hundred Book, Charlesbridge (Watertown, MA), 2003.

(With Peter Alderman) *Soccer Counts!,* illustrated by Paul Estrada, Charlesbridge (Watertown, MA), 2003.

The M&M's Brand Addition Book, Charlesbridge (Watertown, MA), 2004.

M&M's Count around the Circle, Charlesbridge (Watertown, MA), 2004.

The Little Green Witch, illustrated by Martha Alexander, Charlesbridge (Watertown, MA), 2005.

The M&M's Brand Subtraction Book, Charlesbridge (Watertown, MA), 2005.

Contributor to local newspapers.

Some of McGrath's titles have been published in bilingual English/Spanish editions.

Sidelights

Barbara Barbieri McGrath studied early education in college, and her books reflect both her sense of fun and her desire to help young learners grasp concepts such as counting, addition, subtraction, and colors. *The M&M's Brand Chocolate Candies Counting Book* was considered such a valuable addition to educational titles that it was selected for a Teacher's Choice Award. Incorporating popular candies and cereals into their text, McGrath's books endeavor to make learning math skills fun for young readers.

Though McGrath started her counting books using M&M's chocolate candies, her books incorporate diminutive delicacies such as Cheerios, Goldfish crackers,

and Froot Loops as well. Of *The Cheerios Counting Book,* Hazel Rochman noted in *Booklist* that, "As young preschoolers munch and play and tally, they will find a delicious world they recognize in a book."

Other math titles created by McGrath use sports as their topic. In *The Baseball Counting Book* she incorporates rhyme and rhythm as well as baseball themes to teach numbers one through twenty. "The book is full of counting opportunities and is a springboard for many other learning experiences," wrote AnneMarie Hornyak in *Teaching Children Mathematics.* With Peter Alderman, McGrath wrote *Soccer Counts!,* a book that teaches counting drills and the history of soccer at the same time. "This soccer-centered counting book is sure to be a winner with fans young and old," assured a *Kirkus Reviews* contributor. Noting that the reading level may be too easy for many beginning soccer players, Blair Christolon explained in *School Library Journal* that English-as-a-second-language "students may be the best audience for this mixture." However, Sarah Olague, writing in *Teaching Children Mathematics,* thought that "both teachers and their students will learn a lot about soccer from this book."

Aside from her books on counting and mathematics, McGrath has penned a book on phonics, *I Love Words,* and a picture book telling the story of "The Little Red Hen" with a new cast of characters. In *The Little Green Witch* the witch of the title wants her friends to help her make a pumpkin pie, but the ghost, the bat, and the gremlin are all too busy to help. Though the story follows the traditional tale of the little red hen, right up to the witch's refusal to share the results of her hard work, it has an additional twist at the end, "one that will make readers laugh out loud," promised Susan Weitz in *School Library Journal.*

McGrath once told *SATA:* "I taught preschool for sixteen years while writing public-interest articles for local newspapers. Then I focused on making learning fun—using a 'fun' subject to make the lesson memorable. I use brand-name products to teach hands-on lessons."

Biographical and Critical Sources

PERIODICALS

Booklist, October 1, 1998, Hazel Rochman, review of *The Cheerios Counting Book,* p. 333; February 15, 1999, Kathy Broderick, review of *The Baseball Counting Book,* p. 1072.
Canadian Review of Materials, May 21, 1999, review of *The Cheerios Counting Book;* May 26, 2000, review of *The Cheerios Counting Book.*
Kirkus Reviews, June 15, 2003, review of *Soccer Counts!,* p. 861; June 15, 2005, review of *The Little Green Witch,* p. 687.
Publishers Weekly, June 6, 1994, review of *The M&M's Brand Chocolate Candies Counting Book,* p. 64; November 16, 1998, review of *More M&M's Brand*

Echoing the story of the Little Red Hen, The Little Green Witch *finds a young witch getting few offers of help in making the pumpkin pie everyone want to nibble on. (Illustration by Martha Alexander.)*

Chocolate Candies Math, p. 77; April 24, 2000, review of *The Cheerios Counting Book,* p. 92; December 11, 2000, "Volumes of Valentines," p. 86; June 25, 2001, review of *Kellogg's Froot Loops Color Fun Book,* p. 75; February 11, 2002, review of *The M&M's Brand Color Pattern Book,* p. 189; August 11, 2003, review of *The M&M's Count-to-One Hundred Book,* p. 281.
School Library Journal, September, 1998, p. 194; April, 2001, Ilene Abramson, review of *Skittles Riddles Math,* p. 132; September, 2003, Blair Christolon, review of *Soccer Counts!,* p. 202; January, 2004, Tali Balas, review of *I Love Words,* p. 120; August, 2005, Susan Weitz, review of *The Little Green Witch,* p. 100.
Science Books & Film, November, 2003, review of *The M&M's Count to One Hundred Book,* p. 273; July-August, 2005, Charles Mercer, review of *The M&M's Subtraction Book,* p. 168.
Teaching Children Mathematics, December, 1999, Anne-Marie Hornyak, review of *The Baseball Counting Book,* p. 266; September, 2004, Sarah Olague, review of *Soccer Counts!* p. 110.

ONLINE

Barbara McGrath Home Page, http://www.barbaramcgrath.com (March 23, 2006).*

*   *   *

MOED-KASS, Pnina

Personal

Born in Antwerp, Belgium; daughter of David (an architect) and Shifra Golomb (a physician) Moed. *Education:* Attended Hunter College, City University of New York.

Moed-Kass's contemporary novel finds a German teen working at an Israeli kibbutz where an act of politically motivated violence reveals facts about the boy's grandfather's past as a Nazi officer. (Cover photography by Stockbytel/Picturequest.)

Addresses

Agent—Deborah Harris, 9 Yael St., Jerusalem 9350, Israel.

Career

Writer and educator. Formerly on staff of *Opera News* magazine; worked in advertising in New York, NY; teacher of English in New York, NY.

Member

Society of Children's Book Writers and Illustrators, Authors Guild, Association of Jewish Libraries.

Awards, Honors

International Reading Association Award for Best Young-Adult Short Story; Sydney Taylor Award, 2004, for *Real Time.*

Writings

FOR CHILDREN

Stevie's Tricycle, illustrated by Lorna Tomai, Golden Press (New York, NY), 1982.

Tommy's New Bed, illustrated by Turi MacCombie, Western Publishing (Racine, WI), 1984.
Real Time (young-adult novel), Clarion (New York, NY) 2004.

OTHER

(Editor) Leon Fine, *Will the Real Israel Please Stand Up?,* Pelmas/Massada (Givatayim, Israel), 1980.

Author of "Berele" series (in Hebrew), for Keter Publising (Israel), c. 1980s. Writings included in anthologies *Lines of Sand: New Writing on War and Peace,* Frances Lincoln; and *Celebrate Cricket: Thirty Years of Stories and Art,* Cricket Books, 2003.

Sidelights

Pnina Moed-Kass is a freelance writer who, while born in Belgium and educated in the United States, now lives and works in Israel. While writing in a wide variety of formats, for both adults and younger readers, Moed-Kass is most noted in the United States for her award-winning 2004 novel *Real Time.* In addition, she has produced a number of picture books written in both English and Hebrew, including a popular series of educational readers featuring a tiny snail named Berele that has been used by teachers of younger special-education students in Israel.

Inspired by actual events in modern Israel and taking place in Jerusalem, *Real Time* focuses on a terrorist attack on a city bus and examines the events both leading up to and following the tragedy. The bomber—a poor, undereducated Palestinian teen who hopes to attain martyrdom through his act—as well as the bus passengers—who have followed a variety of paths leading them to share this traumatic experience—comprise "deeply developed and painfully sympathetic" characters, according to *School Library Journal* reviewer Mary R. Hofmann. While a *Kirkus Reviews* writer noted that the "complicated threads of pain, fear, memory, and despair" embodied by Moed-Kass's characters "create unique voices" representing many facets of Israeli society, Hofmann praised *Real Time* as "an exhausting but illuminating read." In *Booklist* Hazel Rochman described the author's depiction of "grief and the chaos of the bombing and its aftermath" as "unforgettable," while a *Publishers Weekly* contributor maintained that because of the novel's "graphic portrayal of violence and dark ironies" and Moed-Kass's "strongly political" themes, *Real Time* "is best suited for mature readers well-versed in Middle Eastern politics."

"No day could be more different than the seemingly ordinary Sunday that starts my novel *Real Time,*" Moed-Kass explained to *SATA.* "For the characters I write about, the act of a sixteen-year-old suicide bomber will change the course of their lives. The rhythm of the book is defined by the movement of minutes and hours, not by chapters.

"In the six days of *Real Time,* the reader is drawn into the past and present of the many people touched by the catastrophic event. . . . Sameh, the young Palestinian who becomes a suicide bomber, is the pivotal figure in this drama. His Israeli employer, his mother and brothers, his girlfriend—all are part of the tragic web of life and death in Israel. The characters, Israeli and Palestinian, their lives intertwined, will be marked physically and emotionally by the shock waves of the event.

"This is not a novel that suggests or implies solutions or deals with ideology, politics, or right and wrong," the author added. "My overwhelming desire was to tell the story behind the headlines and sound bites. Its theme is the universality of the dreams and ambitions of ordinary people, wherever they are from and whatever age." As Moed-Kass explained her motivation for writing the novel to an interviewer for the Association of Jewish Libraries Web site: "There was a period when it seemed all of us were 'drowning' in these suicide bombings. Writing seemed to be my only act of release from feelings of overwhelming sadness, bitterness and incomprehension." *Real Time* has been published in Italy, Germany, and France in addition to Israel and the United States.

Regarding her career as a freelance writer, Moed-Kass once explained: "I've done all sorts of writing—I guess you'd call me a wordsmith. In New York I was a lyricist of rock 'n' roll songs (a member of ASCAP), did promotional material for a record company, worked for *Opera News* magazine, worked for an advertising agency, taught English in an inner-city school (the Bronx), and wrote comedy material.

"In Israel I've taught high-school English, written a series (in English) for educational television, translated and written catalogues for documentary film festivals, written English textbooks, advertising copy, and have also done movie dubbing. I also freelance as an editor and proofreader.

"When I'm writing at home my half-schnauzer/half-terrier lies on a comfortable old couch and keeps me company. I read and perform my stories at kindergartens and libraries and frequently speak to parents' groups about writing for children."

Biographical and Critical Sources

PERIODICALS

Booklist, February 1, 2005, Hazel Rochman, review of *Real Time,* p. 955.

Kirkus Reviews, October 1, 2004, review of *Real Time,* p. 963.

Kliatt, September, 2004, Janis Flint-Ferguson, review of *Real Time,* p. 12.

Publishers Weekly, November 22, 2004, review of *Real Time,* p. 61.

School Library Journal, October, 2004, Mary R. Hofmann, review of *Real Time,* p. 169.

ONLINE

Association of Jewish Libraries Web site, http://www.ajh.org/ (April 12, 2006), interview with Moed-Kass.*

*   *   *

MONACO, Octavia 1963-

Personal

Born 1963, in Thionville, France; immigrated to Italy, 1970. *Education:* Academy of Fine Arts of Bologna, graduated, 1991.

Addresses

Home—Italy. *Agent*—c/o Author Mail, Barefoot Books U.S., 2067 Massachusetts Ave., Cambridge, MA 02140. *E-mail*—octaviamonaco@interfree.it.

Career

Illustrator, educator, and goldsmith. School of Arts, Bologna, Italy, instructor in illustration, beginning 2005; art teacher in workshops for adults and children.

Awards, Honors

Premio Andersen (Italy), 2004, for illustration.

Illustrator

Oscar Wilde, *Il compleanno dell-Infanta* (translation of *The Birth of the Infanta*), Edizioni C'era una volta (Italy), 1994.

Brothers Grimm, *Messer Babau e altre diavolerie,* Edizioni C'era una volta (Italy), 1994.

Brothers Grimm, *Il gigante e il sarto,* Edizioni C'era una volta (Italy), 1995.

Brothers Grimm, *Biancaveve,* Edizioni C'era una volta (Italy), 1997.

Julianna Bethem, *La strega di ghiaccio e l'unicorno,* Tango Books (Italy), 1997.

Beatrice Masini, *Una principessa piccola così ma,* Edizioni ARKA (Italy), 1999, translated by Diane Handley as *A Brave Little Princess,* Barefoot Books (New York, NY), 2000.

Beatrice Masisni, *Ciro in cerca d'amore,* Edizioni Arka (Italy), 2000.

Guido Visconti, *Bianca e Neve,* Edizioni ARKA (Italy), 2001.

Graziella Favaro, *Il sale e lo zucchero,* Carthusia (Italy), 2002.

Stefano Bordiglioni, *La principessa che sognava il mare,* Edizioni EMME (Italy), 2002.

Beatrice Masini, *Signore e Signorine, Corale greca,* Edizioni Elle (Italy), 2002.

Nicola Cinguietti, reteller, *Giulietta e Romeo,* Edizioni ARKA (Italy), 2003.

Beatrice Masini, *La spada e il cuire, Donne della bibbia,* Edizioni ELLE (Italy), 2003.

Berénice Capatti, *Ví presento Klimt,* Edizioni ARKA, 2004, translated and adapted by Shannon A. White as *Klimt and His Cat,* Eerdmans Books for Young Readers (Grand Rapids, MI), 2005.

Pino Assandri-Elena Mutti, *In volo* (anthology), Zanichelli Editore (Italy), 2004.

La bussola perditempo: guida per piccoli viaggiatori, Comune di Rimini (Italy), 2004.

Guiseppe Pontremoli, *Ballate per tutto l'anno e altre storie,* Nuove Edizioni Romane, 2004.

Roberto Piumini, *La favola del mercante,* Edizioni ELLE (Italy), 2004.

Angela Nanetti, *Azzurrina,* Einaudi Ragazzi (Italy), 2005.

Beatrice Masini, *Re Artù Ginevra e Lancillotto,* Edizioni ARKA (Italy), 2005.

Roberto Piumini, *Seme di Amacem,* Einaudi Ragazzi (Italy), 2005.

Bruno Concina, *Il mammo dei gatti,* Città aperta edizioni (Italy), 2005.

Matteo Corradini, *Fragole a teatro,* Tip.Le.Co. (Italy), 2005.

Encilopedia de ragazzi, Edizioni Treccanti (Italy), 2005.

Josè Jorge Letria, *Versos com gatos,* Livros horizonte (Italy), 2005.

Emanuela Nava, *La storia di Kiara,* Garda Cartiere (Italy), 2006.

Berenice Capatti, *Noi, bambini di Picasso,* Edizioni ARKA (Italy), 2006.

Contributor to books, including *60 Testimonianze partigiane, illustrate da 30 artisti italiani,* Zoolibri, 2005.

Works including Monaco's artwork have been published in Spanish, Finnish, Portuguese, French, Korean, Japanese, and English.

Biographical and Critical Sources

PERIODICALS

School Library Journal, February, 2001, Laura Santoro, review of *A Brave Little Princess,* p. 104.

ONLINE

Octavia Monaco Home Page, http://www.octaviamonaco.it (February 24, 2006).*

*   *   *

MORREALE-de la GARZA, Phyllis
See De la GARZA, Phyllis

P

PARKER, Toni Trent 1947-2005

OBITUARY NOTICE— See index for *SATA* sketch: Born July 10, 1947, in Winston-Salem, NC; died of a brain tumor, September 15, 2005, in Stamford, CT. Publisher and author. Parker was a leading advocate promoting multicultural literature; she published guides to African-American books and wrote a number of picture books that feature African-American characters. A student of history, she graduated from Oberlin College in 1970 and then pursued graduate courses in African-American history at the University of California, Berkeley. She did not begin promoting black literature until the 1990s, however. Teaming up with friends Sheila Foster and Donna Rand, the three founded Black Books Galore!, which issued four guides to African-American literature from 1998 to 2001. One of these, *Black Books Galore! Guide to Great African-American Children's Books,* was nominated for an National Association for the Advancement of Colored People award for children's literature. In 1998 Parker also founded Kids Cultural Books, a nonprofit organization intended to establish minority book festivals around the country. Parker herself added to the relatively small but growing genre of minority-centered children's books by writing six picture books herself. Among these are *Painted Eggs and Chocolate Bunnies* (2002), *Snowflake Kisses and Gingerbread Smiles* (2002), and her last, *Sienna's Scrapbook* (2005). Parker was recognized for her contributions with a Parenting Leaders award from *Parents* magazine in 1998.

OBITUARIES AND OTHER SOURCES:

PERIODICALS

News & Record (Piedmont Triad, NC), September 24, 2005, p. B8.
New York Times, September 19, 2005, p. A25.

PARKS, Rosa 1913-2005
(Rosa Louise Lee Parks)

OBITUARY NOTICE— See index for *SATA* sketch: Born February 4, 1913, in Tuskegee, AL; died October 24, 2005, in Detroit, MI. Activist and author. Widely hailed as the mother of the African-American anti-segregation movement, Parks became famous in 1955 when her refusal to give up her bus seat to a white man in Montgomery, Alabama, sparked the bus strike and the civil rights movement led by the Reverend Martin Luther King, Jr. Growing up in Tuskegee, Alabama, she developed a finely honed sense of right and wrong even as a little girl. In 1990's *The Autobiography of Rosa Parks,* which was released two years later as *Rosa Parks: My Story,* she recalled an early incident when a white boy threatened her with racial slurs. The young Parks picked up a brick and dared him to come after her, but he retreated. Alabama in the 1920s was a dangerous place for many blacks, and Parks also recalled how her father kept a gun in the house in case the Ku Klux Klan threatened them. Educated at home by her mother until she was eleven, Parks later attended the Montgomery Industrial School, an institution for the education of blacks where the white staff was also subjected to attacks by racists. When she was of college age, she attended what is now Alabama State University, but she had to leave school before graduating in order to take care of her ailing grandmother and, later, her mother. Parks took on a number of jobs, including domestic servant and aide in a hospital; she also married Raymond Parks, a member of the National Association for the Advancement of Colored People (NAACP). Living in Montgomery, Parks endured the entrenched racism and segregationist policies of the area for many years. One of the laws there restricted black people to sitting in the back rows of a bus; the front rows were reserved for white people, and even if those seats were empty black people were not allowed to use them. Finally, on December 1, 1955, Parks had had enough. Boarding a bus driven by James Blake, a man with whom she had had an unpleasant en-

counter years before, she sat in one of the middle rows. When the front rows filled up with white passengers, a white man demanded that she move so he could sit down. When Blake gave her an ultimatum to either move or be arrested, she told him to go ahead and call the police. He did so, and what followed would go down in history. Parks, actually, had not been the first black woman in Montgomery to refuse to such demands; two other women had acted similarly. However, because of her exemplary personal history as a working, married woman who regularly attended church, Parks was chosen by the local NAACP as a rallying point; at the time, she was secretary of the Montgomery NAACP branch. When Parks's case went to the courts, the city's black population organized a bus strike. Since two-thirds of the bus passengers in Montgomery were black, the city's public transportation system was soon in a financial crisis. Parks helped work on the strike by serving as a dispatcher, organizing ways for blacks with cars to carpool with others, while the Reverend King was selected to lead the strike. By the end of 1956, the U.S. Supreme Court had ruled Alabama's bus law unconstitutional. The bus strike in Montgomery ended, but it soon spread through other cities in the South. White reaction to the protests was violent and often bloody, and Parks and her husband faced repeated threats against their lives. Afraid for the worst, they decided to leave Alabama in 1957 and move to Detroit, Michigan, where some of Parks's relatives lived. In Detroit, Parks continued to work for the movement, and, among other activities, was present at the 1963 march led by King in Washington, DC. In 1975, she was hired by U.S. Representative John Conyers, Jr. to work on his staff, which she did until retiring in 1988. By this time, she had long been recognized as an icon in the civil rights movement. Many honors were bestowed upon her, including a Martin Luther King, Jr. Leadership Award in 1987, the Medal of Freedom in 1996, and the Congressional Gold Medal in 1999. In 2000, a museum and library were dedicated in her name in Montgomery, and the bus where she made her famous stand is now housed at the Henry Ford Museum in Detroit. Parks continued to work on worthy causes until her health began to fail. During the 1990s, she also coauthored several books, including *Quiet Strength: The Faith, the Hope, and the Heart of a Woman Who Changed a Nation* (1994), *Dear Mrs. Parks: A Dialogue with Today's Youth* (1996), and *I Am Rosa Parks* (1997). Among her important causes later in life was the founding of the Rosa and Raymond Parks Institute, which helped young blacks in the areas of education and improving self-esteem. At her death Parks became the first black woman to lie in state at the rotunda of the Lincoln Memorial.

OBITUARIES AND OTHER SOURCES:

BOOKS

Parks, Rosa, and Jim Haskins, *Rosa Parks: My Story,* Dial Books (New York, NY), 1992.

Parks, Rosa, and Gregory J. Reed, *Quiet Strength: The Faith, the Hope, and the Heart of a Woman Who Changed a Nation,* Zondervan (Grand Rapids, MI), 1994.
Parks, Rosa, and Jim Haskins, *I Am Rosa Parks,* Dial Books for Young Readers (New York, NY), 1997.

PERIODICALS

Chicago Tribune, October 25, 2005, section 1, pp. 1, 16.
Los Angeles Times, October 25, 2005, pp. A1, A12-13.
New York Times, October 26, 2005, p. C24.
Times (London, England), October 26, 2005, p. 70.

*   *   *

PARKS, Rosa Louise Lee
See PARKS, Rosa

*   *   *

PENNER, Fred 1946-
(Frederick Ralph Cornelius Penner)

Personal

Born November 6, 1946, in Winnipeg, Manitoba, Canada; son of Edward William (an accountant) and Lydia (a homemaker; maiden name, Winter) Penner; married Odette Graziella Heyn (a homemaker, dancer, and choreographer), August 23, 1981; children: four. *Education:* University of Winnipeg, B.A. (economics and psychology), 1970. *Hobbies and other interests:* Raising children, photography, racquetball, skiing, canoeing.

Addresses

Office—Oak Street Music, Ste. 108, 93 Lombard Ave., Winnipeg, Manitoba R3B 3B1, Canada. *Agent*—Paquin Entertainment, 395 Notre Dame Ave., Winnipeg, Manitoba R3B 1R2, Canada.

Career

Children's entertainer and television performer. Worked in residential treatment centers for children, 1969-72; toured with Kornstock (musical-comedy troupe) c. 1970s; performer with Manitoba Theatre Workshop (now Prairie Theatre Exchange) and Rainbow Stage in productions, including *Pippin,* 1977, *The King and I* and *Death of a Salesman* in 1978, and *Hello, Dolly!,* 1979; Sundance (children's dance theatre company), resident musician with wife, Odette Heyn-Penner, 1977-79; host of *Fred Penner's Place,* Canadian Broadcasting Corporation, beginning 1984, and MTV/Nickelodeon, beginning 1989; Oak Street Music (music publishing and recording label), Winnipeg, president, 1987. Composer of music for *Tippi Tales* (television

program). Host of television documentary *The Simple Way;* guest on numerous television specials, telethons, and concert broadcasts; performer in festivals and concerts throughout the United States and Canada, including Philadelphia International Theatre Festival for Children, 1987, Concert for Kids, Centennial Concert Hall, 1988, Wolf Trap Farm, Lehman Centre for the Performing Arts, and Los Angeles Amphitheatre. Chair, National Conference on Down Syndrome. Keynote speaker for early childhood education conferences in United States and Canada; spokesperson for organizations, including UNESCO, UNICEF, and World Vision.

Member

Association of Canadian Television and Radio Artists, American Federation of Musicians, Actors Equity.

Awards, Honors

Eight Juno award nominations, Canadian Academy of Recording Arts and Sciences, including 1979, for *The Cat Came Back,* 1981, for *Polka Dot Pony,* 1983, for *Special Delivery,* 1986, for *A House for Me,* and 1990, for *The Season;* Juno award, 1988, for *Fred Penner's Place* (television series), and for Best Children's Album, 2002, for *Sing with Fred;* four Parents' Choice Awards, Parents' Choice Foundation, including 1983, for *Special Delivery,* 1986, for *A House for Me,* 1989, for *Collections*; *The Cat Came Back* achieved Canadian gold certification status, 1985; Prairie Music Award for Outstanding Children's Recording; Canadian Institute of Child Health Award, 2000, for contribution to well-being and safety of children; named to Order of Canada.

Writings

SOUND RECORDINGS

The Cat Came Back (also see below), Troubadour (Willowdale, Ontario, Canada), 1979, re-released, Casablanca Kids (Toronto, Ontario, Canada), 2000.
The Polka Dot Pony, Troubadour (Willowdale, Ontario, Canada), 1981.
Special Delivery, Troubadour (Willowdale, Ontario, Canada), 1983.
A House for Me, Shoreline (Hollywood, CA), 1985.
(With Rafi and Chris and Ken Whiteley) *A Children's Sampler,* A & M (Hollywood. CA), 1986.
Fred Penner's Place, A & M (Hollywood, CA), 1988.
Collections, A & M (Hollywood, CA), 1989.
The Season, Oak Street Music (Winnipeg, Manitoba, Canada), 1990.
Happy Feet, Oak Street Music (Don Mills, Ontario, Canada), 1991, Dino Music (Beverly Hills, CA), 1992.
Poco, Oak Street Music (Winnipeg, Manitoba, Canada), 1991.
A Circle of Songs, Sony Entertainment (Don Mills, Ontario, Canada), 1991.

What a Day!, Oak Street Music (Don Mills, Ontario, Canada), 1994.
Moonlight Express, Oak Street Music (Winnipeg, Manitoba, Canada), 1996.
One—Two—Three Pack, Oak Street Music (Winnipeg, Manitoba, Canada), 1996.
Fred's Favourites, Casablanca Kids (Toronto, Ontario, Canada), 2001.
Sing with Fred, Casablanca Kids (Toronto, Ontario, Canada), 2002.
I'm Growing!, Casablanca Kids (Toronto, Ontario, Canada), 2004.
Storytime, Casablanca Kids (Toronto, Ontario, Canada), 2004.
My First Adventures, Casablanca Kids (Toronto, Ontario, Canada), 2004.
Rhyme a Word or Two, Casablanca Kids (Toronto, Ontario, Canada), 2004.
Christmastime, Casablanca Kids (Toronto, Ontario, Canada), 2004.

VIDEOS

The Cat Came Back (live concert; with Cat's Meow Band), 1990.
(With Len Udow and others) *A Circle of Songs,* 1991.
(With Al Simmons) *What a Day!,* Sony, 1993.

Also performer in videos *Sing with Fred, Growing, Company's Coming, Treasure Hunt,* and *Lights, Camera, Action!*

PICTURE BOOKS

The Bump, illustrated by Barbara Hicks, Hyperion Press (Winnipeg, Manitoba, Canada), 1984.
Ebeneezer Sneezer, illustrated by Barbara Hicks, Hyperion Press (Winnipeg, Manitoba, Canada), 1985.
Rollerskating, illustrated by Barbara Hicks, Hyperion Press (Winnipeg, Manitoba, Canada), 1987.
(Composer) Sheldon Oberman, *Julie Gerond and the Polka Dot Pony,* illustrated by Alan Pakarnyk, Hyperion Press (Winnipeg, Manitoba, Canada), 1988.
Fred Penner's Sing Along Play Along (activity book; contains songs from Penner's first four sound recordings), illustrated by Barbara Hicks, McGraw-Hill Ryerson (Toronto, Ontario, Canada), 1990.
Proud, illustrated by Vickey Bolling, Longstreet Press (Atlanta, GA), 1997.
The Cat Came Back, illustrated by Renée Reichert, Roaring Brook Press (New Milford, CT), 2005.

Sidelights

With his entertaining mix of songs, stories, jokes, and fun, Fred Penner entertains both children and adults with his energetic performances. An award-winning performer, Penner combines story and song in his many recordings and videos, as well as spin-off picture books, entertaining audiences, listeners, and readers alike while also spreading knowledge about the world. In record-

FRED PENNER

THE CAT CAME BACK

ILLUSTRATIONS BY RENÉE REICHERT

Canadian-based storyteller and author Fred Penner infuses a traditional folk song with new life and a healthy dose of humor in this 2005 book.

ings such as his Juno award-winning *Sing with Fred* and *The Cat Came Back,* as well as in videos such as *Growing, Treasure Hunt,* and *what a Day!,* Penner's baritone vocals intermix a variety of musical styles with tidbits of information on everything from animal habitats to techniques for fending off the common cold. "As a parent and performer for young children," Penner once remarked to *SATA,* "I feel it is important to take advantage of the love that children naturally have for music. It can be so much more than simply background music; movement and song provide a powerful impetus for learning." Praised for his decades-long work with children, Penner was praised by *Los Angeles Parent* magazine as the "Canadian Minister of Positivity," while *Billboard* magazine dubbed him "Mr. MultiMedia" due to his work in film and on stage and television, according to a writer on the Paquin Entertainment Web site.

Born in 1946, in Winnipeg, Manitoba, Canada, Penner began playing the guitar and singing while he was a high-school student. He sang in choirs and folk groups and performed in theatre while studying economics and psychology at the University of Winnipeg. Penner's sister Susie, who had a form of mental retardation called Down's syndrome, had responded positively to music before her death at age twelve, and this also inspired his belief in the power of song. As he related to *Star-*

week, "I gained more understanding about the importance of music through her than through any other human being, because she loved music in the purest sense."

After graduation, Penner found himself pulled toward a career dealing directly with people, and he took a series of jobs with troubled children, working in residential youth treatment centers. Though many young people he encountered in these centers were socially withdrawn, they came to life when Penner played his guitar. "Music was able to cut through any of the problems they were having," Penner recalled to Jonathan Takiff in the *Philadelphia Daily News.*

Searching for the best way to use his talents, Penner began his professional performing career as an actor in musicals and dramas. He also toured with Kornstock, a musical comedy troupe, and later became a musician in Sundance, a dance company for children founded by his wife. Beginning in 1977 Penner performed on television specials and concert broadcasts, and two years later the music he created for a Sundance production was recorded as his first album, *The Cat Came Back.* A number of other recordings for children have followed, including 1983's *Special Delivery,* 1996's *Moonlight Express,* and 2002's *Sing with Fred,* all which combine traditional tunes and original songs. "Penner's picks all have hummable tunes, focused lyrics with memorable choruses, and most display a positive moral tone— delivering lessons about perseverance, self-confidence, tolerance, and honest patriotism—without talking down to the listeners," judged Takiff in the *Philadelphia Daily News.*

Penner has performed for capacity crowds throughout the United States and Canada, and has gained recognition for his exuberance, originality, and spontaneity. He frequently surprises his audiences with imaginative entrances—by speeding out atop a skateboard or by tossing a series of frisbees across the stage before entering. Gaining full audience participation is of prime importance, and Penner mixes favorite sing-along tunes such as "Michael, Row the Boat Ashore" and "Zip-a-dee-doo-dah" with original selections such as "Poco" or "A House Is a House for Me." Between songs he engages his audience in activities ranging from stretching exercises to auditorium-wide "waves." He also incorporates unusual activities into his shows; during one production Penner and his Cat's Meow Band formed chickens from folded towels.

Of prime importance to Penner is incorporating lessons on values and morals into his entertainments. "The bottom line when working with children is the honesty and integrity that you present an audience," he noted to a Vancouver, British Columbia *TV Guide* contributor. "You must realize that a child learns from everything you do. It's easy enough to get up on-stage and sing a couple of songs, but that is not where it stops; it's a life commitment." "There is no doubt Penner knows how to entertain kids in fine style," declared Gloria Kelly in

the *Halifax Herald,* reviewing one of Penner's concert. "They cheered when he came on stage and were still cheering and clapping when his hour long show was finished."

In the mid-1980s Penner's celebrity spread from his native Canada south to the United States when he began hosting a children's television series. Called *Fred Penner's Place,* the show was viewed by its creator as a way of providing an alternative to advertisement-and violence-filled programming. Airing five times a week for twelve seasons on both Canadian television and the U.S. cable network Nickelodeon, *Fred Penner's Place* featured Penner climbing out from a hollow log to greet his audience, then singing, playing his guitar, and telling stories in each segment. The program was filmed in secluded woodland locations in both Vancouver, British Columbia and Winnipeg, Manitoba, Canada. According to Sandy Greer in *Starweek,* Penner traveled to these remote settings because children enjoy having secret places where they feel protected. "That journey captures the imagination," Penner explained to Greer, adding that it added "a vital quality and feeling."

Although Penner's career has primarily been as an entertainer, he has also taken on the role of author by adapting some of his songs into picture books. Beginning with 1984's *The Bump,* his picture books include *Proud* and *The Cat Came Back,* as well as the song-and-activity book *Sing Along Play Along. Proud* is a lullaby that introduces young children to the concepts of personal development and accomplishment through its focus on young children learning to walk, talk, read, and help a friend. A well-known nineteenth-century folk song about a persistent feline is the focus of *The Cat Came Back,* a picture book illustrated by Renée Reichert that a *Kirkus Reviews* contributor praised by noting that, "unlike many songs, [Penner's] . . . lyrics work equally well read or sung." Citing the book's "jaunty, comic tone," a *Publishers Weekly* reviewer deemed the book a "purrfectly perky rendition" about a scruffy orange cat that continues to stray onto a frustrated farmer's doorstep. *School Library Journal* reviewer Jane Marino called the book "loads of fun," and Jennifer Mattson wrote in *Booklist* that Penner's text "retains traces of the traditional song's irreverent, macabre humor."

Continuing to produce CD recordings, books, concerts, and videos, Penner helps young people to learn about the world and discover their dreams through an upbeat presentation that is captured in his signature song "Happy Feet." Encouraging their participation through sing-alongs, mental challenges such as riddles, and creating songs that incorporate audience participation, Penner realizes that having fun is an integral part of learning, especially during his concerts. "Part of the fun is sharing a musical moment," Penner told Barbara S. Rothschild in the *New Jersey Courier-Post,* discussing his performances. "At the end of the show, parents and children alike feel they've shared a positive musical experience." Reviewing Penner's video recording *What a Day!,* a *Publishers Weekly* wrote that the entertainer's "feel-good voice shows its versatility in performances that range from silly to polished," creating a "lively pacing."

Penner once told *SATA:* "We all have opinions, thoughts, and ideas that turn around and around in our minds and sometimes come out in many wonderful ways: stories, music, pictures, etc. When someone sings you a song or reads you a book, that can help your feelings to start to grow and give your imagination an extra nudge.

"Sharing thoughts and ideas with others is what I do in my life. My own family helps me to discover new feelings all the time, and that way I learn what is important to me and what I would like to share with others. Through radio and TV we are able to see and hear people trying to express themselves to us. But there is so much to choose from; the hard part is deciding what we want to be part of our lives. That is where parents come in; our job is to make choices that will enrich the lives of our children."

Biographical and Critical Sources

PERIODICALS

Booklist, November 1, 2005, Jennifer Mattson, review of *The Cat Came Back,* p. 54.
Canadian Book Review Annual, 1997, review of *Proud,* p. 39.
Citizen (Ottawa, Ontario, Canada), February 20, 1987; February 23, 1987.
Halifax Herald, January 20, 1986.
Kirkus Reviews, August 1, 2005, review of *The Cat Came Back,* p. 856.
New Jersey Courier-Post, May 17, 1987.
Philadelphia Daily News, May, 1987.
Quill & Quire, October, 1997, review of *Proud,* p. 39.
Publishers Weekly, December 20, 1993, review of *What a Day!* (video), p. 36; May 16, 1994, review of *What a Day!* (sound recording), p. 30; August 22, 2005, review of *The Cat Came Back,* p. 64.
Resource Links, February, 1998, review of *Proud,* p. 103.
School Library Journal, August, 1994, Rob Reid, review of *What a Day!,* p. 113; October, 2005, Jane Marino, review of *The Cat Came Back,* p. 144.
Starweek (Toronto, Ontario, Canada), April 5-12, 1986.
TV Guide (Vancouver, British Columbia, Canada), October 31-November 6, 1987, p. 2.
Winnipeg Free Press, December 12, 1984; March 14, 1988.

ONLINE

Fred Penner Home Page, http://www.fredpenner.com (March 28, 2006).
Paquin Entertainment Web site, http://www.paquinentertainment.com/ (March 28, 2006), "Fred Penner."*

PENNER, Frederick Ralph Cornelius
    See PENNER, Fred

*   *   *

PETERS, Andrew
    See PETERS, Andrew Fusek

*   *   *

PETERS, Andrew Fusek 1965-
    (Andrew Peters)

Personal

Born July 2, 1965, in Hildesheim, Germany; son of Frederick Maxwell (a geologist) and Vera Anna Fusek (an actress) Peters; married July 13, 1991; wife's name Polly Anne (a drama teacher and writer); children: Rosalind, Asa. *Education:* Attended Corpus Christi College, Oxford, 1984. *Politics:* "Liberal." *Religion:* "Open minded."

Addresses

Home—The Old Chapel, Lydbury North, Shropshire SY7 8AU, England. *E-mail*—tallpoet@compuserve. com.

Career

Writer, broadcaster, and musician. Creative writing tutor, 1987—; author, 1992—. Presenter and writer for broadcast media, including British Broadcasting Corporation (BBC) Radio 4, BBC-1 poetry television series *Wham Bam Strawberry Jam,* and documentaries for Carlton & Central Television.

Member

Poetry Society, National Association of Writers in Education, Society for Storytelling, Performing Rights Society, MCPS.

Awards, Honors

West Midland Arts Valuing the Arts Award, 1996; BBC Radio 4 Write Out Loud Award, 1997; West Midland Arts Creative Ambition Award, 1998; Arts Council Translation Award, 1999, for *Sheep Don't Go to School;* North East Book Award shortlist, Stockton Schools Book Award shortlist, and Carnegie Medal nomination, all 2005, all for *Crash.*

Writings

FOR CHILDREN

Word Whys (poetry), Sherbourne (Oswestry, England), 1992.

Andrew Fusek Peters

(Reteller) *Salt Is Sweeter than Gold* (picture book), illustrated by Zdenka Kabatova-Taborska, Barefoot Books (Bath, England), 1994.

The House That Learned to Swim, Ginn (Oxford, England), 1996.

The Goat-Eared King, and Other Czech Tales, Collins Educational (London, England), 1996.

The Weather's Getting Verse: The Stomping and Storming Poems of Andrew Peters, illustrated by Alan Larkins, Sherbourne (Oswestry, England), 1996.

(Reteller) *The Barefoot Book of Strange and Spooky Stories,* illustrated by Zdenka Kabatova-Taborska, Barefoot Books (Bath, England), 1997, published as *Strange and Spooky Stories,* Millbrook Press (Minneapolis, MN), 1998.

The Moon Is on the Microphone: The Wild and Wacky Poems of Andrew Fusek Peters, illustrated by Danny Bradford, Sherbourne (Oswestry, England), 1997.

(Editor) *Sheep Don't Go to School: Mad and Magical Children's Poetry,* illustrated by Marketa Prachaticka, Bloodaxe Books (Tarset, Northumberland, England), 1999.

(Editor) *The upside down Frown* (shape poems), Wayland/ Young McDonald Books (London, England), 1999.

(Compiler) *Poems about Seasons,* illustrated by Kelly Waldek, Hodder (London, England), 2000.

(Compiler) *Poems about Festivals,* illustrated by Kelly Waldek, Hodder (London, England), 2000.

(Compiler) *The Unidentified Frying Omlette* (poetry), Hodder (London, England), 2000.

(With wife, Polly Peters) *Angelcake*, Wayland (London, England), 2001.

(With Polly Peters) *Dragon Chaser*, Wayland (London, England), 2001.

(With Polly Peters) *Much Ado about Clubbing*, Wayland (London, England), 2001.

(With Polly Peters) *Twisted*, Hodder (London, England), 2001.

(With Polly Peters) *Sadderday and Funday*, Hodder (London, England), 2001.

Dragon and Mousie, illustrated by Gini Wade, Lolfa (Talybont, Wales), 2002.

Monkey's Clever Tale, illustrated by Amanda Montgomery-Higham, Child's Play (Auburn, ME), 2003.

(Compiler) *Hubble Bubble: A Potent Brew of Magical Poems*, Hodder (London, England), 2003.

The Tiger and the Wise Man, illustrated by Diana Mayo, Child's Play (Swindon, England), 2004, Child's Play (Auburn, ME), 2005.

Bear and Turtle and the Great Lake Race, illustrated by Alison Edgson, Child's Play (Swindon, England), 2005.

(Coeditor with Jane Yolen) *My Very First Book of Poetry*, illustrated by Polly Dunbar, Candlewick (Cambridge, MA), 2006.

Also author of *A Pint of Unleaded Please* (poetry). Poems published in anthologies, including *Jugular Defences*, Oscar's Press, 1993, *Custard Pie*, Macmillan, 1995, *A Faber Book of First Verse*, Faber & Faber, 1995, *The Young Poetry Pack*, Radio 4/Poetry Society, 1995, and *Friends*, Macmillan. Contributor of articles to periodicals, including *Junior Education*.

FOR YOUNG ADULTS

(With brother, Mark Peters) *May the Angels Be with Us* (poetry), Shropshire County Council Education Services, 1994.

(With Polly Peters) *Poems with Attitude*, Hodder (London, England), 2000.

(Compiler) *Out of Order* (poetry), illustrated by Clive Goodyear, Evans Brothers (London, England), 2002.

(With Stephen Player) *Ed and the Witchblood* (graphic novel), Hodder (London, England), 2003.

(With Polly Peters) *Crash: A Novel of Love and Death* (verse novel), Hodder (London, England), 2004.

(With Polly Peters) *Love, Hate, and My Best Mate* (poetry), Hodder (London, England), 2005.

(With Stephen Player) *Ed and the River of the Damned* (graphic novel; sequel to *Ed and the Witchblood*), Hodder (London, England), 2005.

(With Polly Peters) *Roar, Bull, Roar!*, Francis Lincoln (London, England), 2006.

OTHER

(Author of lyrics; and performer) *Colour People-Didjeridu* (sound recording), Sonoton, 1990.

When I Come to the Dark Country: Poems of Land, Love, and Loss (adult poetry), illustrated by Jackie Astbury, Abbotsford (Lichfield, England), 1997.

Author, with Sue Harris, of lyrics for *Tales from under the Puddle* (sound recording), 1992.

Work in Progress

Ed and the Devil's Chair, the third part of a (graphic-novel trilogy; *Spies Unlimited, Ghosts Unlimited*, and *The Poetry Archive*, all poetry collections; *Animals Abroad!*, a picture book.

Sidelights

British writer Andrew Fusek Peters is a poet and storyteller whose interest in Czech folk tales was kindled hearing the history of his mother's family. Peters' picture book *Salt Is Sweeter than Gold* retells a traditional Czech fairy tale about an old king who asks his three daughters to express their love for him. While the older two flatter him with extravagant claims, the youngest announces only that she loves her father more than salt. The king angrily banishes the girl, asserting that he will welcome her return only when salt becomes more valuable than gold. *School Librarian* critic David Lewis noted similarities between these opening scenes and Shakespeare's play *King Lear*; in Peters' story the young princess finds a home with a wise old woman in the forest who helps her become reunited with her father. "This picture book will appeal to children seeking 'princess books,'" predicted *Booklist* reviewer Carolyn Phelan.

Peters includes a traditional story from Czechoslovakia in his nine-tale compilation *Strange and Spooky Stories*. Also included are legends from North America, the British Isles, and Central Europe, each with an element of the magical in them. Reviewers were quick to distinguish between the content and style of these stories, which were published in Great Britain under the title *The Barefoot Book of Strange and Spooky Stories*, and include the kind of tales usually presented to American children as "scary." A *Children's Book Review Service* contributor maintained that "readers will be captured by the strange, silly and spooky tales." "Peters writes in a simple, almost conversational style that should appeal to storytellers," observed Julie Corsaro in *Booklist*. A *Times Educational Supplement* commentator similarly asserted: "Peters' skill as an oral storyteller is evident in his retellings. . . . [You] could read these stories aloud in the classroom with enormous pleasure."

Peters has drawn on folk tales for some of his picture books as well, including *The Tiger and the Wise Man*. Set in East India, the story tells of a wise man who frees a tiger from a trap. The tiger then captures the man and plans to eat him. When the man calls to the banyan tree, the eagle, and the crocodile to defend him and convince the tiger to free him, they all turn away, saying that humans have been cruel to them and the en-

vironment. Jackal comes along at the last minute and convinces the tiger to let the wise man go—only to capture the man for himself. "This well-paced trickster tale has charm," wrote Linda Perkins in *Booklist.* "Peters, billed as 'Britain's tallest storyteller,' writes with a conversational fluency," according to a *Kirkus Reviews* contributor. *Bear and Turtle and the Great Lake Race* is a spin off of a Native American tale with a twist at the end.

In addition to his own original works, Peters has teamed with his wife, writer Polly Peters, on several poetry titles, including *Poems with Attitude,* the only poetry collection ever to make the Carnegie Medal long list, and the verse novel *Crash: A Novel of Love and Death,* which was nominated for several awards. When asked on his home page how the couple work together, Peters explained: "Our writing relationship is very fluid, so sometimes it's hard to say when one of us ends and the other begins." This fluidity is evident in *Crash,* which tells the story of a group of seventeen year olds whose mutual friend dies in a car accident. The book shifts from one perspective to the next, capturing the pain and sadness of each of the book's characters. *Crash* "is original to its core in both telling and the tale," wrote Jo Kalce in the *Times Educational Supplement,* while Sue Roe noted in *School Librarian* that the novel's "pace is fast, the emotions raw, and the narrative voices ring true."

Another collaboration by the Peters', the poetry collection *Poems with Attitude*, captures some of the same raw emotions dealt with in *Crash.* Here the collected poems are divided among such themes as "Snogging" and "Family," each corresponding to emotions familiar to teens. "I cannot emphasise how much every school needs this," wrote a reviewer for *School Librarian.* The Peters have also recorded some of their work for the British Library in a project called *The Poetry Archive,* which features sound recordings of poetry by British authors.

Along with picture books and poetry, Peters has also worked with illustrator Stephen Player on a graphic-novel trilogy, beginning with *Ed and the Witchblood.* The series tells the story of the trials of Ed, who thinks his life cannot get any worse. However, ancient legends are moving in Ed's life, and something waits for him under a stone circle. It may be all Ed can do to survive. In *Ed and the River of the Damned* Ed's troubles follow him to London, where a series of underground tunnels reveal dark forces brewing beneath the city. A critic for *School Librarian* considered the second volume of the trilogy to be "a strange and compelling mixture of close-to-the-edge teen-angst 'realism' and new-age-ish fantasy."

Peters once told *SATA:* "What interests me as a writer? That language is a craft and we have to serve our apprenticeship. It is something that takes time, patience and much work and it is a job. I used to get asked *but*

With illustrations by Amanda Montgomery-Higham, Peters' adaptation of an Afro-Caribbean tale about a hungry Crocodile and his quest for dinner is gleefully retold in **Monkey's Clever Tale.**

what is your day job? as if writing were some kind of hobby—my books dashed off in a couple of hours! I am very much a perfectionist as I draft, whether it is stories, poems, or a piece for television. In poetry, as well as writing free verse, I love traditional forms—sonnet, sestina, roundel—and fitting modern-day language into these historical structures. I have even written a *Garland of Sonnets!*

"I mainly write for children. As an author and performer, I love to entertain, and write a lot of material that has a surreal sense of imagination, as well as throwing in the odd piece about bogies or kissing. But I am aware that children are sophisticated humans with the whole range of human emotions. Children's publishers often shy away from any of the big issues—such as grief, bullying, falling in love, etc.—yet this is the material that has often gone down well with readers and critics. I have been reading and admiring a lot of American children's poetry recently—and though I love the zany use of language, some of it seems to play safe.

"When my brother Mark died of AIDS in America, in 1993, I put together a book of his and my poems for teenagers that was successfully published. *May the Angels Be with Us* deals with all the joy of growing up together, and the fights, and the illness, and death and finally the healing of time. As a collection, it had a huge response in Britain, with features in the London *Guardian,* the *Times Educational Supplement,* and on the BBC

Radio Four arts program *Kaleidoscope,* as well as support from actors such as Sir Ian McKellan and well-known children's poet Brian Patten. Poetry, in this instance, became a powerful medium to express a universal message of loss, and the book reached out to all those who had lost a loved one in whatever circumstances.

"My wife and I have completed a collection of adolescent poems. I do a lot of work with this age group, performing and running writing workshops. It seems that there is very little published work that deals with their experiences of growing up, especially not in poetry. You could say there was a gap in the market, or that once again, publishers have been reluctant to tackle a difficult area. The poems we have written deal with bullying, drug addiction, dysfunctional families, abuse, alcoholism, sexuality, and falling in love—issues that affect many young people these days. Trialling these poems has been a joy. To see tough kids from an inner-city area who normally hate poetry fall completely silent as I read the poems showed me that I had touched a nerve. Poetry doesn't just have to be about swaying trees!

"My other interest as a writer is how to get across the sense of the magical and lyrical to my audience. *Strange and Spooky Stories* is a collection of traditional tales gleaned from my mother's Czech upbringing, and from storytellers worldwide. There is something very powerful about traditional tales: the repeated motifs, events happening in threes, the impossible becoming everyday, and good triumphing over bad. In a sense, they are poetry in narrative form. The trick is to convey an atmosphere in your words that carries the reader for a while far from this world, to the place where imagination sings."

Biographical and Critical Sources

PERIODICALS

Booklist, January 1, 1995, Carolyn Phelan, review of *Salt Is Sweeter than Gold,* p. 824; February 1, 1998, Julie Corsaro, review of *Strange and Spooky Stories,* p. 916; August, 2005, Linda Perkins, review of *The Tiger and the Wiseman,* p. 2032.

Children's Book Review Service, February, 1998, review of *Strange and Spooky Stories,* pp. 78-79.

Kirkus Reviews, March 1, 2005, review of *The Tiger and the Wise Man,* p. 293.

School Librarian, November, 1994, David Lewis, review of *Salt Is Sweeter than Gold,* p. 147; winter, 2000, review of *Poems with Attitude,* p. 209; winter, 2003, review of *Hubble Bubble: A Potent Brew of Magical Poems,* p. 207; spring, 2004, Mel Gibson, review of *Ed and the Witchblood,* p. 44; winter, 2004, Ann Trevenen Jenkin, review of *The Tiger and the Wiseman,* p. 188, and Sue Roe, review of *Crash,* p. 216; spring, 2005, review of *Love, Hate, and My Best Mate,* p. 43; spring, 2005, review of *Crash,* p. 43; summer, 2005, Andy Sawyer, review of *Ed and the River of the Damned,* p. 104.

School Library Journal, August, 2002, Sharon Korbeck, review of *Out of Order,* p. 214; January, 2004, Gay Lynn Van Vleck, review of *Monkey's Clever Tale,* p. 116; June, 2005, Rita Soltan, review of *The Tiger and the Wise Man,* p. 142.

Times Educational Supplement, January 30, 1998, review of *The Barefoot Book of Strange and Spooky Stories,* p. 15; October 1, 1999, review of *Sheep Don't Go to School: Mad and Magical Children's Poetry,* p. 41; May 12, 2000, review of *Poems about Seasons* and *Poems about Festivals,* p. 23; October 5, 2001, review of *Dragon Chaser, Much Ado about Clubbing, Twisted,* and *Angelcake,* p. 22; May 30, 2003, John Mole, "Magic Moments," p. 24; October 17, 2003, Gillian Maynard, "Chat and Mouse," review of *Dragon and Mousie,* p. 20; August 6, 2004, Jane Doonan, "A Little Retell Therapy," p. 24; November 26, 2004, Jo Klaces, "Matters of the Heart."

ONLINE

Andrew Fusek Peters and Polly Peters Home Page, http://www.tallpoet.com (March 23, 2006).*

R

REES, Douglas 1947-

Personal

Born October 19, 1947, in Riverside, CA; son of Norman (a career sergeant) and Agnes (a nurse) Rees; married Bonnie Rostonovich (marriage ended 1977); married; second wife's name JoAnn (a librarian); children: Philip Rostonovich. *Politics:* "Liberal." *Religion:* "High-church Episcopalian."

Addresses

Home—Sunnyvale, CA. *Agent*—c/o Author Mail, Watson-Guptill Publications, 770 Broadway, New York, NY 10003. *E-mail*—zeppelinpilot@yahoo.com.

Career

Fiction writer and librarian. San Jose Public Library, San Jose, CA, librarian.

Awards, Honors

Notable Book designation, American Library Association (ALA), and New York Public Library Best Book for the Teen Age designation, both 1999, both for *Lightning Time;* Best Children's Book of the Year nomination, Bay Area Book Reviewers, 1999, for *Lightning Time,* and 2003, for *Vampire High;* Quick Pick for Reluctant Readers citation, ALA, 2004, for *Vampire High.*

Writings

Lightning Time (novel), Dorling Kindersley (New York, NY), 1997.
Vampire High (novel), Delacorte (New York, NY), 2003.
Grandy Thaxter's Helper (picture book), illustrated by S.D. Schindler, Atheneum (New York, NY), 2004.
Smoking Mirror: An Encounter with Paul Gauguin (novel), Watson-Guptill (New York, NY), 2005.

Douglas Rees

The Janus Gate: An Encounter with John Singer Sargent (novel), Watson-Guptill (New York, NY), 2006.

Vampire High has been translated into French and German.

Work in Progress

Jeannette Claus's Difficult Christmas Eve, a picture book, and *Uncle Pirate,* an early cpater book, both to be published by Margaret K. McElderry Books; *Gideon's Remnant,* a novel for young adults about the

Spanish-American War; and *Starbridge, TX,* a comic science-fiction story set in West Texas.

Sidelights

"Until I was six, I wanted to be a fireman," wrote children's book author Douglas Rees on his home page. "Between six and twelve, I wanted to be a paleontologist. When I was twelve, I decided I wanted to be a writer. I still haven't outgrown that." Rees has authored novels for children and young adults as well as a picture book. When not working on his novels, Rees also works at the Rose Garden branch of the San Jose, California, Public Library System.

Rees's first book, *Lightning Time,* is a novel for young adults about the exploits of notorious abolitionist John Brown, who attacked a U.S. military arsenal at Harpers Ferry, Virginia and helped spark the U.S. Civil War. Narrator Theodore is fourteen years old when he meets the charismatic Brown, and is drawn into Brown's cause. Theodore's decision to leave his family to follow Brown is a difficult one for the teen, but his convictions strengthen throughout the course of the novel. "Theodore makes a sympathetic narrator," noted Carolyn Phelan in *Booklist,* while Elizabeth S. Watson wrote in *Horn Book* that "Rees has created a fine historical novel that explores the complexities of the abolitionist cause."

After *Lightning Time* Rees decided to explore the horror genre. "I've always wanted to write a horror story," he explained on his home page. "The only horror stories anyone is reading these days involve vampires, and I don't like vampires. All that self-pity and morbid sexuality are annoying. I mean—and I really did think it exactly this way—surely there must be some decent chaps among the vampires. They must go to high school—and suddenly I saw the kids of Vlad Dracul walking silently up and down the marble halls, and I was off and away." Vlad Dracul High School is an elite magnet school attended almost entirely by vampires. When fifteen-year-old Cody transfers there, it is only a matter of time before he figures out who his classmates are. Unlike the other non-blood-sucking teens attending Vlad Dracul, Cody sets out to challenge the school's standards and social hierarchy, determined to be treated like the other students, regardless of his non-vampire status.

"There's barely a false note in this rollicking tale of horror, humor, and light romance," complimented *Booklist* reviewer Frances Bradburn. A *Publishers Weekly* critic commented on Rees's "bold, almost hyperbolic humor," while Lauren Adams wrote in *Horn Book* that the tale is "a light, engaging parable with a reader-pleasing happy ending." *Vampire High* includes "amusing twists on the fantasy tropes about vampires," according to a *Kirkus Reviews* contributor, and Paula Rohrlick noted in *Kliatt* that "snappy dialogue and the age-old appeal of the vampire make this comedy a winner."

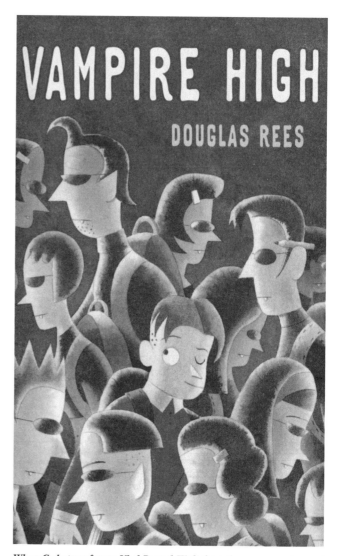

When Cody transfers to Vlad Dracul High the only course requirement is water polo, and his nocturnally inclined classmates soon tip him off to the truth in Rees's amusing teen novel. (Cover illustration by Greg Clarke.)

Rees combines two folktale motifs in his picture book *Grandy Thaxter's Helper.* Set against an early American backdrop—a new setting for the traditional tale—the book tells how Grandy Thaxter outwits Death by explaining that she can only go with him if she gets all her work done. Since it will surely go faster if Death helps, she enlists him in her chores. At the end of the day, Death is far too tired to take Grandy Thaxter away. After two more increasingly exhausting tries, he says he will come back when she is no longer so busy. "*Grandy Thaxter's Helper* will be a welcome storytime visitor," recommended Kitty Flynn in *Horn Book.* "For pure entertainment value, this book is hard to beat," agreed a critic for *Publishers Weekly.* "What makes this rendition of a classic theme interesting, slyly funny, and informative is its Colonial setting," explained Marge Loch-Wouters in *School Library Journal,* the critic pointing out that each chore of Grandy Thaxter's, such as making soap or mush, includes details from the setting.

In Grandy Thaxter's Helper *an appointment with Death is postponed when the elderly woman works the grim reaper himself to exhaustion while trying to finish all her chores.* (Illustration by S.D. Schindler.)

Several of Rees's books introduce historical information to readers, among them *Smoking Mirror: An Encounter with Paul Gauguin* and *The Janus Gate: An Encounter with John Singer Sargent.* As part of the "Art Encounters" series from publisher Watson-Guptill, these books tell fictional stories that capture moments in the lives of famous artists. Paul Gauguin is the featured artist in *Smoking Mirror,* the story about fifteen-year-old Joe Sloan who runs away to Tahiti. There, he meets Gauguin and ends up forming a friendship based on mutual need and admiration. The novel gives readers "an intimate peek at Gauguin's creative process," according to a *Kirkus Reviews* contributor. Ken Marantz, writing in *School Arts,* commented on the "suspenseful story," while *Booklist* reviewer Gillian Engberg praised Rees for his ability to "weave . . . biographical facts about a famous artist into a compelling novel." *The Janus Gate* features portrait painter John Singer Sargent in a fictional supernatural thriller in which the artist must decide whether or not to help the girls who are the subjects of one of his paintings.

On his home page, Rees offered the following advice to young writers: "Just write. Don't worry about the odds against ever getting published. Just do it. The odds are impossible anyway."

Biographical and Critical Sources

PERIODICALS

Booklist, January 1, 1998, Carolyn Phelan, review of *Lightning Time,* p. 794; August, 2003, Frances Bradburn, review of *Vampire High,* p. 1973; March 15, 2005, Gillian Engberg, review of *Smoking Mirror: An Encounter with Paul Gauguin,* p. 1285.

Bulletin of the Center for Children's Books, January, 1998, review of *Lightning Time,* p. 173; October, 2004, Timnah Card, review of *Grandy Thaxter's Helper,* p. 97.

Horn Book, January-February, 1998, Elizabeth S. Watson, review of *Lighting Time,* p. 80; September-October,

2003, Lauren Adams, review of *Vampire High*, p. 617; November-December, 2004, Kitty Flynn, review of *Grandy Thaxter's Helper*, p. 700.

Kirkus Reviews, September 1, 2003, review of *Vampire High*, p. 1129; September 15, 2004, review of *Grandy Thaxter's Helper*, p. 919; January 1, 2005, review of *Smoking Mirror*, p. 56.

Kliatt, September, 2003, Paula Rohrlick, review of *Vampire High*, p. 11.

Library Media Connection, March, 2004, review of *Vampire High*, p. 65.

New York Times, March 13, 2005, Beth Gutcheon, review of *Grandy Thaxter's Helper*.

Publishers Weekly, April 12, 1999, review of *Lightning Time*, p. 78; August 4, 2003, review of *Vampire High*, p. 81; September 20, 2004, review of *Grandy Thaxter's Helper*, p. 61.

School Arts, February, 2005, Ken Marantz, review of *Smoking Mirror*, p. 55.

School Library Journal, December, 1997, Peggy Morgan, review of *Lightning Time*, p. 129; November, 2003, Lynn Evarts, review of *Vampire High*, p. 146; November, 2004, Marge Loch-Wouters, review of *Grandy Thaxter's Helper*, p. 116; March, 2005, Heather E. Miller, review of *Smoking Mirror*, p. 217.

Voice of Youth Advocates, April, 1998, review of *Lightning Time*, p. 47; February, 2004, Jennifer Bromann, review of *Vampire High*, p. 506; April, 2004, "Best Science Fiction, Fantasy, and Horror 2003," p. 14.

ONLINE

Douglas Rees Home Page, http://www.douglasrees.com (March 22, 2006).

Riverside Public Library Web site, http://www.riversideca.gov/library/ (March 22, 2006), interview with Rees.

*   *   *

RICHARDS, Justin

Personal

Married; children: two sons.

Addresses

Home—Warwick, England. *Agent*—Miles Stott Children's Literary Agency, East Hook Farm, Lower Quay Rd., Hook, Haverfordwest SA62 4LR, Wales. *E-mail*—info@invisible-detective.com.

Career

Novelist, editor, technical writer, and software designer. Worked as a software designer for multinational computer company for 14 years; British Broadcasting Corporation (BBC), London, England, creative director for BBC Worldwide.

Writings

The Death Collector (novel), Bloomsbury Children's Books (New York, NY), 2006.

Also author of film and television scripts.

"BENNY SUMMERFIELD" NOVEL SERIES

Dragons' Wrath, Virgin Books (London, England), 1997.
The Medusa Effect, Virgin Books (London, England), 1998.
The Joy Device, Virgin Books (London, England), 1999.
Tears of the Oracle, Virgin Books (London, England), 1999.
Professor Bernice Summerfield and the Doomsday Manuscript, Big Finish (Maidenhead, England), 2000.

"DOCTOR WHO" NOVEL SERIES; BASED ON THE TELEVISION SERIES

Theatre of War ("New Adventures" cycle), Virgin Books (London, England), 1994.
System Shock ("Missing Adventures" series), Virgin Books (London, England), 1995.
(Editor with Andy Lane) *Decalog 3—Consequences: Ten Stories, Seven Doctors, One Chain of Events*, BBC Books (London, England), 1996.
The Sands of Time ("Missing Adventures" series), Virgin Books (London, England), 1996.
(Editor with Andy Lane, and contributor) *Decalog 4—Re-Generations: Ten Stories, a Thousand Years, One Family*, BBC Books (London, England), 1997.
(With Andrew Martin) *Dr. Who: The Book of Lists*, BBC Books (London, England), 1997.
Option Lock, BBC Books (London, England), 1998.
Dreams of Empire, BBC Books (London, England), 1998.
Demontage, BBC Books (London, England), 1999.
Millennium Shock, BBC Books (London, England), 1999.
Grave Matter, BBC Books (London, England), 2000.
(With Andy Lane) *The Banquo Legacy*, BBC Worldwide (London, England), 2000.
The Burning, BBC Books (London, England), 2000.
The Shadow in the Glass, BBC Books (London, England), 2001.
Time Zero, BBC Worldwide (London, England), 2002.
Doctor Who, the Legend: 40 Years of Time Travel, BBC Books (London, England), 2003.
Sometime Never—, BBC Books (London, England), 2004.
The Clockwise Man, BBC Books (London, England), 2005.
Monsters and Villains (reference book), BBC Books (London, England), 2005.
The Deviant Strain, BBC Books (London, England), 2005.
The Legend Continues, BBC Books (London, England), 2005.
The Resurrection Casket, BBC Books (London, England), 2006.

Also author of "Dr. Who" audio plays *Whispers of Terror, Red Dawn, The Time of the Daleks*, 2002, *The Inquiry*, 2004, *Pandora*, 2005, and *Mindbomb*, 2006.

"INVISIBLE DETECTIVE" NOVEL SERIES

The Paranormal Puppet Show, Pocket (London, England), 2003, published as *Double Life,* Putnam's (New York, NY), 2005.

The Shadow Beast, Pocket (London, England), 2003, Putnam's (New York, NY), 2005.

Ghost Soldiers, Pocket (London, England), 2003.

Killing Time, Simon & Schuster (London, England), 2004, Putnam's (New York, NY), 2007.

The Faces of Evil, Pocket (London, England), 2004.

Web of Anubis, Pocket (London, England), 2004.

Stage Fright, Pocket (London, England), 2005.

Legion of the Dead, Pocket (London, England), 2005.

Adaptations

The first two books in the "Invisible Detective" series were adapted as audiobooks by Chivers Audio, 2004; *The Death Collector* was adapted as an audiobook, Random House Audio, 2006; *Dr. Who: The Resurrection Casket* was adapted as an audiobook, including an interview with Richards, 2006.

Sidelights

A former tech writer and software designer, Justin Richards is known for the novels he has written based on the popular, long-running *Doctor Who* television series, produced by the British Broadcasting Corporation. In addition to these sci-fi novels, Richards has also penned the "Invisible Detective" series, which includes *Double Life, The Shadow Beast,* and *Ghost Soldiers.* In the "Invisible Detective" series, mysterious sleuth Brandon Lake solves crime in 1930s London. Lake is not a single person, however; he is actually the creation of four imaginative teens: Art, Meg, Johnny, and Flinch, who are helped in their effort by Art's policeman father. Time travel elements also figure in the series; a parallel story taking place in modern times finds a boy named Art discovering the chronicles of the detectives, only to realize that the decades-old document seems to be written in his own handwriting.

The "Invisible Detective" series begins with *Double Life*—published in England as *The Paranormal Puppet Show*—as the Invisible Detective band investigates missing persons and an exhibition of strange, life-like mannequins, while also unearthing a plot against the duke of York. In the second book, *The Shadow Beast,* the four teens follow clues leading them to the maze of underground tunnels below London, where they encounter a vicious, rat-like beast that is controlled by the same man who has masterminded recent bank robberies. "The dark and menacing world beneath the streets of London is richly evoked, and the detectives' encounter with a mass of scurrying rats is guaranteed to give plenty of kids the creeps," commented *Booklist* critic Todd Morning. In *School Library Journal* Dana Pierce wrote that the first two books in the series are "fast-paced, action-packed stories" that should interest teen mystery buffs.

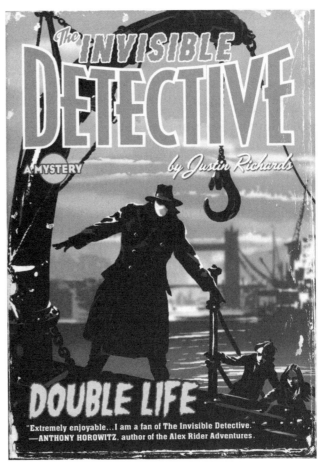

In this installment in Richards' popular crime-fighter series, the young crime solvers must track some sinister puppets that seem to be taking the place of real people. (Cover illustration by David Frankland.)

Biographical and Critical Sources

PERIODICALS

Booklist, August, 2005, Todd Morning, review of *The Shadow Beast,* p. 2030.

Kliatt, March, 2005, Julie Scordato, review of *The Paranormal Puppet Show,* p. 53.

School Librarian, winter, 2004, Chris Brown, review of *Web of Anubis,* p. 204.

School Library Journal, July, 2005, B. Allison Gray, review of *The Invisible Detective* (audiobook), p. 58; October, 2005, Dana Pierce, review of *Double Life,* p. 172.

Voice of Youth Advocates, August, 2005, Mary Arnold, review of *Double Life,* p. 237.

ONLINE

Fantastic Fiction Web site, http://www.fantasticfiction.co.uk/ (December 14, 2005), "Justin Richards."

Invisible Detective Web site, http://www.invisible-detective.com/ (February 24, 2006).

Outpost Gallifrey Web site, http://www.fallifreyone.com/ (December 14, 2005), interview with Richards.

ROSS, Katharine Reynolds
See ROSS, Kathy

*   *   *

ROSS, Kathy 1948-
(Katharine Reynolds Ross)

Personal
Born July 10, 1948, in Saginaw, MI; daughter of Frederick Perry (an engineer) and Katharine (a homemaker; maiden name, Edwards) Reynolds; married Thomas Byron Ross (a company vice president in charge of advertising), June 15, 1968; children: Greyson Reynolds, Allison Ashley. *Education:* Attended Lake Erie College, 1966-68. *Religion:* Episcopalian. *Hobbies and other interests:* Collecting antique paper dolls, reading children's literature, animals.

Addresses
Home—121 The Vineyard, Oneida, NY 13421. *E-mail*—tross1@twcny.rr.com.

Career
Ross Educational Systems, Inc., Oneida, NY, owner, president, and nursery school teacher, beginning 1983. Preschool consultant for *Highlights for Children;* song writer for McMillan Sing-and-Learn Program. Lay eucharistic minister.

Member
People for the Ethical Treatment of Animals, Sherrill-Kenwool Free Library, Progress Club (Oneida, NY).

Awards, Honors
Pewter Plate Award, *Highlights for Children,* 1990; *Every Day Is Earth Day* named an American Booksellers Association Pick of the List, 1995.

Writings

Gifts to Make for Your Favorite Grownups, illustrated by Anne Canevari Green, Millbrook Press (Minneapolis, MN), 1996.

The Jewish Holiday Craft Book, illustrated by Melinda Levine, Millbrook Press (Brookfield, CT), 1997.

Make Yourself a Monster!, illustrated by Sharon Hawkins Vargo, Millbrook Press (Brookfield, CT), 1999.

The Best Birthday Parties Ever!: A Kid's Do-It-Yourself Guide, illustrated by Sharon Lane Holm, Millbrook Press (Brookfield, CT), 1999.

(Editor) *Look What You Can Make with Plastic Bottles and Tubs,* photographs by Hank Schneider, Boyds Mills Press (Honesdale, PA), 2001.

Kathy Ross

(Editor) *Look What You Can Make with Newspapers, Magazines, and Greeting Cards,* photographs by Hank Schneider, Boyds Mills Press (Honesdale, PA), 2001.

Crafts That Celebrate Black History, illustrated by Jenny Stow, Millbrook Press (Brookfield, CT), 2002.

(Editor) *Look What You Can Make with Dozens of Household Items!,* photographs by Hank Schneider, Boyds Mills Press (Honesdale, PA), 2002.

Things to Make for Your Doll, illustrated by Elaine Garvin, Millbrook Press (Brookfield, CT), 2003.

The Storytime Craft Book, illustrated by Vicki Enright and Elaine Garvin, Millbrook Press (Brookfield, CT), 2003.

Star-Spangled Crafts, illustrated by Sharon Lane Holm, Millbrook Press (Brookfield, CT), 2003.

All-Girl Crafts, illustrated by Elaine Garvin, Millbrook Press (Minneapolis, MN), 2005.

The Scrapbooker's Idea Book, illustrated by Nichole in den Bosch, Millbrook Press (Minneapolis, MN), 2007.

The Girlfriends' Pajama Party Craft Book, illustrated by Nichole in den Bosch, Millbrook Press (Minneapolis, MN), 2007.

Creator of over eight hundred crafts published in *Highlights for Children;* contributor of craft column to *Oneida Daily Dispatch.*

"HOLIDAY CRAFTS FOR KIDS" SERIES

Crafts for Halloween, illustrated by Sharon Lane Holm, Millbrook Press (Minneapolis, MN), 1994.

Crafts for Kwanzaa, illustrated by Sharon Lane Holm, Millbrook Press (Minneapolis, MN), 1994.

Every Day Is Earth Day: A Craft Book, illustrated by Sharon Lane Holm, Millbrook Press (Minneapolis, MN), 1995.

Crafts for Valentine's Day, illustrated by Sharon Lane Holm, Millbrook Press (Minneapolis, MN), 1995.

Crafts for Easter, illustrated by Sharon Lane Holm, Millbrook Press (Minneapolis, MN), 1995.

Crafts for Thanksgiving, illustrated by Sharon Lane Holm, Millbrook Press (Minneapolis, MN), 1995.

Crafts for Christmas, illustrated by Sharon Lane Holm, Millbrook Press (Minneapolis, MN), 1995.

Crafts for Hanukkah, illustrated by Sharon Lane Holm, Millbrook Press (Minneapolis, MN), 1996.

The Best Holiday Crafts Ever, illustrated by Sharon Lane Holm, Millbrook Press (Brookfield, CT), 1997.

Crafts for St. Patrick's Day, illustrated by Sharon Lane Holm, Millbrook Press (Brookfield, CT), 1999.

More Best Holiday Crafts Ever!, illustrated by Sharon Lane Holm, Millbrook Press (Brookfield, CT), 2003.

"ALL-NEW HOLIDAY CRAFTS FOR KIDS" SERIES

All-New Crafts for Valentine's Day, illustrated by Barbara Leonard, Millbrook Press (Brookfield, CT), 2002.

All-New Crafts for Halloween, illustrated by Barbara Leonard, Millbrook Press (Brookfield, CT), 2002.

All-New Crafts for Thanksgiving, illustrated by Sharon Lane Holm, Millbrook Press (Brookfield, CT), 2004.

All-New Crafts for Easter, illustrated by Sharon Lane Holm, Millbrook Press (Brookfield, CT), 2004.

All-New Crafts for Earth Day, illustrated by Sharon Lane Holm, Millbrook Press (Minneapolis, MN), 2006.

All-New Crafts for Kwanzaa, illustrated by Sharon Lane Holm, Millbrook Press (Minneapolis, MN), 2007.

"CRAFTS FROM YOUR FAVORITE SONGS AND STORIES" SERIES

Crafts from Your Favorite Fairy Tales, illustrated by Vicky Enright, Millbrook Press (Brookfield, CT), 1997.

Crafts from Your Favorite Bible Stories, illustrated by Sharon Lane Holm, Millbrook Press (Brookfield, CT), 2000.

Crafts from Your Favorite Children's Stories, illustrated by Elaine Garvin, Millbrook Press (Brookfield, CT), 2001.

Crafts from Your Favorite Children's Songs, illustrated by Vicky Enright, Millbrook Press (Brookfield, CT), 2001.

Crafts from Your Favorite Nursery Rhymes, illustrated by Elaine Garvin, Millbrook Press (Brookfield, CT), 2002.

"CRAFTS FOR KIDS WHO ARE WILD ABOUT . . ." SERIES

Crafts for Kids Who Are Wild about the Rainforest, illustrated by Sharon Lane Holm, Millbrook Press (Brookfield, CT), 1997.

Crafts for Kids Who Are Wild about Insects, illustrated by Sharon Lane Holm, Millbrook Press (Brookfield, CT), 1997.

Crafts for Kids Who Are Wild about Dinosaurs, illustrated by Sharon Lane Holm, Millbrook Press (Brookfield, CT), 1997.

Crafts for Kids Who Are Wild about the Wild, illustrated by Sharon Lane Holm, Millbrook Press (Brookfield, CT), 1998.

Crafts for Kids Who Are Wild about Reptiles, illustrated by Sharon Lane Holm, Millbrook Press (Brookfield, CT), 1998.

Crafts for Kids Who Are Wild about Polar Life, illustrated by Sharon Lane Holm, Millbrook Press (Brookfield, CT), 1998.

Crafts for Kids Who Are Wild about Oceans, illustrated by Sharon Lane Holm, Millbrook Press (Brookfield, CT), 1998.

Crafts for Kids Who Are Wild about Deserts, illustrated by Sharon Lane Holm, Millbrook Press (Brookfield, CT), 1998.

"CRAFTS FOR ALL SEASONS" SERIES

Crafts to Make in the Spring, illustrated by Vicky Enright, Millbrook Press (Brookfield, CT), 1998.

Crafts to Make in the Fall, illustrated by Vicky Enright, Millbrook Press (Brookfield, CT), 1998.

Crafts to Make in the Winter, illustrated by Vicki Enright, Millbrook Press (Brookfield, CT), 1999.

Crafts to Make in the Summer, illustrated by Vicki Enright, Millbrook Press (Brookfield, CT), 1999.

Crafts for All Seasons, illustrated by Vicky Enright, Millbrook Press (Brookfield, CT), 2000.

"CHRISTMAS CRAFTS FOR KIDS" SERIES

Christmas Ornaments Kids Can Make, illustrated by Sharon Lane Holm, Millbrook Press (Brookfield, CT), 1998.

Christmas Decorations Kids Can Make, illustrated by Sharon Lane Holm, Millbrook Press (Brookfield, CT), 1999.

More Christmas Ornaments Kids Can Make, illustrated by Sharon Lane Holm, Millbrook Press (Brookfield, CT), 2000.

Christmas Presents Kids Can Make, illustrated by Sharon Lane Holm, Millbrook Press (Brookfield, CT), 2001.

The Best Christmas Crafts Ever, illustrated by Sharon Lane Holm, Millbrook Press (Brookfield, CT), 2002.

"CHRISTIAN CRAFTS FOR KIDS" SERIES

Crafts for Christian Values, illustrated by Sharon Lane Holm, Millbrook Press (Brookfield, CT), 2000.

Crafts to Celebrate God's Creation, illustrated by Sharon Lane Holm, Millbrook Press (Brookfield, CT), 2001.

Christian Crafts for Christmastime, illustrated by Sharon Lane Holm, Millbrook Press (Brookfield, CT), 2001.

The Big Book of Christian Crafts, illustrated by Sharon Lane Holm, Millbrook Press (Brookfield, CT), 2002.

"PLAY-DOH CRAFTS" SERIES

Play-Doh Halloween, illustrated by Sharon Vargo, Millbrook Press (Brookfield, CT), 2001.

Play-Doh Art Projects, illustrated by Sharon Hawkins Vargo, Millbrook Press (Brookfield, CT), 2002.

Play-Doh Animal Fun, illustrated by Sharon Hawkins Vargo, Millbrook Press (Brookfield, CT), 2002.

Play-Doh Fun and Games, illustrated by Sharon Hawkins Vargo, Millbrook Press (Brookfield, CT), 2003.

"EARLY LEARNING CRAFTS"

Kathy Ross Crafts Letter Sounds, illustrated by Jan Barger, Millbrook Press (Brookfield, CT), 2002.

Kathy Ross Crafts Letter Shapes, illustrated by Jan Barger, Millbrook Press (Brookfield, CT), 2002.

Kathy Ross Crafts Triangles, Rectangles, Circles, and Squares, illustrated by Jan Barger, Millbrook Press (Brookfield, CT), 2002.

Kathy Ross Crafts Numbers, illustrated by Jan Barger, Millbrook Press (Brookfield, CT), 2003.

Kathy Ross Crafts Colors, illustrated by Jan Barger, Millbrook Press (Brookfield, CT), 2003.

"CRAFTS FOR KIDS WHO ARE LEARNING ABOUT . . ." SERIES

Crafts for Kids Who Are Learning about Community Workers, illustrated by Jan Barger, Millbrook Press (Minneapolis, MN), 2005.

Crafts for Kids Who Are Learning about the Weather, illustrated by Jan Barger, Millbrook Press (Minneapolis, MN), 2006.

Crafts for Kids Who Are Learning about Transportation, illustrated by Jan Barger, Millbrook Press (Minneapolis, MN), 2007.

Sidelights

Kathy Ross has enjoyed dolls, paper dolls, gum-ball machine charms, and making things since she was a young girl. On her home page, Ross noted: "I *still* like dolls, paper dolls, and gum ball machine charms . . . and I still like to MAKE THINGS!" Ross's enthusiasm for creating has led her to write more than sixty books chock full of crafty projects geared for young readers. "Ross has become a synonym for creative," wrote Kelly Milner Halls in a *Booklist* review of Ross's *Christmas Presents Kids Can Make.* The author also takes her creativity beyond the printed page, offering summer workshops for teachers and traveling to schools to make presentations to students.

Many of Ross's craft collections appear in series focusing on specific themes, such as holidays, seasons, stories, and songs. The "Crafts for Kids Who Are Wild about . . ." series features different climates and types of animals, including rainforests, insects, and dinosaurs. In a review of *Crafts for Kids Who Are Wild about Oceans,* Carolyn Phelan, in *Booklist,* said of the series that, "Upbeat and practical, these books will please." In *Booklist,* Phelan wrote of two other entries in the series that they serve as "an attractive source of practical ideas."

Several of Ross's books focus on the holidays. Her *Christmas Ornaments Kids Can Make* features crafts kids can make on their own, without help from adults. "Ross has some great ideas for using household items," wrote Lauren Peterson in a *Booklist* review. The sequel, *More Christmas Ornaments Kids Can Make,* is "both practical and satisfying" according to Susan Dove Lempke in *Booklist. Christmas Presents Kids Can Make* focuses on hand-made gifts to be given during the Christmas holiday. Though there are a number of such craft books available, according to a *School Library Journal* reviewer, "this one holds a rare place among them." Ross's "All-New Holiday Crafts for Kids" series introduces an assortment of holiday crafts not featured in earlier books. "Children looking for new ideas need look no further," wrote Susannah Price in *School Library Journal.*

Broadening beyond specific holidays, Ross's "Crafts for All Seasons" series uses seasonal tie-ins as topics for the crafts. Of *Crafts to Make in the Winter,* Shelle Rosenfeld wrote in *Booklist* that the author's "multicultural, religiously inclusive book features some unusual and fun ideas." *Crafts for All Seasons,* which draws on the other titles of the series, was described by Phelan as "an attractive and economical way to bolster craft collections."

The "Crafts from Your Favorite Stories and Songs" series takes ideas from familiar stories and songs for classroom or at-home projects. *Crafts from Your Favorite Bible Stories* "provides practical craft ideas for religious settings," wrote Phelan in *Booklist.* In a review of *Crafts from Your Favorite Nursery Rhymes* in the same publication, Phelan noted that "librarians may want to dip into this book for preschool program ideas."

The "Christian Crafts for Kids" books provide craft ideas specifically geared toward a Christian audience. *Crafts to Celebrate God's Creation* is based on the creation story in Genesis. *Booklist* reviewer Phelan considered it "a useful resource for Sunday-school teachers." Of *Crafts for Christian Values,* which features projects based on traditional Christian virtues, Patricia Pearl Dole noted in a *School Library Journal* review that "church-school teachers and parents will find these craft ideas useful and fun to create."

Educational projects with Play-Doh are the focus of the "Play-Doh Crafts" series. *Play-Doh Animal Fun* introduces concepts of animal habitats through crafts. "With a wide variety of ideas, the book encourages creativity," wrote Mary Elam in *School Library Journal.* Another of Ross's educational series is "Early Learning Crafts," designed for the very young. Of the series, which includes *Kathy Ross Crafts Letter Shapes,* Rita Hunt Smith wrote in *School Library Journal* that "these attractive books present hands-on projects to accompany phonics and letter recognition lessons." *Kathy Ross Crafts Numbers* is "a worthy collection of crafts that incorporates early math skills" according to Susannah Price in *School Library Journal.*

Ross also has several stand alone titles, some geared toward a specific female audience, others focused on historic figures. *Crafts That Celebrate Black History* offers crafts about black history, and after each craft, Ross "includes an interesting fact about these historic figures," noted Lynda Jones in *Black Issues Book Review*. *All-Girl Crafts* and *The Girlfriends' Pajama Party Craft Book* both feature crafts to specifically appeal to girls. Of the former, Augusta R. Malvagno wrote in *School Library Journal* that "this book is sure to please children and the adults who assist them."

Ross once told *SATA:* "I was never even close to the best drawer in art class. I could not sew well, knit, or needlepoint, and I still can't seem to manage those skills. It never bothered me. For as long as I can remember, I have loved to make things. And I still do. I have a cellar full of materials that people have saved for me. I definitely have a reputation for turning throwaways into fun and useful projects.

"I also love to sing. Again, I'm not a great singer and I can't read music, but I have written several songs for small children that are enjoyed in schools across the country.

"In this highly competitive day and age, I think that many children are discouraged from pursuing areas that they simply enjoy because they do not display an obvious talent. If you love doing something, do it. The happiness found in doing what you truly enjoy is immeasurable, and you never know where it might lead you. The success of my books and records has put me in a state of delighted amazement. I'm having a great time."

Biographical and Critical Sources

PERIODICALS

Black Issues Book Review, January-February, 2003, Lynda Jones, review of *Crafts That Celebrate Black History,* p. 66.

Booklist, October 15, 1994, p. 433; April 15, 1998, Carolyn Phelan, review of *Crafts for Kids Who Are Wild about Oceans,* p. 1443; October 15, 1998, Lauren Peterson, review of *Christmas Ornaments Kids Can Make,* p. 419; March 15, 1999, Carolyn Phelan, review of *Crafts for Kids Who Are Wild about Polar Life* and *Crafts for Kids Who Are Wild about Deserts,* p. 1328; December 15, 1998, Carolyn Phelan, review of *Christmas Decorations Kids Can Make,* p. 783, and Shelle Rosenfeld, review of *Crafts to Make in the Winter,* p. 788; June 1, 2000, Carolyn Phelan, review of *Crafts from Your Favorite Bible Stories,* p. 1888; September 1, 2000, Susan Dove Lempke, review of *More Christmas Ornaments Kids Can Make,* p. 128; October 15, 2000, Carolyn Phelan, review of *Crafts for All Seasons,* p. 62; January 1, 2001, Carolyn Phelan, review of *Crafts to Celebrate God's Creation,* p. 946; September 15, 2001, Kelly Milner Halls, review of *Christmas Presents Kids Can Make,* p. 234; December 15, 2002, Stephanie Zvirin, review of *Look What You Can Make with Dozens of Household Items!,* p. 762; January 1, 2003, Carolyn Phelan, review of *Crafts from Your Favorite Nursery Rhymes,* p. 885; April 15, 2003, Carolyn Phelan, review of *Kathy Ross Crafts Numbers,* p. 1473; December 15, 2003, Hazel Rochman, review of *Things to Make for Your Doll,* p. 756; October 1, 2005, Carolyn Phelan, review of *All-New Crafts for Thanksgiving,* p. 54.

Instructor, April, 1995, p. 14.

Library Media Connection, October, 2003, review of *Star-Spangled Crafts,* p. 75.

Library Talk, November, 1994, p. 32; May, 1995, p. 23.

Publishers Weekly, May 18, 1998, review of *Crafts from Your Favorite Fairy Tales,* p. 82; January 14, 2002, review of *Kathy Ross Crafts Letter Shapes,* p. 63; January 6, 2003, review of *Look What You Can Make with Dozens of Household Items!,* p. 62.

School Library Journal, January, 1995, p. 105; April, 1995, p. 128; May, 1995, p. 102; October, 1998, Lisa Falk, review of *Christmas Ornaments Kids Can Make,* p. 44; April, 2000, Teri Markson, review of *Make Yourself a Monster!,* p. 125; August, 2000, Patricia Pearl Dole, review of *Crafts from Your Favorite Bible Stories,* p. 175; October, 2000, Susannah Price, review of *More Christmas Ornaments Kids Can Make,* p. 62; February, 2001, Patricia Pearl Dole, review of *Crafts for Christian Values,* p. 114; May, 2001, Dona J. Helmer, review of *Crafts from Your Favorite Children's Songs,* p. 145, and Patricia Pearl Dole, review of *Crafts to Celebrate God's Creation,* p. 146; September, 2001, Lynda Ritterman, review of *Crafts from Your Favorite Children's Stories,* p. 221; October, 2001, review of *Christian Crafts for Christmastime,* p. 68, and review of *Christmas Presents Kids Can Make,* p. 69; April, 2002, Lynda Ritterman, review of *Look What You Can Make with Newspapers, Magazines, and Greeting Cards,* p. 132; May, 2002, Mary Elam, review of *Play-Doh Animal Fun,* p. 144; June, 2002, Rita Hunt Smith, review of *Kathy Ross Crafts Letter Shapes* and *Kathy Ross Shapes Letter Sounds,* p. 124; November, 2002, Susannah Price, review of *All-New Crafts for Valentine's Day,* p. 147; December, 2002, Genevieve Gallagher, review of *Crafts from Your Favorite Nursery Rhymes,* p. 128; January, 2003, review of *Kathy Ross Crafts Triangles, Rectangles, Circles, and Squares,* p. 128; July, 2003, Marion F. Gallivan, review of *Star-Spangled Crafts,* p. 148; October, 2003, Susannah Price, review of *Kathy Ross Crafts Numbers,* p. 156; October, 2005, Augusta R. Malvagno, review of *All-Girl Crafts,* p. 144.

Science Books and Films, May, 1995, p. 113.

ONLINE

Kathy Ross Home Page, http://www.kathyross.com (March 22, 2006).*

ROTNER, Shelley 1951-

Personal

Born January 1, 1951, in New York, NY; daughter of William and Babette (an author and guidance counselor) Rotner; married Stephen Calcagnino (an arts administrator), January 31, 1981; children: Emily. *Education:* Attended Syracuse University Extension Program, 1972; Syracuse University, B.A., 1972; postgraduate study at Columbia University, 1977; Bank Street College of Education, M.A., 1979.

Addresses

Home—48 Ward Ave., Northampton, MA 01060. *E-mail*—Shellro243@aol.com.

Career

Photographer, writer, and educator. Aggasiz Community School District, Cambridge, MA, photography instructor, 1975; Learning Guild, Boston, MA, photography instructor, 1975-76; Lincoln Community School System, Cambridge, MA, photography instructor, 1975-76; International Center of Photography, New York, NY, assistant photography instructor, 1977; Bank Street School for Children, New York, NY, photography instructor, 1977-78; U.N. Photo Library, New York, NY, photo researcher, 1977-78; International Center of Photography, New York, NY, curatorial assistant, 1977-78; American Museum of Natural History, New York, NY, photography instructor, 1979; United Nations and UNICEF, New York, NY, photographer, 1979—. *Exhibitions:* Photographs exhibited at galleries and museums in Holyoke, MA; Springfield, MA; Boston, MA; New York, NY; Seattle, WA; and Portland, ME, including American Museum of Natural History and International Center of Photography.

Awards, Honors

Grand Prize, *Natural History* magazine photo competition, 1979; Third Prize, World Photographic Society, 1983, for color photographs of children; Northampton, MA, Arts Lottery, 1984, 1985; Grand Emmy Award, Polaroid Corporation, 1986; *Parade*/Kodak award finalist, 1988; First Prize, Zone Gallery, Springfield, MA, for color portraits.

Writings

(With Marjorie N. Allen) *Changes,* Macmillan (New York, NY), 1991.
Nature Spy, Macmillan (New York, NY), 1992.
Action Alphabet, Picture Book Studio, 1993.
City Streets, Orchard (New York, NY), 1993.
(And photographer, with Ken Kreisler) *Citybook,* Orchard (New York, NY), 1994.

(And photographer, with Ken Kreisler) *Faces,* Macmillan (New York, NY), 1994.
Wheels Around, Houghton Mifflin (Boston, MA), 1995.
(And photographer, with Julia Pemberton Hellums) *Hold the Anchovies!: A Book about Pizza,* Orchard (New York, NY), 1996.
(And photographer, with Richard Olivo) *Close, Closer, Closest,* Atheneum (New York, NY), 1997.
Boats Afloat, Orchard (New York, NY), 1998.
(With Cheo García) *Pick a Pet,* Orchard (New York, NY), 1999.
(And photographer, with Steve Calcagnino) *The Body Book,* Orchard (New York, NY), 2000.
(And photographer) *Parts,* Walker (New York, NY), 2001.
(And photographer, with Ken Kreisler) *Everybody Works,* Millbrook Press (Brookfield, CT), 2003.
Lots of Feelings, Millbrook Press (Brookfield, CT), 2003.
(And photographer, with Gary Goss) *Where Does Food Come From?,* Millbrook Press (Minneapolis, MN), 2006.
(And photographer) *Senses at the Seashore,* Millbrook Press (Minneapolis, MN), 2006.

AND PHOTOGRAPHER; WITH SHEILA M. KELLY

Lots of Moms, Dial (New York, NY), 1996.
Lots of Dads, DK (New York, NY), 1997.
About Twins, DK (New York, NY), 1999.
The A.D.D. Book for Kids, Millbrook Press (Brookfield, CT), 2000.
Feeling Thankful, Millbrook Press (Brookfield, CT), 2000.
Lots of Grandparents, Millbrook Press (Brookfield, CT), 2001.
What Can You Do?: A Book about Discovering What You Do Well, Millbrook Press (Brookfield, CT), 2001.
Good-byes, Millbrook Press (Brookfield, CT), 2002.
Something's Different, Millbrook Press (Brookfield, CT), 2002.
Many Ways: How Many Families Practice Their Beliefs and Religions, Millbrook Press (Minneapolis, MN), 2006.

PHOTOGRAPHER

Ellen Jackson, *Sometimes Bad Things Happen,* Millbrook Press (Brookfield, CT), 2002.

Sidelights

Shelley Rotner worked as a teacher, a photographer, and a curatorial assistant before she became involved in the creation of children's books. As she once told *SATA:* "After several years as an educator both in the classroom and in museum settings and after the birth of my daughter, I started to think about ideas for children's books. My daughter always loved to look at books and as she grew I started to think and write about the subjects that interested her." These subjects have varied from families and traditions, to feelings, to machines. As both an author and a photographer, Rotner has worked on many titles for young readers that celebrate differences or answer common questions asked by children.

Rotner's early works combine action and description with vivid photographs, sometimes taken by Rotner herself. Her book *Action Alphabet* helps young readers identify verbs; each letter of the alphabet is matched up with an action shown in the accompanying photograph. Annie Ayres recommended the title in her *Booklist* review, commenting, "Consider P for Purchasing." Another of Rotner's early titles, *Wheels Around,* describes both wheels and vehicles, from bicycles to dump trucks. Rotner focuses on variety, showing a wide range of machines that make use of wheels. *Horn Book* contributor Elizabeth S. Watson considered the title "a neatly crafted, spectacularly graphic study of wheels and the vehicles they support." As *Booklist* contributor Hazel Rochman noted, "eager vehicle-watchers will love the action" in the book. Like *Wheels Around, Boats Afloat* shows young readers a variety of sailing vessels, from canoes and jet skies to larger motor boats. Carolyn Phelan, writing in *Booklist,* called the title "clear and well composed."

Parts, which features both Rotner's words and photographs, is a puzzle book wherein readers try to identify a whole object from the parts shown in the photograph. Designed for the pre-school audience, the book is structured as a guessing game. "Sharp, colorful close-up pictures fill the pages, while a snappy text offers hints about the answer," wrote Beth Tegart of *School Library Journal.* Carolyn Phelan wrote in *Booklist* that the "guessing game approach, the familiar objects, and the clear colorful photographs . . . make this fun."

Fellow writer Sheila M. Kelly teams up with Rotner for a number of titles, Rotner serving as photographer and coauthor. Their *Lots of Moms* is a photo-essay about the loving relationship between mothers and their children. "The photos . . . emphasize the intimacy of the mother-child bond," commented a *Publishers Weekly* reviewer, who noted the racial diversity of the featured mother-child pairs. The coauthors continue their collaboration with *Lots of Dads,* this time celebrating the father's role in the parent-child relationship. "Whatever kind of dad a kid is blessed with, he can be found in this utterly winning photo-essay," wrote GraceAnne A. DeCandido in *Booklist.*

Siblings are the topic of Kelly and Rotner's *About Twins.* The text explains how twins are different from other types of siblings, and features many portraits of twins of different ages. "The photographs will compel youngsters to study these children and note their differences," commented Kathy Broderick in a review for *Booklist.* Rotner and Kelly have also written a title about grandparents in *Lots of Grandparents,* as well as a book focusing on diverse family traditions with *Many Ways: How Families Practice Their Beliefs and Religions. Booklist* writer Carolyn Phelan found the latter title to be "a fine visual introduction to a basic American freedom."

Kelly and Rotner also offer advice to children trying to understand Attention Deficit Disorder (ADD), wondering how to describe what they are thankful for, hoping to discover their own talents, or dealing with a change in their family life. *The A.D.D. Book for Kids* uses quotes from children who have A.D.D. and describes symptoms of the disorder, as well as strategies to cope with it. "Crisp, clear, well-chosen photos . . . make for an eye-catching and uncluttered format," commented Kay Weisman in *Booklist. Feeling Thankful* encourages children through words and pictures to identify the things in their life they have to be thankful for. "Overall, an appealing selection," Karen Scott said of the title in her *School Library Journal* review. *Booklist* contributor Ilene Cooper commented on the "very crisp, joyful pictures," and noted: "There will be a myriad of ways to use this."

What Can You Do?: A Book about Discovering What You Can Do Well helps young people identify their strengths. "The message [everyone is good at something] comes through strongly," wrote *Booklist* contributor Kay Weisman. In *Something's Different,* Rotner and Kelly describe the thought process of a boy whose parents are struggling in their marriage and may be preparing to divorce. "Hand-tinted photos capture the boy's changing emotions," *Booklist* contributor Shelle Rosenfeld noted of the artwork. Linda Beck, writing in *School Library Journal,* felt that the book takes "an interesting approach to an issue not often explored in juvenile nonfiction."

With cowriter Julia Pemberton Hellums, Rotner celebrates America's love affair with pizza in *Hold the Anchovies!: A Book about Pizza* another title featuring Rotner's photography. The book follows the process of making a pizza from scratch, and includes a recipe for basic pizza at the end of the book. Readers will "feast visually on this scrumptious treat," wrote April Judge in *Booklist.* With Richard Olivo, Rotner designed a skewed perspective book, showing household items at three different distances. The extreme close-ups show a microscopic view of the object. Lolly Robinson, reviewing the title for *Horn Book,* praised the book's "striking presentation." Though *Booklist* contributor Hazel Rochman felt that the concepts might be difficult for young readers to appreciate, she nonetheless noted: "once they get the idea . . . they will have fun discovering the hidden worlds around them."

Cheo García worked with Rotner on *Pick a Pet,* a picture book about a girl named Patty who imagines what type of pet she would like to have. "Kids will like the animals, both real and fanciful," assured *Booklist* reviewer Denia Hester. With Steve Calcagnino, Rotner has produced *The Body Book,* which describes the parts of the body and what they do. *Booklist* contributor Carolyn Phelan called the book "upbeat, brief, and to the point."

Along with her work as a photo-illustrator and writer, Rotner offers presentations to schools, taking listeners

through the process of making a book "from start to finish," according to her home page. She makes her home in western Massachusetts.

Biographical and Critical Sources

PERIODICALS

Booklist, November 1, 1995, Hazel Rochman, review of *Wheels Around,* p. 475; April 1, 1996, review of *Lots of Moms,* p. 1369; August, 1996, Annie Ayres, review of *Action Alphabet,* p. 1903; September 15, 1996, April Judge, review of *Hold the Anchovies!: A Book about Pizza,* p. 244; April 1, 1997, Hazel Rochman, review of *Close, Closer, Closest,* p. 1336; August, 1997, GraceAnne A. DeCandido, review of *Lots of Dads,* p. 1904; November 1, 1998, Carolyn Phelan, review of *Boats Afloat,* p. 499; June 1, 1999, Kathy Broderick, review of *About Twins,* p. 1835; July, 1999, Denia Hester, review of *Pick a Pet,* p. 1954; March 1, 2000, Carolyn Phelan, review of *The Body Book,* p. 1246; April 15, 2000, Kay Weisman, review of *The A.D.D. Book for Kids,* p. 1549; December 1, 2000, Ilene Cooper, review of *Feeling Thankful,* p. 716; April 15, 2001, Kay Weisman, review of *What Can You Do?: A Book about Discovering What You Do Well,* p. 1562; June 1, 2001, Carolyn Phelan, review of *Parts,* p. 1895; March 1, 2002, Shelle Rosenfeld, review of *Something's Different,* p. 1144; October 1, 2005, Carolyn Phelan, review of *Many Ways: How Families Practice Their Beliefs and Religions,* p. 70.
Bulletin of the Center for Children's Books, April, 1997, review of *Close, Closer, Closest,* p. 294; April, 1999, review of *About Twins,* p. 292.
Horn Book, January-February, 2006, Elizabeth S. Watson, review of *Wheels Around,* p. 93; May-June, 1997, Lolly Robinson, review of *Close, Closer, Closest,* p. 311.
Publishers Weekly, May 6, 1996, review of *Lots of Moms,* p. 79; May 6, 1996, review of *Lots of Moms,* p. 79; November 25, 1996, review of *Colors around Us,* p. 77; November 2, 1998, review of *Boats Afloat,* p. 85.
School Library Journal, December, 1998, Stephani Hutchinson, review of *Boats Afloat,* p. 112; May, 2000, Christine Lindsey, review of *The Body Book,* p. 164; July, 2000, Martha Gordon, review of *The A.D.D. Book for Kids,* p. 97; December, 2000, Karen Scott, review of *Feeling Thankful,* p. 136; May, 2001, review of *Parts,* p. 133; September, 2001, Pamela K. Bomboy, review of *What Can You Do?,* p. 222; August, 2002, Linda Beck, review of *Something's Different,* p. 179; February, 2003, Lucinda Snyder Whitehurst, review of *Sometimes Bad Things Happen,* p. 132; July, 2003, Daryl Grabarek, review of *Everybody Works,* p. 117; October, 2003, review of *Something's Different,* p. S28; April, 2004, Phyllis M. Simon, review of *Lots of Feelings,* p. 142, and review of *Everybody Works,* p. S18; October, 2004, review of *Lots of Feelings,* p. S24.

ONLINE

Shelley Rotner Home Page, http://www.author-illustrsource.com/ShelleyRotner.htm (February 12, 2006).*

ROYSTON, Angela 1945-

Personal

Born February 8, 1945, in Bridlington, Yorkshire, England; daughter of Richard Elsworthy (a chartered accountant) and Chloe Lomas (Locking) Wilkinson; married Robert Royston (a psychotherapist and playwright), September 8, 1979; children: Miranda, Jack. *Ethnicity:* "White." *Education:* University of Edinburgh, M.A., 1966. *Politics:* Green Party. *Religion:* "Agnostic."

Addresses

Home and office—82 Tufnell Park Rd., London N7 0DT, England.

Career

Writer. Worked as a secretary in London, England, 1967-73; Macdonald Educational, London, children's nonfiction editor, 1973-78; Grisewood & Dempsey, London, children's nonfiction editor, 1978-82; freelance writer and editor, 1982—. Writer-in-residence at a primary school in London.

Member

Amnesty International.

Writings

FOR CHILDREN

Picture Word Book, illustrated by Colin Maclean, Moira Maclean, and Liz Graham-Yooll, St. Michael (London, England), 1982.
My First Library Road Travel, Macdonald (London, England), 1986.
Just Look at Road Transport, Macdonald (London, England), 1987, published as *Road Transport,* Rourke Enterprises (Vero Beach, FL), 1988.
Birthday Party ("Stepping Stones 123" series), Warwick (New York, NY), 1988.
Shopping ("Stepping Stones 123" series), Warwick (New York, NY), 1988.
My Family ("Stepping Stones 123" series), Warwick (New York, NY), 1988.
(With Graham Thompson) *Monster Road Builders,* Barron's (New York, NY), 1989.
(With Graham Thompson) *Monster Building Machines,* Barron's (New York, NY), 1990.
Car: See How It Works ("Tell Me About . . ." series), illustrated by Colin King, Frances Lincoln (London, England), 1990, published as *My Lift-the-Flap Car Book,* Barron's (New York, NY), 1991.
(With Terry Pastor) *The A-to-Z Book of Cars,* Barron's (New York, NY), 1991.
Buildings, Bridges, and Tunnels, Warwick Press (New York, NY), 1991.

Flowers, Trees, and Other Plants, Warwick Press (New York, NY), 1991.

The Human Body and How It Works, illustrated by Rob Shone and Chris Forsey, Warwick Press (New York, NY), 1991.

People and Places, Warwick (New York, NY), 1991.

The Senses: A Lift-the-Flap Body Book, illustrated by Edwina Riddell, Barron's (Hauppauge, NY), 1993.

Big Machines, illustrated by Terry Pastor, Little, Brown (Boston, MA), 1994.

(With David Bellamy) *How Green Are You?,* Frances Lincoln (London, England), 1994.

Getting Better, Frances Lincoln (London, England), 1994.

Whirrs, Watts, and Whooshes: The Stories of 14 Inventions That Changed the World, David Bennett Books (London, England), 1994.

Healthy Me (lift-the-flap book), illustrated by Edwina Riddell, Barron's (Hauppauge, NY), 1995.

A First Atlas, Scholastic (New York, NY), 1995.

You and Your Body: 101 Questions and Answers, Facts on File (New York, NY), 1995.

Where Do Babies Come From?, DK Publishing (New York, NY), 1996.

(Translator and adaptor, with Ghislaine Nouvion Severs and others) Christine Lazier, *Wild Animals,* Creative Education (Mankato, MN), 1997.

One Hundred Greatest Medical Discoveries, Grolier Educational (Danbury, CT), 1997.

One Hundred Greatest Women, Grolier Educational (Danbury, CT), 1997.

Fire Fighters!, DK Publishing (New York, NY), 1998.

Digesting: How We Fuel the Body ("Under the Microscope" series), Grolier Educational (Danbury, CT), 1998.

Truck Trouble ("Eyewitness" series), DK Publishing (New York, NY), 1998.

Space Shuttle Mission 7, Ginn (New York, NY), 1998.

Transportation ("Environment Starts Here" series), Raintree-Steck-Vaughn (Austin, TX), 1999.

Recycling ("Environment Starts Here" series), Raintree-Steck-Vaughn (Austin, TX), 1999.

On the Move, Kingfisher (New York, NY), 2000.

Volcanoes, Reader's Digest (Pleasantville, NY), 2000.

Pyramids, Reader's Digest (Pleasantville, NY), 2000.

Mighty Machines: Stories of Machines at Work, Kingfisher (New York, NY), 2000.

Space Station: Accident on Mir, DK Publishing (New York, NY), 2000.

Blue Whales ("Amazing Animals" series), Weigl Publishers (Mankato, MN), 2003.

Junior Science Diagrams on File, Volumes 1-2, Facts on File (New York, NY), 2003.

Alligators and Crocodiles ("Amazing Animals" series), Weigl Publishers (Mankato, MN), 2004.

Wolves ("Amazing Animals" series), Smart Apple Media (Mankato, MN), 2004.

The Life and Times of a Drop of Water: The Water Cycle, Raintree (Chicago, IL), 2006.

The Day the Sun Went Out: The Sun's Energy, Raintree (Chicago, IL), 2006.

Alien Neighbors?: The Solar System, Raintree (Chicago, IL), 2006.

"ANIMAL LIFE STORIES" SERIES

The Deer, illustrated by Bernard Robinson, Warwick (New York, NY), 1988.

The Duck, illustrated by Maurice Pledger and Bernard Robinson, Warwick (New York, NY), 1988.

The Fox, illustrated by Bernard Robinson, Warwick (New York, NY), 1988.

The Otter, illustrated by Bernard Robinson, Warwick (New York, NY), 1988.

The Penguin, illustrated by Trevor Boyer, Warwick (New York, NY), 1988.

The Tiger, illustrated by Graham Allen, Warwick (New York, NY), 1988.

The Elephant, Warwick (New York, NY), 1989.

The Frog, illustrated by Bernard Robinson, Warwick (New York, NY), 1989.

The Hedgehog, illustrated by Maurice Pledger, Warwick (New York, NY), 1989.

The Mouse, illustrated by Maurice Pledger, Warwick (New York, NY), 1989.

The Squirrel, illustrated by Maurice Pledger, Warwick (New York, NY), 1989.

The Whale, illustrated by Jim Channel, Warwick (New York, NY), 1989.

"FARM ANIMAL STORIES" SERIES

Cow, illustrated by Bob Bampton, Warwick (New York, NY), 1990.

Goat, illustrated by Eric Robson, Warwick (New York, NY), 1990.

Hen, illustrated by Dave Cook, Warwick (New York, NY), 1990.

Pig, illustrated by Jim Channel, Warwick (New York, NY), 1990.

Pony, illustrated by Bob Bampton, Warwick (New York, NY), 1990.

Sheep, illustrated by Josephine Martin, Warwick (New York, NY), 1990.

"WHAT'S INSIDE" SERIES

Small Animals, DK Books (New York, NY), 1991.

Insects, DK Books (New York, NY), 1991.

Shells, DK Books (New York, NY), 1991.

Toys, DK Books (New York, NY), 1991.

My Body, DK Books (New York, NY), 1991.

Plants, DK Books (New York, NY), 1991.

"EYE OPENER" SERIES

Cars, photographs by Tim Ridley, illustrated by Jane Cradock-Watson and Dave Hopkins, Aladdin Books (New York, NY), 1991.

Diggers and Dump Trucks, photographs by Tim Ridley, illustrated by Jane Cradock-Watson and Dave Hopkins, Aladdin Books (New York, NY), 1991.

Dinosaurs, photographs by Colin Keates, illustrated by Jane Cradock-Watson and Dave Hopkins, Aladdin Books (New York, NY), 1991.

Jungle Animals, photographs by Philip Dowell, Dave King, and Jerry Young, illustrated by Martine Blaney and Dave Hopkins, Aladdin Books (New York, NY), 1991.

Night-Time Animals, photographs by Dave King, illustrated by Jane Cradock-Watson and Dave Hopkins, Aladdin Books (New York, NY), 1992.

Ships and Boats, photographs by Tim Ridley, illustrated by Jane Cradock-Watson and Dave Hopkins, Aladdin Books (New York, NY), 1992.

Planes, Aladdin Books (New York, NY), 1992.

Sea Animals, photographs by Steve Shott, illustrated by Jane Cradock-Watson and Dave Hopkins, Aladdin Books (New York, NY), 1992.

Insects and Crawly Creatures, photographs by Jerry Young, illustrated by Jane Cradock-Watson and Dave Hopkins, Aladdin Books (New York, NY), 1992.

Trains, photographs by Dave King, illustrated by Jane Cradock-Watson and Dave Hopkins, Aladdin Books (New York, NY), 1992.

Birds, photographs by Dave King, illustrated by Jane Cradock-Watson and Dave Hopkins, Aladdin Books (New York, NY), 1992.

Baby Animals, photographs by Steve Shott and Jane Burton, illustrated by Jane Cradock-Watson and Dave Hopkins, Aladdin Books (New York, NY), 1992.

"SEE HOW THEY GROW" SERIES

Puppy, DK Books (New York, NY), 1991.

Chick, photographs by Jane Burton, Lodestar Books (New York, NY), 1991.

Kitten, photographs by Jane Burton, Lodestar Books (New York, NY), 1991.

Frog, photographs by Kim Taylor and Jane Burton, Lodestar Books (New York, NY), 1991.

Duck, photographs by Barrie Watts, Lodestar Books (New York, NY), 1991.

Mouse, photographs by Barrie Watts, Lodestar Books (New York, NY), 1992.

Rabbit, photographs by Barrie Watts, illustrated by Rowan Clifford, Lodestar Books (New York, NY), 1992.

Lamb, photographs by Gordon Clayton, illustrated by Jane Cradock-Watson, Lodestar Books (New York, NY), 1992.

EDITOR; "SCIENCE NATURE GUIDES" SERIES

Wild Flowers of North America, Thunder Bay Press (San Diego, CA), 1994.

Birds of North America, Thunder Bay Press (San Diego, CA), 1994.

Trees of North America, illustrated by David More, Thunder Bay Press (San Diego, CA), 1994.

John Burton, *Mammals of North America*, illustrated by Jim Channell, Thunder Bay Press (San Diego, CA), 1995.

"BODY SYSTEMS" SERIES

(With Jackie Hardie) *Moving,* Rigby Interactive Library (Crystal Lake, IL), 1997.

Reproduction and Birth, Rigby Interactive Library (Crystal Lake, IL), 1997.

Eating and Digestion, Rigby Interactive Library (Crystal Lake, IL), 1997.

Thinking and Feeling, Rigby Interactive Library (Crystal Lake, IL), 1997.

"GEOGRAPHY STARTS HERE" SERIES

Weather around You, Raintree-Steck-Vaughn (Austin, TX), 1998.

Where People Live, Raintree Steck-Vaughn (Austin, TX), 1998.

Maps and Symbols, Raintree-Steck-Vaughn (Austin, TX), 1999.

"FIRST LIBRARY" SERIES

Life Cycle of a Bean, Heinemann Library (Des Plaines, IL), 1998.

Life Cycle of a Butterfly, Heinemann Library (Des Plaines, IL), 1998.

Life Cycle of a Chicken, Heinemann Library (Des Plaines, IL), 1998.

Life Cycle of a Frog, Heinemann Library (Des Plaines, IL), 1998.

Life Cycle of a Kangaroo, Heinemann Library (Des Plaines, IL), 1998.

Life Cycle of a Guinea Pig, Heinemann Library (Des Plaines, IL), 1998.

Life Cycle of a Sunflower, Heinemann Library (Des Plaines, IL), 1998.

Life Cycle of an Apple, Heinemann Library (Des Plaines, IL), 1998.

Life Cycle of an Oak Tree, Heinemann Library (Des Plaines, IL), 2000.

Life Cycle of a Dog, Heinemann Library (Des Plaines, IL), 2000.

Life Cycle of a Mushroom, Heinemann Library (Des Plaines, IL), 2000.

Life Cycle of a Salmon, Heinemann Library (Des Plaines, IL), 2000.

"INSIDE AND OUT" SERIES

Stars and Planets, illustrated by Stephen Maturin and Roger Stewart, Heinemann Library (Des Plaines, IL), 1998.

Emergency Rescue, illustrated by Roger Stewart, Heinemann Library (Des Plaines, IL), 1998.

Horses and Ponies, Heinemann Library (Des Plaines, IL), 1998.

Flying Machines, illustrated by Sebastian Quigley, Heinemann Library (Des Plaines, IL), 1998.

Boats and Ships, illustrated by John Downes, Heinemann Library (Des Plaines, IL), 1998.

The Earth, illustrated by Jonathan Adams, Heinemann Library (Des Plaines, IL), 1998.

Cars, illustrated by Roger Stewart, Heinemann Library (Des Plaines, IL), 1998.

Under the Sea, Heinemann Library (Des Plaines, IL), 1998.

Trucks, illustrated by Chris Forsey, Heinemann Library (Des Plaines, IL), 1998.

Pets, Heinemann Library (Des Plaines, IL), 1998.

Tractors, illustrated by Terry Gabbey, Heinemann Library (Des Plaines, IL), 1998.

"PLANTS" SERIES

Plants and Us, Heinemann Library (Des Plaines, IL), 1999.

Strange Plants, Heinemann Library (Des Plaines, IL), 1999.

British Plants, Heinemann Library (Des Plaines, IL), 1999.

Trees, Heinemann Library (Des Plaines, IL), 1999.

Flowers, Fruits, and Seeds, Heinemann Library (Des Plaines, IL), 1999.

How Plants Grow, Heinemann Library (Des Plaines, IL), 1999.

"SAFE AND SOUND" SERIES

Fit and Strong, Heinemann Library (Des Plaines, IL), 1999.

Safety First, Heinemann Library (Des Plaines, IL), 2000.

Clean and Healthy, Heinemann Library (Des Plaines, IL), 2000.

Eat Well, Heinemann Library (Des Plaines, IL), 2000.

A Healthy Body, Heinemann Library (Des Plaines, IL), 2000.

"ON THE MOVE" SERIES

The Digger, Kingfisher (New York, NY), 2000.

The Truck, Kingfisher (New York, NY), 2000.

The Tractor, Kingfisher (New York, NY), 2000.

The Tugboat, Kingfisher (New York, NY), 2000.

The Helicopter, Kingfisher (New York, NY), 2000.

The Jumbo Jet, Kingfisher (New York, NY), 2000.

"LEARN TO SAY NO!" SERIES

Tobacco, Heinemann Library (Chicago, IL), 2000.

Alcohol, Heinemann Library (Chicago, IL), 2000.

Marijuana, Heinemann Library (Chicago, IL), 2000.

Inhalants, Heinemann Library (Chicago, IL), 2000.

"IT'S CATCHING" SERIES

Pink Eye, Heinemann Library (Chicago, IL), 2000.

Warts, Heinemann Library (Chicago, IL), 2000.

Chicken Pox, Heinemann Library (Chicago, IL), 2002.

Colds, Heinemann Library (Chicago, IL), 2002.

Head Lice, Heinemann Library (Chicago, IL), 2002.

"MY WORLD OF SCIENCE" SERIES

Using Electricity, Heinemann Library (Chicago, IL), 2001.

Solids, Liquids, and Gasses, Heinemann Library (Chicago, IL), 2001.

Water, Heinemann Library (Chicago, IL), 2001.

Sound and Hearing, Heinemann Library (Chicago, IL), 2001.

Materials, Heinemann Library (Chicago, IL), 2001.

Magnets, Heinemann Library (Chicago, IL), 2001.

Light and Dark, Heinemann Library (Chicago, IL), 2001.

Color, Heinemann Library (Chicago, IL), 2001.

Forces and Motion, Heinemann Library (Chicago, IL), 2001.

Hot and Cold, Heinemann Library (Chicago, IL), 2001.

Bendy and Rigid, Heinemann Library (Chicago, IL), 2003.

Conductors and Insulators, Heinemann Library (Chicago, IL), 2003.

Heavy and Light, Heinemann Library (Chicago, IL), 2003.

Human Growth, Heinemann Library (Chicago, IL), 2003.

Living and Nonliving, Heinemann Library (Chicago, IL), 2003.

Magnetic and Non-Magnetic, Heinemann Library (Chicago, IL), 2003.

Natural and Man-Made, Heinemann Library (Chicago, IL), 2003.

Shiny and Dull, Heinemann Library (Chicago, IL), 2003.

Smooth and Rough, Heinemann Library (Chicago, IL), 2003.

Soft and Hard, Heinemann Library (Chicago, IL), 2003.

Transparent and Opaque, Heinemann Library (Chicago, IL), 2003.

"MACHINES IN ACTION" SERIES

Wheels and Cranks, Heinemann Library (Chicago, IL), 2001.

Pulleys and Gears, Heinemann Library (Chicago, IL), 2001.

Springs, Heinemann Library (Chicago, IL), 2001.

Ramps and Wedges, Heinemann Library (Chicago, IL), 2001.

Levers, Heinemann Library (Chicago, IL), 2001.

Screws, Heinemann Library (Chicago, IL), 2001.

"IN TOUCH" SERIES

Internet and E-mail, Heinemann Library (Chicago, IL), 2002.

Post, Heinemann Library (Chicago, IL), 2002.

Telephone and Fax, Heinemann Library (Chicago, IL), 2002.

"LIVING NATURE" SERIES

Amphibians, Chrysalis Education (North Mankato, MN), 2003.

Birds, Chrysalis Education (North Mankato, MN), 2003.

Fish, Chrysalis Education (North Mankato, MN), 2003.

Flowers, Chrysalis Education (North Mankato, MN), 2003.

Insects, Chrysalis Education (North Mankato, MN), 2003.
Mammals, Chrysalis Education (North Mankato, MN), 2003.
Reptiles, Chrysalis Education (North Mankato, MN), 2003.

"BODY NEEDS" SERIES

Vitamins and Minerals for a Healthy Body, Heinemann Library (Chicago, IL), 2003.
Water and Fiber for a Healthy Body, Heinemann Library (Chicago, IL), 2003.
Proteins for a Healthy Body, Heinemann Library (Chicago, IL), 2003.

"EXTREME SURVIVAL" SERIES

Space, Raintree (Chicago, IL), 2003.
Deserts, Raintree (Chicago, IL), 2004.
Mountains, Raintree (Chicago, IL), 2004.

"LOOK AFTER YOURSELF" SERIES

Get Some Exercise!, Heinemann Library (Chicago, IL), 2003.
Get Some Rest!, Heinemann Library (Chicago, IL), 2003.
Healthy Ears and Eyes, Heinemann Library (Chicago, IL), 2003.
Healthy Food, Heinemann Library (Chicago, IL), 2003.
Healthy Hair, Heinemann Library (Chicago, IL), 2003.
Healthy Skin, Heinemann Library (Chicago, IL), 2003.
Healthy Teeth, Heinemann Library (Chicago, IL), 2003.
Keep Healthy!, Heinemann Library (Chicago, IL), 2003.

"BODY MATTERS" SERIES

Why Do Bones Break? and Other Questions about Bones and Muscles, Heinemann Library (Chicago, IL), 2003.
Why Do Bruises Change Color? and Other Questions about Blood, Heinemann Library (Chicago, IL), 2003.
Why Do I Get a Sunburn? and Other Questions about Skin, Heinemann Library (Chicago, IL), 2003.
Why Do I Get a Toothache? and Other Questions about Nerves, Heinemann Library (Chicago, IL), 2003.
Why Do I Sneeze? and Other Questions about Breathing, Heinemann Library (Chicago, IL), 2003.
Why Do I Vomit? and Other Questions about Digestion, Heinemann Library (Chicago, IL), 2003.
Why Do My Eyes Itch? and Other Questions about Allergies, Heinemann Library (Chicago, IL), 2003.
Why Does My Body Smell? and Other Questions about Hygiene, Heinemann Library (Chicago, IL), 2003.
Why Do We Need to Eat?, Heinemann Library (Chicago, IL), 2006.
Why Do We Need to Be Active?, Heinemann Library (Chicago, IL), 2006.
What Should We Eat?, Heinemann Library (Chicago, IL), 2006.

"BABY ANIMALS" SERIES

Chick, Chrysalis Education (North Mankato, MN), 2004.
Kitten, Chrysalis Education (North Mankato, MN), 2004.
Lamb, Chrysalis Education (North Mankato, MN), 2004.
Puppy, Chrysalis Education (North Mankato, MN), 2004.
Rabbit, Chrysalis Education (North Mankato, MN), 2004.

"IT'S NOT CATCHING" SERIES

Allergies, Heinemann Library (Chicago, IL), 2004.
Asthma, Heinemann Library (Chicago, IL), 2004.
Broken Bones, Heinemann Library (Chicago, IL), 2004.
Bumps and Bruises, Heinemann Library (Chicago, IL), 2004.
Burns and Blisters, Heinemann Library (Chicago, IL), 2004.
Cuts and Grazes, Heinemann Library (Chicago, IL), 2004.
Stings and Bites, Heinemann Library (Chicago, IL), 2004.
Tooth Decay, Heinemann Library (Chicago, IL), 2004.
Using a Wheelchair, Heinemann Library (Chicago, IL), 2005.
Down's Syndrome, Heinemann Library (Chicago, IL), 2005.
Deafness, Heinemann Library (Chicago, IL), 2005.
Cancer, Heinemann Library (Chicago, IL), 2005.
Blindness, Heinemann Library (Chicago, IL), 2005.

"MY AMAZING BODY" SERIES

Breathing, Raintree (Chicago, IL), 2004.
Eating, Raintree (Chicago, IL), 2004.
Growing, Raintree (Chicago, IL), 2004.
Moving, Raintree (Chicago, IL), 2004.
Senses, Raintree (Chicago, IL), 2004.
Staying Healthy, Raintree (Chicago, IL), 2004.

"MY WORLD OF GEOGRAPHY" SERIES

Coasts, Heinemann Library (Oxford, England), 2004, Heinemann Library (Chicago, IL), 2005.
Forests, Heinemann Library (Oxford, England), 2004, Heinemann Library (Chicago, IL), 2005.
Islands, Heinemann Library (Oxford, England), 2004, Heinemann Library (Chicago, IL), 2005.
Deserts, Heinemann Library (Chicago, IL), 2005.
Lakes, Heinemann Library (Chicago, IL), 2005.
Mountains, Heinemann Library (Chicago, IL), 2005.
Oceans, Heinemann Library (Chicago, IL), 2005.
Rivers, Heinemann Library (Chicago, IL), 2005.

"FIVE SENSES" SERIES

Hearing, Chrysalis (North Mankato, MN), 2005.
Touch, Chrysalis (North Mankato, MN), 2005.
Taste, Chrysalis (North Mankato, MN), 2005.
Smell, Chrysalis (North Mankato, MN), 2005.
Sight, Chrysalis (North Mankato, MN), 2005.

"HOW ARE THINGS MADE?" SERIES

How Is Chocolate Made?, Heinemann Library (Chicago, IL), 2005.

How Is a Soccer Ball Made?, Heinemann Library (Chicago, IL), 2005.

How Is a Pencil Made?, Heinemann Library (Chicago, IL), 2005.

How Is a Bicycle Made?, Heinemann Library (Chicago, IL), 2005.

How Is a Book Made?, Heinemann Library (Chicago, IL), 2005.

"LET'S LOOK AT" SERIES

Water: Let's Look at a Puddle, Heinemann Library (Chicago, IL), 2005.

Wood: Let's Look at a Baseball Bat, Heinemann Library (Chicago, IL), 2006.

Soil: Let's Look at a Garden, Heinemann Library (Chicago, IL), 2006.

Rock: Let's Look at Pebbles, Heinemann Library (Chicago, IL), 2006.

Plastic: Let's Look at a Frisbee, Heinemann Library (Chicago, IL), 2006.

Paper: Let's Look at a Comic Book, Heinemann Library (Chicago, IL), 2006.

Metal: Let's Look at a Knife and Fork, Heinemann Library (Chicago, IL), 2006.

Glass: Let's Look at Marbles, Heinemann Library (Chicago, IL), 2006.

All of the titles in the "Let's Look At" series have also been published in Spanish.

OTHER

Henry VIII, Pitkin Unichrome (Andover, Hampshire, England), 1999.

The Six Wives of Henry VIII, Pitkin Unichrome (Andover, Hampshire, England), 1999.

Mary Queen of Scots, Pitkin Unichrome (Andover, Hampshire, England), 1999.

Best of York, Pitkin Unichrome (Andover, Hampshire, England), 1999.

Pitkin Guide to the City of York, Pitkin Unichrome (Andover, Hampshire, England), 1999.

Sidelights

A prolific writer, Angela Royston is the author of numerous nonfiction books for young readers on topics ranging from the human body to the life cycle of a kangaroo to the functioning of a lever. The British author creates books for readers from preschool to the middle grades and, as she once told *SATA,* "I moved into writing from editing and very much enjoy the challenge of writing about a wide variety of subjects." For Royston, it seems, no challenge is too much, and she has taken on subjects as technical as bridge building or the facts of digestion, translating such processes into age-appropriate language. "I had a broad education," Royston explained, "both at school and university, and feel able to tackle almost any subject, provided I can find good research material."

Born in 1945 in the north of England, in Yorkshire, she was educated at the University of Edinburgh where she earned her master's degree in 1966. After graduation, Royston migrated south to London, where she worked as a secretary for seven years, and then found work as a nonfiction editor for children's books in 1973, first with Macdonald Educational and then with Grisewood and Dempsey. This proved an excellent introduction to writing her own nonfiction books for children, and when she began her family, Royston decided to go freelance as a writer and editor full time. With many contacts in the publishing industry, she has worked mostly on commissioned books.

For preschoolers, Royston has written both stand-alone titles and series. Her *Where Do Babies Come From?* is typical Royston, as she "dishes up just the right amount" of information in simplified and concise language, according to a *Publishers Weekly* reviewer. As the same writer further noted, "Royston's matter-of-fact presentation is informative, reassuring and discreet." A contributor for *Kirkus Reviews* called the same book an "outstanding introduction for preschoolers who are already starting to ask a lot of questions about reproduction." This reviewer also commented, "A brief text and stunning full-color photographs provide just enough information to satisfy young questioners." Royston also provides preschoolers with mechanical know-how in both *My Lift-the-Flap Car Book,* which kids "will adore," according to *Booklist* contributor Ilene Cooper, and *Monster Road-Builders* is a look at nine huge machines used in building roads. As *School Library Journal* critic Susan Hepler noted, "Each page features several information-laden sentences," along with double-page spreads of the machines in question.

Royston's series titles for preschoolers include "Stepping Stones 123" and "Farm Animal Stories." Reviewing the six titles in the latter series, *The Cow, The Goat, The Hen, The Pony, The Pig,* and *The Sheep,* Diane Nunn noted in *School Library Journal* that Royston's "narration is in simple story form, relating both daily and seasonal activities of the animals from mating behaviors and birth through adulthood." Nunn felt that the "basic facts are accurate," but warned readers to "be aware that these books depict farm animals in an idyllic rural setting that has disappeared in most areas of the [United States]."

The majority of Royston's books for young readers come in the five-to-seven-year-old category. Popular series for this age group include "Eye Openers," "See How They Grow," "Inside and Out," and "Animal Life Stories," among many others. In "Eye Openers," photographs and drawings are blended with simple text to il-

lustrate and explicate topics from the area of machines such as cars and airplanes, to animals such as dinosaurs and birds. Reviewing *Cars, Diggers and Dump Trucks, Dinosaurs,* and *Jungle Animals* in *School Library Journal,* Steven Engelfried called the series a "winning visual package" with "just enough [information] to satisfy readers or listeners while they pore over the exciting illustrations." In another round-up review of *Baby Animals, Planes, Sea Animals,* and *Ships and Boats,* Dorcas Hand noted in *School Library Journal* that these are "four pleasing offerings for board-book graduates." Hand also remarked, "Each double-page spread. . . . offers a descriptive paragraph and a large, excellent-quality, full-color photograph of the subject." Reviewing *Baby Animals* and *Sea Animals* in *School Librarian,* Joan Hamilton Jones commented that the series "is designed to be both educational and entertaining," and does so "by combining bright photographs with large printed texts." Jones concluded that "The child is led into a world of fascinating information," while Joan Feltwell, also writing in *School Librarian,* praised the series for containing "a feast of fine photographs designed to enthrall and capture the imagination of three-to six-year-olds." *School Library Journal* reviewer Eldon Younce, in a review of Royston's book on trains in the series, thought that "young train enthusiasts will find this slim volume right on track."

Another popular Royston series for beginning readers is "See How They Grow," a group of eight books that focuses on various baby animals and show how they develop, using a story format to inform. Owen Edwards, reviewing the entire series in *Entertainment Weekly,* commented that virtual reality was still only virtual, "but until the nerds catch up with the need, there are the "See How They Grow" books," which "offer lots of pictures, information—and charm." A critic for *Kirkus Reviews* called *Rabbit,* one of the eight books in the series, "an unusually attractive informational book for the youngest." Reviewing *Lamb* and *Mouse* in *School Librarian,* Mary Crawford called the production values of the series "superb," and Crawford concluded: "These books will be popular with a wide range of children as they are both informative and lovely to look at." The "See How They Grow" series shares some qualities with Royston's "First Library" series, which explains the life cycles of various plant and animal species. *Booklist* contributor Carolyn Phelan considered *Life Cycle of a Bean* and other titles in the series to be "useful for primary classrooms studying individual species or life cycles."

Royston's "Inside and Out" series, originally published in England as "A First Look Through," continues this informative look at everyday objects and animals, but with a slightly different twist. The books in this series blend short descriptive paragraphs with acetate double spreads. In "Animal Life Stories," Royston features twelve different creatures: the deer, otter, duck, frog, fox, hedgehog, squirrel, mouse, whale, tiger, elephant, and penguin, in titles named after the animal in question. *Booklist* contributor Isabel Schon, in a review of the Spanish translation of *The Squirrel* (*La Ardilla*), called the entire series "an excellent introduction to the study of these animals," and further remarked that "appealing and informative watercolor illustrations complement the explicit texts." A writer for *Appraisal,* reviewing *The Whale,* dubbed the "Animal Life" series as "aptly named" because the "text consists of factual material, but reads like a story." The same reviewer concluded that *The Whale* "would be appropriate for the beginning reader and for reading aloud." In a round-up review of *The Elephant, The Mouse,* and *The Squirrel,* J.J. Votapka wrote in *School Library Journal:* "Charming full-color illustrations highlight these rather slight stories about the lifestyle of the animals cited in the title," but further noted that the "obvious predictability" of the story format in each title "is apt to wear thin with most children." Another contributor for *Appraisal,* however, praised Royston's "very readable style" in a collective review of *The Fox, The Duck, The Tiger, The Otter,* and *The Penguin.* "Animals are universally the favorite science subject of the five to eight age group," the same reviewer concluded. "These colorful, interesting books are recommended to help fill the need."

Royston has also authored, amongst others, a beginning-reader series that features flora rather than fauna, titled "Plants," and a series that takes a look at human health and well-being titled "Safe and Sound." Reviewing *Flowers, Fruits, and Seeds, How Plants Grow,* and *Strange Plants,* in *School Library Journal,* Katherine Borchert called the three titles "serviceable additions for collections in need of easy nonfiction." Kit Vaughan, also writing in *School Library Journal,* felt that two titles in the "Safe and Sound Series," *Eat Well* and *A Healthy Body,* "inform and educate readers" by the use of "short sentences and a limited vocabulary." Royston's titles for DK's "Eyewitness" series are also aimed at beginning readers; *Truck Trouble* follows a driver trying to make a delivery on a day when nature and his truck seem to be working against his schedule. Susan Dove Lempke of *Booklist* commented on the "little zip of suspense" in the title, as readers wonder if the driver will make his delivery on time. Focusing on smaller, simple machines in her "Machines in Action" series, Royston explains how screws, levers, pulleys, and springs make work easier. Reviewing *Screws* and *Springs* for *School Library Journal,* Maren Ostergard considered these books to be "clear introductions to very specific topics."

In Addition to series titles for young readers, Royston has penned a number of stand-alone books as well as series for middle-grade students. Popular individual titles include *The A-to-Z Book of Cars* and *100 Greatest Medical Discoveries.* In the former book, Royston presents a "browsing guide to automobiles," according to *Booklist* critic Julie Corsaro. Though Corsaro thought that the writing "is nothing special," she still felt that "the book is likely to burn rubber in the circulation department" because of its appealing topic. A writer for

Science Books and Films, reviewing the same title, commented that it is a "wonderful road book." Royston covers more than a hundred medical topics in *100 Greatest Medical Discoveries,* a book that "teems with information by both word and picture," according to a contributor for *Junior Bookshelf.* The same writer remarked that, although the book is aimed at ten to fourteen year olds, it could be "enjoyed by both younger and older groups." Royston's *Big Machines* is a stand-alone title for younger readers, providing "a colorful introduction to nine machines," including the backhoe, street cleaner, and combine, according to Karen Harvey of *Booklist.*

Royston serves up series with both easy and standard reading texts for middle-grade readers. For children with reading difficulties she developed the "First Look At" series, with each title focusing on a different animal species or plant. Delvene Barnett, reviewing Royston's *Fish* in *School Librarian,* found it "inspiring," and one that "could also be used with slow learners and older less able children." Royston's "Science Nature Guides" books also present introductions to wild flowers, trees, birds, and mammals of Great Britain and of North America in separate editions. Each book includes not only text and illustrations, but also activities, such as making a cast of animal footprints in *Mammals of North America.* Reviewing that title in *School Librarian,* Ann Jenkin concluded that "this book is extremely good value and will be enjoyed by 8 to 12-year-olds at school or at home." Reviewing *The Human Body and How It Works,* a writer for *Appraisal* noted that it "includes detailed drawings of the human skeleton, of a developing baby, and experiments that are both appropriate for and of interest to elementary children."

In the "Body Matters" and "It's Not Catching" series, Royston answers questions about natural body functions and diseases for young readers. Titles such as *Why Do I Vomit? And Other Questions about Digestion* and *Why Do My Eyes Itch? And Other Questions about Allergies* address common concerns children have, as well as provide enough information for students needing to write reports about functions of the human body. A reviewer for *School Library Journal* considered the books in this series "accessible introductions." The "It's Not Catching" series illuminates illnesses like *Allergies* and *Tooth Decay,* which people cannot catch from each other. Reviewing *Asthma, Broken Bones,* and *Stings and Bites* for *School Library Journal,* Donna Marie Wagner considered them "concise, informative books filled with facts." Royston's "Look After Yourself" series gives advice to young readers on how to best care for their bodies. "The writing is clear and direct," Joyce Adams Burner of *School Library Journal* said of the series in her review of *Get Some Exercise!* and *Get Some Rest!* In a review of *Healthy Hair* and other titles in the series, Kate Kohlbeck of *School Library Journal* wrote, "These guides provide the basics."

Royston has also investigated how common objects are made in the "How Are Things Made?" series, and

looked at materials and substances through household items in the "Let's Look At" series. Describing objects such as marbles or pebbles to illuminate glass and rock, or considering a puddle to discuss water, the "Let's Look At" series contains such books as *Paper: Let's Look at a Comic Book,* and *Metal: Let's Look at a Knife and Fork.* The "How Are Things Made?" series delves into the creation of soccer balls, books, and chocolate. Reviewing *How Is Chocolate Made?* for *Booklist,* Hazel Rochman noted that the title "covers quite a lot in its step-by-step account of the manufacturing process."

Royston has made a winning combination of simplified text along with well-selected illustrations to come up with individual titles and series that both entertain and inform young readers. In doing so, she follows her own golden rule, as she once explained to *SATA:* "I most like to work on books which are 'fun' and always try to find an interesting approach to explaining or describing things. I always become interested in the subjects of the books I work on, and I hope to stimulate that interest in the reader."

Royston also added to *SATA:* "I am interested in environmental issues, Third World issues, and the work of Amnesty International. I went freelance in 1982 in order to continue my work and expand my career into writing, while at the same time being able to look after and bring up my children. The books I write have all been commissioned by the publishers and, so far, have been mainly for younger children and young readers. I always become interested in the subjects of the books I work on, and I hope to stimulate that interest in the reader."

Later Royston added: "I have recently been a writer-in-residence at a London primary school. I worked with two classes of nine-year-olds and their teachers, and together we produced 500 copies of a twenty-eight page book called *What Can Forces Do?,* written by the children and illustrated with their drawings and with photographs of them carrying out experiments and demonstrating concepts being explained. The book looks very professional and has been well received, much to the children's delight. I found the experience challenging and very rewarding. It was extremely stimulating and informative to be working directly with children as they grappled with understanding and expressing the scientific ideas covered in the book."

Biographical and Critical Sources

PERIODICALS

Appraisal: Science Books for Young People, summer, 1989, review of *The Fox,* p. 82; summer, 1990, review of *The Whale,* pp. 46-47; autumn, 1991, review of *The Human Body and How It Works,* p. 98.
Booklist, February 1, 1991, Isabel Schon, review of *The Squirrel (La Ardilla),* p. 1136; September 15, 1991, Ilene Cooper, review of *My Lift-the-Flap Car Book,* p.

Answering an important question pondered by every sweet tooth, Royston's **How Is Chocolate Made?** *takes readers on a tour of the candy-bar business, from beans to wrapper.*

154; October 15, 1991, Julie Corsaro, review of *The A-to-Z Car Book,* pp. 434-435; January 1, 1994, review of *My Lift-the-Flap Plane Book,* p. 837; March 15, 1994, Karen Harvey, review of *Big Machines,* p. 1369; April 15, 1998, Carolyn Phelan, review of *Life Cycle of a Bean,* p. 1449; July, 1998, Susan Dove Lempke, review of *Fire Fighters* and *Truck Trouble,* p. 189.

Books for Keeps, November, 1994, p. 21.

Entertainment Weekly, April 10, 1992, Owen Edwards, review of "See How They Grow" series, p. 70.

Junior Bookshelf, August, 1995, review of *100 Greatest Medical Discoveries,* p. 150.

Kirkus Reviews, December 15, 1991, review of *Rabbit,* pp. 1597-1598; May 1, 1996, review of *Where Do Babies Come From?,* p. 692.

Library Media Connection, November, 2003, review of *Water and Fiber for a Healthy Body,* p. 79.

Magpies, May, 1994, review of *Plane: See How It Works,* p. 37.

Observer (London, England), July 23, 1995, p. 13.

Publishers Weekly, May 27, 1996, review of *Where Do Babies Come From?,* p. 78.

School Librarian, August, 1992, Joan Hamilton Jones, review of *Baby Animals* and *Sea Animals,* p. 98; August, 1992, Mary Crawford, review of *Lamb* and *Mouse,* p. 98; November, 1992, Joan Feltwell, review

of *Night-Time Animals,* p. 143; November, 1994, Ann Jenkin, review of *Mammals,* p. 158; February, 1997, Delvene Barnett, review of *Fish,* p. 40; summer, 1998, p. 96; spring, 2000, review of *Life Cycle of a Mushroom,* p. 20; summer, 2003, review of *Why Do Bruises Change Color? and Other Questions about Blood,* p. 76.

School Library Journal, February, 1990, J.J. Votapka, review of *The Elephant,* p. 85; May, 1990, Susan Hepler, review of *Monster Road Builders,* pp. 100-101; November, 1990, Diane Nunn, review of *The Cow,* p. 107; January, 1992, Steven Engelfried, review of *Cars,* p. 97; October, 1992, Dorcas Hand, review of *Baby Animals,* p. 109; February, 1993, Eldon Younce, review of *Trains,* p. 86; March, 1993, Karey Wehner, review of *Insects and Crawly Creatures,* p. 194; May, 1994, Eldon Younce, review of *Big Machines,* p. 110; November, 1995, John Peters, review of *A First Atlas,* p. 134; August, 1996, p. 141; October, 1997, p. 154; May, 1998, Frances E. Millhouser, review of *Under the Sea,* p. 137; July, 1998, p. 90; February, 1999, Eldon Younce, review of *Life Cycle of a Sunflower* and *Life Cycle of a Chicken,* p. 101; January, 2000, Katherine Borchert, review of *Flowers, Fruits, and Seeds,* p. 126; January, 2000, Kit Vaughan, review of *Eat Well,* p. 126; April, 2001, Maren Ostergard, review of *Screws* and *Springs,* p. 134; April, 2003, Christine A. Moesch, review of *Why Do I Vomit? and*

Other Questions about Digestion and *Why Do My Eyes Itch? and Other Questions about Allergies,* p. 154; July, 2003, Joyce Adams Burner, review of *Where Do Babies Come From?,* p. 78; February, 2004, Joyce Adams Burner, review of *Get Some Exercise!* and *Get Some Rest!,* p. 138; February, 2004, Kate Kohlbeck, review of *Healthy Food, Healthy Hair,* and *Healthy Teeth,* p. 138; April, 2004, review of *Why Do I Vomit? And Other Questions about Digestion* and *Why Do My Eyes Itch? And Other Questions about Allergies,* p. 21; December, 2004, Donna Marie Wagner, review of *Asthma, Broken Bones,* and *Stings and Bites,* p. 137; August, 2005, Christine A. Moesch, review of *Cancer, Down's Syndrome,* and *Using a Wheelchair,* p. 116.

Science Books and Films, June-July, 1991, review of *The A-to-Z Book of Cars,* p. 131; June, 1995, review of *The Mouse, The Hedgehog,* and *The Elephant,* p. 156; August, 1995, review of *You and Your Body: 101 Questions and Answers,* p. 180; September, 1999, review of *Maps and Symbols,* p. 218; January, 2000, review of *A Healthy Body* and *Clean and Healthy,* p. 37; July, 2002, review of *Solids, Liquids, and Gases* and *Hot and Cold,* p. 468; May, 2003, review of *Why Do I Sneeze? and Other Questions about Breathing* p. 132; November, 2003, review of *Wolves,* p. 277.

Times Educational Supplement, April 13, 2001, Jon O'Connor, review of *Levers, Ramps and Wedges, Springs, Pulleys and Gears, Screws,* and *Wheels and Cranks,* p. 22.*

S

SAUNDERS-SMITH, Gail 1952-

Personal

Born November 23, 1952, in Pittsburgh, PA; married Charles D. Smith, 1974 (deceased). *Education:* Kent State University, B.S., M.A., 1977; Youngstown State University, M.S., 1980; University of Akron, Ph.D., 1994.

Addresses

Agent—c/o Author Mail, Red Brick Press, c/o Capstone Press, 151 Good Counsel Dr., P.O. Box 669, Mankato, MN 56002. *E-mail*—gssmithphd@aol.com.

Career

Educator and writer. Elementary school teacher in Ohio, for ten years; Summit County Board of Education, Akron, OH, curriculum supervisor; currently writer and staff developer.

Member

International Reading Association, ASCD, Phi Delta Kappa, Kappa Delta Pi, Pi Lambda Theta.

Writings

NONFICTION; FOR CHILDREN

Carrots, Pebble Books (Mankato, MN), 1998.
Autumn Leaves, Pebble Books (Mankato, MN), 1998.
Beans, Pebble Books (Mankato, MN), 1998.
Boats, Pebble Books (Mankato, MN), 1998.
Butterflies, Pebble Books (Mankato, MN), 1998.
Cars, Pebble Books (Mankato, MN), 1998.
Chickens, Pebble Books (Mankato, MN), 1998.
Children, Pebble Books (Mankato, MN), 1998.
Clouds, Pebble Books (Mankato, MN), 1998.

Communities, Capstone Press (Mankato, MN), 1998.
The Doctor's Office, Pebble Books (Mankato, MN), 1998.
Flowers, Pebble Books (Mankato, MN), 1998.
Frogs, Pebble Books (Mankato, MN), 1998.
Apple Trees, Pebble Books (Mankato, MN), 1998.
From Bud to Blossom, Pebble Books (Mankato, MN), 1998.
From Blossom to Fruit, Pebble Books (Mankato, MN), 1998.
Picking Apples, Pebble Books (Mankato, MN), 1998.
Eating Apples, Pebble Books (Mankato, MN), 1998.
Koalas, Pebble Books (Mankato, MN), 1998.
Leaves, Pebble Books (Mankato, MN), 1998.
Lightning, Pebble Books (Mankato, MN), 1998.
Parents, Pebble Books (Mankato, MN), 1998.
Rain, Pebble Books (Mankato, MN), 1998.
Airplanes, Pebble Books (Mankato, MN), 1998.
Animals in the Fall, Pebble Books (Mankato, MN), 1998.
Autumn, Pebble Books (Mankato, MN), 1998.
Seeds, Pebble Books (Mankato, MN), 1998.
Spring, Pebble Books (Mankato, MN), 1998.
Stems, Pebble Books (Mankato, MN), 1998.
Summer, Pebble Books (Mankato, MN), 1998.
Sunflowers, Pebble Books (Mankato, MN), 1998.
Sunshine, Pebble Books (Mankato, MN), 1998.
The Supermarket, Pebble Books (Mankato, MN), 1998.
Trucks, Pebble Books (Mankato, MN), 1998.
Warm Clothes, Pebble Books (Mankato, MN), 1998.
Winter, Pebble Books (Mankato, MN), 1998.
Fall Harvest, Pebble Books (Mankato, MN), 1998.
Families, Pebble Books (Mankato, MN), 1998.
The Fire Station, Pebble Books (Mankato, MN), 1998.
The Farm, Pebble Books (Mankato, MN), 1999.
The Universe, Steck-Vaughn (Austin, TX), 2000.

OTHER

The Ultimate Guided Reading How-to Book: Building Literacy through Small-Group Instruction, Zephyr Press (Tucson, AZ), 2003.
The Ultimate Small-Group Reading How-to Book: Building Comprehension through Small-Group Instruction, Zephyr Press (Chicago, IL), 2005.

Consulting editor on several series books for Capstone Press.

Sidelights

Gail Saunders-Smith told *SATA:* "Books, books, books! So many! Paper, paper, paper! So much! I love to read. I hate to write, but love when it's done. I love to read because I get to go places and meet people and do things I would never have the chance otherwise. I guess I don't r-e-a-l-l-y hate to write. But I like reading much better.

"Names fascinate me. I collect names. I hear names and write them down. I have lists and lists of names. Names of people, places, even things. I once thought up this moss that grows into fabric—it's vloss. I made up that name.

"I love books with beautiful illustrations. The author uses words as paint to make the pictures in the readers' mind. The illustrator uses real paint to make the pictures in the readers' eyes. Together the author and the illustrator paint a multidimensional story. The only thing missing is music. And sound effects. Maybe not, because then it'd be a movie.

"So many stories float around in my mind. Just scraps of stories—a character, a place, weather, a room. It takes work to stitch the scraps into a whole. And work takes time. We have to decide what to do with the time given to us. Read? Write? Sleep? Go for a walk? Talk with a friend? At least we have a choice, right?"

*　　*　　*

SELWAY, Martina 1940-

Personal

Born June 20, 1940, in Worcestershire, England; married John Aston (head of graphic design for television); children: Sophie, Gemma. *Education:* Shrewsbury College of Art, degree in printmaking and design, 1962. *Hobbies and other interests:* Travel in Europe, watercolors, sailing, hillwalking.

Addresses

Home—Surrey, England; southern France. *Agent*—c/o Author Mail, Hutchinson Books, Random House UK, 20 Vauxhall Bridge Rd., London SW1V 2SA, England.

Career

Author and illustrator. Stylist for still photographer in London, England, 1963-64; artist for advertising agency, 1964-66; freelance illustrator, 1966—. Background illustrator for animated film *Beatles Yellow Submarine,* 1967.

Member

Chelsea Arts Club, Ariel Sailing Club (London, England).

Awards, Honors

National Diploma in Design.

Writings

SELF-ILLUSTRATED

The Grunts: What a Day!, World's Work (Tadworth, England), 1982.
The Grunts Go on a Picnic, World's Work (Tadworth, England), 1982.
Greedyguts, Hutchinson (London, England), 1990.
Don't Forget to Write, Hutchinson (London, England), 1991, Ideals Publishing (Nashville, TN), 1992.
I Hate Roland Roberts (sequel to *Don't Forget to Write*), Hutchinson (London, England), 1993, Ideals Children's Books (Nashville, TN), 1994.
Wish You Were Here (sequel to *I Hate Roland Roberts*), Hutchinson (London, England), 1994, Ideals Children's Books (Nashville, TN), 1996.
What Can I Write?, Hutchinson (London, England), 1997.
So Many Babies: A Fun-to-Count Book, Hutchinson (London, England), 2001.

ILLUSTRATOR

Judith Miles, *Beauty and the Beast* (reader), Longman (Harlow, England), 1979.
Judith Miles, *Needles, Nuts, and Nails* (reader), Longman (Harlow, England), 1979.
Patricia Gray, *Hello Tiger* (reader), Longman (London, England), 1981.
Patricia Gray, *Hello Panda* (reader), Longman (London, England), 1981.
Patricia Gray, *Hello Koala* (reader), Longman (London, England), 1981.
Patricia Gray, *Hello Elephant* (reader), Longman (London, England), 1981.
Ann Cook, *My Holiday at Home Scrapbook,* Longman (London, England), 1981.
Ann Cook, *My Holiday away Scrapbook,* Longman (London, England), 1981.
Mr Tod and the Birthday Cake; and, Mr Tod and the Riddle (reader), Macmillan Education (London, England), 1982.
Diane Wilmer, *Playing Soldiers* (reader), Longman (Harlow, England), 1983.
Alison M. Wildbore, *Merci de la lettre,* Edward Arnold (London, England), 1983.
Nicci Crowther, *Dressing Up* (reader), Longman (Harlow, England), 1983.
Pauline Burke and Eric Albany, *Bronto's Number Rhyme Activity Book,* Longman (Harlow, England), 1984.
Pauline Burke and Eric Albany, *Bronto's Furniture Cart,* Longman (Harlow, England), 1984.
Pauline Burke and Eric Albany, *Bronto's Counting Book,* Longman (Harlow, England), 1984.
Pauline Burke and Eric Albany, *Bronto Moves into His Cave,* Longman (Harlow, England), 1984.

Pauline Burke and Eric Albany, *Bronto Paints His Cave,* Longman (Harlow, England), 1984.

Pauline Burke and Eric Albany, *Bronto Meets Bird and Frog,* Longman (Harlow, England), 1984.

Elizabeth Adams and Andrew Ross, *At the Zoo* (activity book), Longman (Harlow, England), 1985.

Elizabeth Adams and Andrew Ross, *In the Town* (activity book), Longman (Harlow, England), 1985.

Elizabeth Adams and Andrew Ross, *At the Seaside* (activity book), Longman (Harlow, England), 1985.

Elizabeth Adams and Andrew Ross, *On the Farm* (activity book), Longman (Harlow, England), 1985.

Pat Edwards, *Atishoo* (reader), Longman (Harlow, England), 1987.

Pat Edwards, *The Trumpet* (reader), Longman (Harlow, England), 1987.

Pat Edwards, *Tea Time* (reader), Longman (Harlow, England), 1987.

Pat Edwards, *Fred Makes a Shelf* (reader), Longman (Harlow, England), 1987.

Pat Edwards, *Fred's Birthday* (reader), Longman (Harlow, England), 1987.

Pat Edwards, *Fred's Mess* (reader), Longman (Harlow, England), 1987.

Pat Edwards, *Goodnight* (reader), Longman (Harlow, England), 1987.

Pat Edwards, *Fred's Friends* (reader), Longman (Harlow, England), 1987.

Pat Edwards, *The Joggers* (reader), Longman (Harlow, England), 1987.

Pat Edwards, *Pancakes* (reader), Longman (Harlow, England), 1987.

Pat Edwards, *The Sandwich* (reader), Longman (Harlow, England), 1987.

Pat Edwards, *The Picnic* (reader), Longman (Harlow, England), 1987.

Pat Edwards, *Get Some Bread, Fred* (reader), Longman (Harlow, England), 1987.

Wendy Body, *Fred's Snowman* (reader), Longman (Harlow, England), 1987.

Wendy Body, *The Jumper* (reader), Longman (Harlow, England), 1987.

Wendy Body, *Christmas* (reader), Longman (Harlow, England), 1987.

Pat Edwards, *Fred's Photo Album* (reader), Longman (Harlow, England), 1990.

Pat Edwards, *The Skateboard* (reader), Longman (Harlow, England), 1990.

Pat Edwards, *Fred in Space* (reader), Longman (Harlow, England), 1990.

Pat Edwards, *The Wasp* (reader), Longman (Harlow, England), 1990.

Pat Edwards, *A Sunflower Named Burt* (reader), Longman (Harlow, England), 1990.

Pat Edwards, *Something Nasty!,* Sundance (Littleton, MA), 1999.

Pat Edwards, *What's That?,* Sundance (Littleton, MA), 1999.

Pat Edwards, *The Photograph,* Sundance (Littleton, MA), 1999.

Pat Edwards, *Fred's Cold,* Sundance (Littleton, MA), 1999.

Pat Edwards, *Fred Fixes a Faucet,* Sundance (Littleton, MA), 1999.

Pat Edwards, *Clean out the Fridge, Fred!,* Sundance (Littleton, MA), 1999.

Pat Edwards, *A Visit to Cousin Boris,* Sundance (Littleton, MA), 1999.

Pat Edwards, *The Visitor,* Sundance (Littleton, MA), 1999.

Anna Perera, *Lolly Woe,* Oxford University Press (Oxford, England), 2001.

Rebecca Whitford, *Little Yoga: A Toddler's First Book of Yoga,* Henry Holt (New York, NY), 2005.

Colorist for Charles E. Brock's illustrations for *Gulliver's Travels: My Adventures in Lilliput, by Lemuel Gulliver, Retold by Jonathan Swift,* Castle Books, 1979. Illustrator for "You and Me Storybooks" series and other readers, Longman Group, beginning 1979; and "Maths Storybooks" series, Longman Cheshire Australia, 1991.

Sidelights

Martina Selway is a British author and illustrator who has worked in advertising, photography, and animated films in addition to establishing a long career in children's publishing. While much of her illustration work has appeared in educational readers such as the long-running "Fred" series by Pat Edwards, Selway has also produces the self-illustrated books *Don't Forget to Write, Wish You Were Here,* and *I Hate Roland Roberts* as well as the picture book *So Many Babies: A Fun-to-Count Book.* Based on the tradition nursery rhyme about the old woman who lives in a shoe, *So Many Babies* finds Mrs. Badger frustrated by the fact that her habit of adopting orphaned animal babies has left her with no room in which to live. In *Don't Forget to Write* and its sequel, a letter written by Rosie while taking her first trip away from home shows the young girl's gradual adjustment to life in the country and her growing affection for her loving grandparents. In *Publishers Weekly* a reviewer praised the book's "reassuring message and its portrayal of the strength of a grandparent's hospitality and love." Selway's artwork is a strength of Rebecca Whitford's 2005 picture book *Little Yoga: A Toddler's First Book of Yoga.* DeAnn Tabuchi described the book's illustrations as "playful" and "brightly hued" in her review for *School Library Journal,* while *Booklist* contributor Gillian Engberg maintained that Selway's "cheerfully designed" and heavily outlined drawings of toddlers in basic yoga poses combine with Whitford's text to arm parents with "new ideas for channeling toddler energy."

Selway once told *SATA:* "I left art college and came to London where I initially found work as a stylist for a well-known stills photographer at the beginning of the swinging 1960s. I quickly moved on to work as a visualiser with one of the big advertising agencies. While there, I began to specialize in illustration jobs. During this time, freelance commissions started to roll in and soon I had to quit my full-time job. I did a series of

Colors and counting are just a few of the concepts addressed in Selway's fanciful and colorful self-illustrated picture book So Many Babies: A Fun-to-Count Book.

posters for the National Savings Bank and the London Transport Authority. I also began work on a major commission for the British Broadcasting Corporation (BBC) to produce nearly five hundred drawings for a series of French-language teaching programs.

"Educational publishing was expanding rapidly during this period, and I worked with many of the well-known publishers, including Cambridge University Press, Oxford University Press, Macmillan, Collins, and the Longman Group. These publishers are still some of my biggest clients.

"In 1967 my work was seen by the director of Television Cartoons, Ltd., who invited me to join a small team of background artists for the animated feature film *Beatles Yellow Submarine*. This was a great experience. I got to work with many talented people, including the great Canadian animator George Dunning and the German designer Heinz Edelmann, whose work in the pages of *Twen* magazine greatly influenced the London scene at the time.

"My first daughter, Sophie, was born in 1970, and Gemma followed in 1973. Children and homebuilding had to take precedence over my career for a while. The film experience, however, led to other commissions for more manageable children's programmes by BBC-TV and Thames Television. The work was fun and was seen by millions of children. My own kids soon became my severest critics. The Longman Group began to publish tie-in books that corresponded to the television programs. My involvement with books for small children grew when they asked me to illustrate a number of books by their own authors.

"My first books as an author/illustrator were two volumes about a family of pigs, the Grunts, that were published by Worlds Work. Little did I know that my pigs would become the role model for Fred Pig, the central character in a reading scheme authored by Pat Edwards. Fred appears in a series of dozens of books published by Longman Group, including *Fred's Photo Album*, *Fred Makes a Shelf*, and *Fred's Friends*. I took my next idea to Hutchinson Children's Books and in 1990 they published *Greedyguts*, the story of a greedy, bullying giant defeated by a clever little boy who gets his village to work together as a team."

Biographical and Critical Sources

PERIODICALS

Booklist, June 1, 1992, Carolyn Phelan, review of *Don't Forget to Write*, p. 1765; October 1, 2005, Gillian Engberg, review of *Little Yoga: A Toddler's First Book of Yoga*, p. 60.
Publishers Weekly, April 20, 1992, review of *Don't Forget to Write*, p. 55.
School Librarian, February, 1994, review of *I Hate Roland Roberts*, p. 17.
School Library Journal, November, 2001, Melinda Piehler, review of *So Many Babies: A Fun-to-Count Book*, p. 136; November, 2005, DeAnn Tabuchi, review of *Little Yoga*, p. 122.*

STANDIFORD, Natalie 1961-
(Jesse Harris, a house pseudonym, Emily James)

Personal

Born November 20, 1961, in Baltimore, MD; daughter of John Willard Eagleston (a pediatrician) and Natalie Elizabeth (a public television documentary producer; maiden name, Cusack) Standiford; married Robert Craig Tracy (a banker), April 29, 1989. *Education:* Brown University, B.A., 1983. *Hobbies and other interests:* Travel, movies, going to the beach, all kinds of music, reading, staying up late.

Addresses

Agent—c/o Sarah Burnes, The Gernert Company, 136 E. 57th St., New York, NY 10022. *E-mail*—natstand@ aol.com.

Career

Shakespeare and Co. Bookstore, New York, NY, clerk, 1983; Random House, New York, NY, editorial assistant, 1984-85, assistant editor in Books for Young Readers division, 1985-87; freelance writer, 1987—. Member of New York City Author Read-Aloud Program, beginning 1992.

Member

Society of Children's Book Writers and Illustrators, Authors' Guild, Authors League of America, Authors Support Intellectual Freedom.

Awards, Honors

Fifty Books of the Year citation, Federation of Children's Book Groups (United Kingdom), 1992, for *Space Dog the Hero;* Puffin Award, Alaska Association of School Librarians, 1992, for *The Bravest Dog Ever: The True Story of Balto;* American Library Association Quick Pick for Reluctant Readers designation, 2005, for *The Dating Game* and *Breaking up Is Really, Really Hard to Do.*

Writings

The Best Little Monkeys in the World, illustrated by Hilary Knight, Random House (New York, NY), 1987.

Dollhouse Mouse (picture book), illustrated by Denise Fleming, Random House (New York, NY), 1989.

The Bravest Dog Ever: The True Story of Balto, illustrated by Donald Cook, Random House (New York, NY), 1989.

(Adaptor) *The Headless Horseman* (based on Washington Irving's "The Legend of Sleepy Hollow"), illustrated by Donald Cook, Random House (New York, NY), 1992.

(Under pseudonym Emily James) *Santa's Surprise* (picture book), illustrated by Ethel Gold, Bantam (New York, NY), 1992.

(Under pseudonym Emily James) *Jafar's Curse* (chapter book; based on the movie *Aladdin*), Disney, 1993.

(Under pseudonym Emily James) *Aladdin's Quest* (chapter book; based on the movie *Aladdin*), illustrated by Kenny Thompkins and Raymond Zibach, Mega-Books (New York, NY), 1993.

(Under pseudonym Emily James) *The Mixed-Up Witch* (picture book), illustrated by Stephanie Britt, Bantam (New York, NY), 1993.

(Under pseudonym Emily James) *Fifteen: Hillside Live!* (middle-grade novel; based on the television series *Fifteen*), Grosset & Dunlap (New York, NY), 1993.

Brave Maddie Egg, Random House (New York, NY), 1995.

Astronauts Are Sleeping (picture book), Knopf (New York, NY), 1996.

The Stone Giant: The Hoax That Fooled America, illustrated by Bob Doucet, Golden Books (New York, NY), 2001.

Odd Girl In (middle-grade novel), Hyperion (New York, NY), 2007.

Author's books have been translated into Hebrew.

"SPACE DOG" SERIES; FOR CHILDREN

Space Dog and Roy, illustrated by Kelly Oechsli, Avon (New York, NY), 1990, illustrated by Kathleen Collins Howell, Random House (New York, NY), 1998.

Space Dog and the Pet Show, illustrated by Kelly Oechsli, Avon (New York, NY), 1990, illustrated by Kathleen Collins Howell, Random House (New York, NY), 1998.

Space Dog in Trouble, illustrated by Kathleen Collins Howell, Avon (New York, NY), 1991.

Space Dog the Hero, illustrated by Kathleen Collins Howell, Avon (New York, NY), 1991.

The "Space Dog" series has been translated into Dutch; foreign editions feature illustrations by Tony Ross.

"THE POWER" SERIES, YOUNG-ADULT HORROR; UNDER HOUSE PSEUDONYM JESSE HARRIS

The Witness, Knopf (New York, NY), 1992.

The Diary, Knopf (New York, NY), 1992.

Vampire's Kiss, Knopf (New York, NY), 1992.

"DATING GAME" SERIES; YOUNG-ADULT NOVELS

The Dating Game, Little, Brown (New York, NY), 2005.

Breaking up Is Really, Really Hard to Do, Little, Brown (New York, NY), 2005.

Can True Love Survive High School?, Little, Brown (New York, NY), 2005.

Ex-Rating, Little, Brown (New York, NY), 2006.

Speed Dating, Little, Brown (New York, NY), 2006.

Parallel Parking, Little, Brown (New York, NY), 2006.

Series has been translated into Japanese.

"ELLE WOODS" SERIES; YOUNG-ADULT NOVELS; BASED ON FILM "LEGALLY BLONDE"

Blonde at Heart, Hyperion (New York, NY), 2006.
Beach Blonde, Hyperion (New York, NY), 2006.
Vote Blonde, Hyperion (New York, NY), 2006.
Blonde Love, Hyperion (New York, NY), 2006.

Sidelights

Natalie Standiford, author of the popular "Space Dog" and "Dating Game" series, has written picture books, nonfiction, chapter books, teen novels, and even horror novels for young adults. Writing under the pseudonym Emily James she has published titles to tie in with Disney movies and television shows, while under the pseudonym Jesse Harris she wrote the teen horror series "The Power," released in both the United States and Great Britain. Standiford's "Dating Game" series, beginning with *The Dating Game* in 2005, has drawn a loyal following among adolescent girls. Along with her writing career, Standiford also plays bass in the rock band Ruffian.

"I first began to write stories in the third grade, and I've wanted to be a writer ever since," Standiford once recalled to *SATA*. "I never planned to be a children's writer in particular; in college I, like so many people, looked down on children's books. But now I can see that I'm very lucky to have found my literary niche, and writing for children is it.

"I fell into the world of children's-book publishing a few months after college graduation. I had moved to New York and heard, through an acquaintance, about a job at Random House. It was an editorial assistant position in the juvenile division. I accepted the job, thinking that in six months or a year I'd move into the adult trade division. Needless to say, I never moved.

"I would recommend working in publishing to anyone who wants to write books. Not only do you learn to see things from an editor's point of view, you make a lot of helpful contacts. And in some cases you learn how to write and analyze your writing on the job. It doesn't pay well, but the experience, for me, was more than worth it. Still, I couldn't stand office work for *too* long. I left to freelance after three years."

It was during this period of freelance work that Standiford began writing children's books. Among her early publications for young readers are the books in the "Space Dog" series. In series opener *Space Dog and Roy,* Roy is bullied at school and longs for a dog to join him in his daily adventures. Roy's wish is fulfilled when an extraterrestrial hound crashes his spaceship in Roy's backyard. The dog, whose name is Qrxztlq, hails from a planet where dogs lead enlightened lives, speaking, wearing clothes, and walking on their hind legs. Space Dog grudgingly allows himself to be adopted by Roy, and the rest of the story details Roy's humorous attempts to introduce Qrxztlq to the ways of earthbound dogs. "Space Dog has a delightfully sharp tongue," ob-

In **The Stone Giant** *Standiford introduces budding readers to a mid-eighteenth-century hoax that tricked people into believing that a giant had been unearthed in upstate New York. (Illustration by Bob Doucet.)*

served a *Publishers Weekly* reviewer, who also characterized several of the episodes between Roy and Space Dog as "hilarious." A *Booklist* reviewer noted the series' potentially appealing "blend of humor and fantasy," and, similarly, a *Growing Point* critic praised the first book's "notable tangle of comic absurdities."

While the other books in the "Space Dog" series entertain readers with the further escapades of Roy and his so-called "pet" Qrxztlq, an earlier work by Standiford features a real canine character. *The Bravest Dog Ever: The True Story of Balto* recounts the tale of a sled dog who led his team across the Alaskan wilderness to deliver a shipment of desperately needed medicine. *School Library Journal* contributor Sharron McElmeel called the story "proud and heroic," and asserted that it would find a broad audience among young readers.

Astronauts Are Sleeping returns to space, but this time features a trio of real-world astronauts, and imagines what they might see in their dreams. The picture book is in a quiet tone, geared toward bedtime telling for young children, and the language is poetic. "The tranquil cadences of the elegant prose cast a hypnotic spell," commented a *Publishers Weekly* contributor.

With *The Stone Giant: The Hoax That Fooled America,* Standiford adds to her nonfiction oeuvre, recounting the story of two men who "discovered" a petrified human

giant in 1869. The spectacle was nothing but a hoax, but it was so successful at drawing in a paying crowd that even P.T. Barnum of circus fame followed suit, making a second copy of the stone giant to pass it off as the real thing. Laid out as a chapter book, *The Stone Giant* is written in short segments to encourage even reluctant readers to delve into the historical event. "This small slice of American history is tantalizing," wrote Mary Ann Carcich in *School Library Journal.*

With *The Dating Game* and its sequels, Standiford targeted a new audience: teen girls. The young-adult novels follow the exploits of tenth-grade classmates Madison, Lina, and Holly, as they deal with school, romance, and their families. In *The Dating Game,* the girls design an online dating service for their interpersonal human dynamics class, taught by too-cute-to-be-a-teacher Dan. While Dan becomes the object of Lina's affections, Holly's biggest concern is that her large breasts have earned her the nickname "Boobmeister," and Madison longs to go out with senior Sean, the best-looking guy on the swim team. "Overall, readers will probably find enough to laugh about and relate to as the trio plans—and plays—the Dating Game," a *Publishers Weekly* reviewer commented. *Booklist* contributor Cindy Welch was unconvinced by the treatment of teen issues in the book, but compared it to two other popular teen series, noting that "Girls waiting for a new 'A List' or 'Gossip Girl,' . . . will be well pleased." As *Kliatt* critic Samantha Musher noted, "while it's certainly fluff, it's high quality fluff—the characters are mostly realistic, the dialog is funny and believable, and nothing gets wrapped up too tidily at the end." Nicole Marcucculli Mills, in *School Library Journal,* called *The Dating Game* "Easy reading for fans of Francine Pascal's 'Sweet Valley High.'"

With the success of Holly, Lina, and Madison's dating service, the girls' adventures continue in *Breaking up Is Really, Really Hard to Do* and *Can True Love Survive High School?* In the former, Holly wonders if her boyfriend Rob is really the guy for her and thinks that breaking up might be the only answer; Lina continues to pine after teacher Dan; and as Madison works on an art project with Sean at the center, she finds herself attracted to a brooding eleventh-grade artist. The third book in the series reveals that Dan is not only dating another teacher at school, he is also planning to leave at the end of the year. Lina is determined not to let him get away without a fight and begins to plot ways to attract his attention outside of school. Meanwhile, Holly makes friend Britta her new project, and is determined to find the shy girl the right guy. Madison begins a diary on the Dating Game Web site, revealing details about her life and the play her mother has written; although she is still dating the boy she started seeing in book two, she cannot help wondering if there is a better match out there for her. The series continues with *Ex-Rating,* in which a new feature on the Dating Game Web site—being able to rate your ex-boyfriends and ex-girlfriends—causes a real shake-up at high school. *Speed Dating* continues the teen saga.

"Whatever led me to work in children's books, I think of it as fate," Standiford once confessed to *SATA.* "Even in college, when I spent my time writing short stories for adults, my characters were often children. My writing style, no matter who my audience is, tends to be simple and clear, easy words and short sentences. And my memories of childhood have always been strong and vivid and important to me. My brothers and sisters and I still spend a lot of time rehashing the details of our childhood with each other—we enjoy it, and I'm grateful to have other people around me who are as obsessed with those details as I am.

"We had some children's books at home, but mostly we went to the library. My mother took us to the library every week, and we spent hours picking out books. My mother seemed to enjoy it as much as we did. Our local library was modern, well-stocked, and beautiful.

"Humor is, for me, one of the most important elements of any story. My favorite kind of book, whether for children or adults, is sad but funny (or funny but sad), like J.D. Salinger's *The Catcher in the Rye.* The humor in that novel makes it so sad, and so memorable, and so much fun to read."

Biographical and Critical Sources

PERIODICALS

Booklist, December 15, 1990, review of *Space Dog and the Pet Show* and *Spacedog in Trouble,* p. 865; March 15, 2005, Cindy Welch, review of *The Dating Game,* p. 1285.
Bulletin of the Center for Children's Books, February, 1997, review of *Astronauts Are Sleeping,* p. 223.
Growing Point, May, 1991, review of *Space Dog and Roy,* pp. 5519-20.
Instructor, October, 1996, review of *Astronauts Are Sleeping,* p. 68.
Kliatt, May, 2005, Samantha Musher, review of *The Dating Game,* p. 30.
Publishers Weekly, November 9, 1990, review of *Space Dog and Roy,* p. 58; November 25, 1996, review of *Astronauts Are Sleeping,* p. 74; February 14, 2005, review of *The Dating Game,* p. 77.
School Library Journal, February, 1990, Sharron McElmeel, review of *The Bravest Dog Ever: The True Story of Balto,* p. 86; December, 1996, John Peters, review of *Astronauts Are Sleeping,* p. 106; August, 2001, Mary Ann Carcich, review of *The Stone Giant: The Hoax That Fooled America,* p. 172; August, 2005, Nicole Marcuccilli Mills, review of *The Dating Game,* p. 136.

ONLINE

Natalie Standiford Home Page, http://www.nataliestandi-ford.com (March 20, 2006).

T-U

TAYLOR, Debbie A. 1955-

Personal
Born 1955, in OH; married Charles L. Taylor (a university instructor and writer), 1992; children: Erika, Elaina. *Ethnicity:* "African American." *Education:* Case Western Reserve University, B.A. (English), 1980; Cleveland State University, M.A. (English), 1991. *Hobbies and other interests:* Reading, kite-making, museums, botanical gardens, zoos.

Addresses
Agent—c/o Author Mail, Lee & Low Books, 95 Madison Ave., New York, NY 10016. *E-mail*—dpoet@umich.edu.

Career
Writer and placement officer. University of Michigan, Ann Arbor, in office of Career Planning and Placement, 1992-97, part of graduate experience project, 1997-2000, recruitment coordinator, 2000-01, director of women in Engineering program, 2002—. Cleveland Children's Museum, assistant manager of volunteers; formerly worked as a preschool teacher. Family Book Club, member of board; Matthaei Botanical Garden, member of education committee.

Member
Society of Children's Book Writers and Illustrators, Author's Guild, Authors League.

Writings
Sweet Music in Harlem, illustrated by Frank Morrison, Lee & Low Books (New York, NY), 2004.

Contributor to numerous periodicals, including *Cricket, Spider, Pockets, New Moon,* and *Whiskey Island,* and to professional journals *Careers and the Minority Under-*

Debbie A. Taylor

graduate, Diversity Careers in Engineering and Information Technology, and *Journal of Career Planning and Placement.*

Work in Progress
Vine Street Basketball, Slip through the Dark Woods, Elzada Clover/Lois Jotter, and *Idlewild, Michigan.*

Sidelights
Debbie A. Taylor told *SATA:* "Of course every writer's process is unique, but I suppose for many, the research would come before the writing, or in tandem. On some

projects, and with *Sweet Music in Harlem* in particular, I put the cart before the horse. For that picture book, the plot emerged before I conducted the research. I actually wrote the story a year before I could identify more than a few people in the photograph. Only later did I learn of the historical significance of the photograph and the real story behind that picture.

"For me, a story idea may be triggered by a location, phrase, song lyrics or as in *Sweet Music in Harlem,* a photograph. In general, I write most freely when I simply scribble down the whole story and focus on structure first. Then I return multiple times to revise specific sections. I create a 'dummy book' from folded construction paper. Later I solicit feedback by sharing it with other writers and young readers.

"I hope to always write an interesting story that features engaging language. I hope my books will encourage readers to appreciate family, friends and community. I want readers to consider how they could and should interact with others. I want my characters to encourage readers to solve problems, make decisions, and make the best of any situation. Hopefully, the stories will contribute to a reader's resourcefulness.

"In *Sweet Music in Harlem* I set out to tell a story about a youngster who searches for his uncle's lost possession. I knew it would be a quest tale. Then, of course, as often happens, the story took over. The character's story grew into a tribute to family, to the fine musicians in the photograph and to the great photographer Art Kane.

"Read widely. Read dozens and dozens of books in the genre to which you hope to contribute. Invest time in

With a journalist coming to photograph jazz trumpeter Uncle Click, young C.J. goes on a hunt through the neighborhood, searching for the noted musician's misplaced lucky hat in Taylor's **Sweet Music in Harlem.** *(Illustration by Frank Morrison.)*

developing your craft by taking courses and joining a supportive and honest critique group. As you write, stay open to new directions of the story. Approach each project with openness and anticipation so you can enjoy the process."

Biographical and Critical Sources

PERIODICALS

Black Issues Book Review, September-October, 2004, Vance Garcia, review of *Sweet Music in Harlem,* p. 59.
Kirkus Reviews, April 15, 2004, review of *Sweet Music in Harlem,* p. 402.
Publishers Weekly, May 24, 2004, review of *Sweet Music in Harlem,* p. 61.
School Library Journal, July, 2004, Jane Marino, review of *Sweet Music in Harlem,* p. 89.

ONLINE

Debbie A. Taylor Home Page, http://www.sweetmusicin-harlem.com (April 15, 2006).

* * *

TETZNER, Lisa 1894-1963

Personal

Born November 10, 1894, in Zittau, Germany; immigrated to Switzerland, 1933; naturalized Swiss citizen, 1948; died July 2, 1963, in Corona, Switzerland; father a physician; married Kurt Kläber (a children's author under pen name Kurt Held), 1924. *Education:* Attended Social Women's School (Berlin, Germany); studied acting with Max Reinhardt.

Career

Writer and broadcaster. Berlin Broadcasting Service, Berlin, Germany, founder and producer of *Children's Hour,* beginning 1924.

Writings

Im Land der Industrie zwischen Rein und Ruhr: ein Buntes Buch von Zeit und Menschen, E. Diederichs (Jena, Germany), 1923.
(Compiler) *Die schunsten Marchen der Welt für 365 und 1 Tag,* E. Diederichs (Jena, Germany), 1926.
Hans Urian: The Story of a Journey around the World (in German), [Berlin, Germany], 1929.
. . . Was am See Geschach; die Geschichte von Rosmarin und Thymian, H. Stuffer (Baden-Baden, Germany), 1935.

(With Kurt Held) *Die schwarzen Bruder: Erlebnisse und Aventeuer eines kleinen Tessiners,* Maier (Ravensburg, Germany), 1941, reprinted, 1980, published as *Die Schwarzen Bruder: Roman in Bildern,* edited and illustrated by Hannes Binder, Sauerlander (Düsseldorf, Germany), 2002, translated by Peter F. Neumeyer as *The Black Brothers: A Novel in Pictures,* Front Street Books (Asheville, NC), 2004

Der Gang ins Leben; die Erzahlung einer Kindheit, H.R. Sauerlander (Aarau, Germany), 1954.

Das Madchen in der Glaskutche, illustrations by Horst Lemke, C. Dressler (Berlin, Germany) 1957.

Das Fuchslein und der Zornig Lowe; Tiermarchen aus aller Welt, H.R. Sauerlander (Aarau, Germany), 1958.

Marchen, Gesammelt und Nacherzahlt, illustrations by Regina Ackermann-Ophuls, Fischer Bucherei (Frankfurt am Main, Germany), 1958.

Das War Kurt Held; vierzig Jahr Leben mit Ihm, H.R. Sauerlander (Aarau, Germany), 1961.

Das Marchen und Lisa Tetzner, H.R. Sauerlander (Aarau, Germany), 1966.

War Paul schuldig?: Kindheit und Jugend im Dritten Reich, with material by Dagmar Grenz, E. Klett (Stuttgart, Germany), 1982.

Tetzner's books have been translated into eight languages.

"CHILDREN FROM NO. 67" SERIES; NOVELS

(With Kurt Held) *Erwin kommt nach Schweden,* H.R. Sauerlander (Aarau, Germany), 1944.

(With Kurt Held) *Als ich Wiederkam,* H.R. Sauerlander (Aarau, Germany), 1946.

(With Kurt Held) *Erwin und Paul,* H.R. Sauerlander (Aarau, Germany), 1947.

(With Kurt Held) *Das Madchen aus dem Vordenrhaus,* H.R. Sauerlander (Aarau, Germany), 1948.

(With Kurt Held) *Der Neue Bund,* H.R. Sauerland (Aarau, Germany), 1949.

"Children from No. 67" series originally published in 9 volumes, 1933-49, volumes 1-8 reprinted in several editions, new editions, including all 9 volumes, 1990.

Adaptations

"The Children from No. 67" series was adapted for film in Germany, 1979.

Sidelights

Born in 1894, Lisa Tetzner was a German writer who was raised in a secure, middle-class family and spent much of her life collecting and promoting interest in fairy tales. An author, she also worked in radio, producing the program *Children's Hour* for the Berlin Broadcast Service during the late 1920s. The author of fairytale collections as well as of original tales, she is best known for her nine-volume "Children from No. 67" series, which reflects her worries over the rising tide of National Socialism in her native country following

First published in 1940, The Black Brothers, *Tetzner's story of a Italian boy who is sold into a dangerous servitude as a chimney sweep, is brought to life through woodcut illustrations by German artist Hannes Binder.*

World War I. Ultimately persecuted by the Nazi party, Tetzner and her husband, fellow children's writer Kurt Held, immigrated to Switzerland, where they lived for the remainder of their lives. While many of Tetzner's books have since fallen out of print, her "Children from No. 67" books have remained in print in Germany and have also been translated into eight languages. The series, coauthored by Held, follows a group of children who live in a Berlin tenement as their lives change as a result of the rise of Adolf Hitler's Nazi government, then make their separate escapes from Germany, traveling throughout the world until they are reunited in Switzerland. Because of the somewhat dated nature of the final volume, which presents a dated and overly idealized view of European society, the series was reprinted as volumes one through eight until 1990, when the concluding volume was re-added.

Another of Tetzner's books to receive interest among more modern readers is *The Black Brothers: A Novel in Pictures.* Also coauthored with Held and originally published in 1941, the book was edited and re-illustrated with woodcuts by artist Hannes Binder in 2002 and translated for English-speaking readers in 2004. Taking place in Italy during the 1800s, the book introduces

thirteen-year-old Giorgio, a poor boy who is traded to a chimney sweep in need of an assistant in exchange for the cash needed to pay his ill mother's doctor bills. Moving to Milan, he faces the brutal life of the city, mistreatment at the hands of his employer, and the danger of his job climbing down chimneys. Ultimately, he becomes involved in a secret club, the Black Brothers, and this association helps Giorgio in changing his life for the better. Describing the book as "an industrial novel," a *Kirkus Reviews* writer praised the book as a "haunting, praiseworthy effort that deserves recognition." Praising Binder's artwork, *Booklist* contributor Francisca Goldsmith noted that Tetzner and Held's text "has much to offer readers interested in how a writer uses fiction to increase social awareness."

Biographical and Critical Sources

PERIODICALS

Booklist, September 1, 2004, Francisca Goldsmith, review of *The Black Brothers: A Novel in Pictures,* p. 109.
Kirkus Reviews, October 1, 2004, review of *The Black Brothers,* p. 970.
School Library Journal, November, 2004, Karen T. Bilton, review of *The Black Brothers,* p. 154.*

* * *

TULLOCH, Shirley

Personal

Born in United Kingdom; married Jonathan Tulloch (a writer), 1977 (divorced, 1997); children: Aidan. *Education:* Bachelor's degree (education). *Politics:* "Green." *Religion:* Roman Catholic.

Addresses

Agent—Rosemary Canter, P.F.D., 34-43 Russell St., London WC2B 5HA, England.

Career

Writer and editor. Volunteer in Zimbabwe and South Africa, c. 1990-92, 1997; community worker and educator.

Writings

Who Made Me?, illustrated by Cathie Felstead, Augsburg (Minneapolis, MS), 2000.
(With husband, Jonathan Tulloch) *I Am a Cloud, I Can Blow Anywhere* (novel), Egmont (London, England), 2007.

Work in Progress

Another picture book.

Sidelights

An author and editor, Shirley Tulloch published her first picture book, *Who Made Me?*, in 2000. Released in both Tulloch's native England and the United States, *Who Made Me?* is a creation story that takes place in a small African village. One night, while staring up at the moon, young Zanele ponders the question "Who made me?" She asks this question of seven of her animal friends, including a lion, giraffe, zebra, eagle, and baboon, and each time the girl receives a different answer. Praising the "rich, multitextured illustrations" by Cathie Felstead, *School Library Journal* critic Patricia Pearl Dole cited Tulloch's text as "conversational, varied, and expressive," adding that it "reads aloud especially well." A *Publishers Weekly* critic also enjoyed Tulloch's debut, calling *Who Made Me?* "welcoming and insightful," while in *Booklist* Hazel Rochman deemed it a "gentle fable" in which a "child feels closely connected to the animals in a wide universe."

Tulloch told *SATA:* "Stuck in the African bush with no electricity, no 24-hour water supply, and a broken-down truck to boot . . . anyone would begin writing. But that was 1990-1992 and it wasn't until 2000 that *Who Made Me?* was published. What often might seem short in terms of word count actually draws on the whole life of a writer. *I Am a Cloud, I Can Blow Anywhere* is co-written with my husband, award-winning writer Jonathan Tulloch, and this is also inspired by my voluntary work in southern Africa; two years in rural Zimbabwe (where I met two Roman Catholic priests from Ohio who introduced me to the subtleties of American geography starting with Ohio being the Buckeye State) and one year in Johannesburg.

"I have also worked with young people (in and out of school); the homeless; travelers; and prisoners and their families. There is nothing like a story. It is the inheritance of every child in our world."

Biographical and Critical Sources

PERIODICALS

Booklist, April 15, 2000, Hazel Rochman, review of *Who Made Me?,* p. 1554.
Publishers Weekly, December 20, 1999, review of *Who Made Me?,* p. 78.
School Librarian, summer, 2000, review of *Who Made Me?,* p. 78.
School Library Journal, August, 2000, Patricia Pearl Dole, review of *Who Made Me?,* p. 166.

ONLINE

Books of the Bible Web site, http://www.booksofthebible. com/ (February 24, 2006), review of *Who Made Me?*
PFD Web site, http://www.pfd.co.uk/ (February 24, 2006), "Shirley Tulloch."

USLAN, Michael E. 1951-

Personal

Born 1951, in NJ; son of Joseph (a mason contractor) and Lillian (a bookkeeper) Uslan; married; wife's name Nancy; children: David, Sarah. *Education:* Indiana University, A.B. (history), 1973, M.S. (urban education), 1975, J.D., 1976.

Addresses

Home—NJ. *Agent*—Branded Entertainment, 333 Crestmont Rd., Cedar Grove, NJ 07009.

Career

Writer, producer of motion pictures, television, and animation, and motivational speaker. United Artists, New York, NY, motion-picture attorney, 1976-80. Television work includes: (executive producer) *Three Sovereigns for Sarah,* 1985; (executive producer and creator) *Dinosaucers* (animated series), 1987-93; (executive producer, with others) *1998 Summer Olympics,* 1988; (executive producer) *Swamp Thing* (animated series), 1991-93; (executive producer) *Swamp Thing* (series), 1991-99; (executive producer) *Fish Police* (animated series), 1992; (executive producer) *Robin Cook's "Harmful Intent,"* 1993; (producer) *Teaching Tolerance* (special), 1994; and (executive producer) *Where on Earth Is Carmen Sandiego?,* 1994-97. Film work includes: (producer) *Swamp Thing,* 1982; (producer) *The Return of Swamp Thing,* 1989; (executive producer with Benjamin Melniker) *Batman,* 1989; (executive producer) *Batman Returns,* 1992; (producer) *Batman: Mask of the Phantasm* (animated film), 1993; (director and producer) *The Great Train Robbery, The Kiss, The Sneeze, Streetcar Chivalry, Smashing a Jersey Mosquito,* and *The Barbershop* (remake of Thomas Edison's films), all 1993; (executive producer) *Little Orphan Annie's Very Animated Christmas,* 1995; (executive producer, *Batman Forever,* 1995; (executive producer) *Batman and Robin,* 1997; (executive producer) *Batman and Mr. Freeze: Sub-Zero,* 1998; (executive producer) *Batman Beyond: Return of the Joker* (animated), 2000; (executive producer) *Batman: Mystery of the Batwoman* (animated), 2003; (executive producer) *The Marvel Superheroes Guide to New York City,* 2004; (executive producer) *Catwoman,* 2004; (associate producer) *National Treasure,* 2004; (producer) *Constantine,* 2005; (executive producer) *Batman Begins,* 2005; *Shazam; Way of the Rat; The Spirit;* and *The Lone Ranger: Way of the Mask.* Producer of video *The First National Trivia Quiz;* director of play *Casablanca Revisited.* Appeared in films, including documentary series *Shadows of the Bat: The Cinematic Legacy of the Dark Knight,* 2005; and *In a Single Bound,* 2006. Indiana University, Bloomington, instructor in first accredited course on comic books, 1971. Vice chairman, New Jersey Motion Picture and Television Commission. Former member of National Endowment for the Humanities Youth Grants Panel; member, board of trustees, Thomas A. Edison Media Arts Consortium/Black Maria Film Festival,

1992-2002, and Center for Excellence in Education, 1993-99; member of board of directors, Wild Brain Animation Studio, 1999-2005; member of advisory board, Discovery Channel Global Education Fund, 2003-05.

Awards, Honors

Emmy Award for Best Animated Series (with others), for *Where on Earth Is Carmen Sandiego?;* Hoagy Carmichael Creative Achievement Award, 1989; People's Choice Award for Favorite Motion Picture (with others), 1989, for *Batman;* Annie Award for outstanding achievement in animated movie (with others), 2000, for *Batman Beyond: Return of the Joker;* Distinguished Hoosier Award, 2001; President's Circle Award, 2002; Independent Spirit Award, Garden State Film Festival, 2005; Academy of Law fellow, 2006.

Writings

The Comic Book in America (text book), Indiana University (Bloomington, IN), 1971.
(With Bruce Solomon) *The Pow! Zap! Wham! Comic-Book Trivia Quiz: 1,001 Questions and Answers,* Morrow (New York, NY), 1977.
(With Bruce Solomon) *The Rock 'n' Roll Trivia Quiz Book,* Simon & Schuster (New York, NY), 1978.
(With Bruce Solomon) *The TV Trivia Quiz Book,* Harmony Books (New York, NY), 1979.
(Editor) *America at War: The Best of DC War Comics,* Simon & Schuster (New York, NY), 1979.
(Editor) *Mysteries in Space: The Best of DC Science-Fiction Comics,* Simon & Schuster (New York, NY), 1980.
(Editor with Jeffrey Mendel) John Goldwater, *The Best of Archie,* Putnam (New York, NY), 1980.
(With Bruce Solomon) *Dick Clark's The First 25 Years of Rock & Roll,* Dell (New York, NY), 1981.
(With Bruce Solomon) *The TV Commercial Trivia Quiz Book,* Arbor House (New York, NY), 1985.
(With Bruce Solomon) *The Gossip Trivia Quiz Book,* Arbor House (New York, NY), 1985.
(With Bruce Solomon) *The All-New TV Trivia Quiz Book,* Harmony Books (New York, NY), 1985.
(And director) *Casablanca Revisited,* produced 1997.
Batman: Detective No. 27 (graphic novel; based on the character by Bob Kane), art by Peter Snejbjerg, DC Comics (New York, NY), 2003.
Chatterbox, the Bird Who Wore Glasses (for children), illustrated by John Steven Gurney, EE Publishing 2006.

Also author of *The Comic Book Revolution,* Indiana University Press. Author of introduction to comic-book compilations, including *Superman in Action Comic Archives,* Volume 3, *Batman in the 1950s; Shazam Archives,* Volume 3; *Thunder Agents Archives,* Volumes 1 and 2; *The Mighty Crusaders Archives, Superman: The Greatest Stories Ever Told; Comic Cavalcade Archives,* Volume 1, *Catwoman: 9 Lives of a Feline Fatale; Brave and Bold Team-up Archives,* Volume 1; *The Spirit Archives,* Volume 16; *Batman: The Greatest Stories Ever*

Told; Enemy Ace Archives, Volume 2; *Dynamic Duo Archives,* Volume 2; *Adam Strange Archives,* Volume 2; and *Just Imagine; Stan Lee Creating the DC Universe,* Volumes 1-3. Writer for television. Scripter for *Batman* and *The Shadow* comic-book series, c. 1970s; writer for "Terry and the Pirates" comic strip, 1994-96; initiator and contributor to "Just Imagine" comic-book series (re-adaptation of comics by Stan Lee), DC Comics, 2001-02.

Biographical and Critical Sources

PERIODICALS

Booklist, February 1, 2004, Ray Olson, review of *Batman: Detective No. 27,* p. 986.

Hollywood Reporter, January 21, 2004, Chris Marlowe, "Comic Book Characters Live via Producer Uslan," p. 10.

Library Journal, January 15, 1982, review of *Dick Clark's The First 25 Years of Rock & Roll,* p. 179.

School Library Journal, August, 1982, review of *Dick Clark's The First 25 Years of Rock & Roll,* p. 136.

ONLINE

Chatterbox, the Bird Who Wore Glasses Web site, http://www.chatterboxthebirdwhoworeglasses.com/ (April 3, 2006).

Comicon.com, http://www.comicon.com (August 27, 2004), Jennifer M. Contino, interview with Uslan.

W-Z

WALLACE, Bill 1947-
(William Keith Wallace)

Personal

Born August 1, 1947, in Chickasha, OK; son of Keith and Mabel Wallace; married Carol Ann Priddle (an author and former teacher); children: Laurie Beth, Amanda Nicole, Justin Keith. *Education:* University of Science and Arts of Oklahoma, B.S., 1971; Southwestern State University, M.S. (elementary administration), 1974; attended University of Oklahoma.

Addresses

Home—Near Chickasha, OK. *Agent*—c/o Author Mail, Holiday House, Inc., 425 Madison Ave., New York, NY 10017.

Career

Educator and author. Chickasha, OK, public schools, teacher at fourth-grade center, 1971-74, kindergarten teacher, 1974, assistant principal at ninth-grade center, 1976, principal and physical education teacher at West Elementary School, 1977-88; writer and public speaker, 1988—.

Awards, Honors

Sequoyah Children's Book Award, and Texas Bluebonnet Award, both 1983, and Nebraska Golden Sower Award, 1985, all for *A Dog Called Kitty;* Nebraska Golden Sower Award, and South Carolina Children's Award, both 1989, both for *Ferret in the Bedroom, Lizards in the Fridge;* Utah Children's Book Award, 1989, Sunshine State Young Reader's Award, 1990, and Wyoming Soaring Eagle Award, 1991, all for *Trapped in Death Cave;* Sequoyah Children's Book Award, and William Allen White Award, both 1991, both for *Beauty;* KC Three Award, 1991-92, and Texas Bluebonnet Award, and South Carolina Children's Award, both 1992, all for *Snot Stew;* Pacific Northwest Territory Award, and Young Reader's Choice Award, both 1992, and Maryland Children's Choice Award, 1994, all for *Danger in Quicksand Swamp;* Connecticut Nutmeg Children's Choice Award, 1995, for *The Biggest Klutz in the Fifth Grade;* Arizona Children's Choice Book Award, 1995, for *Totally Disgusting;* Sunshine State Children's Award, 1996, for *Blackwater Swamp;* Oklahoma Book Award finalist, 1996, and Utah Children's Book Award and Wyoming Indian Paintbrush Books Award, both 1997, all for *Watchdog and the Coyotes;* Oklahoma Book Award finalist, 1998, for *Aloha Summer,* and 2005, for *No Dogs Allowed!;* Arrell M. Gibson Lifetime Achievement Award, 2000, from Oklahoma Center for the Book; Maryland Children's Book Award Intermediate Level, 2004, for *Goosed;* West Elementary School, Chickasha, OK, was renamed Bill Wallace Early Childhood Center.

Writings

FOR CHILDREN

A Dog Called Kitty, Holiday House (New York, NY), 1980.
Trapped in Death Cave, Holiday House (New York, NY), 1984.
Shadow on the Snow, Holiday House (New York, NY), 1985, published as *Danger on Panther Peak,* Pocket (New York, NY), 1989.
Ferret in the Bedroom, Lizards in the Fridge, Holiday House (New York, NY), 1986.
Red Dog, Holiday House (New York, NY), 1987, reprinted, Aladdin (New York, NY), 2002.
Beauty, Holiday House (New York, NY), 1988.
Danger in Quicksand Swamp, Holiday House (New York, NY), 1989.
Snot Stew, illustrated by Lisa McCue, Holiday House (New York, NY), 1989.
The Christmas Spurs, Holiday House (New York, NY), 1990.
Totally Disgusting, illustrated by Leslie Morrill, Holiday House (New York, NY), 1991.

The Biggest Klutz in the Fifth Grade, Holiday House (New York, NY), 1992.

Buffalo Gal, Holiday House (New York, NY), 1992.

Never Say Quit, Holiday House (New York, NY), 1993.

Blackwater Swamp, Holiday House (New York, NY), 1994.

True Friends, Holiday House (New York, NY), 1994.

Watchdog and the Coyotes, illustrated by David Slonim, Pocket (New York, NY), 1995.

Journey into Terror, Pocket (New York, NY), 1996.

The Final Freedom, Pocket (New York, NY), 1997.

Aloha Summer, Holiday House (New York, NY), 1997.

The Backward Bird Dog, Pocket (New York, NY), 1997.

Upchuck and the Rotten Willy, Pocket (New York, NY), 1998.

Upchuck and the Rotten Willy: The Great Escape, Pocket (New York, NY), 1998.

(With wife, Carol Wallace) *The Flying Flea, Callie, and Me,* Pocket (New York, NY), 1999.

Eye of the Great Bear, Pocket (New York, NY), 1999.

(With Carol Wallace) *That Furball Puppy and Me,* illustrated by Jason Wolf, Pocket (New York, NY), 1999.

Upchuck and the Rotten Willy: Running Wild, Pocket (New York, NY), 2000.

Coyote Autumn, Holiday House (New York, NY), 2000.

(With Carol Wallace) *Chomps, Flea, and Gray Cat (That's Me!),* illustrated by John Steven Gurney, Pocket (New York, NY), 2001.

Goosed!, illustrated by Jacqueline Rogers, Holiday House (New York, NY), 2002.

(With Carol Wallace) *Bub Moose,* illustrated by Steven Gurney, Simon & Schuster (New York, NY), 2002.

(With Carol Wallace) *Bub, Snow, and the Burly Bear Scare,* illustrated by Steven Gurney, Simon & Schuster (New York, NY), 2002.

Skinny-Dipping at Monster Lake, Simon & Schuster (New York, NY), 2003.

(With Carol Wallace) *The Meanest Hound Around,* Simon & Schuster (New York, NY), 2003.

No Dogs Allowed!, Holiday House (New York, NY), 2004.

The Pick of the Litter, Holiday House (New York, NY), 2005.

The Legend of Thunderfoot, Simon & Schuster (New York, NY), 2006.

Contributor of short stories to periodicals, including *Western Horseman, Hunting Dog,* and *Horse Lovers.*

Sidelights

Bill Wallace is the author of many award-winning novels for grade-school and middle-grade readers. His stories, some set in the historic Old West and others taking place in the present day, offer adventure and a dash of comedy for young audiences. In many cases, animals play key roles, and sometimes are even the main characters of Wallace's books.

Wallace's first novel has the intriguing title of *A Dog Called Kitty.* A boy named Ricky has a fear of dogs, until he adopts a stray that has been beaten up by the cats on his family's farm. Ricky mocks the dog by calling him "Kitty," but he quickly grows fond of his new pet. Then, one day, a pack of wild dogs attacks Ricky and Kitty, but the heroes bravely fend off the attack. Ricky, now recovered from a fear of dogs that had been caused by a dog attach years before, faces tragedy when Kitty later dies in an accident. *Booklist* contributor Judith Goldberger remarked that while the plot is not entirely credible, "Ricky is real, as are his family and friends, and there is no lack of action."

The theme of death is also explored in several of Wallace's other books, among them *Beauty* and *The Christmas Spurs. Beauty* is the story of eleven-year-old Luke, who must learn to adjust to a new life in Oklahoma with his grouchy grandfather. Luke's spirits are lifted when he befriends a loving horse named Beauty. The conclusion, in which Luke must kill the horse after she is critically injured, hearkens back to Fred Gipson's *Old Yeller,* as well as to Mary O'Hara's *My Friend Flicka.* Luke comes to accept the painful changes that sometimes occur in life, and by the end of the book is able to start working with Beauty's granddaughter. Denise M. Wilms commented in *Booklist* that "horse lovers in particular will appreciate the relationship Luke has with Beauty," and *Bulletin of the Center for Children's Books* reviewer Roger Sutton said that the book's "death scene . . . will leave few genre fans unmoved." Charlene Strickland, writing in *School Library Journal,* further complimented Wallace's "smooth writing," which she noted successfully blends "action scenes with Luke's thoughts."

The Christmas Spurs approaches death in a different context, an incurable disease, as Nick's brother, Jimmy, suffers from leukemia. When Jimmy later dies from the illness, Nick has a difficult time handling the loss. However, he finds one of the spurs Jimmy got for Christmas when they received a horse as a gift, and placing the spur on the new Christmas tree in remembrance of his brother is a comfort.

Addressing grim issues such as death is only one aspect of Wallace's work, however; he has also written several very lighthearted novels for young readers. *Ferret in the Bedroom, Lizards in the Fridge* is a comical romp that also makes a point. Liz Robbins's father is a quirky zoologist who likes to keep a menagerie of animals at home. This quirky home life unfortunately gets in the way of Liz's plan to run against pretty and popular Jo Donna Hunt in the election for sixth-grade class president. When Liz tries to hold a meeting in her house, the animals get in the way, with comical results. Liz asks her father to keep his animals somewhere else, which he kindly agrees to do to help his daughter. Gaining a "normal" life does not help Liz win the election, however, but by the end of the story she has forged a stronger relationship with both her parents. Blending humor with a message about peer pressure makes *Ferret in the Bedroom, Lizards in the Fridge* successful, according to several critics. A contributor to the *Bulletin of the Center for Children's Books* wrote that young readers will find some scenes "hilarious" and concluded that "Wal-

lace gains points for having his protagonist find self-acceptance." Genevieve Stuttaford, writing in *Publishers Weekly,* asserted that "young readers should relate to and enjoy this story."

Another humorous tale by Wallace is 1992's *The Biggest Klutz in Fifth Grade,* the story of clumsy Patrick Berry and his friends. Pat bets Neal Moffett that he can survive the summer without hurting himself; if he fails he has to kiss overweight Kristine Plimpton. Neal, of course, spends the summer trying to make Pat mess up, while Pat tries to thwart these attempts on his physical welfare. Meanwhile, Pat and Kristine eventually realize they like each other, and in the end Pat throws the bet to kiss Kristine. While Eunice Weech, writing in *School Library Journal,* objected to Wallace's portrayal of girls as "passive" characters who serve only as "backdrops," she nonetheless complimented the author for his sense of humor and "brisk pace, helped by snappy dialogue." *Bulletin of the Center for Children's Books* contributor Deborah Stevenson similarly faulted "the book's occasionally unpleasant relish of girls' having 'curves in all the right places,'" but concluded that young readers will enjoy the "slapstick" humor.

Wallace has also delved into historical novels, blending his love for animals in the books *Red Dog* and *Buffalo Gal. Red Dog,* set in the 1860s, hearkens back to *A Dog Called Kitty* in its tale of a boy's bond with a dog. The main character, twelve-year-old Adam, carries a grudge about having to move to a new home, just like Luke in *Beauty.* When Adam's stepfather, Sam, takes the family from Tennessee to the Wyoming wilderness, the boy finds some companionship in a puppy. While Adam is left in charge after Sam leaves on an extended trip, a group of men hoping to acquire the gold on the family's land attack the boy and his dog. Adam escapes and is pursued by the greedy gold seekers, who ultimately meet a surprising foe. Reviewers praised Wallace for his honest portrayal of the rugged, difficult way of life in a frontier wilderness. Susan Rice, writing in *Voice of Youth Advocates,* compared *Red Dog* to Jim Kjelgaard's *Big Red* in its combination of coming-of-age tale and animal story, and deemed Wallace's novel "recommended reading for any elementary or junior high reader." *School Library Journal* reviewer Barbara Chatton similarly pointed out that *Red Dog* has "special appeal to reluctant readers."

Buffalo Gal is also a historical coming-of-age story, though this time the story features a young female protagonist. The novel also differs from Wallace's earlier works in that Amanda Guthridge, the fifteen-year-old central character, is older than the writer's usual preteen protagonists. Again, the reader is presented with a character who is suddenly relocated to an unfamiliar setting. In 1904, Amanda is taken from her comfortable home in San Francisco to Texas, where her wealthy mother decides to work toward saving endangered buffalo herds. In Oklahoma Amanda meets David Talltree, who is half white, half Native American. She finds him both repulsive and intriguing—repulsive because of his condescending attitude toward her, and intriguing because he is different from the other boys she has known. David does not respect the rich city girl until she demonstrates her riding skills. Many Wild West adventures follow, including encounters with dangerous animals and hazardous storms, and in the end Amanda is a wiser girl, blossoming into a woman. Reviewers generally found *Buffalo Gal* to be an exciting story, Chatton concluding in *School Library Journal* that Wallace's "fast-paced novel" will appeal to readers and could lead them to think more about the lives of women in the Old West. The reviewer pointed out, however, the slim chance "that greenhorns, particularly women alone, would have received the polite treatment given the Guthridges."

Goosed! features a canine protagonist. T.P., a bird-dog named after an incident in the family bathroom, is not sure how to deal with the arrival of a new puppy named Mocha. T.P. tries to ignoring Mocha, but as a result he does not spend as much time with Jeff, his boy, who loves the new puppy. When Mocha is threatened by a wild goose, T.P. comes to the rescue, learning that his role in the relationship is to mentor the younger dog. A *Kirkus Reviews* contributor commented on the "engagingly doggy spirit of this upbeat animal tale," while Susan Hepler noted in *School Library Journal* that Wallace's "beginning chapter book should appeal to fans of talking animal stories and those looking for a light and humorous read."

Some of Wallace's novels are adventure stories, including *Trapped in Death Cave, Danger in Quicksand Swamp,* and *Journey into Terror.* Treasure hunts and life-threatening situations are typical features of these books; in *Danger in Quicksand Swamp,* for example, friends Ben and Jake think they are on a treasure hunt when they suddenly find themselves in a crocodile-infested swamp, led there by a man who wants them dead. The boys manage to get rescued and then figure out a way to prove the evil intent of their would-be murderer.

In *Blackwater Swamp* Ted and his family move to a small Louisiana town, where Ted learns about an elderly African-American woman who lives alone in the swamp and is rumored to be a witch. Questions arise in Ted's mind when his new friend Jimmy tells him that the "witch" is behind a series of burglaries that have been going on in town. The elderly woman, whose name is Martha Timms, is not really a witch at all, and in the process of defending her, Ted comes to know Timms and share her love of animals. *Voice of Youth Advocates* contributor Diane Tuccillo called *Blackwater Swamp* a "well-written" story that teaches "important lessons about friendship and accepting others' differences."

Wallace returns to the theme of interracial differences in *Aloha Summer,* in which the main character makes friends with a Hawaiian native. *True Friends* is also about differences, but in this case the differences are

BILL WALLACE

Author of *A Dog Called Kitty*

COYOTE AUTUMN

All he ever wanted was a pet. . . .

ALADDIN FICTION

When a young boy moves to the country after his mother dies, an orphaned coyote takes the place of the dog he always wanted in Wallace's inspiring middle-grade novel. (Cover illustration by Richard Cowdrey.)

handicaps, both physical and economic. Judy Baird suffers from cerebral palsy and comes from a poor family. On the other hand, Courtney Brown's family is well off, which makes it easy for her to buddy up to the "in" crowd. However, when Courtney's family's fortunes take a turn for the worse, she discovers who her true friends are. Some reviewers considered the plot to be "overloaded" with messages, as Sutton described it in *Bulletin of the Center for Children's Books.* However, according to Nancy Zachary in *Voice of Youth Advocates,* "Good values like kindness and friendship prevail in a neat conclusion that extols family loyalty."

Many of Wallace's protagonists are average kids with some spunk, but in some cases he writes about quirky characters, such as Patrick in *The Biggest Klutz in Fifth Grade,* or the misfits in *Never Say Quit.* "Misfits," in fact, is the name the fifth and sixth graders give their soccer team in this tale. The title comes from their coach's insistence that no one in the team can quit for at least two years. The kids learn a lot about dedication, teamwork, and loyalty from Coach Reiner, and use these values to help their coach when his problems with alcoholism get the better of him. Although Deborah Abbott

wrote in *Booklist* that the story gets "melodramatic" at times, she praised the book for addressing issues that make for good "discussion opportunities."

Another quirky character, twelve-year-old Bailey, lives at the turn of the twentieth century and is the hero of *Eye of the Great Bear.* Scared of strange noises and easily startled, Bailey is more afraid of fear than the things that cause him to jump, and has trouble calming his jitters. When told by a carnival mystic that the cure to his concerns will involve a bear, Bailey is not sure whether to be relieved or more worried. However, when the moment comes, he can stand between his younger sister and danger in the form of a charging grizzly. "The tale is vigorously told," wrote John Peters and Jack Helbig in their review for *Booklist,* concluding that Wallace's novel is "both entertaining and suspenseful."

In *Coyote Autumn* protagonist Brad has many qualities in common with the heroes of *Big Red* and *A Dog Called Kitty,* primarily his devotion to his pet. But in Brad's case, this pet is a coyote pup that he hides from his family, hoping to nurse it to health after hunters kill its entire family. When Brad's father gives him a dog, however, it is not long before his family discovers the truth, and Brad is faced with a difficult decision. The coyote is a wild animal and needs its freedom. Can Brad bear to part with him and take him to a wildlife refuge? "Wallace has written a book that displays his talent for creating true-to-life people and the lessons they learn from nature," wrote Jane Halsall in *School Library Journal.* Roger Leslie, in *Booklist,* noted that "Wallace handles the ending with aplomb, infusing just a touch of sentimentality" into the tale.

In *Skinny-Dipping at Monster Lake* a group of eight boys who enjoy camping, fishing, and horseback riding take an overnight trip to a local lake. Kent is certain he has seen the monster rumored to live in the lake, and he decides to see if he can track it down. With the help of his father, a paramedic trained in underwater rescue, Kent discovers the truth about the monster and manages to track down a buried treasure as well. Julie Cummins, writing in *Booklist,* noted that the novel is full of "suspense and humor that boys will surely appreciate," while in *School Library Journal* Barbara Auerbach noted that "readers will admire Kent's insight and courage."

Kristine is still mourning the death of her beloved horse when her family tries to cheer her with the gift of a puppy in *No Dogs Allowed!* Not wanting to become attached to the puppy and risk being hurt again, Kristine keeps the dog but refuses to pay attention to it. As her grandfather grows increasingly ill and her baby sister also has health concerns, Kristine learns how to manage her fear of loss, finally allowing the puppy to win her over. "Wallace skillfully builds bibliotherapeutic text rife with internal struggle," commented a critic for *Kirkus Reviews.* Lauren Peterson, writing in *Booklist,*

A dog is no replacement for a beloved horse: at least that's what Kristine believes until a new puppy charms his way into her heart in Wallace's 2004 novel. (Cover illustration by Kevin Torline.)

noted that while the first-person narration is sometimes awkward, "the dilemmas she faces and the way she deals with them will ring true to many young readers." Alison Grant, in *School Library Journal*, considered Kristine a "likeable and realistic" narrator, and Lenore Sandel of *Childhood Education* considered the novel "a wonderful read for the preteen."

The relationship between a boy and his dog is again explored in *Pick of the Litter,* in which Tom helps his grandfather raise and train a litter of hunting dogs. When one of the puppies and Tom form a special bond, the boy is tempted to find a way to keep the pup for himself, even though his grandfather has promised the pick of the litter to the breeder. "Wallace promotes traditional values here, using a first-person narrative delivered by a likeable protagonist," noted Shelle Rosenfeld in a review for *Booklist*.

Along with his solo novels and middle-grade readers, Wallace sometimes teams up with his wife, Carol Wallace, to produce chapter books and short novels. With *The Flying Flea, Callie, and Me* and its sequels *That Furball Puppy and Me* and *Chomps, Flea, and Gray*

Cat (That's Me!), the Wallaces introduce readers to Gray, a family cat. The series of chapter books begins when Gray moves in and learns the ropes involved in being a first-class mouser from his mentor, Callie. When a baby bird falls out of its nest, however, Gray is determined to teach the baby, who he names Flea, to fly. The cat's adventures continue when his family brings a puppy home. Sure that the puppy will take all of the attention, Gray manages to get the newcomer banished to the barn. Realizing that the barn rats may put the puppy in danger, Gray does his best to undo the family's decision. "The plot revolves around such issues as fear, a new sibling, and doing the right thing," noted Elaine Lesh Morgan in *School Library Journal.*

Chapter books *Bub Moose* and *Bub, Snow, and the Burly Bear Scare* feature the adventures of a group of woodland friends. In the first title, Bub befriends a wolf pup named Snow; in the sequel, he faces a difficult winter, as he and his mother struggle to find food and must deal with humans in their territory and the threat of a dangerous grizzly. Along with telling the story, the Wallaces wrap some science information into the text, explaining nature concepts like animal territories. Accord-

After a trying year at school, a summer job working at his grandfather's kennel helps twelve-year-old Tom sort out his feelings and learn about responsibility. (Cover illustration by Kevin Torline.)

ing to Arwen Marshall in *School Library Journal, Bub, Snow, and the Burly Bear Scare* "will appeal mainly to fans of the first book and others looking for a light, funny read."

The Wallaces' 2003 collaboration, *The Meanest Hound Around,* tells the story of house dog Freddy, who finds himself homeless when his boy's father abandons him in the woods. Freddy has never learned how to take care of himself, and the world of the junkyard where he hopes to find shelter is anything but a cozy environment. There he meets Spike, a mean junkyard dog who would give anything to leave the cruelty of his master behind. Freddy manages to help Spike escape, and the two travel together in hopes of finding a new family. A *Kirkus Reviews* contributor called the novel "gently written with a sweetness that does not give way to saccharinity," while Cynde Suite noted in *School Library Journal* that, "for early readers who like animal stories, this one is a good choice."

Wallace once told *SATA:* "When I started teaching, I read a story to my class called *Old Yeller.* They really liked it and, when we finished, they wanted me to read another book. I tried three others that they *wouldn't* listen to. Trying to read to my class when they weren't listening wasn't much fun!

"One of my students asked if I would tell stories about things that happened when I was their age. When I ran out of tales about me, they asked if I could make up some. These 'made up' stories got long enough to be books. My students really liked them and after I would read the manuscripts, they wanted to read them too. Finally, they talked me into sending the stories off to get somebody to make *real* books out of them. It took ten years before a company in New York City named Holiday House decided to publish one of my stories.

"I have been very blessed that kids throughout the country have voted my books their 'favorites' and given me numerous state awards. After trying for ten years and having grown-ups tell me the stories weren't any good, and reading some reviews where other grown-ups don't really like the stories all that much—it's really *wonderful* to have kids (for whom I wrote them in the first place) tell me that they like my books!

"I get my ideas from lots of places. I remember things that happened when I was growing up. I listened to my kids when I was teaching school or doing lunchroom duty. At home, my own children sometimes give me ideas. My wife Carol used to teach second grade, but now she's a writer too. We work together in our home near Chickasha, Oklahoma. We have three kids: Justin, our son, Nikki, our middle daughter (she will have her first book published in 2000), and Laurie, our oldest. She has two daughters of her own: Kristine and Bethany. We also have five dogs: April, Mush, Midog, J.C., and Mike; one cat named Gray; and one horse, Dandy."

In **The Meanest Hound Around** *two canine runaways struggle to stay alive by their wits while dreaming of finding a new home where dogs won't be mistreated. (Illustration by John Steven Gurney.)*

Biographical and Critical Sources

PERIODICALS

Booklist, February 1, 1981, Judith Goldberger, review of *A Dog Called Kitty,* pp. 755-756; June 1, 1987, p. 1526; February 1, 1989, Denise M. Wilms, review of *Beauty,* p. 943; April 1, 1991, Leone McDermott, review of *Totally Disgusting,* p. 1569; June 15, 1992, p. 1827; December 1, 1992, p. 671; April 15, 1993, Deborah Abbott, review of *Never Say Quit,* pp. 1516-1517; June 1, 1994, p. 1823; December 15, 1995, Ellen Mandel, review of *Watchdog and the Coyotes,* p. 706; October 1, 1997, p. 320; February 1, 1999, John Peters and Jack Helbig, review of *Eye of the Great Bear,* p. 975; December, 15, 2000, Roger Leslie, review of *Coyote Autumn,* p. 822; May 15, 2003, Julie Cummins, review of *Skinny-Dipping at Monster Lake,* p. 1662; July, 2004, Lauren Peterson, review of *No Dogs Allowed!,* p. 1845; August, 2005, Shelle Rosenfeld, review of *Pick of the Litter,* p. 2032.

Bulletin of the Center for Children's Books, January, 1981, p. 102; July-August, 1986, review of *Ferret in the Bedroom, Lizards in the Fridge,* pp. 218-219; Novem-

ber, 1988, Roger Sutton, review of *Beauty,* p. 88; March, 1990, p. 177; June, 1991, p. 252; July-August, 1992, p. 307; January, 1993, Deborah Stevenson, review of *The Biggest Klutz in Fifth Grade,* pp. 158-159; May, 1994, p. 304; November, 1994, Roger Sutton, review of *True Friends,* p. 108; November, 2000, review of *Coyote Autumn,* p. 124.

Childhood Education, 2005, Lenore Sandel, review of *No Dogs Allowed!*

Five Owls, December, 1990; March, 2000, review of *Never Say Quit,* p. 88.

Kirkus Reviews, December 15, 1989, p. 1831; November 15, 1994, p. 1545; January 15, 2003, review of *The Meanest Hound Around,* p. 148; October 15, 2002, review of *Goosed!,* p. 1539; May 15, 2004, review of *No Dogs Allowed!,* p. 499.

New York Times Book Review, February 8, 1981, Jane Langton, review of *A Dog Called Kitty,* p. 20.

Publishers Weekly, October 17, 1980, pp. 65-66; April 25, 1986, Genevieve Stuttaford, review of *Ferret in the Bedroom, Lizards in the Fridge,* p. 81; April 27, 1992, pp. 269-270.

School Library Journal, August, 1986, pp. 97-98; June-July, 1987, Barbara Chatton, review of *Red Dog,* p. 102; October, 1988, Charlene Strickland, review of *Beauty,* p. 149; October, 1989, p. 122; October, 1990, p. 40; June, 1991, p. 92; May, 1992, Barbara Chatton, review of *Buffalo Gal,* pp. 134-135; December, 1992, Eunice Weech, review of *The Biggest Klutz in Fifth Grade,* p. 114; April, 1993, p. 144; April, 1994, p. 132; November, 1995, Cheryl Cufari, review of *Watchdog and the Coyotes,* p. 107; March, 1998, Lucy Rafael, review of *Upchuck and the Rotten Willy,* p. 189; May, 1999, Nancy P. Reeder, review of *Eye of the Great Bear,* p. 131; August, 1999, Cheryl Cufari, review of *The Flying Flea, Callie, and Me,* p. 142; April, 2000, Elaine Lesh Morgan, review of *That Furball Puppy and Me,* p. 116; October, 2000, Jane Halsall, review of *Coyote Autumn,* p. 173; January, 2001, Barb Lawler, review of *Upchuck and the Rotten Willy: Running Wild,* p. 110; December, 2002, Susan Hepler, review of *Goosed!,* p. 110; January, 2003, Arwen Marshall, review of *Bub, Snow, and the Burly Bear Scare,* p. 114; April, 2003, Cynde Suite, review of *The Meanest Hound Around,* p. 142; August, 2003, Barbara Auerbach, review of *Skinny-Dipping at Monster Lake,* p. 168; August, 2004, Alison Grant, review of *No Dogs Allowed!,* p. 130; July, 2005, Tina Zubak, review of *Pick of the Litter,* p. 110.

Voice of Youth Advocates, August-September, 1987, Susan Rice, review of *Red Dog,* p. 124; October, 1993, p. 220; October, 1994, Diane Tuccillo, review of *Blackwater Swamp,* p. 219; April, 1995, Nancy Zachary, review of *True Friends,* p. 28.

ONLINE

Bill Wallace's Home Page, http://wallacebooks.com (March 20, 2006).

*   *   *

WALLACE, William Keith
See WALLACE, Bill

WALLACE-BRODEUR, Ruth 1941-
(Ruth Wallace Brodeur)

Personal

Born August 25, 1941, in Springfield, MA; daughter of Emery Lincoln (a minister) and Dorothy Helen (a teacher; maiden name, Blume) Wallace; married Paul Wallace-Brodeur (a health policy analyst), September 1, 1962; children: Jennifer, Jeremy, Rachel, Sarah. *Education:* University of Massachusetts, B.S., 1962. *Hobbies and other interests:* Bicycling, Nordic skiing, gardening, quilting, painting.

Addresses

Home—4 Pleasant St., Montpelier, VT 05602.

Career

Writer, 1975—. Pineland Hospital and Training Center, Pownal, ME, member of psychology staff, 1962-63.

Member

Society of Children's Book Writers and Illustrators, American Civil Liberties Union, Southern Poverty Law Center, Green Mountain Club, Unitarian Universalist Association, Nature Conservancy, Vermont Land Trust.

Awards, Honors

Publishers Weekly and *Booklist* Best-of-the-Year selections, and Intermediate Young Hoosier Book Award nomination, 2006, all for *Blue Eyes Better;* several Dorothy Canfield Fisher awards list titles.

Writings

The Kenton Year (middle-grade novel), Atheneum (New York, NY), 1980.

One April Vacation (young-adult novel), Atheneum (New York, NY), 1981.

Callie's Way (middle-grade novel), Atheneum (New York, NY), 1984.

Steps in Time (middle-grade novel), Atheneum (New York, NY), 1986.

Stories from the Big Chair, Macmillan (New York, NY), 1989.

Home by Five (picture book), illustrated by Mark Graham, Macmillan (New York, NY), 1992.

The Godmother Tree (middle-grade novel), HarperCollins (New York, NY), 1992.

Goodbye, Mitch (picture book), illustrated by Kathryn Mitter, Albert Whitman (Morton Grove, IL), 1995.

Blue Eyes Better (middle-grade novel), Dutton (New York, NY), 2002.

Heron Cove (middle-grade novel), Dutton (New York, NY), 2005.

Ruth Wallace-Brodeur

Also contributor to magazines and newspapers, including *Cricket, Highlights for Children, Boys' Life, Pennywhistle Press, Child Life, Backpacker, Family Journal, Vermont Life, Christian Science Monitor,* and *Vermont Woman.*

Sidelights

Vermont-based writer Ruth Wallace-Brodeur likes to piece quilts from scraps of fabric. In her books for middle-grade readers, such as *Callie's Way, Blue Eyes Better,* and *Heron Cove,* she focuses on pre-teens dealing with family complications, fitting personalities and sometimes conflicting emotions together like the pieces of one of her quilts.

In *Callie's Way* Wallace-Brodeur introduces a pre-teen who feels like the odd one out in her family. Callie has dark eyes, while everyone else in her family has blue eyes; unlike her mother and sister she has no musical or artistic talent; and while her father is a minister, Callie is beginning to question the faith she was raised in. Her emotional alienation prevents her from sharing her feelings or her problems involving her middle-school friends and her relationship with boys with her family. When Callie begins a relationship with Megal, a stroke victim living in a nursing home who cannot talk, she begins to express and assert herself, and she eventually makes some tough decisions about her life and her faith. Wallace-Brodeur's "well-told story gets high marks for believability," Ilene Cooper wrote in a *Booklist* review of *Callie's Way.* "Flaws notwithstanding, readers will identify with Callie's feelings of not belonging and her skirmishes with family and teachers," Kathleen Brachmann noted in *School Library Journal.*

Like *Callie's Way,* the young-adult novel *Steps in Time* also involves a relationship between a teen and an elderly woman. In this case, however, the relationship is familial and distant. When sixteen-year old Evangeline (nicknamed Evan) is sent to spend the summer at her grandmother's house on an island off the Maine coast, she is unhappy. Her grandfather has just died, and because Evan was his favorite grandchild, she worries that her presence will upset Gram. As the summer progresses, Evan explores the island, learns how to dive, goes lobstering, and develops a friendship with a handsome young man. She also helps her widowed Gram learn to enjoy life as an independent woman, building a close bond with her older relative in the process. "With the simple beauty of a conch shell held up to the ear, the story is evocative and satisfying," Karen Jameyson wrote in *Horn Book,* while a *Kirkus Reviews* critic described *Steps in Time* as a "complex, thoughtful novel, with the well-drawn characters we've come to expect from Ruth Wallace-Brodeur."

Described by a *Publishers Weekly* reviewer as "a trenchant tale about belonging, hurt and healing," *Heron Cove* focuses on twelve-year-old Sage, who lives with her free-spirited mother. When Mom decides to attend a six-week summer herbal workshop in Vermont, two elderly great aunts volunteer to take Sage in for the duration. Traveling to Heron Cove, Maine, the girl soon

During a summer spent with two loving great aunts in Maine, Sage finally feels like she has a family, but worries about the end of vacation and her return to an empty home with her distracted single mom. (Cover illustration by Robert Gantt Steele.)

feels at home with Bea and Addie, and begins to love her great aunts' seaside home as well as the sense of family and community she has been missing. She also learns why she has never been told about her dead father, and begins to sort out her tangled family history. Wallace-Brodeur's "sweet, old-fashioned story has an appealing main character and a mostly smooth writing style," according to Lauralyn Persson in a *School Library Journal* review, the critic adding that "Sage's wistful yearning for stability rings true." According to Persson, the author "clearly—and affectingly—knows how to make stories matter," while in *Kirkus Reviews* a critic praised *Heron Cove* for its portrayal of "village life, realistic emotions, imperfect parents and . . . the need to belong."

In addition to her young-adult titles, Wallace-Brodeur has also written several books for younger readers. *Goodbye Mitch,* which focuses on a young boy whose pet cat dies from a tumor, was described by *Booklist* contributor Leone McDermott as "a useful point of departure" for parents helping "a child cope with a dying pet." Written for the Vermont Migrant Education Program and designed to reflect the experiences of migrant children from ages eight to twelve, *The Godmother Tree* tells the story of a young girl whose family relocates when Laura Cate's father finds a new job on a farm. At the beginning of the summer, the Cate family travels to the other side of the county and takes up residence in a house for the first time in Laura's life. Although the Cate children are far from their friends and have many chores to do, Laura and her brother Luther adjust to their new life. Laura also develops a relationship with her grandmother, enjoys the country, and visits a favorite tree, which she names the "godmother tree." Laura's fourteen-year-old brother, Ryan is not as happy as his siblings, however; meanwhile, someone—or something—is clipping the buttons from the family's clothes, misplacing belongings, and making mischief in the garden. Carolyn Phelan remarked in *Booklist* that *The Godmother Tree* is "quietly satisfying," and as "mesmerizing as a summer day." *School Library Journal* contributor Phyllis G. Sidorsky described the character of Laura as "an admirable heroine, sensitive yet sensible."

Also for younger readers, *Stories from the Big Chair* was described by a *Kirkus Reviews* critic as a "nicely crafted collection of brief, easily read chapters." As the book begins, Molly tells her mother that she is tired of her little sister, Susan. When Mama proposes that Molly tell stories about herself each day for one week, Molly sits in the family's big chair with one of her parents and tells a story. The first story is about how Molly lost a tooth, the second about taking a bear to school. Gradually, the stories involve Susan and Molly eventually realizes the love and affection she really has for her small sister. Denise Wilms commented in *Booklist* that Wallace-Brodeur's "portrayals of sisterly dynamics are on the mark."

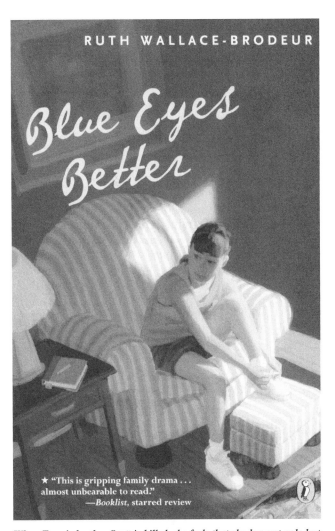

RUTH WALLACE-BRODEUR

Blue Eyes Better

★ "This is gripping family drama . . . almost unbearable to read."
—*Booklist*, starred review

When Tessa's brother Scott is killed, she feels that she has not only lost a sibling; now she is losing her grieving mother as well, in Wallace-Brodeur's sensitive YA novel. (Cover illustration by William Low.)

The picture book *Home by Five* features a curious, thoughtful young protagonist. Rosie ice-skates until the rink closes at 4:30. Promising her parents that she would be home by 5:00, Rosie starts her four-block walk home, but she is distracted first by a friend, then by doughnuts in a window, by snowflakes, and by a friendly cat. When she arrives home half an hour late, Rosie's parents are worried but understanding, and they help the girl find a way to stay on time. Rachel Fox asserted in a *School Library Journal* review that *Home by Five* "is a warm story of a young girl with good intentions," and a *Kirkus Reviews* critic described it as "perceptive and simply told." Stephanie Zvirin observed in *Booklist* that Wallace-Brodeur's "narrative . . . captures time through the eyes of a child . . . genuinely," while a *Publishers Weekly* critic wrote that in *Home by Five* Wallace-Brodeur "skillfully portrays a deep, dreamy, and creative child."

In *Blue Eyes Better* the death of a sixteen year old in a drunk-driving accident leaves the victim's ten-year-old sister full of guilt and sadness. Tessa Drummond feels responsible because she knew her brother Scott was not

telling the truth about where he was going on the night of his death, but she did not tell her parents. Now, the girl's depressed mother leaves the family to stay with a sister on Cape Cod, leaving Tessa to realize that she will never be able to fill the void left by her favored older brother. Fortunately, an elderly neighbor becomes the girl's emotional support and takes on a grandmotherly role, while Tessa's music teacher Ms. Dunn also becomes a confidante. When Ms. Dunn suddenly leaves her job, Tessa must come to terms with her own anger and feelings of abandonment. Praising *Blue Eyes Better* as a "touching first-person problem novel," a *Kirkus Reviews* writer noted that the author's "skill and perception" transforms "a rather conventional pat ending into a moving moment," while in *Publishers Weekly* a critic cited the book as "a fine choice for any middle-grader coping with grief or a grieving parent, and an exquisite example of spare, honest prose." Noting that Wallace-Brodeur's story is optimistic despite its somber theme, Adele Greenlee praised it in *School Library Journal* as "a convincing portrait of a girl and her family rebuilding their lives after tragedy." In *Booklist* Hazel Rochman dubbed the book a "small, beautiful novel rooted in hard fact" in which the author creates "images [that] are simple poetry."

Biographical and Critical Sources

PERIODICALS

Booklist, October 1, 1984, Ilene Cooper, review of *Callie's Way,* p. 252; April 15, 1986, p. 1204; October 15, 1989, Denise Wilms, review of *Stories from the Big Chair,* p. 465; July, 1992, Carolyn Phelan, review of *The Godmother Tree;* September 1, 1992, Stephanie Zvirin, review of *Home by Five;* June 1, 1995, Leone McDermott, review of *Goodbye, Mitch,* p. 1789; November 4, 2002, review of *Blue Eyes Better,* p. 40.

Bulletin of the Center for Children's Books, March, 2002, review of *Blue Eyes Better,* p. 260.

Horn Book, September, 1986, Karen Jameyson, review of *Steps in Time,* pp. 601-602.

Kirkus Reviews, May 1, 1986, review of *Steps in Time,* p. 720; August 1, 1989, review of *Stories from the Big Chair,* p. 1170; September 1, 1992, review of *Home by Five;* December 15, 2001, review of *Blue Eyes Better,* p. 1763; May 1, 2005, review of *Heron Cove,* p. 548.

Publishers Weekly, August 31, 1992, review of *Home by Five;* December 24, 2001, review of *Blue Eyes Better,* p. 65; May 9, 2005, review of *Heron Cove,* p. 71.

School Library Journal, January, 1985, Kathleen Brachmann, review of *Callie's Way,* p. 88; November, 1989, p. 96; May, 1992, Phyllis Sidorsky, review of *The Godmother Tree;* September, 1992, Rachel Fox, review of *Home by Five;* August, 1995, Margaret Chatham, review of *Good-bye, Mitch,* p. 130; January, 2002, Adele Greenlee, review of *Blue Eyes Better,* p. 140; August, 2005, Lauralyn Persson, review of *Heron Cove,* p. 137.

Voice of Youth Advocates, April, 1985, p. 52.

WAUGH, Sylvia 1935-

Personal

Born 1935; married; children: three.

Addresses

Home—Gateshead, England. *Agent*—c/o Author Mail, Delacorte Press, Bantam Dell, 1745 Broadway, New York, NY 10019. *E-mail*—sylvia@waugh-1.freeserve.co.uk.

Career

Children's book author. Formerly worked as a grammar teacher for seventeen years; retired.

Awards, Honors

Birmingham Readers and Writers Children's Book Award, *Guardian* Children's Fiction Prize, Carnegie Award shortlist, Reading Matic Award Top-Ten designation, *Parenting* magazine, Silver Kiss award (Netherlands), and Children's Books of Distinction designation, *Hungry Mind Review,* all 1994, all for *The Mennyms;* Kinderbuchpreis, 2000, for "Mennyms" series.

Writings

"MENNYMS" SERIES

The Mennyms, Julia MacRae (London, England), 1993, Greenwillow (New York, NY), 1994.

Mennyms in the Wilderness, Julia MacRae (London, England), 1994, Greenwillow (New York, NY), 1995.

Mennyms under Siege, Julia MacRae (London, England), 1995, Greenwillow (New York, NY), 1996.

Mennyms Alone, Greenwillow (New York, NY), 1996.

Mennyms Alive, Julia MacRae (London, England), 1996, Greenwillow (New York, NY), 1997.

"ORMINGAT" TRILOGY

Space Race, Delacorte (New York, NY), 2000.

Earthborn, Delacorte (New York, NY), 2002.

Who Goes Home?, Bodley Head (London, England), 2003, Delacorte (New York, NY), 2004.

OTHER

Waugh's books have been translated into Japanese, Polish, Hungarian, Lithuanian, Thai, Hebrew, French, German, Italian, Danish, Swedish, and Spanish.

Work in Progress

An autobiography, titled *Bombs and Butterflies.*

Sidelights

Although writing has always been a central part of her life, British author Sylvia Waugh began her career as a children's book author in her late forties, while working

full-time as a teacher, and her first published book, 1993's *The Mennyms,* immediately captivated both readers and reviewers. The story of a family of life-size, animated rag dolls who pretend to be human, *The Mennyms* became the first book in a series focusing on Waugh's imaginative characters. In addition to the "Mennyms" books, Waugh has also authored three novels in the "Ormingat" series, which also focuses on things that are not what they seem: in this case, as one teen discovers in *Who Goes Home?,* space aliens from the planet Ormingat could be your neighbor, your parent, or even you!

The rag-doll family in Waugh's "Mennyms" books were created by a talented elderly seamstress named Kate Penshaw, and they come magically to life after their creator's death. Now they inhabit an ordinary-looking house, on an ordinary street, in a typical English town, where they go about their business undisturbed. The teenaged dolls Pilbeam and Appleby behave like typical teens, Sir Magnus like a typical grandfather, baby Googles like a typical infant, and Appleby's parents like typical parents. For forty years, in fact, the family has lived at 5 Brocklehurst Grove, London, but because they never age and remain hidden away, each of the Mennyms has become a bit bored in his or her own way. However, boredom changes to anxiety when a letter arrives from Australia announcing that the flat's owner is coming for a visit.

Waugh, who wrote her book because, as she told *Entertainment Weekly* contributor Lois Alter Mark, "the world is too cynical, too lacking in magic," suddenly found herself a bit of a celebrity when *The Mennyms* was hailed by critics in both her native England and the United States. In *Horn Book* Maeve Visser Knoth praised it as "an entertaining story rich in detail and imagination," while also noting the subtleties of Waugh's characters and the fact that "every other detail follows logically" from the fact that the main characters are cloth beings who cannot eat, sleep, or grow old. Praising *The Mennyms* as a "wonderfully eccentric debut," a *Publishers Weekly* reviewer cited the book as "good, old-fashioned fantasy at its finest."

The adventures of the Mennyms continue in several other novels. In *Mennyms in the Wilderness* the dolls find a human friend in Albert Pond, grand nephew of their creator, who arrives in London after being beckoned by the ghost of his great-great-aunt Kate Albert finds that the Mennyms' house is threatened by the construction of a new highway. With his help the dolls make a new home in the country, the dismal Comus House, until the disruption in their home life rights itself and they can return to London again. A *Publishers Weekly* reviewer praised Waugh's second novel "just as good as *The Mennyms* and maybe even better" due to the author's "blend of delicious whimsy and rigorous logic." Noting that the book's fantasy narrative will engage readers, *Horn Book* contributor Martha V. Parravano also noted that the "Mennyms" books have a deeper side: in *Mennyms in the Wilderness,* for example,

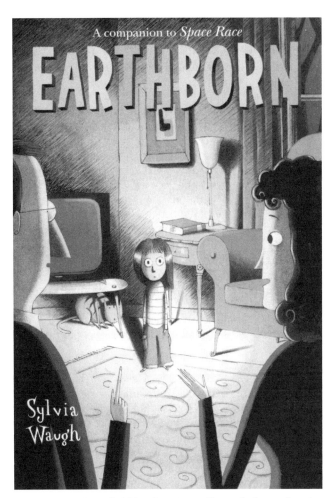

While some children feel like aliens, Nesta Gwynn finds out she actually IS one . . . but when it comes to beaming her up to the mother ship and leaving her friends, she digs in her human heels with a resounding "NO WAY!" in Waugh's 2002 installment in her "Ormingat" series. *(Cover illustration by Martin Matje.)*

Waugh explores "such issues as prejudice and belonging as well as into the more metaphysical questions of existence." As the five-volume series continues, the dolls are rejoined by the ghostly Aunt Kate, are forced into dormancy when their beloved home is reoccupied by Kate's human descendants, and ultimately return to life and reunite in a new home, where they continue their quiet ways, bringing the popular fantasy series to a comfortable conclusion.

Since completing her "Mennyms" books, Waugh has continued her focus, as Parravano noted, on "what it means to be human by exploring the lives of those who are not." In *Space Race,* the first installment in her "Ormingat" trilogy, she introduces alien Patrick (Vateelin) and his son Thomas (Tonitheen), who are visiting Earth and living as humans while on a five-year spying mission for their home planet. Living on Earth almost half of his eleven years, Thomas dreads the fact that the family will be sent home soon, but when a tragedy befalls the pair on their way to retrieve their space ship, he ultimately learns to accept his true identity. "Waugh beams out the message that the driving force in the universe is love—no matter what planet you're from,"

noted Parravano in a *Horn Book* review of *Space Race,* while in *School Library Journal* Susan L. Rogers predicted that "readers will enjoy the exciting plot and fast-moving action" in addition to Waugh's "thoughtful examination of friendship, loyalty, and love."

As the "Ormingat" series continues, other Ormingatrigs are confronted by the prospect of severing their long-term ties with human society. In *Earthborn* stubborn twelve-year-old Nesta has too much to deal with when she finds out that not only are her parents NOT from Boston (they're from the planet Ormingat), but the whole family is scheduled to blast off for the home planet in only a few days' time. Half-human Jacob, in *Who Goes Home?,* is put in a more complex situation because of his mixed heritage when the time comes for his Ormingatrig father to leave Earth. In *Booklist* Carolyn Phelan praised *Earthborn* as "original and involving," while in *Horn Book* Parravano wrote that, in ending the trilogy, Waugh creates in *Who Goes Home?* "a thought-provoking and sometimes heartbreaking exploration of the ties that bind and the ones we can bear to dissolve."

Waugh told *SATA:* "Before *The Mennyms* I had already written a children's novel: *The Shadow People* (unpublished), and before that I was (and still am) an unpublished poet. I have also written many short stories. Writing has been a lifelong interest. My book *Bombs and Butterflies* (not yet published) contains autobiographical material about my own infancy and the stories I was told about my family, stretching back into the nineteenth century.

"Surprisingly, from the reviews I've read, no one seems to have noticed the clever bit of *Who Goes Home?* (or perhaps they have and I just don't know about it). Part of the joy in writing that book was taking events from the first two novels in the series and looking at them from a different perspective! Each book does exist independently, but readers of all three should enjoy this connection—I hope!"

Biographical and Critical Sources

PERIODICALS

Booklist, May 1, 1995, Carolyn Phelan, review of *Mennyms in the Wilderness,* p. 1576; March 15, 1996, Carolyn Phelan, review of *Mennyms under Siege,* p. 1264; September 15, 1996, Carolyn Phelan, review of *Mennyms Alone,* p. 242; September 15, 1997, Carolyn Phelan, review of *Mennyms Alive,* p. 236; July, 2000, Michael Cart, review of *Space Race,* p. 2026; September 1, 2002, Carolyn Phelan, review of *Earthborn,* p. 125; June, 2004, Carolyn Phelan, review of *Who Goes Home?,* p. 1457.

Entertainment Weekly, April 8, 1994, Louis Alter Mark, review of *The Mennyms,* p. 69.

Horn Book, July-August, 1994, Maeve Visser Knoth, review of *The Mennyms,* p. 456; July-August, 1995, Martha V. Parravano, review of *Mennyms in the Wil-*

Jacob never asked to have a life-threatening disease, and he did not ask to be part alien either; but when his dad asks for help doing his job keeping other aliens safe on Earth, Jacob begins to rethink his stubbornly held views. (Cover illustration by Martin Matje.)

derness, p. 462; January-February, 1997, Sarah Guille, review of *Mennyms Alone,* p. 69; July, 2000, Martha V. Parravano, review of *Space Race,* p. 469; September-October, 2002, Martha V. Parravano, review of *Earthborn,* p. 583; March-April, 2004, Martha V. Parravano, review of *Who Goes Home?,* p. 190.

Kirkus Reviews, July 15, 2002, review of *Earthborn,* p. 1047; March 15, 2004, review of *Who Goes Home?,* p. 279.

Publishers Weekly, April 4, 1994, review of *The Mennyms,* p. 81; May 8, 1995, review of *Mennyms in the Wilderness,* p. 296; May 22, 1995, Kit Alderdice, "From Rags to Riches: British Author Sylvia Waugh Delights in Spinning Stories about a Magical Rag Doll Family," p. 25; August 7, 2000, review of *Space Race,* p. 96.

School Library Journal, August, 2000, Susan L. Rogers, review of *Space Race,* p. 190; September, 2002, Eva Mitnick, review of *Earthborn,* p. 236; June, 2004, Jean Gaffney, review of *Who Goes Home?,* p. 152.

ONLINE

Fantastic Fiction Web site, http://www.fantasticfiction.co.uk/ (May 8, 2006), "Sylvia Waugh."

WICKSTROM, Sylvie 1960-

Personal

Born March 17, 1960, in Casablanca, Morocco; daughter of Maurice Kantorovitz (a teachers inspector) and Esther Anahory (a teacher); married Thor Wickstrom, May, 1983 (divorced, 2001); children: Sosha. *Education:* École Normale de Beauvais, degree (French); attended Arts Students' League (New York, NY), and École des Beaux Arts (Paris, France). *Hobbies and other interests:* Reading, listening to music, biking, going to plays, concerts, movies, art shows, and galleries.

Addresses

Home—NY. *Agent*—Linda Pratt, Sheldon Fogelman Agency, 10 E. 40th St., New York, NY 10016. *E-mail*—sylvie@sylviewickstrom.com.

Career

Painter and illustrator, beginning 1987.

Writings

Sylvie Wickstrom

SELF-ILLUSTRATED

Mothers Can't Get Sick, Crown (New York, NY), 1989.
Turkey on the Loose!, Dial (New York, NY), 1990.
I Love You, Mister Bear, HarperCollins (New York, NY), 2004.

ILLUSTRATOR

Raffi, *The Wheels on the Bus,* Random House (New York, NY), 1988.
Clyde Robert Bulla, *The Christmas Coat,* Knopf (New York, NY), 1989.
Roberta Edwards, *Five Silly Fishermen,* Random House (New York, NY), 1989, reprinted, 2003.
Lillian Morrison, compiler, *Yours till Niagara Falls: A Book of Autograph Verses,* new edition, Thomas Y. Crowell (New York, NY), 1990.
Laura Simms, *The Squeaky Door,* Crown (New York, NY), 1991.
Mary Elise Monsell, *Armadillo,* Atheneum (New York, NY), 1991.
Karen Ackerman, *This Old House,* Atheneum (New York, NY), 1992.
Barbara A. Moe, *Dog Days for Dudley,* Bradbury Press (New York, NY), 1994.
Betty Miles, *Hey! I'm Reading!: A How-to-Read Book for Beginners,* Knopf (New York, NY), 1995.
Amy Goldman Koss, *The Baby,* Open Court Publisher (Chicago, IL), 1995.
Deborah Hautzig, *Walter the Warlock,* Random House (New York, NY), 1996.

Deborah Hautzig, *Little Witch Goes to School,* Random House (New York, NY), 1998.
Stuart J. Murphy, *Room for Ripley,* HarperCollins (New York, NY), 1999.
Ann Whitford Paul, *Silly Sadie, Silly Samuel* (reader), Simon & Schuster (New York, NY), 2000.
Deborah Hautzig, *Little Witch's Bad Dream,* Random House (New York, NY), 2000.
Deborah Hautzig, *Little Witch Takes Charge!,* Random House (New York, NY), 2002.
Anna Jane Hayes, *Silly Sara: A Phonics Reader,* Random House (New York, NY), 2002.
Deborah Hautzig, *Little Witch Goes to Camp,* Random House (New York, NY), 2002.
Deborah Hautzig, *Little Witch Learns to Read,* Random House (New York, NY), 2003.
Deborah Hautzig, *Little Witch Loves to Write,* Random House (New York, NY), 2004.
Lola M. Shaefer, *Loose Tooth* (reader), HarperCollins (New York, NY), 2004.
Graham Tether, *The Knee Book* (reader), Random House (New York, NY), 2005.
Anna Jane Hayes, *Smarty Sara,* Random House (New York, NY), 2006.
Natasha Wing, *Go to Bed, Monster,* Harcourt (New York, NY), 2007.

Contributor of illustrations to periodicals, including *Click* and *NAEYC Magazine.*

Sidelights

Primarily an illustrator, Sylvie Wickstrom is noted for her work in collaboration with writer Deborah Hautzig on Hautzing's "Little Witch" novels for younger readers. In addition to the "Little Witch" books, Wickstrom has illustrated books by several other writers, such as Amy Goldman Koss, Stuart J. Murphy, and Clyde Robert Bulla, and has even donned the "author" hat by creating both text and illustrations for the picture books *Mothers Can't Get Sick, Turkey on the Loose!,* and *I Love You, Mister Bear.* Reviewing Wickstrom's work for Mary Elise Monsell's picture book *Armadillo,* a *Publishers Weekly* contributor wrote that "young readers will be . . . charmed by the soft, warm-toned watercolors," while in a *Booklist* review of Ann Whitford Paul's farm-themed picture book *Silly Sadie, Silly Samuel,* Hazel Rochman praised Wickstrom's play on painter Grant Wood's famous picture *American Gothic,* adding that the book's "innocent slapstick nonsense" is reflected in the book's "colorful cartoons."

In *I Love You, Mister Bear* a scruffy, well-worn teddy bear looking for a new home at a yard sale finds one when Sosha—named for the author's daughter—feels sorry for the tattered toy. Bringing the bear home, the girl watches as a bath and a suit of new clothes created with the help of Sosha's mother accomplishes a transformation, and Mister Bear turns out to be quite dapper indeed. Praising Wickstrom's text as "endearing" and "simply told," Carolyn Phelan wrote in *Booklist* that the picture book is "illustrated with affection and panache," while in *School Library Journal* Marge Loch-Wouters described Wickstrom's "quiet story" as "perfect for beginning readers or one-on-one sharing." The author/ illustrator "makes every picture and line resonate with Sosha's forthright love," concluded a *Publishers Weekly* reviewer, adding that the art reflects "the pride all children take in their own redemptive powers."

Wickstrom told *SATA:* "I grew up in France. Besides being an avid reader, I always loved to draw and paint. Although proud of my artistic production, my parents did not favor a career in art. After high school, I tried a year of commercial studies. It was a nightmare. I then followed in my parents' footsteps and became a school teacher. After one year of teaching, the need to create took over and there came the chance to study for one year at the Arts Students' League in New York City. It was heaven. I painted, drew, met my future husband, and discovered the wonderful and magic world of picture books. (They were often close to the art books in bookstores.) Returning to France, I went to the Beaux Arts in Paris, married Thor Wickstrom, painted some more, and started a portfolio of illustrations. Back in the United States in 1985, I took my portfolio around to publishers in New York City and eventually was offered a chance to illustrate Raffi's *The Wheels on the Bus.*

"After a few more illustrated books and a move upstate, I had a daughter who required an enormous amount of being read to. She also loved improvised stories about

Focusing on a circumstance many youngsters can relate to, Wickstrom's I Love You, Mister Bear *describes how a tattered toy can capture a child's compassionate heart.*

herself. The idea of writing my own stories had already taken seed but Sosha was the fertilizer. It took many years and many rewrites before *I Love You, Mister Bear* came out in 2004.

"I am still writing, although at this date, no story of mine is under contract. I am still illustrating, of course. And I am also painting, using my maiden name Sylvie Kantorovitz as my painter's name.

"When I illustrate, I enjoy being able to create characters undergoing a whole range of feelings, and families where parents are present and all-loving . . . not as it was for me. Being a child is a very difficult time of life and a time that will shape what we adults are. It is therefore important to me to describe a range of emotions—albeit in a cartoony way—that I think children go through every day. I wish I had been taught that sadness, jealousy, anger, pain, longing were valid feelings. I've wondered if my love for the world of picture books is a way for me to re-create a childhood for myself.

"As far as my style is concerned, I strive for simplicity. The 'less is more' phrase could be my motto. I enjoy varying the medium and trying different approaches with every title. I never feel I've achieved my goal, though. . . . I guess it is good as it keeps me reaching for more."

Biographical and Critical Sources

PERIODICALS

Booklist, October 15, 1992, Ilene Cooper, review of *This Old House,* p. 436; October 1, 1994, Hazel Rochman,

review of *Dog Days for Dudley,* p. 329; December 1, 1999, Hazel Rochman, review of *Silly Sadie, Silly Samuel,* p. 716; January 1, 2004, Carolyn Phelan, review of *I Love You, Mister Bear,* p. 884.

Horn Book, July-August, 1988, Karen Jameyson, review of *The Wheels on the Bus,* p. 483; November-December, 1989, Ellen Fader, review of *Mothers Can't Get Sick,* p. 765.

Kirkus Reviews, November 15, 2003, review of *I Love You, Mister Bear,* p. 1365.

Publishers Weekly, February 12, 1988, review of *The Wheels on the Bus,* p. 83; July 14, 1989, review of *Mothers Can't Get Sick,* p. 75; August 23, 1991, review of *Armadillo,* p. 61; August 31, 1992, review of *This Old House,* p. 78; January 19, 2004, review of *I Love You, Mister Bear,* p. 74.

School Library Journal, June-July, 1988, Jennifer Smith, review of *The Wheels on the Bus,* p. 98; September, 1989, Patricia Homer, review of *Mothers Can't Get Sick,* p. 235; April, 1990, Sharon McEmeel, review of *Five Silly Fishermen,* p. 88; October, 1990, Susan Hepler, review of *The Christmas Coat,* p. 34; March, 1991, Leslie Barban, review of *Turkey on the Loose!,* p. 180; May, 1991, Luann Toth, review of *The Squeaky Door,* p. 84; November, 1991, Virginia E. Jeschelnig, review of *Armadillo,* p. 104; October, 1994, Christina Door, review of *Dog Days for Dudley,* p. 94; March, 2000, Diane Janoff, review of *Silly Sadie, Silly Samuel,* p. 211; January, 2004, Marge Loch-Wouters, review of *I Love You, Mister Bear,* p. 107.

ONLINE

Sylvie Wickstrom Home Page, http://www.sylviewickstrom. com (April 12, 2006).

*   *   *

WILSON, Troy 1970-

Personal

Born June 4, 1970, in Port Alberni, British Columbia, Canada; son of Ken Wilson (an electrician) and Heather Richmond (a waitress, realtor, and homemaker). *Education:* Attended Malaspina College (now University-College), 1988-90; attended University of Victoria, 1990-94; Camosun College, Diploma (applied communication), 2000.

Addresses

Home—1011-1147 Quadra St., Victoria, British Columbia V8W 2K5, Canada. *E-mail*—troyagain@shaw.ca.

Career

Writer. Summer camp counselor in British Columbia, Canada, 1990-98, 2000-01; British Columbia Ferries, customer sales and service representatives, 2002-04.

Troy Wilson

Awards, Honors

Blue Spruce Award nomination, 2005, and Chocolate Lily Book Award nomination, and Florida Reading Association Children's Book Award nomination, both 2005-06, all for *Perfect Man.*

Writings

Perfect Man, illustrated by Dean Griffiths, Orca Book Publisher (Custer, WA), 2004.
Frosty Is a Stupid Name, illustrated by Dean Griffiths, Orca Book Publishers (Custer, WA), 2005.

Contributor to periodicals, including *ChickaDee* and Victoria, British Columbia's *Monday Magazine.*

Work in Progress

The picture books *Save My Cat!* and *Snowless in Seattle.*

Sidelights

Canadian writer Troy Wilson told *SATA:* "It's ironic, really. I was born and raised in Port Alberni, British Columbia, Canada. Surrounded on all sides by stunning natural beauty. Mountains, forests, crystal clear lakes, oceans—you name it. But I couldn't have cared less about that stuff. My three favorite activities were reading, writing, and cartooning. Heck, they were practically my *only* activities. I spent as much time in my room as I did outside. As long as I had a steady supply of books, comics, paper, and pens, I was as happy as a colt in clover. I wanted to be a cartoonist or a writer when I grew up or both. Partly because I loved comics and stories. And partly because I didn't believe I could do anything else.

"When I was very young, I sold comic stories to my mother and grandmother Nana. As time went on, though, I crafted fewer and fewer stories at home, saving my creative energy for school. Then, between sixth and tenth grade, my teachers didn't ask for stories, so I didn't create any. At Mt. Klitska Junior High School I drew a comic strip for the school paper called "The Roaming Reporter," in which a reporter interviewed various teachers and staff with comedic results. At home, I drew a comic about a monkey with super powers, As for writing, I did manage to get my first letter published in a comic-book letter column—a big thrill for me! It appeared in Marvel's *Rom, Space Knight.*

"When my family moved an hour south to Nanaimo, British Columbia, my writing took off. In grades 11 and 12, I took journalism, creative writing, and every other English-related elective I could. I even won a couple of prizes in a district-wide writing contest. As I entered the education faculty at Malaspina College, I landed my first publishing credit: a humorous essay in the now-defunct comics magazine, *Amazing Heroes.*

"When I transferred to the University of Victoria, I discovered I wasn't cut out to be a teacher and eventually I dropped out of the program. I wandered the employment landscape, working as a burger flipper, day care worker, summer camp counselor, Internet trainer, market surveyor, radio DJ/ producer, and customer service and sales representative.

"Nearing the end of 2000, I decided to get serious about my creative-writing endeavors. By the end of 2001, I'd won third place in the Victoria School of Writing's postcard fiction competition, published my first opinion piece in *Monday Magazine,* an alternative weekly in Victoria, and signed a contract with Orca Book Publishers for *Perfect Man.* A year later, I signed the contract for *Frosty Is a Stupid Name.*

"In *Perfect Man* Michael Maxwell McAllum learns lessons that I wished I'd learned at his age. He's too obsessed with a superhero named Perfect Man (just as I was too obsessed with comic books) until a teacher named Mr. Clark talks some sense into him and suggest he start living his life. Mr. Clark's advice to Michael is pretty much the only advice that might have convinced me (as a boy) to mix a few more real-world activities into my all-comics, all-the-time diet. But none of the adults in my life ever made their cases in quite the way Mr. Clark does. And even if they had, I probably wouldn't have listened anyway! The fact that *Perfect Man* was praised by one of my childhood idols, Stan 'The Man' Lee (co-creator of Spider-Man, Hulk, Fantastic Four, etc.) means more to me than any award the book has received."

On his home page, Wilson had this advice for budding writers: "Don't be afraid to make mistakes, because not only are mistakes inevitable, they are absolutely crucial. The goal is not to prevent all mistakes. (Prevent some? Sure. Prevent all? Fuhgeddaboudit!) The goal is to stop repeating the *same* mistakes again and again. The goal is to make new ones. You want to make as many *different kinds* of mistakes as you possibly can."

Biographical and Critical Sources

PERIODICALS

Kirkus Reviews, May 1, 2004, review of *Perfect Man,* p. 451.
Resource Links, April, 2004, Linda Ludke, review of *Perfect Man,* p. 10.
School Library Journal, November, 2005, Lisa S. Schindler, review of *Frosty Is a Stupid Name,* p. 110.

ONLINE

Troy Wilson Home Page, http://www.troywilson.ca (April 12, 2006).

When Michael's favorite real-world superhero hangs up his cape for good in Wilson's novel **Perfect Man,** *the preteen is convinced that the man will come back into his life in another guise: but as who? (Illustration by Dean Griffiths.)*

* * *

WOOLFE, Angela 1976-

Personal

Born October, 1976, in Warwickshire, England. *Education:* Cambridge University, graduated; postgraduate study in journalism. *Hobbies and other interests:* Music, theatre.

Addresses

Home—London, England. *Agent*—c/o Rod Hall Agency Limited, 6th Fl., Fairgate House, 78 New Oxford St., London WC1A 1HB, England.

Career

Journalist and author. *Vogue* magazine, London, England, member of staff; freelance writer.

Writings

Avril Crump and Her Amazing Clones, Egmont (London, England), 2004, Orchard (New York, NY), 2005.
Avril Crump and the Slumber Code, Egmont (London, England), 2005, published as *Avril Crump and the Clone Countdown,* Orchard Books (New York, NY), 2006.
Avril Crump and the Lucky Thirteen, Egmont (London, England), 2006.

Biographical and Critical Sources

PERIODICALS

Booklist, March 1, 2005, Ilene Cooper, review of *Avril Crump and Her Amazing Clones,* p. 1199.
Kirkus Reviews, February 1, 2005, review of *Avril Crump and Her Amazing Clones,* p. 183.
School Librarian, autumn, 2004, Lesley Martin, review of *Avril Crump and Her Amazing Clones,* p. 148.
School Library Journal, April, 2005, Eva Mitnick, review of *Avril Crump and Her Amazing Clones,* p. 144.
Voice of Youth Advocates, June, 2005, Cindy Faughnan, review of *Avril Crump and Her Amazing Clones,* p. 154.

ONLINE

Egmont Books Web site, http://www.egmont.co.uk/ (April 17, 2006), "Angela Woolfe."*

*   *   *

ZIMMER, Tracie Vaughn

Personal

Born in Hamilton, OH; married; husband's name Randy; children: Cole, Abbie. *Education:* Ohio State University, degree (special education); Miami University of Ohio, M.A. (reading). *Hobbies and other interests:* Reading, gardening, managing her Web site.

Addresses

Home—Charlotte, NC. *Agent*—c/o Author Mail, Clarion Books, 215 Park Ave. S, New York, NY 10003. *E-mail*—tracievzimmer@yahoo.com.

Career

Educator and writer. Teacher in Ohio public schools for ten years; instructor at community colleges; speaker at schools.

Writings

Sketches from a Spy Tree, illustrated by Andrew Glass, Clarion Books (New York, NY), 2005.
Reaching for Sun,, Bloomsbury (New York, NY), 2006.

Author of teacher's guides and curricula.

Work in Progress

A poetry collection for Clarion Books, due 2008.

Sidelights

Born and raised in Ohio, Tracie Vaughn Zimmer taught in Ohio public schools, where her passion for reading and writing, as well as her training in special education, inspired her young students. In addition to working as a speaker for schools and as the author of instructional guides and teaching materials, Zimmer has also added to the wealth of books for young readers with her poetry collection *Sketches from a Spy Tree.*

In Zimmer's book she introduces Anne Marie, a girl who, like Zimmer herself, is an identical twin. In verse, Anne Marie describes many aspects of her life, from

Comprised of a series of interlinked poems, Zimmer's **Sketches from a Spy Tree** *reflects a girl's changing perspective on her friends and neighbors over the span of a year. (Illustration by Andrew Glass.)*

her family and friends to her neighborhood. In addition to people and places, Anne Marie also attempts to express her opinions regarding her parents' divorce, her mother's remarriage, her feelings—good and bad—about being a twin, and her everyday ups and downs. Illustrator Andrew Glass uses a variety of techniques, including photo collage and colored pencil, to compliment Zimmer's revealing poems, and a *Kirkus Reviews* critic commented that *Sketches from a Spy Tree* should be "of special interest to readers who may themselves be facing a shift in family structure." Lee Bock, writing in *School Library Journal,* added that, "with each turn of the page, readers encounter . . . delightfully energized illustrations that complement the subject and mood of each poem well." In *Booklist,* Carolyn Phelan praised the work, noting that Zimmer's poems "chart the shifting movements of Anne Marie's heart" in a book that combines "free verse and freewheeling art with distinction."

A novel told in free verse, *Reaching for Sun* focuses on Josie Watt, who knows what it means to be different. As Zimmer told *SATA,* "Her family's small farmhouse seems to shrink each time another mansion grows up behind it; she lives with her study-obsessed mom and opinionated Gran, and has never known her father; and even if she can forget that she has cerebral palsy, her mom can't seem to let it go. So, when a strange new boy moves into one of the houses nearby—Jordan, who's younger, brighter, and never seems to notice all the things that area supposed to make Josie different—she finds herself reaching out to him."

"I can't imagine my life without books," Zimmer added. "Since childhood, books have sheltered me. It is my honor and privilege to write them for children and my greatest hope that my young readers might find refuge with me in words."

Biographical and Critical Sources

PERIODICALS

Booklist, August, 2005, Carolyn Phelan, review of *Sketches from a Spy Tree,* p. 2032.
Bulletin of the Center for Children's Books, September, 2005, Deborah Stevenson, review of *Sketches from a Spy Tree,* p. 59.
Kirkus Reviews, June 15, 2005, review of *Sketches from a Spy Tree,* p. 693.
School Library Journal, August, 2005, Lee Bock, review of *Sketches from a Spy Tree,* p. 140.

ONLINE

Tracie Vaughn Zimmer Home Page, http://www.tracievaughnzimmer.com (December 14, 2005).

Illustrations Index

(In the following index, the number of the *volume* in which an illustrator's work appears is given *before* the colon, and the *page number* on which it appears is given *after* the colon. For example, a drawing by Adams, Adrienne appears in Volume 2 on page 6, another drawing by her appears in Volume 3 on page 80, another drawing in Volume 8 on page 1, and so on and so on. . . .)

YABC

Index references to *YABC* refer to listings appearing in the two-volume *Yesterday's Authors of Books for Children,* also published by Thomson Gale. *YABC* covers prominent authors and illustrators who died prior to 1960.

A

Aas, Ulf *5:* 174
Abbe, S. van
   See van Abbe, S.
Abel, Raymond *6:* 122; *7:* 195; *12:* 3; *21:* 86; *25:* 119
Abelliera, Aldo *71:* 120
Abolafia, Yossi *60:* 2; *93:* 163; *152:* 202
Abrahams, Hilary *26:* 205; *29:* 24-25; *53:* 61
Abrams, Kathie *36:* 170
Abrams, Lester *49:* 26
Abulafia, Yossi *154:* 67
Accorsi, William *11:* 198
Acs, Laszlo *14:* 156; *42:* 22
Adams, Adrienne *2:* 6; *3:* 80; *8:* 1; *15:* 107; *16:* 180; *20:* 65; *22:* 134-135; *33:* 75; *36:* 103, 112; *39:* 74; *86:* 54; *90:* 2, 3
Adams, Connie J. *129:* 68
Adams, John Wolcott *17:* 162
Adams, Lynn *96:* 44
Adams, Norman *55:* 82
Adams, Pam *112:* 1, 2
Adams, Sarah *98:* 126
Adamson, George *30:* 23, 24; *69:* 64
Addams, Charles *55:* 5
Ade, Rene *76:* 198
Adinolfi, JoAnn *115:* 42
Adkins, Alta *22:* 250
Adkins, Jan *8:* 3; *69:* 4; *144:* 2, 3, 4
Adler, Peggy *22:* 6; *29:* 31
Adler, Ruth *29:* 29
Adlerman, Daniel *163:* 2
Adragna, Robert *47:* 145
Agard, Nadema *18:* 1
Agee, Jon *116:* 8, 9, 10; *157:* 4
Agre, Patricia *47:* 195
Aguirre, Alfredo *152:* 218
Ahl, Anna Maria *32:* 24
Ahlberg, Allan *68:* 6-7, 9; *165:* 5
Ahlberg, Janet *68:* 6-7, 9
Aicher-Scholl, Inge *63:* 127
Aichinger, Helga *4:* 5, 45
Aitken, Amy *31:* 34
Akaba, Suekichi *46:* 23; *53:* 127
Akasaka, Miyoshi *YABC 2:* 261
Akino, Fuku *6:* 144
Alain *40:* 41
Alajalov *2:* 226
Alborough, Jez *86:* 1, 2, 3; *149:* 3

Albrecht, Jan *37:* 176
Albright, Donn *1:* 91
Alcala, Alfredo *91:* 128
Alcorn, John *3:* 159; *7:* 165; *31:* 22; *44:* 127; *46:* 23, 170
Alcorn, Stephen *110:* 4; *125:* 106; *128:* 172; *150:* 97; *160:* 188; *165:* 48
Alcott, May *100:* 3
Alda, Arlene *44:* 24; *158:* 2
Alden, Albert *11:* 103
Aldridge, Andy *27:* 131
Aldridge, George *105:* 125
Alex, Ben *45:* 25, 26
Alexander, Ellen *91:* 3
Alexander, Lloyd *49:* 34
Alexander, Martha *3:* 206; *11:* 103; *13:* 109; *25:* 100; *36:* 131; *70:* 6, 7; *136:* 3, 4, 5; *169:* 120
Alexander, Paul *85:* 57; *90:* 9
Alexeieff, Alexander *14:* 6; *26:* 199
Alfano, Wayne *80:* 69
Aliki
   See Brandenberg, Aliki
Allamand, Pascale *12:* 9
Allan, Judith *38:* 166
Alland, Alexandra *16:* 255
Allen, Gertrude *9:* 6
Allen, Graham *31:* 145
Allen, Jonathan B. *131:* 3, 4
Allen, Pamela *50:* 25, 26-27, 28; *81:* 9, 10; *123:* 4-5
Allen, Rowena *47:* 75
Allen, Thomas B. *81:* 101; *82:* 248; *89:* 37; *104:* 9
Allen, Tom *85:* 176
Allender, David *73:* 223
Alley, R.W. *80:* 183; *95:* 187; *156:* 100, 153; *169:* 4-5
Allison, Linda *43:* 27
Allon, Jeffrey *119:* 174
Allport, Mike *71:* 55
Almquist, Don *11:* 8; *12:* 128; *17:* 46; *22:* 110
Aloise, Frank *5:* 38; *10:* 133; *30:* 92
Althea
   See Braithwaite, Althea
Altschuler, Franz *11:* 185; *23:* 141; *40:* 48; *45:* 29; *57:* 181
Alvin, John *117:* 5
Ambrus, Victor G. *1:* 6-7, 194; *3:* 69; *5:* 15; *6:* 44; *7:* 36; *8:* 210; *12:* 227; *14:* 213; *15:* 213; *22:* 209; *24:* 36; *28:* 179; *30:* 178; *32:* 44,

46; *38:* 143; *41:* 25, 26, 27, 28, 29, 30, 31, 32; *42:* 87; *44:* 190; *55:* 172; *62:* 30, 144, 145, 148; *86:* 99, 100, 101; *87:* 66, 137; *89:* 162; *134:* 160
Ames, Lee J. *3:* 12; *9:* 130; *10:* 69; *17:* 214; *22:* 124; *151:* 13
Amon, Aline *9:* 9
Amoss, Berthe *5:* 5
Amstutz, Andre *152:* 102
Amundsen, Dick *7:* 77
Amundsen, Richard E. *5:* 10; *24:* 122
Ancona, George *12:* 11; *55:* 144; *145:* 7
Andersen, Bethanne *116:* 167; *162:* 189
Anderson, Alasdair *18:* 122
Anderson, Bob *139:* 16
Anderson, Brad *33:* 28
Anderson, C.W. *11:* 10
Anderson, Carl *7:* 4
Anderson, Catherine Corley *72:* 2
Anderson, Cecil *127:* 152
Anderson, David Lee *118:* 176
Anderson, Derek *169:* 9
Anderson, Doug *40:* 111
Anderson, Erica *23:* 65
Anderson, Laurie *12:* 153, 155
Anderson, Lena *99:* 26
Anderson, Scoular *138:* 13
Anderson, Susan *90:* 12
Anderson, Wayne *23:* 119; *41:* 239; *56:* 7; *62:* 26; *147:* 6
Andreasen, Daniel *86:* 157; *87:* 104; *103:* 201, 202; *159:* 75; *167:* 106, 107
Andrew, Ian *111:* 37; *116:* 12
Andrew, John *22:* 4
Andrews, Benny *14:* 251; *31:* 24; *57:* 6, 7
Anelay, Henry *57:* 173
Angel, Marie *47:* 22
Angelo, Valenti *14:* 8; *18:* 100; *20:* 232; *32:* 70
Anglund, Joan Walsh *2:* 7, 250-251; *37:* 198, 199, 200
Anholt, Catherine *74:* 8; *131:* 7; *141:* 5
Anholt, Laurence *141:* 4
Anno, Mitsumasa *5:* 7; *38:* 25, 26-27, 28, 29, 30, 31, 32; *77:* 3, 4; *157:* 10, 11
Antal, Andrew *1:* 124; *30:* 145
Antram, David *152:* 133
Apostolou, Christy Hale
   See Hale, Christy

Apple, Margot *33:* 25; *35:* 206; *46:* 81; *53:* 8; *61:* 109; *64:* 21, 22, 24, 25, 27; *71:* 176; *77:* 53; *82:* 245; *92:* 39; *94:* 180; *96:* 107; *152:* 4, 5; *162:* 192-194
Appleyard, Dev *2:* 192
Aragones, Sergio *48:* 23, 24, 25, 26, 27
Araneus *40:* 29
Arbo, Cris *103:* 4
Archambault, Matthew *85:* 173; *138:* 19, 20; *143:* 33; *145:* 144
Archer, Janet *16:* 69
Ardizzone, Edward *1:* 11, 12; *2:* 105; *3:* 258; *4:* 78; *7:* 79; *10:* 100; *15:* 232; *20:* 69, 178; *23:* 223; *24:* 125; *28:* 25, 26, 27, 28, 29, 30, 31, 33, 34, 35, 36, 37; *31:* 192, 193; *34:* 215, 217; *60:* 173; *64:* 145; *87:* 176; *YABC 2:* 25
Arenella, Roy *14:* 9
Argent, Kerry *103:* 56; *138:* 17; *158:* 134
Arisman, Marshall *162:* 50
Armer, Austin *13:* 3
Armer, Laura Adams *13:* 3
Armer, Sidney *13:* 3
Armitage, David *47:* 23; *99:* 5; *155:* 4
Armitage, Eileen *4:* 16
Armstrong, George *10:* 6; *21:* 72
Armstrong, Shelagh *102:* 114
Arno, Enrico *1:* 217; *2:* 22, 210; *4:* 9; *5:* 43; *6:* 52; *29:* 217, 219; *33:* 152; *35:* 99; *43:* 31, 32, 33; *45:* 212, 213, 214; *72:* 72; *74:* 166; *100:* 169
Arnold, Emily *76:* 7, 9, 10
Arnold, Katya *115:* 11
Arnold, Tedd *116:* 14; *133:* 152; *160:* 5
Arnosky, James Edward *22:* 20; *70:* 9, 10, 11; *118:* 3, 5; *160:* 8, 10
Arnsteen, Katy Keck *105:* 97; *116:* 145
Arrowood, Clinton *12:* 193; *19:* 11; *65:* 210
Artell, Mike *89:* 8
Arting, Fred J. *41:* 63
Artzybasheff, Boris *13:* 143; *14:* 15; *40:* 152, 155
Aruego, Ariane *6:* 4
Aruego, Jose *4:* 140; *6:* 4; *7:* 64; *33:* 195; *35:* 208; *68:* 16, 17; *75:* 46; *93:* 91, 92; *94:* 197; *109:* 65, 67; *125:* 2, 3, 4, 5; *127:* 188; *143:* 25
Asare, Meshack *86:* 9; *139:* 19
Ascensios, Natalie *105:* 139
Asch, Frank *5:* 9; *66:* 2, 4, 6, 7, 9, 10; *102:* 18, 19, 21; *154:* 12
Ashby, Gail *11:* 135
Ashby, Gil *146:* 4
Ashby, Gwynneth *44:* 26
Ashley, C.W. *19:* 197
Ashmead, Hal *8:* 70
Aska, Warabe *56:* 10
Assel, Steven *44:* 153; *77:* 22, 97
Astrop, John *32:* 56
Atene, Ann *12:* 18
Atherton, Lisa *38:* 198
Atkinson, Allen *60:* 5
Atkinson, J. Priestman *17:* 275
Atkinson, Janet *86:* 147; *103:* 138
Atkinson, Mike *127:* 74
Atkinson, Wayne *40:* 46
Attebery, Charles *38:* 170
Atwell, Debby *150:* 6
Atwood, Ann *7:* 9
Aubrey, Meg Kelleher *77:* 159
Augarde, Steve *25:* 22; *159:* 7
Austerman, Miriam *23:* 107
Austin, Margot *11:* 16
Austin, Robert *3:* 44
Austin, Virginia *81:* 205; *127:* 221
Auth, Tony *51:* 5
Avendano, Dolores *158:* 74
Avedon, Richard *57:* 140
Averill, Esther *1:* 17; *28:* 39, 40, 41
Axeman, Lois *2:* 32; *11:* 84; *13:* 165; *22:* 8; *23:* 49; *61:* 116; *101:* 124

Axtel, David *155:* 110
Ayer, Jacqueline *13:* 7
Ayer, Margaret *15:* 12; *50:* 120
Ayers, Alan *91:* 58; *107:* 169
Ayliffe, Alex *95:* 164
Ayto, Russell *111:* 5; *112:* 54
Azarian, Mary *112:* 9, 10; *114:* 129; *117:* 171; *137:* 163

B

B.T.B.
  See Blackwell, Basil T.
Babbitt, Bradford *33:* 158
Babbitt, Natalie *6:* 6; *8:* 220; *68:* 20; *70:* 242, 243
Baca, Maria *104:* 5
Bacchus, Andy *94:* 87
Bacha, Andy *109:* 169
Bachem, Paul *48:* 180; *67:* 65; *144:* 206
Back, Adam *63:* 125
Back, George *31:* 161
Backhouse, Colin *78:* 142
Bacon, Bruce *4:* 74
Bacon, Paul *7:* 155; *8:* 121; *31:* 55; *50:* 42; *56:* 175; *62:* 82, 84
Bacon, Peggy *2:* 11, 228; *46:* 44
Baek, Matthew J. *169:* 95
Baer, Julie *161:* 2
Bailey, Peter *58:* 174; *87:* 221
Bailey, Sheila *155:* 11
Baker, Alan *22:* 22; *61:* 134; *93:* 11-12; *146:* 6, 7, 10
Baker, Charlotte *2:* 12
Baker, Garin *89:* 65
Baker, Jeannie *23:* 4; *88:* 18, 19, 20
Baker, Jim *22:* 24
Baker, Joe *82:* 188; *111:* 55; *124:* 70
Baker, Leslie *112:* 214; *132:* 103, 246
Baldridge, Cyrus LeRoy *19:* 69; *44:* 50
Baldus, Zachary *152:* 231
Balet, Jan *11:* 22
Balian, Lorna *9:* 16; *91:* 16
Balit, Christina *102:* 24; *159:* 9; *162:* 118, 119
Ballantyne, R.M. *24:* 34
Ballis, George *14:* 199
Baltzer, Hans *40:* 30
Banbery, Fred *58:* 15
Banfill, A. Scott *98:* 7; *112:* 59
Bang, Molly Garrett *24:* 37, 38; *69:* 8, 9, 10; *111:* 7, 9, 10, 11; *140:* 11; *158:* 37-39
Banik, Yvette Santiago *21:* 136
Banner, Angela
  See Maddison, Angela Mary
Bannerman, Helen *19:* 13, 14
Bannon, Laura *6:* 10; *23:* 8
Bantock, Nick *74:* 229; *95:* 6
Baptist, Michael *37:* 208
Baracca, Sal *135:* 206
Barasch, Lynne *126:* 16
Barbarin, Lucien C., Jr. *89:* 88
Barbour, Karen *96:* 5; *74:* 209
Bare, Arnold Edwin *16:* 31
Bare, Colleen Stanley *32:* 33
Barger, Jan *147:* 11
Bargery, Geoffrey *14:* 258
Barkat, Jonathan *149:* 177
Barker, Carol *31:* 27
Barker, Cicely Mary *49:* 50, 51
Barkley, James *4:* 13; *6:* 11; *13:* 112
Barks, Carl *37:* 27, 28, 29, 30-31, 32, 33, 34
Barling, Joy *62:* 148
Barling, Tom *9:* 23
Barlow, Gillian *62:* 20
Barlow, Perry *35:* 28
Barlowe, Dot *30:* 223
Barlowe, Wayne *37:* 72; *84:* 43; *105:* 5
Barnard, Bryn *88:* 53; *13:* 55; *169:* 13
Barner, Bob *29:* 37; *128:* 33; *136:* 19, 20

Barnes, Hiram P. *20:* 28
Barnes, Tim *137:* 28
Barnes-Murphy, Rowan *88:* 22
Barnett, Ivan *70:* 14
Barnett, Moneta *16:* 89; *19:* 142; *31:* 102; *33:* 30, 31, 32; *41:* 153; *61:* 94, 97
Barney, Maginel Wright *39:* 32, 33, 34; *YABC 2:* 306
Barnum, Jay Hyde *11:* 224; *20:* 5; *37:* 189, 190
Baron, Alan *80:* 3; *89:* 123
Barr, George *60:* 74; *69:* 64
Barragan, Paula S. *134:* 116
Barrall, Tim *115:* 152
Barrauds *33:* 114
Barrer-Russell, Gertrude *9:* 65; *27:* 31
Barret, Robert *85:* 134
Barrett, Angela *40:* 136, 137; *62:* 74; *75:* 10; *76:* 142; *144:* 137; *145:* 14
Barrett, Jennifer *58:* 149
Barrett, John E. *43:* 119
Barrett, Moneta *74:* 10
Barrett, Peter *55:* 169; *86:* 111
Barrett, Robert *62:* 145; *77:* 146; *82:* 35
Barrett, Ron *14:* 24; *26:* 35
Barron, John N. *3:* 261; *5:* 101; *14:* 220
Barrow, Ann *136:* 27
Barrows, Walter *14:* 268
Barry, Ethelred B. *37:* 79; *YABC 1:* 229
Barry, James *14:* 25
Barry, Katharina *2:* 159; *4:* 22
Barry, Robert E. *6:* 12
Barry, Scott *32:* 35
Bartenbach, Jean *40:* 31
Barth, Ernest Kurt *2:* 172; *3:* 160; *8:* 26; *10:* 31
Bartlett, Alison *101:* 88; *165:* 93
Barton, Byron *8:* 207; *9:* 18; *23:* 66; *80:* 181; *90:* 18, 19, 20, 21; *126:* 29, 30
Barton, Harriett *30:* 71
Barton, Jill *129:* 108; *135:* 120; *145:* 185, 189
Bartram, Robert *10:* 42
Bartsch, Jochen *8:* 105; *39:* 38
Bascove, Barbara *45:* 73
Base, Graeme *101:* 15, 16, 17, 18; *162:* 8, 10, 12
Bash, Barbara *132:* 9
Baskin, Leonard *30:* 42, 43, 46, 47; *49:* 125, 126, 128, 129, 133
Bass, Saul *49:* 192
Bassett, Jeni *40:* 99; *64:* 30
Basso, Bill *99:* 139
Batchelor, Joy *29:* 41, 47, 48
Bate, Norman *5:* 16
Bates, Leo *24:* 35
Batet, Carmen *39:* 134
Batherman, Muriel *31:* 79; *45:* 185
Battaglia, Aurelius *50:* 44
Batten, John D. *25:* 161, 162
Batten, Mary *162:* 14, 15
Battles, Asa *32:* 94, 95
Bauer, Jutta *150:* 32
Bauernschmidt, Marjorie *15:* 15
Baum, Allyn *20:* 10
Baum, Willi *4:* 24-25; *7:* 173
Bauman, Leslie *61:* 121
Baumann, Jill *34:* 170
Baumhauer, Hans *11:* 218; *15:* 163, 165, 167
Baxter, Glen *57:* 100
Baxter, Leon *59:* 102
Baxter, Robert *87:* 129
Bayley, Dorothy *37:* 195
Bayley, Nicola *40:* 104; *41:* 34, 35; *69:* 15; *129:* 33, 34, 35
Baylin, Mark *158:* 233
Baynes, Pauline *2:* 244; *3:* 149; *13:* 133, 135, 137-141; *19:* 18, 19, 20; *32:* 208, 213, 214; *36:* 105, 108; *59:* 12, 13, 14, 16, 17, 18, 20; *100:* 158, 159, 243; *133:* 3, 4
Beach, Lou *150:* 150
Beame, Rona *12:* 40

Bear's Heart *73:* 215
Beard, Dan *22:* 31, 32
Beard, J.H. *YABC 1:* 158
Bearden, Romare *9:* 7; *22:* 35
Beardshaw, Rosalind *169:* 22
Beardsley, Aubrey *17:* 14; *23:* 181; *59:* 130, 131
Bearman, Jane *29:* 38
Beaton, Cecil *24:* 208
Beaton, Clare *125:* 28
Beauce, J.A. *18:* 103
Beaujard, Sophie *81:* 54
Beck, Charles *11:* 169; *51:* 173
Beck, Ian *138:* 27
Beck, Ruth *13:* 11
Becker, Harriet *12:* 211
Beckett, Sheilah *25:* 5; *33:* 37, 38
Beckhoff, Harry *1:* 78; *5:* 163
Beckman, Kaj *45:* 38, 39, 40, 41
Beckman, Per *45:* 42, 43
Beddows, Eric *72:* 70
Bedford, F.D. *20:* 118, 122; *33:* 170; *41:* 220, 221, 230, 233
Bee, Joyce *19:* 62
Beeby, Betty *25:* 36
Beech, Carol *9:* 149
Beek *25:* 51, 55, 59
Beekman, Doug *125:* 146, 148
Beerbohm, Max *24:* 208
Beeson, Bob *108:* 57
Begin, Maryjane *82:* 13
Behr, Joyce *15:* 15; *21:* 132; *23:* 161
Behrens, Hans *5:* 97
Beier, Ellen *135:* 170; *139:* 47
Beinicke, Steve *69:* 18
Beisner, Monika *46:* 128, 131; *112:* 127
Belden, Charles J. *12:* 182
Belina, Renate *39:* 132
Bell, Corydon *3:* 20
Bell, Graham *54:* 48
Bell, Julia *151:* 214
Bell, Julie *159:* 172; *165:* 18
Bell, Thomas P. *76:* 182
Bellamy, Glen *127:* 15
Beltran, Alberto *43:* 37
Bemelmans, Ludwig *15:* 19, 21; *100:* 27
Ben-Ami, Doron *75:* 96; *84:* 107; *108:* 132; *110:* 63; *159:* 157
Bendall-Brunello, John *150:* 4; *157:* 163
Benda, Wladyslaw T. *15:* 256; *30:* 76, 77; *44:* 182
Bender, Robert *77:* 162; *79:* 13; *160:* 23
Bendick, Jeanne *2:* 24; *68:* 27, 28
Benioff, Carol *121:* 42
Benner, Cheryl *80:* 11
Bennett, Charles H. *64:* 6
Bennett, Erin Susanne *165:* 216
Bennett, F.I. *YABC 1:* 134
Bennett, James *146:* 240
Bennett, Jill *26:* 61; *41:* 38, 39; *45:* 54
Bennett, Rainey *15:* 26; *23:* 53
Bennett, Richard *15:* 45; *21:* 11, 12, 13; *25:* 175
Bennett, Susan *5:* 55
Benny, Mike *142:* 78
Benoit, Elise *77:* 74
Benson, Linda *60:* 130; *62:* 91; *75:* 101; *79:* 156; *134:* 129
Benson, Patrick *68:* 162; *147:* 17-19, 20
Bentley, Carolyn *46:* 153
Bentley, James *149:* 30
Bentley, Roy *30:* 162
Benton, Thomas Hart *2:* 99
Berelson, Howard *5:* 20; *16:* 58; *31:* 50
Berenstain, Jan *12:* 47; *64:* 33, 34, 36, 37, 38, 40, 42, 44; *135:* 25, 28, 31, 35
Berenstain, Stan *12:* 47; *64:* 33, 34, 36, 37, 38, 40, 42, 44; *135:* 25, 28, 31, 35
Berenzy, Alix *65:* 13; *73:* 6; *78:* 115
Berg, Joan *1:* 115; *3:* 156; *6:* 26, 58
Berg, Ron *36:* 48, 49; *48:* 37, 38; *67:* 72

Bergen, David *115:* 44
Berger, Barbara *77:* 14
Berger, William M. *14:* 143; *YABC 1:* 204
Bergherr, Mary *74:* 170; *151:* 123
Bergin, Mark *114:* 8, 9; *143:* 95; *160:* 26, 27
Bergstreser, Douglas *69:* 76
Bergum, Constance R. *121:* 14, 15
Bering, Claus *13:* 14
Berkeley, Jon *139:* 218
Berkowitz, Jeanette *3:* 249
Berman, Paul *66:* 14
Bernal, Richard *154:* 176
Bernadette
　　See Watts, Bernadette
Bernardin, James *112:* 24; *167:* 94
Bernath, Stefen *32:* 76
Bernhard, Durga *80:* 13
Bernstein, Michel J. *51:* 71
Bernstein, Ted *38:* 183; *50:* 131
Bernstein, Zena *23:* 46
Berridge, Celia *86:* 63
Berrill, Jacquelyn *12:* 50
Berry, Erick
　　See Best, Allena
Berry, William D. *14:* 29; *19:* 48
Berry, William A. *6:* 219
Berson, Harold *2:* 17, 18; *4:* 28, 29, 220; *9:* 10; *12:* 19; *17:* 45; *18:* 193; *22:* 85; *34:* 172; *44:* 120; *46:* 42; *80:* 240
Berton, Patsy *99:* 16
Bertschmann, Harry *16:* 1
Besco, Don *70:* 99
Beskow, Elsa *20:* 13, 14, 15
Bess, Clayton *63:* 94
Best, Allena *2:* 26; *34:* 76
Betera, Carol *74:* 68
Bethell, Thomas N. *61:* 169
Bethers, Ray *6:* 22
Bettina
　　See Ehrlich, Bettina
Betts, Ethel Franklin *17:* 161, 164, 165; *YABC 2:* 47
Betz, Rudolf *59:* 161
Bewick, Thomas *16:* 40-41, 43-45, 47; *54:* 150; *YABC 1:* 107
Beyer, Paul J. III *74:* 24
Bezencon, Jacqueline *48:* 40
Biamonte, Daniel *40:* 90
Bianchi, John *91:* 19
Bianco, Pamela *15:* 31; *28:* 44, 45, 46
Bible, Charles *13:* 15
Bice, Clare *22:* 40
Bierman, Don *57:* 184
Biggers, John *2:* 123
Bileck, Marvin *3:* 102; *40:* 36, 37
Bilibin, Ivan *61:* 8, 9, 12, 13, 14, 15, 151, 152, 154, 162
Billington, Patrick *98:* 71
Billout, Guy *144:* 38, 39
Bimen, Levent *5:* 179
Binch, Caroline *81:* 18; *140:* 15, 16; *144:* 115
Binder, Hannes *169:* 163
Bing, Christopher *126:* 34
Binger, Bill *121:* 46
Binks, Robert *25:* 150
Binzen, Bill *24:* 47
Birch, Reginald *15:* 150; *19:* 33, 34, 35, 36; *37:* 196, 197; *44:* 182; *46:* 176; *YABC 1:* 84; *2:* 34, 39
Birchall, Mark *123:* 188
Bird, Esther Brock *1:* 36; *25:* 66
Birdsong, Keith *167:* 85
Birkett, Rachel *78:* 206
Birling, Paul *109:* 30
Birmingham, Christian *132:* 243; *143:* 114
Birmingham, Lloyd P. *12:* 51; *83:* 13
Biro, Val *1:* 26; *41:* 42; *60:* 178; *67:* 23, 24; *84:* 242, 243
Bischoff, Ilse *44:* 51
Bishop, Gavin *97:* 17, 18; *144:* 42, 44
Bishop, Kathleen Wong *115:* 67

Bishop, Rich *56:* 43
Bite, I. *60:* 14
Bittinger, Ned *93:* 117
Bjorklund, Lorence *3:* 188, 252; *7:* 100; *9:* 113; *10:* 66; *19:* 178; *33:* 122, 123; *35:* 36, 37, 38, 39, 41, 42, 43; *36:* 185; *38:* 93; *47:* 106; *66:* 194; *YABC 1:* 242
Bjorkman, Steve *91:* 199; *160:* 110
Blackburn, Loren H. *63:* 10
Blackford, John *137:* 105
Blackwell, Basil T. *YABC 1:* 68, 69
Blackwood, Gary L. *118:* 17
Blades, Ann *16:* 52; *37:* 213; *50:* 41; *69:* 21; *99:* 215
Blair, Jay *45:* 46; *46:* 155
Blaisdell, Elinore *1:* 121; *3:* 134; *35:* 63
Blake, Robert J. *160:* 28, 29
Blake, Quentin *3:* 170; *10:* 48; *13:* 38; *21:* 180; *26:* 60; *28:* 228; *30:* 29, 31; *40:* 108; *45:* 219; *46:* 165, 168; *48:* 196; *52:* 10, 11, 12, 13, 14, 15, 16, 17; *73:* 41, 43; *78:* 84, 86; *80:* 250, 251; *84:* 210, 211, 212; *87:* 177; *96:* 24, 26, 28; *124:* 79; *125:* 32, 34
Blake, Robert J. *37:* 90; *53:* 67; *54:* 23
Blake, William *30:* 54, 56, 57, 58, 59, 60
Blanchard, N. Taylor *82:* 140
Blass, Jacqueline *8:* 215
Blazek, Scott R. *91:* 71
Bleck, Cathie *118:* 116
Blegvad, Erik *2:* 59; *3:* 98; *5:* 117; *7:* 131; *11:* 149; *14:* 34, 35; *18:* 237; *32:* 219; *60:* 106; *66:* 16, 17, 18, 19; *70:* 233; *76:* 18; *82:* 106; *87:* 45; *100:* 188; *129:* 125; *132:* 17, 18, 19, 20; *YABC 1:* 201
Blessen, Karen *93:* 126
Bliss, Corinne Demas *37:* 38
Bloch, Lucienne *10:* 12
Blondon, Herve *129:* 48
Bloom, Lloyd *35:* 180; *36:* 149; *47:* 99; *62:* 117; *68:* 231; *72:* 136; *75:* 185; *83:* 99; *108:* 19
Blossom, Dave *34:* 29
Blumenschein, E.L. *YABC 1:* 113, 115
Blumer, Patt *29:* 214
Blundell, Kim *29:* 36
Bluthenthal, Diana Cain *93:* 32; *104:* 106
Blythe, Benjamin *128:* 7
Blythe, Gary *112:* 52
Boardman, Gwenn *12:* 60
Bober, Richard *125:* 145; *132:* 40
Bobri *30:* 138; *47:* 27
Bock, Vera *1:* 187; *21:* 41
Bock, William Sauts *8:* 7; *14:* 37; *16:* 120; *21:* 141; *36:* 177; *62:* 203
Bodecker, N(iels) M(ogens) *8:* 13; *14:* 2; *17:* 55-57; *73:* 22, 23, 24
Boehm, Linda *40:* 31
Bogacki, Tomek *138:* 31, 32; *144:* 123
Bogdan, Florentina *107:* 43
Bohdal, Susi *22:* 44; *101:* 20
Bohlen, Nina *58:* 13
Boies, Alex *96:* 53
Bolam, Emily *101:* 216; *159:* 12
Bolian, Polly *3:* 270; *4:* 30; *13:* 77; *29:* 197
Bolle, Frank *87:* 100
Bollen, Roger *79:* 186; *83:* 16
Bolling, Vickey *114:* 44
Bollinger, Peter *101:* 7; *128:* 198
Bolognese, Don *2:* 147, 231; *4:* 176; *7:* 146; *17:* 43; *23:* 192; *24:* 50; *34:* 108; *36:* 133; *71:* 24, 25; *103:* 131; *129:* 39, 40
Bolton, A.T. *57:* 158
Bond, Arnold *18:* 116
Bond, Barbara Higgins *21:* 102
Bond, Bruce *52:* 97
Bond, Felicia *38:* 197; *49:* 55, 56; *89:* 170; *90:* 171; *126:* 37
Bonn, Pat *43:* 40
Bonners, Susan *41:* 40; *85:* 36; *94:* 99, 100; *151:* 105, 106
Bonsall, Crosby *23:* 6

Boon, Debbie *103:* 6; *144:* 188
Boon, Emilie *86:* 23, 24
Boone, Debbie *165:* 77
Boore, Sara *60:* 73
Bootman, Colin *155:* 13; *159:* 35
Booth, Franklin *YABC 2:* 76
Booth, Graham *32:* 193; *37:* 41, 42
Borda, Juliette *102:* 188
Bordier, Georgette *16:* 54
Boren, Tinka *27:* 128
Borges, Jose Francisco *119:* 62
Borja, Robert *22:* 48
Born, Adolf *49:* 63
Bornstein, Ruth *14:* 44; *88:* 45, 46; *107:* 30
Borten, Helen *3:* 54; *5:* 24
Bosin, Blackbear *69:* 104
Bossom, Naomi *35:* 48
Bostock, Mike *83:* 221; *114:* 14
Boston, Peter *19:* 42
Bosustow, Stephen *34:* 202
Boszko, Ron *75:* 47
Bottner, Barbara *14:* 46
Boucher, Joelle *41:* 138
Boulat, Pierre *44:* 40
Boulet, Susan Seddon *50:* 47
Bouma, Paddy *118:* 25; *128:* 16
Bour, Daniele *66:* 145
Bourke-White, Margaret *15:* 286-287; *57:* 102
Boutet de Monvel, M. *30:* 61, 62, 63, 65
Bowen, Betsy *105:* 222
Bowen, Richard *42:* 134
Bowen, Ruth *31:* 188
Bower, Ron *29:* 33
Bowers, David *95:* 38; *115:* 20; *127:* 169, 170; *165:* 57
Bowman, Eric *151:* 23
Bowman, Leslie *85:* 203; *105:* 108; *116:* 76; *128:* 234
Bowman, Peter *146:* 214, 215; *150:* 115
Bowser, Carolyn Ewing *22:* 253
Boyd, Aaron *158:* 242
Boyd, Patti *45:* 31
Boyle, Eleanor Vere *28:* 50, 51
Boynton, Sandra *57:* 13, 14, 15; *107:* 36, 37; *152:* 12, 13, 14
Bozzo, Frank *4:* 154
Brabbs, Derry *55:* 170
Brace, Eric *132:* 193, 194; *152:* 71
Brackers de Hugo, Pierre *115:* 21
Bradford, June *158:* 138
Bradford, Ron *7:* 157
Bradley, David P. *69:* 105
Bradley, Richard D. *26:* 182
Bradley, William *5:* 164
Brady, Irene *4:* 31; *42:* 37; *68:* 191
Bragg, Michael *32:* 78; *46:* 31
Bragg, Ruth Gembicki *77:* 18
Brainerd, John W. *65:* 19
Braithwaite, Althea *23:* 12-13; *119:* 16
Brak, Syd *146:* 187
Bralds, Braldt *90:* 28; *91:* 151
Bram, Elizabeth *30:* 67
Bramley, Peter *4:* 3
Brandenberg, Aliki *2:* 36-37; *24:* 222; *35:* 49, 50, 51, 52, 53, 54, 56, 57; *75:* 15, 17; *92:* 205; *113:* 18, 19, 20; *157:* 28; *156:* 111
Brandenburg, Alexa *75:* 19
Brandenburg, Jim *47:* 58; *150:* 212
Brandi, Lillian *31:* 158
Brandon, Brumsic, Jr. *9:* 25
Bransom, Paul *17:* 121; *43:* 44
Braren, Loretta Trezzo *87:* 193
Braun, Wendy *80:* 17, 18
Brautigam, Don *115:* 175, 176
Brazell, Derek *75:* 105; *79:* 9
Breathed, Berkeley *86:* 27, 28, 29; *161:* 13, 14
Brennan, Steve *83:* 230; *101:* 184
Brenner, Fred *22:* 85; *36:* 34; *42:* 34
Brett, Bernard *22:* 54
Brett, Harold M. *26:* 98, 99, 100

Brett, Jan *30:* 135; *42:* 39; *71:* 31, 32; *130:* 23, 24, 25, 26, 27
Brewer, Paul *106:* 115; *145:* 202
Brewer, Sally King *33:* 44
Brewster, Patience *40:* 68; *45:* 22, 183; *51:* 20; *66:* 144; *89:* 4; *97:* 30, 31
Brick, John *10:* 15
Brickman, Robin D. *131:* 88; *142:* 150; *155:* 18
Bridge, David R. *45:* 28
Bridgman, L.J. *37:* 77
Bridwell, Norman *4:* 37; *138:* 36, 37, 40
Brierley, Louise *91:* 22; *96:* 165
Briggs, Raymond *10:* 168; *23:* 20, 21; *66:* 29, 31, 32; *131:* 28, 29
Brigham, Grace A. *37:* 148
Bright, Robert *24:* 55
Brighton, Catherine *107:* 39
Brinckloe, Julie *13:* 18; *24:* 79, 115; *29:* 35; *63:* 140; *81:* 131
Brion *47:* 116
Brisley, Joyce L. *22:* 57
Brisson, James F. *110:* 60
Brittingham, Geoffrey *88:* 37
Brix-Henker, Silke *81:* 194
Brock, Charles E. *15:* 97; *19:* 247, 249; *23:* 224, 225; *36:* 88; *42:* 41, 42, 43, 44, 45; *100:* 189; *YABC 1:* 194, 196, 203
Brock, Emma *7:* 21
Brock, Henry Matthew *15:* 81; *16:* 141; *19:* 71; *34:* 115; *40:* 164; *42:* 47, 48, 49; *49:* 66
Brocksopp, Arthur *57:* 157
Broda, Ron *136:* 180
Brodkin, Gwen *34:* 135
Brodovitch, Alexi *52:* 22
Bromhall, Winifred *5:* 11; *26:* 38
Bromley, Lizzy *159:* 179
Bronson, Linda *150:* 210
Brooke, L. Leslie *16:* 181-183, 186; *17:* 15-17; *18:* 194
Brooker, Christopher *15:* 251
Brooker, Krysten *111:* 94; *140:* 28; *162:* 111
Brooks, Maya Itzna *92:* 153
Brooks, Ron *94:* 15
Broomfield, Maurice *40:* 141
Brotman, Adolph E. *5:* 21
Brown, Buck *45:* 48
Brown, Christopher *62:* 124, 125, 127, 128
Brown, Craig McFarland *73:* 28; *84:* 65
Brown, Dan *61:* 167; *115:* 183, 184; *116:* 28, 29
Brown, David *7:* 47; *48:* 52
Brown, Denise *11:* 213
Brown, Ford Madox *48:* 74
Brown, Judith Gwyn *1:* 45; *7:* 5; *8:* 167; *9:* 182, 190; *20:* 16, 17, 18; *23:* 142; *29:* 117; *33:* 97; *36:* 23, 26; *43:* 184; *48:* 201, 223; *49:* 69; *86:* 227; *110:* 188; *153:* 7
Brown, Kathryn *98:* 26
Brown, Laurie Krasny *99:* 30
Brown, Marc (Tolon) *10:* 17, 197; *14:* 263; *51:* 18; *53:* 11, 12, 13, 15, 16-17; *75:* 58; *80:* 24, 25, 26; *82:* 261; *99:* 29; *145:* 22, 23, 25, 27; *162:* 198
Brown, Marcia *7:* 30; *25:* 203; *47:* 31, 32, 33, 34, 35, 36-37, 38, 39, 40, 42, 43, 44; *YABC 1:* 27
Brown, Margery W. *5:* 32-33; *10:* 3
Brown, Martin *101:* 43
Brown, Mary Barrett *97:* 74
Brown, Palmer *36:* 40
Brown, Paul *25:* 26; *26:* 107
Brown, Richard *61:* 18; *67:* 30
Brown, Rick *78:* 71; *150:* 154
Brown, Robert S. *85:* 33
Brown, Rod *157:* 142
Brown, Ruth *55:* 165; *86:* 112, 113; *105:* 16, 17, 18
Brown, Trevor *99:* 160; *139:* 247
Browne, Anthony *45:* 50, 51, 52; *61:* 21, 22, 23, 24, 25; *105:* 21, 22, 23, 25

Browne, Dik *8:* 212; *67:* 32, 33, 35, 37, 39
Browne, Gordon *16:* 97; *64:* 114, 116, 117, 119, 121
Browne, Hablot K. *15:* 65, 80; *21:* 14, 15, 16, 17, 18, 19, 20; *24:* 25
Browne, Jane *165:* 222
Browning, Coleen *4:* 132
Browning, Mary Eleanor *24:* 84
Bruce, Robert *23:* 23
Brude, Dick *48:* 215
Brule, Al *3:* 135
Brumbeau, Jeff *157:* 29
Bruna, Dick *43:* 48, 49, 50; *76:* 27, 28
Brundage, Frances *19:* 244
Brunhoff, Jean de *24:* 57, 58
Brunhoff, Laurent de *24:* 60; *71:* 35, 36, 37
Brunkus, Denise *84:* 50; *123:* 117
Brunson, Bob *43:* 135
Bryan, Ashley F. *31:* 44; *72:* 27, 28, 29; *107:* 92; *116:* 192; *132:* 24
Bryant, Michael *93:* 74
Brychta, Alex *21:* 21
Bryer, Diana *107:* 121
Bryson, Bernarda *3:* 88, 146; *39:* 26; *44:* 185; *131:* 40
Buba, Joy *12:* 83; *30:* 226; *44:* 56
Buchanan, Lilian *13:* 16
Bucholtz-Ross, Linda *44:* 137
Buchs, Thomas *40:* 38
Buck, Margaret Waring *3:* 30
Buehner, Mark *104:* 12, 15; *105:* 160; *119:* 98; *157:* 188; *159:* 39, 40, 43
Buehr, Walter *3:* 31
Buff, Conrad *19:* 52, 53, 54
Buff, Mary *19:* 52, 53
Bull, Charles Livingston *18:* 207; *88:* 175, 176
Bullen, Anne *3:* 166, 167
Bullock, Kathleen *77:* 24
Bumgarner-Kirby, Claudia *77:* 194
Burbank, Addison *37:* 43
Burchard, Peter Duncan *3:* 197; *5:* 35; *6:* 158, 218; *143:* 17
Burckhardt, Marc *94:* 48; *110:* 89
Burger, Carl *3:* 33; *45:* 160, 162
Burgeson, Marjorie *19:* 31
Burgess, Anne *76:* 252
Burgess, Gelett *32:* 39, 42
Burgess, Mark *157:* 31
Burke, Phillip *95:* 117
Burkert, Nancy Ekholm *18:* 186; *22:* 140; *24:* 62, 63, 64, 65; *26:* 53; *29:* 60, 61; *46:* 171; *YABC 1:* 46
Burkhardt, Bruce *142:* 86
Burkhardt, Melissa A. *142:* 86
Burleson, Joe *104:* 35
Burn, Doris *6:* 172
Burn, Jeffrey *89:* 125; *152:* 132
Burn, Ted
See Burn, Thomas E.
Burn, Thomas E. *151:* 41
Burnard, Damon *115:* 23
Burnett, Virgil *44:* 42
Burningham, John *9:* 68; *16:* 60-61; *59:* 28, 29, 30, 31, 32, 33, 35; *111:* 18, 19, 21; *160:* 37
Burns, Howard M. *12:* 173
Burns, Jim *47:* 70; *86:* 32; *91:* 197; *123:* 16
Burns, M.F. *26:* 69
Burns, Raymond *9:* 29
Burns, Robert *24:* 106
Burr, Dan *65:* 28; *108:* 134
Burr, Dane *12:* 2
Burra, Edward *YABC 2:* 68
Burrell, Galen *56:* 76
Burri, Rene *41:* 143; *54:* 166
Burridge, Marge Opitz *14:* 42
Burris, Burmah *4:* 81
Burroughs, John Coleman *41:* 64
Burroughs, Studley O. *41:* 65
Burton, Marilee Robin *46:* 33

Burton, Virginia Lee *2:* 43; *44:* 49, 51; *100:* 46, 47; *YABC 1:* 24; *147:* 56
Busoni, Rafaello *1:* 186; *3:* 224; *6:* 126; *14:* 5; *16:* 62-63
Butchkes, Sidney *50:* 58
Butler, Geoff *94:* 20
Butler, Ralph *116:* 212
Butterfield, Ned *1:* 153; *27:* 128; *79:* 63
Butterworth, Nick *106:* 43, 44; *149:* 34
Buxton, John *123:* 12
Buzelli, Christopher *105:* 149
Buzonas, Gail *29:* 88
Buzzell, Russ W. *12:* 177
Byard, Carole *39:* 44; *57:* 18, 19, 20; *60:* 60; *61:* 93, 96; *69:* 210; *78:* 246; *79:* 227
Byars, Betsy *46:* 35
Byfield, Barbara Ninde *8:* 18
Byfield, Graham *32:* 29
Byrd, Robert *13:* 218; *33:* 46; *158:* 70
Byrd, Samuel *123:* 104

C

Cabat, Erni *74:* 38
Cabban, Vanessa *138:* 73
Cabrera, Jane *103:* 24; *152:* 27
Caddy, Alice *6:* 41
Cady, Harrison *17:* 21, 23; *19:* 57, 58
Caffrey, Aileen *72:* 223; *141:* 154
Caldecott, Randolph *16:* 98, 103; *17:* 32-33, 36, 38-39; *26:* 90; *100:* 49, 50; *YABC 2:* 172
Calder, Alexander *18:* 168
Calderon, W. Frank *25:* 160
Caldwell, Ben *105:* 75; *149:* 60
Caldwell, Clyde *98:* 100; *116:* 39
Caldwell, Doreen *23:* 77; *71:* 41
Caldwell, John *46:* 225
Call, Greg *126:* 135; *165:* 49
Callahan, Kevin *22:* 42
Callahan, Philip S. *25:* 77
Callan, Jamie *59:* 37
Calvin, James *61:* 92
Camburn-Bracalente, Carol A. *118:* 22
Cameron, Julia Margaret *19:* 203
Cameron, Scott *99:* 18
Camm, Martin *140:* 208, 209, 210
Campbell, Ann *11:* 43; *123:* 182
Campbell, Bill *89:* 39
Campbell, Ken *126:* 143
Campbell, Robert *55:* 120
Campbell, Rod *51:* 27; *98:* 34
Campbell, Walter M. *YABC 2:* 158
Camps, Luis *28:* 120-121; *66:* 35
Cann, Helen *124:* 50; *141:* 78
Cannon, Janell *78:* 25; *128:* 40
Canright, David *36:* 162
Canty, Thomas *85:* 161; *92:* 47; *113:* 192; *134:* 60
Canyon, Christopher *150:* 44; *151:* 112
Caporale, Wende *70:* 42
Capp, Al *61:* 28, 30, 31, 40, 41, 43, 44
Cappon, Manuela *154:* 64
Caras, Peter *36:* 64
Caraway, Caren *57:* 22
Caraway, James *3:* 200-201
Carbe, Nino *29:* 183
Cares, Linda *67:* 176
Carigiet, Alois *24:* 67
Carle, Eric *4:* 42; *11:* 121; *12:* 29; *65:* 32, 33, 34, 36; *73:* 63, 65; *163:* 55, 56
Carlson, Nancy L. *41:* 116; *56:* 25; *90:* 45; *144:* 48, 50
Carmi, Giora *79:* 35; *149:* 40
Carpenter, Nancy *76:* 128; *86:* 173; *89:* 171; *131:* 186; *134:* 8; *138:* 215; *153:* 204; *159:* 93; *165:* 232
Carr, Archie *37:* 225

Carrick, Donald *5:* 194; *39:* 97; *49:* 70; *53:* 156; *63:* 15, 16, 17, 18, 19, 21; *80:* 131; *86:* 151; *118:* 24
Carrick, Malcolm *28:* 59, 60
Carrick, Paul *118:* 26
Carrick, Valery *21:* 47
Carrier, Lark *71:* 43
Carroll, Jim *88:* 211; *140:* 177; *153:* 99
Carroll, Lewis
    See Dodgson, Charles L.
Carroll, Michael *72:* 5
Carroll, Pamela *84:* 68; *128:* 214
Carroll, Ruth *7:* 41; *10:* 68
Carter, Abby *81:* 32; *97:* 121; *102:* 61; *163:* 139
Carter, Barbara *47:* 167, 169
Carter, David A. *114:* 24, 25
Carter, Don *124:* 54
Carter, Harry *22:* 179
Carter, Helene *15:* 38; *22:* 202, 203; *YABC 2:* 220-221
Cartlidge, Michelle *49:* 65; *96:* 50, 51
Cartwright, Reg *63:* 61, 62; *78:* 26; *143:* 4
Carty, Leo *4:* 196; *7:* 163; *58:* 131
Cary *4:* 133; *9:* 32; *20:* 2; *21:* 143
Cary, Page *12:* 41
Casale, Paul *71:* 63; *109:* 122; *136:* 28
Case, Sandra E. *16:* 2
Caseley, Judith *87:* 36; *159:* 47, 48, 49
Casilla, Robert *78:* 7; *167:* 124
Casino, Steve *85:* 193
Cassel, Lili
    See Wronker, Lili Cassel
Cassel-Wronker, Lili
    See Wronker, Lili Cassel
Cassels, Jean *8:* 50; *150:* 119
Cassen, Melody *140:* 51
Cassity, Don *104:* 24
Cassler, Carl *75:* 137, 138; *82:* 162
Casson, Hugh *65:* 38, 40, 42, 43
Castellon, Federico *48:* 45, 46, 47, 48
Castle, Jane *4:* 80
Castro, Antonio *84:* 71
Catalano, Dominic *94:* 79; *163:* 60, 61; *162:* 54
Catalanotto, Peter *63:* 170; *70:* 23; *71:* 182; *72:* 96; *74:* 114; *76:* 194, 195; *77:* 7; *79:* 157; *80:* 28, 67; *83:* 157; *85:* 27; *108:* 11; *113:* 30, 31, 33, 34, 36; *114:* 27, 28, 29; *117:* 53; *124:* 168; *159:* 54, 55
Catania, Tom *68:* 82
Cather, Carolyn *3:* 83; *15:* 203; *34:* 216
Catrow, David *117:* 179; *152:* 31, 33
Cauley, Lorinda Bryan *44:* 135; *46:* 49
Cayard, Bruce *38:* 67
Cazet, Denys *52:* 27; *99:* 39, 40; *163:* 65, 66
Cecil, Randy *127:* 132, 133
Cellini, Joseph *2:* 73; *3:* 35; *16:* 116; *47:* 103
Cepeda, Joe *90:* 62; *109:* 91; *134:* 172; *159:* 57, 58, 164
Chabrian, Debbi *45:* 55
Chabrian, Deborah *51:* 182; *53:* 124; *63:* 107; *75:* 84; *79:* 85; *82:* 247; *89:* 93; *101:* 197
Chagnon, Mary *37:* 158
Chalmers, Mary *3:* 145; *13:* 148; *33:* 125; *66:* 214
Chamberlain, Christopher *45:* 57
Chamberlain, Margaret *46:* 51; *106:* 89
Chamberlain, Nigel *78:* 140
Chambers, C.E. *17:* 230
Chambers, Dave *12:* 151
Chambers, Jill *134:* 110
Chambers, Mary *4:* 188
Chambliss, Maxie *42:* 186; *56:* 159; *93:* 163, 164; *103:* 178
Champlin, Dale *136:* 124
Chan, Harvey *96:* 236; *99:* 153; *143:* 218
Chandler, David P. *28:* 62
Chaney, Howard *139:* 27
Chang, Warren *101:* 209
Chapel, Jody *68:* 20

Chapman, C.H. *13:* 83, 85, 87
Chapman, Frederick T. *6:* 27; *44:* 28
Chapman, Gaynor *32:* 52, 53
Chapman, Jane *145:* 186; *150:* 56
Chappell, Warren *3:* 172; *21:* 56; *27:* 125
Charles, Donald *30:* 154, 155
Charlip, Remy *4:* 48; *34:* 138; *68:* 53, 54; *119:* 29, 30
Charlot, Jean *1:* 137, 138; *8:* 23; *14:* 31; *48:* 151; *56:* 21
Charlot, Martin *64:* 72
Charlton, Michael *34:* 50; *37:* 39
Charmatz, Bill *7:* 45
Chartier, Normand *9:* 36; *52:* 49; *66:* 40; *74:* 220; *145:* 169
Chase, Lynwood M. *14:* 4
Chast, Roz *97:* 39, 40
Chastain, Madye Lee *4:* 50
Chateron, Ann *152:* 19
Chatterton, Martin *68:* 102; *152:* 19
Chau, Tungwai *140:* 35
Chauncy, Francis *24:* 158
Chayka, Doug *145:* 97
Chee, Cheng-Khee *79:* 42; *81:* 224
Chen, Chih-sien *90:* 226
Chen, Tony *6:* 45; *19:* 131; *29:* 126; *34:* 160
Cheney, T.A. *11:* 47
Cheng, Judith *36:* 45; *51:* 16
Chermayeff, Ivan *47:* 53
Cherry, David *93:* 40
Cherry, Lynne *34:* 52; *65:* 184; *87:* 111; *99:* 46, 47
Chesak, Lina *135:* 118
Chess, Victoria *12:* 6; *33:* 42, 48, 49; *40:* 194; *41:* 145; *69:* 80; *72:* 100; *92:* 33, 34; *104:* 167
Chessare, Michele *41:* 50; *56:* 48; *69:* 145
Chesterton, G.K. *27:* 43, 44, 45, 47
Chestnutt, David *47:* 217
Chesworth, Michael *75:* 24, 152; *88:* 136; *94:* 25; *98:* 155; *160:* 42
Chetham, Celia *134:* 34
Chetwin, Grace *86:* 40
Cheung, Irving *158:* 96
Chevalier, Christa *35:* 66
Chew, Ruth *7:* 46; *132:* 147
Chewning, Randy *92:* 206
Chichester Clark, Emma *72:* 121; *77:* 212; *78:* 209; *87:* 143; *117:* 37, 39, 40; *144:* 138; *156:* 24, 25
Chifflart *47:* 113, 127
Child, Lauren *119:* 32
Chin, Alex *28:* 54
Chitwood, Susan Tanner *163:* 16
Cho, Shinta *8:* 126
Chodos-Irvine, Margaret *52:* 102, 103, 107; *152:* 44
Chollick, Jay *25:* 175
Choma, Christina *99:* 169
Chorao, Kay *7:* 200-201; *8:* 25; *11:* 234; *33:* 187; *35:* 239; *69:* 35; *70:* 235; *123:* 174
Chowdhury, Subrata *62:* 130; *162:* 22, 23
Christelow, Eileen *38:* 44; *83:* 198, 199; *90:* 57, 58
Christensen, Bonnie *93:* 100; *153:* 67
Christensen, Gardell Dano *1:* 57
Christensen, James C. *140:* 226
Christiana, David *90:* 64; *135:* 13
Christiansen, Per *40:* 24
Christie, R. Gregory *116:* 107; *127:* 20, 21; *162:* 179; *165:* 137
Christy, Howard Chandler *17:* 163-165, 168-169; *19:* 186, 187; *21:* 22, 23, 24, 25
Chronister, Robert *23:* 138; *63:* 27; *69:* 167
Church, Frederick *YABC 1:* 155
Chute, Marchette *1:* 59
Chwast, Jacqueline *1:* 63; *2:* 275; *6:* 46-47; *11:* 125; *12:* 202; *14:* 235
Chwast, Seymour *3:* 128-129; *18:* 43; *27:* 152; *92:* 79; *96:* 56, 57, 58; *146:* 32, 33

Cieslawksi, Steve *101:* 142; *127:* 116; *158:* 169, 171
Cinelli, Lisa *146:* 253
Cirlin, Edgard *2:* 168
Clairin, Georges *53:* 109
Clapp, John *105:* 66; *109:* 58; *126:* 7; *129:* 148; *130:* 165
Clark, Brenda *119:* 85; *153:* 55
Clark, David *77:* 164; *134:* 144, 145
Clark, Emma Chichester
    See Chichester Clark, Emma
Clark, Victoria *35:* 159
Clarke, Greg *169:* 134
Clarke, Gus *72:* 226; *134:* 31
Clarke, Harry *23:* 172, 173
Clarke, Peter *75:* 102
Claverie, Jean *38:* 46; *88:* 29
Clayton, Elaine *159:* 60
Clayton, Robert *9:* 181
Cleaver, Elizabeth *8:* 204; *23:* 36
Cleland, T.M. *26:* 92
Clemens, Peter *61:* 125
Clement, Charles *20:* 38
Clement, Rod *97:* 42
Clement, Stephen *88:* 3
Clementson, John *84:* 213
Clevin, Jorgen *7:* 50
Clifford, Judy *34:* 163; *45:* 198
Clokey, Art *59:* 44
Clouse, James *84:* 15
Clouse, Nancy L. *78:* 31; *114:* 90
Clover, Peter *152:* 45
Cneut, Carll *156:* 166; *165:* 67
Coalson, Glo *9:* 72, 85; *25:* 155; *26:* 42; *35:* 212; *53:* 31; *56:* 154; *94:* 37, 38, 193
Cober, Alan E. *17:* 158; *32:* 77; *49:* 127
Cober-Gentry, Leslie *92:* 111
Cocca-Leffler, Maryann *80:* 46; *136:* 60; *139:* 193
Cochran, Bobbye *11:* 52
CoConis, Ted *4:* 41; *46:* 41; *51:* 104
Cocozza, Chris *87:* 18; *110:* 173; *111:* 149
Cockroft, Jason *152:* 20
Coerr, Eleanor *1:* 64; *67:* 52
Coes, Peter *35:* 172
Cogancherry, Helen *52:* 143; *69:* 131; *77:* 93; *78:* 220; *109:* 204; *110:* 129
Coggins, Jack *2:* 69
Cohen, Alix *7:* 53
Cohen, Miriam *155:* 23, 24
Cohen, Nancy R. *165:* 35
Cohen, Sheldon *105:* 33, 34
Cohen, Vincent O. *19:* 243
Cohen, Vivien *11:* 112
Coker, Paul *51:* 172
Colbert, Anthony *15:* 41; *20:* 193
Colby, C.B. *3:* 47
Cole, Babette *58:* 172; *96:* 63, 64; *155:* 29
Cole, Brock *68:* 223; *72:* 36, 37, 38, 192; *127:* 23; *136:* 64, 65
Cole, Gwen *87:* 185
Cole, Herbert *28:* 104
Cole, Michael *59:* 46
Cole, Olivia H.H. *1:* 134; *3:* 223; *9:* 111; *38:* 104
Colin, Paul *102:* 59; *123:* 118; *126:* 152
Collicott, Sharleen *98:* 39; *143:* 29, 30
Collier, Bryan *126:* 54; *151:* 166
Collier, David *13:* 127
Collier, John *27:* 179
Collier, Steven *50:* 52
Collins, Heather *66:* 84; *67:* 68; *81:* 40; *98:* 192, 193; *129:* 95, 96, 98
Collins, Matt *167:* 90
Collins, Ross *140:* 23, 24
Colman, Audrey *146:* 161
Colon, Raul *108:* 112; *113:* 5; *117:* 167; *134:* 112; *146:* 23; *159:* 92
Colonna, Bernard *21:* 50; *28:* 103; *34:* 140; *43:* 180; *78:* 150
Comport, Sally Wern *117:* 169; *169:* 104

Conde, J.M. *100:* 120
Condon, Grattan *54:* 85 *Condon, Ken 161:* 44
Cone, Ferne Geller *39:* 49
Cone, J. Morton *39:* 49
Conklin, Paul *43:* 62
Connolly, Howard *67:* 88
Connolly, Jerome P. *4:* 128; *28:* 52
Connolly, Peter *47:* 60
Conoly, Walle *110:* 224
Conover, Chris *31:* 52; *40:* 184; *41:* 51; *44:* 79
Contreras, Gerry *72:* 9
Converse, James *38:* 70
Conway *62:* 62
Conway, Michael *69:* 12; *81:* 3; *92:* 108
Cook, G.R. *29:* 165
Cook, Joel *108:* 160
Cookburn, W.V. *29:* 204
Cooke, Donald E. *2:* 77
Cooke, Tom *52:* 118
Coomaraswamy, A.K. *50:* 100
Coombs, Charles *43:* 65
Coombs, Deborah *139:* 175
Coombs, Patricia *2:* 82; *3:* 52; *22:* 119; *51:* 32, 33, 34, 35, 36-37, 38, 39, 40, 42, 43
Cooney, Barbara *6:* 16-17, 50; *12:* 42; *13:* 92; *15:* 145; *16:* 74, 111; *18:* 189; *23:* 38, 89, 93; *32:* 138; *38:* 105; *59:* 48, 49, 51, 52, 53; *74:* 222; *81:* 100; *91:* 25; *96:* 71, 72, 74; *100:* 149; *YABC 2:* 10
Cooper, Elisha *157:* 38, 39
Cooper, Floyd *79:* 95; *81:* 45; *84:* 82; *85:* 74; *91:* 118; *96:* 77, 78; *103:* 149; *144:* 54; *145:* 151; *159:* 198
Cooper, Heather *50:* 39
Cooper, Helen *102:* 42, 43, 44
Cooper, Mario *24:* 107
Cooper, Marjorie *7:* 112
Cope, Jane *61:* 201; *108* 52
Copelman, Evelyn *8:* 61; *18:* 25
Copley, Heather *30:* 86; *45:* 57
Corbett, Grahame *30:* 114; *43:* 67
Corbino, John *19:* 248
Corcos, Lucille *2:* 223; *10:* 27; *34:* 66
Corey, Robert *9:* 34
Corlass, Heather *10:* 7
Cornell, James *27:* 60
Cornell, Jeff *11:* 58
Cornell, Laura *94:* 179; *95:* 25
Corrigan, Barbara *8:* 37
Corrigan, Patrick *145:* 149
Corwin, Judith Hoffman *10:* 28
Cory, Fanny Y. *20:* 113; *48:* 29
Cosentino, Ralph *169:* 32
Cosgrove, Margaret *3:* 100; *47:* 63; *82:* 133
Costabel, Eva Deutsch *45:* 66, 67
Costanza, John *58:* 7, 8, 9
Costello, Chris *86:* 78
Costello, David F. *23:* 55
Cote, Nancy *126:* 139; *156:* 101
Couch, Greg *94:* 124; *110:* 13; *162:* 31
Councell, Ruth Tietjen *79:* 29
Courtney, Cathy *58:* 69, 144; *59:* 15; *61:* 20, 87
Courtney, R. *35:* 110
Counihan, Claire *133:* 106
Cousineau, Normand *89:* 180; *112:* 76
Couture, Christin *41:* 209
Covarrubias, Miguel *35:* 118, 119, 123, 124, 125
Coville, Katherine *32:* 57; *36:* 167; *92:* 38
Covington, Neverne *113:* 87
Cowdrey, Richard *169:* 170
Cowell, Cressida *140:* 39
Cowell, Lucinda *77:* 54
Cox *43:* 93
Cox, Charles *8:* 20
Cox, David *56:* 37; *90:* 63; *119:* 38
Cox, Palmer *24:* 76, 77
Cox, Steve *140:* 96
Coxe, Molly *69:* 44
Coxon, Michele *158:* 80

Crabb, Gordon *70:* 39
Crabtree, Judith *98:* 42
Craft, Kinuko *22:* 182; *36:* 220; *53:* 122, 123, 148, 149; *74:* 12; *81:* 129; *86:* 31; *89:* 139; *127:* 27, 28, 29; *132:* 142; *139:* 38
Craig, David *136:* 198
Craig, Helen *49:* 76; *62:* 70, 71, 72; *69:* 141; *94:* 42, 43, 44; *112:* 53; *135:* 101, 102
Crane, Alan H. *1:* 217
Crane, H.M. *13:* 111
Crane, Jack *43:* 183
Crane, Walter *18:* 46-49, 53, 54, 56-57, 59-61; *22:* 128; *24:* 210, 217; *100:* 70, 71
Cravath, Lynne W. *98:* 45
Crawford, Denise *137:* 213
Crawford, Will *43:* 77
Credle, Ellis *1:* 69
Czernecki, Stefan *154:* 104
Crespi, Francesca *87:* 90
Cressy, Michael *124:* 55
Crews, Donald *32:* 59, 60; *76:* 42, 43, 44
Crews, Nina *97:* 49
Crichlow, Ernest *74:* 88; *83:* 203
Croft, James *150:* 57
Crofut, Bob *80:* 87; *81:* 47
Crofut, Susan *23:* 61
Croll, Carolyn *80:* 137; *102:* 52
Cross, Peter *56:* 78; *63:* 60, 65
Crowe, Elizabeth *88:* 144
Crowell, Pers *3:* 125
Cruikshank, George *15:* 76, 83; *22:* 74, 75, 76, 77, 78, 79, 80, 81, 82, 84, 137; *24:* 22, 23
Crump, Fred H. *11:* 62
Cruz, Ray *6:* 55; *70:* 234; *123:* 173
Csatari, Joe *44:* 82; *55:* 152; *63:* 25, 28; *102:* 58
Cuetara, Mittie *158:* 85
Cuffari, Richard *4:* 75; *5:* 98; *6:* 56; *7:* 13, 84, 153; *8:* 148, 155; *9:* 89; *11:* 19; *12:* 55, 96, 114; *15:* 51, 202; *18:* 5; *20:* 139; *21:* 197; *22:* 14, 192; *23:* 15, 106; *25:* 97; *27:* 133; *28:* 196; *29:* 54; *30:* 85; *31:* 35; *36:* 101; *38:* 171; *42:* 97; *44:* 92, 192; *45:* 212, 213; *46:* 36, 198; *50:* 164; *54:* 80, 136, 137, 145; *56:* 17; *60:* 63; *66:* 49, 50; *70:* 41; *71:* 132; *77:* 157; *78:* 58, 149; *79:* 120; *85:* 2, 152
Cugat, Xavier *19:* 120
Cumings, Art *35:* 160
Cummings, Chris *29:* 167
Cummings, Michael *159:* 142
Cummings, Pat *42:* 61; *61:* 99; *69:* 205; *71:* 57, 58; *78:* 24, 25; *93:* 75; *107:* 49, 50
Cummings, Richard *24:* 119
Cunette, Lou *20:* 93; *22:* 125
Cunningham, Aline *25:* 180
Cunningham, David *11:* 13
Cunningham, Imogene *16:* 122, 127
Cupples, Pat *107:* 12; *126:* 109
Curlee, Lynn *98:* 48; *141:* 39
Curry, John Steuart *2:* 5; *19:* 84; *34:* 36; *144:* 126
Curry, Tom *127:* 131
Curtis, Bruce *23:* 96; *30:* 88; *36:* 22
Curtis, Neil *167:* 30
Cusack, Margaret *58:* 49, 50, 51
Cushman, Doug *65:* 57; *101:* 39, 40; *133:* 179; *157:* 45
Cyrus, Kurt *132:* 39
Czechowski, Alicia *95:* 21
Czernecki, Stefan *117:* 173

D

Dabcovich, Lydia *25:* 105; *40:* 114; *99:* 75, 76
Dacey, Bob *82:* 175; *152:* 65
d'Achille, Gino *127:* 175, 176
Dailey, Don *78:* 197
Dain, Martin J. *35:* 75
Dale, Penny *127:* 224; *151:* 57; *160:* 89

Dale, Rae *72:* 197
Daley, Joann *50:* 22
Dalton, Anne *40:* 62; *63:* 119
Daly, Deborah M. *74:* 213
Daly, Jim *103:* 60; *150:* 48
Daly, Jude *138:* 118, 119
Daly, Nicholas *37:* 53; *76:* 48, 49
Daly, Niki *107:* 15; *114:* 38, 39, 40
Daly, Paul *97:* 205
Dalziel, Brothers *33:* 113
D'Amato, Alex *9:* 48; *20:* 25
D'Amato, Janet *9:* 48; *20:* 25; *26:* 118
Danalis, Johnny *167:* 27
Daniel, Alan *23:* 59; *29:* 110; *76:* 50, 53, 55, 56; *153:* 76 *115:* 74; *134:* 70
Daniel, Lea *76:* 53, 55; *153:* 76
Daniel, Lewis C. *20:* 216
Daniels, Beau *73:* 4
Daniels, Steve *22:* 16
Daniels, Stewart *56:* 12
Dann, Bonnie *31:* 83
Dann, Penny *82:* 128
Danska, Herbert *24:* 219
Danyell, Alice *20:* 27
Darley, F.O.C. *16:* 145; *19:* 79, 86, 88, 185; *21:* 28, 36; *35:* 76, 77, 78, 79, 80-81; *YABC 2:* 175
Darling, Lois *3:* 59; *23:* 30, 31
Darling, Louis *1:* 40-41; *2:* 63; *3:* 59; *23:* 30, 31; *43:* 54, 57, 59; *121:* 53
Darrow, David R. *84:* 101
Darrow, Whitney, Jr. *13:* 25; *38:* 220, 221
Darwin, Beatrice *43:* 54
Darwin, Len *24:* 82
Dastolfo, Frank *33:* 179
Dauber, Liz *1:* 22; *3:* 266; *30:* 49
Daugherty, James *3:* 66; *8:* 178; *13:* 27-28, 161; *18:* 101; *19:* 72; *29:* 108; *32:* 156; *42:* 84; *YABC 1:* 256; *2:* 174
d'Aulaire, Edgar Parin *5:* 51; *66:* 53
d'Aulaire, Ingri Parin *5:* 51; *66:* 53
Davalos, Felipe *99:* 197; *159:* 66
Davenier, Christine *125:* 88; *127:* 32; *128:* 152
Davick, Linda *151:* 124
David, Jonathan *19:* 37
Davidson, Kevin *28:* 154
Davidson, Raymond *32:* 61
Davie, Helen K. *77:* 48, 49
Davis, Allen *20:* 11; *22:* 45; *27:* 222; *29:* 157; *41:* 99; *47:* 99; *50:* 84; *52:* 105
Davis, Bette J. *15:* 53; *23:* 95
Davis, Dimitris *45:* 95
Davis, Hendon *151:* 122
Davis, Jack E. *145:* 139
Davis, Jim *32:* 63, 64
Davis, Katie *152:* 52, 53, 54
Davis, Lambert *110:* 23, 24
Davis, Marguerite *31:* 38; *34:* 69, 70; *100:* 34; *YABC 1:* 126, 230
Davis, Nelle *69:* 191
Davis, Paul *78:* 214
Davis, Yvonne LeBrun *94:* 144
Davisson, Virginia H. *44:* 178
DaVolls, Andy *85:* 53
Dawson, Diane *24:* 127; *42:* 126; *52:* 130; *68:* 104
Day, Alexandra *67:* 59; *97:* 54; *169:* 40
Day, Larry *169:* 88
Day, Rob *94:* 110; *127:* 24
Dean, Bob *19:* 211
de Angeli, Marguerite *1:* 77; *27:* 62, 65, 66, 67, 69, 70, 72; *100:* 75, 76; *YABC 1:* 166
DeArmond, Dale *70:* 47
Deas, Michael *27:* 219, 221; *30:* 156; *67:* 134; *72:* 24; *75:* 155; *84:* 206; *88:* 124
Debon, Nicolas *151:* 60
de Bosschere, Jean *19:* 252; *21:* 4
De Bruyn, M(onica) G. *13:* 30-31
De Cuir, John F. *1:* 28-29
Deeter, Catherine *74:* 110; *103:* 150; *137:* 50

Degen, Bruce *40:* 227, 229; *57:* 28, 29; *56:* 156; *75:* 229; *76:* 19; *81:* 36, 37; *92:* 26; *93:* 199; *97:* 56, 58, 59; *124:* 40; *147:* 39-41
De Grazia *14:* 59; *39:* 56, 57
DeGrazio, George *88:* 40
deGroat, Diane *9:* 39; *18:* 7; *23:* 123; *28:* 200-201; *31:* 58, 59; *34:* 151; *41:* 152; *43:* 88; *46:* 40, 200; *49:* 163; *50:* 89; *52:* 30, 34; *54:* 43; *63:* 5; *70:* 136; *71:* 99; *73:* 117, 156; *77:* 34; *85:* 48; *86:* 201; *87:* 142; *90:* 72, 73, 143; *95:* 182; *111:* 123; *118:* 160; *126:* 8; *130:* 130; *138:* 93, 94; *169:* 46-47
de Groot, Lee *6:* 21
Deines, Brian *110:* 139
DeJohn, Marie *89:* 78
Dekhteryov, B. *61:* 158
de Kiefte, Kees *94:* 107
Delacre, Lulu *36:* 66; *156:* 35
Delaney, A. *21:* 78
Delaney, Molly *80:* 43
Delaney, Ned *28:* 68; *56:* 80; *102:* 11
DeLapine, Jim *79:* 21
De La Roche Saint Andre, Anne *75:* 37
de Larrea, Victoria *6:* 119, 204; *29:* 103; *72:* 203; *87:* 199
Delessert, Etienne *7:* 140; *46:* 61, 62, 63, 65, 67, 68; *130:* 38, 39, 40, 41, 42; *YABC 2:* 209
DeLorenzo, Christopher *154:* 149
Delulio, John *15:* 54
DeLuna, Tony *88:* 95
Demarest, Chris L. *45:* 68-69, 70; *73:* 172, 173, 176; *78:* 106; *82:* 48, 49; *89:* 212; *92:* 86; *128:* 57, 58
De Mejo, Oscar *40:* 67
Demi *11:* 135; *15:* 245; *66:* 129, 130; *89:* 216; *102:* 66, 67, 68
Denetsosie, Hoke *13:* 126; *82:* 34
Denise, Christopher *147:* 43-44
Dennis, Morgan *18:* 68-69; *64:* 89
Dennis, Wesley *2:* 87; *3:* 111; *11:* 132; *18:* 71-74; *22:* 9; *24:* 196, 200; *46:* 178; *69:* 94, 96; *129:* 62
Denslow, W.W. *16:* 84-87; *18:* 19-20, 24; *29:* 211; *100:* 21
Denton, Kady MacDonald *110:* 82; *130:* 70
Denton, Terry *72:* 163
DePalma, Mary Newell *132:* 114; *139:* 75
de Paola, Tomie *8:* 95; *9:* 93; *11:* 69; 25; 103; *28:* 157; *29:* 80; *39:* 52-53; *40:* 226; *46:* 187; *59:* 61, 62, 63, 64, 65, 66, 67, 68, 69, 71, 72, 74; *62:* 19; *108:* 63, 67, 68, 70; *155:* 62, 64, 66
Deraney, Michael J. *77:* 35; *78:* 148
deRosa, Dee *70:* 48; *71:* 210; *91:* 78
Dervaux, Isabelle *111:* 117
De Saulles, Tony *119:* 39
de Seve, Peter *146:* 261
Deshaprabhu, Meera Dayal *86:* 192
Desimini, Lisa *86:* 68; *94:* 47; *96:* 7; *104:* 107; *125:* 194; *131:* 180
de St. Menin, Charles *70:* 17
Detmold, Edward J. *22:* 104, 105, 106, 107; *35:* 120; *64:* 5; *YABC 2:* 203
Detrich, Susan *20:* 133
Deutermann, Diana *77:* 175
DeVelasco, Joseph E. *21:* 51
de Veyrac, Robert *YABC 2:* 19
DeVille, Edward A. *4:* 235
de Visser, John *55:* 119
Devito, Bert *12:* 164
Devlin, Harry *11:* 74; *74:* 63, 65; *136:* 77, 78
Dewan, Ted *108:* 73; *157:* 55; *165:* 129
Dewar, Nick *133:* 122
Dewey, Ariane *7:* 64; *33:* 195; *35:* 208; *68:* 16, 17; *75:* 46; *93:* 91; *94:* 197; *109:* 65, 66, 67; *125:* 2, 3, 4, 5; *127:* 188; *143:* 25
Dewey, Jennifer (Owings) *58:* 54; *64:* 214; *65:* 207; *88:* 169; *103:* 45
Dewey, Kenneth *39:* 62; *51:* 23; *56:* 163
de Zanger, Arie *30:* 40

Diamond, Donna *21:* 200; *23:* 63; *26:* 142; *35:* 83, 84, 85, 86-87, 88, 89; *38:* 78; *40:* 147; *44:* 152; *50:* 144; *53:* 126; *69:* 46, 47, 48, 201; *71:* 133; *123:* 19
Dias, Ron *71:* 67
Diaz, David *80:* 213; *96:* 83, 84; *108:* 228; *110:* 29; *149:* 106; *150:* 63
Dibley, Glin *138:* 83; *141:* 128
DiCesare, Joe *70:* 38; *71:* 63, 106; *79:* 214; *93:* 147; *116:* 217; *143:* 111
Dick, John Henry *8:* 181
Dickens, Frank *34:* 131
Dickey, Robert L. *15:* 279
Dickson, Mora *84:* 21
Dietz, James *128:* 223
di Fate, Vincent *37:* 70; *90:* 11; *93:* 60; *109:* 219, 220
Di Fiori, Lawrence *10:* 51; *12:* 190; *27:* 97; *40:* 219; *93:* 57; *130:* 45
Digby, Desmond *97:* 180
Di Grazia, Thomas *32:* 66; *35:* 241
Dillard, Annie *10:* 32
Dillard, Sarah *136:* 186
Dillon, Corinne B. *1:* 139
Dillon, Diane *4:* 104, 167; *6:* 23; *13:* 29; *15:* 99; *26:* 148; *27:* 136, 201; *51:* 29, 48, 51, 52, 53, 54, 55, 56-57, 58, 59, 60, 61, 62; *54:* 155; *56:* 69; *58:* 127, 128; *61:* 95; *62:* 27; *64:* 46; *68:* 3; *69:* 209; *74:* 89; *79:* 92; *86:* 89; *92:* 28, 177; *93:* 7, 210; *94:* 239, 240; *97:* 167; *106:* 58, 59, 61, 64; *107:* 3; *139:* 246; *167:* 77
Dillon, Leo *4:* 104, 167; *6:* 23; *13:* 29; *15:* 99; *26:* 148; *27:* 136, 201; *51:* 29, 48, 51, 52, 53, 54, 55, 56-57, 58, 59, 60, 61, 62; *54:* 155; *56:* 69; *58:* 127, 128; *61:* 95; *62:* 27; *64:* 46; *68:* 3; *69:* 209; *74:* 89; *79:* 92; *86:* 89; *92:* 28, 177; *93:* 7, 210; *94:* 239, 240; *97:* 167; *106:* 58, 59, 61, 64; *107:* 3; *139:* 246; *167:* 77
Dillon, Sharon Saseen *59:* 179, 188
DiMaccio, Gerald *121:* 80
DiMaggio, Joe *36:* 22
DiMassi, Gina *169:* 17
Dinan, Carol *25:* 169; *59:* 75
Dines, Glen *7:* 66-67
Dinesen, Thomas *44:* 37
Dinh, Pham Viet *167:* 184
Dinnerstein, Harvey *42:* 63, 64, 65, 66, 67, 68; *50:* 146
Dinsdale, Mary *10:* 65; *11:* 171
Dinyer, Eric *86:* 148; *109:* 163; *110:* 239; *124:* 11; *150:* 69
DiSalvo-Ryan, DyAnne *59:* 77; *62:* 185; *117:* 46; *144:* 64; *150:* 153
Disney, Walt *28:* 71, 72, 73, 76, 77, 78, 79, 80, 81, 87, 88, 89, 90, 91, 94
DiTerlizzi, Tony *105:* 7; *147:* 22; *154:* 31, 32, 33
Divito, Anna *83:* 159
Dixon, Don *74:* 17; *109:* 196
Dixon, Larry *127:* 125
Dixon, Maynard *20:* 165
Doares, Robert G. *20:* 39
Dobias, Frank *22:* 162
Dobrin, Arnold *4:* 68
Dobson, Steven Gaston *102:* 103
Dockray, Tracy *139:* 77
Docktor, Irv *43:* 70
Dodd, Ed *4:* 69
Dodd, Julie *74:* 73
Dodd, Lynley *35:* 92; *86:* 71; *132:* 45, 46, 47
Dodge, Bill *96:* 36; *118:* 7, 8, 9; *133:* 135
Dodgson, Charles L. *20:* 148; *33:* 146; *YABC 2:* 98
Dodson, Bert *9:* 138; *14:* 195; *42:* 55; *54:* 8; *60:* 49; *101:* 125
Dodson, Liz Brenner *105:* 117; *111:* 15
Dohanos, Stevan *16:* 10
Dolce, J. Ellen *74:* 147; *75:* 41
Dolch, Marguerite P. *50:* 64

Dolesch, Susanne *34:* 49
Dollar, Diane *57:* 32
Dolobowsky, Mena *81:* 54
Dolson, Hildegarde *5:* 57
Domanska, Janina *6:* 66-67; *YABC 1:* 166
Domi *134:* 113
Dominguez, El *53:* 94
Domjan, Joseph *25:* 93
Domm, Jeffrey C. *84:* 69; *135:* 70
Donahey, William *68:* 209
Donahue, Dorothy *76:* 170
Donahue, Vic *2:* 93; *3:* 190; *9:* 44
Donald, Elizabeth *4:* 18
Donalty, Alison *149:* 195, 196, 197
Donato *85:* 59; *149:* 204
Doney, Todd L.W. *87:* 12; *93:* 112; *98:* 135; *101:* 57; *104:* 40; *118:* 163; *135:* 162, 163; *151:* 18
Donna, Natalie *9:* 52
Donohue, Dorothy *95:* 2; *132:* 30
Dooling, Michael *82:* 19; *105:* 55; *106:* 224; *125:* 135
Doran, Ben-Ami *128:* 189
Dore, Gustave *18:* 169, 172, 175; *19:* 93, 94, 95, 96, 97, 98, 99, 100, 101, 102, 103, 104, 105; *23:* 188; *25:* 197, 199
Doremus, Robert *6:* 62; *13:* 90; *30:* 95, 96, 97; *38:* 97
Dorfman, Ronald *11:* 128
Doriau *86:* 59; *91:* 152
Dorros, Arthur *78:* 42, 43; *91:* 28
Doruyter, Karel *165:* 105
dos Santos, Joyce Audy *57:* 187, 189
Doty, Roy *28:* 98; *31:* 32; *32:* 224; *46:* 157; *82:* 71; *142:* 7
Doucet, Bob *132:* 238; *169:* 159
Dougherty, Charles *16:* 204; *18:* 74
Doughty, Thomas *118:* 31; *140:* 60
Douglas, Aaron *31:* 103
Douglas, Carole Nelson *73:* 48
Douglas, Goray *13:* 151
Dow, Brian *150:* 92
Dowd, Jason *132:* 51, 52
Dowd, Vic *3:* 244; *10:* 97
Dowden, Anne Ophelia *7:* 70-71; *13:* 120
Dowdy, Mrs. Regera *29:* 100
Downing, Julie *60:* 140; *81:* 50; *86:* 200; *99:* 129
Doyle, Janet *56:* 31
Doyle, Richard *21:* 31, 32, 33; *23:* 231; *24:* 177; *31:* 87
Draper, Angie *43:* 84
Drath, Bill *26:* 34
Drawson, Blair *17:* 53; *126:* 65
Drescher, Henrik *105:* 60, 62, 63
Drescher, Joan *30:* 100, 101; *35:* 245; *52:* 168; *137:* 52
Drew, Patricia *15:* 100
Drummond, V.H. *6:* 70
Drury, Christian Potter *105:* 97
Dubanevich, Arlene *56:* 44
Ducak, Danilo *99:* 130; *108:* 214
Duchesne, Janet *6:* 162; *79:* 8
Duda, Jana *102:* 155
Dudash, Michael *32:* 122; *77:* 134; *82:* 149
Duer, Douglas *34:* 177
Duffy, Daniel Mark *76:* 37; *101:* 196; *108:* 147, 148
Duffy, Joseph *38:* 203
Duffy, Pat *28:* 153
Dugin, Andrej *77:* 60
Dugina, Olga *77:* 60
Duke, Chris *8:* 195; *139:* 164
Duke, Kate *87:* 186; *90:* 78, 79, 80, 81
Duke, Marion *165:* 87
Dulac, Edmund *19:* 108, 109, 110, 111, 112, 113, 114, 115, 117; *23:* 187; *25:* 152; *YABC 1:* 37; *2:* 147
Dulac, Jean *13:* 64
Dumas, Philippe *52:* 36, 37, 38, 39, 40-41, 42, 43, 45; *119:* 40, 41, 42

Dunaway, Nancy *108:* 161
Dunbar, James *76:* 63
Duncan, Beverly *72:* 92
Duncan, John *116:* 94
Dunn, H.T. *62:* 196
Dunn, Harvey *34:* 78, 79, 80, 81
Dunn, Iris *5:* 175
Dunn, Phoebe *5:* 175
Dunne, Jeanette *72:* 57, 173, 222
Dunn-Ramsey, Marcy *117:* 131
Dunnington, Tom *3:* 36; *18:* 281; *25:* 61; *31:* 159; *35:* 168; *48:* 195; *79:* 144; *82:* 230
Dunrea, Olivier *59:* 81; *118:* 53, 54; *124:* 43
Duntze, Dorothee *88:* 28; *160:* 76
Dupasquier, Philippe *86:* 75; *104:* 76; *151:* 63
DuQuette, Keith *90:* 83; *155:* 73, 74
Duroussy, Nathalie *146:* 150
Durrell, Julie *82:* 62; *94:* 62
Dutz *6:* 59
Duvoisin, Roger *2:* 95; *6:* 76-77; *7:* 197; *28:* 125; *30:* 101, 102, 103, 104, 105, 107; *47:* 205; *84:* 254
Dyer, Dale *141:* 71
Dyer, Jane *75:* 219; *129:* 28; *147:* 49-51
Dypold, Pat *15:* 37

E

E.V.B.
    See Boyle, Eleanor Vere (Gordon)
Eachus, Jennifer *29:* 74; *82:* 201
Eadie, Bob *63:* 36
Eagle, Bruce *95:* 119
Eagle, Ellen *82:* 121; *89:* 3
Eagle, Jeremy *141:* 71
Eagle, Michael *11:* 86; *20:* 9; *23:* 18; *27:* 122; *28:* 57; *34:* 201; *44:* 189; *73:* 9; *78:* 235; *85:* 43
Earl-Bridges, Michele *159:* 128
Earle, Edwin *56:* 27
Earle, Olive L. *7:* 75
Earle, Vana *27:* 99
Early, Lori *132:* 2
Early, Margaret *72:* 59
East, Stella *131:* 223
Eastman, P.D. *33:* 57
Easton, Reginald *29:* 181
Eaton, Tom *4:* 62; *6:* 64; *22:* 99; *24:* 124
Ebel, Alex *11:* 89
Ebert, Len *9:* 191; *44:* 47
Echevarria, Abe *37:* 69
Eckersley, Maureen *48:* 62
Eckert, Horst *72:* 62
Ede, Janina *33:* 59
Edens, Cooper *49:* 81, 82, 83, 84, 85; *112:* 58
Edens, John *109:* 115
Edgar, Sarah E. *41:* 97
Edliq, Emily S. *131:* 107
Edrien *11:* 53
Edwards, Freya *45:* 102
Edwards, George Wharton *31:* 155
Edwards, Gunvor *2:* 71; *25:* 47; *32:* 71; *54:* 106
Edwards, Jeanne *29:* 257
Edwards, Linda Strauss *21:* 134; *39:* 123; *49:* 88-89
Edwards, Michelle *152:* 62, 63
Egan, Tim *155:* 76, 77, 78
Egge, David *102:* 71
Eggenhofer, Nicholas *2:* 81
Eggleton, Bob *74:* 40; *81:* 190, 191; *105:* 6; *121:* 183; *149:* 203
Egielski, Richard *11:* 90; *16:* 208; *33:* 236; *38:* 35; *49:* 91, 92, 93, 95, 212, 213, 214, 216; *79:* 122; *106:* 67, 68, 69; *134:* 135; *144:* 244; *163:* 82, 84
Ehlert, Lois *35:* 97; *69:* 51; *112:* 7; *113:* 208; *128:* 63, 64, 65
Ehrlich, Bettina *1:* 83

Eitan, Ora *160:* 165
Eichenberg, Fritz *1:* 79; *9:* 54; *19:* 248; *23:* 170; *24:* 200; *26:* 208; *50:* 67, 68, 69, 70, 71, 72, 73, 74, 75, 77, 79, 80, 81; *60:* 165; *100:* 137; *YABC 1:* 104-105; *2:* 213
Einsel, Naiad *10:* 35; *29:* 136
Einsel, Walter *10:* 37
Einzig, Susan *3:* 77; *43:* 78; *67:* 155; *129:* 154
Eisner, Will *165:* 82-83
Eitzen, Allan *9:* 56; *12:* 212; *14:* 226; *21:* 194; *38:* 162; *76:* 218
Eldridge, H. *54:* 109
Eldridge, Harold *43:* 83
Elgaard, Greta *19:* 241
Elgin, Kathleen *9:* 188; *39:* 69
Ellacott, S.E. *19:* 118
Elliott, Mark *93:* 69; *105:* 108; *107:* 123; *140:* 53; *165:* 189
Elliott, Sarah M. *14:* 58
Ellis, Dianne *130:* 208
Ellis, Jan Davey *88:* 50; *115:* 80
Ellis, Richard *130:* 47, 48
Ellison, Pauline *55:* 21
Elmer, Richard *78:* 5
Elmore, Larry *90:* 8
Elwell, Tristan *110:* 39; *121:* 182; *127:* 46; *137:* 144; *141:* 173; *151:* 236; *158:* 264; *167:* 119-121; *169:* 20
Elzbieta *88:* 80, 81
Emberley, Ed *8:* 53; *70:* 53, 54; *146:* 65, 69, 70
Emberley, Michael *34:* 83; *80:* 72; *119:* 47, 48; *147:* 100; *158:* 115
Emerling, Dorothy *104:* 27
Emery, Leslie *49:* 187
Emmett, Bruce *49:* 147; *80:* 175; *101:* 206
Emry-Perrott, Jennifer *61:* 57
Engel, Diana *70:* 57
Engle, Mort *38:* 64
Englebert, Victor *8:* 54
English, Mark *101:* 207
Enik, Ted *142:* 39
Enos, Randall *20:* 183
Enright, Maginel Wright *19:* 240, 243; *39:* 31, 35, 36
Enrique, Romeo *34:* 135
Epstein, Stephen *50:* 142, 148
Erdrich, Louise *141:* 62
Erhard, Walter *1:* 152
Erickson, Phoebe *11:* 83; *59:* 85
Erikson, Mel *31:* 69
Eriksson, Eva *63:* 88, 90, 92, 93
Ering, Timothy Basil *131:* 100
Ernst, Lisa Campbell *47:* 147; *95:* 47; *154:* 46, 47, 48
Esco, Jo *61:* 103
Escourido, Joseph *4:* 81
Escriva, Vivi *119:* 51
Este, Kirk *33:* 111
Estep, David *73:* 57
Estes, Eleanor *91:* 66
Estoril, Jean *32:* 27
Estrada, Pau *74:* 76
Estrada, Ric *5:* 52, 146; *13:* 174
Etchemendy, Teje *38:* 68
Etheredges, the *73:* 12
Etienne, Kirk-Albert *145:* 184
Ets, Marie Hall *2:* 102
Eulalie *YABC 2:* 315
Evans, Greg *73:* 54, 55, 56; *143:* 40, 41
Evans, Katherine *5:* 64
Evans, Leslie *144:* 227
Evans, Shane *142:* 160; *160:* 190
Everitt, Betsy *151:* 110
Ewart, Claire *76:* 69; *145:* 59, 60
Ewing, Carolyn *66:* 143; *79:* 52
Ewing, Juliana Horatia *16:* 92
Eyolfson, Norman *98:* 154

F

Fabian, Limbert *136:* 114
Facklam, Paul *132:* 62
Falconer, Ian *125:* 66
Falconer, Pearl *34:* 23
Falkenstern, Lisa *70:* 34; *76:* 133; *78:* 171; *127:* 16
Falls, C.B. *1:* 19; *38:* 71, 72, 73, 74
Falter, John *40:* 169, 170
Falwell, Cathryn *118:* 77; *137:* 185
Fancher, Lou *138:* 219; *141:* 64; *144:* 199
Fanelli, Sara *89:* 63; *126:* 69
Faria, Rosana *150:* 143
Farmer, Andrew *49:* 102
Farmer, Peter *24:* 108; *38:* 75
Farnsworth, Bill *93:* 189; *116:* 147; *124:* 8; *135:* 52; *146:* 242, 243, 244
Farquharson, Alexander *46:* 75
Farrell, David *40:* 135
Farris, David *74:* 42
Fasolino, Teresa *118:* 145
Fatigati, Evelyn *24:* 112
Faul-Jansen, Regina *22:* 117
Faulkner, Jack *6:* 169
Faulkner, Matt *161:* 174; *167:* 75
Fava, Rita *2:* 29
Fax, Elton C. *1:* 101; *4:* 2; *12:* 77; *25:* 107
Fay *43:* 93
Fearnley, Jan *153:* 82, 83
Fearrington, Ann *146:* 80
Federspiel, Marian *33:* 51
Fedorov, Nickolai Ivanovich *110:* 102
Feelings, Tom *5:* 22; *8:* 56; *12:* 153; *16:* 105; *30:* 196; *49:* 37; *61:* 101; *69:* 56, 57; *93:* 74; *105:* 88
Fehr, Terrence *21:* 87
Feiffer, Jules *3:* 91; *8:* 58; *61:* 66, 67, 70, 74, 76, 77, 78; *111:* 47, 48, 49, 50; *132:* 122; *157:* 62
Feigeles, Neil *41:* 242
Feldman, Elyse *86:* 7
Feller, Gene *33:* 130
Fellows, Muriel H. *10:* 42
Felstead, Cathie *116:* 85
Felts, Shirley *33:* 71; *48:* 59
Fennelli, Maureen *38:* 181
Fenton, Carroll Lane *5:* 66; *21:* 39
Fenton, Mildred Adams *5:* 66; *21:* 39
Ferguson, Walter W. *34:* 86
Fernandes, Eugenie *77:* 67
Fernandes, Stanislaw *70:* 28
Fernandez, Fernando *77:* 57
Fernandez, Laura *77:* 153; *101:* 117; *131:* 222
Fetz, Ingrid *11:* 67; *12:* 52; *16:* 205; *17:* 59; *29:* 105; *30:* 108, 109; *32:* 149; *43:* 142; *56:* 29; *60:* 34; *85:* 48; *87:* 146
Fiammenghi, Gioia *9:* 66; *11:* 44; *12:* 206; *13:* 57, 59; *52:* 126, 129; *66:* 64; *85:* 83; *91:* 161
Fiedler, Joseph Daniel *96:* 42; *113:* 173; *129:* 164; *146:* 17; *159:* 68; *162:* 104
Field, Rachel *15:* 113
Fielding, David *70:* 124
Fieser, Stephen *152:* 36
Fine, Howard *145:* 159; *159:* 64; *165:* 134
Fine, Peter K. *43:* 210
Finger, Helen *42:* 81
Fink, Sam *18:* 119
Finlay, Winifred *23:* 72
Finney, Pat *79:* 215
Fiore, Peter *99:* 196; *125:* 139; *144:* 225; *160:* 169
Fiorentino, Al *3:* 240
Firmin, Charlotte *29:* 75; *48:* 70
Firmin, Peter *58:* 63, 64, 65, 67, 68, 70, 71
Firth, Barbara *81:* 208; *127:* 218
Fischel, Lillian *40:* 204
Fischer, Hans *25:* 202
Fischer-Nagel, Andreas *56:* 50

Fischer-Nagel, Heiderose *56:* 50
Fisher, Carolyn *154:* 50
Fisher, Chris *79:* 62; *158:* 248
Fisher, Cynthia *117:* 45; *137:* 118
Fisher, Jeffrey *142:* 80
Fisher, Leonard Everett *3:* 6; *4:* 72, 86; *6:* 197; *9:* 59; *16:* 151, 153; *23:* 44; *27:* 134; *29:* 26; *34:* 87, 89, 90, 91, 93, 94, 95, 96; *40:* 206; *50:* 150; *60:* 158; *73:* 68, 70, 71, 72, 73; *YABC 2:* 169
Fisher, Lois *20:* 62; *21:* 7
Fisk, Nicholas *25:* 112
Fitschen, Marilyn *2:* 20-21; *20:* 48
Fitzgerald, F.A. *15:* 116; *25:* 86-87
Fitzhugh, Louise *1:* 94; *9:* 163; *45:* 75, 78
Fitzgerald, Joanne *157:* 153, 154
Fitzhugh, Susie *11:* 117
Fitzpatrick, Jim *109:* 130
Fitzpatrick, Marie-Louise *125:* 69, 70
Fitzsimmons, Arthur *14:* 128
Fix, Philippe *26:* 102
Flack, Marjorie *21:* 67; *100:* 93; *YABC 2:* 122
Flagg, James Montgomery *17:* 227
Flavin, Teresa *132:* 115
Flax, Zeona *2:* 245
Fleishman, Seymour *14:* 232; *24:* 87
Fleming, Denise *71:* 179; *81:* 58; *126:* 71, 72, 73
Fleming, Guy *18:* 41
Flesher, Vivienne *85:* 55
Fletcher, Claire *80:* 106; *157:* 159
Flint, Russ *74:* 80
Floate, Helen *111:* 163
Floca, Brian *155:* 88, 89
Floethe, Richard *3:* 131; *4:* 90
Floherty, John J., Jr. *5:* 68
Flook, Helen *160:* 81
Flora, James *1:* 96; *30:* 111, 112
Florian, Douglas *19:* 122; *83:* 64, 65; *125:* 71, 72, 74, 76; *128:* 130
Flory, Jane *22:* 111
Flower, Renee *125:* 109
Floyd, Gareth *1:* 74; *17:* 245; *48:* 63; *62:* 35, 36, 37, 39, 40, 41; *74:* 245; *79:* 56
Fluchere, Henri A. *40:* 79
Flynn, Barbara *7:* 31; *9:* 70
Fogarty, Thomas *15:* 89
Folger, Joseph *9:* 100
Folkard, Charles *22:* 132; *29:* 128, 257-258
Foott, Jeff *42:* 202
Forberg, Ati *12:* 71, 205; *14:* 1; *22:* 113; *26:* 22; *48:* 64, 65
Ford, George *24:* 120; *31:* 70, 177; *58:* 126; *81:* 103; *107:* 91; *136:* 100
Ford, H.J. *16:* 185-186
Ford, Pamela Baldwin *27:* 104
Foreman, Michael *2:* 110-111; *67:* 99; *73:* 78, 79, 80, 81, 82; *93:* 146; *135:* 55, 56, 57
Forrester, Victoria *40:* 83
Forsey, Chris *140:* 210
Fortnum, Peggy *6:* 29; *20:* 179; *24:* 211; *26:* 76, 77, 78; *39:* 78; *58:* 19, 21, 23, 27; *YABC 1:* 148
Foster, Brad W. *34:* 99
Foster, Genevieve *2:* 112
Foster, Gerald *7:* 78
Foster, Jon *146:* 18
Foster, Laura Louise *6:* 79
Foster, Marian Curtis *23:* 74; *40:* 42
Foster, Sally *58:* 73, 74
Foucher, Adele *47:* 118
Fowler, Mel *36:* 127
Fowler, Richard *87:* 219
Fowles, Selley *165:* 127
Fox, Charles Phillip *12:* 84
Fox, Jim *6:* 187
Fox-Davies, Sarah *76:* 150
Frace, Charles *15:* 118
Frailey, Joy *72:* 108

Frame, Paul *2:* 45, 145; *9:* 153; *10:* 124; *21:* 71; *23:* 62; *24:* 123; *27:* 106; *31:* 48; *32:* 159; *34:* 195; *38:* 136; *42:* 55; *44:* 139; *60:* 39, 40, 41, 42, 43, 44, 46; *73:* 183
Frampton, David *85:* 72; *102:* 33; *139:* 182; *152:* 37
Francois, Andre *25:* 117
Francoise
    See Seignobosc, Francoise
Frank, Lola Edick *2:* 199
Frank, Mary *4:* 54; *34:* 100
Franke, Phil *45:* 91
Frankel, Alona *66:* 70
Frankel, Julie *40:* 84, 85, 202
Frankenberg, Robert *22:* 116; *30:* 50; *38:* 92, 94, 95; *68:* 111
Frankfeldt, Gwen *84:* 223; *110:* 92
Frankland, David *169:* 137
Franklin, Ashton *165:* 144
Franklin, John *24:* 22
Franson, Leanne R. *111:* 57, 58; *151:* 7
Frascino, Edward *9:* 133; *29:* 229; *33:* 190; *48:* 80, 81, 82, 83, 84-85, 86
Frasconi, Antonio *6:* 80; *27:* 208; *53:* 41, 43, 45, 47, 48; *68:* 145; *73:* 226; *131:* 68
Fraser, Betty *2:* 212; *6:* 185; *8:* 103; *31:* 72, 73; *43:* 136; *111:* 76
Fraser, Eric *38:* 78; *41:* 149, 151
Fraser, F.A. *22:* 234
Fraser, Mary Ann *137:* 63
Frasier, Debra *69:* 60; *112:* 67
Fraustino, Lisa Rowe *146:* 87
Frazee, Marla *72:* 98; *105:* 79, 80; *151:* 67, 68
Frazetta, Frank *41:* 72; *58:* 77, 78, 79, 80, 81, 82, 83
Freas, John *25:* 207
Fredrickson, Mark *103:* 33
Freeland, Michael J. *118:* 115
Freeman, Don *2:* 15; *13:* 249; *17:* 62-63, 65, 67-68; *18:* 243; *20:* 195; *23:* 213, 217; *32:* 155; *55:* 129
Freeman, Irving *67:* 150
Freeman, Laura *144:* 111
Freeman, Pietri *140:* 223
Freeman, Tom *167:* 118
Fregosi, Claudia *24:* 117
Fremaux, Charlotte Murray *138:* 29; *141:* 95
French, Fiona *6:* 82-83; *75:* 61; *109:* 170; *132:* 79, 80, 81, 82
French, Martin *163:* 4
Frendak, Rodney *126:* 97, 98
Freynet, Gilbert *72:* 221
Friedman, Judith *43:* 197; *131:* 221
Friedman, Marvin *19:* 59; *42:* 86
Frinta, Dagmar *36:* 42
Frith, Michael K. *15:* 138; *18:* 120
Fritz, Ronald *46:* 73; *82:* 124
Fromm, Lilo *29:* 85; *40:* 197
Frost, A.B. *17:* 6-7; *19:* 123, 124, 125, 126, 127, 128, 129, 130; *100:* 119; *YABC 1:* 156-157, 160; *2:* 107
Frost, Kristi *118:* 113
Frost, Michael *151:* 209
Froud, Brian *150:* 82, 83
Froud, Wendy *151:* 237
Fry, Guy *2:* 224
Fry, Rosalie *3:* 72; *YABC 2:* 180-181
Fry, Rosalind *21:* 153, 168
Fryer, Elmer *34:* 115
Fuchs, Bernie *110:* 10; *162:* 46
Fuchs, Erich *6:* 84
Fuchshuber, Annegert *43:* 96
Fufuka, Mahiri *32:* 146
Fuge, Charles *144:* 91, 93
Fujikawa, Gyo *39:* 75, 76; *76:* 72, 73, 74
Fulford, Deborah *23:* 159
Fuller, Margaret *25:* 189
Fulweiler, John *93:* 99
Funai, Mamoru *38:* 105
Funk, Tom *7:* 17, 99
Furchgott, Terry *29:* 86

Furness, William Henry, Jr. *94:* 18
Furukawa, Mel *25:* 42

G

Gaadt, David *78:* 212; *121:* 166
Gaadt, George *71:* 9
Gaber, Susan *99:* 33; *115:* 57, 58; *169:* 61-63
Gaberell, J. *19:* 236
Gabler, Mirko *99:* 71
Gackenbach, Dick *19:* 168; *41:* 81; *48:* 89, 90, 91, 92, 93, 94; *54:* 105; *79:* 75, 76, 77
Gad, Victor *87:* 161
Gaetano, Nicholas *23:* 209
Gaffney-Kessell, Walter *94:* 219
Gag, Flavia *17:* 49, 52
Gag, Wanda *100:* 101, 102; *YABC 1:* 135, 137-138, 141, 143
Gagnon, Cecile *11:* 77; *58:* 87
Gal, Laszlo *14:* 127; *52:* 54, 55, 56; *65:* 142; *68:* 150; *81:* 185; *96:* 104, 105
Galazinski, Tom *55:* 13
Galdone, Paul *1:* 156, 181, 206; *2:* 40, 241; *3:* 42, 144; *4:* 141; *10:* 109, 158; *11:* 21; *12:* 118, 210; *14:* 12; *16:* 36-37; *17:* 70-74; *18:* 111, 230; *19:* 183; *21:* 154; *22:* 150, 245; *33:* 126; *39:* 136, 137; *42:* 57; *51:* 169; *55:* 110; *66:* 80, 82, 139; *72:* 73; *100:* 84
Gale, Cathy *140:* 22; *143:* 52
Gallagher, S. Saelig *105:* 154
Gallagher, Sears *20:* 112
Galloway, Ewing *51:* 154
Galouchko, Annouchka Gravel *95:* 55
Galster, Robert *1:* 66
Galsworthy, Gay John *35:* 232
Galvez, Daniel *125:* 182
Gamble, Kim *112:* 64, 65; *124:* 77
Gammell, Stephen *7:* 48; *13:* 149; *29:* 82; *33:* 209; *41:* 88; *50:* 185, 186-187; *53:* 51, 52-53, 54, 55, 56, 57, 58; *54:* 24, 25; *56:* 147, 148, 150; *57:* 27, 66; *81:* 62, 63; *87:* 88; *89:* 10; *106:* 223; *126:* 2; *128:* 71, 73, 74, 77; *154:* 34
Gamper, Ruth *84:* 198
Gampert, John *58:* 94
Ganly, Helen *56:* 56
Gannett, Ruth Chrisman *3:* 74; *18:* 254; *33:* 77, 78
Gantschev, Ivan *45:* 32
Garafano, Marie *73:* 33
Garbot, Dave *131:* 106
Garbutt, Bernard *23:* 68
Garcia *37:* 71
Garcia, Manuel *74:* 145
Gardner, Earle *45:* 167
Gardner, Joan *40:* 87
Gardner, Joel *40:* 87, 92
Gardner, John *40:* 87
Gardner, Lucy *40:* 87
Gardner, Richard
    See Cummings, Richard
Gargiulo, Frank *84:* 158
Garland, Michael *36:* 29; *38:* 83; *44:* 168; *48:* 78, 221, 222; *49:* 161; *60:* 139; *71:* 6, 11; *72:* 229; *74:* 142; *89:* 187; *93:* 183; *104:* 110; *131:* 55; *139:* 209
Garland, Peggy *60:* 139
Garland, Sarah *62:* 45; *135:* 67, 68
Garn, Aimee *75:* 47
Garner, Joan *128:* 170
Garneray, Ambroise Louis *59:* 140
Garnett, Eve *3:* 75
Garnett, Gary *39:* 184
Garns, Allen *80:* 125; *84:* 39; *165:* 231
Garraty, Gail *4:* 142; *52:* 106
Garrett, Agnes *46:* 110; *47:* 157
Garrett, Edmund H. *20:* 29
Garrett, Tom *107:* 194
Garrick, Jacqueline *67:* 42, 43; *77:* 94

Garrison, Barbara *19:* 133; *104:* 146; *109:* 87
Garro, Mark *108:* 131; *128:* 210
Garvey, Robert *98:* 222
Garza, Carmen Lomas *80:* 211
Gates, Frieda *26:* 80
Gaughan, Jack *26:* 79; *43:* 185
Gaver, Becky *20:* 61
Gawing, Toby *72:* 52
Gay, Marie-Louise *68:* 76-77, 78; *102:* 136; *126:* 76, 78, 81, 83; *127:* 55, 56
Gay, Zhenya *19:* 135, 136
Gaydos, Tim *62:* 201
Gazsi, Ed *80:* 48
Gazso, Gabriel *73:* 85
Geary, Clifford N. *1:* 122; *9:* 104; *51:* 74
Geary, Rick *142:* 44, 46
Gee, Frank *33:* 26
Geehan, Wayne *157:* 181
Geer, Charles *1:* 91; *3:* 179; *4:* 201; *6:* 168; *7:* 96; *9:* 58; *10:* 72; *12:* 127; *39:* 156, 157, 158, 159, 160; *42:* 88, 89, 90, 91; *55:* 111, 116
Gehm, Charlie *36:* 65; *57:* 117; *62:* 60, 138
Geisel, Theodor Seuss *1:* 104-105, 106; *28:* 108, 109, 110, 111, 112, 113; *75:* 67, 68, 69, 70, 71; *89:* 127, 128; *100:* 106, 107, 108
Geisert, Arthur *92:* 67, 68; *133:* 72, 73, 74; *165:* 97-98
Geldart, William *15:* 121; *21:* 202
Genia *4:* 84
Gentry, Cyrille R. *12:* 66
Genzo, John Paul *136:* 74
George, Jean *2:* 113
George, Lindsay Barrett *95:* 57; *155:* 97, 98
Geraghty, Paul *130:* 60, 61
Gerard, Jean Ignace *45:* 80
Gerard, Rolf *27:* 147, 150
Gerber, Mark *61:* 105
Gerber, Mary Jane *112:* 124
Gerber, Stephanie *71:* 195
Gerdstein, Mordecai *169:* 105
Gergely, Tibor *54:* 15, 16
Geritz, Franz *17:* 135
Gerlach, Geff *42:* 58
Gerrard, Roy *47:* 78; *90:* 96, 97, 98, 99
Gershinowitz, George *36:* 27
Gerstein, Mordicai *31:* 117; *47:* 80, 81, 82, 83, 84, 85, 86; *51:* 173; *69:* 134; *107:* 122; *142:* 49, 52; *165:* 209
Gervase *12:* 27
Geter, Tyrone *146:* 249; *150:* 86
Getz, Arthur *32:* 148
Gewirtz, Bina *61:* 81
Giancola, Donato *95:* 146
Gibbons, Gail *23:* 78; *72:* 77, 78, 79; *82:* 182; *104:* 65; *160:* 99, 100
Gibbs, Tony *40:* 95
Gibran, Kahlil *32:* 116
Gider, Iskender *81:* 193
Giesen, Rosemary *34:* 192-193
Giffard, Hannah *83:* 70
Giguere, George *20:* 111
Gilbert, John *19:* 184; *54:* 115; *YABC 2:* 287
Gilbert, W.S. *36:* 83, 85, 96
Gilbert, Yvonne *116:* 70; *128:* 84; *149:* 119
Gilchrist, Jan Spivey *72:* 82, 83, 84-85, 87; *77:* 90; *105:* 89, 91; *130:* 63, 64; *155:* 105, 107
Giles, Will *41:* 218
Gili, Phillida *70:* 73
Gill, Margery *4:* 57; *7:* 7; *22:* 122; *25:* 166; *26:* 146, 147
Gillen, Denver *28:* 216
Gillette, Henry J. *23:* 237
Gilliam, Stan *39:* 64, 81
Gillies, Chuck *62:* 31
Gilliland, Jillian *87:* 58
Gillman, Alec *98:* 105
Gilman, Esther *15:* 124
Gilman, Phoebe *104:* 70, 71
Ginsberg, Sari *111:* 184

Ginsburg, Max *62:* 59; *68:* 194 *Girard, Roge 161:* 30
Girouard, Patrick *155:* 100
Giovanopoulos, Paul *7:* 104; *60:* 36
Giovine, Sergio *79:* 12; *93:* 118; *139:* 118
Githens, Elizabeth M. *5:* 47
Gladden, Scott *99:* 108; *103:* 160
Gladstone, Gary *12:* 89; *13:* 190
Gladstone, Lise *15:* 273
Glanzman, Louis S. *2:* 177; *3:* 182; *36:* 97, 98; *38:* 120, 122; *52:* 141, 144; *71:* 191; *91:* 54, 56
Glaser, Byron *154:* 59, 60
Glaser, Milton *3:* 5; *5:* 156; *11:* 107; *30:* 26; *36:* 112; *54:* 141; *151:* 70
Glass, Andrew *36:* 38; *44:* 133; *48:* 205; *65:* 3; *68:* 43, 45; *90:* 104, 105; *150:* 89
Glass, Marvin *9:* 174
Glasser, Judy *41:* 156; *56:* 140; *69:* 79; *72:* 101
Glattauer, Ned *5:* 84; *13:* 224; *14:* 26
Glauber, Uta *17:* 76
Gleeson, J.M. *YABC 2:* 207
Glegg, Creina *36:* 100
Glienke, Amelie *63:* 150
Gliewe, Unada *3:* 78-79; *21:* 73; *30:* 220
Gliori, Debi *72:* 91; *138:* 82; *162:* 37
Glovach, Linda *7:* 105
Gobbato, Imero *3:* 180-181; *6:* 213; *7:* 58; *9:* 150; *18:* 39; *21:* 167; *39:* 82, 83; *41:* 137, 251; *59:* 177
Goble, Paul *25:* 121; *26:* 86; *33:* 65; *69:* 68-69; *131:* 79, 80
Goble, Warwick *46:* 78, 79
Godal, Eric *36:* 93
Godkin, Celia *145:* 84, 86
Godfrey, Michael *17:* 279
Goembel, Ponder *42:* 124
Goffe, Toni *61:* 83, 84, 85; *89:* 11; *90:* 124
Goffstein, M.B. *8:* 71; *70:* 75, 76, 77
Golbin, Andre *15:* 125
Goldfeder, Cheryl *11:* 191
Goldsborough, June *5:* 154-155; *8:* 92; *14:* 226; *19:* 139; *54:* 165
Goldsmith, Robert *110:* 77
Goldstein, Leslie *5:* 8; *6:* 60; *10:* 106
Goldstein, Nathan *1:* 175; *2:* 79; *11:* 41, 232; *16:* 55
Goldstrom, Robert *98:* 36; *145:* 51, 52
Golembe, Carla *79:* 80, 81; *136:* 91; *144:* 113
Golin, Carlo *74:* 112
Gomez, Elizabeth *127:* 70; *133:* 76
Gomi, Taro *64:* 102; *103:* 74, 76
Gon, Adriano *101:* 112
Gonzalez, Maya Christina *104:* 3; *136:* 92
Goodall, John S. *4:* 92-93; *10:* 132; *66:* 92, 93; *YABC 1:* 198
Goode, Diane *15:* 126; *50:* 183; *52:* 114-115, 76; *195; *84:* 94; *99:* 141; *114:* 76, 77, 78
Goodelman, Aaron *40:* 203
Goodenow, Earle *40:* 97
Goodfellow, Peter *62:* 95; *94:* 202
Goodman, Joan Elizabeth *50:* 86
Goodman, Vivienne *82:* 251; *146:* 181, 182
Goodnow, Patti *117:* 33
Goodwin, Harold *13:* 74
Goodwin, Philip R. *18:* 206
Goor, Nancy *39:* 85, 86
Goor, Ron *39:* 85, 86
Gorbachev, Valeri *89:* 96; *112:* 97; *143:* 63, 64
Gordon, Gwen *12:* 151
Gordon, Margaret *4:* 147; *5:* 48-49; *9:* 79
Gordon, Mike *101:* 62, 63, 64
Gordon, Russell *136:* 204; *137:* 214
Gordon, Walter *138:* 9
Gore, Leonid *89:* 51; *94:* 74; *136:* 8; *158:* 117
Gorecka-Egan, Erica *18:* 35

Gorey, Edward *1:* 60-61; *13:* 169; *18:* 192; *20:* 201; *29:* 90, 91, 92-93, 94, 95, 96, 97, 98, 99, 100; *30:* 129; *32:* 90; *34:* 200, *65:* 48; *68:* 24, 25; *69:* 79; *70:* 80, 82, 83, 84; *85:* 136; *127:* 62
Gorsline, Douglas *1:* 98; *6:* 13; *11:* 113; *13:* 104; *15:* 14; *28:* 117, 118; *YABC 1:* 15
Gorton, Julia *108:* 94
Gosfield, Josh *118:* 165, 166; *149:* 67
Gosner, Kenneth *5:* 135
Gosney, Joy *167:* 142
Gotlieb, Jules *6:* 127
Goto, Scott *115:* 86; *136:* 69
Gottlieb, Dale *67:* 162; *107:* 16; *149:* 6
Goudey, Ray *97:* 86
Gough, Alan *91:* 57
Gough, Philip *23:* 47; *45:* 90
Gould, Chester *49:* 112, 113, 114, 116, 117, 118
Gould, Jason *151:* 232
Govern, Elaine R. *26:* 94
Gower, Teri *102:* 184
Gowing, Toby *60:* 25; *63:* 33; *78:* 70, 252; *83:* 228; *86:* 187; *93:* 145; *108:* 133; *110:* 217
Grabianski *20:* 144
Grabianski, Janusz *39:* 92, 93, 94, 95
Graboff, Abner *35:* 103, 104
Graef, Renee *61:* 188; *72:* 207
Grafe, Max *156:* 173
Graham, A.B. *11:* 61
Graham, Bob *101:* 66, 67, 68; *151:* 74, 75
Graham, L. *7:* 108
Graham, Margaret Bloy *11:* 120; *18:* 305, 307
Graham, Mark *88:* 208; *159:* 153
Grahame-Johnstone, Janet *13:* 61
Grahame-Johnstone, Anne *13:* 61
Grainger, Sam *42:* 95
Gramatky, Hardie *1:* 107; *30:* 116, 119, 120, 122, 123
Granahan, Julie *84:* 84
GrandPre, Mary *84:* 131; *109:* 199; *118:* 76
Grandville, J.J. *45:* 81, 82, 83, 84, 85, 86, 87, 88; *47:* 125; *64:* 10
Granger, Paul *39:* 153
Granström, Brita *162:* 35; *167:* 46
Grant, (Alice) Leigh *10:* 52; *15:* 131; *20:* 20; *26:* 119; *48:* 202
Grant, Gordon *17:* 230, 234; *25:* 123, 124, 125, 126; *52:* 69; *YABC 1:* 164
Grant, Melvin *159:* 186, 187
Grant, Renee *77:* 40
Grant, Shirley *109:* 45
Graves, Elizabeth *45:* 101
Graves, Keith *167:* 89
Gray, Harold *33:* 87, 88
Gray, Les *82:* 76; *83:* 232
Gray, Reginald *6:* 69
Greder, Armin *76:* 235
Green, Ann Canevari *62:* 48
Green, Eileen *6:* 97
Green, Elizabeth Shippen *139:* 109
Green, Jonathan *86:* 135; *105:* 109
Green, Ken *111:* 68
Green, Michael *32:* 216
Green, Robina *87:* 138
Green, Jonathan *157:* 105
Greene, Jeffrey *117:* 93
Greenaway, Kate *17:* 275; *24:* 180; *26:* 107; *41:* 222, 232; *100:* 115, 116; *YABC 1:* 88-89; *2:* 131, 133, 136, 138-139, 141
Greenberg, Melanie Hope *72:* 93; *80:* 125; *101:* 174; *133:* 180
Greenstein, Elaine *150:* 100
Greenwald, Sheila *1:* 34; *3:* 99; *8:* 72
Greger, Carol *76:* 86
Gregorian, Joyce Ballou *30:* 125
Gregory, Fran *130:* 4; *140:* 93
Gregory, Frank M. *29:* 107
Greiffenhagen, Maurice *16:* 137; *27:* 57; *YABC 2:* 288
Greiner, Robert *6:* 86

Gretter, J. Clemens *31:* 134
Gretz, Susanna *7:* 114
Gretzer, John *1:* 54; *3:* 26; *4:* 162; *7:* 125; *16:* 247; *18:* 117; *28:* 66; *30:* 85, 211; *33:* 235; *56:* 16
Grey Owl *24:* 41
Gri *25:* 90
Grieder, Walter *9:* 84
Griesbach/Martucci *59:* 3
Grifalconi, Ann *2:* 126; *3:* 248; *11:* 18; *13:* 182; *46:* 38; *50:* 145; *66:* 99, 100, 101, 104, 106; *69:* 38; *70:* 64; *87:* 128; *90:* 53; *93:* 49; *128:* 48; *133:* 79, 81
Griffin, Gillett Good *26:* 96
Griffin, James *30:* 166
Griffin, John Howard *59:* 186
Griffin, Rachel *131:* 23
Griffith, Gershom *94:* 214
Griffiths, Dave *29:* 76
Griffiths, Dean *169:* 182
Grimsdell, Jeremy *83:* 75
Grimwood, Brian *82:* 89
Gringhuis, Dirk *6:* 98; *9:* 196
Gripe, Harald *2:* 127; *74:* 98
Grisha *3:* 71
Grohmann, Susan *84:* 97
Gropper, William *27:* 93; *37:* 193
Gros *60:* 199
Grose, Helen Mason *YABC 1:* 260; *2:* 150
Grossman, Nancy *24:* 130; *29:* 101
Grossman, Robert *11:* 124; *46:* 39
Groth, John *15:* 79; *21:* 53, 54; *83:* 230
Grubb, Lisa *160:* 116
Gruelle, Johnny *35:* 107
Gschwind, William *11:* 72
Guay, Rebecca *110:* 95, 96; *135:* 240
Guback, Georgia *88:* 102
Guerguerion, Claudine *105:* 73
Guevara, Susan *97:* 87; *167:* 49
Guggenheim, Hans *2:* 10; *3:* 37; *8:* 136
Guilbeau, Honore *22:* 69
Guillette, Joseph *137:* 37
Guisewite, Cathy *57:* 52, 53, 54, 56, 57
Gukova, Julia *95:* 104; *154:* 103
Gundersheimer, Karen *35:* 240; *82:* 100
Gunderson, Nick *57:* 120
Gurney, James *76:* 97; *86:* 32
Gurney, John Steven *75:* 39, 82; *110:* 175; *143:* 67, 68; *169:* 172
Gusman, Annie *38:* 62
Gustafson, Scott *34:* 111; *43:* 40
Gustavson, Adam *104:* 10
Guthridge, Bettina *108:* 79
Guthrie, R. Dale *64:* 143
Guthrie, Robin *20:* 122
Gutierrez, Alan *136:* 31, 32
Gutierrez, Rudy *97:* 162
Gutmann, Bessie Pease *73:* 93, 94
Gwynne, Fred *41:* 94, 95
Gyberg, Bo-Erik *38:* 131

H

Haas, Irene *17:* 77; *87:* 46; *96:* 117
Hack, Konrad *51:* 127
Hader, Berta H. *16:* 126
Hader, Elmer S. *16:* 126
Haeffele, Deborah *76:* 99
Haemer, Alan *62:* 109
Hafner, Marylin *22:* 196, 216; *24:* 44; *30:* 51; *35:* 95; *51:* 25, 160, 164; *86:* 16; *105:* 196; *121:* 93, 94; *149:* 208, 209
Hagerty, Sean *62:* 181
Hague, Michael *32:* 128; *48:* 98, 99, 100-101, 103, 105, 106-107, 108, 109, 110; *49:* 121; *51:* 105; *64:* 14, 15; *79:* 134; *80:* 91, 92; *83:* 135; *100:* 241; *102:* 29; *129:* 101, 103, 104
Hair, Jonathan *115:* 135
Halas, John *29:* 41, 47, 48

Haldane, Roger *13:* 76; *14:* 202
Hale, Christy *79:* 124; *84:* 200; *114:* 201; *128:* 2, 3; *146:* 203; *158:* 243; *167:* 99
Hale, Irina *26:* 97
Hale, James Graham *88:* 207
Hale, Kathleen *17:* 79; *66:* 114, 116, 118
Haley, Gail E. *43:* 102, 103, 104, 105; *78:* 65, 67; *136:* 106, 107
Hall, Amanda *96:* 110
Hall, Chuck *30:* 189
Hall, Douglas *15:* 184; *43:* 106, 107; *86:* 100; *87:* 82; *129:* 72
Hall, H. Tom *1:* 227; *30:* 210
Hall, Melanie *116:* 48, 49; *169:* 77-78
Hall, Sydney P. *31:* 89
Hall, Vicki *20:* 24
Hallinan, P.K. *39:* 98
Hallman, Tom *98:* 166
Hally, Greg *101:* 200; *151:* 224
Halperin, Wendy Anderson *96:* 151; *125:* 96, 97, 98, 99; *139:* 22; *140:* 84
Halpern, Joan *10:* 25
Halsey, Megan *96:* 172; *114:* 185
Halstead, Virginia *125:* 105
Halverson, Janet *49:* 38, 42, 44
Hallensleben, Georg *134:* 5, 6
Hamanaka, Sheila *71:* 100
Hamann, Brad *78:* 151
Hamann, Sigune *104:* 115
Hamberger, John *6:* 8; *8:* 32; *14:* 79; *34:* 136; *88:* 78
Hamil, Tom *14:* 80; *43:* 163
Hamilton, Bill and Associates *26:* 215
Hamilton, Helen S. *2:* 238
Hamilton, J. *19:* 83, 85, 87
Hamilton, Laurie *116:* 210
Hamilton, Todd Cameron *84:* 15
Hamlin, Janet *97:* 136; *124:* 90; *137:* 157
Hamlin, Louise *71:* 135
Hammond, Chris *21:* 37
Hammond, Elizabeth *5:* 36, 203
Hampshire, Michael *5:* 187; *7:* 110-111; *48:* 150; *51:* 129
Hampson, Denman *10:* 155; *15:* 130
Hampton, Blake *41:* 244
Handford, Martin *64:* 105, 106-07, 109
Handforth, Thomas *42:* 100, 101, 102, 103, 104, 105, 107
Handville, Robert *1:* 89; *38:* 76; *45:* 108, 109
Hane, Roger *17:* 239; *44:* 54
Haney, Elizabeth Mathieu *34:* 84
Hanke, Ted *71:* 10
Hanley, Catherine *8:* 161
Hann, Jacquie *19:* 144
Hanna, Cheryl *91:* 133
Hanna, Wayne A. *67:* 145
Hannon, Mark *38:* 37
Hansen, Gabby *159:* 11
Hansen, Mia *149:* 76
Hanson, Joan *8:* 76; *11:* 139
Hanson, Peter E. *52:* 47; *54:* 99, 100; *73:* 21; *84:* 79; *116:* 144
Hansson, Gunilla *64:* 111, 112
Hardcastle, Nick *121:* 82
Hardy, David A. *9:* 96; *119:* 74
Hardy, Paul *YABC 2:* 245 Haring, Keith *145:* 65
Harlan, Jerry *3:* 96
Harlin, Greg *89:* 194; *103:* 82; *118:* 161; *121:* 167
Harness, Cheryl *106:* 80; *131:* 87
Harnischfeger *18:* 121
Harper, Arthur *YABC 2:* 121
Harper, Betty *126:* 90
Harper, Piers *79:* 27; *105:* 102; *161:* 67
Harrington, Glenn *82:* 18; *94:* 66, 68
Harrington, Jack *83:* 162
Harrington, Richard *5:* 81
Harris, Jim *127:* 130
Harris, John *83:* 25
Harris, Nick *86:* 177

Harris, Susan Yard *42:* 121
Harrison, Florence *20:* 150, 152
Harrison, Harry *4:* 103
Harrison, Jack *28:* 149
Harrison, Mark *105:* 157; *165:* 190
Harrison, Ted *56:* 73
Harsh, Fred *72:* 107
Harston, Jerry *105:* 143
Hart, Lewis *98:* 115
Hart, William *13:* 72
Hartung, Susan Kathleen *150:* 107, 108
Hartelius, Margaret *10:* 24
Hartshorn, Ruth *5:* 115; *11:* 129
Harvey, Amanda *145:* 44
Harvey, Bob *48:* 219
Harvey, Gerry *7:* 180
Harvey, Lisa *97:* 21
Harvey, Paul *88:* 74
Harvey, Roland *71:* 88; *123:* 63
Hassall, Joan *43:* 108, 109
Hassell, Hilton *YABC 1:* 187
Hassett, John *162:* 59
Hasselriis, Else *18:* 87; *YABC 1:* 96
Hastings, Glenn *89:* 183
Hastings, Ian *62:* 67
Hauman, Doris *2:* 184; *29:* 58, 59; *32:* 85, 86, 87
Hauman, George *2:* 184; *29:* 58, 59; *32:* 85, 86, 87
Hausherr, Rosmarie *15:* 29
Hawkes, Kevin *78:* 72; *104:* 198; *105:* 197; *112:* 109; *126:* 87; *144:* 88; *149:* 210; *150:* 110, 135; *156:* 94
Hawkins, Jacqui *112:* 86; *162:* 64
Hawkinson, John *4:* 109; *7:* 83; *21:* 64
Hawkinson, Lucy *21:* 64
Hawthorne, Mike *140:* 228
Haxton, Elaine *28:* 131
Haydock, Robert *4:* 95
Hayes, Geoffrey *26:* 111; *44:* 133; *91:* 85
Haynes, Max *72:* 107
Hays, Michael *73:* 207; *83:* 93; *139:* 197; *146:* 202, 250
Haywood, Carolyn *1:* 112; *29:* 104
Heale, Jonathan *104:* 117
Healy, Daty *12:* 143
Healy, Deborah *58:* 181, 182; *101:* 111
Heap, Sue *102:* 207; *150:* 113, 114
Hearn, Diane Dawson *79:* 99; *113:* 13
Hearon, Dorothy *34:* 69
Heaslip, William *57:* 24, 25
Hechtkopf, H. *11:* 110
Hedderwick, Mairi *30:* 127; *32:* 47; *36:* 104; *77:* 86; *145:* 91, 93, 95
Hefferman, Phil *146:* 197
Hefter, Richard *28:* 170; *31:* 81, 82; *33:* 183
Hehenberger, Shelly *126:* 91
Heigh, James *22:* 98
Heighway, Richard *25:* 160; *64:* 4
Heighway-Bury, Robin *159:* 89
Heine, Helme *67:* 86; *135:* 91, 92
Heinly, John *45:* 113
Hellard, Susan *81:* 21
Hellebrand, Nancy *26:* 57
Heller, Linda *46:* 86
Heller, Ruth M. *66:* 125; *77:* 30, 32
Hellmuth, Jim *38:* 164
Helms, Georgeann *33:* 62
Helquist, Brett *142:* 203; *146:* 133, 134; *156:* 10
Helweg, Hans *41:* 118; *50:* 93; *58:* 22, 26
Henba, Bobbie *90:* 195
Henderson, Dave *73:* 76; *75:* 191, 192, 193, 194; *82:* 4
Henderson, Douglas *103:* 68
Henderson, Kathy *55:* 32; *155:* 118
Henderson, Keith *35:* 122
Henderson, Meryl *127:* 58, 60; *169:* 81
Hendry, Linda *80:* 104; *83:* 83
Hengeveld, Dennis *142:* 86
Henkes, Kevin *43:* 111; *108:* 106, 107, 108

Henneberger, Robert *1:* 42; *2:* 237; *25:* 83
Henriksen, Harold *35:* 26; *48:* 68
Henriquez, Celeste *103:* 137
Henriquez, Elsa *82:* 260
Henriquez, Emile F. *89:* 88
Henry, Everett *29:* 191
Henry, Matthew *117:* 58
Henry, Paul *93:* 121
Henry, Thomas *5:* 102
Hensel *27:* 119
Henshaw, Jacqui *141:* 127
Henstra, Friso *8:* 80; *36:* 70; *40:* 222; *41:* 250; *73:* 100, 101
Henterly, Jamichael *93:* 4
Heo, Yumi *89:* 85, 86; *94:* 89, 90; *146:* 40, 137, 138; *163:* 227
Hepple, Norman *28:* 198
Herbert, Helen *57:* 70
Herbert, Wally *23:* 101
Herbster, Mary Lee *9:* 33
Herge
    See Remi, Georges
Hermansen, Pal *133:* 113
Hermanson, Dennis *10:* 55
Hermes, Gertrude *54:* 161
Herr, Margo *57:* 191
Herr, Susan *83:* 163
Herriman, George *140:* 74, 75, 76, 77, 78
Herriman, Lisa *87:* 190
Herring, Michael *121:* 76
Herrington, Roger *3:* 161
Herscovici, C. *165:* 240
Hescox, Richard *85:* 86; *90:* 30; *139:* 35
Heslop, Mike *38:* 60; *40:* 130
Hess, Lydia J. *85:* 17
Hess, Mark *111:* 146; *113:* 207
Hess, Paul *134:* 47
Hess, Richard *42:* 31
Hester, Ronnie *37:* 85
Heuser, Olga J. *121:* 116
Heustis, Louise L. *20:* 28
Hewison, Jennifer *74:* 119; *124:* 167
Hewitt, Kathryn *80:* 126; *149:* 105
Hewitt, Margaret *84:* 112
Heyduck-Huth, Hilde *8:* 82
Heyer, Carol *74:* 122; *130:* 72, 73
Heyer, Hermann *20:* 114, 115
Heyer, Marilee *102:* 108
Heyman, Ken *8:* 33; *34:* 113
Heyne, Ulrike *146:* 151
Heywood, Karen *48:* 114
Hickling, P.B. *40:* 165
Hickman, Steve *85:* 58; *136:* 33
Hierstein, Judy *56:* 40; *162:* 168
Higashi, Sandra *154:* 59, 60
Higginbottom, J. Winslow *8:* 170; *29:* 105, 106
Higgins, Chester *101:* 79
Higham, David *50:* 104
Hildebrandt, Greg *8:* 191; *55:* 35, 36, 38, 39, 40, 42, 46
Hildebrandt, Tim *8:* 191; *55:* 44, 45, 46
Hilder, Rowland *19:* 207
Hill, Eric *66:* 127, 128; *133:* 91
Hill, Gregory *35:* 190
Hill, Pat *49:* 120
Hillenbrand, Will *84:* 115; *92:* 76, 80; *93:* 131; *104:* 168; *128:* 137; *145:* 187; *146:* 184; *147:* 105-107; *152:* 59
Hillier, Matthew *45:* 205
Hillman, Priscilla *48:* 115
Hills, Tad *113:* 4; *137:* 147
Himler, Ronald *6:* 114; *7:* 162; *8:* 17, 84, 125; *14:* 76; *19:* 145; *26:* 160; *31:* 43; *38:* 116; *41:* 44, 79; *43:* 52; *45:* 120; *46:* 43; *54:* 44, 83; *58:* 180; *59:* 38; *68:* 146; *69:* 231; *70:* 98; *71:* 177, 178; *77:* 219; *79:* 212; *83:* 62; *89:* 5; *91:* 160; *92:* 91, 92, 93; *94:* 93; *95:* 69, 174, 194; *99:* 99, 112; *113:* 92; *118:* 114; *137:* 73, 74, 77, 167; *163:* 99; *165:* 138

Himmelman, John *47:* 109; *65:* 87; *94:* 96, 97; *159:* 85
Hinds, Bill *37:* 127, 130
Hines, Anna Grossnickle *51:* 90; *74:* 124; *95:* 78, 79, 80, 81
Hines, Bob *135:* 149, 150
Hiroko *99:* 61
Hiroshige *25:* 71
Hirsh, Marilyn *7:* 126
Hiscock, Bruce *137:* 80, 81
Hissey, Jane *103:* 90; *130:* 81
Hitch, Jeff *99:* 206; *128:* 86
Hitz, Demi *11:* 135; *15:* 245; *66:* 129, 130; *152:* 94, 95
Hnizdovsky, Jacques *32:* 96; *76:* 187
Ho, Kwoncjan *15:* 132
Hoban, Lillian *1:* 114; *22:* 157; *26:* 72; *29:* 53; *40:* 105, 107, 195; *41:* 80; *69:* 107, 108; *71:* 98; *77:* 168; *106:* 50; *113:* 86; *136:* 118
Hoban, Tana *22:* 159; *104:* 82, 83, 85
Hoberman, Norman *5:* 82
Hobson, Sally *77:* 185
Hockerman, Dennis *39:* 22; *56:* 23
Hodgell, P.C. *42:* 114
Hodges, C. Walter *2:* 139; *11:* 15; *12:* 25; *23:* 34; *25:* 96; *38:* 165; *44:* 197; *45:* 95; *100:* 57; *YABC 2:* 62-63
Hodges, David *9:* 98
Hodgetts, Victoria *43:* 132
Hofbauer, Imre *2:* 162
Hoff, Syd *9:* 107; *10:* 128; *33:* 94; *72:* 115, 116, 117, 118; *138:* 114, 115
Hoffman, Rosekrans *15:* 133; *50:* 219; *63:* 97
Hoffman, Sanford *38:* 208; *76:* 174; *88:* 160, 161; *151:* 156
Hoffmann, Felix *9:* 109
Hoffnung, Gerard *66:* 76, 77
Hofsinde, Robert *21:* 70
Hogan, Inez *2:* 141
Hogarth, Burne *41:* 58; *63:* 46, 48, 49, 50, 52, 53, 54, 55, 56
Hogarth, Paul *41:* 102, 103, 104; *YABC 1:* 16
Hogarth, William *42:* 33
Hogenbyl, Jan *1:* 35
Hogner, Nils *4:* 122; *25:* 144
Hogrogian, Nonny *3:* 221; *4:* 106-107; *5:* 166; *7:* 129; *15:* 2; *16:* 176; *20:* 154; *22:* 146; *25:* 217; *27:* 206; *74:* 127, 128, 129, 149, 152; *127:* 99; *YABC 2:* 84, 94
Hokanson, Lars *93:* 111
Hokusai *25:* 71
Hol, Colby *126:* 96
Holberg, Richard *2:* 51
Holbrook, Kathy *107:* 114
Holdcroft, Tina *38:* 109
Holden, Caroline *55:* 159
Holder, Heidi *36:* 99; *64:* 9
Holder, Jimmy *151:* 224
Holiday, Henry *YABC 2:* 107
Holl, F. *36:* 91
Holland, Brad *45:* 59, 159
Holland, Gay W. *128:* 105
Holland, Janice *18:* 118
Holland, Marion *6:* 116
Holldobler, Turid *26:* 120
Holliday, Keaf *144:* 236
Holling, Holling C. *15:* 136-137
Hollinger, Deanne *12:* 116
Holm, Sharon Lane *114:* 84; *115:* 52
Holmes, B. *3:* 82
Holmes, Bea *7:* 74; *24:* 156; *31:* 93
Holmes, Dave *54:* 22
Holmes, Lesley *135:* 96
Holmgren, George Ellen *45:* 112
Holmlund, Heather D. *150:* 140
Holt, Norma *44:* 106
Holt, Pater *151:* 188
Holtan, Gene *32:* 192
Holub, Joan *149:* 72
Holyfield, John *149:* 231
Holz, Loretta *17:* 81

Hom, Nancy 79: 195
Homar, Lorenzo 6: 2
Homer, Winslow 128: 8; YABC 2: 87
Honey, Elizabeth 112: 95, 96; 137: 93, 94
Honeywood, Varnette P. 110: 68, 70
Hong, Lily Toy 76: 104
Honigman, Marian 3: 2
Honore, Paul 42: 77, 79, 81, 82
Hood, Alun 69: 145, 218; 72: 41; 80: 226; 87: 4; 95: 139
Hood, Susan 12: 43
Hook, Christian 104: 103
Hook, Frances 26: 188; 27: 127
Hook, Jeff 14: 137; 103: 105
Hook, Richard 26: 188
Hooks 63: 30
Hoover, Carol A. 21: 77
Hoover, Russell 12: 95; 17: 2; 34: 156
Hope, James 141: 116
Hopkins, Chris 99: 127
Hoppin, Augustus 34: 66
Horacek, Petr 163: 117
Horder, Margaret 2: 108; 73: 75
Horen, Michael 45: 121
Horne, Daniel 73: 106; 91: 153; 109: 127; 110: 232
Horne, Richard 111: 80
Horse, Harry 128: 195; 169: 86
Horvat, Laurel 12: 201
Horvath, Ferdinand Kusati 24: 176
Horvath, Maria 57: 171
Horwitz, Richard 57: 174
Hotchkiss, De Wolfe 20: 49
Hough, Charlotte 9: 112; 13: 98; 17: 83; 24: 195
Houlihan, Ray 11: 214
Housman, Laurence 25: 146, 147
Houston, James 13: 107; 74: 132, 134, 135
Hovland, Gary 88: 172
Hoyt, Eleanor 158: 231
How, W.E. 20: 47
Howard, Alan 16: 80; 34: 58; 45: 114
Howard, Arthur 165: 111-112
Howard, J.N. 15: 234
Howard, John 33: 179
Howard, Kim 116: 71
Howard, Paul 142: 126, 129; 144: 187
Howard, Rob 40: 161
Howe, John 115: 47
Howe, John F. 79: 101; 80: 150
Howe, Phillip 79: 117
Howe, Stephen 1: 232
Howell, Karen 119: 123
Howell, Pat 15: 139
Howell, Troy 23: 24; 31: 61; 36: 158; 37: 184; 41: 76, 235; 48: 112; 56: 13; 57: 3; 59: 174; 63: 5; 74: 46; 89: 188; 90: 231; 95: 97; 98: 130; 99: 189; 153: 156, 157, 158
Howes, Charles 22: 17
Hoyt, Ard 145: 141
Hranilovich, Barbara 127: 51
Hu, Ying-Hwa 116: 107; 152: 236
Huang, Benrei 137: 55
Huang, Zhong-Yang 117: 30, 32
Hubbard, Woodleigh Marx 98: 67; 115: 79; 160: 138
Hubley, Faith 48: 120-121, 125, 130, 131, 132, 134
Hubley, John 48: 125, 130, 131, 132, 134
Hudak, Michal 143: 74
Hudnut, Robin 14: 62
Huerta, Catherine 76: 178; 77: 44, 45; 90: 182
Huffaker, Sandy 10: 56
Huffman, Joan 13: 33
Huffman, Tom 13: 180; 17: 212; 21: 116; 24: 132; 33: 154; 38: 59; 42: 147
Hughes, Arthur 20: 148, 149, 150; 33: 114, 148, 149
Hughes, Darren 95: 44
Hughes, David 36: 197

Hughes, Shirley 1: 20, 21; 7: 3; 12: 217; 16: 163; 29: 154; 63: 118; 70: 102, 103, 104; 73: 169; 88: 70; 110: 118, 119; 159: 103
Hugo, Victor 47: 112
Hull, Cathy 78: 29
Hull, Richard 95: 120; 123: 175
Hulsmann, Eva 16: 166
Hummel, Berta 43: 137, 138, 139
Hummel, Lisl 29: 109; YABC 2: 333-334
Humphrey, Henry 16: 167
Humphreys, Graham 25: 168
Humphries, Tudor 76: 66; 80: 4; 124: 4, 5
Hunt, James 2: 143
Hunt, Jonathan 84: 120
Hunt, Paul 119: 104; 129: 135; 139: 160
Hunt, Robert 110: 206, 235; 147: 136-137
Hunter, Anne 133: 190
Hurd, Clement 2: 148, 149; 64: 127, 128, 129, 131, 133, 134, 135, 136; 100: 37, 38
Hurd, Peter 24: 30, 31,; YABC 2: 56
Hurd, Thacher 46: 88-89; 94: 114, 115, 116; 123: 81-82, 84
Hurlimann, Ruth 32: 99
Hussar, Michael 114: 113; 117: 159
Hustler, Tom 6: 105
Hutchins, Laurence 55: 22
Hutchins, Pat 15: 142; 70: 106-107, 108
Hutchinson, Sascha 95: 211
Hutchinson, William M. 6: 3, 138; 46: 70
Hutchison, Paula 23: 10
Hutton, Clarke YABC 2: 335
Hutton, Kathryn 35: 155; 89: 91
Hutton, Warwick 20: 91
Huyette, Marcia 29: 188
Hyatt, John 54: 7
Hyde, Maureen 82: 17; 121: 145, 146
Hyman, David 117: 64
Hyman, Trina Schart 1: 204; 2: 194; 5: 153; 6: 106; 7: 138, 145; 8: 22; 10: 196; 13: 96; 14: 114; 15: 204; 16: 234; 20: 82; 22: 133; 24: 151; 25: 79, 82; 26: 82; 29: 83; 31: 37, 39; 34: 104; 38: 84, 100, 128; 41: 49; 43: 146; 46: 91, 92, 93, 95, 96, 97, 98, 99, 100, 101, 102, 103, 104-105, 108, 109, 111, 197; 48: 60, 61; 52: 32; 60: 168; 66: 38; 67: 214; 72: 74; 75: 92; 79: 57; 82: 95, 238; 89: 46; 95: 91, 92, 93; 100: 33, 199; 132: 12; 147: 33, 35, 36; 167: 58, 60

Ibarra, Rosa 147: 91
Ibatoulline, Bagram 156: 48
Ichikawa, Satomi 29: 152; 41: 52; 47: 133, 134, 135, 136; 78: 93, 94; 80: 81; 146: 143, 145, 146
Ide, Jacqueline YABC 1: 39
Ilsley, Velma 3: 1; 7: 55; 12: 109; 37: 62; 38: 184
in den Bosch, Nicole 150: 204
Inga 1: 142
Ingman, Bruce 134: 50
Ingpen, Robert 109: 103, 104; 132: 138; 137: 177
Ingraham, Erick 21: 177; 84: 256; 103: 66
Inkpen, Mick 99: 104, 105; 106: 44
Innerst, Stacy 149: 104
Innocenti, Roberto 21: 123; 96: 122; 159: 111, 197
Inoue, Yosuke 24: 118
Iofin, Michael 97: 157
Iosa, Ann 63: 189
Ipcar, Dahlov 1: 124-125; 49: 137, 138, 139, 140-141, 142, 143, 144, 145; 147: 122, 124, 126
Irvin, Fred 13: 166; 15: 143-144; 27: 175
Irving, Jay 45: 72
Irving, Laurence 27: 50
Isaac, Joanne 21: 76

Isadora, Rachel 43: 159, 160; 54: 31; 79: 106-107, 108; 121: 100, 102; 165: 116-117
Ishmael, Woodi 24: 111; 31: 99
Ives, Ruth 15: 257
Iwai, Melissa 149: 233

J

Jabar, Cynthia 101: 201
Jackness, Andrew 94: 237
Jackson, Julian 91: 104, 106
Jackson, Michael 43: 42
Jackson, Shelley 79: 71; 99: 109
Jacob, Murv 89: 30
Jacobi, Kathy 62: 118
Jacobs, Barbara 9: 136
Jacobs, Lou, Jr. 9: 136; 15: 128
Jacobson, Rick 131: 222
Jacobus, Tim 79: 140; 109: 126; 129: 180
Jacques, Robin 1: 70; 2: 1; 8: 46; 9: 20; 15: 187; 19: 253; 32: 102, 103, 104; 43: 184; 73: 135; YABC 1: 42
Jaffee, Al 66: 131, 132
Jagr, Miloslav 13: 197
Jahn-Clough, Lisa 88: 114; 152: 104
Jahnke, Robert 84: 24
Jainschigg, Nicholas 80: 64; 91: 138; 95: 63; 99: 25; 108: 50
Jakesavic, Nenad 85: 102
Jakobsen, Kathy 116: 83
Jakubowski, Charles 14: 192
Jambor, Louis YABC 1: 11
James, Ann 73: 50; 82: 113; 158: 61
James, Brian 140: 91
James, Derek 35: 187; 44: 91; 61: 133; 74: 2; 80: 57; 86: 88; 130: 30
James, Gilbert YABC 1: 43
James, Harold 2: 151; 3: 62; 8: 79; 29: 113; 51: 195; 74: 90
James, Kennon 126: 211
James, Robin 50: 106; 53: 32, 34, 35
James, Will 19: 150, 152, 153, 155, 163
Janosch
See Eckert, Horst
Janovitch, Marilyn 68: 168
Janovitz, Marilyn 87: 187; 130: 198
Jansons, Inese 48: 117
Jansson, Tove 3: 90; 41: 106, 108, 109, 110, 111, 113, 114
Jaques, Faith 7: 11, 132-33; 21: 83, 84; 69: 114, 116; 73: 170
Jaques, Frances Lee 29: 224
Jauss, Anne Marie 1: 139; 3: 34; 10: 57, 119; 11: 205; 23: 194
Jay, Alison 158: 97, 98
Jeffers, Susan 17: 86-87; 25: 164-165; 26: 112; 50: 132, 134-135; 70: 111, 112-113; 137: 107, 108, 109, 110, 111
Jefferson, Louise E. 4: 160
Jenkin-Pearce, Susie 78: 16
Jenkins, Debra Reid 85: 202; 114: 89
Jenkins, Jean 98: 79, 102
Jenkins, Leonard 157: 169; 167: 128
Jenkins, Patrick 72: 126
Jenkins, Steve 124: 177; 154: 90, 91, 92, 93
Jenks, Aleta 73: 117; 124: 225
Jenkyns, Chris 51: 97
Jensen, Bruce 95: 39
Jensinius, Kirsten 56: 58
Jeram, Anita 89: 135; 102: 122, 123; 129: 112; 154: 96, 97, 98
Jernigan, E. Wesley 85: 92
Jerome, Karen A. 72: 194
Jeruchim, Simon 6: 173; 15: 250
Jeschke, Susan 20: 89; 39: 161; 41: 84; 42: 120
Jessel, Camilla 29: 115
Jessel, Tim 159: 3
Jiang, Cheng An 109: 108

Jiang, Wei *109:* 108
Jimenez, Maria *77:* 158; *93:* 127
Jobling, Curtis *138:* 74
Jocelyn, Marthe *118:* 83; *137:* 219; *163:* 119, 120
Joerns, Consuelo *38:* 36; *44:* 94
John, Diana *12:* 209
John, Helen *1:* 215; *28:* 204
Johns, Elizabeth *127:* 33
Johns, Jasper *61:* 172
Johns, Jeanne *24:* 114
Johnson, Adrian *143:* 50
Johnson, Bruce *9:* 47
Johnson, Cathy *92:* 136
Johnson, Crockett
See Leisk, David
Johnson, D. William *23:* 104
Johnson, Gillian *119:* 175
Johnson, Harper *1:* 27; *2:* 33; *18:* 302; *19:* 61; *31:* 181; *44:* 46, 50, 95
Johnson, Ingrid *37:* 118
Johnson, James Ralph *1:* 23, 127
Johnson, James David *12:* 195
Johnson, Jane *48:* 136
Johnson, Joel Peter *98:* 18; *128:* 111
Johnson, John E. *34:* 133
Johnson, Kevin *72:* 44
Johnson, Kevin Eugene *109:* 215
Johnson, Larry *47:* 56; *123:* 107; *159:* 203
Johnson, Margaret S. *35:* 131
Johnson, Meredith Merrell *71:* 181; *83:* 158; *89:* 103; *104:* 88
Johnson, Milton *1:* 67; *2:* 71; *26:* 45; *31:* 107; *60:* 112; *68:* 96
Johnson, Pamela *16:* 174; *52:* 145; *62:* 140; *73:* 116; *85:* 64
Johnson, Paul Brett *83:* 95; *132:* 119
Johnson, Stephen T. *80:* 15; *131:* 35; *141:* 96; *145:* 40
Johnson, Steve *138:* 219; *141:* 64; *144:* 199
Johnson, William R. *38:* 91
Johnson-Petrov, Arden *115:* 206
Johnston, David McCall *50:* 131, 133
Johnston, Lynne *118:* 85, 87, 89
Johnstone, Anne *8:* 120; *36:* 89
Johnstone, Janet Grahame *8:* 120; *36:* 89
Jonas, Ann *50:* 107, 108, 109; *135:* 113
Jones, Bob *71:* 5; *77:* 199
Jones, Carol *5:* 131; *72:* 185, 186; *153:* 111, 112
Jones, Chuck *53:* 70, 71
Jones, Davy *89:* 176
Jones, Elizabeth Orton *18:* 124, 126, 128-129
Jones, Harold *14:* 88; *52:* 50
Jones, Holly *127:* 3
Jones, Jeff *41:* 64
Jones, Laurian *25:* 24, 27
Jones, Margaret *74:* 57
Jones, Randy *131:* 104
Jones, Richard *127:* 222
Jones, Robert *25:* 67
Jones, Wilfred *35:* 115; *YABC 1:* 163
Jordan, Charles *89:* 58
Jordan, Jess *158:* 136
Jordan, Martin George *84:* 127
Jordan, Richard *84:* 36
Jorgenson, Andrea *91:* 111
Jorisch, Stephane *153:* 56, 193
Joseph, James *53:* 88
Joudrey, Ken *64:* 145; *78:* 6
Joyce, William *72:* 131, 132, 133, 134; *73:* 227; *145:* 37
Joyner, Jerry *34:* 138
Jucker, Sita *5:* 93
Judkis, Jim *37:* 38
Juhasz, Victor *31:* 67
Jullian, Philippe *24:* 206; *25:* 203
Jung, Tom *91:* 217
Junge, Walter *67:* 150
Jupo, Frank *7:* 148-149

Jurisch, Stephane *154:* 105
Justice, Martin *34:* 72

K

Kabatova-Taborska, Zdenka *107:* 153
Kachik, John *165:* 230
Kaczman, James *156:* 98
Kahl, David *74:* 95; *97:* 35; *109:* 174; *110:* 213
Kahl, M.P. *37:* 83
Kahl, Virginia *48:* 138
Kahn, Katherine Janus *90:* 135
Kakimoo, Kozo *11:* 148
Kalett, Jim *48:* 159, 160, 161
Kalin, Victor *39:* 186
Kalman, Maira *96:* 131, 132; *137:* 115
Kalmenoff, Matthew *22:* 191
Kalow, Gisela *32:* 105
Kamen, Gloria *1:* 41; *9:* 119; *10:* 178; *35:* 157; *78:* 236; *98:* 82
Kaminsky, Jef *102:* 153
Kandell, Alice *35:* 133
Kane, Henry B. *14:* 90; *18:* 219-220
Kane, Robert *18:* 131
Kanfer, Larry *66:* 141
Kappes, Alfred *28:* 104
Karalus, Bob *41:* 157
Karas, G. Brian *80:* 60; *99:* 179; *115:* 41; *118:* 50; *136:* 168; *145:* 166; *149:* 245; *159:* 65
Karasz, Ilonka *128:* 163
Karlin, Eugene *10:* 63; *20:* 131
Karlin, Nurit *63:* 78; *103:* 110
Karpinski, Tony *134:* 160
Kasamatsu, Shiro *139:* 155
Kasparavicius, Kestutis *139:* 210
Kassian, Olena *64:* 94
Kastner, Jill *79:* 135; *117:* 84, 85
Kasuya, Masahiro *41:* 206-207; *51:* 100
Katona, Robert *21:* 85; *24:* 126
Katz, Karen *158:* 123
Kauffer, E. McKnight *33:* 103; *35:* 127; *63:* 67
Kaufman, Angelika *15:* 156
Kaufman, Joe *33:* 119
Kaufman, John *13:* 158
Kaufman, Stuart *62:* 64; *68:* 226; *137:* 44
Kaufmann, John *1:* 174; *4:* 159; *8:* 43, 1; *10:* 102; *18:* 133-134; *22:* 251
Kaye, Graham *1:* 9; *67:* 7, 8
Kaye, M.M. *62:* 95
Kazalovski, Nata *40:* 205
Keane, Bil *4:* 135
Kearney, David *72:* 47; *121:* 83
Keating, Pamel T. *77:* 37
Keats, Ezra Jack *3:* 18, 105, 257; *14:* 101, 102; *33:* 129; *57:* 79, 80, 82, 83, 84, 87
Keegan, Marcia *9:* 122; *32:* 93
Keeler, Patricia A. *81:* 56
Keely, Jack *119:* 95
Keely, John *26:* 104; *48:* 214
Keen, Eliot *25:* 213
Keeping, Charles *9:* 124, 185; *15:* 28, 134; *18:* 115; *44:* 194, 196; *47:* 25; *52:* 3; *54:* 156; *69:* 123, 124; *74:* 56; *155:* 9
Keith, Eros *4:* 98; *5:* 138; *31:* 29; *43:* 220; *52:* 91, 92, 93, 94; *56:* 64, 66; *60:* 37; *79:* 93
Keleinikov, Andrei *65:* 101, 102
Kelen, Emery *13:* 115
Keller, A.J. *62:* 198
Keller, Arthur I. *26:* 106
Keller, Dick *36:* 123, 125
Keller, Holly *45:* 79; *76:* 118, 119, 120, 121, 108; *137:* 137, 138, 140; *157:* 117, 118, 119
Keller, Katie *79:* 222; *93:* 108
Keller, Ronald *45:* 208
Kelley, True *41:* 114, 115; *42:* 137; *75:* 35; *92:* 104, 105; *124:* 62; *130:* 100, 101

Kellogg, Steven *8:* 96; *11:* 207; *14:* 130; *20:* 58; *29:* 140-141; *30:* 35; *41:* 141; *57:* 89, 90, 92, 93, 94, 96; *59:* 182; *73:* 141; *77:* 129; *130:* 105, 106; *YABC 1:* 65, 73
Kelly, Billy *158:* 143
Kelly, Geoff *97:* 196; *112:* 25
Kelly, Irene *147:* 134
Kelly, Kathleen M. *71:* 109
Kelly, Laura *89:* 217
Kelly, True *163:* 87
Kelly, Walt *18:* 136-141, 144-146, 148-149
Kemble, E.W. *34:* 75; *44:* 178; *YABC 2:* 54, 59
Kemp-Welsh, Lucy *24:* 197; *100:* 214
Kendall, Jane *150:* 105
Kendall, Peter *152:* 85
Kendrick, Dennis *79:* 213
Kennaway, Adrienne *60:* 55, 56
Kennedy, Paul Edward *6:* 190; *8:* 132; *33:* 120
Kennedy, Richard *3:* 93; *12:* 179; *44:* 193; *100:* 15; *YABC 1:* 57
Kent, Jack *24:* 136; *37:* 37; *40:* 81; *84:* 89; *86:* 150; *88:* 77
Kent, Rockwell *5:* 166; *6:* 129; *20:* 225, 226, 227, 229; *59:* 144
Kenyon, Tony *81:* 201; *127:* 74
Kepes, Juliet *13:* 119
Kerins, Anthony *76:* 84
Kerr, Judity *24:* 137
Kerr, Phyllis Forbes *72:* 141
Kessler, Leonard *1:* 108; *7:* 139; *14:* 107, 227; *22:* 101; *44:* 96; *67:* 79; *82:* 123
Kesteven, Peter *35:* 189
Ketcham, Hank *28:* 140, 141, 142
Kettelkamp, Larry *2:* 164
Key, Alexander *8:* 99
Khalsa, Dayal Kaur *62:* 99
Kiakshuk *8:* 59
Kidd, Chip *94:* 23
Kidd, Richard *152:* 110
Kidd, Tom *64:* 199; *81:* 189
Kiddell-Monroe, Joan *19:* 201; *55:* 59, 60; *87:* 174; *121:* 112
Kidder, Harvey *9:* 105; *80:* 41
Kidwell, Carl *43:* 145
Kieffer, Christa *41:* 89
Kiesler, Kate *110:* 105; *136:* 142
Kiff, Ken *40:* 45
Kilbride, Robert *37:* 100
Kilby, Don *141:* 144
Kim, Glenn *99:* 82
Kimball, Anton *78:* 114; *119:* 105
Kimball, Yeffe *23:* 116; *37:* 88
Kincade, Orin *34:* 116
Kindersley, Barnabas *96:* 110
Kindred, Wendy *7:* 151
King, Colin *53:* 3
King, Robin *10:* 164-165
King, Stephen Michael *141:* 31
King, Tara Calahan *139:* 172
King, Tony *39:* 121
Kingman, Dong *16:* 287; *44:* 100, 102, 104
Kingsley, Charles *YABC 2:* 182
Kingston, Julie *147:* 14
Kingston, Maxine Hong *53:* 92
Kipling, John Lockwood *YABC 2:* 198
Kipling, Rudyard *YABC 2:* 196
Kipniss, Robert *29:* 59
Kirchherr, Astrid *55:* 23
Kirchhoff, Art *28:* 136
Kirk, Daniel *153:* 115, 116, 117
Kirk, David *117:* 88, 89; *161:* 97, 98
Kirk, Ruth *5:* 96
Kirk, Tim *32:* 209, 211; *72:* 89; *83:* 49
Kirmse, Marguerite *15:* 283; *18:* 153
Kirsch, Vincent X. *124:* 207
Kirschner, Ruth *22:* 154
Kish, Ely *73:* 119; *79:* 2
Kitamura, Satoshi *62:* 102; *98:* 91; *101:* 147; *138:* 2; *143:* 83, 85, 86
Kitchel, JoAnn E. *133:* 32

Kitchen, Herbert Thomas *70:* 126
Kittelsen, Theodor *62:* 14
Kiuchi, Tatsuro *114:* 71
Klapholz, Mel *13:* 35
Klein, Bill *89:* 105
Klein, Robert *55:* 77
Klein, Suzanna *63:* 104
Kleinman, Zalman *28:* 143
Kliban, B. *35:* 137, 138
Kline, Michael *127:* 66
Knabel, Lonnie *73:* 103; *75:* 187, 228
Kneen, Maggie *140:* 139
Knight, Ann *34:* 143
Knight, Christopher *13:* 125
Knight, Hilary *1:* 233; *3:* 21; *15:* 92, 158-159; *16:* 258-260; *18:* 235; *19:* 169; *35:* 242; *46:* 167; *52:* 116; *69:* 126, 127; *132:* 129; *YABC 1:* 168-169, 172
Knorr, Peter *126:* 92, 93
Knotts, Howard *20:* 4; *25:* 170; *36:* 163
Knutson, Barbara *112:* 134
Knutson, Kimberley *115:* 90
Kobayashi, Ann *39:* 58
Kocsis, J.C.
   See Paul, James
Koehn, Ilse *34:* 198; *79:* 123
Koelsch, Michael *99:* 182; *107:* 164; *109:* 239; *138:* 142; *150:* 94
Koering, Ursula *3:* 28; *4:* 14; *44:* 5; *64:* 140, 141; *85:* 46
Koerner, Henry
   See Koerner, W.H.D.
Koerner, W.H.D. *14:* 216; *21:* 88, 89, 90, 91; *23:* 211
Koffler, Camilla *36:* 113
Kogan, Deborah Ray *161:* 101, 102
Koide, Yasuko *50:* 114
Kolado, Karen *102:* 228
Komoda, Kiyo *9:* 128; *13:* 214
Kompaneyets, Marc *169:* 92
Konashevich, Vladimir *61:* 160
Konashevicha, V. *YABC 1:* 26
Konigsburg, E.L. *4:* 138; *48:* 141, 142, 144, 145; *94:* 129, 130; *126:* 129, 130, 131
Kooiker, Leonie *48:* 148
Koonook, Simon *65:* 157
Koontz, Robin Michal *136:* 155
Koopmans, Loek *101:* 121
Kopelke, Lisa *154:* 107
Kopper, Lisa *72:* 152, 153; *105:* 135, 136
Korach, Mimi *1:* 128-129; *2:* 52; *4:* 39; *5:* 159; *9:* 129; *10:* 21; *24:* 69
Koren, Edward *5:* 100; *65:* 65, 67
Koscielniak, Bruce *99:* 122; *153:* 120, 121, 122
Koshkin, Alexander *92:* 180
Kossin, Sandy *10:* 71; *23:* 105
Kostin, Andrej *26:* 204
Kotzky, Brian *68:* 184
Kovacevic, Zivojin *13:* 247
Kovalski, Maryann *58:* 120; *84:* 88; *97:* 124, 125, 126; *158:* 3
Krahn, Fernando *2:* 257; *34:* 206; *49:* 152
Kramer, Anthony *33:* 81
Kramer, David *96:* 162; *109:* 132; *150:* 220
Kramer, Frank *6:* 121
Krantz, Kathy *35:* 83
Kratter, Paul *139:* 65
Kraus, Robert *13:* 217; *65:* 113; *93:* 93, 94
Kredel, Fritz *6:* 35; *17:* 93-96; *22:* 147; *24:* 175; *29:* 130; *35:* 77; *YABC 2:* 166, 300
Krementz, Jill *17:* 98; *49:* 41
Krenina, Katya *117:* 106; *125:* 133
Kresin, Robert *23:* 19
Krieger, Salem *54:* 164
Kriegler, Lyn *73:* 29
Krommes, Beth *128:* 141; *149:* 136
Krone, Mike *101:* 71
Kronheimer, Ann *135:* 119
Krosoczka, Jarrett J. *155:* 142
Kruck, Gerald *88:* 181

Krupinski, Loretta *67:* 104; *102:* 131; *161:* 105, 106
Krupp, Robin Rector *53:* 96, 98
Krush, Beth *1:* 51, 85; *2:* 233; *4:* 115; *9:* 61; *10:* 191; *11:* 196; *18:* 164-165; *32:* 72; *37:* 203; *43:* 57; *60:* 102, 103, 107, 108, 109
Krush, Joe *2:* 233; *4:* 115; *9:* 61; *10:* 191; *11:* 196; *18:* 164-165; *32:* 72, 91; *37:* 203; *43:* 57; *60:* 102, 103, 107, 108, 109
Krych, Duane *91:* 43
Krykorka, Vladyana *96:* 147; *143:* 90, 91
Kubick, Dana *165:* 91
Kubinyi, Laszlo *4:* 116; *6:* 113; *16:* 118; *17:* 100; *28:* 227; *30:* 172; *49:* 24, 28; *54:* 23; *167:* 149
Kubricht, Mary *73:* 118
Kucharik, Elena *139:* 31
Kuchera, Kathleen *84:* 5
Kuhn, Bob *17:* 91; *35:* 235
Kulikov, Boris *163:* 185
Kukalis, Romas *90:* 27; *139:* 37
Kuklin, Susan *63:* 82, 83, 84
Kunhardt, Dorothy *53:* 101
Kunhardt, Edith *67:* 105, 106
Kunstler, Mort *10:* 73; *32:* 143
Kurchevsky, V. *34:* 61
Kurczok, Belinda *121:* 118
Kurelek, William *8:* 107
Kuriloff, Ron *13:* 19
Kurisu, Jane *160:* 120
Kuskin, Karla *2:* 170; *68:* 115, 116; *111:* 116
Kutzer, Ernst *19:* 249
Kuzma, Steve *57:* 8; *62:* 93
Kuznetsova, Berta *74:* 45
Kvasnosky, Laura McGee *93:* 103; *142:* 83
Kyong, Yunmee *165:* 139

L

LaBlanc, Andre *24:* 146
Laboccetta, Mario *27:* 120
LaBrose, Darcie *157:* 134
Labrosse, Darcia *58:* 88; *108:* 77
LaCava, Vince *95:* 118
Laceky, Adam *32:* 121
Lacis, Astra *85:* 117
La Croix *YABC 2:* 4
Ladwig, Tim *98:* 212; *117:* 76
La Farge, Margaret *47:* 141
LaFave, Kim *64:* 177; *72:* 39; *97:* 146; *99:* 172; *106:* 123; *149:* 126
Lafontaine, Roger *167:* 158
Lagarrigue, Jerome *136:* 102
Laimgruber, Monika *11:* 153
Laite, Gordon *1:* 130-131; *8:* 209; *31:* 113; *40:* 63; *46:* 117
Laliberté, Louise-Andrée *169:* 98
LaMarche, Jim *46:* 204; *61:* 56; *94:* 69; *114:* 22; *129:* 163; *162:* 78, 80
Lamb, Jim *10:* 117
Lambase, Barbara *101:* 185; *150:* 221
Lambert, J.K. *38:* 129; *39:* 24
Lambert, Sally Anne *133:* 191
Lambert, Saul *23:* 112; *33:* 107; *54:* 136
Lambert, Stephen *109:* 33
Lambo, Don *6:* 156; *35:* 115; *36:* 146
Lamut, Sonja *57:* 193
Lamut, Sonya *85:* 102
Landa, Peter *11:* 95; *13:* 177; *53:* 119
Landau, Jacob *38:* 111
Landis, Joan *104:* 23
Landon, Lucinda *79:* 31
Landshoff, Ursula *13:* 124
Landström, Lena *146:* 165, 166
Landström, Olof *146:* 166, 168
Lane, Daniel *112:* 60
Lane, John R. *8:* 145
Lane, John *15:* 176-177; *30:* 146
Lang, G.D. *48:* 56

Lang, Gary *73:* 75
Lang, Jerry *18:* 295
Lange, Dorothea *50:* 141
Langley, Jonathan *162:* 128
Langner, Nola *8:* 110; *42:* 36
Lanino, Deborah *105:* 148
Lantz, Paul *1:* 82, 102; *27:* 88; *34:* 102; *45:* 123
Larkin, Bob *84:* 225
Laroche, Giles *126:* 140; *146:* 81
Larrecq, John *44:* 108; *68:* 56
Larsen, Suzanne *1:* 13
Larson, Gary *57:* 121, 122, 123, 124, 125, 126, 127
Larsson, Carl *35:* 144, 145, 146, 147, 148-149, 150, 152, 153, 154
Larsson, Karl *19:* 177
Lartitegui, Ana G. *105:* 167
LaRue, Jenna *167:* 20
La Rue, Michael D. *13:* 215
Lasker, Joe *7:* 186-187; *14:* 55; *38:* 115; *39:* 47; *83:* 113, 114, 115
Latham, Barbara *16:* 188-189; *43:* 71
Lathrop, Dorothy *14:* 117, 118-119; *15:* 109; *16:* 78-79, 81; *32:* 201, 203; *33:* 112; *YABC 2:* 301
Lattimore, Eleanor Frances *7:* 156
Lauden, Claire *16:* 173
Lauden, George, Jr. *16:* 173
Laune, Paul *2:* 235; *34:* 31
Laure, Jason *49:* 53; *50:* 122
Lauter, Richard *63:* 29; *67:* 111; *77:* 198
Lavallee, Barbara *74:* 157; *92:* 154; *96:* 126; *145:* 193
Lave, Fitz Hugh *59:* 139
Lavis, Stephen *43:* 143; *87:* 137, 164, 165
Layton, Neal *152:* 120, 121
Lawrence, John *25:* 131; *30:* 141; *44:* 198, 200
Lawrence, Stephen *20:* 195
Lawson, Carol *6:* 38; *42:* 93, 131
Lawson, George *17:* 280
Lawson, Robert *5:* 26; *6:* 94; *13:* 39; *16:* 11; *20:* 100, 102, 103; *54:* 3; *66:* 12; *100:* 144, 145; *YABC 2:* 222, 224-225, 227-235, 237-241
Layfield, Kathie *60:* 194
Lazare, Jerry *44:* 109; *74:* 28
Lazarevich, Mila *17:* 118
Lazarus, Claire *103:* 30
Lazarus, Keo Felker *21:* 94
Lazzaro, Victor *11:* 126
Lea, Tom *43:* 72, 74
Leacroft, Richard *6:* 140
Leaf, Munro *20:* 99
Leake, Donald *70:* 41
Leander, Patricia *23:* 27
Lear, Edward *18:* 183-185
Lear, Rebecca *149:* 46
Lebenson, Richard *6:* 209; *7:* 76; *23:* 145; *44:* 191; *87:* 153
Le Cain, Errol *6:* 141; *9:* 3; *22:* 142; *25:* 198; *28:* 173; *68:* 128, 129; *86:* 49
Lechon, Daniel *113:* 211
Leder, Dora *129:* 172
Leduc, Bernard *102:* 36
Lee, Alan *62:* 25, 28
Lee, Bryce *99:* 60; *101:* 195
Lee, Dom *83:* 118, 120; *93:* 123; *121:* 121, 126; *146:* 174, 175, 206, 207
Lee, Doris *13:* 246; *32:* 183; *44:* 111
Lee, Hector Viveros *115:* 96
Lee, Jeanne M. *158:* 56
Lee, Jared *93:* 200; *157:* 229
Lee, Jody *81:* 121; *82:* 225; *91:* 155; *100:* 182
Lee, Jody A. *127:* 124, 126, 127
   See also Lee, Jody
Lee, Manning de V. *2:* 200; *17:* 12; *27:* 87; *37:* 102, 103, 104; *YABC 2:* 304
Lee, Marie G. *138:* 157

Lee, Paul *97:* 100; *105:* 72, 209; *109:* 177; *128:* 113
Lee, Robert J. *3:* 97; *67:* 124
Lee, Victor *96:* 228; *105:* 182; *140:* 196
Leech, Dorothy *98:* 76
Leech, John *15:* 59
Leedy, Loreen *84:* 142; *128:* 144, 145, 146
Leeman, Michael *44:* 157
Leeming, Catherine *87:* 39
Lees, Harry *6:* 112
LeFever, Bill *88:* 220, 221
Legenisel *47:* 111
Legrand, Edy *18:* 89, 93
Lehman, Barbara *73:* 123
Lehrman, Rosalie *2:* 180
Leichman, Seymour *5:* 107
Leighton, Clare *25:* 130; *33:* 168; *37:* 105, 106, 108, 109
Leisk, David *1:* 140-141; *11:* 54; *30:* 137, 142, 143, 144
Leister, Brian *89:* 45; *106:* 37; *114:* 67; *149:* 236
Leloir, Maurice *18:* 77, 80, 83, 99
Lematire, Pascal *144:* 175
Lemieux, Michele *100:* 148; *139:* 153
Lemke, Horst *14:* 98; *38:* 117, 118, 119
Lemke, R.W. *42:* 162
Lemon, David Gwynne *9:* 1
LeMoult, Adolph *82:* 116
Lenn, Michael *136:* 89
Lennon, John *114:* 100
Lennox, Elsie *95:* 163; *143:* 160
Lenski, Lois *1:* 144; *26:* 135, 137, 139, 141; *100:* 153, 154
Lent, Blair *1:* 116-117; *2:* 174; *3:* 206-207; *7:* 168-169; *34:* 62; *68:* 217; *133:* 101
Leonard, Richard *91:* 128
Leone, Leonard *49:* 190
Lerner, Carol *86:* 140, 141, 142
Lerner, Judith *116:* 138
Lerner, Sharon *11:* 157; *22:* 56
Leroux-Hugon, Helene *132:* 139
Leslie, Cecil *19:* 244
Lessac, Frane *80:* 182, 207; *96:* 182
Lessing, Erich *167:* 52
Lester, Alison *50:* 124; *90:* 147, 148; *129:* 130
Le Tord, Bijou *49:* 156; *95:* 112
Leutz, Emanuel *165:* 27
Levai, Blaise *39:* 130
Levin, Ted *12:* 148
Levine, David *43:* 147, 149, 150, 151, 152; *64:* 11
Levine, Joe *71:* 88
Levine, Marge *81:* 127
Levit, Herschel *24:* 223
Levstek, Ljuba *131:* 192; *134:* 216; *149:* 65
Levy, Jessica Ann *19:* 225; *39:* 191
Levy, Lina *117:* 126
Lewin, Betsy *32:* 114; *48:* 177; *90:* 151; *91:* 125; *92:* 85; *115:* 105; *169:* 110-111
Lewin, Ted *4:* 168; *20:* 110; *21:* 99, 100; *27:* 110; 28; 96, 97; *31:* 49; *45:* 55; *48:* 223; *60:* 20, 119, 120; *62:* 139; *66:* 108; *71:* 12; *72:* 21; *74:* 226; *76:* 139, 140; *77:* 82; *79:* 87; *85:* 49, 177; *86:* 55; *88:* 182; *93:* 28, 29; *94:* 34, 182, 194; *99:* 156; *104:* 8; *115:* 123; *118:* 74; *119:* 114, 116; *131:* 54; *145:* 99; *165:* 151
Lewis, Allen *15:* 112
Lewis, E.B. *88:* 143; *93:* 109; *119:* 79; *124:* 113; *128:* 49; *151:* 167
Lewis, J. Patrick *162:* 83
Lewis, Jan *81:* 22
Lewis, Kim *136:* 165
Lewis, Richard W. *52:* 25
Lewis, Robin Baird *98:* 193
Leydon, Rita Floden *21:* 101
Lichtenheld, Tom *152:* 125, 126
Lieblich, Irene *22:* 173; *27:* 209, 214
Lieder, Rick *108:* 197
Lies, Brian *92:* 40; *141:* 101; *150:* 138

Liese, Charles *4:* 222
Life, Kay *79:* 49
Lifton, Robert Jay *66:* 154
Lightburn, Ron *86:* 153; *91:* 122
Lightfoot, Norman R. *45:* 47
Lignell, Lois *37:* 114
Lill, Debra *121:* 70
Lilly, Charles *8:* 73; *20:* 127; *48:* 53; *72:* 9, 16; *77:* 98; *102:* 94
Lilly, Ken *37:* 224
Lim, John *43:* 153
Limona, Mercedes *51:* 183
Lin, Grace *143:* 217; *162:* 86, 87
Lincoln, Patricia Henderson *27:* 27; *78:* 127
Lindahn, Ron *84:* 17
Lindahn, Val *84:* 17
Lindberg, Howard *10:* 123; *16:* 190
Lindberg, Jeffrey *64:* 77; *77:* 71; *79:* 54; *80:* 149
Linden, Seymour *18:* 200-201; *43:* 140
Lindenbaum, Pija *144:* 143
Linder, Richard *27:* 119
Lindman, Maj *43:* 154
Lindsay, Norman *67:* 114
Lindsay, Vachel *40:* 118
Lindstrom, Jack *145:* 118
Line, Les *27:* 143
Linell
  See Smith, Linell
Lionni, Leo *8:* 115; *72:* 159, 160, 161
Lipinsky, Lino *2:* 156; *22:* 175
Lippincott, Gary A. *70:* 35; *119:* 118
Lippman, Peter *8:* 31; *31:* 119, 120, 160
Lisi, Victoria *89:* 145
Lisker, Emily *164:* 114
Lisker, Sonia O. *16:* 274; *31:* 31; *44:* 113, 114
Lisowski, Gabriel *47:* 144; *49:* 157
Lissim, Simon *17:* 138
Little, Ed *89:* 145; *151:* 53
Little, Harold *16:* 72
Little, Mary E. *28:* 146
Littlewood, Karen *165:* 126
Litty, Julie *111:* 63
Litzinger, Rosanne *151:* 101
Liu, Lesley *143:* 72
Lively, Lorna *19:* 216
Livingston, Susan *95:* 22
Llerena, Carlos Antonio *19:* 181
Lloyd, Errol *11:* 39; *22:* 178
Lloyd, Megan *77:* 118; *80:* 113; *97:* 75; *117:* 94, 95
Lo, Beth *165:* 154
Lo, Koon-chiu *7:* 134
Loates, Glen *63:* 76
Lobel, Anita *6:* 87; *9:* 141; *18:* 248; *55:* 85, 86, 87, 88, 93, 104; *60:* 67; *78:* 263; *82:* 110; *96:* 157, 159; *101:* 84; *132:* 35; *162:* 93, 94
Lobel, Arnold *1:* 188-189; *5:* 12; *6:* 147; *7:* 167, 209; *18:* 190-191; *25:* 39, 43; *27:* 40; *29:* 174; *52:* 127; *55:* 89, 91, 94, 95, 97, 98, 99, 100, 101, 102, 103, 105, 106; *60:* 18, 31; *66:* 181, 183; *75:* 57; *82:* 246; *136:* 146
Locker, Thomas *109:* 134
Lodge, Bernard *107:* 125, 126; *153:* 93
Loeb, Jeph *153:* 177
Lodge, Jo *112:* 119
Loefgren, Ulf *3:* 108
Loescher, Ann *20:* 108
Loescher, Gil *20:* 108
Loew, David *93:* 184
Lofting, Hugh *15:* 182-183; *100:* 161, 162
Lofts, Pamela *60:* 188
Loh, George *38:* 88
Lomberg, Jon *58:* 160
Lonette, Reisie *11:* 211; *12:* 168; *13:* 56; *36:* 122; *43:* 155
Long, Laurel *162:* 135
Long, Loren *99:* 176
Long, Melinda *152:* 128
Long, Miles *115:* 174

Long, Sally *42:* 184
Long, Sylvia *74:* 168; *132:* 63
Longoni, Eduardo *73:* 85
Longtemps, Ken *17:* 123; *29:* 221; *69:* 82
Looser, Heinz *YABC 2:* 208
Lopshire, Robert *6:* 149; *21:* 117; *34:* 166; *73:* 13
Lord, John Vernon *21:* 104; *23:* 25; *51:* 22
Lorenz, Albert *40:* 146; *115:* 127
Loretta, Sister Mary *33:* 73
Lorraine, Walter H. *3:* 110; *4:* 123; *16:* 192; *103:* 119
Los, Marek *146:* 22
Loss, Joan *11:* 163
Louderback, Walt *YABC 1:* 164
Lousada, Sandra *40:* 138
Louth, Jack *149:* 252; *151:* 191, 192
Low, Joseph *14:* 124, 125; *18:* 68; *19:* 194; *31:* 166; *80:* 239
Low, William *62:* 175; *80:* 147; *112:* 194; *150:* 202; *169:* 175
Lowenheim, Alfred *13:* 65-66
Lowenstein, Sallie *116:* 90, 91
Lowitz, Anson *17:* 124; *18:* 215
Lowrey, Jo *8:* 133
Lubach, Vanessa *142:* 152
Lubell, Winifred *1:* 207; *3:* 15; *6:* 151
Lubin, Leonard B. *19:* 224; *36:* 79, 80; *45:* 128, 129, 131, 132, 133, 134, 135, 136, 137, 139, 140, 141; *70:* 95; *YABC 2:* 96
Lucht, Irmgard *82:* 145
Ludwig, Helen *33:* 144, 145
Lufkin, Raymond *38:* 138; *44:* 48
Luhrs, Henry *7:* 123; *11:* 120
Lujan, Tonita *82:* 33
Lupo, Dom *4:* 204
Lustig, Loretta *30:* 186; *46:* 134, 135, 136, 137
Luxbacher, Irene *153:* 145
Luzak, Dennis *52:* 121; *99:* 142
Lydbury, Jane *82:* 98
Lydecker, Laura *21:* 113; *42:* 53
Lynch, Charles *16:* 33
Lynch, Marietta *29:* 137; *30:* 171
Lynch, P.J. *126:* 228; *129:* 110; *132:* 247
Lyon, Carol *102:* 26
Lyon, Elinor *6:* 154
Lyon, Fred *14:* 16
Lyons, Oren *8:* 193
Lyster, Michael *26:* 41

M

Maas, Dorothy *6:* 175
Maas, Julie *47:* 61
Macaulay, David *46:* 139, 140-141, 142, 143, 144-145, 147, 149, 150; *72:* 167, 168, 169; *137:* 129, 130, 131, 132
MacCarthy, Patricia *69:* 141
Macdonald, Alister *21:* 55
Macdonald, Roberta *19:* 237; *52:* 164
MacDonald, Norman *13:* 99
MacDonald, Suse *54:* 41; *109* 138; *130:* 156
Mace, Varian *49:* 159
Macguire, Robert Reid *18:* 67
Machetanz, Fredrick *34:* 147, 148
MacInnes, Ian *35:* 59
MacIntyre, Elisabeth *17:* 127, 128
Mack, Jeff *161:* 128
Mack, Stan *17:* 129; *96:* 33
Mackay, Donald *17:* 60
MacKaye, Arvia *32:* 119
Mackenzie, Stuart *73:* 213
MacKenzie, Garry *33:* 159
Mackie, Clare *87:* 134
Mackinlay, Miguel *27:* 22
MacKinstry, Elizabeth *15:* 110; *42:* 139, 140, 141, 142, 143, 144, 145
MacLeod, Lee *91:* 167

Maclise, Daniel *YABC 2:* 257
Madden, Don *3:* 112-113; *4:* 33, 108, 155; *7:* 193; *78:* 12; *YABC 2:* 211
Maddison, Angela Mary *10:* 83
Madsen, Jim *146:* 259; *152:* 237
Maestro, Giulio *8:* 124; *12:* 17; *13:* 108; *25:* 182; *54:* 147; *59:* 114, 115, 116, 117, 118, 121, 123, 124, 125, 126, 127; *68:* 37, 38; *106:* 129, 130, 131, 136, 137, 138
Maffia, Daniel *60:* 200
Maggio, Viqui *58:* 136, 181; *74:* 150; *75:* 90; *85:* 159; *90:* 158; *109:* 184
Magnus, Erica *77:* 123
Magnuson, Diana *28:* 102; *34:* 190; *41:* 175
Magovern, Peg *103:* 123
Maguire, Sheila *41:* 100
Magurn, Susan *91:* 30
Mahony, Will *37:* 120
Mahony, Will *85:* 116
Mahood, Kenneth *24:* 141
Maik, Henri *9:* 102
Maione, Heather Harms *106:* 5
Maisto, Carol *29:* 87
Maitland, Antony *1:* 100, 176; *8:* 41; *17:* 246; *24:* 46; *25:* 177, 178; *32:* 74; *60:* 65, 195; *67:* 156; *87:* 131; *101:* 110
Majewski, Dawn W. *169:* 95
Mak, Kam *72:* 25; *75:* 43; *87:* 186; *97:* 24; *102:* 154; *149:* 195
Makie, Pam *37:* 117
Maktima, Joe *116:* 191
Maland, Nick *99:* 77
Male, Alan *132:* 64
Malone, James Hiram *84:* 161
Malone, Nola Langner *82:* 239
Malsberg, Edward *51:* 175
Malvern, Corinne *2:* 13; *34:* 148, 149
Manchess, Gregory *165:* 241
Mancusi, Stephen *63:* 198, 199
Mandelbaum, Ira *31:* 115
Manders, John *138:* 152, 155
Manet, Edouard *23:* 170
Mangurian, David *14:* 133
Manham, Allan *42:* 109; *77:* 180; *80:* 227
Manley, Matt *103:* 167; *117:* 98
Manniche, Lise *31:* 121
Manning, Jane *96:* 203
Manning, Jo *63:* 154
Manning, Samuel F. *5:* 75
Mantel, Richard *57:* 73; *63:* 106; *82:* 255
Maraja *15:* 86; *YABC 1:* 28; *2:* 115
Marcellino, Fred *20:* 125; *34:* 222; *53:* 125; *58:* 205; *61:* 64, 121, 122; *68:* 154, 156-157, 158, 159; *72:* 25; *86:* 184; *98:* 181; *118:* 129, 130, 131; *149:* 218
Marchesi, Stephen *34:* 140; *46:* 72; *50:* 147; *66:* 239; *70:* 33; *73:* 18, 114, 163; *77:* 47, 76, 147; *78:* 79; *80:* 30; *81:* 6; *89:* 66; *93:* 21, 130; *94:* 94; *97:* 66; *98:* 96; *114:* 115, 116
Marchiori, Carlos *14:* 60
Marciano, John Bemelmans *118:* 133; *167:* 110-112
Marcus, Barry David *139:* 248; *145:* 18
Margules, Gabriele *21:* 120
Mariana
    See Foster, Marian Curtis
Mariano, Michael *52:* 108
Marino, Dorothy *6:* 37; *14:* 135
Mario, Heide Stetson *101:* 202
Maris, Ron *71:* 123
Maritz, Nicolaas *85:* 123
Mark, Mona *65:* 105; *68:* 205; *116:* 213
Markham, R.L. *17:* 240
Marks, Alan *104:* 104; *109:* 182
Marks, Cara *54:* 9
Marokvia, Artur *31:* 122
Marquez, Susan *108:* 121
Marrella, Maria Pia *62:* 116

Marriott, Pat *30:* 30; *34:* 39; *35:* 164, 165, 166; *44:* 170; *48:* 186, 187, 188, 189, 191, 192, 193; *91:* 92
Mars, W.T. *1:* 161; *3:* 115; *4:* 208, 225; *5:* 92, 105, 186; *8:* 214; *9:* 12; *13:* 121; *27:* 151; *31:* 180; *38:* 102; *48:* 66; *62:* 164, 165; *64:* 62; *68:* 229; *79:* 55
Marschall, Ken *85:* 29
Marsh, Christine *3:* 164
Marsh, James *73:* 137
Marsh, Reginald *17:* 5; *19:* 89; *22:* 90, 96
Marshall, Anthony D. *18:* 216
Marshall, James *6:* 160; *40:* 221; *42:* 24, 25, 29; *51:* 111, 112, 113, 114, 115, 116, 117, 118, 119, 120, 121; *64:* 13; *75:* 126, 127, 128, 129; *102:* 10, 12
Marshall, Janet *97:* 154
Marstall, Bob *55:* 145; *84:* 153, 170; *104:* 145; *154:* 166, 167, 168
Martchenko, Michael *50:* 129, 153, 155, 156, 157; *83:* 144, 145; *154:* 137, 138, 139
Marten, Ruth *129:* 52
Martin, Charles E. *70:* 144
Martin, David Stone *24:* 232; *62:* 4
Martin, Fletcher *18:* 213; *23:* 151
Martin, Rene *7:* 144; *42:* 148, 149, 150
Martin, Richard E. *51:* 157; *131:* 203
Martin, Ron *32:* 81
Martin, Stefan *8:* 68; *32:* 124, 126; *56:* 33
Martinez, Ed *58:* 192; *72:* 231; *77:* 33; *80:* 214; *167:* 123
Martinez, John *6:* 113; *118:* 13; *139:* 143
Martinez, Sergio *158:* 190
Marton, Jirina *95:* 127, 128; *144:* 145
Martorell, Antonio *84:* 6; *97:* 161
Martucci, Griesbach *52:* 106
Marvin, Frederic *83:* 86
Marx, Robert F. *24:* 143
Masefield, Judith *19:* 208, 209
Masheris, Robert *78:* 51
Mason, George F. *14:* 139
Mason, Robert *84:* 96
Massey, Barbara *68:* 142
Massie, Diane Redfield *16:* 194
Massie, Kim *31:* 43
Mataya, David *121:* 66
Mathers, Petra *119:* 135; *163:* 104
Mathewuse, James *51:* 143
Mathieu, Joseph *14:* 33; *39:* 206; *43:* 167; *56:* 180; *79:* 126; *94:* 147
Matje, Martin *169:* 177-178
Matsubara, Naoko *12:* 121
Matsuda, Shizu *13:* 167
Matte, L'Enc *22:* 183
Mattelson, Marvin *36:* 50, 51
Matthews, F. Leslie *4:* 216
Mattingly, David *71:* 76, 77; *82:* 64; *91:* 216, 217; *109:* 25
Matulay, Laszlo *5:* 18; *43:* 168
Matus, Greta *12:* 142
Mauldin, Bill *27:* 23
Mauterer, Erin Marie *119:* 5
Mawicke, Tran *9:* 137; *15:* 191; *47:* 100
Mawson, Matt *74:* 115
Max, Peter *45:* 146, 147, 148-149, 150
Maxie, Betty *40:* 135
Maxwell, John Alan *1:* 148
Mayan, Earl *7:* 193
Mayer, Danuta *117:* 103
Mayer, Marianna *32:* 132
Mayer, Mercer *11:* 192; *16:* 195-196; *20:* 55, 57; *32:* 129, 130, 132, 133, 134; *41:* 144, 248, 252; *58:* 186; *73:* 140, 142, 143; *137:* 137, 138
Mayhew, James *85:* 121; *138:* 187; *149:* 140
Mayhew, Richard *3:* 106
Mayo, Gretchen Will *38:* 81; *84:* 166
Mays, Victor *5:* 127; *8:* 45, 153; *14:* 245; *23:* 50; *34:* 155; *40:* 79; *45:* 158; *54:* 91; *66:* 240
Mazal, Chanan *49:* 104

Maze, Deborah *71:* 83
Mazellan, Ron *75:* 97, 98
Mazetti, Alan *112:* 72
Mazille, Capucine *96:* 168
Mazza, Adriana Saviozzi *19:* 215
Mazzella, Mary Jo *82:* 165
Mazzetti, Alan *45:* 210
McAfee, Steve *135:* 146; *167:* 176
McAlinden, Paul *112:* 128
McBride, Angus *28:* 49; *103:* 40
McBride, Will *30:* 110
McCaffery, Janet *38:* 145
McCallum, Graham *78:* 78
McCallum, Stephen *141:* 143; *156:* 5
McCann, Gerald *3:* 50; *4:* 94; *7:* 54; *41:* 121
McCauley, Adam *157:* 36
McCay, Winsor *41:* 124, 126, 128-129, 130-131; *134:* 77, 79
McClary, Nelson *1:* 111
McClintock, Barbara *57:* 135; *95:* 130; *146:* 190
McClintock, Theodore *14:* 141
McCloskey, Robert *1:* 184-185; *2:* 186-187; *17:* 209; *39:* 139, 140, 141, 142, 143, 146, 147, 148; *85:* 150, 151; *100:* 172, 173, 174
McClung, Robert *2:* 189; *68:* 166, 167
McClure, Gillian *31:* 132; *150:* 53
McConnel, Jerry *31:* 75, 187
McConnell, Mary *102:* 49
McCord, Kathleen Garry *78:* 236
McCormack, John *66:* 193
McCormick, A.D. *35:* 119
McCormick, Dell J. *19:* 216
McCrady, Lady *16:* 198; *39:* 127
McCrea, James *3:* 122; *33:* 216
McCrea, Ruth *3:* 122; *27:* 102; *33:* 216
McCue, Lisa *65:* 148, 149; *77:* 54; *80:* 132
McCully, Emily Arnold *2:* 89; *4:* 120-121, 146, 197; *5:* 2, 129; *7:* 191; *11:* 122; *15:* 210; *33:* 23; *35:* 244; *37:* 122; *39:* 88; *40:* 103; *50:* 30, 31, 32, 33, 34, 35, 36-37; *52:* 89, 90; *57:* 6; *62:* 3; *70:* 195; *86:* 82; *96:* 192; *97:* 93; *110:* 143, 144; *117:* 47; *167:* 96
McCurdy, Michael *13:* 153; *24:* 85; *81:* 160; *82:* 157, 158; *86:* 125; *97:* 92; *117:* 178; *132:* 6; *147:* 159-160
McCusker, Paul *99:* 19
McDaniel, Jerry *132:* 135
McDaniel, Preston *160:* 206
McDermott, Beverly Brodsky *11:* 180
McDermott, Gerald *16:* 201; *74:* 174-175; *163:* 150-151
McDermott, Mike *96:* 187
McDonald, Jill *13:* 155; *26:* 128
McDonald, Mercedes *169:* 118
McDonald, Ralph J. *5:* 123, 195
McDonnell, Flora *146:* 199, 200
McDonough, Don *10:* 163
McElmurry, Jill *137:* 148; *163:* 141
McElrath-Eslick, Lori *129:* 145; *142:* 21
McEntee, Dorothy *37:* 124
McEwan, Keith *88:* 116; *165:* 122-123
McEwen, Katharine *169:* 34
McFall, Christie *12:* 144
McFeely, Daniel *160:* 213
McGaw, Laurie *109:* 243; *143:* 216
McGee, Barbara *6:* 165
McGee, Marni *163:* 153
McGillvray, Kim *158:* 171; *165:* 213
McGinley-Nally, Sharon *131:* 19
McGinnis, Robert *110:* 113
McGovern, Tara *98:* 171
McGraw, Sheila *83:* 146
McGregor, Malcolm *23:* 27
McGuirk, Leslie *152:* 159
McHale, John *138:* 190
McHugh, Tom *23:* 64
McIntosh, Jon *42:* 56
McKay, Donald *2:* 118; *32:* 157; *45:* 151, 152
McKean, Dave *150:* 71
McKeating, Eileen *44:* 58

McKee, David *10:* 48; *21:* 9; *70:* 154, 155;
  107: 139, 140, 141; *134:* 218; *158:* 148-151
McKee, Diana *109:* 185
McKie, Roy *7:* 44
McKillip, Kathy *30:* 153
McKinney, Ena *26:* 39
McKinnon, James *136:* 75
McLachlan, Edward *5:* 89
McLaren, Chesley *133:* 53
McLaren, Kirsty *123:* 99; *124:* 226
Mclean, Andrew *113:* 117, 118, 120, 121
McLean, Meg *94:* 196
McLean, Sammis *32:* 197
McLean, Wilson *90:* 29; *113:* 195
McLoughlin, John C. *47:* 149
McLoughlin, Wayne *102:* 230; *134:* 178
McMahon, Robert *36:* 155; *69:* 169
McManus, Shawn *85:* 71
McMenemy, Sarah *156:* 139
McMillan, Bruce *22:* 184
McMullan, James *40:* 33; *67:* 172; *87:* 142;
  99: 63, 64
McMullen, Nigel *146:* 177
McNeely, Tom *162:* 55
McNaught, Harry *12:* 80; *32:* 136
McNaughton, Colin *39:* 149; *40:* 108; *92:* 144,
  145, 146; *134:* 104, 106
McNicholas, Maureen *38:* 148
McPhail, David *14:* 105; *23:* 135; *37:* 217,
  218, 220, 221; *47:* 151, 152, 153, 154, 155,
  156, 158-159, 160, 162-163, 164; *71:* 211;
  81: 139, 140, 142; *86:* 123; *132:* 150; *140:*
  129, 131, 132
McPhee, Richard B. *41:* 133
McPheeters, Neal *78:* 132; *86:* 90; *99:* 162;
  111: 141; *142:* 162
McQuade, Jacqueline *124:* 223
McQueen, Lucinda *28:* 149; *41:* 249; *46:* 206;
  53: 103
McQuillan, Mary *153:* 97
McVay, Tracy *11:* 68
McVicker, Charles *39:* 150
Mead, Ben Carlton *43:* 75
Meade, Holly *90:* 102; *94:* 101; *149:* 8; *151:*
  107
Mecray, John *33:* 62
Meddaugh, Susan *20:* 42; *29:* 143; *41:* 241;
  77: 50; *84:* 173, 174, 175, 176-77, 178; *125:*
  160, 161, 162
Meehan, Dennis B. *56:* 144
Meents, Len W. *73:* 147, 150
Meers, Tony *99:* 113
Meisel, Paul *98:* 137; *124:* 18; *162:* 180
Melanson, Luc *149:* 229
Melendez, Francisco *72:* 180
Melnychuk, Monika *153:* 65
Melo, John *16:* 285; *58:* 203
Meloni, Maria Teresa *98:* 62
Meltzer, Ericka
  See O'Rourke, Ericka
Menasco, Milton *43:* 85
Mendelson, Steven T. *86:* 154
Mendelssohn, Felix *19:* 170
Mendola, Christopher *88:* 223
Meng, Heinz *13:* 158
Merian, Maria Sibylla *140:* 88
Mero, Lee *34:* 68
Merrill, Frank T. *16:* 147; *19:* 71; *YABC 1:*
  226, 229, 273
Merriman, Rachel *98:* 108; *114:* 122; *149:* 142
Meryman, Hope *27:* 41
Meryweather, Jack *10:* 179
Messick, Dale *64:* 150, 151, 152
Meth, Harold *24:* 203
Meyer, Herbert *19:* 189
Meyer, Renate *6:* 170
Meyers, Bob *11:* 136
Meynell, Louis *37:* 76
Micale, Albert *2:* 65; *22:* 185
Miccuci, Charles *82:* 163; *144:* 150
Middleton-Sandford, Betty *2:* 125

Mieke, Anne *45:* 74
Mighell, Patricia *43:* 134
Miglio, Paige *101:* 203; *151:* 223
Mikolaycak, Charles *9:* 144; *12:* 101; *13:* 212;
  21: 121; *22:* 168; *30:* 187; *34:* 103, 150; *37:*
  183; *43:* 179; *44:* 90; *46:* 115, 118-119; *49:*
  25; *78:* 121, 122, 205, 207; *81:* 4
Milelli, Pascal *129:* 66; *135:* 153
Miles, Elizabeth *117:* 77
Miles, Jennifer *17:* 278
Milgrim, David *158:* 157
Milhous, Katherine *15:* 193; *17:* 51
Millais, John E. *22:* 230, 231
Millar, H.R. *YABC 1:* 194-195, 203
Millard, C.E. *28:* 186
Millard, Kerry *105:* 124
Miller, Don *15:* 195; *16:* 71; *20:* 106; *31:* 178
Miller, Edna *29:* 148
Miller, Edward *115:* 64
Miller, Frank J. *25:* 94
Miller, Grambs *18:* 38; *23:* 16
Miller, Ian *99:* 128
Miller, Jane *15:* 196
Miller, Marcia *13:* 233
Miller, Marilyn *1:* 87; *31:* 69; *33:* 157
Miller, Mitchell *28:* 183; *34:* 207
Miller, Shane *5:* 140
Miller, Virginia *81:* 206
Mills, Elaine *72:* 181
Mills, Judith Christine *130:* 168, 169
Mills, Lauren *92:* 170
Mills, Yaroslava Surmach *35:* 169, 170; *46:*
  114
Millsap, Darrel *51:* 102
Milone, Karen *89:* 169
Milord, Susan *147:* 163-164
Milton, Debbie *162:* 161
Miner, Julia *98:* 69
Minor, Wendell *39:* 188; *52:* 87; *56:* 171; *58:*
  116; *62:* 56; *66:* 109; *74:* 93; *78:* 129; *94:*
  67; *117:* 12, 13; *124:* 84, 86; *136:* 121
Mirocha, Paul *81:* 133
Mitchell, Judith *109:* 117
Mitchell, Mark *91:* 208
Mitgutsch, Ali *76:* 161
Mitsuhashi, Yoko *45:* 153
Miyake, Yoshi *38:* 141
Mizumura, Kazue *10:* 143; *18:* 223; *36:* 159
Mochi, Ugo *8:* 122; *38:* 150
Mock, Paul *55:* 83; *123:* 32
Modarressi, Mitra *90:* 236; *126:* 168
Modell, Frank *39:* 152
Mogenson, Jan *74:* 183
Mohn, Susan *89:* 224
Mohr, Mark *133:* 201
Mohr, Nicholasa *8:* 139; *113:* 127
Molan, Christine *60:* 177; *84:* 183
Moldon, Peter L. *49:* 168
Molk, Laurel *92:* 150
Momaday, N. Scott *48:* 159
Mombourquette, Paul *112:* 91; *126:* 142
Monks, Julie *165:* 231
Montgomery, Lucy *150:* 126
Montgomery-Higham, Amanda *169:* 131
Montiel, David *69:* 106; *84:* 145
Montresor, Beni *2:* 91; *3:* 138; *38:* 152, 153,
  154, 155, 156-157, 158, 159, 160; *68:* 63
Montserrat, Pep *128:* 135
Moon, Carl *25:* 183, 184, 185
Moon, Eliza *14:* 40
Moon, Ivan *22:* 39; *38:* 140
Moore, Adrienne *67:* 147
Moore, Agnes Kay Randall *43:* 187
Moore, Cyd *117:* 107, 108; *159:* 137, 138
Moore, Gustav *127:* 181, 182
Moore, Jackie *128:* 79
Moore, Janet *63:* 153
Moore, Mary *29:* 160
Moore, Yvette *101:* 11, 12; *154:* 141
Mora, Raul Mina *20:* 41
Moraes, Odilon *102:* 144

Morales, Yuyi *154:* 144
Moran, Rosslyn *111:* 26
Moran, Tom *60:* 100
Mordvinoff, Nicolas *15:* 179
Moreno, René King *169:* 59
Morgan, Barbara *169:* 116
Morgan, Jacqui *58:* 57
Morgan, Mary *114:* 133, 134, 135; *123:* 11
Morgan, Tom *42:* 157
Morgenstern, Michael *158:* 7, 57
Morice, Dave *93:* 142
Morin, Paul *73:* 132; *79:* 130; *88:* 140; *137:*
  143
Morozumi, Atsuko *110:* 155
Morrill, Leslie *18:* 218; *29:* 177; *33:* 84; *38:*
  147; *42:* 127; *44:* 93; *48:* 164, 165, 167,
  168, 169, 170, 171; *49:* 162; *63:* 136, 180;
  70: 72; *71:* 70, 91, 92; *72:* 228; *80:* 163,
  164, 165; *90:* 121; *121:* 88
Morrill, Rowena A. *84:* 16; *98:* 163
Morris *47:* 91
Morris, Frank *55:* 133; *60:* 28; *76:* 2
Morris, Harry O. *119:* 138
Morris, Jackie *128:* 194; *144:* 119; *151:* 146
Morris, Oradel Nolen *128:* 180
Morris, Tony *62:* 146; *70:* 97
Morrison, Bill *42:* 116; *66:* 170; *69:* 40
Morrison, Gordon *87:* 150; *113:* 93; *128:* 181,
  182
Morrison, Frank *169:* 162
Morrison, Taylor *159:* 144, 145
Morrow, Gray *2:* 64; *5:* 200; *10:* 103, 114; *14:*
  175
Morton, Lee Jack *32:* 140
Morton, Marian *3:* 185
Mosberg, Hilary *117:* 195; *118:* 164; *149:* 55
Moser, Barry *56:* 68, 117, 118, 119, 120, 121,
  122, 123, 124; *59:* 141; *60:* 160; *79:* 91,
  147, 149, 151, 152; *82:* 81; *90:* 118; *91:* 35;
  95: 210; *97:* 91, 93; *102:* 152; *126:* 4; *128:*
  175; *133:* 141; *138:* 167, 171, 174; *153:* 205
Moser, Cara *90:* 118; *138:* 167
Moses, Grandma *18:* 228
Moskof, Martin Stephen *27:* 152
Mosley, Francis *57:* 144
Moss, Donald *11:* 184
Moss, Geoffrey *32:* 198
Moss, Marissa *71:* 130; *104:* 127; *163:* 156
Most, Bernard *48:* 173; *91:* 142, 143; *134:* 120
Mowry, Carmen *50:* 62
Moxley, Sheila *96:* 174; *169:* 26
Moyers, William *21:* 65
Moyler, Alan *36:* 142
Mozley, Charles *9:* 87; *20:* 176, 192, 193; *22:*
  228; *25:* 205; *33:* 150; *43:* 170, 171, 172,
  173, 174; *YABC 2:* 89
Mueller, Hans Alexander *26:* 64; *27:* 52, 53
Mugnaini, Joseph *11:* 35; *27:* 52, 53; *35:* 62
Mujica, Rick *72:* 67; *88:* 95; *111:* 53
Muller, Robin *86:* 161
Muller, Steven *32:* 167
Muller, Jorg *35:* 215; *67:* 138, 139
Mulock, Julie *163:* 112
Mullins, Edward S. *10:* 101
Mullins, Patricia *51:* 68
Multer, Scott *80:* 108
Munari, Bruno *15:* 200
Munch, Edvard *140:* 143
Munowitz, Ken *14:* 148; *72:* 178, 179
Munro, Roxie *58:* 134; *136:* 177; *137:* 218
Munsinger, Lynn *33:* 161; *46:* 126; *71:* 92; *82:*
  80; *89:* 218; *92:* 125; *94:* 157, 158, 159,
  160; *98:* 196; *103:* 198; *142:* 143; *145:*
  133-134, 136; *153:* 203
Munson, Russell *13:* 9
Munoz, William *42:* 160
Munzar, Barbara *149:* 75
Murdocca, Salvatore *73:* 212; *98:* 132; *111:*
  168; *157:* 228
Murphy, Bill *5:* 138; *130:* 170
Murphy, Jill *37:* 142; *70:* 166; *142:* 132, 134

Murphy, Kelly *130:* 212; *143:* 119
Murr, Karl *20:* 62
Murray, Ossie *43:* 176
Mussino, Attilio *29:* 131; *100:* 164
Mutchler, Dwight *1:* 25
Myers, Bernice *9:* 147; *36:* 75; *81:* 146, 147, 148
Muth, Jon J. *165:* 169; *167:* 109
Myers, Duane O. *99:* 145
Myers, Tim *147:* 168
Myers, V.G. *142:* 41
Myers, Lou *11:* 2

N

Nachreiner, Tom *29:* 182
Nacht, Merle *65:* 49
Nadler, Ellis *88:* 91
Najaka, Marlies *62:* 101
Nakai, Michael *30:* 217; *54:* 29
Nakata, Hiroe *157:* 156; *162:* 30
Nakatani, Chiyoko *12:* 124
Narahashi, Keiko *77:* 188; *82:* 213; *115:* 142, 143, 144
Nascimbene, Yan *133:* 128
Nash, Lesa *87:* 135
Nash, Linell *46:* 175
Nash, Scott *130:* 36
Naso, John *33:* 183
Nason, Thomas W. *14:* 68
Nasser, Muriel *48:* 74
Nast, Thomas *21:* 29; *28:* 23; *51:* 132, 133, 134, 135, 136, 137, 138, 139, 141
Nasta, Vincent *78:* 185
Natale, Vincent *76:* 3; *78:* 125; *112:* 47
Natchev, Alexi *96:* 177
Nathan, Charlott *125:* 151
Nathan, Cheryl *150:* 104
Natti, Susanna *20:* 146; *32:* 141, 142; *35:* 178; *37:* 143; *71:* 49; *93:* 98; *125:* 166, 168; *126:* 228; *151:* 6
Navarra, Celeste Scala *8:* 142
Naylor, Penelope *10:* 104
Nazz, James *72:* 8
Nebel, M. *45:* 154
Neebe, William *7:* 93
Needler, Jerry *12:* 93
Neel, Alice *31:* 23
Neely, Beth *119:* 184
Neely, Keith R. *46:* 124
Neff, Leland *78:* 74
Negri, Rocco *3:* 213; *5:* 67; *6:* 91, 108; *12:* 159
Neidigh, Sherry *128:* 53
Neill, John R. *18:* 8, 10-11, 21, 30; *100:* 22
Neilsen, Terese *116:* 74
Neilson, Cliff *158:* 131
Nelson, Craig *62:* 151; 153
Nelson, Gail White *68:* 140
Nelson, Jennifer *129:* 152
Nelson, Kadir *151:* 185; *154:* 146, 147; *157:* 189, 222
Nelson, S.D. *131:* 34
Ness, Evaline *1:* 164-165; *2:* 39; *3:* 8; *10:* 147; *12:* 53; *26:* 150, 151, 152, 153; *49:* 30, 31, 32; *56:* 30; *60:* 113
Neville, Vera *2:* 182
Nevwirth, Allan *79:* 168
Newberry, Clare Turlay *1:* 170
Newbold, Greg *108:* 125; *145:* 199; *151:* 23
Newfeld, Frank *14:* 121; *26:* 154
Newman, Andy *149:* 61
Newman, Ann *43:* 90
Newsham, Ian *143:* 162
Newsom, Carol *40:* 159; *44:* 60; *47:* 189; *65:* 29; *70:* 192; *80:* 36; *85:* 137, 138; *92:* 167
Newsom, Tom *49:* 149; *71:* 13, 62; *75:* 156; *91:* 113
Newton, Jill *83:* 105

Ng, Michael *29:* 171
Ng, Simon *167:* 7
Nicholson, William *15:* 33-34; *16:* 48
Nickens, Bessie *104:* 153
Nicklaus, Carol *45:* 194; *62:* 132, 133
Nickless, Will *16:* 139
Nicholas, Corasue *154:* 20
Nicolas *17:* 130, 132-133; *YABC 2:* 215
Niebrugge, Jane *6:* 118
Nielsen, Cliff *95:* 207, 208; *105:* 58; *114:* 112; *124:* 12; *125:* 91, 92; *132:* 224; *135:* 187; *136:* 40; *137:* 168; *145:* 54; *149:* 28; *158:* 129; *165:* 64, 158
Nielsen, Jon *6:* 100; *24:* 202
Nielsen, Kay *15:* 7; *16:* 211-213, 215, 217; *22:* 143; *YABC 1:* 32-33
Niland, Deborah *25:* 191; *27:* 156; *135:* 50
Niland, Kilmeny *25:* 191; *75:* 143
Nino, Alex *59:* 145
Ninon *1:* 5; *38:* 101, 103, 108
Nissen, Rie *44:* 35
Nithael, Mark *158:* 237
Nivola, Claire A. *78:* 126; *140:* 147
Nixon, K. *14:* 152
Noble, Louise *61:* 170
Noble, Marty *97:* 168; *125:* 171
Noble, Trinka Hakes *39:* 162; *84:* 157
Noguchi, Yoshie *30:* 99
Nolan, Dennis *42:* 163; *67:* 163; *78:* 189; *82:* 225; *83:* 26; *92:* 169, 170; *103:* 166; *111:* 35; *112:* 213; *127:* 171
Noll, Sally *82:* 171
Nolte, Larry *121:* 63, 65
Nones, Eric Jon *61:* 111; *76:* 38; *77:* 177
Noonan, Daniel *100:* 224
Noonan, Julia *4:* 163; *7:* 207; *25:* 151; *91:* 29; *95:* 149
Norcia, Ernie *108:* 155; *140:* 47
Nordenskjold, Birgitta *2:* 208
Norling, Beth *149:* 153, 154
Norman, Elaine *77:* 72, 176; *94:* 35; *136:* 63
Norman, Mary *36:* 138, 147
Norman, Michael *12:* 117; *27:* 168
Northway, Jennifer *85:* 96
Nostlinger, Christiana *162:* 131
Novak, Matt *104:* 132, 133; *165:* 173-174
Novelli, Luca *61:* 137
Nugent, Cynthia *106:* 189
Numeroff, Laura Joffe *28:* 161; *30:* 177
Nussbaumer, Paul *16:* 219; *39:* 117
Nutt, Ken *72:* 69; *97:* 170
Nyce, Helene *19:* 219
Nygren, Tord *30:* 148; *127:* 164

O

Oakley, Graham *8:* 112; *30:* 164, 165; *84:* 188, 189, 190, 191, 192
Oakley, Thornton *YABC 2:* 189
Oberheide, Heide *118:* 37
Obligado, Lilian *2:* 28, 66-67; *6:* 30; *14:* 179; *15:* 103; *25:* 84; *61:* 138, 139, 140, 141, 143
Obrant, Susan *11:* 186
O'Brien, Anne Sibley *53:* 116, 117; *155:* 115
O'Brien, John *41:* 253; *72:* 12; *89:* 59, 60; *98:* 16; *161:* 185; *169:* 16
O'Brien, Teresa *87:* 89
O'Brien, Tim *93:* 25; *136:* 94; *169:* 57
O'Clair, Dennis *127:* 25
Odell, Carole *35:* 47
Odem, Mel *99:* 164; *167:* 84, 87
O'Donohue, Thomas *40:* 89
Oechsli, Kelly *5:* 144-145; *7:* 115; *8:* 83, 183; *13:* 117; *20:* 94; *81:* 199
Offen, Hilda *42:* 207
Ogden, Bill *42:* 59; *47:* 55
Ogg, Oscar *33:* 34
Ogle, Nancy Gray *163:* 144
Ohi, Ruth *90:* 175, 177; *131:* 63; *135:* 106

Ohlsson, Ib *4:* 152; *7:* 57; *10:* 20; *11:* 90; *19:* 217; *41:* 246; *82:* 106; *92:* 213
Ohtomo, Yasuo *37:* 146; *39:* 212, 213
O'Keefe, Jennifer *136:* 184
O'Kelley, Mattie Lou *36:* 150
Olbinski, Rafal *149:* 27; *158:* 77
Oliver, Jenni *23:* 121; *35:* 112
Oliver, Narelle *152:* 192
Oller, Erika *128:* 186; *134:* 126
Olschewski, Alfred *7:* 172
Olsen, Ib Spang *6:* 178-179; *81:* 164
Olson, Alan *77:* 229
Olugebefola, Ademola *15:* 205
O'Malley, Kevin *94:* 180; *106:* 8; *113:* 108; *136:* 70; *157:* 193
O'Neil, Dan IV *7:* 176
O'Neill, Catharine *72:* 113; *84:* 78; *134:* 153
O'Neill, Jean *22:* 146
O'Neill, Michael J. *54:* 172
O'Neill, Rose *48:* 30, 31
O'Neill, Steve *21:* 118
Ono, Chiyo *7:* 97
Orbaan, Albert *2:* 31; *5:* 65, 171; *9:* 8; *14:* 241; *20:* 109
Orbach, Ruth *21:* 112
Orfe, Joan *20:* 81
Org, Ed *119:* 93
Ormai, Stella *72:* 129
Ormerod, Jan *55:* 124; *70:* 170, 171; *90:* 39; *132:* 172, 173, 174; *147:* 98
Ormsby, Virginia H. *11:* 187
O'Rourke, Ericka *108:* 216; *117:* 194; *111:* 142; *119:* 194; *137:* 152; *150:* 134; *167:* 64
O'Rourke, Ericka Meltzer
    See O'Rourke, Ericka
Orozco, Jose Clemente *9:* 177
Orr, Forrest W. *23:* 9
Orr, N. *19:* 70
Ortiz, Vilma *88:* 158
Osborn, Cathy *152:* 232
Osborn, Robert *65:* 49
Osborne, Billie Jean *35:* 209
Osmond, Edward *10:* 111
O'Sullivan, Tom *3:* 176; *4:* 55; *78:* 195
Otani, June *124:* 42; *156:* 53
Ottley, Matt *147:* 221
Otto, Svend *22:* 130, 141; *67:* 188, 189
Oudry, J.B. *18:* 167
Oughton, Taylor *5:* 23; *104:* 136
Overeng, Johannes *44:* 36
Overlie, George *11:* 156
Owens, Carl *2:* 35; *23:* 521
Owens, Gail *10:* 170; *12:* 157; *19:* 16; *22:* 70; *25:* 81; *28:* 203, 205; *32:* 221, 222; *36:* 132; *46:* 40; *47:* 57; *54:* 66, 67, 68, 69, 70, 71, 72, 73; *71:* 100; *73:* 64; *77:* 157; *80:* 32; *82:* 3; *99:* 226
Owens, Mary Beth *113:* 202, 203
Owens, Nubia *84:* 74
Oxenbury, Helen *3:* 150-151; *24:* 81; *68:* 174, 175, 176; *81:* 209; *84:* 213, 245; *129:* 56; *149:* 159
Oz, Robin *88:* 167

P

Padgett, Jim *12:* 165
Page, Homer *14:* 145
Page, Mark *162:* 70
Paget, Sidney *24:* 90, 91, 93, 95, 97
Paget, Walter *64:* 122
Pajouhesh, Noushin *160:* 121
Pak *12:* 76
Pak, Yu Cha *86:* 174
Paladino, Lance *134:* 30
Palazzo, Tony *3:* 152-153
Palecek, Josef *56:* 136; *89:* 158
Palen, Debbie *135:* 88

Palencar, John Jude *84:* 12, 45; *85:* 87; *92:* 187; *99:* 128; *110:* 204; *150:* 122
Palin, Nicki *81:* 201; *89:* 161
Palladini, David *4:* 113; *40:* 176, 177, 178-179, 181, 224-225; *50:* 138; *78:* 186
Pallarito, Don *43:* 36
Palmer, Carol *158:* 230
Palmer, Heidi *15:* 207; *29:* 102
Palmer, Jan *42:* 153; *82:* 161
Palmer, Judd *153:* 160, 161
Palmer, Juliette *6:* 89; *15:* 208
Palmer, Kate Salley *104:* 143; *154:* 169
Palmer, Lemuel *17:* 25, 29
Palmisciano, Diane *110:* 62; *162:* 26
Palmquist, Eric *38:* 133
Panesis, Nicholas *3:* 127
Panton, Doug *52:* 99
Paparone, Pamela *129:* 174
Papas, William *11:* 223; *50:* 160
Papin, Joseph *26:* 113
Papish, Robin Lloyd *10:* 80
Paradis, Susan *40:* 216
Paraquin, Charles H. *18:* 166
Paris, Peter *31:* 127
Parisi, Elizabeth B. *141:* 82
Park, Nick *113:* 143
Park, Seho *39:* 110
Park, W.B. *22:* 189
Parker, Ant *82:* 87, 88; *104:* 121
Parker, Lewis *2:* 179
Parker, Nancy Winslow *10:* 113; *22:* 164; *28:* 47, 144; *52:* 7; *69:* 153; *91:* 171, 174; *132:* 175
Parker, Robert *4:* 161; *5:* 74; *9:* 136; *29:* 39
Parker, Robert Andrew *11:* 81; *29:* 186; *39:* 165; *40:* 25; *41:* 78; *42:* 123; *43:* 144; *48:* 182; *54:* 140; *74:* 141; *91:* 24; *111:* 115; *151:* 201; *154:* 156
Parker-Rees, Guy *149:* 145
Parkin, Trevor *140:* 151
Parkins, David *114:* 123; *146:* 176
Parkinson, Kathy *71:* 143; *144:* 234
Parkinson, Keith *70:* 66
Parks, Gordon, Jr. *33:* 228
Parnall, Peter *5:* 137; *16:* 221; *24:* 70; *40:* 78; *51:* 130; *69:* 17, 155; *136:* 22, 23, 24
Parnall, Virginia *40:* 78
Parow, Lorraine *158:* 127
Parr, Todd *134:* 139, 140
Parrish, Anne *27:* 159, 160
Parrish, Dillwyn *27:* 159
Parrish, Maxfield *14:* 160, 161, 164, 165; *16:* 109; *18:* 12-13; *YABC 1:* 149, 152, 267; *2:* 146, 149
Parry, David *26:* 156
Parry, Marian *13:* 176; *19:* 179
Partch, Virgil *45:* 163, 165
Pascal, David *14:* 174
Pasquier, J.A. *16:* 91
Pasternak, Robert *119:* 53
Paterson, Diane *13:* 116; *39:* 163; *59:* 164, 165, 166, 167; *72:* 51, 53; *129:* 175
Paterson, Helen *16:* 93
Patkau, Karen *112:* 123
Paton, Jane *15:* 271; *35:* 176
Patrick, John *139:* 190
Patrick, Pamela *90:* 160; *93:* 211; *105:* 12
Patterson, Geoffrey *54:* 75
Patterson, Robert *25:* 118
Patz, Nancy *111:* 40; *154:* 161
Paul, James *4:* 130; *23:* 161
Paul, Korky *102:* 85
Paull, Grace *24:* 157; *87:* 127
Paulsen, Ruth Wright *79:* 160, 164
Pavlov, Elena *80:* 49
Payne, Adam S. *135:* 166
Payne, C.F. *145:* 138, 140
Payne, Joan Balfour *1:* 118
Payson, Dale *7:* 34; *9:* 151; *20:* 140; *37:* 22
Payzant, Charles *21:* 147
Peacock, Ralph *64:* 118

Peake, Mervyn *22:* 136, 149; *23:* 162, 163, 164; *YABC 2:* 307
Pearson, Larry *38:* 225
Pearson, Tracey Campbell *64:* 163, 164, 167, 168, 169; *118:* 51; *156:* 169, 171, 172; *163:* 140
Peat, Fern B. *16:* 115
Peck, Anne Merriman *18:* 241; *24:* 155
Peck, Beth *66:* 242; *79:* 166; *80:* 136; *91:* 34; *95:* 9; *101:* 77
Pedersen, Judy *66:* 217; *121:* 36
Pedersen, Vilhelm *YABC 1:* 40
Pederson, Sharleen *12:* 92
Pedlar, Elaine *161:* 45
Peek, Merle *39:* 168
Peet, Bill *2:* 203; *41:* 159, 160, 161, 162, 163; *78:* 158, 159, 160, 161
Peguero, Adrian *116:* 133
Peguero, Gerard *116:* 133
Pels, Winslow Pinney *55:* 126
Peltier, Leslie C. *13:* 178
Pendle, Alexy *7:* 159; *13:* 34; *29:* 161; *33:* 215; *86:* 62
Pendola, Joanne *76:* 203; *81:* 125; *105:* 181
Pene du Bois, William *4:* 70; *10:* 122; *26:* 61; *27:* 145, 211; *35:* 243; *41:* 216; *68:* 180, 181; *73:* 45
Penfound, David *102:* 185
Pennington, Eunice *27:* 162
Peppe, Mark *28:* 142
Peppe, Rodney *4:* 164-165; *74:* 187, 188, 189
Pepper, Hubert *64:* 143
Percy, Graham *63:* 2
Perkins, David *60:* 68
Perkins, Lucy Fitch *72:* 199
Perl, Susan *2:* 98; *4:* 231; *5:* 44-45, 118; *6:* 199; *8:* 137; *12:* 88; *22:* 193; *34:* 54-55; *52:* 128; *YABC 1:* 176
Perrone, Donna *78:* 166
Perry, Marie Fritz *165:* 180
Perry, Patricia *29:* 137; *30:* 171
Perry, Roger *27:* 163
Perske, Martha *46:* 83; *51:* 108, 147
Pesek, Ludek *15:* 237
Petach, Heidi *149:* 166
Peters, David *72:* 205
Petersham, Maud *17:* 108, 147-153
Petersham, Miska *17:* 108, 147-153
Peterson, Eric *109:* 125
Peterson, Nisse *99:* 27
Peterson, R.F. *7:* 101
Peterson, Russell *7:* 130
Petie, Haris *2:* 3; *10:* 41, 118; *11:* 227; *12:* 70
Petricic, Dusan *153:* 75, 76, 77
Petrides, Heidrun *19:* 223
Petrone, Valeria *159:* 160
Petruccio, Steven James *67:* 159; *127:* 5
Pettingill, Ondre *64:* 181; *70:* 64
Peyo *40:* 56, 57
Peyton, K.M. *15:* 212
Pfeifer, Herman *15:* 262
Pfister, Marcus *83:* 165, 166, 167; *146:* 152; *150:* 160
Pfloog, Jan *124:* 60
Pham, LeUyen *160:* 48
Phillips, Craig *70:* 151
Phillips, Douglas *1:* 19
Phillips, F.D. *6:* 202
Phillips, Louise *133:* 67
Phillips, Thomas *30:* 55
Philpot, Glyn *54:* 46
Phiz
    See Browne, Hablot K.
Piatti, Celestino *16:* 223
Pica, Steve *115:* 181
Picarella, Joseph *13:* 147
Picart, Gabriel *121:* 165
Pickard, Charles *12:* 38; *18:* 203; *36:* 152
Picken, George A. *23:* 150
Pickens, David *22:* 156

Pienkowski, Jan *6:* 183; *30:* 32; *58:* 140, 141, 142, 143, 146, 147; *73:* 3; *87:* 156, 157; *131:* 189
Pignataro, Anna *163:* 220 *Pileggi, Steve 145:* 122
Pilkey, Dav *68:* 186; *115:* 164, 166
Pimlott, John *10:* 205
Pincus, Harriet *4:* 186; *8:* 179; *22:* 148; *27:* 164, 165; *66:* 202
Pini, Wendy *89:* 166
Pinkett, Neil *60:* 8
Pinkney, Brian *81:* 184, 185; *94:* 107; *113:* 146, 147; *117:* 121, 166; *132:* 145; *158:* 108, 191; *160:* 189
Pinkney, Jerry *8:* 218; *10:* 40; *15:* 276; *20:* 66; *24:* 121; *33:* 109; *36:* 222; *38:* 200; *41:* 165, 166, 167, 168, 169, 170, 171, 173, 174; *44:* 198; *48:* 51; *53:* 20; *56:* 61, 68; *58:* 184; *60:* 59; *61:* 91; *71:* 146, 148, 149; *72:* 17; *73:* 149; *74:* 159, 192; *75:* 45; *80:* 206; *81:* 44; *85:* 144; *95:* 50; *107:* 158, 159, 160; *108:* 164; *112:* 114, 115; *133:* 58
Pinkwater, Daniel Manus *46:* 180, 181, 182, 185, 188, 189, 190; *151:* 161 *76:* 178, 179, 180
Pinkwater, Manus *8:* 156; *46:* 180
    See also Pinkwater, Daniel Manus
Pinkwater, Jill *114:* 160, 161; *158:* 179
Pinto, Ralph *10:* 131; *45:* 93
Pinon, Mark *74:* 22
Pistolesi *73:* 211
Pittman, Helena Clare *71:* 151
Pitz, Henry C. *4:* 168; *19:* 165; *35:* 128; *42:* 80; *YABC 2:* 95, 176
Pitzenberger, Lawrence J. *26:* 94
Player, Stephen *82:* 190
Plecas, Jennifer *84:* 201; *106:* 124; *149:* 168
Plowden, David *52:* 135, 136
Plummer, William *32:* 31
Podwal, Mark *56:* 170, 173; *101:* 154, 155, 157; *149:* 176; *160:* 194
Pogany, Willy *15:* 46, 49; *19:* 222, 256; *25:* 214; *44:* 142, 143, 144, 145, 146, 147, 148
Pohrt, Tom *67:* 116; *104:* 80; *152:* 199
Poirson, V.A. *26:* 89
Polacco, Patricia *74:* 195, 196-197, 198; *123:* 121-123
Polgreen, John *21:* 44
Politi, Leo *1:* 178; *4:* 53; *21:* 48; *47:* 173, 174, 176, 178, 179, 180, 181
Pollema-Cahill, Phyllis *123:* 126
Pollen, Samson *64:* 80
Polonsky, Arthur *34:* 168
Polseno, Jo *1:* 53; *3:* 117; *5:* 114; *17:* 154; *20:* 87; *32:* 49; *41:* 245
Pomaska, Anna *117:* 148
Ponter, James *5:* 204
Poole, Colin *111:* 27
Poortvliet, Rien *6:* 212; *65:* 165, 166-67
Popp, Wendy *72:* 122; *158:* 68
Poppel, Hans *71:* 154, 155
Porfirio, Guy *76:* 134
Portal, Colette *6:* 186; *11:* 203
Porter, George *7:* 181
Porter, Janice Lee *136:* 175
Porter, John *113:* 47
Porter, Pat Grant *84:* 112; *125:* 101
Porter, Sue *146:* 246, 247
Porter, Walter *124:* 175
Posthuma, Sieb *150:* 163
Postma, Lidia *79:* 17
Potter, Beatrix *100:* 194, 195; *132:* 179, 180, 181, 182; *YABC 1:* 208-210, 212, 213
Potter, Giselle *117:* 123; *143:* 44; *144:* 170, 197; *149:* 7; *150:* 165
Potter, Katherine *104:* 147
Potter, Miriam Clark *3:* 162
Poulin, Stephane *98:* 140, 141
Poullis, Nick *146:* 210
Powell, Gary *151:* 208
Powell, Ivan *67:* 219

Power, Margaret *105:* 122
Powers, Daniel *161:* 173
Powers, Richard M. *1:* 230; *3:* 218; *7:* 194; *26:* 186
Powledge, Fred *37:* 154
Powzyk, Joyce *74:* 214
Poydar, Nancy *96:* 149
Pracher, Richard *91:* 166
Prachaticka, Marketa *126:* 126
Prater, John *103:* 142, 143, 144; *149:* 172
Pratt, Charles *23:* 29
Pratt, George *116:* 208
Pratt, Pierre *150:* 73
Prebenna, David *73:* 174
Preiss-Glasser, Robin *123:* 176; *152* 40
Press, Jenny *116:* 95
Preston, Mark *152:* 162
Pretro, Korinna *91:* 126
Price, Christine *2:* 247; *3:* 163, 253; *8:* 166
Price, Cynthia *118:* 156
Price, Edward *33:* 34
Price, Garrett *1:* 76; *2:* 42
Price, Hattie Longstreet *17:* 13
Price, Norman *YABC 1:* 129
Price, Willard *48:* 184
Priceman, Marjorie *81:* 171; *136:* 169; *156:* 200
Primavera, Elise *26:* 95; *58:* 151; *73:* 37; *80:* 79; *86:* 156; *105:* 161
Primrose, Jean *36:* 109
Prince, Alison *86:* 188, 189
Prince, Leonora E. *7:* 170
Pritchett, Shelley *116:* 148
Prittie, Edwin J. *YABC 1:* 120
Prosmitsky, Jenya *132:* 33
Provensen, Alice *37:* 204, 215, 222; *70:* 176, 177, 178, 180; *71:* 213; *147:* 184
Provensen, Martin *37:* 204, 215, 222; *70:* 176, 177, 178, 180; *71:* 213
Pucci, Albert John *44:* 154
Pudlo *8:* 59
Pulver, Harry, Jr. *129:* 159
Pulver, Robin *160:* 4
Punchatz, Don *99:* 57
Purdy, Susan *8:* 162
Pursell, Weimer *55:* 18
Purtscher, Alfons *97:* 6
Puskas, James *5:* 141
Pyk, Jan *7:* 26; *38:* 123
Pyle, Chuck *99:* 149
Pyle, Howard *16:* 225-228, 230-232, 235; *24:* 27; *34:* 124, 125, 127, 128; *59:* 132; *100:* 198

Q

Quackenbush, Robert *4:* 190; *6:* 166; *7:* 175, 178; *9:* 86; *11:* 65, 221; *41:* 154; *43:* 157; *70:* 185, 186; *71:* 137; *85:* 47; *92:* 148; *133:* 154, 164, 169
Quennell, Marjorie (Courtney) *29:* 163, 164
Quidor, John *19:* 82
Quirk, John *62:* 170
Quirk, Thomas *12:* 81

R

Rackham, Arthur *15:* 32, 78, 214-227; *17:* 105, 115; *18:* 233; *19:* 254; *20:* 151; *22:* 129, 131, 132, 133; *23:* 175; *24:* 161, 181; *26:* 91; *32:* 118; *64:* 18; *100:* 9, 16, 203, 204; *YABC 1:* 25, 45, 55, 147; *2:* 103, 142, 173, 210
Racz, Michael *56:* 134
Radcliffe, Andrew *82:* 215
Rader, Laura *101:* 219

Rafilson, Sidney *11:* 172
Raglin, Tim *125:* 24
Raible, Alton *1:* 202-203; *28:* 193; *35:* 181; *110:* 207
Raine, Patricia *82:* 74; *88:* 154
Ramhorst, John *117:* 11
Ramsey, James *16:* 41
Ramsey, Marcy Dunn *82:* 11
Ramus, Michael *51:* 171
Rand, Paul *6:* 188
Rand, Ted *67:* 9, 10, 121, 123; *74:* 190; *84:* 170; *103:* 170; *112:* 6; *114:* 73; *139:* 168; *143:* 194; *156:* 154; *161:* 9, 10
Randazzo, Tony *81:* 98
Randell, William *55:* 54
Rane, Walter *93:* 144; *143:* 109
Rankin, Joan *163:* 40
Ransome, Arthur *22:* 201
Ransome, James E. *74:* 137; *75:* 80; *84:* 181; *94:* 108; *117:* 115; *123:* 128-130; *158:* 101, 102; *159:* 205
Rantz, Don *119:* 184
Rao, Anthony *28:* 126
Raphael, Elaine *23:* 192; *71:* 24, 25
Rappaport, Eva *6:* 190
Raschka, Chris *80:* 187, 189, 190; *97:* 211; *115:* 210; *117:* 151, 152, 153, 154; *143:* 195; *145:* 153
Rash, Andy *158:* 178; *162:* 172
Raskin, Ellen *2:* 208-209; *4:* 142; *13:* 183; *22:* 68; *29:* 139; *36:* 134; *38:* 173, 174, 175, 176, 177, 178, 179, 180, 181; *60:* 163; *86:* 81
Rathmann, Peggy *93:* 32; *94:* 168; *157:* 212, 214
Ratkus, Tony *77:* 133
Ratzkin, Lawrence *40:* 143
Rau, Margaret *9:* 157
Raverat, Gwen *YABC 1:* 152
Ravid, Joyce *61:* 73
Ravielli, Anthony *1:* 198; *3:* 168; *11:* 143
Ravilious, Robin *77:* 169
Rawlins, Donna *72:* 198; *73:* 15, 129
Rawlins, Janet *76:* 79
Rawlings, Steve *143:* 139; *151:* 54
Rawlinson, Debbie *75:* 132
Ray, Deborah Kogan *8:* 164; *29:* 238; *50:* 112, 113; *62:* 119; *78:* 191
Ray, Jane *96:* 166; *97:* 104; *152:* 208
Ray, Ralph *2:* 239; *5:* 73
Rayann, Omar *162:* 205
Rayevsky, Robert *64:* 17; *70:* 173; *80:* 204; *117:* 79
Raymond, Larry *31:* 108; *97:* 109
Rayner, Hugh *151:* 170
Rayner, Mary *22:* 207; *47:* 140; *72:* 191; *87:* 171, 172
Rayner, Shoo
    See Rayner, Hugh
Raynes, John *71:* 19
Raynor, Dorka *28:* 168
Raynor, Paul *24:* 73
Rayyan, Omar *110:* 222; *112:* 17; *125:* 131
Razzi, James *10:* 127
Read, Alexander D. *20:* 45
Reader, Dennis *71:* 157
Reasoner, Charles *53:* 33, 36, 37
Reczuch, Karen *115:* 132; *145:* 131
Redlich, Ben *163:* 221
Reed, Joseph *116:* 139
Reed, Lynn Rowe *115:* 173
Reed, Tom *34:* 171
Reeder, Colin *74:* 202; *77:* 113
Rees, Mary *134:* 219
Reese, Bob *60:* 135
Reeves, Eira B. *130:* 173, 174; *141:* 151
Regan, Dana *117:* 116
Regan, Laura *103:* 198; *153:* 206
Reichert, Renée *169:* 127
Reid, Barbara *82:* 178; *92:* 17; *93:* 169, 170
Reid, Stephen *19:* 213; *22:* 89

Reim, Melanie *104:* 151; *150:* 98
Reinert, Kirk *89:* 138
Reinertson, Barbara *44:* 150; *62:* 103
Reiniger, Lotte *40:* 185
Reisberg, Mira *119:* 2
Reisch, Jesse *158:* 130
Reiser, Lynn *81:* 175; *138:* 184
Reiss, John J. *23:* 193
Relf, Douglas *3:* 63
Relyea, C.M. *16:* 29; *31:* 153
Remi, Georges *13:* 184
Remington, Frederic *19:* 188; *41:* 178, 179, 180, 181, 183, 184, 185, 186, 187, 188; *62:* 197
Remkiewicz, Frank *67:* 102; *77:* 171; *80:* 130; *113:* 107; *152:* 116; *152:* 211, 212; *157:* 148
Rendon, Maria *116:* 141; *192; 134:* 152
Renfro, Ed *79:* 176
Renlie, Frank *11:* 200
Reschofsky, Jean *7:* 118
Rethi *60:* 181
Rethi, Lili *2:* 153; *36:* 156
Reusswig, William *3:* 267
Rex, Adam *156:* 172; *169:* 91
Rex, Michael *157:* 147
Rey, H.A. *1:* 182; *26:* 163, 164, 166, 167, 169; *69:* 172, 173, 174, 175; *86:* 195, 196, 197; *100:* 211; *YABC 2:* 17
Reynolds, Doris *5:* 71; *31:* 77
Reynolds, Peter *142:* 12
Rhead, Louis *31:* 91; *100:* 228
Rhodes, Andrew *38:* 204; *50:* 163; *54:* 76; *61:* 123, 124; *87:* 200
Ribbons, Ian *3:* 10; *37:* 161; *40:* 76
Ricci, Regolo *93:* 22
Rice, Elizabeth *2:* 53, 214
Rice, Eve *34:* 174, 175; *91:* 172
Rice, James *22:* 210; *93:* 173
Richards, George *40:* 116, 119, 121; *44:* 179
Richards, Henry *YABC 1:* 228, 231
Richardson, Ernest *2:* 144
Richardson, Frederick *18:* 27, 31
Richardson, John *110:* 88
Richman, Hilda *26:* 132
Richmond, George *24:* 179
Riddell, Chris *114:* 170, 195
Riddle, Tohby *74:* 204; *151:* 179
Riding, Peter *63:* 195
Rieniets, Judy King *14:* 28
Riger, Bob *2:* 166
Riggio, Anita *73:* 191; *85:* 63; *137:* 184
Riley, Jon *74:* 70
Riley, Kenneth *22:* 230
Riley-Webb, Charlotte *153:* 143
Rinaldi, Angelo *165:* 60, 69
Ringgold, Faith *71:* 162; *114:* 173, 174, 176
Ringi, Kjell *12:* 171
Rios, Tere
    See Versace, Marie
Ripper, Charles L. *3:* 175
Ripplinger, Henry *117:* 31
Ritchie, William *74:* 183
Ritz, Karen *41:* 117; *72:* 239; *87:* 125; *102:* 7; *106:* 6
Rivkin, Jay *15:* 230
Rivoche, Paul *45:* 125
Roach, Marilynne *9:* 158
Robbin, Jodi *44:* 156, 159
Robbins, Frank *42:* 167
Robbins, Ken *147:* 191-192
Robbins, Ruth *52:* 102
Roberts, Cliff *4:* 126
Roberts, David *154:* 4, 6
Roberts, Doreen *4:* 230; *28:* 105
Roberts, Jim *22:* 166; *23:* 69; *31:* 110
Roberts, Tony *109:* 195, 214
Roberts, W. *22:* 2, 3
Robins, Arthur *137:* 172; *151:* 225
Robinson, Aminah Brenda Lynn *86:* 205; *103:* 55; *159:* 175

Robinson, Charles [1870-1937] *17:* 157, 171, 172, 173, 175, 176; *24:* 207; *25:* 204; *YABC 2:* 308, 309, 310, 331
Robinson, Charles *3:* 53; *5:* 14; *6:* 193; *7:* 150; *7:* 183; *8:* 38; *9:* 81; *13:* 188; *14:* 248-249; *23:* 149; *26:* 115; *27:* 48; *28:* 191; *32:* 28; *35:* 210; *36:* 37; *48:* 96; *52:* 33; *53:* 157; *56:* 15; *62:* 142; *77:* 41; *111:* 148
Robinson, Jerry *3:* 262
Robinson, Joan G. *7:* 184
Robinson, Lolly *90:* 227
Robinson, T.H. *17:* 179, 181-183; *29:* 254
Robinson, W. Heath *17:* 185, 187, 189, 191, 193, 195, 197, 199, 202; *23:* 167; *25:* 194; *29:* 150; *YABC 1:* 44; *2:* 183
Roche, Christine *41:* 98
Roche, Denis *99:* 184
Roche, P.K. *57:* 151, 152
Rocker, Fermin *7:* 34; *13:* 21; *31:* 40; *40:* 190, 191
Rocklen, Margot *101:* 181
Rockwell, Anne *5:* 147; *33:* 171, 173; *71:* 166, 167, 168; *114:* 183, 184
Rockwell, Gail *7:* 186
Rockwell, Harlow *33:* 171, 173, 175
Rockwell, Lizzy *114:* 182; *162:* 182
Rockwell, Norman *23:* 39, 196, 197, 199, 200, 203, 204, 207; *41:* 140, 143; *123:* 47; *YABC 2:* 60
Rockwood, Richard *119:* 75
Rodanas, Kristina *156:* 183, 184
Rodegast, Roland *43:* 100
Rodgers, Frank *69:* 177
Rodriguez, Joel *16:* 65
Rodriguez, Robert *145:* 145
Roeckelein, Katrina *134:* 223
Roennfeldt, Robert *66:* 243
Roever, J.M. *4:* 119; *26:* 170
Roffey, Maureen *33:* 142, 176, 177
Rogasky, Barbara *46:* 90
Rogers, Carol *2:* 262; *6:* 164; *26:* 129
Rogers, Chris M. *150:* 59
Rogers, Forest *87:* 160; *101:* 76
Rogers, Frances *10:* 130
Rogers, Gregory *104:* 76; *126:* 57
Rogers, Jacqueline *78:* 249; *80:* 34; *86:* 54 *103:* 70; *115:* 72; *129:* 173; *131:* 57, 225; *143:* 211; *153:* 100
Rogers, Walter S. *31:* 135, 138; *67:* 65, 168; *100:* 81
Rogers, William A. *15:* 151, 153-154; *33:* 35
Rogoff, Barbara *95:* 20
Rohmann, Eric *103:* 152
Rojankovsky, Feodor *6:* 134, 136; *10:* 183; *21:* 128, 129, 130; *25:* 110; *28:* 42; *68:* 120
Rolfsen, Alf *62:* 15
Romain, Trevor *134:* 157
Roman, Barbara J. *103:* 171
Romas *114:* 111; *165:* 63
Romano, Robert *64:* 68
Root, Barry *80:* 212; *90:* 196; *146:* 78; *156:* 165; *159:* 161
Root, Kimberly Bulcken *86:* 72; *98:* 21; *108:* 111; *127:* 114; *159:* 162
Roper, Bob *65:* 153
Roraback, Robin *111:* 156
Rorer, Abigail *43:* 222; *85:* 155
Rosales, Melodye *80:* 35
Rosamilia, Patricia *36:* 120
Rose, Carl *5:* 62
Rose, David S. *29:* 109; *70:* 120
Rose, Gerald *68:* 200, 201; *86:* 48
Rose, Ted *93:* 178
Rosenbaum, Jonathan *50:* 46
Rosenberg, Amye *74:* 207, 208
Rosenberry, Vera *87:* 22, 26; *144:* 212, 213; *158:* 120
Rosenblum, Richard *11:* 202; *18:* 18
Rosier, Lydia *16:* 236; *20:* 104; *21:* 109; *22:* 125; *30:* 151, 158; *42:* 128; *45:* 214; *77:* 227, 228

Rosing, Jens *85:* 142
Ross
  See Thomson, Ross
Ross, Christine *83:* 172-173
Ross, Clare Romano *3:* 123; *21:* 45; *48:* 199
Ross, Dave *32:* 152; *57:* 108
Ross, Herbert *37:* 78
Ross, John *3:* 123; *21:* 45
Ross, Johnny *32:* 190
Ross, Larry *47:* 168; *60:* 62
Ross, Ruth *109:* 233
Ross, Tony *17:* 204; *56:* 132; *65:* 176, 177, 179; *90:* 123; *123:* 186-187, 190; *130:* 188, 190, 191, 192; *132:* 242
Rossetti, Dante Gabriel *20:* 151, 153
Roth, Arnold *4:* 238; *21:* 133
Roth, Marci *135:* 223
Roth, Rob *105:* 98; *146:* 41
Roth, Roger *61:* 128
Roth, Stephanie *136:* 171, 172
Roth, Susan L. *80:* 38; *93:* 78; *134:* 165, 166
Rothenberg, Joani Keller *162:* 190, 191
Rothman, Michael *139:* 62 Rotman, *Jeffrey L. 145:* 30
Rotondo, Pat *32:* 158
Roughsey, Dick *35:* 186
Rounds, Glen *8:* 173; *9:* 171; *12:* 56; *32:* 194; *40:* 230; *51:* 161, 162, 166; *56:* 149; *70:* 198, 199; *YABC 1:* 1-3; *112:* 163
Roundtree, Katherine *114:* 88
Rowan, Evadne *52:* 51
Rowe, Eric *111:* 161
Rowe, Gavin *27:* 144; *72:* 47; *88:* 201
Rowe, John *132:* 70, 71
Rowell, Kenneth *40:* 72
Rowen, Amy *52:* 143
Rowena *116:* 101
Rowland, Jada *83:* 73
Rowles, Daphne *58:* 24
Roy, Jeroo *27:* 229; *36:* 110
Royo *118:* 32; *144:* 105, 106, 108; *165:* 19
Rubel, Nicole *18:* 255; *20:* 59; *81:* 66, 67; *95:* 169, 170; *119:* 60; *135:* 177, 179, 180; *169:* 68
Rubel, Reina *33:* 217
Rud, Borghild *6:* 15
Ruddell, Gary *110:* 238; *116:* 207
Rudolph, Norman Guthrie *17:* 13
Rue, Leonard Lee III *37:* 164
Ruelle, Karen Gray *126:* 193
Ruff, Donna *50:* 173; *72:* 203; *78:* 49; *80:* 120, 121; *93:* 162
Ruffins, Reynold *10:* 134-135; *41:* 191, 192-193, 194-195, 196; *125:* 187, 188, 189; *162:* 197
Ruhlin, Roger *34:* 44
Ruiz, Art *95:* 154; *110:* 91
Runnerstroem, Bengt Arne *75:* 161
Ruse, Margaret *24:* 155
Rush, Ken *98:* 74
Rush, Peter *42:* 75
Russell, Charles M. *167:* 171
Russell, E.B. *18:* 177, 182
Russell, Jim *53:* 134
Russell, P. Craig *80:* 196; *146:* 102; *162:* 186
Russo, Marisabina *84:* 51; *106:* 164; *151:* 183
Russo, Susan *30:* 182; *36:* 144
Russon, Mary *87:* 145
Ruth, Rod *9:* 161
Rutherford, Alexa *110:* 108
Rutherford, Jenny *78:* 5
Rutherford, Meg *25:* 174; *34:* 178, 179; *69:* 73; *72:* 31
Rutland, Jonathan *31:* 126
Ruurs, Margriet *147:* 195
Ruzzier, Sergio *159:* 176, 177; *163:* 184
Ryan, Will *86:* 134
Ryden, Hope *8:* 176
Rylant, Cynthia *112:* 170, 172

Rymer, Alta M. *34:* 181
Rystedt, Rex *49:* 80

S

Saaf, Chuck *49:* 179
Saaf, Donald *101:* 220; *124:* 180
Sabaka, Donna R. *21:* 172
Sabin, Robert *45:* 35; *60:* 30; *99:* 161
Sacker, Amy *16:* 100
Saelig, S.M. *129:* 73
Saffioti, Lino *36:* 176; *48:* 60
Saflund, Birgitta *94:* 2
Sagsoorian, Paul *12:* 183; *22:* 154; *33:* 106; *87:* 152
Sahlberg, Myron *57:* 165
Saidens, Amy *145:* 162
Saint Exupery, Antoine de *20:* 157
Saint James, Synthia *152:* 220
Saldutti, Denise *39:* 186; *57:* 178
Sale, Morton *YABC 2:* 31
Sale, Tim *153:* 177
Salerno, Steven *150:* 79
Salter, George *72:* 128, 130
Saltzberg, Barney *135:* 184, 185
Saltzman, David *86:* 209
Salwowski, Mark *71:* 54
Salzman, Yuri *86:* 12
Sambourne, Linley *YABC 2:* 181
Sampson, Katherine *9:* 197
Samson, Anne S. *2:* 216
San Souci, Daniel *40:* 200; *96:* 199, 200; *113:* 171; *157:* 149
Sancha, Sheila *38:* 185
Sanchez, Enrique O. *155:* 84
Sand, George X. *45:* 182
Sandberg, Lasse *15:* 239, 241
Sanders, Beryl *39:* 173
Sanderson, Ruth *21:* 126; *24:* 53; *28:* 63; *33:* 67; *41:* 48, 198, 199, 200, 201, 202, 203; *43:* 79; *46:* 36, 44; *47:* 102; *49:* 58; *62:* 121, 122; *85:* 3; *109:* 207, 208, 209, 210
Sandia *119:* 74
Sandin, Joan *4:* 36; *6:* 194; *7:* 177; *12:* 145, 185; *20:* 43; *21:* 74; *26:* 144; *27:* 142; *28:* 224, 225; *38:* 86; *41:* 46; *42:* 35; *59:* 6; *80:* 136; *94:* 188; *140:* 116; *153:* 179, 180
Sandland, Reg *39:* 215
Sandoz, Edouard *26:* 45, 47
Sanford, John *66:* 96, 97
Sankey, Tom *72:* 103
sano, Kazuhiko *153:* 208
Santore, Charles *54:* 139
Santoro, Christopher *74:* 215
Santos, Jesse J. *99:* 24
Sapieha, Christine *1:* 180
Saport, Linda *123:* 137-138
Sara
  See De La Roche Saint Andre, Anne
Sarg, Tony *YABC 2:* 236
Sargent, Claudia *64:* 181
Sargent, Robert *2:* 217
Saris *1:* 33
Sarony *YABC 2:* 170
Sasek, Miroslav *16:* 239-242
Sassman, David *9:* 79
Satty *29:* 203, 205
Sauber, Robert *40:* 183; *76:* 256; *78:* 154; *87:* 92
Saunders, Dave *85:* 163, 164, 165
Savadier, Elivia *84:* 50; *145:* 45
Savage, Naomi *56:* 172
Savage, Steele *10:* 203; *20:* 77; *35:* 28
Savio *76:* 4
Savitt, Sam *8:* 66, 182; *15:* 278; *20:* 96; *24:* 192; *28:* 98
Sawyer, Kem Knapp *84:* 228, 229
Say, Allen *28:* 178; *69:* 182, 183, 232; *110:* 194, 195, 196; *161:* 154, 155

Sayles, Elizabeth *82:* 93; *105:* 155; *109:* 116

Scabrini, Janet *13:* 191; *44:* 128

Scanlan, Peter *83:* 27; *153:* 165

Scanlon, Paul *83:* 87

Scannell, Reece *105:* 105

Scarry, Huck *35:* 204-205

Scarry, Richard *2:* 220-221; *18:* 20; *35:* 193, 194-195, 196, 197, 198, 199, 200-201, 202; *75:* 165, 167, 168

Schachner, Judith Byron *88:* 180; *92:* 163; *93:* 102; *142:* 82

Schaeffer, Mead *18:* 81, 94; *21:* 137, 138, 139; *47:* 128

Schaffer, Amanda *90:* 206

Schanzer, Rosalyn *138:* 192, 193

Scharl, Josef *20:* 132; *22:* 128

Scheel, Lita *11:* 230

Scheib, Ida *29:* 28

Schermer, Judith *30:* 184

Schick, Eleanor *82:* 210, 211; *144:* 222

Schick, Joel *16:* 160; *17:* 167; *22:* 12; *27:* 176; *31:* 147, 148; *36:* 23; *38:* 64; *45:* 116, 117; *52:* 5, 85; *104:* 159

Schields, Gretchen *75:* 171, 203

Schindelman, Joseph *1:* 74; *4:* 101; *12:* 49; *26:* 51; *40:* 146; *56:* 158; *73:* 40

Schindler, Edith *7:* 22

Schindler, S.D. *38:* 107; *46:* 196; *74:* 162; *75:* 172, 173; *99:* 133; *112:* 177; *118:* 185, 186; *121:* 71; *136:* 159; *143:* 45; *149:* 120; *156:* 30; *169:* 135

Schlesinger, Bret *7:* 77

Schmid, Eleanore *12:* 188; *126:* 196, 197

Schmiderer, Dorothy *19:* 224

Schmidt, Bill *73:* 34; *76:* 220, 222, 224

Schmidt, Elizabeth *15:* 242

Schmidt, George Paul *132:* 122

Schmidt, Karen Lee *54:* 12; *71:* 174; *92:* 56; *94:* 190, 191; *127:* 103

Schmidt, Lynette *76:* 205

Schneider, Rex *29:* 64; *44:* 171

Schoberle, Cecile *80:* 200; *92:* 134

Schoenherr, Ian *32:* 83

Schoenherr, John *1:* 146-147, 173; *3:* 39, 139; *17:* 75; *29:* 72; *32:* 83; *37:* 168, 169, 170; *43:* 164, 165; *45:* 160, 162; *51:* 127; *66:* 196, 197, 198; *68:* 83; *72:* 240; *75:* 225; *88:* 176

Scholder, Fritz *69:* 103

Schomburg, Alex *13:* 23

Schongut, Emanuel *4:* 102; *15:* 186; *47:* 218, 219; *52:* 147, 148, 149, 150

Schoonover, Frank *17:* 107; *19:* 81, 190, 233; *22:* 88, 129; *24:* 189; *31:* 88; *41:* 69; *YABC 2:* 282, 316

Schottland, Miriam *22:* 172

Schramm, Ulrik *2:* 16; *14:* 112

Schreiber, Elizabeth Anne *13:* 193

Schreiber, Ralph W. *13:* 193

Schreiter, Rick *14:* 97; *23:* 171; *41:* 247; *49:* 131

Schroeder, Binette *56:* 128, 129

Schroeder, E. Peter *12:* 112

Schroeder, Ted *11:* 160; *15:* 189; *30:* 91; *34:* 43

Schrotter, Gustav *22:* 212; *30:* 225

Schubert, Dieter *101:* 167, 168

Schubert-Gabrys, Ingrid *101:* 167, 168

Schucker, James *31:* 163

Schuett, Stacey *72:* 137

Schulder, Lili *146:* 29

Schulke, Debra *57:* 167

Schulke, Flip *57:* 167

Schulz, Barbara *167:* 24

Schulz, Charles M. *10:* 137-142; *118:* 192, 193, 194, 196, 199

Schutzer, Dena *109:* 32

Schwark, Mary Beth *51:* 155; *72:* 175

Schwartz, Amy *47:* 191; *82:* 100; *83:* 178, 179, 180, 181; *129:* 107; *131:* 197, 198

Schwartz, Carol *124:* 41; *130:* 199

Schwartz, Charles *8:* 184

Schwartz, Daniel *46:* 37

Schwartz, Joanie *124:* 170

Schwartzberg, Joan *3:* 208

Schweitzer, Iris *2:* 137; *6:* 207

Schweninger, Ann *29:* 172; *82:* 246; *159:* 202

Schwinger, Laurence *84:* 44; *91:* 61

Scofield, Penrod *61:* 107; *62:* 160

Scott, Anita Walker *7:* 38

Scott, Art *39:* 41

Scott, Frances Gruse *38:* 43

Scott, Julian *34:* 126

Scott, Roszel *33:* 238

Scott, Sally *87:* 27

Scott, Trudy *27:* 172

Scrace, Carolyn *143:* 95, 96

Scribner, Joanne *14:* 236; *29:* 78; *33:* 185; *34:* 208; *78:* 75

Scrofani, Joseph *31:* 65; *74:* 225

Seaman, Mary Lott *34:* 64

Searle, Ronald *24:* 98; *42:* 172, 173, 174, 176, 177, 179; *66:* 73, 74; *70:* 205, 206, 207

Searle, Townley *36:* 85

Sebree, Charles *18:* 65

Sedacca, Joseph M. *11:* 25; *22:* 36

Seder, Jason *108:* 102

Seeley, Laura L. *97:* 105

Segar, E.C. *61:* 179, 181

Segur, Adrienne *27:* 121

Seibold, J. Otto *83:* 188, 190, 191; *149:* 212, 214, 215, 216

Seignobosc, Francoise *21:* 145, 146

Sejima, Yoshimasa *8:* 187

Selig, Sylvie *13:* 199

Seltzer, Isadore *6:* 18; *133:* 59

Seltzer, Meyer *17:* 214

Selven, Maniam *144:* 133

Selway, Martina *169:* 157

Selznick, Brian *79:* 192; *104:* 25; *117:* 175; *126:* 156; *134:* 171; *158:* 76, 78; *169:* 70

Sempe, Jean-Jacques *47:* 92; *YABC 2:* 109

Sendak, Maurice *1:* 135, 190; *3:* 204; *7:* 142; *15:* 199; *17:* 210; *27:* 181, 182, 183, 185, 186, 187, 189, 190-191, 192, 193, 194, 195, 197, 198, 199, 203; *28:* 181, 182; *32:* 108; *33:* 148, 149; *35:* 238; *44:* 180, 181; *45:* 97, 99; *46:* 174; *73:* 225; *91:* 10, 11 *YABC 1:* 167; *113:* 163, 165, 167, 168; *118:* 153; *127:* 161

Sengler, Johanna *18:* 256

Senn, Steve *60:* 145

Seredy, Kate *1:* 192; *14:* 20-21; *17:* 210

Sergeant, John *6:* 74

Servello, Joe *10:* 144; *24:* 139; *40:* 91; *70:* 130, 131; *146:* 159

Seton, Ernest Thompson *18:* 260-269, 271

Seuss, Dr.
See Geisel, Theodor

Severin, John Powers *7:* 62

Sewall, Marcia *15:* 8; *22:* 170; *37:* 171, 172, 173; *39:* 73; *45:* 209; *62:* 117; *69:* 185, 186; *71:* 212; *90:* 232; *96:* 127; *102:* 101; *107:* 129; *119:* 176, 177, 178, 180

Seward, James *70:* 35

Seward, Prudence *16:* 243

Sewell, Helen *3:* 186; *15:* 308; *33:* 102; *38:* 189, 190, 191, 192

Seymour, Stephen *54:* 21

Shachat, Andrew *82:* 179

Shahn, Ben *39:* 178; *46:* 193

Shalansky, Len *38:* 167

Shanks, Anne Zane *10:* 149

Shannon, David *57:* 137; *107:* 184; *112:* 216; *135:* 12; *152:* 223, 224, 225; *158:* 192

Sharp, Paul *52:* 60

Sharp, William *6:* 131; *19:* 241; *20:* 112; *25:* 141

Sharratt, Nick *102:* 207, 208; *104:* 163; *153:* 198

Shaw, Barclay *74:* 14, 16; *118:* 138

Shaw, Charles *21:* 135; *38:* 187; *47:* 124; *126:* 219

Shaw, Charles G. *13:* 200

Shaw-Smith, Emma *144:* 117

Shea, Edmund *56:* 19

Shearer, Ted *43:* 193, 194, 195, 196

Shecter, Ben *16:* 244; *25:* 109; *33:* 188, 191; *41:* 77

Shed, Greg *74:* 94; *84:* 204; *129:* 149, *167:* 91

Sheeban, Chris *144:* 190; *158:* 163

Shefcik, James *48:* 221, 222; *60:* 141

Shefelman, Karl *58:* 168

Shefts, Joelle *48:* 210

Shein, Bob *139:* 189

Shekerjian, Haig *16:* 245

Shekerjian, Regina *16:* 245; *25:* 73

Shemie, Bonnie *96:* 207

Shenton, Edward *45:* 187, 188, 189; *YABC 1:* 218-219, 221

Shepard, Ernest H. *3:* 193; *4:* 74; *16:* 101; *17:* 109; *25:* 148; *33:* 152, 199, 200, 201, 202, 203, 204, 205, 206, 207; *46:* 194; *98:* 114; *100:* 111, 178, 179, 217, 219, 220, 221; *YABC 1:* 148, 153, 174, 176, 180-181

Shepard, Mary *4:* 210; *22:* 205; *30:* 132, 133; *54:* 150, 152, 153, 157, 158; *59:* 108, 109, 111; *100:* 246

Shepperson, Rob *96:* 153

Sherman, Theresa *27:* 167

Sherwan, Earl *3:* 196

Shields, Charles *10:* 150; *36:* 63

Shields, Leonard *13:* 83, 85, 87

Shiffman, Lena *139:* 167

Shigley, Neil K. *66:* 219

Shillabeer, Mary *35:* 74

Shilston, Arthur *49:* 61; *62:* 58

Shimin, Symeon *1:* 93; *2:* 128-129; *3:* 202; *7:* 85; *11:* 177; *12:* 139; *13:* 202-203; *27:* 138; *28:* 65; *35:* 129; *36:* 130; *48:* 151; *49:* 59; *56:* 63, 65, 153

Shine, Andrea *104:* 165; *128:* 34

Shinn, Everett *16:* 148; *18:* 229; *21:* 149, 150, 151; *24:* 218

Shinn, Florence Scovel *63:* 133, 135

Shore, Robert *27:* 54; *39:* 192, 193; *YABC 2:* 200

Shortall, Leonard *4:* 144; *8:* 196; *10:* 166; *19:* 227, 228-229, 230; *25:* 78; *28:* 66, 167; *33:* 127; *52:* 125; *73:* 12, 212

Shortt, T.M. *27:* 36

Shpitalnik, Vladimir *83:* 194

Shtainments, Leon *32:* 161

Shulevitz, Uri *3:* 198-199; *17:* 85; *22:* 204; *27:* 212; *28:* 184; *50:* 190, 191, 192, 193, 194-195, 196, 197, 198, 199, 201; *106:* 181, 182, 183; *165:* 203, 205

Shupe, Bobbi *139:* 80, 81

Shute, A.B. *67:* 196

Shute, Linda *46:* 59; *74:* 118

Siberell, Anne *29:* 193

Sibley, Don *1:* 39; *12:* 196; *31:* 47

Sibthorp, Fletcher *94:* 111, 112

Sidjakov, Nicolas *18:* 274

Siebel, Fritz *3:* 120; *17:* 145

Siebold, J. Otto *158:* 227

Siegel, Hal *74:* 246

Siegl, Helen *12:* 166; *23:* 216; *34:* 185, 186

Sill, John *140:* 194; *141:* 157

Sills, Joyce *5:* 199

Silva, Simon *108:* 122

Silver, Maggie *85:* 210

Silveria, Gordon *96:* 44

Silverstein, Alvin *8:* 189

Silverstein, Shel *33:* 211; *92:* 209, 210

Silverstein, Virginia *8:* 189

Silvey, Joe *135:* 203

Simard, Remy *95:* 156

Simmons, Elly *110:* 2; *127:* 69; *134:* 181

Simon, Eric M. *7:* 82

Simon, Hilda *28:* 189

Simon, Howard 2: 175; 5: 132; 19: 199; 32: 163, 164, 165
Simont, Marc 2: 119; 4: 213; 9: 168; 13: 238, 240; 14: 262; 16: 179; 18: 221; 26: 210; 33: 189, 194; 44: 132; 58: 122; 68: 117; 73: 204, 205, 206; 74: 221; 126: 199, 200; 133: 195
Sims, Agnes 54: 152
Sims, Blanche 44: 116; 57: 129; 75: 179, 180; 77: 92; 104: 192; 152: 117; 156: 160; 160: 70
Singer, Edith G. 2: 30
Singer, Gloria 34: 56; 36: 43
Singer, Julia 28: 190
Siomades, Lorianne 134: 45
Simont, Marc 163: 40
Siracusa, Catherine 68: 135; 82: 218
Sis, Peter 67: 179, 181, 183, 184, 185; 96: 96, 98; 106: 193, 194, 195; 149: 224, 226
Sivard, Robert 26: 124
Sivertson, Liz 116: 84
Skardinski, Stanley 23: 144; 32: 84; 66: 122; 84: 108
Slackman, Charles B. 12: 201
Slade, Paul 61: 170
Slark, Albert 99: 212
Slater, Rod 25: 167
Sloan, Joseph 16: 68
Sloane, Eric 21: 3; 52: 153, 154, 155, 156, 157, 158, 160
Slobodkin, Louis 1: 200; 3: 232; 5: 168; 13: 251; 15: 13, 88; 26: 173, 174, 175, 176, 178, 179; 60: 180
Slobodkina, Esphyr 1: 201
Small, David 50: 204-205; 79: 44; 95: 189, 190, 191; 126: 203, 204; 136: 119; 143: 201, 202, 203; 144: 246; 150: 5; 161: 176
Small, W. 33: 113
Smalley, Janet 1: 154
Smedley, William T. 34: 129
Smee, David 14: 78; 62: 30
Smee, Nicola 167: 156
Smith, A.G., Jr. 35: 182
Smith, Alvin 1: 31, 229; 13: 187; 27: 216; 28: 226; 48: 149; 49: 60
Smith, Anne Warren 41: 212
Smith, Barry 75: 183
Smith, Carl 36: 41
Smith, Cat Bowman 146: 39
Smith, Craig 97: 197
Smith, Doris Susan 41: 139
Smith, E. Boyd 19: 70; 22: 89; 26: 63; YABC 1: 4-5, 240, 248-249
Smith, Edward J. 4: 224
Smith, Elwood H. 157: 231
Smith, Eunice Young 5: 170
Smith, Gary 113: 216
Smith, George 102: 169
Smith, Howard 19: 196
Smith, J. Gerard 95: 42
Smith, Jacqueline Bardner 27: 108; 39: 197
Smith, Jay J. 61: 119
Smith, Jeff 93: 191
Smith, Jessie Willcox 15: 91; 16: 95; 18: 231; 19: 57, 242; 21: 29, 156, 157, 158, 159, 160, 161; 34: 65; 100: 223; YABC 1: 6; 2: 180, 185, 191, 311, 325
Smith, Jos. A. 52: 131; 72: 120; 74: 151; 84: 147, 148; 85: 146; 87: 96; 94: 219; 96: 97; 104: 33; 108: 126, 127, 128; 111: 140; 136: 145
Smith, Kenneth R. 47: 182
Smith, Kevin Warren 89: 112
Smith, L.H. 35: 174
Smith, Lane 76: 211, 213; 88: 115; 105: 202, 203, 204, 205; 131: 207; 160: 217, 221
Smith, Lee 29: 32
Smith, Linell Nash 2: 195
Smith, Maggie Kaufman 13: 205; 35: 191; 110: 158
Smith, Mavis 101: 219

Smith, Moishe 33: 155
Smith, Philip 44: 134; 46: 203
Smith, Ralph Crosby 2: 267; 49: 203
Smith, Robert D. 5: 63
Smith, Sally J. 84: 55
Smith, Susan Carlton 12: 208
Smith, Terry 12: 106; 33: 158
Smith, Virginia 3: 157; 33: 72
Smith, William A. 1: 36; 10: 154; 25: 65
Smith-Moore, J.J. 98: 147
Smolinski, Dick 84: 217
Smoljan, Joe 112: 201
Smollin, Mike 39: 203
Smyth, Iain 105: 207
Smyth, M. Jane 12: 15
Smythe, Fiona 151: 213
Smythe, Theresa 141: 37
Sneed, Brad 125: 25
Snyder, Andrew A. 30: 212
Snyder, Jerome 13: 207; 30: 173
Snyder, Joel 28: 163
So, Meilo 162: 201
Soentpiet, Chris K. 97: 208; 110: 33; 159: 184; 161: 10; 163: 130
Sofia 1: 62; 5: 90; 32: 166; 86: 43
Sofilas, Mark 93: 157
Sokol, Bill 37: 178; 49: 23
Sokolov, Kirill 34: 188
Solbert, Ronni 1: 159; 2: 232; 5: 121; 6: 34; 17: 249
Solonevich, George 15: 246; 17: 47
Soma, Liana 81: 118
Soman, David 90: 122; 102: 126; 140: 120; 93
Sommer, Robert 12: 211
Sorel, Edward 4: 61; 36: 82; 65: 191, 193; 126: 214
Sorensen, Henrik 62: 16
Sorensen, Svend Otto 22: 130, 141; 67: 188, 189
Sorra, Kristin 155: 80
Sotomayor, Antonio 11: 215
Souhami, Jessica 112: 128
Souza, Diana 71: 139
Sovak, Jan 115: 190
Soyer, Moses 20: 177
Spaenkuch, August 16: 28
Spafford, Suzy 160: 228
Spain, Valerie 105: 76
Spain, Sunday Sahara 133: 204
Spalenka, Greg 149: 69; 151: 228
Spanfeller, James 1: 72, 149; 2: 183; 19: 230, 231, 232; 22: 66; 36: 160, 161; 40: 75; 52: 166; 76: 37
Sparks, Mary Walker 15: 247
Speidel, Sandra 78: 233; 94: 178; 134: 180
Speirs, John 67: 178
Spence, Geraldine 21: 163; 47: 196
Spence, Jim 38: 89; 50: 102
Spencer, Laurie 113: 12
Spencer, Mark 57: 170
Spengler, Kenneth J. 146: 256
Sperling, Andrea 133: 182
Spiegel, Doris 29: 111
Spiegelman, Art 109: 227
Spier, Jo 10: 30
Spier, Peter 3: 155; 4: 200; 7: 61; 11: 78; 38: 106; 54: 120, 121, 122-123, 124-125, 126, 127, 128-129, 130, 131, 132-133, 134
Spilka, Arnold 5: 120; 6: 204; 8: 131
Spirin, Gennady 95: 196, 197; 113: 172; 128: 9; 129: 49; 134: 210; 153: 9
Spivak, I. Howard 8: 10; 13: 172
Spohn, David 72: 233
Spohn, Kate 87: 195; 147: 201-202
Spollen, Christopher J. 12: 214
Spooner, Malcolm 40: 142
Spowart, Robin 82: 228; 92: 149; 133: 131
Sprague, Kevin 150: 60
Sprattler, Rob 12: 176
Spring, Bob 5: 60
Spring, Ira 5: 60

Springer, Harriet 31: 92
Spudvilas, Anne 110: 74
Spurll, Barbara 78: 199; 88: 141, 142; 99: 215
Spurrier, Steven 28: 198
Spuvilas, Anne 85: 114
Spy
    See Ward, Leslie
Squires, Stuart 127: 74
St. John, J. Allen 41: 62
Stabin, Victor 101: 131
Stadler, John 62: 33
Staffan, Alvin E. 11: 56; 12: 187
Stahl, Ben 5: 181; 12: 91; 49: 122; 71: 128; 87: 206; 112: 107
Stair, Gobin 35: 214
Stallwood, Karen 73: 126
Stamaty, Mark Alan 12: 215
Stammen, JoEllen McAllister 113: 14
Stampnick, Ken 51: 142
Stanbridge, Joanne 150: 91
Stanley, Diane 3: 45; 37: 180; 80: 217, 219
Stanley, Sanna 145: 228
Starcke, Helmut 86: 217
Starr, Branka 73: 25
Stasiak, Krystyna 49: 181; 64: 194
Staub, Leslie 103: 54
Staunton, Ted 112: 192
Stead, L. 55: 51, 56
Steadman, Broeck 97: 185, 186; 99: 56; 121: 48
Steadman, Ralph 32: 180; 123: 143, 145
Steckler, June 90: 178
Steele, Robert Gantt 169: 174
Steichen, Edward 30: 79
Steig, William 18: 275-276; 70: 215, 216, 217, 218; 111: 173, 174, 175, 176, 177
Stein, Harve 1: 109
Steinberg, Saul 47: 193
Steinel, William 23: 146
Steiner, Charlotte 45: 196
Steiner, Joan 110: 219
Steirnagel, Michael 80: 56
Stemp, Eric 60: 184
Stephens, Alice Barber 66: 208, 209
Stephens, Charles H. YABC 2: 279
Stephens, Pat 126: 110; 128: 101
Stephens, William M. 21: 165
Steptoe, Javaka 151: 203, 204
Steptoe, John 8: 197; 57: 9; 63: 158, 159, 160, 161, 163, 164, 165, 166, 167; 96: 4; 105: 87
Stern, Simon 15: 249-250; 17: 58; 34: 192-193
Sterret, Jane 53: 27
Stetsios, Debbie 165: 108-109
Steven, Kat 158: 237
Stevens, David 62: 44
Stevens, Janet 40: 126; 57: 10, 11; 80: 112; 90: 221, 222; 109: 156; 130: 34
Stevens, Mary 11: 193; 13: 129; 43: 95
Stevenson, Harvey 66: 143; 80: 201, 221; 153: 60
Stevenson, James 42: 182, 183; 51: 163; 66: 184; 71: 185, 187, 188; 78: 262; 87: 97; 113: 182, 183, 184, 185; 161: 182, 183
Stevenson, Sucie 92: 27; 104: 194, 195; 112: 168; 160: 202
Stewart, April Blair 75: 210
Stewart, Arvis 33: 98; 36: 69; 60: 118; 75: 91; 127: 4
Stewart, Charles 2: 205
Stewart, Joel 151: 205
Stiles, Fran 26: 85; 78: 56; 82: 150
Stillman, Susan 44: 130; 76: 83
Stimpson, Tom 49: 171
Stinemetz, Morgan 40: 151
Stinson, Paul 110: 86
Stirnweis, Shannon 10: 164
Stites, Joe 86: 96
Stobbs, William 1: 48, 49; 3: 68; 6: 20; 17: 117, 217; 24: 150; 29: 250; 60: 179; 87: 204, 205, 206

Stock, Catherine *37:* 55; *65:* 198; *72:* 7; *99:* 225; *114:* 197, 198, 199; *126:* 3; *145:* 161; *161:* 82
Stockman, Jack *113:* 24
Stoeke, Janet Morgan *90:* 225; *136:* 196
Stoerrle, Tom *55:* 147
Stolp, Jaap *49:* 98
Stolp, Todd *89:* 195
Stone, David L. *87:* 154
Stone, David *9:* 173
Stone, David K. *4:* 38; *6:* 124; *9:* 180; *43:* 182; *60:* 70
Stone, Helen V. *6:* 209
Stone, Helen *44:* 121, 122, 126
Stone, Kazuko G. *134:* 43
Stone, Phoebe *86:* 212; *134:* 213; *162:* 188
Stone, Tony *150:* 34, 35
Stoud, Virginia A. *89:* 31
Stover, Jill *82:* 234
Stratton, Helen *33:* 151
Stratton-Porter, Gene *15:* 254, 259, 263-264, 268-269
Streano, Vince *20:* 173
Street, Janet Travell *84:* 235
Streeter, Clive *121:* 2
Stringer, Lauren *129:* 187; *154:* 172, 173; *161:* 127
Strodl, Daniel *47:* 95
Strogart, Alexander *63:* 139
Stromoski, Rick *111:* 179; *124:* 161, 190
Strong, Joseph D., Jr. *YABC 2:* 330
Stroyer, Poul *13:* 221
Strugnell, Ann *27:* 38
Struzan, Drew *117:* 6
Stubbs, William *73:* 196
Stubis, Talivaldis *5:* 182, 183; *10:* 45; *11:* 9; *18:* 304; *20:* 127
Stubley, Trevor *14:* 43; *22:* 219; *23:* 37; *28:* 61; *87:* 26
Stuck, Marion *104:* 44
Stuecklen, Karl W. *8:* 34, 65; *23:* 103
Stull, Betty *11:* 46
Stutzman, Mark *119:* 99
Stutzmann, Laura *73:* 185
Suarez, Maribel *162:* 208
Suba, Susanne *4:* 202-203; *14:* 261; *23:* 134; *29:* 222; *32:* 30
Sueling, Barbara *98:* 185
Sueling, Gwenn *98:* 186
Sugarman, Tracy *3:* 76; *8:* 199; *37:* 181, 182
Sugita, Yutaka *36:* 180-181
Suh, John *80:* 157
Sullivan, Dorothy *89:* 113
Sullivan, Edmund J. *31:* 86
Sullivan, James F. *19:* 280; *20:* 192
Sully, Tom *104:* 199, 200
Sumichrast, Jozef *14:* 253; *29:* 168, 213
Sumiko *46:* 57
Summers, Leo *1:* 177; *2:* 273; *13:* 22
Summers, Mark *118:* 144
Sutton, Judith *94:* 164
Svarez, Juan *56:* 113
Svolinsky, Karel *17:* 104
Swain, Su Zan Noguchi *21:* 170
Swan, Susan *22:* 220-221; *37:* 66; *60:* 146; *145:* 205
Swann, Susan *86:* 55
Swanson, Karl *79:* 65; *89:* 186
Swayne, Sam *53:* 143, 145
Swayne, Zoa *53:* 143, 145
Swearingen, Greg *152:* 56; *165:* 135
Sweat, Lynn *25:* 206; *57:* 176; *73:* 184
Sweet, Darrell K. *60:* 9; *69:* 86; *74:* 15; *75:* 215; *76:* 130, 131; *81:* 96, 122; *82:* 253; *83:* 11; *84:* 14; *85:* 37; *89:* 140; *90:* 6; *91:* 137, 139; *95:* 160, 161; *126:* 25
Sweet, Darryl *1:* 163; *4:* 136
Sweet, Melissa *71:* 94; *72:* 172; *111:* 82; *139:* 53, 58; *141:* 88; *142:* 231; *155:* 121; *159:* 121, 122
Sweet, Ozzie *31:* 149, 151, 152

Sweetland, Robert *12:* 194
Swiatkowska, Gabi *132:* 43
Swope, Martha *43:* 160; *56:* 86, 87, 89
Sylvada, Peter *154:* 174
Sylvester, Natalie G. *22:* 222
Szafran, Gene *24:* 144
Szasz, Susanne *13:* 55, 226; *14:* 48
Szekeres, Cyndy *2:* 218; *5:* 185; *8:* 85; *11:* 166; *14:* 19; *16:* 57, 159; *26:* 49, 214; *34:* 205; *60:* 150, 151, 152, 153, 154; *73:* 224; *74:* 218; *131:* 213, 215
Szpura, Beata *81:* 68; *119:* 65

T

Taback, Simms *40:* 207; *52:* 120; *57:* 34; *80:* 241; *104:* 202, 203
Taber, Patricia *75:* 124
Tabor, Nancy Maria Grande *89:* 210; *161:* 188
Taddei, Richard *112:* 13, 14
Tadgell, Nicole *150:* 77; *161:* 20
Tadiello, Ed *133:* 200
Tafuri, Nancy *39:* 210; *75:* 199, 200; *92:* 75; *130:* 215, 216, 217
Tailfeathers, Gerald *86:* 85
Tait, Douglas *12:* 220; *74:* 105, 106
Takabayashi, Mari *113:* 112; *130:* 22; *156:* 169
Takahashi, Hideko *160:* 160
Takakjian, Portia *15:* 274
Takashima, Shizuye *13:* 228
Talarczyk, June *4:* 173
Talbott, Hudson *84:* 240; *163:* 100
Tallarico, Tony *116:* 197
Tallon, Robert *2:* 228; *43:* 200, 201, 202, 203, 204, 205, 206, 207, 209
Tamas, Szecsko *29:* 135
Tamburine, Jean *12:* 222
Tandy, H.R. *13:* 69
Tandy, Russell H. *65:* 9; *100:* 30, 131
Tang, Charles *81:* 202; *90:* 192
Tang, Susan *80:* 174; *108:* 158
Tang, You-shan *63:* 100
Tankersley, Paul *69:* 206; *133:* 219
Tannenbaum, Robert *48:* 181
Tanner, Jane *87:* 13; *97:* 37
Tanner, Tim *72:* 192; *84:* 35
Tanobe, Miyuki *23:* 221
Tarabay, Sharif *110:* 149; *113:* 123; *169:* 83
Tarkington, Booth *17:* 224-225
Tarlow, Phyllis *61:* 198
Tate, Don *159:* 141, 191
Tauss, Herbert *95:* 179
Tauss, Marc *117:* 160; *126:* 155
Tavares, Matt *159:* 192, 193
Taylor, Ann *41:* 226
Taylor, Dahl *129:* 157
Taylor, Geoff *93:* 156
Taylor, Isaac *41:* 228
Taylor, Mike *143:* 99, 100
Teague, Mark *83:* 6; *139:* 241
Teale, Edwin Way *7:* 196
Teason, James *1:* 14
Teeple, Lyn *33:* 147
Tee-Van, Helen Damrosch *10:* 176; *11:* 182
Teicher, Dick *50:* 211
Teichman, Mary *77:* 220; *124:* 208; *127:* 22
Temertey, Ludmilla *96:* 232; *104:* 43, 45; *109:* 244
Tempest, Margaret *3:* 237, 238; *88:* 200
Temple, Frances *85:* 185, 186, 187
Temple, Herbert *45:* 201
Templeton, Owen *11:* 77
Tenggren, Gustaf *18:* 277-279; *19:* 15; *28:* 86; *YABC 2:* 145
Tennent, Julie *81:* 105
Tenneson, Joyce *153:* 166
Tenney, Gordon *24:* 204
Tenniel, John *74:* 234, 235; *100:* 89; *YABC 2:* 99; *153:* 63

Tepper, Matt *116:* 80
Terkel, Ari *103:* 162
Terry, Will *131:* 73
Teskey, Donald *71:* 51
Thacher, Mary M. *30:* 72
Thackeray, William Makepeace *23:* 224, 228
Thamer, Katie *42:* 187
Tharlet, Eve *146:* 149
Thelwell, Norman *14:* 201
Theobalds, Prue *40:* 23
Theurer, Marilyn Churchill *39:* 195
Thiesing, Lisa *89:* 134; *95:* 202; *156:* 190; *159:* 195
Thiewes, Sam *133:* 114
Thistlethwaite, Miles *12:* 224
Thollander, Earl *11:* 47; *18:* 112; *22:* 224
Thomas, Allan *22:* 13
Thomas, Art *48:* 217
Thomas, Eric *28:* 49
Thomas, Harold *20:* 98
Thomas, Jacqui *125:* 95
Thomas, Mark *42:* 136
Thomas, Martin *14:* 255
Thompson, Arthur *34:* 107
Thompson, Carol *85:* 189; *95:* 75; *102:* 86; *147:* 166
Thompson, Colin *95:* 204
Thompson, Ellen *51:* 88, 151; *60:* 33; *67:* 42; *77:* 148; *78:* 75, 219; *79:* 122, 170; *84:* 219; *85:* 97; *87:* 37; *88:* 192, 194; *89:* 80; *93:* 37; *98:* 59; *132:* 14
Thompson, George W. *22:* 18; *28:* 150; *33:* 135
Thompson, John *58:* 201; *102:* 226; *124:* 154; *128:* 228; *129:* 157; *150:* 49
Thompson, Julie *44:* 158
Thompson, Katherine *132:* 146
Thompson, K. Dyble *84:* 6
Thompson, Miles *152:* 77
Thompson, Sharon *74:* 113; *158:* 60; *165:* 87
Thomson, Arline K. *3:* 264
Thomson, Hugh *26:* 88
Thomson, Ross *36:* 179
Thorkelson, Gregg *95:* 183, 184; *98:* 58; *165:* 30-31
Thornberg, Dan *104:* 125
Thornburgh, Rebecca McKillip *143:* 37
Thorne, Diana *25:* 212
Thornhill, Jan *77:* 213
Thorpe, Peter *58:* 109
Thorvall, Kerstin *13:* 235
Threadgall, Colin *77:* 215
Thurber, James *13:* 239, 242-245, 248-249
Thurman, Mark *63:* 173
Tibbles, Jean-Paul *115:* 200
Tibbles, Paul *45:* 23
Tibo, Gilles *67:* 207; *107:* 199, 201
Tichenor, Tom *14:* 207
Tichnor, Richard *90:* 218
Tiegreen, Alan *36:* 143; *43:* 55, 56, 58; *77:* 200; *94:* 216, 217; *121:* 54, 59
Tierney, Tom *113:* 198, 200, 201
Tilley, Debbie *102:* 134; *133:* 226; *137:* 101; *159:* 96
Tilney, F.C. *22:* 231
Timbs, Gloria *36:* 90
Timmins, Harry *2:* 171
Tinkelman, Murray *12:* 225; *35:* 44
Titherington, Jeanne *39:* 90; *58:* 138; *75:* 79; *135:* 161
Tobin, Nancy *145:* 197
Tolbert, Jeff *128:* 69
Tolford, Joshua *1:* 221
Tolkien, J.R.R. *2:* 243; *32:* 215
Tolmie, Ken *15:* 292
Tomei, Lorna *47:* 168, 171
Tomes, Jacqueline *2:* 117; *12:* 139

Tomes, Margot *1:* 224; *2:* 120-121; *16:* 207; *18:* 250; *20:* 7; *25:* 62; *27:* 78, 79; *29:* 81, 199; *33:* 82; *36:* 186, 187, 188, 189, 190; *46:* 129; *56:* 71; *58:* 183; *70:* 228; *75:* 73, 75; *80:* 80; *83:* 97; *90:* 205
Toner, Raymond John *10:* 179
Tong, Gary *66:* 215
Tongier, Stephen *82:* 32
Toothill, Harry *6:* 54; *7:* 49; *25:* 219; *42:* 192
Toothill, Ilse *6:* 54
Topolski, Feliks *44:* 48
Torbert, Floyd James *22:* 226
Torgersen, Don *55:* 157
Torline, Kevin *169:* 171
Torres, Leyla *156:* 199, 201
Torrey, Helen *87:* 41
Torrey, Marjorie *34:* 105
Toschik, Larry *6:* 102
Totten, Bob *13:* 93
Toy, Julie *128:* 112
Trachok, Cathy *131:* 16
Tracy, Libba *82:* 24
Trago, Keith *158:* 253
Trail, Lee *55:* 157
Trang, To Ngoc *167:* 180
Trang, Winson *89:* 151
Trapani, Iza *116:* 202
Travers, Bob *49:* 100; *63:* 145
Treatner, Meryl *95:* 180
Tremain, Ruthven *17:* 238
Tresilian, Stuart *25:* 53; *40:* 212
Trez, Alain *17:* 236
Trezzo, Loretta *86:* 45
Trier, Walter *14:* 96
Trimby, Elisa *47:* 199
Trinkle, Sally *53:* 27
Tripp, F.J. *24:* 167
Tripp, Wallace *2:* 48; *7:* 28; *8:* 94; *10:* 54, 76; *11:* 92; *31:* 170, 171; *34:* 203; *42:* 57; *60:* 157; *73:* 182
Trivas, Irene *53:* 4; *54:* 168; *82:* 46, 101
Trnka, Jiri *22:* 151; *43:* 212, 213, 214, 215; *YABC 1:* 30-31
Troughton, Joanna *37:* 186; *48:* 72
Troyer, Johannes *3:* 16; *7:* 18
Trudeau, G.B. *35:* 220, 221, 222; *48:* 119, 123, 126, 127, 128-129, 133
Trueman, Matthew *165:* 208
Truesdell, Sue *55:* 142; *108:* 219, 220
Tryon, Leslie *84:* 7; *139:* 214; *143:* 10
Tseng, Jean *72:* 195; *94:* 102; *119:* 126; *151:* 106
Tseng, Mou-sien *72:* 195; *94:* 102; *119:* 126; *151:* 106
Tsinajinie, Andy *2:* 62
Tsugami, Kyuzo *18:* 198-199
Tucker, Ezra *156:* 31
Tuckwell, Jennifer *17:* 205
Tudor, Bethany *7:* 103
Tudor, Tasha *18:* 227; *20:* 185, 186, 187; *36:* 111; *69:* 196, 198; *100:* 44; *YABC 2:* 46, 314; *160:* 234
Tuerk, Hanne *71:* 201
Tulloch, Maurice *24:* 79
Tunis, Edwin *1:* 218-219; *28:* 209, 210, 211, 212
Tunnicliffe, C.F. *62:* 176; *177;* 178, 179; 181
Turkle, Brinton *1:* 211, 213; *2:* 249; *3:* 226; *11:* 3; *16:* 209; *20:* 22; *50:* 23; *67:* 50; *68:* 65; *79:* 205, 206, 207; *128:* 47; *YABC 1:* 79
Turnbull, Christopher J. *143:* 99, 100
Turner, Gwenda *59:* 195
Turska, Krystyna *12:* 103; *31:* 173, 174-175; *56:* 32, 34; *100:* 66
Tusa, Tricia *72:* 242; *111:* 180, 181; *157:* 165
Tusan, Stan *6:* 58; *22:* 236-237
Tworkov, Jack *47:* 207
Tyers, Jenny *89:* 220
Tylden-Wright, Jenny *114:* 119
Tyrol, Adelaide Murphy *103:* 27

Tyrrell, Frances *107:* 204
Tzimoulis, Paul *12:* 104

U

Uchida, Yoshiko *1:* 220
Uderzo *47:* 88
Ueno, Noriko *59:* 155
Ulm, Robert *17:* 238
Ulrich, George *73:* 15; *75:* 136, 139; *99:* 150
Ulriksen, Mark *101:* 58
Unada *84:* 67
    See Gliewe, Unada
Underhill, Liz *53:* 159
Underwood, Clarence *40:* 166
Unger, Jim *67:* 208
Ungerer, Tomi *5:* 188; *9:* 40; *18:* 188; *29:* 175; *33:* 221, 222-223, 225; *71:* 48; *106:* 209, 210, 211, 212
Unwin, Nora S. *3:* 65, 234-235; *4:* 237; *44:* 173, 174; *YABC 1:* 59; *2:* 301
Upitis, Alvis *145:* 179
Urban, Helle *149:* 243
Urbanovic, Jackie *86:* 86
Uris, Jill *49:* 188, 197
Ursell, Martin *50:* 51
Utpatel, Frank *18:* 114
Utz, Lois *5:* 190

V

Vagin, Vladimir *66:* 10; *142:* 215
Vaillancourt, Francois *107:* 199
Vainio, Pirkko *123:* 157-158
Vallejo, Boris *62:* 130; *72:* 212; *91:* 38; *93:* 61
Van Abbe, S. *16:* 142; *18:* 282; *31:* 90; *YABC 2:* 157, 161
Van Allsburg, Chris *37:* 205, 206; *53:* 161, 162, 163, 165, 166, 167, 168, 169, 170-171; *105:* 215, 216, 217, 218; *156:* 176, 177, 178
Vance, James *65:* 28
Van Der Linde, Henry *99:* 17
van der Meer, Ron *98:* 204, 205
van der Meer, Atie *98:* 204, 205
Vandivert, William *21:* 175
Van Dongen, H.R. *81:* 97
Van Everen, Jay *13:* 160; *YABC 1:* 121
Van Fleet, John *165:* 12, 13
Van Frankenhuyzen, Gijsbert *145:* 230; *149:* 164
van Genechten, Guido *165:* 226
Van Horn, William *43:* 218
van Lawick, Hugo *62:* 76, 79
Van Loon, Hendrik Willem *18:* 285, 289, 291
Van Munching, Paul *83:* 85
Van Rynbach, Iris *102:* 192
Van Sciver, Ruth *37:* 162
VanSeveren, Joe *63:* 182
Van Stockum, Hilda *5:* 193
Van Wely, Babs *16:* 50; *79:* 16
Van Wright, Cornelius *72:* 18; *102:* 208; *116:* 107; *152:* 236
Van Zyle, Jon *103:* 125; *160:* 181, 182
Vardzigulyants, Ruben *90:* 54
Varga, Judy *29:* 196
Vargo, Kurt *79:* 224
Varley, Susan *61:* 199; *63:* 176, 177; *101:* 148; *134:* 220
Vasconcellos, Daniel *80:* 42
Vasiliu, Mircea *2:* 166, 253; *9:* 166; *13:* 58; *68:* 42
Vaughn, Frank *34:* 157
Vavra, Robert *8:* 206
Vawter, Will *17:* 163
Vayas, Diana *71:* 61
Vazquez, Carlos *125:* 184

Veeder, Larry *18:* 4
Velasquez, Eric *45:* 217; *61:* 45; *63:* 110, 111; *88:* 162; *90:* 34, 144; *94:* 213; *107:* 147; *132:* 192; *138:* 213; *159:* 126
Velasquez, Jose A. *63:* 73
Velez, Walter *71:* 75; *91:* 154; *121:* 181
Velthuijs, Max *110:* 228, 229
Vendrell, Carme Sole *42:* 205
Venezia, Mike *54:* 17
Venti, Anthony Bacon *124:* 103; *126:* 26
Venturo, Piero *61:* 194, 195
Ver Beck, Frank *18:* 16-17
Verkaaik, Ben *110:* 209
Verling, John *71:* 27
Verney, John *14:* 225; *75:* 8
Verrier, Suzanne *5:* 20; *23:* 212
Versace, Marie *2:* 255
Verstraete, Randy *108:* 193
Vestal, H.B. *9:* 134; *11:* 101; *27:* 25; *34:* 158
Vicatan *59:* 146
Vickrey, Robert *45:* 59, 64
Victor, Joan Berg *30:* 193
Viereck, Ellen *3:* 242; *14:* 229
Vigna, Judith *15:* 293; *102:* 194, 195, 196, 197
Vilato, Gaspar E. *5:* 41
Villiard, Paul *51:* 178
Vimnera, A. *23:* 154
Vincent, Eric *34:* 98
Vincent, Felix *41:* 237
Vincent, Gabrielle *121:* 175
Vip *45:* 164
Viskupic, Gary *83:* 48
Vitale, Stefano *109:* 71, 107; *114:* 219, 220; *123:* 106; *138:* 232
Vivas, Julie *51:* 67, 69; *96:* 225
Voake, Charlotte *114:* 221, 222
Vo-Dinh, Mai *16:* 272; *60:* 191
Vogel, Ilse-Margret *14:* 230
Voigt, Erna *35:* 228
Vojnar, Kamil *95:* 31; *114:* 4; *115:* 62; *121:* 90; *124:* 72; *130:* 31; *141:* 81; *146:* 196; *150:* 123; *158:* 5, 6; *158:* 154
Vojtech, Anna *42:* 190; *108:* 222, 223; *150:* 203
von Buhler, Cynthia *149:* 237; *162:* 177
von Roehl, Angela *126:* 191
von Schmidt, Eric *8:* 62; *50:* 209, 210
von Schmidt, Harold *30:* 80
Vosburgh, Leonard *1:* 161; *7:* 32; *15:* 295, 296; *23:* 110; *30:* 214; *43:* 181
Voss, Tom *127:* 104
Voter, Thomas W. *19:* 3, 9
Vroman, Tom *10:* 29
Vulliamy, Clara *72:* 65

W

Waber, Bernard *47:* 209, 210, 211, 212, 213, 214; *95:* 215, 216, 217; *156:* 203, 205, 206, 207
Wack, Jeff *95:* 140; *110:* 90
Wagner, John *8:* 200; *52:* 104
Wagner, Ken *2:* 59
Waide, Jan *29:* 225; *36:* 139
Wainwright, Jerry *14:* 85
Wakeen, Sandra *47:* 97
Waldherr, Kris *81:* 186
Waldman, Bruce *15:* 297; *43:* 178
Waldman, Neil *35:* 141; *50:* 163; *51:* 180; *54:* 78; *77:* 112; *79:* 162; *82:* 174; *84:* 5, 56, 106; *94:* 232, 233, 234; *96:* 41; *111:* 139; *113:* 9; *118:* 30; *142:* 220, 223
Waldrep, Richard *111:* 147
Walker, Brian *144:* 128
Walker, Charles *1:* 46; *4:* 59; *5:* 177; *11:* 115; *19:* 45; *34:* 74; *62:* 168; *72:* 218
Walker, Dugald Stewart *15:* 47; *32:* 202; *33:* 112
Walker, Gil *8:* 49; *23:* 132; *34:* 42

Walker, Jeff 55: 154; 123: 116
Walker, Jim 10: 94
Walker, Mort 8: 213
Walker, Norman 41: 37; 45: 58
Walker, Stephen 12: 229; 21: 174
Wallace, Beverly Dobrin 19: 259
Wallace, Cly 87: 93
Wallace, Ian 53: 176, 177; 56: 165, 166; 58:
  4; 98: 4; 101: 191; 112: 124; 141: 197, 198,
  199, 200; 151: 212
Wallace, John 105: 228
Wallace, Nancy Elizabeth 141: 204
Wallenta, Adam 123: 180
Waller, S.E. 24: 36
Wallner, Alexandra 15: 120; 156: 183
Wallner, John C. 9: 77; 10: 188; 11: 28; 14:
  209; 31: 56, 118; 37: 64; 51: 186, 187,
  188-189, 190-191, 192-193, 194, 195; 52:
  96; 53: 23, 26; 71: 99; 73: 158; 89: 215;
  141: 9
Wallner, John 162: 17
Wallower, Lucille 11: 226
Walotsky, Ron 93: 87
Walsh, Ellen Stoll 99: 209; 147: 219
Walsh, Rebecca 158: 193
Walsh, Vivian 149: 215; 158: 227
Walters, Audrey 18: 294
Walther, Tom 31: 179
Walton, Garry 69: 149
Walton, Tony 11: 164; 24: 209; 153: 8
Waltrip, Lela 9: 195
Waltrip, Mildred 3: 209; 37: 211
Waltrip, Rufus 9: 195
Wan 12: 76
Warburton, Sarah 154: 187
Wappers, G. 121: 40
Ward, Fred 52: 19
Ward, Helen 72: 244; 144: 240, 242
Ward, John 42: 191; 96: 54; 97: 110; 123:
  105; 124: 71
Ward, Keith 2: 107; 132: 69
Ward, Leslie 34: 126; 36: 87
Ward, Lynd 1: 99, 132, 133, 150; 2: 108, 158,
  196, 259; 18: 86; 27: 56; 29: 79, 187, 253,
  255; 36: 199, 200, 201, 202, 203, 204, 205,
  206, 207, 209; 43: 34; 56: 28; 60: 116; 100:
  65
Ward, Peter 37: 116
Warhola, James 92: 5; 115: 85, 87; 118: 174,
  175, 177
Warner, Ben 159: 171
Warner, Peter 14: 87
Warnick, Elsa 113: 223
Warren, Betsy 2: 101
Warren, Jim 85: 81
Warren, Marion Cray 14: 215
Warshaw, Jerry 30: 197, 198; 42: 165
Wasden, Kevin 102: 162
Washington, Nevin 20: 123
Washington, Phyllis 20: 123
Wasserman, Amy L. 92: 110
Waterman, Stan 11: 76
Watkins-Pitchford, D.J. 6: 215, 217
Watling, James 67: 210; 78: 112; 101: 81;
  117: 189, 190; 127: 119, 120
Watson, Aldren A. 2: 267; 5: 94; 13: 71; 19:
  253; 32: 220; 42: 193, 194, 195, 196, 197,
  198, 199, 200, 201; YABC 2: 202
Watson, G. 83: 162
Watson, Gary 19: 147; 36: 68; 41: 122; 47:
  139
Watson, J.D. 22: 86
Watson, Karen 11: 26
Watson, Mary 117: 193
Watson, Richard Jesse 62: 188, 189
Watson, Wendy 5: 197; 13: 101; 33: 116; 46:
  163; 64: 12; 74: 242, 243; 91: 21; 142: 228
Watt, Melanie 136: 206
Watterson, Bill 66: 223, 225, 226
Watts, Bernadette 4: 227; 103: 182, 183
Watts, James 59: 197; 74: 145; 86: 124

Watts, John 37: 149
Watts, Leslie Elizabeth 150: 207; 165: 106
Watts, Stan 116: 205
Weatherby, Mark Alan 77: 141
Webb, Jennifer 110: 79
Webb, Lanny 142: 175
Webb, Sophie 135: 214
Webber, Helen 3: 141
Webber, Irma E. 14: 238
Weber, Erik 56: 19, 20
Weber, Florence 40: 153
Weber, Jill 127: 227, 228
Weber, Roland 61: 204
Weber, William J. 14: 239
Webster, Jean 17: 241
Weeks, Sarah 162: 39
Wegman, William 78: 243
Wegner, Fritz 14: 250; 20: 189; 44: 165; 86:
  62
Weidenear, Reynold H. 21: 122
Weihs, Erika 4: 21; 15: 299; 72: 201; 107:
  207, 208
Weil, Lisl 7: 203; 10: 58; 21: 95; 22: 188,
  217; 33: 193
Weiman, Jon 50: 162, 165; 52: 103; 54: 78,
  79, 81; 78: 80; 82: 107; 93: 82; 97: 69; 105:
  179
Weiner, Sandra 14: 240
Weiner, Scott 55: 27
Weinhaus, Karen Ann 53: 90; 71: 50; 86: 124
Weisgard, Leonard 1: 65; 2: 191, 197, 204,
  264-265; 5: 108; 21: 42; 30: 200, 201, 203,
  204; 41: 47; 44: 125; 53: 25; 85: 196, 198,
  200, 201; 100: 139, 207; YABC 2: 13
Weiss, Ellen 44: 202
Weiss, Emil 1: 168; 7: 60
Weiss, Harvey 1: 145, 223; 27: 224, 227; 68:
  214; 76: 245, 246, 247
Weiss, Nicki 33: 229
Weissman, Bari 49: 72; 90: 125; 139: 142
Welch, Sheila Kelly 130: 221
Welkes, Allen 68: 218
Wellington, Monica 99: 223; 157: 259, 260,
  261
Welliver, Norma 76: 94
Wellner, Fred 127: 53
Wells, Frances 1: 183
Wells, H.G. 20: 194, 200
Wells, Haru 53: 120, 121
Wells, Rosemary 6: 49; 18: 297; 60: 32; 66:
  203; 69: 215, 216; 114: 227; 118: 149, 150;
  156: 188, 189, 190, 191
Wells, Rufus III 56: 111, 113
Wells, Susan 22: 43
Wendelin, Rudolph 23: 234
Wengenroth, Stow 37: 47
Werenskiold, Erik 15: 6; 62: 17
Werner, Honi 24: 110; 33: 41; 88: 122
Werth, Kurt 7: 122; 14: 157; 20: 214; 39: 128
West, Harry A. 124: 38
Westcott, Nadine Bernard 68: 46; 84: 49; 86:
  133; 106: 199; 111: 78; 113: 111; 130: 224;
  139: 54; 158: 256
Westerberg, Christine 29: 226
Westerduin, Anne 105: 229
Westerman, Johanna 162: 206
Weston, Martha 29: 116; 30: 213; 33: 85, 100;
  53: 181, 182, 183, 184; 77: 95; 80: 152;
  119: 196, 197, 198, 199; 127: 189; 133: 196
Wetherbee, Margaret 5: 3
Wexler, Jerome 49: 73; 150: 129
Whalley, Peter 50: 49
Wheatley, Arabelle 11: 231; 16: 276
Wheeler, Cindy 49: 205
Wheeler, Dora 44: 179
Wheelright, Rowland 15: 81; YABC 2: 286
Whelan, Michael 56: 108; 70: 27, 29, 67, 68,
  148; 74: 18; 84: 14; 91: 195, 196; 95: 147;
  98: 150, 151; 106: 157; 113: 218, 220; 116:
  99, 100
Whelan, Patrick 135: 145

Whistler, Rex 16: 75; 30: 207, 208
White, Craig 110: 130; 119: 193; 130: 33
White, David Omar 5: 56; 18: 6
White, Joan 83: 225
White, Martin 51: 197; 85: 127
Whitear 32: 26
Whitehead, Beck 86: 171
Whitehead, S.B. 154: 132
Whithorne, H.S. 7: 49
Whitney, George Gillett 3: 24
Whitney, Jean 99: 53
Whitson, Paul 102: 161
Whittam, Geoffrey 30: 191
Whyte, Mary 96: 127
Wiberg, Harald 38: 127; 93: 215
Wick, Walter 77: 128
Wickstrom, Sylvie 106: 87; 169: 180
Widener, Terry 105: 230; 106: 7; 163: 23
Wiese, Kurt 3: 255; 4: 206; 14: 17; 17: 18-19;
  19: 47; 24: 152; 25: 212; 32: 184; 36: 211,
  213, 214, 215, 216, 217, 218; 45: 161; 100:
  92
Wiesner, David 33: 47; 51: 106; 57: 67; 58:
  55; 64: 78, 79, 81; 69: 233; 72: 247, 248-49,
  251, 252-53, 254; 83: 134; 104: 31; 117:
  197, 199, 200, 202; 139: 223, 224; 151: 51
Wiesner, William 4: 100; 5: 200, 201; 14: 262
Wiggins, George 6: 133
Wijngaard, Juan 111: 36; 114: 124
Wikkelsoe, Otto 45: 25, 26
Wikland, Ilon 5: 113; 8: 150; 38: 124, 125,
  130; 127: 162
Wikler, Madeline 114: 233
Wilbur, C. Keith, M.D. 27: 228
Wilburn, Kathy 53: 102; 68: 234
Wilcox, Cathy 105: 123
Wilcox, J.A.J. 34: 122
Wilcox, R. Turner 36: 219
Wild, Jocelyn 46: 220-221, 222; 80: 117
Wilde, George 7: 139
Wildsmith, Brian 16: 281-282; 18: 170-171;
  66: 25; 69: 224-225, 227; 77: 103; 83: 218;
  124: 214, 217, 219
Wildsmith, Mike 140: 229
Wilhelm, Hans 58: 189, 191; 73: 157; 77:
  127; 135: 229, 230, 233, 234
Wilkin, Eloise 36: 173; 49: 208, 209, 210
Wilkinson, Barry 50: 213
Wilkinson, Gerald 3: 40
Wilkon, Jozef 31: 183, 184; 71: 206, 207, 209;
  133: 222
Wilks, Mike 34: 24; 44: 203
Willems, Mo 154: 245, 246, 247
Willey, Bee 103: 129; 139: 159
Willhoite, Michael A. 71: 214
Williams, Berkeley, Jr. 64: 75
Williams, Ferelith Eccles 22: 238
Williams, Garth 1: 197; 2: 49, 270; 4: 205;
  15: 198, 302-304, 307; 16: 34; 18: 283,
  298-301; 29: 177, 178, 179, 232-233,
  241-245, 248; 40: 106; 66: 229, 230, 231,
  233, 234; 71: 192; 73: 218, 219, 220; 78:
  261; 100: 251, 252, 255; 136: 117; YABC 2:
  15-16, 19
Williams, J. Scott 48: 28
Williams, Jennifer 102: 201
Williams, Jenny 60: 202; 81: 21; 88: 71
Williams, Kit 44: 206-207, 208, 209, 211, 212
Williams, Marcia 97: 214; 159: 208, 209
Williams, Maureen 12: 238
Williams, Patrick 14: 218
Williams, Richard 44: 93; 72: 229; 74: 133;
  78: 155, 237; 91: 178; 110: 212; 136: 201,
  202, 203; 152: 115
Williams, Sam 124: 222; 153: 11
Williams, Sophy 135: 236
Williams, Vera B. 53: 186, 187, 188, 189; 102:
  201, 202, 203
Williamson, Mel 60: 9
Willingham, Fred 104: 206; 154: 157
Willmore, J.T. 54: 113, 114

Wilson, Anne *160:* 114
Wilson, Charles Banks *17:* 92; *43:* 73
Wilson, Connie *113:* 179
Wilson, Dagmar *10:* 47
Wilson, Dawn *67:* 161; *81:* 120; *113:* 158
Wilson, Edward A. *6:* 24; *16:* 149; *20:* 220-221; *22:* 87; *26:* 67; *38:* 212, 214, 215, 216, 217
Wilson, Forrest *27:* 231
Wilson, Gahan *35:* 234; *41:* 136
Wilson, George *76:* 87
Wilson, Helen Miranda *140:* 61
Wilson, Jack *17:* 139
Wilson, Janet *77:* 154; *96:* 114; *99:* 219, 220; *153:* 64 *106:* 122; *130:* 210; *145:* 178
Wilson, John *22:* 240
Wilson, Maurice *46:* 224
Wilson, Patten *35:* 61
Wilson, Peggy *15:* 4; *84:* 20
Wilson, Rowland B. *30:* 170
Wilson, Sarah *50:* 215
Wilson, Tom *33:* 232
Wilson, W.N. *22:* 26
Wilton, Nicholas *103:* 52
Wilwerding, Walter J. *9:* 202
Wimmer, Mike *63:* 6; *70:* 121; *75:* 186; *76:* 21, 22, 23; *91:* 114; *97:* 45, 68; *98:* 28; *107:* 130; *146:* 21; *149:* 47
Winborn, Marsha *78:* 34; *99:* 70
Winch, John *165:* 233
Winchester, Linda *13:* 231
Wind, Betty *28:* 158
Windham, Kathryn Tucker *14:* 260
Winfield, Alison *115:* 78
Winfield, Wayne *72:* 23
Wing, Gary *64:* 147
Wing, Ron *50:* 85
Wingerter, Linda S. *132:* 199
Winick, Judd *124:* 227, 228, 229
Winslow, Will *21:* 124
Winsten, Melanie Willa *41:* 41
Winter, Jeanette *151:* 240, 241, 242
Winter, Milo *15:* 97; *19:* 221; *21:* 181, 203, 204, 205; *64:* 19; *YABC 2:* 144
Winter, Paula *48:* 227
Winter, Susan *163:* 177
Winters, Greg *70:* 117
Winters, Nina *62:* 194
Wise, Louis *13:* 68
Wiseman, Ann *31:* 187
Wiseman, B. *4:* 233
Wishnefsky, Phillip *3:* 14
Wiskur, Darrell *5:* 72; *10:* 50; *18:* 246
Wisniewski, David *95:* 220, 221
Wisniewski, Robert *95:* 10; *119:* 192
Witschonke, Alan *153:* 149, 150
Witt, Dick *80:* 244
Wittmann, Patrick *162:* 204
Wittman, Sally *30:* 219
Wittner, Dale *99:* 43
Wittwer, Hala *158:* 267
Woehr, Lois *12:* 5
Wohlberg, Meg *12:* 100; *14:* 197; *41:* 255
Wohnoutka, Mike *137:* 68
Wojtowycz, David *167:* 168
Woldin, Beth Weiner *34:* 211
Wolf, Elizabeth *133:* 151
Wolf, J. *16:* 91
Wolf, Janet *78:* 254
Wolf, Linda *33:* 163
Wolfe, Corey *72:* 213
Wolff, Ashley *50:* 217; *81:* 216; *156:* 216, 217
Wondriska, William *6:* 220
Wong, Janet S. *98:* 225; *152:* 43
Wonsetler, John C. *5:* 168

Wood, Audrey *50:* 221, 222, 223; *81:* 219, 221
Wood, Don *50:* 220, 225, 226, 228-229; *81:* 218, 220; *139:* 239, 240
Wood, Grant *19:* 198
Wood, Heather *133:* 108
Wood, Ivor *58:* 17
Wood, Muriel *36:* 119; *77:* 167
Wood, Myron *6:* 220
Wood, Owen *18:* 187; *64:* 202, 204-05, 206, 208, 210
Wood, Ruth *8:* 11
Woodbridge, Curtis *133:* 138
Wooding, Sharon L. *66:* 237
Woodruff, Liza *132:* 239
Woods, John, Jr. *109:* 142
Woodson, Jack *10:* 201
Woodson, Jacqueline *94:* 242
Woodward, Alice *26:* 89; *36:* 81
Wool, David *26:* 27
Woolley, Janet *112:* 75
Woolman, Steven *106:* 47; *163:* 73
Wooten, Vernon *23:* 70; *51:* 170
Worboys, Evelyn *1:* 166-167
Word, Reagan *103:* 204
Wormell, Christopher *154:* 251
Worth, Jo *34:* 143
Worth, Wendy *4:* 133
Wosmek, Frances *29:* 251
Wrenn, Charles L. *38:* 96; *YABC 1:* 20, 21
Wright, Barbara Mullarney *98:* 161
Wright, Dare *21:* 206
Wright-Frierson, Virginia *58:* 194; *110:* 246
Wright, George *YABC 1:* 268
Wright, Joseph *30:* 160
Wronker, Lili Cassel *3:* 247; *10:* 204; *21:* 10
Wummer, Amy *154:* 181
Wyant, Alexander Helwig *110:* 19
Wyatt, David *97:* 9; *101:* 44; *114:* 194; *140:* 20; *167:* 13
Wyatt, Stanley *46:* 210
Wyeth, Andrew *13:* 40; *YABC 1:* 133-134
Wyeth, Jamie *41:* 257
Wyeth, N.C. *13:* 41; *17:* 252-259, 264-268; *18:* 181; *19:* 80, 191, 200; *21:* 57, 183; *22:* 91; *23:* 152; *24:* 28, 99; *35:* 61; *41:* 65; *100:* 206; *YABC 1:* 133, 223; *2:* 53, 75, 171, 187, 317
Wyman, Cherie R. *91:* 42

X

Xuan, YongSheng *119:* 202, 207, 208; *140:* 36

Y

Yaccarino, Dan *141:* 208, 209; *147:* 171
Yakovetic, Joe *59:* 202; *75:* 85
Yalowitz, Paul *93:* 33
Yamaguchi, Marianne *85:* 118
Yamasaki, James *167:* 93
Yang, Jay *1:* 8; *12:* 239
Yap, Weda *6:* 176
Yaroslava
 See Mills, Yaroslava Surmach
Yashima, Taro *14:* 84
Yates, John *74:* 249, 250
Yee, Wong Herbert *115:* 216, 217
Yeo, Brad *135:* 121
Yezerski, Thomas F. *162:* 29
Ylla
 See Koffler, Camilla

Yohn, F.C. *23:* 128; *YABC 1:* 269
Yorinks, Adrienne *144:* 248
Yorke, David *80:* 178
Yoshida, Toshi *77:* 231
Youll, Paul *91:* 218
Youll, Stephen *92:* 227; *118:* 136, 137
Young, Cybéle *167:* 9
Young, Ed *7:* 205; *10:* 206; *40:* 124; *63:* 142; *74:* 250, 251, 252, 253; *75:* 227; *81:* 159; *83:* 98; *94:* 154; *115:* 160; *137:* 162; *YABC 2:* 242
Young, Mary O'Keefe *77:* 95; *80:* 247; *134:* 214; *140:* 213
Young, Noela *8:* 221; *89:* 231; *97:* 195
Young, Selina *153:* 12
Yun, Cheng Mung *60:* 143

Z

Zacharow, Christopher *88:* 98
Zacks, Lewis *10:* 161
Zadig *50:* 58
Zaffo, George *42:* 208
Zagwyn, Deborah Turney *138:* 227
Zaid, Barry *50:* 127; *51:* 201
Zaidenberg, Arthur *34:* 218, 219, 220
Zalben, Jane Breskin *7:* 211; *79:* 230, 231, 233
Zallinger, Jean *4:* 192; *8:* 8, 129; *14:* 273; *68:* 36; *80:* 254; *115:* 219, 220, 222
Zallinger, Rudolph F. *3:* 245
Zebot, George *83:* 214
Zeck, Gerry *40:* 232
Zeifert, Harriet *154:* 265, 267
Zeiring, Bob *42:* 130
Zeldich, Arieh *49:* 124; *62:* 120
Zeldis, Malcah *86:* 239; *94:* 198; *146:* 265, 266
Zelinsky, Paul O. *14:* 269; *43:* 56; *49:* 218, 219, 220, 221, 222-223; *53:* 111; *68:* 195; *102:* 219, 220, 221, 222; *154:* 255, 256, 257
Zelvin, Diana *72:* 190; *76:* 101; *93:* 207
Zemach, Kaethe *149:* 250
Zemach, Margot *3:* 270; *8:* 201; *21:* 210-211; *27:* 204, 205, 210; *28:* 185; *49:* 22, 183, 224; *53:* 151; *56:* 146; *70:* 245, 246; *92:* 74
Zeman, Ludmila *153* 212
Zemsky, Jessica *10:* 62
Zepelinsky, Paul *35:* 93
Zerbetz, Evon *127:* 34; *158:* 109
Zhang, Ange *101:* 190
Zhang, Son Nang *163:* 113
Ziegler, Jack *84:* 134
Zimdars, Berta *129:* 155
Zimet, Jay *147:* 94; *152:* 74
Zimic, Tricia *72:* 95
Zimmer, Dirk *38:* 195; *49:* 71; *56:* 151; *65:* 214; *84:* 159; *89:* 26; *147:* 224
Zimmer, Tracie Vaughn *169:* 183
Zimmermann, H. Werner *101:* 223; *112:* 197
Zimnik, Reiner *36:* 224
Zinkeisen, Anna *13:* 106
Zinn, David *97:* 97
Zoellick, Scott *33:* 231
Zonia, Dhimitri *20:* 234-235
Zorn, Peter A., Jr. *142:* 157
Zudeck, Darryl *58:* 129; *63:* 98; *80:* 52
Zug, Mark *88:* 131
Zuma *99:* 36
Zvorykin, Boris *61:* 155
Zweifel, Francis *14:* 274; *28:* 187
Zwerger, Lisbeth *54:* 176, 178; *66:* 246, 247, 248; *130:* 230, 231, 232, 233
Zwinger, Herman H. *46:* 227
Zwolak, Paul *67:* 69, 71, 73, 74

Author Index

The following index gives the number of the volume in which an author's biographical sketch, Autobiography Feature, Brief Entry, or Obituary appears.

This index includes references to all entries in the following series, which are also published by The Gale Group.

YABC—*Yesterday's Authors of Books for Children: Facts and Pictures about Authors and Illustrators of Books for Young People from Early Times to 1960*
CLR—*Children's Literature Review: Excerpts from Reviews, Criticism, and Commentary on Books for Children*
SAAS—*Something about the Author Autobiography Series*

A

Aaron, Chester 1923- *74*
  Earlier sketch in SATA *9*
  See also SAAS *12*
Aaseng, Nate
  See Aaseng, Nathan
Aaseng, Nathan 1953- *88*
  Brief entry *38*
  Earlier sketch in SATA *51*
  See also CLR *54*
  See also SAAS *12*
Abbas, Jailan 1952- *91*
Abbey, Lynn
  See Abbey, Marilyn Lorraine
Abbey, Marilyn Lorraine 1948- *156*
Abbott, Alice
  See Borland, Kathryn Kilby
  and Speicher, Helen Ross S(mith)
Abbott, Jacob 1803-1879 .... *22*
Abbott, Manager Henry
  See Stratemeyer, Edward L.
Abbott, R(obert) Tucker 1919-1995 .... *61*
  Obituary *87*
Abbott, Sarah
  See Zolotow, Charlotte (Gertrude) S(hapiro)
Abbott, Tony 1952- *159*
Abdelsayed, Cindy 1962- *123*
Abdul, Raoul 1929- *12*
Abel, Raymond 1911- *12*
Abell, Kathleen 1938- *9*
Abelove, Joan *110*
Abels, Harriette S(heffer) 1926- *50*
Abercrombie, Barbara (Mattes) 1939- *16*
Abernethy, Robert G(ordon) 1927- *5*
Abisch, Roslyn Kroop 1927- *9*
Abisch, Roz
  See Abisch, Roslyn Kroop
Abodaher, David J. (Naiph) 1919- *17*
Abolafia, Yossi 1944- *60*
  Brief entry *46*
Abrahall, Clare Hoskyns
  See Hoskyns-Abrahall, Clare (Constance Drury)
Abrahams, Hilary (Ruth) 1938- *29*
Abrahams, Robert David 1905-1998 .... *4*
Abrams, Joy 1941- *16*
Abrams, Lawrence F. *58*
  Brief entry *47*

Abrashkin, Raymond 1911-1960 .... *50*
Achebe, (Albert) Chinua(lumogu) 1930- *40*
  Brief entry *38*
  Earlier sketch in SATA *38*
  See also CLR *20*
Ackerman, Diane 1948- *102*
Ackerman, Eugene (Francis) 1888-1974 ..... *10*
Ackerman, Karen 1951- *126*
Ackerman, Susan Yoder 1945- *92*
Ackison, Wendy Wassink 1956- *103*
Ackley, Peggy Jo 1955- *58*
Ackroyd, Peter 1949- *153*
Acorn, John (Harrison) 1958- *79*
Acredolo, Linda (Potter) 1947- *159*
Acs, Laszlo (Bela) 1931- *42*
  Brief entry *32*
Acuff, Selma Boyd 1924- *45*
Ada, Alma Flor 1938- *143*
  Earlier sketches in SATA *43, 84*
  See also CLR *62*
Adair, Gilbert 1944- *98*
Adair, Ian 1942- *53*
Adair, Margaret Weeks (?)-1971 .... *10*
Adam, Cornel
  See Lengyel, Cornel Adam
Adam, Mark
  See Alexander, Marc
Adam, Robert 1948- *93*
Adams, Adrienne 1906- *90*
  Earlier sketch in SATA *8*
  See also CLR *73*
Adams, Andy 1859-1935
  See YABC *1*
Adams, Barbara Johnston 1943- *60*
Adams, Bruin
  See Ellis, Edward S(ylvester)
Adams, Captain Bruin
  See Ellis, Edward S(ylvester)
Adams, Captain J. F. C.
  See Ellis, Edward S(ylvester)
Adams, Dale
  See Quinn, Elisabeth
Adams, Daniel
  See Nicole, Christopher (Robin)
Adams, Debra
  See Speregen, Devra Newberger
Adams, Douglas (Noel) 1952-2001 .... *116*
  Obituary *128*

Adams, Edith
  See Shine, Deborah
Adams, Florence 1932- *61*
Adams, Harriet S(tratemeyer) 1892(?)-1982 . *1*
  Obituary *29*
Adams, Harrison
  See Rathborne, St. George (Henry)
  and Stratemeyer, Edward L.
Adams, Hazard 1926- *6*
Adams, Hazard Simeon
  See Adams, Hazard
Adams, John Anthony 1944- *67*
Adams, Laurie 1941- *33*
Adams, Lowell
  See Joseph, James (Herz)
Adams, Nicholas
  See Pine, Nicholas
Adams, Nicholas
  See Smith, Sherwood
Adams, Nicholas
  See Doyle, Debra
  and Macdonald, James D.
Adams, Pam 1919- *112*
Adams, Richard (George) 1920- *69*
  Earlier sketch in SATA *7*
  See also CLR *20*
Adams, Ruth Joyce *14*
Adams, William Taylor 1822-1897 .... *28*
Adam Smith, Janet (Buchanan) 1905-1999
  .... *63*
Adamson, Gareth 1925-1982(?) *46*
  Obituary *30*
Adamson, George (Worsley) 1913-2005 ..... *30*
Adamson, Graham
  See Groom, Arthur William
Adamson, Joy(-Friederike Victoria) 1910-1980
  .... *11*
  Obituary *22*
Adamson, Wendy Writson 1942- *22*
Addona, Angelo F. 1925- *14*
Addy, Sharon Hart 1943- *108*
Addy, Ted
  See Winterbotham, R(ussell) R(obert)
Adelberg, Doris
  See Orgel, Doris
Adelson, Leone 1908- *11*

Adkins, Jan 1944- *144*
  Earlier sketches in SATA *8, 69*
  See also CLR *77*
  See also SAAS *19*
Adler, C(arole) S(chwerdtfeger) 1932- *126*
  Earlier sketches in SATA *26, 63, 102*
  See also CLR *78*
  See also SAAS *15*
Adler, David A. 1947- *151*
  Earlier sketches in SATA *14, 70, 106*
  See also CLR *108*
Adler, Irene
  See Penzler, Otto
  and Storr, Catherine (Cole)
Adler, Irving 1913- *29*
  Autobiography Feature *164*
  Earlier sketch in SATA *1*
  See also CLR *27*
  See also SAAS *15*
Adler, Larry 1939- *36*
Adler, Peggy *22*
Adler, Ruth 1915-1968 .... *1*
Adlerman, Daniel (Ezra) 1963- *163*
  Earlier sketch in SATA *96*
Adlerman, Kim
  See Adlerman, Kimberly M(arie)
Adlerman, Kimberly M(arie) 1964- *163*
  Earlier sketch in SATA *96*
Adoff, Arnold 1935- *96*
  Earlier sketches in SATA *5, 57*
  See also CLR *7*
  See also SAAS *15*
Adoff, Jaime (Levi) *163*
Adorjan, Carol (Madden) 1934- *71*
  Earlier sketch in SATA *10*
Adrian, Frances
  See Polland, Madeleine A(ngela Cahill)
Adrian, Mary
  See Jorgensen, Mary Venn
Adshead, Gladys L(ucy) 1896-1985 .... *3*
Aesop 620(?)B.C.-560(?)B.C. *64*
  See also CLR *14*
Aesop, Abraham
  See Newbery, John
Affabee, Eric
  See Stine, R.L.
Agapida, Fray Antonio
  See Irving, Washington
Agard, John 1949- *138*
Agard, Nadema 1948- *18*
Agarwal, Deepa 1947- *141*
Agee, Jon 1960- *157*
  Earlier sketch in SATA *116*
Agell, Charlotte 1959- *150*
  Earlier sketch in SATA *99*
Agent Orange
  See Moseley, James W(illett)
Aghill, Gordon
  See Garrett, (Gordon) Randall (Phillip)
  and Silverberg, Robert
Agle, Nan Hayden 1905- *3*
  See also SAAS *10*
Agnew, Edith J(osephine) 1897-1988 .... *11*
Ahern, Margaret McCrohan 1921- *10*
Ahl, Anna Maria 1926- *32*
Ahlberg, Allan 1938- *165*
  Brief entry *35*
  Earlier sketches in SATA *68, 120*
  See also CLR *18*
Ahlberg, Janet 1944-1994 .... *120*
  Brief entry *32*
  Obituary *83*
  Earlier sketch in SATA *68*
  See also CLR *18*
Aichinger, Helga 1937- *4*
Aiken, Clarissa (M.) Lorenz 1899-1992 ..... *12*
  Obituary *109*
Aiken, Conrad (Potter) 1889-1973 .... *30*
  Earlier sketch in SATA *3*

Aiken, Joan (Delano) 1924-2004 .... *73*
  Autobiography Feature *109*
  Obituary *152*
  Earlier sketches in SATA *2, 30*
  See also CLR *90*
  See also SAAS *1*
Ainsley, Alix
  See Steiner, Barbara A(nnette)
Ainsworth, Catherine Harris 1910- *56*
Ainsworth, Norma *9*
Ainsworth, Ruth (Gallard) 1908- *73*
  Earlier sketch in SATA *7*
Ainsworth, William Harrison 1805-1882 ..... *24*
Aistrop, Jack 1916- *14*
Aitken, Amy 1952- *54*
  Brief entry *40*
Aitken, Dorothy 1916- *10*
Aitmatov, Chingiz (Torekulovich) 1928- *56*
  See Aytmatov, Chingiz
Akaba, Suekichi 1910- *46*
Akers, Floyd
  See Baum, L(yman) Frank
Aks, Patricia 1926-1994 .... *68*
Alagoa, Ebiegberi Joe 1933- *108*
Alain
  See Brustlein, Daniel
Alan, David
  See Horsfield, Alan
Alan, Robert
  See Silverstein, Robert Alan
Alarcon, Francisco X(avier) 1954- *104*
Albert, Burton 1936- *22*
Albert, Louise 1928- *157*
Albert, Richard E. 1909-1999 .... *82*
Albert, Susan Wittig 1940- *107*
Alberts, Frances Jacobs 1907-1989 .... *14*
Albertson, Susan
  See Wojciechowski, Susan
Albion, Lee Smith *29*
Alborough, Jez 1959- *149*
  Earlier sketch in SATA *86*
Albrecht, Lillie (Vanderveer H.) 1894-1985
  .... *12*
Albyn, Carole Lisa 1955- *83*
Alcock, Gudrun 1908- *56*
  Brief entry *33*
Alcock, Vivien (Dolores) 1924-2003 .... *76*
  Brief entry *38*
  Obituary *148*
  Earlier sketch in SATA *45*
  See also CLR *26*
Alcorn, John 1935- *31*
  Brief entry *30*
Alcorn, Stephen 1958- *110*
Alcott, Louisa May 1832-1888 .... *100*
  See also YABC *1*
  See also CLR *109*
Alda, Arlene 1933- *158*
  Brief entry *36*
  Earlier sketches in SATA *44, 106*
  See also CLR *93*
Alden, Isabella (Macdonald) 1841-1930 ... *115*
  See also YABC *2*
Alden, Sue
  See Francis, Dorothy Brenner
Alderman, Clifford Lindsey 1902-1988 .... *3*
Alderson, Sue Ann 1940- *59*
  Brief entry *48*
Alding, Peter
  See Jeffries, Roderic (Graeme)
Aldis, Dorothy (Keeley) 1896-1966 .... *2*
Aldiss, Brian W(ilson) 1925- *34*
Aldon, Adair
  See Meigs, Cornelia Lynde
Aldous, Allan (Charles) 1911- *27*
Aldrich, Ann
  See Meaker, Marijane (Agnes)
Aldrich, Bess Streeter 1881-1954
  See CLR *70*
Aldrich, Thomas (Bailey) 1836-1907 .... *114*
  Earlier sketch in SATA *17*

Aldridge, (Harold Edward) James 1918- *87*
Aldridge, Josephine Haskell *14*
Alegria, Ricardo E(nrique) 1921- *6*
Aleksin, Anatolii Georgievich 1924- *36*
Alenov, Lydia 1948- *61*
Alex, Ben (a pseudonym) 1946- *45*
Alex, Marlee (a pseudonym) 1948- *45*
Alexander, Anna B(arbara Cooke) 1913- *1*
Alexander, Anne
  See Alexander, Anna B(arbara Cooke)
Alexander, Ellen 1938- *91*
Alexander, Frances (Laura) 1888-1979 .... *4*
Alexander, Jocelyn Anne Arundel 1930- *22*
Alexander, Linda 1935- *2*
Alexander, Lloyd (Chudley) 1924- *135*
  Earlier sketches in SATA *3, 49, 81, 129*
  See also CLR *48*
  See also SAAS *19*
Alexander, Marc 1929- *117*
Alexander, Martha 1920- *136*
  Earlier sketches in SATA *11, 70*
Alexander, Rae Pace
  See Alexander, Raymond Pace
Alexander, Raymond Pace 1898-1974 .... *22*
Alexander, Rod
  See Pellowski, Michael (Joseph)
Alexander, Sally Hobart 1943- *84*
Alexander, Sue 1933- *136*
  Earlier sketches in SATA *12, 89*
  See also SAAS *15*
Alexeieff, Alexandre A. 1901-1979 .... *14*
Alger, Horatio, Jr.
  See Stratemeyer, Edward L.
Alger, Horatio, Jr. 1832-1899 .... *16*
  See also CLR *87*
Alger, Leclaire (Gowans) 1898-1969 .... *15*
Aliki
  See CLR *71*
  See Brandenberg, Aliki (Liacouras)
Alkema, Chester Jay 1932- *12*
Al-Khalili, Jim 1962- *124*
Alkiviades, Alkis 1953- *105*
Allaby, John Michael
  See Allaby, Michael
Allaby, Michael 1933- *167*
Allamand, Pascale 1942- *12*
Allan, Mabel Esther 1915-1998 .... *75*
  Earlier sketches in SATA *5, 32*
  See also CLR *43*
  See also SAAS *11*
Allan, Nicholas 1956- *123*
  Earlier sketch in SATA *79*
Allan-Meyer, Kathleen 1918- *51*
  Brief entry *46*
Allard, Harry
  See Allard, Harry G(rover), Jr.
Allard, Harry G(rover), Jr. 1928- *102*
  Earlier sketch in SATA *42*
  See also CLR *85*
Allee, Marjorie Hill 1890-1945 .... *17*
Allen, Adam
  See Epstein, Beryl (M. Williams)
  and Epstein, Samuel
Allen, Alex B.
  See Heide, Florence Parry
Allen, Allyn
  See Eberle, Irmengarde
Allen, Betsy
  See Harrison, Elizabeth (Allen) Cavanna
Allen, Bob 1961- *76*
Allen, Gertrude E(lizabeth) 1888-1984 .... *9*
Allen, Grace
  See Hogarth, Grace (Weston Allen)
Allen, Jeffrey (Yale) 1948- *42*
Allen, John
  See Perry, Ritchie (John Allen)
Allen, Jonathan B(urgess) 1957- *131*
  See Allen, Jonathan Dean
Allen, Jonathan Dean
  See Allen, Jonathan B(urgess)

Allen, Judy (Christina) 1941- *124*
  Earlier sketch in SATA *80*
Allen, Kenneth S. 1913-1981 .... *56*
Allen, Leroy 1912- *11*
Allen, Linda 1925- *33*
Allen, Marjorie 1931- *22*
Allen, Maury 1932- *26*
Allen, Merritt Parmelee 1892-1954 .... *22*
Allen, Nancy Kelly 1949- *127*
Allen, Nina (Stroemgren) 1935- *22*
Allen, Pamela (Kay) 1934- *123*
  Earlier sketches in SATA *50, 81*
  See also CLR *44*
Allen, Rodney F. 1938-1999 .... *27*
Allen, Roger MacBride 1957- *105*
Allen, Ruth
  See Peterson, Esther (Allen)
Allen, Samuel W(ashington) 1917- *9*
Allen, T. D.
  See Allen, Terril Diener
Allen, Terril Diener 1908- *35*
  See Allen, T. D.
Allen, Terry D.
  See Allen, Terril Diener
Allen, Thomas B(enton) 1929- *140*
  Earlier sketch in SATA *45*
Allen, Tom
  See Allen, Thomas B(enton)
Allende, Isabel 1942- *163*
  See also CLR *99*
Allerton, Mary
  See Govan, (Mary) Christine Noble
Alley, Robert W.
  See Alley, R.W.
Alley, R.W. *169*
Alleyn, Ellen
  See Rossetti, Christina
Allington, Richard L(loyd) 1947- *39*
  Brief entry *35*
Allison, Amy 1956- *138*
Allison, Bob *14*
Allison, Diane Worfolk *78*
Allison, Linda 1948- *43*
Allman, Barbara 1950- *137*
Allmendinger, David F(rederick), Jr. 1938-
  .... *35*
Allred, Alexandra Powe 1965- *144*
Allred, Gordon T(hatcher) 1930- *10*
Allsop, Kenneth 1920-1973 .... *17*
Almedingen, E. M. *3*
  See Almedingen, Martha Edith von
Almon, Russell
  See Clevenger, William R(ussell)
  and Downing, David A(lmon)
Almond, David 1951- *158*
  Earlier sketch in SATA *114*
  See also CLR *85*
Almquist, Don 1929- *11*
Alphin, Elaine Marie 1955- *139*
  Autobiography Feature *139*
  Earlier sketches in SATA *80, 130*
Alsop, Mary O'Hara 1885-1980 .... *34*
  Obituary *24*
  Earlier sketch in SATA *2*
  See O'Hara, Mary
Alter, Anna 1974- *135*
Alter, Judith (MacBain) 1938- *101*
  Earlier sketch in SATA *52*
Alter, Judy
  See Alter, Judith (MacBain)
Alter, Robert Edmond 1925-1965 .... *9*
Althea
  See Braithwaite, Althea
Altman, Linda Jacobs 1943- *21*
Altman, Suzanne
  See Orgel, Doris
  and Schecter, Ellen
Alton, Steve *169*
Altschuler, Franz 1923- *45*
Altsheler, Joseph A(lexander) 1862-1919
  See YABC *1*

Alvarez, John
  See del Rey, Lester
Alvarez, Joseph A. 1930- *18*
Alvarez, Julia 1950- *129*
al-Windawi, Thura
  See Windawi, Thura al-
Alyer, Philip A.
  See Stratemeyer, Edward L.
Amann, Janet 1951- *79*
Amato, Carol A. 1942- *92*
Amato, Mary 1961- *140*
Ambrose, Stephen E(dward) 1936-2002 ... *138*
  Earlier sketch in SATA *40*
Ambrus, Gyozo Laszlo 1935- *41*
  See Ambrus, Victor G.
Ambrus, Victor G. *1*
  See also SAAS *4*
  See Ambrus, Gyozo Laszlo
Amend, Bill 1962- *147*
Amerman, Lockhart 1911-1969 .... *3*
Ames, Evelyn 1908-1990 .... *13*
  Obituary *64*
Ames, Gerald 1906-1993 .... *11*
  Obituary *74*
Ames, Lee J(udah) 1921- *151*
  Earlier sketch in SATA *3*
Ames, Mildred 1919-1994 .... *85*
  Earlier sketches in SATA *22, 81*
Ammon, Richard 1942- *124*
Amon, Aline 1928- *9*
Amoss, Berthe 1925- *112*
  Earlier sketch in SATA *5*
Anastasio, Dina 1941- *94*
  Brief entry *30*
  Earlier sketch in SATA *37*
Anckarsvard, Karin Inez Maria 1915-1969 ... *6*
Ancona, George 1929- *145*
  Earlier sketches in SATA *12, 85*
  See also SAAS *18*
Anders, C. J.
  See Bennett, Cherie
Anders, Isabel 1946- *101*
Andersdatter, Karla M(argaret) 1938- *34*
Andersen, Hans Christian 1805-1875 .... *100*
  See also YABC *1*
  See also CLR *6*
Andersen, Ted
  See Boyd, Waldo T.
Andersen, Yvonne 1932- *27*
Anderson, Bernice G(oudy) 1894-1997 ...... *33*
Anderson, Bob 1944- *139*
  Earlier sketch in SATA *136*
Anderson, Brad(ley Jay) 1924- *33*
  Brief entry *31*
Anderson, C. C.
  See Anderson, Catherine Corley
Anderson, C(larence) W(illiam) 1891-1971
  .... *11*
Anderson, Catherine C.
  See Anderson, Catherine Corley
Anderson, Catherine Corley 1909-2001 ...... *72*
Anderson, Clifford
  See Gardner, Richard (M.)
Anderson, Daryl Shon 1963- *93*
Anderson, Dave
  See Anderson, David (Poole)
Anderson, David (Poole) 1929- *60*
Anderson, Derek 1969- *169*
Anderson, Eloise Adell 1927- *9*
Anderson, George
  See Groom, Arthur William
Anderson, Grace Fox 1932- *43*
Anderson, J(ohn) R(ichard) L(ane) 1911-1981
  .... *15*
  Obituary *27*
Anderson, Joy 1928- *1*
Anderson, Kevin J(ames) 1962- *117*
  Earlier sketch in SATA *74*
Anderson, Kirsty 1978- *108*
Anderson, Laurie Halse 1961- *132*
  Earlier sketch in SATA *95*

Anderson, LaVere Francis Shoenfelt 1907-1998
  .... *27*
Anderson, Leone Castell 1923- *53*
  Brief entry *49*
Anderson, Lisa G. 1963- *108*
Anderson, Lonzo *2*
  See Anderson, John L(onzo)
Anderson, Lucia (Lewis) 1922- *10*
Anderson, M(atthew) T(obin) 1968- *146*
  Earlier sketch in SATA *97*
Anderson, Madelyn Klein *28*
Anderson, Margaret J(ean) 1931- *27*
  See also SAAS *8*
Anderson, Marilyn D. 1943- *144*
Anderson, Mary 1939- *82*
  Earlier sketch in SATA *7*
  See also SAAS *23*
Anderson, Mona 1910-2004 .... *40*
Anderson, Mrs. Melvin
  See Anderson, Catherine Corley
Anderson, Norman Dean 1928- *22*
Anderson, Peggy Perry 1953- *84*
Anderson, Poul (William) 1926-2001 .... *90*
  Autobiography Feature *106*
  Brief entry *39*
  See also CLR *58*
Anderson, Rachel 1943- *86*
  Earlier sketch in SATA *34*
  See also SAAS *18*
Anderson, Richard
  See Anderson, J(ohn) R(ichard) L(ane)
Anderson, (Tom) Scoular *138*
Anderson, Susan 1952- *90*
Anderson, W. B.
  See Schultz, James Willard
Anderson, Wayne 1946- *147*
  Earlier sketch in SATA *56*
Andre, Evelyn M(arie) 1924- *27*
Andreassen, Karl
  See Boyd, Waldo T.
Andreassi, K. Robert
  See DeCandido, Keith R.A.
Andrew, Ian 1962- *166*
  Earlier sketch in SATA *116*
Andrew, Ian Peter
  See Andrew, Ian
Andrew, Prudence (Hastings) 1924- *87*
Andrews, Benny 1930- *31*
Andrews, Eleanor Lattimore
  See Lattimore, Eleanor Frances
Andrews, Elton V.
  See Pohl, Frederik
Andrews, F(rank) Emerson 1902-1978 .... *22*
Andrews, J(ames) S(ydney) 1934- *4*
Andrews, Jan 1942- *167*
  Brief entry *49*
  Earlier sketches in SATA *58, 98*
Andrews, Julie 1935- *153*
  Earlier sketch in SATA *7*
  See also CLR *85*
Andrews, Roy Chapman 1884-1960 .... *19*
Andrews, Tamra 1959- *129*
Andrews, Wendy
  See Sharmat, Marjorie Weinman
Andrews, William G(eorge) 1930- *74*
Andrezel, Pierre
  See Blixen, Karen (Christentze Dinesen)
Andriani, Renee
  See Williams-Andriani, Renee
Andrist, Ralph K. 1914-2004 .... *45*
Andryszewski, Tricia 1956- *148*
  Earlier sketch in SATA *88*
Angel, Marie 1923- *47*
Angeles, Peter A. 1931- *40*
Angeletti, Roberta 1964- *124*
Angeli, Marguerite (Lofft) de
  See de Angeli, Marguerite (Lofft)
Angell, Madeline 1919- *18*
Angelo, Valenti 1897- *14*

Angelou, Maya 1928- *136*
  Earlier sketch in SATA *49*
  See also CLR *53*
Angier, Bradford -1997 .... *12*
Anglund, Joan Walsh 1926- *2*
  See also CLR *94*
Ango, Fan D.
  See Longyear, Barry B(rookes)
Angrist, Stanley W(olff) 1933- *4*
Anholt, Catherine 1958- *131*
  Earlier sketch in SATA *74*
Anholt, Laurence 1959- *141*
  Earlier sketch in SATA *74*
Anita
  See Daniel, Anita
Anmar, Frank
  See Nolan, William F(rancis)
Annett, Cora
  See Scott, Cora Annett (Pipitone)
Annie-Jo
  See Blanchard, Patricia
  and Suhr, Joanne
Annixter, Jane
  See Sturtzel, Jane Levington
Annixter, Paul
  See Sturtzel, Howard A(llison)
Anno, Mitsumasa 1926- *157*
  Earlier sketches in SATA *5, 38, 77*
  See also CLR *14*
Anrooy, Francine Van
  See Van Anrooy, Francine
Ansary, Mir Tamim 1948- *140*
Anstey, Caroline 1958- *81*
Antell, Will D. 1935- *31*
Anthony, Barbara
  See Barber, Antonia
Anthony, C. L.
  See Smith, Dorothy Gladys
Anthony, Edward 1895-1971 .... *21*
Anthony, John
  See Beckett, Ronald Brymer
  and Ciardi, John (Anthony)
  and Sabini, John Anthony
Anthony, Joseph Patrick 1964- *103*
Anthony, Patricia 1947- *109*
Anthony, Piers 1934- *129*
  Autobiography Feature *129*
  Earlier sketch in SATA *84*
  See also SAAS *22*
Anthony, Susan C(arol) 1953- *87*
Anticaglia, Elizabeth 1939- *12*
Antle, Nancy 1955- *102*
Anton, Michael J(ames) 1940- *12*
Antonacci, Robert J(oseph) 1916- *45*
  Brief entry *37*
Anvil, Christopher
  See Crosby, Harry C., Jr.
Aoki, Hisako 1942- *45*
Apfel, Necia H(alpern) 1930- *51*
  Brief entry *41*
Aphrodite, J.
  See Livingston, Carole
Apikuni
  See Schultz, James Willard
Apostolou, Christine Hale 1955- *128*
  Earlier sketch in SATA *82*
Appel, Allen (R.) 1945- *115*
Appel, Benjamin 1907-1977 .... *39*
  Obituary *21*
Appel, Martin E(liot) 1948- *45*
Appel, Marty
  See Appel, Martin E(liot)
Appelbaum, Diana Muir Karter 1953- *132*
Appelt, Kathi 1954- *129*
  Earlier sketch in SATA *83*
Apperley, Dawn 1969- *135*
Appiah, Peggy 1921-2006 .... *84*
  Earlier sketch in SATA *15*
  See also SAAS *19*

Apple, Margot *152*
  Brief entry *42*
  Earlier sketch in SATA *64*
Applebaum, Stan 1922- *45*
Applegate, K. A.
  See CLR *90*
  See Applegate, Katherine (Alice)
Applegate, Katherine (Alice) 1956- *162*
  Earlier sketch in SATA *109*
  See Applegate, K. A.
Appleton, Victor *67*
  Earlier sketch in SATA *1*
  See Barrett, Neal, Jr.
  and Doyle, Debra
  and Macdonald, James D.
  and Rotsler, (Charles) William
  and Stratemeyer, Edward L.
  and Vardeman, Robert E(dward)
Appleton, Victor II *67*
  Earlier sketch in SATA *1*
  See Goulart, Ron(ald Joseph)
Apsler, Alfred 1907-1982 .... *10*
Aragones, Sergio 1937- *48*
  Brief entry *39*
Araujo, Frank P. 1937- *86*
Arbo, Cris 1950- *103*
Arbuthnot, May Hill 1884-1969 .... *2*
Archambault, John *163*
  Earlier sketches in SATA *67, 112*
Archbold, Rick 1950- *97*
Archer, Colleen Rutherford 1949- *164*
Archer, Jules 1915- *85*
  Earlier sketch in SATA *4*
  See also SAAS *5*
Archer, Marion Fuller 1917- *11*
Archibald, Joe
  See Archibald, Joseph S(topford)
Archibald, Joseph S(topford) 1898-1986 ...... *3*
  Obituary *47*
Ardagh, Philip 1961- *154*
Ardai, Charles 1969- *85*
Arden, Barbi
  See Stoutenburg, Adrien (Pearl)
Arden, William
  See Lynds, Dennis
Ardizzone, Edward (Jeffrey Irving) 1900-1979
  .... *28*
  Obituary *21*
  Earlier sketch in SATA *1*
  See also CLR *3*
Ardley, Neil (Richard) 1937- *121*
  Earlier sketch in SATA *43*
Arehart-Treichel, Joan 1942- *22*
Arena, Felice 1968- *151*
Arenella, Roy 1939- *14*
Argent, Kerry 1960- *138*
Arkin, Alan (Wolf) 1934- *59*
  Brief entry *32*
Arksey, Neil *158*
Arlen, Leslie
  See Nicole, Christopher (Robin)
Arley, Robert
  See Jackson, Mike
Armer, Alberta (Roller) 1904-1986 .... *9*
Armer, Laura Adams 1874-1963 .... *13*
Armistead, John 1941- *130*
Armitage, David 1943- *155*
  Brief entry *38*
  Earlier sketch in SATA *99*
Armitage, Frank
  See Carpenter, John (Howard)
Armitage, Ronda (Jacqueline) 1943- *155*
  Brief entry *38*
  Earlier sketches in SATA *47, 99*
Armour, Richard (Willard) 1906-1989 ...... *14*
  Obituary *61*
Armstrong, George D. 1927- *10*
Armstrong, Gerry (Breen) 1929- *10*
Armstrong, Jeannette (C.) 1948- *102*

Armstrong, Jennifer 1961- *165*
  Autobiography Feature *120*
  Earlier sketches in SATA *77, 111*
  See also CLR *66*
  See also SAAS *24*
Armstrong, Louise *43*
  Brief entry *33*
Armstrong, Martin Donisthorpe 1882-1974
  .... *115*
Armstrong, Ralph Richard
  See Armstrong, Richard
Armstrong, Richard 1903-1986 .... *11*
Armstrong, William H(oward) 1914-1999 .... *4*
  Obituary *111*
  See also CLR *1*
  See also SAAS *7*
Armstrong-Ellis, Carey (Fraser) 1956- *145*
Arndt, Ursula (Martha H.) *56*
  Brief entry *39*
Arneson, D(on) J(on) 1935- *37*
Arnett, Caroline
  See Cole, Lois Dwight
Arnett, Jack
  See Goulart, Ron(ald Joseph)
Arnette, Robert
  See Silverberg, Robert
Arno, Enrico 1913-1981 .... *43*
  Obituary *28*
Arnold, Caroline 1944- *131*
  Brief entry *34*
  Earlier sketches in SATA *36, 85*
  See also CLR *61*
  See also SAAS *23*
Arnold, Elizabeth 1944- *164*
Arnold, Elliott 1912-1980 .... *5*
  Obituary *22*
Arnold, Emily 1939- *76*
  Earlier sketch in SATA *50*
  See McCully, Emily Arnold
Arnold, Katya 1947- *168*
  Earlier sketches in SATA *82, 115*
Arnold, Marsha Diane 1948- *147*
  Earlier sketch in SATA *93*
Arnold, Nick 1961- *113*
Arnold, Oren 1900-1980 .... *4*
Arnold, Susan (Riser) 1951- *58*
Arnold, Tedd 1949- *160*
  Earlier sketches in SATA *69, 116*
Arnoldy, Julie
  See Bischoff, Julia Bristol
Arnosky, James Edward 1946- *160*
  Earlier sketch in SATA *22*
  See also CLR *93*
  See Arnosky, Jim
Arnosky, Jim *118*
  Earlier sketch in SATA *70*
  See also CLR *93*
  See Arnosky, James Edward
Arnott, Kathleen 1914- *20*
Arnov, Boris, Jr. 1926- *12*
Arnow, Harriette (Louisa) Simpson 1908-1986
  .... *42*
  Obituary *47*
Arnsteen, Katy Keck 1934- *68*
Arnstein, Helene S(olomon) 1915- *12*
Arntson, Herbert E(dward) 1911-1982 ...... *12*
Aroner, Miriam *82*
Aronson, Marc 1948- *126*
Aronson, Virginia 1954- *122*
Arora, Shirley (Lease) 1930- *2*
Arrigan, Mary 1943- *142*
Arrington, Stephen L(ee) 1948- *97*
Arrley, Richmond
  See Delany, Samuel R(ay), Jr.
Arrowood, (McKendrick Lee) Clinton 1939-
  .... *19*
Artell, Mike 1948- *134*
  Earlier sketch in SATA *89*
Arthur, Robert (Andrew) 1909-1969
  See Arthur, Robert, (Jr.)

Arthur, Robert, (Jr.) 1909-1969 .... *118*
  See Arthur, Robert (Andrew)
Arthur, Ruth M(abel) 1905-1979 .... *26*
  Earlier sketch in SATA *7*
Artis, Vicki Kimmel 1945- *12*
Artzybasheff, Boris (Miklailovich) 1899-1965
  .... *14*
Aruego, Ariane
  See Dewey, Ariane
Aruego, Jose (Espiritu) 1932- *125*
  Earlier sketches in SATA *6, 68*
  See also CLR *5*
Arundel, Honor (Morfydd) 1919-1973 .... *4*
  Obituary *24*
  See also CLR *35*
Arundel, Jocelyn
  See Alexander, Jocelyn Anne Arundel
Arvey, Michael 1948- *79*
Asare, Meshack (Yaw) 1945- *139*
  Earlier sketch in SATA *86*
Asaro, Catherine Ann 1955- *165*
  Earlier sketch in SATA *101*
Asay, Donna Day 1945- *127*
Asbjornsen, Peter Christen 1812-1885 .... *15*
  See also CLR *104*
  See Asbjornsen and Moe
Asch, Frank 1946- *154*
  Earlier sketches in SATA *5, 66, 102*
Ash, Jutta 1942- *38*
Ashabranner, Brent 1921- *166*
  Earlier sketches in SATA *1, 67, 130*
  See also CLR *28*
  See also SAAS *14*
Ashabranner, Brent Kenneth
  See Ashabranner, Brent
Ashbless, William
  See Powers, Tim(othy Thomas)
Ashby, Gil 1958- *146*
Ashby, Gwynneth 1922- *44*
Ashby, Yvonne 1955- *121*
Ashe, Arthur (Robert, Jr.) 1943-1993 .... *65*
  Obituary *87*
Ashe, Geoffrey (Thomas) 1923- *17*
  Autobiography Feature *125*
Ashe, Mary Ann
  See Lewis, Mary (Christianna)
Asher, Sandra Fenichel 1942- *158*
  Autobiography Feature *158*
  Earlier sketch in SATA *118*
  See Asher, Sandy
Asher, Sandy *71*
  Brief entry *34*
  Earlier sketch in SATA *36*
  See also SAAS *13*
  See Asher, Sandra Fenichel
Asheron, Sara
  See Moore, Lilian
Ashey, Bella
  See Breinburg, Petronella
Ashford, Daisy
  See Ashford, Margaret Mary
Ashford, Jeffrey
  See Jeffries, Roderic (Graeme)
Ashford, Margaret Mary 1881-1972 .... *10*
Ashley, Bernard (John) 1935- *155*
  Brief entry *39*
  Earlier sketches in SATA *47, 79*
  See also CLR *4*
Ashley, Elizabeth
  See Salmon, Annie Elizabeth
Ashley, Ray
  See Abrashkin, Raymond
Ashman, Linda 1960- *150*
Ashton, Lorayne
  See Gottfried, Theodore Mark
Ashton, Warren T.
  See Adams, William Taylor
Asimov, Isaac 1920-1992 .... *74*
  Earlier sketches in SATA *1, 26*
  See also CLR *79*
Asinof, Eliot 1919- *6*

Aska, Warabe *56*
  See Masuda, Takeshi
Asprin, Robert L(ynn) 1946- *92*
Asquith, Cynthia Mary Evelyn (Charteris)
  1887-1960 .... *107*
Asquith, Ros *153*
Astley, Juliet
  See Lofts, Norah (Robinson)
Aston, James
  See White, T(erence) H(anbury)
Ata, Te 1895-1995 .... *119*
Atene, Ann
  See Atene, (Rita) Anna
Atene, (Rita) Anna 1922- *12*
Atheling, William, Jr.
  See Blish, James (Benjamin)
Atkins, Catherine *160*
Atkins, Jeannine 1953- *113*
Atkinson, Allen G. 1953(?)-1987 .... *60*
  Brief entry *46*
  Obituary *55*
Atkinson, M. E.
  See Frankau, Mary Evelyn Atkinson
Atkinson, Margaret Fleming *14*
Attema, Martha 1949- *156*
  Earlier sketch in SATA *94*
Atticus
  See Davies, Hunter
  and Fleming, Ian (Lancaster)
  and Pawle, Gerald Strachan
  and Wilson, (Thomas) Woodrow
Atwater, Florence (Hasseltine Carroll)
  1896-1979 .... *66*
  Earlier sketch in SATA *16*
  See also CLR *19*
Atwater, Montgomery Meigs 1904-1976 .... *15*
Atwater, Richard (Tupper) 1892-1948 .... *66*
  Brief entry *27*
  Earlier sketch in SATA *54*
  See also CLR *19*
Atwater-Rhodes, Amelia 1984- *124*
Atwell, Debby 1953- *150*
  Earlier sketch in SATA *87*
Atwood, Ann (Margaret) 1913-1992 .... *7*
Atwood, Margaret 1939- *50*
Atwood, Margaret Eleanor
  See Atwood, Margaret
Aubrey, Meg Kelleher 1963- *83*
Aubry, Claude B. 1914-1984 .... *29*
  Obituary *40*
Auch, Mary Jane *138*
Auclair, Joan 1960- *68*
Auel, Jean M(arie) 1936- *91*
Auer, Martin 1951- *77*
Augarde, Steve 1950- *159*
  Earlier sketch in SATA *25*
Augelli, John P(at) 1921- *46*
Augustine, Mildred
  See Benson, Mildred (Augustine Wirt)
Ault, Phil
  See Ault, Phillip H(alliday)
Ault, Phillip H(alliday) 1914- *23*
Ault, Rosalie Sain 1942- *38*
Ault, Roz
  See Ault, Rosalie Sain
Aung, (Maung) Htin 1909- *21*
Aunt Weedy
  See Alcott, Louisa May
Auseon, Andrew 1976- *166*
Austen, Carrie
  See Bennett, Cherie
Austin, Carrie
  See Seuling, Barbara
Austin, Elizabeth S. 1907-1977 .... *5*
Austin, Harry
  See McInerny, Ralph (Matthew)
Austin, Margot 1909(?)-1990 .... *11*
  Obituary *66*
Austin, Oliver L(uther), Jr. 1903-1988 .... *7*
  Obituary *59*
Austin, Patricia 1950- *137*

Austin, R. G.
  See Gelman, Rita Golden
  and Lamb, Nancy
Austin, Virginia 1951- *152*
  Earlier sketch in SATA *80*
Auteur, Hillary
  See Gottfried, Theodore Mark
Auth, Tony
  See Auth, William Anthony, Jr.
Auth, William Anthony, Jr. 1942- *51*
Autry, Gloria Diener
  See Allen, Terril Diener
Auvil, Peggy A(ppleby) 1954- *122*
Averill, Esther (Holden) 1902-1992 .... *28*
  Obituary *72*
  Earlier sketch in SATA *1*
Avery, A. A.
  See Montgomery, Rutherford George
Avery, Al
  See Montgomery, Rutherford George
Avery, Gillian (Elise) 1926- *137*
  Autobiography Feature *137*
  Earlier sketches in SATA *7, 75*
  See also SAAS *6*
Avery, Kay 1908- *5*
Avery, Lorraine
  See Older, Effin
  and Older, Jules
Avery, Lynn
  See Cole, Lois Dwight
Avi *108*
  Earlier sketch in SATA *71*
  See also CLR *68*
  See Wortis, Avi
Avishai, Susan 1949- *82*
Awdry, Christopher Vere 1940- *67*
Awdry, Wilbert Vere 1911-1997 .... *94*
  See also CLR *23*
Axelrod, Amy *131*
Axelsen, Stephen 1953- *165*
Axton, David
  See Koontz, Dean R.
Ayars, James S(terling) 1898-1986 .... *4*
Aye, A. K.
  See Edwards, Hazel (Eileen)
Ayer, Eleanor H. 1947-1998 .... *121*
  Earlier sketch in SATA *78*
Ayer, Jacqueline 1930- *13*
Ayer, Margaret (?)-1981 .... *15*
Aylesworth, Jim 1943- *139*
  Earlier sketches in SATA *38, 89*
  See also CLR *89*
Aylesworth, Thomas G(ibbons) 1927-1995 . *88*
  Earlier sketch in SATA *4*
  See also CLR *6*
  See also SAAS *17*
Aylward, Marcus
  See Alexander, Marc
Aymar, Brandt 1911- *22*
Ayme, Marcel (Andre) 1902-1967 .... *91*
  See also CLR *25*
Ayres, Becky
  See Hickox, Rebecca (Ayres)
Ayres, Pam 1947- *90*
Aytmatov, Chingiz
  See Aitmatov, Chingiz (Torekulovich)
Ayto, Russell 1960- *166*
  Earlier sketch in SATA *111*
Azaid
  See Zaidenberg, Arthur
Azar, Penny 1952- *121*
Azarian, Mary 1940- *112*

B

Baastad, Babbis Friis
  See Friis-Baastad, Babbis Ellinor
Bab
  See Gilbert, W(illiam) S(chwenck)

Babbis, Eleanor
 See Friis-Baastad, Babbis Ellinor
Babbitt, Lucy Cullyford 1960- *85*
Babbitt, Natalie (Zane Moore) 1932- *106*
 Earlier sketches in SATA *6, 68*
 See also CLR *53*
 See also SAAS *5*
Babcock, Chris 1963- *83*
Babcock, Dennis Arthur 1948- *22*
Baber, Carolyn Stonnell 1936- *96*
Baca, Maria 1951- *104*
Bach, Alice (Hendricks) 1942- *93*
 Brief entry *27*
 Earlier sketch in SATA *30*
Bach, Bellamy
 See Windling, Terri
Bach, Mary 1960- *125*
Bach, Richard 1936- *13*
Bach, Richard David
 See Bach, Richard
Bache, Ellyn 1942- *124*
Bachel, Beverly K. 1957- *142*
Bachman, Fred 1949- *12*
Bachman, Richard
 See King, Stephen
Bachrach, Deborah *80*
Bacmeister, Rhoda W(arner) 1893-1991 ..... *11*
Bacon, Betty
 See Bacon, Elizabeth
Bacon, Elizabeth 1914-2001 .... *3*
 Obituary *131*
Bacon, Joan Chase
 See Bowden, Joan Chase
Bacon, Josephine Dodge (Daskam) 1876-1961
 .... *48*
Bacon, Margaret Frances
 Obituary *50*
 See Bacon, Peggy
Bacon, Margaret Hope 1921- *6*
Bacon, Martha Sherman 1917-1981 .... *18*
 Obituary *27*
 See also CLR *3*
Bacon, Melvin (L.) 1950- *93*
Bacon, Peggy 1895-1987 .... *2*
 See Bacon, Margaret Frances
Bacon, R(onald) L(eonard) 1924- *84*
 Earlier sketch in SATA *26*
Baden, Robert 1936- *70*
Baden-Powell, Robert (Stephenson Smyth)
 1857-1941 .... *16*
Badt, Karin L(uisa) 1963- *91*
Baehr, Kingsley M. 1937- *89*
Baehr, Patricia (Goehner) 1952- *65*
Baer, Jill
 See Gilbert, (Agnes) Joan (Sewell)
Baer, Judy 1951- *71*
Baer, Julie 1960- *161*
Baerg, Harry J(ohn) 1909-1996 .... *12*
Baeten, Lieve 1954- *83*
Bagert, Brod 1947- *80*
Baggette, Susan K. 1942- *126*
Bagnold, Enid 1889-1981 .... *25*
 Earlier sketch in SATA *1*
Bahlke, Valerie Worth 1933-1994 .... *81*
 See Worth, Valerie
Bahous, Sally 1939- *86*
Bahr, Mary (Madelyn) 1946- *95*
Bahr, Robert 1940- *38*
Bahti, Tom 1926-1972 .... *57*
 Brief entry *31*
Bailey, Alice Cooper 1890-1978 .... *12*
Bailey, Anne 1958- *71*
Bailey, Bernadine (Freeman) 1901-1995 ..... *14*
Bailey, Carolyn Sherwin 1875-1961 .... *14*
Bailey, Debbie 1954- *123*
Bailey, Donna (Veronica Anne) 1938- *68*
Bailey, Jane H(orton) 1916- *12*
Bailey, John (Robert) 1940- *52*
Bailey, Linda 1948- *107*
Bailey, Maralyn Collins (Harrison) 1941- ... *12*

Bailey, Matilda
 See Radford, Ruby L(orraine)
Bailey, Maurice Charles 1932- *12*
Bailey, Pearl (Mae) 1918-1990 .... *81*
Bailey, Ralph Edgar 1893-1982 .... *11*
Bailey, Sheila (Lucas) 1960- *155*
Baillie, Allan (Stuart) 1943- *151*
 Earlier sketch in SATA *87*
 See also CLR *49*
 See also SAAS *21*
Baines, John (David) 1943- *71*
Bains, Larry
 See Sabin, Louis
Baird, Alison 1963- *138*
Baird, Bil 1904-1987 .... *30*
 Obituary *52*
Baird, Thomas (P.) 1923-1990 .... *45*
 Brief entry *39*
 Obituary *64*
Baird, William Britton
 See Baird, Bil
Baity, Elizabeth Chesley 1907-1989 .... *1*
Baiul, Oksana 1977- *108*
Bakeless, John (Edwin) 1894-1978 .... *9*
Bakeless, Katherine Little 1895-1992 .... *9*
Baker, Alan 1951- *146*
 Earlier sketches in SATA *22, 93*
Baker, Augusta 1911-1998 .... *3*
Baker, Betty Lou 1928-1987 .... *73*
 Obituary *54*
 Earlier sketch in SATA *5*
Baker, Carin Greenberg 1959- *79*
Baker, Charlotte 1910- *2*
Baker, Christopher W. 1952- *144*
Baker, (Mary) Elizabeth (Gillette) 1923- *7*
Baker, Gayle Cunningham 1950- *39*
Baker, James W. 1924- *65*
 Earlier sketch in SATA *22*
Baker, James W. 1926- *122*
Baker, Janice E(dla) 1941- *22*
Baker, Jeannie 1950- *156*
 Earlier sketches in SATA *23, 88*
 See also CLR *28*
Baker, Jeffrey J(ohn) W(heeler) 1931- *5*
Baker, Jim
 See Baker, James W.
Baker, Ken 1962- *133*
Baker, Laura Nelson 1911- *3*
Baker, Margaret 1890-1965 .... *4*
Baker, Margaret J(oyce) 1918- *12*
 See also SAAS *8*
Baker, Mary Gladys Steel 1892-1974 .... *12*
Baker, (Robert) Michael (Graham) 1938- *4*
Baker, Nina (Brown) 1888-1957 .... *15*
Baker, Pamela J. 1947- *66*
Baker, Rachel 1904-1978 .... *2*
 Obituary *26*
Baker, Rosalie F. 1945- *166*
Baker, Samm Sinclair 1909-1997 .... *12*
 Obituary *96*
Baker, Susan (Catherine) 1942-1991 .... *29*
Balaam
 See Lamb, G(eoffrey) F(rederick)
Balan, Bruce 1959- *113*
Balcavage, Dynise 1965- *137*
Balch, Glenn 1902-1989 .... *3*
 Obituary *83*
 See also SAAS *11*
Balderose, Nancy Ward 1952- *93*
Balderson, Margaret 1935- *151*
Baldry, Cherith 1947- *167*
 Earlier sketch in SATA *72*
Balducci, Carolyn (Feleppa) 1946- *5*
Baldwin, Alex
 See Butterworth, W.E.
Baldwin, Anne Norris 1938- *5*
Baldwin, Clara *11*
Baldwin, Gordo
 See Baldwin, Gordon C(ortis)
Baldwin, Gordon C(ortis) 1908-1983 .... *12*
Baldwin, James 1841-1925 .... *24*

Baldwin, James (Arthur) 1924-1987 .... *9*
 Obituary *54*
Baldwin, Louis 1919- *110*
Baldwin, Margaret
 See Weis, Margaret Edith
Baldwin, Stan(ley C.) 1929- *62*
 Brief entry *28*
Bales, Carol Ann 1940- *57*
 Brief entry *29*
Balet, Jan (Bernard) 1913- *11*
Balgassi, Haemi 1971- *131*
Balian, Lorna 1929- *91*
 Earlier sketch in SATA *9*
Balit, Christina 1961- *159*
 Earlier sketch in SATA *102*
Ball, Duncan 1941- *73*
Ball, Zachary
 See Janas, Frankie-Lee
 and Masters, Kelly R(ay)
Ballantine, Lesley Frost
 See Frost, Lesley
Ballantyne, R(obert) M(ichael) 1825-1894 . *24*
Ballard, J(ames) G(raham) 1930- *93*
Ballard, Jane
 See Gorman, Carol
Ballard, John 1945- *110*
Ballard, Lowell C(lyne) 1904-1986 .... *12*
 Obituary *49*
Ballard, (Charles) Martin 1929- *1*
Ballard, Mignon F(ranklin) 1934- *64*
 Brief entry *49*
Ballard, Robert D(uane) 1942- *85*
 See also CLR *60*
Ballard, Robin 1965- *126*
Balliett, Blue 1955- *156*
Ballinger, Bryan 1968- *161*
Ballouhey, Pierre 1944- *90*
Balogh, Penelope 1916-1975 .... *1*
 Obituary *34*
Balow, Tom 1931- *12*
Baltazzi, Evan S(erge) 1921- *90*
Baltimore, J.
 See Catherall, Arthur
Baltzer, Hans (Adolf) 1900- *40*
Bambara, Toni Cade 1939-1995 .... *112*
Bamfylde, Walter
 See Bevan, Tom
Bamman, Henry A. 1918- *12*
Banat, D. R.
 See Bradbury, Ray (Douglas)
Bancroft, Griffing 1907-1999 .... *6*
Bancroft, Laura
 See Baum, L(yman) Frank
Bandel, Betty 1912- *47*
Baner, Skulda Vanadis 1897-1964 .... *10*
Banfill, A. Scott 1956- *98*
Bang, Betsy 1912- *48*
 Brief entry *37*
Bang, Garrett
 See Bang, Molly Garrett
Bang, Molly Garrett 1943- *158*
 Earlier sketches in SATA *24, 69, 111*
 See also CLR *8*
Bang-Campbell, Monika *140*
Banjo, The
 See Paterson, A(ndrew) B(arton)
Banke, Cecile de
 See de Banke, Cecile
Banks, Kate 1960- *134*
Banks, Lynne Reid
 See CLR *86*
 See Reid Banks, Lynne
Banks, Michael A. 1951- *101*
Banks, Sara (Jeanne Gordon Harrell) *26*
 See Harrell, Sara (Jeanne) Gordon
Bannatyne-Cugnet, (Elizabeth) Jo(-Anne)
 1951- *101*
Banner, Angela
 See CLR *24*
 See Maddison, Angela Mary

Bannerman, Helen (Brodie Cowan Watson)
  1862(?)-1946 19
  See also CLR 21
Banning, Evelyn I. 1903-1993 36
Bannon, Laura (?)-1963 6
Bannor, Brett 1959- 143
Bantock, Nick 1950(?)- 95
Barasch, Lynne 1939- 126
  Earlier sketch in SATA 74
Barbalet, Margaret 1949- 77
Barbary, James
  See Beeching, Jack
Barbash, Shepard 1957- 84
Barbe, Walter Burke 1926- 45
Barber, Antonia 1932- 163
  Earlier sketch in SATA 29
Barber, Lynda
  See Graham-Barber, Lynda
Barber, Lynda Graham
  See Graham-Barber, Lynda
Barber, Richard (William) 1941- 35
Barbera, Joe
  See Barbera, Joseph Roland
Barbera, Joseph Roland 1911- 51
Barberis, Juan C(arlos) 1920- 61
Barbour, Karen 1956- 121
  Earlier sketch in SATA 63
Barbour, Ralph Henry 1870-1944 16
Barclay, Bill
  See Moorcock, Michael
Barclay, Isabel
  See Dobell, I(sabel) M(arian) B(arclay)
Barclay, William Ewert
  See Moorcock, Michael
Bardhan-Quallen, Sudipta 168
Bare, Arnold Edwin 1920- 16
Bare, Colleen Stanley 32
Bargar, Gary W. 1947-1985 63
Barger, Jan 1948- 147
Barish, Matthew 1907-2000 12
Barkan, Joanne 127
  Earlier sketch in SATA 77
Barker, Albert W. 1900- 8
Barker, Carol (Minturn) 1938- 31
Barker, Cicely Mary 1895-1973 49
  Brief entry 39
  See also CLR 88
Barker, Melvern 1907-1989 11
Barker, S(quire) Omar 1894-1985 10
Barker, Will 1913-1983 8
Barkin, Carol 1944- 52
  Earlier sketch in SATA 42
Barklem, Jill 1951- 96
  See also CLR 31
Barkley, James Edward 1941- 6
Barks, Carl 1901-2000 37
Barley, Janet Crane 1934- 95
Barnaby, Ralph S(tanton) 1893-1986 9
Barnard, A. M.
  See Alcott, Louisa May
Barnard, Bryn 1956- 169
  Earlier sketch in SATA 115
Barne, Kitty
  See Barne, Marion Catherine
Barne, Marion Catherine 1883-1957 97
  See Barne, Kitty
Barner, Bob 1947- 136
  Earlier sketch in SATA 29
Barnes, (Frank) Eric Wollencott 1907-1962
  22
Barnes, Joyce Annette 1958- 85
Barnes, Laura T. 1958- 119
Barnes, Loutricia
  See Barnes-Svarney, Patricia L(ou)
Barnes, Michael 1934- 55
Barnes-Murphy, Frances 1951- 88
Barnes-Murphy, Rowan 1952- 88
Barnes-Svarney, Patricia L(ou) 1953- ... 67
Barnet, Nancy 1954- 84
Barnett, Ivan 1947- 70
Barnett, Lincoln (Kinnear) 1909-1979 ... 36

Barnett, Moneta 1922-1976 33
Barnett, Naomi 1927- 40
Barney, Maginel Wright 1881(?)-1966 ... 39
  Brief entry 32
Barnhart, Clarence L(ewis) 1900-1993 .. 48
  Obituary 78
Barnouw, Victor 1915-1989 43
  Brief entry 28
Barnstone, Willis 1927- 20
Barnum, Jay Hyde 1888(?)-1962 20
Barnum, P. T., Jr.
  See Stratemeyer, Edward L.
Barnum, Richard 67
  Earlier sketch in SATA 1
Barnum, Theodore
  See Stratemeyer, Edward L.
Baron, Kathy 1954- 90
Baron, Virginia Olsen 1931- 46
  Brief entry 28
Barr, Donald 1921-2004 20
  Obituary 152
Barr, George 1907-1992 2
Barr, Jene 1922-1985 16
  Obituary 42
  See Cohen, Jene Barr
Barr, Nevada 1952- 126
  Earlier sketch in SATA 115
Barrer, Gertrude
  See Barrer-Russell, Gertrude
Barrer-Russell, Gertrude 1921- 27
Barrett, Angela (Jane) 1955- 145
  Earlier sketch in SATA 75
Barrett, Ethel 87
  Brief entry 44
Barrett, Joyce Durham 1943- 138
Barrett, Judi
  See Barrett, Judith
Barrett, Judith 1941- 26
  See also CLR 98
Barrett, Robert T(heodore) 1949- 92
Barrett, Ron 1937- 14
Barrett, Susan (Mary) 1938- 113
Barrett, Tracy 1955- 156
  Earlier sketches in SATA 84, 115
Barrie, J(ames) M(atthew) 1860-1937 ... 100
  See also YABC 1
  See also CLR 16
Barringer, William 1940-1996 153
Barrington, Michael
  See Moorcock, Michael
Barris, George 1925- 47
Barrol, Grady
  See Bograd, Larry
Barron, Rex 1951- 84
Barron, T(homas) A(rchibald) 1952- ... 126
  Earlier sketch in SATA 83
  See also CLR 86
Barron, Tom
  See Barron, T(homas) A(rchibald)
Barrow, Lloyd H. 1942- 73
Barry, Dana (Marie Malloy) 1949- 139
Barry, James P(otvin) 1918- 14
Barry, Katharina Watjen 1936- 4
Barry, Robert (Everett) 1931- 6
Barry, Scott 1952- 32
Barry, Sheila Anne -2003 91
Bartenbach, Jean 1918- 40
Barth, Edna 1914-1980 7
  Obituary 24
Barth, Kelly L. 1964- 152
Barthelme, Donald 1931-1989 7
  Obituary 62
Bartholomew, Barbara 1941- 86
  Brief entry 42
Bartholomew, Jean
  See Beatty, Patricia (Robbins)
Bartlett, Alison 153
Bartlett, Philip A. 1
Bartlett, Robert Merrill 1899-1995 12
Bartoletti, Susan Campbell 1958- 135
  Earlier sketches in SATA 88, 129

Barton, Byron 1930- 126
  Earlier sketches in SATA 9, 90
Barton, Jill(ian) 1940- 75
Barton, May Hollis 67
  Earlier sketch in SATA 1
Barton, Pat 59
  See Arrowsmith, Pat
Bartos-Hoeppner, Barbara 1923- 5
Bartram, Simon 156
Bartsch, Jochen 1906- 39
Baruch, Dorothy W(alter) 1899-1962 21
Barunga, Albert 1912(?)-1977 120
Bas, Rutger
  See Rutgers van der Loeff-Basenau, An(na)
  Maria Margaretha
Base, Graeme (Rowland) 1958- 162
  Earlier sketches in SATA 67, 101
  See also CLR 22
Bash, Barbara 1948- 132
Bashevis, Isaac
  See Singer, Isaac Bashevis
Baskin, Leonard 1922-2000 120
  Brief entry 27
  Earlier sketch in SATA 30
Baskin, Nora Raleigh 1961- 129
Bason, Lillian 1913- 20
Bass, L. G.
  See Geringer, Laura
Bassett, Jeni 1959- 64
  Brief entry 43
Bassett, John Keith
  See Keating, Lawrence A.
Bassett, Lisa 1958- 61
Bassil, Andrea 1948- 96
Bastyra, Judy 108
Bat-Ami, Miriam 1950- 150
  Autobiography Feature 150
  Earlier sketches in SATA 82, 122
Bate, Lucy 1939- 18
Bate, Norman (Arthur) 1916- 5
Bateman, Teresa 1957- 168
  Earlier sketch in SATA 112
Bates, Barbara S(nedeker) 1919- 12
Bates, Betty 19
  See Bates, Elizabeth
Bates, Dianne 1948- 147
Bates, Katharine Lee 1859-1929 113
  See Lincoln, James
Bateson, Catherine 1960- 157
Batey, Tom 1946- 52
  Brief entry 41
Batherman, Muriel
  See Sheldon, Muriel
Batson, Larry 1930- 35
Batt, Tanya Robyn 1970- 131
Battaglia, Aurelius 1910- 50
  Brief entry 33
Batten, H(arry) Mortimer 1888-1958 25
Batten, Mary 1937- 162
  Earlier sketches in SATA 5, 102
Batterberry, Ariane Ruskin 1935- 13
Batterberry, Michael Carver 1932- 32
Battle-Lavert, Gwendolyn 1951- 155
  Earlier sketch in SATA 85
  See Lavert, Gwendolyn Battle
Battles, (Roxy) Edith 1921- 7
Baudouy, Michel-Aime 1909- 7
Bauer, Caroline Feller 1935- 98
  Brief entry 46
  Earlier sketch in SATA 52
  See also SAAS 24
Bauer, Fred 1934- 36
Bauer, Helen 1900-1988 2
Bauer, Joan 1951- 160
  Earlier sketch in SATA 117
Bauer, Jutta 1955- 150
Bauer, Marion Dane 1938- 144
  Autobiography Feature 144
  Earlier sketches in SATA 20, 69, 113
  See also SAAS 9
Bauer, Michael Gerard 1955(?)- 167

Bauer, Steven 1948- 125
Bauerschmidt, Marjorie 1926- 15
Baughman, Dorothy 1940- 61
Baum, Allyn Z(elton) 1924-1997 98
  Earlier sketch in SATA 20
Baum, L. Frank
  See Thompson, Ruth Plumly
Baum, L(yman) Frank 1856-1919 100
  Earlier sketch in SATA 18
  See also CLR 107
Baum, Louis 1948- 64
  Brief entry 52
Baum, Louis F.
  See Baum, L(yman) Frank
Baum, Willi 1931- 4
Baumann, Amy (Brown) Beeching 1922- ... 10
Baumann, Hans 1914- 2
  See also CLR 35
Baumann, Kurt 1935- 21
Baumgartner, Barbara 1939- 86
Baurys, Flo(rence) 1938- 122
Bawden, Nina (Mary Mabey) 1925- 72
  Earlier sketch in SATA 4
  See also CLR 51
  See also SAAS 16
  See Kark, Nina Mary
Bay, Jeanette Graham 1928- 88
Bayer, Harold
  See Gregg, Andrew K.
Bayley, Nicola 1949- 129
  Earlier sketches in SATA 41, 69
Baylor, Byrd 1924- 136
  Earlier sketches in SATA 16, 69
  See also CLR 3
Baynes, Pauline (Diana) 1922- 133
  Earlier sketches in SATA 19, 59
BB
  See Watkins-Pitchford, Denys James
Beach, Charles
  See Reid, (Thomas) Mayne
Beach, Charles Amory 1
Beach, Edward L. 1918-2002 12
  Obituary 140
Beach, Edward Latimer
  See Beach, Edward L.
Beach, Lisa 1957- 111
Beach, Lynn
  See Lance, Kathryn
Beach, Stewart T(aft) 1899-1979 23
Beachcroft, Nina 1931- 18
Beagle, Peter S(oyer) 1939- 130
  Earlier sketch in SATA 60
Beaglehole, Helen 1946- 117
Beale, Fleur 107
Bealer, Alex W(inkler III) 1921-1980 8
  Obituary 22
Beales, Valerie 1915- 74
Beals, Carleton 1893-1979 12
Beame, Rona 1934- 12
Beamer, (George) Charles (Jr.) 1942- 43
Bean, Normal
  See Burroughs, Edgar Rice
Beaney, Jan
  See Udall, Jan Beaney
Beaney, Jane
  See Udall, Jan Beaney
Bear, Carolyn
  See Rayban, Chloe
Bear, Greg(ory Dale) 1951- 105
  Earlier sketch in SATA 65
Bearanger, Marie
  See Messier, Claire
Beard, Charles A(ustin) 1874-1948 18
Beard, Dan(iel Carter) 1850-1941 22
Beard, Darleen Bailey 1961- 96
Bearden, Romare (Howard) 1914(?)-1988 .. 22
  Obituary 56
Beardmore, Cedric
  See Beardmore, George
Beardmore, George 1908-1979 20
Beardsley, Martyn R. 1957- 150

Bearman, Jane (Ruth) 1917- 29
Beaton, Clare 1947- 125
Beatty, Elizabeth
  See Holloway, Teresa (Bragunier)
Beatty, Hetty Burlingame 1907-1971 5
Beatty, Jerome, Jr. 1918- 5
Beatty, John (Louis) 1922-1975 6
  Obituary 25
Beatty, Patricia (Robbins) 1922-1991 73
  Obituary 68
  Earlier sketches in SATA 1, 30
  See also SAAS 4
Beaty, Mary (T.) 1947- 146
Bechard, Margaret 1953- 164
  Earlier sketch in SATA 85
Bechtel, Louise Seaman 1894-1985 4
  Obituary 43
Beck, Barbara L. 1927- 12
Beck, Ian (Archibald) 1947- 138
Becker, Beril 1901-1999 11
Becker, Deborah Zimmett 1955- 138
Becker, Helaine 1961- 142
Becker, John (Leonard) 1901- 12
Becker, John E(mil) 1942- 148
Becker, Joyce 1936- 39
Becker, May Lamberton 1873-1958 33
Becker, Neesa 1951- 123
Beckett, Sheilah 1913- 33
Beckman, Delores 1914-1994 51
Beckman, Gunnel 1910- 6
  See also CLR 25
  See also SAAS 9
Beckman, Kaj
  See Beckman, Karin
Beckman, Karin 1913- 45
Beckman, Per (Frithiof) 1913- 45
Bedard, Michael 1949- 154
  Earlier sketch in SATA 93
  See also CLR 35
Beddows, Eric
  See Nutt, Ken
Bedford, A. N.
  See Watson, Jane Werner
Bedford, Annie North
  See Watson, Jane Werner
Bedford, David 159
Bedoukian, Kerop 1907-1981 53
Bee, Jay
  See Brainerd, John W(hiting)
Beebe, B(urdetta) F(aye) 1
  See Johnson, B(urdetta) F(aye)
Beebe, (Charles) William 1877-1962 19
Beeby, Betty 1923- 25
Beech, Webb
  See Butterworth, W.E.
Beecham, Jahnna 161
Beechcroft, William
  See Hallstead, William F(inn III)
Beeching, Jack 1922- 14
Beeke, Tiphanie 163
Beeler, Janet
  See Shaw, Janet
Beeler, Nelson F(rederick) 1910-1978 13
Beere, Peter 1951- 97
Beers, Dorothy Sands 1917- 9
Beers, Lorna 1897-1989 14
Beers, V(ictor) Gilbert 1928- 130
  Earlier sketch in SATA 9
Beeton, Max
  See Redding, Robert Hull
Begay, Shonto 1954- 137
Begaye, Lisa Shook
  See Beach, Lisa
Begin, Maryjane 1963- 82
Begin-Callanan, Maryjane
  See Begin, Maryjane
Begley, Kathleen A(nne) 1948- 21
Behan, Leslie
  See Gottfried, Theodore Mark
Behler, Deborah A. 1947- 145
Behler, John L. 1943-2006 145

Behn, Harry 1898-1973 2
  Obituary 34
Behnke, Frances L. 8
Behr, Joyce 1929- 15
Behrens, June York 1925- 19
Behrman, Carol H(elen) 1925- 144
  Earlier sketch in SATA 14
Beifuss, John, (Jr.) 1959- 92
Beil, Karen Magnuson 1950- 124
Beiler, Edna 1923- 61
Beinicke, Steve 1956- 69
Beirne, Barbara 1933- 71
Beiser, Arthur 1931- 22
Beiser, Germaine 1931- 11
Belair, Richard L. 1934- 45
Belaney, Archibald Stansfeld 1888-1938 ... 24
  See Grey Owl
Belbin, David 1958- 164
  Earlier sketch in SATA 106
Belden, Wilanne Schneider 1925- 56
Belfrage, Sally 1936-1994 65
  Obituary 79
Belknap, B. H.
  See Ellis, Edward S(ylvester)
Belknap, Boynton
  See Ellis, Edward S(ylvester)
Belknap, Boynton M.D.
  See Ellis, Edward S(ylvester)
Bell, Anthea 1936- 148
  Earlier sketch in SATA 88
Bell, Clare (Louise) 1952- 99
Bell, Corydon Whitten 1894-1980 3
Bell, David Owen 1949- 99
Bell, Emerson
  See Stratemeyer, Edward L.
Bell, Emily Mary
  See Cason, Mabel Earp
Bell, Frank
  See Benson, Mildred (Augustine Wirt)
Bell, Gertrude (Wood) 1911-1987 12
Bell, Hilari 1958- 151
Bell, Jadrien
  See Golden, Christie
Bell, Janet
  See Clymer, Eleanor
Bell, Janet Cheatham 1937- 127
Bell, Krista (Anne Blakeney) 1950- 126
Bell, Margaret E(lizabeth) 1898-1990 2
Bell, Mary Reeves 1946- 88
Bell, Norman (Edward) 1899- 11
Bell, Raymond Martin 1907-1999 13
Bell, Thelma Harrington 1896-1985 3
Bell, William 1945- 90
  See also CLR 91
Bellairs, John (Anthony) 1938-1991 160
  Obituary 66
  Earlier sketches in SATA 2, 68
  See also CLR 37
Beller, Susan Provost 1949- 128
  Earlier sketch in SATA 84
  See also CLR 106
Bellingham, Brenda 1931- 99
  Brief entry 51
Bello, Rosario de
  See De Bello, Rosario
Belloc, (Joseph) Hilaire (Pierre Sebastien Rene
  Swanton) 1870-1953 112
  See also YABC 1
  See also CLR 102
Belloc, Joseph Peter Rene Hilaire
  See Belloc, (Joseph) Hilaire (Pierre Sebastien
  Rene Swanton)
Belloc, Joseph Pierre Hilaire
  See Belloc, (Joseph) Hilaire (Pierre Sebastien
  Rene Swanton)
Belloli, Andrea P. A. 1947- 86
Bellville, Cheryl Walsh 1944- 54
  Brief entry 49
Belpre, Pura 1899-1982 16
  Obituary 30
Belting, Natalia Maree 1915-1997 6

Belton, John Raynor 1931- 22
Belton, Sandra (Yvonne) 1939- 134
  Earlier sketch in SATA 85
Beltran, Alberto 1923- 43
Beltran-Hernandez, Irene 1945- 74
Belvedere, Lee
  See Grayland, Valerie (Merle Spanner)
Bemelmans, Ludwig 1898-1962 100
  Earlier sketch in SATA 15
  See also CLR 93
Benander, Carl D. 1941- 74
Benary, Margot
  See Benary-Isbert, Margot
Benary-Isbert, Margot 1889-1979 2
  Obituary 21
  See also CLR 12
Benasutti, Marion 1908-1992 6
Benatar, Raquel 1955- 167
Benchley, Nathaniel (Goddard) 1915-1981 . 25
  Obituary 28
  Earlier sketch in SATA 3
Benchley, Peter 1940-2006 164
  Earlier sketches in SATA 3, 89
Benchley, Peter Bradford
  See Benchley, Peter
Bender, Edna 1941- 92
Bender, Esther 1942- 88
Bender, Lucy Ellen 1942- 22
Bender, Robert 1962- 160
  Earlier sketch in SATA 79
Bendick, Jeanne 1919- 135
  Earlier sketches in SATA 2, 68
  See also CLR 5
  See also SAAS 4
Bendick, Robert L(ouis) 1917- 11
Benedict, Andrew
  See Arthur, Robert, (Jr.)
Benedict, Dorothy Potter 1889-1979 11
  Obituary 23
Benedict, Lois Trimble 1902-1967 12
Benedict, Rex 1920-1995 8
Benedict, Stewart H(urd) 1924- 26
Beneduce, Ann Keay 128
Benet, Laura 1884-1979 3
  Obituary 23
Benet, Stephen Vincent 1898-1943
  See YABC 1
Benet, Sula 1906-1982 21
  Obituary 33
Ben-Ezer, Ehud 1936- 122
Benezra, Barbara (Beardsley) 1921- 10
Benham, Leslie 1922- 48
Benham, Lois (Dakin) 1924- 48
Benham, Mary Lile 1914-1991 55
Benjamin, E. M. J.
  See Bache, Ellyn
Benjamin, Nora
  See Kubie, Nora Gottheil Benjamin
Benjamin, Saragail Katzman 1953- 86
Benner, Cheryl 1962- 80
Benner, Judith Ann 1942- 94
Bennett, Alice
  See Ziner, Florence
Bennett, Cherie 1960- 158
  Earlier sketch in SATA 97
Bennett, Dorothea
  See Young, Dorothea Bennett
Bennett, James (W.) 1942- 153
  Autobiography Feature 153
  Earlier sketches in SATA 93, 148
Bennett, Jay 1912- 87
  Brief entry 27
  Earlier sketch in SATA 41
  See also SAAS 4
Bennett, Jill (Crawford) 1934- 41
Bennett, John 1865-1956
  See YABC 1
Bennett, Penelope (Agnes) 1938- 94
Bennett, Rachel
  See Hill, Margaret (Ohler)

Bennett, Rainey 1907-1998 15
  Obituary 111
Bennett, Richard 1899- 21
Bennett, Russell H(oradley) 1896- 25
Bennett, William (John) 1943- 102
Benning, Elizabeth
  See Rice, Bebe Faas
Benson, Elizabeth P(olk) 1924- 65
Benson, Kathleen 1947- 111
  Earlier sketch in SATA 62
Benson, Linda M(aria) 1959- 84
Benson, Mildred (Augustine Wirt) 1905-2002
  100
  Obituary 135
  Earlier sketch in SATA 65
  See Keene, Carolyn
Benson, Mildred Wirt
  See Benson, Mildred (Augustine Wirt)
Benson, Millie
  See Benson, Mildred (Augustine Wirt)
Benson, Patrick 1956- 147
Benson, Sally 1900-1972 35
  Obituary 27
  Earlier sketch in SATA 1
Bentley, Judith (McBride) 1945- 89
  Earlier sketch in SATA 40
Bentley, Nancy (L.) 1946- 78
Bentley, Phyllis Eleanor 1894-1977 6
  Obituary 25
Bentley, Roy 1947- 46
Bentley, William (George) 1916- 84
ben Uzair, Salem
  See Horne, Richard Henry Hengist
Bercaw, Edna Coe 1961- 124
Berck, Judith 1960- 75
Berelson, Howard 1940- 5
Berends, Polly Berrien 1939- 50
  Brief entry 38
Berenstain, Jan 1923- 135
  Earlier sketches in SATA 12, 64, 129
  See also CLR 19
  See also SAAS 20
Berenstain, Janice
  See Berenstain, Jan
Berenstain, Michael 1951- 45
Berenstain, Stan 1923-2005 135
  Obituary 169
  Earlier sketches in SATA 12, 64, 129
  See also CLR 19
  See also SAAS 20
Berenstain, Stanley
  See Berenstain, Stan
Berenzy, Alix 1957- 168
  Earlier sketch in SATA 65
Beresford, Elisabeth 1928- 141
  Earlier sketches in SATA 25, 86
  See also SAAS 20
Berg, Adriane G(ilda) 1948- 152
Berg, Dave
  See Berg, David
Berg, David 1920-2002 27
  Obituary 137
Berg, Elizabeth 1948- 104
Berg, Jean Horton 1913-1995 6
Berg, Joan
  See Victor, Joan Berg
Berg, Ron 1952- 48
Bergaust, Erik 1925-1978 20
Bergel, Colin J. 1963- 137
Bergen, Joyce 1949- 95
Berger, Barbara (Helen) 1945- 77
Berger, Gilda 1935- 88
  Brief entry 42
Berger, Josef 1903-1971 36
Berger, Melvin H. 1927- 158
  Autobiography Feature 124
  Earlier sketches in SATA 5, 88
  See also CLR 32
  See also SAAS 2
Berger, Phil 1942-2001 62
Berger, Samantha (Allison) 1969- 140

Berger, Terry 1933- 8
Bergey, Alyce (Mae) 1934- 45
Bergin, Mark 1961- 160
  Earlier sketch in SATA 114
Bergman, Donna 1934- 73
Bergman, Tamar 1939- 95
Bergsma, Jody Lynn 163
Bergum, Constance R. 1952- 121
Berkey, Barry Robert 1935- 24
Berkowitz, Freda Pastor 1908-1994 12
Berkus, Clara Widess 1909- 78
Berlan, Kathryn Hook 1946- 78
Berlfein, Judy Reiss 1958- 79
Berliner, Don 1930- 33
Berliner, Franz 1930- 13
Berlitz, Charles (L. Frambach) 1914-2003 . 32
  Obituary 151
Berman, Linda 1948- 38
Berman, Paul (Lawrence) 1949- 66
Berna, Paul 1910-1994 15
  Obituary 78
  See also CLR 19
Bernadette
  See Watts, (Anna) Bernadette
Bernard, Bruce 1928-2000 78
  Obituary 124
Bernard, George I. 1949- 39
Bernard, Jacqueline (de Sieyes) 1921-1983 .. 8
  Obituary 45
Bernard, Patricia 1942- 106
Bernardin, James (B.) 1966- 112
Bernards, Neal 1963- 71
Bernays, Anne 1930- 32
Bernhard, Durga T. 1961- 80
Bernhard, Emery 1950- 80
Bernstein, Daryl (Evan) 1976- 81
Bernstein, Joanne E(ckstein) 1943- 15
Bernstein, Margery 1933- 114
Bernstein, Theodore M(enline) 1904-1979 . 12
  Obituary 27
Berrien, Edith Heal
  See Heal, Edith
Berrill, Jacquelyn (Batsel) 1905- 12
Berrington, John
  See Brownjohn, Alan
Berry, B. J.
  See Berry, Barbara J.
Berry, Barbara J. 1937- 7
Berry, Erick
  See Best, (Evangel) Allena Champlin
Berry, James 1925- 110
  Earlier sketch in SATA 67
  See also CLR 22
Berry, Joy
  See Berry, Joy Wilt
Berry, Joy Wilt 1944- 58
  Brief entry 46
Berry, William D(avid) 1926- 14
Bersani, Shennen 1961- 164
Berson, Harold 1926- 4
Bertagna, Julie 1962- 151
Bertin, Charles-Francois
  See Berlitz, Charles (L. Frambach)
Bertolet, Paul
  See McLaughlin, Frank
Berton, Pierre (Francis de Marigny) 1920-2004
  99
  Obituary 158
Bertrand, Cecile 1953- 76
Bertrand, Diane Gonzales 1956- 106
Bertrand, Lynne 1963- 164
  Earlier sketch in SATA 81
Beskow, Elsa (Maartman) 1874-1953 20
  See also CLR 17
Bess, Clayton
  See CLR 39
  See Locke, Robert
Best, (Evangel) Allena Champlin 1892-1974
  2
  Obituary 25

Best, Cari 1951- *149*
  Earlier sketch in SATA *107*
Best, (Oswald) Herbert 1894-1980 .... *2*
Bestall, A(lfred) E(dmeades) 1892-1986 ..... *97*
  Obituary *48*
Betancourt, Jeanne 1941- *148*
  Brief entry *43*
  Earlier sketches in SATA *55, 96*
Beth, Mary
  See Miller, Mary Beth
Bethancourt, T. Ernesto *11*
  See also CLR *3*
  See Paisley, Tom
Bethel, Dell 1929- *52*
Bethell, Jean (Frankenberry) 1922- *8*
Bethers, Ray 1902-1973 .... *6*
Bethke, Bruce Raymond 1955- *114*
Bethlen, T. D.
  See Silverberg, Robert
Bethune, J. G.
  See Ellis, Edward S(ylvester)
Bethune, J. H.
  See Ellis, Edward S(ylvester)
Betteridge, Anne
  See Potter, Margaret (Newman)
Bettina
  See Ehrlich, Bettina Bauer
Bettmann, Otto Ludwig 1903-1998 .... *46*
Betts, James
  See Haynes, Betsy
Betz, Eva Kelly 1897-1968 .... *10*
Bevan, Tom 1868-1930(?)
  See YABC *2*
Bewick, Thomas 1753-1828 .... *16*
Beyer, Audrey White 1916- *9*
Beyer, Paul J. III 1950- *74*
Beynon, John
  See Harris, John (Wyndham Parkes Lucas)
  Beynon
Bezencon, Jacqueline (Buxcel) 1924- *48*
Bial, Morrison David 1917- *62*
Bial, Raymond 1948- *165*
  Earlier sketches in SATA *76, 116*
Biala
  See Brustlein, Janice Tworkov
Biale, Rachel 1952- *99*
Bialk, Elisa
  See Krautter, Elisa (Bialk)
Bianchi, John 1947- *91*
Bianchi, Robert S(teven) 1943- *92*
Bianco, Margery
  See Bianco, Margery Williams
Bianco, Margery Williams 1881-1944 .... *15*
  See also CLR *19*
Bianco, Pamela 1906- *28*
Bibby, Violet 1908- *24*
Bible, Charles 1937- *13*
Bibo, Bobette
  See Gugliotta, Bobette
Bice, Clare 1909-1976 .... *22*
Bickerstaff, Isaac
  See Swift, Jonathan
Biegel, Paul 1925- *79*
  Earlier sketch in SATA *16*
  See also CLR *27*
  See also SAAS *18*
Biemiller, Carl L(udwig), Jr.) 1912-1979 .... *40*
  Obituary *21*
Bienenfeld, Florence L(ucille) 1929- *39*
Bierhorst, John (William) 1936- *149*
  Autobiography Feature *149*
  Earlier sketches in SATA *6, 91*
  See also SAAS *10*
Biggar, Joan R(awlins) 1936- *120*
Biggle, Lloyd, Jr. 1923-2002 .... *65*
Bilal, Abdel W(ahab) 1970- *92*
Bilbrough, Norman 1941- *111*
Bileck, Marvin 1920- *40*
Bilibin, Ivan (Iakolevich) 1876-1942 .... *61*
Bill, Alfred Hoyt 1879-1964 .... *44*
Billam, Rosemary 1952- *61*

Billings, Charlene W(interer) 1941- *41*
Billingsley, Franny 1954- *132*
Billington, Elizabeth T(hain) *50*
  Brief entry *43*
Billout, Guy (Rene) 1941- *144*
  Earlier sketch in SATA *10*
  See also CLR *33*
Bilson, Geoffrey 1938-1987 .... *99*
Binch, Caroline (Lesley) 1947- *140*
  Earlier sketch in SATA *81*
Bing, Christopher (H.) *126*
Bingham, Caroline 1962- *158*
Bingham, Jane M. 1941- *163*
Bingham, Jane Marie
  See Bingham, Jane M.
Bingham, Sam(uel A.) 1944- *96*
Bingley, Margaret (Jane Kirby) 1947- *72*
Binkley, Anne
  See Rand, Ann (Binkley)
Binzen, Bill *24*
  See Binzen, William
Birch, David (W.) 1913-1996 .... *89*
Birch, Reginald B(athurst) 1856-1943 .... *19*
Birchman, David 1949- *72*
Birchmore, Daniel A. 1951- *92*
Bird, Carmel 1940- *124*
Bird, E(lzy) J(ay) 1911- *58*
Birdseye, Tom 1951- *148*
  Earlier sketches in SATA *66, 98*
Birenbaum, Barbara 1941- *65*
Birmingham, Lloyd P(aul) 1924- *83*
  Earlier sketch in SATA *12*
Birney, Betty G. 1947- *169*
  Earlier sketch in SATA *98*
Biro, B.
  See Biro, B(alint) S(tephen)
Biro, B(alint) S(tephen) 1921- *67*
  See Biro, Val
Biro, Val *1*
  See also CLR *28*
  See also SAAS *13*
  See Biro, B(alint) S(tephen)
Bischoff, Julia Bristol 1909-1970 .... *12*
Bishop, Bonnie 1943- *37*
Bishop, Claire Huchet 1899(?)-1993 .... *14*
  Obituary *74*
  See also CLR *80*
Bishop, Courtney
  See Ruemmler, John D(avid)
Bishop, Curtis (Kent) 1912-1967 .... *6*
Bishop, Gavin 1946- *144*
  Earlier sketch in SATA *97*
Bishop, Kathleen Wong 1954- *120*
Bishop, Kathy
  See Bishop, Kathleen Wong
Bishop, Nic 1955- *161*
  Earlier sketch in SATA *107*
Bisset, Donald 1910-1995 .... *86*
  Earlier sketch in SATA *7*
Bisson, Terry (Ballantine) 1942- *99*
Bitter, Gary G(len) 1940- *22*
Bixby, William (Courtney) 1920-1986 .... *6*
  Obituary *47*
Bjoerk, Christina 1938- *99*
  Earlier sketch in SATA *67*
  See also CLR *22*
Bjork, Christina
  See Bjoerk, Christina
Bjorklund, Lorence F. 1913-1978 .... *35*
  Brief entry *32*
Bjorkman, Steve *163*
Black, Algernon David 1900-1993 .... *12*
  Obituary *76*
Black, Holly 1971- *147*
Black, Irma Simonton 1906-1972 .... *2*
  Obituary *25*
Black, Mansell
  See Trevor, Elleston
Black, MaryAnn
  See Easley, MaryAnn
Black, Susan Adams 1953- *40*

Blackall, Bernie 1956- *126*
Blackburn, Claire
  See Altman, Linda Jacobs
Blackburn, John(ny) Brewton 1952- *15*
Blackburn, Joyce Knight 1920- *29*
Blackett, Veronica Heath 1927- *12*
Blackie, Jean Cutler 1943- *79*
Blacklin, Malcolm
  See Chambers, Aidan
Blacklock, Dyan 1951- *112*
Blackman, Malorie 1962- *128*
  Earlier sketch in SATA *83*
Blackton, Peter
  See Wilson, Lionel
Blackwood, Alan 1932- *70*
Blackwood, Gary L. 1945- *169*
  Earlier sketches in SATA *72, 118*
Blade, Alexander
  See Garrett, (Gordon) Randall (Phillip)
  and Hamilton, Edmond
  and Silverberg, Robert
Blades, Ann (Sager) 1947- *69*
  Earlier sketch in SATA *16*
  See also CLR *15*
Bladow, Suzanne Wilson 1937- *14*
Blaine, John
  See Goodwin, Harold L(eland)
Blaine, Marge
  See Blaine, Margery Kay
Blaine, Margery Kay 1937- *11*
Blair, Alison
  See Lerangis, Peter
Blair, Anne Denton 1914-1993 .... *46*
Blair, David Nelson 1954- *80*
Blair, Eric (Arthur) 1903-1950 .... *29*
  See Orwell, George
Blair, Jay 1953- *45*
Blair, Lucile
  See Yeakley, Marjory Hall
Blair, Margaret Whitman 1951- *124*
Blair, Pauline Hunter
  See Clarke, Pauline
Blair, Ruth Van Ness 1912-1999 .... *12*
Blair, Shannon
  See Kaye, Marilyn
Blair, Walter 1900-1992 .... *12*
  Obituary *72*
Blaisdell, Bob
  See Blaisdell, Robert
Blaisdell, Robert 1959- *105*
Blake, Bronwyn 1940- *149*
Blake, Jon 1954- *78*
Blake, Olive
  See Supraner, Robyn
Blake, Quentin (Saxby) 1932- *125*
  Earlier sketches in SATA *9, 52, 96*
  See also CLR *31*
Blake, Robert 1949- *42*
Blake, Robert J. *160*
Blake, Walker E.
  See Butterworth, W.E.
Blake, William 1757-1827 .... *30*
  See also CLR *52*
Blakely, Gloria 1950- *139*
Blakely, Roger K. 1922- *82*
Blakeney, Jay D.
  See Chester, Deborah
Blakey, Nancy 1955- *94*
Blanc, Esther S. 1913-1997 .... *66*
Blanchard, Patricia *125*
Blanchet, M(uriel) Wylie 1891-1961 .... *106*
Blanco, Richard L(idio) 1926- *63*
Bland, E.
  See Nesbit, E(dith)
Bland, Edith Nesbit
  See Nesbit, E(dith)
Bland, Fabian
  See Nesbit, E(dith)
Blank, Clarissa Mabel 1915-1965 .... *62*

Blassingame, Wyatt Rainey 1909-1985 .... *34*
  Obituary *41*
  Earlier sketch in SATA *1*
Blatchford, Claire H. 1944- *94*
Blauer, Ettagale 1940- *49*
Bledsoe, Glen L(eonard) 1951- *108*
Bledsoe, Karen E. 1962- *167*
  Earlier sketch in SATA *108*
Bledsoe, Karen Elizabeth
  See Bledsoe, Karen E.
Bledsoe, Lucy Jane 1957- *162*
  Earlier sketch in SATA *97*
Bleeker, Sonia *2*
  Obituary *26*
  See Zim, Sonia Bleeker
Blegen, Daniel M. 1950- *92*
Blegvad, Erik 1923- *132*
  Earlier sketches in SATA *14, 66*
Blegvad, Lenore 1926- *66*
  Earlier sketch in SATA *14*
Blish, James (Benjamin) 1921-1975 .... *66*
Blishen, Edward (William) 1920-1996 .... *66*
  Obituary *93*
  Earlier sketch in SATA *8*
Bliss, Corinne Demas 1947- *37*
  See Demas, Corinne
Bliss, Frederick
  See Card, Orson Scott
Bliss, Harry 1964- *156*
Bliss, Reginald
  See Wells, H(erbert) G(eorge)
Bliss, Ronald G(ene) 1942- *12*
Bliven, Bruce, Jr. 1916-2002 .... *2*
Blixen, Karen (Christentze Dinesen)
  1885-1962 .... *44*
  See Dinesen, Isak
Blizzard, Gladys S. (?)-1992 .... *79*
Blobaum, Cindy 1966- *123*
Bloch, Lucienne 1909-1999 .... *10*
Bloch, Marie Halun 1910-1998 .... *6*
  See also SAAS *9*
Bloch, Robert (Albert) 1917-1994 .... *12*
  Obituary *82*
Blochman, Lawrence G(oldtree) 1900-1975
  .... *22*
Block, Francesca Lia 1962- *158*
  Earlier sketches in SATA *80, 116*
  See also CLR *33*
  See also SAAS *21*
Block, Irvin 1917- *12*
Blomgren, Jennifer (Alice) 1954- *136*
Blood, Charles Lewis 1929- *28*
Bloom, Barbara Lee 1943- *146*
Bloom, Freddy 1914-2000 .... *37*
  Obituary *121*
Bloom, Lloyd 1947- *108*
  Brief entry *43*
Bloomfield, Michaela 1966- *70*
Bloor, Edward (William) 1950- *155*
  Earlier sketch in SATA *98*
Blos, Joan W(insor) 1928- *153*
  Autobiography Feature *153*
  Brief entry *27*
  Earlier sketches in SATA *33, 69, 109*
  See also CLR *18*
  See also SAAS *11*
Blough, Glenn O(rlando) 1907-1995 .... *1*
Blue, Rose 1931- *166*
  Autobiography Feature *117*
  Earlier sketches in SATA *5, 91, 93*
  See also SAAS *24*
Blue, Zachary
  See Stine, R.L.
Bluggage, Oranthy
  See Alcott, Louisa May
Blumberg, Leda 1956- *59*
Blumberg, Rhoda 1917- *123*
  Earlier sketches in SATA *35, 70*
  See also CLR *21*

Blume, Judy (Sussman) 1938- *142*
  Earlier sketches in SATA *2, 31, 79*
  See also CLR *69*
Blumenthal, Deborah *161*
Blumenthal, Shirley 1943- *46*
Blutig, Eduard
  See Gorey, Edward (St. John)
Bly, Janet (Chester) 1945- *43*
Bly, Stephen A(rthur) 1944- *116*
  Earlier sketch in SATA *43*
Blyler, Allison Lee 1966- *74*
Blyton, Carey 1932-2002 .... *9*
  Obituary *138*
Blyton, Enid (Mary) 1897-1968 .... *25*
  See also CLR *31*
Boardman, Fon Wyman, Jr. 1911-2000 .... *6*
Boardman, Gwenn R. *12*
  See Petersen, Gwenn Boardman
Boase, Wendy 1944-1999 .... *28*
  Obituary *110*
Boatner, Mark Mayo III 1921- *29*
Bobbe, Dorothie de Bear 1905-1975 .... *1*
  Obituary *25*
Bober, Natalie S. 1930- *134*
  Earlier sketch in SATA *87*
  See also SAAS *23*
Bobette, Bibo
  See Gugliotta, Bobette
Bobritsky, Vladimir *47*
  Brief entry *32*
  See Bobri, Vladimir V.
Bochak, Grayce 1956- *76*
Bock, Hal
  See Bock, Harold I.
Bock, Harold I. 1939- *10*
Bock, William Sauts Netamux'we 1939- *14*
Bode, Janet 1943-1999 .... *96*
  Obituary *118*
  Earlier sketch in SATA *60*
Bodecker, N(iels) M(ogens) 1922-1988 ..... *73*
  Obituary *54*
  Earlier sketch in SATA *8*
Boden, Hilda
  See Bodenham, Hilda Morris
Bodenham, Hilda Morris 1901- *13*
Bodett, Tom *70*
  See Bodett, Thomas Edward
Bodie, Idella F(allaw) 1925- *89*
  Earlier sketch in SATA *12*
Bodker, Cecil 1927- *133*
  Earlier sketch in SATA *14*
  See also CLR *23*
Bodker, Cecil 1927-
  See Bodker, Cecil
Bodsworth, (Charles) Fred(erick) 1918- *27*
Boeckman, Charles 1920- *12*
Boelts, Maribeth 1964- *163*
  Earlier sketch in SATA *78*
Boerst, William J. 1939- *121*
Boesch, Mark J(oseph) 1917- *12*
Boesen, Victor 1908- *16*
Bogacki, Tomek 1950- *138*
Bogaerts, Gert 1965- *80*
Bogan, Paulette 1960- *129*
Bogart, Jo Ellen 1945- *92*
  See also CLR *59*
Boggs, Ralph Steele 1901-1994 .... *7*
Bograd, Larry 1953- *89*
  Earlier sketch in SATA *33*
  See also SAAS *21*
Bohdal, Susi 1951- *101*
  Earlier sketch in SATA *22*
Bohlen, Nina 1931- *58*
Bohlmeijer, Arno 1956- *94*
Bohner, Charles (Henry) 1927- *62*
Bohnhoff, Maya Kaathryn 1954- *88*
Boissard, Janine 1932- *59*
Bojunga, Lygia
  See Nunes, Lygia Bojunga
Bojunga-Nunes, Lygia
  See Nunes, Lygia Bojunga

Boland, Janice *98*
Bolden, Tonya (Wilyce) 1959- *138*
  Earlier sketch in SATA *79*
Boles, Paul Darcy 1916-1984 .... *9*
  Obituary *38*
Bolian, Polly 1925- *4*
Bollen, Roger 1941(?)- *83*
  Brief entry *29*
Bolliger, Max 1929- *7*
Bollinger, Max 1929- *167*
Bolognese, Don(ald Alan) 1934- *129*
  Earlier sketches in SATA *24, 71*
Bolotin, Norman (Phillip) 1951- *93*
Bolton, Carole 1926- *6*
Bolton, Elizabeth
  See St. John, Nicole
Bolton, Evelyn
  See Bunting, (Anne) Eve(lyn)
Bonar, Veronica
  See Bailey, Donna (Veronica Anne)
Bond, B. J.
  See Heneghan, James
Bond, Bruce 1939- *61*
Bond, Felicia 1954- *126*
  Earlier sketch in SATA *49*
Bond, Gladys Baker 1912- *14*
Bond, Higgins 1951- *83*
Bond, J. Harvey
  See Winterbotham, R(ussell) R(obert)
Bond, (Thomas) Michael 1926- *157*
  Earlier sketches in SATA *6, 58*
  See also CLR *95*
  See also SAAS *3*
Bond, Nancy (Barbara) 1945- *159*
  Autobiography Feature *159*
  Earlier sketches in SATA *22, 82*
  See also CLR *11*
  See also SAAS *13*
Bond, Rebecca 1972- *130*
Bond, Ruskin 1934- *87*
  Earlier sketch in SATA *14*
Bondie, J. D.
  See Cunningham, Chet
Bone, Ian 1956- *158*
  Earlier sketch in SATA *117*
Bonehill, Captain Ralph
  See Stratemeyer, Edward L.
Bonham, Barbara Thomas 1926- *7*
Bonham, Frank 1914-1989 .... *49*
  Obituary *62*
  Earlier sketch in SATA *1*
  See also SAAS *3*
Boniface, William 1963- *102*
Bonn, Pat
  See Bonn, Patricia Carolyn
Bonn, Patricia Carolyn 1948- *43*
Bonner, Mary Graham 1890-1974 .... *19*
Bonner, Mike 1951- *121*
Bonners, Susan 1947- *85*
  Brief entry *48*
Bonning, Tony 1948- *169*
Bonsall, Crosby Barbara (Newell) 1921-1995
  .... *23*
  Obituary *84*
Bonsall, Joseph S. 1948- *119*
Bonsignore, Joan 1959- *140*
Bontemps, Arna(ud Wendell) 1902-1973 .... *44*
  Obituary *24*
  Earlier sketch in SATA *2*
  See also CLR *6*
Bonzon, Paul-Jacques 1908-1978 .... *22*
Boock, Paula 1964- *134*
Booher, Dianna Daniels 1948- *33*
Book, Rick 1949- *119*
Book, Rita
  See Holub, Joan
Bookman, Charlotte
  See Zolotow, Charlotte (Gertrude) S(hapiro)
Boon, Debbie 1960- *103*
Boon, Emilie (Laetitia) 1958- *86*

Boone, Charles Eugene
  See Boone, Pat
Boone, Pat 1934- *7*
Boorman, Linda (Kay) 1940- *46*
Boorstin, Daniel J(oseph) 1914-2004 .... *52*
Booth, Ernest Sheldon 1915-1984 .... *43*
Booth, Graham (Charles) 1935- *37*
Bootman, Colin *159*
Borden, Louise (Walker) 1949- *141*
  Autobiography Feature *141*
  Earlier sketches in SATA *68, 104*
Bordier, Georgette 1924- *16*
Borgman, James (Mark) 1954- *122*
Borgman, Jim
  See Borgman, James (Mark)
Boring, Mel 1939- *168*
  Earlier sketch in SATA *35*
Borja, Corinne 1929- *22*
Borja, Robert 1923- *22*
Borland, Hal *5*
  Obituary *24*
  See Borland, Harold Glen
Borland, Kathryn Kilby 1916- *16*
Borlenghi, Patricia 1951- *79*
Born, Adolf 1930- *49*
Bornstein, Ruth Lercher
  Autobiography Feature *107*
  See Bornstein-Lercher, Ruth
Bornstein-Lercher, Ruth 1927- *88*
  Earlier sketch in SATA *14*
  See Bornstein, Ruth Lercher
Borski, Lucia Merecka *18*
Borten, Helen Jacobson 1930- *5*
Bortolotti, Dan 1969- *157*
Borton, Elizabeth
  See Trevino, Elizabeth B(orton) de
Borton, Lady 1942- *98*
Borton de Trevino, Elizabeth
  See Trevino, Elizabeth B(orton) de
Bortstein, Larry 1942- *16*
Bortz, Alfred B(enjamin) 1944- *139*
  Earlier sketch in SATA *74*
Bortz, Fred
  See Bortz, Alfred B(enjamin)
Bosco, Jack
  See Holliday, Joseph
Boshell, Gordon 1908- *15*
Boshinski, Blanche 1922- *10*
Bosman, Paul 1929- *107*
Bosse, Malcolm (Joseph, Jr.) 1926-2002 .. *136*
  Earlier sketch in SATA *35*
Bosserman, (Charles) Phillip 1931- *84*
Bossom, Naomi 1933- *35*
Bostock, Mike 1962- *114*
Boston, L(ucy) M(aria Wood) 1892-1990 ... *19*
  Obituary *64*
  See also CLR *3*
Bostrom, Kathleen (Susan) Long 1954- *139*
Bostrom, Kathy
  See Bostrom, Kathleen (Susan) Long
Bosworth, J. Allan 1925- *19*
Bothwell, Jean (?)-1977 .... *2*
Botkin, B(enjamin) A(lbert) 1901-1975 ...... *40*
Botsford, Ward 1927-2004 .... *66*
Botting, Douglas (Scott) 1934- *43*
Bottner, Barbara 1943- *93*
  Autobiography Feature *121*
  Earlier sketch in SATA *14*
  See also SAAS *26*
Bottone, Frank G., Jr. 1969- *141*
Bouchard, David 1952- *117*
Boucher, (Clarence) Carter 1954- *129*
Boudelang, Bob
  See Pell, Ed(ward)
Boughton, Richard 1954- *75*
Boulet, Susan Seddon 1941- *50*
Boulle, Pierre (Francois Marie-Louis)
  1912-1994 .... *22*
  Obituary *78*
Boulton, Jane 1921- *91*
Bouma, Paddy 1947- *128*

Bour, Daniele 1939- *62*
Bourdon, David 1934-1998 .... *46*
Bourgeois, Paulette 1951- *153*
Bourne, Lesley
  See Marshall, Evelyn
Bourne, Miriam Anne 1931-1989 .... *16*
  Obituary *63*
Boutet de Monvel, (Louis) M(aurice)
  1850(?)-1913 .... *30*
  See also CLR *32*
Bova, Ben(jamin William) 1932- *133*
  Earlier sketches in SATA *6, 68*
  See also CLR *96*
Bovaird, Anne E(lizabeth) 1960- *90*
Bow, Patricia 1946- *168*
Bowden, Joan Chase 1925- *51*
  Brief entry *38*
Bowen, Alexandra Russell *97*
Bowen, Andy Russell
  See Bowen, Alexandra Russell
Bowen, Betty Morgan
  See West, Betty
Bowen, Catherine (Shober) Drinker 1897-1973
  .... *7*
Bowen, David
  See Bowen, Joshua David
Bowen, Fred 1953- *136*
Bowen, Joshua David 1930- *22*
Bowen, Rhys
  See Quin-Harkin, Janet
Bowen, Robert Sydney 1900-1977 .... *52*
  Obituary *21*
Bowermaster, Jon 1954- *135*
  Earlier sketch in SATA *77*
Bowers, Terrell L. 1945- *101*
Bowers, Terry
  See Bowers, Terrell L.
Bowie, C. W.
  See Old, Wendie C(orbin)
  and Wirths, Claudine (Turner) G(ibson)
Bowie, Jim
  See Norwood, Victor G(eorge) C(harles)
  and Stratemeyer, Edward L.
Bowkett, Stephen 1953- *67*
Bowler, Jan Brett
  See Brett, Jan (Churchill)
Bowler, Tim 1953- *149*
Bowman, Crystal 1951- *105*
Bowman, James Cloyd 1880-1961 .... *23*
Bowman, John S(tewart) 1931- *16*
Bowman, Kathleen (Gill) 1942- *52*
  Brief entry *40*
Boyce, George A(rthur) 1898- *19*
Boyd, Candy Dawson 1946- *72*
  See also CLR *50*
Boyd, Pauline
  See Schock, Pauline
Boyd, Selma
  See Acuff, Selma Boyd
Boyd, Waldo T. 1918- *18*
Boyden, Linda 1948- *143*
Boyer, Allen B. 1963- *153*
Boyer, Robert E(rnst) 1929- *22*
Boyes, Vivien (Elizabeth) 1952- *106*
Boyle, Ann (Peters) 1916- *10*
Boyle, Eleanor Vere (Gordon) 1825-1916 .. *28*
Boyle, Robert H. 1928- *65*
Boylston, Helen Dore 1895-1984 .... *23*
  Obituary *39*
Boynton, Sandra (Keith) 1953- *152*
  Brief entry *38*
  Earlier sketches in SATA *57, 107*
  See also CLR *105*
Boz
  See Dickens, Charles (John Huffam)
Bracken, Charles
  See Pellowski, Michael (Joseph)
Brackers de Hugo, Pierre 1960- *115*
Brackett, Dolli Tingle 1911-1993 .... *137*
Brackett, Virginia 1950- *166*
  Earlier sketch in SATA *121*

Brackett, Virginia Roberts Meredith
  See Brackett, Virginia
Bradbury, Bianca (Ryley) 1908-1982 .... *56*
  Earlier sketch in SATA *3*
Bradbury, Edward P.
  See Moorcock, Michael
Bradbury, Ray (Douglas) 1920- *123*
  Earlier sketches in SATA *11, 64*
Bradby, Marie *161*
Bradfield, Carl 1942- *91*
Bradford, Ann (Liddell) 1917- *56*
  Brief entry *38*
Bradford, Barbara Taylor 1933- *66*
Bradford, Karleen 1936- *96*
  Earlier sketch in SATA *48*
Bradford, Lois J(ean) 1936- *36*
Bradford, Richard (Roark) 1932-2002 .... *59*
  Obituary *135*
Bradley, Duane
  See Sanborn, Duane
Bradley, Marion Zimmer 1930-1999 .... *139*
  Obituary *116*
  Earlier sketch in SATA *90*
  See Chapman, Lee
  and Dexter, John
  and Gardner, Miriam
  and Ives, Morgan
  and Rivers, Elfrida
Bradley, Virginia 1912- *23*
Bradley, Will
  See Strickland, (William) Brad(ley)
Bradman, Tony 1954- *152*
  Earlier sketch in SATA *81*
Bradshaw, Gillian (Joan) 1949- *118*
Bradshaw, Gillian (Marucha) 1956- *127*
Bradstreet, T. J.
  See Thesman, Jean
Brady, Esther Wood 1905-1987 .... *31*
  Obituary *53*
Brady, Irene 1943- *4*
Brady, Kimberley S(mith) 1953- *101*
Brady, Lillian 1902- *28*
Bragdon, Elspeth MacDuffie 1897-1980 ..... *6*
Bragdon, Lillian Jacot *24*
Brager, Bruce L. 1949- *146*
Bragg, Mabel Caroline 1870-1945 .... *24*
Bragg, Michael 1948- *46*
Bragg, Ruth Gembicki 1943- *77*
Brahm, Sumishta 1954- *58*
Brailsford, Frances
  See Wosmek, Frances
Brainerd, John W(hiting) 1918- *65*
Braithwaite, Althea 1940- *23*
  Autobiography Feature *119*
  See also SAAS *24*
Bram, Elizabeth 1948- *30*
Brancato, Robin F(idler) 1936- *97*
  See also CLR *32*
  See also SAAS *9*
Branch, Muriel Miller 1943- *152*
  Earlier sketch in SATA *94*
Brand, Christianna
  See Lewis, Mary (Christianna)
Brand, Rebecca
  See Charnas, Suzy McKee
Brandel, Marc 1919- *71*
Brandenberg, Alexa (Demetria) 1966- *97*
Brandenberg, Aliki (Liacouras) 1929- *157*
  Earlier sketches in SATA *2, 35, 75, 113*
  See Aliki
Brandenberg, Franz 1932- *75*
  Earlier sketches in SATA *8, 35*
Brandenburg, Jim 1945- *87*
Brandhorst, Carl T(heodore) 1898-1988 ..... *23*
Brandis, Marianne 1938- *149*
  Earlier sketches in SATA *59, 96*
Brandon, Brumsic, Jr. 1927- *9*
Brandon, Curt
  See Bishop, Curtis (Kent)
Brandreth, Gyles 1948- *28*
Brandt, Catharine 1905-1997 .... *40*

Brandt, Keith
  See Sabin, Louis
Brandt, Sue R(eading) 1916- *59*
Branfield, John (Charles) 1931- *11*
Branford, Henrietta 1946-1999 .... *106*
Branley, Franklyn M(ansfield) 1915-2002
  .... *136*
  Earlier sketches in SATA *4, 68*
  See also CLR *13*
  See also SAAS *16*
Branscum, Robbie (Tilley) 1937-1997 .... *72*
  Obituary *96*
  Earlier sketch in SATA *23*
  See also SAAS *17*
Bransom, (John) Paul 1885-1979 .... *43*
Brashares, Ann 1967- *145*
Bratton, Helen 1899-1986 .... *4*
Bratun, Katy 1950- *160*
  Earlier sketch in SATA *83*
Braude, Michael 1936- *23*
Braun, Lilian Jackson 1916(?)- *109*
Brautigan, Richard (Gary) 1935-1984 .... *56*
Bray, Libba *159*
Braymer, Marjorie Elizabeth 1911-1988 .... *6*
Breathed, Berke 1957- *161*
  Earlier sketch in SATA *86*
Breathed, Guy Berkeley
  See Breathed, Berke
Brecht, Edith 1895-1975 .... *6*
  Obituary *25*
Breck, Vivian
  See Breckenfeld, Vivian Gurney
Breckenfeld, Vivian Gurney 1895-1992 .... *1*
Breda, Tjalmar
  See DeJong, David C(ornel)
Bredeson, Carmen 1944- *163*
  Earlier sketch in SATA *98*
Breinburg, Petronella 1927- *11*
  See also CLR *31*
Breisky, William J(ohn) 1928- *22*
Brennan, Gale (Patrick) 1927- *64*
  Brief entry *53*
Brennan, Herbie
  See Brennan, J(ames) H(erbert)
Brennan, J(ames) H(erbert) 1940- *140*
Brennan, Jan
  See Brennan, J(ames) H(erbert)
Brennan, Joseph Lomas 1903-2000 .... *6*
Brennan, Linda Crotta 1952- *130*
Brenner, Anita 1905-1974 .... *56*
Brenner, Barbara (Johnes) 1925- *124*
  Earlier sketches in SATA *4, 42, 76*
  See also SAAS *14*
Brenner, Fred 1920- *36*
  Brief entry *34*
Brent, Stuart *14*
Breslin, Theresa *128*
  Autobiography Feature *128*
  Earlier sketch in SATA *70*
Breslow, Maurice (A.) 1935- *72*
Breslow, Susan 1951- *69*
Brett, Bernard 1925- *22*
Brett, Grace N(eff) 1900-1975 .... *23*
Brett, Jan (Churchill) 1949- *130*
  Earlier sketches in SATA *42, 71*
  See also CLR *27*
Brewer, James D. 1951- *108*
Brewer, Sally King 1947- *33*
Brewster, Benjamin
  See Folsom, Franklin (Brewster)
Brewster, Hugh 1950- *95*
Brewster, Patience 1952- *97*
Brewton, John E(dmund) 1898-1982 .... *5*
Brian, Janeen (Paulette) 1948- *141*
Brick, John 1922-1973 .... *10*
Brickman, Robin D. 1954- *155*
Bride, Nadja
  See Nobisso, Josephine

Bridgers, Sue Ellen 1942- *90*
  Autobiography Feature *109*
  Earlier sketch in SATA *22*
  See also CLR *18*
  See also SAAS *1*
Bridges, Laurie
  See Bruck, Lorraine
Bridges, Ruby (Nell) 1954- *131*
Bridges, William (Andrew) 1901-1984 .... *5*
Bridwell, Norman (Ray) 1928- *138*
  Earlier sketches in SATA *4, 68*
  See also CLR *96*
Brier, Howard M(axwell) 1903-1969 .... *8*
Brierley, (Louise) 1958- *59*
Briggs, Katharine Mary 1898-1980 .... *101*
  Obituary *25*
Briggs, Peter 1921-1975 .... *39*
  Obituary *31*
Briggs, Raymond 1934- *131*
  Earlier sketches in SATA *23, 66*
  See also CLR *10*
Briggs, Raymond Redvers
  See Briggs, Raymond
Bright, Robert (Douglas Sr.) 1902-1988 ..... *63*
  Obituary *60*
  Earlier sketch in SATA *24*
Bright, Sarah
  See Shine, Deborah
Brightfield, Richard 1927- *65*
  Brief entry *53*
Brightfield, Rick
  See Brightfield, Richard
Brighton, Catherine 1943- *107*
  Earlier sketch in SATA *65*
Brill, Marlene Targ 1945- *124*
  Earlier sketch in SATA *77*
Brimberg, Stanlee 1947- *9*
Brimner, Larry Dane 1949- *79*
  Autobiography Feature *112*
Brin, David 1950- *65*
Brin, Ruth Firestone 1921- *22*
Brinckloe, Julie (Lorraine) 1950- *13*
Brindel, June (Rachuy) 1919- *7*
Brindle, Max
  See Fleischman, (Albert) Sid(ney)
Brindze, Ruth 1903-1984 .... *23*
Brink, Carol Ryrie 1895-1981 .... *100*
  Obituary *27*
  Earlier sketches in SATA *1, 31*
  See also CLR *30*
Brinsmead, H. F.
  See Brinsmead, H(esba) F(ay)
Brinsmead, H. F(ay)
  See Aalben, Patrick
  and Brinsmead, H(esba) F(ay)
Brinsmead, H(esba) F(ay) 1922- *78*
  Earlier sketch in SATA *18*
  See also CLR *47*
  See also SAAS *5*
Briquebec, John
  See Rowland-Entwistle, (Arthur) Theodore
  (Henry)
Brisbane, Henry R.
  See Ellis, Edward S(ylvester)
Brisco, P. A.
  See Matthews, Patricia (Anne)
Brisco, Patty
  See Matthews, Patricia (Anne)
  and Matthews, Clayton (Hartley)
Briscoe, Jill (Pauline) 1935- *56*
  Brief entry *47*
Brisley, Joyce Lankester 1896-1978 .... *22*
  Obituary *84*
Brissenden, Connie
  See Brissenden, Constance
Brissenden, Constance 1947- *150*
Brisson, Pat 1951- *133*
  Autobiography Feature *133*
  Earlier sketches in SATA *67, 128*
Britt, Dell 1934- *1*

Brittain, Bill
  See SAAS *7*
  See Brittain, William (E.)
Brittain, C. Dale 1948- *82*
Brittain, William (E.) 1930- *76*
  Earlier sketch in SATA *36*
  See Brittain, Bill
Brittingham, Geoffrey (Hugh) 1959- *76*
Britton, Kate *49*
  See Stegeman, Janet Allais
Britton, Louisa
  See McGuire, Leslie (Sarah)
Britton, Rick 1952- *82*
Bro, Margueritte (Harmon) 1894-1977 .... *19*
  Obituary *27*
Broadhead, Helen Cross 1913- *25*
Brochmann, Elizabeth 1938- *41*
Brock, Betty (Carter) 1923-2003 .... *4*
  Obituary *150*
Brock, C(harles) E(dmund) 1870-1938 .... *42*
  Brief entry *32*
Brock, Delia
  See Ephron, Delia
Brock, Emma L(illian) 1886-1974 .... *8*
Brock, H(enry) M(atthew) 1875-1960 .... *42*
Brockett, Eleanor Hall 1913-1967 .... *10*
Brockman, C(hristian) Frank 1902-1985 ..... *26*
Broderick, Dorothy M. 1929- *5*
Brodeur, Ruth Wallace
  See Wallace-Brodeur, Ruth
Brodie, Sally
  See Cavin, Ruth (Brodie)
Brodsky, Beverly
  See McDermott, Beverly Brodsky
Brody, Wendy
  See Staub, Wendy Corsi
Broeger, Achim 1944- *31*
Broekel, Rainer Lothar 1923- *38*
Broekel, Ray
  See Broekel, Rainer Lothar
Broekstra, Lorette 1964- *124*
Broger, Achim
  See Broeger, Achim
Broida, Marian *154*
Brokamp, Marilyn 1920- *10*
Broman, Fred
  See Moseley, James W(illett)
Bromhall, Winifred *26*
Brommer, Gerald F(rederick) 1927- *28*
Brondfield, Jerome 1913-1998 .... *22*
Brondfield, Jerry
  See Brondfield, Jerome
Bronner, Stephen Eric 1949- *101*
Bronowski, Jacob 1908-1974 .... *55*
Bronson, Lynn
  See Lampman, Evelyn Sibley
Brook, Judith (Penelope) 1926- *59*
  Brief entry *51*
Brook, Judy
  See Brook, Judith (Penelope)
Brooke, L(eonard) Leslie 1862-1940 .... *17*
  See also CLR *20*
Brooke, William J. 1946- *139*
Brooke-Haven, P.
  See Wodehouse, P(elham) G(renville)
Brookins, Dana 1931- *28*
Brooks, Anita *5*
  See Abramovitz, Anita (Zeltner Brooks)
Brooks, Bill 1939- *59*
Brooks, Bruce 1950- *112*
  Brief entry *53*
  Earlier sketch in SATA *72*
  See also CLR *25*
Brooks, Caryl 1924- *84*
Brooks, Charlotte K(endrick) 1918-1998 .... *24*
  Obituary *112*
Brooks, Erik 1972- *152*
Brooks, George
  See Baum, L(yman) Frank

Brooks, Gwendolyn (Elizabeth) 1917-2000 .. 6
  Obituary 123
  See also CLR 27
Brooks, Jerome 1931- 23
Brooks, Kevin M. 1959- 150
Brooks, Lester 1924- 7
Brooks, Martha 1944- 134
  Autobiography Feature 134
  Earlier sketches in SATA 68, 121
Brooks, Maurice (Graham) 1900- 45
Brooks, Polly Schoyer 1912- 12
Brooks, Ron(ald George) 1948- 94
  Brief entry 33
Brooks, Terry 1944- 60
Brooks, Walter R(ollin) 1886-1958 17
Brooks-Hill, Helen (Mason) 1908-1994 59
Broome, Errol 1937- 158
  Earlier sketch in SATA 105
Brophy, Nannette 1963- 73
Brosnan, James Patrick 1929- 14
Brosnan, Jim
  See Brosnan, James Patrick
Brostoff, Anita 1931- 132
Brothers Grimm
  See Grimm, Jacob Ludwig Karl
  and Grimm, Wilhelm Karl
Brothers Hildebrandt, The
  See Hildebrandt, Greg
  and Hildebrandt, Tim(othy)
Broun, Emily
  See Sterne, Emma Gelders
Brouwer, S. W.
  See Brouwer, Sigmund (W.)
Brouwer, Sigmund (W.) 1959- 109
Brow, Thea 1934- 60
Brower, Millicent 8
Brower, Pauline 1929- 22
Browin, Frances Williams 1898-1986 5
Brown, Alexis
  See Baumann, Amy (Brown) Beeching
Brown, Anne Ensign 1937- 61
Brown, Beverly Swerdlow 97
Brown, Bill
  See Brown, William L(ouis)
Brown, Billye Walker
  See Cutchen, Billye Walker
Brown, Bob
  See Brown, Robert Joseph
Brown, Buck 1936- 45
Brown, Cassie 1919-1986 55
Brown, Conrad 1922- 31
Brown, Craig McFarland 1947- 73
Brown, David
  See Brown, David A(lan)
  and Myller, Rolf
Brown, Dee 1908-2002 110
  Obituary 141
  Earlier sketch in SATA 5
Brown, Dee Alexander
  See Brown, Dee
Brown, Drew T. III 1955- 83
Brown, Drollene P. 1939- 53
Brown, Eleanor Frances 1908-1987 3
Brown, Elizabeth Ferguson 1937- 153
Brown, Elizabeth M(yers) 1915- 43
Brown, Fern G. 1918- 34
Brown, (Robert) Fletch 1923- 42
Brown, Fornan 1901-1996 71
  Obituary 88
Brown, George Earl 1883-1964 11
Brown, George Mackay 1921-1996 35
Brown, Irene Bennett 1932- 3
Brown, Irving
  See Adams, William Taylor
Brown, Ivor (John Carnegie) 1891-1974 5
  Obituary 26
Brown, Jane Clark 1930- 81
Brown, Janet Mitsui 87
Brown, Joanne 1933- 147
Brown, Joe David 1915-1976 44

Brown, Joseph E(dward) 1929- 59
  Brief entry 51
Brown, Judith Gwyn 1933- 20
Brown, Kathryn 1955- 168
  Earlier sketch in SATA 98
Brown, Kathy
  See Brown, Kathryn
Brown, Ken (James) 129
Brown, Kevin 1960- 101
Brown, Laurene Krasny 1945- 99
  Earlier sketch in SATA 54
Brown, Laurie Krasny
  See Brown, Laurene Krasny
Brown, Lloyd Arnold 1907-1966 36
Brown, Mahlon A.
  See Ellis, Edward S(ylvester)
Brown, Marc (Tolon) 1946- 145
  Earlier sketches in SATA 10, 53, 80
  See also CLR 29
Brown, Marcia (Joan) 1918- 47
  Earlier sketch in SATA 7
  See also CLR 12
Brown, Margaret Wise 1910-1952 100
  See also YABC 2
  See also CLR 107
Brown, Margery (Wheeler) 78
  Earlier sketch in SATA 5
Brown, Marion Marsh 1908-2001 6
Brown, Myra Berry 1918- 6
Brown, Palmer 1919- 36
Brown, Pamela (Beatrice) 1924-1989 5
  Obituary 61
Brown, Reeve Lindbergh
  See Lindbergh, Reeve
Brown, Richard E. 1946- 61
Brown, Robert Joseph 1907-1989 14
Brown, Roderick (Langmere) Haig-
  See Haig-Brown, Roderick (Langmere)
Brown, Rosalie 9
  See Moore, Rosalie (Gertrude)
Brown, Roswell
  See Webb, Jean Francis (III)
Brown, Roy (Frederick) 1921-1982 51
  Obituary 39
Brown, Ruth 1941- 105
Brown, Scott 1971- 134
Brown, Sue Ellen 1954- 81
Brown, Tricia 1954- 114
Brown, Vinson 1912-1991 19
Brown, Walter R(eed) 1929- 19
Brown, Will
  See Ainsworth, William Harrison
Brown, William L(ouis) 1910-1964 5
Browne, Anthony (Edward Tudor) 1946- . 163
  Brief entry 44
  Earlier sketches in SATA 45, 61, 105
  See also CLR 19
Browne, Dik
  See Browne, Richard Arthur Allen
Browne, Hablot Knight 1815-1882 21
Browne, Matthew
  See Rands, William Brighty
Browne, Nicky Matthews
  See Browne, N.M.
Browne, N.M. 1960- 167
Browne, Richard Arthur Allen 1917-1989 .. 67
  Brief entry 38
  See Browne, Dik
Browne, Vee F(rances) 1956- 90
Browning, Robert 1812-1889
  See YABC 1
  See also CLR 97
Brownjohn, Alan 1931- 6
Brownlee, Walter 1930- 62
Brownlie, Betty 1946- 159
Brownlow, Kevin 1938- 65
Brownridge, William R(oy) 1932- 94
Bruce, (William) Harry 1934- 77
Bruce, Mary 1927- 1

Bruchac, Joseph III 1942- 131
  Earlier sketches in SATA 42, 89
  See also CLR 46
Bruck, Lorraine 1921- 55
  Brief entry 46
  See Bridges, Laurie
Bruel, Nick 166
Bruemmer, Fred 1929- 47
Brugman, Alyssa (F.) 1974- 152
Brumbeau, Jeff 1955- 157
Bruna, Dick 1927- 76
  Brief entry 30
  Earlier sketch in SATA 43
  See also CLR 7
Brunhoff, Jean de 1899-1937 24
  See also CLR 4
Brunhoff, Laurent de 1925- 150
  Earlier sketches in SATA 24, 71
  See also CLR 4
Brunskill, Elizabeth Ann Flatt 1966- 88
Brush, Karen A(lexandra) 1960- 85
Brussel-Smith, Bernard 1914- 58
Brust, Steven K. (Zoltan) 1955- 121
  Earlier sketch in SATA 86
Brustlein, Daniel 1904- 40
Brustlein, Janice Tworkov -2000 40
  Obituary 126
Brutschy, Jennifer 1960- 84
Bryan, Ashley F. 1923- 132
  Earlier sketches in SATA 31, 72
  See also CLR 66
Bryant, Bernice (Morgan) 1908-1976 11
Bryant, Jennifer F(isher) 1960- 94
Brychta, Alex 1956- 21
Brynie, Faith H(ickman) 1946- 113
Bryson, Bernarda 1903-2004 9
  See Shahn, Bernarda Bryson
Buba, Joy Flinsch 1904- 44
Buchan, Bryan 1945- 36
Buchan, John 1875-1940
  See YABC 2
Buchanan, Debby 1952- 82
Buchanan, Deborah Leevonne
  See Buchanan, Debby
Buchanan, Jane 1956- 160
Buchanan, Paul 1959- 116
Buchanan, Sue 1939- 139
Buchheimer, Naomi Barnett
  See Barnett, Naomi
Buchignani, Walter 1965- 84
Buchwald, Art(hur) 1925- 10
Buchwald, Emilie 1935- 7
Buck, Gisela 1941- 101
Buck, Lewis 1925- 18
Buck, Margaret Waring 1905-1997 3
Buck, Pearl S(ydenstricker) 1892-1973 25
  Earlier sketch in SATA 1
Buck, Siegfried 1941- 101
Buckeridge, Anthony (Malcolm) 1912-2004
  85
  Earlier sketch in SATA 6
Buckholtz, Eileen (Garber) 1949- 54
  Brief entry 47
Buckler, Ernest 1908-1984 47
Buckless, Andrea K. 1968- 117
Buckley, Helen E(lizabeth) 1918- 90
  Earlier sketch in SATA 2
Buckley, James, Jr. 1963- 166
  Earlier sketch in SATA 114
Buckmaster, Henrietta 6
  See Stephens, Henrietta Henkle
Bucks, Brad
  See Holub, Joan
Budd, E. S.
  See Sirimarco, Elizabeth
Budd, Lillian (Peterson) 1897-1989 7
Buehler, Stephanie Jona 1956- 83
Buehner, Caralyn (M.) 1963- 159
  Earlier sketch in SATA 104
Buehner, Mark 1959- 159
  Earlier sketch in SATA 104

Buehr, Walter Franklin 1897-1971 .... *3*
Buell, Janet 1952- *106*
Buergel, Paul-Hermann H. 1949- *83*
Buettner, Dan 1960- *95*
Buff, Conrad 1886-1975 .... *19*
Buff, Mary (E. Marsh) 1890-1970 .... *19*
Buffett, Jimmy 1946- *110*
Earlier sketch in SATA *76*
Buffie, Margaret 1945- *161*
Earlier sketches in SATA *71, 107*
See also CLR *39*
Bugni, Alice 1951- *122*
Bujold, Lois McMaster 1949- *136*
Bulfinch, Thomas 1796-1867 .... *35*
Bulion, Leslie 1958- *161*
Bull, Angela (Mary) 1936- *45*
Bull, Emma 1954- *99*
Autobiography Feature *103*
Bull, Norman John 1916- *41*
Bull, Schuyler M. 1974- *138*
Bulla, Clyde Robert 1914- *139*
Earlier sketches in SATA *2, 41, 91*
See also SAAS *6*
Bullard, Lisa 1961- *142*
Bullock, Kathleen (Mary) 1946- *77*
Bullock, Robert (D.) 1947- *92*
Bulpin, (Barbara) Vicki *92*
Bumstead, Kathleen Mary 1918-1987 .... *53*
Bundles, A'Lelia Perry 1952- *76*
Bunin, Catherine 1967- *30*
Bunin, Sherry 1925- *30*
Bunkers, Suzanne L. 1950- *136*
Bunting, A. E.
   See Bunting, (Anne) Eve(lyn)
Bunting, Eve
   See Bunting, (Anne) Eve(lyn)
Bunting, (Anne) Eve(lyn) 1928- *158*
Earlier sketches in SATA *18, 64, 110*
See also CLR *82*
See Bunting, Eve
Bunting, Glenn (Davison) 1957- *22*
Burack, Sylvia K. 1916-2003 .... *35*
Obituary *143*
Burbank, Addison (Buswell) 1895-1961 ..... *37*
Burch, Joann J(ohansen) *75*
Burch, Robert J(oseph) 1925- *74*
Earlier sketch in SATA *1*
See also CLR *63*
Burchard, Peter Duncan 1921- *143*
Earlier sketches in SATA *5, 74*
See also SAAS *13*
Burchard, S. H.
   See Burchard, Sue
Burchard, Sue 1937- *22*
Burchardt, Nellie 1921- *7*
Burdett, Lois *117*
Burdick, Eugene (Leonard) 1918-1965 .... *22*
Burford, Eleanor
   See Hibbert, Eleanor Alice Burford
Burgan, Michael 1960- *167*
Earlier sketch in SATA *118*
Burger, Carl 1888-1967 .... *9*
Burgess, Ann Marie
   See Gerson, Noel Bertram
Burgess, Barbara Hood 1926- *69*
Burgess, Em
   See Burgess, Mary Wyche
Burgess, (Frank) Gelett 1866-1951 .... *32*
Brief entry *30*
Burgess, Mark *157*
Burgess, Mary Wyche 1916- *18*
Burgess, Melvin 1954- *146*
Earlier sketch in SATA *96*
Burgess, Michael
   See Gerson, Noel Bertram
Burgess, Robert F(orrest) 1927- *4*
Burgess, Thornton Waldo 1874-1965 .... *17*
Burgess, Trevor
   See Trevor, Elleston
Burgwyn, Mebane Holoman 1914-1992 .... *7*
Burke, David 1927- *46*

Burke, Diana G.
   See Gallagher, Diana G.
Burke, Diana Gallagher
   See Gallagher, Diana G.
Burke, Dianne O'Quinn 1940- *89*
Burke, Janine 1952- *139*
Burke, Katie 1953- *168*
Burke, Patrick 1958- *114*
Burke, Ralph
   See Garrett, (Gordon) Randall (Phillip)
   and Silverberg, Robert
Burkert, Nancy Ekholm 1933- *24*
See also SAAS *14*
Burke-Weiner, Kimberly 1962- *95*
Burks, Brian 1955- *95*
Burland, Brian (Berkeley) 1931- *34*
Burland, C. A.
   See Burland, Cottie (Arthur)
Burland, Cottie (Arthur) 1905-1983 .... *5*
Burleigh, Robert 1936- *146*
Earlier sketches in SATA *55, 98*
Burlingame, (William) Roger 1889-1967 ...... *2*
Burman, Ben Lucien 1896-1984 .... *6*
Obituary *40*
Burn, Doris 1923- *1*
Burn, Ted
   See Burn, Thomas E.
Burn, Thomas E. 1940- *150*
Burnard, Damon 1963- *115*
Burnett, Constance Buel 1893-1975 .... *36*
Burnett, Frances (Eliza) Hodgson 1849-1924
   .... *100*
See also YABC *2*
See also CLR *24*
Burnford, Sheila (Philip Cochrane Every)
   1918-1984 .... *3*
Obituary *38*
See also CLR *2*
Burnham, Nicole 1970- *161*
Burnham, Niki
   See Burnham, Nicole
Burnham, Sophy 1936- *65*
Burningham, John (Mackintosh) 1936- *160*
Earlier sketches in SATA *16, 59, 111*
See also CLR *9*
Burns, Diane L. 1950- *81*
See also SAAS *24*
Burns, Eloise Wilkin
   See Wilkin, Eloise
Burns, Florence M. 1905-1988 .... *61*
Burns, Khephra 1950- *92*
Burns, Marilyn 1941- *96*
Brief entry *33*
Burns, Olive Ann 1924-1990 .... *65*
Burns, Paul C. *5*
Burns, Ray
   See Burns, Raymond (Howard)
Burns, Raymond (Howard) 1924- *9*
Burns, Theresa 1961- *84*
Burns, William A. 1909-1999 .... *5*
Burr, Dan 1951- *65*
Burr, Lonnie 1943- *47*
Burrell, Roy E(ric) C(harles) 1923- *72*
Burroughs, Edgar Rice 1875-1950 .... *41*
Burroughs, Jean Mitchell 1908- *28*
Burroughs, Polly 1925- *2*
Burroway, Janet (Gay) 1936- *23*
Burstein, Chaya M(alamud) 1923- *64*
Burstein, Fred 1950- *83*
Burstein, John 1949- *54*
Brief entry *40*
Bursztynski, Sue 1953- *114*
Burt, Jesse Clifton 1921-1976 .... *46*
Obituary *20*
Burt, Olive Woolley 1894-1981 .... *4*
Burton, Gennett 1945- *95*
Burton, Hester (Wood-Hill) 1913-2000 .... *74*
Earlier sketch in SATA *7*
See also CLR *1*
See also SAAS *8*

Burton, Leslie
   See McGuire, Leslie (Sarah)
Burton, Marilee Robin 1950- *82*
Earlier sketch in SATA *46*
Burton, Maurice 1898-1992 .... *23*
Burton, Robert (Wellesley) 1941- *22*
Burton, Virginia Lee 1909-1968 .... *100*
Earlier sketch in SATA *2*
See also CLR *11*
Burton, William H(enry) 1890-1964 .... *11*
Busby, Cylin 1970- *118*
Buscaglia, (Felice) Leo(nardo) 1924-1998 .. *65*
See Buscaglia, Leo F.
Buscaglia, Leo F.
   See Buscaglia, (Felice) Leo(nardo)
Busch, Phyllis S. 1909- *30*
Bush, Anne Kelleher
   See Kelleher, Anne
Bush, Catherine 1961- *128*
Bushnell, Jack 1952- *86*
Busoni, Rafaello 1900-1962 .... *16*
Buss, Helen M.
   See Clarke, Margaret
Busselle, Rebecca 1941- *80*
Butcher, Kristin 1951- *140*
Butenko, Bohdan 1931- *90*
Butler, Beverly Kathleen 1932- *7*
Butler, Bill
   See Butler, William (Arthur) Vivian
   and Butler, Ernest Alton
   and Butler, William Huxford
Butler, Charles (Cadman) 1963- *121*
Butler, Dori Hillestad 1965- *164*
Butler, Dorothy 1925- *73*
Butler, Geoff 1945- *94*
Butler, M. Christina 1934- *72*
Butler, Octavia E. 1947-2006 .... *84*
See also CLR *65*
Butler, Octavia Estelle
   See Butler, Octavia E.
Butler, Vivian
   See Butler, William (Arthur) Vivian
Butler, William
   See Butler, William (Arthur) Vivian
Butler, William (Arthur) Vivian 1927-1987
   .... *79*
See Marric, J. J.
Butters, Dorothy Gilman *5*
See Gilman, Dorothy
Butterworth, Emma Macalik 1928- *43*
Butterworth, Nick 1946- *149*
Earlier sketch in SATA *106*
Butterworth, Oliver 1915-1990 .... *1*
Obituary *66*
Butterworth, W.E. 1929- *5*
See Griffin, W. E. B.
Butterworth, William Edmund III
   See Butterworth, W.E.
Butts, Ellen R(ubinstein) 1942- *93*
Buxton, Ralph
   See Silverstein, Alvin
   and Silverstein, Virginia B(arbara Opshelor)
Buzzeo, Toni 1951- *135*
Byalick, Marcia 1947- *141*
Earlier sketch in SATA *97*
Byard, Carole (Marie) 1941- *57*
Byars, Betsy 1928- *163*
Autobiography Feature *108*
Earlier sketches in SATA *4, 46, 80*
See also CLR *72*
See also SAAS *1*
Byars, Betsy Cromer
   See Byars, Betsy
Byfield, Barbara Ninde 1930- *8*
Byman, Jeremy 1944- *129*
Bynum, Janie *133*
Byrd, Elizabeth 1912-1989 .... *34*
Byrd, Nicole
   See Zach, Cheryl (Byrd)

Byrd, Robert (John) 1942- *158*
  Earlier sketches in SATA *33, 112*
Byrne, Mary Gregg 1951- *162*

C

C. 3. 3.
  See Wilde, Oscar (Fingal O'Flahertie Wills)
Cabaniss, J(ames) Allen 1911-1997 .... *5*
Cabat, Erni 1914- *74*
Cable, Mary 1920- *9*
Cabot, Meg 1967- *127*
  See also CLR *85*
Cabot, Meggin
  See Cabot, Meg
Cabot, Patricia
  See Cabot, Meg
Cabral, O. M.
  See Cabral, Olga
Cabral, Olga 1909- *46*
Cabrera, Jane 1968- *152*
  Earlier sketch in SATA *103*
Cabrera, Marcela 1966- *90*
Cade, Toni
  See Bambara, Toni Cade
Cadmus and Harmonia
  See Buchan, John
Cadnum, Michael 1949- *165*
  Earlier sketches in SATA *87, 121*
  See also CLR *78*
Caduto, Michael J. 1955- *103*
Cadwallader, Sharon 1936- *7*
Cady, (Walter) Harrison 1877(?)-1970 .... *19*
Caffey, Donna (J.) 1954- *110*
Cagle, Malcolm W(infield) 1918- *32*
Cahn, Rhoda 1922- *37*
Cahn, William 1912-1976 .... *37*
Cain, Arthur H(omer) 1913-1981 .... *3*
Caine, Geoffrey
  See Walker, Robert W(ayne)
Caines, Jeannette (Franklin) 1938- *78*
  Brief entry *43*
  See also CLR *24*
Cairns, Trevor 1922- *14*
Calabro, Marian 1954- *79*
Caldecott, Moyra 1927- *22*
Caldecott, Randolph (J.) 1846-1886 .... *100*
  Earlier sketch in SATA *17*
  See also CLR *110*
Calder, Charlotte 1952- *125*
Calder, David 1932-1997 .... *105*
Calder, Lyn
  See Calmenson, Stephanie
Calder, Marie D(onais) 1948- *96*
Calderone-Stewart, Lisa
  See Calderone-Stewart, Lisa-Marie
Calderone-Stewart, Lisa-Marie 1958- *123*
Caldwell, Doreen (Mary) 1942- *71*
Caldwell, John C(ope) 1913-1984 .... *7*
Calhoun, B. B. 1961- *98*
Calhoun, Chad
  See Barrett, Neal, Jr.
  and Cunningham, Chet
  and Goulart, Ron(ald Joseph)
Calhoun, Dia 1959- *129*
Calhoun, Mary *2*
  See also CLR *42*
  See Wilkins, Mary Huiskamp
Calhoun, T. B.
  See Bisson, Terry (Ballantine)
Calif, Ruth 1922- *67*
Calkins, Franklin
  See Stratemeyer, Edward L.
Call, Hughie Florence 1890-1969 .... *1*
Callahan, Dorothy M(onahan) 1934- *39*
  Brief entry *35*
Callahan, Philip Serna 1923- *25*
Callan, Jamie 1954- *59*
Callaway, Bernice (Anne) 1923- *48*

Callaway, Kathy 1943- *36*
Callen, Larry
  See Callen, Lawrence Willard, Jr.
Callen, Lawrence Willard, Jr. 1927- *19*
Calley, Karin 1965- *92*
Calmenson, Stephanie 1952- *139*
  Brief entry *37*
  Earlier sketches in SATA *51, 84*
Calvert, Elinor H.
  See Lasell, Elinor H.
Calvert, John
  See Leaf, (Wilbur) Munro
Calvert, Patricia 1931- *132*
  Earlier sketches in SATA *45, 69*
  See also SAAS *17*
Camburn, Carol A.
  See Camburn-Bracalente, Carol A.
Camburn-Bracalente, Carol A. 1962- *118*
Cameron, Ann 1943- *129*
  Earlier sketches in SATA *27, 89*
  See also SAAS *20*
Cameron, Edna M. 1905-1999 .... *3*
Cameron, Eleanor (Frances) 1912-1996 ...... *25*
  Obituary *93*
  Earlier sketch in SATA *1*
  See also CLR *72*
  See also SAAS *10*
Cameron, Elizabeth
  See Nowell, Elizabeth Cameron
Cameron, Elizabeth Jane 1910-1976 .... *32*
  Obituary *30*
Cameron, Ian
  See Payne, Donald Gordon
Cameron, M(alcolm) G(ordon) Graham
  See Graham-Cameron, M(alcolm) G(ordon)
Cameron, M. Graham
  See Graham-Cameron, M(alcolm) G(ordon)
Cameron, Mike Graham
  See Graham-Cameron, M(alcolm) G(ordon)
Cameron, Polly 1928- *2*
Cameron, Scott 1962- *84*
Camp, Lindsay 1957- *133*
Camp, Walter (Chauncey) 1859-1925
  See YABC *1*
Campbell, (Elizabeth) Andrea 1963- *50*
Campbell, Ann R. 1925- *11*
Campbell, Bill 1960- *89*
Campbell, Bruce
  See Epstein, Samuel
Campbell, Camilla 1905-1992 .... *26*
Campbell, Carole R. 1939- *125*
Campbell, Hope 1925- *20*
Campbell, Hugh 1930- *90*
Campbell, Jane
  See Edwards, Jane Campbell
Campbell, Julie
  See Tatham, Julie Campbell
Campbell, Patricia J(ean) 1930- *45*
Campbell, Patty
  See Campbell, Patricia J(ean)
Campbell, Peter A. 1948- *99*
Campbell, R. W.
  See Campbell, Rosemae Wells
Campbell, Robin
  See Strachan, Ian
Campbell, Rod 1945- *98*
  Brief entry *44*
  Earlier sketch in SATA *51*
Campbell, Rosemae Wells 1909- *1*
Campion, Nardi Reeder 1917- *22*
Campling, Elizabeth 1948- *53*
Campoy, F. Isabel (Coronado) 1946- *143*
Camps, Luis 1928- *66*
Canales, Viola 1957- *141*
Canfield, Dorothea F.
  See Fisher, Dorothy (Frances) Canfield
Canfield, Dorothea Frances
  See Fisher, Dorothy (Frances) Canfield
Canfield, Dorothy
  See Fisher, Dorothy (Frances) Canfield
Canfield, Jack 1944- *164*

Canfield, Jane White 1897-1984 .... *32*
  Obituary *38*
Canfield, Muriel 1935- *94*
Cann, Helen 1969- *124*
Cann, Kate 1954- *152*
  Earlier sketch in SATA *103*
Cannan, Joanna *82*
  See Pullein-Thompson, Joanna Maxwell
Cannon, A(nn) E(dwards) *163*
  Earlier sketch in SATA *93*
Cannon, Bettie (Waddell) 1922- *59*
Cannon, Curt
  See Hunter, Evan
Cannon, Eileen E(mily) 1948- *119*
Cannon, Frank
  See Mayhar, Ardath
Cannon, Janell 1957- *128*
  Earlier sketch in SATA *78*
Cannon, Marian G. 1923- *85*
Cannon, Taffy
  See Cannon, Eileen E(mily)
Canusi, Jose
  See Barker, S(quire) Omar
Canyon, Christopher 1966- *150*
  Earlier sketch in SATA *104*
Capek, Michael 1947- *142*
  Earlier sketch in SATA *96*
Capes, Bernard (Edward Joseph) 1854-1918
  .... *116*
Caponigro, John Paul 1965- *84*
Capote, Truman 1924-1984 .... *91*
Capp, Al *61*
  See Caplin, Alfred Gerald
Cappel, Constance 1936- *22*
Cappetta, Cynthia 1949- *125*
Cappo, Nan Willard 1955- *143*
Capps, Benjamin (Franklin) 1922- *9*
Captain Kangaroo
  See Keeshan, Robert J.
Captain Wheeler
  See Ellis, Edward S(ylvester)
Captain Young of Yale
  See Stratemeyer, Edward L.
Capucilli, Alyssa Satin 1957- *163*
  Earlier sketch in SATA *115*
Capucine
  See Mazille, Capucine
Caraher, Kim(berley Elizabeth) 1961- *105*
Caraker, Mary 1929- *74*
Caras, Roger A(ndrew) 1928-2001 .... *12*
  Obituary *127*
Caravantes, Peggy 1935- *140*
Caraway, Caren 1939- *57*
Carbone, Elisa
  See Carbone, Elisa Lynn
Carbone, Elisa Lynn 1954- *137*
  Earlier sketch in SATA *81*
Carbonnier, Jeanne 1894-1974 .... *3*
  Obituary *34*
Card, Orson Scott 1951- *127*
  Earlier sketch in SATA *83*
Carew, Jan (Rynveld) 1925- *51*
  Brief entry *40*
Carey, Bonnie
  See Marshall, Bonnie C.
Carey, Ernestine Gilbreth 1908- *2*
Carey, Lisa *110*
Carey, M. V.
  See Carey, Mary V(irginia)
Carey, Mary V(irginia) 1925-1994 .... *44*
  Brief entry *39*
Carey, Peter 1943- *94*
Carey, Valerie Scho 1949- *60*
Carigiet, Alois 1902-1985 .... *24*
  Obituary *47*
  See also CLR *38*
Carini, Edward 1923- *9*
Carkeet, David 1946- *75*

Carle, Eric 1929- *163*
  Earlier sketches in SATA *4, 65, 120*
  See also CLR *72*
  See also SAAS *6*
Carleton, Captain L. C.
  See Ellis, Edward S(ylvester)
Carleton, Captain Latham C.
  See Ellis, Edward S(ylvester)
Carleton, Latham C.
  See Ellis, Edward S(ylvester)
Carling, Amelia Lau 1949- *164*
  Earlier sketch in SATA *119*
Carlisle, Carolyn
  See Hawes, Louise
Carlisle, Clark
  See Holding, James (Clark Carlisle, Jr.)
Carlisle, Olga Andreyev 1930- *35*
Carlsen, G(eorge) Robert 1917- *30*
Carlsen, Ruth C(hristoffer) 1918- *2*
Carlson, Bernice Wells 1910- *8*
Carlson, Dale (Bick) 1935- *1*
Carlson, Daniel (Bick) 1960- *27*
Carlson, Laurie (Winn) 1952- *101*
Carlson, Melody 1956- *113*
Carlson, Nancy L.
  See Carlson, Nancy L(ee)
Carlson, Nancy L(ee) 1953- *144*
  Brief entry *45*
  Earlier sketches in SATA *56, 90*
Carlson, Natalie Savage 1906-1997 .... *68*
  Earlier sketch in SATA *2*
  See also SAAS *4*
Carlson, Susan Johnston 1953- *88*
Carlson, Vada F. 1897- *16*
Carlstrom, Nancy White 1948- *156*
  Brief entry *48*
  Earlier sketches in SATA *53, 92*
Carlton, Keith
  See Robertson, Keith (Carlton)
Carlyon, Richard *55*
Carman, Patrick *161*
Carmer, Carl (Lamson) 1893-1976 .... *37*
  Obituary *30*
Carmer, Elizabeth Black 1904- *24*
Carmi, Giora 1944- *149*
  Earlier sketch in SATA *79*
Carmichael, Carrie *40*
  See Carmichael, Harriet
Carmody, Isobelle 1958- *161*
Carmody, Isobelle Jane
  See Carmody, Isobelle
Carol, Bill J.
  See Knott, William C(ecil, Jr.)
Caron, Romi
  See Caron-Kyselkova', Romana
Caron-Kyselkova', Romana 1967- *94*
Caroselli, Remus F(rancis) 1916- *36*
Carpelan, Bo (Gustaf Bertelsson) 1926- *8*
Carpenter, (John) Allan 1917- *81*
  Earlier sketch in SATA *3*
Carpenter, Angelica Shirley 1945- *153*
  Earlier sketch in SATA *71*
Carpenter, Frances 1890-1972 .... *3*
  Obituary *27*
Carpenter, John (Howard) 1948- *58*
Carpenter, Johnny
  See Carpenter, John (Howard)
Carpenter, Patricia (Healy Evans) 1920- *11*
Carr, Glyn
  See Styles, (Frank) Showell
Carr, Harriett H(elen) 1899-1977 .... *3*
Carr, Jan 1953- *132*
  Earlier sketch in SATA *89*
Carr, M. J.
  See Carr, Jan
Carr, Mary Jane 1899-1988 .... *2*
  Obituary *55*
Carr, Philippa
  See Hibbert, Eleanor Alice Burford
Carr, Roger Vaughan 1937- *95*
Carrel, Annette Felder 1929- *90*

Carrick, Carol (Hatfield) 1935- *118*
  Earlier sketches in SATA *7, 63*
  See also SAAS *18*
Carrick, Donald (F.) 1929-1989 .... *63*
  Earlier sketch in SATA *7*
Carrick, Malcolm 1945- *28*
Carrier, Lark 1947- *71*
  Brief entry *50*
Carrier, Roch 1937- *166*
  Earlier sketch in SATA *105*
Carrighar, Sally 1898-1985 .... *24*
Carrington, G. A.
  See Cunningham, Chet
Carrington, Marsha Gray 1954- *168*
  Earlier sketch in SATA *111*
Carris, Joan Davenport 1938- *44*
  Brief entry *42*
Carroll, Curt
  See Bishop, Curtis (Kent)
Carroll, Elizabeth
  See Barkin, Carol
  and James, Elizabeth
Carroll, Jenny
  See Cabot, Meg
Carroll, (Archer) Latrobe 1894-1996 .... *7*
Carroll, Laura
  See Parr, Lucy
Carroll, Lewis
  See CLR *108*
  See Dodgson, Charles L(utwidge)
Carroll, Raymond 1924- *86*
  Brief entry *47*
Carruth, Hayden 1921- *47*
Carryl, Charles E(dward) 1841-1920 .... *114*
Carse, Robert 1902-1971 .... *5*
Carson, J(ohn) Franklin 1920-1981 .... *1*
  Obituary *107*
Carson, Mary Kay 1964- *150*
Carson, Rachel
  See Carson, Rachel Louise
Carson, Rachel Louise 1907-1964 .... *23*
  See Carson, Rachel
Carson, Rosalind
  See Chittenden, Margaret
Carson, S. M.
  See Gorsline, (Sally) Marie
Carson, William C. 1928- *154*
Carter, Alden R(ichardson) 1947- *137*
  Earlier sketch in SATA *67*
  See also CLR *22*
  See also SAAS *18*
Carter, Andy 1948- *134*
Carter, Angela (Olive) 1940-1992 .... *66*
  Obituary *70*
Carter, Anne Laurel 1953- *135*
Carter, Asa Earl
  See Carter, Forrest
Carter, Avis Murton
  See Allen, Kenneth S.
Carter, Bruce
  See Hough, Richard (Alexander)
Carter, Carol S(hadis) 1948- *124*
Carter, David A. 1957- *114*
Carter, Don 1958- *124*
Carter, Dorothy Sharp 1921- *8*
Carter, Forrest 1927(?)-1979 .... *32*
Carter, Helene 1887-1960 .... *15*
Carter, (William) Hodding, Jr. 1907-1972 .... *2*
  Obituary *27*
Carter, James Earl, Jr.
  See Carter, Jimmy
Carter, Jimmy 1924- *79*
Carter, Katharine J(ones) 1905-1984 .... *2*
Carter, Lin(wood Vrooman) 1930-1988 ...... *91*
Carter, Mike 1936- *138*

Carter, Nick
  See Avallone, Michael (Angelo, Jr.)
  and Ballard, (Willis) Todhunter
  and Crider, (Allen) Bill(y)
  and Cassiday, Bruce (Bingham)
  and Chastain, Thomas
  and Dey, Frederic (Merrill) Van Rensselaer
  and Garside, (Clifford) Jack
  and Hayes, Ralph E(ugene)
  and Henderson, M(arilyn) R(uth)
  and Lynds, Dennis
  and Lynds, Gayle (Hallenbeck)
  and Randisi, Robert J(oseph)
  and Rasof, Henry
  and Stratemeyer, Edward L.
  and Smith, Martin Cruz
  and Swain, Dwight V(reeland)
  and Vardeman, Robert E(dward)
  and Wallmann, Jeffrey M(iner)
  and White, Lionel
Carter, Peter 1929- *57*
Carter, Phyllis Ann
  See Eberle, Irmengarde
Carter, Samuel (Thomson) III 1904-1988 ... *37*
  Obituary *60*
Carter, William E. 1926-1983 .... *1*
  Obituary *35*
Cartlidge, Michelle 1950- *96*
  Brief entry *37*
  Earlier sketch in SATA *49*
Cartner, William Carruthers 1910- *11*
Cartwright, Ann 1940- *78*
Cartwright, Reg(inald Ainsley) 1938- *64*
Cartwright, Sally 1923- *9*
Carusone, Al 1949- *89*
Carver, John
  See Gardner, Richard (M.)
Carwell, L'Ann
  See McKissack, Patricia C.
Cary
  See Cary, Louis F(avreau)
Cary, Louis F(avreau) 1915- *9*
Caryl, Jean
  See Kaplan, Jean Caryl Korn
Casanova, Mary 1957- *136*
  Earlier sketch in SATA *94*
Cascone, A.G.
  See Cascone, Annette
  and Cascone, Gina
Cascone, Annette 1960- *103*
Cascone, Gina 1955- *103*
Case, Marshal T(aylor) 1941- *9*
Case, Michael
  See Howard, Robert West
Caseley, Judith 1951- *159*
  Brief entry *53*
  Earlier sketch in SATA *87*
Casewit, Curtis W(erner) 1922-2002 .... *4*
Casey, Barbara (Louise) 1944- *147*
  Earlier sketch in SATA *79*
Casey, Brigid 1950- *9*
Casey, Tina 1959- *141*
Cash, Megan Montague *160*
Casilla, Robert 1959- *146*
  Earlier sketch in SATA *75*
Cason, Mabel Earp 1892-1965 .... *10*
Cass, Joan E(velyn) *1*
Cass-Beggs, Barbara 1904- *62*
Cassedy, Patrice (Rinaldo) 1953- *149*
Cassedy, Sylvia 1930-1989 .... *77*
  Obituary *61*
  Earlier sketch in SATA *27*
  See also CLR *26*
Cassel, Lili
  See Wronker, Lili Cassel
Cassidy, Anne 1952- *166*
Casson, Hugh Maxwell 1910-1999 .... *65*
  Obituary *115*
Cassutt, Michael (Joseph) 1954- *78*
Castaldo, Nancy Fusco 1962- *151*
  Earlier sketch in SATA *93*

Castaneda, Omar S. 1954- *71*
Castell, Megan
  See Williams, Jeanne
Castellanos, Jane Mollie Robinson 1913-2001
  .... *9*
Castellon, Federico 1914-1971 .... *48*
Castillo, Edmund L. 1924-2005 .... *1*
  Obituary *167*
Castle, Lee
  See Ogan, George F.
  and Ogan, Margaret E. (Nettles)
Castle, Paul
  See Howard, Vernon (Linwood)
Castle, Robert
  See Hamilton, Edmond
Caswell, Brian 1954- *97*
Caswell, Helen (Rayburn) 1923- *12*
Catalano, Dominic 1956- *163*
  Earlier sketch in SATA *76*
Catalano, Grace (A.) 1961- *99*
Catalanotto, Peter 1959- *159*
  Autobiography Feature *113*
  Earlier sketches in SATA *70, 114*
  See also CLR *68*
  See also SAAS *25*
Cate, Dick
  See Cate, Richard Edward Nelson
Cate, Richard Edward Nelson 1932- *28*
Cather, Willa (Sibert) 1873-1947 .... *30*
  See also CLR *98*
Catherall, Arthur 1906-1980 .... *74*
  Earlier sketch in SATA *3*
  See Ruthin, Margaret
Cathon, Laura E(lizabeth) 1908-1991 ...... *27*
Catlett, Elizabeth 1919(?)- *82*
Catlin, Wynelle 1930- *13*
Cato, Heather *105*
Cato, Sheila *114*
Catrow, David
  See Catrow, David J. III
Catrow, David J. III *152*
Catt, Louis
  See French, Vivian
Cattell, James 1954- *123*
Catton, (Charles) Bruce 1899-1978 .... *2*
  Obituary *24*
Catz, Max
  See Glaser, Milton
Caudell, Marian 1930- *52*
Caudill, Rebecca 1899-1985 .... *1*
  Obituary *44*
Cauley, Lorinda Bryan 1951- *46*
  Brief entry *43*
Cauman, Samuel 1910-1971 .... *48*
Causley, Charles (Stanley) 1917-2003 ...... *66*
  Obituary *149*
  Earlier sketch in SATA *3*
  See also CLR *30*
Cavallaro, Ann (Abelson) 1918- *62*
Cavallo, Diana 1931- *7*
Cavanagh, Helen (Carol) 1939- *98*
  Brief entry *37*
  Earlier sketch in SATA *48*
Cavanah, Frances 1899-1982 .... *31*
  Earlier sketch in SATA *1*
Cavanna, Betty *30*
  Earlier sketch in SATA *1*
  See also SAAS *4*
  See Harrison, Elizabeth (Allen) Cavanna
Cavanna, Elizabeth
  See Harrison, Elizabeth (Allen) Cavanna
Cave, Kathryn 1948- *123*
  Earlier sketch in SATA *76*
Cavendish, Peter
  See Horler, Sydney
Cavin, Ruth (Brodie) 1918- *38*
Cavoukian, Raffi 1948- *68*
Cawley, Winifred 1915- *13*
Caxton, Pisistratus
  See Lytton, Edward G(eorge) E(arle) L(ytton)
  Bulwer-Lytton Baron

Cazeau, Charles J(ay) 1931- *65*
Cazet, Denys 1938- *163*
  Brief entry *41*
  Earlier sketches in SATA *52, 99*
Cazzola, Gus 1934- *73*
Cebulash, Mel 1937- *91*
  Earlier sketch in SATA *10*
Ceder, Georgiana Dorcas -1985 .... *10*
Celenza, Anna Harwell *133*
Celestino, Martha Laing 1951- *39*
Cepeda, Joe *159*
Cerf, Bennett (Alfred) 1898-1971 .... *7*
Cerf, Christopher (Bennett) 1941- *2*
Cerullo, Mary M. 1949- *145*
  Earlier sketch in SATA *86*
Cervon, Jacqueline
  See Moussard, Jacqueline
Cetin, Frank Stanley 1921- *2*
Chabon, Michael 1963- *145*
Chaconas, D(oris) J. 1938- *145*
Chaconas, Dori
  See Chaconas, D(oris) J.
Chadwick, Lester *67*
  Earlier sketch in SATA *1*
Chaffee, Allen *3*
Chaffin, Lillie D(orton) 1925- *4*
Chaikin, Miriam 1924- *152*
  Earlier sketches in SATA *24, 102*
Chall, Marsha Wilson *150*
Challand, Helen J(ean) 1921- *64*
Challans, Mary 1905-1983 .... *23*
  Obituary *36*
  See Renault, Mary
Chalmers, Mary (Eileen) 1927- *6*
  See also SAAS *14*
Chamberlain, Margaret 1954- *46*
Chamberlin, Kate 1945- *105*
Chambers, Aidan 1934- *108*
  Earlier sketches in SATA *1, 69*
  See also SAAS *12*
Chambers, Catherine E.
  See St. John, Nicole
Chambers, John W. 1933- *57*
  Brief entry *46*
Chambers, Kate
  See St. John, Nicole
Chambers, Margaret Ada Eastwood 1911- *2*
Chambers, Peggy
  See Chambers, Margaret Ada Eastwood
Chambers, Robert W(illiam) 1865-1933 ... *107*
Chan, Gillian 1954- *147*
  Earlier sketch in SATA *102*
Chance, James T.
  See Carpenter, John (Howard)
Chance, John T.
  See Carpenter, John (Howard)
Chance, Stephen
  See Turner, Philip (William)
Chandler, Caroline A(ugusta) 1906-1979 .... *22*
  Obituary *24*
Chandler, David P(orter) 1933- *28*
Chandler, Edna Walker 1908-1982 .... *11*
  Obituary *31*
Chandler, Jennifer
  See Westwood, Jennifer
Chandler, Karen 1959- *122*
Chandler, Linda S(mith) 1929- *39*
Chandler, Robert 1953- *40*
Chandler, Ruth Forbes 1894-1978 .... *2*
  Obituary *26*
Chandonnet, Ann F. 1943- *92*
Chaney, Jill 1932- *87*
Chang, Chih-Wei 1966- *111*
Chang, Cindy 1968- *90*
Chang, Margaret (Scrogin) 1941- *71*
Chang, Raymond 1939- *142*
  Earlier sketches in SATA *71, 142 PEN*
Chanin, Michael 1952- *84*
Channel, A. R.
  See Catherall, Arthur
Chapian, Marie 1938- *29*

Chapin, Tom 1945- *83*
Chapman, Allen *67*
  Earlier sketch in SATA *1*
Chapman, Cheryl O(rth) 1948- *80*
Chapman, (Constance) Elizabeth (Mann) 1919-
  .... *10*
Chapman, Gaynor 1935- *32*
Chapman, Gillian 1955- *120*
Chapman, Jane 1970- *122*
Chapman, Jean *104*
  Earlier sketch in SATA *34*
  See also CLR *65*
Chapman, Lee
  See Bradley, Marion Zimmer
Chapman, Lynne F(erguson) 1963- *150*
  Earlier sketch in SATA *94*
Chapman, Vera (Ivy May) 1898-1996 ...... *33*
Chapman, Walker
  See Silverberg, Robert
Chappell, Audrey 1954- *72*
Chappell, Warren 1904-1991 .... *68*
  Obituary *67*
  Earlier sketch in SATA *6*
  See also SAAS *10*
Charbonneau, Eileen 1951- *118*
  Earlier sketch in SATA *84*
Charbonnet, Gabrielle 1961- *81*
Chardiet, Bernice (Kroll) 1927(?)- *27*
Charles, Donald
  See Meighan, Donald Charles
Charles, Louis
  See Stratemeyer, Edward L.
Charles, Nicholas J.
  See Kuskin, Karla
Charles, Norma *153*
Charlip, Remy 1929- *119*
  Earlier sketches in SATA *4, 68*
  See also CLR *8*
Charlot, Jean 1898-1979 .... *8*
  Obituary *31*
Charlot, Martin (Day) 1944- *64*
Charlton, Michael (Alan) 1923- *34*
Charmatz, Bill 1925-2005 .... *7*
Charnas, Suzy McKee 1939- *110*
  Earlier sketch in SATA *61*
Charosh, Mannis 1906- *5*
Chartier, Normand L. 1945- *66*
Chase, Alice
  See McHargue, Georgess
Chase, Alyssa 1965- *92*
Chase, Andra 1942- *91*
Chase, Emily
  See Aks, Patricia
  and Garwood, Julie
  and Sachs, Judith
  and White, Carol
Chase, Mary (Coyle) 1907-1981 .... *17*
  Obituary *29*
Chase, Mary Ellen 1887-1973 .... *10*
Chase, Richard 1904-1988 .... *64*
  Obituary *56*
Chase, Samantha
  See Glick, Ruth (Burtnick)
Chast, Roz 1954- *97*
Chastain, Madye Lee 1908-1989 .... *4*
Chataway, Carol 1955- *140*
Chatterjee, Debjani 1952- *83*
Chauncy, Nan(cen Beryl Masterman)
  1900-1970 .... *6*
  See also CLR *6*
Chaundler, Christine 1887-1972 .... *1*
  Obituary *25*
Chbosky, Stephen 1972- *164*
Chee, Cheng-Khee 1934- *79*
Cheese, Chloe 1952- *118*
Chekhonte, Antosha
  See Chekhov, Anton (Pavlovich)
Chekhov, Anton (Pavlovich) 1860-1904 .... *90*
Chen, Anthony 1929- *6*
Chen, Chih-Yuan 1975- *155*
Chen, Ju-Hong 1941- *78*

Chen, Sara
    See Odgers, Sally Farrell
Chen, Tony
    See Chen, Anthony
Chen, Yuan-tsung 1932- 65
Chenault, Nell
    See Smith, Linell Nash
Chenery, Janet (Dai) 1923- 25
Cheney, Cora 1916-1999 3
    Obituary 110
Cheney, Glenn (Alan) 1951- 99
Cheney, Lynne V. 1941- 152
Cheney, Ted
    See Cheney, Theodore Albert
Cheney, Theodore A. Rees
    See Cheney, Theodore Albert
Cheney, Theodore Albert 1928- 11
Cheng, Andrea 1957- 128
Cheng, Christopher 1959- 106
Cheng, Judith 1955- 36
Cheng, Shan
    See Jiang, Cheng An
Cheripko, Jan 1951- 155
    Earlier sketch in SATA 83
Chermayeff, Ivan 1932- 47
Chernoff, Dorothy A.
    See Ernst, (Lyman) John
Chernoff, Goldie Taub 1909- 10
Cherry, Carolyn Janice 93
    See Cherryh, C. J.
Cherry, Lynne 1952- 99
    Earlier sketch in SATA 34
Cherryholmes, Anne
    See Price, Olive
Chesler, Bernice 1932-2002 59
Chess, Victoria (Dickerson) 1939- 92
    Earlier sketch in SATA 33
Chester, Deborah 1957- 85
Chester, Kate
    See Guccione, Leslie Davis
Chesterton, G(ilbert) K(eith) 1874-1936 27
Chesworth, Michael 160
Chetin, Helen 1922- 6
Chetwin, Grace 86
    Brief entry 50
Chevalier, Christa 1937- 35
Chevalier, Tracy 1962- 128
Chew, Ruth 1920- 7
Chichester Clark, Emma 1955- 156
    Earlier sketch in SATA 117
    See Clark, Emma Chichester
Chidsey, Donald Barr 1902-1981 3
    Obituary 27
Chiefari, Janet D. 1942- 58
Chien-min, Lin
    See Rumford, James
Child, L. Maria
    See Child, Lydia Maria
Child, Lauren 1965- 160
    Earlier sketch in SATA 119
Child, Lincoln B. 1957- 113
Child, Lydia Maria 1802-1880 67
Child, Mrs.
    See Child, Lydia Maria
Child, Philip 1898-1978 47
Children's Shepherd, The
    See Westphal, Arnold Carl
Childress, Alice 1920-1994 81
    Earlier sketches in SATA 7, 48
    See also CLR 14
Childs, H(alla) Fay (Cochrane) 1890-1971 ... 1
    Obituary 25
Chilton, Charles (Frederick William) 1917-
    102
Chimaera
    See Farjeon, Eleanor
Chin, Richard (M.) 1946- 52
Chinery, Michael 1938- 26
Chin-Lee, Cynthia D. 1958- 102
Chippendale, Lisa A. 158

Chipperfield, Joseph Eugene 1912-1980(?) . 87
    Earlier sketch in SATA 2
Chisholm, P. F.
    See Finney, Patricia
Chislett, Gail (Elaine) 1948- 58
Chittenden, Elizabeth F. 1903-1999 9
Chittenden, Margaret 1935- 28
Chittum, Ida 1918- 7
Chitwood, Suzanne Tanner 1958- 160
Chmielarz, Sharon Lee 1940- 72
Choate, Judith (Newkirk) 1940- 30
Chocolate, Debbi 1954- 96
Chocolate, Deborah M. Newton
    See Chocolate, Debbi
Chodos-Irvine, Margaret 152
Choi, Sook Nyul 1937- 73
    Autobiography Feature 126
    See also CLR 53
Choldenko, Gennifer 1957- 135
Chorao, (Ann Mc)Kay (Sproat) 1936- 162
    Earlier sketches in SATA 8, 69
Choron, Sandra (Zena Samelson) 1950- ... 146
Chown, Marcus 1959- 137
Choyce, Lesley 1951- 165
    Earlier sketch in SATA 94
Chrisman, Arthur Bowie 1889-1953 124
    See also YABC 1
Christelow, Eileen 1943- 90
    Autobiography Feature 120
    Brief entry 35
    Earlier sketch in SATA 38
Christensen, Bonnie 1951- 157
    Earlier sketch in SATA 110
Christensen, Gardell Dano 1907-1991 1
Christensen, Laurie
    See Steding, Laurie
Christesen, Barbara 1940- 40
Christgau, Alice Erickson 1902-1977 13
Christian, Mary Blount 1933- 9
Christie, Agatha (Mary Clarissa) 1890-1976
    36
Christie, Gregory
    See Christie, R. Gregory
Christie, Philippa 129
    Earlier sketches in SATA 1, 67
    See also CLR 9
    See Pearce, Philippa
Christie, R. Gregory 1971- 127
Christopher, John
    See CLR 2
    See Youd, (Christopher) Samuel
Christopher, Louise
    See Hale, Arlene
Christopher, Matt(hew Frederick) 1917-1997
    80
    Obituary 99
    Earlier sketches in SATA 2, 47
    See also CLR 33
    See also SAAS 9
Christopher, Milbourne 1914(?)-1984 46
Christy, Howard Chandler 1873-1952 21
Chrystie, Frances N(icholson) 1904-1986 ... 60
Chu, Daniel 1933- 11
Chukovsky, Kornei (Ivanovich) 1882-1969
    34
    Earlier sketch in SATA 5
Church, Richard 1893-1972 3
Churchill, E(lmer) Richard 1937- 11
Churchill, Elizabeth
    See Hough, Richard (Alexander)
Chute, B(eatrice) J(oy) 1913-1987 2
    Obituary 53
Chute, Marchette (Gaylord) 1909-1994 1
Chwast, Jacqueline 1932- 6
Chwast, Seymour 1931- 146
    Earlier sketches in SATA 18, 96
Ciardi, John (Anthony) 1916-1986 65
    Obituary 46
    Earlier sketch in SATA 1
    See also CLR 19
    See also SAAS 26

Ciccone, Madonna Louise Veronica
    See Madonna
Ciment, James D. 1958- 140
Citra, Becky 1954- 137
Clair, Andree 19
Clampett, Robert 44
    See Clampett, Bob
Clapp, John 1968- 109
Clapp, Patricia 1912- 74
    Earlier sketch in SATA 4
    See also SAAS 4
Clare, Ellen
    See Sinclair, Olga
Clare, Helen
    See Clarke, Pauline
Claremont, Chris(topher Simon) 1950- 87
Clark, Ann Nolan 1896-1995 82
    Obituary 87
    Earlier sketch in SATA 4
    See also CLR 16
    See also SAAS 16
Clark, Champ 1923-2002 47
Clark, Christopher (Anthony) Stuart
    See Stuart-Clark, Christopher (Anthony)
Clark, Clara Gillow 1951- 154
    Earlier sketch in SATA 84
Clark, David
    See Hardcastle, Michael
Clark, David Allen
    See Ernst, (Lyman) John
Clark, Emma Chichester 69
    See Chichester Clark, Emma
Clark, Frank J(ames) 1922- 18
Clark, Garel
    See Garelick, May
Clark, Halsey
    See Deming, Richard
Clark, Joan
    See Benson, Mildred (Augustine Wirt)
Clark, Joan 1934- 96
    Earlier sketch in SATA 59
Clark, Leonard 1905-1981 30
    Obituary 29
Clark, M. R.
    See Clark, Mavis Thorpe
Clark, Margaret (D.) 1943- 126
Clark, Margaret Goff 1913- 82
    Earlier sketch in SATA 8
Clark, Mary Higgins 1929- 46
Clark, Mavis Thorpe 1909-1999 74
    Earlier sketch in SATA 8
    See also CLR 30
    See also SAAS 5
Clark, Merle
    See Gessner, Lynne
Clark, Patricia Denise 1921- 117
    See Lorrimer, Claire
Clark, Patricia Finrow 1929- 11
Clark, Ronald William 1916-1987 2
    Obituary 52
Clark, Sherryl 1956- 149
Clark, Van D(eusen) 1909-1974 2
Clark, Virginia
    See Gray, Patricia (Clark)
Clark, Walter Van Tilburg 1909-1971 8
Clarke, Arthur C(harles) 1917- 115
    Earlier sketches in SATA 13, 70
Clarke, Clorinda 1917- 7
Clarke, Gus 1948- 134
Clarke, J.
    See Clarke, Judith
Clarke, James Hall
    See Rowland-Entwistle, (Arthur) Theodore
    (Henry)
Clarke, Joan B. 1921- 42
    Brief entry 27
Clarke, John
    See Laklan, Carli
    and Sontup, Dan(iel)

Clarke, Judith 1943- *164*
  Earlier sketches in SATA *75, 110*
  See also CLR *61*
Clarke, Julia 1950- *138*
Clarke, Kenneth 1957- *107*
Clarke, Lea
  See Rowland-Entwistle, (Arthur) Theodore
  (Henry)
Clarke, Margaret 1941-
  See CLR *99*
Clarke, Mary Stetson 1911-1994 .... *5*
Clarke, Michael
  See Newlon, (Frank) Clarke
Clarke, Pauline 1921- *131*
  See also CLR *28*
  See Clare, Helen
  and Hunter Blair, Pauline
Clarke-Rich, Elizabeth L. 1934- *103*
Clarkson, E(dith) Margaret 1915- *37*
Clarkson, Ewan 1929- *9*
Claudia, Susan
  See Goulart, Ron(ald Joseph)
  and Johnston, William
Claverie, Jean 1946- *38*
Clay, Patrice 1947- *47*
Claypool, Jane *103*
  See Miner, Jane Claypool
Clayton, Elaine 1961- *159*
  Earlier sketch in SATA *94*
Clayton, Lawrence (Otto, Jr.) 1945- *75*
Clayton, Sandra 1951- *110*
Cleary, Beverly (Atlee Bunn) 1916- *121*
  Earlier sketches in SATA *2, 43, 79*
  See also CLR *72*
  See also SAAS *20*
Cleary, Brian P. 1959- *132*
  Earlier sketch in SATA *93*
Cleaver, Bill *22*
  Obituary *27*
  See also CLR *6*
  See Cleaver, William J(oseph)
Cleaver, Carole 1934- *6*
Cleaver, Elizabeth (Ann Mrazik) 1939-1985
  .... *23*
  Obituary *43*
  See also CLR *13*
Cleaver, Hylton Reginald 1891-1961 .... *49*
Cleaver, Vera (Allen) 1919-1993 .... *76*
  Earlier sketch in SATA *22*
  See also CLR *6*
Cleishbotham, Jebediah
  See Scott, Sir Walter
Cleland, Mabel
  See Widdemer, Mabel Cleland
Clem, Margaret H(ollingsworth) 1923- *90*
Clemens, Samuel Langhorne 1835-1910 ... *100*
  See also YABC *2*
  See Twain, Mark
Clemens, Virginia Phelps 1941- *35*
Clement, Rod *97*
Clements, Andrew 1949- *158*
  Earlier sketch in SATA *104*
Clements, Bruce 1931- *94*
  Earlier sketch in SATA *27*
Clemons, Elizabeth
  See Nowell, Elizabeth Cameron
Clerk, N. W.
  See Lewis, C.S.
Cleveland-Peck, Patricia *80*
Cleven, Cathrine
  See Cleven, Kathryn Seward
Cleven, Kathryn Seward *2*
Clevenger, William R(ussell) 1954- *84*
Clevin, Joergen 1920- *7*
Clevin, Jorgen
  See Clevin, Joergen
Clewes, Dorothy (Mary) 1907-2003 .... *86*
  Obituary *138*
  Earlier sketch in SATA *1*
Clifford, David
  See Rosenberg, Eth(el) Clifford

Clifford, Eth *92*
  See also SAAS *22*
  See Rosenberg, Eth(el) Clifford
Clifford, Harold B(urton) 1893-1988 .... *10*
Clifford, Margaret Cort 1929- *1*
Clifford, Martin
  See Hamilton, Charles (Harold St. John)
Clifford, Mary Louise Beneway 1926- *23*
Clifford, Peggy
  See Clifford, Margaret Cort
Clifford, Rachel Mark
  See Lewis, Brenda Ralph
Clifton, (Thelma) Lucille 1936- *128*
  Earlier sketches in SATA *20, 69*
  See also CLR *5*
Climo, Shirley 1928- *166*
  Autobiography Feature *110*
  Brief entry *35*
  Earlier sketches in SATA *39, 77*
  See also CLR *69*
Clinton, Cathryn
  See Hoellwarth, Cathryn Clinton
Clinton, Dirk
  See Silverberg, Robert
Clinton, Jon
  See Prince, J(ack) H(arvey)
Clish, (Lee) Marian 1946- *43*
Clive, Clifford
  See Hamilton, Charles (Harold St. John)
Clokey, Art 1921- *59*
Cloudsley-Thompson, J(ohn) L(eonard) 1921-
  .... *19*
Clouse, Nancy L. 1938- *78*
Clover, Peter 1952- *152*
Clutha, Janet Paterson Frame 1924-2004 .. *119*
  See Frame, Janet
Clymer, Eleanor 1906-2001 .... *85*
  Obituary *126*
  Earlier sketch in SATA *9*
  See also SAAS *17*
Clyne, Patricia (Edwards) *31*
Coalson, Glo 1946- *94*
  Earlier sketch in SATA *26*
Coates, Anna 1958- *73*
Coates, Belle 1896-1986 .... *2*
Coates, Ruth Allison 1915- *11*
Coats, Alice M(argaret) 1905-1976 .... *11*
Coatsworth, Elizabeth (Jane) 1893-1986 ... *100*
  Obituary *49*
  Earlier sketches in SATA *2, 56*
  See also CLR *2*
Cobalt, Martin
  See Mayne, William (James Carter)
Cobb, Mary 1931- *88*
Cobb, Vicki 1938- *136*
  Autobiography Feature *136*
  Earlier sketches in SATA *8, 69, 131*
  See also CLR *2*
  See also SAAS *6*
Cobbett, Richard
  See Pluckrose, Henry (Arthur)
Cober, Alan E(dwin) 1935-1998 .... *7*
  Obituary *101*
Cobham, Sir Alan
  See Hamilton, Charles (Harold St. John)
Coburn, Jake 1978- *155*
Cocagnac, Augustin Maurice(-Jean) 1924- ... *7*
Cocca-Leffler, Maryann 1958- *136*
  Earlier sketch in SATA *80*
Cochran, Bobbye A. 1949- *11*
Cockett, Mary *3*
Coddell, Esme Raji
  See Codell, Esme Raji
Codell, Esme Raji 1968- *160*
Cody, C. S.
  See Waller, Leslie
Cody, Jess
  See Cunningham, Chet
Coe, Anne (E.) 1949- *95*

Coe, Douglas
  See Epstein, Beryl (M. Williams)
  and Epstein, Samuel
Coen, Rena Neumann 1925- *20*
Coerr, Eleanor (Beatrice) 1922- *67*
  Earlier sketch in SATA *1*
Cofer, Judith Ortiz 1952- *164*
  Earlier sketch in SATA *110*
  See Ortiz Cofer, Judith
Coffey, Brian
  See Koontz, Dean R.
Coffin, Geoffrey
  See Mason, F(rancis) van Wyck
Coffin, M. T.
  See Stanley, George Edward
Coffman, Ramon Peyton 1896-1989 .... *4*
Cogan, Karen 1954- *125*
Coggins, Jack (Banham) 1914- *2*
Cohen, Barbara 1932-1992 .... *77*
  Obituary *74*
  Earlier sketch in SATA *10*
  See also SAAS *7*
Cohen, Daniel (E.) 1936- *70*
  Earlier sketch in SATA *8*
  See also CLR *43*
  See also SAAS *4*
Cohen, Jan Barger
  See Barger, Jan
Cohen, Jene Barr
  See Barr, Jene
Cohen, Joan Lebold 1932- *4*
Cohen, Judith Love 1933- *78*
Cohen, Miriam 1926-1955 .... *155*
  Earlier sketches in SATA *29, 106*
  See also SAAS *11*
Cohen, Nora *75*
Cohen, Paul S. 1945- *58*
Cohen, Peter Zachary 1931- *150*
  Earlier sketch in SATA *4*
Cohen, Robert Carl 1930- *8*
Cohen, Sholom 1951- *94*
Cohn, Angelo 1914-1997 .... *19*
Cohn, Rachel 1968- *161*
Coit, Margaret Louise 1922-2003 .... *2*
  Obituary *142*
Colbert, Anthony 1934- *15*
Colbert, Nancy A. 1936- *139*
Colby, C(arroll) B(urleigh) 1904-1977 .... *35*
  Earlier sketch in SATA *3*
Colby, Jean Poindexter 1909-1993 .... *23*
Cole, Annette
  See Steiner, Barbara A(nnette)
Cole, Babette 1949- *155*
  Earlier sketches in SATA *61, 96*
Cole, Betsy 1940- *83*
Cole, Brock 1938- *136*
  Earlier sketch in SATA *72*
  See also CLR *18*
Cole, Davis
  See Elting, Mary
Cole, Hannah 1954- *74*
Cole, Jack -1974
  See Stewart, John (William)
Cole, Jackson
  See Curry, Thomas Albert
  and Germano, Peter B.
  and Heckelmann, Charles N(ewman)
  and Newton, D(wight) B(ennett)
  and Schisgall, Oscar
Cole, Jennifer
  See Zach, Cheryl (Byrd)
Cole, Joanna 1944- *168*
  Brief entry *37*
  Earlier sketches in SATA *49, 81, 120*
  See also CLR *40*
Cole, Lois Dwight 1903-1979 .... *10*
  Obituary *26*
Cole, Michael 1947- *59*
Cole, Sheila R(otenberg) 1939- *95*
  Earlier sketch in SATA *24*
Cole, Stephen 1971- *161*

Cole, William (Rossa) 1919-2000 .... *71*
  Earlier sketch in SATA *9*
  See also SAAS *9*
Coleman, Andrew
  See Pine, Nicholas
Coleman, Clare
  See Bell, Clare (Louise)
  and Easton, M(alcolm) Coleman
Coleman, Loren 1947- *164*
Coleman, Loren Elwood, Jr.
  See Coleman, Loren
Coleman, Mary Ann 1928- *83*
Coleman, Michael (Lee) 1946- *133*
  Autobiography Feature *133*
  Earlier sketch in SATA *108*
Coleman, William L(eRoy) 1938- *49*
  Brief entry *34*
Coles, Robert (Martin) 1929- *23*
Colfer, Eoin 1965- *148*
  See also CLR *112*
Colin, Ann
  See Ure, Jean
Collard, Sneed B. III 1959- *139*
  Earlier sketch in SATA *84*
Colledge, Anne 1939- *142*
Collicott, Sharleen 1937- *143*
  Earlier sketch in SATA *98*
Collier, Bryan *126*
Collier, Christopher 1930- *70*
  Earlier sketch in SATA *16*
Collier, Ethel 1903-1999 .... *22*
Collier, James Lincoln 1928- *166*
  Earlier sketches in SATA *8, 70*
  See also CLR *3*
  See also SAAS *21*
Collier, Jane
  See Collier, Zena
Collier, Steven 1942- *61*
Collier, Zena 1926- *23*
  See Collier, Jane
Collings, Gillian 1939- *102*
Collington, Peter 1948- *99*
  Earlier sketch in SATA *59*
Collins, Ace 1953- *82*
Collins, Andrew J.
  See Collins, Ace
Collins, David R(aymond) 1940-2001 ...... *121*
  Earlier sketch in SATA *7*
Collins, Heather 1946- *81*
Collins, Hunt
  See Hunter, Evan
Collins, Michael
  See Lynds, Dennis
Collins, Michael 1930- *58*
Collins, Pat(ricia) Lowery 1932- *151*
  Earlier sketch in SATA *31*
Collins, Paul 1954- *126*
Collinson, A. S.
  See Collinson, Alan S.
Collinson, Alan S. 1934- *80*
Collinson, Roger (Alfred) 1936- *133*
Collodi, Carlo
  See CLR *5*
  See Lorenzini, Carlo
Colloms, Brenda 1919- *40*
Colman, Hila *53*
  Earlier sketch in SATA *1*
  See also SAAS *14*
Colman, Penny (Morgan) 1944- *160*
  Autobiography Feature *160*
  Earlier sketches in SATA *77, 114*
Colman, Warren (David) 1944- *67*
Colombo, John Robert 1936- *50*
Colon, Raul *156*
Colonius, Lillian 1911-1992 .... *3*
Colorado, Antonio J.
  See Colorado (Capella), Antonio J(ulio)
Colorado (Capella), Antonio J(ulio) 1903-1994
  .... *23*
  Obituary *79*
Colquhoun, Glenn 1964- *165*

Colston, Fifi E. 1960- *150*
Colt, Martin
  See Epstein, Beryl (M. Williams)
  and Epstein, Samuel
Colum, Padraic 1881-1972 .... *15*
  See also CLR *36*
Columbus, Chris(topher) 1959- *97*
Columella
  See Moore, Clement Clarke
Colver, Anne 1908- *7*
Colvin, James
  See Moorcock, Michael
Colwell, Eileen (Hilda) 1904-2002 .... *2*
Coman, Carolyn *127*
Combs, Lisa M.
  See McCourt, Lisa
Combs, Robert
  See Murray, John
Comfort, Jane Levington
  See Sturtzel, Jane Levington
Comfort, Mildred Houghton 1886-1976 .... *3*
Comins, Ethel M(ae) *11*
Comins, Jeremy 1933- *28*
Commager, Henry Steele 1902-1998 .... *23*
  Obituary *102*
Compere, Mickie
  See Davidson, Margaret
Compestine, Ying Chang 1963- *140*
Compton, Patricia A. 1936- *75*
Comte, The Great
  See Hawkesworth, Eric
Comus
  See Ballantyne, R(obert) M(ichael)
Comyns, Nance
  See Comyns-Toohey, Nantz
Comyns-Toohey, Nantz 1956- *86*
Conan Doyle, Arthur
  See Doyle, Sir Arthur Conan
Condit, Martha Olson 1913- *28*
Condon, Bill 1949- *142*
Condon, Judith *83*
Condy, Roy 1942- *96*
Cone, Ferne Geller 1921- *39*
Cone, Molly (Lamken) 1918- *151*
  Autobiography Feature *151*
  Earlier sketches in SATA *1, 28, 115*
  See also SAAS *11*
Cone, Patrick 1954- *89*
Coney, Michael G. 1932-2005 .... *61*
Coney, Michael Greatrex
  See Coney, Michael G.
Coney, Mike
  See Coney, Michael G.
Conford, Ellen 1942- *162*
  Earlier sketches in SATA *6, 68, 110*
  See also CLR *71*
Conger, Lesley
  See Suttles, Shirley (Smith)
Conklin, Gladys Plemon 1903- *2*
Conklin, Paul S. 1929(?)-2003 .... *43*
  Brief entry *33*
  Obituary *147*
Conkling, Hilda 1910-1986 .... *23*
Conlan, Kathleen Elizabeth 1950- *145*
Conlan, Kathy
  See Conlan, Kathleen Elizabeth
Conley-Weaver, Robyn 1963- *125*
Conlon-McKenna, Marita 1956- *71*
Conly, Jane Leslie 1948- *164*
  Earlier sketches in SATA *80, 112*
Conly, Robert Leslie 1918(?)-1973 .... *23*
  See O'Brien, Robert C.
Connolly, Jerome P(atrick) 1931- *8*
Connolly, Pat 1943- *74*
Connolly, Peter 1935- *105*
  Earlier sketch in SATA *47*
Conover, Chris 1950- *31*
Conquest, Owen
  See Hamilton, Charles (Harold St. John)
Conrad, Joseph 1857-1924 .... *27*

Conrad, Pam 1947-1996 .... *133*
  Brief entry *49*
  Obituary *90*
  Earlier sketches in SATA *52, 80*
  See also CLR *18*
  See also SAAS *19*
Conroy, Jack *19*
  See Conroy, John Wesley
Conroy, Robert
  See Goldston, Robert (Conroy)
Constant, Alberta Wilson 1908-1981 .... *22*
  Obituary *28*
Conway, Diana C(ohen) 1943- *91*
Conway, Gordon
  See Hamilton, Charles (Harold St. John)
Cook, Bernadine 1924- *11*
Cook, Fred J(ames) 1911-2003 .... *2*
  Obituary *145*
Cook, Glen (Charles) 1944- *108*
Cook, Hugh (Walter Gilbert) 1956- *85*
Cook, Jean Thor 1930- *94*
Cook, Joel 1934- *79*
Cook, Joseph Jay 1924- *8*
Cook, Lisa Broadie *157*
Cook, Lyn
  See Waddell, Evelyn Margaret
Cook, Roy
  See Silverberg, Robert
Cooke, Ann
  See Cole, Joanna
Cooke, Arthur
  See Lowndes, Robert A(ugustine) W(ard)
Cooke, Barbara
  See Alexander, Anna B(arbara Cooke)
Cooke, David Coxe 1917- *2*
Cooke, Donald Ewin 1916-1985 .... *2*
  Obituary *45*
Cooke, Frank E. 1920- *87*
Cooke, Jean (Isobel Esther) 1929- *74*
Cooke, John Estes
  See Baum, L(yman) Frank
Cooke, Trish 1962- *129*
Cookson, Catherine (McMullen) 1906-1998 . *9*
  Obituary *116*
Coolidge, Olivia E(nsor) 1908- *26*
  Earlier sketch in SATA *1*
Cooling, Wendy *169*
  Earlier sketch in SATA *111*
Coombs, Charles I(ra) 1914-1994 .... *43*
  Earlier sketch in SATA *3*
  See also SAAS *15*
Coombs, Chick
  See Coombs, Charles I(ra)
Coombs, Patricia 1926- *51*
  Earlier sketch in SATA *3*
  See also SAAS *22*
Cooney, Barbara 1917-2000 .... *96*
  Obituary *123*
  Earlier sketches in SATA *6, 59*
  See also CLR *23*
Cooney, Caroline B. 1947- *130*
  Brief entry *41*
  Earlier sketches in SATA *48, 80, 113*
Cooney, Nancy Evans 1932- *42*
Coontz, Otto 1946- *33*
Cooper, Ann (Catharine) 1939- *104*
Cooper, Elisha 1971- *157*
  Earlier sketch in SATA *99*
Cooper, Elizabeth Keyser -1992 .... *47*
Cooper, Floyd *144*
  Earlier sketch in SATA *96*
  See also CLR *60*
Cooper, Gordon 1932- *23*
Cooper, Helen 1963- *169*
  Earlier sketch in SATA *102*
Cooper, Henry S(potswood) F(enimore), Jr.
  1933- *65*
Cooper, Ilene 1948- *145*
  Earlier sketches in SATA *66, 97*
Cooper, James Fenimore 1789-1851 .... *19*
  See also CLR *105*

Cooper, John R. *1*
Cooper, Kay 1941- *11*
Cooper, Lee Pelham 1926- *5*
Cooper, Lester (Irving) 1919-1985 .... *32*
   Obituary *43*
Cooper, Lettice (Ulpha) 1897-1994 .... *35*
   Obituary *82*
Cooper, Louise 1952- *152*
Cooper, M. E.
   See Lerangis, Peter
Cooper, Melrose
   See Kroll, Virginia L.
Cooper, Michael L. 1950- *117*
   Earlier sketch in SATA *79*
Cooper, Patrick 1949- *134*
Cooper, Susan (Mary) 1935- *151*
   Earlier sketches in SATA *4, 64, 104*
   See also CLR *67*
   See also SAAS *6*
Cope, Jane U(rsula) 1949- *108*
Copeland, Helen 1920- *4*
Copeland, Paul W. *23*
Coplans, Peta 1951- *84*
Copley (Diana) Heather Pickering 1918- *45*
Coppard, A(lfred) E(dgar) 1878-1957
   See YABC *1*
Coralie
   See Anderson, Catherine Corley
Corbett, Grahame *43*
   Brief entry *36*
Corbett, Scott 1913- *42*
   Earlier sketch in SATA *2*
   See also CLR *1*
   See also SAAS *2*
Corbett, W(illiam) J(esse) 1938- *102*
   Brief entry *44*
   Earlier sketch in SATA *50*
   See also CLR *19*
Corbin, Sabra Lee
   See Malvern, Gladys
Corbin, William
   See McGraw, William Corbin
Corby, Dan
   See Catherall, Arthur
Corcoran, Barbara (Asenath) 1911- *77*
   Autobiography Feature *125*
   Earlier sketch in SATA *3*
   See also CLR *50*
   See also SAAS *20*
Corcos, Lucille 1908-1973 .... *10*
Cordell, Alexander
   See Graber, Alexander
Cordell, Alexander
   See Graber, (George) Alexander
Corder, Zizou
   See Young, Louisa
Corella, Joseph
   See Odgers, Sally Farrell
Coren, Alan 1938- *32*
Corey, Dorothy *23*
Corey, Shana 1974- *133*
Corfe, Thomas Howell 1928- *27*
Corfe, Tom
   See Corfe, Thomas Howell
Corfield, Robin Bell 1952- *74*
Corlett, William 1938-2005 .... *46*
   Brief entry *39*
Cormack, M(argaret) Grant 1913- *11*
Cormack, Maribelle B. 1902-1984 .... *39*
Cormier, Robert (Edmund) 1925-2000 .... *83*
   Obituary *122*
   Earlier sketches in SATA *10, 45*
   See also CLR *55*
Cornelius, Carol 1942- *40*
Cornelius, Kay 1933- *157*
Cornell, J.
   See Cornell, Jeffrey
Cornell, James (Clayton, Jr.) 1938- *27*
Cornell, Jean Gay 1920- *23*
Cornell, Jeffrey 1945- *11*
Cornish, Sam(uel James) 1935- *23*

Cornwall, Nellie
   See Sloggett, Nellie
Correy, Lee
   See Stine, G(eorge) Harry
Corrick, James A. 1945- *76*
Corrigan, (Helen) Adeline 1909- *23*
Corrigan, Barbara 1922- *8*
Corrigan, Eireann 1977- *163*
Corrin, Sara 1918- *86*
   Brief entry *48*
Corrin, Stephen *86*
   Brief entry *48*
Cort, M. C.
   See Clifford, Margaret Cort
Cort, Margaret
   See Clifford, Margaret Cort
Corwin, Judith H(offman) 1946- *10*
Cory, Rowena
   See Lindquist, Rowena Cory
Cosby, Bill
   See Cosby, William Henry, Jr.
Cosby, William Henry, Jr. 1937- *110*
   Earlier sketch in SATA *66*
   See Cosby, Bill
Cosentino, Ralph *169*
Cosgrove, Margaret (Leota) 1926- *47*
Cosgrove, Stephen E(dward) 1945- *53*
   Brief entry *40*
Coskey, Evelyn 1932- *7*
Cosner, Shaaron 1940- *43*
Cossi, Olga 1921- *102*
   Earlier sketch in SATA *67*
Costabel, Eva Deutsch 1924- *45*
Costabel-Deutsch, Eva
   See Costabel, Eva Deutsch
Costello, David F(rancis) 1904-1990 .... *23*
Cott, Jonathan 1942- *23*
Cottam, Clarence 1899-1974 .... *25*
Cottle, Joan 1960- *135*
Cottler, Joseph 1899-1996 .... *22*
Cottonwood, Joe 1947- *92*
Cottrell, Leonard 1913-1974 .... *24*
Cottringer, Anne 1952- *150*
   Earlier sketch in SATA *97*
Coulman, Valerie 1969- *161*
Counsel, June 1926- *70*
Countryman, The
   See Whitlock, Ralph
Courlander, Harold 1908-1996 .... *6*
   Obituary *88*
Coursen, Valerie 1965(?)- *102*
Courtney, Dayle
   See Goldsmith, Howard
Cousins, Linda 1946- *90*
Cousins, Margaret 1905-1996 .... *2*
   Obituary *92*
Cousteau, Jacques-Yves 1910-1997 .... *98*
   Earlier sketch in SATA *38*
Couture, Christin 1951- *73*
Coville, Bruce 1950- *155*
   Autobiography Feature *155*
   Earlier sketches in SATA *32, 77, 118*
Covington, Dennis *109*
Covington, Linda
   See Windsor, Linda
Cowan, Catherine *121*
Cowell, Cressida 1966- *140*
Cowen, Eve
   See Werner, Herma
Cowen, Ida 1898-1993 .... *64*
Cowie, Leonard W(allace) 1919- *4*
Cowles, Kathleen
   See Krull, Kathleen
Cowley, (Cassia) Joy 1936- *90*
   Autobiography Feature *118*
   Earlier sketch in SATA *4*
   See also CLR *55*
   See also SAAS *26*
Cowley, Joy 1936- *164*
Cowley, Marjorie 1925- *111*
Cox, (Christopher) Barry 1931- *62*

Cox, Clinton 1934- *108*
   Earlier sketch in SATA *74*
Cox, David (Dundas) 1933- *56*
Cox, Donald William 1921- *23*
Cox, Jack
   See Cox, John Roberts
Cox, John Roberts 1915-1981 .... *9*
Cox, Judy 1954- *160*
   Earlier sketch in SATA *117*
Cox, Palmer 1840-1924 .... *24*
   See also CLR *24*
Cox, Vic 1942- *88*
Cox, Vicki 1945- *158*
Cox, Victoria
   See Garretson, Victoria Diane
Cox, Wally 1924- *25*
   See Cox, Wallace (Maynard)
Cox, William R(obert) 1901-1988 .... *46*
   Brief entry *31*
   Obituary *57*
   See Ward, Jonas
Coxe, Molly 1959- *101*
   Earlier sketch in SATA *69*
Coxon, Michele 1950- *158*
   Earlier sketch in SATA *76*
Coy, Harold 1902-1986 .... *3*
Coy, John 1958- *120*
Craats, Rennay 1973- *131*
Crabtree, Judith 1928- *98*
   Earlier sketch in SATA *63*
Cracker, Edward E.B.
   See Odgers, Sally Farrell
Craft, K. Y.
   See Craft, Kinuko Y(amabe)
Craft, Kinuko
   See Craft, Kinuko Y(amabe)
Craft, Kinuko Y(amabe) 1940- *127*
   Earlier sketch in SATA *65*
Craft, Ruth 1935- *87*
   Brief entry *31*
Craig, A. A.
   See Anderson, Poul (William)
Craig, Alisa
   See MacLeod, Charlotte (Matilda)
Craig, Helen 1934- *94*
   Earlier sketches in SATA *46, 49*
Craig, John Eland
   See Chipperfield, Joseph Eugene
Craig, John Ernest 1921- *23*
Craig, Kit
   See Reed, Kit
Craig, M. F.
   See Craig, Mary (Francis) Shura
Craig, M. Jean *17*
Craig, M. S.
   See Craig, Mary (Francis) Shura
Craig, Margaret (Maze) 1911-1964 .... *9*
Craig, Mary
   See Craig, Mary (Francis) Shura
Craig, Mary Shura
   See Craig, Mary (Francis) Shura
Craig, Mary (Francis) Shura 1923-1991 ..... *86*
   Obituary *65*
   Earlier sketch in SATA *6*
   See also SAAS *7*
Craig, Ruth 1922- *95*
Craik, Mrs.
   See Craik, Dinah Maria (Mulock)
Craik, Dinah Maria (Mulock) 1826-1887 ... *34*
   See Craik, Mrs.
   and Mulock, Dinah Maria
Crandell, Rachel 1943- *152*
Crane, Barbara (Joyce) 1934- *31*
Crane, Caroline 1930- *11*
Crane, M. A.
   See Wartski, Maureen (Ann Crane)
Crane, Stephen (Townley) 1871-1900
   See YABC *2*
Crane, Walter 1845-1915 .... *100*
   Earlier sketch in SATA *18*
   See also CLR *56*

Crane, William D(wight) 1892-1976 .... *1*
Cranfield, Ingrid 1945- *74*
Cranshaw, Stanley
  See Fisher, Dorothy (Frances) Canfield
Crary, Elizabeth (Ann) 1942- *99*
  Brief entry *43*
Crary, Margaret (Coleman) 1906-1986 .... *9*
Cravath, Lynne W(oodcock) 1951- *148*
  Earlier sketch in SATA *98*
Craven, Thomas 1889-1969 .... *22*
Crawford, Charles P. 1945- *28*
Crawford, Deborah 1922- *6*
Crawford, John E(dmund) 1904-1971 .... *3*
Crawford, K(aren) Michael 1959- *155*
Crawford, Mel 1925- *44*
  Brief entry *33*
Crawford, Phyllis 1899- *3*
Cray, Roberta
  See Emerson, Ru
Crayder, Dorothy *7*
Crayder, Teresa
  See Colman, Hila
Crayon, Geoffrey
  See Irving, Washington
Craz, Albert G. 1926- *24*
Crebbin, June 1938- *169*
  Earlier sketch in SATA *80*
Crecy, Jeanne
  See Williams, Jeanne
Credle, Ellis 1902-1998 .... *1*
Creech, Sharon 1945- *139*
  Earlier sketch in SATA *94*
  See also CLR *89*
Creeden, Sharon 1938- *91*
Creighton, Jill 1949- *96*
Crenson, Victoria 1952- *159*
  Earlier sketch in SATA *88*
Cresp, Gael 1954- *119*
Crespo, George 1962- *82*
Cresswell, Helen 1934-2005 .... *79*
  Obituary *168*
  Earlier sketches in SATA *1, 48*
  See also CLR *18*
  See also SAAS *20*
Cressy, Michael 1955- *124*
Cressy, Mike
  See Cressy, Michael
Cretan, Gladys (Yessayan) 1921- *2*
Cretzmeyer, Stacy (Megan) 1959- *124*
Crew, Gary 1947- *163*
  Earlier sketches in SATA *75, 110*
  See also CLR *42*
Crew, Helen (Cecilia) Coale 1866-1941
  See YABC *2*
Crew, Linda (Jean) 1951- *137*
  Earlier sketch in SATA *71*
Crews, Donald 1938- *76*
  Brief entry *30*
  Earlier sketch in SATA *32*
  See also CLR *7*
Crews, Nina 1963- *158*
  Earlier sketch in SATA *97*
Crichton, (John) Michael 1942- *88*
  Earlier sketch in SATA *9*
Crider, (Allen) Bill(y) 1941- *99*
Crilley, Mark 1966- *148*
  Autobiography Feature *148*
  Earlier sketch in SATA *120*
Crisman, Ruth 1914- *73*
Crisp, Marta Marie 1947- *128*
Crisp, Marty
  See Crisp, Marta Marie
Crispin, A(nn) C(arol) 1950- *86*
Crist, James J. *168*
Cristall, Barbara *79*
Crist-Evans, Craig 1954- *153*
Crofford, Emily (Ardell) 1927- *61*
Crofut, William E. III 1934- *23*
Croll, Carolyn 1945- *102*
  Brief entry *52*
  Earlier sketch in SATA *56*

Croman, Dorothy Young
  See Rosenberg, Dorothy
Cromie, Alice Hamilton 1914-2000 .... *24*
Cromie, William J(oseph) 1930- *4*
Crompton, Anne Eliot 1930- *73*
  Earlier sketch in SATA *23*
Crompton, Richmal
  See Lamburn, Richmal Crompton
Cronbach, Abraham 1882-1965 .... *11*
Crone, Ruth 1919-2003 .... *4*
Cronin, A(rchibald) J(oseph) 1896-1981 ..... *47*
  Obituary *25*
Cronin, Doreen (A.) *125*
  See also CLR *105*
Crook, Beverly Courtney *38*
  Brief entry *35*
Crook, Connie Brummel 1930- *168*
  Earlier sketch in SATA *98*
Crook, Constance
  See Crook, Connie Brummel
Crosby, Alexander L. 1906-1980 .... *2*
  Obituary *23*
Crosby, Harry C., Jr. *102*
Crosby, Margaret
  See CLR *77*
  See Rathmann, Peggy
Crosher, G. R. *14*
Cross, Gilbert B. 1939- *60*
  Brief entry *51*
Cross, Gillian 1945- *165*
  Earlier sketches in SATA *38, 71, 110*
  See also CLR *28*
Cross, Gillian Clare
  See Cross, Gillian
Cross, Helen Reeder
  See Broadhead, Helen Cross
Cross, Peter 1951- *95*
Cross, Tom 1954- *146*
Cross, Verda 1914- *75*
Cross, Wilbur Lucius III 1918- *2*
Crossland, Caroline 1964- *83*
Crossley-Holland, Kevin 1941- *165*
  Earlier sketches in SATA *5, 74, 120*
  See also CLR *84*
  See also SAAS *20*
Crossley-Holland, Kevin John William
  See Crossley-Holland, Kevin
Crouch, Marcus 1913-1996 .... *4*
Crout, George C(lement) 1917- *11*
Crow, Donna Fletcher 1941- *40*
Crowe, Andrew *111*
Crowe, John
  See Lynds, Dennis
Crowe, (Bettina) Peter Lum 1911- *6*
Crowell, Grace Noll 1877-1969 .... *34*
Crowell, Pers 1910-1990 .... *2*
Crowell, Robert Leland 1909-2001 .... *63*
Crowfield, Christopher
  See Stowe, Harriet (Elizabeth) Beecher
Crowley, Arthur McBlair 1945- *38*
Crowley, John 1942- *140*
  Earlier sketch in SATA *65*
Crownfield, Gertrude 1867-1945
  See YABC *1*
Crowther, James Gerald 1899-1983 .... *14*
Crowther, Robert 1948- *163*
Cruikshank, George 1792-1878 .... *22*
  See also CLR *63*
Crum, Shutta *134*
Crummel, Susan Stevens 1949- *130*
Crump, Fred H., Jr. 1931- *76*
  Earlier sketch in SATA *11*
Crump, J(ames) Irving 1887-1979 .... *57*
  Obituary *21*
Crump, William D(rake) 1949- *138*
Crunden, Reginald
  See Cleaver, Hylton Reginald
Crunk, T.
  See Crunk, Tony
Crunk, Tony 1956- *130*

Crutcher, Chris(topher C.) 1946- *153*
  Earlier sketches in SATA *52, 99*
  See also CLR *28*
Cruz, Ray(mond) 1933- *6*
Cruz Martinez, Alejandro (?)-1987 .... *74*
Crystal, Billy 1947- *154*
Cuetara, Mittie 1957- *158*
  Earlier sketch in SATA *106*
Cuffari, Richard 1925-1978 .... *66*
  Obituary *25*
  Earlier sketch in SATA *6*
Cullen, Countee 1903-1946 .... *18*
Culliford, Pierre 1928-1992 .... *40*
  Obituary *74*
Cullinan, Bernice E(llinger) 1926- *135*
Culp, Louanna McNary 1901-1965 .... *2*
Culper, Felix
  See McCaughrean, Geraldine
Cumbaa, Stephen 1947- *72*
Cumming, Peter 1951- *168*
Cumming, Primrose Amy 1915- *24*
Cumming, Robert 1945- *65*
Cummings, Betty Sue 1918- *15*
  See also SAAS *9*
Cummings, Parke 1902-1987 .... *2*
  Obituary *53*
Cummings, Pat (Marie) 1950- *107*
  Earlier sketches in SATA *42, 71*
  See also CLR *48*
  See also SAAS *13*
Cummings, Phil 1957- *123*
  Earlier sketch in SATA *74*
Cummings, Priscilla 1951- *129*
Cummings, Richard
  See Gardner, Richard (M.)
Cummins, Maria Susanna 1827-1866
  See YABC *1*
Cuneo, Mary Louise -2001 .... *85*
Cunliffe, John Arthur 1933- *86*
  Earlier sketch in SATA *11*
Cunliffe, Marcus (Falkner) 1922-1990 .... *37*
  Obituary *66*
Cunningham, Bob
  See May, Julian
Cunningham, Captain Frank
  See Glick, Carl (Cannon)
Cunningham, Cathy
  See Cunningham, Chet
Cunningham, Chet 1928- *23*
Cunningham, Dale S(peers) 1932- *11*
Cunningham, Dru *91*
Cunningham, E. V.
  See Fast, Howard (Melvin)
Cunningham, Julia (Woolfolk) 1916- *132*
  Earlier sketches in SATA *1, 26*
  See also SAAS *2*
Cunningham, Lawrence J. 1943- *125*
Cunningham, Virginia
  See Holmgren, Virginia C(unningham)
Curiae, Amicus
  See Fuller, Edmund (Maybank)
Curie, Eve 1904- *1*
Curlee, Lynn 1947- *141*
  Earlier sketch in SATA *98*
Curley, Daniel 1918-1988 .... *23*
  Obituary *61*
Curley, Marianne 1959- *131*
Currie, Robin 1948- *120*
Currie, Stephen 1960- *132*
  Earlier sketch in SATA *82*
Curry, Ann (Gabrielle) 1934- *72*
Curry, Jane L(ouise) 1932- *138*
  Autobiography Feature *138*
  Earlier sketches in SATA *1, 52, 90*
  See also CLR *31*
  See also SAAS *6*
Curry, Peggy Simson 1911-1987 .... *8*
  Obituary *50*
Curtis, Bruce (Richard) 1944- *30*
Curtis, Chara M(ahar) 1950- *78*

Curtis, Christopher Paul 1954(?)- *140*
    Earlier sketch in SATA *93*
    See also CLR 68
Curtis, Gavin 1965- *107*
Curtis, Jamie Lee 1958- *144*
    Earlier sketch in SATA *95*
    See also CLR 88
Curtis, Marci *160*
Curtis, Patricia 1921- *101*
    Earlier sketch in SATA *23*
Curtis, Peter
    See Lofts, Norah (Robinson)
Curtis, Philip (Delacourt) 1920- *62*
Curtis, Richard (Alan) 1937- *29*
Curtis, Richard Hale
    See Deming, Richard
    and Levinson, Leonard
    and Rothweiler, Paul Roger
Curtis, Wade
    See Pournelle, Jerry (Eugene)
Curtiss, A(rlene) B. 1934- *90*
Cusack, Margaret 1945- *58*
Cushman, Doug 1953- *157*
    Earlier sketches in SATA *65, 101*
Cushman, Jerome *2*
Cushman, Karen 1941- *147*
    Earlier sketch in SATA *89*
    See also CLR 55
Cusick, Richie Tankersley 1952- *140*
    Earlier sketch in SATA *67*
Cutchen, Billye Walker 1930- *15*
Cutchins, Judy 1947- *59*
Cutler, Daniel S(olomon) 1951- *78*
Cutler, Ebbitt 1923- *9*
Cutler, Ivor 1923-2006 .... *24*
Cutler, Jane 1936- *162*
    Earlier sketches in SATA *75, 118*
Cutler, May Ebbitt
    See Cutler, Ebbitt
Cutler, Samuel
    See Folsom, Franklin (Brewster)
Cutlip, Kimbra L(eigh-Ann) 1964- *128*
Cutrate, Joe
    See Spiegelman, Art
Cutt, W(illiam) Towrie 1898-1981 .... *16*
    Obituary *85*
Cuyler, Margery S(tuyvesant) 1948- *156*
    Earlier sketches in SATA *39, 99*
Cuyler, Stephen
    See Bates, Barbara S(nedeker)
Cyrus, Kurt 1954- *132*

D

Dabcovich, Lydia *99*
    Brief entry *47*
    Earlier sketch in SATA *58*
Dace, Dolores B(oelens) 1929- *89*
Dadey, Debbie 1959- *136*
    Earlier sketch in SATA *73*
Dahl, Borghild (Margarethe) 1890-1984 .... *7*
    Obituary *37*
Dahl, Roald 1916-1990 .... *73*
    Obituary *65*
    Earlier sketches in SATA *1, 26*
    See also CLR *111*
Dahlstedt, Marden (Stewart) 1921-1983 .... *8*
    Obituary *110*
Dain, Martin J. 1924-2000 .... *35*
Dakos, Kalli 1950- *115*
    Earlier sketch in SATA *80*
Dale, Gary
    See Reece, Colleen L.
Dale, George E.
    See Asimov, Isaac
Dale, Jack
    See Holliday, Joseph
Dale, Kim 1957- *123*
Dale, Margaret J(essy) Miller 1911- *39*

Dale, Norman
    See Denny, Norman (George)
Dale, Penny 1954- *151*
    Earlier sketch in SATA *70*
Dalgliesh, Alice 1893-1979 .... *17*
    Obituary *21*
    See also CLR 62
Dalkey, Kara (Mia) 1953- *132*
Dallas, Ruth
    See Mumford, Ruth
Dalmas, John
    See Jones, John R(obert)
Dalton, Annie 1948- *140*
    Earlier sketch in SATA *40*
Dalton, Kit
    See Cunningham, Chet
Dalton, Pamela
    See Johnson, Pamela
Dalton, Sean
    See Chester, Deborah
Dalton, Sheila 1949- *108*
Daly, Jim
    See Stratemeyer, Edward L.
Daly, Kathleen N(orah) *124*
    Brief entry *37*
Daly, Maureen 1921- *129*
    Earlier sketch in SATA *2*
    See also CLR 96
    See also SAAS *1*
Daly, Nicholas 1946- *164*
    Earlier sketches in SATA *37, 76, 114*
    See also CLR 41
    See Daly, Niki
Daly, Niki
    See SAAS *21*
    See Daly, Nicholas
D'Amato, Alex 1919- *20*
D'Amato, Janet (Potter) 1925- *9*
Damerow, Gail (Jane) 1944- *83*
Damrell, Liz 1956- *77*
Damrosch, Helen
    See Tee-Van, Helen Damrosch
Dana, Barbara 1940- *22*
Dana, Richard Henry, Jr. 1815-1882 .... *26*
Danachair, Caoimhin O
    See Danaher, Kevin
Danaher, Kevin 1913-2002 .... *22*
Danakas, John 1963- *94*
D'Andrea, Kate
    See Steiner, Barbara A(nnette)
Dangerfield, Balfour
    See McCloskey, (John) Robert
Daniel, Alan 1939- *76*
    Brief entry *53*
Daniel, Anita 1893(?)-1978 .... *23*
    Obituary *24*
Daniel, Anne
    See Steiner, Barbara A(nnette)
Daniel, Becky 1947- *56*
Daniel, Claire 1949- *164*
Daniel, Colin
    See Windsor, Patricia
Daniel, Hawthorne 1890- *8*
Daniel, (Donna) Lee 1944- *76*
Daniel, Rebecca
    See Daniel, Becky
Daniels, Guy 1919-1989 .... *11*
    Obituary *62*
Daniels, Lucy
    See Oldfield, Jenny
Daniels, Max
    See Gellis, Roberta (Leah Jacobs)
Daniels, Olga
    See Sinclair, Olga
Daniels, Patricia 1955- *93*
Daniels, Zoe
    See Laux, Constance
Dank, Gloria Rand 1955- *56*
    Brief entry *46*
Dank, Leonard D(ewey) 1929- *44*
Dank, Milton 1920- *31*

Dann, Max 1955- *62*
Dantz, William R.
    See Philbrick, (W.) Rodman
Danziger, Paula 1944-2004 .... *149*
    Brief entry *30*
    Obituary *155*
    Earlier sketches in SATA *36, 63, 102*
    See also CLR 20
Darby, Gene Kegley
    See Darby, Jean (Kegley)
Darby, J. N.
    See Govan, (Mary) Christine Noble
Darby, Jean (Kegley) 1921- *68*
Darby, Patricia (Paulsen) *14*
Darby, Ray(mond) 1912-1982 .... *7*
d'Arcy, Willard
    See Cox, William R(obert)
Dare, Geena
    See McNicoll, Sylvia (Marilyn)
Darian, Shea 1959- *97*
Daringer, Helen Fern 1892-1986 .... *1*
Darke, Marjorie 1929- *87*
    Earlier sketch in SATA *16*
Darley, F(elix) O(ctavius) C(arr) 1822-1888
    .... *35*
Darling, David J. 1953- *60*
    Brief entry *44*
Darling, Kathy
    See Darling, Mary Kathleen
Darling, Lois (MacIntyre) 1917-1989 .... *3*
    Obituary *64*
Darling, Louis, (Jr.) 1916-1970 .... *3*
    Obituary *23*
Darling, Mary Kathleen 1943- *124*
    Earlier sketches in SATA *9, 79*
Darling, Sandra Louise Woodward
    See Day, Alexandra
Darnell, K(athryn) L(ynne) 1955- *150*
Darroll, Sally
    See Odgers, Sally Farrell
Darrow, Whitney, (Jr.) 1909-1999 .... *13*
    Obituary *115*
Darwin, Len
    See Darwin, Leonard
Darwin, Leonard 1916- *24*
Dasent, Sir George Webbe 1817-1896 .... *62*
    Brief entry *29*
Dash, Joan 1925- *142*
Daskam, Josephine Dodge
    See Bacon, Josephine Dodge (Daskam)
D'ath, Justin 1953- *106*
Dauer, Rosamond 1934- *23*
Daugherty, Charles Michael 1914- *16*
Daugherty, James (Henry) 1889-1974 .... *13*
    See also CLR 78
Daugherty, Richard D(eo) 1922- *35*
d'Aulaire, Edgar Parin 1898-1986 .... *66*
    Obituary *47*
    Earlier sketch in SATA *5*
    See also CLR 21
d'Aulaire, Ingri (Mortenson Parin) 1904-1980
    .... *66*
    Obituary *24*
    Earlier sketch in SATA *5*
    See also CLR 21
Dave, Dave
    See Berg, David
Daveluy, Paule Cloutier 1919- *11*
Davenier, Christine 1961- *127*
Davenport, John 1960- *156*
Daves, Michael 1938- *40*
David, A. R.
    See David, A(nn) Rosalie
David, A(nn) Rosalie 1946- *103*
David, Jonathan
    See Ames, Lee J(udah)
David, Lawrence 1963- *165*
    Earlier sketch in SATA *111*
David, Peter (Allen) 1956- *72*
    See Peters, David

David, Rosalie
   See David, A(nn) Rosalie
Davidson, Alice Joyce 1932- *54*
   Brief entry *45*
Davidson, Basil 1914- *13*
Davidson, (Marie) Diane 1924- *91*
Davidson, Hugh
   See Hamilton, Edmond
Davidson, Jessica 1915-1986 .... *5*
Davidson, Judith 1953- *40*
Davidson, Lionel 1922- *87*
Davidson, Margaret 1936- *5*
Davidson, Marion
   See Garis, Howard R(oger)
Davidson, Mary R. 1885-1973 .... *9*
Davidson, Mary S. 1940- *61*
Davidson, Mickie
   See Davidson, Margaret
Davidson, Nicole
   See Jensen, Kathryn
Davidson, R.
   See Davidson, Raymond
Davidson, Raymond 1926- *32*
Davidson, Rosalie 1921- *23*
Davie, Helen K(ay) 1952- *148*
   Earlier sketch in SATA *77*
Davies, Andrew (Wynford) 1936- *27*
Davies, Bettilu D(onna) 1942- *33*
Davies, Hunter 1936- *55*
   Brief entry *45*
Davies, Jacqueline 1962- *155*
Davies, Joan 1934- *50*
   Brief entry *47*
Davies, Nicola 1958- *150*
   Earlier sketch in SATA *99*
Davies, Peter J(oseph) 1937- *52*
Davies, Sumiko 1942- *46*
Davis, (A.) Aubrey 1949- *153*
Davis, Bette J. 1923- *15*
Davis, Burke 1913- *4*
Davis, Christopher 1928- *6*
Davis, D(elbert) Dwight 1908-1965 .... *33*
Davis, Daniel S(heldon) 1936- *12*
Davis, David R. 1948- *106*
Davis, Donald 1944- *169*
   Earlier sketch in SATA *93*
Davis, Donald D.
   See Davis, Donald
Davis, Gibbs 1953- *102*
   Brief entry *41*
   Earlier sketch in SATA *46*
Davis, Grania 1943- *88*
   Brief entry *50*
Davis, H(arold) L(enoir) 1896-1960 .... *114*
Davis, Hubert J(ackson) 1904-1997 .... *31*
Davis, James Robert 1945- *32*
   See Davis, Jim
Davis, Jenny 1953- *74*
Davis, Jim
   See Davis, James Robert
Davis, Julia 1900(?)-1993 .... *6*
   Obituary *75*
Davis, Karen (Elizabeth) 1944- *109*
Davis, Katie 1959(?)- *152*
Davis, Leslie
   See Guccione, Leslie Davis
Davis, Louise Littleton 1921- *25*
Davis, Maggie S. 1943- *57*
Davis, Marguerite 1889- *34*
Davis, Mary L(ee) 1935- *9*
Davis, Mary Octavia 1901-1976 .... *6*
Davis, Nelle 1958- *73*
Davis, Ossie 1917-2005 .... *81*
   See also CLR *56*
Davis, Paxton 1925-1994 .... *16*
Davis, Robert 1881-1949
   See YABC *1*
Davis, Robin W(orks) 1962- *87*
Davis, Russell Gerard 1922- *3*
Davis, Tim(othy N.) 1957- *94*
Davis, Verne Theodore 1889-1973 .... *6*

Davis, Yvonne 1927- *115*
Davol, Marguerite W. 1928- *146*
   Earlier sketch in SATA *82*
DaVolls, Andy (P.) 1967- *85*
DaVolls, Linda 1966- *85*
Davys, Sarah
   See Manning, Rosemary (Joy)
Dawes, Claiborne 1935- *111*
Dawson, Elmer A. *67*
   Earlier sketch in SATA *1*
Dawson, Imogen (Zoe) 1948-
   See Dawson, Imogen (Zoe)
Dawson, Imogen (Zoe) 1948- *126*
   Earlier sketch in SATA *90*
Dawson, Mary 1919- *11*
Day, A(rthur) Grove 1904-1994 .... *59*
Day, Alexandra 1941- *169*
   Earlier sketches in SATA *67, 97*
   See also CLR *22*
   See also SAAS *19*
Day, Beth (Feagles) 1924- *33*
Day, Donna
   See Asay, Donna Day
Day, Edward C. 1932- *72*
Day, Jon 1936(?)- *79*
Day, Nancy 1953- *140*
Day, Nancy Raines 1951- *148*
   Earlier sketch in SATA *93*
Day, Shirley 1962- *94*
Day, Thomas 1748-1789
   See YABC *1*
Day, Trevor 1955- *124*
Dazey, Agnes J(ohnston) *2*
Dazey, Frank M. *2*
Deacon, Alexis 1978- *139*
Deacon, Eileen
   See Geipel, Eileen
Deacon, Richard
   See McCormick, (George) Donald (King)
Deak, Erzsi 1959- *152*
Dean, Anabel 1915- *12*
Dean, Carolee 1962- *148*
Dean, Karen Strickler 1923- *49*
Dean, Ruth (Brigham) 1947- *145*
Dean, Zoey
   See Bennett, Cherie
de Angeli, Marguerite (Lofft) 1889-1987 .. *100*
   Obituary *51*
   Earlier sketches in SATA *1, 27*
   See also CLR *1*
Deans, Sis Boulos 1955- *136*
   Earlier sketch in SATA *78*
DeArmand, Frances Ullmann 1904(?)-1984
   .... *10*
   Obituary *38*
DeArmond, Dale 1914- *70*
DeArmond, Dale Burlison
   See DeArmond, Dale
Deary, Terry 1946- *101*
   Brief entry *41*
   Earlier sketch in SATA *51*
Deaver, Julie Reece 1953- *68*
de Banke, Cecile 1889-1965 .... *11*
De Bello, Rosario 1923- *89*
Debon, Nicolas *151*
de Bono, Edward 1933- *66*
de Brissac, Malcolm
   See Dickinson, Peter (Malcolm de Brissac)
de Brunhoff, Jean
   See Brunhoff, Jean de
De Brunhoff, Laurent
   See Brunhoff, Laurent de
de Bruyn, Monica (Jean) G(rembowicz) 1952-
   .... *13*
DeBry, Roger K. 1942- *91*
de Camp, Catherine Crook 1907-2000 .... *83*
   Earlier sketch in SATA *12*
de Camp, L(yon) Sprague 1907-2000 .... *83*
   Earlier sketch in SATA *9*
DeCandido, Keith R.A. *112*
Dechausay, Sonia E. *94*

Decker, Duane 1910-1964 .... *5*
DeClements, Barthe (Faith) 1920- *131*
   Earlier sketches in SATA *35, 71*
   See also CLR *23*
de Conte, Sieur Louis
   See Clemens, Samuel Langhorne
Dedman, Stephen *108*
Dee, Catherine 1964- *138*
Dee, Ruby *77*
   See Wallace, Ruby Ann
Deedy, John 1923- *24*
Deegan, Paul Joseph 1937- *48*
   Brief entry *38*
Deem, James M. 1950- *134*
   Earlier sketch in SATA *75*
Deeter, Catherine 1947- *137*
DeFelice, Cynthia 1951- *165*
   Earlier sketches in SATA *79, 121*
DeFelice, Cynthia C.
   See DeFelice, Cynthia
Defoe, Daniel 1660(?)-1731 .... *22*
   See also CLR *61*
DeFord, Deborah H. *123*
deFrance, Anthony
   See DiFranco, Anthony (Mario)
Degen, Bruce 1945- *147*
   Brief entry *47*
   Earlier sketches in SATA *57, 97*
DeGering, Etta (Belle) Fowler 1898-1996 .... *7*
De Goldi, Kate
   See De Goldi, Kathleen Domenica
De Goldi, Kathleen Domenica 1959- *123*
De Grazia, Ted *39*
   See De Grazia, Ettore
deGroat, Diane 1947- *169*
   Earlier sketches in SATA *31, 90*
deGros, J. H.
   See Villiard, Paul
de Grummond, Lena Young *62*
   Earlier sketch in SATA *6*
de Hamel, Joan Littledale 1924- *86*
De Haven, Tom 1949- *72*
de Hugo, Pierre
   See Brackers de Hugo, Pierre
Deiss, Joseph Jay 1915- *12*
de Jenkins, Lyll Becerra 1925-1997 .... *102*
DeJong, David C(ornel) 1905-1967 .... *10*
de Jong, Dola 1911-2003 .... *7*
   Obituary *149*
   See de Jong, Dorothea Rosalie
DeJong, Meindert 1906-1991 .... *2*
   Obituary *68*
   See also CLR *73*
DeJonge, Joanne E. 1943- *56*
Deka, Connie
   See Laux, Constance
de Kay, Ormonde (Jr.) 1923-1998 .... *7*
   Obituary *106*
de Kiriline, Louise
   See Lawrence, Louise de Kiriline
Dekker, Carl
   See Laffin, John (Alfred Charles)
   and Lynds, Dennis
deKruif, Paul (Henry) 1890-1971 .... *50*
   Earlier sketch in SATA *5*
Delacre, Lulu 1957- *156*
   Earlier sketch in SATA *36*
DeLaCroix, Alice 1940- *75*
De la Garza, Phyllis 1942- *169*
De Lage, Ida 1918- *11*
de la Mare, Walter (John) 1873-1956 .... *16*
   See also CLR *23*
Delaney, Harry 1932- *3*
Delaney, Michael 1955- *96*
Delaney, Ned *28*
   See Delaney, Thomas Nicholas III
Delano, Hugh 1933- *20*
Delany, Samuel R(ay), Jr. 1942- *92*
De la Ramee, Marie Louise (Ouida) 1839-1908
   .... *20*
   See Ouida

de la Roche, Mazo 1879-1961 .... *64*
De La Roche Saint Andre, Anne 1950- ... *75*
Delaune, (Jewel) Lynn (de Grummond) *7*
DeLaurentis, Louise Budde 1920- *12*
Delderfield, Eric R(aymond) 1909-1995 ..... *14*
Delderfield, Ronald Frederick 1912-1972 ... *20*
DeLeeuw, Adele (Louise) 1899-1988 .... *30*
  Obituary *56*
  Earlier sketch in SATA *1*
De Leon, Nephtali 1945- *97*
Delessert, Etienne 1941- *130*
  Brief entry *27*
  Earlier sketch in SATA *46*
  See also CLR *81*
Delgado, James P. 1958- *122*
de Lint, Charles (Henri Diederick Hofsmit)
  1951- *157*
  Earlier sketch in SATA *115*
Delmar, Roy
  See Wexler, Jerome (LeRoy)
Deloria, Vine, Jr. 1933-2005 .... *21*
Deloria, Vine Victor
  See Deloria, Vine, Jr.
del Rey, Lester 1915-1993 .... *22*
  Obituary *76*
Delrio, Martin
  See Doyle, Debra
  and Macdonald, James D.
Delton, Judy 1931-2001 .... *77*
  Obituary *130*
  Earlier sketch in SATA *14*
  See also SAAS *9*
Delulio, John 1938- *15*
Delving, Michael
  See Williams, Jay
Demarest, Chris(topher) L(ynn) 1951- *128*
  Brief entry *44*
  Earlier sketches in SATA *45, 82*
Demarest, Doug
  See Barker, Will
Demas, Corinne *131*
  See Bliss, Corinne Demas
Demas, Vida 1927- *9*
De Mejo, Oscar 1911-1992 .... *40*
de Messieres, Nicole 1930- *39*
Demi
  See Hitz, Demi
Demijohn, Thom
  See Disch, Thomas M(ichael)
  and Sladek, John
Deming, Richard 1915-1983 .... *24*
  See Queen, Ellery
Demuth, Patricia Brennan 1948- *84*
  Brief entry *51*
Dendinger, Roger E. 1952- *158*
Dengler, Marianna (Herron) 1935- *103*
Dengler, Sandy 1939- *54*
  Brief entry *40*
Denim, Sue
  See Pilkey, Dav
Denise, Christopher 1968- *147*
Denmark, Harrison
  See Zelazny, Roger (Joseph)
Dennard, Deborah 1953- *136*
  Earlier sketch in SATA *78*
Denney, Diana 1910-2000 .... *25*
  Obituary *120*
Dennis, Morgan 1891(?)-1960 .... *18*
Dennis, Wesley 1903-1966 .... *18*
Denny, Norman (George) 1901-1982 .... *43*
Denslow, Sharon Phillips 1947- *142*
  Earlier sketch in SATA *68*
Denslow, W(illiam) W(allace) 1856-1915 .. *16*
  See also CLR *15*
Denton, Kady MacDonald *110*
  Earlier sketch in SATA *66*
  See also CLR *71*
Denver, Walt
  See Redding, Robert Hull
  and Sherman, Jory (Tecumseh)

Denzel, Justin F(rancis) 1917-1999 .... *46*
  Brief entry *38*
Denzer, Ann Wiseman
  See Wiseman, Ann (Sayre)
DePalma, Mary Newell 1961- *139*
dePaola, Thomas Anthony 1934- *155*
  Earlier sketches in SATA *11, 59, 108*
  See dePaola, Tomie
dePaola, Tomie
  See CLR *81*
  See also SAAS *15*
  See dePaola, Thomas Anthony
deParrie, Paul 1949- *74*
DePauw, Linda Grant 1940- *24*
DeRan, David 1946- *76*
Derby, Sally 1934- *132*
  Earlier sketch in SATA *89*
de Regniers, Beatrice Schenk (Freedman)
  1914-2000 .... *68*
  Obituary *123*
  Earlier sketch in SATA *2*
  See also SAAS *6*
Dereske, Jo 1947- *72*
Derleth, August (William) 1909-1971 .... *5*
Derman, Martha (Winn) *74*
Derman, Sarah Audrey 1915- *11*
DeRoberts, Lyndon
  See Silverstein, Robert Alan
de Roo, Anne Louise 1931-1997 .... *84*
  Earlier sketch in SATA *25*
  See also CLR *63*
deRosa, Dee *70*
Derrick, Lionel
  See Cunningham, Chet
Derrickson, Jim 1959- *141*
Derry Down Derry
  See Lear, Edward
Dervaux, Isabelle 1961- *106*
Derwent, Lavinia *14*
Desai, Anita 1937- *126*
  Earlier sketch in SATA *63*
De Saulles, Tony 1958- *119*
Desbarats, Peter 1933- *39*
de Selincourt, Aubrey 1894-1962 .... *14*
Deshpande, Chris 1950- *69*
Desimini, Lisa 1964- *148*
  Earlier sketch in SATA *86*
Desjarlais, John (J.) 1953- *71*
Desmoinaux, Christel 1967- *149*
  Earlier sketch in SATA *103*
Desmond, Adrian J(ohn) 1947- *51*
Desmond, Alice Curtis 1897-1990 .... *8*
DeSpain, Pleasant 1943- *87*
Desputeaux, Helene 1959- *95*
Dessen, Sarah 1970- *120*
Detine, Padre
  See Olsen, Ib Spang
de Trevino, Elizabeth B.
  See Trevino, Elizabeth B(orton) de
de Trevino, Elizabeth Borton
  See Trevino, Elizabeth B(orton) de
Detwiler, Susan Dill 1956- *58*
Deuker, Carl 1950- *150*
  Earlier sketch in SATA *82*
Deutsch, Babette 1895-1982 .... *1*
  Obituary *33*
Deutsch, Eva Costabel
  See Costabel, Eva Deutsch
Deutsch, Helen 1906-1992 .... *76*
Deutsch, Kurt
  See Singer, Kurt D.
Devaney, John 1926-1994 .... *12*
de Varennes, Monique 1947- *168*
de Varona, Frank J. 1943- *83*
Devereux, Frederick L(eonard), Jr. 1914-1993
  .... *9*
Devi, Nila
  See Woody, Regina Jones
deVinck, Christopher 1951- *85*
DeVito, Cara 1956- *80*

Devlin, Harry 1918-2001 .... *136*
  Earlier sketches in SATA *11, 74*
Devlin, (Dorothy) Wende 1918-2002 .... *74*
  Earlier sketch in SATA *11*
Devon, Paddie 1953- *92*
Devons, Sonia 1974- *72*
Devorah-Leah *111*
de Vos, Gail 1949- *122*
DeVries, Douglas 1933- *122*
De Waard, E(lliott) John 1935- *7*
Dewan, Ted 1961- *157*
  Earlier sketch in SATA *108*
Dewdney, Selwyn (Hanington) 1909-1979 . *64*
DeWeese, Gene
  See DeWeese, Thomas Eugene
DeWeese, Jean
  See DeWeese, Thomas Eugene
DeWeese, Thomas Eugene 1934- *46*
  Brief entry *45*
Dewey, Ariane 1937- *109*
  Earlier sketch in SATA *7*
Dewey, Jennifer (Owings) 1941- *103*
  Brief entry *48*
  Earlier sketch in SATA *58*
Dewey, Kenneth Francis 1940- *39*
deWit, Dorothy (May Knowles) 1916-1980
  .... *39*
  Obituary *28*
Dexter, Alison 1966- *125*
Dexter, John
  See Bradley, Marion Zimmer
Deyneka, Anita 1943- *24*
Deyrup, Astrith Johnson 1923- *24*
Dhami, Narinder 1958- *152*
Dhondy, Farrukh 1944- *152*
  Earlier sketch in SATA *65*
  See also CLR *41*
Diamond, Arthur 1957- *76*
Diamond, Donna 1950- *69*
  Brief entry *30*
  Earlier sketch in SATA *35*
Diamond, Petra
  See Sachs, Judith
Diamond, Rebecca
  See Sachs, Judith
Dias, Earl Joseph 1916- *41*
Dias, Ron 1937- *71*
Diaz, David 1959(?)- *150*
  Earlier sketch in SATA *96*
  See also CLR *65*
DiCamillo, Kate 1964- *163*
  Earlier sketch in SATA *121*
Di Certo, J(oseph) J(ohn) 1933- *60*
DiCianni, Ron 1952- *107*
Dick, Trella Lamson 1889-1974 .... *9*
Dickens, Charles (John Huffam) 1812-1870
  .... *15*
  See also CLR *95*
Dickens, Frank
  See Huline-Dickens, Frank William
Dickens, Monica (Enid) 1915-1992 .... *4*
  Obituary *74*
Dickinson, Emily (Elizabeth) 1830-1886 .... *29*
Dickinson, Mary 1949- *48*
  Brief entry *41*
Dickinson, Mary-Anne
  See Rodda, Emily
Dickinson, Peter (Malcolm de Brissac) 1927-
  .... *150*
  Earlier sketches in SATA *5, 62, 95*
  See also CLR *29*
Dickinson, Susan 1931- *8*
Dickinson, Terence 1943- *102*
Dickinson, W(illiam) Croft 1897-1963 .... *13*
Dickson, Gordon R(upert) 1923-2001 .... *77*
Dickson, Naida 1916- *8*
Diehn, Gwen 1943- *80*
Dieterich, Michele M. 1962- *78*
Dietz, David H(enry) 1897-1984 .... *10*
  Obituary *41*

Dietz, Lew 1907-1997 .... *11*
　Obituary *95*
Diffily, Deborah *159*
Di Fiori, Larry
　See Di Fiori, Lawrence
Di Fiori, Lawrence 1934- *130*
DiFranco, Anthony (Mario) 1945- *42*
Digby, Anne 1935- *72*
Digges, Jeremiah
　See Berger, Josef
D'Ignazio, Fred(erick) 1949- *39*
　Brief entry *35*
Di Grazia, Thomas (?)-1983 .... *32*
Dikty, Julian May
　See May, Julian
Dillard, Annie 1945- *140*
　Earlier sketch in SATA *10*
Dillard, Kristine 1964- *113*
Dillard, Polly Hargis 1916- *24*
Diller, Harriett 1953- *78*
Dillon, Barbara 1927- *44*
　Brief entry *39*
Dillon, Diane (Claire) 1933- *106*
　Earlier sketches in SATA *15, 51*
　See also CLR *44*
Dillon, Eilis 1920-1994 .... *74*
　Autobiography Feature *105*
　Obituary *83*
　Earlier sketch in SATA *2*
　See also CLR *26*
Dillon, Jana (a pseudonym) 1952- *117*
Dillon, Leo 1933- *106*
　Earlier sketches in SATA *15, 51*
　See also CLR *44*
Dillon, Sharon Saseen
　See Saseen, Sharon (Dillon)
Dils, Tracey E. 1958- *83*
Dilson, Jesse 1914-1988 .... *24*
Dinan, Carolyn *59*
　Brief entry *47*
Dines, (Harry) Glen 1925-1996 .... *7*
Dinesen, Isak
　See Blixen, Karen (Christentze Dinesen)
Dinessi, Alex
　See Schembri, Jim
Dinneen, Betty 1929- *61*
Dinnerstein, Harvey 1928- *42*
Dinsdale, Tim(othy Kay) 1924-1987 .... *11*
Diouf, Sylviane A. 1952- *168*
Diouf, Sylviane Anna
　See Diouf, Sylviane A.
DiPucchio, Kelly *159*
Dirk
　See Gringhuis, Richard H.
Dirks, Wilhelmina 1916- *59*
Dirks, Willy
　See Dirks, Wilhelmina
DiSalvo, DyAnne 1960- *144*
　Earlier sketch in SATA *59*
DiSalvo-Ryan, DyAnne
　See DiSalvo, DyAnne
Disch, Thomas M(ichael) 1940- *92*
　See also CLR *18*
　See also SAAS *15*
　See Disch, Tom
Disch, Tom
　See Disch, Thomas M(ichael)
Disher, Garry 1949- *125*
　Earlier sketch in SATA *81*
Disney, Walt(er Elias) 1901-1966 .... *28*
　Brief entry *27*
DiTerlizzi, Tony 1969- *154*
Divakaruni, Chitra Banerjee 1956- *160*
Di Valentin, Maria (Amelia) Messuri
　1911-1985 .... *7*
Dixon, Ann R(enee) 1954- *127*
　Earlier sketch in SATA *77*
Dixon, Dougal 1947- *127*
　Earlier sketch in SATA *45*

Dixon, Franklin W. *100*
　Earlier sketches in SATA *1, 67*
　See also CLR *61*
　See Barrett, Neal, Jr.
　and Goulart, Ron(ald Joseph)
　and Lantz, Francess L(in)
　and McFarlane, Leslie (Charles)
　and Stanley, George Edward
　and Stratemeyer, Edward L.
Dixon, Jeanne 1936- *31*
Dixon, Paige
　See Corcoran, Barbara (Asenath)
Dixon, Peter L(ee) 1931- *6*
Dixon, Rachel 1952- *74*
Djoleto, (Solomon Alexander) Amu 1929- . *80*
d'lacey, Chris 1949- *165*
Doak, Annie
　See Dillard, Annie
Doane, Pelagie 1906-1966 .... *7*
Dobell, I(sabel) M(arian) B(arclay) 1909-1998
　... *11*
Dobie, J(ames) Frank 1888-1964 .... *43*
Dobler, Lavinia G. 1910- *6*
Dobrin, Arnold 1928- *4*
Dobson, Jill 1969- *140*
Dobson, Julia 1941- *48*
Dobson, Mary 1954- *117*
Dockery, Wallene T. 1941- *27*
Dockray, Tracy 1962- *139*
Dockrey, Karen 1955- *103*
Doctor, Bernard
　See Doctor, Bernard Aquina
Doctor, Bernard Aquina 1950- *81*
Doctor X
　See Nourse, Alan E(dward)
Dodd, Ed(ward Benton) 1902-1991 .... *4*
　Obituary *68*
Dodd, Lynley (Stuart) 1941- *132*
　Earlier sketches in SATA *35, 86*
　See also CLR *62*
Dodd, Marty 1921- *142*
Dodd, Quentin 1972- *137*
Dodds, Bill 1952- *78*
Dodds, Dayle Ann 1952- *150*
　Earlier sketch in SATA *75*
Dodge, Bertha S(anford) 1902-1995 .... *8*
Dodge, Fremont
　See Grimes, Lee
Dodge, Gil
　See Hano, Arnold
Dodge, Mary (Elizabeth) Mapes 1831(?)-1905
　... *100*
　Earlier sketch in SATA *21*
　See also CLR *62*
Dodgson, Charles L(utwidge) 1832-1898 . *100*
　See also YABC *2*
　See also CLR *2*
　See Carroll, Lewis
Dodson, Kenneth MacKenzie 1907-1999 .... *11*
Dodson, Susan 1941- *50*
　Brief entry *40*
Dogyear, Drew
　See Gorey, Edward (St. John)
Doherty, Berlie 1943- *111*
　Earlier sketch in SATA *72*
　See also CLR *21*
　See also SAAS *16*
Doherty, Charles Hugh 1913- *6*
Doherty, Craig A. 1951- *169*
　Earlier sketch in SATA *83*
Doherty, Katherine M(ann) 1951- *83*
Doherty, Kieran 1945- *164*
Dokey, Cameron 1956- *97*
Dolan, Edward F(rancis), Jr. 1924- *94*
　Brief entry *31*
　Earlier sketch in SATA *45*
Dolan, Ellen M(eara) 1929-1998 .... *88*
Dolan, Sean J. 1958- *74*
Dolce, J. Ellen 1948- *75*
Dolch, Edward William 1889-1961 .... *50*
Dolch, Marguerite Pierce 1891-1978 .... *50*

Dollar, Diane (Hills) 1933- *57*
Dolson, Hildegarde *5*
　See Lockridge, Hildegarde (Dolson)
Domanska, Janina 1913(?)-1995 .... *68*
　Obituary *84*
　Earlier sketch in SATA *6*
　See also CLR *40*
　See also SAAS *18*
Dominguez, Angel 1953- *76*
Domino, John
　See Averill, Esther (Holden)
Domjan, Joseph (Spiri) 1907-1992 .... *25*
Domm, Jeffrey C. 1958- *84*
Donald, Rhonda Lucas 1962- *147*
Donalds, Gordon
　See Shirreffs, Gordon D(onald)
Donaldson, Bryna
　See Stevens, Bryna
Donaldson, Gordon 1913-1993 .... *64*
　Obituary *76*
Donaldson, Joan 1953- *78*
Donaldson, Julia 1948- *132*
　Earlier sketch in SATA *82*
Donaldson, Stephen R(eeder) 1947- *121*
Doner, Kim 1955- *91*
Doney, Todd L. W. 1959- *104*
Donkin, Nance (Clare) 1915- *95*
Donna, Natalie 1934-1979 .... *9*
Donnelly, Elfie 1950-
　See CLR *104*
Donnelly, Jennifer 1963- *154*
Donnelly, Matt 1972- *148*
Donoghue, Emma 1969- *101*
Donoughue, Carol 1935- *139*
Donovan, John 1928-1992 .... *72*
　Brief entry *29*
　See also CLR *3*
Donovan, Mary Lee 1961- *86*
Donze, Mary Terese 1911- *89*
Doob, Leonard W(illiam) 1909-2000 .... *8*
Dooley, Norah 1953- *74*
Dooling, Michael 1958- *105*
Dor, Ana
　See Ceder, Georgiana Dorcas
Dore, (Louis Christophe Paul) Gustave
　1832-1883 .... *19*
Doremus, Robert 1913- *30*
Doren, Marion (Walker) 1928- *57*
Dorenkamp, Michelle 1957- *89*
Dorflinger, Carolyn 1953- *91*
Dorian, Edith M(cEwen) 1900-1983 .... *5*
Dorian, Harry
　See Hamilton, Charles (Harold St. John)
Dorian, Marguerite *7*
Dorin, Patrick C(arberry) 1939- *59*
　Brief entry *52*
Dorman, Michael 1932- *7*
Dorman, N. B. 1927- *39*
Dorris, Michael (Anthony) 1945-1997 .... *75*
　Obituary *94*
　See also CLR *58*
Dorris, Michael A.
　See Dorris, Michael (Anthony)
Dorritt, Susan
　See Schlein, Miriam
Dorros, Arthur 1950- *168*
　Earlier sketches in SATA *78, 122*
　See also CLR *42*
　See also SAAS *20*
Dorros, Arthur M.
　See Dorros, Arthur
Dorson, Richard M(ercer) 1916-1981 .... *30*
Doss, Helen (Grigsby) 1918- *20*
Doss, Margot Patterson *6*
Dothers, Anne
　See Chess, Victoria (Dickerson)
Dottig
　See Grider, Dorothy
Dotts, Maryann J. 1933- *35*
Doty, Jean Slaughter 1929- *28*
Doty, Roy 1922- *28*

Doubtfire, Dianne (Abrams) 1918- *29*
Doucet, Sharon Arms 1951- *144*
  Autobiography Feature *144*
  Earlier sketch in SATA *125*
Dougherty, Charles 1922- *18*
Dougherty, Terri (L.) 1964- *146*
Douglas, Blaise 1960- *101*
Douglas, Carole Nelson 1944- *73*
Douglas, Garry
  See Kilworth, Garry
Douglas, James McM.
  See Butterworth, W.E.
Douglas, Kathryn
  See Ewing, Kathryn
Douglas, Leonard
  See Bradbury, Ray (Douglas)
Douglas, Marjory Stoneman 1890-1998 ..... *10*
Douglas, Michael
  See Bright, Robert (Douglas Sr.)
Douglas, Michael
  See Crichton, (John) Michael
Douglass, Barbara 1930- *40*
Douglass, Frederick 1817(?)-1895 .... *29*
Douglass, Keith
  See Cunningham, Chet
Douty, Esther M(orris) 1909-1978 .... *8*
  Obituary *23*
Dow, Emily R. 1904-1987 .... *10*
Dow, Vicki
  See McVey, Vicki
Dowd, John David 1945- *78*
Dowdell, Dorothy (Florence) Karns 1910- . *12*
Dowden, Anne Ophelia 1907- *7*
  See also SAAS *10*
Dowdey, Landon Gerald 1923- *11*
Dowdy, Mrs. Regera
  See Gorey, Edward (St. John)
Dowell, Frances O'Roark *157*
Dowling, Terry 1947- *101*
Downer, Ann 1960- *155*
Downer, Marion 1892(?)-1971 .... *25*
Downey, Fairfax D(avis) 1893-1990 .... *3*
  Obituary *66*
Downie, John 1931- *87*
Downie, Mary Alice (Dawe) 1934- *87*
  Earlier sketch in SATA *13*
Downing, David A(lmon) 1958- *84*
Downing, Julie 1956- *148*
  Earlier sketch in SATA *81*
Downing, Paula E. 1951- *80*
Downing, Warwick 1931- *138*
Downing, Wick
  See Downing, Warwick
Doyle, A. Conan
  See Doyle, Sir Arthur Conan
Doyle, Sir Arthur Conan 1859-1930 .... *24*
  See also CLR *106*
  See Conan Doyle, Arthur
Doyle, Brian 1935- *156*
  Earlier sketches in SATA *67, 104*
  See also CLR *22*
  See also SAAS *16*
Doyle, Charlotte (Lackner) 1937- *94*
Doyle, Conan
  See Doyle, Sir Arthur Conan
Doyle, Debra 1952- *165*
  Earlier sketch in SATA *105*
  See Appleton, Victor
Doyle, John
  See Graves, Robert (von Ranke)
Doyle, Malachy 1954- *165*
  Earlier sketch in SATA *120*
  See also CLR *83*
Doyle, Richard 1824-1883 .... *21*
Doyle, Sir A. Conan
  See Doyle, Sir Arthur Conan
Dr. A
  See Asimov, Isaac
  and Silverstein, Alvin
  and Silverstein, Virginia B(arbara Opshelor)

Dr. Alphabet
  See Morice, Dave
Dr. Fred
  See Bortz, Alfred B(enjamin)
Dr. Laura
  See Schlessinger, Laura (Catherine)
Dr. Seuss
  See CLR *100*
  See Geisel, Theodor Seuss
  and LeSieg, Theo.
  and Seuss, Dr.
  and Stone, Rosetta
Dr. Zed
  See Penrose, Gordon
Drabble, Margaret 1939- *48*
Drackett, Phil(ip Arthur) 1922- *53*
Draco, F.
  See Davis, Julia
Dracup, Angela 1943- *74*
Dragisic, Patricia *116*
Dragonwagon, Crescent 1952- *133*
  Earlier sketches in SATA *11, 41, 75*
  See also SAAS *14*
Drake, David (Allen) 1945- *85*
Drake, Frank
  See Hamilton, Charles (Harold St. John)
Drake, Jane 1954- *82*
Drakeford, Dale B(enjamin) 1952- *113*
Draper, Hastings
  See Jeffries, Roderic (Graeme)
Draper, Sharon M(ills) *146*
  Autobiography Feature *146*
  Earlier sketch in SATA *98*
  See also CLR *57*
Drapier, M. B.
  See Swift, Jonathan
Drawson, Blair 1943- *126*
  Earlier sketch in SATA *17*
Dresang, Eliza (Carolyn Timberlake) 1941-
  .... *19*
Drescher, Henrik 1955- *105*
  Earlier sketch in SATA *67*
  See also CLR *20*
Drescher, Joan E(lizabeth) 1939- *137*
  Earlier sketch in SATA *30*
Drew, Patricia (Mary) 1938- *15*
Drewery, Mary 1918- *6*
Drewery, Melanie 1970- *165*
Drewry, Henry N(athaniel) 1924- *138*
Drial, J. E.
  See Laird, Jean E(louise)
Drimmer, Frederick 1916-2000 .... *60*
  Obituary *124*
Driskill, J. Lawrence 1920- *90*
Driskill, Larry
  See Driskill, J. Lawrence
Driving Hawk, Virginia
  See Sneve, Virginia Driving Hawk
Drucker, Malka 1945- *111*
  Brief entry *29*
  Earlier sketch in SATA *39*
Drucker, Olga Levy 1927- *79*
Drummond, V(iolet) H(ilda) 1911-2000 .... *6*
Drummond, Walter
  See Silverberg, Robert
Drury, Clare Marie
  See Hoskyns-Abrahall, Clare (Constance
  Drury)
Drury, Roger W(olcott) 1914-1996 .... *15*
Druse, Eleanor
  See King, Stephen
Dryden, Pamela
  See St. John, Nicole
D.T., Hughes
  See Hughes, Dean
Duane, Diane (Elizabeth) 1952- *145*
  Brief entry *46*
  Earlier sketches in SATA *58, 95*
Dubanevich, Arlene 1950- *56*
Dubelaar, Thea 1947- *60*

du Blane, Daphne
  See Groom, Arthur William
Duble, Kathleen Benner 1958- *164*
Du Bois, Shirley Graham 1907(?)-1977 ..... *24*
  See Graham, Shirley
Du Bois, W(illiam) E(dward) B(urghardt)
  1868-1963 .... *42*
du Bois, William Pene
  See Pene du Bois, William (Sherman)
Duboise, Novella 1911-1999 .... *88*
Dubosarsky, Ursula (Bridget) 1961- *147*
  Earlier sketch in SATA *107*
DuBose, LaRocque (Russ) 1926- *2*
Dubrovin, Vivian 1931- *139*
  Earlier sketch in SATA *65*
Ducey, Jean Sparks 1915- *93*
Du Chaillu, Paul (Belloni) 1835(?)-1903 .... *26*
Ducharme, Dede Fox
  See Ducharme, Lilian Fox
Ducharme, Lilian Fox 1950- *122*
Ducornet, Erica 1943- *7*
Ducornet, Rikki
  See Ducornet, Erica
Duden, Jane 1947- *136*
Duder, Tessa 1940- *117*
  Earlier sketch in SATA *80*
  See also CLR *43*
  See also SAAS *23*
Dudley, Helen
  See Hope Simpson, Jacynth
Dudley, Nancy
  See Cole, Lois Dwight
Dudley, Robert
  See Baldwin, James
Dudley, Ruth H(ubbell) 1905-2001 .... *11*
Dudley-Smith, T.
  See Trevor, Elleston
Due, Linnea A. 1948- *64*
Dueck, Adele 1955- *97*
Dueland, Joy V(ivian) *27*
Duerr, Gisela 1968- *89*
Duey, Kathleen 1950- *132*
Dufault, Joseph Ernest Nephtali
  See James, Will(iam Roderick)
Duff, Maggie
  See Duff, Margaret K(app)
Duff, Margaret K(app) 1916-2003 .... *37*
  Obituary *144*
Duffey, Betsy (Byars) 1953- *131*
  Earlier sketch in SATA *80*
Duffie, Charles 1960- *144*
Duffield, Katy S. 1961- *147*
Duffy, Carol Ann 1955- *165*
  Earlier sketch in SATA *95*
Dugan, Jack
  See Butterworth, W.E.
Dugan, Michael (Gray) 1947- *15*
Duggan, Alfred Leo 1903-1964 .... *25*
Duggan, Maurice (Noel) 1922-1974 .... *40*
  Obituary *30*
Duggleby, John 1952- *94*
Dugin, Andrej 1955- *77*
Dugina, Olga 1964- *77*
du Jardin, Rosamond Neal 1902-1963 .... *2*
Duke, Kate 1956- *148*
  Earlier sketch in SATA *90*
  See also CLR *51*
Duke, Will
  See Gault, William Campbell
Dulac, Edmund 1882-1953 .... *19*
Dumas, Alexandre (pere) 1802-1870 .... *18*
Dumas, Jacqueline 1946- *55*
Dumas, Philippe 1940- *119*
  Earlier sketch in SATA *52*
du Maurier, Daphne 1907-1989 .... *27*
  Obituary *60*
Dumbleton, Mike 1948- *124*
  Earlier sketch in SATA *73*
Dunbar, Fiona 1961- *167*
Dunbar, Joyce 1944- *162*
  Earlier sketches in SATA *76, 112*

Dunbar, Paul Laurence 1872-1906 .... *34*
Dunbar, Robert E(verett) 1926- *32*
Duncan, Alexandra
  See Moore, Ishbel (Lindsay)
Duncan, Alice Faye 1967- *168*
  Earlier sketch in SATA *95*
Duncan, Gregory
  See McClintock, Marshall
Duncan, Jane
  See Cameron, Elizabeth Jane
Duncan, Julia K. *1*
  See Benson, Mildred (Augustine Wirt)
Duncan, Lois 1934- *141*
  Autobiography Feature *141*
  Earlier sketches in SATA *1, 36, 75, 133*
  See also CLR *29*
  See also SAAS *2*
Duncan, Norman 1871-1916
  See YABC *1*
Duncan, Terence
  See Nolan, William F(rancis)
Duncombe, Frances (Riker) 1900-1994 ...... *25*
  Obituary *82*
Dunham, Montrew 1919- *162*
Dunham, Montrew Goetz
  See Dunham, Montrew
Dunkle, Clare B. 1964- *155*
Dunlap, Julie 1958- *84*
Dunleavy, Deborah 1951- *133*
Dunlop, Agnes M. R. (?)-1982 .... *87*
  See Kyle, Elisabeth
Dunlop, Eileen (Rhona) 1938- *76*
  Earlier sketch in SATA *24*
  See also SAAS *12*
Dunn, Anne M. 1940- *107*
Dunn, Harvey T(homas) 1884-1952 .... *34*
Dunn, Herb
  See Gutman, Dan
Dunn, John M. (III) 1949- *93*
Dunn, Judy
  See Spangenberg, Judith Dunn
Dunn, Mary Lois 1930- *6*
Dunnahoo, Terry Janson 1927- *7*
Dunne, Jeanette 1952- *72*
Dunne, Kathleen 1933- *126*
Dunne, Marie
  See Clark, Ann Nolan
Dunne, Mary Collins 1914- *11*
Dunne, Mary Jo
  See Dunne, Mary Collins
Dunnett, Margaret (Rosalind) 1909-1977 ... *42*
Dunrea, Olivier (Jean-Paul Dominique) 1953-
  .... *160*
  Brief entry *46*
  Earlier sketches in SATA *59, 118*
Dunton, Dorothy 1912- *92*
Dupasquier, Philippe 1955- *151*
  Earlier sketch in SATA *86*
DuPrau, Jeanne 1944- *144*
Dupuy, T(revor) N(evitt) 1916-1995 .... *4*
  Obituary *86*
DuQuette, Keith 1960- *155*
  Earlier sketch in SATA *90*
Duranceau, Suzanne 1952- *162*
Durant, Alan 1958- *165*
  Earlier sketch in SATA *121*
Durant, John 1902- *27*
Durbin, William 1951- *143*
Durell, Ann 1930- *66*
Durrant, Lynda 1954- *148*
  Earlier sketch in SATA *96*
Durrell, Gerald (Malcolm) 1925-1995 .... *8*
  Obituary *84*
Durrell, Julie 1955- *94*
Durrett, Deanne 1940- *144*
  Earlier sketch in SATA *92*
Du Soe, Robert C. 1892-1958
  See YABC *2*
Dussling, Jennifer 1970- *143*
  Earlier sketch in SATA *96*
DuTemple, Lesley A. 1952- *113*

Dutz
  See Davis, Mary Octavia
Duval, Katherine
  See James, Elizabeth
Duvall, Aimee
  See Thurlo, Aimee
  and Thurlo, David
Duvall, Evelyn Millis 1906- *9*
Duvall, Jill D(onovan) 1932- *102*
Duvoisin, Roger (Antoine) 1904-1980 .... *30*
  Obituary *23*
  Earlier sketch in SATA *2*
  See also CLR *23*
Dwiggins, Don(ald J.) 1913-1988 .... *4*
  Obituary *60*
Dwight, Allan
  See Cole, Lois Dwight
Dwyer, Deanna
  See Koontz, Dean R.
Dwyer, K. R.
  See Koontz, Dean R.
Dyck, Peter J. 1914- *75*
Dyer, James (Frederick) 1934- *37*
Dyer, Jane *147*
Dyess, John (Foster) 1939- *76*
Dygard, Thomas J. 1931-1996 .... *97*
  Obituary *92*
  Earlier sketch in SATA *24*
  See also SAAS *15*
Dyke, John 1935- *35*

E

E. V. L.
  See Lucas, E(dward) V(errall)
Eagar, Frances (Elisabeth Stuart) 1940-1978
  .... *11*
  Obituary *55*
Eager, Edward (McMaken) 1911-1964 .... *17*
  See also CLR *43*
Eager, George 1921- *56*
  See Eager, George B.
Eager, George B.
  See Eager, George
Eagle, Ellen 1953- *61*
Eagle, Kin
  See Adlerman, Daniel (Ezra)
  and Adlerman, Kimberly M(arie)
Eagle, Mike 1942- *11*
Earle, Olive L(ydia) 1888-1982 .... *7*
Earle, William
  See Johns, W(illiam) E(arle)
Earls, Nick 1963- *156*
  Earlier sketch in SATA *95*
Early, Jack
  See Scoppettone, Sandra
Early, Jon
  See Johns, W(illiam) E(arle)
Early, Margaret 1951- *72*
Earnshaw, Brian 1929- *17*
Earnshaw, Micky
  See Earnshaw, Spencer Wright
Earnshaw, Spencer Wright 1939- *88*
Easley, MaryAnn *94*
Eastman, Charles A(lexander) 1858-1939
  See YABC *1*
Eastman, P(hilip) D(ey) 1909-1986 .... *33*
  Obituary *46*
Easton, Kelly 1960- *141*
Eastwick, Ivy (Ethel) O(live) *3*
Eaton, Anne T(haxter) 1881-1971 .... *32*
Eaton, Anthony 1971- *167*
Eaton, George L.
  See Verral, Charles Spain
Eaton, Janet
  See Givens, Janet E(aton)
Eaton, Jeanette 1886-1968 .... *24*
Eaton, Tom 1940- *22*
Ebel, Alex 1927- *11*

Eber, Dorothy (Margaret) Harley 1930- *27*
Eberle, Irmengarde 1898-1979 .... *2*
  Obituary *23*
Eble, Diane 1956- *74*
Eboch, Chris *113*
Echlin, Kim 1955- *166*
Eckblad, Edith Berven 1923- *23*
Eckert, Allan W. 1931- *91*
  Brief entry *27*
  Earlier sketch in SATA *29*
  See also SAAS *21*
Eckert, Horst 1931- *72*
  Earlier sketch in SATA *8*
  See Janosch
Ecklar, Julia (Marie) 1964- *112*
Eddings, David (Carroll) 1931- *91*
Ede, Janina 1937- *33*
Edell, Celeste *12*
Edelman, Lily (Judith) 1915-1981 .... *22*
Edelson, Edward 1932- *51*
Edens, Cooper 1945- *166*
  Earlier sketches in SATA *49, 112*
Edens, (Bishop) David 1926- *39*
Edey, Maitland A(rmstrong) 1910-1992 ...... *25*
  Obituary *71*
Edgeworth, Maria 1768-1849 .... *21*
Edgy, Wardore
  See Gorey, Edward (St. John)
Edison, Theodore
  See Stratemeyer, Edward L.
Edler, Tim(othy) 1948- *56*
Edmiston, Jim 1948- *80*
Edmonds, I(vy) G(ordon) 1917- *8*
Edmonds, Walter D(umaux) 1903-1998 ...... *27*
  Obituary *99*
  Earlier sketch in SATA *1*
  See also SAAS *4*
Edmund, Sean
  See Pringle, Laurence P(atrick)
Edsall, Marian (Stickney) 1920- *8*
Edwards, Al
  See Nourse, Alan E(dward)
Edwards, Anne 1927- *35*
Edwards, Audrey 1947- *52*
  Brief entry *31*
Edwards, Becky (Jane) 1966- *125*
Edwards, Bertram
  See Edwards, Herbert Charles
Edwards, Bronwen Elizabeth
  See Rose, Wendy
Edwards, Cecile Pepin 1916- *25*
Edwards, Dorothy 1914-1982 .... *88*
  Obituary *31*
  Earlier sketch in SATA *4*
Edwards, F. E.
  See Nolan, William F(rancis)
Edwards, Frank B. 1952- *93*
Edwards, Gunvor *32*
Edwards, Harvey 1929- *5*
Edwards, Hazel (Eileen) 1945- *135*
Edwards, Herbert Charles 1912- *12*
Edwards, Jane Campbell 1932- *10*
Edwards, Julia
  See Stratemeyer, Edward L.
Edwards, Julie
  See Andrews, Julie
Edwards, Julie Andrews
  See Andrews, Julie
Edwards, Linda Strauss 1948- *49*
  Brief entry *42*
Edwards, Michelle 1955- *152*
  Earlier sketch in SATA *70*
Edwards, Monica le Doux Newton 1912-1998
  .... *12*
Edwards, Olwen
  See Gater, Dilys
Edwards, Page (Lawrence, Jr.) 1941-1999 .. *59*
Edwards, R. T.
  See Goulart, Ron(ald Joseph)
Edwards, Sally (Cary) 1929- *7*

Edwards, Samuel
  See Gerson, Noel Bertram
Egan, E(dward) W(elstead) 1922- 35
Egan, Lorraine Hopping 1960- 134
  Earlier sketch in SATA 91
Egan, Tim 1957- 155
  Earlier sketch in SATA 89
Egermeier, Elsie E(milie) 1890-1986 65
Eggenberger, David 1918- 6
Eggleston, Edward 1837-1902 27
Egielski, Richard 1952- 163
  Earlier sketches in SATA 11, 49, 106
Egypt, Ophelia Settle 1903-1984 16
  Obituary 38
Ehlert, Lois (Jane) 1934- 128
  Earlier sketches in SATA 35, 69
  See also CLR 28
Ehling, Katalin Olah 1941- 93
Ehrenfreund, Norbert 1921- 86
Ehrlich, Amy 1942- 132
  Earlier sketches in SATA 25, 65, 96
Ehrlich, Bettina Bauer 1903-1985 1
Ehrlich, H. M.
  See Ziefert, Harriet
Eichenberg, Fritz 1901-1990 50
  Earlier sketch in SATA 9
Eichler, Margrit 1942- 35
Eichner, James A. 1927- 4
Eidson, Thomas 1944- 112
Eifert, Virginia (Louise) S(nider) 1911-1966
  2
Eige, (Elizabeth) Lillian 1915- 65
Eiken, J. Melia 1967- 125
Einsel, Naiad 10
Einsel, Walter 1926- 10
Einzig, Susan 1922- 43
Eiseman, Alberta 1925- 15
Eisenberg, Azriel (Louis) 1903-1985 12
Eisenberg, Lisa 1949- 155
  Brief entry 50
  Earlier sketch in SATA 57
Eisenberg, Phyllis Rose 1924- 41
Eisner, Vivienne
  See Margolis, Vivienne
Eisner, Will 1917-2005 165
  Earlier sketch in SATA 31
Eisner, William Erwin
  See Eisner, Will
Eitzen, Allan 1928- 9
Eitzen, Ruth (Carper) 1924- 9
Ekwensi, C. O. D.
  See Ekwensi, Cyprian (Odiatu Duaka)
Ekwensi, Cyprian (Odiatu Duaka) 1921- 66
Elam, Richard M(ace, Jr.) 1920- 9
Elborn, Andrew
  See Clements, Andrew
  and Clements, Andrew
Elboz, Stephen 1956- 152
Eldin, Peter 1939- 154
Eldon, Kathy 1946- 107
Elfman, Blossom 1925- 8
Elgin, Kathleen 1923- 39
Elia
  See Lamb, Charles
Eliot, A. D.
  See Jewett, (Theodora) Sarah Orne
Eliot, Alice
  See Jewett, (Theodora) Sarah Orne
Eliot, Anne
  See Cole, Lois Dwight
Eliot, Dan
  See Silverberg, Robert
Elish, Dan 1960- 129
  Earlier sketch in SATA 68
Elisha, Ron 1951- 104
Elkin, Benjamin 1911-1995 3
Elkins, Dov Peretz 1937- 5
Ellacott, S(amuel) E(rnest) 1911- 19
Elleman, Barbara 1934- 147
Ellen, Jaye
  See Nixon, Joan Lowery

Eller, Scott
  See Holinger, William (Jacques)
  and Shepard, James R.
Ellestad, Myrvin H. 1921- 120
Elliot, David 1952- 122
Elliott, Bruce
  See Field, Edward
Elliott, David 1952- 163
Elliott, Don
  See Silverberg, Robert
Elliott, Elizabeth Shippen Green
  See Green, Elizabeth Shippen
Elliott, Janice 1931-1995 119
Elliott, Joey
  See Houk, Randy
Elliott, Louise 111
Elliott, Odette 1939- 75
Elliott, Sarah M(cCarn) 1930- 14
Elliott, (Robert) Scott 1970- 153
Elliott, William
  See Bradbury, Ray (Douglas)
Ellis, (Mary) Amabel (Nassau Strachey)
  Williams
  See Williams-Ellis, (Mary) Amabel (Nassau
  Strachey)
Ellis, Anyon
  See Rowland-Entwistle, (Arthur) Theodore
  (Henry)
Ellis, Deborah 1961- 129
Ellis, E. S.
  See Ellis, Edward S(ylvester)
Ellis, Edward S(ylvester) 1840-1916
  See YABC 1
Ellis, Ella Thorp 1928- 127
  Earlier sketch in SATA 7
  See also SAAS 9
Ellis, Harry Bearse 1921-2004 9
Ellis, Herbert
  See Wilson, Lionel
Ellis, Mel(vin Richard) 1912-1984 7
  Obituary 39
Ellis, Richard 1938- 130
Ellis, Sarah 1952- 131
  Earlier sketch in SATA 68
  See also CLR 42
Ellison, Emily 114
Ellison, Lucile Watkins 1907(?)-1979 50
  Obituary 22
Ellison, Virginia H(owell) 1910- 4
Ellsberg, Edward 1891-1983 7
Ellsworth, Mary Ellen (Tressel) 1940- 146
Elmer, Robert 1958- 154
  Earlier sketch in SATA 99
Elmore, (Carolyn) Patricia 1933- 38
  Brief entry 35
El-Moslimany, Ann P(axton) 1937- 90
Elspeth
  See Bragdon, Elspeth MacDuffie
Elster, Jean Alicia 1953- 150
Elting, Mary 1906- 88
  Earlier sketch in SATA 2
  See also SAAS 20
Elwart, Joan Potter 1927- 2
Elwood, Ann 1931- 55
  Brief entry 52
Elwood, Roger 1943- 58
Elya, Susan M(iddleton) 1955- 159
  Earlier sketch in SATA 106
Elzbieta 88
Emberley, Barbara A(nne) 1932- 146
  Earlier sketches in SATA 8, 70
  See also CLR 5
Emberley, Ed(ward Randolph) 1931- 146
  Earlier sketches in SATA 8, 70
  See also CLR 81
Emberley, Michael 1960- 119
  Earlier sketches in SATA 34, 80
Embry, Margaret Jacob 1919-1975 5
Emecheta, (Florence Onye) Buchi 1944- 66

Emerson, Alice B. 67
  Earlier sketch in SATA 1
  See Benson, Mildred (Augustine Wirt)
Emerson, Kathy Lynn 1947- 63
Emerson, Ru 1944- 107
  Earlier sketch in SATA 70
Emerson, Sally 1952- 111
Emerson, William K(eith) 1925- 25
Emert, Phyllis R(aybin) 1947- 93
Emery, Anne (McGuigan) 1907- 33
  Earlier sketch in SATA 1
Emmens, Carol Ann 1944- 39
Emmett, Jonathan 1965- 138
Emory, Jerry 1957- 96
Emrich, Duncan (Black Macdonald)
  1908-1970(?) 11
Emslie, M. L.
  See Simpson, Myrtle L(illias)
Ende, Michael (Andreas Helmuth) 1929-1995
  130
  Brief entry 42
  Obituary 86
  Earlier sketch in SATA 61
  See also CLR 14
Enderle, Dotti 1954- 145
Enderle, Judith (Ann) Ross 1941- 89
  Autobiography Feature 114
  Earlier sketch in SATA 38
  See also SAAS 26
Enell, Trinka (Gochenour) 1951- 79
Enfield, Carrie
  See Smith, Susan Vernon
Engdahl, Sylvia Louise 1933- 4
  Autobiography Feature 122
  See also CLR 2
  See also SAAS 5
Engel, Diana 1947- 70
Engelbreit, Mary 1952- 169
Engelhart, Margaret S. 1924- 59
Engelmann, Kim (V.) 1959- 87
England, George Allan 1877-1936 102
Englart, Mindi Rose 1965- 146
Engle, Eloise
  See Paananen, Eloise (Katherine)
Englebert, Victor 1933- 8
English, James W(ilson) 1915- 37
Engstrom, Elizabeth 1951- 110
Enright, D(ennis) J(oseph) 1920-2002 25
  Obituary 140
Enright, Elizabeth (Wright) 1909-1968 9
  See also CLR 4
Ensor, Robert (T.) 1922- 93
Entwistle, (Arthur) Theodore (Henry) Rowland
  See Rowland-Entwistle, (Arthur) Theodore
  (Henry)
Enys, Sarah L.
  See Sloggett, Nellie
Epanya, Christian A(rthur Kingue) 1956- ... 91
Ephraim, Shelly S(chonebaum) 1952- 97
Ephron, Delia 1944- 65
  Brief entry 50
Epler, Doris M. 1928- 73
Epp, Margaret A(gnes) 1913- 20
Epple, Anne Orth 1927- 20
Epstein, Anne Merrick 1931- 20
Epstein, Beryl (M. Williams) 1910- 31
  Earlier sketch in SATA 1
  See also CLR 26
  See also SAAS 17
Epstein, Perle S(herry) 1938- 27
Epstein, Rachel S. 1941- 102
Epstein, Samuel 1909-2000 31
  Earlier sketch in SATA 1
  See also CLR 26
  See also SAAS 17
Erdman, Loula Grace 1905(?)-1976 1
Erdoes, Richard 1912- 33
  Brief entry 28
Erdrich, Karen Louise
  See Erdrich, Louise

Erdrich, Louise 1954- *141*
  Earlier sketch in SATA *94*
Erickson, Betty J. 1923- *97*
Erickson, Betty Jean
  See Erickson, Betty J.
Erickson, John R. 1943- *136*
  Earlier sketch in SATA *70*
Erickson, Jon 1948- *141*
Erickson, Phoebe *59*
Erickson, Russell E(verett) 1932- *27*
Erickson, Sabra Rollins 1912-1995 .... *35*
Erickson, Walter
  See Fast, Howard (Melvin)
Ericson, Walter
  See Fast, Howard (Melvin)
Erikson, Mel 1937- *31*
Erlanger, Baba
  See Trahey, Jane
Erlbach, Arlene 1948- *160*
  Earlier sketches in SATA *78, 115*
Erlich, Lillian (Feldman) 1910-1983 .... *10*
Ernst, (Lyman) John 1940- *39*
Ernst, Kathleen A. 1959- *162*
Ernst, Kathryn (Fitzgerald) 1942- *25*
Ernst, Lisa Campbell 1957- *154*
  Brief entry *44*
  Earlier sketches in SATA *55, 95*
Ervin, Janet Halliday 1923- *4*
Erwin, Will
  See Eisner, Will
Esbensen, Barbara J(uster) 1925-1996 .... *97*
  Brief entry *53*
  Earlier sketch in SATA *62*
Eschbacher, Roger *160*
Eseki, Bruno
  See Mphahlele, Ezekiel
Eshmeyer, R. E. *29*
  See Eschmeyer, R(einhart) E(rnst)
Eskridge, Ann E. 1949- *84*
Espeland, Pamela (Lee) 1951- *128*
  Brief entry *38*
  Earlier sketch in SATA *52*
Espriella, Don Manuel Alvarez
  See Southey, Robert
Espy, Willard R(ichardson) 1910-1999 .... *38*
  Obituary *113*
Essrig, Harry 1912- *66*
Estep, Irene Compton *5*
Esterl, Arnica 1933- *77*
Estes, Eleanor (Ruth) 1906-1988 .... *91*
  Obituary *56*
  Earlier sketch in SATA *7*
  See also CLR *70*
Estoril, Jean
  See Allan, Mabel Esther
Estrada, Pau 1961- *74*
Etchemendy, Nancy 1952- *166*
  Earlier sketch in SATA *38*
Etchemendy, Nancy Elise Howell
  See Etchemendy, Nancy
Etchison, Birdie L(ee) 1937- *38*
Etchison, Craig 1945- *133*
Etherington, Frank 1945- *58*
Ets, Marie Hall 1893-1984 .... *2*
  See also CLR *33*
Eunson, (John) Dale 1904-2002 .... *5*
  Obituary *132*
Evan, Frances Y. 1951- *167*
Evanoff, Vlad 1916- *59*
Evans, Douglas 1953- *144*
  Earlier sketch in SATA *93*
Evans, Eva (Knox) 1905-1998 .... *27*
Evans, Freddi Williams 1957- *134*
Evans, Greg 1947- *143*
  Earlier sketch in SATA *73*
Evans, Hubert Reginald 1892-1986 .... *118*
  Obituary *48*
Evans, Katherine (Floyd) 1901-1964 .... *5*
Evans, Larry
  See Evans, Laurence Chubb
Evans, Laurence Chubb 1939- *88*

Evans, Lawrence Watt *75*
  See Watt-Evans, Lawrence
Evans, Mari 1923- *10*
Evans, Mark *19*
Evans, Nancy 1950- *65*
Evans, Patricia Healy
  See Carpenter, Patricia (Healy Evans)
Evans, (Alice) Pearl 1927- *83*
Evans, Shirlee 1931- *58*
Evans, Tabor
  See Cameron, Lou
  and Knott, William C(ecil, Jr.)
  and Wallmann, Jeffrey M(iner)
  and Whittington, Harry (Benjamin)
Evarts, Esther
  See Benson, Sally
Evarts, Hal G., (Jr.) 1915-1989 .... *6*
Everett, Gail
  See Hale, Arlene
Evernden, Margery 1916- *5*
Eversole, Robyn Harbert 1971- *74*
Evslin, Bernard 1922-1993 .... *83*
  Brief entry *28*
  Obituary *77*
  Earlier sketch in SATA *45*
Ewart, Claire 1958- *145*
  Earlier sketch in SATA *76*
Ewen, David 1907-1985 .... *4*
  Obituary *47*
Ewing, Juliana (Horatia Gatty) 1841-1885 . *16*
  See also CLR *78*
Ewing, Kathryn 1921- *20*
Eyerly, Jeannette (Hyde) 1908- *86*
  Earlier sketch in SATA *4*
  See also SAAS *10*
Eyre, Dorothy
  See McGuire, Leslie (Sarah)
Eyre, Katherine Wigmore 1901-1970 .... *26*
Ezzell, Marilyn 1937- *42*
  Brief entry *38*

F

Fabe, Maxene 1943- *15*
Faber, Doris (Greenberg) 1924- *78*
  Earlier sketch in SATA *3*
Faber, Harold 1919- *5*
Fabre, Jean Henri (Casimir) 1823-1915 ...... *22*
Facklam, Margery (Metz) 1927- *132*
  Earlier sketches in SATA *20, 85*
Fadiman, Clifton (Paul) 1904-1999 .... *11*
  Obituary *115*
Fahs, Sophia Blanche Lyon 1876-1978 ..... *102*
Fair, David 1952- *96*
Fair, Sylvia 1933- *13*
Fairfax-Lucy, Brian (Fulke Cameron-Ramsay)
  1898-1974 .... *6*
  Obituary *26*
Fairfield, Flora
  See Alcott, Louisa May
Fairman, Joan A(lexandra) 1935- *10*
Faithfull, Gail 1936- *8*
Falcone, L(ucy) M. 1951- *155*
Falconer, Ian 1959- *125*
  See also CLR *90*
Falconer, James
  See Kirkup, James
Falconer, Lee N.
  See May, Julian
Falk, Lee
  See Copper, Basil
  and Goulart, Ron(ald Joseph)
Falkner, Leonard 1900-1977 .... *12*
Fall, Andrew
  See Arthur, Robert, (Jr.)
Fall, Thomas
  See Snow, Donald Clifford
Falls, C(harles) B(uckles) 1874-1960 .... *38*
  Brief entry *27*

Falstein, Louis 1909-1995 .... *37*
Fanelli, Sara 1969- *126*
  Earlier sketch in SATA *89*
Fanning, Leonard M(ulliken) 1888-1967 ...... *5*
Faralla, Dana 1909- *9*
Faralla, Dorothy W.
  See Faralla, Dana
Farb, Peter 1929-1980 .... *12*
  Obituary *22*
Farber, Norma 1909-1984 .... *75*
  Obituary *38*
  Earlier sketch in SATA *25*
Farish, Terry 1947- *146*
  Earlier sketch in SATA *82*
Farjeon, (Eve) Annabel 1919-2004 .... *11*
  Obituary *153*
Farjeon, Eleanor 1881-1965 .... *2*
  See also CLR *34*
Farley, Carol (J.) 1936- *137*
  Earlier sketch in SATA *4*
Farley, Terri *165*
Farley, Walter (Lorimer) 1915-1989 .... *132*
  Earlier sketches in SATA *2, 43*
Farlow, James O(rville, Jr.) 1951- *75*
Farmer, Nancy 1941- *161*
  Earlier sketches in SATA *79, 117*
Farmer, Patti 1948- *79*
Farmer, Penelope (Jane) 1939- *105*
  Brief entry *39*
  Earlier sketch in SATA *40*
  See also CLR *8*
  See also SAAS *22*
Farmer, Peter 1950- *38*
Farmer, Philip Jose 1918- *93*
Farnham, Burt
  See Clifford, Harold B(urton)
Farnsworth, Bill 1958- *135*
  Earlier sketch in SATA *84*
Farquhar, Margaret C(utting) 1905-1988 .... *13*
Farquharson, Alexander 1944- *46*
Farquharson, Martha
  See Finley, Martha
Farr, Diana (Pullein-Thompson) *82*
  See Pullein-Thompson, Diana
Farr, Finis (King) 1904-1982 .... *10*
Farrar, Jill
  See Morris, Jill
Farrar, Susan Clement 1917- *33*
Farrell, Ben
  See Cebulash, Mel
Farrell, Patrick
  See Odgers, Sally Farrell
Farrell, Sally
  See Odgers, Sally Farrell
Farrer, Vashti *167*
Farrington, S(elwyn) Kip, Jr. 1904-1983 .... *20*
Farshtey, Greg(ory T.) 1965- *148*
Farthing, Alison 1936- *45*
  Brief entry *36*
Farthing-Knight, Catherine 1933- *92*
Fassler, Joan (Grace) 1931- *11*
Fast, Howard (Melvin) 1914-2003 .... *7*
  Autobiography Feature *107*
Fasulo, Michael 1963- *83*
Fatchen, Max 1920- *84*
  Earlier sketch in SATA *20*
  See also SAAS *20*
Fate, Marilyn
  See Collins, Paul
Father Goose
  See Ghigna, Charles
Fatigati, (Frances) Evelyn 1948- *24*
Fatio, Louise 1904-1993 .... *6*
Faulhaber, Martha 1926- *7*
Faulkner, Anne Irvin 1906- *23*
Faulkner, Frank
  See Ellis, Edward S(ylvester)
Faulkner, Nancy
  See Faulkner, Anne Irvin
Faulknor, Cliff(ord Vernon) 1913- *86*
Favole, Robert J(ames) 1950- *125*

Fax, Elton Clay 1909-1993 25
Faxon, Lavinia
   See Russ, Lavinia (Faxon)
Feagles, Anita M(acRae) 1927- 9
Feagles, Elizabeth
   See Day, Beth (Feagles)
Feague, Mildred H. 1915- 14
Fearnley, Jan 1965- 153
Fearrington, Ann (Peyton) 1945- 146
Fecher, Constance
   See Heaven, Constance (Christina)
Feder, Chris Welles 1938- 81
Feder, Harriet K. 1928- 73
Feder, Paula (Kurzband) 1935- 26
Feelings, Muriel (Lavita Grey) 1938- 16
   See also CLR 5
   See also SAAS 8
Feelings, Thomas 1933-2003 8
   Obituary 148
   See Feelings, Tom
Feelings, Tom 69
   See also CLR 58
   See also SAAS 19
   See Feelings, Thomas
Fehler, Gene 1940- 74
Fehrenbach, T(heodore) R(eed, Jr.) 1925- .. 33
Feiffer, Jules (Ralph) 1929- 157
   Earlier sketches in SATA 8, 61, 111
Feig, Barbara Krane 1937- 34
Feikema, Feike
   See Manfred, Frederick (Feikema)
Feil, Hila 1942- 12
Feilen, John
   See May, Julian
Feinberg, Barbara Jane 1938- 58
   See Feinberg, Barbara Silberdick
Feinberg, Barbara Silberdick 123
   See Feinberg, Barbara Jane
Feinstein, John 1956- 163
Feldman, Anne (Rodgers) 1939- 19
Feldman, Elane 79
Felix
   See Vincent, Felix
Fell, Derek 1939- 167
Fell, Derek John
   See Fell, Derek
Fellows, Muriel H. 10
Felsen, Henry Gregor 1916-1995 1
   See also SAAS 2
Feltenstein, Arlene (H.) 1934- 119
Felton, Harold William 1902-1991 1
Felton, Ronald Oliver 1909- 3
Felts, Shirley 1934- 33
Fenderson, Lewis H., Jr. 1907-1983 47
   Obituary 37
Fenner, Carol (Elizabeth) 1929-2002 89
   Obituary 132
   Earlier sketch in SATA 7
   See also SAAS 24
Fenner, Phyllis R(eid) 1899-1982 1
   Obituary 29
Fensham, Elizabeth 169
Fenten, Barbara D(oris) 1935- 26
Fenten, D(onald) X. 1932- 4
Fenton, Carroll Lane 1900-1969 5
Fenton, Edward 1917-1995 7
   Obituary 89
Fenton, Mildred Adams 1899-1995 21
Fenwick, Patti
   See Grider, Dorothy
Feravolo, Rocco Vincent 1922- 10
Ferber, Edna 1887-1968 7
Fergus, Charles 114
Ferguson, Alane 1957- 85
Ferguson, Bob
   See Ferguson, Robert Bruce
Ferguson, Cecil 1931- 45
Ferguson, Robert Bruce 1927-2001 13
Ferguson, Sarah (Margaret) 1959- 110
   Earlier sketch in SATA 66
Ferguson, Walter (W.) 1930- 34

Fergusson, Erna 1888-1964 5
Fermi, Laura 1907-1977 6
   Obituary 28
Fern, Eugene A. 1919-1987 10
   Obituary 54
Fernandes, Eugenie 1943- 139
   Earlier sketch in SATA 77
Ferrari, Maria 123
Ferreiro, Carmen 1958- 158
Ferrell, Nancy Warren 1932- 70
Ferrier, Lucy
   See Penzler, Otto
Ferris, Helen Josephine 1890-1969 21
Ferris, James Cody 1
   See McFarlane, Leslie (Charles)
Ferris, Jean 1939- 149
   Brief entry 50
   Earlier sketches in SATA 56, 105
Ferris, Jeri Chase 1937- 84
Ferry, Charles 1927- 92
   Earlier sketch in SATA 43
   See also CLR 34
   See also SAAS 20
Fetz, Ingrid 1915- 30
Feydy, Anne Lindbergh
   Brief entry 32
   See Sapieyevski, Anne Lindbergh
Fiammenghi, Gioia 1929- 66
   Earlier sketch in SATA 9
Fiarotta, Noel 15
   See Ficarotta, Noel
Fiarotta, Phyllis 15
   See Ficarotta, Phyllis
Fichter, George S. 1922-1993 7
Fidler, Kathleen (Annie) 1899-1980 87
   Obituary 45
   Earlier sketch in SATA 3
Fiedler, Jean(nette Feldman) 4
Fiedler, Joseph Daniel 159
Field, Dorothy 1944- 97
Field, Edward 1924- 109
   Earlier sketch in SATA 8
Field, Eugene 1850-1895 16
Field, Gans T.
   See Wellman, Manly Wade
Field, James 1959- 113
Field, Peter
   See Drago, Harry Sinclair
   and Dresser, Davis
   and Mann, E(dward) B(everly)
Field, Rachel (Lyman) 1894-1942 15
   See also CLR 21
Fielding, Kate
   See Oldfield, Jenny
Fienberg, Anna 1956- 112
Fife, Dale (Odile Hollerbach) 1901- 18
Fighter Pilot, A
   See Johnston, H(ugh) A(nthony) S(tephen)
Figler, Jeanie 1949- 123
Figley, Marty Rhodes 1948- 158
   Earlier sketch in SATA 88
Figueredo, D(anilo) H. 1951- 155
Figueroa, Pablo 1938- 9
Fijan, Carol 1918- 12
Filderman, Diane E(lizabeth) 1959- 87
Files, Meg 1946- 107
Fillmore, Parker H(oysted) 1878-1944
   See YABC 1
Filstrup, Chris
   See Filstrup, E(dward) Christian
Filstrup, E(dward) Christian 1942- 43
Finchler, Judy 1943- 93
Finder, Martin
   See Salzmann, Siegmund
Findlay, Jamieson 1958- 169
Findon, Joanne 1957- 161
Fine, Anne 1947- 160
   Earlier sketches in SATA 29, 72, 111
   See also CLR 25
   See also SAAS 15
Fine, Edith Hope 169

Fine, Jane
   See Ziefert, Harriet
Finger, Charles J(oseph) 1869(?)-1941 42
Fink, William B(ertrand) 1916- 22
Finke, Blythe Foote 1922- 26
Finkel, George (Irvine) 1909-1975 8
Finkelstein, Norman H. 1941- 137
   Earlier sketch in SATA 73
Finlay, Alice Sullivan 1946- 82
Finlay, Winifred Lindsay Crawford
   (McKissack) 1910-1989 23
Finlayson, Ann 1925- 8
Finley, Martha 1828-1909 43
Finley, Mary Peace 1942- 83
Finney, Jack 109
   See Finney, Walter Braden
Finney, Patricia 1958- 163
Finney, Shan 1944- 65
Firer, Ben Zion
   See Firer, Benzion
Firer, Benzion 1914- 64
Fireside, Bryna J. 1932- 73
Firmin, Charlotte 1954- 29
Firmin, Peter 1928- 58
   Earlier sketch in SATA 15
Fischbach, Julius 1894-1988 10
Fischer, John
   See Fluke, Joanne
Fischer, R. J.
   See Fluke, Joanne
Fischer-Nagel, Andreas 1951- 56
Fischer-Nagel, Heiderose 1956- 56
Fischler, Shirley (Walton) 66
Fischler, Stan(ley I.) 66
   Brief entry 36
Fisher, Aileen (Lucia) 1906-2002 73
   Obituary 143
   Earlier sketches in SATA 1, 25
   See also CLR 49
Fisher, Barbara 1940- 44
   Brief entry 34
Fisher, Carolyn 1968- 154
Fisher, Catherine 1957- 155
Fisher, Chris 1958- 80
Fisher, Clavin C(argill) 1912- 24
Fisher, Dorothy (Frances) Canfield 1879-1958
   See YABC 1
   See also CLR 71
Fisher, Gary L. 1949- 86
Fisher, John (Oswald Hamilton) 1909- 15
Fisher, Laura Harrison 1934- 5
Fisher, Leonard Everett 1924- 120
   Autobiography Feature 122
   Earlier sketches in SATA 4, 34, 73
   See also CLR 18
   See also SAAS 1
Fisher, Lois I. 1948- 38
   Brief entry 35
Fisher, Margery (Turner) 1913-1992 20
   Obituary 74
Fisher, Marshall Jon 1963- 113
Fisher, Nikki
   See Strachan, Ian
Fisher, Robert (Tempest) 1943- 47
Fisher, Suzanne
   See Staples, Suzanne Fisher
Fishman, Cathy Goldberg 1951- 106
Fisk, Nicholas 25
   See Higginbottom, David
Fisk, Pauline 1948- 160
   Earlier sketch in SATA 66
Fiske, Tarleton
   See Bloch, Robert (Albert)
Fisscher, Catharina G. M. 1958- 142
Fisscher, Tiny
   See Fisscher, Catharina G. M.
Fitch, Clarke
   See Sinclair, Upton
Fitch, John IV
   See Cormier, Robert (Edmund)
Fitch, Sheree 1956- 108

Fitschen, Dale 1937- 20
Fitzalan, Roger
   See Trevor, Elleston
Fitzgerald, Captain Hugh
   See Baum, L(yman) Frank
Fitzgerald, Edward Earl 1919-2001 20
Fitzgerald, F(rancis) A(nthony) 1940- 15
Fitzgerald, John D(ennis) 1907(?)-1988 20
   Obituary 56
   See also CLR 1
Fitzgerald, Merni Ingrassia 1955- 53
Fitzgibbon, Terry 1948- 121
Fitzhardinge, Joan Margaret 1912- 73
   Earlier sketch in SATA 2
   See Phipson, Joan
Fitzhugh, Louise (Perkins) 1928-1974 45
   Obituary 24
   Earlier sketch in SATA 1
   See also CLR 72
Fitzhugh, Percy Keese 1876-1950 65
Fitzpatrick, Marie-Louise 1962- 125
FitzRalph, Matthew
   See McInerny, Ralph (Matthew)
Fitz-Randolph, Jane (Currens) 1915- 51
Fitzsimons, Cecilia 1952- 97
Fitzsimons, Cecilia A.L.
   See Fitzsimons, Cecilia
Flack, Marjorie 1897-1958 100
   See also YABC 2
   See also CLR 28
Flack, Naomi John White -1999 40
   Brief entry 35
Flake, Sharon G. 166
Flannery, Kate
   See De Goldi, Kathleen Domenica
Flatt, Lizann
   See Brunskill, Elizabeth Ann Flatt
Fleagle, Gail S(hatto) 1940- 117
Fleetwood, Jenni 1947- 80
Fleischer, Jane
   See Oppenheim, Joanne
Fleischhauer-Hardt, Helga 1936- 30
Fleischman, John 1948- 145
Fleischman, Paul 1952- 156
   Brief entry 32
   Earlier sketches in SATA 39, 72, 110
   See also CLR 66
   See also SAAS 20
Fleischman, (Albert) Sid(ney) 1920- 148
   Earlier sketches in SATA 8, 59, 96
   See also CLR 15
Fleischner, Jennifer 1956- 93
Fleisher, Paul 1948- 132
   Earlier sketch in SATA 81
Fleisher, Robbin 1951-1977 52
   Brief entry 49
Fleishman, Seymour 1918- 66
   Brief entry 32
Fleming, A. A.
   See Arthur, Robert, (Jr.)
Fleming, Alice Mulcahey 1928- 9
Fleming, Candace 1962- 143
   Earlier sketch in SATA 94
Fleming, Denise 1950- 126
   Earlier sketch in SATA 81
Fleming, Ian (Lancaster) 1908-1964 9
Fleming, Ronald Lee 1941- 56
Fleming, Stuart
   See Knight, Damon (Francis)
Fleming, Susan 1932- 32
Fleming, Thomas (James) 1927- 8
Fleming, Virginia (Edwards) 1923- 84
Flesch, Y.
   See Flesch, Yolande (Catarina)
Flesch, Yolande (Catarina) 1950- 55
Fletcher, Charlie May Hogue 1897-1977 3
Fletcher, Colin 1922- 28
Fletcher, Dirk
   See Cunningham, Chet
Fletcher, George U.
   See Pratt, (Murray) Fletcher

Fletcher, Helen Jill 1910- 13
Fletcher, Ralph (J.) 1953- 149
   Earlier sketch in SATA 105
   See also CLR 104
Fletcher, Susan (Clemens) 1951- 110
   Earlier sketch in SATA 70
Fleur, Paul
   See Pohl, Frederik
Flexner, James Thomas 1908-2003 9
Flinn, Alex 1966- 159
Flint, Helen 1952- 102
Flint, Russ 1944- 74
Flitner, David P(erkins), Jr. 1949- 7
Floca, Brian 155
Floethe, Louise Lee 1913-1988 4
Floethe, Richard 1901-1998 4
Floherty, John Joseph 1882-1964 25
Flood, Bo
   See Flood, Nancy Bo
Flood, Nancy Bo 1945- 130
Flood, Pansie Hart 1964- 140
Flood, William 1942- 129
Flooglebuckle, Al
   See Spiegelman, Art
Flora, James (Royer) 1914-1998 30
   Obituary 103
   Earlier sketch in SATA 1
   See also SAAS 6
Florian, Douglas 1950- 125
   Earlier sketches in SATA 19, 83
Flory, Jane Trescott 1917- 22
Flournoy, Valerie (Rose) 1952- 95
Flowerdew, Phyllis -1994 33
Flowers, Pam 1946- 136
Flowers, Sarah 1952- 98
Floyd, Gareth 1940- 62
   Brief entry 31
Fluchere, Henri 1914-1991 40
Fluke, Joanne 88
Flynn, Barbara 1928- 9
Flynn, Jackson
   See Bensen, Donald R.
   and Shirreffs, Gordon D(onald)
Flynn, Nicholas
   See Odgers, Sally Farrell
Flynn, Rachel 1953- 109
Flynn, Warren (G.) 1950- 154
Fodor, R(onald) V(ictor) 1944- 25
Fogelin, Adrian 1951- 129
Foley, (Anna) Bernice Williams 1902-1987
   28
Foley, June 1944- 44
Foley, (Mary) Louise Munro 1933- 106
   Brief entry 40
   Earlier sketch in SATA 54
Folke, Will
   See Bloch, Robert (Albert)
Folsom, Franklin (Brewster) 1907-1995 5
   Obituary 88
Folsom, Michael (Brewster) 1938-1990 40
   Obituary 88
Fontenot, Mary Alice 1910- 91
   Earlier sketch in SATA 34
Foon, Dennis 1951- 119
Fooner, Michael 22
Foote, Timothy (Gilson) 1926- 52
Forberg, Ati 22
   See Forberg, Beate Gropius
Forbes, Anna 1954- 101
Forbes, Bryan 1926- 37
Forbes, Cabot L.
   See Hoyt, Edwin P(almer), Jr.
Forbes, Esther 1891-1967 100
   Earlier sketch in SATA 2
   See also CLR 27
Forbes, Graham B. 1
Forbes, Kathryn
   See McLean, Kathryn (Anderson)
Forbes, Robert
   See Arthur, Robert, (Jr.)

Ford, Albert Lee
   See Stratemeyer, Edward L.
Ford, Barbara 56
   Brief entry 34
Ford, Brian J(ohn) 1939- 49
Ford, Carolyn (Mott) 1938- 98
Ford, Elbur
   See Hibbert, Eleanor Alice Burford
Ford, Ellen 1949- 89
Ford, George (Jr.) 31
Ford, Hilary
   See Youd, (Christopher) Samuel
Ford, Hildegarde
   See Morrison, Velma Ford
Ford, Jerome W. 1949- 78
Ford, Jerry
   See Ford, Jerome W.
Ford, Juwanda G(ertrude) 1967- 102
Ford, Marcia
   See Radford, Ruby L(orraine)
Ford, Peter 1936- 59
Ford, S. M.
   See Uhlig, Susan
Foreman, Michael 1938- 135
   Earlier sketches in SATA 2, 73, 129
   See also CLR 32
   See also SAAS 21
Foreman, Wilmoth 1939- 153
Forest, Dial
   See Gault, William Campbell
Forest, Heather 1948- 120
Forester, C(ecil) S(cott) 1899-1966 13
Forman, Brenda 1936- 4
Forman, James
   See Forman, James D(ouglas)
Forman, James D(ouglas) 1932- 70
   Earlier sketch in SATA 8
Forrest, Elizabeth
   See Salsitz, Rhondi Vilott
Forrest, Mary
   See Pausacker, Jenny
Forrest, Sybil
   See Markun, Patricia Maloney
Forrestal, Elaine 1941- 165
   Earlier sketch in SATA 117
Forrester, Helen 48
   See Bhatia, Jamunadevi
Forrester, Jade
   See Pausacker, Jenny
Forrester, Marian
   See Schachtel, Roger (Bernard)
Forrester, Sandra 1949- 166
   Earlier sketch in SATA 90
Forrester, Victoria 1940- 40
   Brief entry 35
Forsee, (Frances) Aylesa -1986 1
Forsey, Chris 1950- 59
Forshay-Lunsford, Cin 1965- 60
Forster, E(dward) M(organ) 1879-1970 57
Forsyth, Kate 1966- 154
Fort, Paul
   See Stockton, Francis Richard
Forte, Maurizio 1961- 110
Fortey, Richard (Alan) 1946- 109
Forth, Melissa D(eal) 96
Fortnum, Peggy 26
   See Nuttall-Smith, Margaret Emily Noel
Forward, Robert L(ull) 1932-2002 82
Foster, Alan Dean 1946- 70
Foster, Brad W. 1955- 34
Foster, Doris Van Liew 1899-1993 10
Foster, E(lizabeth) C(onnell) 1902- 9
Foster, Elizabeth 1902- 12
Foster, Elizabeth 1905-1963 10
Foster, F. Blanche 1919- 11
Foster, G(eorge) Allen 1907-1969 26
Foster, Genevieve (Stump) 1893-1979 2
   Obituary 23
   See also CLR 7
Foster, Hal
   See Foster, Harold (Rudolf)

Foster, Harold (Rudolf) 1892-1982 .... *31*
  See Foster, Hal
Foster, Jeanne
  See Williams, Jeanne
Foster, John
  See Foster, John L(ouis)
    and Furcolo, Foster
Foster, John (Thomas) 1925- *8*
Foster, John L(ouis) 1941- *102*
Foster, Laura Louise (James) 1918- *6*
Foster, Leila Merrell 1929- *73*
Foster, Lynne 1937- *74*
Foster, Marian Curtis 1909-1978 .... *23*
Foster, Sally *58*
Foulds, E. V.
  See Foulds, Elfrida Vipont
Foulds, Elfrida Vipont 1902-1992 .... *52*
  See Vipont, Elfrida
Fourie, Corlia 1944- *91*
Fourth Brother, The
  See Aung, (Maung) Htin
Fowke, Edith (Margaret) 1913-1996 .... *14*
Fowles, John 1926-2005 .... *22*
Fowles, John Robert
  See Fowles, John
Fox, Aileen 1907-2005 .... *58*
Fox, Charles Philip 1913-2003 .... *12*
  Obituary *150*
Fox, Eleanor
  See St. John, Wylly Folk
Fox, Freeman
  See Hamilton, Charles (Harold St. John)
Fox, Geoffrey 1941- *73*
Fox, Grace
  See Anderson, Grace Fox
Fox, Larry *30*
Fox, Lorraine 1922-1976 .... *27*
  Earlier sketch in SATA *11*
Fox, Louisa
  See Kroll, Virginia L.
Fox, Mary Virginia 1919- *152*
  Brief entry *39*
  Earlier sketches in SATA *44, 88*
Fox, Mem *103*
  See also CLR *23*
  See Fox, Merrion Frances
Fox, Merrion Frances 1946- *155*
  Earlier sketch in SATA *51*
  See also CLR *80*
  See Fox, Mem
Fox, Michael W(ilson) 1937- *15*
Fox, Paula 1923- *167*
  Earlier sketches in SATA *17, 60, 120*
  See also CLR *96*
Fox, Robert J. 1927- *33*
Fradin, Dennis
  See Fradin, Dennis Brindell
Fradin, Dennis Brindell 1945- *135*
  Earlier sketches in SATA *29, 90*
Fradin, Judith (Bernette) Bloom 1945- *152*
  Earlier sketch in SATA *90*
Frailey, Paige (Menefee) 1965- *82*
Frame, Janet
  See Clutha, Janet Paterson Frame
Frame, Paul 1913-1994 .... *60*
  Brief entry *33*
  Obituary *83*
Frances, Miss
  See Horwich, Frances R(appaport)
Franchere, Ruth *18*
Francis, Charles
  See Holme, Bryan
Francis, Dee
  See Haas, Dorothy F.
Francis, Dorothy Brenner 1926- *127*
  Earlier sketch in SATA *10*
Francis, Jaye
  See Pausacker, Jenny
Francis, Pamela (Mary) 1926- *11*
Franck, Eddie
  See Cooke, Frank E.

Franco, Betsy *150*
Franco, Eloise (Bauder) 1910- *62*
Franco, Johan (Henri Gustave) 1908-1988 . *62*
Franco, Marjorie *38*
Francois, Andre 1915-2005 .... *25*
Francoise
  See Seignobosc, Francoise
Frank, Anne(lies Marie) 1929-1945 .... *87*
  Brief entry *42*
  See also CLR *101*
Frank, Daniel B. 1956- *55*
Frank, E(mily) R. 1967- *157*
Frank, Helene
  See Vautier, Ghislaine
Frank, Hillary 1976- *148*
Frank, Josette 1893-1989 .... *10*
  Obituary *63*
Frank, Lucy 1947- *166*
  Earlier sketch in SATA *94*
Frank, Mary 1933- *34*
Frank, R., Jr.
  See Ross, Frank (Xavier), Jr.
Frankau, Mary Evelyn Atkinson 1899-1974 . *4*
Frankel, Alona 1937- *66*
Frankel, Bernice *9*
Frankel, Edward 1910- *44*
Frankel, Ellen 1951- *78*
Frankel, Julie 1947- *40*
  Brief entry *34*
Frankenberg, Robert 1911- *22*
Franklin, Cheryl J. 1955- *70*
Franklin, Harold 1926- *13*
Franklin, Kristine L. 1958- *124*
  Earlier sketch in SATA *80*
Franklin, Lance
  See Lantz, Francess L(in)
Franklin, Max
  See Deming, Richard
Franklin, Steve
  See Stevens, Franklin
Franson, Leanne R. 1963- *111*
Franzen, Nils-Olof 1916- *10*
Frascino, Edward *48*
  Brief entry *33*
  See also SAAS *9*
Frasconi, Antonio 1919- *131*
  Earlier sketches in SATA *6, 53*
  See also SAAS *11*
Fraser, Betty
  See Fraser, Elizabeth Marr
Fraser, Elizabeth Marr 1928- *31*
Fraser, Eric (George) 1902-1983 .... *38*
Fraser, Mary Ann 1959- *137*
  Earlier sketch in SATA *76*
  See also SAAS *23*
Fraser, Wynnette (McFaddin) 1925- *90*
Frasier, Debra 1953- *112*
  Earlier sketch in SATA *69*
Fraustino, Lisa Rowe 1961- *146*
  Autobiography Feature *146*
  Earlier sketch in SATA *84*
Frazee, Marla 1958- *151*
  Earlier sketch in SATA *105*
Frazetta, Frank 1928- *58*
Frazier, Neta (Osborn) Lohnes 1890-1990 .... *7*
Frederic, Mike
  See Cox, William R(obert)
Fredericks, Anthony D. 1947- *113*
Freed, Alvyn M. 1913-1993 .... *22*
Freedman, Benedict 1919- *27*
Freedman, Jeff 1953- *90*
Freedman, Nancy 1920- *27*
Freedman, Russell (Bruce) 1929- *123*
  Earlier sketches in SATA *16, 71*
  See also CLR *71*
Freeman, Barbara C(onstance) 1906- *28*
Freeman, Bill
  See Freeman, William Bradford
Freeman, Don 1908-1978 .... *17*
  See also CLR *90*
Freeman, Ira Maximilian 1905-1987 .... *21*

Freeman, Lucy (Greenbaum) 1916-2004 .... *24*
Freeman, Mae (Blacker) 1907- *25*
Freeman, Marcia S. 1937- *102*
Freeman, Martha 1956- *152*
  Earlier sketch in SATA *101*
Freeman, Nancy 1932- *61*
Freeman, Peter J.
  See Calvert, Patricia
Freeman, Sarah (Caroline) 1940- *66*
Freeman, Tor 1977- *164*
Freeman, VicToria
  See Freeman, Tor
Freeman, William Bradford 1938- *58*
  Brief entry *48*
Fregosi, Claudia (Anne Marie) 1946- *24*
French, Allen 1870-1946
  See YABC *1*
French, Dorothy Kayser 1926- *5*
French, Fiona 1944- *132*
  Earlier sketches in SATA *6, 75*
  See also CLR *37*
  See also SAAS *21*
French, Jackie *139*
  Autobiography Feature *139*
  Earlier sketch in SATA *108*
  See French, Jacqueline Anne
French, Kathryn
  See Mosesson, Gloria R(ubin)
French, Michael 1944- *49*
  Brief entry *38*
French, Paul
  See Asimov, Isaac
French, Simon 1957- *147*
  Earlier sketch in SATA *86*
French, Vivian *165*
Frenette, Liza *126*
Freschet, Gina 1960- *139*
Frewer, Glyn (M.) 1931- *11*
Frey, Darcy *98*
Freymann-Weyr, (Rhoda) Garret (Michaela)
  1965- *145*
Frick, C. H.
  See Irwin, Constance (H.) Frick
Frick, Constance
  See Irwin, Constance (H.) Frick
Fricke, Aaron 1962- *89*
Fridell, Ron 1943- *124*
Friedlander, Joanne K(ohn) 1930- *9*
Friedman, Debra 1955- *150*
Friedman, Estelle (Ehrenwald) 1920- *7*
Friedman, Frieda 1905- *43*
Friedman, Ina R(osen) 1926- *136*
  Brief entry *41*
  Earlier sketch in SATA *49*
Friedman, Jerrold David
  See Gerrold, David
Friedman, Judi 1935- *59*
Friedman, Laurie 1964- *138*
Friedman, Marvin 1930- *42*
  Brief entry *33*
Friedman, Robin 1968- *162*
Friedmann, Stan 1953- *80*
Friedrich, Otto (Alva) 1929-1995 .... *33*
Friedrich, Priscilla 1927- *39*
Friendlich, Dick
  See Friendlich, Richard J.
Friendlich, Richard J. 1909- *11*
Friermood, Elisabeth Hamilton 1903-1992 ... *5*
Friesen, Bernice (Sarah Anne) 1966- *105*
Friesen, Gayle 1960- *109*
Friesner, Esther M. 1951- *168*
  Earlier sketch in SATA *71*
Friis-Baastad, Babbis Ellinor 1921-1970 .... *7*
Frimmer, Steven 1928- *31*
Frischmuth, Barbara 1941- *114*
Friskey, Margaret (Richards) 1901-1995 ..... *5*
Fritts, Mary Bahr
  See Bahr, Mary (Madelyn)

Fritz, Jean (Guttery) 1915- *163*
 Autobiography Feature *122*
 Earlier sketches in SATA *1, 29, 72, 119*
 See also CLR *96*
 See also SAAS *2*
Froehlich, Margaret W(alden) 1930- *56*
Frois, Jeanne 1953- *73*
Froissart, Jean 1338(?)-1410(?) *28*
Froman, Elizabeth Hull 1920-1975 .... *10*
Froman, Robert (Winslow) 1917- *8*
Fromm, Lilo 1928- *29*
Frommer, Harvey 1937- *41*
Frost, A(rthur) B(urdett) 1851-1928 .... *19*
Frost, Erica
 See Supraner, Robyn
Frost, Helen 1949- *157*
Frost, Lesley 1899-1983 .... *14*
 Obituary *34*
Frost, Robert (Lee) 1874-1963 .... *14*
 See also CLR *67*
Frost, Shelley 1960- *138*
Froud, Brian 1947- *150*
Fry, Annette R(iley) *89*
Fry, Christopher 1907-2005 .... *66*
Fry, Edward Bernard 1925- *35*
Fry, Rosalie Kingsmill 1911-1992 .... *3*
 See also SAAS *11*
Fry, Virginia Lynn 1952- *95*
Frye, Sally
 See Moore, Elaine
Fuchs, Bernie 1932- *162*
 Earlier sketch in SATA *95*
Fuchs, Erich 1916- *6*
Fuchshuber, Annegert 1940- *43*
Fuerst, Jeffrey B. 1956- *143*
Fuertes, Gloria 1918-1998 .... *115*
Fuge, Charles 1966- *144*
 Earlier sketch in SATA *74*
Fujikawa, Gyo 1908-1998 .... *76*
 Brief entry *30*
 Obituary *110*
 Earlier sketch in SATA *39*
 See also CLR *25*
 See also SAAS *16*
Fujita, Tamao 1905-1999 .... *7*
Fujiwara, Kim 1957- *81*
Fujiwara, Michiko 1946- *15*
Fuller, Catherine Leuthold 1916- *9*
Fuller, Edmund (Maybank) 1914- *21*
Fuller, Iola
 See McCoy, Iola Fuller
Fuller, John G(rant, Jr.) 1913-1990 .... *65*
Fuller, Kathleen
 See Gottfried, Theodore Mark
Fuller, Lois Hamilton 1915- *11*
Fuller, Margaret
 See Ossoli, Sarah Margaret (Fuller)
Fuller, Maud
 See Petersham, Maud (Sylvia Fuller)
Fuller, Roy (Broadbent) 1912-1991 .... *87*
Fuller, Sarah Margaret
 See Ossoli, Sarah Margaret (Fuller)
Fuller, Sarah Margaret
 See Ossoli, Sarah Margaret (Fuller)
Fults, John Lee 1932- *33*
Funk, Thompson 1911- *7*
Funk, Tom
 See Funk, Thompson
Funke, Cornelia (Caroline) 1958- *154*
Funke, Lewis 1912-1992 .... *11*
Fuqua, Jonathon Scott 1966- *141*
Furbee, Mary R.
 See Furbee, Mary Rodd
Furbee, Mary Rodd 1954- *138*
Furchgott, Terry 1948- *29*
Furlong, Monica (Mavis) 1930-2003 .... *86*
 Obituary *142*
Furman, Gertrude Lerner Kerman 1909- *21*
Furniss, Tim 1948- *49*
Furukawa, Toshi 1924- *24*
Fusillo, Archimede 1962- *137*

Futcher, Jane P. 1947- *76*
Fyleman, Rose (Amy) 1877-1957 .... *21*
Fyson, J(enny) G(race) 1904- *42*

G

Gaan, Margaret 1914- *65*
Gaber, Susan 1956- *169*
 Earlier sketch in SATA *115*
Gaberman, Judie Angell 1937- *78*
 Earlier sketch in SATA *22*
 See also CLR *33*
Gabhart, Ann 1947- *75*
Gabler, Mirko 1951- *77*
Gabriel, Adriana
 See Rojany, Lisa
Gabrys, Ingrid Schubert
 See Schubert-Gabrys, Ingrid
Gackenbach, Dick 1927- *79*
 Brief entry *30*
 Earlier sketch in SATA *48*
Gadd, Jeremy 1949- *116*
Gaddis, Vincent H. 1913-1997 .... *35*
Gadler, Steve J. 1905-1985 .... *36*
Gaeddert, Lou Ann (Bigge) 1931- *103*
 Earlier sketch in SATA *20*
Gaeddert, Louann
 See Gaeddert, Lou Ann (Bigge)
Gaer, Joseph 1897-1969 .... *118*
Gaer, Yossef
 See Gaer, Joseph
Gaetz, Dayle Campbell 1947- *138*
Gaffney, Timothy R. 1951- *69*
Gaffron, Norma (Bondeson) 1931- *97*
Gag, Wanda (Hazel) 1893-1946 .... *100*
 See also YABC *1*
 See also CLR *4*
Gage, Brian *162*
Gage, Wilson
 See Steele, Mary Q(uintard Govan)
Gagliano, Eugene M. 1946- *150*
Gagnon, Cecile 1936- *58*
Gaiman, Neil (Richard) 1960- *146*
 Earlier sketch in SATA *85*
 See also CLR *109*
Gainer, Cindy 1962- *74*
Gaines, Ernest J(ames) 1933- *86*
 See also CLR *62*
Gaither, Gloria 1942- *127*
Gal, Laszlo 1933- *96*
 Brief entry *32*
 Earlier sketch in SATA *52*
 See also CLR *61*
Galbraith, Kathryn O(sebold) 1945- *85*
Galdone, Paul 1907(?)-1986 .... *66*
 Obituary *49*
 Earlier sketch in SATA *17*
 See also CLR *16*
Galinsky, Ellen 1942- *23*
Gallagher, Diana G. 1946- *153*
Gallagher, Lurlene Nora
 See McDaniel, Lurlene
Gallant, Roy A(rthur) 1924- *110*
 Earlier sketches in SATA *4, 68*
 See also CLR *30*
Gallardo, Evelyn 1948- *78*
Gallaz, Christophe 1948- *162*
Gallico, Paul (William) 1897-1976 .... *13*
Gallo, Donald R(obert) 1938- *112*
 Autobiography Feature *104*
Galloway, Owateka (S.) 1981- *121*
Galloway, Priscilla 1930- *112*
 Earlier sketch in SATA *66*
Gallup, Joan 1957- *128*
Galouchko, Annouchka Gravel 1960- *95*
Galt, Thomas Franklin, Jr. 1908-1989 .... *5*
Galt, Tom
 See Galt, Thomas Franklin, Jr.
Galvin, Matthew R(eppert) 1950- *93*

Gamble, Kim 1952- *124*
 Earlier sketch in SATA *81*
Gambrell, Jamey *82*
Gamerman, Martha 1941- *15*
Gammell, Stephen 1943- *128*
 Earlier sketches in SATA *53, 81*
 See also CLR *83*
Ganly, Helen (Mary) 1940- *56*
Gannett, Ruth Chrisman (Arens) 1896-1979
 .... *33*
Gannett, Ruth Stiles 1923- *3*
Gannon, Robert Haines 1931- *8*
Gano, Lila 1949- *76*
Gans, Roma 1894-1996 .... *45*
 Obituary *93*
Gant, Matthew
 See Hano, Arnold
Gantner, Susan (Verble) 1939- *63*
Gantos, Jack 1951- *169*
 Earlier sketches in SATA *20, 81, 119*
 See also CLR *85*
Gantos, John Bryan, Jr.
 See Gantos, Jack
Ganz, Yaffa 1938- *61*
 Brief entry *52*
Garafano, Marie 1942- *84*
Garant, Andre J. 1968- *123*
Garbe, Ruth Moore
 See Moore, Ruth (Ellen)
Garcia, Yolanda P(acheco) 1952- *113*
Gard, Janice
 See Latham, Jean Lee
Gard, Joyce
 See Reeves, Joyce
Gard, Robert Edward 1910-1992 .... *18*
 Obituary *74*
Gardam, Jane (Mary) 1928- *130*
 Brief entry *28*
 Earlier sketches in SATA *39, 76*
 See also CLR *12*
 See also SAAS *9*
Gardella, Tricia 1944- *96*
Garden, Nancy 1938- *147*
 Autobiography Feature *147*
 Earlier sketches in SATA *12, 77, 114*
 See also CLR *51*
 See also SAAS *8*
Gardiner, John Reynolds 1944-2006 .... *64*
Gardiner, Lindsey 1971- *144*
Gardner, Craig Shaw 1949- *99*
Gardner, Dic
 See Gardner, Richard (M.)
Gardner, Graham *159*
Gardner, Jane Mylum 1946- *83*
Gardner, Jeanne LeMonnier 1925- *5*
Gardner, John (Champlin), Jr. 1933-1982 ... *40*
 Obituary *31*
Gardner, Martin 1914- *142*
 Earlier sketch in SATA *16*
Gardner, Miriam
 See Bradley, Marion Zimmer
Gardner, Richard (M.) 1931- *24*
Gardner, Richard A(lan) 1931-2003 .... *13*
 Obituary *144*
Gardner, Sandra 1940- *70*
Gardner, Scot 1968- *143*
Gardner, Sheldon 1934- *33*
Gardner, Ted
 See Gardner, Theodore Roosevelt II
Gardner, Theodore Roosevelt II 1934- *84*
Garelick, May 1910-1989 .... *19*
Garfield, James B. 1881-1984 .... *6*
 Obituary *38*
Garfield, Leon 1921-1996 .... *76*
 Obituary *90*
 Earlier sketches in SATA *1, 32*
 See also CLR *21*
Garis, Howard R(oger) 1873-1962 .... *13*
Garland, Mark (A.) 1953- *79*
Garland, Michael 1952- *168*

Garland, Sarah 1944- 135
    Earlier sketch in SATA 62
Garland, Sherry 1948- 145
    Autobiography Feature 145
    Earlier sketches in SATA 73, 114
Garner, Alan 1934- 69
    Autobiography Feature 108
    Earlier sketch in SATA 18
    See also CLR 20
Garner, David 1958- 78
Garner, Eleanor Ramrath 1930- 122
Garner, James Finn 1960(?)- 92
Garnet, A. H.
    See Slote, Alfred
Garnett, Eve C. R. 1900-1991 3
    Obituary 70
Garou, Louis P.
    See Bowkett, Stephen
Garraty, John A(rthur) 1920- 23
Garren, Devorah-Leah
    See Devorah-Leah
Garret, Maxwell R. 1917- 39
Garretson, Victoria Diane 1945- 44
Garrett, Helen 1895- 21
Garrett, Richard 1920- 82
Garrigue, Sheila 1931- 21
Garrison, Barbara 1931- 163
    Earlier sketch in SATA 19
Garrison, Frederick
    See Sinclair, Upton
Garrison, Mary 1952- 146
Garrison, Webb B(lack) 1919-2000 25
Garrity, Jennifer Johnson 1961- 124
Garrity, Linda K. 1947- 128
Garst, Doris Shannon 1894-1981 1
Garst, Shannon
    See Garst, Doris Shannon
Garth, Will
    See Hamilton, Edmond
    and Kuttner, Henry
Garthwaite, Marion H(ook) 1893-1981 7
Gascoigne, Bamber 1935- 62
Gaskins, Pearl Fuyo 1957- 134
Gasperini, Jim 1952- 54
    Brief entry 49
Gater, Dilys 1944- 41
Gates, Doris 1901-1987 34
    Obituary 54
    Earlier sketch in SATA 1
    See also SAAS 1
Gates, Frieda 1933- 26
Gates, Susan 1950- 153
Gates, Viola R. 1931- 101
Gathorne-Hardy, Jonathan G. 1933- 124
    Earlier sketch in SATA 26
Gatti, Anne 1952- 103
Gatty, Juliana Horatia
    See Ewing, Juliana (Horatia Gatty)
Gauch, Patricia Lee 1934- 80
    Earlier sketch in SATA 26
    See also CLR 56
    See also SAAS 21
Gaul, Randy 1959- 63
Gault, Clare 1925- 36
Gault, Frank 1926-1982 36
    Brief entry 30
Gault, William Campbell 1910-1995 8
Gauthier, Gail 1953- 160
    Earlier sketch in SATA 118
Gaver, Becky
    See Gaver, Rebecca
Gaver, Rebecca 1952- 20
Gavin, Jamila 1941- 125
    Earlier sketch in SATA 96
Gay, Amelia
    See Hogarth, Grace (Weston Allen)
Gay, Kathlyn 1930- 144
    Earlier sketch in SATA 9

Gay, Marie-Louise 1952- 126
    Earlier sketch in SATA 68
    See also CLR 27
    See also SAAS 21
Gay, Michel 1947- 162
Gay, Zhenya 1906-1978 19
Gaze, Gillian
    See Barklem, Jill
Gear, Kathleen M. O'Neal
    See Gear, Kathleen O'Neal
Gear, Kathleen O'Neal 1954- 166
    Earlier sketch in SATA 71
Gear, W. Michael 1955- 166
    Earlier sketch in SATA 71
Geary, Rick 1946- 142
Geason, Susan 1946- 122
Gedalof, Robin
    See McGrath, Robin
Gedge, Pauline (Alice) 1945- 101
Gee, Maurice (Gough) 1931- 101
    Earlier sketch in SATA 46
    See also CLR 56
Geehan, Wayne (E.) 1947- 107
Geer, Charles 1922- 42
    Brief entry 32
Geeslin, Campbell 1925- 163
    Earlier sketch in SATA 107
Gehman, Mary W. 1923- 86
Gehr, Mary 1910(?)-1997 32
    Obituary 99
Geipel, Eileen 1932- 30
Geis, Darlene Stern 1918(?)-1999 7
    Obituary 111
Geisel, Helen 1898-1967 26
Geisel, Theodor Seuss 1904-1991 100
    Obituary 67
    Earlier sketches in SATA 1, 28, 75
    See also CLR 100
    See Dr. Seuss
Geisert, Arthur (Frederick) 1941- 133
    Brief entry 52
    Earlier sketches in SATA 56, 92
    See also CLR 87
    See also SAAS 23
Geisert, Bonnie 1942- 165
    Earlier sketch in SATA 92
Geldart, William 1936- 15
Gelinas, Paul J. 1904-1996 10
Gellis, Roberta (Leah Jacobs) 1927- 128
Gellman, Marc 112
Gelman, Amy 1961- 72
Gelman, Jan 1963- 58
Gelman, Rita Golden 1937- 131
    Brief entry 51
    Earlier sketch in SATA 84
Gelman, Steve 1934- 3
Gemming, Elizabeth 1932- 11
Gennaro, Joseph F(rancis), Jr. 1924- 53
Gentile, Petrina 1969- 91
Gentle, Mary 1956- 48
Gentleman, David (William) 1930- 7
Geoghegan, Adrienne 1962- 143
George, Barbara
    See Katz, Bobbi
George, Emily
    See Katz, Bobbi
George, Gail
    See Katz, Bobbi
George, Jean
    See George, Jean Craighead
George, Jean Craighead 1919- 124
    Earlier sketches in SATA 2, 68
    See also CLR 1, 80
George, John L(othar) 1916- 2
George, Kristine O'Connell 1954- 156
    Earlier sketch in SATA 110
George, Lindsay Barrett 1952- 155
    Earlier sketch in SATA 95
George, S(idney) C(harles) 1898- 11
George, Sally
    See Orr, Wendy

George, Twig C. 1950- 114
Georgiou, Constantine 1927- 7
Georgiou, Theo
    See Odgers, Sally Farrell
Geraghty, Paul 1959- 130
Gerard, Jean Ignace Isidore 1803-1847 45
Geras, Adele (Daphne Weston) 1944- 129
    Earlier sketches in SATA 23, 87
    See also SAAS 21
    See Geras, Adele (Daphne Weston)
Geras, Adele (Daphne Weston) 1944-
    See Geras, Adele (Daphne Weston)
Gerber, Merrill Joan 1938- 127
    Earlier sketch in SATA 64
Gerber, Perren 1933- 104
Gerberg, Mort 1931- 64
Gergely, Tibor 1900-1978 54
    Obituary 20
Geringer, Laura 1948- 164
    Earlier sketches in SATA 29, 94
Gerler, William R(obert) 1917-1996 47
Gerrard, Jean 1933- 51
Gerrard, Roy 1935-1997 90
    Brief entry 45
    Obituary 99
    Earlier sketch in SATA 47
    See also CLR 23
Gerrold, David 1944- 144
    Earlier sketch in SATA 66
Gershator, Phillis 1942- 158
    Earlier sketch in SATA 90
Gerson, Corinne 1927- 37
Gerson, Mary-Joan 136
    Earlier sketch in SATA 79
Gerson, Noel Bertram 1914-1988 22
    Obituary 60
Gerstein, Mordicai 1935- 142
    Brief entry 36
    Earlier sketches in SATA 47, 81
    See also CLR 102
Gertridge, Allison 1967- 132
Gervais, Bernadette 1959- 80
Gesner, Clark 1938-2002 40
    Obituary 143
Gessner, Lynne 1919- 16
Geter, Tyrone 150
Getz, David 1957- 91
Getzinger, Donna 1968- 128
Gevirtz, Eliezer 1950- 49
Gewe, Raddory
    See Gorey, Edward (St. John)
Ghan, Linda (R.) 1947- 77
Ghent, Natale 1962- 148
Gherman, Beverly 1934- 123
    Earlier sketch in SATA 68
Ghigna, Charles 1946- 153
    Earlier sketch in SATA 108
Giambastiani, Kurt R. A. 1958- 141
Giannini, Enzo 1946- 68
Gibbons, Alan 1953- 124
Gibbons, Faye 1938- 103
    Earlier sketch in SATA 65
Gibbons, Gail (Gretchen) 1944- 160
    Earlier sketches in SATA 23, 72, 104
    See also CLR 8
    See also SAAS 12
Gibbons, Kaye 1960- 117
Gibbs, Adrea 1960- 126
Gibbs, Alonzo (Lawrence) 1915-1992 5
Gibbs, Tony
    See Gibbs, Wolcott, Jr.
Gibbs, Wolcott, Jr. 1935- 40
Giblin, James Cross 1933- 122
    Earlier sketches in SATA 33, 75
    See also CLR 29
    See also SAAS 12
Gibson, Andrew (William) 1949- 72
Gibson, Betty 1911- 75
Gibson, Jo
    See Fluke, Joanne
Gibson, William 1914- 66

Gidal, Nachum
    See Gidal, Tim Nachum
Gidal, Sonia (Epstein) 1922- 2
Gidal, Tim Nachum 1909-1996 2
Gidalewitsch, Nachum
    See Gidal, Tim Nachum
Giegling, John A(llan) 1935- 17
Gifaldi, David 1950- 76
Giff, Patricia Reilly 1935- 160
    Earlier sketches in SATA *33, 70, 121*
Giffard, Hannah 1962- 83
Gifford, Griselda 1931- 42
Gifford, Kerri 1961- 91
Gilbert, Ann
    See Taylor, Ann
Gilbert, Anne Yvonne 1951- 128
Gilbert, Barbara Snow 1954- 97
Gilbert, Frances
    See Collings, Gillian
Gilbert, Harriett 1948- 30
Gilbert, (Agnes) Joan (Sewell) 1931- 10
Gilbert, John (Raphael) 1926- 36
Gilbert, Nan
    See Gilbertson, Mildred Geiger
Gilbert, Roby Goodale 1966- 90
Gilbert, Ruth Gallard Ainsworth
    See Ainsworth, Ruth (Gallard)
Gilbert, Sara (Dulaney) 1943- 82
    Earlier sketch in SATA *11*
Gilbert, Sheri L. 157
Gilbert, Suzie 1956- 97
Gilbert, W(illiam) S(chwenck) 1836-1911 .. 36
Gilbert, Yvonne
    See Gilbert, Anne Yvonne
Gilbertson, Mildred Geiger 1908-1988 2
Gilbreath, Alice 1921- 12
Gilbreth, Frank B(unker), Jr. 1911-2001 2
Gilchrist, Jan Spivey 1949- 130
    Earlier sketch in SATA *72*
Gilden, Mel 1947- 97
Giles, Gail 152
Gilfond, Henry 2
Gilge, Jeanette 1924- 22
Gili, Phillida 1944- 70
Gill, Derek (Lewis Theodore) 1919-1997 9
Gill, Margery Jean 1925- 22
Gill, Stephen 1932- 63
Gillespie, Carol Ann 1951- 158
Gillett, Mary (Bledsoe) 7
Gillette, Henry Sampson 1915- 14
Gillette, J(an) Lynett 1946- 103
Gillham, Bill
    See Gillham, W(illiam) E(dwin) C(harles)
Gillham, W(illiam) E(dwin) C(harles) 1936-
    42
Gilliam, Stan 1946- 39
    Brief entry 35
Gilliland, Alexis A(rnaldus) 1931- 72
Gilliland, (Cleburne) Hap 1918- 92
Gillmor, Don 1954- 127
Gilman, Esther 1925- 15
Gilman, Phoebe 1940-2002 104
    Obituary 141
    Earlier sketch in SATA *58*
Gilmore, Iris 1900-1982 22
Gilmore, Kate 1931- 87
Gilmore, Mary (Jean Cameron) 1865-1962
    49
Gilmore, Susan 1954- 59
Gilroy, Beryl (Agatha) 1924- 80
Gilson, Barbara
    See Gilson, Charles James Louis
Gilson, Charles James Louis 1878-1943
    See YABC 2
Gilson, Jamie 1933- 91
    Brief entry 34
    Earlier sketch in SATA *37*
Ginsburg, Mirra 1909-2000 92
    Earlier sketch in SATA *6*
    See also CLR *45*

Giovanni, Nikki 1943- 107
    Earlier sketch in SATA *24*
    See also CLR *73*
Giovanopoulos, Paul (Arthur) 1939- 7
Gipson, Fred(erick Benjamin) 1908-1973 2
    Obituary 24
Girard, Linda (Walvoord) 1942- 41
Girion, Barbara 1937- 78
    Earlier sketch in SATA *26*
    See also SAAS *14*
Girouard, Patrick 1957- 155
Girzone, Joseph F(rancis) 1930- 76
Gise, Joanne
    See Mattern, Joanne
Gittings, Jo (Grenville) Manton 1919- 3
Gittings, Robert (William Victor) 1911-1992
    6
    Obituary 70
Givens, Janet E(aton) 1932- 60
Gladstone, Eve
    See Werner, Herma
Gladstone, Gary 1935- 12
Gladstone, M(yron) J. 1923- 37
Glanville, Brian (Lester) 1931- 42
Glanzman, Louis S. 1922- 36
Glaser, Byron 1954- 154
Glaser, Dianne E(lizabeth) 1937- 50
    Brief entry 31
Glaser, Isabel Joshlin 1929- 94
Glaser, Milton 1929- 151
    Earlier sketch in SATA *11*
Glaser, Shirley 151
Glaspell, Susan 1882(?)-1948
    See YABC 2
Glass, Andrew 1949- 150
    Brief entry 46
    Earlier sketch in SATA *90*
Glasscock, Amnesia
    See Steinbeck, John (Ernst)
Glassman, Bruce 1961- 76
Glauber, Uta (Heil) 1936- 17
Glazer, Thomas (Zachariah) 1914-2003 9
Glazer, Tom
    See Glazer, Thomas (Zachariah)
Gleasner, Diana (Cottle) 1936- 29
Gleason, Judith 1929- 24
Gleason, Katherine (A.) 1960- 104
Gleeson, Libby 1950- 142
    Autobiography Feature 142
    Earlier sketches in SATA *82, 118*
Gleiter, Jan 1947- 111
Gleitzman, Morris 1953- 156
    Earlier sketch in SATA *88*
    See also CLR *88*
Glen, Maggie 1944- 88
Glendinning, Richard 1917-1988 24
Glendinning, Sally
    See Glendinning, Sara W(ilson)
Glendinning, Sara W(ilson) 1913-1993 24
Glenn, Mel 1943- 93
    Brief entry 45
    Earlier sketch in SATA *51*
    See also CLR *51*
Glenn, Patricia Brown 1953- 86
Glenn, Sharlee 159
Glenn, Sharlee Mullins
    See Glenn, Sharlee
Glennon, Karen M. 1946- 85
Gles, Margaret Breitmaier 1940- 22
Glick, Carl (Cannon) 1890-1971 14
Glick, Ruth (Burtnick) 1942- 125
Gliewe, Unada (Grace) 1927- 3
Glimmerveen, Ulco 1958- 85
Glines, Carroll V(ane), Jr. 1920- 19
Gliori, Debi 1959- 138
    Earlier sketch in SATA *72*
Globe, Leah Ain 1900- 41
Glori Ann
    See Blakely, Gloria
Glovach, Linda 1947- 105
    Earlier sketch in SATA *7*

Glover, Denis (James Matthews) 1912-1980
    7
Glubok, Shirley (Astor) 146
    Autobiography Feature 146
    Earlier sketches in SATA *6, 68*
    See also CLR *1*
    See also SAAS 7
Glyman, Caroline A. 1967- 103
Glynne-Jones, William 1907-1977 11
Gobbato, Imero 1923- 39
Gobbletree, Richard
    See Quackenbush, Robert M(ead)
Goble, Dorothy 26
Goble, Paul 1933- 131
    Earlier sketches in SATA *25, 69*
    See also CLR *21*
Goble, Warwick (?)-1943 46
Godden, (Margaret) Rumer 1907-1998 36
    Obituary 109
    Earlier sketch in SATA *3*
    See also CLR *20*
    See also SAAS *12*
Gode, Alexander
    See Gode von Aesch, Alexander (Gottfried Friedrich)
Gode von Aesch, Alexander (Gottfried
    Friedrich) 1906-1970 14
Godfrey, Jane
    See Bowden, Joan Chase
Godfrey, Martyn
    See Godfrey, Martyn N.
    and Godfrey, Martyn N.
Godfrey, Martyn N. 1949-2000 95
    See also CLR *57*
    See Godfrey, Martyn
Godfrey, William
    See Youd, (Christopher) Samuel
Godkin, Celia (Marilyn) 1948- 145
    Earlier sketch in SATA *66*
Goedecke, Christopher (John) 1951- 81
Goekler, Susan
    See Wooley, Susan Frelick
Goettel, Elinor 1930- 12
Goetz, Delia 1898-1996 22
    Obituary 91
Goffe, Toni 1936- 61
Goffstein, Brooke
    See Goffstein, M(arilyn) B(rooke)
Goffstein, M(arilyn) B(rooke) 1940- 70
    Earlier sketch in SATA *8*
    See also CLR *3*
Goforth, Ellen
    See Francis, Dorothy Brenner
Gogol, Sara 1948-2004 80
Goh, Chan Hon 1969- 145
Going, K(elly) L. 156
Golann, Cecil Paige 1921-1995 11
Golbin, Andree 1923- 15
Gold, Alison Leslie 1945- 104
Gold, Bernice 150
Gold, Phyllis 21
    See Goldberg, Phyllis
Gold, Robert S(tanley) 1924- 63
Gold, Sharlya 9
Gold, Susan
    See Gold, Susan Dudley
Gold, Susan Dudley 1949- 147
Goldberg, Grace 1956- 78
Goldberg, Herbert S. 1926- 25
Goldberg, Jacob 1943- 94
Goldberg, Jake
    See Goldberg, Jacob
Goldberg, Jan 123
    See Curran, Jan Goldberg
Goldberg, Stan J. 1939- 26
Goldberg, Susan 1948- 71
Goldberg, Whoopi 1955- 119
Golden, Christie 1963- 167
    Earlier sketch in SATA *116*
Goldentyer, Debra 1960- 84

Goldfeder, Cheryl
  See Pahz, (Anne) Cheryl Suzanne
Goldfeder, James
  See Pahz, James Alon
Goldfeder, Jim
  See Pahz, James Alon
Goldfrank, Helen Colodny 1912- 6
Goldin, Augusta 1906-1999 13
Goldin, Barbara Diamond 1946- 129
  Autobiography Feature 129
  Earlier sketch in SATA 92
  See also SAAS 26
Goldin, David 1963- 101
Golding, Theresa Martin 1960- 150
Golding, William (Gerald) 1911-1993
  See CLR 94
Goldman, Alex J. 1917- 65
Goldman, E(leanor) M(aureen) 1943- 103
Goldman, Elizabeth 1949- 90
Goldring, Ann 1937- 149
Goldsborough, June 1923- 19
Goldsmith, Connie 1945- 147
Goldsmith, Howard 1943- 108
  Earlier sketch in SATA 24
Goldsmith, Oliver 1730-1774 26
Goldsmith, Ruth M. 1919- 62
Goldstein, Nathan 1927- 47
Goldstein, Philip 1910-1997 23
Goldston, Robert (Conroy) 1927- 6
Goldstone, Lawrence A.
  See Treat, Lawrence
Golembe, Carla 1951- 79
Golenbock, Peter 1946- 99
Goll, Reinhold W(eimar) 1897-1993 26
Gollub, Matthew 1960- 134
  Earlier sketch in SATA 83
Gomez, Elizabeth 133
Gomez-Freer, Elizabeth
  See Gomez, Elizabeth
Gomi, Taro 1945- 103
  Earlier sketch in SATA 64
  See also CLR 57
Gondosch, Linda 1944- 58
Gonzalez, Catherine Troxell 1917-2000 87
Gonzalez, Christina
  See Gonzalez, Maya Christina
Gonzalez, Gloria 1940- 23
Gonzalez, Maya
  See Gonzalez, Maya Christina
Gonzalez, Maya Christina 1964- 115
Gonzalez, Rigoberto 1970- 147
Goobie, Beth 1959- 128
Good, Alice 1950- 73
Goodall, Daphne Machin
  See Machin Goodall, Daphne (Edith)
Goodall, Jane 1934- 111
Goodall, John S(trickland) 1908-1996 66
  Obituary 91
  Earlier sketch in SATA 4
  See also CLR 25
Goodbody, Slim
  See Burstein, John
Goode, Diane (Capuozzo) 1949- 114
  Earlier sketches in SATA 15, 84
Goode, Stephen Ray 1943- 55
  Brief entry 40
Goodenow, Earle 1913- 40
Goodhart, Pippa 1958- 153
Goodhue, Thomas W. 1949- 143
Goodin, Sallie (Brown) 1953- 74
Goodman, Alison 1966- 111
Goodman, Deborah Lerme 1956- 50
  Brief entry 49
Goodman, Elaine 1930- 9
Goodman, Joan Elizabeth 1950- 162
  Earlier sketches in SATA 50, 94
Goodman, Walter 1927-2002 9
Goodrich, Samuel Griswold 1793-1860 23
GoodWeather, Harley
  See King, Thomas

Goodwin, Hal
  See Goodwin, Harold L(eland)
Goodwin, Harold L(eland) 1914-1990 51
  Obituary 65
  Earlier sketch in SATA 13
Goodwin, William 1943- 117
Goor, Nancy (Ruth Miller) 1944- 39
  Brief entry 34
Goor, Ron(ald Stephen) 1940- 39
  Brief entry 34
Goossen, Agnes
  See Epp, Margaret A(gnes)
Gorbachev, Valeri 1944- 143
  Autobiography Feature 143
  Earlier sketch in SATA 98
Gordion, Mark
  See Turtledove, Harry
Gordon, Ad
  See Hano, Arnold
Gordon, Amy 1949- 156
  Earlier sketch in SATA 115
Gordon, Bernard Ludwig 1931- 27
Gordon, Colonel H. R.
  See Ellis, Edward S(ylvester)
Gordon, Donald
  See Payne, Donald Gordon
Gordon, Dorothy 1893-1970 20
Gordon, Esther S(aranga) 1935- 10
Gordon, Frederick 1
Gordon, Gaelyn 1939-1997
  See CLR 75
Gordon, Gary
  See Edmonds, I(vy) G(ordon)
Gordon, Hal
  See Goodwin, Harold L(eland)
Gordon, Jeffie Ross
  See Enderle, Judith (Ann) Ross
  and Gordon, Stephanie Jacob
Gordon, John
  See Gesner, Clark
Gordon, John (William) 1925- 84
Gordon, Lew
  See Baldwin, Gordon C(ortis)
Gordon, Margaret (Anna) 1939- 9
Gordon, Mike 1948- 101
Gordon, Selma
  See Lanes, Selma Gordon
Gordon, Sheila 1927- 88
  See also CLR 27
Gordon, Shirley 1921- 48
  Brief entry 41
Gordon, Sol 1923- 11
Gordon, Stephanie Jacob 1940- 89
  Autobiography Feature 114
  Earlier sketch in SATA 64
  See also SAAS 26
Gordon, Stewart
  See Shirreffs, Gordon D(onald)
Gorelick, Molly C(hernow) 1920-2003 9
  Obituary 153
Gorey, Edward (St. John) 1925-2000 70
  Brief entry 27
  Obituary 118
  Earlier sketch in SATA 29
  See also CLR 36
Gorham, Charles Orson 1868-1936 36
Gorham, Michael
  See Folsom, Franklin (Brewster)
Gorman, Carol 150
Gorman, Jacqueline Laks 1955- 148
Gormley, Beatrice 1942- 127
  Brief entry 35
  Earlier sketch in SATA 39
Gorog, Judith (Katharine Allen) 1938- 75
  Earlier sketch in SATA 39
Gorsline, Douglas (Warner) 1913-1985 11
  Obituary 43
Gorsline, (Sally) Marie 1928- 28
Gorsline, S. M.
  See Gorsline, (Sally) Marie

Gorton, Kaitlyn
  See Emerson, Kathy Lynn
Goryan, Sirak
  See Saroyan, William
Goscinny, Rene 1926-1977 47
  Brief entry 39
  See also CLR 37
Goss, Clay(ton E.) 1946- 82
Goss, Gary 1947- 124
Gottesman, S. D.
  See Kornbluth, C(yril) M.
  and Lowndes, Robert A(ugustine) W(ard)
  and Pohl, Frederik
Gottfried, Ted
  See Gottfried, Theodore Mark
Gottfried, Theodore Mark 1928- 150
  Earlier sketch in SATA 85
Gottlieb, Gerald 1923- 7
Gottlieb, William P. 1917-2006 24
Gottlieb, William Paul
  See Gottlieb, William P.
Goudey, Alice E(dwards) 1898-1993 20
Goudge, Eileen 1950- 88
Goudge, Elizabeth (de Beauchamp) 1900-1984
  2
  Obituary 38
  See also CLR 94
Gough, Catherine 24
  See Mulgan, Catherine
Gough, Philip 1908- 45
Gough, Sue 1940- 106
Goulart, Ron(ald Joseph) 1933- 138
  Earlier sketch in SATA 6
  See Dixon, Franklin W.
  and Keene, Carolyn
Gould, Alberta 1945- 96
Gould, Chester 1900-1985 49
  Obituary 43
Gould, Jean R(osalind) 1909-1993 11
  Obituary 77
Gould, Lilian 6
Gould, Marilyn 1928- 76
  Earlier sketch in SATA 15
Gould, Robert 154
Gould, Steven (Charles) 1955- 95
Gourley, Catherine 1950- 95
Gourse, (Roberta) Leslie 1939-2004 89
Govan, (Mary) Christine Noble 1898-1985 .. 9
Gove, Doris 1944- 72
Govern, Elaine 1939- 26
Gowen, L. Kris 1968- 156
Graaf, Peter
  See Youd, (Christopher) Samuel
Graber, Alexander 1914-1997 98
  Earlier sketch in SATA 7
Graber, (George) Alexander 1914-1997 98
Graber, Richard (Fredrick) 1927- 26
Grabianski, Janusz 1928-1976 39
  Obituary 30
Graboff, Abner 1919-1986 35
Grace, Fran(ces Jane) 45
Grace, Theresa
  See Mattern, Joanne
Gracza, Margaret Young 1928- 56
Graduate of Oxford, A
  See Ruskin, John
Graeber, Charlotte Towner 106
  Brief entry 44
  Earlier sketch in SATA 56
Graeme, Roderic
  See Jeffries, Roderic (Graeme)
Graf, Michael
  See Graf, Mike
Graf, Mike 1960- 164
Graff, Polly Anne Colver
  See Colver, Anne
Graff, (S.) Stewart 1908- 9
Graham, Ada 1931- 11
Graham, Alastair 1945- 74
Graham, Arthur Kennon
  See Harrison, David L(ee)

Graham, Bob 1942- *151*
  Earlier sketches in SATA *63, 101*
  See also CLR *31*
Graham, Brenda Knight 1942- *32*
Graham, Charlotte
  See Bowden, Joan Chase
Graham, Eleanor 1896-1984 .... *18*
  Obituary *38*
Graham, Ennis
  See Molesworth, Mary Louisa
Graham, Frank, Jr. 1925- *11*
Graham, Ian 1953- *112*
Graham, John 1926- *11*
Graham, Kennon
  See Harrison, David L(ee)
Graham, Larry
  See Graham, Lawrence (Otis)
Graham, Lawrence (Otis) 1962- *63*
Graham, Linda
  See Graham-Barber, Lynda
Graham, Lorenz (Bell) 1902-1989 .... *74*
  Obituary *63*
  Earlier sketch in SATA *2*
  See also CLR *10*
  See also SAAS *5*
Graham, Margaret Bloy 1920- *11*
Graham, Robin Lee 1949- *7*
Graham, Shirley 1896(?)-1977
  See Du Bois, Shirley Graham
Graham-Barber, Lynda 1944- *159*
  Earlier sketch in SATA *42*
Graham-Cameron, M.
  See Graham-Cameron, M(alcolm) G(ordon)
Graham-Cameron, M(alcolm) G(ordon) 1931-
  .... *53*
  Brief entry *45*
Graham-Cameron, Mike
  See Graham-Cameron, M(alcolm) G(ordon)
Grahame, Kenneth 1859-1932 .... *100*
  See also YABC *1*
  See also CLR *5*
Gralley, Jean *166*
Gramatky, Hardie 1907-1979 .... *30*
  Obituary *23*
  Earlier sketch in SATA *1*
  See also CLR *22*
Grambling, Lois G. 1927- *148*
  Earlier sketch in SATA *71*
Grambo, Rebecca L(ynn) 1963- *109*
Grammer, June Amos 1927- *58*
Grand, Samuel 1912-1988 .... *42*
Grandville, J. J.
  See Gerard, Jean Ignace Isidore
Grandville, Jean Ignace Isidore Gerard
  See Gerard, Jean Ignace Isidore
Granfield, Linda 1950- *160*
  Earlier sketch in SATA *96*
Grange, Peter
  See Nicole, Christopher (Robin)
Granger, Michele 1949- *88*
Granowsky, Alvin 1936- *101*
Granstaff, Bill 1925- *10*
Granstrom, Brita 1969- *167*
  Earlier sketch in SATA *111*
Grant, Bruce 1893-1977 .... *5*
  Obituary *25*
Grant, Cynthia D. 1950- *147*
  Earlier sketches in SATA *33, 77*
Grant, Eva 1907-1996 .... *7*
Grant, Gordon 1875-1962 .... *25*
Grant, Gwen(doline Ellen) 1940- *47*
Grant, (Alice) Leigh 1947- *10*
Grant, Matthew G.
  See May, Julian
Grant, Maxwell
  See Gibson, Walter B(rown)
  and Lynds, Dennis
Grant, Myrna (Lois) 1934- *21*
Grant, Neil 1938- *154*
  Earlier sketch in SATA *14*

Grant, Nicholas
  See Nicole, Christopher (Robin)
Grant, Richard 1948- *80*
Grant, Skeeter
  See Spiegelman, Art
Grater, Michael 1923- *57*
Gravel, Fern
  See Hall, James Norman
Gravelle, Karen 1942- *166*
  Earlier sketch in SATA *78*
Graves, Charles Parlin 1911-1972 .... *4*
Graves, Keith *156*
Graves, Robert (von Ranke) 1895-1985 ..... *45*
Graves, Valerie
  See Bradley, Marion Zimmer
Gray, Betsy
  See Poole, Gray Johnson
Gray, Caroline
  See Nicole, Christopher (Robin)
Gray, Elizabeth Janet
  See Vining, Elizabeth Gray
Gray, Genevieve S(tuck) 1920-1995 .... *4*
Gray, Harold (Lincoln) 1894-1968 .... *33*
  Brief entry *32*
Gray, Jenny
  See Gray, Genevieve S(tuck)
Gray, John Lee
  See Jakes, John (William)
Gray, Judith A(nne) 1949- *93*
Gray, Keith *151*
Gray, Kes 1960- *153*
Gray, Les 1929- *82*
Gray, Libba Moore 1937- *83*
Gray, Luli 1945- *149*
  Earlier sketch in SATA *90*
Gray, Marian
  See Pierce, Edith Gray
Gray, Nicholas Stuart 1922-1981 .... *4*
  Obituary *27*
Gray, Nigel 1941- *104*
  Earlier sketch in SATA *33*
Gray, (Lucy) Noel (Clervaux) 1898-1983 ... *47*
Gray, Patricia (Clark) *7*
Gray, Patsey
  See Gray, Patricia (Clark)
Graydon, Shari 1958- *158*
Grayland, V. Merle
  See Grayland, Valerie (Merle Spanner)
Grayland, Valerie (Merle Spanner) *7*
Grayson, Devin (Kalile) 1970- *119*
Grayson, Kristine
  See Rusch, Kristine Kathryn
Grayson, Paul 1946- *79*
Graystone, Lynn
  See Brennan, Joseph Lomas
Great Comte, The
  See Hawkesworth, Eric
Greaves, Margaret 1914-1995 .... *87*
  Earlier sketch in SATA *7*
Greaves, Nick 1955- *77*
Gree, Alain 1936- *28*
Green, Adam
  See Weisgard, Leonard (Joseph)
Green, Anne Canevari 1943- *62*
Green, Brian
  See Card, Orson Scott
Green, Cliff(ord) 1934- *126*
Green, Connie Jordan 1938- *80*
Green, D.
  See Casewit, Curtis W(erner)
Green, Elizabeth Shippen 1871-1954 .... *139*
Green, Hannah
  See Greenberg, Joanne (Goldenberg)
Green, Jane 1937- *9*
Green, Mary Moore 1906- *11*
Green, Morton 1937- *8*
Green, Norma B(erger) 1925- *11*
Green, Phyllis 1932- *20*
Green, Roger (Gilbert) Lancelyn 1918-1987
  .... *2*
  Obituary *53*

Green, (James Le)Roy 1948- *89*
Green, Sheila Ellen 1934- *148*
  Earlier sketch in SATA *8, 87*
Green, Timothy 1953- *91*
Greenaway, Kate 1846-1901 .... *100*
  See also YABC *2*
  See also CLR *111*
Greenbank, Anthony Hunt 1933- *39*
Greenberg, Harvey R. 1935- *5*
Greenberg, Jan 1942- *125*
  Earlier sketch in SATA *61*
Greenberg, Joanne (Goldenberg) 1932- *25*
Greenberg, Melanie Hope 1954- *72*
Greenberg, Polly 1932- *52*
  Brief entry *43*
Greenblat, Rodney Alan 1960- *106*
Greenburg, Dan 1936- *102*
Greene, Bette 1934- *161*
  Earlier sketches in SATA *8, 102*
  See also CLR *2*
  See also SAAS *16*
Greene, Carla 1916- *67*
  Earlier sketch in SATA *1*
Greene, Carol *102*
  Brief entry *44*
  Earlier sketch in SATA *66*
Greene, Constance C(larke) 1924- *72*
  Earlier sketch in SATA *11*
  See also CLR *62*
  See also SAAS *11*
Greene, Ellin 1927- *23*
Greene, Graham (Henry) 1904-1991 .... *20*
Greene, Jacqueline Dembar 1946- *131*
  Earlier sketch in SATA *76*
Greene, Laura Offenhartz 1935- *38*
Greene, Meg
  See Malvasi, Meg Greene
Greene, Rhonda Gowler 1955- *160*
  Earlier sketch in SATA *101*
Greene, Stephanie 1953- *127*
Greene, Wade 1933- *11*
Greene, Yvonne
  See Flesch, Yolande (Catarina)
Greenfeld, Howard (Scheinman) 1928- *140*
  Earlier sketch in SATA *19*
Greenfeld, Josh(ua Joseph) 1928- *62*
Greenfield, Eloise 1929- *155*
  Earlier sketches in SATA *19, 61, 105*
  See also CLR *38*
  See also SAAS *16*
Greening, Hamilton
  See Hamilton, Charles (Harold St. John)
Greenlaw, M. Jean 1941- *107*
Greenleaf, Barbara Kaye 1942- *6*
Greenleaf, Peter 1910-1997 .... *33*
Greenlee, Sharon 1935- *77*
Greeno, Gayle 1949- *81*
Greenseid, Diane 1948- *93*
Greenspun, Adele Aron 1938- *142*
  Earlier sketch in SATA *76*
Greenstein, Elaine 1959- *150*
  Earlier sketch in SATA *82*
Greenwald, Sheila
  See Green, Sheila Ellen
Greenwood, Barbara 1940- *129*
  Earlier sketch in SATA *90*
Greenwood, Pamela D. 1944- *115*
Greer, Richard
  See Garrett, (Gordon) Randall (Phillip)
  and Silverberg, Robert
Gregg, Andrew K. 1929- *81*
Gregg, Charles T(hornton) 1927- *65*
Gregg, Walter H(arold) 1919- *20*
Gregor, Arthur 1923- *36*
Gregor, Lee
  See Pohl, Frederik
Gregori, Leon 1919- *15*
Gregorian, Joyce Ballou 1946-1991 .... *30*
  Obituary *83*
Gregorich, Barbara 1943- *66*
Gregorowski, Christopher 1940- *30*

Gregory, Diana (Jean) 1933- *49*
  Brief entry *42*
Gregory, Harry
  See Gottfried, Theodore Mark
Gregory, Jean
  See Ure, Jean
Gregory, Kristiana 1951- *136*
  Earlier sketch in SATA *74*
Gregory, Nan 1944- *148*
Gregory, Philippa 1954- *122*
Gregory, Stephen
  See Penzler, Otto
Gregory, Valiska 1940- *82*
Greisman, Joan Ruth 1937- *31*
Grendon, Stephen
  See Derleth, August (William)
Grenville, Pelham
  See Wodehouse, P(elham) G(renville)
Gretz, Susanna 1937- *7*
Gretzer, John *18*
Grewdead, Roy
  See Gorey, Edward (St. John)
Grey, Carol
  See Lowndes, Robert A(ugustine) W(ard)
Grey, Jerry 1926- *11*
Grey, Mini *166*
Greybeard the Pirate
  See Macintosh, Brownie
Grey Owl
  See CLR *32*
  See Belaney, Archibald Stansfeld
Gri
  See Denney, Diana
Gribbin, John (R.) 1946- *159*
Grice, Frederick 1910-1983 .... *6*
Grider, Dorothy 1915- *31*
Gridley, Marion E(leanor) 1906-1974 .... *35*
  Obituary *26*
Grieco-Tiso, Pina 1954- *108*
Grieder, Walter 1924- *9*
Griego, Tony A. 1955- *77*
Griese, Arnold A(lfred) 1921- *9*
Griessman, Annette 1962- *116*
Grieve, James 1934- *146*
Grifalconi, Ann 1929- *133*
  Earlier sketches in SATA *2, 66*
  See also CLR *35*
  See also SAAS *16*
Griffin, Adele 1970- *153*
  Earlier sketch in SATA *105*
Griffin, Elizabeth May 1985- *89*
Griffin, Gillett Good 1928- *26*
Griffin, Judith Berry *34*
Griffin, Kitty 1951- *137*
Griffin, Peni R(ae Robinson) 1961- *99*
  Earlier sketch in SATA *67*
Griffin, Steven A(rthur) 1953- *89*
Griffin, W. E. B.
  See Butterworth, W.E.
Griffith, Connie 1946- *89*
Griffith, Gershom 1960- *85*
Griffith, Helen V(irginia) 1934- *87*
  Autobiography Feature *107*
  Earlier sketch in SATA *39*
Griffith, Jeannette
  See Eyerly, Jeannette (Hyde)
Griffiths, Andy 1961- *152*
Griffiths, Helen 1939- *86*
  Earlier sketch in SATA *5*
  See also CLR *75*
  See also SAAS *5*
Grigson, Jane (McIntire) 1928-1990 .... *63*
Grimes, Lee 1920- *68*
Grimes, Nikki 1950- *136*
  Earlier sketch in SATA *93*
  See also CLR *42*
Grimm, Jacob Ludwig Karl 1785-1863 ...... *22*
  See also CLR *112*
  See Grimm and Grimm

Grimm, Wilhelm Karl 1786-1859 .... *22*
  See also CLR *112*
  See Grimm and Grimm
Grimm, William C(arey) 1907-1992 .... *14*
Grimm Brothers
  See Grimm, Jacob Ludwig Karl
  and Grimm, Wilhelm Karl
Grimsdell, Jeremy 1942- *83*
Grimshaw, Nigel (Gilroy) 1925- *23*
Grimsley, Gordon
  See Groom, Arthur William
Grindley, (Jane) Sally 1953- *148*
Gringhuis, Dirk
  See Gringhuis, Richard H.
Gringhuis, Richard H. 1918-1974 .... *6*
  Obituary *25*
Grinnell, George Bird 1849-1938 .... *16*
Grinspoon, David H. 1959- *156*
Gripe, Maria 1923- *74*
  Earlier sketch in SATA *2*
  See also CLR *5*
Gripe, Maria Kristina
  See Gripe, Maria
Groch, Judith (Goldstein) 1929- *25*
Grode, Redway
  See Gorey, Edward (St. John)
Groener, Carl
  See Lowndes, Robert A(ugustine) W(ard)
Groening, Matt 1954- *116*
  Earlier sketch in SATA *81*
Grohmann, Susan 1948- *84*
Grohskopf, Bernice *7*
Grol, Lini R(icharda) 1913- *9*
Grollman, Earl A. 1925- *22*
Groom, Arthur William 1898-1964 .... *10*
Grooms, Duffy 1964- *169*
Gross, Alan 1947- *54*
  Brief entry *43*
Gross, Ernie 1913- *67*
Gross, Philip 1952- *164*
  Earlier sketch in SATA *84*
Gross, Philip John
  See Gross, Philip
Gross, Ruth Belov 1929- *33*
Gross, Sarah Chokla 1906-1976 .... *9*
  Obituary *26*
Grosser, Morton 1931- *74*
Grosser, Vicky 1958- *83*
Grossman, Bill 1948- *126*
  Earlier sketch in SATA *72*
Grossman, Nancy 1940- *29*
Grossman, Patricia 1951- *73*
Grossman, Robert 1940- *11*
Grote, JoAnn A. 1951- *113*
Groten, Dallas 1951- *64*
Groth, John (August) 1908-1988 .... *21*
  Obituary *56*
Groth-Fleming, Candace
  See Fleming, Candace
Grove, Vicki 1948- *151*
  Autobiography Feature *151*
  Earlier sketch in SATA *122*
Grover, Lorie Ann 1964- *168*
Grover, Wayne 1934- *69*
Groves, Georgina
  See Symons, (Dorothy) Geraldine
Groves, Maketa 1950- *107*
Groves, Seli *77*
Grubb, Lisa *160*
Gruber, Terry (deRoy) 1953- *66*
Gruelle, John (Barton) 1880-1938 .... *35*
  Brief entry *32*
  See Gruelle, Johnny
Gruelle, Johnny
  See CLR *34*
  See Gruelle, John (Barton)
Gruenberg, Sidonie Matsner 1881-1974 .... *2*
  Obituary *27*
Gruhzit-Hoyt, Olga (Margaret) 1922- *127*
  Earlier sketch in SATA *16*
Grummer, Arnold E(dward) 1923- *49*

Grunewalt, Pine
  See Kunhardt, Edith
Grunwell, Jeanne Marie 1971- *147*
Grupper, Jonathan *137*
Gryski, Camilla 1948- *72*
Guarino, Dagmar
  See Guarino, Deborah
Guarino, Deborah 1954- *68*
Guay, Georgette (Marie Jeanne) 1952- *54*
Guback, Georgia *88*
Guccione, Leslie Davis 1946- *111*
  Earlier sketch in SATA *72*
Guck, Dorothy 1913-2002 .... *27*
Guerny, Gene
  See Gurney, Gene
Guest, Elissa Haden 1953- *125*
Guest, Jacqueline 1952- *135*
Guevara, Susan *167*
  Earlier sketch in SATA *97*
Gugler, Laurel Dee *95*
Gugliotta, Bobette 1918-1994 .... *7*
Guianan, Eve 1965- *102*
Guiberson, Brenda Z. 1946- *124*
  Earlier sketch in SATA *71*
Guile, Melanie 1949- *152*
  Earlier sketch in SATA *104*
Guillaume, Jeanette G. Flierl 1899-1990 ...... *8*
Guillot, Rene 1900-1969 .... *7*
  See also CLR *22*
Guisewite, Cathy (Lee) 1950- *57*
Gulbis, Stephen 1959- *142*
Gulley, Judie 1942- *58*
Gump, P. Q.
  See Card, Orson Scott
Gundrey, Elizabeth 1924- *23*
Gunn, James E(dwin) 1923- *35*
Gunn, Robin Jones 1955- *84*
Gunning, Monica Olwen 1930- *161*
Gunston, Bill
  See Gunston, William Tudor
Gunston, William Tudor 1927- *9*
Gunther, John 1901-1970
Guravich, Dan 1918- *74*
Gurko, Leo 1914- *9*
Gurko, Miriam 1910(?)-1988 .... *9*
  Obituary *58*
Gurney, Gene 1924- *65*
Gurney, James 1958- *120*
  Earlier sketch in SATA *76*
Gurney, John Steven 1962- *143*
  Earlier sketch in SATA *75*
Gustafson, Sarah R.
  See Riedman, Sarah R(egal)
Gustafson, Scott 1956- *34*
Guthrie, A(lfred) B(ertram), Jr. 1901-1991 . *62*
  Obituary *67*
Guthrie, Anne 1890-1979 .... *28*
Guthrie, Donna W. 1946- *105*
  Earlier sketch in SATA *63*
Gutman, Bill *128*
  Brief entry *43*
  Earlier sketch in SATA *67*
Gutman, Dan 1955- *139*
  Earlier sketch in SATA *77*
Gutmann, Bessie Pease 1876-1960 .... *73*
Guy, Geoffrey 1942- *153*
Guy, Rosa (Cuthbert) 1925- *122*
  Earlier sketches in SATA *14, 62*
  See also CLR *13*
Guy, Susan 1948- *149*
Guymer, (Wilhelmina) Mary 1909- *50*
Guzman, Lila 1952- *168*
Guzman, Rick 1957- *168*
Gwynne, Fred(erick Hubbard) 1926-1993 .. *41*
  Brief entry *27*
  Obituary *75*
Gwynne, Oscar A.
  See Ellis, Edward S(ylvester)
Gwynne, Oswald A.
  See Ellis, Edward S(ylvester)

H

Haab, Sherri 1964- *169*
　Earlier sketch in SATA *91*
Haar, Jaap ter
　See CLR *15*
　See ter Haar, Jaap
Haas, Carolyn Buhai 1926- *43*
Haas, Dan 1957- *105*
Haas, Dorothy F. *46*
　Brief entry *43*
　See also SAAS *17*
Haas, Irene 1929- *96*
　Earlier sketch in SATA *17*
Haas, James E(dward) 1943- *40*
Haas, (Katherine) Jessie 1959- *135*
　Autobiography Feature *135*
　Earlier sketch in SATA *98*
Habenstreit, Barbara 1937- *5*
Haber, Karen 1955- *78*
Haber, Louis 1910-1988 .... *12*
Hackett, John Winthrop 1910-1997 .... *65*
Haddix, Margaret Peterson 1964- *125*
　Earlier sketch in SATA *94*
Haddon, Mark 1962- *155*
Hader, Berta (Hoerner) 1891(?)-1976 .... *16*
Hader, Elmer (Stanley) 1889-1973 .... *16*
Hadithi, Mwenye
　See Hobson, Bruce
Hadley, Franklin
　See Winterbotham, R(ussell) R(obert)
Hadley, Lee 1934-1995 .... *89*
　Brief entry *38*
　Obituary *86*
　Earlier sketch in SATA *47*
　See also CLR *40*
　See Irwin, Hadley
Haeffele, Deborah 1954- *76*
Haenel, Wolfram 1956- *89*
　See also CLR *64*
Hafner, Marylin 1925- *121*
　Earlier sketch in SATA *7*
Hager, Betty 1923- *89*
Hager, Tom 1953- *119*
Haggard, H(enry) Rider 1856-1925 .... *16*
Haggerty, James J(oseph) 1920- *5*
Hagon, Priscilla
　See Allan, Mabel Esther
Hague, (Susan) Kathleen 1949- *49*
　Brief entry *45*
Hague, Michael R. 1948- *129*
　Brief entry *32*
　Earlier sketches in SATA *48, 80*
Hahn, Emily 1905-1997 .... *3*
　Obituary *96*
Hahn, Hannelore *8*
Hahn, James (Sage) 1947- *9*
Hahn, (Mona) Lynn 1949- *9*
Hahn, Mary Downing 1937- *157*
　Autobiography Feature *157*
　Brief entry *44*
　Earlier sketches in SATA *50, 81, 138*
　See also SAAS *12*
Hahn, Michael T. 1953- *92*
Haig-Brown, Roderick (Langmere) 1908-1976
　.. *12*
　See also CLR *31*
Haight, Rip
　See Carpenter, John (Howard)
Haight, Sandy 1949- *79*
Haij, Vera
　See Jansson, Tove (Marika)
Haines, Gail Kay 1943- *11*
Haining, Peter (Alexander) 1940- *14*
Hains, Harriet
　See Watson, Carol
Hajdusiewicz, Babs Bell *163*
Hakim, Joy 1931- *83*
Halacy, D(aniel) S(tephen), Jr. 1919-2002 .. *36*
　See Halacy, Dan

Halacy, Dan
　See SAAS *8*
　See Halacy, D(aniel) S(tephen), Jr.
Halam, Ann
　See Jones, Gwyneth A(nn)
Haldane, Roger John 1945- *13*
Hale, Arlene 1924-1982 .... *49*
Hale, Bruce 1957- *123*
Hale, Christy
　See Apostolou, Christine Hale
Hale, Edward Everett 1822-1909 .... *16*
Hale, Glenn
　See Walker, Robert W(ayne)
Hale, Helen
　See Mulcahy, Lucille Burnett
Hale, Irina 1932- *26*
Hale, Kathleen 1898-2000 .... *66*
　Obituary *121*
　Earlier sketch in SATA *17*
Hale, Linda (Howe) 1929- *6*
Hale, Lucretia P.
　See Hale, Lucretia Peabody
Hale, Lucretia Peabody 1820-1900 .... *26*
　See also CLR *105*
Hale, Nancy 1908-1988 .... *31*
　Obituary *57*
Hale, Shannon *158*
Haley, Gail E(inhart) 1939- *161*
　Autobiography Feature *161*
　Brief entry *28*
　Earlier sketches in SATA *43, 78, 136*
　See also CLR *21*
　See also SAAS *13*
Haley, Neale *52*
Hall, Adam
　See Trevor, Elleston
Hall, Adele 1910- *7*
Hall, Anna Gertrude 1882-1967 .... *8*
Hall, Barbara 1960- *68*
Hall, Beverly B. 1918- *95*
Hall, Borden
　See Yates, Raymond F(rancis)
Hall, Brian P(atrick) 1935- *31*
Hall, Cameron
　See del Rey, Lester
Hall, Caryl
　See Hansen, Caryl (Hall)
Hall, Donald (Andrew, Jr.) 1928- *97*
　Earlier sketch in SATA *23*
Hall, Douglas 1931- *43*
Hall, Elizabeth 1929- *77*
Hall, Elvajean 1910-1984 .... *6*
Hall, Francie 1940- *166*
Hall, James Norman 1887-1951 .... *21*
Hall, Jesse
　See Boesen, Victor
Hall, Katy
　See McMullan, Kate
Hall, Kirsten Marie 1974- *67*
Hall, Lynn 1937- *79*
　Earlier sketches in SATA *2, 47*
　See also SAAS *4*
Hall, Malcolm 1945- *7*
Hall, Marjory
　See Yeakley, Marjory Hall
Hall, Melanie W. 1949- *169*
　Earlier sketches in SATA *78, 116*
Hall, Patricia 1940- *136*
Hall, Rosalys Haskell 1914- *7*
Hall, Willis 1929-2005 .... *66*
Hallard, Peter
　See Catherall, Arthur
Hallas, Richard
　See Knight, Eric (Mowbray)
Hall-Clarke, James
　See Rowland-Entwistle, (Arthur) Theodore
　(Henry)
Haller, Dorcas Woodbury 1946- *46*
Hallett, Mark 1947- *83*
Halliburton, Richard 1900-1939(?) *81*
Halliburton, Warren J. 1924- *19*

Halliday, Brett
　See Dresser, Davis
　and Johnson, (Walter) Ryerson
　and Terrall, Robert
Halliday, William R(oss) 1926- *52*
Hallin, Emily Watson *6*
Hallinan, P(atrick) K(enneth) 1944- *39*
　Brief entry *37*
Hallman, Ruth 1929- *43*
　Brief entry *28*
Hallowell, Tommy
　See Hill, Thomas
Hall-Quest, (Edna) Olga W(ilbourne)
　1899-1986 .... *11*
　Obituary *47*
Halls, Kelly Milner 1957- *131*
Hallstead, William F(inn III) 1924- *11*
Hallward, Michael 1889-1982 .... *12*
Halperin, Michael *156*
Halperin, Wendy Anderson 1952- *125*
　Earlier sketch in SATA *80*
Halpin, Marlene 1927- *88*
Halsell, Grace (Eleanor) 1923-2000 .... *13*
Halter, Jon C(harles) 1941- *22*
Halvorson, Marilyn 1948- *123*
Hamalian, Leo 1920- *41*
Hamberger, John 1934- *14*
Hamblin, Dora Jane 1920- *36*
Hambly, Barbara 1951- *108*
Hamer, Martyn
　See Eldin, Peter
Hamerstrom, Frances 1907-1998 .... *24*
Hamil, Thomas Arthur 1928- *14*
Hamill, Ethel
　See Webb, Jean Francis (III)
Hamilton, (John) Alan 1943- *66*
Hamilton, Alice
　See Cromie, Alice Hamilton
Hamilton, Anita 1919- *92*
Hamilton, Buzz
　See Hemming, Roy G.
Hamilton, Carol (Jean Barber) 1935- *94*
Hamilton, Charles (Harold St. John) 1876-1961
　.. *13*
Hamilton, Charles 1913-1996 .... *65*
　Obituary *93*
Hamilton, Clive
　See Lewis, C.S.
Hamilton, Dorothy (Drumm) 1906-1983 .... *12*
　Obituary *35*
Hamilton, Edith 1867-1963 .... *20*
Hamilton, Edmond 1904-1977 .... *118*
Hamilton, (Muriel) Elizabeth (Mollie) 1906-
　.. *23*
Hamilton, Franklin
　See Silverberg, Robert
Hamilton, Gail
　See Corcoran, Barbara (Asenath)
　and Dodge, Mary Abigail
Hamilton, Kersten 1958- *134*
Hamilton, Martha 1953- *123*
Hamilton, Mary (E.) 1927- *55*
Hamilton, Mollie
　See Kaye, M(ary) M(argaret)
Hamilton, Morse 1943-1998 .... *101*
　Earlier sketch in SATA *35*
Hamilton, Peter F. 1960- *109*
Hamilton, Priscilla
　See Gellis, Roberta (Leah Jacobs)
Hamilton, Ralph
　See Stratemeyer, Edward L.
Hamilton, Virginia (Esther) 1936-2002 ..... *123*
　Obituary *132*
　Earlier sketches in SATA *4, 56, 79*
　See also CLR *40*
Hamilton-Paterson, James 1941- *82*
Hamlet, Ova
　See Lupoff, Richard A(llen)

Hamley, Dennis 1935- *69*
  Earlier sketch in SATA *39*
  See also CLR *47*
  See also SAAS *22*
Hamlin, Peter J. 1970- *84*
Hamm, Diane Johnston 1949- *78*
Hammer, Charles 1934- *58*
Hammer, Richard 1928- *6*
Hammerman, Gay M(orenus) 1926- *9*
Hammond, Ralph
  See Hammond Innes, Ralph
Hammond, Winifred G(raham) 1899-1992 . *29*
  Obituary *107*
Hammond Innes, Ralph 1913-1998 .... *116*
  See Innes, (Ralph) Hammond
Hammontree, Marie (Gertrude) 1913- *13*
Hample, Zack 1977- *161*
Hampshire, Joyce Gregorian
  See Gregorian, Joyce Ballou
Hampshire, Susan 1942- *98*
Hampson, (Richard) Denman 1929- *15*
Hampton, Wilborn *156*
Hamre, Leif 1914- *5*
Hamsa, Bobbie 1944- *52*
  Brief entry *38*
Han, Lu
  See Stickler, Soma Han
Han, Soma
  See Stickler, Soma Han
Han, Suzanne Crowder 1953- *89*
Hancock, Mary A. 1923- *31*
Hancock, Sibyl 1940- *9*
Hand, Elizabeth 1957- *167*
  Earlier sketch in SATA *118*
Handford, Martin (John) 1956- *64*
  See also CLR *22*
Handforth, Thomas (Schofield) 1897-1948 . *42*
Handler, Daniel
  See CLR *79*
  See Snicket, Lemony
Handville, Robert (Tompkins) 1924- *45*
Hanel, Wolfram
  See Haenel, Wolfram
Haney, Lynn 1941- *23*
Hanff, Helene 1916-1997 .... *97*
  Earlier sketch in SATA *11*
Hanley, Boniface Francis 1924- *65*
Hanlon, Emily 1945- *15*
Hann, Jacquie 1951- *19*
Hann, Judith 1942- *77*
Hanna, Bill
  See Hanna, William (Denby)
Hanna, Cheryl 1951- *84*
Hanna, Jack (Bushnell) 1947- *74*
Hanna, Nell(ie L.) 1908- *55*
Hanna, Paul R(obert) 1902-1988 .... *9*
Hanna, William (Denby) 1910-2001 .... *51*
  Obituary *126*
Hannam, Charles 1925- *50*
Hannon, Ezra
  See Hunter, Evan
Hann-Syme, Marguerite *127*
Hano, Arnold 1922- *12*
Hano, Renee Roth
  See Roth-Hano, Renee
Hanover, Terri
  See Huff, Tanya (Sue)
Hansen, Ann Larkin 1958- *96*
Hansen, Brooks 1965- *104*
Hansen, Caryl (Hall) 1929- *39*
Hansen, Ian V. 1929- *113*
Hansen, Jennifer 1972- *156*
Hansen, Joyce (Viola) 1942- *101*
  Brief entry *39*
  Earlier sketch in SATA *46*
  See also CLR *21*
  See also SAAS *15*
Hansen, Mark Victor *112*
Hansen, Ron(ald Thomas) 1947- *56*
Hanser, Richard (Frederick) 1909-1981 ...... *13*
Hanson, Joan 1938- *8*

Hanson, Warren 1949- *155*
Hansson, Gunilla 1939- *64*
Harald, Eric
  See Boesen, Victor
Hard, Charlotte (Ann) 1969- *98*
Hardcastle, Michael 1933- *47*
  Brief entry *38*
Harding, Lee 1937- *32*
  Brief entry *31*
Hardt, Helga Fleischhauer
  See Fleischhauer-Hardt, Helga
Hardwick, Richard Holmes, Jr. 1923- *12*
Hardy, Alice Dale *67*
  Earlier sketch in SATA *1*
Hardy, David A(ndrews) 1936- *9*
Hardy, Jon 1958- *53*
Hardy, LeAnne 1951- *154*
Hardy, Stuart
  See Schisgall, Oscar
Hare, Norma Q(uarles) 1924- *46*
  Brief entry *41*
Harel, Nira 1936- *154*
Harford, Henry
  See Hudson, W(illiam) H(enry)
Hargrave, Leonie
  See Disch, Thomas M(ichael)
Hargrove, James 1947- *57*
  Brief entry *50*
Hargrove, Jim
  See Hargrove, James
Hariton, Anca I. 1955- *79*
Hark, Mildred
  See McQueen, Mildred Hark
Harkaway, Hal
  See Stratemeyer, Edward L.
Harkins, Philip 1912-1997 .... *6*
  Obituary *129*
Harlan, Elizabeth 1945- *41*
  Brief entry *35*
Harlan, Glen
  See Cebulash, Mel
Harlan, Judith 1949- *135*
  Earlier sketch in SATA *74*
  See also CLR *81*
Harland, Richard 1947- *152*
Harlee, J. V.
  See Leese, Jennifer L.B.
Harler, Ann
  See Van Steenwyk, Elizabeth (Ann)
Harley, Bill 1954- *87*
Harlow, Joan Hiatt 1932- *157*
Harmelink, Barbara (Mary) *9*
Harmer, Mabel 1894-1992 .... *45*
Harmon, Dan
  See Harmon, Daniel E(lton)
Harmon, Daniel E(lton) 1949- *157*
Harmon, Margaret 1906- *20*
Harmon, William (Ruth) 1938- *65*
Harnan, Terry 1920- *12*
Harness, Cheryl 1951- *131*
Harnett, Cynthia (Mary) 1893-1981 .... *5*
  Obituary *32*
Harper, Anita 1943- *41*
Harper, Betty 1946- *126*
Harper, Elaine
  See Hallin, Emily Watson
Harper, Ellen
  See Noble, Marty
Harper, Jessica (R.) 1949- *148*
Harper, Jo 1932- *169*
  Earlier sketch in SATA *97*
Harper, Mary Wood
  See Dixon, Jeanne
Harper, Piers 1966- *161*
  Earlier sketch in SATA *105*
Harper, Wilhelmina 1884-1973 .... *4*
  Obituary *26*
Harrah, Madge 1931- *154*
Harrah, Michael 1940- *41*
Harrah, Monique
  See Harrah, Madge

Harrar, George E. 1949- *124*
Harrell, Beatrice Orcutt 1943- *93*
Harrell, Janice 1945- *70*
Harries, Joan 1922- *39*
Harrill, Ronald 1950- *90*
Harrington, Denis J(ames) 1932- *88*
Harrington, Lyn *5*
  See Harrington, Evelyn Davis
Harris, Alan 1944- *71*
Harris, Aurand 1915-1996 .... *37*
  Obituary *91*
Harris, Carol Flynn 1933- *135*
Harris, Catherine
  See Ainsworth, Catherine Harris
Harris, Christie
  See Harris, Christie (Lucy) Irwin
Harris, Christie (Lucy) Irwin 1907-2002 .... *74*
  Autobiography Feature *116*
  Earlier sketch in SATA *6*
  See also CLR *47*
  See also SAAS *10*
Harris, Christine 1955- *105*
Harris, Colver
  See Colver, Anne
Harris, David (William) 1942- *118*
Harris, Dorothy Joan 1931- *153*
  Earlier sketch in SATA *13*
Harris, Geraldine (Rachel) 1951- *54*
Harris, Jacqueline L. 1929- *62*
Harris, Janet 1932-1979 .... *4*
  Obituary *23*
Harris, Jesse
  See Standiford, Natalie
Harris, Joan 1946- *146*
Harris, Joel Chandler 1848-1908 .... *100*
  See also YABC *1*
  See also CLR *49*
Harris, John (Wyndham Parkes Lucas) Beynon
  1903-1969 .... *118*
  See Wyndham, John
Harris, Johnson
  See Harris, John (Wyndham Parkes Lucas)
  Beynon
Harris, Jonathan 1921-1997 .... *52*
Harris, Larry Vincent 1939- *59*
Harris, Lavinia
  See St. John, Nicole
Harris, Leon A., Jr. 1926-2000 .... *4*
Harris, Lorle K(empe) 1912-2001 .... *22*
Harris, Marilyn
  See Springer, Marilyn Harris
Harris, Mark Jonathan 1941- *84*
  Earlier sketch in SATA *32*
Harris, Mary K(athleen) 1905-1966 .... *119*
Harris, Robie H. 1940- *147*
  Brief entry *53*
  Earlier sketch in SATA *90*
Harris, Robin
  See Shine, Deborah
Harris, Rosemary (Jeanne) *82*
  Earlier sketch in SATA *4*
  See also CLR *30*
  See also SAAS *7*
Harris, Ruth Elwin 1935- *164*
Harris, Sherwood 1932- *25*
Harris, Steven Michael 1957- *55*
Harris, Trudy 1949- *128*
Harris-Filderman, Diane
  See Filderman, Diane E(lizabeth)
Harrison, C(hester) William 1913-1994 ...... *35*
Harrison, Carol
  See Harrison, Carol Thompson
Harrison, Carol Thompson *113*
Harrison, David L(ee) 1937- *150*
  Earlier sketches in SATA *26, 92*
Harrison, Deloris 1938- *9*
Harrison, Edward Hardy 1926- *56*
Harrison, Elizabeth (Allen) Cavanna
  1909-2001 .... *142*
  See Cavanna, Betty
Harrison, Harry (Max) 1925- *4*

Harrison, Mette Ivie 1970- *149*
Harrison, Michael 1939- *106*
Harrison, Molly (Hodgett) 1909-2002 .... *41*
Harrison, Sarah 1946- *63*
Harrison, Ted
　　See Harrison, Edward Hardy
Harsh, Fred (T.) 1925- 72
Harshaw, Ruth H(etzel) 1890-1968 27
Harshman, Marc 1950- *109*
　　Earlier sketch in SATA *71*
Hart, Alison
　　See Leonhardt, Alice
Hart, Bruce 1938-2006 57
　　Brief entry *39*
Hart, Carole 1943- 57
　　Brief entry *39*
Hart, Carolyn 1936- 74
Hart, Carolyn G.
　　See Hart, Carolyn
Hart, Carolyn Gimpel
　　See Hart, Carolyn
Hart, Jan Siegel 1940- 79
Hart, Joyce 1954- *148*
Hart, Virginia 1949- 83
Harte, (Francis) Bret(t) 1836(?)-1902 26
Harter, Debbie 1963- *107*
Hartfield, Claire 1957- *147*
Hartinger, Brent 1964- *145*
Hartley, Ellen (Raphael) 1915-1980 23
Hartley, Fred Allan III 1953- *41*
Hartley, William B(rown) 1913-1980 23
Hartling, Peter
　　See CLR 29
　　See Hartling, Peter
Hartling, Peter 1933- 66
　　See Hartling, Peter
Hartman, Evert 1937- 38
　　Brief entry 35
Hartman, Jane E(vangeline) 1928- 47
Hartman, Louis F(rancis) 1901-1970 22
Hartman, Victoria 1942- 91
Hartnett, Sonya 1968- *130*
　　Earlier sketch in SATA *93*
Hartshorn, Ruth M. 1928- *11*
Hartung, Susan Kathleen *150*
Hartwig, Manfred 1950- 81
Harvey, Brett 1936- 61
Harvey, Karen D. 1935- 88
Harvey, Roland 1945- *123*
　　Earlier sketch in SATA *71*
Harwick, B. L.
　　See Keller, Beverly L(ou)
Harwin, Brian
　　See Henderson, LeGrand
Harwood, Pearl Augusta (Bragdon) 1903-1998
　　.. 9
Haseley, Dennis 1950- *157*
　　Brief entry *44*
　　Earlier sketches in SATA *57, 105*
Hashmi, Kerri 1955- *108*
Haskell, Arnold L(ionel) 1903-1981(?) 6
Haskins, James
　　See Haskins, James S.
Haskins, James S. 1941-2005 .... *132*
　　Autobiography Feature *132*
　　Earlier sketches in SATA *9, 69, 105*
　　See also CLR 39
　　See Haskins, Jim
Haskins, Jim
　　See SAAS 4
　　See Haskins, James S.
Hasler, Joan 1931- 28
Hass, Robert 1941- 94
Hassall, Joan 1906-1988 43
　　Obituary 56
Hassett, Ann 1958- *162*
Hassett, John *162*
Hassler, Jon (Francis) 1933- 19
Hastings, Beverly
　　See Barkin, Carol
　　and James, Elizabeth

Hastings, Graham
　　See Jeffries, Roderic (Graeme)
Hastings, Ian 1912- 62
Hatch, Lynda S. 1950- 90
Hathaway, Barbara *164*
Hathorn, Libby 1943- *156*
　　Autobiography Feature *156*
　　Earlier sketches in SATA *74, 120*
　　See Hathorn, Elizabeth Helen
Haugaard, Erik Christian 1923- 68
　　Earlier sketch in SATA *4*
　　See also CLR *11*
　　See also SAAS *12*
Haugaard, Kay *117*
Haugen, Tormod 1945- 66
Hauman, Doris 1898-1984 32
Hauman, George 1890-1961 32
Hauptly, Denis J(ames) 1945- 57
Hauser, Jill Frankel 1950- *127*
Hauser, Margaret L(ouise) 1909- 10
Hausherr, Rosmarie 1943- 86
Hausman, Gerald 1945- *132*
　　Earlier sketches in SATA *13, 90*
　　See also CLR *89*
Hausman, Gerry
　　See Hausman, Gerald
Hauth, Katherine B. 1940- 99
Hautman, Pete(r Murray) 1952- *128*
　　Earlier sketch in SATA *82*
Hautzig, Deborah 1956- *106*
　　Earlier sketch in SATA *31*
Hautzig, Esther Rudomin 1930- *148*
　　Earlier sketches in SATA *4, 68*
　　See also CLR *22*
　　See also SAAS *15*
Havel, Geoff 1955- *152*
Havel, Jennifer
　　See Havill, Juanita
Havelin, Kate 1961- *143*
Havighurst, Walter (Edwin) 1901-1994 .... *1*
　　Obituary 79
Haviland, Virginia 1911-1988 6
　　Obituary 54
Havill, Juanita 1949- *155*
　　Earlier sketch in SATA *74*
Hawes, Judy 1913- *4*
Hawes, Louise 1943- 60
Hawke, Rosanne 1953- *165*
　　Earlier sketch in SATA *124*
Hawke, Rosanne Joy
　　See Hawke, Rosanne
Hawkes, Kevin (Cliff) 1959- *150*
　　Earlier sketch in SATA *78*
Hawkes, Nigel 1943- *119*
Hawkesworth, Eric 1921- 13
Hawkins, Arthur 1903-1985 19
Hawkins, Colin 1945- *162*
　　Earlier sketch in SATA *112*
Hawkins, Jacqui *162*
　　Earlier sketch in SATA *112*
Hawkins, Laura 1951- 74
Hawkins, (Helena Ann) Quail 1905-2002 6
　　Obituary *141*
Hawkinson, John (Samuel) 1912-1994 .... *4*
Hawkinson, Lucy (Ozone) 1924-1971 21
Hawks, Robert 1961- 85
Hawley, Mabel C. 67
　　Earlier sketch in SATA *1*
Hawthorne, Captain R. M.
　　See Ellis, Edward S(ylvester)
Hawthorne, Nathaniel 1804-1864
　　See YABC *2*
　　See also CLR *103*
Hay, Jeff T. *154*
Hay, John 1915- 13
Hay, Timothy
　　See Brown, Margaret Wise
Hayashi, Leslie Ann 1954- *115*
Hayashi, Nancy 1939- 80
Haycock, Kate 1962- 77

Haycraft, Howard 1905-1991 6
　　Obituary 70
Haycraft, Molly Costain 1911- 6
Hayden, Gwendolen Lampshire 1904- 35
Hayden, Robert C(arter), Jr. 1937- 47
　　Brief entry 28
Hayden, Robert E(arl) 1913-1980 19
　　Obituary 26
Hayden, Torey L. 1951- *163*
　　Earlier sketch in SATA *65*
Hayden, Torey Lynn
　　See Hayden, Torey L.
Hayes, Carlton J(oseph) H(untley) 1882-1964
　　.. *11*
Hayes, Daniel 1952- *109*
　　Earlier sketch in SATA *73*
Hayes, Geoffrey 1947- 91
　　Earlier sketch in SATA *26*
Hayes, Joe 1945- *131*
　　Earlier sketch in SATA *88*
Hayes, John F. 1904-1980 .... *11*
Hayes, Rosemary *158*
Hayes, Sheila 1937- 51
　　Brief entry 50
Hayes, Will 7
Hayes, William D(imitt) 1913-1976 8
Haynes, Betsy 1937- 94
　　Brief entry 37
　　Earlier sketch in SATA *48*
　　See also CLR *90*
Haynes, David 1955- 97
Haynes, Linda
　　See Swinford, Betty (June Wells)
Haynes, Mary 1938- 65
Haynes, Max 1956- 72
Hays, H(offmann) R(eynolds) 1904-1980 ... 26
Hays, Thomas Anthony 1957- 84
Hays, Tony
　　See Hays, Thomas Anthony
Hays, Wilma Pitchford 1909- 28
　　Earlier sketch in SATA *1*
　　See also CLR *59*
　　See also SAAS *3*
Hayward, Linda 1943- *101*
　　Brief entry *39*
Haywood, Carolyn 1898-1990 75
　　Obituary 64
　　Earlier sketches in SATA *1, 29*
　　See also CLR *22*
Hazell, Rebecca (Eileen) 1947- *141*
Hazen, Barbara Shook 1930- 90
　　Earlier sketch in SATA *27*
Head, Gay
　　See Hauser, Margaret L(ouise)
Head, Tom 1978- *167*
Headley, Elizabeth
　　See Harrison, Elizabeth (Allen) Cavanna
Headstrom, (Birger) Richard 1902-1985 8
Heady, Eleanor B(utler) 1917-1979 8
Heagy, William D. 1964- 76
Heal, Edith 1903-1995 7
Heal, Gillian 1934- 89
Heale, Jay (Jeremy Peter Wingfield) 1937-
　　.. 84
Healey, Brooks
　　See Albert, Burton
Healey, Larry 1927- 44
　　Brief entry 42
Heap, Sue 1954- *150*
Heaps, Willard A(llison) 1908-1987 26
Hearn, Diane Dawson 1952- 79
Hearn, Emily
　　See Valleau, Emily
Hearn, Julie *152*
Hearn, Lian
　　See Rubinstein, Gillian (Margaret)
Hearn, Sneed
　　See Gregg, Andrew K.
Hearne, Betsy Gould 1942- *146*
　　Earlier sketches in SATA *38, 95*
Heath, Charles D(ickinson) 1941- 46

Heath, Veronica
    See Blackett, Veronica Heath
Heaven, Constance (Christina) 1911- 7
Hebert-Collins, Sheila 1948- 111
Hecht, Henri Joseph 1922- 9
Hechtkopf, Henryk 1910- 17
Heck, Bessie (Mildred) Holland 1911-1995
    26
Heckert, Connie K(aye Delp) 1948- 82
Hedderwick, Mairi 1939- 145
    Earlier sketches in SATA *30, 77*
Hedges, Sid(ney) G(eorge) 1897-1974 28
Heelan, Jamee Riggio 1965- 146
Heerboth, Sharon
    See Leon, Sharon
Heffernan, John 1949- 168
    Earlier sketch in SATA *121*
Heffron, Dorris 1944- 68
Hefter, Richard 1942- 31
Hegarty, Reginald Beaton 1906-1973 10
Hehenberger, Shelly 1968- 126
Heidbreder, Robert K. 1947- 130
Heide, Florence Parry 1919- 118
    Earlier sketches in SATA *32, 69*
    See also CLR *60*
    See also SAAS *6*
Heiderstadt, Dorothy 1907-2001 6
Heidi Louise
    See Erdrich, Louise
Heidler, David S(tephen) 1955- 132
Heidler, Jeanne T. 1956- 132
Heilbroner, Joan Knapp 1922- 63
Heiligman, Deborah 1958- 144
    Earlier sketch in SATA *90*
Heilman, Joan Rattner 50
Heimann, Rolf 1940- 164
    Earlier sketch in SATA *120*
Hein, Lucille Eleanor 1915-1994 20
Heine, Helme 1941- 135
    Earlier sketch in SATA *67*
    See also CLR *18*
Heinlein, Robert A(nson) 1907-1988 69
    Obituary 56
    Earlier sketch in SATA *9*
    See also CLR *75*
Heins, Ethel L(eah) 1918-1997 101
Heins, Paul 1909- 13
Heintze, Carl 1922- 26
Heinz, Brian J(ames) 1946- 95
Heinz, W(ilfred) C(harles) 1915- 26
Heinzen, Mildred
    See Masters, Mildred
Heisel, Sharon E(laine) 1941- 125
    Earlier sketch in SATA *84*
Heitzmann, William Ray 1948- 73
Heitzmann, Wm. Ray
    See Heitzmann, William Ray
Helberg, Shirley Adelaide Holden 1919- .. 138
Helfman, Elizabeth S(eaver) 1911-2001 3
Helfman, Harry Carmozin 1910-1995 3
Hellberg, Hans-Eric 1927- 38
Heller, Linda 1944- 46
    Brief entry 40
Heller, Mike
    See Hano, Arnold
Heller, Ruth M. 1924- 112
    Earlier sketch in SATA *66*
Hellman, Hal
    See Hellman, Harold
Hellman, Harold 1927- 4
Helman, Andrea (Jean) 1946- 160
    Earlier sketch in SATA *107*
Helmer, Diana Star 1962- 86
Helmer, Marilyn 160
    Earlier sketch in SATA *112*
Helps, Racey 1913-1971 2
    Obituary 25
Helquist, Brett 146
Helweg, Hans H. 1917- 50
    Brief entry 33

Helyar, Jane Penelope Josephine 1933- *138*
    Autobiography Feature *138*
    Earlier sketch in SATA *82*
    See Poole, Josephine
Hemmant, Lynette 1938- 69
Hemming, Roy G. 1928-1995 .... *11*
    Obituary 86
Hemphill, Kris (Harrison) 1963- 118
Hemphill, Martha Locke 1904-1973 37
Henba, Bobbie 1926- 87
Henbest, Nigel 1951- 55
    Brief entry 52
Henderley, Brooks *1*
Henderson, Aileen Mary
    See Fox, Aileen
Henderson, Gordon 1950- 53
Henderson, Kathy 1949- 155
    Brief entry 53
    Earlier sketches in SATA *55, 95*
Henderson, LeGrand 1901-1965 9
Henderson, Nancy Wallace 1916- 22
Henderson, Zenna (Chlarson) 1917-1983 5
Hendrickson, Walter Brookfield, Jr. 1936- 9
Hendry, Diana 1941- 106
    Earlier sketch in SATA *68*
Hendry, Frances Mary 1941- 110
Hendry, Linda (Gail) 1961- 83
Heneghan, James 1930- 160
    Earlier sketches in SATA *53, 97*
Henkes, Kevin 1960- 154
    Earlier sketches in SATA *43, 76, 108*
    See also CLR *108*
Henney, Carolee Wells 1928- 102
Henriod, Lorraine 1925- 26
Henriquez, Emile F. 1937- 89
Henry, Ernest 1948- 107
Henry, Joanne Landers 1927- 6
Henry, Maeve 1960- 75
Henry, Marguerite 1902-1997 100
    Obituary 99
    See also CLR *4*
    See also SAAS *7*
Henry, Marie H. 1935- 65
Henry, Marilyn 1939- 117
Henry, Marion
    See del Rey, Lester
Henry, O.
    See Porter, William Sydney
Henry, Oliver
    See Porter, William Sydney
Henry, T. E.
    See Rowland-Entwistle, (Arthur) Theodore
    (Henry)
Henschel, Elizabeth Georgie 56
Henson, James Maury
    See Henson, Jim
Henson, Jim 1936-1990 43
    Obituary 65
Henstra, Friso 1928- 73
    Earlier sketch in SATA *8*
    See also SAAS *14*
Hentoff, Nat(han Irving) 1925- 133
    Brief entry 27
    Earlier sketches in SATA *42, 69*
    See also CLR *52*
Henty, G(eorge) A(lfred) 1832-1902 64
    See also CLR *76*
Heo, Yumi 1964- 146
    Earlier sketch in SATA *94*
Herald, Kathleen
    See Peyton, Kathleen Wendy (Herald)
Herb, Angela M. 1970- 92
Herbert, Cecil
    See Hamilton, Charles (Harold St. John)
Herbert, Don(ald Jeffrey) 1917- 2
Herbert, Frank (Patrick) 1920-1986 37
    Obituary 47
    Earlier sketch in SATA *9*
Herbert, Helen (Jean) 1947- 57
Herbert, Janis 1956- 139

Herbert, Wally
    See Herbert, Walter William
Herbert, Walter William 1934- 23
Herbst, Judith 1947- 74
Herda, D.J. 1948- 80
Herge
    See CLR *6*
    See Remi, Georges
Heritage, Martin
    See Horler, Sydney
Herkimer, L(awrence) R(ussell) 1925(?)- ... 42
Herlihy, Dirlie Anne 1935- 73
Herman, Charlotte 1937- 99
    Earlier sketch in SATA *20*
Hermanson, Dennis (Everett) 1947- 10
Hermes, Jules 1962- 92
Hermes, Patricia (Mary) 1936- 141
    Earlier sketches in SATA *31, 78*
Hernandez, Natalie Nelson 1929- 123
Herndon, Ernest 91
Herold, Ann Bixby 1937- 72
Herrera, Juan Felipe 1948- 127
Herrick, Steven 1958- 156
    Earlier sketch in SATA *103*
Herriman, George (Joseph) 1880-1944 140
Herriot, James 1916-1995 135
    Earlier sketch in SATA *86*
    See also CLR *80*
    See Wight, James Alfred
Herrmanns, Ralph 1933- *11*
Herrold, Tracey
    See Dils, Tracey E.
Herron, Edward A(lbert) 1912- 4
Herschler, Mildred Barger 130
Hersey, John (Richard) 1914-1993 25
    Obituary 76
Hershberger, Priscilla (Gorman) 1951- 81
Hershenhorn, Esther 1945- 151
Hershey, Kathleen M. 1934- 80
Hersom, Kathleen 1911- 73
Hertz, Grete Janus 1915- 23
Herzig, Alison Cragin 1935- 87
Herzog, Brad 1968- 131
Heslewood, Juliet 1951- 82
Hess, Lilo 1916- 4
Hess, Paul 1961- 134
Hesse, Hermann 1877-1962 50
Hesse, Karen 1952- 158
    Autobiography Feature 113
    Earlier sketches in SATA *74, 103*
    See also CLR *54*
    See also SAAS *25*
Hest, Amy 1950- 129
    Earlier sketches in SATA *55, 82*
Heuer, Kenneth John 1927- 44
Heuman, William 1912-1971 21
Heuston, Kimberley 1960- 167
Heuston, Kimberley Burton
    See Heuston, Kimberley
Hewes, Agnes Danforth 1874-1963 35
Hewett, Anita 1918-1989 13
Hewett, Joan 1930- 140
    Earlier sketch in SATA *81*
Hewett, Richard 1929- 81
Hewitson, Jennifer 1961- 97
Hewitt, Margaret 1961- 84
Hewitt, Sally 1949- 127
Hext, Harrington
    See Phillpotts, Eden
Hey, Nigel S(tewart) 1936- 20
Heyduck-Huth, Hilde 1929- 8
Heyer, Carol 1950- 130
    Earlier sketch in SATA *74*
Heyer, Marilee 1942- 102
    Earlier sketch in SATA *64*
Heyerdahl, Thor 1914-2002 52
    Earlier sketch in SATA *2*
Heyes, (Nancy) Eileen 1956- 150
    Earlier sketch in SATA *80*
Heyliger, William 1884-1955
    See YABC *1*

Heyman, Ken(neth Louis) 1930- *114*
  Earlier sketch in SATA *34*
Heyward, (Edwin) DuBose 1885-1940 ..... *21*
Heywood, Karen 1946- *48*
Hezlep, William (Earl) 1936- *88*
Hibbert, Christopher 1924- *4*
Hibbert, Eleanor Alice Burford 1906-1993 ... *2*
  Obituary *74*
  See Holt, Victoria
Hickman, Estella (Lee) 1942- *111*
Hickman, Janet 1940- *127*
  Earlier sketch in SATA *12*
Hickman, Martha Whitmore 1925- *26*
Hickman, Pamela M. 1958- *128*
Hickock, Will
  See Harrison, C(hester) William
Hickok, Lorena A. 1893-1968 .... *20*
Hickox, Rebecca (Ayres) *116*
Hicks, Barbara Jean 1953- *165*
Hicks, Clifford B. 1920- *50*
Hicks, Eleanor B.
  See Coerr, Eleanor (Beatrice)
Hicks, Harvey
  See Stratemeyer, Edward L.
Hicks, Peter 1952- *111*
Hicyilmaz, Gaye 1947- *157*
  Earlier sketch in SATA *77*
Hieatt, Constance B(artlett) 1928- *4*
Hiebert, Ray Eldon 1932- *13*
Higdon, Hal 1931- *4*
Higginbottom, David 1923- *87*
  See Fisk, Nicholas
Higginbottom, J(effrey) Winslow 1945- *29*
Higgins, Joanna 1945- *125*
Higgins, Simon (Richard) 1958- *105*
Higginsen, Vy *79*
High, Linda Oatman 1958- *145*
  Earlier sketch in SATA *94*
High, Philip E(mpson) 1914- *119*
Higham, David (Michael) 1949- *50*
Higham, Jon Atlas
  See Higham, Jonathan Huw
Higham, Jonathan Huw 1960- *59*
Highet, Helen
  See MacInnes, Helen (Clark)
Hightower, Florence Cole 1916-1981 .... *4*
  Obituary *27*
Highwater, Jamake (Mamake) 1942(?)-2001
  .... *69*
  Brief entry *30*
  Earlier sketch in SATA *32*
  See also CLR *17*
Hildebrandt, Greg 1939- *55*
  Brief entry *33*
Hildebrandt, Tim(othy) 1939- *55*
  Brief entry *33*
Hildebrandts, The
  See Hildebrandt, Greg
  and Hildebrandt, Tim(othy)
Hilder, Rowland 1905-1993 .... *36*
  Obituary *77*
Hildick, E. W.
  See SAAS *6*
  See Hildick, (Edmund) Wallace
Hildick, (Edmund) Wallace 1925-2001 .... *68*
  Earlier sketch in SATA *2*
  See Hildick, E. W.
Hilgartner, Beth 1957- *58*
Hill, Alexis
  See Craig, Mary (Francis) Shura
  and Glick, Ruth (Burtnick)
Hill, Anthony R. 1942- *164*
  Earlier sketch in SATA *91*
Hill, Anthony Robert
  See Hill, Anthony R.
Hill, David 1942- *152*
  Earlier sketch in SATA *103*
Hill, Donna (Marie) 1921- *124*
  Earlier sketch in SATA *24*
Hill, Douglas (Arthur) 1935- *78*
  Earlier sketch in SATA *39*

Hill, Elizabeth Starr 1925- *143*
  Earlier sketch in SATA *24*
Hill, Eric 1927- *133*
  Brief entry *53*
  Earlier sketch in SATA *66*
  See also CLR *13*
Hill, Gordon
  See Eldin, Peter
Hill, Grace Brooks *67*
  Earlier sketch in SATA *1*
Hill, Grace Livingston 1865-1947
  See YABC *2*
Hill, Helen M(orey) 1915- *27*
Hill, John
  See Koontz, Dean R.
Hill, Johnson
  See Kunhardt, Edith
Hill, Judy I. R.
  See Roberts, Judy I.
Hill, Kathleen Louise 1917- *4*
Hill, Kay
  See Hill, Kathleen Louise
Hill, Kirkpatrick 1938- *126*
  Earlier sketch in SATA *72*
Hill, Lee Sullivan 1958- *96*
Hill, Lorna 1902-1991 .... *12*
Hill, Margaret (Ohler) 1915- *36*
Hill, Meg
  See Hill, Margaret (Ohler)
Hill, Meredith
  See Craig, Mary (Francis) Shura
Hill, Monica
  See Watson, Jane Werner
Hill, Pamela Smith 1954- *112*
Hill, Ralph Nading 1917-1987 .... *65*
Hill, Robert W(hite) 1919-1982 .... *12*
  Obituary *31*
Hill, Ruth A.
  See Viguers, Ruth Hill
Hill, Ruth Livingston
  See Munce, Ruth Hill
Hill, Thomas 1960- *82*
Hillcourt, William 1900-1992 .... *27*
Hillenbrand, Will 1960- *147*
  Earlier sketch in SATA *84*
Hiller, Ilo (Ann) 1938- *59*
Hillerman, Tony 1925- *6*
Hillert, Margaret 1920- *91*
  Earlier sketch in SATA *8*
Hillman, Elizabeth 1942- *75*
Hillman, John 1952- *120*
Hillman, Martin
  See Hill, Douglas (Arthur)
Hillman, Priscilla 1940- *48*
  Brief entry *39*
Hills, C(harles) A(lbert) R(eis) 1955- *39*
Hilton, Irene Pothus -1979 .... *7*
Hilton, James 1900-1954 .... *34*
Hilton, Margaret Lynette 1946- *105*
  Earlier sketch in SATA *68*
  See Hilton, Nette
Hilton, Nette
  See CLR *25*
  See also SAAS *21*
  See Hilton, Margaret Lynette
Hilton, Ralph 1907-1982 .... *8*
Hilton, Suzanne 1922- *4*
Hilton-Bruce, Anne
  See Hilton, Margaret Lynette
Himelstein, Shmuel 1940- *83*
Himler, Ann 1946- *8*
Himler, Ronald (Norbert) 1937- *137*
  Earlier sketches in SATA *6, 92*
Himmelman, John C(arl) 1959- *159*
  Earlier sketches in SATA *47, 94*
Hinckley, Helen
  See Jones, Helen Hinckley
Hind, Dolores (Ellen) 1931- *53*
  Brief entry *49*
Hindin, Nathan
  See Bloch, Robert (Albert)

Hindley, Judy 1940- *120*
Hinds, P(atricia) Mignon *98*
Hines, Anna Grossnickle 1946- *141*
  Brief entry *45*
  Earlier sketches in SATA *51, 95*
  See also SAAS *16*
Hines, Gary (Roger) 1944- *136*
  Earlier sketch in SATA *74*
Hinojosa, Maria (de Lourdes) 1961- *88*
Hinton, Nigel 1941- *166*
Hinton, S(usan) E(loise) 1950- *160*
  Earlier sketches in SATA *19, 58, 115*
  See also CLR *23*
Hinton, Sam 1917- *43*
Hintz, Martin 1945- *128*
  Brief entry *39*
  Earlier sketch in SATA *47*
Hintz, Stephen V. 1975- *129*
Hippopotamus, Eugene H.
  See Kraus, (Herman) Robert
Hirano, Cathy 1957- *68*
Hirsch, Karen 1941- *61*
Hirsch, Odo *157*
  Earlier sketch in SATA *111*
Hirsch, Phil 1926- *35*
Hirsch, S. Carl 1913-1990 .... *2*
  See also SAAS *7*
Hirschfelder, Arlene B. 1943- *138*
  Earlier sketch in SATA *80*
Hirschi, Ron 1948- *95*
  Earlier sketch in SATA *56*
Hirschmann, Linda (Ann) 1941- *40*
Hirsh, Marilyn 1944-1988 .... *7*
  Obituary *58*
Hirshberg, Al(bert Simon) 1909-1973 .... *38*
Hiscock, Bruce 1940- *137*
  Earlier sketch in SATA *57*
Hiser, Constance 1950- *71*
Hiser, Iona Seibert -1998 .... *4*
Hislop, Julia Rose Catherine 1962- *74*
Hissey, Jane (Elizabeth) 1952- *130*
  Autobiography Feature *130*
  Earlier sketches in SATA *58, 103*
Hitchcock, Alfred (Joseph) 1899-1980 .... *27*
  Obituary *24*
Hite, Sid 1954- *136*
  Earlier sketch in SATA *75*
Hitte, Kathryn 1919- *16*
Hitz, Demi 1942- *152*
  Earlier sketches in SATA *11, 66, 102*
  See also CLR *58*
  See Demi
Hitzeroth, Deborah L. 1961- *78*
Hnizdovsky, Jacques 1915- *32*
Ho, Minfong 1951- *151*
  Earlier sketches in SATA *15, 94*
  See also CLR *28*
Hoagland, Edward (Morley) 1932- *51*
Hoare, Robert J(ohn) 1921-1975 .... *38*
Hoban, Lillian 1925-1998 .... *69*
  Obituary *104*
  Earlier sketch in SATA *22*
  See also CLR *67*
Hoban, Russell (Conwell) 1925- *136*
  Earlier sketches in SATA *1, 40, 78*
  See also CLR *69*
Hoban, Tana 1917(?)-2006 .... *104*
  Earlier sketches in SATA *22, 70*
  See also CLR *76*
  See also SAAS *12*
Hobart, Lois (Elaine) *7*
Hobbie, Holly 1944-
  See CLR *88*
Hobbs, Leigh 1953- *166*
Hobbs, Valerie 1941- *145*
  Autobiography Feature *145*
  Earlier sketch in SATA *93*
Hobbs, Will(iam Carl) 1947- *110*
  Autobiography Feature *127*
  Earlier sketch in SATA *72*
  See also CLR *59*

Hoberman, Mary Ann 1930- *158*
    Earlier sketches in SATA *5, 72, 111*
    See also CLR *22*
    See also SAAS *18*
Hobson, Bruce 1950- *62*
Hobson, Burton (Harold) 1933- *28*
Hobson, Laura Z(ametkin) 1900-1986 .... *52*
Hobson, Sally 1947- *84*
Hochschild, Arlie Russell 1940- *11*
Hockaby, Stephen
    See Mitchell, Gladys (Maude Winifred)
Hockenberry, Hope
    See Newell, Hope Hockenberry
Hodge, Deborah 1954- *163*
    Earlier sketch in SATA *122*
Hodge, P. W.
    See Hodge, Paul W(illiam)
Hodge, Paul W(illiam) 1934- *12*
Hodgell, P(atricia) C(hristine) 1951- *42*
Hodges, C(yril) Walter 1909-2004 .... *2*
    Obituary *158*
Hodges, Carl G. 1902-1964 .... *10*
Hodges, Elizabeth Jamison *1*
Hodges, Margaret
    See Hodges, Margaret Moore
Hodges, Margaret Moore 1911-2005 .... *167*
    Earlier sketches in SATA *1, 33, 75, 117*
    See also SAAS *9*
Hodgetts, Blake Christopher 1967- *43*
Hodgson, Harriet (W.) 1935- *84*
Hoehne, Marcia 1951- *89*
Hoellwarth, Cathryn Clinton 1957- *136*
Hoestlandt, Jo(celyne) 1948- *94*
Hoexter, Corinne K. 1927- *6*
Hoeye, Michael 1947- *136*
Hoff, Carol 1900-1979 .... *11*
Hoff, Mary (King) 1956- *157*
    Earlier sketch in SATA *74*
Hoff, Syd(ney) 1912-2004 .... *138*
    Obituary *154*
    Earlier sketches in SATA *9, 72*
    See also CLR *83*
    See also SAAS *4*
Hoffman, Edwin D. *49*
Hoffman, Mary (Margaret) 1945- *144*
    Earlier sketches in SATA *59, 97*
    See also SAAS *24*
    See Lassiter, Mary
Hoffman, Mat 1972- *150*
Hoffman, Nina Kiriki 1955- *160*
Hoffman, Phyllis M(iriam) 1944- *4*
Hoffman, Rosekrans 1926- *15*
Hoffmann, E(rnst) T(heodor) A(madeus)
    1776-1822 .... *27*
Hoffmann, Felix 1911-1975 .... *9*
Hoffmann, Heinrich 1809-1894
    See CLR *70*
Hoffmann, Margaret Jones 1910- *48*
Hoffmann, Peggy
    See Hoffmann, Margaret Jones
Hofher, Catherine Baxley 1954- *130*
Hofher, Cathy
    See Hofher, Catherine Baxley
Hofmeyr, Dianne (Louise) *138*
Hofsepian, Sylvia A. 1932- *74*
Hofsinde, Robert 1902-1973 .... *21*
Hogan, Bernice Harris 1929- *12*
Hogan, Inez 1895-1973 .... *2*
Hogan, James P(atrick) 1941- *81*
Hogan, Linda 1947- *132*
Hogarth, Burne 1911-1996 .... *89*
    Earlier sketch in SATA *63*
Hogarth, Grace (Weston Allen) 1905-1995 . *91*
Hogarth, Jr.
    See Kent, Rockwell
Hogarth, (Arthur) Paul 1917-2001 .... *41*
Hogg, Garry 1902-1976 .... *2*
Hogg, Gary 1957- *105*
Hogner, Dorothy Childs *4*
Hogner, Nils 1893-1970 .... *25*

Hogrogian, Nonny 1932- *74*
    Autobiography Feature *127*
    Earlier sketch in SATA *7*
    See also CLR *95*
    See also SAAS *1*
Hoh, Diane 1937- *102*
    Brief entry *48*
    Earlier sketch in SATA *52*
Hoke, John (Lindsay) 1925- *7*
Hol, Coby 1943- *126*
Holabird, Katharine 1948- *135*
    Earlier sketch in SATA *62*
Holaday, Bobbie 1922- *153*
Holbeach, Henry
    See Rands, William Brighty
Holberg, Ruth L(angland) 1889-1984 .... *1*
Holbrook, Kathy 1963- *107*
Holbrook, Peter
    See Glick, Carl (Cannon)
Holbrook, Sabra
    See Erickson, Sabra Rollins
Holbrook, Sara *131*
Holbrook, Stewart Hall 1893-1964 .... *2*
Holcomb, Jerry (Leona) Kimble 1927- *113*
Holcomb, Nan
    See McPhee, Norma H.
Holden, Elizabeth Rhoda
    See Lawrence, Louise
Holding, James (Clark Carlisle, Jr.) 1907-1997
    .... *3*
Holeman, Linda 1949- *136*
    Autobiography Feature *136*
    Earlier sketch in SATA *102*
Holinger, William (Jacques) 1944- *90*
Holisher, Desider 1901-1972 .... *6*
Holl, Adelaide Hinkle 1910- *8*
Holl, Kristi D(iane) 1951- *51*
Holland, Gay W. 1941- *128*
Holland, Isabelle (Christian) 1920-2002 ..... *70*
    Autobiography Feature *103*
    Obituary *132*
    Earlier sketch in SATA *8*
    See also CLR *57*
Holland, Janice 1913-1962 .... *18*
Holland, John L(ewis) 1919- *20*
Holland, Joyce
    See Morice, Dave
Holland, Julia 1954- *106*
Holland, Lynda (H.) 1959- *77*
Holland, Lys
    See Gater, Dilys
Holland, Marion 1908-1989 .... *6*
    Obituary *61*
Hollander, John 1929- *13*
Hollander, Nicole 1940(?)- *101*
Hollander, Paul
    See Silverberg, Robert
Hollander, Phyllis 1928- *39*
Hollander, Zander 1923- *63*
Holldobler, Turid 1939- *26*
Holliday, Joe
    See Holliday, Joseph
Holliday, Joseph 1910- *11*
Holling, Holling C(lancy) 1900-1973 .... *15*
    Obituary *26*
    See also CLR *50*
Hollingsworth, Alvin C(arl) 1930- *39*
Hollingsworth, Mary 1947- *166*
    Earlier sketch in SATA *91*
Holloway, Teresa (Bragunier) 1906- *26*
Holm, (Else) Anne (Lise) 1922-1998 .... *1*
    See also CLR *75*
    See also SAAS *7*
Holm, Jennifer L. 1968(?)- *163*
    Earlier sketch in SATA *120*
Holm, Sharon Lane 1955- *114*
    Earlier sketch in SATA *78*
Holman, Felice 1919- *82*
    Earlier sketch in SATA *7*
    See also SAAS *17*

Holm and Hamel
    See Holm, Jennifer L.
Holme, Bryan 1913-1990 .... *26*
    Obituary *66*
Holmes, Barbara Ware 1945- *127*
    Earlier sketch in SATA *65*
Holmes, John
    See Souster, (Holmes) Raymond
Holmes, Marjorie (Rose) 1910-2002 .... *43*
Holmes, Martha 1961- *72*
Holmes, Mary Z(astrow) 1943- *80*
Holmes, Oliver Wendell 1809-1894 .... *34*
Holmes, Peggy 1898- *60*
Holmes, Raymond
    See Souster, (Holmes) Raymond
Holmes, Rick
    See Hardwick, Richard Holmes, Jr.
Holmgren, Helen Jean 1930- *45*
Holmgren, Sister George Ellen
    See Holmgren, Helen Jean
Holmgren, Virginia C(unningham) 1909- ... *26*
Holmquist, Eve 1921- *11*
Holt, Kimberly Willis 1960- *122*
Holt, Margaret 1937- *4*
Holt, Margaret Van Vechten (Saunders)
    1899-1963 .... *32*
Holt, Michael (Paul) 1929- *13*
Holt, Rackham
    See Holt, Margaret Van Vechten (Saunders)
Holt, Rochelle L. *41*
    See DuBois, Rochelle (Lynn) Holt
Holt, Stephen
    See Thompson, Harlan (Howard)
Holt, Victoria
    See Hibbert, Eleanor Alice Burford
Holton, Leonard
    See Wibberley, Leonard (Patrick O'Connor)
Holtze, Sally Holmes 1952- *64*
Holtzman, Jerome 1926- *57*
Holub, Joan 1956- *149*
    Earlier sketch in SATA *99*
Holubitsky, Katherine 1955- *165*
    Earlier sketch in SATA *121*
Holyer, Erna Maria 1925- *22*
Holyer, Ernie
    See Holyer, Erna Maria
Holz, Loretta (Marie) 1943- *17*
Homel, David 1952- *97*
Homze, Alma C. 1932- *17*
Honey, Elizabeth 1947- *137*
    Autobiography Feature *137*
    Earlier sketch in SATA *112*
Honeycutt, Natalie 1945- *97*
Hong, Lily Toy 1958- *76*
Honig, Donald 1931- *18*
Honness, Elizabeth H. 1904- *2*
Hoobler, Dorothy 1941- *161*
    Earlier sketches in SATA *28, 109*
Hoobler, Thomas *161*
    Earlier sketches in SATA *28, 109*
Hood, Joseph F. 1925- *4*
Hood, Robert E. 1926- *21*
Hood, Sarah
    See Killough, (Karen) Lee
Hook, Brendan 1963- *105*
Hook, Frances 1912-1983 .... *27*
Hook, Geoffrey R(aynor) 1928- *103*
Hook, Jeff
    See Hook, Geoffrey R(aynor)
Hook, Martha 1936- *27*
Hooker, Richard
    See Heinz, W(ilfred) C(harles)
Hooker, Ruth 1920-1998 .... *21*
hooks, bell
    See Watkins, Gloria Jean
Hooks, William H(arris) 1921- *94*
    Earlier sketch in SATA *16*
Hoon, Patricia Easterly 1954- *90*
Hooper, Mary 1944- *160*
Hooper, Maureen Brett 1927- *76*

Hooper, Meredith (Jean) 1939- *159*
　Earlier sketches in SATA *28, 101*
Hooper, Patricia 1941- *95*
Hoopes, Lyn Littlefield 1953- *49*
　Brief entry *44*
Hoopes, Ned E(dward) 1932- *21*
Hoopes, Roy 1922- *11*
Hoose, Phillip M. 1947- *137*
Hoover, H(elen) M(ary) 1935- *132*
　Brief entry *33*
　Earlier sketches in SATA *44, 83*
　See also SAAS *8*
Hoover, Helen (Drusilla Blackburn) 1910-1984
　.. *12*
　Obituary *39*
Hope, Christopher (David Tully) 1944- *62*
Hope, Laura Lee *67*
　Earlier sketch in SATA *1*
　See Goulart, Ron(ald Joseph)
　and Stanley, George Edward
Hope Simpson, Jacynth 1930- *12*
Hopf, Alice (Martha) L(ightner) 1904-1988 . *5*
　Obituary *55*
Hopkins, C. M.
　See Hopkins, Cathy
Hopkins, Cathy 1953- *165*
Hopkins, Cathy M.
　See Hopkins, Cathy
Hopkins, Ellen L. 1955- *128*
Hopkins, Jackie (Mims) 1952- *92*
Hopkins, Joseph G(erard) E(dward) 1909- .. *11*
Hopkins, Lee Bennett 1938- *168*
　Earlier sketches in SATA *3, 68, 125*
　See also CLR *44*
　See also SAAS *4*
Hopkins, Lyman
　See Folsom, Franklin (Brewster)
Hopkins, Marjorie 1911-1999 .... *9*
Hopkins, Mary R(ice) 1956- *97*
Hopkinson, Amanda 1948- *84*
Hopkinson, Deborah 1952- *159*
　Earlier sketches in SATA *76, 108*
Hoppe, Joanne 1932- *42*
Hoppe, Matthias 1952- *76*
Hopper, Nancy J. 1937- *38*
　Brief entry *35*
Hopping, Lorraine Jean
　See Egan, Lorraine Hopping
Horacek, Petr *163*
Horenstein, Henry 1947- *108*
Horgan, Paul (George Vincent O'Shaughnessy)
　1903-1995 .... *13*
　Obituary *84*
Horlak, E. E.
　See Tepper, Sheri S.
Horler, Sydney 1888-1954 .... *102*
Horn, Sandra Ann 1944- *154*
Hornblow, Arthur, Jr. 1893-1976 .... *15*
Hornblow, Leonora 1920-2005 .... *18*
Hornblow, Leonora Schinasi
　See Hornblow, Leonora
Horne, Constance 1927- *149*
Horne, Richard Henry Hengist 1802(?)-1884
　.. *29*
Horner, Althea (Jane) 1926- *36*
Horner, Dave 1934- *12*
Horner, Jack
　See Horner, John R(obert)
Horner, John R(obert) 1946- *106*
Hornik, Laurie Miller *159*
Horniman, Joanne 1951- *167*
　Earlier sketch in SATA *98*
Hornos, Axel 1907-1994 .... *20*
Hornstein, Reuben Aaron 1912- *64*
Horowitz, Anthony 1955- *137*
Horowitz, Ruth 1957- *136*
Horrocks, Anita 1958- *169*
Horse, Harry 1960- *169*
　Earlier sketch in SATA *111*
Horse, Richard George Anthony
　See Horse, Harry

Horsfield, Alan 1939- *153*
Horton, Madelyn (Stacey) 1962- *77*
Horvath, Betty 1927- *4*
Horvath, Polly 1957- *140*
　Earlier sketch in SATA *85*
　See also CLR *90*
Horwich, Frances R(appaport) 1908-2001 .. *11*
　Obituary *130*
Horwitz, Elinor Lander *45*
　Brief entry *33*
Horwood, William 1944- *85*
Hosford, Dorothy (Grant) 1900-1952 .... *22*
Hosford, Jessie 1892-1990 .... *5*
Hoshi, Shin'ichi 1926- *101*
Hoskyns-Abrahall, Clare (Constance
　Drury) *13*
Hossack, Sylvia 1939- *83*
Hossack, Sylvie Adams
　See Hossack, Sylvia
Hosseini, Khaled 1965- *156*
Hossell, Karen Price
　See Price, Karen
Hostetler, Marian 1932- *91*
Houck, Carter 1924- *22*
Hough, (Helen) Charlotte 1924- *9*
Hough, Judy Taylor 1932- *63*
　Brief entry *51*
　Earlier sketch in SATA *56*
Hough, Richard (Alexander) 1922-1999 ..... *17*
Houghton, Eric 1930- *7*
Houk, Randy 1944- *97*
Houlehen, Robert J. 1918- *18*
Household, Geoffrey (Edward West)
　1900-1988 .... *14*
　Obituary *59*
Housman, Laurence 1865-1959 .... *25*
Houston, Dick 1943- *74*
Houston, Gloria *138*
　Autobiography Feature *138*
　Earlier sketch in SATA *81*
Houston, James A(rchibald) 1921-2005 ...... *74*
　Obituary *163*
　Earlier sketch in SATA *13*
　See also CLR *3*
　See also SAAS *17*
Houston, James D. 1933- *78*
Houston, Jeanne Toyo Wakatsuki
　See Houston, Jeanne Wakatsuki
Houston, Jeanne Wakatsuki 1934- *168*
　Autobiography Feature *168*
　Earlier sketch in SATA *78*
Houston, Juanita C. 1921- *129*
Houton, Kathleen
　See Kilgore, Kathleen
Houts, Amy E. *164*
Hovey, Kate *158*
Howard, Alan 1922- *45*
Howard, Alyssa
　See Buckholtz, Eileen (Garber)
　and Glick, Ruth (Burtnick)
　and Titchener, Louise
Howard, Arthur 1948- *165*
Howard, Arthur Charles
　See Howard, Arthur
Howard, Elizabeth Fitzgerald 1927- *119*
　Earlier sketch in SATA *74*
Howard, Ellen 1943- *99*
　Earlier sketch in SATA *67*
Howard, Jane R(uble) 1924- *87*
Howard, Norman Barry 1949- *90*
Howard, P. M.
　See Howard, Pauline Rodriguez
Howard, Paul 1967- *118*
Howard, Pauline Rodriguez 1951- *124*
Howard, Prosper
　See Hamilton, Charles (Harold St. John)
Howard, Robert West 1908-1988 .... *5*
Howard, Todd 1964- *135*
Howard, Tristan
　See Currie, Stephen

Howard, Vernon (Linwood) 1918-1992 ...... *40*
　Obituary *73*
Howard, Warren F.
　See Pohl, Frederik
Howarth, David (Armine) 1912-1991 .... *6*
　Obituary *68*
Howarth, Lesley 1952- *94*
Howe, Deborah 1946-1978 .... *29*
Howe, James 1946- *161*
　Earlier sketches in SATA *29, 71, 111*
　See also CLR *9*
Howe, John F. 1957- *79*
Howe, Norma 1930- *126*
Howell, Pat 1947- *15*
Howell, S.
　See Styles, (Frank) Showell
Howell, Virginia
　See Ellison, Virginia H(owell)
Howes, Barbara 1914-1996 .... *5*
Howie, Diana (Melson) 1945- *122*
Howker, Janni 1957- *72*
　Brief entry *46*
　See also CLR *14*
　See also SAAS *13*
Howland, Ethan 1963- *131*
Hoy, Linda 1946- *65*
Hoy, Nina
　See Roth, Arthur J(oseph)
Hoyle, Geoffrey 1942- *18*
Hoyt, Edwin P(almer), Jr. 1923- *28*
Hoyt, Erich 1950- *140*
　Earlier sketch in SATA *65*
Hoyt, Olga
　See Gruhzit-Hoyt, Olga (Margaret)
Hrdlitschka, Shelley 1956- *167*
　Earlier sketch in SATA *111*
Hrdlitschka, Shelley Joanne
　See Hrdlitschka, Shelley
Htin Aung, U.
　See Aung, (Maung) Htin
Huang, Benrei 1959- *86*
Hubalek, Linda K. 1954- *111*
Hubbard, Michelle Calabro 1953- *122*
Hubbard, Patricia 1945- *124*
Hubbard, Woodleigh Marx *160*
　Earlier sketch in SATA *98*
Hubbell, Patricia 1928- *132*
　Earlier sketch in SATA *8*
Hubley, Faith Elliot 1924-2001 .... *48*
　Obituary *133*
Hubley, John 1914-1977 .... *48*
　Obituary *24*
Huck, Charlotte S. 1922- *136*
　Earlier sketch in SATA *82*
Hudak, Michal 1956- *143*
Hudson, Cheryl Willis 1948- *160*
　Earlier sketch in SATA *81*
Hudson, Jan 1954-1990 .... *77*
　See also CLR *40*
Hudson, Jeffrey
　See Crichton, (John) Michael
Hudson, (Margaret) Kirsty 1947- *32*
Hudson, Margaret
　See Shuter, Jane (Margaret)
Hudson, W(illiam) H(enry) 1841-1922 .... *35*
Hudson, Wade 1946- *162*
　Earlier sketch in SATA *74*
Huelsmann, Eva 1928- *16*
Huff, Barbara A. 1929- *67*
Huff, T. S.
　See Huff, Tanya (Sue)
Huff, Tanya (Sue) 1957- *85*
Huff, Vivian 1948- *59*
Huffaker, Sandy 1943- *10*
Huffman, Tom *24*
Huggins, Nathan Irvin 1927-1989 .... *63*
Hughes, Carol 1955- *108*
Hughes, Dean 1943- *139*
　Earlier sketches in SATA *33, 77*
　See also CLR *76*

Hughes, Eden
    See Butterworth, W.E.
Hughes, Edward James
    See Hughes, Ted
Hughes, (James Mercer) Langston 1902-1967
    33
    Earlier sketch in SATA *4*
    See also CLR *17*
Hughes, Libby 71
Hughes, Matilda
    See MacLeod, Charlotte (Matilda)
Hughes, Monica 1925-2003 162
    Earlier sketches in SATA *15, 70, 119*
    See also CLR *60*
    See also SAAS *11*
Hughes, Monica Ince
    See Hughes, Monica
Hughes, Richard (Arthur Warren) 1900-1976
    8
    Obituary 25
Hughes, Sara
    See Saunders, Susan
Hughes, Shirley 1927- 159
    Earlier sketches in SATA *16, 70, 110*
    See also CLR *15*
Hughes, Ted 1930-1998 49
    Brief entry 27
    Obituary 107
    See also CLR *3*
    See Hughes, Edward James
Hughes, Thomas 1822-1896 31
Hughes, Virginia
    See Campbell, Hope
Hughes, Walter (Llewellyn) 1910-1993 26
Hughey, Roberta 1942- 61
Hugo, Pierre Brackers de
    See Brackers de Hugo, Pierre
Hugo, Victor (Marie) 1802-1885 47
Huline-Dickens, Frank William 1931- 34
Hull, Eleanor (Means) 1913- 21
Hull, Eric Traviss
    See Harnan, Terry
Hull, H. Braxton
    See Jacobs, Helen Hull
Hull, Jesse Redding
    See Hull, Jessie Redding
Hull, Jessie Redding 1932- 51
Hull, Katharine 1921-1977 23
Hull, Lise (E.) 1954- 148
Hull, Maureen 1949- 142
Hulme, Joy N. 1922- 161
    Earlier sketches in SATA *74, 112*
Hults, Dorothy Niebrugge 1898-2000 6
Humble, Richard 1945- 60
Hume, Lotta Carswell 7
Hume, Ruth Fox 1922-1980 26
    Obituary 22
Hume, Stephen Eaton 1947- 136
Hummel, Berta 1909-1946 43
Hummel, Sister Maria Innocentia
    See Hummel, Berta
Humphrey, Carol Sue 1956- 167
Humphrey, Henry (III) 1930- 16
Humphrey, Kate
    See Forsyth, Kate
Humphrey, Sandra McLeod 1936- 95
Humphreys, Martha 1943- 71
Humphreys, Susan L.
    See Lowell, Susan
Hundal, Nancy 1957- 128
Huneck, Stephen 1949- 129
Hungerford, Hesba Fay
    See Brinsmead, H(esba) F(ay)
Hungerford, Pixie
    See Brinsmead, H(esba) F(ay)
Hunkin, Timothy Mark Trelawney 1950- ... 53
Hunt, Angela Elwell 1957- 159
    Earlier sketch in SATA *75*
Hunt, Francesca
    See Holland, Isabelle (Christian)

Hunt, Irene 1907-2001 91
    Earlier sketch in SATA *2*
    See also CLR *1*
Hunt, Janie Louise 1963- 102
Hunt, Jonathan 1966- 84
Hunt, Joyce 1927- 31
Hunt, Linda 1940- 39
Hunt, Lisa B(ehnke) 1967- 84
Hunt, Mabel Leigh 1892-1971 1
    Obituary 26
Hunt, Morton M(agill) 1920- 22
Hunt, Nigel
    See Greenbank, Anthony Hunt
Hunt, Peter (Leonard) 1945- 76
Hunter, Anne B. 1966- 118
Hunter, Bernice Thurman 1922-2002 85
    Brief entry 45
Hunter, Bobbi Dooley 1945- 89
Hunter, Captain Marcy
    See Ellis, Edward S(ylvester)
Hunter, Chris
    See Fluke, Joanne
Hunter, Clingham M.D.
    See Adams, William Taylor
Hunter, Dawe
    See Downie, Mary Alice (Dawe)
Hunter, Edith Fisher 1919- 31
Hunter, Evan 1926-2005 25
    Obituary 167
    See McBain, Ed
Hunter, George E.
    See Ellis, Edward S(ylvester)
Hunter, Hilda 1921- 7
Hunter, Jim 1939- 65
Hunter, Kristin
    See Lattany, Kristin (Elaine Eggleston) Hunter
Hunter, Leigh
    See Etchison, Birdie L(ee)
Hunter, Lieutenant Ned
    See Ellis, Edward S(ylvester)
Hunter, Mel 1927-2004 39
Hunter, Mollie 1922- 139
    Autobiography Feature 139
    Earlier sketches in SATA *54, 106*
    See also CLR *25*
    See also SAAS *7*
    See McIlwraith, Maureen Mollie Hunter
Hunter, Ned
    See Ellis, Edward S(ylvester)
Hunter, Norman (George Lorimer) 1899-1995
    84
    Earlier sketch in SATA *26*
Hunter, Ryan Ann
    See Greenwood, Pamela D.
    and Macalaster, Elizabeth G.
Hunter, Sara Hoagland 1954- 98
Hunter Blair, Pauline 3
    See Clarke, Pauline
Huntington, Amy 1956- 138
Huntington, Geoffrey 145
Huntington, Harriet E(lizabeth) 1909- 1
Huntsberry, William E(mery) 1916- 5
Hurd, Clement (G.) 1908-1988 64
    Obituary 54
    Earlier sketch in SATA *2*
    See also CLR *49*
Hurd, Edith Thacher 1910-1997 64
    Obituary 95
    Earlier sketch in SATA *2*
    See also CLR *49*
    See also SAAS *13*
Hurd, (John) Thacher 1949- 94
    Autobiography Feature 123
    Brief entry 45
    Earlier sketch in SATA *46*
Hurlimann, Bettina 39
    Obituary 34
    See Huerlimann, Bettina
Hurlimann, Ruth 32
    Brief entry 31
    See Huerlimann, Ruth

Hurmence, Belinda 1921- 77
    See also CLR *25*
    See also SAAS *20*
Hurst, Carol Otis 1933- 130
Hurt-Newton, Tania 1968- 84
Hurwitz, Johanna 1937- 113
    Earlier sketches in SATA *20, 71*
    See also SAAS *18*
Hurwood, Bernhardt J. 1926-1987 12
    Obituary 50
Husain, Shahrukh 1950- 108
Huser, Glen 1943- 151
Hutchens, Paul 1902-1977 31
Hutchins, Carleen Maley 1911- 9
Hutchins, Hazel J. 1952- 135
    Brief entry 51
    Earlier sketch in SATA *81*
    See also SAAS *24*
Hutchins, Pat 1942- 111
    Earlier sketches in SATA *15, 70*
    See also CLR *20*
    See also SAAS *16*
Hutchins, Ross Elliott 1906- 4
Hutchison, Linda 1942- 152
Huthmacher, J. Joseph 1929- 5
Hutto, Nelson (Allen) 1904-1985 20
Hutton, Kathryn 1915- 89
Hutton, Warwick 1939-1994 20
    Obituary 83
    See also SAAS *17*
Huxley, Aldous (Leonard) 1894-1963 63
Huxley, Elspeth (Josceline Grant) 1907-1997
    62
    Obituary 95
Hyde, Catherine R(yan) 1955- 141
Hyde, Dayton O(gden) 9
Hyde, Hawk
    See Hyde, Dayton O(gden)
Hyde, Margaret O(ldroyd) 1917- 139
    Earlier sketches in SATA *1, 42, 76*
    See also CLR *23*
    See also SAAS *8*
Hyde, Shelley
    See Reed, Kit
Hyde, Wayne Frederick 1922- 7
Hylander, Clarence J(ohn) 1897-1964 7
Hyman, Robin P(hilip) 1931- 12
Hyman, Trina Schart 1939-2004 95
    Obituary 158
    Earlier sketches in SATA *7, 46*
    See also CLR *50*
Hymes, Lucia M(anley) 1907-1998 7
Hyndman, Jane Andrews Lee 1912-1978 ... 46
    Obituary 23
    Earlier sketch in SATA *1*
Hyndman, Robert Utley 1906-1973 18
Hynes, Pat 98

I

Iannone, Jeanne 7
    See Balzano, Jeanne (Koppel)
Ibbitson, John Perrie 1955- 102
Ibbotson, Eva 1925- 156
    Earlier sketches in SATA *13, 103*
Ibbotson, M. C(hristine) 1930- 5
Icenoggle, Jodi 1967- 168
Icenoggle, Jodi O.
    See Icenoggle, Jodi
Ichikawa, Satomi 1949- 146
    Brief entry 36
    Earlier sketches in SATA *47, 78*
    See also CLR *62*
Ignoffo, Matthew 1945- 92
Igus, Toyomi 1953- 112
    Earlier sketch in SATA *76*
Ihimaera, Witi (Tame) 1944- 148
Ikeda, Daisaku 1928- 77
Ilowite, Sheldon A. 1931- 27

Ilsley, Velma (Elizabeth) 1918- *12*
Imai, Miko 1963- *90*
Imershein, Betsy 1953- *62*
Immel, Mary Blair 1930- *28*
Immell, Myra H. 1941- *92*
Impey, Rose 1947- *152*
  Earlier sketch in SATA *69*
Ingelow, Jean 1820-1897 .... *33*
Ingermanson, Randall (Scott) 1958- *134*
Ingersoll, Norman 1928- *79*
Ingham, Colonel Frederic
  See Hale, Edward Everett
Ingman, Bruce 1963- *134*
Ingman, Nicholas 1948- *52*
Ingold, Jeanette *128*
Ingpen, Robert 1936- *166*
  Earlier sketch in SATA *109*
Ingpen, Robert Roger
  See Ingpen, Robert
Ingraham, Erick 1950- *145*
Ingraham, Leonard W(illiam) 1913-2003 ..... *4*
Ingram, Scott 1948- *167*
  Earlier sketch in SATA *92*
Ingram, W. Scott
  See Ingram, Scott
Ingrams, Doreen 1906-1997 .... *97*
  Earlier sketch in SATA *20*
Ingrid, Charles
  See Salsitz, Rhondi Vilott
Ingves, Gunilla (Anna Maria Folkesdotter)
  1939- *101*
Inkpen, Mick 1952- *154*
  Earlier sketch in SATA *99*
Innes, (Ralph) Hammond
  See Hammond Innes, Ralph
Innes, Ralph Hammond
  See Hammond Innes, Ralph
Innocenti, Roberto 1940- *159*
  Earlier sketch in SATA *96*
  See also CLR *56*
Inyart, Gene *6*
  See Namovicz, Gene Inyart
Ionesco, Eugene 1912-1994 .... *7*
  Obituary *79*
Ipcar, Dahlov (Zorach) 1917- *147*
  Autobiography Feature *147*
  Earlier sketches in SATA *1, 49*
  See also SAAS *8*
Ireland, Karin *151*
  Earlier sketch in SATA *101*
Ironside, Jetske 1940- *60*
Irvin, Fred 1914- *15*
Irvine, Georgeanne 1955- *72*
Irvine, Joan 1951- *80*
Irving, Alexander
  See Hume, Ruth Fox
Irving, Robert
  See Adler, Irving
Irving, Washington 1783-1859
  See YABC *2*
  See also CLR *97*
Irwin, Ann(abelle Bowen) 1915-1998 .... *89*
  Brief entry *38*
  Obituary *106*
  Earlier sketch in SATA *44*
  See also CLR *40*
  See Irwin, Hadley
Irwin, Constance (H.) Frick 1913-1995 .... *6*
Irwin, Hadley
  See CLR *40*
  See also SAAS *14*
  See Hadley, Lee
  and Irwin, Ann(abelle Bowen)
Irwin, Keith Gordon 1885-1964 .... *11*
Isaac, Joanne 1934- *21*
Isaacs, Anne 1949- *90*
Isaacs, Jacob
  See Kranzler, George G(ershon)
Isaacson, Philip M(arshal) 1924- *87*

Isadora, Rachel 1953(?)- *165*
  Brief entry *32*
  Earlier sketches in SATA *54, 79, 121*
  See also CLR *7*
Isbell, Rebecca T(emple) 1942- *125*
Isham, Charlotte H(ickock) 1912- *21*
Ish-Kishor, Judith 1892-1972 .... *11*
Ish-Kishor, Sulamith 1896-1977 .... *17*
Ishmael, Woodi 1914-1995 .... *31*
  Obituary *109*
Isle, Sue 1963- *105*
Israel, Elaine 1945- *12*
Iterson, S(iny) R(ose) Van
  See Van Iterson, S(iny) R(ose)
Ivanko, John D(uane) 1966- *111*
Iverson, Carol (L.) 1941- *145*
Iverson, Diane 1950- *122*
Iverson, Eric G.
  See Turtledove, Harry
Ivery, Martha M. 1948- *124*
Ives, Morgan
  See Bradley, Marion Zimmer
Iwamatsu, Jun Atsushi 1908-1994 .... *81*
  Earlier sketch in SATA *14*
  See Yashima, Taro
Iwasaki (Matsumoto), Chihiro 1918-1974
  See CLR *18*

J

Jac, Lee
  See Morton, Lee Jack, Jr.
Jacka, Martin 1943- *72*
Jackson, Alison 1953- *160*
  Earlier sketches in SATA *73, 108*
Jackson, C(aary) Paul 1902-1991 .... *6*
Jackson, Caary
  See Jackson, C(aary) Paul
Jackson, Dave
  See Jackson, J. David
Jackson, Ellen B. 1943- *167*
  Earlier sketches in SATA *75, 115*
Jackson, Garnet Nelson 1944- *87*
Jackson, Gina
  See Fluke, Joanne
Jackson, Guida M. 1930- *71*
Jackson, J. David 1944- *91*
Jackson, Jacqueline 1928- *65*
Jackson, Jacqueline Dougan
  See Jackson, Jacqueline
Jackson, Jesse 1908-1983 .... *29*
  Obituary *48*
  Earlier sketch in SATA *2*
  See also CLR *28*
Jackson, Marjorie 1928- *127*
Jackson, Melanie 1956- *141*
Jackson, Mike 1946- *91*
Jackson, Neta J. 1944- *91*
Jackson, O. B.
  See Jackson, C(aary) Paul
Jackson, Robert B(lake) 1926- *8*
Jackson, Sally
  See Kellogg, Jean (Defrees)
Jackson, Shirley 1919-1965 .... *2*
Jackson, Woody 1948- *92*
Jacob, Helen Pierce 1927- *21*
Jacobs, Flora Gill 1918- *5*
Jacobs, Francine 1935- *150*
  Brief entry *42*
  Earlier sketch in SATA *43*
Jacobs, Frank 1929- *30*
Jacobs, Helen Hull 1908-1997 .... *12*
Jacobs, Joseph 1854-1916 .... *25*
Jacobs, Judy 1952- *69*
Jacobs, Laurie A. 1956- *89*
Jacobs, Leah
  See Gellis, Roberta (Leah Jacobs)
Jacobs, Leland Blair 1907-1992 .... *20*
  Obituary *71*

Jacobs, Linda
  See Altman, Linda Jacobs
Jacobs, Lou(is), Jr. 1921- *2*
Jacobs, Shannon K. 1947- *77*
Jacobs, Susan *30*
  See Quinn, Susan
Jacobs, William Jay 1933- *89*
  Earlier sketch in SATA *28*
Jacobson, Daniel 1923- *12*
Jacobson, Morris K(arl) 1906- *21*
Jacopetti, Alexandra *14*
  See Hart, Alexandra
Jacques, Brian 1939- *138*
  Earlier sketches in SATA *62, 95*
  See also CLR *21*
Jacques, Robin 1920-1995 .... *32*
  Brief entry *30*
  Obituary *86*
  See also SAAS *5*
Jaekel, Susan M. 1948- *89*
Jaffee, Al(lan) 1921- *66*
  Earlier sketch in SATA *37*
Jagendorf, Moritz (Adolf) 1888-1981 .... *2*
  Obituary *24*
Jahn, Michael
  See Jahn, (Joseph) Michael
Jahn, (Joseph) Michael 1943- *28*
Jahn, Mike
  See Jahn, (Joseph) Michael
Jahn-Clough, Lisa 1967- *152*
  Earlier sketch in SATA *88*
Jahsmann, Allan Hart 1916- *28*
Jakes, John (William) 1932- *62*
James, Andrew
  See Kirkup, James
James, Ann 1952- *168*
  Earlier sketches in SATA *82, 117*
James, Brian 1976- *140*
James, Bronte
  See Nash, Renea Denise
James, Captain Lew
  See Stratemeyer, Edward L.
James, Dynely
  See Mayne, William (James Carter)
James, Edwin
  See Gunn, James E(dwin)
James, Elizabeth 1942- *97*
  Earlier sketches in SATA *39, 45, 52*
James, Emily
  See Standiford, Natalie
James, Harry Clebourne 1896-1978 .... *11*
James, J. Alison 1962- *146*
  Earlier sketch in SATA *83*
James, Josephine
  See Sterne, Emma Gelders
James, Mary
  See Meaker, Marijane (Agnes)
James, Philip
  See del Rey, Lester
  and Moorcock, Michael
James, Robin (Irene) 1953- *50*
James, Tegan
  See Odgers, Sally Farrell
James, Will(iam Roderick) 1892-1942 .... *19*
Jameson, W. C. 1942- *93*
Jamieson, Ian R.
  See Goulart, Ron(ald Joseph)
Jamiolkowski, Raymond M. 1953- *81*
Jane, Mary Childs 1909- *6*
Jane, Pamela *158*
Janeczko, Paul B(ryan) 1945- *155*
  Earlier sketches in SATA *53, 98*
  See also CLR *47*
  See also SAAS *18*
Janes, Edward C. 1908- *25*
Janes, J(oseph) Robert 1935- *148*
  Brief entry *50*
  Earlier sketch in SATA *101*
Janeway, Elizabeth (Hall) 1913-2005 .... *19*
Janger, Kathleen N. 1940- *66*

Janice
  See Brustlein, Janice Tworkov
Janosch
  See CLR 26
  See Eckert, Horst
Janover, Caroline (Davis) 1943- *141*
  Earlier sketch in SATA *89*
Jansen, Jared
  See Cebulash, Mel
Janson, Dora Jane (Heineberg) 1916- *31*
Janson, H(orst) W(oldemar) 1913-1982 .... *9*
Jansson, Tove (Marika) 1914-2001 .... *41*
  Earlier sketch in SATA *3*
  See also CLR 2
Janus, Grete
  See Hertz, Grete Janus
Jaques, Faith 1923-1997 .... *97*
  Earlier sketches in SATA *21, 69*
Jaquith, Priscilla 1908- *51*
Jaramillo, Mari-Luci 1928- *139*
Jarman, Julia 1946- *133*
Jarman, Rosemary Hawley 1935- *7*
Jarrell, Mary Von Schrader 1914- *35*
Jarrell, Randall 1914-1965 .... *7*
  See also CLR *111*
Jarrett, Roxanne
  See Werner, Herma
Jarrow, Gail 1952- *84*
Jarvis, E. K.
  See Ellison, Harlan (Jay)
Jaskol, Julie 1958- *127*
Jasner, W. K.
  See Watson, Jane Werner
Jassem, Kate
  See Oppenheim, Joanne
Jauss, Anne Marie 1902(?)-1991 .... *10*
  Obituary *69*
Javernick, Ellen 1938- *89*
Jayne, Lieutenant R. H.
  See Ellis, Edward S(ylvester)
Jaynes, Clare
  See Mayer, Jane Rothschild
Jeake, Samuel, Jr.
  See Aiken, Conrad (Potter)
Jean-Bart, Leslie 1954- *121*
Jefferds, Vincent H(arris) 1916- *59*
  Brief entry *49*
Jefferies, (John) Richard 1848-1887 .... *16*
Jeffers, Susan 1942- *137*
  Earlier sketches in SATA *17, 70, 129*
  See also CLR *30*
Jefferson, Sarah
  See Farjeon, (Eve) Annabel
Jeffries, Roderic (Graeme) 1926- *4*
Jenkin-Pearce, Susie 1943- *80*
Jenkins, Debra Reid
  See Reid Jenkins, Debra
Jenkins, Emily 1967- *144*
Jenkins, Jean *98*
Jenkins, Jerry B(ruce) 1949- *149*
Jenkins, Marie M(agdalen) 1909- *7*
Jenkins, Patrick 1955- *72*
Jenkins, Steve 1952- *154*
Jenkins, William A(twell) 1922-1998 .... *9*
Jenkyns, Chris 1924- *51*
Jennings, Coleman A(lonzo) 1933- *64*
Jennings, Dana Andrew 1957- *93*
Jennings, Elizabeth (Joan) 1926-2001 .... *66*
Jennings, Gary (Gayne) 1928-1999 .... *9*
  Obituary *117*
Jennings, Patrick 1962- *160*
  Earlier sketch in SATA *96*
Jennings, Paul 1943- *165*
  Earlier sketch in SATA *88*
  See also CLR *40*
Jennings, Richard (W.) 1945- *136*
Jennings, Robert
  See Hamilton, Charles (Harold St. John)
Jennings, S. M.
  See Meyer, Jerome Sydney
Jennings, Sharon (Elizabeth) 1954- *95*

Jennison, C. S.
  See Starbird, Kaye
Jennison, Keith Warren 1911-1995 .... *14*
Jensen, Kathryn 1949- *81*
Jensen, Kristine Mary 1961- *78*
Jensen, Niels 1927- *25*
Jensen, Vickie (Dee) 1946- *81*
Jensen, Virginia Allen 1927- *8*
Jenson-Elliott, Cynthia L(ouise) 1962- *143*
Jeram, Anita 1965- *154*
  Earlier sketches in SATA *71, 102*
Jerman, Jerry 1949- *89*
Jernigan, E. Wesley 1940- *85*
Jernigan, Gisela (Evelyn) 1948- *85*
Jeschke, Susan 1942- *42*
  Brief entry *27*
Jessel, Camilla (Ruth) 1937- *143*
  Earlier sketch in SATA *29*
Jessey, Cornelia
  See Sussman, Cornelia Silver
Jewel
  See Kilcher, Jewel
Jewell, Nancy 1940- *109*
  Brief entry *41*
Jewett, Eleanore Myers 1890-1967 .... *5*
Jewett, (Theodora) Sarah Orne 1849-1909 . *15*
Jezard, Alison 1919- *57*
  Brief entry *34*
Jiang, Cheng An 1943- *109*
Jiang, Ji-li 1954- *101*
Jiang, Zheng An
  See Jiang, Cheng An
Jiler, John 1946- *42*
  Brief entry *35*
Jimenez, Francisco 1943- *108*
Jinks, Catherine 1963- *155*
  Earlier sketch in SATA *94*
Jobb, Jamie 1945- *29*
Jobling, Curtis *131*
Jocelyn, Ann Henning 1948- *92*
Jocelyn, Marthe 1956- *163*
  Earlier sketch in SATA *118*
Joerns, Consuelo *44*
  Brief entry *33*
Joey D
  See Macaulay, Teresa (E.)
Johansen, K(rista) V(ictoria) 1968- *129*
Johansson, Philip *163*
John, Joyce *59*
Johns, Avery
  See Cousins, Margaret
Johns, Elizabeth 1943- *88*
Johns, Janetta
  See Quin-Harkin, Janet
Johns, W(illiam) E(arle) 1893-1968 .... *55*
Johns, Captain W. E.
  See Johns, W(illiam) E(arle)
Johnson, A.
  See Johnson, Annabell (Jones)
Johnson, A. E.
  See Johnson, Annabell (Jones)
  and Johnson, Edgar (Raymond)
Johnson, Angela 1961- *150*
  Earlier sketches in SATA *69, 102*
  See also CLR 33
Johnson, Annabel
  See Johnson, Annabell (Jones)
Johnson, Annabell (Jones) 1921- *72*
  Earlier sketch in SATA *2*
  See Johnson, Annabel
Johnson, Art 1946- *123*
Johnson, Benjamin F., of Boone
  See Riley, James Whitcomb
Johnson, Bettye 1858-1919
  See Rogers, Bettye
Johnson, Caryn
  See Goldberg, Whoopi
Johnson, Caryn E.
  See Goldberg, Whoopi
Johnson, Charles R. 1925- *11*

Johnson, Charlotte Buel *46*
  See von Wodtke, Charlotte Buel Johnson
Johnson, Chuck
  See Johnson, Charles R.
Johnson, Crockett
  See CLR 98
  See Leisk, David (Johnson)
Johnson, D(onald) B. 1944- *146*
Johnson, D(ana) William 1945- *23*
Johnson, Daniel Shahid 1954- *73*
Johnson, Dinah *130*
  See Johnson, Dianne
Johnson, Dolores 1949- *69*
Johnson, Dorothy M(arie) 1905-1984 .... *6*
  Obituary *40*
Johnson, E(ugene) Harper *44*
Johnson, Edgar (Raymond) 1912-1990 .... *72*
  Earlier sketch in SATA *2*
Johnson, Elizabeth 1911-1984 .... *7*
  Obituary *39*
Johnson, Eric W(arner) 1918-1994 ....
  Obituary *82*
  Earlier sketch in SATA *8*
Johnson, Evelyne 1922- *20*
Johnson, Fred 19(?)-1982 .... *63*
Johnson, Gaylord 1884-1972 .... *7*
Johnson, Gerald White 1890-1980 .... *19*
  Obituary *28*
Johnson, Harper
  See Johnson, E(ugene) Harper
Johnson, James Ralph 1922- *1*
Johnson, James Weldon 1871-1938 .... *31*
  See also CLR 32
Johnson, Jane 1951- *48*
Johnson, Joan J. 1942- *59*
Johnson, John E(mil) 1929- *34*
Johnson, Johnny 1901-1995
  See Johnson, (Walter) Ryerson
Johnson, La Verne B(ravo) 1925- *13*
Johnson, Lee Kaiser 1962- *78*
Johnson, Lissa H(alls) 1955- *65*
Johnson, Lois Smith 1894-1993 .... *6*
Johnson, Lois Walfrid 1936- *130*
  Earlier sketches in SATA *22, 91*
Johnson, Margaret S(weet) 1893-1964 .... *35*
Johnson, Marguerite Annie
  See Angelou, Maya
Johnson, Meredith Merrell 1952- *104*
Johnson, Milton 1932- *31*
Johnson, Neil 1954- *135*
  Earlier sketch in SATA *73*
Johnson, Pamela 1949- *71*
Johnson, Patricia Polin 1956- *84*
Johnson, Paul Brett 1947- *132*
  Earlier sketch in SATA *83*
Johnson, Rebecca L. 1956- *147*
  Earlier sketch in SATA *67*
Johnson, Rick L. 1954- *79*
Johnson, (Walter) Ryerson 1901-1995 .... *10*
  Obituary *106*
  See Halliday, Brett
Johnson, Scott 1952- *119*
  Earlier sketch in SATA *76*
Johnson, Sherrie 1948- *87*
Johnson, Shirley K(ing) 1927- *10*
Johnson, Spencer 1938- *145*
  Brief entry *38*
Johnson, Stephen T. 1964- *141*
  Earlier sketch in SATA *84*
Johnson, Sue Kaiser 1963- *78*
Johnson, Sylvia A. *166*
  Brief entry *52*
  Earlier sketch in SATA *104*
Johnson, William R. *38*
Johnson, William Weber 1909-1992 .... *7*
Johnston, Agnes Christine
  See Dazey, Agnes J(ohnston)
Johnston, Annie Fellows 1863-1931 .... *37*
Johnston, Dorothy Grunbock 1915-1979 .... *54*
Johnston, Ginny 1946- *60*

Johnston, H(ugh) A(nthony) S(tephen)
1913-1967 .... *14*
Johnston, Janet 1944- *71*
Johnston, Johanna 1914(?)-1982 .... *12*
Obituary *33*
Johnston, Julie 1941- *110*
Autobiography Feature *128*
Earlier sketch in SATA *78*
See also CLR *41*
See also SAAS *24*
Johnston, Lynn (Beverley) 1947- *118*
Johnston, Norma *29*
See St. John, Nicole
Johnston, Portia
See Takakjian, Portia
Johnston, Susan Taylor 1942- *128*
Earlier sketch in SATA *83*
See Johnston, Tony
Johnston, Tim(othy Patrick) 1962- *146*
Johnston, Tony *8*
See Johnston, Susan Taylor
Joinson, Carla *160*
Jonas, Ann 1932- *135*
Brief entry *42*
Earlier sketch in SATA *50*
See also CLR *74*
Jonell, Lynne *109*
Jones, Adrienne 1915-2000 .... *82*
Earlier sketch in SATA *7*
See also SAAS *10*
Jones, Annabel
See Lewis, Mary (Christianna)
Jones, Betty Millsaps 1940- *54*
Jones, Carol 1942- *153*
Earlier sketch in SATA *79*
Jones, Charles M(artin) 1912-2002 .... *53*
Obituary *133*
See Jones, Chuck
Jones, Charlotte Foltz 1945- *122*
Earlier sketch in SATA *77*
Jones, Chuck
See Jones, Charles M(artin)
Jones, Constance 1961- *112*
Jones, Diana Wynne 1934- *160*
Earlier sketches in SATA *9, 70, 108*
See also CLR *23*
See also SAAS *7*
Jones, Douglas C(lyde) 1924-1998 .... *52*
Jones, Elizabeth McDavid *155*
Jones, Elizabeth Orton 1910-2005 .... *18*
Obituary *164*
Jones, Evan 1915-1996 .... *3*
Jones, Geraldine
See McCaughrean, Geraldine
Jones, Gillingham
See Hamilton, Charles (Harold St. John)
Jones, Gwyneth A(nn) 1952- *159*
Jones, Harold 1904-1992 .... *14*
Obituary *72*
Jones, Helen Hinckley 1903-1991 .... *26*
Jones, Hettie 1934- *42*
Brief entry *27*
Jones, Hortense P. 1918- *9*
Jones, J(on) Sydney 1948- *101*
Jones, Jennifer (Berry) 1947- *90*
Jones, John R(obert) 1926- *76*
Jones, Marcia Thornton 1958- *115*
Earlier sketch in SATA *73*
Jones, Martha T(annery) 1931- *130*
Jones, Mary Alice 1898(?)-1980 .... *6*
Jones, McClure *34*
Jones, Patrick 1961- *136*
Jones, Penelope 1938- *31*
Jones, Rebecca C(astaldi) 1947- *99*
Earlier sketch in SATA *33*
Jones, Robin D(orothy) 1959- *80*
Jones, Sanford W.
See Thorn, John
Jones, Terence Graham Parry 1942- *127*
See Jones, Terry
and Monty Python

Jones, Terry *67*
Brief entry *51*
See Jones, Terence Graham Parry
Jones, Tim(othy) Wynne
See Wynne-Jones, Tim(othy)
Jones, V(ictoria) M(ary) 1958- *147*
Jones, Veda Boyd 1948- *119*
Jones, Volcano
See Mitchell, Adrian
Jones, Weyman (B.) 1928- *4*
See also SAAS *11*
Jones, William Glynne
See Glynne-Jones, William
Jonk, Clarence 1906-1987 .... *10*
Jonsberg, Barry 1951- *168*
Joos, Francoise 1956- *78*
Joos, Frederic 1953- *78*
Joosse, Barbara M. 1949- *164*
Earlier sketches in SATA *52, 96*
Joosse, Barbara Monnot
See Joosse, Barbara M.
Jordan, Alexis Hill
See Glick, Ruth (Burtnick)
and Titchener, Louise
Jordan, Anne Devereaux 1943- *80*
Jordan, Don
See Howard, Vernon (Linwood)
Jordan, Hope Dahle 1905-1995 .... *15*
Jordan, Jael (Michal) 1949- *30*
Jordan, June (Meyer) 1936-2002 .... *136*
Earlier sketch in SATA *4*
See also CLR *10*
Jordan, Lee
See Scholefield, Alan
Jordan, Martin George 1944- *84*
Jordan, Robert
See Rigney, James Oliver, Jr.
Jordan, Sherryl 1949- *122*
Earlier sketch in SATA *71*
See also SAAS *23*
Jordan, Shirley 1930- *154*
Jordan, Tanis 1946- *84*
Jorgensen, Mary Venn -1995 .... *36*
Jorgensen, Norman 1954- *157*
Jorgenson, Ivar
See Silverberg, Robert
Joseph, Anne
See Coates, Anna
Joseph, James (Herz) 1924- *53*
Joseph, Joan 1939- *34*
Joseph, Joseph M(aron) 1903-1979 .... *22*
Joseph, Patrick
See O'Malley, Kevin
Josephs, Rebecca
See Talbot, Toby
Josh
See Clemens, Samuel Langhorne
Joshua, Peter
See Stone, Peter
Joslin, Sesyle *2*
See Hine, Sesyle Joslin
Joyce, Bill
See Joyce, William
Joyce, J(ames) Avery 1902-1987 .... *11*
Obituary *50*
Joyce, Peter 1937- *127*
Joyce, William 1957- *118*
Brief entry *46*
Earlier sketch in SATA *72*
See also CLR *26*
Joyner, Jerry 1938- *34*
Juby, Susan 1969- *156*
Jucker, Sita 1921- *5*
Judah, Aaron 1923- *118*
Judd, Cyril
See Kornbluth, C(yril) M.
and Merril, Judith
and Pohl, Frederik
Judd, Denis (O'Nan) 1938- *33*
Judd, Frances K. *1*
See Benson, Mildred (Augustine Wirt)

Jude, Conny *81*
Judson, Clara Ingram 1879-1960 .... *38*
Brief entry *27*
Judy, Stephen
See Tchudi, Stephen N.
Judy, Stephen N.
See Tchudi, Stephen N.
Jukes, Mavis 1947- *111*
Brief entry *43*
Earlier sketch in SATA *72*
See also SAAS *12*
Jules, Jacqueline 1956- *148*
Julian, Jane
See Wiseman, David
Jumpp, Hugo
See MacPeek, Walter G.
Jungman, Ann *165*
Jupo, Frank J. 1904-1981 .... *7*
Jurmain, Suzanne 1945- *169*
Earlier sketch in SATA *72*
Jurmain, Suzanne Tripp
See Jurmain, Suzanne
Juster, Norton 1929- *132*
Earlier sketch in SATA *3*
See also CLR *112*
Justus, May 1898-1989 .... *1*
Obituary *106*
Juvenilia
See Taylor, Ann

K

Kaaberbol, Lene
See Kaaberbol, Lene
Kaaberbol, Lene 1960- *159*
Kabdebo, Tamas
See Kabdebo, Thomas
Kabdebo, Thomas 1934- *10*
Kabibble, Osh
See Jobb, Jamie
Kacer, Kathy 1954- *142*
Kaczman, James *156*
Kadesch, Robert R(udstone) 1922- *31*
Kadohata, Cynthia (Lynn) 1956(?)- *155*
Kaempfert, Wade
See del Rey, Lester
Kaestner, Erich 1899-1974 .... *14*
See also CLR *4*
See Kastner, Erich
Kahl, Jonathan (D.) 1959- *77*
Kahl, M(arvin) P(hilip) 1934- *37*
Kahl, Virginia (Caroline) 1919-2004 .... *48*
Brief entry *38*
Obituary *158*
Kahn, Joan 1914-1994 .... *48*
Obituary *82*
Kahn, Katherine Janus 1942- *167*
Earlier sketch in SATA *90*
Kahn, Peggy
See Katz, Bobbi
Kahn, Roger 1927- *37*
Kahukiwa, Robyn 1940- *134*
Kains, Josephine
See Goulart, Ron(ald Joseph)
Kaizuki, Kiyonori 1950- *72*
Kakimoto, Kozo 1915- *11*
Kalashnikoff, Nicholas 1888-1961 .... *16*
Kalb, Jonah 1926- *23*
Kalbacken, Joan 1925- *96*
Kalechofsky, Roberta 1931- *92*
Kaler, James Otis 1848-1912 .... *15*
Kalish, Claire M. 1947- *92*
Kallen, Stuart A(rnold) 1955- *126*
Earlier sketch in SATA *86*
Kallevig, Christine Petrell 1955- *164*
Kalman, Bobbie 1947- *63*
Kalman, Maira 1949- *137*
Earlier sketch in SATA *96*
See also CLR *32*

Kalnay, Francis 1899-1992 .... *7*
Kaloustian, Rosanne 1955- *93*
Kalow, Gisela 1946- *32*
Kamen, Gloria 1923- *98*
Earlier sketch in SATA 9
Kamerman, Sylvia E.
See Burack, Sylvia K.
Kamm, Josephine (Hart) 1905-1989 .... *24*
Kammerman, Sylvia K.
See Burack, Sylvia K.
Kandel, Michael 1941- *93*
Kandell, Alice S. 1938- *35*
Kane, Bob 1916-1998 .... *120*
Kane, Henry Bugbee 1902-1971 .... *14*
Kane, L. A.
See Mannetti, Lisa
Kane, Robert W. 1910- *18*
Kane, Wilson
See Bloch, Robert (Albert)
Kanefield, Teri 1960- *135*
Kaner, Etta 1947- *126*
Kanetzke, Howard W(illiam) 1932- *38*
Kanoza, Muriel Canfield
See Canfield, Muriel
Kanzawa, Toshiko
See Furukawa, Toshi
Kaplan, Andrew 1960- *78*
Kaplan, Anne Bernays
See Bernays, Anne
Kaplan, Bess 1927- *22*
Kaplan, Boche 1926- *24*
Kaplan, Elizabeth (A.) 1956- *83*
Kaplan, Irma 1900- *10*
Kaplan, Jean Caryl Korn 1926- *10*
Kaplow, Robert 1954- *70*
Karageorge, Michael
See Anderson, Poul (William)
Karen, Ruth 1922-1987 .... *9*
Obituary *54*
Kark, Nina Mary 1925- *132*
Earlier sketch in SATA 4
See Bawden, Nina (Mary Mabey)
Karl, Herb 1938- *73*
Karl, Jean E(dna) 1927-2000 .... *122*
Earlier sketch in SATA 34
See also SAAS 10
Karlin, Bernie 1927- *68*
Karlin, Eugene 1918- *10*
Karlin, Nurit *103*
Earlier sketch in SATA 63
Karnes, Frances A. 1937- *110*
Karp, Naomi J. 1926- *16*
Karpinski, J. Rick
See Karpinski, John Eric
Karpinski, John Eric 1952- *81*
Karpinski, Rick
See Karpinski, John Eric
Karr, Kathleen 1946- *127*
Earlier sketch in SATA 82
Karr, Phyllis Ann 1944- *119*
Karwoski, Gail 1949- *127*
Karwoski, Gail Langer
See Karwoski, Gail
Kashiwagi, Isami 1925- *10*
Kassem, Lou 1931- *62*
Brief entry *51*
Kastel, Warren
See Silverberg, Robert
Kastner, Erich
See Kaestner, Erich
Kastner, Jill (Marie) 1964- *117*
Earlier sketch in SATA 70
Kasuya, Masahiro 1937- *51*
Kasza, Keiko 1951- *124*
Kataphusin
See Ruskin, John
Katchen, Carole 1944- *9*
Kathryn
See Searle, Kathryn Adrienne
Katona, Robert 1949- *21*

Katsarakis, Joan Harries
See Harries, Joan
Katz, Avner 1939- *103*
Katz, Bobbi 1933- *12*
Katz, Fred(eric Phillip) 1938- *6*
Katz, Jane B(resler) 1934- *33*
Katz, Karen 1947- *158*
Katz, Marjorie P.
See Weiser, Marjorie P(hillis) K(atz)
Katz, Susan 1945- *156*
Katz, Welwyn Wilton 1948- *96*
Autobiography Feature *118*
Earlier sketch in SATA 62
See also CLR 45
Katz, William 1940- *98*
Katz, William Loren 1927- *13*
Kaufman, Bel *57*
Kaufman, Jeff 1955- *84*
Kaufman, Joe 1911-2001 .... *33*
Kaufman, Joseph
See Kaufman, Joe
Kaufman, Mervyn D. 1932- *4*
Kaufmann, Angelika 1935- *15*
Kaufmann, John 1931- *18*
Kaula, Edna Mason 1906-1987 .... *13*
Kaur Khalsa, Dayal
See Khalsa, Dayal Kaur
Kavaler, Lucy 1930- *23*
Kavanagh, Jack 1920- *85*
Kavanagh, P(atrick) J(oseph Gregory) 1931-
.... *122*
Kavanaugh, Ian
See Webb, Jean Francis (III)
Kay, Alan N. 1965- *144*
Kay, Elizabeth 1949- *165*
Kay, Guy Gavriel 1954- *167*
Earlier sketch in SATA 121
Kay, Helen
See Goldfrank, Helen Colodny
Kay, Jackie 1961- *165*
Earlier sketch in SATA 97
Kay, Jacqueline Margaret
See Kay, Jackie
Kay, Mara *13*
Kay, Verla 1946- *120*
Kaye, Geraldine (Hughesdon) 1925- *85*
Earlier sketch in SATA 10
Kaye, Judy
See Baer, Judy
Kaye, M(ary) M(argaret) 1908-2004 .... *62*
Obituary *152*
Kaye, Marilyn 1949- *110*
Earlier sketch in SATA 56
Kaye, Mollie
See Kaye, M(ary) M(argaret)
Kaye, Peggy 1948- *143*
Keach, James P. 1950- *125*
Keams, Geri 1951- *117*
Keane, Bil 1922- *4*
Keaney, Brian 1954- *106*
Kearny, Jillian
See Goulart, Ron(ald Joseph)
Keating, Bern
See Keating, Leo Bernard
Keating, Frank 1944- *143*
Keating, Lawrence A. 1903-1966 .... *23*
Keating, Leo Bernard 1915- *10*
Keats, Emma 1899(?)-1979(?) *68*
Keats, Ezra Jack 1916-1983 .... *57*
Obituary *34*
Earlier sketch in SATA 14
See also CLR 35
Keefer, Catherine
See Ogan, George F.
and Ogan, Margaret E. (Nettles)
Keefer, Janice Kulyk *132*
See Kulyk Keefer, Janice
Keegan, Marcia 1943- *104*
Earlier sketch in SATA 9
Keehn, Sally M. 1947- *165*
Earlier sketch in SATA 87

Keel, Frank
See Keeler, Ronald F(ranklin)
Keeler, Ronald F(ranklin) 1913-1983 .... *47*
Keely, Jack 1951- *119*
Keen, Martin L. 1913-1992 .... *4*
Keenan, Sheila 1953- *95*
Keene, Ann T(odd) 1940- *86*
Keene, Carolyn *100*
Earlier sketch in SATA 65
See Benson, Mildred (Augustine Wirt)
and Goulart, Ron(ald Joseph)
and McFarlane, Leslie (Charles)
and Stanley, George Edward
and Stratemeyer, Edward L.
Keens-Douglas, Richardo 1953- *154*
Earlier sketch in SATA 95
Keep, Linda Lowery
See Lowery, Linda
Keeping, Charles (William James) 1924-1988
.... *69*
Obituary *56*
Earlier sketch in SATA 9
See also CLR 34
Keeshan, Robert J. 1927-2004 .... *32*
Obituary *151*
Kehret, Peg 1936- *149*
Autobiography Feature *149*
Earlier sketches in SATA 73, 108
Keillor, Garrison 1942- *58*
Keillor, Gary Edward
See Keillor, Garrison
Keir, Christine
See Pullein-Thompson, Christine
Keister, Douglas 1948- *88*
Keith, Doug 1952- *81*
Keith, Eros 1942- *52*
Keith, Hal 1934- *36*
Keith, Harold (Verne) 1903-1998 .... *74*
Earlier sketch in SATA 2
Keith, Robert
See Applebaum, Stan
Keleinikov, Andrei 1924- *65*
Kelemen, Julie 1959- *78*
Kelen, Emery 1896-1978 .... *13*
Obituary *26*
Kelleam, Joseph E(veridge) 1913-1975 ...... *31*
Kelleher, Anne 1959- *97*
Kelleher, Annette 1950- *122*
Kelleher, Daria Valerian 1955- *79*
Kelleher, Victor (Michael Kitchener) 1939-
.... *129*
Brief entry *52*
Earlier sketch in SATA 75
See also CLR 36
Keller, Beverly L(ou) *91*
Earlier sketch in SATA 13
Keller, Charles 1942- *82*
Earlier sketch in SATA 8
Keller, Debra 1958- *94*
Keller, Dick 1923- *36*
Keller, Emily *96*
Keller, Gail Faithfull
See Faithfull, Gail
Keller, Holly 1942- *157*
Brief entry *42*
Earlier sketches in SATA 76, 108
See also CLR 45
Keller, Irene (Barron) 1927-2002 .... *36*
Obituary *139*
Kelley, Leo P(atrick) 1928- *32*
Brief entry *31*
Kelley, Patrick (G.) 1963- *129*
Kelley, Patte 1947- *93*
Kelley, True (Adelaide) 1946- *130*
Brief entry *39*
Earlier sketches in SATA 41, 92
Kellin, Sally Moffet 1932- *9*
Kelling, Furn L. 1914-2000 .... *37*
Kellogg, Gene
See Kellogg, Jean (Defrees)
Kellogg, Jean (Defrees) 1916-1978 .... *10*

Kellogg, Steven (Castle) 1941- *130*
  Earlier sketches in SATA *8, 57*
  See also CLR *6*
Kellow, Kathleen
  See Hibbert, Eleanor Alice Burford
Kelly, Clint 1950- *140*
Kelly, Eric P(hilbrook) 1884-1960
  See YABC *1*
Kelly, Fiona
  See Coleman, Michael (Lee)
  and Oldfield, Jenny
  and Welford, Sue
Kelly, Irene 1957- *147*
Kelly, Jeff
  See Kelly, Jeffrey
Kelly, Jeffrey 1946- *65*
Kelly, Joanne (W.) 1934- *87*
Kelly, Kate 1958- *91*
Kelly, Kathleen M. 1964- *71*
Kelly, Katy 1955- *169*
Kelly, Lauren
  See Oates, Joyce Carol
Kelly, Laurene 1954- *123*
Kelly, Martha Rose 1914-1983 .... *37*
Kelly, Marty
  See Kelly, Martha Rose
Kelly, Mij *166*
Kelly, Ralph
  See Geis, Darlene Stern
Kelly, Regina Z(immerman) 1898-1986 .... *5*
Kelly, Rosalie (Ruth) *43*
Kelly, Walt(er Crawford) 1913-1973 .... *18*
Kelsey, Alice Geer 1896-1982 .... *1*
Kelsey, Elin *159*
Kemnitz, Thomas Milton, Jr. 1984- *152*
Kemnitz, Tom, Jr.
  See Kemnitz, Thomas Milton, Jr.
Kemp, Gene 1926- *75*
  Earlier sketch in SATA *25*
  See also CLR *29*
Kempner, Mary Jean 1913-1969 .... *10*
Kempton, Jean Welch 1914- *10*
Kenda, Margaret 1942- *71*
Kendall, Carol (Seeger) 1917- *74*
  Earlier sketch in SATA *11*
  See also SAAS *7*
Kendall, Katherine
  See Applegate, Katherine (Alice)
Kendall, Lace
  See Stoutenburg, Adrien (Pearl)
Kendall, Martha E. *87*
Kendall, Russ 1957- *83*
Kenealy, James P. 1927- *52*
  Brief entry *29*
Kenealy, Jim
  See Kenealy, James P.
Kennaway, Adrienne 1945- *60*
Kennedy, Brendan 1970- *57*
Kennedy, Dana Forrest 1917- *74*
Kennedy, Dorothy M(intzlaff) 1931- *53*
Kennedy, Doug(las) 1963- *122*
Kennedy, John Fitzgerald 1917-1963 .... *11*
Kennedy, Joseph Charles 1929- *130*
  Autobiography Feature *130*
  Earlier sketches in SATA *14, 86*
  See Kennedy, X. J.
Kennedy, Pamela (J.) 1946- *87*
Kennedy, Paul E(dward) 1929- *113*
  Earlier sketch in SATA *33*
Kennedy, (Jerome) Richard 1932- *22*
Kennedy, Robert 1938- *63*
Kennedy, T(eresa) A. 1953- *42*
  Brief entry *35*
Kennedy, Teresa
  See Kennedy, T(eresa) A.
Kennedy, William (Joseph) 1928- *57*
Kennedy, X. J.
  See CLR *27*
  See also SAAS *22*
  See Kennedy, Joseph Charles

Kennell, Ruth Epperson 1893-1977 .... *6*
  Obituary *25*
Kennemore, Tim 1957- *133*
Kennett, David 1959- *121*
Kenny, Herbert Andrew 1912-2002 .... *13*
Kenny, Kathryn
  See Bowden, Joan Chase
  and Krull, Kathleen
  and Sanderlin, Owenita (Harrah)
  and Stack, Nicolete Meredith
Kenny, Kevin
  See Krull, Kathleen
Kensinger, George
  See Fichter, George S.
Kensington, Kathryn Wesley
  See Rusch, Kristine Kathryn
Kent, Alexander
  See Reeman, Douglas Edward
Kent, David
  See Lambert, David (Compton)
Kent, Deborah Ann 1948- *155*
  Brief entry *41*
  Earlier sketches in SATA *47, 104*
Kent, Jack
  See Kent, John Wellington
Kent, John Wellington 1920-1985 .... *24*
  Obituary *45*
Kent, Lisa 1942- *90*
Kent, Mallory
  See Lowndes, Robert A(ugustine) W(ard)
Kent, Margaret 1894- *2*
Kent, Rockwell 1882-1971 .... *6*
Kent, Sherman 1903-1986 .... *20*
  Obituary *47*
Kenward, Jean 1920- *42*
Kenworthy, Leonard S. 1912-1991 .... *6*
Kenyon, Karen (Smith) 1938- *145*
Kenyon, Kate
  See Adorjan, Carol (Madden)
  and Ransom, Candice F.
Kenyon, Ley 1913-1990 .... *6*
Keown, Elizabeth *78*
Kepes, Juliet A(ppleby) 1919-1999 .... *13*
Kerby, Mona 1951- *75*
Kerigan, Florence 1896-1984 .... *12*
Kerley, Barbara 1960- *138*
Kerman, Gertrude
  See Furman, Gertrude Lerner Kerman
Kerns, Thelma 1929- *116*
Kerr, Bob 1951- *120*
Kerr, Jessica 1901-1991 .... *13*
Kerr, (Anne-)Judith 1923-1970 .... *24*
Kerr, M. E.
  See CLR *29*
  See also SAAS *1*
  See Meaker, Marijane (Agnes)
Kerr, P.B.
  See Kerr, Philip
Kerr, Philip 1956- *168*
Kerr, Phyllis Forbes 1942- *72*
Kerr, Tom 1950- *77*
Kerry, Frances
  See Kerigan, Florence
Kerry, Lois
  See Duncan, Lois
Kershen, (L.) Michael 1982- *82*
Kerven, Rosalind 1954- *83*
Ker Wilson, Barbara 1929- *121*
  Earlier sketches in SATA *20, 70*
  See also SAAS *18*
Keselman, Gabriela 1953- *128*
Kesey, Ken (Elton) 1935-2001 .... *66*
  Obituary *131*
Kesler, Jay 1935- *65*
Kessel, Joyce Karen 1937- *41*
Kessler, Ethel 1922- *44*
  Brief entry *37*
Kessler, Leonard P. 1921- *14*
Kest, Kristin 1967- *168*
  Earlier sketch in SATA *118*

Kesteven, G. R.
  See Crosher, G. R.
Ketcham, Hank
  See Ketcham, Henry King
Ketcham, Henry King 1920-2001 .... *28*
  Brief entry *27*
  Obituary *128*
Ketcham, Sallie 1963- *124*
Ketchum, Liza 1946- *132*
  See Murrow, Liza Ketchum
Ketner, Mary Grace 1946- *75*
Kettelkamp, Larry (Dale) 1933- *2*
  See also SAAS *3*
Ketteman, Helen 1945- *167*
  Earlier sketches in SATA *73, 115*
Kettle, Peter
  See Glover, Denis (James Matthews)
Kevles, Bettyann Holtzmann 1938- *23*
Key, Alexander (Hill) 1904-1979 .... *8*
  Obituary *23*
Key, Samuel M.
  See de Lint, Charles (Henri Diederick
  Hofsmit)
Keyes, Daniel 1927- *37*
Keyes, Fenton 1915-1999 .... *34*
Keyes, Greg
  See Keyes, J. Gregory
Keyes, J. Gregory 1963- *116*
Keyser, Marcia 1933- *42*
Keyser, Sarah
  See McGuire, Leslie (Sarah)
Khalsa, Dayal Kaur 1943-1989 .... *62*
  See also CLR *30*
  See Kaur Khalsa, Dayal
Khan, Rukhsana 1962- *165*
  Earlier sketch in SATA *118*
Khanshendel, Chiron
  See Rose, Wendy
Kheirabadi, Masoud 1951- *158*
Khemir, Sabiha *87*
Kherdian, David 1931- *74*
  Autobiography Feature *125*
  Earlier sketch in SATA *16*
  See also CLR *24*
Kibbe, Pat (Hosley) *60*
Kidd, Diana 1933-2000 .... *150*
Kidd, Richard 1952- *152*
Kidd, Ronald 1948- *92*
  Earlier sketch in SATA *42*
Kiddell, John 1922- *3*
Kiddell-Monroe, Joan 1908-1972 .... *55*
Kidwell, Carl 1910- *43*
Kiefer, Irene 1926- *21*
Kiefer, Kathleen Balmes 1957- *142*
Kierstead, Vera M. 1913- *121*
Kiesel, Stanley 1925- *35*
Kiesler, Kate (A.) 1971- *152*
  Earlier sketch in SATA *90*
Kihn, Greg 1952- *110*
Kikukawa, Cecily H(arder) 1919- *44*
  Brief entry *35*
Kilcher, Jewel 1974- *109*
Kile, Joan 1940- *78*
Kilgore, Kathleen 1946- *42*
Kilian, Crawford 1941- *35*
Killdeer, John
  See Mayhar, Ardath
Killien, Christi 1956- *73*
Killilea, Marie (Lyons) 1913-1991 .... *2*
Killingback, Julia 1944- *63*
Killough, (Karen) Lee 1942- *64*
Kilreon, Beth
  See Walker, Barbara (Jeanne) K(erlin)
Kilworth, Garry 1941- *94*
Kilworth, Garry D.
  See Kilworth, Garry
Kilworth, Garry Douglas
  See Kilworth, Garry
Kim, Helen 1899-1970 .... *98*
Kimball, Gayle 1943- *90*
Kimball, Violet T(ew) 1932- *126*

Kimball, Yeffe 1914-1978 .... *37*
Kimbrough, Emily 1899-1989 .... *2*
　Obituary *59*
Kimeldorf, Martin (R.) 1948- *121*
Kimenye, Barbara 1940(?)- *121*
Kimmel, Eric A. 1946- *125*
　Earlier sketches in SATA *13, 80*
Kimmel, Margaret Mary 1938- *43*
　Brief entry *33*
Kimmelman, Leslie (Grodinsky) 1958- *156*
　Earlier sketch in SATA *85*
Kincaid, Jamaica 1949-
　See CLR *63*
Kincher, Jonni 1949- *79*
Kindl, Patrice 1951- *128*
　Earlier sketch in SATA *82*
Kindred, Wendy (Good) 1937- *7*
Kines, Pat Decker 1937- *12*
King, Adam
　See Hoare, Robert J(ohn)
King, Alison
　See Martini, Teri
King, (Maria) Anna 1964- *72*
King, Billie Jean 1943- *12*
King, Christopher (L.) 1945- *84*
King, (David) Clive 1924- *144*
　Earlier sketch in SATA *28*
King, Colin 1943- *76*
King, Cynthia 1925- *7*
King, Daniel (John) 1963- *130*
King, Elizabeth 1953- *83*
King, Frank R. 1904-1999 .... *127*
King, Jane
　See Currie, Stephen
King, Jeanette (Margaret) 1959- *105*
King, Larry L. 1929- *66*
King, Laurie R. 1952- *88*
King, Marian 1900(?)-1986 .... *23*
　Obituary *47*
King, Martin Luther, Jr. 1929-1968 .... *14*
King, Mary Ellen 1958- *93*
King, Paul
　See Drackett, Phil(ip Arthur)
King, Paula
　See Downing, Paula E.
King, Stephen 1947- *161*
　Earlier sketches in SATA *9, 55*
King, Stephen Edwin
　See King, Stephen
King, Stephen Michael *157*
King, Steve
　See King, Stephen
King, Thomas 1943- *96*
King, Tony 1947- *39*
Kingman, Dong (Moy Shu) 1911-2000 ...... *44*
Kingman, Lee *67*
　Earlier sketch in SATA *1*
　See also SAAS *3*
　See Natti, (Mary) Lee
Kingsland, Leslie William 1912- *13*
Kingsley, Charles 1819-1875
　See YABC *2*
　See also CLR *77*
Kingsley, Emily Perl 1940- *33*
King-Smith, Dick 1922- *135*
　Brief entry *38*
　Earlier sketches in SATA *47, 80*
　See also CLR *40*
Kingston, Maxine (Ting Ting) Hong 1940-
　.. *53*
Kinney, C. Cle(land) 1915- *6*
Kinney, Harrison 1921- *13*
Kinney, Jean Stout 1912- *12*
Kinsey, Elizabeth
　See Clymer, Eleanor
Kinsey, Helen 1948- *82*
Kinsey-Warnock, Natalie 1956- *167*
　Earlier sketches in SATA *71, 116*
Kinzel, Dorothy 1950- *57*
Kinzel, Dottie
　See Kinzel, Dorothy

Kipling, (Joseph) Rudyard 1865-1936 ...... *100*
　See also YABC *2*
　See also CLR *65*
Kippax, Frank
　See Needle, Jan
Kirby, David K. 1944- *78*
Kirby, David Kirk
　See Kirby, David K.
Kirby, Margaret
　See Bingley, Margaret (Jane Kirby)
Kirby, Margaret
　See Bingley, Margaret (Jane Kirby)
Kirby, Susan E. 1949- *62*
Kirk, Connie Ann 1957- *167*
Kirk, Daniel 1952- *153*
　Earlier sketch in SATA *107*
Kirk, David 1955- *161*
　Earlier sketch in SATA *117*
Kirk, Heather 1949- *166*
Kirk, Ruth (Kratz) 1925- *5*
Kirkham, Dinah
　See Card, Orson Scott
Kirkland, Will
　See Hale, Arlene
Kirkpatrick, Katherine (Anne) 1964- *113*
Kirkup, James 1918- *12*
Kirkwood, Kathryn
　See Fluke, Joanne
Kirshenbaum, Binnie *79*
Kirshner, David S. 1958- *123*
Kish, Eleanor M(ary) 1924- *73*
Kish, Ely
　See Kish, Eleanor M(ary)
Kishida, Eriko 1929- *12*
Kisinger, Grace Gelvin (Maze) 1913-1965 . *10*
Kissin, Eva H. 1923- *10*
Kissinger, Rosemary K.
　See Updyke, Rosemary K.
Kistler, John M. 1967- *160*
Kitamura, Satoshi 1956- *143*
　Earlier sketches in SATA *62, 98*
　See also CLR *60*
Kitchen, Bert
　See Kitchen, Herbert Thomas
Kitchen, Herbert Thomas 1940- *70*
Kite, (L.) Patricia *78*
　See Kite, Pat
Kitt, Tamara
　See de Regniers, Beatrice Schenk (Freedman)
Kittinger, Jo S(usenbach) 1955- *148*
　Earlier sketch in SATA *96*
Kituomba
　See Odaga, Asenath (Bole)
Kitzinger, Sheila 1929- *57*
Kiwak, Barbara 1966- *103*
Kjelgaard, James Arthur 1910-1959 .... *17*
　See also CLR *81*
　See Kjelgaard, Jim
Kjelgaard, Jim
　See Kjelgaard, James Arthur
Kjelle, Marylou Morano 1954- *146*
Klagsbrun, Francine (Lifton) *36*
Klaits, Barrie 1944- *52*
Klaperman, Gilbert 1921- *33*
Klaperman, Libby Mindlin 1921-1982 .... *33*
　Obituary *31*
Klass, David 1960- *142*
　Earlier sketch in SATA *88*
Klass, Morton 1927-2001 .... *11*
Klass, Sheila Solomon 1927- *99*
　Autobiography Feature *126*
　Earlier sketch in SATA *45*
　See also SAAS *26*
Klause, Annette Curtis 1953- *79*
　See also CLR *104*
Klaveness, Jan O'Donnell 1939- *86*
Kleberger, Ilse 1921- *5*
Kleeberg, Irene (Flitner) Cumming 1932- .. *65*
Klein, Aaron E. 1930-1998 .... *45*
　Brief entry *28*
Klein, Bill 1945- *89*

Klein, David 1919-2001 .... *59*
Klein, Frederick C. 1938- *154*
Klein, Gerda Weissmann 1924- *44*
Klein, H(erbert) Arthur *8*
Klein, James 1932- *115*
Klein, Leonore (Glotzer) 1916- *6*
Klein, Mina C(ooper) 1906-1979 .... *8*
Klein, Norma 1938-1989 .... *57*
　Earlier sketch in SATA *7*
　See also CLR *19*
　See also SAAS *1*
Klein, Rachel S. 1953- *105*
Klein, Robin 1936- *164*
　Brief entry *45*
　Earlier sketches in SATA *55, 80*
　See also CLR *21*
Klemin, Diana *65*
Klemm, Barry 1945- *104*
Klemm, Edward G., Jr. 1910-2001 .... *30*
Klemm, Roberta K(ohnhorst) 1884-1975 .... *30*
Kleven, Elisa 1958- *76*
　See also CLR *85*
Klevin, Jill Ross 1935- *39*
　Brief entry *38*
Kliban, B(ernard) 1935-1990 .... *35*
　Obituary *66*
Klimowicz, Barbara 1927- *10*
Kline, Christina Baker 1964- *101*
Kline, James
　See Klein, James
Kline, Jim
　See Kline, Jim
Kline, Lisa Williams 1954- *143*
Kline, Suzy 1943- *152*
　Brief entry *48*
　Earlier sketches in SATA *67, 99*
Kliros, Thea 1935- *106*
Klise, M. Sarah 1961- *128*
Klug, Ron(ald) 1939- *31*
Knaak, Richard A. 1961- *166*
　Earlier sketch in SATA *86*
Knaak, Richard Allen
　See Knaak, Richard A.
Knapp, Edward
　See Kunhardt, Edith
Knapp, Ron 1952- *34*
Knebel, Fletcher 1911-1993 .... *36*
　Obituary *75*
Kneeland, Linda Clarke 1947- *94*
Knickerbocker, Diedrich
　See Irving, Washington
Knifesmith
　See Cutler, Ivor
Knigge, Robert (R.) 1921(?)-1987 .... *50*
Knight, Anne (Katherine) 1946- *34*
Knight, Brenda *112*
Knight, Christopher G. 1943- *96*
Knight, Damon (Francis) 1922-2002 .... *9*
　Obituary *139*
Knight, David C(arpenter) 1925-1984 .... *14*
　See also CLR *38*
Knight, Eric (Mowbray) 1897-1943 .... *18*
Knight, Francis Edgar 1905- *14*
Knight, Frank
　See Knight, Francis Edgar
Knight, Hilary 1926- *132*
　Earlier sketches in SATA *15, 69*
Knight, Joan
　See Knight, Joan (MacPhail)
Knight, Joan (MacPhail) *159*
　Earlier sketch in SATA *82*
Knight, Kathryn Lasky
　See Lasky, Kathryn
Knight, Mallory T.
　See Hurwood, Bernhardt J.
Knight, Theodore O. 1946- *77*
Knobloch, Dorothea 1951- *88*
Knoepfle, John (Ignatius) 1923- *66*
Knott, Bill
　See Knott, William C(ecil, Jr.)

Knott, William C(ecil, Jr.) 1927- 3
  See Knott, Bill
  and Mitchum, Hank
  and Sharpe, Jon
Knotts, Howard (Clayton, Jr.) 1922- 25
Knowles, Anne 1933- 37
Knowles, John 1926-2001 89
  Obituary 134
  Earlier sketch in SATA 8
  See also CLR 98
Knox, Calvin M.
  See Silverberg, Robert
Knox, (Mary) Eleanor Jessie 1909-2000 59
  Earlier sketch in SATA 30
Knox, James
  See Brittain, William (E.)
Knox, Jolyne 1937- 76
Knudsen, James 1950- 42
Knudsen, R. R.
  See SAAS 18
  See Knudson, Rozanne
Knudson, Richard L(ewis) 1930- 34
Knudson, Rozanne 1932- 79
  Earlier sketch in SATA 7
  See Knudson, R. R.
Knutson, Barbara 1959-2005 166
Knutson, Kimberley 115
Knye, Cassandra
  See Disch, Thomas M(ichael)
Koch, Dorothy Clarke 1924- 6
Koch, Kenneth (Jay) 1925-2002 65
Koch, Phyllis (Mae) McCallum 1911- 10
Kocsis, J. C.
  See Paul, James
Koda-Callan, Elizabeth 1944- 140
  Earlier sketch in SATA 67
Koehler, Phoebe 1955- 85
Koehler-Pentacoff, Elizabeth 1957- 160
  Earlier sketch in SATA 96
Koehn, Ilse
  See Van Zwienen, Ilse Charlotte Koehn
Koenig, Viviane 1950- 80
Koering, Ursula 1921-1976 64
Koerner, W(illiam) H(enry) D(avid) 1878-1938
  21
Koertge, Ronald 1940- 131
  Earlier sketches in SATA 53, 92
Koestler-Grack, Rachel A. 1973- 156
Koff, Richard Myram 1926- 62
Koffinke, Carol 1949- 82
Kogan, Deborah 50
  See Kogan Ray, Deborah
Kogan Ray, Deborah 1940- 161
  See Kogan, Deborah
  and Ray, Deborah
Kogawa, Joy Nozomi 1935- 99
Kohl, Herbert 1937- 47
Kohl, MaryAnn F(aubion) 1947- 144
  Earlier sketch in SATA 74
Kohn, Bernice 4
  See Hunt, Bernice (Kohn)
Kohn, Rita (T.) 1933- 89
Kohner, Frederick 1905-1986 10
  Obituary 48
Koide, Tan 1938-1986 50
Koike, Kay 1940- 72
Koja, Kathe 1960- 155
Kolba, St. Tamara 22
Kolibalova, Marketa
  See Kolibalova, Marketa
Kolibalova, Marketa 1953- 126
Koller, Jackie French 1948- 157
  Earlier sketches in SATA 72, 109
  See also CLR 68
Kolodny, Nancy J. 1946- 76
Komaiko, Leah 1954- 164
  Earlier sketch in SATA 97
Komisar, Lucy 1942- 9
Komoda, Beverly 1939- 25
Komoda, Kiyo 1937- 9
Kompaneyets, Marc 1974- 169

Komroff, Manuel 1890-1974 2
  Obituary 20
Konigsburg, E(laine) L(obl) 1930- 126
  Earlier sketches in SATA 4, 48, 94
  See also CLR 81
Koningsberger, Hans 5
  See Koning, Hans
Konkle, Janet Everest 1917- 12
Konzak, Burt 1946- 151
Koob, Theodora (J. Foth) 1918- 23
Kooiker, Leonie
  See Kooyker-Romijn, Johanna Maria
Koons, James
  See Pernu, Dennis
Koontz, Dean R. 1945- 165
  Earlier sketch in SATA 92
Koontz, Dean Ray
  See Koontz, Dean R.
Koontz, Robin Michal 1954- 136
  Earlier sketch in SATA 70
Kooyker, Leonie
  See Kooyker-Romijn, Johanna Maria
Kooyker-Romijn, Johanna Maria 1927- 48
  See Kooyker, Leonie
Kooyker-Romyn, Johanna Maria
  See Kooyker-Romijn, Johanna Maria
Kopelke, Lisa 1963- 154
Kopper, Lisa (Esther) 1950- 105
  Brief entry 51
Koppes, Steven N. 1957- 169
Koppes, Steven Nelson
  See Koppes, Steven N.
Korach, Mimi 1922- 9
Koralek, Jenny 1934- 140
  Earlier sketch in SATA 71
Korczak, Janusz 65
  See Goldszmit, Henryk
Koren, Edward (Benjamin) 1935- 148
  Earlier sketch in SATA 5
Korinets, Iurii Iosifovich
  See Korinetz, Yuri (Iosifovich)
Korinetz, Yuri (Iosifovich) 1923- 9
  See also CLR 4
Korman, Bernice 1937- 78
Korman, Gordon 1963- 167
  Brief entry 41
  Earlier sketches in SATA 49, 81, 119
  See also CLR 25
Korman, Gordon Richard
  See Korman, Gordon
Korman, Justine 1958- 70
Kornblatt, Marc 1954- 147
  Earlier sketch in SATA 84
Korte, Gene J. 1950- 74
Korty, Carol 1937- 15
Koscielniak, Bruce 1947- 153
  Earlier sketches in SATA 67, 99
Koshin, Alexander (A.) 1952- 86
Kositsky, Lynne 1947- 158
Koskenmaki, Rosalie
  See Maggio, Rosalie
Koss, Amy Goldman 1954- 158
  Earlier sketch in SATA 115
Kossin, Sandy (Sanford) 1926- 10
Kossman, Nina 1959- 84
Kotzwinkle, William 1938- 146
  Earlier sketches in SATA 24, 70
  See also CLR 6
Kouhi, Elizabeth 1917- 54
  Brief entry 49
Kouts, Anne 1945- 8
Koutsky, Jan Dale 1955- 146
Kovacs, Deborah 1954- 132
  Earlier sketch in SATA 79
Kovalski, Maryann 1951- 97
  Earlier sketch in SATA 58
  See also CLR 34
  See also SAAS 21
Kowalski, Kathiann M. 1955- 151
  Earlier sketch in SATA 96
Kraft, Betsy Harvey 1937- 157

Krahn, Fernando 1935- 49
  Brief entry 31
  See also CLR 3
Krakauer, Hoong Yee Lee 1955- 86
Krakauer, Jon 1954- 108
Kramer, George
  See Heuman, William
Kramer, Nora 1896(?)-1984 26
  Obituary 39
Kramer, Remi (Thomas) 1935- 90
Krantz, Hazel (Newman) 12
Kranzler, George G(ershon) 1916- 28
Kranzler, Gershon
  See Kranzler, George G(ershon)
Krasilovsky, Phyllis 1926- 38
  Earlier sketch in SATA 1
  See also CLR 83
  See also SAAS 5
Krasne, Betty
  See Levine, Betty K(rasne)
Krasner, Steven 1953- 154
Krasno, Rena 1923- 104
Kraus, Joanna Halpert 1937- 87
Kraus, (Herman) Robert 1925-2001 93
  Obituary 130
  Earlier sketches in SATA 4, 65
  See also SAAS 11
Krauss, Ruth (Ida) 1911-1993 30
  Obituary 75
  Earlier sketch in SATA 1
  See also CLR 42
Krautter, Elisa (Bialk) 1912(?)-1990 1
  Obituary 65
Krautwurst, Terry 1946- 79
Kray, Robert Clement 1930- 82
Kredel, Fritz 1900-1973 17
Kreikemeier, Gregory Scott 1965- 85
Krementz, Jill 1940- 134
  Earlier sketches in SATA 17, 71
  See also CLR 5
  See also SAAS 8
Kremer, Marcie
  See Sorenson, Margo
Krenina, Katya 1968- 101
Krensky, Stephen (Alan) 1953- 136
  Brief entry 41
  Earlier sketches in SATA 47, 93
Kresh, Paul 1919-1997 61
  Obituary 94
Kress, Nancy 1948- 147
  Autobiography Feature 147
  Earlier sketch in SATA 85
Kricher, John C. 1944- 113
Krieger, Melanie 96
Kripke, Dorothy Karp 30
Krisher, Trudy (B.) 1946- 160
  Earlier sketch in SATA 86
Krishnaswami, Uma 1956- 144
Kristof, Jane 1932- 8
Kroeber, Theodora (Kracaw) 1897-1979 1
Kroeger, Mary Kay 1950- 92
Krohn, Katherine E(lizabeth) 1961- 125
  Earlier sketch in SATA 84
Kroll, Francis Lynde 1904-1973 10
Kroll, Steven 1941- 135
  Autobiography Feature 135
  Earlier sketches in SATA 19, 66, 125
  See also SAAS 7
Kroll, Virginia L. 1948- 168
  Earlier sketches in SATA 76, 114
Kroll, Virginia Louisa
  See Kroll, Virginia L.
Krommes, Beth 1956- 128
Kronenwetter, Michael 1943- 62
Kroniuk, Lisa
  See Berton, Pierre (Francis de Marigny)
Kropp, Paul (Stephan) 1948- 38
  Brief entry 34
  See also CLR 96
Krosoczka, Jarrett J. 1977- 155

Kruess, James
  See CLR 9
  See Kruss, James
Krull, Kathleen 1952- 149
  Autobiography Feature 106
  Brief entry 39
  Earlier sketches in SATA 52, 80
  See also CLR 44
Krumgold, Joseph (Quincy) 1908-1980 48
  Obituary 23
  Earlier sketch in SATA 1
Krupinski, Loretta 1940- 161
  Earlier sketches in SATA 67, 102
Krupnick, Karen 1947- 89
Krupp, E(dwin) C(harles) 1944- 123
  Earlier sketch in SATA 53
Krupp, Robin Rector 1946- 53
Krush, Beth 1918- 18
Krush, Joe 1918- 18
  See Krush, Joseph P.
Kruss, James 1926-1997 8
  See Kruess, James
Krykorka, Vladyana 1945- 96
Kubie, Eleanor Gottheil
  See Kubie, Nora Gottheil Benjamin
Kubie, Nora Benjamin
  See Kubie, Nora Gottheil Benjamin
Kubie, Nora Gottheil Benjamin 1899-1988
  39
  Obituary 59
Kubinyi, Laszlo 1937- 94
  Earlier sketch in SATA 17
Kudlinski, Kathleen V. 1950- 150
Kuenstler, Morton 1927- 10
Kuharski, Janice 1947- 128
Kuklin, Susan 1941- 163
  Earlier sketches in SATA 63, 95
  See also CLR 51
Kulling, Monica 1952- 89
Kullman, Harry 1919-1982 35
Kumin, Maxine (Winokur) 1925- 12
Kunhardt, Dorothy (Meserve) 1901-1979 ... 53
  Obituary 22
Kunhardt, Edith 1937- 67
Kunjufu, Jawanza 1953- 73
Kunstler, Morton
  See Kuenstler, Morton
Kuntz, J(ohn) L. 1947- 91
Kuntz, Jerry 1956- 133
Kupferberg, Herbert 1918-2001 19
Kuratomi, Chizuko 1939- 12
  See also CLR 32
Kurczok, Belinda 1978- 121
Kurelek, William 1927-1977 8
  Obituary 27
  See also CLR 2
Kurian, George 1928- 65
Kurjian, Judi(th M.) 1944- 127
Kurland, Gerald 1942- 13
Kurland, Michael 1938- 118
  Earlier sketch in SATA 48
Kurland, Michael Joseph
  See Kurland, Michael
Kuroi, Ken 1947- 120
Kurokawa, Mitsuhiro 1954- 88
Kurten, Bjorn (Olof) 1924-1988 64
Kurtz, Jane 1952- 139
  Earlier sketch in SATA 91
Kurtz, Katherine (Irene) 1944- 126
  Earlier sketch in SATA 76
Kurz, Rudolf 1952- 95
Kushner, Donn (J.) 1927- 52
  See also CLR 55
Kushner, Ellen (Ruth) 1955- 98
Kushner, Jill Menkes 1951- 62
Kushner, Lawrence 1943- 169
  Earlier sketch in SATA 83
Kushner, Tony 1956- 160

Kuskin, Karla 1932- 164
  Earlier sketches in SATA 2, 68, 111
  See also CLR 4
  See also SAAS 3
Kuskin, Karla Seidman
  See Kuskin, Karla
Kusugak, Michael (Arvaarluk) 1948- 143
Kuttner, Paul 1922- 18
Kuzma, Kay 1941- 39
Kvale, Velma R(uth) 1898-1979 8
Kvasnosky, Laura McGee 1951- 142
  Earlier sketch in SATA 93
Kwasney, Michelle D. 1960- 162
Kyle, Benjamin
  See Gottfried, Theodore Mark
Kyle, Elisabeth
  See Dunlop, Agnes M. R.
Kyte, Kathy S. 1946- 50
  Brief entry 44

L

L., Barry
  See Longyear, Barry B(rookes)
L., Tommy
  See Lorkowski, Thomas V(incent)
Lace, William W. 1942- 126
Lachner, Dorothea
  See Knobloch, Dorothea
Lackey, Mercedes R. 1950- 127
  Earlier sketch in SATA 81
Lackey, Mercedes Ritchie
  See Lackey, Mercedes R.
Lacoe, Addie 78
Lacome, Julie 1961- 80
Lacy, Leslie Alexander 1937- 6
Ladd, Cheryl (Jean) 1951- 113
Ladd, Louise 1943- 97
Ladd, Veronica
  See Miner, Jane Claypool
Laden, Nina 1962- 148
  Earlier sketch in SATA 85
Lader, Lawrence 1919-2006 6
LaDoux, Rita C. 1951- 74
Lady, A
  See Taylor, Ann
Lady of Quality, A
  See Bagnold, Enid
La Farge, Oliver (Hazard Perry) 1901-1963
  19
La Farge, Phyllis 14
LaFaye, A. 1970- 156
  Earlier sketch in SATA 105
LaFaye, Alexandria R.T.
  See LaFaye, A.
Laffin, John (Alfred Charles) 1922- 31
LaFontaine, Bruce 1948- 114
La Fontaine, Jean de 1621-1695 18
Lager, Claude
  See Lapp, Christiane (Germain)
Lager, Marilyn 1939- 52
Lagercrantz, Rose (Elsa) 1947- 39
Lagerloef, Selma (Ottiliana Lovisa)
  See Lagerlof, Selma (Ottiliana Lovisa)
Lagerlof, Selma (Ottiliana Lovisa) 1858-1940
  15
  See also CLR 7
  See Lagerloef, Selma (Ottiliana Lovisa)
Laguna, Sofie 1968- 158
LaHaye, Tim(othy) F. 1926- 149
Laiken, Deirdre S(usan) 1948- 48
  Brief entry 40
Laimgruber, Monika 1946- 11
Lain, Anna
  See Lamb, Nancy
Laing, Alexander (Kinnan) 1903-1976 117
Laing, Martha
  See Celestino, Martha Laing

Laird, Christa 1944- 108
  Autobiography Feature 120
  See also SAAS 26
Laird, Elizabeth (Mary Risk) 1943- 159
  Earlier sketches in SATA 77, 114
  See also CLR 65
Laird, Jean E(louise) 1930- 38
Laite, Gordon 1925- 31
Lake, Harriet
  See Taylor, Paula (Wright)
Laklan, Carli 1907-1988 5
Laliberte, Louise-Andree 1958- 169
Lalicki, Barbara 61
Lally, Soinbhe 1945- 119
LaMarche, Jim 162
Lamb, Beatrice Pitney 1904-1997 21
Lamb, Charles 1775-1834 17
Lamb, Elizabeth Searle 1917- 31
Lamb, G(eoffrey) F(rederick) 10
Lamb, Harold (Albert) 1892-1962 53
Lamb, Lynton (Harold) 1907-1977 10
Lamb, Mary Ann 1764-1847 17
Lamb, Nancy 1939- 80
Lamb, Robert (Boyden) 1941- 13
Lambert, David (Compton) 1932- 84
  Brief entry 49
Lambert, Janet 1895(?)-1973 25
Lambert, Martha L. 113
Lambert, Saul 1928- 23
Lamburn, Richmal Crompton 1890-1969 5
  See Crompton, Richmal
Lamensdorf, Len
  See Lamensdorf, Leonard
Lamensdorf, Leonard 1930- 120
Laminack, Lester L. 1956- 163
  Earlier sketch in SATA 120
Lamorisse, Albert (Emmanuel) 1922-1970 . 23
Lampert, Emily 1951- 52
  Brief entry 49
Lamplugh, Lois 1921- 17
Lampman, Evelyn Sibley 1907-1980 87
  Obituary 23
  Earlier sketch in SATA 4
Lamprey, Louise 1869-1951
  See YABC 2
Lampton, Chris
  See Lampton, Christopher F.
Lampton, Christopher
  See Lampton, Christopher F.
Lampton, Christopher F. 67
  Brief entry 47
Lamstein, Sarah Marwil 1943- 126
Lanagan, Margo 1960- 163
Lancaster, Bruce 1896-1963 9
Lance, Kathryn 1943- 76
Land, Barbara (Neblett) 1923- 16
Land, Jane
  See Borland, Kathryn Kilby
  and Speicher, Helen Ross S(mith)
Land, Myrick (Ebben) 1922-1998 15
Land, Ross
  See Borland, Kathryn Kilby
  and Speicher, Helen Ross S(mith)
Landau, Elaine 1948- 141
  Earlier sketches in SATA 10, 94
Landau, Jacob 1917- 38
Landeck, Beatrice 1904-1978 15
Landin, Les 1923- 2
Landis, J(ames) D(avid) 1942- 60
  Brief entry 52
Landis, James D.
  See Landis, J(ames) D(avid)
Landis, Jill Marie 1948- 101
Landon, Dena 1978(?)- 168
Landon, Lucinda 1950- 56
  Brief entry 51
Landon, Margaret (Dorothea Mortenson)
  1903-1993 50
Landshoff, Ursula 1908-1989 13
Landstrom, Lena 1943- 146
Landstrom, Olof 1943- 146

Lane, Carolyn 1926-1993 .... *10*
Lane, Dakota 1959- *166*
  Earlier sketch in SATA *105*
Lane, Jerry
  See Martin, Patricia Miles
Lane, John (Richard) 1932- *15*
Lane, Margaret 1907-1994 .... *65*
  Brief entry *38*
  Obituary *79*
Lane, Rose Wilder 1887-1968 .... *29*
  Brief entry *28*
Lanes, Selma Gordon 1929- *3*
Lanfredi, Judy 1964- *83*
Lang, Andrew 1844-1912 .... *16*
  See also CLR *101*
Lang, Aubrey *169*
Lang, Paul 1948- *83*
Lang, Susan S. 1950- *68*
Lang, T.T.
  See Taylor, Theodore
Langdo, Bryan 1973- *138*
Lange, John
  See Crichton, (John) Michael
Lange, Suzanne 1945- *5*
Langley, Andrew 1949- *166*
  Earlier sketch in SATA *104*
Langley, Charles P(itman) III 1949- *103*
Langley, Jonathan 1952- *122*
Langner, Nola *8*
  See Malone, Nola Langner
Langone, John (Michael) 1929- *46*
  Brief entry *38*
Langreuter, Jutta 1944- *122*
Langsen, Richard C. 1953- *95*
Langstaff, John 1920-2005 .... *68*
  Earlier sketch in SATA *6*
  See also CLR *3*
Langstaff, John Meredith
  See Langstaff, John
Langstaff, Launcelot
  See Irving, Washington
Langton, Jane (Gillson) 1922- *140*
  Autobiography Feature *140*
  Earlier sketches in SATA *3, 68, 129*
  See also CLR *33*
  See also SAAS *5*
Lanier, Sidney 1842-1881 .... *18*
Lanier, Sterling E(dmund) 1927- *109*
Lanino, Deborah 1964- *123*
Lankford, Mary D. 1932- *112*
  Earlier sketch in SATA *77*
Lannin, Joanne (A.) 1951- *121*
Lansdale, Joe R(ichard) 1951- *116*
Lansing, Alfred 1921-1975 .... *35*
Lansing, Karen E. 1954- *71*
Lantier-Sampon, Patricia 1952- *92*
Lantz, Fran
  See Lantz, Francess L(in)
Lantz, Francess L(in) 1952-2004 .... *153*
  Autobiography Feature *153*
  Obituary *159*
  Earlier sketches in SATA *63, 109*
  See Dixon, Franklin W.
Lantz, Paul 1908- *45*
Lantz, Walter 1900-1994 .... *37*
  Obituary *79*
Lanza, Barbara 1945- *101*
Lapp, Christiane (Germain) 1948- *74*
Lappin, Peter 1911-1999 .... *32*
Lardy, Philippe 1963- *168*
Larkin, Amy
  See Burns, Olive Ann
Larkin, Maia
  See Wojciechowska, Maia (Teresa)
Laroche, Giles 1956- *126*
  Earlier sketch in SATA *71*
LaRochelle, David 1960- *115*
LaRose, Linda *125*
Larrabee, Lisa 1947- *84*
Larrecq, John M(aurice) 1926-1980 .... *44*
  Obituary *25*

Larrick (Crosby), Nancy 1910-2004 .... *4*
Larsen, Anita 1942- *78*
Larsen, Egon 1904- *14*
Larsen, Rebecca 1944- *54*
Larson, Eve
  See St. John, Wylly Folk
Larson, Gary 1950- *57*
Larson, Ingrid D(ana) 1965- *92*
Larson, Jean Russell 1930- *121*
Larson, Kirby 1954- *96*
Larson, Norita D(ittberner) 1944- *29*
Larson, William H. 1938- *10*
Larsson, Carl (Olof) 1853-1919 .... *35*
LaSalle, Charles A.
  See Ellis, Edward S(ylvester)
LaSalle, Charles E.
  See Ellis, Edward S(ylvester)
Lasell, Elinor H. 1929- *19*
Lasell, Fen H.
  See Lasell, Elinor H.
Lasenby, Jack 1931- *103*
  Earlier sketch in SATA *65*
Laser, Michael 1954- *117*
Lash, Joseph P. 1909-1987 .... *43*
Lasher, Faith B. 1921- *12*
Lasker, David 1950- *38*
Lasker, Joe *83*
  See also SAAS *17*
  See Lasker, Joseph Leon
Lasker, Joseph Leon 1919- *9*
  See Lasker, Joe
Laski, Marghanita 1915-1988 .... *55*
Laskin, Pamela L. 1954- *75*
Lasky, Kathryn 1944- *157*
  Earlier sketches in SATA *13, 69, 112*
  See also CLR *11*
Lasky Knight, Kathryn
  See Lasky, Kathryn
Lass, Bonnie *131*
Lassalle, C. E.
  See Ellis, Edward S(ylvester)
Lassiter, Mary *59*
  See Hoffman, Mary (Margaret)
Lassiter, Rhiannon 1977- *157*
Latham, Barbara 1896- *16*
Latham, Frank B(rown) 1910-2000 .... *6*
Latham, Jean Lee 1902-1995 .... *68*
  Earlier sketch in SATA *2*
  See also CLR *50*
Latham, Mavis
  See Clark, Mavis Thorpe
Latham, Philip
  See Richardson, Robert S(hirley)
Lathrop, Dorothy P(ulis) 1891-1980 .... *14*
  Obituary *24*
Lathrop, Francis
  See Leiber, Fritz (Reuter, Jr.)
Latimer, Jim 1943- *80*
Latta, Rich
  See Latta, Richard
Latta, Richard 1946- *113*
Lattany, Kristin
  See Lattany, Kristin (Elaine Eggleston) Hunter
Lattany, Kristin (Eggleston) Hunter 1931-
  .... *154*
  Autobiography Feature *154*
  Earlier sketch in SATA *132*
Lattany, Kristin (Elaine Eggleston) Hunter
  1931- *132*
  Earlier sketch in SATA *12*
  See also CLR *3*
  See also SAAS *10*
  See Hunter, Kristin
Lattimore, Eleanor Frances 1904-1986 .... *7*
  Obituary *48*
Lattin, Ann
  See Cole, Lois Dwight
Lauber, Patricia (Grace) 1924- *138*
  Earlier sketches in SATA *1, 33, 75*
  See also CLR *16*
Laugesen, Mary E(akin) 1906-1995 .... *5*

Laughbaum, Steve 1945- *12*
Laughlin, Florence Young 1910-2001 .... *3*
Laughlin, Rosemary 1941- *123*
Laure, Ettagale
  See Blauer, Ettagale
Laure, Jason 1940- *50*
  Brief entry *44*
Laurence, Ester Hauser 1935- *7*
Laurie, Rona 1916- *55*
Laurin, Anne
  See McLaurin, Anne
Lauritzen, Jonreed 1902-1979 .... *13*
Lauscher, Hermann
  See Hesse, Hermann
Lauture, Denize 1946- *86*
Laux, Connie
  See Laux, Constance
Laux, Constance 1952- *97*
Laux, Dorothy 1920- *49*
Lavallee, Barbara 1941- *166*
  Earlier sketch in SATA *74*
Lavender, David (Sievert) 1910-2003 .... *97*
  Obituary *145*
  Earlier sketch in SATA *64*
Lavender, William D. 1921- *143*
Lavert, Gwendolyn Battle 1951- *131*
  See Battle-Lavert, Gwendolyn
Laverty, Donald
  See Blish, James (Benjamin)
  and Knight, Damon (Francis)
Lavigne, Louis-Dominique *107*
Lavine, David 1928- *31*
Lavine, Sigmund Arnold 1908-1986 .... *82*
  Earlier sketch in SATA *3*
  See also CLR *35*
Lavond, Paul Dennis
  See Kornbluth, C(yril) M.
  and Lowndes, Robert A(ugustine) W(ard)
  and Pohl, Frederik
Lawhead, Stephen R. 1950- *109*
Lawhead, Steve
  See Lawhead, Stephen R.
Lawlor, Laurie 1953- *137*
  Earlier sketch in SATA *80*
Lawrence, Ann (Margaret) 1942-1987 .... *41*
  Obituary *54*
Lawrence, Iain 1955- *135*
Lawrence, J. T.
  See Rowland-Entwistle, (Arthur) Theodore
  (Henry)
Lawrence, Jerome 1915-2004 .... *65*
Lawrence, John 1933- *30*
Lawrence, Louise 1943- *119*
  Earlier sketches in SATA *38, 78*
Lawrence, Louise de Kiriline 1894-1992 .... *13*
Lawrence, Lynn
  See Garland, Sherry
Lawrence, Margery H. 1889-1969 .... *120*
Lawrence, Michael 1943- *132*
Lawrence, Mildred Elwood 1907-1997 .... *3*
Lawrence, R(onald) D(ouglas) 1921- *55*
Lawrinson, Julia 1969- *141*
Lawson, Amy
  See Gordon, Amy
Lawson, Carol (Antell) 1946- *42*
Lawson, Don(ald Elmer) 1917-1990 .... *9*
Lawson, Joan 1906- *55*
Lawson, Julie 1947- *126*
  Earlier sketch in SATA *79*
  See also CLR *89*
Lawson, Marion Tubbs 1896-1994 .... *22*
Lawson, Robert 1892-1957 .... *100*
  See also YABC *2*
  See also CLR *73*
Lawton, Clive A. 1951- *145*
Laxdal, Vivienne 1962- *112*
Laycock, George (Edwin) 1921- *5*
Layne, Laura
  See Knott, William C(ecil, Jr.)
Layton, Neal (Andrew) 1971- *152*
Lazare, Gerald John 1927- *44*

Lazare, Jerry
  See Lazare, Gerald John
Lazarevich, Mila 1942- *17*
Lazarus, Keo Felker 1913-1993 .... *21*
  Obituary *129*
Lea, Alec 1907- *19*
Lea, Joan
  See Neufeld, John (Arthur)
Leach, Maria 1892-1977 .... *39*
  Brief entry *28*
Leacock, Elspeth 1946- *131*
Leacroft, Helen (Mabel Beal) 1919- *6*
Leacroft, Richard (Vallance Becher) 1914- ... *6*
Leaf, (Wilbur) Munro 1905-1976 .... *20*
  See also CLR *25*
Leaf, VaDonna Jean 1929- *26*
Leah, Devorah
  See Devorah-Leah
Leakey, Richard E(rskine Frere) 1944- *42*
Leander, Ed
  See Richelson, Geraldine
Lear, Edward 1812-1888 .... *100*
  Earlier sketch in SATA *18*
  See also CLR *75*
Lears, Laurie 1955- *127*
Leasor, (Thomas) James 1923- *54*
Leavitt, Jerome E(dward) 1916- *23*
LeBar, Mary E(velyn) 1910-1982 .... *35*
LeBlanc, Annette M. 1965- *68*
LeBlanc, L(ee) 1913- *54*
LeBox, Annette 1943- *145*
Lebrun, Claude 1929- *66*
Le Cain, Errol (John) 1941-1989 .... *68*
  Obituary *60*
  Earlier sketch in SATA *6*
Lecourt, Nancy (Hoyt) 1951- *73*
Ledbetter, Suzann 1953- *119*
Leder, Jane Mersky 1945- *61*
  Brief entry *51*
Lederer, Muriel 1929- *48*
Lederer, William J(ulius) 1912- *62*
Lee, Amanda
  See Baggett, Nancy
  and Buckholtz, Eileen (Garber)
  and Glick, Ruth (Burtnick)
Lee, Benjamin 1921- *27*
Lee, Betsy 1949- *37*
Lee, Carol
  See Fletcher, Helen Jill
Lee, Cora
  See Anderson, Catherine Corley
Lee, Dennis (Beynon) 1939- *102*
  Earlier sketch in SATA *14*
  See also CLR *3*
Lee, Dom 1959- *146*
  Autobiography Feature *121*
  Earlier sketch in SATA *83*
  See also SAAS *26*
Lee, Doris Emrick 1905-1983 .... *44*
  Obituary *35*
Lee, Elizabeth Rogers 1940- *90*
Lee, (Nelle) Harper 1926- *11*
Lee, Hector Viveros 1962- *115*
Lee, Howard N.
  See Goulart, Ron(ald Joseph)
Lee, Howard N.
  See Goulart, Ron(ald Joseph)
Lee, Huy Voun 1969- *129*
Lee, J(oseph) Edward 1953- *130*
Lee, Jeanne M. 1943- *138*
Lee, John R(obert) 1923-1976 .... *27*
Lee, Jordan
  See Scholefield, Alan
Lee, Julian
  See Latham, Jean Lee
Lee, Liz
  See Lee, Elizabeth Rogers
Lee, Lucy
  See Talbot, Charlene Joy
Lee, Lyn 1953- *128*

Lee, Manning de Villeneuve 1894-1980 ..... *37*
  Obituary *22*
Lee, Marian
  See Clish, (Lee) Marian
Lee, Marie G. 1964- *130*
  Earlier sketch in SATA *81*
Lee, Mary Price 1934- *82*
  Earlier sketch in SATA *8*
Lee, Mildred *6*
  See also SAAS *12*
  See Scudder, Mildred Lee
Lee, Richard S. 1927- *82*
Lee, Robert C. 1931- *20*
Lee, Robert E(dwin) 1918-1994 .... *65*
  Obituary *82*
Lee, Robert J. 1921- *10*
Lee, Sally 1943- *67*
Lee, Tammie
  See Townsend, Thomas L.
Lee, Tanith 1947- *134*
  Earlier sketches in SATA *8, 88*
Leech, Ben
  See Bowkett, Stephen
Leedy, Loreen (Janelle) 1959- *128*
  Brief entry *50*
  Earlier sketches in SATA *54, 84*
Lee-Hostetler, Jeri 1940- *63*
Leekley, Thomas B(riggs) 1910-2001 .... *23*
Leeming, Jo Ann
  See Leeming, Joseph
Leeming, Joseph 1897-1968 .... *26*
Leemis, Ralph B. 1954- *72*
Leese, Jennifer L.B. 1970- *163*
Leeson, Muriel 1920- *54*
Leeson, R. A.
  See Leeson, Robert (Arthur)
Leeson, Robert (Arthur) 1928- *76*
  Earlier sketch in SATA *42*
Leffland, Ella 1931- *65*
Lefler, Irene (Whitney) 1917- *12*
Le Gallienne, Eva 1899-1991 .... *9*
  Obituary *68*
Legg, Gerald 1947- *143*
LeGrand
  See Henderson, LeGrand
Le Guin, Ursula K(roeber) 1929- *149*
  Earlier sketches in SATA *4, 52, 99*
  See also CLR *91*
Legum, Colin 1919-2003 .... *10*
Lehman, Barbara 1963- *115*
Lehman, Bob *91*
Lehman, Elaine *91*
Lehn, Cornelia 1920- *46*
Lehne, Judith Logan 1947- *93*
Lehr, Delores 1920- *10*
Lehr, Norma 1930- *71*
Leiber, Fritz (Reuter, Jr.) 1910-1992 .... *45*
  Obituary *73*
Leibold, Jay 1957- *57*
  Brief entry *52*
Leichman, Seymour 1933- *5*
Leigh, Nila K. 1981- *81*
Leigh, Tom 1947- *46*
Leigh-Pemberton, John 1911-1997 .... *35*
Leighton, Clare (Veronica Hope) 1899-1989
  .... *37*
Leighton, Margaret (Carver) 1896-1987 .... *1*
  Obituary *52*
Leiner, Al(an) 1938- *83*
Leiner, Katherine 1949- *93*
Leipold, L. Edmond 1902-1983 .... *16*
Leisk, David (Johnson) 1906-1975 .... *30*
  Obituary *26*
  Earlier sketch in SATA *1*
  See also CLR *98*
  See Johnson, Crockett
Leister, Mary 1917- *29*
Leitch, Patricia 1933- *98*
  Earlier sketch in SATA *11*
Leitner, Isabella 1924- *86*
Leland, Bob 1956- *92*

Leland, Robert E.
  See Leland, Bob
Lember, Barbara Hirsch 1941- *92*
LeMieux, A(nne) C(onnelly) 1954- *125*
  Earlier sketch in SATA *90*
  See LeMieux, Anne
LeMieux, Anne
  See LeMieux, A(nne) C(onnelly)
Lemieux, Michele 1955- *139*
Lemke, Horst 1922- *38*
Lenanton, Carola Mary Anima Oman
  See Oman, Carola (Mary Anima)
L'Engle, Madeleine (Camp Franklin) 1918-
  .... *128*
  Earlier sketches in SATA *1, 27, 75*
  See also CLR *57*
  See also SAAS *15*
Lengyel, Cornel Adam 1915- *27*
Lengyel, Emil 1895-1985 .... *3*
  Obituary *42*
Lennon, John (Ono) 1940-1980 .... *114*
Leno, Jay 1950- *154*
LeNoir, Janice 1941- *89*
Lens, Sidney 1912-1986 .... *13*
  Obituary *48*
Lenski, Lois 1893-1974 .... *100*
  Earlier sketches in SATA *1, 26*
  See also CLR *26*
Lent, Blair *133*
  Earlier sketch in SATA *2*
Lent, Henry Bolles 1901-1973 .... *17*
Lent, John 1948- *108*
Leodhas, Sorche Nic
  See Alger, Leclaire (Gowans)
Leokum, Arkady 1916(?)- *45*
Leon, Sharon 1959- *79*
Leonard, Alison 1944- *70*
Leonard, Constance (Brink) 1923- *42*
  Brief entry *40*
Leonard, Elmore (John, Jr.) 1925- *163*
Leonard, Jonathan N(orton) 1903-1975 ...... *36*
Leonard, Laura 1923- *75*
Leong, Gor Yun
  See Ellison, Virginia H(owell)
Leonhardt, Alice 1950- *152*
Lerangis, Peter 1955- *72*
Lerner, Aaron Bunsen 1920- *35*
Lerner, Carol 1927- *86*
  Earlier sketch in SATA *33*
  See also CLR *34*
  See also SAAS *12*
Lerner, Gerda 1920- *65*
Lerner, Harriet 1944- *101*
Lerner, Marguerite Rush 1924-1987 .... *11*
  Obituary *51*
Lerner, Sharon (Ruth) 1938-1982 .... *11*
  Obituary *29*
Leroe, Ellen W(hitney) 1949- *99*
  Brief entry *51*
  Earlier sketch in SATA *61*
Leroux, Gaston 1868-1927 .... *65*
Leroux-Hugon, Helene 1955- *132*
LeRoy, Gen *52*
  Brief entry *36*
LeShan, Eda J(oan) 1922-2002 .... *21*
  See also CLR *6*
LeSieg, Theo.
  See Dr. Seuss
  and Geisel, Theodor Seuss
  and Seuss, Dr.
  and Stone, Rosetta
Lesinski, Jeanne M. 1960- *120*
Leslie, Robert Franklin 1911-1990 .... *7*
Leslie, Roger 1961- *168*
Leslie, Roger James
  See Leslie, Roger
Leslie, Sarah
  See McGuire, Leslie (Sarah)
LeSourd, Catherine
  See Marshall, (Sarah) Catherine (Wood)

Lessac, Frane
  See Lessac, Frane
Lessac, Frane 1954- 148
  Earlier sketch in SATA *61*
Lessem, Dino Don
  See Lessem, Don
Lessem, Don 1951- 155
  Earlier sketch in SATA *97*
Lesser, Rika 1953- 53
Lester, Alison 1952- 129
  Earlier sketches in SATA *50, 90*
Lester, Helen 1936- 145
  Earlier sketches in SATA *46, 92*
Lester, Julius 1939- 157
  Earlier sketches in SATA *12, 74, 112*
  See also CLR *41*
Lester, Julius Bernard
  See Lester, Julius
Lester, Mike 1955- 131
Le Sueur, Meridel 1900-1996 6
Le Tord, Bijou 1945- 95
  Earlier sketch in SATA *49*
Letts, Billie 1938- 121
Leuck, Laura 1962- 146
  Earlier sketch in SATA *85*
Leutscher, Alfred (George) 1913- 23
Levai, Blaise 1919- 39
Levenkron, Steven 1941- 86
Leverich, Kathleen 1948- 103
LeVert, (William) John 1946- 55
Levete, Sarah 1961- 153
Levin, Betty 1927- 137
  Earlier sketches in SATA *19, 84*
  See also SAAS *11*
Levin, Ira 1929- 66
Levin, Marcia Obrasky 1918- 13
Levin, Meyer 1905-1981 21
  Obituary 27
Levin, Miriam (Ramsfelder) 1962- 97
Levine, Abby 1943- 54
  Brief entry 52
Levine, Betty K(rasne) 1933- 66
Levine, David 1926- 43
  Brief entry 35
Levine, Edna S(imon) 35
Levine, Evan 1962- 77
  Earlier sketch in SATA *74*
Levine, Gail Carson 1947- 161
  Earlier sketch in SATA *98*
  See also CLR *85*
Levine, I(srael) E. 1923-2003 12
  Obituary 146
Levine, Joan Goldman 11
Levine, Joseph 1910- 33
Levine, Marge 1934- 81
Levine, Rhoda 14
Levine, Sarah 1970- 57
Levine, Shar 1953- 131
Levine-Freidus, Gail
  See Provost, Gail Levine
Levinson, Nancy Smiler 1938- 140
  Earlier sketches in SATA *33, 80*
Levinson, Riki 99
  Brief entry 49
  Earlier sketch in SATA *52*
Levithan, David 1972- 166
Levitin, Sonia (Wolff) 1934- 131
  Autobiography Feature 131
  Earlier sketches in SATA *4, 68, 119*
  See also CLR *53*
  See also SAAS *2*
Levitt, Sidney (Mark) 1947- 68
Levon, O. U.
  See Kesey, Ken (Elton)
Levoy, Myron 49
  Brief entry 37
Levy, Barrie 112
Levy, Constance 1931- 140
  Earlier sketch in SATA *73*
  See also SAAS *22*

Levy, Elizabeth 1942- *169*
  Earlier sketches in SATA *31, 69, 107*
  See also SAAS *18*
Levy, Marilyn 1937- 67
Levy, Nathan 1945- 63
Levy, Robert 1945- 82
Lewees, John
  See Stockton, Francis Richard
Lewin, Betsy 1937- *169*
  Autobiography Feature 115
  Earlier sketches in SATA *32, 90*
Lewin, Hugh 1939- 72
  Brief entry 40
  See also CLR *9*
Lewin, Ted 1935- 165
  Autobiography Feature 115
  Earlier sketches in SATA *21, 76, 119*
Lewis, Alice C. 1936- 46
Lewis, Amanda 1955- 80
Lewis, (Joseph) Anthony 1927- 27
Lewis, Anthony 1966- 120
Lewis, Barbara A. 1943- 73
Lewis, Beverly 1949- 80
Lewis, Brenda Ralph 1932- 72
Lewis, Brian 1963- 128
Lewis, Claudia (Louise) 1907-2001 5
Lewis, Clive Staples
  See Lewis, C.S.
Lewis, C.S. 1898-1963 100
  Earlier sketch in SATA *13*
  See also CLR *109*
Lewis, Cynthia Copeland 1960- 111
Lewis, E. M. 123
  Earlier sketch in SATA *20*
Lewis, Earl Bradley
  See Lewis, E.B.
Lewis, E.B. 1956- 168
  Earlier sketches in SATA *93, 124*
Lewis, Elizabeth Foreman 1892-1958 121
  See also YABC *2*
Lewis, Francine
  See Wells, Helen
Lewis, J. Patrick 1942- 162
  Earlier sketches in SATA *69, 104*
Lewis, Jack P(earl) 1919- 65
Lewis, Jean 1924- 61
Lewis, Julinda
  See Lewis-Ferguson, Julinda
Lewis, Kim 1951- 136
  Earlier sketch in SATA *84*
Lewis, Linda (Joy) 1946- 67
Lewis, Lucia Z.
  See Anderson, Lucia (Lewis)
Lewis, Marjorie 1929- 40
  Brief entry 35
Lewis, Mary (Christianna) 1907(?)-1988 64
  Obituary 56
  See Brand, Christianna
Lewis, Mervyn
  See Frewer, Glyn (M.)
Lewis, Michael
  See Untermeyer, Louis
Lewis, Naomi 144
  Earlier sketch in SATA *76*
Lewis, Paul
  See Gerson, Noel Bertram
Lewis, Richard 1935- 3
Lewis, Rob 1962- 72
Lewis, Roger
  See Zarchy, Harry
Lewis, Shannon
  See Llywelyn, Morgan
Lewis, Shari 1934-1998 35
  Brief entry 30
  Obituary 104
Lewis, Sylvan R.
  See Aronson, Virginia
Lewis, Thomas P(arker) 1936- 27
Lewis, Wendy A. 1966- 150
Lewis-Ferguson, Julinda 1955- 85
Lewiton, Mina 1904-1970 2

Lexau, Joan M. *130*
  Earlier sketches in SATA *1, 36*
Ley, Willy 1906-1969 2
Leydon, Rita (Floden) 1949- 21
Leyland, Eric (Arthur) 1911- 37
Li, Xiao Jun 1952- 86
Liatsos, Sandra Olson 1942- 103
Libby, Barbara M. 153
Libby, Bill
  See Libby, William M.
Libby, William M. 1927-1984 5
  Obituary 39
Liberty, Gene 1924- 3
Lichtenheld, Tom 152
Liddell, Kenneth 1912-1975 63
Lidz, Jane 120
Lieberman, E(dwin) James 1934- 62
Liebers, Arthur 1913-1984 12
Lieblich, Irene 1923- 22
Liers, Emil E(rnest) 1890-1975 37
Lies, Brian 1963- 131
Liestman, Vicki 1961- 72
Lietz, Gerald S. 1918- 11
Life, Kay (Guinn) 1930- 83
Lifton, Betty Jean 118
  Earlier sketch in SATA *6*
Lifton, Robert Jay 1926- 66
Lightburn, Ron 1954- 91
Lightburn, Sandra 1955- 91
Lightner, A. M.
  See Hopf, Alice (Martha) L(ightner)
Lightner, Alice
  See Hopf, Alice (Martha) L(ightner)
Lignell, Lois 1911- 37
Liles, Maurine Walpole 1935- 81
Lilley, Stephen R(ay) 1950- 97
Lillington, Kenneth (James) 1916-1998 39
Lilly, Ray
  See Curtis, Richard (Alan)
Lim, John 1932- 43
Liman, Ellen (Fogelson) 1936- 22
Limb, Sue 1946- 158
Limburg, Peter R(ichard) 1929- 13
Lin, Grace 1974- 162
  Earlier sketch in SATA *111*
Lincoln, C(harles) Eric 1924-2000 5
Lincoln, James
  See Bates, Katharine Lee
Lindbergh, Anne 81
  See Sapieyevski, Anne Lindbergh
Lindbergh, Anne (Spencer) Morrow 1906-2001
  33
  Obituary 125
Lindbergh, Charles A(ugustus, Jr.) 1902-1974
  33
Lindbergh, Reeve 1945- 163
  Earlier sketch in SATA *116*
Lindblom, Steven (Winther) 1946- 94
  Brief entry 39
  Earlier sketch in SATA *42*
Linde, Gunnel 1924- 5
Lindenbaum, Pija 1955- 144
  Earlier sketch in SATA *77*
Lindgren, Astrid (Anna Emilia Ericsson)
  1907-2002 38
  Obituary 128
  Earlier sketch in SATA *2*
  See also CLR *39*
Lindgren, Barbro 1937- 120
  Brief entry 46
  Earlier sketch in SATA *63*
  See also CLR *86*
Lindman, Maj (Jan) 1886-1972 43
Lindop, Edmund 1925- 5
Lindquist, Jennie Dorothea 1899-1977 13
Lindquist, Rowena Cory 1958- 98
Lindquist, Willis 1908-1988 20
Lindsay, Norman Alfred William 1879-1969
  67
  See also CLR *8*
Lindsay, (Nicholas) Vachel 1879-1931 40

Lindsey, Kathleen D(orothy) 1949- 153
Line, David
    See Davidson, Lionel
Line, Les 1935- 27
Linfield, Esther 40
Lingard, Joan (Amelia) 1932- 130
    Autobiography Feature 130
    Earlier sketches in SATA 8, 74, 114
    See also CLR 89
    See also SAAS 5
Link, Martin 1934- 28
Linn, Margot
    See Ziefert, Harriet
Linnea, Sharon 1956- 82
Lionni, Leo(nard) 1910-1999 72
    Obituary 118
    Earlier sketch in SATA 8
    See also CLR 71
Lipinsky de Orlov, Lino S. 1908- 22
Lipkind, William 1904-1974 15
Lipman, David 1931- 21
Lipman, Matthew 1923- 14
Lippincott, Gary A. 1953- 119
    Earlier sketch in SATA 73
Lippincott, Joseph W(harton) 1887-1976 17
Lippincott, Sarah Lee 1920- 22
Lippman, Peter J. 1936- 31
Lipsyte, Robert 1938- 161
    Earlier sketches in SATA 5, 68, 113
    See also CLR 76
Lipsyte, Robert Michael
    See Lipsyte, Robert
Lisandrelli, Elaine Slivinski 1951- 94
Lisker, Sonia O. 1933- 44
Lisle, Holly 1960- 98
Lisle, Janet Taylor 1947- 150
    Brief entry 47
    Earlier sketches in SATA 59, 96
    See also SAAS 14
Lisle, Rebecca 162
Lisle, Seward D.
    See Ellis, Edward S(ylvester)
Lisowski, Gabriel 1946- 47
    Brief entry 31
Liss, Howard 1922-1995 4
    Obituary 84
Lisson, Deborah 1941- 110
    Earlier sketch in SATA 71
List, Ilka Katherine 1935- 6
Liston, Robert A. 1927- 5
Litchfield, Ada B(assett) 1916-1999 5
Litchfield, Jo 1973- 116
Lithgow, John (Arthur) 1945- 145
Litowinsky, Olga (Jean) 1936- 26
Littke, Lael J. 1929- 140
    Earlier sketches in SATA 51, 83
Little, A. Edward
    See Klein, Aaron E.
Little, Douglas 1942- 96
Little, (Flora) Jean 1932- 149
    Earlier sketches in SATA 2, 68, 106
    See also CLR 4
    See also SAAS 17
Little, Lessie Jones 1906-1986 60
    Obituary 50
Little, Mary E. 1912-1999 28
Littlechild, George 1958- 85
Littledale, Freya (Lota) 1929-1992 74
    Earlier sketch in SATA 2
Littlefield, Bill 1948- 83
Littlefield, Holly 1963- 97
Littlesugar, Amy 1953- 122
Littleton, Mark R. 1950- 142
    Earlier sketch in SATA 89
Lively, Penelope 1933- 164
    Earlier sketches in SATA 7, 60, 101
    See also CLR 7
Lively, Penelope Margaret
    See Lively, Penelope
Liversidge, (Henry) Douglas 1913- 8
Livesey, Claire (Warner) 1927- 127

Livingston, Carole 1941- 42
Livingston, (M.) Irene 1932- 150
Livingston, Myra Cohn 1926-1996 68
    Obituary 92
    Earlier sketch in SATA 5
    See also CLR 7
    See also SAAS 1
Livingston, Richard R(oland) 1922- 8
Livo, Norma J. 1929- 76
Llerena Aguirre, Carlos (Antonio) 1952- 19
Llewellyn, Claire 1954- 143
    Earlier sketch in SATA 77
Llewellyn, Grace 1964- 110
Llewellyn, Grace Katherine
    See Llewellyn, Grace
Llewellyn, Richard
    See Llewellyn Lloyd, Richard Dafydd Vivian
Llewellyn, Sam 1948- 95
Llewellyn Lloyd, Richard Dafydd Vivian
    1906-1983 11
    Obituary 37
    See Llewellyn, Richard
Llewelyn, T. Harcourt
    See Hamilton, Charles (Harold St. John)
Lloyd, Alan
    See Lloyd, A.R.
Lloyd, Alan Richard
    See Lloyd, A.R.
Lloyd, A.R. 1927- 168
    Earlier sketch in SATA 97
Lloyd, David
    See Lloyd, David T.
Lloyd, David T. 1954- 167
Lloyd, E. James
    See James, Elizabeth
Lloyd, Errol 1943- 22
Lloyd, Hugh
    See Fitzhugh, Percy Keese
Lloyd, James
    See James, Elizabeth
Lloyd, Megan 1958- 117
    Earlier sketch in SATA 77
Lloyd, (Mary) Norris 1908-1993 10
    Obituary 75
Lloyd Webber, Andrew 1948- 56
    See Webber, Andrew Lloyd
Llywelyn, Morgan 1937- 109
Lo, Ginnie 165
Lo, Virginia M.
    See Lo, Ginnie
Lobato, Jose Bento Monteiro 1882-1948 .. 114
Lobel, Anita (Kempler) 1934- 162
    Earlier sketches in SATA 6, 55, 96
Lobel, Arnold (Stark) 1933-1987 55
    Obituary 54
    Earlier sketch in SATA 6
    See also CLR 5
Lobsenz, Amelia 12
Lobsenz, Norman M(itchell) 1919- 6
Lochak, Michele 1936- 39
Lochlons, Colin
    See Jackson, C(aary) Paul
Locke, Clinton W. 1
Locke, Elsie (Violet) 1912-2001 87
Locke, Lucie 1904-1989 10
Locke, Robert 1944- 63
    See Bess, Clayton
Locker, Thomas 1937- 109
    Earlier sketch in SATA 59
    See also CLR 14
Lockridge, Hildegarde (Dolson) 1908-1981
    121
    See Dolson, Hildegarde
Lockwood, Mary
    See Spelman, Mary
Lodge, Bernard 1933- 107
    Earlier sketch in SATA 33
Lodge, Jo 1966- 112
Loeb, Jeffrey 1946- 57
Loeb, Robert H., Jr. 1917- 21
Loefgren, Ulf 1931- 3

Loehfelm, Bill 1969- 153
Loeper, John J(oseph) 1929- 118
    Earlier sketch in SATA 10
Loescher, Ann Dull 1942- 20
Loescher, Gil(burt Damian) 1945- 20
Loewer, Jean Jenkins
    See Jenkins, Jean
Loewer, (Henry) Peter 1934- 98
LoFaro, Jerry 1959- 77
Lofo
    See Heimann, Rolf
Lofting, Hugh (John) 1886-1947 100
    Earlier sketch in SATA 15
    See also CLR 19
Lofts, Norah (Robinson) 1904-1983 8
    Obituary 36
Logan, Jake
    See Knott, William C(ecil, Jr.)
    and Krepps, Robert W(ilson)
    and Pearl, Jacques Bain
    and Riefe, Alan
    and Rifkin, Shepard
    and Smith, Martin Cruz
Logan, Mark
    See Nicole, Christopher (Robin)
Logan, Rochelle 1954- 169
Logston, Anne 1962- 112
Logue, Christopher 1926- 23
Logue, Mary 1952- 161
    Earlier sketch in SATA 112
Loh, Morag 1935- 73
Lohans, Alison 1949- 101
Loken, Newton Clayton 1919- 26
Lomas, Steve
    See Brennan, Joseph Lomas
Lomask, Milton (Nachman) 1909-1991 20
Lombino, Salvatore
    See Hunter, Evan
LoMonaco, Palmyra 1932- 102
London, Jack 1876-1916 18
    See also CLR 108
    See London, John Griffith
London, Jane
    See Geis, Darlene Stern
London, Jonathan (Paul) 1947- 157
    Earlier sketches in SATA 74, 113
Lonergan, (Pauline) Joy (MacLean) 1909- . 10
Lonette, Reisie (Dominee) 1924- 43
Long, Cathryn J. 1946- 89
Long, Earlene (Roberta) 1938- 50
Long, Emmett
    See Leonard, Elmore (John, Jr.)
Long, Helen Beecher 1
Long, Judith Elaine 1953- 20
Long, Judy
    See Long, Judith Elaine
Long, Kim 1949- 69
Long, Loren 1966(?)- 151
Long, Melinda 1960- 152
Long, Sylvia 1948- 120
Longbeard, Frederick
    See Longyear, Barry B(rookes)
Longfellow, Henry Wadsworth 1807-1882 . 19
    See also CLR 99
Longfellow, Layne (A.) 1937- 102
Longman, Harold S. 1919- 5
Longsworth, Polly 1933- 28
Longtemps, Kenneth 1933- 17
Longway, A. Hugh
    See Lang, Andrew
Longyear, Barry B(rookes) 1942- 117
Loomans, Diane 1955- 90
Loomis, Christine 160
    Earlier sketch in SATA 113
Loomis, Jennifer A. 1942- 101
Loomis, Robert D. 5
Lopez, Angelo (Cayas) 1967- 83
Lopez, Barry (Holstun) 1945- 67
Lopshire, Robert M(artin) 1927- 6
Loraine, Connie
    See Reece, Colleen L.

Author Index

Lorbiecki, Marybeth 1959- *121*
Lord, Athena V. 1932- *39*
Lord, Beman 1924-1991 .... *5*
   Obituary *69*
Lord, Bette Bao 1938- *58*
Lord, (Doreen Mildred) Douglas 1904- *12*
Lord, John Vernon 1939- *21*
Lord, Nancy
   See Titus, Eve
Lord, Walter 1917-2002 .... *3*
Lorde, Diana
   See Reno, Dawn E(laine)
Lorenz, Albert 1941- *115*
Lorenzini, Carlo 1826-1890 .... *100*
   Earlier sketch in SATA 29
   See Collodi, Carlo
Lorimer, Janet 1941- *60*
Loring, Emilie (Baker) 1864(?)-1951 .... *51*
Lorkowski, Thomas V(incent) 1950- *92*
Lorkowski, Tom
   See Lorkowski, Thomas V(incent)
Lorraine, Walter (Henry) 1929- *16*
Lorrimer, Claire
   See Clark, Patricia Denise
Loss, Joan 1933- *11*
Lothrop, Harriet Mulford Stone 1844-1924
   .... *20*
Lottridge, Celia Barker 1936- *157*
   Earlier sketch in SATA *112*
LoTurco, Laura 1963- *84*
Lotz, Wolfgang 1912-1981 .... *65*
Louie, Ai-Ling 1949- *40*
   Brief entry *34*
Louis, Pat
   See Francis, Dorothy Brenner
Louisburgh, Sheila Burnford
   See Burnford, Sheila (Philip Cochrane Every)
Louise, Anita
   See Riggio, Anita
Lourie, Helen
   See Storr, Catherine (Cole)
Lourie, Peter (King) 1952- *142*
   Earlier sketch in SATA *82*
Love, Ann 1947- *168*
   Earlier sketch in SATA *79*
Love, D. Anne 1949- *145*
   Earlier sketch in SATA *96*
Love, Douglas 1967- *92*
Love, Katherine (Isabel) 1907- *3*
Love, Kathleen Ann
   See Love, Ann
Love, Sandra (Weller) 1940- *26*
Lovejoy, Jack 1937- *116*
Lovelace, Delos Wheeler 1894-1967 .... *7*
Lovelace, Maud Hart 1892-1980 .... *2*
   Obituary *23*
Lovell, Ingraham
   See Bacon, Josephine Dodge (Daskam)
Loverseed, Amanda (Jane) 1965- *75*
Lovett, Margaret (Rose) 1915- *22*
Low, Alice 1926- *156*
   Earlier sketches in SATA *11, 76*
Low, Elizabeth Hammond 1898-1991 .... *5*
Low, Joseph 1911- *14*
Lowe, Jay, Jr.
   See Loeper, John J(oseph)
Lowell, Susan 1950- *127*
   Earlier sketch in SATA *81*
Lowenstein, Dyno 1914-1996 .... *6*
Lowenstein, Sallie 1949- *116*
Lowery, Linda 1949- *151*
   Earlier sketch in SATA *74*
Lowitz, Anson C. 1901(?)-1978 .... *18*
Lowitz, Sadyebeth Heath 1901-1969 .... *17*
Lowndes, Robert A(ugustine) W(ard)
   1916-1998 .... *117*
Lowrey, Janette Sebring 1892-1986 .... *43*

Lowry, Lois (Hammersburg) 1937- *111*
   Autobiography Feature *127*
   Earlier sketches in SATA 23, 70
   See also CLR 72
   See also SAAS 3
Lowry, Peter 1953- *7*
Loyie, Larry 1933- *150*
Lozansky, Edward D. 1941- *62*
Lozier, Herbert 1915- *26*
Lubar, David 1954- *133*
Lubell, Cecil 1912-2000 .... *6*
Lubell, Winifred (A. Milius) 1914- *6*
Lubin, Leonard
   See Lubin, Leonard B.
Lubin, Leonard B. 1943-1994 .... *45*
   Brief entry *37*
Lubka, S. Ruth 1948- *154*
Luby, Thia 1954- *124*
Lucado, Max (Lee) 1955- *104*
Lucas, Cedric 1962- *101*
Lucas, E(dward) V(errall) 1868-1938 .... *20*
Lucas, Eileen 1956- *113*
   Earlier sketch in SATA 76
Lucas, George 1944- *56*
Lucas, Jerry 1940- *33*
Lucas, Victoria
   See Plath, Sylvia
Lucashenko, Melissa 1967- *104*
Luccarelli, Vincent 1923- *90*
Luce, Celia (Geneva Larsen) 1914- *38*
Luce, Willard (Ray) 1914-1990 .... *38*
Lucht, Irmgard 1937- *82*
Luckett, Dave 1951- *167*
   Earlier sketch in SATA *106*
Luckhardt, Mildred Corell 1898-1990 .... *5*
Ludel, Jacqueline 1945- *64*
Ludlum, Mabel Cleland
   See Widdemer, Mabel Cleland
Ludwig, Helen *33*
Ludwig, Lyndell 1923- *63*
Ludwig, Trudy 1959- *166*
Lueders, Edward (George) 1923- *14*
Luenn, Nancy 1954- *79*
   Earlier sketch in SATA *51*
Lufkin, Raymond H. 1897- *38*
Lugard, Flora Louisa Shaw 1852-1929 .... *21*
Luger, Harriett Mandelay 1914- *23*
Luhrmann, Winifred B(ruce) 1934- *11*
Luis, Earlene W. 1929- *11*
Lum, Peter
   See Crowe, (Bettina) Peter Lum
Lumry, Amanda (R.) *159*
Lund, Deb *157*
Lund, Doris Herold 1919- *12*
Lung, Chang
   See Rigney, James Oliver, Jr.
Lunge-Larsen, Lise 1955- *138*
Lunn, Carolyn (Kowalczyk) 1960- *67*
Lunn, Janet (Louise Swoboda) 1928- *110*
   Earlier sketches in SATA 4, 68
   See also CLR *18*
   See also SAAS *12*
Lunsford, Cin Forshay
   See Forshay-Lunsford, Cin
Lupoff, Dick
   See Lupoff, Richard A(llen)
Lupoff, Richard A(llen) 1935- *60*
Lurie, Alison 1926- *112*
   Earlier sketch in SATA 46
Lurie, Morris 1938- *72*
Lussert, Anneliese 1929- *101*
Lusted, Marcia Amidon 1962- *143*
Lustig, Arnost 1926- *56*
Lustig, Loretta 1944- *46*
Luther, Rebekah (Lyn) S(tiles) 1960- *90*
Luttmann, Gail
   See Damerow, Gail (Jane)
Luttrell, Guy L. 1938- *22*
Luttrell, Ida (Alleene) 1934- *91*
   Brief entry *35*
   Earlier sketch in SATA 40

Luttrell, William (J. III) 1954- *149*
Lutz, Norma Jean 1943- *122*
Lutzeier, Elizabeth 1952- *72*
Lutzker, Edythe 1904-1991 .... *5*
Luxbacher, Irene M. 1970- *153*
Luzadder, Patrick 1954- *89*
Luzzati, Emanuele 1921- *7*
Luzzatto, Paola Caboara 1938- *38*
Lybbert, Tyler 1970- *88*
Lydon, Michael 1942- *11*
Lyfick, Warren
   See Reeves, Lawrence F.
Lyle, Katie Letcher 1938- *8*
Lynch, Chris 1962- *131*
   Earlier sketch in SATA 95
   See also CLR 58
Lynch, Lorenzo 1932- *7*
Lynch, Marietta 1947- *29*
Lynch, P(atrick) J(ames) 1962- *122*
   Earlier sketch in SATA 79
Lynch, Patricia (Nora) 1898-1972 .... *9*
Lynds, Dennis 1924-2005 .... *47*
   Brief entry *37*
Lyngseth, Joan
   See Davies, Joan
Lynn, Elizabeth A(nne) 1946- *99*
Lynn, Mary
   See Brokamp, Marilyn
Lynn, Patricia
   See Watts, Mabel Pizzey
Lyon, Elinor 1921- *6*
Lyon, George Ella 1949- *148*
   Autobiography Feature *148*
   Earlier sketches in SATA *68, 119*
Lyon, Lyman R.
   See de Camp, L(yon) Sprague
Lyons, Dorothy M(arawee) 1907-1997 .... *3*
Lyons, Grant 1941- *30*
Lyons, Marcus
   See Blish, James (Benjamin)
Lyons, Mary E(velyn) 1947- *142*
   Earlier sketch in SATA *93*
Lystad, Mary (Hanemann) 1928- *11*
Lytle, Elizabeth Stewart 1949- *79*
Lytle, Robert A. 1944- *119*
Lyttle, Richard B(ard) 1927- *23*
Lytton, Edward G(eorge) E(arle) L(ytton)
   Bulwer-Lytton Baron 1803-1873 .... *23*

M

Ma, Wenhai 1954- *84*
Maar, Leonard (Frank, Jr.) 1927- *30*
Maartens, Maretha 1945- *73*
Maas, Selve -1997 .... *14*
Mabie, Grace
   See Mattern, Joanne
Mac
   See MacManus, Seumas
   and Maccari, Ruggero
Macalaster, Elizabeth G. 1951- *115*
MacAlister, Katie *159*
MacAodhagain, Eamon
   See Egan, E(dward) W(elstead)
MacArthur-Onslow, Annette Rosemary 1933-
   .... *26*
Macaulay, David (Alexander) 1946- *137*
   Brief entry *27*
   Earlier sketches in SATA *46, 72*
   See also CLR *14*
Macaulay, Teresa (E.) 1947- *95*
MacBeth, George (Mann) 1932-1992 .... *4*
   Obituary *70*
MacBride, Roger Lea 1929-1995 .... *85*
MacCarter, Don 1944- *91*
MacClintock, Dorcas 1932- *8*
MacDonald, Amy 1951- *156*
   Autobiography Feature *156*
   Earlier sketches in SATA *76, 136*

MacDonald, Anne Elizabeth Campbell Bard -1958
  See MacDonald, Betty
MacDonald, Anson
  See Heinlein, Robert A(nson)
MacDonald, Betty 1908-1958
  See YABC *1*
  See MacDonald, Anne Elizabeth Campbell Bard
Macdonald, Blackie
  See Emrich, Duncan (Black Macdonald)
Macdonald, Caroline 1948- 86
  Obituary 111
  See also CLR 60
Macdonald, Dwight 1906-1982 29
  Obituary 33
MacDonald, George 1824-1905 100
  Earlier sketch in SATA *33*
  See also CLR 67
MacDonald, Golden
  See Brown, Margaret Wise
Macdonald, James D. 1954- 165
  Earlier sketches in SATA *81, 114*
  See Appleton, Victor
Macdonald, Marcia
  See Hill, Grace Livingston
MacDonald, Margaret Read 1940- 164
  Earlier sketch in SATA *94*
Macdonald, Marianne 1934- 113
Macdonald, Mary
  See Gifford, Griselda
MacDonald, Maryann 1947- 72
Macdonald, Shelagh 1937- 25
MacDonald, Suse 1940- 109
  Brief entry 52
  Earlier sketch in SATA *54*
Macdonald, Zillah K(atherine) 1885-1979 .. 11
MacDonnell, Megan
  See Stevens, Serita (Deborah)
MacDougal, John
  See Blish, James (Benjamin)
MacDougal, John
  See Blish, James (Benjamin)
  and Lowndes, Robert A(ugustine) W(ard)
Mace, Elisabeth 1933- 27
Mace, Varian 1938- 49
MacEwen, Gwendolyn (Margaret) 1941-1987
  50
  Obituary 55
Macfarlan, Allan A. 1892-1982 35
MacFarlane, Iris 1922- 11
MacGill-Callahan, Sheila 1926-2000 78
MacGregor, Carol Lynn 153
MacGregor, Ellen 1906-1954 39
  Brief entry 27
MacGregor-Hastie, Roy (Alasdhair Niall) 1929- 3
MacGrory, Yvonne 1948- 142
Machado, Ana Maria 1941- 150
Machetanz, Frederick 1908- 34
Machin Goodall, Daphne (Edith) 37
Macht, Norman L(ee) 1929- 122
MacInnes, Helen (Clark) 1907-1985 22
  Obituary 44
Macintosh, Brownie 1950- 98
MacIntyre, Elisabeth 1916- 17
Mack, Stan(ley) 17
Mack, Todd 168
Mack, Tracy 1968- 128
Mackall, Dandi D(aley) 1949- 118
Mackay, Claire 1930- 97
  Autobiography Feature 124
  Earlier sketch in SATA *40*
  See also CLR 43
Mackay, Constance D'Arcy (?)-1966 125
Mackay, Donald 1914-2005 81
Mackay, Donald Alexander
  See Mackay, Donald
MacKaye, Percy (Wallace) 1875-1956 32
Mackel, Kathryn 1950- 162

Mackel, Kathy
  See Mackel, Kathryn
MacKellar, William 1914- 4
Macken, Walter 1915-1967 36
MacKenzie, Jill (Kelly) 1947- 75
Mackey, Ernan
  See McInerny, Ralph (Matthew)
Mackie, Maron
  See McNeely, Jeannette
Mackin, Edward
  See McInerny, Ralph (Matthew)
MacKinnon, Bernie 1957- 69
MacKinnon Groomer, Vera 1915- 57
MacKinstry, Elizabeth 1879-1956 42
Mackler, Carolyn 1973- 156
MacLachlan, Patricia 1938- 168
  Brief entry 42
  Earlier sketches in SATA *62, 107*
  See also CLR *14*
MacLane, Jack
  See Crider, (Allen) Bill(y)
MacLean, Alistair (Stuart) 1922(?)-1987 23
  Obituary 50
Maclean, Art
  See Shirreffs, Gordon D(onald)
MacLean, Glynne 1964- 150
MacLeod, Beatrice 1910- 162
  Earlier sketch in SATA *10*
MacLeod, Beatrice Beach
  See MacLeod, Beatrice
MacLeod, Charlotte (Matilda) 1922-2005 ... 28
  Obituary 160
MacLeod, Doug 1959- 60
MacLeod, Elizabeth 158
MacLeod, Ellen Jane (Anderson) 1916- 14
MacManus, James
  See MacManus, Seumas
MacManus, Seumas 1869-1960 25
MacMaster, Eve (Ruth) B(owers) 1942- 46
MacMillan, Annabelle
  See Quick, Annabelle
MacMillan, Dianne M(arie) 1943- 125
  Earlier sketch in SATA *84*
Macneill, Janet
  See McNeely, Jeannette
MacPeek, Walter G. 1902-1973 4
  Obituary 25
MacPhail, Catherine 1946- 130
MacPherson, Margaret 1908- 9
  See also SAAS *4*
MacPherson, Winnie 1930- 107
Macrae, Travis
  See Feagles, Anita M(acRae)
MacRaois, Cormac 1944- 72
Macumber, Mari
  See Sandoz, Mari(e Susette)
Macy, Sue 1954- 134
  Earlier sketch in SATA *88*
Madaras, Lynda 1947- 151
Madden, Don 1927- 3
Madden, Kerry 1961- 168
Madden-Lunsford, Kerry
  See Madden, Kerry
Maddern, Eric 1950- 166
Maddison, Angela Mary 1923- 10
  See Banner, Angela
Maddock, Reginald (Bertram) 1912-1994 ... 15
Madenski, Melissa (Ann) 1949- 77
Madian, Jon 1941- 9
Madison, Arnold 1937- 6
Madison, Winifred 5
Madonna 1958- 149
Madsen, Ross Martin 1946- 82
Madsen, Susan A(rrington) 1954- 90
Maestro, Betsy (Crippen) 1944- 106
  Brief entry 30
  Earlier sketch in SATA *59*
  See also CLR *45*
Maestro, Giulio 1942- 106
  Earlier sketches in SATA *8, 59*
  See also CLR *45*

Maeterlinck, Maurice 1862-1949 66
Magee, Doug 1947- 78
Magee, Wes 1939- 64
Maggio, Rosalie 1943- 69
Magid, Ken(neth Marshall) 65
Magnus, Erica 1946- 77
Magorian, James 1942- 92
  Earlier sketch in SATA *32*
Magorian, Michelle 1947- 128
  Earlier sketch in SATA *67*
Magovern, Peg 103
Maguire, Anne
  See Nearing, Penny
Maguire, Gregory 1954- 129
  Earlier sketches in SATA *28, 84*
  See also SAAS 22
Maguire, Gregory Peter
  See Maguire, Gregory
Maguire, Jack 1920-2000 74
Maguire, Jesse
  See Smith, Sherwood
Maguire, Jessie
  See Smith, Sherwood
Maher, Ramona 1934- 13
Mahlqvist, (Karl) Stefan 30
  See Maehlqvist, (Karl) Stefan
Mahon, Julia C(unha) 1916- 11
Mahood, Kenneth 1930- 24
Mahy, Margaret (May) 1936- 119
  Earlier sketches in SATA *14, 69*
  See also CLR 78
Maiden, Cecil (Edward) 1902-1981 52
Maidoff, Ilka
  See List, Ilka Katherine
Maifair, Linda Lee 1947- 83
Maik, Henri
  See Hecht, Henri Joseph
Maillu, David G(ian) 1939- 111
Maine, Trevor
  See Catherall, Arthur
Mains, Randolph P. 1946- 80
Maiorano, Robert 1946- 43
Maisner, Heather 1947- 89
Maison, Della
  See Katz, Bobbi
Maitland, Antony Jasper 1935- 25
Maitland, Barbara 102
Major, Kevin (Gerald) 1949- 134
  Earlier sketches in SATA *32, 82*
  See also CLR *11*
Majure, Janet 1954- 96
Makie, Pam 1943- 37
Makowski, Silk
  See Makowski, Silvia Ann
Makowski, Silvia Ann 1940- 101
Malam, John 1957- 152
  Earlier sketch in SATA *89*
Malcolm, Dan
  See Silverberg, Robert
Malcolm, Jahnna N.
  See Beecham, Jahnna
Malcolmson, Anne
  See von Storch, Anne B.
Malcolmson, David 1899-1978 6
Maletta, Dr. Arlene
  See Feltenstein, Arlene (H.)
Mali, Jane Lawrence 1937-1995 51
  Brief entry 44
  Obituary 86
Mallett, Jerry J. 1939- 76
Mallory, Kenneth 1945- 128
Mallowan, Agatha Christie
  See Christie, Agatha (Mary Clarissa)
Malmberg, Carl 1904-1979 9
Malmgren, Dallin 1949- 65
Malo, John W. 1911-2000 4
Malone, James Hiram 1930- 84
Malone, Patricia 1932- 155
Maloney, Pat
  See Markun, Patricia Maloney

Malory, Sir Thomas 1410(?)-1471(?) *59*
  Brief entry *33*
Malvasi, Meg Greene *143*
Malvern, Corinne 1905-1956 .... *34*
Malvern, Gladys (?)-1962 .... *23*
Mama G.
  See Davis, Grania
Mammano, Julie (Lynn) 1962- *107*
Mamonova, Tatyana 1943- *93*
Manchel, Frank 1935- *10*
Manchester, William (Raymond) 1922-2004
  .... *65*
Mandel, Brett H. 1969- *108*
Mandel, Peter (Bevan) 1957-1998 .... *87*
Mandel, Sally (Elizabeth) 1944- *64*
Mandell, Muriel (Hortense Levin) 1921- *63*
Manes, Stephen 1949- *99*
  Brief entry *40*
  Earlier sketch in SATA *42*
Manfred, Frederick (Feikema) 1912-1994 .. *30*
Mangin, Marie France 1940- *59*
Mangione, Jerre *6*
  Obituary *104*
  See Mangione, Gerlando
Mango, Karin N. 1936- *52*
Mangurian, David 1938- *14*
Mania, Cathy 1950- *102*
Mania, Robert (C.) 1952- *102*
Maniatty, Taramesha 1978- *92*
Maniscalco, Joseph 1926- *10*
Manley, Deborah 1932- *28*
Manley, Seon 1921- *15*
  See also CLR *3*
  See also SAAS *2*
Mann, Elizabeth 1948- *153*
Mann, Josephine
  See Pullein-Thompson, Josephine (Mary
  Wedderburn)
Mann, Kenny 1946- *91*
Mann, Pamela 1946- *91*
Mann, Patrick
  See Waller, Leslie
Mann, Peggy *6*
  See Houlton, Peggy Mann
Mannetti, Lisa 1953- *57*
  Brief entry *51*
Mannheim, Grete (Salomon) 1909-1986 ..... *10*
Manniche, Lise 1943- *31*
Manning, Rosemary (Joy) 1911-1988 .... *10*
  See Davys, Sarah
  and Voyle, Mary
Manning, Sarra *162*
Manning-Sanders, Ruth (Vernon) 1895(?)-1988
  .... *73*
  Obituary *57*
  Earlier sketch in SATA *15*
Manson, Ainslie Kertland 1938- *115*
Manson, Beverlie 1945- *57*
  Brief entry *44*
Manthorpe, Helen 1958- *122*
Mantinband, Gerda (B.) 1917- *74*
Manton, Jo
  See Gittings, Jo (Grenville) Manton
Manuel, Lynn 1948- *99*
Manushkin, Fran 1942- *166*
Manushkin, Fran 1942- *166*
  Earlier sketches in SATA *7, 54, 93*
Manushkin, Frances
  See Manushkin, Fran
Man Without a Spleen, A
  See Chekhov, Anton (Pavlovich)
Manzano, Sonia 1950- *167*
Mapes, Mary A.
  See Ellison, Virginia H(owell)
Maple, Marilyn 1931- *80*
Mappin, Strephyn 1956- *109*
Mara, Barney
  See Roth, Arthur J(oseph)
Mara, Jeanette
  See Cebulash, Mel

Marasmus, Seymour
  See Rivoli, Mario
Marbach, Ethel
  See Pochocki, Ethel (Frances)
Marcal, Annette B.
  See Callaway, Bernice (Anne)
Marcelino
  See Agnew, Edith J(osephine)
Marcellino, Fred 1939-2001 .... *118*
  Obituary *127*
  Earlier sketch in SATA *68*
March, Carl
  See Fleischman, (Albert) Sid(ney)
Marchant, Bessie 1862-1941
  See YABC *2*
Marchant, Catherine
  See Cookson, Catherine (McMullen)
Marcher, Marion Walden 1890-1987 .... *10*
Marchesi, Stephen 1951- *114*
Marchesi, Steve
  See Marchesi, Stephen
  and Older, Effin
  and Older, Jules
Marciano, John Bemelmans 1970- *118*
  See also CLR *93*
Marciano, John Bemelmans 1970- *167*
Marco, Lou
  See Gottfried, Theodore Mark
Marcus, Leonard S. 1950- *133*
Marcus, Paul 1953- *82*
Marcus, Rebecca B(rian) 1907- *9*
Marcuse, Aida E. 1934- *89*
Margaret, Karla
  See Andersdatter, Karla M(argaret)
Margolin, Harriet
  See Ziefert, Harriet
Margolis, Jeffrey A. 1948- *108*
Margolis, Richard J(ules) 1929-1991 .... *86*
  Obituary *67*
  Earlier sketch in SATA *4*
Margolis, Vivienne 1922- *46*
Mariana
  See Foster, Marian Curtis
Marie, Geraldine 1949- *61*
Mariner, Scott
  See Pohl, Frederik
Marino, Dorothy Bronson 1912- *14*
Marino, Jan 1936- *114*
Marino, Nick
  See Deming, Richard
Mario, Anna
  See Odgers, Sally Farrell
Marion, Henry
  See del Rey, Lester
Maris, Ron *71*
  Brief entry *45*
Mark, Jan 1943-2006 .... *164*
  Earlier sketches in SATA *22, 69, 114*
  See also CLR *11*
Mark, Janet Marjorie
  See Mark, Jan
Mark, Joan T. 1937- *122*
Mark, Pauline (Dahlin) 1913-1997 .... *14*
Mark, Polly
  See Mark, Pauline (Dahlin)
Mark, Ted
  See Gottfried, Theodore Mark
Markel, Michelle *169*
Marker, Sherry 1941- *76*
Markert, Jennifer 1965- *83*
Markert, Jenny
  See Markert, Jennifer
Markham, Lynne 1947- *102*
Markham, Marion M. 1929- *60*
Markins, W. S.
  See Jenkins, Marie M(agdalen)
Markle, Sandra L(ee) 1946- *148*
  Brief entry *41*
  Earlier sketches in SATA *57, 92*
Marko, Katherine D(olores) *28*

Markoosie
  See CLR *23*
  See Patsauq, Markoosie
Marks, Alan 1957- *151*
  Earlier sketch in SATA *77*
Marks, Burton 1930- *47*
  Brief entry *43*
Marks, Graham *158*
Marks, Hannah K.
  See Trivelpiece, Laurel
Marks, J
  See Highwater, Jamake (Mamake)
Marks, J.
  See Highwater, Jamake (Mamake)
Marks, J(ames) M(acdonald) 1921- *13*
Marks, Laurie J. 1957- *68*
Marks, Mickey Klar -1986 .... *12*
Marks, Peter
  See Smith, Robert Kimmel
Marks, Rita 1938- *47*
Marks, Stan(ley) *14*
Marks-Highwater, J
  See Highwater, Jamake (Mamake)
Marks-Highwater, J.
  See Highwater, Jamake (Mamake)
Markun, Patricia Maloney 1924- *15*
Markusen, Bruce (Stanley Rodriguez) 1965-
  .... *141*
Marley, Louise 1952- *120*
Marlin, Hilda
  See Van Stockum, Hilda
Marlow, Max
  See Nicole, Christopher (Robin)
Marlowe, Amy Bell *67*
  Earlier sketch in SATA *1*
Marney, Dean 1952- *90*
Marokvia, Artur 1909- *31*
Marokvia, Mireille (Journet) 1918- *5*
Marol, Jean-Claude 1946- *125*
Marr, John S(tuart) 1940- *48*
Marric, J. J.
  See Butler, William (Arthur) Vivian
  and Creasey, John
Marrin, Albert 1936- *126*
  Brief entry *43*
  Earlier sketches in SATA *53, 90*
  See also CLR *53*
Marriott, Alice Lee 1910-1992 .... *31*
  Obituary *71*
Marriott, Janice 1946- *134*
Marriott, Pat(ricia) 1920- *35*
Marroquin, Patricio
  See Markun, Patricia Maloney
Mars, W. T.
  See Mars, Witold Tadeusz J.
Mars, Witold Tadeusz J. 1912-1985 .... *3*
Marsden, Carolyn 1950- *140*
Marsden, John 1950- *146*
  Earlier sketches in SATA *66, 97*
  See also CLR *34*
  See also SAAS *22*
Marsh, Carole 1946- *127*
Marsh, Dave 1950- *66*
Marsh, J. E.
  See Marshall, Evelyn
Marsh, James 1946- *73*
Marsh, Jean
  See Marshall, Evelyn
Marsh, Joan F. 1923- *83*
Marsh, Valerie 1954- *89*
Marshall, Anthony D(ryden) 1924- *18*
Marshall, Bonnie C. 1941- *141*
  Earlier sketch in SATA *18*
Marshall, Bridget M(ary) 1974- *103*
Marshall, (Sarah) Catherine (Wood) 1914-1983
  .... *2*
  Obituary *34*
Marshall, Douglas
  See McClintock, Marshall
Marshall, Edward
  See Marshall, James (Edward)

Marshall, Evelyn 1897-1991 11
Marshall, Felicity 1950- 116
Marshall, Garry 1934- 60
Marshall, H. H.
    See Jahn, (Joseph) Michael
Marshall, James (Edward) 1942-1992 75
    Earlier sketches in SATA 6, 51
    See also CLR 21
Marshall, James Vance
    See Payne, Donald Gordon
Marshall, Janet (Perry) 1938- 97
Marshall, Jeff
    See Laycock, George (Edwin)
Marshall, Kim
    See Marshall, Michael (Kimbrough)
Marshall, Michael (Kimbrough) 1948- 37
Marshall, Percy
    See Young, Percy M(arshall)
Marshall, S(amuel) L(yman) A(twood)
    1900-1977 21
Marsoli, Lisa Ann 1958- 101
    Brief entry 53
Marsten, Richard
    See Hunter, Evan
Marston, Elsa 1933- 156
Marston, Hope Irvin 1935- 127
    Earlier sketch in SATA 31
Marszalek, John F., Jr.) 1939- 167
Marszalek, John Francis 1939-
    See Marszalek, John F., Jr.)
Martchenko, Michael 1942- 154
    Earlier sketches in SATA 50, 95
Martel, Aimee
    See Thurlo, Aimee
    and Thurlo, David
Martel, Suzanne 1924- 99
Martin, Ann M(atthews) 1955- 126
    Brief entry 41
    Earlier sketches in SATA 44, 70
    See also CLR 32
Martin, Bill, Jr. 67
    Brief entry 40
    See also CLR 97
    See Martin, William Ivan, Jr.
Martin, Charles E(lmer) 70
    Earlier sketch in SATA 69
    See Mastrangelo, Charles E(lmer)
Martin, Christopher
    See Hoyt, Edwin P(almer), Jr.
Martin, Claire 1933- 76
Martin, David Stone 1913-1992 39
Martin, Donald
    See Honig, Donald
Martin, Dorothy 1921- 47
Martin, Eugene 1
Martin, Eva M. 1939- 65
Martin, Frances M(cEntee) 1906-1998 36
Martin, Francesca 1947- 101
Martin, Fred 1948- 119
Martin, Fredric
    See Christopher, Matt(hew Frederick)
Martin, George R(aymond) R(ichard) 1948-
    118
Martin, J(ohn) P(ercival) 1880(?)-1966 15
Martin, Jacqueline Briggs 1945- 149
    Earlier sketch in SATA 98
Martin, Jane Read 1957- 84
Martin, Jeremy
    See Levin, Marcia Obrasky
Martin, Les
    See Schulman, L(ester) M(artin)
Martin, Linda 1961- 82
Martin, Lynne 1923- 21
Martin, Marcia
    See Levin, Marcia Obrasky
Martin, Marvin 1926- 126
Martin, Melanie
    See Pellowski, Michael (Joseph)
Martin, Nancy
    See Salmon, Annie Elizabeth

Martin, Patricia Miles 1899-1986 43
    Obituary 48
    Earlier sketch in SATA 1
Martin, Peter
    See Chaundler, Christine
Martin, Rene 1891-1977 42
    Obituary 20
Martin, Rupert (Claude) 1905- 31
Martin, S. R.
    See Mappin, Strephyn
Martin, Stefan 1936- 32
Martin, Vicky
    See Storey, Victoria Carolyn
Martin, Webber
    See Silverberg, Robert
Martin, Wendy
    See Martini, Teri
Martin, William Ivan, Jr. 1916-2004 145
    Earlier sketch in SATA 40
    See Martin, Bill, Jr.
Martineau, Harriet 1802-1876
    See YABC 2
Martinet, Jeanne 1958- 80
Martinez, Agnes 167
Martinez, Ed(ward) 1954- 98
Martinez, Elizabeth Coonrod 1954- 85
Martinez, Victor 1954- 95
Martini, Teri 1930- 3
Martini, Therese
    See Martini, Teri
Martinson, Janis
    See Herbert, Janis
Marton, Jirina 1946- 144
    Earlier sketch in SATA 95
Marton, Pierre
    See Stone, Peter
Martson, Del
    See Lupoff, Richard A(llen)
Martyr, Paula (Jane) 57
    See Lawford, Paula Jane
Maruki, Toshi 1912-2000 112
    See also CLR 19
Marvin, Isabel R(idout) 1924- 84
Marx, Patricia Windschill 1948- 160
    Earlier sketch in SATA 112
Marx, Robert F(rank) 1936- 24
Marx, Trish
    See Marx, Patricia Windschill
Marzani, Carl (Aldo) 1912-1994 12
Marzollo, Jean 1942- 130
    Earlier sketches in SATA 29, 77
    See also SAAS 15
Masefield, John (Edward) 1878-1967 19
Masoff, Joy 1951- 118
Mason, Adrienne 1962- 163
Mason, Ernst
    See Pohl, Frederik
Mason, F(rancis) van Wyck 1901-1978 3
    Obituary 26
Mason, Frank W.
    See Mason, F(rancis) van Wyck
Mason, George Frederick 1904-2000 14
Mason, Miriam E(vangeline) 1900-1973 2
    Obituary 26
Mason, Tally
    See Derleth, August (William)
Mason, Van Wyck
    See Mason, F(rancis) van Wyck
Mass, Wendy 1967- 158
Mass, William
    See Gibson, William
Masselman, George 1897-1971 19
Massie, Dianne Redfield 1938- 125
    Earlier sketch in SATA 16
Massie, Elizabeth 108
Masson, Sophie 1959- 133
Masters, Anthony (Richard) 1940-2003 112
    Obituary 145
Masters, Kelly R(ay) 1897-1987 3
Masters, Mildred 1932- 42

Masters, William
    See Cousins, Margaret
Masters, Zeke
    See Bensen, Donald R.
    and Goulart, Ron(ald Joseph)
Matas, Carol 1949- 93
    Autobiography Feature 112
    See also CLR 52
Matchette, Katharine E. 1941- 38
Math, Irwin 1940- 42
Mathabane, Mark 1960- 123
Mather, Kirtley F(letcher) 1888-1978 65
Mathers, Petra 1945- 119
    See also CLR 76
Matheson, Richard (Christian) 1953- 119
Matheson, Shirlee Smith 1942- 155
Mathews, Janet 1914-1992 41
Mathews, Judith 80
    See Goldberger, Judith M.
Mathews, Louise
    See Tooke, Louise Mathews
Mathieu, Joe 1949- 94
    Brief entry 36
    Earlier sketch in SATA 43
Mathieu, Joseph P.
    See Mathieu, Joe
Mathis, Sharon Bell 1937- 58
    Earlier sketch in SATA 7
    See also CLR 3
    See also SAAS 3
Matloff, Gregory 1945- 73
Matott, Justin 1961- 109
Matranga, Frances Carfi 1922- 78
Matray, James I. 1948- 161
Matray, James Irving
    See Matray, James I.
Matson, Emerson N(els) 1926- 12
Matsui, Tadashi 1926- 8
Matsuno, Masako 6
    See Kobayashi, Masako Matsuno
Matte, (Encarnacion) L'Enc 1936- 22
Mattern, Joanne 1963- 122
Matthews, Andrew 1948- 138
Matthews, Caitlin 1952- 122
Matthews, Downs 1925- 71
Matthews, Ellen
    See Bache, Ellyn
Matthews, Ellen 1950- 28
Matthews, Jacklyn Meek
    See Meek, Jacklyn O'Hanlon
Matthews, John (Kentigern) 1948- 116
Matthews, Liz
    See Pellowski, Michael (Joseph)
Matthews, Morgan
    See Pellowski, Michael (Joseph)
Matthews, Nicola
    See Browne, N.M.
Matthews, Patricia (Anne) 1927- 28
Matthews, William Henry III 1919- 45
    Brief entry 28
Matthiessen, Peter 1927- 27
Mattingley, Christobel (Rosemary) 1931- ... 85
    Earlier sketch in SATA 37
    See also CLR 24
    See also SAAS 18
Matulay, Laszlo 1912- 43
Matus, Greta 1938- 12
Maugham, W. S.
    See Maugham, W(illiam) Somerset
Maugham, W(illiam) Somerset 1874-1965 . 54
Maugham, William Somerset
    See Maugham, W(illiam) Somerset
Maurer, Diane Philippoff
    See Maurer-Mathison, Diane V(ogel)
Maurer, Diane Vogel
    See Maurer-Mathison, Diane V(ogel)
Maurer-Mathison, Diane V(ogel) 1944- 89
Mauser, Pat Rhoads
    See McCord, Patricia
Mauser, Patricia Rhoads 37
    See McCord, Patricia

Maves, Mary Carolyn 1916- *10*
Maves, Paul B(enjamin) 1913-1994 .... *10*
Mavor, Salley 1955- *125*
Mawicke, Tran 1911- *15*
Max, Peter 1939- *45*
Maxon, Anne
   See Best, (Evangel) Allena Champlin
Maxwell, Arthur S. 1896-1970 .... *11*
Maxwell, Edith 1923- *7*
Maxwell, Gavin 1914-1969 .... *65*
Maxwell, Katie
   See MacAlister, Katie
Maxwell-Hyslop, Miranda 1968- *154*
May, Charles Paul 1920- *4*
May, Elaine Tyler 1947- *120*
May, J. C.
   See May, Julian
May, Julian 1931- *11*
May, Robert Stephen 1929-1996 .... *46*
May, Robin
   See May, Robert Stephen
Mayberry, Florence V(irginia) Wilson *10*
Maybury, Richard J. 1946- *72*
Mayer, Agatha
   See Maher, Ramona
Mayer, Ann M(argaret) 1938- *14*
Mayer, Danuta 1958- *117*
Mayer, Jane Rothschild 1903-2001 .... *38*
Mayer, Marianna 1945- *132*
   Earlier sketches in SATA *32, 83*
Mayer, Mercer 1943- *137*
   Earlier sketches in SATA *16, 32, 73, 129*
   See also CLR *11*
Mayerson, Charlotte Leon *36*
Mayerson, Evelyn Wilde 1935- *55*
Mayfield, Katherine 1958- *118*
Mayfield, Sue 1963- *146*
   Earlier sketch in SATA *72*
Mayhar, Ardath 1930- *38*
Mayhew, James (John) 1964- *149*
   Earlier sketch in SATA *85*
Maynard, Olga 1920- *40*
Mayne, William (James Carter) 1928- *122*
   Earlier sketches in SATA *6, 68*
   See also CLR *25*
   See also SAAS *11*
Maynes, J. O. Rocky, Jr.
   See Maynes, J. Oscar, Jr.
Maynes, J. Oscar, Jr. 1929- *38*
Mayo, Gretchen Will 1936- *163*
   Earlier sketch in SATA *84*
Mayo, Margaret 1935- *165*
   Earlier sketches in SATA *38, 96*
Mayo, Margaret Mary
   See Mayo, Margaret
Mays, Lucinda L(a Bella) 1924- *49*
Mays, (Lewis) Victor (Jr.) 1927- *5*
Mazer, Anne 1953- *105*
   Earlier sketch in SATA *67*
Mazer, Harry 1925- *167*
   Earlier sketches in SATA *31, 67, 105*
   See also CLR *16*
   See also SAAS *11*
Mazer, Norma Fox 1931- *168*
   Earlier sketches in SATA *24, 67, 105*
   See also CLR *23*
   See also SAAS *1*
Mazille, Capucine 1953- *96*
Mazza, Adriana 1928- *19*
Mazzio, Joann 1926- *74*
Mbugua, Kioi Wa 1962- *83*
McAfee, Carol 1955- *81*
McAllister, Amanda
   See Dowdell, Dorothy (Florence) Karns
   and Hager, Jean
   and Meaker, Eloise
McAllister, Margaret I. 1956- *169*
   Earlier sketch in SATA *117*
McAllister, M.I.
   See McAllister, Margaret I.
McArthur, Nancy *96*

McAvoy, Jim 1972- *142*
McBain, Ed
   See Hunter, Evan
McBratney, Sam 1943- *164*
   Earlier sketch in SATA *89*
   See also CLR *44*
McBrier, Michael
   See Older, Effin
   and Older, Jules
McCafferty, Jim 1954- *84*
McCaffery, Janet 1936- *38*
McCaffrey, Anne 1926- *152*
   Autobiography Feature *152*
   Earlier sketches in SATA *8, 70, 116*
   See also CLR *49*
   See also SAAS *11*
McCaffrey, Anne Inez
   See McCaffrey, Anne
McCaffrey, Mary
   See Szudek, Agnes S(usan) P(hilomena)
McCain, Becky Ray 1954- *138*
McCain, Murray (David, Jr.) 1926-1981 .... *7*
   Obituary *29*
McCall, Edith (Sansom) 1911- *6*
McCall, Virginia Nielsen 1909-2000 .... *13*
McCall Smith, Alexander 1948- *73*
McCallum, Phyllis
   See Koch, Phyllis (Mae) McCallum
McCallum, Stephen 1960- *91*
McCampbell, Darlene Z. 1942- *83*
McCann, Edson
   See del Rey, Lester
   and Pohl, Frederik
McCann, Gerald 1916- *41*
McCann, Helen 1948- *75*
McCannon, Dindga *41*
McCants, William D. 1961- *82*
McCarter, Neely Dixon 1929- *47*
McCarthy, Agnes 1933- *4*
McCarthy, Colin (John) 1951- *77*
McCarthy, Meghan *168*
McCarthy, Ralph F. 1950- *139*
McCarthy-Tucker, Sherri N. 1958- *83*
McCarty, Rega Kramer 1904-1986 .... *10*
McCaslin, Nellie 1914-2005 .... *12*
McCaughrean, Geraldine 1951- *139*
   Earlier sketch in SATA *87*
   See also CLR *38*
McCaughren, Tom 1936- *75*
McCauley, Adam 1965- *128*
McCay, (Zenas) Winsor 1869-1934 .... *134*
   Earlier sketch in SATA *41*
McClafferty, Carla Killough 1958- *137*
McCleery, Patsy R. 1925- *133*
   Earlier sketch in SATA *88*
McClintock, Barbara 1955- *146*
   Earlier sketches in SATA *57, 95*
McClintock, Marshall 1906-1967 .... *3*
McClintock, May Garelick
   See Garelick, May
McClintock, Mike
   See McClintock, Marshall
McClintock, Theodore 1902-1971 .... *14*
McClinton, Leon 1933- *11*
McCloskey, Kevin 1951- *79*
McCloskey, (John) Robert 1914-2003 .... *100*
   Obituary *146*
   Earlier sketches in SATA *2, 39*
   See also CLR *7*
McCloy, James F(loyd) 1941- *59*
McClung, Robert M(arshall) 1916- *135*
   Earlier sketches in SATA *2, 68*
   See also CLR *11*
   See also SAAS *15*
McClure, Gillian Mary 1948- *31*
McColley, Kevin 1961- *80*
   See also SAAS *23*
McConduit, Denise Walter 1950- *89*
McConnell, James Douglas Rutherford
   1915-1988 .... *40*
   Obituary *56*

McCord, Anne 1942- *41*
McCord, David (Thompson Watson)
   1897-1997 .... *18*
   Obituary *96*
   See also CLR *9*
McCord, Jean 1924- *34*
McCord, Pat Mauser
   See McCord, Patricia
McCord, Patricia 1943- *159*
   See Mauser, Patricia Rhoads
McCord, Patricia Sue Rhoads Mauser
   See McCord, Patricia
McCormick, Brooks
   See Adams, William Taylor
McCormick, Dell J. 1892-1949 .... *19*
McCormick, (George) Donald (King)
   1911-1998 .... *14*
McCormick, Edith (Joan) 1934- *30*
McCormick, Kimberly A. 1960- *153*
McCormick, Patricia 1956- *128*
McCourt, Lisa 1964- *159*
   Earlier sketch in SATA *117*
McCourt, Malachy 1931- *126*
McCoy, Iola Fuller *3*
McCoy, J(oseph) J(erome) 1917- *8*
McCoy, Karen Kawamoto 1953- *82*
McCoy, Lois (Rich) 1941- *38*
McCrady, Lady 1951- *16*
McCrea, James (Craig, Jr.) 1920- *3*
McCrea, Ruth (Pirman) 1921- *3*
McCreigh, James
   See Pohl, Frederik
McCrumb, Sharyn 1948- *109*
McCue, Lisa (Emiline) 1959- *65*
McCullen, Andrew
   See Arthur, Robert, (Jr.)
McCullers, (Lula) Carson (Smith) 1917-1967
   .... *27*
McCulloch, John Tyler
   See Burroughs, Edgar Rice
McCulloch, Sarah
   See Ure, Jean
McCullough, David (Gaub) 1933- *62*
McCullough, Frances Monson 1938- *8*
McCullough, Sharon Pierce 1943- *131*
McCully, Emily Arnold *134*
   Autobiography Feature *134*
   Earlier sketches in SATA *5, 110*
   See also CLR *46*
   See also SAAS *7*
   See Arnold, Emily
McCune, Dan
   See Haas, Dorothy F.
McCunn, Ruthanne Lum 1946- *63*
McCurdy, Michael (Charles) 1942- *147*
   Earlier sketches in SATA *13, 82*
McCutcheon, Elsie (Mary Jackson) 1937- .. *60*
McCutcheon, John 1952- *97*
McDaniel, Becky Bring 1953- *61*
McDaniel, Lurlene 1944- *146*
   Earlier sketch in SATA *71*
McDaniels, Pellom III 1968- *121*
McDearmon, Kay *20*
McDermott, Beverly Brodsky 1941- *11*
McDermott, Eleni *156*
McDermott, Gerald (Edward) 1941- *163*
   Earlier sketches in SATA *16, 74*
   See also CLR *9*
McDermott, Michael 1962- *76*
McDevitt, John Charles *155*
   Earlier sketch in SATA *94*
   See McDevitt, Jack
McDole, Carol
   See Farley, Carol (J.)
McDonald, Collin 1943- *79*
McDonald, Gerald D(oan) 1905-1970 .... *3*
McDonald, Jamie
   See Heide, Florence Parry
McDonald, Janet 1953- *148*
McDonald, Jill (Masefield) 1927-1982 .... *13*
   Obituary *29*

McDonald, Joyce 1946- 164
    Earlier sketch in SATA 101
McDonald, Lucile Saunders 1898-1992 10
McDonald, Mary Ann 1956- 84
McDonald, Megan 1959- 151
    Autobiography Feature 151
    Earlier sketches in SATA 67, 99, 148
    See also CLR 94
McDonald, Meme 1954- 112
McDonald, Mercedes 1956- 169
    Earlier sketch in SATA 97
McDonell, Chris 1960- 138
McDonnell, Christine 1949- 115
    Earlier sketch in SATA 34
McDonnell, Flora (Mary) 1963- 146
    Earlier sketch in SATA 90
McDonnell, Lois Eddy 1914-2001 10
McDonough, Yona Zeldis 1957- 73
McElligott, Matt(hew) 1968- 135
McElmeel, Sharron L. 1942- 128
McElmurry, Jill 159
McElrath, William N. 1932- 65
McElrath-Eslick, Lori 1960- 96
McEntee, Dorothy (Layng) 1902- 37
McFadden, Kevin Christopher 1961(?)- 156
    Earlier sketch in SATA 68
    See also CLR 29
    See Pike, Christopher
McFall, Christie 1918- 12
McFarlan, Donald M(aitland) 1915- 59
McFarland, Henry "Hammer"
    See McFarland, Henry O.
McFarland, Henry O. 1934- 143
McFarland, Kenton D(ean) 1920- 11
McFarland, Martha
    See Smith-Ankrom, M. E.
McFarlane, Leslie (Charles) 1902-1977 31
    See Dixon, Franklin W.
    and Ferris, James Cody
    and Keene, Carolyn
    and Rockwood, Roy
McFarlane, Peter (William) 1940- 95
McFarlane, Sheryl P. 1954- 86
McFarlane, Todd 1961- 117
McGaw, Jessie Brewer 1913-1997 10
McGee, Barbara 1943- 6
McGee, Marni 163
McGiffin, (Lewis) Lee (Shaffer) 1908-1978 . 1
McGill, Alice 159
McGill, Ormond 1913- 92
McGinley, Jerry 1948- 116
McGinley, Phyllis 1905-1978 44
    Obituary 24
    Earlier sketch in SATA 2
McGinnis, Lila S(prague) 1924- 44
McGinty, Alice B. 1963- 134
McGivern, Justin 1985- 129
McGivern, Maureen Daly
    See Daly, Maureen
McGough, Elizabeth (Hemmes) 1934- 33
McGovern, Ann 1930- 132
    Earlier sketches in SATA 8, 69, 70
    See also CLR 50
    See also SAAS 17
McGowen, Thomas E. 1927- 109
    Earlier sketch in SATA 2
McGowen, Tom
    See McGowen, Thomas E.
McGrady, Mike 1933- 6
McGrath, Barbara Barbieri 1953- 169
    Earlier sketch in SATA 108
McGrath, Robin 1949- 121
McGrath, Thomas (Matthew) 1916-1990 41
    Obituary 66
McGraw, Eloise Jarvis 1915-2000 67
    Obituary 123
    Earlier sketch in SATA 1
    See also SAAS 6
McGraw, William Corbin 1916-1999 3
McGreal, Elizabeth
    See Yates, Elizabeth

McGregor, Barbara 1959- 82
McGregor, Craig 1933- 8
McGregor, Iona 1929- 25
McGuffey, Alexander Hamilton 1816-1896
    60
McGuigan, Mary Ann 1949- 106
McGuire, Edna 1899- 13
McGuire, Leslie (Sarah) 1945- 94
    Brief entry 45
    Earlier sketch in SATA 52
McGuirk, Leslie (A.) 1960- 152
McGurk, Slater
    See Roth, Arthur J(oseph)
McHargue, Georgess 1941- 77
    Earlier sketch in SATA 4
    See also CLR 2
    See also SAAS 5
McHugh, (Berit) Elisabet 1941- 55
    Brief entry 44
McIlwraith, Maureen Mollie Hunter 2
    See Hunter, Mollie
McInerney, Judith W(hitelock) 1945- 49
    Brief entry 46
McInerny, Ralph (Matthew) 1929- 93
McKaughan, Larry (Scott) 1941- 75
McKay, Donald 1895- 45
McKay, Hilary (Jane) 1959- 145
    Earlier sketch in SATA 92
    See also SAAS 23
McKay, Lawrence, Jr. 1948- 114
McKay, Robert W. 1921- 15
McKay, Sharon E. 1954- 165
McKay, Simon
    See Nicole, Christopher (Robin)
McKeating, Eileen 1957- 81
McKee, David (John) 1935- 158
    Earlier sketches in SATA 70, 107
    See also CLR 38
McKee, Tim 1970- 111
McKeever, Marcia
    See Laird, Jean E(louise)
McKelvey, Carole A. 1942- 78
McKelvy, Charles 1950- 124
McKendrick, Melveena (Christine) 1941- ... 55
McKenna, Colleen O'Shaughnessy 1948- . 136
    Earlier sketch in SATA 76
McKenzie, Ellen Kindt 1928- 80
McKie, Robin 112
McKillip, Patricia A(nne) 1948- 126
    Earlier sketches in SATA 30, 80
McKim, Audrey Margaret 1909-1999 47
McKinley, (Jennifer Carolyn) Robin 1952-
    130
    Brief entry 32
    Earlier sketches in SATA 50, 89
    See also CLR 81
McKinney, Barbara Shaw 1951- 116
McKinney, Nadine 1938- 91
McKissack, Fredrick L. 1939- 162
    Brief entry 53
    Earlier sketches in SATA 73, 117
    See also CLR 55
McKissack, Fredrick Lemuel
    See McKissack, Fredrick L.
McKissack, Patricia C. 1944- 162
    Earlier sketches in SATA 51, 73, 117
    See also CLR 55
McKissack, Patricia L'Ann Carwell
    See McKissack, Patricia C.
McKissack and McKissack
    See McKissack, Fredrick L.
    and McKissack, Patricia C.
McKown, Robin (?)-1976 6
McLaren, Clemence 1938- 158
    Earlier sketch in SATA 105
McLaughlin, Frank 1934- 73
McLaurin, Anne 1953- 27
McLean, Andrew 1946- 113
McLean, J. Sloan
    See Gillette, Virginia M(ary)
    and Wunsch, Josephine (McLean)

McLean, Janet 1946- 113
McLean, Kathryn (Anderson) 1909-1966 9
McLean, Virginia Overton 1946- 90
McLean-Carr, Carol 1948- 122
McLeish, Kenneth 1940-1997 35
McLenighan, Valjean 1947- 46
    Brief entry 40
McLennan, Will
    See Wisler, G(ary) Clifton
McLeod, Chum 1955- 95
McLeod, Emilie Warren 1926-1982 23
    Obituary 31
McLeod, Kirsty
    See Hudson, (Margaret) Kirsty
McLeod, Margaret Vail
    See Holloway, Teresa (Bragunier)
McLerran, Alice 1933- 137
    Earlier sketch in SATA 68
McLoughlin, John C. 1949- 47
McManus, Patrick F. 1933- 46
McManus, Patrick Francis
    See McManus, Patrick F.
McMeekin, Clark
    See McMeekin, Isabel McLennan
McMeekin, Isabel McLennan 1895-1973 3
McMenemy, Sarah 1965- 156
McMillan, Bruce 1947- 129
    Earlier sketches in SATA 22, 70
    See also CLR 47
McMillan, Naomi
    See Grimes, Nikki
McMorey, James L.
    See Moyer, Terry J.
McMorrow, Annalisa 1969- 104
McMullan, Jim 1934- 150
    Earlier sketch in SATA 87
McMullan, K. H.
    See McMullan, Kate
McMullan, Kate
    See McMullan, Kate
McMullan, Kate 1947- 132
    Brief entry 48
    Earlier sketches in SATA 52, 87
McMullan, Kate Hall
    See McMullan, Kate
McMurtrey, Martin A(loysias) 1921- 21
McNabb, Linda 1963- 147
McNair, Kate 3
McNair, Sylvia 1924-2002 74
McNaught, Harry 32
McNaughton, Colin 1951- 134
    Earlier sketches in SATA 39, 92
    See also CLR 54
McNaughton, Janet 1953- 162
    Earlier sketch in SATA 110
McNeely, Jeannette 1918- 25
McNeer, May (Yonge) 1902-1994 81
    Earlier sketch in SATA 1
McNeese, Tim 1953- 139
McNeill, Janet 97
    Earlier sketch in SATA 1
    See Alexander, Janet
McNicoll, Sylvia (Marilyn) 1954- 113
    See also CLR 99
McNulty, Faith 1918-2005 168
    Earlier sketches in SATA 12, 84, 139
McPhail, David M(ichael) 1940- 140
    Brief entry 32
    Earlier sketches in SATA 47, 81
McPhee, Norma H. 1928- 95
McPhee, Richard B(yron) 1934- 41
McPherson, James M(unro) 1936- 141
    Earlier sketch in SATA 16
McQueen, Lucinda 1950- 58
    Brief entry 48
McQueen, Mildred Hark 1908-1978 12
McRae, Russell (William) 1934- 63
McShean, Gordon 1936- 41
Mc Swigan, Marie 1907-1962 24
McVeity, Jen 148
McVey, Vicki 1946- 80

McVicker, Charles (Taggart) 1930- *39*
McVicker, Chuck
  See McVicker, Charles (Taggart)
McWhirter, A(lan) Ross 1925-1975 .... *37*
  Obituary *31*
McWhirter, Norris (Dewar) 1925-2004 .... *37*
McWilliams, Karen 1943- *65*
Mdurvwa, Hajara E. 1962- *92*
Meacham, Margaret 1952- *95*
Meachum, Virginia 1918- *133*
  Earlier sketch in SATA *87*
Mead, Alice 1952- *146*
  Earlier sketch in SATA *94*
Mead, Russell (M., Jr.) 1935- *10*
Meade, Ellen *5*
  See Roddick, Ellen
Meade, Marion 1934- *127*
  Earlier sketch in SATA *23*
Meader, Stephen W(arren) 1892-1977 .... *1*
Meadmore, Susan
  See Sallis, Susan (Diana)
Meadow, Charles T(roub) 1929- *23*
Meadowcroft, Enid LaMonte
  See Wright, Enid Meadowcroft (LaMonte)
Meadows, Graham (W.) 1934- *161*
Meaker, M. J.
  See Meaker, Marijane (Agnes)
Meaker, Marijane (Agnes) 1927- *160*
  Autobiography Feature *111*
  Earlier sketches in SATA *20, 61, 99*
  See Aldrich, Ann
  and James, Mary
  and Kerr, M. E.
  and Packer, Vin
Means, Florence Crannell 1891-1980 .... *1*
  Obituary *25*
  See also CLR *56*
Mearian, Judy Frank 1936- *49*
Mecca, Judy Truesdell 1955- *127*
Medary, Marjorie 1890-1980 .... *14*
Meddaugh, Susan 1944- *125*
  Earlier sketches in SATA *29, 84*
Medearis, Angela Shelf 1956- *123*
  Earlier sketch in SATA *72*
Medearis, Mary 1915- *5*
Medina, Jane 1953- *167*
  Earlier sketch in SATA *122*
Medlicott, Mary 1946- *88*
Mee, Charles L., Jr. 1938- *72*
  Earlier sketch in SATA *8*
Meek, Jacklyn O'Hanlon 1933- *51*
  Brief entry *34*
Meeker, Clare Hodgson 1952- *96*
Meeker, Oden 1919(?)-1976 .... *14*
Meeker, Richard
  See Brown, Fornan
Meeks, Esther MacBain *1*
Meggs, Libby Phillips 1943- *130*
Mehdevi, Alexander (Sinclair) 1947- *7*
Mehdevi, Anne (Marie) Sinclair 1947- *8*
Meidell, Sherry 1951- *73*
Meier, Minta 1906- *55*
Meighan, Donald Charles 1929- *30*
Meigs, Cornelia Lynde 1884-1973 .... *6*
  See also CLR *55*
Meilach, Dona Z(weigoron) 1926- *34*
Meilman, Philip W(arren) 1951- *79*
Meinstereifel, Ronald L. 1960- *134*
Melcher, Marguerite Fellows 1879-1969 .... *10*
Melendez, Francisco 1964- *72*
Melin, Grace Hathaway 1892-1973 .... *10*
Mellersh, H(arold) E(dward) L(eslie) 1897-
  .... *10*

Melmoth, Sebastian
  See Wilde, Oscar (Fingal O'Flahertie Wills)
Melnikoff, Pamela (Rita) *97*
Meltzer, Milton 1915- *128*
  Autobiography Feature *124*
  Earlier sketches in SATA *1, 50, 80*
  See also CLR *13*
  See also SAAS *1*

Melville, Anne
  See Potter, Margaret (Newman)
Melville, Herman 1819-1891 .... *59*
Melwood, Mary
  See Lewis, E. M.
Melzack, Ronald 1929- *5*
Memling, Carl 1918-1969 .... *6*
Mendel, Jo
  See Bond, Gladys Baker
  and Gilbertson, Mildred Geiger
Mendelson, Steven T. 1958-1995 .... *86*
Mendes, Valerie 1939- *157*
Mendez, Raymond A. 1947- *66*
Mendonca, Susan
  Brief entry *45*
  See Smith, Susan Vernon
Mendoza, George 1934- *41*
  Brief entry *39*
  See also SAAS *7*
Menendez, Shirley (C.) 1937- *146*
Meng, Heinz (Karl) 1924- *13*
Mennen, Ingrid 1954- *85*
Menotti, Gian Carlo 1911- *29*
Menuhin, Sir Yehudi 1916-1999 .... *40*
  Obituary *113*
Menville, Douglas 1935- *64*
Menzel, Barbara Jean 1946- *63*
Mercati, Cynthia *164*
Mercati, Cynthia J.
  See Mercati, Cynthia
Mercer, Charles (Edward) 1917-1988 .... *16*
  Obituary *61*
Meredith, David William
  See Miers, Earl Schenck
Meringoff, Laurene Krasny
  See Brown, Laurene Krasny
Meriwether, Louise 1923- *52*
  Brief entry *31*
Merlin, Arthur
  See Blish, James (Benjamin)
Merlin, Christina
  See Heaven, Constance (Christina)
Merriam, Eve 1916-1992 .... *73*
  Earlier sketches in SATA *3, 40*
  See also CLR *14*
Merrill, Jane 1946- *42*
Merrill, Jean (Fairbanks) 1923- *82*
  Earlier sketch in SATA *1*
  See also CLR *52*
Merriman, Alex
  See Silverberg, Robert
Merriman, Rachel 1971- *149*
  Earlier sketch in SATA *98*
Merrit, Elizabeth
  See Goudge, Eileen
Mertz, Barbara 1927- *49*
Mertz, Barbara Gross
  See Mertz, Barbara
Meschel, Susan V. 1936- *83*
Messenger, Charles (Rynd Milles) 1942- *59*
Messick, Dale 1906-2005 .... *64*
  Brief entry *48*
Messier, Claire 1956- *103*
Messieres, Nicole de
  See de Messieres, Nicole
Messmer, Otto 1892(?)-1983 .... *37*
Metcalf, Doris H(unter) *91*
Metcalf, Suzanne
  See Baum, L(yman) Frank
Metos, Thomas H(arry) 1932- *37*
Metter, Bert(ram Milton) 1927- *56*
Metzenthen, David 1958- *167*
  Earlier sketch in SATA *106*
Meyer, Barbara 1939- *77*
Meyer, Carolyn (Mae) 1935- *142*
  Autobiography Feature *142*
  Earlier sketches in SATA *9, 70, 118*
  See also SAAS *9*
Meyer, Edith Patterson 1895-1993 .... *5*
Meyer, F(ranklyn) E(dward) 1932- *9*
Meyer, Jean Shepherd *11*

Meyer, Jerome Sydney 1895-1975 .... *3*
  Obituary *25*
Meyer, June
  See Jordan, June (Meyer)
Meyer, L. A.
  See Meyer, Louis A(lbert), Jr.
Meyer, Louis A(lbert), Jr. 1942- *144*
  Earlier sketch in SATA *12*
Meyer, Renate 1930- *6*
Meyer, Susan E. 1940- *64*
Meyers, Susan 1942- *164*
  Earlier sketches in SATA *19, 108*
Meynier, Yvonne (Pollet) 1908- *14*
Mezey, Robert 1935- *33*
Micale, Albert 1913- *22*
Michael, James
  See Scagnetti, Jack
Michael, Manfred
  See Winterfeld, Henry
Michaels, Barbara
  See Mertz, Barbara
Michaels, Joanne Louise
  See Teitelbaum, Michael
Michaels, Kristin
  See Williams, Jeanne
Michaels, Molly
  See Untermeyer, Louis
Michaels, Neal
  See Teitelbaum, Michael
Michaels, Ski
  See Pellowski, Michael (Joseph)
Michaels, Steve 1955- *71*
Michaels, William M. 1917- *77*
Michel, Anna 1943- *49*
  Brief entry *40*
Michel, Francois 1948- *82*
Micich, Paul *74*
Micklish, Rita 1931- *12*
Micklos, John J., Jr. 1956- *129*
Micucci, Charles (Patrick, Jr.) 1959- *144*
  Earlier sketch in SATA *82*
Middleton, Haydn 1955- *152*
  Earlier sketch in SATA *85*
Miers, Earl Schenck 1910-1972 .... *1*
  Obituary *26*
Migdale, Lawrence 1951- *89*
Mikaelsen, Ben(jamin John) 1952- *107*
  Earlier sketch in SATA *73*
Miklowitz, Gloria D. 1927- *129*
  Earlier sketches in SATA *4, 68*
  See also SAAS *17*
Mikolaycak, Charles 1937-1993 .... *78*
  Obituary *75*
  Earlier sketch in SATA *9*
  See also SAAS *4*
Mild, Warren (Paul) 1922- *41*
Milelli, Pascal 1965- *135*
Miles, Betty 1928- *78*
  Earlier sketch in SATA *8*
  See also SAAS *9*
Miles, Miska
  See Martin, Patricia Miles
Miles, (Mary) Patricia 1930- *29*
Miles, Patricia A.
  See Martin, Patricia Miles
Milgrim, David *158*
Milgrom, Harry 1912-1978 .... *25*
Milhous, Katherine 1894-1977 .... *15*
Milios, Rita 1949- *79*
Militant
  See Sandburg, Carl (August)
Millais, Raoul 1901- *77*
Millar, Barbara F. 1924- *12*
Millar, Margaret (Ellis Sturm) 1915-1994 .. *61*
  Obituary *79*
Millbank, Captain H. R.
  See Ellis, Edward S(ylvester)
Millen, C(ynthia) M. 1955- *114*
Miller, Albert G(riffith) 1905-1982 .... *12*
  Obituary *31*
Miller, Alice Ann 1958- *150*

Miller, Alice P(atricia McCarthy) *22*
Miller, Debbie 1951- *160*
  Earlier sketch in SATA *103*
Miller, Debbie S.
  See Miller, Debbie
Miller, Deborah Uchill 1944- *61*
Miller, Don 1923- *15*
Miller, Doris R.
  See Mosesson, Gloria R(ubin)
Miller, Eddie
  See Miller, Edward
Miller, Edna Anita 1920- *29*
Miller, Edward 1905-1974 .... *8*
Miller, Elizabeth 1933- *41*
Miller, Ellanita 1957- *87*
Miller, Eugene 1925- *33*
Miller, Frances A. 1937- *52*
  Brief entry *46*
Miller, Helen M(arkley) -1984 .... *5*
Miller, Jane (Judith) 1925-1989 .... *15*
Miller, Jewel 1956- *73*
Miller, John
  See Samachson, Joseph
Miller, Judi *117*
Miller, Louise (Rolfe) 1940- *76*
Miller, M. L. *85*
Miller, Madge 1918- *63*
Miller, Margaret J.
  See Dale, Margaret J(essy) Miller
Miller, Marilyn (Jean) 1925- *33*
Miller, Marvin *65*
Miller, Mary Beth 1942- *9*
Miller, Maryann 1943- *73*
Miller, Natalie 1917-1976 .... *35*
Miller, Robert H. 1944- *91*
Miller, Ruth White
  See White, Ruth C.
Miller, Sandy (Peden) *41*
  Brief entry *35*
  See Miller, Sandra (Peden)
Miller, Virginia
  See Austin, Virginia
Miller, William R. 1959- *116*
Milligan, Spike
  See CLR *92*
  See Milligan, Terence Alan
Milligan, Terence Alan 1918-2002 .... *29*
  Obituary *134*
  See Milligan, Spike
Millington, Ada
  See Deyneka, Anita
Millman, Isaac 1933- *140*
Mills, Adam
  See Stanley, George Edward
Mills, Claudia 1954- *145*
  Brief entry *41*
  Earlier sketches in SATA *44, 89*
Mills, Elaine (Rosemary) 1941- *72*
Mills, Joyce C. 1944- *102*
Mills, Judith Christine 1956- *130*
Mills, Yaroslava Surmach 1925- *35*
Millspaugh, Ben P. 1936- *77*
Millstead, Thomas E. *30*
Milne, A(lan) A(lexander) 1882-1956 .... *100*
  See also YABC *1*
  See also CLR *108*
Milne, Lorus J. *5*
  See also CLR *22*
  See also SAAS *18*
Milne, Margery *5*
  See also CLR *22*
  See also SAAS *18*
Milne, Terry
  See Milne, Theresa Ann
Milne, Theresa Ann 1964- *84*
Milnes, Irma McDonough 1924- *101*
Milonas, Rolf
  See Myller, Rolf
Milord, Susan 1954- *147*
  Earlier sketch in SATA *74*

Milotte, Alfred G(eorge) 1904-1989 .... *11*
  Obituary *62*
Milstein, Linda 1954- *80*
Milton, Ann *134*
Milton, Hilary (Herbert) 1920- *23*
Milton, John R(onald) 1924- *24*
Milton, Joyce 1946- *101*
  Brief entry *41*
  Earlier sketch in SATA *52*
Milverton, Charles A.
  See Penzler, Otto
Minahan, John A. 1956- *92*
Minar, Barbra (Goodyear) 1940- *79*
Minard, Rosemary 1939- *63*
Minarik, Else Holmelund 1920- *127*
  Earlier sketch in SATA *15*
  See also CLR *33*
Miner, Jane Claypool 1933- *38*
  Brief entry *37*
  See Claypool, Jane
Miner, Lewis S. 1909-1971 .... *11*
Mines, Jeanette (Marie) 1948- *61*
Minier, Nelson
  See Stoutenburg, Adrien (Pearl)
Minnitt, Ronda Jacqueline
  See Armitage, David
Minor, Wendell G. 1944- *164*
  Earlier sketches in SATA *78, 109*
Mintonye, Grace *4*
Miranda, Anne 1954- *109*
  Earlier sketch in SATA *71*
Mirsky, Jeannette 1903-1987 .... *8*
  Obituary *51*
Mirsky, Reba Paeff 1902-1966 .... *1*
Mishica, Clare 1960- *91*
Miskovits, Christine 1939- *10*
Miss Frances
  See Horwich, Frances R(appaport)
Miss Read
  See Saint, Dora Jessie
Mister Rogers
  See Rogers, Fred McFeely
Mitchard, Jacquelyn 1953- *168*
  Earlier sketch in SATA *98*
Mitchell, Adrian 1932- *166*
  Earlier sketch in SATA *104*
Mitchell, Allison
  See Butterworth, W.E.
Mitchell, B(etty) J(o) 1931- *120*
Mitchell, Clyde
  See Ellison, Harlan (Jay)
Mitchell, Cynthia 1922- *29*
Mitchell, (Sibyl) Elyne (Keith) 1913- *10*
Mitchell, Gladys (Maude Winifred) 1901-1983
  .... *46*
  Obituary *35*
Mitchell, Jay
  See Roberson, Jennifer
Mitchell, Joyce Slayton 1933- *142*
  Brief entry *43*
  Earlier sketch in SATA *46*
Mitchell, K. L.
  See Lamb, Elizabeth Searle
Mitchell, Kathy 1948- *59*
Mitchell, Lori 1961- *128*
Mitchell, Margaree King 1953- *84*
Mitchell, Marianne 1947- *145*
Mitchell, Rhonda *89*
Mitchelson, Mitch
  See Mitchelson, Peter Richard
Mitchelson, Peter Richard 1950- *104*
Mitchison, Naomi (Margaret Haldane)
  1897-1999 .... *24*
  Obituary *112*
Mitchnik, Helen 1901-1982 .... *41*
  Brief entry *35*
Mitchum, Hank
  See Knott, William C(ecil, Jr.)
  and Murray, Stuart A. P.
  and Newton, D(wight) B(ennett)
  and Sherman, Jory (Tecumseh)

Mitgutsch, Ali 1935- *76*
Mitsuhashi, Yoko *45*
  Brief entry *33*
Mitton, Jacqueline 1948- *162*
  Earlier sketches in SATA *66, 115*
Mitton, Simon 1946- *66*
Mitton, Tony 1951- *149*
  Earlier sketch in SATA *104*
Mizner, Elizabeth Howard 1907- *27*
Mizumura, Kazue *18*
Mobley, Joe A. 1945- *91*
Moche, Dinah (Rachel) L(evine) 1936- *44*
  Brief entry *40*
Mochi, Ugo (A.) 1889-1977 .... *38*
Mochizuki, Ken 1954- *146*
  Earlier sketch in SATA *81*
  See also SAAS *22*
Modarressi, Mitra 1967- *126*
Modell, Frank B. 1917- *39*
  Brief entry *36*
Modesitt, Jeanne 1953- *143*
  Earlier sketch in SATA *92*
Modesitt, L. E., Jr. 1943- *164*
  Earlier sketch in SATA *91*
Modesitt, Leland Exton, Jr.
  See Modesitt, L. E., Jr.
Modrell, Dolores 1933- *72*
Moe, Barbara 1937- *20*
Moe, Jorgen (Ingebretsen) 1813-1882
  See CLR *104*
  See Asbjornsen and Moe
Moed-Kass, Pnina *169*
Moerbeek, Kees 1955- *98*
Moeri, Louise 1924- *93*
  Earlier sketch in SATA *24*
  See also SAAS *10*
Moffett, Jami 1952- *84*
Moffett, Martha (Leatherwood) 1934- *8*
Mogensen, Suzanne A(ncher) 1946- *129*
Mohn, Peter B(urnet) 1934- *28*
Mohn, Viola Kohl 1914- *8*
Mohr, Nicholasa 1938- *97*
  Autobiography Feature *113*
  Earlier sketch in SATA *8*
  See also CLR *22*
  See also SAAS *8*
Mok, Esther 1953- *93*
Molan, Christine 1943- *84*
Molarsky, Osmond 1909- *16*
Moldon, Peter L(eonard) 1937- *49*
Mole, John 1941- *103*
  Earlier sketch in SATA *36*
  See also CLR *61*
Molesworth, Mary Louisa 1839-1921 .... *98*
Molin, Charles
  See Mayne, William (James Carter)
Molina, Silvia 1946- *97*
Molk, Laurel 1957- *162*
  Earlier sketch in SATA *92*
Mollel, Tololwa M. 1952- *88*
Molloy, Anne Baker 1907-1999 .... *32*
Molloy, Michael (John) 1940- *162*
Molloy, Paul (George) 1924- *5*
Moloney, James 1954- *144*
  Autobiography Feature *144*
  Earlier sketch in SATA *94*
Momaday, N(avarre) Scott 1934- *48*
  Brief entry *30*
Monaco, Octavia 1963- *169*
Monagle, Bernie 1957- *121*
Moncure, Jane Belk 1926- *23*
Monjo, F(erdinand) N(icholas III) 1924-1978
  .... *16*
  See also CLR *2*
Monk, Isabell 1952- *136*
Monroe, Lyle
  See Heinlein, Robert A(nson)
Monsell, Helen Albee 1895-1971 .... *24*
Monson-Burton, Marianne 1975- *139*
Montenegro, Laura Nyman 1953- *95*
Montero, Gloria 1933- *109*

Montes, Marisa 1951- *144*
Montgomerie, Norah (Mary) 1913- *26*
Montgomery, Constance
　See Cappel, Constance
Montgomery, Elizabeth Rider *34*
　Obituary *41*
　Earlier sketch in SATA *3*
　See Julesberg, Elizabeth Rider Montgomery
Montgomery, Hugh (Edward) 1962- *146*
Montgomery, L(ucy) M(aud) 1874-1942 .. *100*
　See also YABC *1*
　See also CLR *91*
Montgomery, Raymond A. (Jr.) 1936- *39*
Montgomery, Rutherford George 1894-1985
　.. *3*
Montgomery, Sy 1958- *132*
　Autobiography Feature *132*
　Earlier sketch in SATA *114*
Montgomery, Vivian *36*
Montpetit, Charles 1958- *101*
Montresor, Beni 1926-2001 .... *38*
　Earlier sketch in SATA *3*
　See also SAAS *4*
Monty Python
　See Chapman, Graham
　and Cleese, John (Marwood)
　and Gilliam, Terry (Vance)
　and Idle, Eric
　and Jones, Terence Graham Parry
　and Palin, Michael (Edward)
Moodie, Fiona 1952- *133*
Moody, Minerva
　See Alcott, Louisa May
Moody, Ralph Owen 1898-1982 .... *1*
Moon, Carl 1879(?)-1948 .... *25*
Moon, Grace (Purdie) 1877(?)-1947 .... *25*
Moon, Lily
　See Warnes, Tim
Moon, Nicola 1952- *147*
　Earlier sketch in SATA *96*
Moon, Pat 1946- *113*
Moon, Sheila (Elizabeth) 1910-1991 .... *5*
　Obituary *114*
Mooney, Bel 1946- *95*
Mooney, Bill *122*
　See Mooney, William F.
Moor, Emily
　See Deming, Richard
Moorcock, Michael 1939- *166*
　Earlier sketch in SATA *93*
　See Bradbury, Edward P.
Moore, Anne Carroll 1871-1961 .... *13*
Moore, Cheri
　See Ladd, Cheryl (Jean)
Moore, Clement Clarke 1779-1863 .... *18*
Moore, Cyd 1957- *133*
　Earlier sketch in SATA *83*
Moore, Elaine 1944- *86*
Moore, Eva 1942- *103*
　Earlier sketch in SATA *20*
Moore, Ishbel (Lindsay) 1954- *140*
Moore, Jack (William) 1941- *46*
　Brief entry *32*
Moore, Janet Gaylord 1905-1992 .... *18*
Moore, Jim 1946- *42*
Moore, John Travers 1908- *12*
Moore, Lilian 1909-2004 .... *137*
　Obituary *155*
　Earlier sketch in SATA *52*
　See also CLR *15*
Moore, Liz
　See Moore, M. Elizabeth
Moore, M. Elizabeth 1959- *156*
Moore, Margaret R(umberger) 1903- *12*
Moore, Marianne (Craig) 1887-1972 .... *20*
Moore, Patrick (Alfred Caldwell) 1923- *49*
　Brief entry *39*
　See also SAAS *8*
Moore, Regina
　See Dunne, Mary Collins
Moore, Ruth (Ellen) 1908-1989 .... *23*

Moore, Ruth Nulton 1923- *38*
Moore, S(arah) E. *23*
Moore, Sarah Margaret
　See Hodges, Margaret Moore
Moore, Tara 1950- *61*
Moore, Yvette 1958- *154*
　Earlier sketches in SATA *69, 70*
Mooser, Stephen 1941- *75*
　Earlier sketch in SATA *28*
Mora, Francisco X(avier) 1952- *90*
Mora, Pat(ricia) 1942- *134*
　Earlier sketch in SATA *92*
　See also CLR *58*
Morales, Yuyi *154*
Moran, Tom 1943- *60*
Moranville, Sharelle Byars *152*
Moray Williams, Ursula 1911- *142*
　Earlier sketch in SATA *73*
　See also SAAS *9*
　See Williams, Ursula Moray
Mordvinoff, Nicolas 1911-1973 .... *17*
More, Caroline
　See Cone, Molly (Lamken)
　and Strachan, Margaret Pitcairn
Moreton, Andrew Esq.
　See Defoe, Daniel
Morey, Charles
　See Fletcher, Helen Jill
Morey, Walt(er Nelson) 1907-1992 .... *51*
　Obituary *70*
　Earlier sketch in SATA *3*
　See also SAAS *9*
Morgan, Alfred P(owell) 1889-1972 .... *33*
Morgan, Alison (Mary) 1930- *85*
　Earlier sketch in SATA *30*
Morgan, Anne 1954- *121*
Morgan, Douglas
　See Macdonald, James D.
Morgan, Ellen
　See Bumstead, Kathleen Mary
Morgan, Geoffrey 1916- *46*
Morgan, Helen (Gertrude Louise) 1921-1990
　.. *29*
Morgan, Jane
　See Cooper, James Fenimore
　and Franklin, Jane (Morgan)
　and Moren, Sally M(oore)
Morgan, Lenore H. 1908-1976 .... *8*
Morgan, Mary 1957- *114*
　Earlier sketch in SATA *81*
Morgan, Nicola 1961- *161*
Morgan, Nina 1953- *110*
Morgan, Pierr 1952- *122*
　Earlier sketch in SATA *77*
Morgan, Robin (Evonne) 1941- *80*
Morgan, Roxanne
　See Gentle, Mary
Morgan, Sarah (Nicola) 1959- *68*
Morgan, Shirley *10*
　See Kiepper, Shirley Morgan
Morgan, Stacy T(owle) 1959- *104*
Morgan, Stevie
　See Davies, Nicola
Morgan, Tom 1942- *42*
Morgan, Wendy
　See Staub, Wendy Corsi
Morgan-Vanroyen, Mary
　See Morgan, Mary
Morgenstern, Susie Hoch 1945- *133*
Mori, Hana 1909-1990(?) *88*
Mori, Kyoko 1957- *122*
　Autobiography Feature *126*
　See also CLR *64*
　See also SAAS *26*
Moriarty, Jaclyn *162*
Moriarty, William J. 1930- *127*
Morice, Dave 1946- *93*
Morin, Isobel V. 1928- *110*
Morley, Wilfred Owen
　See Lowndes, Robert A(ugustine) W(ard)

Morningstar, Mildred (Whaley) 1912-1997
　.. *61*
　Obituary *114*
Morozumi, Atsuko *110*
Morpurgo, Michael 1943- *143*
　Earlier sketch in SATA *93*
　See also CLR *51*
Morrah, Dave
　See Morrah, David Wardlaw, Jr.
Morrah, David Wardlaw, Jr. 1914-1991 ...... *10*
Morreale-de la Garza, Phyllis
　See De la Garza, Phyllis
Morressy, John 1930-2006 .... *23*
Morrill, Leslie H(olt) 1934-2003 .... *48*
　Brief entry *33*
　Obituary *148*
　See also SAAS *22*
Morris, Chris(topher Crosby) 1946- *66*
Morris, Deborah 1956- *91*
Morris, Desmond (John) 1928- *14*
Morris, Don 1954- *83*
Morris, Gerald (Paul) 1963- *150*
　Earlier sketch in SATA *107*
Morris, Gilbert (Leslie) 1929- *104*
Morris, Jackie *151*
Morris, Janet (Ellen) 1946- *66*
Morris, Jay
　See Tatham, Julie Campbell
Morris, (Margaret) Jean 1924- *98*
Morris, Jeffrey B(randon) 1941- *92*
Morris, Jill 1936- *165*
　Earlier sketch in SATA *119*
Morris, Juddi *85*
Morris, Judy K. 1936- *61*
Morris, Oradel Nolen *128*
Morris, Robert A(da) 1933- *7*
Morris, William 1913-1994 .... *29*
Morrison, Bill 1935- *66*
　Brief entry *37*
Morrison, Chloe Anthony Wofford
　See Morrison, Toni
Morrison, Dorothy Nafus *29*
Morrison, Gordon 1944- *128*
　Earlier sketch in SATA *87*
Morrison, Joan 1922- *65*
Morrison, Lillian 1917- *108*
　Earlier sketch in SATA *3*
Morrison, Lucile Phillips 1896- *17*
Morrison, Martha A. 1948- *77*
Morrison, Meighan 1966- *90*
Morrison, Richard
　See Lowndes, Robert A(ugustine) W(ard)
Morrison, Robert
　See Lowndes, Robert A(ugustine) W(ard)
Morrison, Roberta
　See Webb, Jean Francis (III)
Morrison, Susan Dudley
　See Gold, Susan Dudley
Morrison, Taylor 1971- *159*
　Earlier sketch in SATA *95*
Morrison, Toni 1931- *144*
　Earlier sketch in SATA *57*
　See also CLR *99*
Morrison, Velma Ford 1909- *21*
Morrison, Wilbur Howard 1915- *64*
Morrison, William
　See Samachson, Joseph
Morriss, James E(dward) 1932- *8*
Morrow, Barbara Olenyik 1952- *167*
Morrow, Betty
　See Bacon, Elizabeth
Morse, Carol
　See Yeakley, Marjory Hall
Morse, Flo 1921- *30*
Morse, Tony 1953- *129*
Mort, Vivian
　See Cromie, Alice Hamilton
Mortimer, Anne 1958- *116*
Morton, Alexandra (Hubbard) 1957- *144*
Morton, Anthony
　See Arthur, Robert, (Jr.)

Morton, Jane 1931- 50
Morton, Joseph C. 1932- 156
Morton, Lee Jack, Jr. 1928- 32
Morton, Miriam 1918(?)-1985 9
    Obituary 46
Mosatche, Harriet (S.) 1949- 122
Moscow, Alvin 1925- 3
Mosel, Arlene (Tichy) 1921-1996 7
Moseley, James W(illett) 1931- 139
Moseng, Elisabeth 1967- 90
Moser, Barry (A.) 1940- 138
    Earlier sketches in SATA 56, 79
    See also CLR 49
    See also SAAS 15
Moser, Don(ald Bruce) 1932- 31
Moses, Sheila P. 1961- 168
Moses, Will 1956- 120
Mosesson, Gloria R(ubin) 24
Mosher, Richard 1949- 120
Moskin, Marietta D(unston) 1928- 23
Moskof, Martin Stephen 1930- 27
Mosley, Francis 1957- 57
Moss, Don(ald) 1920- 11
Moss, Elaine (Dora) 1924- 57
    Brief entry 31
Moss, Jeff(rey) 1942-1998 73
    Obituary 106
Moss, Marissa 1959- 163
    Earlier sketches in SATA 71, 104
Moss, Miriam 1955- 140
    Earlier sketch in SATA 76
Moss, Thylias (Rebecca Brasier) 1954- 108
Most, Bernard 1937- 134
    Brief entry 40
    Earlier sketches in SATA 48, 91
Mott, Evelyn Clarke 1962- 133
    Earlier sketch in SATA 75
Motz, Lloyd 1909- 20
Mould, Edwin
    See Whitlock, Ralph
Mouly, Francoise 155
Mountain, Robert
    See Montgomery, Raymond A. (Jr.)
Mountfield, David
    See Grant, Neil
Moussard, Jacqueline 1924- 24
Mowat, Claire (Angel Wheeler) 1933- 123
Mowat, Farley (McGill) 1921- 55
    Earlier sketch in SATA 3
    See also CLR 20
Mowry, Jess 1960- 131
    Autobiography Feature 131
    Earlier sketch in SATA 109
    See also CLR 65
Moxley, Sheila 1966- 96
Moyer, Terry J. 1937- 94
Moyes, Patricia 63
    See Haszard, Patricia Moyes
Moyler, Alan (Frank Powell) 1926- 36
Mozley, Charles 1915- 43
    Brief entry 32
Mphahlele, Es'kia
    See Mphahlele, Ezekiel
Mphahlele, Ezekiel 1919- 119
    See Mphahlele, Es'kia
Mr. McGillicuddy
    See Abisch, Roslyn Kroop
Mr. Sniff
    See Abisch, Roslyn Kroop
Mr. Tivil
    See Lorkowski, Thomas V(incent)
Mr. Wizard
    See Herbert, Don(ald Jeffrey)
Mrs. Fairstar
    See Horne, Richard Henry Hengist
Muchmore, Jo Ann 1937- 103
Mude, O.
    See Gorey, Edward (St. John)
Mudgeon, Apeman
    See Mitchell, Adrian

Mueller, Jorg 1942- 67
    See also CLR 43
Mueller, Virginia 1924- 28
Muggs
    See Watkins, Lois
Muir, Diana
    See Appelbaum, Diana Muir Karter
Muir, Frank (Herbert) 1920-1998 30
Muir, Helen 1937- 65
Mukerji, Dhan Gopal 1890-1936 40
    See also CLR 10
Mulcahy, Lucille Burnett 12
Mulford, Philippa G(reene) 1948- 112
    Earlier sketch in SATA 43
Mulila, Vigad G.
    See Maillu, David G(ian)
Mullen, Michael 1937- 122
Muller, Billex
    See Ellis, Edward S(ylvester)
Muller, Jorg
    See Mueller, Jorg
Muller, (Lester) Robin 1953- 86
Mullin, Caryl Cude 1969- 130
Mullins, Edward S(wift) 1922- 10
Mullins, Hilary 1962- 84
Mulock, Dinah Maria
    See Craik, Dinah Maria (Mulock)
Mulvihill, William Patrick 1923- 8
Mumford, Ruth 1919- 86
    See Dallas, Ruth
Mumy, Bill 1954- 112
Mun
    See Leaf, (Wilbur) Munro
Munari, Bruno 1907-1998 15
    See also CLR 9
Munce, Ruth Hill 1898- 12
Mundy, Simon (Andrew James Hainault) 1954-
    64
Munowitz, Ken 1935-1977 14
Munoz, William 1949- 92
    Earlier sketch in SATA 42
Munro, Alice (Anne) 1931- 29
Munro, Eleanor 1928- 37
Munro, Roxie 1945- 136
    Earlier sketch in SATA 58
Munsch, Bob
    See Munsch, Robert (Norman)
Munsch, Robert (Norman) 1945- 120
    Brief entry 48
    Earlier sketches in SATA 50, 83
    See also CLR 19
Munsinger, Lynn 1951- 94
    Earlier sketch in SATA 33
Munson, Derek 1970- 139
Munson, R. W.
    See Karl, Jean E(dna)
Munson-Benson, Tunie 1946- 15
Munsterberg, Peggy 1921- 102
Munthe, Nelly 1947- 53
Munves, James (Albert) 1922- 30
Munzer, Martha E. 1899-1999 4
Murch, Mel
    See Manes, Stephen
Murdoch, David H(amilton) 1937- 96
Murhall, J(acqueline) J(ane) 1964- 143
Murphy, Barbara Beasley 1933- 130
    Earlier sketch in SATA 5
Murphy, Claire Rudolf 1951- 137
    Earlier sketch in SATA 76
Murphy, E(mmett) Jefferson 1926- 4
Murphy, Jill (Frances) 1949- 142
    Earlier sketches in SATA 37, 70
    See also CLR 39
Murphy, Jim 1947- 124
    Brief entry 32
    Earlier sketches in SATA 37, 77
    See also CLR 53
Murphy, Joseph E., Jr. 1930- 65
Murphy, Kelly 1977- 143
Murphy, Louise 1943- 155

Murphy, Pat
    See Murphy, E(mmett) Jefferson
Murphy, Patricia J. 1963- 132
Murphy, Robert (William) 1902-1971 10
Murphy, Shirley Rousseau 1928- 126
    Earlier sketches in SATA 36, 71
    See also SAAS 18
Murphy, Stuart J. 1942- 157
    Earlier sketch in SATA 115
Murphy, Tim
    See Murphy, Jim
Murray, John 1923- 39
Murray, Kirsty 1960- 165
    Earlier sketch in SATA 108
Murray, Marguerite 1917- 63
Murray, Marian 5
Murray, Martine 1965- 125
Murray, (Judith) Michele (Freedman)
    1933-1974 7
Murray, Ossie 1938- 43
Murrow, Liza Ketchum 1946- 78
    See Ketchum, Liza
Musgrave, Florence 1902-1999 3
Musgrove, Margaret W(ynkoop) 1943- 124
    Earlier sketch in SATA 26
Mussey, Virginia Howell
    See Ellison, Virginia H(owell)
Mussey, Virginia T.H.
    See Ellison, Virginia H(owell)
Mutel, Cornelia F. 1947- 74
Muth, Jon J. 165
Mutz
    See Kuenstler, Morton
My Brother's Brother
    See Chekhov, Anton (Pavlovich)
Myers, Anna 160
Myers, Arthur 1917- 91
    Earlier sketch in SATA 35
Myers, Bernice 81
    Earlier sketch in SATA 9
Myers, Caroline Elizabeth Clark 1887-1980
    28
Myers, Christopher 1975-
    See CLR 97
Myers, Edward 1950- 96
Myers, Elisabeth P(erkins) 1918- 36
Myers, (Mary) Hortense (Powner) 1913-1987
    10
Myers, Jack 1913- 83
Myers, Lou 1915-2005 81
Myers, Louis
    See Myers, Lou
Myers, R(obert) E(ugene) 1924- 119
Myers, Tim (Brian) 1953- 147
Myers, Walter Dean 1937- 157
    Brief entry 27
    Earlier sketches in SATA 41, 71, 109
    See also CLR 110
    See also SAAS 2
Myers, Walter M.
    See Myers, Walter Dean
Myller, Rolf 1926-2006 27
Myra, Harold L(awrence) 1939- 46
    Brief entry 42
Myracle, Lauren 1969- 162
Myrus, Donald (Richard) 1927- 23
Mysterious Traveler, The
    See Arthur, Robert, (Jr.)

N

Na, An 149
Nadel, Laurie 1948- 74
Naden, Corinne J. 1930- 166
    Earlier sketch in SATA 79
Nagel, Andreas Fischer
    See Fischer-Nagel, Andreas
Nagel, Heiderose Fischer
    See Fischer-Nagel, Heiderose

Naidoo, Beverley 1943- *135*
  Earlier sketch in SATA *63*
  See also CLR 29
Nakae, Noriko 1940- *59*
Nakatani, Chiyoko 1930-1981 .... *55*
  Brief entry *40*
  See also CLR 30
Nally, Susan W. 1947- *90*
Namioka, Lensey 1929- *157*
  Autobiography Feature *116*
  Earlier sketches in SATA *27, 89*
  See also CLR 48
  See also SAAS 24
Nanji, Shenaaz 1954- *131*
Nanogak Agnes 1925- *61*
Napier, Mark
  See Laffin, John (Alfred Charles)
Napoli, Donna Jo 1948- *137*
  Earlier sketch in SATA *92*
  See also CLR 51
  See also SAAS 23
Narahashi, Keiko 1959- *115*
  Earlier sketch in SATA *79*
Narayan, R(asipuram) K(rishnaswami)
  1906-2001 .... *62*
Nascimbene, Yan 1949- *133*
Nash, Bruce M(itchell) 1947- *34*
Nash, Linell
  See Smith, Linell Nash
Nash, Mary (Hughes) 1925- *41*
Nash, (Frediric) Ogden 1902-1971 .... *46*
  Earlier sketch in SATA *2*
Nash, Renea Denise 1963- *81*
Nast, Elsa Ruth
  See Watson, Jane Werner
Nast, Thomas 1840-1902 .... *51*
  Brief entry *33*
Nastick, Sharon 1954- *41*
Nathan, Amy *104*
Nathan, Amy *155*
Nathan, Dorothy (Goldeen) (?)-1966 .... *15*
Nathan, Robert (Gruntal) 1894-1985 .... *6*
  Obituary *43*
Nathanson, Laura Walther 1941- *57*
Natti, Susanna 1948- *125*
  Earlier sketch in SATA *32*
Naughton, Bill
  See Naughton, William John (Francis)
Naughton, James Franklin 1957- *85*
Naughton, Jim
  See Naughton, James Franklin
Naughton, William John (Francis) 1910-1992
  .... *86*
  See Naughton, Bill
Navarra, John Gabriel 1927- *8*
Naylor, Penelope 1941- *10*
Naylor, Phyllis 1933-
  See Naylor, Phyllis Reynolds
Naylor, Phyllis Reynolds 1933- *152*
  Autobiography Feature *152*
  Earlier sketches in SATA *12, 66, 102*
  See also CLR 17
  See also SAAS 10
  See Naylor, Phyllis
Nazarian, Nikki
  See Nichols, Cecilia Fawn
Nazaroff, Alexander I(vanovich) 1898-1981 . *4*
Neal, Harry Edward 1906-1993 .... *5*
  Obituary *76*
Neal, Michael
  See Teitelbaum, Michael
Nearing, Penny 1916- *47*
  Brief entry *42*
Nebel, Gustave E. *45*
  Brief entry *33*
Nebel, Mimouca
  See Nebel, Gustave E.
Nee, Kay Bonner *10*
Needham, Kate 1962- *95*

Needle, Jan 1943- *98*
  Earlier sketch in SATA *30*
  See also CLR 43
  See also SAAS 23
Needleman, Jacob 1934- *6*
Neel, David 1960- *82*
Neel, Preston 1959- *93*
Negri, Rocco 1932- *12*
Neier, Aryeh 1937- *59*
Neigoff, Anne *13*
Neigoff, Mike 1920- *13*
Neilson, Frances Fullerton (Jones) 1910-2001
  .... *14*
Neimark, Anne E. 1935- *145*
  Earlier sketch in SATA *4*
Neimark, Paul G. 1934- *80*
  Brief entry *37*
Neitzel, Shirley 1941- *134*
  Earlier sketch in SATA *77*
Nell
  See Hanna, Nell(ie L.)
Nelson, Catherine Chadwick 1926- *87*
Nelson, Cordner (Bruce) 1918- *54*
  Brief entry *29*
Nelson, Drew 1952- *77*
Nelson, Esther L. 1928- *13*
Nelson, Jim A.
  See Stotter, Mike
Nelson, Julie L. 1970- *117*
Nelson, Kadir *154*
Nelson, Kris
  See Rusch, Kristine Kathryn
Nelson, Marilyn 1946- *151*
  See Waniek, Marilyn Nelson
Nelson, Mary Carroll 1929- *23*
Nelson, O. Terry 1941- *62*
Nelson, Peter N. 1953- *73*
Nelson, Richard K(ing) 1941- *65*
Nelson, Robin Laura 1971- *141*
Nelson, Roy Paul 1923- *59*
Nelson, Sharlene (P.) 1933- *96*
Nelson, Ted (W.) 1931- *96*
Nelson, Theresa 1948- *143*
  Autobiography Feature *143*
  Earlier sketch in SATA *79*
Nerlove, Miriam 1959- *53*
  Brief entry *49*
Nesbit, E(dith) 1858-1924 .... *100*
  See also YABC 1
  See also CLR 70
Nesbit, Troy
  See Folsom, Franklin (Brewster)
Nespojohn, Katherine V(eronica) 1912-1975
  .... *7*
Ness, Evaline (Michelow) 1911-1986 .... *26*
  Obituary *49*
  Earlier sketch in SATA *1*
  See also CLR 6
  See also SAAS 1
Nestor, Larry 1940- *149*
Nestor, William P(rodromos) 1947- *49*
Nethery, Mary *93*
Neuberger, Julia (Babette Sarah) 1950- *142*
  Earlier sketch in SATA *78*
Neufeld, John (Arthur) 1938- *131*
  Autobiography Feature *131*
  Earlier sketches in SATA *6, 81*
  See also CLR 52
  See also SAAS 3
Neuhaus, David 1958- *83*
Neumeyer, Peter F(lorian) 1929- *13*
Neurath, Marie (Reidemeister) 1898-1986 .... *1*
Neuschwander, Cindy 1953- *157*
  Earlier sketch in SATA *107*
Neusner, Jacob 1932- *38*
Neville, Charles
  See Bodsworth, (Charles) Fred(erick)
Neville, Emily Cheney 1919- *1*
  See also SAAS 2
Neville, Mary
  See Woodrich, Mary Neville

Nevins, Albert (Francis) J(erome) 1915-1997
  .... *20*
Newberger, Devra
  See Speregen, Devra Newberger
Newberry, Clare Turlay 1903-1970 .... *1*
  Obituary *26*
Newbery, John 1713-1767 .... *20*
Newbery, Linda 1952- *142*
Newcombe, Jack *45*
  Brief entry *33*
  See Newcombe, Eugene A.
Newcome, Robert 1955- *91*
Newcome, Zita 1959- *88*
Newell, Crosby
  See Bonsall, Crosby Barbara (Newell)
Newell, Edythe W(eatherford) 1910-1989 .. *11*
Newell, Hope Hockenberry 1896-1965 .... *24*
Newfeld, Frank 1928- *26*
Newlon, (Frank) Clarke 1905(?)-1982 .... *6*
  Obituary *33*
Newman, Daisy 1904-1994 .... *27*
  Obituary *78*
Newman, Gerald 1939- *46*
  Brief entry *42*
Newman, Jerry 1935- *82*
Newman, Leslea 1955- *134*
  Earlier sketches in SATA *71, 128*
Newman, Margaret
  See Potter, Margaret (Newman)
Newman, Marjorie *146*
Newman, Matthew (Harrison) 1955- *56*
Newman, Nanette 1934- *162*
Newman, Robert (Howard) 1909-1988 .... *87*
  Obituary *60*
  Earlier sketch in SATA *4*
Newman, Shirlee P(etkin) *144*
  Earlier sketches in SATA *10, 90*
Newsom, Carol 1948- *92*
  Earlier sketch in SATA *40*
Newsom, Tom 1944- *80*
Newth, Mette 1942- *140*
Newton, David E(dward) 1933- *67*
Newton, James R(obert) 1935- *23*
Newton, Suzanne 1936- *77*
  Earlier sketch in SATA *5*
Ney, John 1923- *43*
  Brief entry *33*
Nez, John *155*
Ng, Franklin *82*
Nichol, B(arrie) P(hillip) 1944-1988 .... *66*
Nicholas, Louise D.
  See Watkins, Dawn L.
Nicholls, Judith (Ann) 1941- *61*
Nichols, Cecilia Fawn 1906-1987 .... *12*
Nichols, Grace 1950- *164*
  Earlier sketch in SATA *98*
Nichols, Janet (Louise) 1952- *67*
Nichols, Judy 1947- *124*
Nichols, Leigh
  See Koontz, Dean R.
Nichols, Paul
  See Hawks, Robert
Nichols, Peter
  See Youd, (Christopher) Samuel
Nichols, (Joanna) Ruth 1948- *15*
Nicholson, C. R.
  See Nicole, Christopher (Robin)
Nicholson, Christina
  See Nicole, Christopher (Robin)
Nicholson, Joyce Thorpe 1919- *35*
Nicholson, Lois P. 1949- *88*
Nicholson, Robin
  See Nicole, Christopher (Robin)
Nicholson, William 1872-1949
  See CLR 76
Nickell, Joe 1944- *167*
  Earlier sketch in SATA *73*
Nickelsburg, Janet 1893-1983 .... *11*
Nickerson, Elizabeth *14*
  See Nickerson, Betty
Nickl, Barbara (Elisabeth) 1939- *56*

Nicklaus, Carol *62*
  Brief entry *33*
Nickless, Will 1902-1979(?) *66*
Nic Leodhas, Sorche
  See Alger, Leclaire (Gowans)
Nicol, Ann
  See Turnbull, Ann (Christine)
Nicolas
  See Mordvinoff, Nicolas
Nicolay, Helen 1866-1954
  See YABC *1*
Nicole, Christopher (Robin) 1930- *5*
Nicoll, Helen 1937- *87*
Nicolson, Cynthia Pratt 1949- *141*
Ni Dhuibhne, Eilis 1954- *91*
Niehaus, Paddy Bouma
  See Bouma, Paddy
Nields, Nerissa 1967- *166*
Nielsen, Kay (Rasmus) 1886-1957 .... *16*
  See also CLR *16*
Nielsen, Laura F(arnsworth) 1960- *93*
Nielsen, Nancy J. 1951- *77*
Nielsen, Virginia
  See McCall, Virginia Nielsen
Nieuwsma, Milton J(ohn) 1941- *142*
Nightingale, Sandy 1953- *76*
Nikolajeva, Maria 1952- *127*
Nikola-Lisa, W. 1951- *71*
Niland, Deborah 1951- *27*
Niland, Kilmeny *75*
Nilsen, Anna
  See Bassil, Andrea
Nilsson, Eleanor 1939- *117*
  Earlier sketch in SATA *81*
  See also SAAS *23*
Nilsson, Per 1954- *159*
Nimmo, Jenny 1944- *144*
  Earlier sketch in SATA *87*
  See also CLR *44*
Niven, Larry
  See Niven, Laurence Van Cott
Niven, Laurence Van Cott 1938- *95*
  See Niven, Larry
Nivola, Claire A. 1947- *140*
  Earlier sketch in SATA *84*
Nix, Garth 1963- *143*
  Earlier sketch in SATA *97*
  See also CLR *68*
Nixon, Hershell Howard 1923- *42*
Nixon, Joan Lowery 1927-2003 .... *115*
  Obituary *146*
  Earlier sketches in SATA *8, 44, 78*
  See also CLR *24*
  See also SAAS *9*
Nixon, K.
  See Nixon, Kathleen Irene (Blundell)
Nixon, Kathleen Irene (Blundell) 1894-1988(?)
  .... *14*
  Obituary *59*
Nobisso, Josephine 1953- *121*
  Earlier sketch in SATA *78*
Noble, Iris (Davis) 1922-1986 .... *5*
  Obituary *49*
Noble, Marty 1947- *125*
  Earlier sketch in SATA *97*
Noble, Trinka Hakes *123*
  Brief entry *37*
Noda, Takayo 1961- *168*
Nodelman, Perry 1942- *101*
Nodset, Joan L.
  See Lexau, Joan M.
Noel Hume, Ivor 1927- *65*
Noestlinger, Christine
  See Nostlinger, Christine
Noguere, Suzanne 1947- *34*
Nolan, Dennis 1945- *166*
  Brief entry *34*
  Earlier sketches in SATA *42, 92*
Nolan, Han 1956- *157*
  Earlier sketch in SATA *109*
Nolan, Janet 1956- *145*

Nolan, Jeannette Covert 1897-1974 .... *2*
  Obituary *27*
Nolan, Paul T(homas) 1919- *48*
Nolan, William F(rancis) 1928- *88*
  Brief entry *28*
Nolen, Jerdine 1953- *157*
  Earlier sketch in SATA *105*
Noll, Sally 1946- *82*
Noonan, Diana 1960- *146*
Noonan, Julia 1946- *148*
  Earlier sketches in SATA *4, 95*
Norac, Carl 1960- *166*
Nordan, Robert W(arren) 1934-2004 .... *133*
Nordhoff, Charles Bernard 1887-1947 .... *23*
Nordlicht, Lillian *29*
Nordstrom, Ursula 1910-1988 .... *3*
  Obituary *57*
Nordtvedt, Matilda 1926- *67*
Norling, Beth 1969- *149*
Norman, Charles 1904-1996 .... *38*
  Obituary *92*
Norman, Howard
  See Norman, Howard A.
Norman, Howard A. 1949- *81*
Norman, James
  See Schmidt, James Norman
Norman, Jay
  See Arthur, Robert, (Jr.)
Norman, Lilith 1927- *120*
  Earlier sketch in SATA *86*
Norman, Mary 1931- *36*
Norman, Steve
  See Pashko, Stanley
Norment, Lisa 1966- *91*
Norris, Gunilla Brodde 1939- *20*
North, Andrew
  See Norton, Andre
North, Anthony
  See Koontz, Dean R.
North, Captain George
  See Stevenson, Robert Louis (Balfour)
North, Captain George
  See Stevenson, Robert Louis (Balfour)
North, Howard
  See Trevor, Elleston
North, Joan 1920- *16*
North, Milou
  See Erdrich, Louise
North, Robert
  See Withers, Carl A.
North, Sara
  See Bonham, Barbara Thomas
  and Hager, Jean
North, Sterling 1906-1974 .... *45*
  Obituary *26*
  Earlier sketch in SATA *1*
Northeast, Brenda V(ictoria) 1948- *106*
Northmore, Elizabeth Florence 1906-1974
  .... *122*
Norton, Alice Mary *43*
  Earlier sketch in SATA *1*
  See Norton, Andre
Norton, Andre 1912-2005 .... *91*
  See also CLR *50*
  See Norton, Alice Mary
Norton, Browning
  See Norton, Frank R. B(rowning)
Norton, Frank R. B(rowning) 1909-1989 .... *10*
Norton, Mary 1903-1992 .... *60*
  Obituary *72*
  Earlier sketch in SATA *18*
  See also CLR *6*
Nosredna, Trebor
  See Anderson, Bob
Nostlinger, Christine 1936- *162*
  Brief entry *37*
  Earlier sketch in SATA *64*
  See also CLR *12*
Nourse, Alan E(dward) 1928-1992 .... *48*
  See also CLR *33*

Novak, Matt 1962- *165*
  Brief entry *52*
  Earlier sketches in SATA *60, 104*
Novelli, Luca 1947- *61*
Nowell, Elizabeth Cameron *12*
Noyes, Deborah
  See Wayshak, Deborah Noyes
Nugent, Nicholas 1949- *73*
Numeroff, Laura Joffe 1953- *142*
  Earlier sketches in SATA *28, 90*
  See also CLR *85*
Nunes, Lygia Bojunga 1932- *154*
  Earlier sketch in SATA *75*
  See Bojunga, Lygia
Nunn, Laura (Donna) Silverstein 1968- *124*
Nurnberg, Maxwell 1897-1984 .... *27*
  Obituary *41*
Nussbaumer, Paul (Edmund) 1934- *16*
Nutt, Ken 1951- *163*
  Earlier sketch in SATA *97*
Nuygen, Mathieu 1967- *80*
Nyberg, (Everett Wayne) Morgan 1944- *87*
Nyce, (Nellie) Helene von Strecker 1885-1969
  .... *19*
Nyce, Vera 1862-1925 .... *19*
Nye, Naomi Shihab 1952- *147*
  Earlier sketch in SATA *86*
  See also CLR *59*
Nye, Robert 1939- *6*
Nyikos, Stacy A. 1969- *164*
Nystrom, Carolyn 1940- *130*
  Earlier sketch in SATA *67*

O

Oakes, Elizabeth H. 1964- *132*
Oakes, Vanya 1909-1983 .... *6*
  Obituary *37*
Oakley, Don(ald G.) 1927- *8*
Oakley, Graham 1929- *84*
  Earlier sketch in SATA *30*
  See also CLR *7*
Oakley, Helen (McKelvey) 1906- *10*
Oana, Katherine 1929- *53*
  Brief entry *37*
Oates, Eddie H. 1943- *88*
Oates, Joyce Carol 1938- *159*
Oates, Stephen B(aery) 1936- *59*
Obed, Ellen Bryan 1944- *74*
Oberle, Joseph 1958- *69*
Oberman, Sheldon 1949-2004 .... *85*
  Autobiography Feature *114*
  Obituary *153*
  See also CLR *54*
  See also SAAS *26*
Obligado, Lilian (Isabel) 1931- *61*
  Brief entry *45*
Obrant, Susan 1946- *11*
O'Brian, E. G.
  See Clarke, Arthur C(harles)
O'Brien, Anne Sibley 1952- *80*
  Brief entry *48*
  Earlier sketch in SATA *53*
O'Brien, Robert C.
  See CLR *2*
  See Conly, Robert Leslie
O'Brien, Thomas C(lement) 1938- *29*
O'Callaghan, Julie 1954- *113*
O'Callahan, Jay 1938- *88*
O'Carroll, Ryan
  See Markun, Patricia Maloney
Ochiltree, Dianne 1953- *117*
Ockham, Joan Price
  See Price, Joan
O'Connell, Margaret F(orster) 1935-1977 .. *30*
  Obituary *30*
O'Connell, Peg
  See Ahern, Margaret McCrohan
O'Connell, Rebecca 1968- *130*

O'Connor, Barbara 1950- *154*
O'Connor, Francine M(arie) 1930- *90*
O'Connor, Genevieve A. 1914- *75*
O'Connor, Jane 1947- *150*
  Brief entry *47*
  Earlier sketches in SATA *59, 103*
O'Connor, Karen 1938- *89*
  Earlier sketch in SATA *34*
O'Connor, Patrick
  See Wibberley, Leonard (Patrick O'Connor)
O'Conor, Jane 1958- *78*
Odaga, Asenath (Bole) 1937- *130*
  Earlier sketch in SATA *67*
  See also SAAS *19*
O Danachair, Caoimhin
  See Danaher, Kevin
Odanaka, Barbara *159*
O'Daniel, Janet 1921- *24*
O'Day, Cathy
  See Crane, Barbara (Joyce)
O'Dell, Scott 1898-1989 .... *134*
  Earlier sketches in SATA *12, 60*
  See also CLR *16*
Odenwald, Robert P(aul) 1899-1965 .... *11*
Odgers, Sally
  See Odgers, Sally Farrell
Odgers, Sally Farrell 1957- *139*
  Earlier sketch in SATA *72*
O'Donnell, Dick
  See Lupoff, Richard A(llen)
  and Thompson, Don(ald Arthur)
Oechsli, Kelly 1918-1999 .... *5*
Oesterle, Virginia Rorby
  See Rorby, Ginny
Ofek, Uriel 1926- *36*
  See also CLR *28*
Offenbacher, Ami 1958- *91*
Offit, Sidney 1928- *10*
Ofosu-Appiah, L(awrence) H(enry) 1920- .. *13*
Ogan, George F. 1912-1983 .... *13*
Ogan, M. G.
  See Ogan, George F.
  and Ogan, Margaret E. (Nettles)
Ogan, Margaret E. (Nettles) 1923-1979 ...... *13*
Ogburn, Charlton (Jr.) 1911-1998 .... *3*
  Obituary *109*
Ogburn, Jacqueline K. *162*
Ogilvie, Elisabeth May 1917- *40*
  Brief entry *29*
Ogilvy, Gavin
  See Barrie, J(ames) M(atthew)
O'Green, Jennifer
  See Roberson, Jennifer
O'Green, Jennifer Roberson
  See Roberson, Jennifer
O'Hagan, Caroline 1946- *38*
O'Hanlon, Jacklyn
  See Meek, Jacklyn O'Hanlon
O'Hara, Elizabeth
  See Ni Dhuibhne, Eilis
O'Hara, Kenneth
  See Morris, (Margaret) Jean
O'Hara, Mary
  See Alsop, Mary O'Hara
O'Hara (Alsop), Mary
  See Alsop, Mary O'Hara
O'Hare, Jeff(rey A.) 1958- *105*
Ohi, Ruth 1964- *95*
Ohiyesa
  See Eastman, Charles A(lexander)
Ohlsson, Ib 1935- *7*
Ohmi, Ayano 1959- *115*
Ohtomo, Yasuo 1946- *37*
o huigin, sean 1942- *138*
  See also CLR *75*
Oiseau
  See Moseley, James W(illett)
Oke, Janette 1935- *97*
O'Keefe, Susan Heyboer *133*
O'Keeffe, Frank 1938- *99*

O'Kelley, Mattie Lou 1908-1997 .... *97*
  Earlier sketch in SATA *36*
Okimoto, Jean Davies 1942- *103*
  Earlier sketch in SATA *34*
Okomfo, Amasewa
  See Cousins, Linda
Olaleye, Isaac O. 1941- *96*
  See also SAAS *23*
Olcott, Frances Jenkins 1872(?)-1963 .... *19*
Old, Wendie C(orbin) 1943- *154*
Old Boy
  See Hughes, Thomas
Oldenburg, E(gbert) William 1936-1974 ..... *35*
Older, Effin 1942- *114*
Older, Jules 1940- *156*
  Earlier sketch in SATA *114*
Oldfield, Jenny 1949- *140*
Oldfield, Margaret J(ean) 1932- *56*
Oldfield, Pamela 1931- *86*
Oldham, June *70*
Oldham, Mary 1944- *65*
Olds, Elizabeth 1896-1991 .... *3*
  Obituary *66*
Olds, Helen Diehl 1895-1981 .... *9*
  Obituary *25*
Oldstyle, Jonathan
  See Irving, Washington
O'Leary, Brian (Todd) 1940- *6*
O'Leary, Patsy B(aker) 1937- *97*
Oliphant, B. J.
  See Tepper, Sheri S.
Oliver, Burton
  See Burt, Olive Woolley
Oliver, Chad
  See Oliver, Symmes C(hadwick)
Oliver, John Edward 1933- *21*
Oliver, Marilyn Tower 1935- *89*
Oliver, Narelle 1960- *152*
Oliver, Shirley (Louise Dawkins) 1958- *74*
Oliver, Symmes C(hadwick) 1928-1993 ... *101*
  See Oliver, Chad
Oliviero, Jamie 1950- *84*
Olmsted, Lorena Ann 1890-1989 .... *13*
Olney, Ross R. 1929- *13*
Olschewski, Alfred (Erich) 1920- *7*
Olsen, Barbara *148*
Olsen, Carol 1945- *89*
Olsen, Ib Spang 1921- *81*
  Earlier sketch in SATA *6*
Olsen, Violet (Mae) 1922-1991 .... *58*
Olson, Arielle North 1932- *67*
Olson, Gene 1922- *32*
Olson, Helen Kronberg *48*
Olson, Marianne
  See Mitchell, Marianne
Olugebefola, Ademole 1941- *15*
Oluonye, Mary N(kechi) 1955- *111*
Om
  See Gorey, Edward (St. John)
O'Malley, Kevin 1961- *157*
Oman, Carola (Mary Anima) 1897-1978 .... *35*
O'Mara, Carmel 1965- *166*
O'Mara-Horwitz, Carmel
  See O'Mara, Carmel
O'Meara, Walter (Andrew) 1897-1989 .... *65*
Ommanney, F(rancis) D(ownes) 1903-1980
  .... *23*
O Mude
  See Gorey, Edward (St. John)
Oneal, Elizabeth 1934- *82*
  Earlier sketch in SATA *30*
  See Oneal, Zibby
O'Neal, Reagan
  See Rigney, James Oliver, Jr.
Oneal, Zibby
  See CLR *13*
  See Oneal, Elizabeth
O'Neill, Amanda 1951- *111*
O'Neill, Gerard K(itchen) 1927-1992 .... *65*
O'Neill, Judith (Beatrice) 1930- *34*

O'Neill, Mary L(e Duc) 1908(?)-1990 .... *2*
  Obituary *64*
Onslow, Annette Rosemary MacArthur
  See MacArthur-Onslow, Annette Rosemary
Onyefulu, Ifeoma 1959- *157*
  Earlier sketches in SATA *81, 115*
Opie, Iona (Margaret Balfour) 1923- *118*
  Earlier sketches in SATA *3, 63*
  See also SAAS *6*
Opie, Peter (Mason) 1918-1982 .... *118*
  Obituary *28*
  Earlier sketches in SATA *3, 63*
Oppel, Kenneth 1967- *153*
  Earlier sketch in SATA *99*
Oppenheim, Joanne 1934- *136*
  Earlier sketches in SATA *5, 82*
Oppenheimer, Joan L(etson) 1925- *28*
Oppong, Joseph Ransford 1953- *160*
Optic, Oliver
  See Adams, William Taylor
  and Stratemeyer, Edward L.
Oram, Hiawyn 1946- *101*
  Earlier sketch in SATA *56*
Orbach, Ruth Gary 1941- *21*
Orczy, Emma
  See Orczy, Baroness Emmuska
Orczy, Emma Magdalena Rosalia Maria Josefa
  See Orczy, Baroness Emmuska
Orczy, Emmuska
  See Orczy, Baroness Emmuska
Orczy, Baroness Emmuska 1865-1947 .... *40*
  See Orczy, Emma
Orde, A. J.
  See Tepper, Sheri S.
O'Reilly, Jackson
  See Rigney, James Oliver, Jr.
Orenstein, Denise Gosliner 1950- *157*
Orgel, Doris 1929- *148*
  Earlier sketches in SATA *7, 85*
  See also CLR *48*
  See also SAAS *19*
Orleans, Ilo 1897-1962 .... *10*
Orlev, Uri 1931- *135*
  Earlier sketch in SATA *58*
  See also CLR *30*
  See also SAAS *19*
Ormai, Stella *57*
  Brief entry *48*
Ormerod, Jan 1946- *132*
  Brief entry *44*
  Earlier sketches in SATA *55, 70*
  See also CLR *20*
Ormondroyd, Edward 1925- *14*
Ormsby, Virginia H(aire) 1906-1990 .... *11*
Orr, Katherine S(helley) 1950- *72*
Orr, Wendy 1953- *141*
  Earlier sketch in SATA *90*
Orris
  See Ingelow, Jean
Orth, Richard
  See Gardner, Richard (M.)
Ortiz Cofer, Judith
  See Cofer, Judith Ortiz
Orwell, George
  See CLR *68*
  See Blair, Eric (Arthur)
Orwin, Joanna 1944- *141*
Osborn, Elinor 1939- *145*
Osborn, Lois D(orothy) 1915- *61*
Osborne, Charles 1927- *59*
Osborne, Chester G(orham) 1915-1987 .... *11*
Osborne, David
  See Silverberg, Robert
Osborne, George
  See Silverberg, Robert
Osborne, Leone Neal 1914-1996 .... *2*
Osborne, Mary Pope 1949- *144*
  Earlier sketches in SATA *41, 55, 98*
  See also CLR *88*
Osceola
  See Blixen, Karen (Christentze Dinesen)

Osgood, William E(dward) 1926- *37*
O'Shaughnessy, Darren
  See Shan, Darren
O'Shaughnessy, Ellen Cassels 1937- *78*
O'Shea, (Catherine) Pat(ricia Shiels) 1931-
  .... *87*
  See also CLR *18*
Osmond, Edward 1900- *10*
Ossoli, Sarah Margaret (Fuller) 1810-1850
  .... *25*
  See Fuller, Margaret
  and Fuller, Sarah Margaret
Ostendorf, (Arthur) Lloyd, (Jr.) 1921-2000
  .... *65*
  Obituary *125*
Otfinoski, Steven 1949- *116*
  Earlier sketch in SATA 56
Otis, James
  See Kaler, James Otis
O'Toole, Thomas 1941- *71*
O'Trigger, Sir Lucius
  See Horne, Richard Henry Hengist
Otten, Charlotte F(ennema) 1926- *98*
Ottley, Matt 1962- *102*
Ottley, Reginald Leslie 1909-1985 .... *26*
  See also CLR *16*
Otto, Svend
  See Soerensen, Svend Otto
Oughton, Jerrie (Preston) 1937- *131*
  Earlier sketch in SATA 76
Oughton, (William) Taylor 1925- *104*
Ouida
  See De la Ramee, Marie Louise (Ouida)
Ousley, Odille 1896-1976 .... *10*
Outcalt, Todd 1960- *123*
Overmyer, James E. 1946- *88*
Overton, Jenny (Margaret Mary) 1942- *52*
  Brief entry *36*
Owen, Ann
  See Qualey, Marsha
Owen, Annie 1949- *75*
Owen, Caroline Dale
  See Snedeker, Caroline Dale (Parke)
Owen, Clifford
  See Hamilton, Charles (Harold St. John)
Owen, Dilys
  See Gater, Dilys
Owen, (Benjamin) Evan 1918-1984 .... *38*
Owen, (John) Gareth 1936-2002 .... *162*
  Earlier sketch in SATA 83
  See also CLR *31*
  See also SAAS *14*
Owens, Bryant 1968- *116*
Owens, Gail 1939- *54*
Owens, Thomas S(heldon) 1960- *86*
Owens, Tom
  See Owens, Thomas S(heldon)
Oxenbury, Helen 1938- *149*
  Earlier sketches in SATA 3, 68
  See also CLR *70*
Oxendine, Bess Holland 1933- *90*
Oz, Frank (Richard) 1944- *60*
Ozer, Jerome S. 1927- *59*

P

Pace, Lorenzo 1943- *131*
Pace, Mildred Mastin 1907- *46*
  Brief entry *29*
Pachter, Hedwig (?)-1988 .... *63*
Pack, Janet 1952- *77*
Pack, Robert 1929- *118*
Packard, Edward 1931- *148*
  Earlier sketches in SATA 47, 90
Packer, Kenneth L. 1946- *116*
Packer, Vin
  See Meaker, Marijane (Agnes)
Pad, Peter
  See Stratemeyer, Edward L.

Page, Eileen
  See Heal, Edith
Page, Eleanor
  See Coerr, Eleanor (Beatrice)
Page, Jake 1936- *81*
Page, James Keena, Jr.
  See Page, Jake
Page, Lou Williams 1912-1997 .... *38*
Page, Mary
  See Heal, Edith
Page, Robin 1943- *154*
Pagnucci, Susan 1944- *90*
Pahz, (Anne) Cheryl Suzanne 1949- *11*
Pahz, James Alon 1943- *11*
Paice, Margaret 1920- *10*
Paige, Harry W(orthington) 1922- *41*
  Brief entry *35*
Paige, Richard
  See Koontz, Dean R.
Paige, Robin
  See Albert, Susan Wittig
Paine, Penelope Colville 1946- *87*
Paine, Roberta M. 1925- *13*
Paisley, Tom 1932- *78*
  See Bethancourt, T. Ernesto
Palatini, Margie *134*
Palazzo, Anthony D.
  See Palazzo, Tony
Palazzo, Tony 1905-1970 .... *3*
Palder, Edward L. 1922- *5*
Palecek, Josef 1932- *56*
Palecek, Libuse 1937- *89*
Palin, Michael (Edward) 1943- *67*
  See Monty Python
Palladini, David (Mario) 1946- *40*
  Brief entry *32*
Pallas, Norvin 1918-1983 .... *23*
Pallotta-Chiarolli, Maria 1960- *117*
Palmer, Bernard (Alvin) 1914-1998 .... *26*
Palmer, C. Everard 1930- *14*
Palmer, (Ruth) Candida 1926- *11*
Palmer, Cyril Everard
  See Palmer, C. Everard
Palmer, Don
  See Benson, Mildred (Augustine Wirt)
Palmer, Hap 1942- *68*
Palmer, Heidi 1948- *15*
Palmer, Helen Marion
  See Geisel, Helen
Palmer, Jessica 1953- *120*
Palmer, Judd 1972- *153*
Palmer, Juliette 1930- *15*
Palmer, Kate Salley 1946- *97*
Palmer, Maria
  See Brennan, J(ames) H(erbert)
  and Strachan, Ian
Palmer, Robin 1909-2000 .... *43*
Paltrowitz, Donna (Milman) 1950- *61*
  Brief entry *50*
Paltrowitz, Stuart 1946- *61*
  Brief entry *50*
Panagopoulos, Janie Lynn *149*
Panati, Charles 1943- *65*
Panchyk, Richard 1970- *138*
Panetta, George 1915-1969 .... *15*
Panetta, Joseph N. 1953- *96*
Panik, Sharon 1952- *82*
Panowski, Eileen Thompson 1920- *49*
Pansy
  See Alden, Isabella (Macdonald)
Pantell, Dora (Fuchs) *39*
Panter, Carol 1936- *9*
Paolini, Christopher 1983- *157*
  See also CLR *102*
Papas, Bill
  See Papas, William
Papas, William 1927-2000 .... *50*
Papashvily, George 1898-1978 .... *17*
Papashvily, Helen (Waite) 1906-1996 .... *17*
Pape, D. L.
  See Pape, Donna (Lugg)

Pape, Donna (Lugg) 1930- *82*
  Earlier sketch in SATA 2
Paperny, Myra (Green) 1932- *51*
  Brief entry *33*
Paradis, Adrian A(lexis) 1912- *67*
  Earlier sketch in SATA 1
  See also SAAS *8*
Paradis, Marjorie Bartholomew 1886(?)-1970
  .... *17*
Parenteau, Shirley Laurolyn 1935- *47*
  Brief entry *40*
Parish, Margaret (Cecile) 1927-1988 .... *73*
  See Parish, Peggy
Parish, Margaret Holt
  See Holt, Margaret
Parish, Peggy *17*
  Obituary *59*
  See also CLR *22*
  See Parish, Margaret (Cecile)
Park, Barbara 1947- *123*
  Brief entry *35*
  Earlier sketches in SATA 40, 78
  See also CLR *34*
Park, Bill
  See Park, W(illiam) B(ryan)
Park, Janie Jaehyun *150*
Park, Jordan
  See Kornbluth, C(yril) M.
  and Pohl, Frederik
Park, Linda Sue 1960- *127*
  See also CLR *84*
Park, Nick 1958- *113*
Park, (Rosina) Ruth (Lucia) 1923(?)- *93*
  Earlier sketch in SATA 25
  See also CLR *51*
Park, W(illiam) B(ryan) 1936- *22*
Parke, Marilyn 1928- *82*
Parker, Barbara Keevil 1938- *157*
Parker, Elinor Milnor 1906- *3*
Parker, Julie F. 1961- *92*
Parker, Kristy 1957- *59*
Parker, Lois M(ay) 1912-1996 .... *30*
Parker, Margot M. 1937- *52*
Parker, Marjorie Blain 1960- *145*
Parker, Mary Jessie 1948- *71*
Parker, Nancy Winslow 1930- *132*
  Earlier sketches in SATA 10, 69
  See also SAAS *20*
Parker, Richard 1915-1990 .... *14*
Parker, Robert
  See Boyd, Waldo T.
Parker, Toni Trent 1947-2005 .... *142*
  Obituary *169*
Parkes, Lucas
  See Harris, John (Wyndham Parkes Lucas)
  Beynon
Parkhill, John
  See Cox, William R(obert)
Parkinson, Ethelyn M(inerva) 1906-1999 ... *11*
Parkinson, Kathy *71*
  See Parkinson, Kathryn N.
Parks, Deborah A. 1948- *133*
  Earlier sketch in SATA 91
Parks, Edd Winfield 1906-1968 .... *10*
Parks, Gordon 1912-2006 .... *108*
  Earlier sketch in SATA 8
Parks, Gordon Alexander Buchanan
  See Parks, Gordon
Parks, Peggy J. 1951- *143*
Parks, PJ
  See Parks, Peggy J.
Parks, Rosa 1913-2005 .... *83*
  Obituary *169*
Parks, Rosa Louise Lee
  See Parks, Rosa
Parks, Van Dyke 1943- *62*
Parley, Peter
  See Goodrich, Samuel Griswold
Parlin, John
  See Graves, Charles Parlin

Parnall, Peter 1936- 69
Earlier sketch in SATA 16
See also SAAS 11
Parotti, Phillip (Elliott) 1941- 109
Parr, Ann 1943- 144
Parr, Danny
See Parr, Ann
Parr, Letitia (Evelyn) 1906-1985(?) 37
Parr, Lucy 1924- 10
Parr, Todd 134
Parrish, Anne 1888-1957 27
Parrish, Mary
See Cousins, Margaret
Parrish, Maxfield
See Parrish, (Frederick) Maxfield
Parrish, (Frederick) Maxfield 1870-1966 14
Parry, Marian 1924- 13
Parson Lot
See Kingsley, Charles
Parsons, Alexandra 1947- 92
Parsons, Ellen
See Dragonwagon, Crescent
Parsons, Martin (Leslie) 1951- 116
Partch, Virgil Franklin II 1916-1984 39
Obituary 39
Parton, Dolly (Rebecca) 1946- 94
Partridge, Benjamin W(aring), Jr. 1915-2005
.... 28
Obituary 163
Partridge, Cora Cheney
See Cheney, Cora
Partridge, Elizabeth 134
Partridge, Jenny (Lilian) 1947- 52
Brief entry 37
Pasachoff, Naomi 1947- 147
Pascal, David 1918- 14
Pascal, Francine 1938- 143
Brief entry 37
Earlier sketches in SATA 51, 80
See also CLR 25
Paschal, Nancy
See Trotter, Grace V(iolet)
Pascudniak, Pascal
See Lupoff, Richard A(llen)
Pashko, Stanley 1913-1982 29
Passailaigue, Thomas E.
See Paisley, Tom
Pateman, Robert 1954- 84
Patent, Dorothy Hinshaw 1940- 162
Autobiography Feature 162
Earlier sketches in SATA 22, 69, 120
See also CLR 19
See also SAAS 13
Paterson, A(ndrew) B(arton) 1864-1941 97
Paterson, Banjo
See Paterson, A(ndrew) B(arton)
Paterson, Diane (R. Cole) 1946- 59
Brief entry 33
Paterson, John (Barstow) 1932- 114
Paterson, Katherine 1932- 133
Earlier sketches in SATA 13, 53, 92
See also CLR 50
Paterson, Katherine Womeldorf
See Paterson, Katherine
Patience, John 1949- 90
Patneaude, David 1944- 159
Earlier sketch in SATA 85
Paton, Alan (Stewart) 1903-1988 11
Obituary 56
Paton, Jane (Elizabeth) 1934- 35
Paton, Priscilla 1952- 98
Paton Walsh, Gillian 1937- 109
Earlier sketches in SATA 4, 72
See also CLR 65
See also SAAS 3
See Paton Walsh, Jill
and Walsh, Jill Paton
Paton Walsh, Jill
See Paton Walsh, Gillian
Patrick, Susan
See Clark, Patricia Denise

Patron, Susan 1948- 76
Patschke, Steve 1955- 125
Patten, Brian 1946- 152
Earlier sketch in SATA 29
Patterson, Charles 1935- 59
Patterson, Geoffrey 1943- 54
Brief entry 44
Patterson, James 1947- 164
Patterson, James B.
See Patterson, James
Patterson, Lillie G. -1999 88
Earlier sketch in SATA 14
Patterson, Nancy Ruth 1944- 148
Earlier sketch in SATA 72
Pattison, Darcy (S.) 1954- 126
Earlier sketch in SATA 72
Pattou, Edith 164
Patz (Blaustein), Nancy 154
Paul, Aileen 1917- 12
Paul, Ann Whitford 1941- 168
Earlier sketches in SATA 76, 110
Paul, Elizabeth
See Crow, Donna Fletcher
Paul, Hamish Vigne Christie 1951- 151
See also CLR 87
Paul, James 1936- 23
Paul, Korky
See Paul, Hamish Vigne Christie
Paul, Robert
See Roberts, John G(aither)
Paul, Tessa 1944- 103
Pauli, Hertha (Ernestine) 1909-1973 3
Obituary 26
Paull, Grace A. 1898- 24
Paulsen, Gary 1939- 158
Earlier sketches in SATA 22, 50, 54, 79, 111
See also CLR 82
Paulson, Jack
See Jackson, C(aary) Paul
Pauquet, Gina Ruck
See Ruck-Pauquet, Gina
Pausacker, Jenny 1948- 72
See also SAAS 23
Pausewang, Gudrun 1928- 165
Earlier sketch in SATA 104
Pavel, Frances 1907- 10
Paxton, Tom 70
See Paxton, Thomas R.
Payne, Alan
See Jakes, John (William)
Payne, Bernal C., Jr. 1941- 60
Payne, C. D. 1949- 133
Payne, Donald Gordon 1924- 37
Payne, Emmy
See West, Emily Govan
Payne, Nina 135
Payne, Rachel Ann
See Jakes, John (William)
Payson, Dale 1943- 9
Payzant, Charles 18
Paz, A.
See Pahz, James Alon
Paz, Zan
See Pahz, (Anne) Cheryl Suzanne
Peace, Mary
See Finley, Mary Peace
Peake, Mervyn 1911-1968 23
Peale, Norman Vincent 1898-1993 20
Obituary 78
Pearce, Jacqueline 1962- 146
Pearce, Margaret 104
Peare, Catherine Owens 1911- 9
Pearson, Gayle 1947- 119
Earlier sketch in SATA 53
Pearson, Kit 1947- 77
Autobiography Feature 117
See also CLR 26
Pearson, Mary E. 1955- 134
Pearson, Susan 1946- 166
Brief entry 27
Earlier sketches in SATA 39, 91

Pearson, Tracey Campbell 1956- 155
Earlier sketch in SATA 64
Pease, (Clarence) Howard 1894-1974 2
Obituary 25
Peavy, Linda 1943- 54
Peck, Anne Merriman 1884-1976 18
Peck, Beth 1957- 79
Peck, Jan 159
Peck, Jeanie J. 1967- 147
Peck, Marshall III 1951- 92
Peck, Richard (Wayne) 1934- 158
Autobiography Feature 110
Earlier sketches in SATA 18, 55, 97, 110
See also CLR 15
See also SAAS 2
Peck, Robert Newton 1928- 156
Autobiography Feature 108
Earlier sketches in SATA 21, 62, 111
See also CLR 45
See also SAAS 1
Peck, Sylvia 1953- 133
Peck-Whiting, Jeanie J.
See Peck, Jeanie J.
Pederson, Sharleen
See Collicott, Sharleen
Peebles, Anne
See Galloway, Priscilla
Peek, Merle 1938- 39
Peel, John 1954- 79
Peel, Norman Lemon
See Hirsch, Phil
Peeples, Edwin A(ugustus, Jr.) 1915-1994 6
Peers, Judi(th May West) 1956- 119
Peet, Bill
See CLR 12
See Peet, William Bartlett
Peet, Creighton B. 1899-1977 30
Peet, William Bartlett 1915-2002 78
Obituary 137
Earlier sketches in SATA 2, 41
See Peet, Bill
Peguero, Leone 116
Pelaez, Jill 1924- 12
Pelham, David 1938- 70
Pell, Ed(ward) 1950- 157
Pellowski, Anne 1933- 20
Pellowski, Michael (Joseph) 1949- 151
Brief entry 48
Earlier sketch in SATA 88
Pellowski, Michael Morgan
See Pellowski, Michael (Joseph)
Pelta, Kathy 1928- 18
Peltier, Leslie C(opus) 1900-1980 13
Pemberton, John Leigh
See Leigh-Pemberton, John
Pembury, Bill
See Groom, Arthur William
Pemsteen, Hans
See Manes, Stephen
Pendennis, Arthur Esquir
See Thackeray, William Makepeace
Pender, Lydia Podger 1907- 61
Pendery, Rosemary (Schmitz) 7
Pendle, Alexy 1943- 29
Pendleton, Don
See Cunningham, Chet
and Garside, (Clifford) Jack
and Jagninski, Tom
and Krauzer, Steven M(ark)
and Obstfeld, Raymond
Pene du Bois, William (Sherman) 1916-1993
.... 68
Obituary 74
Earlier sketch in SATA 4
See also CLR 1
Penn, Ruth Bonn
See Rosenberg, Eth(el) Clifford
Pennac, Daniel 1944- 155
Pennage, E. M.
See Finkel, George (Irvine)

Penner, Fred 1946- *169*
  Earlier sketch in SATA *67*
Penner, Frederick Ralph Cornelius
  See Penner, Fred
Penney, Grace Jackson 1904-2000 .... *35*
Penney, Ian 1960- *76*
Penney, Sue 1957- *152*
  Earlier sketch in SATA *102*
Pennington, Eunice 1923- *27*
Pennington, Lillian Boyer 1904- *45*
Penrose, Gordon 1925- *66*
Penson, Mary E. 1917- *78*
Penzler, Otto 1942- *38*
Pepe, Phil 1935- *20*
Peppe, Rodney (Darrell) 1934- *74*
  Earlier sketch in SATA *4*
  See also SAAS *10*
Percy, Charles Henry
  See Smith, Dorothy Gladys
Percy, Rachel 1930- *63*
Perdrizet, Marie-Pierre 1952- *79*
Perenyi, Constance (Marie) 1954- *93*
Perera, Hilda 1926- *105*
Perera, Thomas Biddle 1938- *13*
Peretti, Frank E. 1951- *141*
  Earlier sketch in SATA *80*
Perkins, Al(bert Rogers) 1904-1975 .... *30*
Perkins, Lucy Fitch 1865-1937 .... *72*
Perkins, Lynne Rae *131*
Perkins, (Richard) Marlin 1905-1986 .... *21*
  Obituary *48*
Perkins, Mitali 1963- *88*
Perks, Anne-Marie 1955- *122*
Perl, Lila *72*
  Earlier sketch in SATA *6*
Perl, Susan 1922-1983 .... *22*
  Obituary *34*
Perlmutter, O(scar) William 1920-1975 .... *8*
Pernu, Dennis 1970- *87*
Perrault, Charles 1628-1703 .... *25*
  See also CLR *79*
Perret, Gene (Richard) 1937- *76*
Perrine, Mary 1913-1976 .... *2*
Perrins, Lesley 1953- *56*
Perrow, Angeli 1954- *121*
Perry, Andrea 1956- *148*
Perry, Barbara Fisher
  See Fisher, Barbara
Perry, Marie Fritz *165*
Perry, Patricia 1949- *30*
Perry, Phyllis J(ean) 1933- *152*
  Earlier sketches in SATA *60, 101*
Perry, Ritchie (John Allen) 1942- *105*
Perry, Roger 1933- *27*
Perry, Steve(n Carl) 1947- *76*
Pershall, Mary K. 1951- *70*
Pershing, Marie
  See Schultz, Pearle Henriksen
Perske, Robert 1927- *57*
Persun, Morgan Reed
  See Watkins, Dawn L.
Petach, Heidi *149*
Peter
  See Stratemeyer, Edward L.
Peters, Alexander
  See Hollander, Zander
Peters, Andrew Fusek 1965- *169*
  Earlier sketch in SATA *107*
Peters, Caroline
  See Betz, Eva Kelly
Peters, David
  See David, Peter (Allen)
Peters, Elizabeth
  See Mertz, Barbara
Peters, Emma
  See Price, Karen
Peters, Gabriel
  See Matott, Justin
Peters, Julie Anne 1952- *128*
  Earlier sketch in SATA *82*

Peters, Linda
  See Catherall, Arthur
Peters, Lisa Westberg 1951- *161*
  Earlier sketches in SATA *74, 115*
Peters, Patricia 1953- *84*
Peters, Russell M. 1929- *78*
Peters, S. H.
  See Porter, William Sydney
  and Proffitt, Nicholas (Charles)
Petersen, David 1946- *109*
  Earlier sketch in SATA *62*
Petersen, Gwenn Boardman 1924- *61*
  See Boardman, Gwenn R.
Petersen, P(eter) J(ames) 1941- *118*
  Brief entry *43*
  Earlier sketches in SATA *48, 83*
Petersen, Palle 1943- *85*
Petersham, Maud (Sylvia Fuller) 1890-1971
  .... *17*
  See also CLR *24*
Petersham, Miska 1888-1960 .... *17*
  See also CLR *24*
Peterson, Cris 1952- *145*
  Earlier sketch in SATA *84*
Peterson, Dawn 1934- *86*
Peterson, Esther (Allen) 1934- *35*
Peterson, Hans 1922- *8*
Peterson, Harold L(eslie) 1922-1978 .... *8*
Peterson, Helen Stone 1910- *8*
Peterson, Jean Sunde 1941- *108*
Peterson, Jeanne Whitehouse 1939- *159*
  See Whitehouse, Jeanne
Peterson, Kathleen B. 1951- *119*
Peterson, Lorraine 1940- *56*
  Brief entry *44*
Peterson, Shelley 1952- *146*
Petie, Haris *10*
  See Petty, Roberta
Petrides, Heidrun 1944- *19*
Petrie, Catherine 1947- *52*
  Brief entry *41*
Petroski, Catherine (Ann Groom) 1939- *48*
Petrovich, Michael B(oro) 1922- *40*
Petrovskaya, Kyra
  See Wayne, Kyra Petrovskaya
Petruccio, Steven James 1961- *67*
Petry, Ann (Lane) 1908-1997 .... *5*
  Obituary *94*
  See also CLR *12*
Pettit, Jayne 1932- *108*
Pevsner, Stella *131*
  Earlier sketches in SATA *8, 77*
  See also SAAS *14*
Peyo
  See Culliford, Pierre
Peyton, K. M.
  See CLR *3*
  See also SAAS *17*
  See Peyton, Kathleen Wendy (Herald)
Peyton, Kathleen Wendy (Herald) 1929- .. *157*
  Earlier sketches in SATA *15, 62*
  See Peyton, K. M.
Pfanner, (Anne) Louise 1955- *68*
Pfeffer, Susan Beth 1948- *83*
  Earlier sketch in SATA *4*
  See also CLR *11*
  See also SAAS *17*
Pfeffer, Wendy 1929- *142*
  Earlier sketch in SATA *78*
Pfeiffer, Janet (B.) 1949- *96*
Pfister, Marcus *150*
  Earlier sketch in SATA *83*
  See also CLR *42*
Pfitsch, Patricia Curtis 1948- *148*
Pflieger, Pat 1955- *84*
Phelan, Mary Kay 1914- *3*
Phelan, Terry Wolfe 1941- *56*
Phelps, Ethel Johnston 1914-1984 .... *35*
Philbrick, Rodman
  See Philbrick, (W.) Rodman

Philbrick, (W.) Rodman 1951- *163*
  Earlier sketch in SATA *122*
  See Philbrick, W. R.
Philbrick, W. R. *163*
  See Philbrick, (W.) Rodman
Philbrook, Clem(ent E.) 1917- *24*
Phillips, Aileen Paul
  See Paul, Aileen
Phillips, Betty Lou
  See Phillips, Elizabeth Louise
Phillips, Bob 1940- *95*
Phillips, Douglas A. 1949- *161*
Phillips, Elizabeth Louise *58*
  Brief entry *48*
Phillips, Irv(ing W.) 1905-2000 .... *11*
  Obituary *125*
Phillips, Jack
  See Sandburg, Carl (August)
Phillips, Leon
  See Gerson, Noel Bertram
Phillips, Loretta (Hosey) 1893-1987 .... *10*
Phillips, Louis 1942- *102*
  Earlier sketch in SATA *8*
Phillips, Mary Geisler 1881-1964 .... *10*
Phillips, Michael
  See Nolan, William F(rancis)
Phillips, (Woodward) Prentice 1894-1981 .. *10*
Phillpotts, Eden 1862-1960 .... *24*
Phin
  See Thayer, Ernest Lawrence
Phipson, Joan
  See CLR *5*
  See also SAAS *3*
  See Fitzhardinge, Joan Margaret
Phiz
  See Browne, Hablot Knight
Phleger, Fred B. 1909-1993 .... *34*
Phleger, Marjorie Temple 1908(?)-1986 .... *1*
  Obituary *47*
Piatti, Celestino 1922- *16*
Picard, Barbara Leonie 1917- *89*
  Earlier sketch in SATA *2*
  See also SAAS *10*
Pickard, Charles 1932- *36*
Pickering, James Sayre 1897-1969 .... *36*
  Obituary *28*
Pickering, Robert B. 1950- *93*
Pielichaty, Helena 1955- *142*
Pienkowski, Jan (Michal) 1936- *131*
  Earlier sketches in SATA *6, 58*
  See also CLR *6*
Pierce, Edith Gray 1893-1977 .... *45*
Pierce, Katherine
  See St. John, Wylly Folk
Pierce, Meredith Ann 1958- *127*
  Brief entry *48*
  Earlier sketch in SATA *67*
  See also CLR *20*
Pierce, Ruth (Ireland) 1936- *5*
Pierce, Sharon
  See McCullough, Sharon Pierce
Pierce, Tamora 1954- *153*
  Brief entry *49*
  Earlier sketches in SATA *51, 96*
Pierik, Robert 1921- *13*
Piers, Robert
  See Anthony, Piers
Pig, Edward
  See Gorey, Edward (St. John)
Pike, Bob
  See Pike, Robert W(ilson)
Pike, Christopher
  See McFadden, Kevin Christopher
Pike, Deborah 1951- *89*
Pike, E(dgar) Royston 1896-1980 .... *22*
  Obituary *56*
Pike, R. William 1956- *92*
Pike, Robert W(ilson) 1931- *102*
Pilarski, Laura 1926- *13*
Pilgrim, Anne
  See Allan, Mabel Esther

Pilkey, Dav 1966- *166*
　Earlier sketches in SATA *68, 115*
　See also CLR *48*
Pilkey, David Murray, Jr.
　See Pilkey, Dav
Pilkington, Francis Meredyth 1907- *4*
Pilkington, Roger (Windle) 1915-2003 .... *10*
　Obituary *144*
Pincus, Harriet 1938- *27*
Pinczes, Elinor J(ane) 1940- *81*
Pine, Nicholas 1951- *91*
Pine, Tillie S(chloss) 1896-1999 .... *13*
Pini, Richard (Alan) 1950- *89*
Pini, Wendy 1951- *89*
Pinkett, Jada
　See Smith, Jada Pinkett
Pinkney, Andrea Davis 1963- *160*
　Earlier sketch in SATA *113*
Pinkney, (Jerry) Brian 1961- *148*
　Earlier sketch in SATA *74*
　See also CLR *54*
Pinkney, Gloria Jean 1941- *85*
Pinkney, J. Brian
　See Pinkney, (Jerry) Brian
Pinkney, Jerry 1939- *151*
　Brief entry *32*
　Earlier sketches in SATA *41, 71, 107*
　See also CLR *43*
　See also SAAS *12*
Pinkney, John *97*
Pinkney, Sandra L. *128*
Pinkwater, D. Manus
　See Pinkwater, Daniel Manus
Pinkwater, Daniel
　See Pinkwater, Daniel Manus
Pinkwater, Daniel M.
　See Pinkwater, Daniel Manus
Pinkwater, Daniel Manus 1941- *158*
　Earlier sketches in SATA *8, 46, 76, 114*
　See also CLR *4*
　See also SAAS *3*
Pinkwater, Manus
　See Pinkwater, Daniel Manus
Pinner, Joma
　See Werner, Herma
Pioneer
　See Yates, Raymond F(rancis)
Piowaty, Kim Kennelly 1957- *49*
Piper, Roger
　See Fisher, John (Oswald Hamilton)
Pirner, Connie White 1955- *72*
Piro, Richard 1934- *7*
Pirot, Alison Lohans
　See Lohans, Alison
Pirsig, Robert M(aynard) 1928- *39*
Pita
　See Rendon, Maria
Pitcher, Caroline (Nell) 1948- *128*
Pitre, Felix 1949- *84*
Pitrone, Jean Maddern 1920- *4*
Pittman, Helena Clare 1945- *71*
Pitz, Henry C(larence) 1895-1976 .... *4*
　Obituary *24*
Pizer, Vernon 1918- *21*
Place, Marian T(empleton) 1910- *3*
Place, Robin (Mary) 1926- *71*
Plaidy, Jean
　See Hibbert, Eleanor Alice Burford
Plain, Belva 1919- *62*
Plath, Sylvia 1932-1963 .... *96*
Platt, Kin 1911- *86*
　Earlier sketch in SATA *21*
　See also SAAS *17*
Platt, Randall 1948- *95*
Platt, Richard 1953- *166*
　Earlier sketch in SATA *120*
Playfellow, Robin
　See Ellis, Edward S(ylvester)
Playsted, James
　See Wood, James Playsted

Plecas, Jennifer 1966- *149*
　Earlier sketch in SATA *84*
Plimpton, George (Ames) 1927-2003 .... *10*
　Obituary *150*
Plomer, William Charles Franklin 1903-1973
　.. *24*
Plotz, Helen Ratnoff 1913-2000 .... *38*
Plourde, Lynn 1955- *168*
　Earlier sketch in SATA *122*
Plowden, David 1932- *52*
Plowden, Martha Ward 1948- *98*
Plowhead, Ruth Gipson 1877-1967 .... *43*
Plowman, Stephanie 1922- *6*
Pluckrose, Henry (Arthur) 1931- *141*
　Earlier sketch in SATA *13*
Plum, J.
　See Wodehouse, P(elham) G(renville)
Plum, Jennifer
　See Kurland, Michael
Plumme, Don E.
　See Katz, Bobbi
Plummer, Margaret 1911- *2*
Pochocki, Ethel (Frances) 1925- *76*
Podendorf, Illa (E.) 1903(?)-1983 .... *18*
　Obituary *35*
Podwal, Mark 1945- *160*
　Earlier sketch in SATA *101*
Poe, Edgar Allan 1809-1849 .... *23*
Poe, Ty (Christopher) 1975- *94*
Pogany, William Andrew 1882-1955 .... *44*
　See Pogany, Willy
Pogany, Willy
　Brief entry *30*
　See Pogany, William Andrew
Pohl, Frederik 1919- *24*
Pohlmann, Lillian (Grenfell) 1902-1997 ..... *11*
Pohrt, Tom 1953- *152*
　Earlier sketch in SATA *67*
Pointon, Robert
　See Rooke, Daphne (Marie)
Points, Larry (Gene) 1945- *133*
Pokeberry, P. J.
　See Mitchell, B(etty) J(o)
POLA
　See Watson, Pauline
Polacco, Patricia Ann 1944- *123*
　Earlier sketch in SATA *74*
　See also CLR *40*
Polatnick, Florence T. 1923- *5*
Polder, Markus
　See Kruss, James
Polese, Carolyn 1947- *58*
Polese, James 1914- *87*
Polette, Nancy (Jane) 1930- *42*
Polhamus, Jean Burt 1928- *21*
Policoff, Stephen Phillip 1948- *77*
Polikoff, Barbara G. 1929- *162*
　Earlier sketch in SATA *77*
Polikoff, Barbara Garland
　See Polikoff, Barbara G.
Polisar, Barry Louis 1954- *134*
　Earlier sketch in SATA *77*
Politi, Leo 1908-1996 .... *47*
　Obituary *88*
　Earlier sketch in SATA *1*
　See also CLR *29*
Polking, Kirk 1925- *5*
Pollack, Jill S. 1963- *88*
Polland, Barbara K(ay) 1939- *44*
Polland, Madeleine A(ngela Cahill) 1918- .. *68*
　Earlier sketch in SATA *6*
　See also SAAS *8*
Pollema-Cahill, Phyllis 1958- *123*
Pollock, Bruce 1945- *46*
Pollock, Mary
　See Blyton, Enid (Mary)
Pollock, Penny 1935- *137*
　Brief entry *42*
　Earlier sketch in SATA *44*
Pollowitz, Melinda Kilborn 1944- *26*
Polner, Murray 1928- *64*

Polonsky, Arthur 1925- *34*
Polseno, Jo *17*
Pomaska, Anna 1946- *117*
Pomerantz, Charlotte 1930- *80*
　Earlier sketch in SATA *20*
Pomeroy, Pete
　See Roth, Arthur J(oseph)
Pond, Alonzo W(illiam) 1894-1986 .... *5*
Pontiflet, Ted 1932- *32*
Poole, Gray Johnson 1906- *1*
Poole, Josephine *5*
　See also SAAS *2*
　See Helyar, Jane Penelope Josephine
Poole, (Jane Penelope) Josephine
　See Helyar, Jane Penelope Josephine
Poole, Lynn 1910-1969 .... *1*
Poole, Peggy 1925- *39*
Poortvliet, Rien 1932- *65*
　Brief entry *37*
Pope, Elizabeth Marie 1917- *38*
　Brief entry *36*
Popescu, Christine
　See Pullein-Thompson, Christine
Poploff, Michelle 1956- *67*
Popp, K. Wendy *91*
Poppel, Hans 1942- *71*
Portal, Colette 1936- *6*
Porte, Barbara Ann 1943- *152*
　Brief entry *45*
　Earlier sketches in SATA *57, 93*
Porter, A(nthony) P(eyton) 1945- *68*
Porter, Connie (Rose) 1959(?)- *129*
　Earlier sketch in SATA *81*
Porter, Donald Clayton
　See Gerson, Noel Bertram
Porter, Eleanor H(odgman) 1868-1920
　See CLR *110*
Porter, Gene(va Grace) Stratton
　See Stratton-Porter, Gene(va Grace)
Porter, Janice Lee 1953- *108*
　Earlier sketch in SATA *68*
Porter, Katherine Anne 1890-1980 .... *39*
　Obituary *23*
Porter, Kathryn
　See Swinford, Betty (June Wells)
Porter, Sheena 1935- *24*
　See also SAAS *10*
Porter, Sue
　See Limb, Sue
Porter, Sue 1951- *76*
Porter, William Sydney 1862-1910
　See YABC *2*
　See Henry, O.
Porto, Tony 1960- *153*
Posell, Elsa Z(eigerman) -1995 .... *3*
Posten, Margaret L(ois) 1915- *10*
Posthuma, Sieb 1960- *150*
Potok, Chaim 1929-2002 .... *106*
　Obituary *134*
　Earlier sketch in SATA *33*
　See also CLR *92*
Potok, Herbert Harold -2002
　See Potok, Chaim
Potok, Herman Harold
　See Potok, Chaim
Potter, (Helen) Beatrix 1866-1943 .... *132*
　Earlier sketch in SATA *100*
　See also YABC *1*
　See also CLR *73*
Potter, Giselle *150*
Potter, Margaret (Newman) 1926-1998 .... *21*
　Obituary *104*
　See Betteridge, Anne
Potter, Marian 1915- *9*
Potter, Miriam Clark 1886-1965 .... *3*
Poulin, Stephane 1961- *98*
　See also CLR *28*
Poulton, Kimberly 1957(?)- *136*
Pournelle, Jerry (Eugene) 1933- *161*
　Earlier sketches in SATA *26, 91*
Povelite, Kay 1955- *102*

Pow, Tom 1950- 163
Powe-Allred, Alexandra
  See Allred, Alexandra Powe
Powell, A. M.
  See Morgan, Alfred P(owell)
Powell, E. Sandy 1947- 72
Powell, Pamela 1960- 78
Powell, Patricia Hruby 1966- 136
Powell, Randy 1956- 118
Powell, Richard Stillman
  See Barbour, Ralph Henry
Powell, Robert (Stephenson Smyth) Baden
  See Baden-Powell, Robert (Stephenson
  Smyth)
Powell, Stephanie 1953- 93
Power, Margaret (M.) 1945- 125
  Earlier sketch in SATA 75
Powers, Anne
  See Schwartz, Anne Powers
Powers, Bill 1931- 52
  Brief entry 31
Powers, Daniel 1959- 164
Powers, Margaret
  See Heal, Edith
Powers, Tim(othy Thomas) 1952- 107
Powledge, Fred 1935- 37
Poynter, Margaret 1927- 27
Prachaticka, Marketa
  See Kolibalova, Marketa
Prachatika, Marketa
  See Kolibalova, Marketa
Prager, Arthur 44
Prager, Ellen J. 1962- 136
Pratchett, Terry 1948- 139
  Earlier sketch in SATA 82
  See also CLR 64
Prater, John 1947- 149
  Earlier sketches in SATA 72, 103
Pratt, (Murray) Fletcher 1897-1956 102
Pratt, Kristin Joy 1976- 87
Pratt, Pierre 1962- 166
  Earlier sketch in SATA 95
Preiss, Byron 1953-2005 166
  Brief entry 42
  Earlier sketch in SATA 47
Preiss, Byron Cary
  See Preiss, Byron
Preller, James 1961- 88
Prelutsky, Jack 1940- 118
  Earlier sketches in SATA 22, 66
  See also CLR 13
Prentice, Amy
  See Kaler, James Otis
Prescott, Casey
  See Morris, Chris(topher Crosby)
Presnall, Judith (Ann) Janda 1943- 96
Pressler, Mirjam 1940- 155
Preston, Douglas 1956- 113
Preston, Edna Mitchell 40
Preston, Lillian Elvira 1918- 47
Preussler, Otfried 1923- 24
Price, Beverley Joan 1931- 98
Price, Christine (Hilda) 1928-1980 3
  Obituary 23
Price, Jennifer
  See Hoover, Helen (Drusilla Blackburn)
Price, Joan 1931- 124
Price, Jonathan (Reeve) 1941- 46
Price, Karen 1957- 125
Price, Lucie Locke
  See Locke, Lucie
Price, Olive 1903-1991 8
Price, Susan 1955- 128
  Earlier sketches in SATA 25, 85
Price, Willard 1887-1983 48
  Brief entry 38
Price-Groff, Claire 127
Priceman, Marjorie 1958- 168
  Earlier sketches in SATA 81, 120
Prichard, Katharine Susannah 1883-1969 ... 66

Prideaux, Tom 1908-1993 37
  Obituary 76
Priestley, Alice 1962- 95
Priestley, Lee (Shore) 1904-1999 27
Priestly, Doug(las Michael) 1954- 122
Prieto, Mariana Beeching 1912-1999 8
Primavera, Elise 1954- 109
  Brief entry 48
  Earlier sketch in SATA 58
Prime, Derek (James) 1931- 34
Prince, Alison (Mary) 1931- 86
  Earlier sketch in SATA 28
Prince, J(ack) H(arvey) 1908- 17
Prince, Maggie 102
Pringle, Eric 138
Pringle, Laurence P(atrick) 1935- 154
  Earlier sketches in SATA 4, 68, 104
  See also CLR 57
  See also SAAS 6
Prior, Natalie Jane 1963- 106
Pritchett, Elaine H(illyer) 1920- 36
Pritts, Kim Derek 1953- 83
Prochazkova, Iva 1953- 68
Proctor, Everitt
  See Montgomery, Rutherford George
Proeysen, Alf 1914-1970
  See CLR 24
  See Proysen, Alf
Professor Scribbler
  See Hollingsworth, Mary
Prose, Francine 1947- 149
  Earlier sketch in SATA 101
Provensen, Alice 1918- 147
  Earlier sketches in SATA 9, 70
  See also CLR 11
Provensen, Martin (Elias) 1916-1987 70
  Obituary 51
  Earlier sketch in SATA 9
  See also CLR 11
Provenzo, Eugene (F., Jr.) 1949- 142
  Earlier sketch in SATA 78
Provost, Gail Levine 1944- 65
Provost, Gary (Richard) 1944-1995 66
Proysen, Alf 67
  See Proeysen, Alf
Pruett, Candace (J.) 1968- 157
Pryor, Bonnie H. 1942- 69
Pryor, Boori (Monty) 1950- 112
Pryor, Helen Brenton 1897-1972 4
Pryor, Michael 1957- 153
Pucci, Albert John 1920- 44
Pudney, John (Sleigh) 1909-1977 24
Pugh, Ellen (Tiffany) 1920- 7
Pullein-Thompson, Christine 1925-2005 82
  Earlier sketch in SATA 3
Pullein-Thompson, Diana 3
  See Farr, Diana (Pullein-Thompson)
Pullein-Thompson, Josephine (Mary
  Wedderburn) 82
  Earlier sketch in SATA 3
Pullman, Philip (Nicholas) 1946- 150
  Earlier sketches in SATA 65, 103
  See also CLR 84
  See also SAAS 17
Pulver, Harry, Jr. 1960- 129
Pulver, Robin 1945- 133
  Earlier sketch in SATA 76
Puner, Helen W(alker) 1915-1989 37
  Obituary 63
Purdy, Carol 1943- 120
  Earlier sketch in SATA 66
Purdy, Susan G(old) 1939- 8
Purmell, Ann 1953- 147
Purnell, Idella 1901-1982 120
Purscell, Phyllis 1934- 7
Purtill, Richard L. 1931- 53
Pushker, Gloria 1927- 162
  Earlier sketch in SATA 75
Pushker, Gloria Teles
  See Pushker, Gloria

Pushkin, Aleksandr Sergeevich
  See Pushkin, Alexander (Sergeyevich)
Pushkin, Alexander (Sergeyevich) 1799-1837
  61
  See Pushkin, Aleksandr Sergeevich
Putnam, Alice 1916- 61
Putnam, Arthur Lee
  See Alger, Horatio, Jr.
Putnam, Peter B(rock) 1920-1998 30
  Obituary 106
Pyle, Howard 1853-1911 100
  Earlier sketch in SATA 16
  See also CLR 22
Pyle, Katharine 1863-1938 66
Pyne, Mable Mandeville 1903-1969 9
Pyrnelle, Louise-Clarke 1850-1907 114

Q

Quackenbush, Robert M(ead) 1929- 133
  Autobiography Feature 133
  Earlier sketches in SATA 7, 70
  See also SAAS 7
Qualey, Marsha 1953- 124
  Earlier sketch in SATA 79
Quammen, David 1948- 7
Quark, Jason
  See Eldin, Peter
Quarles, Benjamin (Arthur) 1904-1996 12
Quatermass, Martin
  See Carpenter, John (Howard)
Quattlebaum, Mary 1958- 134
  Earlier sketch in SATA 88
Quay, Emma 119
Queen, Ellery
  See Deming, Richard
  and Dannay, Frederic
  and Davidson, Avram (James)
  and Fairman, Paul W.
  and Flora, Fletcher
  and Hoch, Edward D(entinger)
  and Kane, Henry
  and Lee, Manfred B.
  and Marlowe, Stephen
  and Powell, (Oval) Talmage
  and Sheldon, Walter J(ames)
  and Sturgeon, Theodore (Hamilton)
  and Tracy, Don(ald Fiske)
  and Vance, John Holbrook
Queen, Ellery, Jr.
  See Dannay, Frederic
  and Holding, James (Clark Carlisle, Jr.)
  and Lee, Manfred B.
Quennell, Marjorie Courtney 1884-1972 29
Quentin, Brad
  See Bisson, Terry (Ballantine)
Quest, (Edna) Olga W(ilbourne) Hall
  See Hall-Quest, (Edna) Olga W(ilbourne)
Quick, Annabelle 1922-1986 2
Quill, Monica
  See McInerny, Ralph (Matthew)
Quin-Harkin, Janet 1941- 165
  Earlier sketches in SATA 18, 90, 119
  See Bowen, Rhys
Quinlan, Susan E(lizabeth) 1954- 88
Quinn, Elisabeth 1881-1962 22
Quinn, Pat 1947- 130
Quinn, Patrick 1950- 73
Quinn, Rob 1972- 138
Quinn, Theodora K.
  See Kroeber, Theodora (Kracaw)
Quinn, Vernon
  See Quinn, Elisabeth
Quirk, Anne (E.) 1956- 99
Quixley, Jim 1931- 56
Quyth, Gabriel
  See Jennings, Gary (Gayne)

R

Ra, Carol F. 1939- 76
Raab, Evelyn 1951- 129
Rabe, Berniece (Louise) 1928- 148
　Autobiography Feature 148
　Earlier sketches in SATA 7, 77
　See also SAAS 10
Rabe, Olive H(anson) (?)-1968 13
Rabin, Staton 1958- 162
　Earlier sketch in SATA 84
Rabinowich, Ellen 1946- 29
Rabinowitz, Sandy 1954- 52
　Brief entry 39
Rachlin, Carol K(ing) 1919- 64
Rachlin, Harvey (Brant) 1951- 47
Rachlin, Nahid 64
Rackham, Arthur 1867-1939 100
　Earlier sketch in SATA 15
　See also CLR 57
Raczka, Bob 1963- 163
Radencich, Marguerite C. 1952-1998 79
Radford, Ruby L(orraine) 1891-1971 6
Radin, Ruth Yaffe 1938- 107
　Brief entry 52
　Earlier sketch in SATA 56
Radlauer, David 1952- 28
Radlauer, Edward 1921- 15
Radlauer, Ruth Shaw 1926- 98
　Earlier sketch in SATA 15
Radley, Gail 1951- 112
　Earlier sketch in SATA 25
Rae, Gwynedd 1892-1977 37
Raebeck, Lois 1921- 5
Rael, Elsa Okon 1927-
　See CLR 84
Raffi
　See Cavoukian, Raffi
Raftery, Gerald (Bransfield) 1905-1986 11
Ragan-Reid, Gale 1956- 90
Rahaman, Vashanti 1953- 98
Rahn, Joan Elma 1929- 27
Rai, Bali 1971- 152
Raible, Alton (Robert) 1918- 35
Raiff, Stan 1930- 11
Raines, Shirley C(arol) 1945- 128
Rainey, W. B.
　See Blassingame, Wyatt Rainey
Rake, Jody 1961- 157
Ralston, Jan
　See Dunlop, Agnes M. R.
Ramal, Walter
　See de la Mare, Walter (John)
Ramanujan, A(ttipat) K(rishnaswami)
　1929-1993 86
Ramstad, Ralph L. 1919- 115
Rana, Indi
　See Rana, Indira Higham
Rana, Indira Higham 1944- 82
Ranadive, Gail 1944- 10
Rand, Ann (Binkley) 30
Rand, Gloria 1925- 156
　Earlier sketch in SATA 101
Rand, Paul 1914-1996 6
Randall, Carrie
　See Ransom, Candice F.
Randall, David 1972- 167
Randall, Florence Engel 1917-1997 5
Randall, Janet
　See Young, Janet Randall
　and Young, Robert W(illiam)
Randall, Robert
　See Garrett, (Gordon) Randall (Phillip)
　and Silverberg, Robert
Randall, Ruth (Elaine) Painter 1892-1971 3
Randell, Beverley
　See Price, Beverley Joan
Randle, Kristen (Downey) 1952- 92
　Autobiography Feature 119
　See also SAAS 24

Randolph, Boynton M.D.
　See Ellis, Edward S(ylvester)
Randolph, Geoffrey
　See Ellis, Edward S(ylvester)
Randolph, J. H.
　See Ellis, Edward S(ylvester)
Randolph, Lieutenant J. H.
　See Ellis, Edward S(ylvester)
Rands, William Brighty 1823-1882 17
Raney, Ken 1953- 74
Rankin, Joan 1940- 148
　Earlier sketch in SATA 88
Ranney, Agnes V. 1916-1985 6
Ransom, Candice F. 1952- 135
　Brief entry 49
　Earlier sketches in SATA 52, 89
Ransome, Arthur (Michell) 1884-1967 22
　See also CLR 8
Ransome, James E. 1961- 123
　Earlier sketch in SATA 76
　See also CLR 86
Rant, Tol E.
　See Longyear, Barry B(rookes)
Raphael, Elaine 23
　See Bolognese, Elaine (Raphael Chionchio)
Rapp, Adam 1968(?)- 148
Rappaport, Doreen 151
Rappaport, Eva 1924- 6
Rappoport, Ken 1935- 167
　Earlier sketch in SATA 89
Rarick, Carrie 1911-2002 41
Raschka, Chris 1959- 166
　Earlier sketches in SATA 80, 117
Raschka, Christopher
　See Raschka, Chris
Rascol, Sabina I. 159
Rash, Andy 162
Raskin, Edith Lefkowitz 1908-1987 9
Raskin, Ellen 1928-1984 139
　Earlier sketches in SATA 2, 38
　See also CLR 12
Raskin, Joseph 1897-1982 12
　Obituary 29
Rathjen, Carl Henry 1909-1984 11
Rathmann, Peggy 1953- 157
　Earlier sketch in SATA 94
　See Crosby, Margaret
Ratliff, Thomas M. 1948- 118
Rattigan, Jama Kim 1951- 99
Ratto, Linda Lee 1952- 79
Rattray, Simon
　See Trevor, Elleston
Ratz de Tagyos, Paul 1958- 76
Rau, Dana Meachen 1971- 167
　Earlier sketch in SATA 94
Rau, Margaret 1913- 168
　Earlier sketch in SATA 9
　See also CLR 8
Raucher, Herman 1928- 8
Raum, Elizabeth 1949- 155
RavenWolf, Silver 1956- 155
Ravielli, Anthony 1916-1997 3
　Obituary 95
Ravilious, Robin 1944- 77
Rawding, F(rederick) W(illiam) 1930- 55
Rawlings, Marjorie Kinnan 1896-1953 100
　See also YABC 1
　See also CLR 63
Rawls, (Woodrow) Wilson 1913-1984 22
　See also CLR 81
Rawlyk, George Alexander 1935- 64
Rawn, Melanie (Robin) 1954- 98
Ray, Carl 1943-1978 63
Ray, Deborah 8
　See Kogan Ray, Deborah
Ray, Delia 1963- 70
Ray, Irene
　See Sutton, Margaret Beebe
Ray, Jane 1960- 152
　Earlier sketch in SATA 72
Ray, JoAnne 1935- 9

Ray, Mary (Eva Pedder) 1932- 127
　Earlier sketch in SATA 2
Ray, Mary Lyn 1946- 154
　Earlier sketch in SATA 90
Rayban, Chloe 1944- 167
Rayevsky, Robert 1955- 81
Raymond, Robert
　See Alter, Robert Edmond
Rayner, Hugh 151
Rayner, Mary 1933- 87
　Earlier sketch in SATA 22
　See also CLR 41
Rayner, Shoo
　See Rayner, Hugh
Rayner, William 1929- 55
　Brief entry 36
Raynor, Dorka 28
Rayson, Steven 1932- 30
Razzell, Arthur (George) 1925- 11
Razzell, Mary (Catherine) 1930- 102
Razzi, James 1931- 10
Read, Elfreida 1920- 2
Read, Nicholas 1956- 146
Read, Piers Paul 1941- 21
Reade, Deborah 1949- 69
Reader, Dennis 1929- 71
Reading, Richard P(atrick) 1962- 161
Readman, Jo 1958- 89
Ready, Kirk L(ewis) 1943- 39
Reaney, James 1926- 43
Reaver, Chap 1935-1993 69
　Obituary 77
Reaver, Herbert R.
　See Reaver, Chap
Reaves, J. Michael
　See Reaves, (James) Michael
Reaves, (James) Michael 1950- 99
Redding, Robert Hull 1919- 2
Redekopp, Elsa 61
Redway, Ralph
　See Hamilton, Charles (Harold St. John)
Redway, Ridley
　See Hamilton, Charles (Harold St. John)
Reece, Colleen L. 1935- 116
Reece, Gabrielle 1970- 108
Reed, Betty Jane 1921- 4
Reed, E.
　See Evans, Mari
Reed, Gwendolyn E(lizabeth) 1932- 21
Reed, Kit 1932- 116
　Earlier sketch in SATA 34
Reed, Neil 1961- 99
Reed, Talbot Baines 1852-1893
　See CLR 76
Reed, Thomas (James) 1947- 34
Reed, William Maxwell 1871-1962 15
Reeder, Carolyn 1937- 97
　Earlier sketch in SATA 66
　See also CLR 69
Reeder, Colin (Dawson) 1938- 74
Reeder, Colonel Red
　See Reeder, Russell P(otter), Jr.
Reeder, Russell P(otter), Jr. 1902-1998 4
　Obituary 101
Reeder, Stephanie Owen 1951- 102
Reed-Jones, Carol 1955- 112
Reef, Catherine 1951- 128
　Earlier sketch in SATA 73
Reekie, Jocelyn (Margaret) 1947- 145
Reeman, Douglas Edward 1924- 63
　Brief entry 28
Rees, Celia 1949- 124
Rees, David (Bartlett) 1936-1993 69
　Obituary 76
　Earlier sketch in SATA 36
　See also SAAS 5
Rees, Douglas 1947- 169
Rees, Ennis (Samuel, Jr.) 1925- 3
Rees, (George) Leslie (Clarence) 1905-2000
　.. 105
　Obituary 135

Reese, Bob
  See Reese, Robert A.
Reese, Della 1931(?)- 114
Reese, Lyn 64
  See Reese, Carolyn Johnson
Reese, Robert A. 1938- 60
  Brief entry 53
Reese, (John) Terence 1913-1996 59
Reeve, Joel
  See Cox, William R(obert)
Reeve, Kirk 1934- 117
Reeves, Faye Couch 1953- 76
Reeves, James 15
  See Reeves, John Morris
Reeves, Jeni 1947- 111
Reeves, John Morris 1909-1978 87
  See Reeves, James
Reeves, Joyce 1911- 17
Reeves, Lawrence F. 1926- 29
Reeves, Ruth Ellen
  See Ranney, Agnes V.
Regan, Dian Curtis 1950- 149
  Autobiography Feature 149
  Earlier sketches in SATA 75, 133
Regehr, Lydia 1903-1991 37
Reger, James P. 1952- 106
Reggiani, Renee 1925- 18
Rehm, Karl M. 1935- 72
Reich, Ali
  See Katz, Bobbi
Reich, Susanna 1954- 113
Reiche, Dietlof 1941- 159
Reichert, Mickey Zucker
  See Reichert, Miriam Zucker
Reichert, Miriam Zucker 1962- 85
Reichhold, Jane(t E.) 1937- 147
Reid, Alastair 1926- 46
Reid, Barbara 1922- 21
Reid, Barbara (Jane) 1957- 93
  See also CLR 64
Reid, Desmond
  See Moorcock, Michael
  and McNeilly, Wilfred (Glassford)
Reid, Eugenie Chazal 1924- 12
Reid, John Calvin 21
Reid, (Thomas) Mayne 1818-1883 24
Reid, Meta Mayne 1905-1991 58
  Brief entry 36
Reid, Robin (Nicole) 1969- 145
Reid Banks, Lynne 1929- 165
  Earlier sketches in SATA 22, 75, 111
  See also CLR 24
  See Banks, Lynne Reid
Reider, Katja 1960- 126
Reid Jenkins, Debra 1955- 87
Reiff, Stephanie Ann 1948- 47
  Brief entry 28
Reig, June 1933- 30
Reigot, Betty Polisar 1924- 55
  Brief entry 41
Reim, Melanie (K.) 1956- 104
Reinach, Jacquelyn (Krasne) 1930-2000 28
Reiner, Carl 1922- 151
Reiner, William B(uck) 1910-1976 46
  Obituary 30
Reinfeld, Fred 1910-1964 3
Reinhart, Matthew 161
Reiniger, Lotte 1899-1981 40
  Obituary 33
Reinsma, Carol 1949- 91
Reinstedt, Randall A. 1935- 101
Reinstedt, Randy
  See Reinstedt, Randall A.
Reisberg, Mira 1955- 82
Reisberg, Veg
  See Reisberg, Mira
Reiser, Lynn (Whisnant) 1944- 138
  Earlier sketch in SATA 81
Reisgies, Teresa (Maria) 1966- 74
Reiss, Johanna (de Leeuw) 1929(?)- 18
  See also CLR 19

Reiss, John J. 23
Reiss, Kathryn 1957- 144
  Earlier sketch in SATA 76
Reit, Seymour Victory 1918-2001 21
  Obituary 133
Reit, Sy
  See Reit, Seymour Victory
Relf, Patricia 1954- 134
  Earlier sketch in SATA 71
Remi, Georges 1907-1983 13
  Obituary 32
  See Herge
Remington, Frederic S(ackrider) 1861-1909
  41
Remkiewicz, Frank 1939- 152
  Earlier sketch in SATA 77
Remy, Georges
  See Remi, Georges
Renaud, Bernadette 1945- 66
Renault, Mary
  See Challans, Mary
Rendell, Joan 28
Rendina, Laura (Jones) Cooper 1902- 10
Rendon, Marcie R. 1952- 97
Rendon, Maria 1965- 116
Renee, Janina 1956- 140
Renfro, Ed 1924- 79
Renick, Marion (Lewis) 1905-1983 1
Renken, Aleda 1907- 27
Renlie, Frank H. 1936- 11
Rennert, Richard Scott 1956- 67
Rennison, Louise 1951- 149
Reno, Dawn E(laine) 1953- 130
Rensie, Willis
  See Eisner, Will
Renton, Cam
  See Armstrong, Richard
Renvoize, Jean 5
Resciniti, Angelo G. 1952- 75
Resnick, Michael D(iamond) 1942- 159
  Earlier sketches in SATA 38, 106
Resnick, Mike
  See Resnick, Michael D(iamond)
Resnick, Seymour 1920- 23
Retla, Robert
  See Alter, Robert Edmond
Reuter, Bjarne (B.) 1950- 142
  Earlier sketch in SATA 68
Reuter, Carol (Joan) 1931- 2
Revena
  See Wright, Betty Ren
Revsbech, Vicki
  See Liestman, Vicki
Rey, H(ans) A(ugusto) 1898-1977 100
  Earlier sketches in SATA 1, 26, 69
  See also CLR 93
Rey, Margret (Elisabeth) 1906-1996 86
  Obituary 93
  Earlier sketch in SATA 26
  See also CLR 93
Reyher, Becky
  See Reyher, Rebecca Hourwich
Reyher, Rebecca Hourwich 1897-1987 18
  Obituary 50
Reynolds, C. Buck 1957- 107
Reynolds, John
  See Whitlock, Ralph
Reynolds, Madge
  See Whitlock, Ralph
Reynolds, Malvina 1900-1978 44
  Obituary 24
Reynolds, Marilyn (M.) 1935- 121
  See also SAAS 23
Reynolds, Marilynn 1940- 141
  Earlier sketch in SATA 80
Reynolds, Pamela 1923- 34
Reynolds, Peter H. 1961- 128
Rhine, Richard
  See Silverstein, Alvin
  and Silverstein, Virginia B(arbara Opshelor)
Rhoades, Diane 1952- 90

Rhodes, Bennie (Loran) 1927- 35
Rhodes, Donna McKee 1962- 87
Rhodes, Frank Harold Trevor 1926- 37
Rhue, Morton
  See Strasser, Todd
Rhyne, Nancy 1926- 66
Rhynes, Martha E. 1939- 141
Ribbons, Ian 1924- 37
  Brief entry 30
  See also SAAS 3
Ricciuti, Edward R(aphael) 1938- 10
Rice, Alice (Caldwell) Hegan 1870-1942 ... 63
Rice, Bebe Faas 1932- 89
Rice, Dale R(ichard) 1948- 42
Rice, Dick
  See Rice, R. Hugh
Rice, Earle (Wilmont), Jr. 1928- 151
  Earlier sketch in SATA 92
Rice, Edward 1918-2001 47
  Brief entry 42
Rice, Elizabeth 1913-1976 2
Rice, Eve (Hart) 1951- 91
  Earlier sketch in SATA 34
Rice, Inez 1907- 13
Rice, James 1934- 93
  Earlier sketch in SATA 22
Rice, John F. 1958- 82
Rice, R. Hugh 1929- 115
Rice, Richard H.
  See Rice, R. Hugh
Rich, Barbara
  See Graves, Robert (von Ranke)
Rich, Elaine Sommers 1926- 6
Rich, Josephine Bouchard 1912- 10
Rich, Louise Dickinson 1903-1991 54
  Obituary 67
Richard, Adrienne 1921- 5
  See also SAAS 9
Richard, James Robert
  See Bowen, Robert Sydney
Richards, Frank
  See Hamilton, Charles (Harold St. John)
Richards, Hilda
  See Hamilton, Charles (Harold St. John)
Richards, Jackie 1925- 102
Richards, Jean 1940- 135
Richards, Justin 169
Richards, Kay
  See Baker, Susan (Catherine)
Richards, Laura E(lizabeth Howe) 1850-1943
  See YABC 1
  See also CLR 54
Richards, Norman 1932- 48
Richards, R(onald) C(harles) W(illiam) 1923-
  59
  Brief entry 43
Richardson, Andrew (William) 1986- 120
Richardson, Carol 1932- 58
Richardson, Grace Lee
  See Dickson, Naida
Richardson, Jean (Mary) 59
Richardson, Judith Benet 1941- 77
Richardson, Robert S(hirley) 1902-1981 8
Richardson, Sandy 1949- 116
Richardson, Willis 1889-1977 60
Richelson, Geraldine 1922- 29
Richemont, Enid 1940- 82
Richler, Mordecai 1931-2001 98
  Brief entry 27
  Earlier sketch in SATA 44
  See also CLR 17
Richman, Sophia 1941- 142
Rich-McCoy, Lois
  See McCoy, Lois (Rich)
Richmond, Robin 1951- 75
Richoux, Pat(ricia) 1927- 7
Richter, Alice 1941- 30
Richter, Conrad (Michael) 1890-1968 3
Richter, Hans Peter 1925-1993 6
  See also CLR 21
  See also SAAS 11

Rickard, Graham 1949- *71*
Riddell, Chris 1962- *166*
  Earlier sketch in SATA *114*
Riddell, Christopher Barry
  See Riddell, Chris
Riddell, Edwina 1955- *82*
Ridden, Brian (John) 1934- *123*
Riddle, Tohby 1965- *151*
  Earlier sketch in SATA *74*
Riddles, Libby 1956- *140*
Ridge, Antonia (Florence) (?)-1981 .... *7*
  Obituary *27*
Ridge, Martin 1923-2003 .... *43*
Ridley, Philip *88*
Ridlon, Marci *22*
  See Balterman, Marcia Ridlon
Riedman, Sarah R(egal) 1902-1995 .... *1*
Riehecky, Janet 1953- *164*
Riesenberg, Felix, Jr. 1913-1962 .... *23*
Rieu, E(mile) V(ictor) 1887-1972 .... *46*
  Obituary *26*
Rigg, Sharon
  See Creech, Sharon
Riggio, Anita 1952- *148*
  Earlier sketch in SATA *73*
Riggs, Stephanie 1964- *138*
Rigney, James Oliver, Jr. 1948- *95*
  See Jordan, Robert
Rikhoff, Jean 1928- *9*
Rikki
  See Ducornet, Erica
Riley, James A. 1939- *97*
Riley, James Whitcomb 1849-1916 .... *17*
Riley, Jocelyn (Carol) 1949- *60*
  Brief entry *50*
Riley, Linda Capus 1950- *85*
Riley, Martin 1948- *81*
Rimes, (Margaret) LeAnn 1982- *154*
Rinaldi, Ann 1934- *161*
  Brief entry *50*
  Earlier sketches in SATA *51, 78, 117*
  See also CLR *46*
Rinard, Judith E(llen) 1947- *140*
  Earlier sketch in SATA *44*
Rinder, Lenore 1949- *92*
Ring, Elizabeth 1920- *79*
Ringdahl, Mark
  See Longyear, Barry B(rookes)
Ringgold, Faith 1930- *114*
  Earlier sketch in SATA *71*
  See also CLR *30*
Ringi, Kjell (Arne Soerensen) 1939- *12*
Rinkoff, Barbara Jean (Rich) 1923-1975 .... *4*
  Obituary *27*
Rinn, Miriam 1946- *127*
Riordan, James 1936- *95*
Rios, Tere
  See Versace, Marie Teresa Rios
Ripken, Cal(vin Edward), Jr. 1960- *114*
Ripley, Catherine 1957- *82*
Ripley, Elizabeth Blake 1906-1969 .... *5*
Ripper, Charles L(ewis) 1929- *3*
Ripper, Chuck
  See Ripper, Charles L(ewis)
Riq
  See Atwater, Richard (Tupper)
Rish, David 1955- *110*
Riskind, Mary 1944- *60*
Rissinger, Matt 1956- *93*
Rissman, Art
  See Sussman, Susan
Rissman, Susan
  See Sussman, Susan
Ritchie, Barbara Gibbons *14*
Ritter, Felix
  See Kruss, James
Ritter, John H. 1951- *137*
  Earlier sketch in SATA *129*
Ritter, Lawrence S(tanley) 1922-2004 .... *58*
  Obituary *152*
Ritthaler, Shelly 1955- *91*

Ritz, Karen 1957- *80*
Rivera, Geraldo (Miguel) 1943- *54*
  Brief entry *28*
Rivers, Elfrida
  See Bradley, Marion Zimmer
Rivers, Karen 1970- *131*
Riverside, John
  See Heinlein, Robert A(nson)
Rivkin, Ann 1920- *41*
Rivoli, Mario 1943- *10*
Roach, Marilynne K. 1946- *9*
Roach, Marilynne Kathleen
  See Roach, Marilynne K.
Roach, Portia
  See Takakjian, Portia
Robb, Laura 1937- *95*
Robbins, Frank 1917-1994(?) *42*
  Brief entry *32*
Robbins, Ken 1945- *147*
  Brief entry *53*
  Earlier sketch in SATA *94*
Robbins, Raleigh
  See Hamilton, Charles (Harold St. John)
Robbins, Ruth 1917(?)- *14*
Robbins, Tony
  See Pashko, Stanley
Robbins, Wayne
  See Cox, William R(obert)
Robel, S. L.
  See Fraustino, Lisa Rowe
Roberson, Jennifer 1953- *72*
Roberson, John R(oyster) 1930- *53*
Robert, Adrian
  See St. John, Nicole
Roberts, Bethany *133*
Roberts, Bruce (Stuart) 1930- *47*
  Brief entry *39*
Roberts, Charles G(eorge) D(ouglas)
  1860-1943 .... *88*
  Brief entry *29*
  See also CLR *33*
Roberts, David
  See Cox, John Roberts
Roberts, Elizabeth 1944- *80*
Roberts, Elizabeth Madox 1886-1941 .... *33*
  Brief entry *27*
  See also CLR *100*
Roberts, Jim
  See Bates, Barbara S(nedeker)
Roberts, John G(aither) 1913-1993 .... *27*
Roberts, Judy I. 1957- *93*
Roberts, Katherine 1962- *152*
Roberts, M. L.
  See Mattern, Joanne
Roberts, Nancy Correll 1924- *52*
  Brief entry *28*
Roberts, Terence
  See Sanderson, Ivan T(erence)
Roberts, Willo Davis 1928-2004 .... *150*
  Autobiography Feature *150*
  Obituary *160*
  Earlier sketches in SATA *21, 70, 133*
  See also CLR *95*
  See also SAAS *8*
Robertson, Barbara (Anne) 1931- *12*
Robertson, Don 1929-1999 .... *8*
  Obituary *113*
Robertson, Dorothy Lewis 1912- *12*
Robertson, Ellis
  See Ellison, Harlan (Jay)
  and Silverberg, Robert
Robertson, Janet (E.) 1935- *68*
Robertson, Jennifer Sinclair 1942-1998 .... *12*
Robertson, Jenny
  See Robertson, Jennifer Sinclair
Robertson, Keith (Carlton) 1914-1991 .... *85*
  Obituary *69*
  Earlier sketch in SATA *1*
  See also SAAS *15*
Robertson, Stephen
  See Walker, Robert W(ayne)

Robertus, Polly M. 1948- *73*
Robeson, Kenneth
  See Johnson, (Walter) Ryerson
Robeson, Kenneth
  See Dent, Lester
  and Goulart, Ron(ald Joseph)
Robinet, Harriette Gillem 1931- *104*
  Earlier sketch in SATA *27*
  See also CLR *64*
Robins, Deri 1958- *166*
  Earlier sketch in SATA *117*
Robins, Patricia
  See Clark, Patricia Denise
Robins, Rollo, Jr.
  See Ellis, Edward S(ylvester)
Robins, Seelin
  See Ellis, Edward S(ylvester)
Robinson, Adjai 1932- *8*
Robinson, Aminah Brenda Lynn 1940- *159*
  Earlier sketch in SATA *77*
Robinson, Barbara (Webb) 1927- *84*
  Earlier sketch in SATA *8*
Robinson, C(harles) A(lexander), Jr. 1900-1965
  .... *36*
Robinson, Charles 1870-1937 .... *17*
Robinson, Charles 1931- *6*
Robinson, Dorothy W. 1929- *54*
Robinson, Eve
  See Tanselle, Eve
Robinson, Glen(dal P.) 1953- *92*
Robinson, Jan M. 1933- *6*
Robinson, Jean O. 1934- *7*
Robinson, Joan (Mary) G(ale Thomas)
  1910-1988 .... *7*
Robinson, Kim Stanley 1952- *109*
Robinson, Lee 1948- *110*
Robinson, Lloyd
  See Silverberg, Robert
Robinson, Lynda S(uzanne) 1951- *107*
Robinson, Marileta 1942- *32*
Robinson, Maudie Millian Oller 1914- *11*
Robinson, Nancy K(onheim) 1942-1994 ..... *91*
  Brief entry *31*
  Obituary *79*
  Earlier sketch in SATA *32*
Robinson, Ray(mond Kenneth) 1920- *23*
Robinson, Shari
  See McGuire, Leslie (Sarah)
Robinson, Sharon 1950- *162*
Robinson, Spider 1948- *118*
Robinson, Sue
  See Robinson, Susan Maria
Robinson, Susan Maria 1955- *105*
Robinson, Suzanne
  See Robinson, Lynda S(uzanne)
Robinson, T(homas) H(eath) 1869-1950 ..... *17*
Robinson, (Wanda) Veronica 1926- *30*
Robinson, W(illiam) Heath 1872-1944 .... *17*
Robison, Bonnie 1924- *12*
Robison, Nancy L(ouise) 1934- *32*
Robles, Harold E. 1948- *87*
Robottom, John 1934- *7*
Robson, Eric 1939- *82*
Roche, A. K.
  See Abisch, Roslyn Kroop
  and Kaplan, Boche
Roche, Denis (Mary) 1967- *99*
Roche, P(atricia) K. 1935- *57*
  Brief entry *34*
Roche, Terry
  See Poole, Peggy
Rochman, Hazel 1938- *105*
Rock, Maxine 1940- *108*
Rocker, Fermin 1907- *40*
Rocklin, Joanne 1946- *134*
  Earlier sketch in SATA *86*
Rockwell, Anne F(oote) 1934- *162*
  Earlier sketches in SATA *33, 71, 114*
  See also SAAS *19*
Rockwell, Bart
  See Pellowski, Michael (Joseph)

Rockwell, Harlow 1910-1988 .... *33*
  Obituary *56*
Rockwell, Norman (Percevel) 1894-1978 ... *23*
Rockwell, Thomas 1933- *70*
  Earlier sketch in SATA *7*
  See also CLR *6*
Rockwood, Joyce 1947- *39*
Rockwood, Roy *67*
  Earlier sketch in SATA *1*
  See McFarlane, Leslie (Charles)
  and Stratemeyer, Edward L.
Rodanas, Kristina 1952- *155*
Rodari, Gianni 1920-1980
  See CLR *24*
Rodd, Kathleen Tennant *57*
  Obituary *55*
  See Rodd, Kylie Tennant
Rodda, Emily 1948- *146*
  Earlier sketch in SATA *97*
  See also CLR *32*
Roddenberry, Eugene Wesley 1921-1991 .... *45*
  Obituary *69*
  See Roddenberry, Gene
Roddenberry, Gene
  Obituary *69*
  See Roddenberry, Eugene Wesley
Roddie, Shen *153*
Roddy, Lee 1921- *57*
Rodenas, Paula *73*
Rodgers, Frank 1944- *69*
Rodgers, Mary 1931- *130*
  Earlier sketch in SATA *8*
  See also CLR *20*
Rodman, Emerson
  See Ellis, Edward S(ylvester)
Rodman, Eric
  See Silverberg, Robert
Rodman, Maia
  See Wojciechowska, Maia (Teresa)
Rodman, (Cary) Selden 1909-2002 .... *9*
Rodowsky, Colby 1932- *164*
  Earlier sketches in SATA *21, 77, 120*
  See also SAAS *22*
Rodowsky, Colby F.
  See Rodowsky, Colby
Rodriguez, Alejo 1941- *83*
Rodriguez, Luis J. 1954- *125*
Roeder, Virginia Marsh 1926- *98*
Roehrig, Catharine H. 1949- *67*
Roennfeldt, Robert 1953- *78*
Roessel-Waugh, C. C.
  See Waugh, Carol-Lynn Rossel
  and Waugh, Charles G(ordon)
Roets, Lois F. 1937- *91*
Roever, J(oan) M(arilyn) 1935- *26*
Rofes, Eric Edward 1954- *52*
Roffey, Maureen 1936- *33*
Rogak, Lisa Angowski 1962- *80*
Rogasky, Barbara 1933- *144*
  Earlier sketch in SATA *86*
Rogers, (Thomas) Alan (Stinchcombe) 1937-
  .... *81*
  Earlier sketch in SATA *2*
Rogers, Bettye 1858-1919 .... *103*
Rogers, Cindy 1950- *89*
Rogers, Emma 1951- *74*
Rogers, Frances 1888-1974 .... *10*
Rogers, Fred McFeely 1928-2003 .... *33*
  Obituary *138*
Rogers, Hal
  See Sirimarco, Elizabeth
Rogers, Jean 1919- *55*
  Brief entry *47*
Rogers, Matilda 1894-1976 .... *5*
  Obituary *34*
Rogers, Pamela 1927- *9*
Rogers, Paul 1950- *98*
  Earlier sketch in SATA *54*
Rogers, Robert
  See Hamilton, Charles (Harold St. John)
Rogers, W(illiam) G(arland) 1896-1978 ..... *23*

Rohan, M. S.
  See Rohan, Michael Scott
Rohan, Michael Scott 1951- *98*
Rohan, Mike Scott
  See Rohan, Michael Scott
Rohmann, Eric 1957-
  See CLR *100*
Rohmer, Harriet 1938- *56*
Rohrer, Doug 1962- *89*
Rojan
  See Rojankovsky, Feodor (Stepanovich)
Rojankovsky, Feodor (Stepanovich) 1891-1970
  .... *21*
Rojany, Lisa *94*
Rokeby-Thomas, Anna E(lma) 1911- *15*
Roland, Albert 1925-2002 .... *11*
Roland, Mary
  See Lewis, Mary (Christianna)
Roleff, Tamara L. 1959- *143*
Rolerson, Darrell A(llen) 1946- *8*
Roll, Winifred 1909-1998 .... *6*
Rollins, Charlemae Hill 1897-1979 .... *3*
  Obituary *26*
Rollock, Barbara T(herese) 1924- *64*
Romack, Janice Reed
  See LeNoir, Janice
Romain, Trevor *134*
Romanenko, Vitaliy 1962- *101*
Romano, Louis G. 1921- *35*
Romano, Melora A. 1966- *118*
Romijn, Johanna Maria Kooyker
  See Kooyker-Romijn, Johanna Maria
Romyn, Johanna Maria Kooyker
  See Kooyker-Romijn, Johanna Maria
Rongen, Bjoern 1906- *10*
Rongen, Bjorn
  See Rongen, Bjoern
Ronson, Mark
  See Alexander, Marc
Rood, Ronald (N.) 1920- *12*
Rooke, Daphne (Marie) 1914- *12*
Roop, Connie 1951- *167*
  Brief entry *49*
  Earlier sketches in SATA *54, 116*
Roop, Constance Betzer
  See Roop, Connie
Roop, Peter 1951- *167*
  Brief entry *49*
  Earlier sketches in SATA *54, 116*
Roop, Peter G.
  See Roop, Peter
Roos, Stephen 1945- *128*
  Brief entry *41*
  Earlier sketches in SATA *47, 77*
Roose-Evans, James 1927- *65*
Roosevelt, (Anna) Eleanor 1884-1962 .... *50*
Root, Betty *84*
Root, Phyllis 1949- *145*
  Brief entry *48*
  Earlier sketches in SATA *55, 94*
Roper, Laura (Newbold) Wood 1911-2003 . *34*
  Obituary *150*
Roper, Robert 1946- *142*
  Earlier sketch in SATA *78*
Roraback, Robin (Ellan) 1964- *111*
Rorby, Ginny 1944- *94*
Rorer, Abigail 1949- *85*
Rosamel, Godeleine de 1968- *151*
Roscoe, D(onald) T(homas) 1934- *42*
Rose, Anne *8*
Rose, Deborah Lee 1955- *124*
  Earlier sketch in SATA *71*
Rose, Elizabeth (Jane Pretty) 1933- *68*
  Brief entry *28*
Rose, Florella
  See Carlson, Vada F.
Rose, Gerald (Hembdon Seymour) 1935- ... *68*
  Brief entry *30*
Rose, Malcolm 1953- *168*
  Earlier sketch in SATA *107*

Rose, Nancy A.
  See Sweetland, Nancy A(nn)
Rose, Ted 1940- *93*
Rose, Wendy 1948- *12*
Rosen, Lillian (Diamond) 1928- *63*
Rosen, Marvin 1933- *161*
Rosen, Michael (Wayne) 1946- *137*
  Brief entry *40*
  Earlier sketches in SATA *48, 84*
  See also CLR *45*
Rosen, Michael J(oel) 1954- *86*
Rosen, Sidney 1916- *1*
Rosen, Winifred 1943- *8*
Rosenbaum, Maurice 1907- *6*
Rosenberg, Amye 1950- *74*
Rosenberg, Dorothy 1906- *40*
Rosenberg, Eth(el) Clifford 1915- *3*
  See Clifford, Eth
Rosenberg, Jane 1949- *58*
Rosenberg, Liz 1958- *129*
  Earlier sketch in SATA *75*
Rosenberg, Maxine B(erta) 1939- *93*
  Brief entry *47*
  Earlier sketch in SATA *55*
Rosenberg, Nancy (Sherman) 1931- *4*
Rosenberg, Sharon 1942- *8*
Rosenberry, Vera 1948- *144*
  Earlier sketch in SATA *83*
Rosenblatt, Arthur
  See Rosenblatt, Arthur S.
Rosenblatt, Arthur S. 1938- *68*
  Brief entry *45*
Rosenblatt, Lily 1956- *90*
Rosenbloom, Joseph 1928- *21*
Rosenblum, Richard 1928- *11*
Rosenburg, John M. 1918- *6*
Rosenfeld, Dina 1962- *99*
Rosenthal, Harold 1914-1999 .... *35*
Rosenthal, M(acha) L(ouis) 1917-1996 .... *59*
Rosenthal, Mark A(lan) 1946- *64*
Rosman, Steven M(ichael) 1956- *81*
Rosoff, Meg 1956- *160*
Ross, Alan
  See Warwick, Alan R(oss)
Ross, Christine 1950- *83*
Ross, Clare *111*
  Earlier sketch in SATA *48*
  See Romano, Clare
Ross, Dana Fuller
  See Cockrell, Amanda
  and Gerson, Noel Bertram
Ross, Dave *32*
  See Ross, David
Ross, David 1896-1975 .... *49*
  Obituary *20*
Ross, David 1949- *133*
  See Ross, Dave
Ross, Diana
  See Denney, Diana
Ross, Edward S(hearman) 1915- *85*
Ross, Eileen 1950- *115*
Ross, Frank (Xavier), Jr. 1914- *28*
Ross, Jane 1961- *79*
Ross, John 1921- *45*
Ross, Judy 1942- *54*
Ross, Katharine Reynolds
  See Ross, Kathy
Ross, Kathy 1948- *169*
  Earlier sketch in SATA *89*
Ross, Kent 1956- *91*
Ross, Lillian Hammer 1925- *72*
Ross, Michael Elsohn 1952- *127*
  Earlier sketch in SATA *80*
Ross, Pat(ricia Kienzle) 1943- *53*
  Brief entry *48*
Ross, Ramon R(oyal) 1930- *62*
Ross, Stewart 1947- *134*
  Earlier sketch in SATA *92*
  See also SAAS *23*
Ross, Tom 1958- *84*

Ross, Tony 1938- *130*
  Earlier sketches in SATA *17, 65*
Ross, Wilda 1915- *51*
  Brief entry *39*
Rossel, Seymour 1945- *28*
Rossel-Waugh, C. C.
  See Waugh, Carol-Lynn Rossel
Rossetti, Christina 1830-1894 .... *20*
Rossetti, Christina Georgina
  See Rossetti, Christina
Rossi, Joyce 1943- *116*
Rossotti, Hazel Swaine 1930- *95*
Rostkowski, Margaret I. 1945- *59*
Roth, Arnold 1929- *21*
Roth, Arthur J(oseph) 1925-1993 .... *43*
  Brief entry *28*
  Obituary *75*
  See also SAAS *11*
Roth, David 1940- *36*
Roth, Susan L. *134*
Rothberg, Abraham 1922- *59*
Roth-Hano, Renee 1931- *85*
Rothkopf, Carol Z. 1929- *4*
Rothman, Joel 1938- *7*
Rotner, Shelley 1951- *169*
  Earlier sketch in SATA *76*
Rottman, S(usan) L(ynn) 1970- *157*
  Earlier sketch in SATA *106*
Roueche, Berton 1911-1994 .... *28*
Roughsey, Dick 1921(?)-1985 .... *35*
  See also CLR *41*
Roughsey, Goobalathaldin
  See Roughsey, Dick
Rounds, Glen (Harold) 1906-2002 .... *112*
  Obituary *141*
  Earlier sketches in SATA *8, 70*
Rourke, Constance Mayfield 1885-1941
  See YABC *1*
Rowan, Deirdre
  See Williams, Jeanne
Rowe, Jennifer
  See Rodda, Emily
Rowe, John A. 1949- *146*
Rowh, Mark 1952- *90*
Rowland, Florence Wightman 1900-1997 ..... *8*
  Obituary *108*
Rowland-Entwistle, (Arthur) Theodore (Henry)
  1925- *94*
  Earlier sketch in SATA *31*
Rowling, J. K. 1966- *109*
  See also CLR *112*
Rowling, Joanne Kathleen
  See Rowling, J. K.
Rowsome, Frank (Howard), Jr. 1914-1983 . *36*
Roy, Gabrielle 1909-1983 .... *104*
Roy, Jacqueline 1954- *74*
Roy, Liam
  See Scarry, Patricia (Murphy)
Roy, Ron(ald) 1940- *110*
  Brief entry *35*
  Earlier sketch in SATA *40*
Roybal, Laura (Husby) 1956- *85*
Royds, Caroline 1953- *55*
Royston, Angela 1945- *169*
  Earlier sketch in SATA *120*
Rozakis, Laurie E. 1952- *84*
Rubel, Nicole 1953- *135*
  Earlier sketches in SATA *18, 95*
Rubin, Eva Johanna 1925- *38*
Rubin, Susan Goldman 1939- *132*
  Earlier sketch in SATA *84*
Rubinetti, Donald 1947- *92*
Rubinstein, Gillian (Margaret) 1942- *158*
  Autobiography Feature *116*
  Earlier sketches in SATA *68, 105*
  See also CLR *35*
  See also SAAS *25*
Rubinstein, Patricia (Giulia Caulfield Kate)
  -2003 .... *29*
  Obituary *149*
  See Forest, Antonia

Rubinstein, Robert E(dward) 1943- *49*
Rublowsky, John M(artin) 1928- *62*
Ruby, Laura *155*
Ruby, Lois (F.) 1942- *95*
  Autobiography Feature *105*
  Brief entry *34*
  Earlier sketch in SATA *35*
Ruchlis, Hy(man) 1913-1992 .... *3*
  Obituary *72*
Rucker, Mike 1940- *91*
Ruckman, Ivy 1931- *93*
  Earlier sketch in SATA *37*
Ruck-Pauquet, Gina 1931- *40*
  Brief entry *37*
Rudley, Stephen 1946- *30*
Rudolph, Marguerita 1908- *21*
Rudomin, Esther
  See Hautzig, Esther Rudomin
Rue, Leonard Lee III 1926- *142*
  Earlier sketch in SATA *37*
Ruedi, Norma Paul
  See Ainsworth, Norma
Ruelle, Karen Gray 1957- *126*
  Earlier sketch in SATA *84*
Ruemmler, John D(avid) 1948- *78*
Ruepp, Krista 1947- *143*
Ruffell, Ann 1941- *30*
Ruffins, Reynold 1930- *125*
  Earlier sketch in SATA *41*
Rugoff, Milton 1913- *30*
Ruhen, Olaf 1911-1989 .... *17*
Rumbaut, Hendle 1949- *84*
Rumford, James 1948- *116*
Rumsey, Marian (Barritt) 1928- *16*
Rumstuckle, Cornelius
  See Brennan, J(ames) H(erbert)
Runnerstroem, Bengt Arne 1944- *75*
Runyan, John
  See Palmer, Bernard (Alvin)
Runyon, Catherine 1947- *62*
Ruoff, A. LaVonne Brown 1930- *76*
Rusch, Kris
  See Rusch, Kristine Kathryn
Rusch, Kristine Kathryn 1960- *113*
Rush, Alison 1951- *41*
Rush, Peter 1937- *32*
Rushford, Patricia H(elen) 1943- *134*
Rushmore, Helen 1898-1994 .... *3*
Rushmore, Robert (William) 1926-1986 .... *8*
  Obituary *49*
Ruskin, Ariane
  See Batterberry, Ariane Ruskin
Ruskin, John 1819-1900 .... *24*
Russ, Lavinia (Faxon) 1904-1992 .... *74*
Russell, Charlotte
  See Rathjen, Carl Henry
Russell, Ching Yeung 1946- *107*
Russell, Franklin (Alexander) 1926- *11*
Russell, Gertrude Barrer
  See Barrer-Russell, Gertrude
Russell, Helen Ross 1915- *8*
Russell, James 1933- *53*
Russell, Jim
  See Russell, James
Russell, Joan Plummer 1930- *139*
Russell, P(hilip) Craig 1951- *162*
  Earlier sketch in SATA *80*
Russell, Patrick
  See Sammis, John
Russell, Paul (Gary) 1942- *57*
Russell, Sarah
  See Laski, Marghanita
Russell, Sharman Apt 1954- *123*
Russell, Solveig Paulson 1904-1985 .... *3*
Russo, Marisabina 1950- *151*
  Earlier sketch in SATA *106*
Russo, Monica J. 1950- *83*
Russo, Susan 1947- *30*
Rutgers van der Loeff, An
  See Rutgers van der Loeff-Basenau, An(na)
    Maria Margaretha

Rutgers van der Loeff-Basenau, An(na) Maria
  Margaretha 1910- *22*
Ruth, Rod 1912-1987 .... *9*
Rutherford, Douglas
  See McConnell, James Douglas Rutherford
Rutherford, Meg 1932- *34*
Ruthin, Margaret *4*
  See Catherall, Arthur
Rutledge, Jill Zimmerman 1951- *155*
Rutz, Viola Larkin 1932- *12*
Ruurs, Margriet 1952- *147*
  Earlier sketch in SATA *97*
Ruzzier, Sergio 1966- *159*
Ryan, Betsy
  See Ryan, Elizabeth (Anne)
Ryan, Cheli Duran *20*
Ryan, Elizabeth (Anne) 1943- *30*
Ryan, Jeanette Mines
  See Mines, Jeanette (Marie)
Ryan, John (Gerald Christopher) 1921- *22*
Ryan, Margaret 1950- *166*
  Earlier sketch in SATA *78*
Ryan, Mary E. 1953- *61*
Ryan, Mary Elizabeth
  See Ryan, Mary E.
Ryan, Pam(ela) Munoz *134*
Ryan, Patrick 1957- *138*
Ryan, Peter (Charles) 1939- *15*
Ryan-Lush, Geraldine 1949- *89*
Rybakov, Anatoli (Naumovich) 1911-1998 . *79*
  Obituary *108*
  See Rybakov, Anatolii (Naumovich)
Rybakov, Anatolii (Naumovich)
  See Rybakov, Anatoli (Naumovich)
Rybolt, Thomas R(oy) 1954- *62*
Rydberg, Ernest E(mil) 1901-1993 .... *21*
Rydberg, Lou(isa Hampton) 1908- *27*
Rydell, Katy 1942- *91*
Rydell, Wendell
  See Rydell, Wendy
Rydell, Wendy *4*
Ryden, Hope *91*
  Earlier sketch in SATA *8*
Ryder, Joanne (Rose) 1946- *163*
  Brief entry *34*
  Earlier sketches in SATA *65, 122*
  See also CLR *37*
Ryder, Pamela
  See Lamb, Nancy
Rye, Anthony
  See Youd, (Christopher) Samuel
Rylant, Cynthia 1954- *160*
  Brief entry *44*
  Earlier sketches in SATA *50, 76, 112*
  See also CLR *86*
  See also SAAS *13*
Rymer, Alta May 1925- *34*

S

S. L. C.
  See Clemens, Samuel Langhorne
S., Svend Otto
  See Soerensen, Svend Otto
Saaf, Donald W(illiam) 1961- *124*
Saal, Jocelyn
  See Sachs, Judith
Sabbeth, Carol (Landstrom) 1957- *125*
Saberhagen, Fred(erick Thomas) 1930- *89*
  Earlier sketch in SATA *37*
Sabin, Edwin L(egrand) 1870-1952
  See YABC *2*
Sabin, Francene *27*
Sabin, Lou
  See Sabin, Louis
Sabin, Louis 1930- *27*
Sabre, Dirk
  See Laffin, John (Alfred Charles)

Sabuda, Robert (James) 1965- *120*
  Earlier sketch in SATA *81*
Sachar, Louis 1954- *154*
  Brief entry *50*
  Earlier sketches in SATA *63, 104*
  See also CLR *79*
Sachs, Elizabeth-Ann 1946- *48*
Sachs, Judith 1947- *52*
  Brief entry *51*
Sachs, Marilyn 1927- *164*
  Autobiography Feature *110*
  Earlier sketches in SATA *3, 68*
  See also CLR *2*
  See also SAAS *2*
Sachs, Marilyn Stickle
  See Sachs, Marilyn
Sackett, S(amuel) J(ohn) 1928- *12*
Sackson, Sid 1920- *16*
Sacre, Antonio 1968- *152*
Saddler, Allen
  See Richards, R(onald) C(harles) W(illiam)
Saddler, K. Allen
  See Richards, R(onald) C(harles) W(illiam)
Sadie, Stanley (John) 1930-2005 .... *14*
Sadiq, Nazneen 1944- *101*
Sadler, Catherine Edwards 1952- *60*
  Brief entry *45*
Sadler, Marilyn (June) 1950- *79*
Sadler, Mark
  See Lynds, Dennis
Saffer, Barbara *144*
Sagan, Carl (Edward) 1934-1996 .... *58*
  Obituary *94*
Sage, Juniper
  See Brown, Margaret Wise
  and Hurd, Edith Thacher
Sagsoorian, Paul 1923- *12*
Saidman, Anne 1952- *75*
Saint, Dora Jessie 1913- *10*
St. Antoine, Sara L. 1966- *84*
Saint-Exupery, Antoine (Jean Baptiste Marie
  Roger) de 1900-1944 .... *20*
  See also CLR *10*
St. George, Judith 1931- *161*
  Earlier sketches in SATA *13, 99*
  See also CLR *57*
  See also SAAS *12*
St. James, Blakely
  See Gottfried, Theodore Mark
  and Platt, Charles
Saint James, Synthia 1949- *152*
  Earlier sketch in SATA *84*
St. John, Nicole *143*
  Autobiography Feature *143*
  Earlier sketch in SATA *89*
  See also CLR *46*
  See also SAAS *7*
  See Johnston, Norma
St. John, Philip
  See del Rey, Lester
St. John, Wylly Folk 1908-1985 .... *10*
  Obituary *45*
St. Max, E. S.
  See Ellis, Edward S(ylvester)
St. Meyer, Ned
  See Stratemeyer, Edward L.
St. Mox, E. A.
  See Ellis, Edward S(ylvester)
St. Myer, Ned
  See Stratemeyer, Edward L.
St. Tamara
  See Kolba, St. Tamara
Saito, Michiko
  See Fujiwara, Michiko
Sakers, Don 1958- *72*
Sakharnov, S.
  See Sakharnov, Svyatoslav
Sakharnov, Svyatoslav 1923- *65*
Saksena, Kate *148*
Sakurai, Gail 1952- *153*
  Earlier sketch in SATA *87*

Salassi, Otto R(ussell) 1939-1993 .... *38*
  Obituary *77*
Salat, Cristina *82*
Saldutti, Denise 1953- *39*
Sale, Tim 1956- *153*
Salem, Kay 1952- *92*
Salinger, J(erome) D(avid) 1919- *67*
  See also CLR *18*
Salisbury, Graham 1944- *161*
  Earlier sketches in SATA *76, 108*
Salisbury, Joyce E(llen) 1944- *138*
Salkey, (Felix) Andrew (Alexander) 1928-1995
  .... *118*
  Earlier sketch in SATA *35*
Salley, Coleen *166*
Sallis, Susan (Diana) 1929- *55*
Salmon, Annie Elizabeth 1899- *13*
Salsi, Lynn 1947- *130*
Salsitz, R. A. V.
  See Salsitz, Rhondi Vilott
Salsitz, Rhondi Vilott *115*
  See Salsitz, R. A. V.
Salten, Felix
  See Salzmann, Siegmund
Salter, Cedric
  See Knight, Francis Edgar
Saltman, Judith 1947- *64*
Saltzberg, Barney 1955- *135*
Saltzman, David (Charles Laertes) 1967-1990
  .... *86*
Salvadori, Mario (George) 1907-1997 .... *97*
  Earlier sketch in SATA *40*
Salwood, F. K.
  See Kilworth, Garry
Salzer, L. E.
  See Wilson, Lionel
Salzman, Marian 1959- *77*
Salzmann, Siegmund 1869-1945 .... *25*
  See Salten, Felix
Samachson, Dorothy (Mirkin) 1914-1997 ..... *3*
Samachson, Joseph 1906-1980 .... *3*
  Obituary *52*
Sammis, John 1942- *4*
Sampson, Emma (Keats) Speed 1868-1947
  .... *68*
Sampson, Fay (Elizabeth) 1935- *151*
  Brief entry *40*
  Earlier sketch in SATA *42*
Sampson, Michael 1952- *143*
  Earlier sketch in SATA *95*
Samson, Anne S(tringer) 1933- *2*
Samson, Joan 1937-1976 .... *13*
Samson, Suzanne M. 1959- *91*
Samuels, Charles 1902-1982 .... *12*
Samuels, Cynthia K(alish) 1946- *79*
Samuels, Gertrude 1910(?)-2003 .... *17*
  Obituary *147*
Sanborn, Duane 1914-1996 .... *38*
Sancha, Sheila 1924- *38*
Sanchez, Alex 1957- *151*
Sanchez, Sonia 1934- *136*
  Earlier sketch in SATA *22*
  See also CLR *18*
Sanchez-Silva, Jose Maria 1911- *132*
  Earlier sketch in SATA *16*
  See also CLR *12*
Sand, George X. *45*
Sandak, Cass R(obert) 1950-2001 .... *51*
  Brief entry *37*
Sandberg, (Karin) Inger 1930- *15*
Sandberg, Karl C. 1931- *35*
Sandberg, Lasse (E. M.) 1924- *15*
Sandburg, Carl (August) 1878-1967 .... *8*
  See also CLR *67*
Sandburg, Charles
  See Sandburg, Carl (August)
Sandburg, Charles A.
  See Sandburg, Carl (August)
Sandburg, Helga 1918- *3*
  See also SAAS *10*
Sander, Heather L. 1947- *157*

Sanderlin, George 1915- *4*
Sanderlin, Owenita (Harrah) 1916- *11*
Sanders, Nancy I. 1960- *141*
  Earlier sketch in SATA *90*
Sanders, Scott Russell 1945- *109*
  Earlier sketch in SATA *56*
Sanders, Winston P.
  See Anderson, Poul (William)
Sanderson, Irma 1912- *66*
Sanderson, Ivan T(erence) 1911-1973 .... *6*
Sanderson, Margaret Love
  See Keats, Emma
  and Sampson, Emma (Keats) Speed
Sanderson, Ruth (L.) 1951- *109*
  Earlier sketch in SATA *41*
Sandin, Joan 1942- *153*
  Earlier sketches in SATA *12, 94*
Sandison, Janet
  See Cameron, Elizabeth Jane
Sandler, Martin W. *160*
Sandoz, Mari(e Susette) 1900-1966 .... *5*
Sanford, Agnes (White) 1897-1976 .... *61*
Sanford, Doris 1937- *69*
Sanger, Marjory Bartlett 1920- *8*
San Jose, Christine 1929- *167*
Sankey, Alice (Ann-Susan) 1910- *27*
San Souci, Daniel *96*
San Souci, Robert D. 1946- *158*
  Earlier sketches in SATA *40, 81, 117*
  See also CLR *43*
Santiago, Esmeralda 1948- *129*
Santos, Helen
  See Griffiths, Helen
Santrey, Louis
  See Sabin, Louis
Santucci, Barbara 1948- *130*
Sapieyevski, Anne Lindbergh 1940-1993 ... *78*
  Earlier sketch in SATA *35*
  See Feydy, Anne Lindbergh
  and Lindbergh, Anne
Saport, Linda 1954- *123*
Sapp, Allen 1929- *151*
Sarac, Roger
  See Caras, Roger A(ndrew)
Sarah, Duchess of York
  See Ferguson, Sarah (Margaret)
Sarasin, Jennifer
  See Sachs, Judith
Sarg, Anthony Frederick
  See Sarg, Tony
Sarg, Tony 1882-1942
  See YABC *1*
Sargent, Pamela 1948- *78*
  Earlier sketch in SATA *29*
Sargent, Robert 1933- *2*
Sargent, Sarah 1937- *44*
  Brief entry *41*
Sargent, Shirley 1927-2004 .... *11*
Sarnoff, Jane 1937- *10*
Saroyan, William 1908-1981 .... *23*
  Obituary *24*
Sarton, (Eleanor) May 1912-1995 .... *36*
  Obituary *86*
Saseen, Sharon (Dillon) 1949- *59*
Sasek, Miroslav 1916-1980 .... *16*
  Obituary *23*
  See also CLR *4*
Sasso, Sandy Eisenberg 1947- *162*
  Earlier sketches in SATA *86, 116*
Sathre, Vivian 1952- *133*
  Earlier sketch in SATA *79*
Satterfield, Charles
  See del Rey, Lester
  and Pohl, Frederik
Sattgast, L. J.
  See Sattgast, Linda J.
Sattgast, Linda J. 1953- *91*
Sattler, Helen Roney 1921-1992 .... *74*
  Earlier sketch in SATA *4*
  See also CLR *24*

Sauer, Julia Lina 1891-1983 .... *32*
  Obituary *36*
Sauerwein, Leigh 1944- *155*
Saul, Carol P. 1947- *117*
  Earlier sketch in SATA *78*
Saul, John (W. III) 1942- *98*
Saul, (Ellen) Wendy 1946- *42*
Saulnier, Karen Luczak 1940- *80*
Saunders, Caleb
  See Heinlein, Robert A(nson)
Saunders, Dave 1939- *85*
Saunders, Julie 1939- *85*
Saunders, (William) Keith 1910-1994 .... *12*
Saunders, Rubie (Agnes) 1929- *21*
Saunders, Susan 1945- *96*
  Brief entry *41*
  Earlier sketch in SATA *46*
Saunders-Smith, Gail 1952- *169*
Sauvain, Philip Arthur 1933- *111*
Savadier, Elivia 1950- *164*
  Earlier sketch in SATA *79*
Savage, Alan
  See Nicole, Christopher (Robin)
Savage, Blake
  See Goodwin, Harold L(eland)
Savage, Candace (M.) 1949- *142*
Savage, Deborah 1955- *76*
Savage, Jeff 1961- *97*
Savageau, Cheryl 1950- *96*
Savery, Constance (Winifred) 1897-1999 ..... *1*
Saville, Andrew
  See Taylor, Andrew
Saville, (Leonard) Malcolm 1901-1982 ...... *23*
  Obituary *31*
Saviozzi, Adriana
  See Mazza, Adriana
Savitt, Sam 1917(?)-2000 .... *8*
  Obituary *126*
Savitz, Harriet May 1933- *72*
  Earlier sketch in SATA *5*
  See also SAAS *26*
Sawicki, Mary 1950- *90*
Sawyer, (Frederick) Don(ald) 1947- *72*
Sawyer, Kem Knapp 1953- *84*
Sawyer, Robert J(ames) 1960- *149*
  Earlier sketch in SATA *81*
Sawyer, Ruth 1880-1970 .... *17*
  See also CLR *36*
Saxby, H. M.
  See Saxby, (Henry) Maurice
Saxby, (Henry) Maurice 1924- *71*
Saxon, Andrew
  See Arthur, Robert, (Jr.)
Saxon, Antonia
  See Sachs, Judith
Say, Allen 1937- *161*
  Earlier sketches in SATA *28, 69, 110*
  See also CLR *22*
Sayers, Frances Clarke 1897-1989 .... *3*
  Obituary *62*
Sayles, Elizabeth 1956- *163*
  Earlier sketch in SATA *108*
Saylor-Marchant, Linda 1963- *82*
Sayre, April Pulley 1966- *131*
  Earlier sketch in SATA *88*
Sazer, Nina 1949- *13*
Scabrini, Janet 1953- *13*
Scagell, Robin 1946- *107*
Scagnetti, Jack 1924- *7*
Scamell, Ragnhild 1940- *77*
Scanlon, Marion Stephany *11*
Scannell, Vernon 1922- *59*
Scarborough, Elizabeth (Ann) 1947- *98*
Scarf, Maggi
  See Scarf, Maggie
Scarf, Maggie 1932- *5*
Scariano, Margaret M. 1924- *86*
Scarlett, Susan
  See Streatfeild, (Mary) Noel
Scarry, Huck
  See Scarry, Richard McClure, Jr.

Scarry, Patricia (Murphy) 1924- *2*
Scarry, Patsy
  See Scarry, Patricia (Murphy)
Scarry, Richard (McClure) 1919-1994 .... *75*
  Obituary *90*
  Earlier sketches in SATA *2, 35*
  See also CLR *41*
Scarry, Richard McClure, Jr. 1953- *35*
Schachner, Judith Byron 1951- *88*
Schachtel, Roger (Bernard) 1949- *38*
Schaedler, Sally *116*
Schaefer, Jack (Warner) 1907-1991 .... *66*
  Obituary *65*
  Earlier sketch in SATA *3*
Schaefer, Lola M. 1950- *144*
  Earlier sketch in SATA *91*
Schaeffer, Mead 1898- *21*
Schaeffer, Susan Fromberg 1941- *22*
Schaer, Brigitte 1958- *112*
Schaller, George B(eals) 1933- *30*
Schanzer, Rosalyn (Good) 1942- *138*
  Earlier sketch in SATA *77*
Schatell, Brian *66*
  Brief entry *47*
Schechter, Betty (Goodstein) 1921- *5*
Schecter, Ellen 1944- *85*
Scheeder, Louis 1946- *141*
Scheer, Julian (Weisel) 1926-2001 .... *8*
Scheffler, Victor B(lanchard) 1906- *6*
Scheffler, Ursel 1938- *81*
Scheffrin-Falk, Gladys 1928- *76*
Scheidl, Gerda Marie 1913- *85*
Scheier, Michael 1943- *40*
  Brief entry *36*
Schell, Mildred 1922- *41*
Schell, Orville (Hickok) 1940- *10*
Scheller, Melanie 1953- *77*
Schellie, Don 1932- *29*
Schembri, Jim 1962- *124*
Schemm, Mildred Walker 1905-1998 .... *21*
  Obituary *103*
  See Walker, Mildred
Schenker, Dona 1947- *133*
  Earlier sketch in SATA *68*
Scher, Paula 1948- *47*
Scherf, Margaret 1908-1979 .... *10*
Schermer, Judith (Denise) 1941- *30*
Schertle, Alice 1941- *145*
  Earlier sketches in SATA *36, 90*
Schick, Alice 1946- *27*
Schick, Eleanor 1942- *144*
  Earlier sketches in SATA *9, 82*
Schick, Joel 1945- *31*
  Brief entry *30*
Schields, Gretchen 1948- *75*
Schiff, Ken(neth Roy) 1942- *7*
Schiller, Andrew 1919- *21*
Schiller, Barbara (Heyman) 1928- *21*
Schiller, Pamela (Byrne) *127*
Schindel, John 1955- *115*
  Earlier sketch in SATA *77*
Schindelman, Joseph 1923- *67*
  Brief entry *32*
Schindler, S(teven) D. 1952- *118*
  Brief entry *50*
  Earlier sketch in SATA *75*
Schinto, Jeanne 1951- *93*
Schisgall, Oscar 1901-1984 .... *12*
  Obituary *38*
Schlaepfer, Gloria G. 1931- *154*
Schlee, Ann 1934- *44*
  Brief entry *36*
Schleichert, Elizabeth 1945- *77*
Schlein, Miriam 1926-2004 .... *130*
  Obituary *159*
  Earlier sketches in SATA *2, 87*
  See also CLR *41*
Schlesinger, Arthur M(eier), Jr. 1917- *61*
Schlessinger, Laura (Catherine) 1947- *160*
  Earlier sketch in SATA *110*
Schloat, G. Warren, Jr. 1914-2000 .... *4*

Schmid, Eleonore 1939- *126*
  Earlier sketches in SATA *12, 84*
Schmiderer, Dorothy 1940- *19*
Schmidt, Annie M. G. 1911-1995 .... *67*
  Obituary *91*
  See also CLR *22*
Schmidt, Diane 1953- *70*
Schmidt, Elizabeth 1915- *15*
Schmidt, Gary D. 1957- *135*
  Earlier sketch in SATA *93*
Schmidt, James Norman 1912-1983 .... *21*
Schmidt, Karen Lee 1953- *94*
Schmidt, Lynette 1952- *76*
Schneider, Antonie 1954- *167*
  Earlier sketch in SATA *89*
Schneider, Christine M. 1972(?)- *120*
Schneider, Elisa
  See Kleven, Elisa
Schneider, Herman 1905-2003 .... *7*
  Obituary *148*
Schneider, Laurie
  See Adams, Laurie
Schneider, Nina 1913- *2*
Schneider, Rex 1937- *44*
Schnirel, James R. 1931- *14*
Schnitter, Jane T. 1958- *88*
Schnitzlein, Danny *134*
Schnur, Steven 1952- *144*
  Earlier sketch in SATA *95*
Schoberle, Cecile 1949- *80*
Schock, Pauline 1928- *45*
Schoell, William 1951- *160*
Schoen, Barbara (Taylor) 1924-1993 .... *13*
Schoenherr, John (Carl) 1935- *66*
  Earlier sketch in SATA *37*
  See also SAAS *13*
Schofield, Sandy
  See Rusch, Kristine Kathryn
Scholastica, Sister Mary
  See Jenkins, Marie M(agdalen)
Scholefield, A. T.
  See Scholefield, Alan
Scholefield, Alan 1931- *66*
Scholefield, Edmund O.
  See Butterworth, W.E.
Scholey, Arthur 1932- *28*
Schone, Virginia *22*
Schongut, Emanuel 1936- *52*
  Brief entry *36*
Schoonover, Frank (Earle) 1877-1972 .... *24*
Schoor, Gene 1921- *3*
Schories, Pat 1952- *164*
  Earlier sketch in SATA *116*
Schotter, Roni *149*
  Earlier sketch in SATA *105*
Schraff, Anne E(laine) 1939- *92*
  Earlier sketch in SATA *27*
Schram, Peninnah 1934- *119*
Schrecengost, Maity
  See Schrecengost, S. Maitland
Schrecengost, S. Maitland 1938- *118*
Schrecker, Judie 1954- *90*
Schreiber, Elizabeth Anne (Ferguson) 1947-
  .... *13*
Schreiber, Ralph W(alter) 1942- *13*
Schreiner, Samuel A(gnew), Jr. 1921- *70*
Schroeder, Alan 1961- *98*
  Earlier sketch in SATA *66*
Schroeder, Binette
  See Nickl, Barbara (Elisabeth)
Schroeder, Russell (K.) 1943- *146*
Schubert, Dieter 1947- *101*
  Earlier sketch in SATA *62*
Schubert-Gabrys, Ingrid 1953- *101*
  Earlier sketch in SATA *62*
Schuerger, Michele R. *110*
Schuett, Stacey 1960- *168*
  Earlier sketch in SATA *75*
Schulke, Flip Phelps Graeme 1930- *57*
Schulman, Arlene 1961- *105*

Schulman, Janet 1933- 137
  Earlier sketch in SATA 22
Schulman, L(ester) M(artin) 1934- 13
Schulte, Elaine L(ouise) 1934- 36
Schultz, Betty K(epka) 1932- 125
Schultz, Gwendolyn 21
Schultz, James Willard 1859-1947
  See YABC 1
Schultz, Pearle Henriksen 1918- 21
Schulz, Charles M. 1922-2000 10
  Obituary 118
Schulz, Charles Monroe
  See Schulz, Charles M.
Schumaker, Ward 1943- 96
Schuman, Michael A. 1953- 134
  Earlier sketch in SATA 85
Schur, Maxine
  See Schur, Maxine Rose
Schur, Maxine Rose 1948- 135
  Autobiography Feature 135
  Brief entry 49
  Earlier sketches in SATA 53, 98
Schurfranz, Vivian 1925- 13
Schutzer, A. I. 1922- 13
Schuyler, Pamela R. 1948- 30
Schwager, Tina 1964- 110
Schwandt, Stephen (William) 1947- 61
Schwark, Mary Beth 1954- 51
Schwartz, Alvin 1927-1992 56
  Obituary 71
  Earlier sketch in SATA 4
  See also CLR 89
Schwartz, Amy 1954- 131
  Brief entry 41
  Earlier sketches in SATA 47, 83
  See also CLR 25
  See also SAAS 18
Schwartz, Anne Powers 1913-1987 10
Schwartz, Carol 1954- 77
Schwartz, Charles W(alsh) 1914- 8
Schwartz, David M(artin) 1951- 110
  Earlier sketch in SATA 59
Schwartz, Elizabeth Reeder 1912- 8
Schwartz, Ellen 1949- 117
Schwartz, Jerome L.
  See Lawrence, Jerome
Schwartz, Joel L. 1940- 54
  Brief entry 51
Schwartz, Joyce R. 1950- 93
Schwartz, Julius 1907-2004 45
Schwartz, Perry 1942- 75
Schwartz, Sheila (Ruth) 1929- 27
Schwartz, Stephen (Lawrence) 1948- 19
Schwartz, Virginia Frances 1950- 131
Schwarz, (Silvia Tessa) Viviane 1977- 141
Schweitzer, Byrd Baylor
  See Baylor, Byrd
Schweitzer, Iris 59
  Brief entry 36
Schweninger, Ann 1951- 168
  Earlier sketches in SATA 29, 98
Schwerin, Doris H(alpern) 1922- 64
Scieszka, Jon 1954- 160
  Earlier sketches in SATA 68, 105
  See also CLR 107
Scillian, Devin 128
Scioscia, Mary (Hershey) 1926- 63
Scofield, Penrod 1933- 62
  Obituary 78
Scoggin, Margaret C(lara) 1905-1968 47
  Brief entry 28
Scoltock, Jack 1942- 141
  Earlier sketch in SATA 72
Scoppettone, Sandra 1936- 92
  Earlier sketch in SATA 9
  See Early, Jack
Scot, Michael
  See Rohan, Michael Scott
Scotland, Jay
  See Jakes, John (William)

Scott, Alastair
  See Allen, Kenneth S.
Scott, Ann Herbert 1926- 140
  Autobiography Feature 140
  Brief entry 29
  Earlier sketches in SATA 56, 94
Scott, Bill
  See Scott, William N(eville)
Scott, Cora Annett (Pipitone) 1931- 11
Scott, Dan
  See Barker, S(quire) Omar
Scott, Elaine 1940- 164
  Earlier sketches in SATA 36, 90
Scott, Jack Denton 1915-1995 83
  Earlier sketch in SATA 31
  See also CLR 20
  See also SAAS 14
Scott, Jane (Harrington) 1931- 55
Scott, John 1912-1976 14
Scott, John Anthony 1916- 23
Scott, John M(artin) 1913- 12
Scott, Mary
  See Mattern, Joanne
Scott, Melissa 1960- 109
Scott, Richard
  See Rennert, Richard Scott
Scott, Roney
  See Gault, William Campbell
Scott, Sally 1909-1978 43
Scott, Sally (Elisabeth) 1948- 44
Scott, W. N.
  See Scott, William N(eville)
Scott, Sir Walter 1771-1832
  See YABC 2
Scott, Warwick
  See Trevor, Elleston
Scott, William N(eville) 1923- 87
Scotti, Anna
  See Coates, Anna
Scribner, Charles, Jr. 1921-1995 13
  Obituary 87
Scribner, Joanne L. 1949- 33
Scribner, Kimball 1917- 63
Scrimger, Richard 1957- 164
  Earlier sketch in SATA 119
Scroder, Walter K. 1928- 82
Scruggs, Sandy 1961- 89
Scudder, Brooke 1959- 154
Scull, Marie-Louise 1943-1993 77
Scuro, Vincent 1951- 21
Seabrooke, Brenda 1941- 148
  Earlier sketches in SATA 30, 88
Seaman, Augusta Huiell 1879-1950 31
Seamands, Ruth 1916- 9
Searcy, Margaret Zehmer 1926- 54
  Brief entry 39
Searight, Mary W(illiams) 1918- 17
Searle, Kathryn Adrienne 1942- 10
Searle, Ronald (William Fordham) 1920- ... 70
  Earlier sketch in SATA 42
Sears, Stephen W. 1932- 4
Sebastian, Lee
  See Silverberg, Robert
Sebestyen, Igen
  See Sebestyen, Ouida
Sebestyen, Ouida 1924- 140
  Earlier sketch in SATA 39
  See also CLR 17
  See also SAAS 10
Sebrey, Mary Ann 1951- 62
Sechrist, Elizabeth Hough 1903-1991 2
Sedges, John
  See Buck, Pearl S(ydenstricker)
Sedgwick, Marcus 1968- 160
Seed, Cecile Eugenie 1930- 86
  See Seed, Jenny
Seed, Jenny 8
  See also CLR 76
  See Seed, Cecile Eugenie
Seeger, Pete(r R.) 1919- 139
  Earlier sketch in SATA 13

Seeley, Laura L. 1958- 71
Seever, R.
  See Reeves, Lawrence F.
Sefozo, Mary 1925- 82
Sefton, Catherine
  See Waddell, Martin
Segal, Joyce 1940- 35
Segal, Lore 1928- 163
  Earlier sketches in SATA 4, 66
  See also SAAS 11
Segal, Lore Groszmann
  See Segal, Lore
Segar, E(lzie) C(risler) 1894-1938 61
Seguin, Marilyn W(eymouth) 1951- 91
Seguin-Fontes, Marthe 1924- 109
Seibold, J. Otto 1960- 149
  Earlier sketch in SATA 83
  See also SAAS 22
Seidel, Ross 95
Seidelman, James Edward 1926- 6
Seiden, Art(hur) 107
  Brief entry 42
Seidler, Ann (G.) 1925- 131
Seidler, Tor 1952- 149
  Brief entry 46
  Earlier sketches in SATA 52, 98
Seidman, Laurence Ivan 1925- 15
Seigel, Kalman 1917-1998 12
  Obituary 103
Seignobosc, Francoise 1897-1961 21
Seinfeld, Jerry 1954- 146
Seitz, Jacqueline 1931- 50
Seixas, Judith S. 1922- 17
Sejima, Yoshimasa 1913- 8
Selberg, Ingrid (Maria) 1950- 68
Selden, George
  See CLR 8
  See Thompson, George Selden
Selden, Neil R(oy) 1931- 61
Self, Margaret Cabell 1902-1996 24
Selig, Sylvie 1942- 13
Sellers, Naomi
  See Flack, Naomi John White
Selman, LaRue W. 1927- 55
Selsam, Millicent E(llis) 1912-1996 29
  Obituary 92
  Earlier sketch in SATA 1
  See also CLR 1
Seltzer, Meyer 1932- 17
Seltzer, Richard (Warren, Jr.) 1946- 41
Selway, Martina 1940- 169
  Earlier sketch in SATA 74
Selznick, Brian 1966- 117
  Earlier sketch in SATA 79
Semel, Nava 1954- 107
Semloh
  See Holmes, Peggy
Sendak, Jack 1924(?)-1995 28
Sendak, Maurice 1928- 165
  Earlier sketches in SATA 1, 27, 113
  See also CLR 74
Sendak, Maurice Bernard
  See Sendak, Maurice
Sender, Ruth M(insky) 1926- 62
Sengler, Johanna 1924- 18
Senisi, Ellen B(abinec) 1951- 116
Senn, J(oyce) A(nn) 1941- 115
Senn, Steve 1950- 60
  Brief entry 48
Serage, Nancy 1924- 10
Seredy, Kate 1899-1975 1
  Obituary 24
  See also CLR 10
Seroff, Victor I(ilyitch) 1902-1979 12
  Obituary 26
Serraillier, Ian (Lucien) 1912-1994 73
  Obituary 83
  Earlier sketch in SATA 1
  See also CLR 2
  See also SAAS 3
Servello, Joe 1932- 10

Service, Pamela F. 1945- *64*
Service, Robert
    See Service, Robert W(illiam)
Service, Robert W(illiam) 1874(?)-1958 ..... *20*
    See Service, Robert
Serwadda, W(illiam) Moses 1931- *27*
Serwer-Bernstein, Blanche L(uria) 1910-1997
    .... *10*
Sescoe, Vincent E. 1938- *123*
Seth, Mary
    See Lexau, Joan M.
Seton, Anya 1904(?)-1990 .... *3*
    Obituary *66*
Seton, Ernest (Evan) Thompson 1860-1946
    .... *18*
    See also CLR *59*
Seton-Thompson, Ernest
    See Seton, Ernest (Evan) Thompson
Seuling, Barbara 1937- *145*
    Earlier sketches in SATA *10, 98*
    See also SAAS *24*
Seuss, Dr.
    See Dr. Seuss
    and Geisel, Theodor Seuss
    and LeSieg, Theo.
    and Stone, Rosetta
Severn, Bill
    See Severn, William Irving
Severn, David
    See Unwin, David S(torr)
Severn, William Irving 1914- *1*
Sewall, Marcia 1935- *119*
    Earlier sketches in SATA *37, 69*
Seward, Prudence 1926- *16*
Sewell, Anna 1820-1878 .... *100*
    Earlier sketch in SATA *24*
    See also CLR *17*
Sewell, Helen (Moore) 1896-1957 .... *38*
Sexton, Anne (Harvey) 1928-1974 .... *10*
Seymour, Alta Halverson *10*
Seymour, Jane 1951- *139*
Seymour, Tres 1966- *164*
    Earlier sketch in SATA *82*
Shachtman, Tom 1942- *49*
Shackleton, C. C.
    See Aldiss, Brian W(ilson)
Shader, Rachel
    See Sofer, Barbara
Shadow, Jak
    See Sutherland, Jon
Shadyland, Sal
    See Cooper, Louise
Shafer, Robert E(ugene) 1925- *9*
Shaffer, Terea 1968- *79*
Shahan, Sherry 1949- *134*
    Earlier sketch in SATA *92*
Shahn, Bernarda Bryson
    See Bryson, Bernarda
Shaik, Fatima *114*
Shalant, Phyllis 1949- *150*
Shan, Darren 1972- *168*
    Earlier sketch in SATA *129*
Shanberg, Karen
    See Shragg, Karen (I.)
Shane, Harold Gray 1914-1993 .... *36*
    Obituary *76*
Shange, Ntozake 1948- *157*
Shanks, Ann Zane (Kushner) *10*
Shannon, David 1959- *152*
    Earlier sketch in SATA *107*
    See also CLR *87*
Shannon, George (William Bones) 1952- . *143*
    Earlier sketches in SATA *35, 94*
Shannon, Jacqueline *63*
Shannon, Margaret
    See Silverwood, Margaret Shannon
Shannon, Monica 1905(?)-1965 .... *28*
Shannon, Terry *21*
    See Mercer, Jessie
Shannon, Terry Miller 1951- *148*
Shapiro, Irwin 1911-1981 .... *32*

Shapiro, Milton J. 1926- *32*
Shapiro, Tricia
    See Andryszewski, Tricia
Shapp, Martha Glauber 1910- *3*
Sharfman, Amalie *14*
Sharma, Partap 1939- *15*
Sharma, Rashmi
    See Singh, Rashmi Sharma
Sharman, Alison
    See Leonard, Alison
Sharmat, Marjorie Weinman 1928- *133*
    Earlier sketches in SATA *4, 33, 74*
Sharmat, Mitchell 1927- *127*
    Earlier sketch in SATA *33*
Sharp, Anne Wallace 1947- *144*
Sharp, Luke
    See Alkiviades, Alkis
Sharp, Margery 1905-1991 .... *29*
    Obituary *67*
    Earlier sketch in SATA *1*
    See also CLR *27*
Sharpe, Jon
    See Duncan, Alice
    and Knott, William C(ecil, Jr.)
    and Messman, Jon
Sharpe, Mitchell R(aymond) 1924- *12*
Sharpe, Susan 1946- *71*
Sharratt, Nick 1962- *153*
    Earlier sketch in SATA *104*
Shasha, Mark 1961- *80*
Shattuck, Roger 1923-2005 .... *64*
Shattuck, Roger Whitney
    See Shattuck, Roger
Shaw, Arnold 1909-1989 .... *4*
    Obituary *63*
Shaw, Carolyn V. 1934- *91*
Shaw, Charles (Green) 1892-1974 .... *13*
Shaw, Evelyn S. 1927- *28*
Shaw, Flora Louisa
    See Lugard, Flora Louisa Shaw
Shaw, Janet 1937- *146*
    Earlier sketch in SATA *61*
    See also CLR *96*
Shaw, Janet Beeler
    See Shaw, Janet
Shaw, Margret 1940- *68*
Shaw, Nancy 1946- *162*
    Earlier sketch in SATA *71*
Shaw, Ray *7*
Shaw, Richard 1923- *12*
Shawn, Frank S.
    See Goulart, Ron(ald Joseph)
Shay, Art
    See Shay, Arthur
Shay, Arthur 1922- *4*
Shay, Lacey
    See Shebar, Sharon Sigmond
Shea, George 1940- *54*
    Brief entry *42*
Shea, Pegi Deitz 1960- *137*
    Earlier sketch in SATA *77*
Shearer, John 1947- *43*
    Brief entry *27*
    See also CLR *34*
Shearer, Ted 1919- *43*
Shebar, Sharon Sigmond 1945- *36*
Shecter, Ben 1935- *16*
Shedd, Warner 1934- *147*
    Earlier sketch in SATA *87*
Sheedy, Alexandra Elizabeth 1962- *39*
    Earlier sketch in SATA *19*
Sheehan, Ethna 1908-2000 .... *9*
Sheehan, Patty 1945- *77*
Sheehan, Sean 1951- *154*
    Earlier sketch in SATA *86*
Sheen, Barbara 1949- *143*
Shefelman, Janice Jordan 1930- *129*
    Earlier sketch in SATA *58*
Shefelman, Tom (Whitehead) 1927- *58*
Sheffer, H. R.
    See Abels, Harriette S(heffer)

Sheffield, Charles 1935-2002 .... *109*
Sheffield, Janet N. 1926- *26*
Sheikh, Nazneen
    See Sadiq, Nazneen
Shekerjian, Regina Tor *16*
Shelby, Anne 1948- *85*
    Autobiography Feature *121*
    See also SAAS *26*
Sheldon, Ann *67*
    Earlier sketch in SATA *1*
Sheldon, Ann
    See Antle, Nancy
Sheldon, Aure 1917-1976 .... *12*
Sheldon, John
    See Bloch, Robert (Albert)
Sheldon, Muriel 1926- *45*
    Brief entry *39*
Shelley, Frances
    See Wees, Frances Shelley
Shelley, Mary Wollstonecraft (Godwin)
    1797-1851 .... *29*
Shelton, William Roy 1919-1995 .... *5*
    Obituary *129*
Shemie, Bonnie (Jean Brenner) 1949- *96*
Shemin, Margaretha (Hoeneveld) 1928- *4*
Shenton, Edward 1895-1977 .... *45*
Shepard, Aaron 1950- *113*
    Earlier sketch in SATA *75*
Shepard, Ernest Howard 1879-1976 .... *100*
    Obituary *24*
    Earlier sketches in SATA *3, 33*
    See also CLR *27*
Shepard, James R. *164*
    Earlier sketch in SATA *90*
Shepard, Jim
    See Shepard, James R.
Shepard, Mary
    See Knox, (Mary) Eleanor Jessie
Shephard, Esther 1891-1975 .... *5*
    Obituary *26*
Shepherd, Donna Walsh
    See Walsh Shepherd, Donna
Shepherd, Elizabeth *4*
Sherburne, Zoa (Lillian Morin) 1912-1995 ... *3*
    See also SAAS *18*
Sherlock, Patti *71*
Sherman, D(enis) R(onald) 1934- *48*
    Brief entry *29*
Sherman, Diane (Finn) 1928- *12*
Sherman, Elizabeth
    See Friskey, Margaret (Richards)
Sherman, Harold (Morrow) 1898-1987 .... *37*
    Obituary *137*
Sherman, Josepha *163*
    Earlier sketch in SATA *75*
Sherman, Michael
    See Lowndes, Robert A(ugustine) W(ard)
Sherman, Nancy
    See Rosenberg, Nancy (Sherman)
Sherman, Peter Michael
    See Lowndes, Robert A(ugustine) W(ard)
Sherrard, Valerie (Anne) 1957- *141*
Sherrod, Jane
    See Singer, Jane Sherrod
Sherry, Clifford J. 1943- *84*
Sherry, (Dulcie) Sylvia 1932- *122*
    Earlier sketch in SATA *8*
Sherwan, Earl 1917- *3*
Sherwood, Jonathan
    See London, Jonathan (Paul)
Shetterly, Will(iam Howard) 1955- *78*
    Autobiography Feature *106*
Shiefman, Vicky 1942- *22*
Shields, Brenda Desmond (Armstrong) 1914-
    .... *37*
Shields, Charles 1944- *10*
Shiels, Barbara
    See Adams, Barbara Johnston
Shiffman, Lena 1957- *101*
Shiina, Makoto 1944- *83*
Shimin, Symeon 1902-1984 .... *13*

Shine, Andrea 1955- *104*
Shine, Deborah 1932- *71*
Shinn, Everett 1876-1953 .... *21*
Shinn, Sharon 1957- *164*
  Earlier sketch in SATA *110*
Shippen, Katherine B(inney) 1892-1980 .... *1*
  Obituary *23*
  See also CLR *36*
Shippey, T(homas) A(lan) 1943- *143*
Shipton, Eric Earle 1907-1977 .... *10*
Shirer, William L(awrence) 1904-1993 .... *45*
  Obituary *78*
Shirley, Gayle C(orbett) 1955- *96*
Shirley, Jean 1919- *70*
Shirreffs, Gordon D(onald) 1914-1996 .... *11*
Shirts, Morris A(lpine) 1922- *63*
Shlichta, Joe 1968- *84*
Shmurak, Carole B. 1944- *118*
Shore, June Lewis *30*
Shore, Nancy 1960- *124*
Shore, Robert 1924- *39*
Short, Michael 1937- *65*
Short, Roger
  See Arkin, Alan (Wolf)
Shortall, Leonard W. *19*
Shortt, Tim(othy Donald) 1961- *96*
Shotwell, Louisa Rossiter 1902-1993 .... *3*
Shoup, Barbara 1947- *156*
  Earlier sketch in SATA *86*
  See also SAAS *24*
Showalter, Jean B(reckinridge) *12*
Showell, Ellen Harvey 1934- *33*
Showers, Paul C. 1910-1999 .... *92*
  Obituary *114*
  Earlier sketch in SATA *21*
  See also CLR *6*
  See also SAAS *7*
Shpakow, Tanya 1959(?)- *94*
Shpitalnik, Vladimir 1964- *83*
Shragg, Karen (I.) 1954- *142*
Shreeve, Elizabeth 1956- *156*
Shreve, Susan
  See Shreve, Susan Richards
Shreve, Susan Richards 1939- *152*
  Brief entry *41*
  Earlier sketches in SATA *46, 95*
Shriver, Jean Adair 1932- *75*
Shriver, Maria (Owings) 1955- *134*
Shrode, Mary
  See Hollingsworth, Mary
Shtainmets, Leon *32*
Shub, Elizabeth 1915(?)-2004 .... *5*
Shuken, Julia 1948- *84*
Shulevitz, Uri 1935- *165*
  Earlier sketches in SATA *3, 50, 106*
  See also CLR *61*
Shulman, Alix Kates 1932- *7*
Shulman, Dee 1957- *146*
Shulman, Irving 1913-1995 .... *13*
Shulman, Neil B(arnett) 1945- *89*
Shumsky, Zena
  See Collier, Zena
Shura, Mary Francis
  See Craig, Mary (Francis) Shura
Shusterman, Neal 1962- *140*
  Autobiography Feature *140*
  Earlier sketches in SATA *85, 121*
Shuter, Jane (Margaret) 1955- *151*
  Earlier sketch in SATA *90*
Shuttlesworth, Dorothy Edwards *3*
Shwartz, Susan (Martha) 1949- *94*
Shyer, Christopher 1961- *98*
Shyer, Marlene Fanta *13*
Siberell, Anne *29*
Sibley, Don 1922- *12*
Siburt, Ruth 1951- *121*
Siculan, Daniel 1922- *12*
Sidgwick, Ethel 1877-1970 .... *116*
Sidjakov, Nicolas 1924- *18*
Sidman, Joyce 1956- *145*

Sidney, Frank
  See Warwick, Alan R(oss)
Sidney, Margaret
  See Lothrop, Harriet Mulford Stone
Siegal, Aranka 1930- *88*
  Brief entry *37*
Siegel, Beatrice *36*
Siegel, Helen
  See Siegl, Helen
Siegel, Robert (Harold) 1939- *39*
Siegelson, Kim L. 1962- *114*
Siegl, Helen 1924- *34*
Siepmann, Mary Aline
  See Wesley, Mary (Aline)
Sierra, Judy 1945- *162*
  Earlier sketch in SATA *104*
Sieswerda, Paul L. 1942- *147*
Sievert, Terri
  See Dougherty, Terri (L.)
Silas
  See McCay, (Zenas) Winsor
Silcock, Sara Lesley 1947- *12*
Sill, Cathryn 1953- *141*
  Earlier sketch in SATA *74*
Sill, John 1947- *140*
  Earlier sketch in SATA *74*
Sillitoe, Alan 1928- *61*
Sills, Leslie (Elka) 1948- *129*
Silly, E. S.
  See Kraus, (Herman) Robert
Silsbe, Brenda 1953- *73*
Silva, Joseph
  See Goulart, Ron(ald Joseph)
Silver, Ruth
  See Chew, Ruth
Silverberg, Robert 1935- *91*
  Autobiography Feature *104*
  Earlier sketch in SATA *13*
  See also CLR *59*
Silverman, Erica 1955- *165*
  Earlier sketches in SATA *78, 112*
Silverman, Janis L. 1946- *127*
Silverman, Mel(vin Frank) 1931-1966 .... *9*
Silverman, Robin L(andrew) 1954- *96*
Silverstein, Alvin 1933- *124*
  Earlier sketches in SATA *8, 69*
  See also CLR *25*
Silverstein, Herma 1945- *106*
Silverstein, Robert Alan 1959- *124*
  Earlier sketch in SATA *77*
Silverstein, Shel(don Allan) 1932-1999 ...... *92*
  Brief entry *27*
  Obituary *116*
  Earlier sketch in SATA *33*
  See also CLR *96*
Silverstein, Virginia B(arbara Opshelor) 1937-
  .... *124*
  Earlier sketches in SATA *8, 69*
  See also CLR *25*
Silverthorne, Elizabeth 1930- *35*
Silverwood, Margaret Shannon 1966- *137*
  Earlier sketch in SATA *83*
Silvey, Diane F. 1946- *135*
Sim, David 1953- *162*
Sim, Dorrith M. 1931- *96*
Simard, Remy 1959- *168*
Simmie, Lois (Ann) 1932- *106*
Simmonds, Posy 1945- *130*
  See also CLR *23*
Simmons, Andra 1939- *141*
Simmons, Elly 1955- *134*
Simms, Laura 1947- *117*
Simner, Janni Lee *113*
Simon, Charlie May
  See Fletcher, Charlie May Hogue
Simon, Francesca 1955- *111*
Simon, Gabriel 1972- *118*
Simon, Hilda Rita 1921- *28*
  See also CLR *39*
Simon, Howard 1903-1979 .... *32*
  Obituary *21*

Simon, Joe
  See Simon, Joseph H.
Simon, Joseph H. 1913- *7*
Simon, Martin P(aul William) 1903-1969 ... *12*
Simon, Mina Lewiton
  See Lewiton, Mina
Simon, Norma (Feldstein) 1927- *129*
  Earlier sketches in SATA *3, 68*
Simon, Seymour 1931- *138*
  Earlier sketches in SATA *4, 73*
  See also CLR *63*
Simon, Shirley (Schwartz) 1921- *11*
Simon, Solomon 1895-1970 .... *40*
Simonetta, Linda 1948- *14*
Simonetta, Sam 1936- *14*
Simons, Barbara B(rooks) 1934- *41*
Simont, Marc 1915- *126*
  Earlier sketches in SATA *9, 73*
Simpson, Colin 1908-1983 .... *14*
Simpson, Harriette
  See Arnow, Harriette (Louisa) Simpson
Simpson, Jacynth Hope
  See Hope Simpson, Jacynth
Simpson, Lesley 1963- *150*
Simpson, Margaret 1943- *128*
Simpson, Myrtle L(illias) 1931- *14*
Sims, Blanche *168*
  Earlier sketch in SATA *75*
Sims, Blanche L.
  See Sims, Blanche
Simundsson, Elva 1950- *63*
Sinclair, Clover
  See Gater, Dilys
Sinclair, Emil
  See Hesse, Hermann
Sinclair, Jeff 1958- *77*
Sinclair, Olga 1923- *121*
Sinclair, Rose
  See Smith, Susan Vernon
Sinclair, Upton 1878-1968 .... *9*
Sinclair, Upton Beall
  See Sinclair, Upton
Singer, A. L.
  See Lerangis, Peter
Singer, Arthur 1917-1990 .... *64*
Singer, Isaac
  See Singer, Isaac Bashevis
Singer, Isaac Bashevis 1904-1991 .... *27*
  Obituary *68*
  Earlier sketch in SATA *3*
  See also CLR *1*
Singer, Jane Sherrod 1917-1985 .... *4*
  Obituary *42*
Singer, Julia 1917- *28*
Singer, Kurt D. 1911-2005 .... *38*
Singer, Marilyn 1948- *158*
  Autobiography Feature *158*
  Brief entry *38*
  Earlier sketches in SATA *48, 80, 125*
  See also CLR *48*
  See also SAAS *13*
Singer, Muff 1942-2005 .... *104*
  Obituary *160*
Singer, Susan (Mahler) 1941- *9*
Singh, Rashmi Sharma 1952- *90*
Singleton, Linda Joy 1957- *166*
  Earlier sketch in SATA *88*
Singleton, L.J.
  See Singleton, Linda Joy
Sinykin, Sheri(l Terri) Cooper 1950- *142*
  Autobiography Feature *142*
  Earlier sketches in SATA *72, 133*
Sipiera, Paul P., (Jr.) 1948- *144*
  Earlier sketch in SATA *89*
Siracusa, Catherine (Jane) 1947- *82*
Sirett, Dawn (Karen) 1966- *88*
Sirimarco, Elizabeth 1966- *158*
Sirof, Harriet 1930- *94*
  Earlier sketch in SATA *37*
Sirois, Allen L. 1950- *76*
Sirvaitis (Chernyaev), Karen (Ann) 1961- .. *79*

Sis, Peter 1949- *106*
　Earlier sketch in SATA *67*
　See also CLR *110*
　See Sis, Peter
Sis, Peter 1949- *149*
　See also CLR *110*
　See Sis, Peter
Sisson, Rosemary Anne 1923- *11*
Sister Mary Terese
　See Donze, Mary Terese
Sita, Lisa 1962- *87*
Sitomer, Harry 1903-1985 .... *31*
Sitomer, Mindel 1903-1987 .... *31*
Sittenfeld, Curtis 1976(?)- *164*
Sive, Helen R(obinson) 1951- *30*
Sivulich, Sandra (Jeanne) Stroner 1941- *9*
Skarmeta, Antonio 1940- *57*
Skelly, James R(ichard) 1927- *17*
Skinner, Constance Lindsay 1877-1939
　See YABC *1*
Skinner, Cornelia Otis 1901-1979 .... *2*
Skipper, G. C. 1939- *46*
　Brief entry *38*
Sklansky, Amy E(dgar) 1971- *145*
Skofield, James *95*
　Brief entry *44*
Skold, Betty Westrom 1923- *41*
Skorpen, Liesel Moak 1935- *3*
Skott, Maria
　See Nikolajeva, Maria
Skrypuch, Marsha Forchuk 1954- *134*
Skurzynski, Gloria (Joan) 1930- *145*
　Autobiography Feature *145*
　Earlier sketches in SATA *8, 74, 122*
　See also SAAS *9*
Skutch, Robert 1925- *89*
Skye, Maggie
　See Werner, Herma
Slackman, Charles B. 1934- *12*
Slade, Arthur G(regory) 1967- *149*
　Earlier sketch in SATA *106*
Slade, Richard 1910-1971 .... *9*
Slangerup, Erik Jon 1969- *130*
Slate, Joseph (Frank) 1928- *122*
　Earlier sketch in SATA *38*
Slater, Ray
　See Lansdale, Joe R(ichard)
Slaughter, Hope 1940- *84*
Slaughter, Jean
　See Doty, Jean Slaughter
Slaughter, Tom 1955- *152*
Slavicek, Louise Chipley 1956- *144*
Slavin, Bill 1959- *148*
　Earlier sketch in SATA *76*
Slaymaker, Melissa Eskridge 1958- *158*
Sleator, William (Warner III) 1945- *161*
　Earlier sketches in SATA *3, 68, 118*
　See also CLR *29*
Slegers, Liesbet 1975- *154*
Sleigh, Barbara 1906-1982 .... *86*
　Obituary *30*
　Earlier sketch in SATA *3*
Slepian, Jan(ice B.) 1921- *85*
　Brief entry *45*
　Earlier sketch in SATA *51*
　See also SAAS *8*
Slicer, Margaret O. 1920- *4*
Slier, Debby
　See Shine, Deborah
Sloan, Carolyn 1937- *116*
　Earlier sketch in SATA *58*
Sloan, Glenna (Davis) 1930- *120*
Sloane, Eric 1910(?)-1985 .... *52*
　Obituary *42*
Sloane, Todd 1955- *88*
Sloat, Teri 1948- *164*
　Earlier sketches in SATA *70, 106*
Slobodkin, Florence Gersh 1905-1994 .... *5*
　Obituary *107*
Slobodkin, Louis 1903-1975 .... *26*
　Earlier sketch in SATA *1*

Slobodkina, Esphyr 1908-2002 .... *1*
　Obituary *135*
　See also SAAS *8*
Sloggett, Nellie 1851-1923 .... *44*
Sloss, Lesley Lord 1965- *72*
Slote, Alfred 1926- *72*
　Earlier sketch in SATA *8*
　See also CLR *4*
　See also SAAS *21*
Slote, Elizabeth 1956- *80*
Small, David 1945- *126*
　Brief entry *46*
　Earlier sketches in SATA *50, 95*
　See also CLR *53*
Small, Ernest
　See Lent, Blair
Small, Mary 1932- *165*
Small, Terry 1942- *75*
Smallcomb, Pam 1954- *159*
Smalls, Irene
　See Smalls-Hector, Irene
Smalls-Hector, Irene 1950- *146*
　Earlier sketch in SATA *73*
　See also CLR *103*
Smaridge, Norah (Antoinette) 1903-1994 ..... *6*
Smee, Nicola 1948- *167*
　Earlier sketch in SATA *76*
Smiley, Virginia Kester 1923- *2*
Smith, Anne Warren 1938- *41*
　Brief entry *34*
Smith, Barry (Edward Jervis) 1943- *75*
Smith, Beatrice S(chillinger) *12*
Smith, Betsy Covington 1937- *55*
　Earlier sketch in SATA *43*
Smith, Betty (Wehner) 1904-1972 .... *6*
Smith, Bradford 1909-1964 .... *5*
Smith, Brenda 1946- *82*
Smith, C. Pritchard
　See Hoyt, Edwin P(almer), Jr.
Smith, Caesar
　See Trevor, Elleston
Smith, Charles R., (Jr.) 1969- *159*
Smith, Craig 1955- *117*
　Earlier sketch in SATA *81*
Smith, Cynthia Leitich 1967- *152*
Smith, Datus C(lifford), Jr. 1907-1999 .... *13*
　Obituary *116*
Smith, Debra 1955- *89*
Smith, Derek 1943- *141*
Smith, Dick King
　See King-Smith, Dick
Smith, Dodie
　See Smith, Dorothy Gladys
Smith, Doris Buchanan 1934-2002 .... *75*
　Obituary *140*
　Earlier sketch in SATA *28*
　See also SAAS *10*
Smith, Dorothy Gladys 1896-1990 .... *82*
　Obituary *65*
　See Smith, Dodie
Smith, Dorothy Stafford 1905- *6*
Smith, E(lmer) Boyd 1860-1943
　See YABC *1*
Smith, E(dric) Brooks 1917- *40*
Smith, Emma 1923- *52*
　Brief entry *36*
Smith, (Katherine) Eunice (Young) 1902-1993
　.. *5*
Smith, Frances C(hristine) 1904-1986 .... *3*
Smith, Gary R. 1932- *14*
Smith, Geof 1969- *102*
Smith, George Harmon 1920- *5*
Smith, Greg Leitich *152*
Smith, Helene 1937- *142*
Smith, Howard E(verett), Jr. 1927- *12*
Smith, Hugh L(etcher) 1921-1968 .... *5*
Smith, Imogene Henderson 1922- *12*
Smith, Jacqueline B. 1937- *39*
Smith, Jada Pinkett 1971- *161*
Smith, Janet (Buchanan) Adam
　See Adam Smith, Janet (Buchanan)

Smith, Janice Lee 1949- *155*
　Earlier sketch in SATA *54*
Smith, Jean
　See Smith, Frances C(hristine)
Smith, Jean Pajot 1945- *10*
Smith, Jeff(rey Alan) 1958- *161*
　Earlier sketch in SATA *93*
Smith, Jeff Allen
　See Smith, Jeff(rey Alan)
Smith, Jenny 1963- *90*
Smith, Jessie
　See Kunhardt, Edith
Smith, Jessie Willcox 1863-1935 .... *21*
　See also CLR *59*
Smith, Joan (Mary) 1933- *54*
　Brief entry *46*
Smith, Johnston
　See Crane, Stephen (Townley)
Smith, Jos(eph) A. 1936- *120*
　Earlier sketch in SATA *73*
Smith, Judie R. 1936- *80*
Smith, Lafayette
　See Higdon, Hal
Smith, Lane 1959- *131*
　Earlier sketch in SATA *76*
　See also CLR *47*
Smith, Lee
　See Albion, Lee Smith
Smith, Lendon H(oward) 1921- *64*
Smith, Linell Nash 1932- *2*
Smith, Lucia B. 1943- *30*
Smith, Marion Hagens 1913- *12*
Smith, Marion Jaques 1899-1987 .... *13*
Smith, Mary Ellen *10*
Smith, Marya 1945- *78*
Smith, Mike
　See Smith, Mary Ellen
Smith, Nancy Covert 1935- *12*
Smith, Norman F. 1920- *70*
　Earlier sketch in SATA *5*
Smith, Patricia Clark 1943- *96*
Smith, Pauline C.
　See Arthur, Robert, (Jr.)
Smith, Pauline C(oggeshall) 1908-1994 ...... *27*
Smith, Philip Warren 1936- *46*
Smith, Rebecca 1946- *123*
Smith, Robert Kimmel 1930- *77*
　Earlier sketch in SATA *12*
Smith, Robert Paul 1915-1977 .... *52*
　Obituary *30*
Smith, Roland 1951- *161*
　Earlier sketch in SATA *115*
Smith, Rosamond
　See Oates, Joyce Carol
Smith, Ruth Leslie 1902- *2*
Smith, Sandra Lee 1945- *75*
Smith, Sarah Stafford
　See Smith, Dorothy Stafford
Smith, Sharon 1947- *82*
Smith, Sherri L. 1971- *156*
Smith, Sherwood 1951- *140*
　Earlier sketch in SATA *82*
Smith, Shirley Raines
　See Raines, Shirley C(arol)
Smith, Susan Carlton 1923- *12*
Smith, Susan Mathias 1950- *43*
　Brief entry *35*
Smith, Susan Vernon 1950- *48*
　See Mendonca, Susan
Smith, Tim(othy R.) 1945- *151*
Smith, Ursula 1934- *54*
Smith, Vian (Crocker) 1920-1969 .... *11*
Smith, Wanda VanHoy 1926- *65*
Smith, Ward
　See Goldsmith, Howard
Smith, William A. 1918- *10*
Smith, William Jay 1918- *154*
　Autobiography Feature *154*
　Earlier sketches in SATA *2, 68*
　See also SAAS *22*
Smith, Winsome 1935- *45*

Smith, Z. Z.
  See Westheimer, David
Smith-Ankrom, M. E. 1942- *130*
Smith-Griswold, Wendy 1955- *88*
Smith-Rex, Susan J. 1950- *94*
Smithsen, Richard
  See Pellowski, Michael (Joseph)
Smits, Teo
  See Smits, Theodore R(ichard)
Smits, Theodore R(ichard) 1905-1996 .... *45*
  Brief entry *28*
Smolinski, Dick 1932- *86*
Smothers, Ethel Footman 1944- *149*
  Earlier sketch in SATA *76*
Smucker, Barbara (Claassen) 1915- *130*
  Earlier sketches in SATA *29, 76*
  See also CLR *10*
  See also SAAS *11*
Smyth, Iain 1959- *105*
Snedeker, Caroline Dale (Parke) 1871-1956
  See YABC *2*
Snell, Nigel (Edward Creagh) 1936- *57*
  Brief entry *40*
Snellgrove, L(aurence) E(rnest) 1928- *53*
Snelling, Dennis (Wayne) 1958- *84*
Sneve, Virginia Driving Hawk 1933- *95*
  Earlier sketch in SATA *8*
  See also CLR *2*
Snicket, Lemony 1970- *126*
  See Handler, Daniel
Snodgrass, Mary Ellen 1944- *75*
Snodgrass, Quentin Curtius
  See Clemens, Samuel Langhorne
Snodgrass, Thomas Jefferson
  See Clemens, Samuel Langhorne
Snook, Barbara (Lillian) 1913-1976 .... *34*
Snow, Donald Clifford 1917-1979 .... *16*
Snow, Dorothea J(ohnston) 1909- *9*
Snow, Richard F(olger) 1947- *52*
  Brief entry *37*
Snyder, Anne 1922-2001 .... *4*
  Obituary *125*
Snyder, Bernadette McCarver 1930- *97*
Snyder, Carol 1941- *35*
Snyder, Gerald S(eymour) 1933- *48*
  Brief entry *34*
Snyder, Midori 1954- *106*
Snyder, Paul A. 1946- *125*
Snyder, Zilpha Keatley 1927- *163*
  Autobiography Feature *163*
  Earlier sketches in SATA *1, 28, 75, 110*
  See also CLR *31*
  See also SAAS *2*
Snyderman, Reuven K. 1922- *5*
So, Meilo *162*
Sobel, June 1950- *149*
Soble, Jennie
  See Cavin, Ruth (Brodie)
Sobol, Donald J. 1924- *132*
  Earlier sketches in SATA *1, 31, 73*
  See also CLR *4*
Sobol, Harriet Langsam 1936- *47*
  Brief entry *34*
Sobol, Rose 1931- *76*
Sobott-Mogwe, Gaele 1956- *97*
Soderlind, Arthur E(dwin) 1920- *14*
Soentpiet, Chris K. 1970- *159*
  Earlier sketch in SATA *97*
Soerensen, Svend Otto 1916- *67*
Sofer, Barbara 1949- *109*
Sofer, Rachel
  See Sofer, Barbara
Softly, Barbara Frewin 1924- *12*
Sohl, Frederic J(ohn) 1916- *10*
Sokol, Bill
  See Sokol, William
Sokol, William 1923- *37*
Sokolov, Kirill 1930- *34*
Solbert, Romaine G. 1925- *2*
Solbert, Ronni
  See Solbert, Romaine G.

Solheim, James *133*
Solomon, Joan 1930- *51*
  Brief entry *40*
Solomons, Ikey Esquir
  See Thackeray, William Makepeace
Solonevich, George 1915-2003 .... *15*
Solot, Mary Lynn 1939- *12*
Somerlott, Robert 1928-2001 .... *62*
Somervill, Barbara A(nn) 1948- *140*
Sommer, Angela
  See Sommer-Bodenburg, Angela
Sommer, Carl 1930- *126*
Sommer, Elyse 1929- *7*
Sommer, Robert 1929- *12*
Sommer-Bodenburg, Angela 1948- *63*
Sommer-Bodenburg, Angela 1948- *113*
Sommerdorf, Norma (Jean) 1926- *131*
Sommerfelt, Aimee 1892-1975 .... *5*
Son, John *160*
Sones, Sonya *131*
Sonneborn, Ruth (Cantor) 1899-1974 .... *4*
  Obituary *27*
Sonnenmark, Laura A. 1958- *73*
Sopko, Eugen 1949- *58*
Sorel, Edward 1929- *126*
  Brief entry *37*
  Earlier sketch in SATA *65*
Sorensen, Henri 1950- *115*
  Earlier sketch in SATA *77*
Sorensen, Svend Otto
  See Soerensen, Svend Otto
Sorensen, Virginia 1912-1991 .... *2*
  Obituary *72*
  See also SAAS *15*
Sorenson, Jane 1926- *63*
Sorenson, Margo 1946- *96*
Sorley Walker, Kathrine *41*
Sorrentino, Joseph N. 1937- *6*
Sortor, June Elizabeth 1939- *12*
Sortor, Toni
  See Sortor, June Elizabeth
Soskin, V. H.
  See Ellison, Virginia H(owell)
Soto, Gary 1952- *120*
  Earlier sketch in SATA *80*
  See also CLR *38*
Sotomayor, Antonio 1902-1985 .... *11*
Souci, Robert D. San
  See San Souci, Robert D.
Soudley, Henry
  See Wood, James Playsted
Soule, Gardner (Bosworth) 1913-2000 .... *14*
Soule, Jean Conder 1919- *10*
Souster, (Holmes) Raymond 1921- *63*
South, Sheri Cobb 1959- *82*
Southall, Ivan (Francis) 1921- *134*
  Autobiography Feature *134*
  Earlier sketches in SATA *3, 68*
  See also CLR *2*
  See also SAAS *3*
Southey, Robert 1774-1843 .... *54*
Southgate, Vera *54*
Sovak, Jan 1953- *115*
Sowden, Celeste
  See Walters, Celeste
Sowter, Nita *69*
Spafford, Suzy 1945- *160*
Spagnoli, Cathy 1950- *134*
  Earlier sketch in SATA *79*
Spain, Sahara Sunday 1991- *133*
Spalding, Andrea 1944- *150*
  Earlier sketch in SATA *101*
Spanfeller, James J(ohn) 1930- *19*
  See Spanfeller, Jim
Spanfeller, Jim
  See SAAS *8*
  See Spanfeller, James J(ohn)
Spangenberg, Judith Dunn 1942- *5*
Spanyol, Jessica 1965- *137*
Spar, Jerome 1918- *10*
Sparks, Barbara 1942- *78*

Sparks, Beatrice (Mathews) 1918- *44*
  Brief entry *28*
Sparks, Mary W. 1920- *15*
Spaulding, Douglas
  See Bradbury, Ray (Douglas)
Spaulding, Leonard
  See Bradbury, Ray (Douglas)
Spaulding, Norma *107*
Speare, Elizabeth George 1908-1994 .... *62*
  Obituary *83*
  Earlier sketch in SATA *5*
  See also CLR *8*
Spearing, Judith (Mary Harlow) 1922- *9*
Speck, Nancy 1959- *104*
Specking, Inez 1890-1960(?) *11*
Speed, Nell
  See Keats, Emma
  and Sampson, Emma (Keats) Speed
Speed, Nell (Ewing) 1878-1913 .... *68*
Speer, Bonnie Stahlman 1929- *113*
Speer-Lyon, Tammie L. 1965- *89*
Speicher, Helen Ross S(mith) 1915- *8*
Speir, Nancy 1958- *81*
Spellman, John W(illard) 1934- *14*
Spellman, Roger G.
  See Cox, William R(obert)
Spelman, Cornelia Maude 1946- *144*
  Earlier sketch in SATA *96*
Spelman, Mary 1934- *28*
Spence, Cynthia
  See Eble, Diane
Spence, Eleanor (Rachel) 1928- *21*
  See also CLR *26*
Spence, Geraldine 1931- *47*
Spencer, Ann 1918- *10*
Spencer, Cornelia
  See Yaukey, Grace S(ydenstricker)
Spencer, Donald D(ean) 1931- *41*
Spencer, Elizabeth 1921- *14*
Spencer, Leonard G.
  See Garrett, (Gordon) Randall (Phillip)
  and Silverberg, Robert
Spencer, William 1922- *9*
Spencer, Zane A(nn) 1935- *35*
Sper, Emily 1957- *142*
Speregen, Devra Newberger 1964- *84*
Sperling, Dan(iel Lee) 1949- *65*
Sperry, Armstrong W. 1897-1976 .... *1*
  Obituary *27*
Sperry, Raymond
  See Garis, Howard R(oger)
Sperry, Raymond, Jr. *1*
Spetter, Jung-Hee 1969- *134*
Spicer, Dorothy Gladys -1975 .... *32*
Spiegelman, Art 1948- *158*
  Earlier sketch in SATA *109*
Spiegelman, Judith M. *5*
Spielberg, Steven 1947- *32*
Spier, Peter (Edward) 1927- *54*
  Earlier sketch in SATA *4*
  See also CLR *5*
Spilhaus, Athelstan (Frederick) 1911-1998 . *13*
  Obituary *102*
Spilka, Arnold 1917- *6*
Spillane, Frank Morrison 1918- *66*
  See Spillane, Mickey
Spillane, Mickey
  See Spillane, Frank Morrison
Spinelli, Eileen 1942- *150*
  Earlier sketches in SATA *38, 101*
Spinelli, Jerry 1941- *158*
  Earlier sketches in SATA *39, 71, 110*
  See also CLR *82*
Spink, Reginald (William) 1905-1994 ...... *11*
Spinka, Penina Keen 1945- *72*
Spinner, Stephanie 1943- *132*
  Earlier sketches in SATA *38, 91*
Spinossimus
  See White, William, Jr.
Spires, Elizabeth 1952- *111*
  Earlier sketch in SATA *71*

Spirin, Gennadii
   See Spirin, Gennady
Spirin, Gennadij
   See Spirin, Gennady
Spirin, Gennady 1948- *134*
   Earlier sketch in SATA 95
   See also CLR 88
Spivak, Dawnine *101*
Spohn, David 1948- *72*
Spohn, Kate 1962- *147*
   Earlier sketch in SATA 87
Spollen, Christopher 1952- *12*
Spooner, Michael (Tim) 1954- *92*
Spowart, Robin 1947- *82*
Sprague, Gretchen (Burnham) 1926- *27*
Sprigge, Elizabeth (Miriam Squire) 1900-1974
   .... *10*
Spring, (Robert) Howard 1889-1965 .... *28*
Springer, Margaret 1941- *78*
Springer, Marilyn Harris 1931- *47*
Springer, Nancy 1948- *110*
   Earlier sketch in SATA 65
Springstubb, Tricia 1950- *78*
   Brief entry *40*
   Earlier sketch in SATA 46
Spudvilas, Anne 1951- *94*
Spurll, Barbara 1952- *78*
Spykman, E(lizabeth) C(hoate) 1896-1965 . *10*
   See also CLR 35
Spyri, Johanna (Heusser) 1827-1901 .... *100*
   Earlier sketch in SATA 19
   See also CLR 13
Squires, Phil
   See Barker, S(quire) Omar
Srba, Lynne *98*
Sreenivasan, Jyotsna 1964- *101*
S-Ringi, Kjell
   See Ringi, Kjell (Arne Soerensen)
Stacey, Cherylyn 1945- *96*
Stacy, Donald
   See Pohl, Frederik
Stadtler, Bea 1921- *17*
Stafford, Liliana 1950- *141*
Stafford, Paul 1966- *116*
Stahl, Ben(jamin) 1910-1987 .... *5*
   Obituary *54*
Stahl, Hilda 1938-1993 .... *48*
   Obituary *77*
Stahler, David, Jr. *162*
Stair, Gobin (John) 1912- *35*
Stalder, Valerie *27*
Stamaty, Mark Alan 1947- *12*
Stambler, Irwin 1924- *5*
Standiford, Natalie 1961- *169*
   Earlier sketch in SATA 81
Stanek, Lou Willett 1931- *63*
Stang, Judit 1921-1977 .... *29*
Stang, Judy
   See Stang, Judit
Stangl, (Mary) Jean 1928- *67*
Stanhope, Eric
   See Hamilton, Charles (Harold St. John)
Stankevich, Boris 1928- *2*
Stanley, Diane 1943- *164*
   Brief entry *32*
   Earlier sketches in SATA 37, 80, 115
   See also CLR 46
   See also SAAS 15
Stanley, George Edward 1942- *157*
   Earlier sketches in SATA 53, 111
   See Dixon, Franklin W.
   and Hope, Laura Lee
   and Keene, Carolyn
Stanley, Jerry 1941- *127*
   Earlier sketch in SATA 79
Stanley, Mandy *165*
Stanley, Robert
   See Hamilton, Charles (Harold St. John)
Stanley, Sanna 1962- *145*
Stanli, Sue
   See Meilach, Dona Z(weigoron)

Stanstead, John
   See Groom, Arthur William
Stanton, Schuyler
   See Baum, L(yman) Frank
Staples, Suzanne Fisher 1945- *151*
   Earlier sketches in SATA 70, 105
   See also CLR 60
Stapleton, Marjorie (Winifred) 1932- *28*
Stapp, Arthur D(onald) 1906-1972 .... *4*
Starbird, Kaye 1916- *6*
   See also CLR 60
Stark, Evan 1942- *78*
Stark, James
   See Goldston, Robert (Conroy)
Stark, Ulf 1944- *124*
Starke, Ruth (Elaine) 1946- *129*
Starkey, Marion L(ena) 1901-1991 .... *13*
Starr, Ward
   See Manes, Stephen
Starret, William
   See McClintock, Marshall
Starr Taylor, Bridget 1959- *99*
Stasiak, Krystyna *49*
Staub, Frank (Jacob) 1949- *116*
Staub, Wendy Corsi 1964- *114*
Stauffacher, Sue 1961- *155*
Staunton, Schuyler
   See Baum, L(yman) Frank
Staunton, Ted 1956- *167*
   Earlier sketch in SATA 112
Steadman, Ralph (Idris) 1936- *123*
   Earlier sketch in SATA 32
Stearman, Kaye 1951- *118*
Stearns, Monroe (Mather) 1913-1987 .... *5*
   Obituary *55*
Steckler, Arthur 1921-1985 .... *65*
Steding, Laurie 1953- *119*
Steel, Danielle 1947- *66*
Steel, Danielle Fernande
   See Steel, Danielle
Steele, Addison II
   See Lupoff, Richard A(llen)
Steele, Alexander 1958- *116*
Steele, Henry Maxwell
   See Steele, Max
Steele, Mary 1930- *94*
Steele, Mary Q(uintard Govan) 1922-1992 . *51*
   Obituary *72*
   Earlier sketch in SATA 3
Steele, Max 1922-2005 .... *168*
   Earlier sketch in SATA 10
Steele, Philip 1948- *140*
   Earlier sketch in SATA 81
Steele, William O(wen) 1917-1979 .... *51*
   Obituary *27*
   Earlier sketch in SATA 1
Steelhammer, Ilona 1952- *98*
Steelsmith, Shari 1962- *72*
Stefanik, Alfred T. 1939- *55*
Steffanson, Con
   See Cassiday, Bruce (Bingham)
   and Goulart, Ron(ald Joseph)
Steffens, Bradley 1955- *166*
   Earlier sketch in SATA 77
Stegeman, Janet Allais 1923- *53*
   Brief entry *49*
   See Britton, Kate
Steig, William (H.) 1907-2003 .... *111*
   Obituary *149*
   Earlier sketches in SATA 18, 70
   See also CLR 103
Stein, M(eyer) L(ewis) 1920- *6*
Stein, Mini *2*
Stein, R(ichard) Conrad 1937- *154*
   Earlier sketches in SATA 31, 82
Stein, Wendy 1951- *77*
Steinbeck, John (Ernst) 1902-1968 .... *9*
Steinberg, Alfred 1917-1995 .... *9*
Steinberg, Fannie 1899-1990 .... *43*
Steinberg, Fred J. 1933- *4*
Steinberg, Phillip Orso 1921- *34*

Steinberg, Rafael (Mark) 1927- *45*
Steinberg, Saul 1914-1999 .... *67*
Steiner, Barbara A(nnette) 1934- *83*
   Earlier sketch in SATA 13
   See also SAAS 13
Steiner, Charlotte 1900-1981 .... *45*
Steiner, George 1929- *62*
Steiner, Joan *110*
Steiner, Jorg
   See Steiner, Jorg
Steiner, Jorg 1930- *35*
Steiner, K. Leslie
   See Delany, Samuel R(ay), Jr.
Steiner, Stan(ley) 1925-1987 .... *14*
   Obituary *50*
Steins, Richard 1942- *79*
Stem, Jacqueline 1931- *110*
Steneman, Shep 1945- *132*
Stengel, Joyce A. 1938- *158*
Stephanie, Gordon
   See Gordon, Stephanie Jacob
Stephens, Alice Barber 1858-1932 .... *66*
Stephens, Casey
   See Wagner, Sharon B.
Stephens, Mary Jo 1935- *8*
Stephens, Rebecca 1961- *141*
Stephens, Reed
   See Donaldson, Stephen R(eeder)
Stephens, William M(cLain) 1925- *21*
Stephensen, A. M.
   See Manes, Stephen
Stepp, Ann 1935- *29*
Stepto, Michele 1946- *61*
Steptoe, Javaka 1971- *151*
Steptoe, John (Lewis) 1950-1989 .... *63*
   Earlier sketch in SATA 8
   See also CLR 12
Sterling, Brett
   See Bradbury, Ray (Douglas)
   and Hamilton, Edmond
   and Samachson, Joseph
Sterling, Dorothy 1913- *83*
   Autobiography Feature *127*
   Earlier sketch in SATA 1
   See also CLR 1
   See also SAAS 2
Sterling, Philip 1907-1989 .... *8*
   Obituary *63*
Sterling, Shirley (Anne) 1948- *101*
Stern, Ellen Norman 1927- *26*
Stern, Judith M. 1951- *75*
Stern, Madeleine B(ettina) 1912- *14*
Stern, Maggie 1953- *156*
Stern, Philip Van Doren 1900-1984 .... *13*
   Obituary *39*
Stern, Simon 1943- *15*
Sterne, Emma Gelders 1894- *6*
Steurt, Marjorie Rankin 1888-1978 .... *10*
Stevens, Bryna 1924- *65*
Stevens, Carla M(cBride) 1928- *13*
Stevens, Chambers 1968- *128*
Stevens, Diane 1939- *94*
Stevens, Franklin 1933- *6*
Stevens, Greg
   See Cook, Glen (Charles)
Stevens, Gwendolyn 1944- *33*
Stevens, Jan Romero 1953- *95*
Stevens, Janet 1953- *148*
   Earlier sketch in SATA 90
Stevens, Kathleen 1936- *49*
Stevens, Leonard A. 1920- *67*
Stevens, Lucile Vernon 1899-1994 .... *59*
Stevens, Margaret Dean
   See Aldrich, Bess Streeter
Stevens, Patricia Bunning 1931- *27*
Stevens, Peter
   See Geis, Darlene Stern
Stevens, Serita (Deborah) 1949- *70*
Stevens, Shira
   See Stevens, Serita (Deborah)
Stevenson, Anna (M.) 1905- *12*

Stevenson, Augusta 1869(?)-1976 2
  Obituary 26
Stevenson, Burton Egbert 1872-1962 25
Stevenson, Drew 1947- 60
Stevenson, Harvey 1960- 148
  Earlier sketch in SATA 80
Stevenson, James 1929- 161
  Brief entry 34
  Earlier sketches in SATA 42, 71, 113
  See also CLR 17
Stevenson, Janet 1913- 8
Stevenson, Robert Louis (Balfour) 1850-1894
  100
  See also YABC 2
  See also CLR 107
Stevenson, Sucie 1956- 104
Stewart, A(gnes) C(harlotte) 15
Stewart, Chantal 1945- 121
Stewart, Charles
  See Zurhorst, Charles (Stewart, Jr.)
Stewart, Eleanor
  See Porter, Eleanor H(odgman)
Stewart, Elisabeth J(ane) 1927- 93
Stewart, Elizabeth Laing 1907- 6
Stewart, Gail B. 1949- 141
Stewart, George Rippey 1895-1980 3
  Obituary 23
Stewart, Jennifer J(enkins) 1960- 128
Stewart, Joel 151
Stewart, John (William) 1920- 14
  See Cole, Jack
Stewart, Mary (Florence Elinor) 1916- 12
Stewart, Mary Rainbow
  See Stewart, Mary (Florence Elinor)
Stewart, Melissa 1968- 167
  Earlier sketch in SATA 111
Stewart, Paul 1955- 163
  Earlier sketch in SATA 114
Stewart, Robert Neil 1891-1972 7
Stewart, Sarah 143
Stewart, Scott
  See Zaffo, George J.
Stewart, W(alter) P. 1924- 53
Stewart, Whitney 1959- 167
  Earlier sketch in SATA 92
Stewig, John Warren 1937- 162
  Earlier sketches in SATA 26, 110
Stickler, Soma Han 1942- 128
Stidworthy, John 1943- 63
Stiles, Martha Bennett 108
  Earlier sketch in SATA 6
Still, James 1906-2001 29
  Obituary 127
Stille, Darlene R(uth) 1942- 126
Stillerman, Marci 104
Stillerman, Robbie 1947- 12
Stilley, Frank 1918- 29
Stilton, Geronimo 158
Stimpson, Gerald
  See Mitchell, Adrian
Stine, Catherine 165
Stine, G(eorge) Harry 1928-1997 136
  Earlier sketch in SATA 10
Stine, Jovial Bob
  See Stine, R.L.
Stine, R.L. 1943- 129
  Earlier sketches in SATA 31, 76
  See also CLR 111
Stine, Robert Lawrence
  See Stine, R.L.
Stinetorf, Louise (Allender) 1900-1992 10
Stinson, Kathy 1952- 98
Stirling, Arthur
  See Sinclair, Upton
Stirling, Ian 1941- 77
Stirling, Nora B(romley) 1900-1997 3
Stirnweis, Shannon 1931- 10
Stobbs, William 1914-2000 17
  Obituary 120
Stock, Carolmarie 1951- 75

Stock, Catherine 1952- 158
  Earlier sketches in SATA 65, 114
Stockdale, Susan 1954- 98
Stockham, Peter (Alan) 1928- 57
Stockton, Francis Richard 1834-1902 44
  See Stockton, Frank R.
Stockton, Frank R.
  Brief entry 32
  See Stockton, Francis Richard
Stockwell-Moniz, Marc J. 1954- 164
Stoddard, Edward G. 1923- 10
Stoddard, Hope 1900-1987 6
Stoddard, Sandol 1927- 98
  See Warburg, Sandol Stoddard
Stoehr, Shelley 1969- 107
Stoeke, Janet Morgan 1957- 136
  Earlier sketch in SATA 90
Stoiko, Michael 1919- 14
Stojic, Manya 1967- 156
Stoker, Abraham 1847-1912 29
  See Stoker, Bram
Stoker, Bram
  See Stoker, Abraham
Stokes, Cedric
  See Beardmore, George
Stokes, Jack (Tilden) 1923- 13
Stokes, Olivia Pearl 1916- 32
Stolz, Mary (Slattery) 1920- 133
  Earlier sketches in SATA 10, 71
  See also SAAS 3
Stone, Alan
  See Svenson, Andrew E(dward)
Stone, David K(arl) 1922- 9
Stone, David Lee 1978- 166
Stone, Eugenia 1879-1971 7
Stone, Gene
  See Stone, Eugenia
Stone, Helen V(irginia) 6
Stone, Idella Purnell
  See Purnell, Idella
Stone, Ikey
  See Purnell, Idella
Stone, Irving 1903-1989 3
  Obituary 64
Stone, Jon 1931-1997 39
  Obituary 95
Stone, Josephine Rector
  See Dixon, Jeanne
Stone, Lesley
  See Trevor, Elleston
Stone, Peter 1930-2003 65
  Obituary 143
Stone, Phoebe 134
Stone, Raymond 1
Stone, Rosetta
  See Dr. Seuss
  and Geisel, Theodor Seuss
  and LeSieg, Theo.
  and Seuss, Dr.
Stonehouse, Bernard 1926- 140
  Earlier sketches in SATA 13, 80
Stones, (Cyril) Anthony 1934- 72
Stong, Phil(ip Duffield) 1899-1957 32
Stoops, Erik D(aniel) 1966- 142
  Earlier sketch in SATA 78
Stoppelmoore, Cheryl Jean
  See Ladd, Cheryl (Jean)
Stops, Sue 1936- 86
Storad, Conrad J. 1957- 119
Storey, Margaret 1926- 9
Storey, Victoria Carolyn 1945- 16
Storme, Peter
  See Stern, Philip Van Doren
Storr, Catherine (Cole) 1913-2001 87
  Obituary 122
  Earlier sketch in SATA 9
Story, Josephine
  See Loring, Emilie (Baker)
Stotko, Mary-Ann 1960- 154
Stott, Dorothy (M.) 1958- 99
  Earlier sketch in SATA 67

Stott, Dot
  See Stott, Dorothy (M.)
Stotter, Mike 1957- 108
Stout, William 1949- 132
Stoutenburg, Adrien (Pearl) 1916-1982 3
Stoutland, Allison 1963- 130
Stover, Allan C(arl) 1938- 14
Stover, Jill (Griffin) 1958- 82
Stover, Marjorie Filley 1914- 9
Stowe, Harriet (Elizabeth) Beecher 1811-1896
  See YABC 1
Stowe, Leland 1899-1994 60
  Obituary 78
Stowe, Rosetta
  See Ogan, George F.
  and Ogan, Margaret E. (Nettles)
Strachan, Ian 1938- 85
Strachan, Linda 167
Strachan, Margaret Pitcairn 1908-1998 14
Strahinich, H. C.
  See Strahinich, Helen C.
Strahinich, Helen C. 1949- 78
Strait, Treva Adams 1909- 35
Strand, Mark 1934- 41
Stranger, Joyce
  See SAAS 24
  See Wilson, Joyce M(uriel Judson)
Strangis, Joel 1948- 124
Strannigan, Shawn (Alyne) 1956- 93
Strasser, Todd 1950- 153
  Earlier sketches in SATA 41, 45, 71, 107
  See also CLR 11
Stratemeyer, Edward L. 1862-1930 100
  Earlier sketches in SATA 1, 67
  See Adams, Harrison
  and Appleton, Victor
  and Dixon, Franklin W.
  and Keene, Carolyn
  and Rockwood, Roy
  and Young, Clarence
Stratford, Philip 1927- 47
Stratton, J. M.
  See Whitlock, Ralph
Stratton, Thomas
  See Coulson, Robert S(tratton)
  and DeWeese, Thomas Eugene
Stratton-Porter, Gene(va Grace) 1863-1924
  15
  See also CLR 87
  See Porter, Gene(va Grace) Stratton
Strauss, Gwen 1963- 77
Strauss, Joyce 1936- 53
Strauss, Linda Leopold 1942- 127
Strauss, Susan (Elizabeth) 1954- 75
Strayer, E. Ward
  See Stratemeyer, Edward L.
Streano, Vince(nt Catello) 1945- 20
Streatfeild, (Mary) Noel 1897(?)-1986 20
  Obituary 48
  See also CLR 83
Street, Janet Travell 1959- 84
Street, Julia Montgomery 1898-1993 11
Streissguth, Thomas 1958- 116
Strelkoff, Tatiana 1957- 89
Stren, Patti 1949- 88
  Brief entry 41
  See also CLR 5
Strete, Craig Kee 1950- 96
  Earlier sketch in SATA 44
Stretton, Barbara (Humphrey) 1936- 43
  Brief entry 35
Strickland, (William) Brad(ley) 1947- 142
  Earlier sketches in SATA 83, 137
Strickland, Craig (A.) 1956- 102
Strickland, Dorothy S(alley) 1933- 89
Strickland, Michael R. 1965- 144
  Earlier sketch in SATA 83
Striegel, Jana 1955- 140
Striegel-Wilson, Jana
  See Striegel, Jana

Striker, Lee
    See Clark, Margaret (D.)
Striker, Susan 1942- 63
Stringer, Lauren 1957- 129
Stroeyer, Poul 1923- 13
Stromoski, Rick 1958- 111
Strong, Charles
    See Epstein, Beryl (M. Williams)
    and Epstein, Samuel
Strong, David
    See McGuire, Leslie (Sarah)
Strong, J. J.
    See Strong, Jeremy
Strong, Jeremy 1949- 105
    Earlier sketch in SATA 36
Strong, Pat
    See Hough, Richard (Alexander)
Strong, Stacie 1965- 74
Stroud, Bettye 1939- 165
    Earlier sketch in SATA 96
Stroud, Jonathan 1970- 159
    Earlier sketch in SATA 102
Stroyer, Poul
    See Stroeyer, Poul
Strug, Kerri 1977- 108
Stryker, Daniel
    See Morris, Chris(topher Crosby)
    and Stump, Jane Barr
Stuart, David
    See Hoyt, Edwin P(almer), Jr.
Stuart, Derek
    See Foster, John L(ouis)
Stuart, Forbes 1924- 13
Stuart, Ian
    See MacLean, Alistair (Stuart)
Stuart, Jesse (Hilton) 1906-1984 2
    Obituary 36
Stuart, Ruth McEnery 1849(?)-1917 116
Stuart, Sheila
    See Baker, Mary Gladys Steel
Stuart-Clark, Christopher (Anthony) 1940- . 32
Stubis, Talivaldis 1926- 5
Stubley, Trevor (Hugh) 1932- 22
Stucky, Naomi R. 1922- 72
Stucley, Elizabeth
    See Northmore, Elizabeth Florence
Stultifer, Morton
    See Curtis, Richard (Alan)
Sture-Vasa, Mary
    See Alsop, Mary O'Hara
Sturtevant, Katherine 1950- 130
Sturton, Hugh
    See Johnston, H(ugh) A(nthony) S(tephen)
Sturtzel, Howard A(llison) 1894-1985 1
Sturtzel, Jane Levington 1903-1996 1
Stutley, D(oris) J(ean) 1959- 142
Stutson, Caroline 1940- 104
Stuve-Bodeen, Stephanie 1965- 158
    Earlier sketch in SATA 114
Stux, Erica 1929- 140
Styles, (Frank) Showell 1908- 10
Stynes, Barbara White 133
Suba, Susanne 4
Subond, Valerie
    See Grayland, Valerie (Merle Spanner)
Sudbery, Rodie 1943- 42
Suen, Anastasia 1956(?)- 157
Sufrin, Mark 1925- 76
Sugarman, Joan G. 1917- 64
Sugarman, Tracy 1921- 37
Sugita, Yutaka 1930- 36
Suhl, Yuri (Menachem) 1908-1986 8
    Obituary 50
    See also CLR 2
    See also SAAS 1
Suhr, Joanne 129
Suid, Murray 1942- 27
Sullivan, George (Edward) 1927- 147
    Earlier sketches in SATA 4, 89
Sullivan, Jody
    See Rake, Jody

Sullivan, Kathryn A. 1954- 141
Sullivan, Mary Ann 1954- 63
Sullivan, Mary W(ilson) 1907- 13
Sullivan, Pat
    See Messmer, Otto
Sullivan, Paul 1939- 106
Sullivan, Silky
    See Makowski, Silvia Ann
Sullivan, Sue
    See Sullivan, Susan E.
Sullivan, Susan E. 1962- 123
Sullivan, Thomas Joseph, Jr. 1947- 16
Sullivan, Tom
    See Sullivan, Thomas Joseph, Jr.
Sully, Tom 1959- 104
Sumichrast, Jozef 1948- 29
Sumiko
    See Davies, Sumiko
Summerforest, Ivy B.
    See Kirkup, James
Summers, James L(evingston) 1910-1973 .. 57
    Brief entry 28
Summertree, Katonah
    See Windsor, Patricia
Sun, Chyng Feng 1959- 90
Sunderlin, Sylvia (S.) 1911-1997 28
    Obituary 99
Sung, Betty Lee 26
Supeene, Shelagh Lynne 1952- 153
Supraner, Robyn 1930- 101
    Earlier sketch in SATA 20
Supree, Burt(on) 1941-1992 73
Surface, Mary Hall 1958- 126
Surge, Frank 1931- 13
Susac, Andrew 1929- 5
Susi, Geraldine Lee 1942- 98
Sussman, Cornelia Silver 1914-1999 59
Sussman, Irving 1908-1996 59
Sussman, Susan 1942- 48
Sutcliff, Rosemary 1920-1992 78
    Obituary 73
    Earlier sketches in SATA 6, 44
    See also CLR 37
Sutcliffe, Jane 1957- 138
Sutherland, Colleen 1944- 79
Sutherland, Efua (Theodora Morgue)
    1924-1996 25
Sutherland, Jon 1958- 167
Sutherland, Jonathan D.
    See Sutherland, Jon
Sutherland, Margaret 1941- 15
Sutherland, Zena Bailey 1915-2002 37
    Obituary 137
Suttles, Shirley (Smith) 1922- 21
Sutton, Ann (Livesay) 1923- 31
Sutton, Eve(lyn Mary) 1906-1992 26
Sutton, Felix 1910(?)-1973 31
Sutton, Jane 1950- 52
    Brief entry 43
Sutton, Larry M(atthew) 1931- 29
Sutton, Margaret Beebe 1903-2001 1
    Obituary 131
Sutton, Myron Daniel 1925- 31
Sutton, Roger 1956- 93
Suzanne, Jamie
    See Hawes, Louise
    and Lantz, Francess L(in)
    and Singleton, Linda Joy
    and Zach, Cheryl (Byrd)
Suzuki, David T(akayoshi) 1936- 138
Svendsen, Mark (Nestor) 1962- 120
Svenson, Andrew E(dward) 1910-1975 2
    Obituary 26
Swain, Gwenyth 1961- 134
    Earlier sketch in SATA 84
Swain, Ruth
    See Swain, Ruth Freeman
Swain, Ruth Freeman 1951- 161
    Earlier sketch in SATA 119
Swain, Su Zan (Noguchi) 1916- 21
Swamp, Jake 1941- 98

Swan, Susan 1944- 108
    Earlier sketch in SATA 22
Swann, Brian (Stanley Frank) 1940- 116
Swann, E. L.
    See Lasky, Kathryn
Swann, Ruth Rice 1920- 84
Swanson, Helen M(cKendry) 1919- 94
Swanson, June 1931- 76
Swanson, Wayne 1942- 167
Swarthout, Glendon (Fred) 1918-1992 26
Swarthout, Kathryn 1919- 7
Swayne, Sam(uel F.) 1907- 53
Swayne, Zoa (Lourana) 1905- 53
Sweat, Lynn 1934- 168
    Earlier sketch in SATA 57
Swede, George 1940- 67
Sweeney, James B(artholomew) 1910-1999
    21
Sweeney, Joyce 1955- 167
    Earlier sketches in SATA 65, 68, 108
Sweeney, Joyce Kay
    See Sweeney, Joyce
Sweeney, Karen O'Connor
    See O'Connor, Karen
Sweeney, Matthew (Gerard) 1952- 156
Sweet, Sarah C.
    See Jewett, (Theodora) Sarah Orne
Sweetland, Nancy A(nn) 1934- 48
Swenson, Allan A(rmstrong) 1933- 21
Swenson, May 1919-1989 15
Swentzell, Rina 1939- 79
Swift, Bryan
    See Knott, William C(ecil, Jr.)
Swift, David
    See Kaufmann, John
Swift, Jonathan 1667-1745 19
    See also CLR 53
Swift, Merlin
    See Leeming, Joseph
Swiger, Elinor Porter 1927- 8
Swinburne, Laurence (Joseph) 1924- 9
Swinburne, Stephen R. 1952- 150
Swinburne, Steve
    See Swinburne, Stephen R.
Swindells, Robert (Edward) 1939- 150
    Brief entry 34
    Earlier sketches in SATA 50, 80
    See also SAAS 14
Swinford, Betty (June Wells) 1927- 58
Swinford, Bob
    See Swinford, Betty (June Wells)
Swithen, John
    See King, Stephen
Switzer, Ellen 1923- 48
Swope, Sam 156
    See Swope, Samuel
Swope, Samuel
    See Swope, Sam
Sybesma, Jetske
    See Ironside, Jetske
Sydney, Frank
    See Warwick, Alan R(oss)
Sylvester, Natalie G(abry) 1922- 22
Syme, (Neville) Ronald 1913-1992 87
    Earlier sketch in SATA 2
Symes, R. F. 77
Symons, (Dorothy) Geraldine 1909- 33
Symons, Stuart
    See Stanley, George Edward
Symynkywicz, Jeffrey B(ruce) 1954- 87
Synge, (Phyllis) Ursula 1930- 9
Sypher, Lucy Johnston 1907- 7
Szasz, Suzanne (Shorr) 1915-1997 13
    Obituary 99
Szekeres, Cyndy 1933- 157
    Autobiography Feature 157
    Earlier sketches in SATA 5, 60, 131
    See also SAAS 13
Szekessy, Tanja 98
Szpura, Beata 1961- 93

Szudek, Agnes S(usan) P(hilomena) *57*
  Brief entry *49*
Szulc, Tad 1926-2001 .... *26*
Szydlow, Jarl
  See Szydlowski, Mary Vigliante
Szydlowski, Mary Vigliante 1946- *94*
Szymanski, Lois 1957- *91*

T

Taback, Simms 1932- *104*
  Brief entry *36*
  Earlier sketch in SATA *40*
  See also CLR *100*
Tabor, Nancy Maria Grande 1949- *161*
  Earlier sketch in SATA *89*
Tabrah, Ruth Milander 1921- *14*
Tackach, James 1953- *123*
Tafuri, Nancy (E.) 1946- *130*
  Earlier sketches in SATA *39, 75*
  See also CLR *74*
  See also SAAS *14*
Tagg, Christine Elizabeth 1962- *138*
Taha, Karen T(erry) 1942- *156*
  Earlier sketch in SATA *71*
Tai, Sharon O. 1963- *153*
Tait, Douglas 1944- *12*
Takabayashi, Mari 1960- *156*
  Earlier sketch in SATA *115*
Takahashi, Rumiko 1957- *163*
Takakjian, Portia 1930- *15*
Takashima, Shizuye 1928- *13*
Takayama, Sandi 1962- *106*
Takeda, Pete(r M.) 1964- *148*
Talbert, Marc (Alan) 1953- *154*
  Autobiography Feature *154*
  Earlier sketches in SATA *68, 99*
Talbot, Charlene Joy 1928- *10*
Talbot, Toby 1928- *14*
Talbott, Hudson 1949- *131*
  Earlier sketch in SATA *84*
Talifero, Gerald 1950- *75*
Talker, T.
  See Rands, William Brighty
Tallarico, Tony 1933- *116*
Tallcott, Emogene *10*
Tallis, Robyn
  See Coville, Bruce
  and Doyle, Debra
  and Macdonald, James D.
  and Smith, Sherwood
  and Zambreno, Mary Frances
Tallon, Robert 1939- *43*
  Brief entry *28*
Talmadge, Marian *14*
Tamar, Erika 1934- *150*
  Earlier sketches in SATA *62, 101*
Tamarin, Alfred H. 1913-1980 .... *13*
Tamburine, Jean 1930- *12*
Tames, Richard (Lawrence) 1946- *102*
  Earlier sketch in SATA *67*
Tamminga, Frederick W(illiam) 1934- *66*
Tan, Amy (Ruth) 1952- *75*
Tanaka, Beatrice 1932- *76*
Tanaka, Shelley *136*
Tang, Charles 1948- *81*
Tang, You-Shan 1946- *53*
Tania B.
  See Blixen, Karen (Christentze Dinesen)
Tannen, Mary 1943- *37*
Tannenbaum, Beulah Goldstein 1916- *3*
Tannenbaum, D(onald) Leb 1948- *42*
Tanner, Jane 1946- *74*
Tanner, Louise S(tickney) 1922-2000 .... *9*
Tanobe, Miyuki 1937- *23*
Tanselle, Eve 1933- *125*
Tapio, Pat Decker
  See Kines, Pat Decker

Tapp, Kathy Kennedy 1949- *88*
  Brief entry *50*
Tarbescu, Edith 1939- *107*
Tarkington, (Newton) Booth 1869-1946 ..... *17*
Tarpley, Natasha A(nastasia) 1971- *147*
Tarr, Judith 1955- *149*
  Earlier sketch in SATA *64*
Tarry, Ellen 1906- *16*
  See also CLR *26*
  See also SAAS *16*
Tarshis, Jerome 1936- *9*
Tarsky, Sue 1946- *41*
Tashjian, Janet 1956- *151*
  Earlier sketch in SATA *102*
Tashjian, Virginia A. 1921- *3*
Tasker, James 1908- *9*
Tate, Don(ald E.) *159*
Tate, Eleanora E(laine) 1948- *94*
  Earlier sketch in SATA *38*
  See also CLR *37*
Tate, Ellalice
  See Hibbert, Eleanor Alice Burford
Tate, Joan 1922- *86*
  Earlier sketch in SATA *9*
  See also SAAS *20*
Tate, Mary Anne
  See Hale, Arlene
Tate, Nikki *134*
Tate, Richard
  See Masters, Anthony (Richard)
Tate, Suzanne 1930- *91*
Tatham, Betty *142*
Tatham, Campbell
  See Elting, Mary
Tatham, Julie
  See Tatham, Julie Campbell
Tatham, Julie Campbell 1908-1999 .... *80*
Tavares, Matt *159*
Taves, Isabella 1915- *27*
Taylor, Alastair 1959- *130*
Taylor, Andrew 1951- *70*
Taylor, Andrew John Robert
  See Taylor, Andrew
Taylor, Ann 1782-1866 .... *41*
  Brief entry *35*
Taylor, Audilee Boyd 1931- *59*
Taylor, Barbara J. 1927- *10*
Taylor, Ben
  See Strachan, Ian
Taylor, Carl 1937- *14*
Taylor, Cheryl Munro 1957- *96*
Taylor, Cora (Lorraine) 1936- *103*
  Earlier sketch in SATA *64*
  See also CLR *63*
Taylor, Dave 1948- *78*
Taylor, David
  See Taylor, Dave
Taylor, David 1900-1965 .... *10*
Taylor, Debbie A. 1955- *169*
Taylor, Elizabeth 1912-1975 .... *13*
Taylor, Florance Walton *9*
Taylor, Florence M(arian Tompkins) 1892-1983
  .... *9*
Taylor, G(raham) P(eter) 1959(?)- *156*
Taylor, Gage 1942-2000 .... *87*
Taylor, Graham
  See Taylor, G(raham) P(eter)
Taylor, Herb(ert Norman, Jr.) 1942-1987 .... *22*
  Obituary *54*
Taylor, J. David
  See Taylor, Dave
Taylor, Jane 1783-1824 .... *41*
  Brief entry *35*
Taylor, Jerry D(uncan) 1938- *47*
Taylor, John Robert
  See Taylor, Andrew
Taylor, Judy
  See Hough, Judy Taylor
Taylor, Kenneth N. 1917-2005 .... *26*
Taylor, Kenneth Nathaniel
  See Taylor, Kenneth N.

Taylor, L(ester) B(arbour), Jr. 1932- *27*
Taylor, Lois Dwight Cole
  See Cole, Lois Dwight
Taylor, Louise Todd 1939- *47*
Taylor, Margaret 1950- *106*
Taylor, Mark 1927- *32*
  Brief entry *28*
Taylor, Mildred D(elois) 1943- *135*
  See also CLR *90*
  See also SAAS *5*
Taylor, Paula (Wright) 1942- *48*
  Brief entry *33*
Taylor, Robert Lewis 1912-1998 .... *10*
Taylor, Sydney (Brenner) 1904(?)-1978 ...... *28*
  Obituary *26*
  Earlier sketch in SATA *1*
Taylor, Theodore 1921- *128*
  Earlier sketches in SATA *5, 54, 83*
  See also CLR *30*
  See also SAAS *4*
Taylor, William 1938- *164*
  Earlier sketches in SATA *78, 113*
  See also CLR *63*
Tazewell, Charles 1900-1972 .... *74*
Tchana, Katrin Hyman 1963- *125*
Tchekhov, Anton
  See Chekhov, Anton (Pavlovich)
Tchen, Richard *120*
Tchudi, Stephen N. 1942- *55*
Teague, Bob
  See Teague, Robert
Teague, Mark 1963- *99*
  Earlier sketch in SATA *68*
Teague, Mark Christopher
  See Teague, Mark
Teague, Robert 1929- *32*
  Brief entry *31*
Teal, Val(entine M.) 1902-1997 .... *10*
  Obituary *114*
Teale, Edwin Way 1899-1980 .... *7*
  Obituary *25*
Teasdale, Sara 1884-1933 .... *32*
Tebbel, John (William) 1912-2004 .... *26*
Teensma, Lynne Bertrand
  See Bertrand, Lynne
Tee-Van, Helen Damrosch 1893-1976 .... *10*
  Obituary *27*
Tegner, Bruce 1928- *62*
Teitelbaum, Michael 1953- *116*
  Earlier sketch in SATA *59*
Tejima
  See Tejima, Keizaburo
Tejima, Keizaburo 1931- *139*
  See also CLR *20*
Telander, Todd (G.) 1967- *88*
Teleki, Geza 1943- *45*
Telemaque, Eleanor Wong 1934- *43*
Telescope, Tom
  See Newbery, John
Temkin, Sara Anne Schlossberg 1913-1996
  .... *26*
Temko, Florence *13*
Templar, Maurice
  See Groom, Arthur William
Temple, Charles 1947- *79*
Temple, Frances (Nolting) 1945-1995 .... *85*
Temple, Herbert 1919- *45*
Temple, Paul
  See McConnell, James Douglas Rutherford
Temple, William F(rederick) 1914-1989 ... *107*
Tenggren, Gustaf 1896-1970 .... *18*
  Obituary *26*
Tennant, Kylie *6*
  See Rodd, Kylie Tennant
Tennant, Veronica 1947- *36*
Tenneshaw, S. M.
  See Beaumont, Charles
  and Garrett, (Gordon) Randall (Phillip)
  and Silverberg, Robert

Tenniel, John 1820-1914 74
  Brief entry 27
  See also CLR *18*
Tepper, Sheri S. 1929- *113*
Terada, Alice M. 1928- *90*
Terban, Marvin 1940- *54*
  Brief entry 45
ter Haar, Jaap 1922- *6*
  See Haar, Jaap ter
Terhune, Albert Payson 1872-1942 ... *15*
Terkel, Susan N(eiburg) 1948- *103*
  Earlier sketch in SATA *59*
Terlouw, Jan (Cornelis) 1931- *30*
Terris, Susan 1937- *77*
  Earlier sketch in SATA *3*
Terry, Luther L(eonidas) 1911-1985 .... *11*
  Obituary 42
Terry, Margaret
  See Dunnahoo, Terry Janson
Terry, Walter 1913-1982 .... *14*
Terzian, James P. 1915- *14*
Tessendorf, K(enneth) C(harles) 1925-2003
  .... *75*
  Obituary *142*
Tessler, Stephanie Gordon
  See Gordon, Stephanie Jacob
Tester, Sylvia Root 1939- *64*
  Brief entry 37
Tether, (Cynthia) Graham 1950- *46*
  Brief entry 36
Tetzner, Lisa 1894-1963 .... *169*
Thacher, Mary McGrath 1933- *9*
Thackeray, William Makepeace 1811-1863
  .... *23*
Thaler, Michael C.
  See Thaler, Mike
Thaler, Mike 1936- *93*
  Brief entry 47
  Earlier sketch in SATA *56*
Thaler, Shmuel 1958- *126*
  Earlier sketch in SATA *72*
Thamer, Katie 1955- *42*
Thane, Elswyth 1900-1984(?) *32*
Tharp, Louise (Marshall) Hall 1898-1992 .... *3*
  Obituary *129*
Thayer, Ernest Lawrence 1863-1940 .... *60*
Thayer, Jane
  See Woolley, Catherine
Thayer, Marjorie 1908-1992 .... *74*
  Brief entry 37
Thayer, Peter
  See Wyler, Rose
Thelwell, Norman 1923-2004 .... *14*
Themerson, Stefan 1910-1988 .... *65*
Thermes, Jennifer 1966- *155*
Theroux, Paul (Edward) 1941- *109*
  Earlier sketch in SATA *44*
Thesman, Jean *124*
  Earlier sketch in SATA *74*
Thieda, Shirley Ann 1943- *13*
Thiele, Colin (Milton) 1920- *125*
  Earlier sketches in SATA *14, 72*
  See also CLR *27*
  See also SAAS *2*
Thiesing, Lisa 1958- *159*
  Earlier sketch in SATA *95*
Thiry, Joan (Marie) 1926- *45*
Thistlethwaite, Miles 1945- *12*
Thollander, Earl 1922- *22*
Thomas, Abigail 1941- *112*
Thomas, Andrea
  See Hill, Margaret (Ohler)
Thomas, Art(hur Lawrence) 1952- *48*
  Brief entry 38
Thomas, Carroll
  See Ratliff, Thomas M.
  and Shmurak, Carole B.
Thomas, Dylan (Marlais) 1914-1953 .... *60*
Thomas, Egbert S.
  See Ellis, Edward S(ylvester)
Thomas, Estelle Webb 1899-1982 .... *26*

Thomas, Frances 1943- *92*
Thomas, H. C.
  See Keating, Lawrence A.
Thomas, Ianthe 1951- *139*
  Brief entry 42
  See also CLR *8*
Thomas, Jane Resh 1936- *90*
  Earlier sketch in SATA *38*
Thomas, Jerry D. 1959- *91*
Thomas, Joan Gale
  See Robinson, Joan (Mary) G(ale Thomas)
Thomas, Joyce Carol 1938- *137*
  Autobiography Feature *137*
  Earlier sketches in SATA *40, 78, 123*
  See also CLR *19*
  See also SAAS *7*
Thomas, Lowell Jackson, Jr. 1923- *15*
Thomas, Meredith 1963- *119*
Thomas, Michael
  See Wilks, Michael Thomas
Thomas, Patricia J. 1934- *51*
Thomas, Rob 1965- *97*
Thomas, Scott 1959- *147*
Thomas, Vernon (Arthur) 1934- *56*
Thomas, Victoria
  See DeWeese, Thomas Eugene
  and Kugi, Constance Todd
Thomasma, Kenneth R. 1930- *90*
Thomassie, Tynia 1959- *92*
Thompson, Brenda 1935- *34*
Thompson, Carol 1951- *85*
Thompson, China
  See Lewis, Mary (Christianna)
Thompson, Colin (Edward) 1942- *163*
  Earlier sketch in SATA *95*
Thompson, David H(ugh) 1941- *17*
Thompson, Eileen
  See Panowski, Eileen Thompson
Thompson, George Selden 1929-1989 .... *73*
  Obituary *63*
  Earlier sketch in SATA *4*
  See Selden, George
Thompson, Harlan (Howard) 1894-1987 .... *10*
  Obituary *53*
  See Holt, Stephen
Thompson, Hilary 1943- *56*
  Brief entry 49
Thompson, Julian F(rancis) 1927- *155*
  Brief entry 40
  Earlier sketches in SATA *55, 99*
  See also CLR *24*
  See also SAAS *13*
Thompson, K(athryn Carolyn) Dyble 1952-
  .... *82*
Thompson, Kay 1912(?)-1998 .... *16*
  See also CLR *22*
Thompson, Lauren (Stevens) 1962- *132*
Thompson, Ruth Plumly 1891-1976 .... *66*
Thompson, Sharon (Elaine) 1952- *119*
Thompson, Stith 1885-1976 .... *57*
  Obituary *20*
Thompson, Vivian L(aubach) 1911- *3*
Thomson, David (Robert Alexander)
  1914-1988 .... *40*
  Obituary *55*
Thomson, Pat 1939- *122*
  Earlier sketch in SATA *77*
Thomson, Peggy 1922- *31*
Thon, Melanie Rae 1957- *132*
Thorn, John 1947- *59*
Thorndyke, Helen Louise *67*
  Earlier sketch in SATA *1*
  See Benson, Mildred (Augustine Wirt)
Thorne, Ian
  See May, Julian
Thorne, Jean Wright
  See May, Julian
Thornhill, Jan 1955- *148*
  Earlier sketch in SATA *77*
Thornton, Hall
  See Silverberg, Robert

Thornton, W. B.
  See Burgess, Thornton Waldo
Thornton, Yvonne S(hirley) 1947- *96*
Thorpe, E(ustace) G(eorge) 1916- *21*
Thorpe, J. K.
  See Nathanson, Laura Walther
Thorvall, Kerstin 1925- *13*
Thorvall-Falk, Kerstin
  See Thorvall, Kerstin
Thrasher, Crystal (Faye) 1921- *27*
Threadgall, Colin 1941- *77*
Three Little Pigs
  See Lantz, Francess L(in)
Thum, Gladys 1920- *26*
Thum, Marcella *28*
  Earlier sketch in SATA *3*
Thundercloud, Katherine
  See Witt, Shirley Hill
Thurber, James (Grover) 1894-1961 .... *13*
Thurlo, Aimee *161*
Thurlo, David *161*
Thurman, Judith 1946- *33*
Thurman, Mark (Gordon Ian) 1948- *63*
Thwaite, Ann (Barbara Harrop) 1932- *14*
Tibbetts, Peggy *127*
Tibbles, Jean-Paul 1958- *115*
Tibo, Gilles 1951- *107*
  Earlier sketch in SATA *67*
Tiburzi, Bonnie 1948- *65*
Ticheburn, Cheviot
  See Ainsworth, William Harrison
Tichenor, Tom 1923-1992 .... *14*
Tichnor, Richard 1959- *90*
Tichy, William 1924- *31*
Tickle, Jack
  See Chapman, Jane
Tiegreen, Alan F. 1935- *94*
  Brief entry 36
Tierney, Frank M. 1930- *54*
Tierney, Tom 1928- *113*
Tiffault, Benette W. 1955- *77*
Tiller, Ruth L. 1949- *83*
Tilly, Nancy 1935- *62*
Tilton, Madonna Elaine 1929- *41*
Tilton, Rafael
  See Tilton, Madonna Elaine
Timberlake, Amy *156*
Timberlake, Carolyn
  See Dresang, Eliza (Carolyn Timberlake)
Timmins, William F(rederick) *10*
Tiner, John Hudson 1944- *32*
Tingle, Dolli (?)-
  See Brackett, Dolli Tingle
Tingum, Janice 1958- *91*
Tinkelman, Murray 1933- *12*
Tinkle, (Julien) Lon 1906-1980 ..... *36*
Tinling, Marion (Rose) 1904- *140*
Tipene, Tim 1972- *141*
Tippett, James S(terling) 1885-1958 .... *66*
Tirone Smith, Mary-Ann 1944- *143*
Titler, Dale M(ilton) 1926- *35*
  Brief entry 28
Titmarsh, Michael Angelo
  See Thackeray, William Makepeace
Titus, Eve 1922- *2*
Tjong Khing, The 1933- *76*
Tobias, Katherine
  See Gottfried, Theodore Mark
Tobias, Tobi 1938- *82*
  Earlier sketch in SATA *5*
  See also CLR *4*
Todd, Anne Ophelia
  See Dowden, Anne Ophelia
Todd, Barbara K(eith) 1917- *10*
Todd, H(erbert) E(atton) 1908-1988 .... *84*
  Earlier sketch in SATA *11*
Todd, Loreto 1942- *30*
Todd, Pamela 1950- *124*
Todd, Peter
  See Hamilton, Charles (Harold St. John)
Toews, Miriam 1964- *165*

Tofel, Richard J. 1957- *140*
Tolan, Stephanie S. 1942- *142*
    Earlier sketches in SATA *38, 78*
Toland, John (Willard) 1912-2004 .... *38*
Tolbert, Steve 1944- *143*
Tolkien, J(ohn) R(onald) R(euel) 1892-1973
    .... *100*
    Obituary *24*
    Earlier sketches in SATA *2, 32*
    See also CLR *56*
Toll, Emily
    See Cannon, Eileen E(mily)
Toll, Nelly S. 1935- *78*
Tolland, W. R.
    See Heitzmann, William Ray
Tolles, Martha 1921- *76*
    Earlier sketch in SATA *8*
Tolliver, Ruby C(hangos) 1922- *110*
    Brief entry *41*
    Earlier sketch in SATA *55*
Tolmie, Kenneth Donald 1941- *15*
Tolstoi, Lev
    See Tolstoy, Leo (Nikolaevich)
Tolstoy, Leo (Nikolaevich) 1828-1910 .... *26*
    See Tolstoi, Lev
Tolstoy, Count Leo
    See Tolstoy, Leo (Nikolaevich)
Tomalin, Ruth *29*
Tomaselli, Rosa
    See Pausacker, Jenny
Tomes, Margot (Ladd) 1917-1991 .... *70*
    Brief entry *27*
    Obituary *69*
    Earlier sketch in SATA *36*
Tomey, Ingrid 1943- *77*
Tomfool
    See Farjeon, Eleanor
Tomkins, Jasper
    See Batey, Tom
Tomline, F. Latour
    See Gilbert, W(illiam) S(chwenck)
Tomlinson, Jill 1931-1976 .... *3*
    Obituary *24*
Tomlinson, Theresa 1946- *165*
    Earlier sketch in SATA *103*
    See also CLR *60*
Tompert, Ann 1918- *139*
    Earlier sketches in SATA *14, 89*
Toner, Raymond John 1908-1986 .... *10*
Tong, Gary S. 1942- *66*
Took, Belladonna
    See Chapman, Vera (Ivy May)
Tooke, Louise Mathews 1950- *38*
Toonder, Martin
    See Groom, Arthur William
Toothaker, Roy Eugene 1928- *18*
Tooze, Ruth (Anderson) 1892-1972 .... *4*
Topek, Susan Remick 1955- *78*
Topping, Audrey R(onning) 1928- *14*
Tor, Regina
    See Shekerjian, Regina Tor
Torbert, Floyd James 1922- *22*
Torgersen, Don Arthur 1934- *55*
    Brief entry *41*
Torley, Luke
    See Blish, James (Benjamin)
Torres, Daniel 1958- *102*
Torres, John A. 1965- *163*
    Earlier sketch in SATA *94*
Torres, John Albert
    See Torres, John A.
Torres, Laura 1967- *146*
    Earlier sketch in SATA *87*
Torres, Leyla 1960- *155*
Torrie, Malcolm
    See Mitchell, Gladys (Maude Winifred)
Toten, Teresa 1955- *99*
Totham, Mary
    See Breinburg, Petronella
Touponce, William F. 1948- *114*
Tournier, Michel 1924- *23*

Tournier, Michel Edouard
    See Tournier, Michel
Towle, Wendy 1963- *79*
Towne, Mary
    See Spelman, Mary
Townsend, Brad W. 1962- *91*
Townsend, John Rowe 1922- *132*
    Autobiography Feature *132*
    Earlier sketches in SATA *4, 68*
    See also CLR *2*
    See also SAAS *2*
Townsend, Sue *93*
    Brief entry *48*
    Earlier sketch in SATA *55*
    See Townsend, Susan Lilian
Townsend, Thomas L. 1944- *59*
Townsend, Tom
    See Townsend, Thomas L.
Townson, Hazel *134*
Toye, William Eldred 1926- *8*
Traherne, Michael
    See Watkins-Pitchford, Denys James
Trahey, Jane 1923-2000 .... *36*
    Obituary *120*
Trapani, Iza 1954- *116*
    Earlier sketch in SATA *80*
Trapp, Maria Augusta von *16*
    See von Trapp, Maria Augusta
Travers, P(amela) L(yndon) 1899-1996 .... *100*
    Obituary *90*
    Earlier sketches in SATA *4, 54*
    See also CLR *93*
    See also SAAS *2*
Travis, Lucille *133*
    Earlier sketch in SATA *88*
Treadgold, Mary 1910- *49*
Trease, (Robert) Geoffrey 1909-1998 .... *60*
    Obituary *101*
    Earlier sketch in SATA *2*
    See also CLR *42*
    See also SAAS *6*
Treat, Lawrence 1903-1998 .... *59*
Tredez, Alain 1926- *17*
Tredez, Denise 1930- *50*
Treece, Henry 1912-1966 .... *2*
    See also CLR *2*
Tregarthen, Enys
    See Sloggett, Nellie
Tregaskis, Richard 1916-1973 .... *3*
    Obituary *26*
Treherne, Katie Thamer 1955- *76*
Trell, Max 1900-1996 .... *14*
    Obituary *108*
Tremain, Ruthven 1922- *17*
Trembath, Don 1963- *168*
    Earlier sketch in SATA *96*
Tremens, Del
    See MacDonald, Amy
Trent, Robbie 1894-1988 .... *26*
Trent, Timothy
    See Malmberg, Carl
Treseder, Terry Walton 1956- *68*
Tresilian, (Cecil) Stuart 1891-(?) *40*
Tresselt, Alvin 1916-2000 .... *7*
    See also CLR *30*
Trevino, Elizabeth B(orton) de 1904- *29*
    Earlier sketch in SATA *1*
    See also SAAS *5*
Trevor, Elleston 1920-1995 .... *28*
    See Hall, Adam
Trevor, Frances
    See Teasdale, Sara
Trevor, Glen
    See Hilton, James
Trevor, (Lucy) Meriol 1919-2000 .... *113*
    Obituary *122*
    Earlier sketch in SATA *10*
Trez, Alain
    See Tredez, Alain
Trez, Denise
    See Tredez, Denise

Trezise, Percy (James) 1923-
    See CLR *41*
Triggs, Tony D. 1946- *70*
Trimble, Marshall I(ra) 1939- *93*
Trimby, Elisa 1948- *47*
    Brief entry *40*
Tripp, Eleanor B(aldwin) 1936- *4*
Tripp, Janet 1942- *108*
Tripp, John
    See Moore, John Travers
Tripp, Nathaniel 1944- *101*
Tripp, Paul 1916-2002 .... *8*
    Obituary *139*
Tripp, Valerie 1951- *168*
    Earlier sketch in SATA *78*
Tripp, Wallace (Whitney) 1940- *31*
Trivelpiece, Laurel 1926- *56*
    Brief entry *46*
Trivett, Daphne Harwood 1940- *22*
Trivizas, Eugene 1946- *84*
Trnka, Jiri 1912-1969 .... *43*
    Brief entry *32*
Trollope, Anthony 1815-1882 .... *22*
Trost, Lucille W(ood) 1938- *149*
    Earlier sketch in SATA *12*
Trott, Betty 1933- *91*
Trotter, Grace V(iolet) 1900-1991 .... *10*
Trottier, Maxine 1950- *131*
Troughton, Joanna (Margaret) 1947- *37*
Trout, Kilgore
    See Farmer, Philip Jose
Trout, Richard E. *123*
Trudeau, Garretson Beekman
    See Trudeau, G.B.
Trudeau, Garry
    See Trudeau, G.B.
Trudeau, Garry B.
    See Trudeau, G.B.
Trudeau, G.B. 1948- *168*
    Earlier sketch in SATA *35*
    See Trudeau, Garry B.
Trueman, Terry 1947- *132*
Truesdell, Judy
    See Mecca, Judy Truesdell
Truesdell, Sue
    See Truesdell, Susan G.
Truesdell, Susan G. *108*
    Brief entry *45*
Trumbauer, Lisa (Trutkoff) 1963- *149*
Truss, Jan 1925- *35*
Tryon, Leslie *139*
Tubb, Jonathan N. 1951- *78*
Tubby, I. M.
    See Kraus, (Herman) Robert
Tucker, Caroline
    See Nolan, Jeannette Covert
Tudor, Tasha 1915- *160*
    Earlier sketches in SATA *20, 69*
    See also CLR *13*
Tuerk, Hanne 1951- *71*
Tulloch, Richard (George) 1949- *76*
Tulloch, Shirley *169*
Tully, John (Kimberley) 1923- *14*
Tumanov, Vladimir A. 1961- *138*
Tung, Angela 1972- *109*
Tunis, Edwin (Burdett) 1897-1973 .... *28*
    Obituary *24*
    Earlier sketch in SATA *1*
    See also CLR *2*
Tunis, John R(oberts) 1889-1975 .... *37*
    Brief entry *30*
Tunnell, Michael
    See Tunnell, Michael O('Grady)
Tunnell, Michael O('Grady) 1950- *157*
    Earlier sketch in SATA *103*
Tunnicliffe, C(harles) F(rederick) 1901-1979
    .... *62*
Turck, Mary C. 1950- *144*
Turk, Hanne
    See Tuerk, Hanne
Turk, Ruth 1917- *82*

Turkle, Brinton 1915- *79*
    Earlier sketch in SATA *2*
Turlington, Bayly 1919-1977 .... *5*
    Obituary *52*
Turnbull, Agnes Sligh 1888-1982 .... *14*
Turnbull, Ann (Christine) 1943- *160*
    Earlier sketch in SATA *18*
Turner, Alice K. 1940- *10*
Turner, Ann W(arren) 1945- *113*
    Earlier sketches in SATA *14, 77*
Turner, Bonnie 1932- *75*
Turner, Elizabeth 1774-1846
    See YABC 2
Turner, Glennette Tilley 1933- *71*
Turner, Josie
    See Crawford, Phyllis
Turner, Megan Whalen 1965- *94*
Turner, Philip (William) 1925- *83*
    Earlier sketch in SATA *11*
    See also CLR 89
    See also SAAS 6
Turner, Robyn 1947- *77*
Turngren, Ellen (?)-1964 .... *3*
Turska, Krystyna (Zofia) 1933- *31*
    Brief entry *27*
Turteltaub, H.N.
    See Turtledove, Harry
Turtledove, Harry 1949- *166*
    Earlier sketch in SATA *116*
Turtledove, Harry Norman
    See Turtledove, Harry
Tusa, Tricia 1960- *111*
    Earlier sketch in SATA *72*
Tusiani, Joseph 1924- *45*
Twain, Mark
    See CLR 66
    See Clemens, Samuel Langhorne
Tweit, Susan J(oan) 1956- *94*
Tweton, D. Jerome 1933- *48*
Twinem, Neecy 1958- *92*
Tworkov, Jack 1900-1982 .... *47*
    Obituary *31*
Tyers, Jenny 1969- *89*
Tyers, Kathy 1952- *82*
Tyler, Anne 1941- *90*
    Earlier sketch in SATA *7*
Tyler, Linda
    See Tyler, Linda W(agner)
Tyler, Linda W(agner) 1952- *65*
Tyler, Vicki 1952- *64*
Tyne, Joel
    See Schembri, Jim
Tyrrell, Frances 1959- *107*

U

Ubell, Earl 1926- *4*
Uchida, Yoshiko 1921-1992 .... *53*
    Obituary *72*
    Earlier sketch in SATA *1*
    See also CLR 56
    See also SAAS 1
Udall, Jan Beaney 1938- *10*
Uden, (Bernard Gilbert) Grant 1910- *26*
Uderzo, Albert 1927-
    See CLR 37
Udry, Janice May 1928- *152*
    Earlier sketch in SATA *4*
Uegaki, Chieri 1969- *153*
Ueno, Noriko
    See Nakae, Noriko
Uhlig, Susan 1955- *129*
Ulam, S(tanislaw) M(arcin) 1909-1984 .... *51*
Ullman, James Ramsey 1907-1971 .... *7*
Ulm, Robert 1934-1977 .... *17*
Ulmer, Louise 1943- *53*
Ulyatt, Kenneth 1920- *14*
Umansky, Kaye 1946- *158*

Unada
    See Gliewe, Unada (Grace)
Uncle Carter
    See Boucher, (Clarence) Carter
Uncle Gus
    See Rey, H(ans) A(ugusto)
Uncle Ray
    See Coffman, Ramon Peyton
Uncle Shelby
    See Silverstein, Shel(don Allan)
Underhill, Alice Mertie (Waterman) 1900-1971
    .... *10*
Underhill, Liz 1948- *53*
    Brief entry *49*
Unger, Harlow G. 1931- *75*
Unger, Jim 1937- *67*
Ungerer, (Jean) Thomas 1931- *106*
    Earlier sketches in SATA *5, 33*
    See Ungerer, Tomi
Ungerer, Tomi 1931-
    See CLR 77
    See Ungerer, (Jean) Thomas
Unkelbach, Kurt 1913-1992 .... *4*
Unnerstad, Edith (Totterman) 1900-1982 ...... *3*
    See also CLR 36
Unobagha, Uzo *139*
Unrau, Ruth 1922- *9*
Unstead, R(obert) J(ohn) 1915-1988 .... *12*
    Obituary *56*
Unsworth, Walt(er) 1928- *4*
Untermeyer, Bryna Ivens 1909-1985 .... *61*
Untermeyer, Louis 1885-1977 .... *37*
    Obituary *26*
    Earlier sketch in SATA *2*
Unwin, David S(torr) 1918- *14*
Unwin, Nora S(picer) 1907-1982 .... *3*
    Obituary *49*
Unzner, Christa 1958- *141*
    Earlier sketch in SATA *80*
Unzner-Fischer, Christa
    See Unzner, Christa
Updyke, Rosemary K. 1924- *103*
Upitis, Alvis *109*
Urban, Helle (Denise) 1957- *149*
Ure, Jean 1943- *129*
    Earlier sketches in SATA *48, 78*
    See also CLR 34
    See also SAAS 14
U'Ren, Andrea 1968- *142*
Uris, Leon (Marcus) 1924-2003 .... *49*
    Obituary *146*
Ury, Allen B. 1954- *98*
Uschan, Michael V. 1948- *129*
Usher, Margo Scegge
    See McHargue, Georgess
Uslan, Michael E. 1951- *169*
Uston, Ken(neth Senzo) 1935-1987 .... *65*
Uttley, Alice Jane (Taylor) 1884-1976 .... *88*
    Obituary *26*
    Earlier sketch in SATA *3*
    See Uttley, Alison
Uttley, Alison
    See Uttley, Alice Jane (Taylor)
Utz, Lois (Marie) 1932-1986 .... *5*
    Obituary *50*

V

Vaeth, J(oseph) Gordon 1921- *17*
Vagin, Vladimir (Vasilevich) 1937- *142*
Vail, Rachel 1966- *163*
    Earlier sketch in SATA *94*
Vainio, Pirkko 1957- *123*
    Earlier sketch in SATA *76*
Valen, Nanine 1950- *21*
Valencak, Hannelore *42*
    See Mayer, Hannelore Valencak
Valens, Amy 1946- *70*
Valens, E(vans) G(ladstone), Jr. 1920-1992 .. *1*

Valentine, Johnny *72*
Valgardson, W(illiam) D(empsey) 1939- .. *151*
    Earlier sketch in SATA *101*
Valleau, Emily 1925- *51*
Van Abbe, Salaman 1883-1955 .... *18*
Van Allsburg, Chris 1949- *156*
    Earlier sketches in SATA *37, 53, 105*
    See also CLR 13
Van Anrooy, Francine 1924- *2*
Van Anrooy, Frans
    See Van Anrooy, Francine
Vance, Eleanor Graham 1908-1985 .... *11*
Vance, Gerald
    See Garrett, (Gordon) Randall (Phillip)
    and Silverberg, Robert
Vance, Marguerite 1889-1965 .... *29*
VanCleave, Janice 1942- *116*
    Autobiography Feature *123*
    Earlier sketch in SATA *75*
Vandenburg, Mary Lou 1943- *17*
Vander Boom, Mae M. *14*
Vander-Els, Betty 1936- *63*
van der Linde, Laurel 1952- *78*
van der Meer, Ron 1945- *98*
Van der Veer, Judy 1912-1982 .... *4*
    Obituary *33*
Vanderwerff, Corrine 1939- *117*
Vander Zee, Ruth *159*
Vande Velde, Vivian 1951- *141*
    Earlier sketches in SATA *62, 95*
Vandivert, Rita (Andre) 1905-1986 .... *21*
Van Draanen, Wendelin *122*
Van Duyn, Janet 1910- *18*
Van Dyne, Edith
    See Baum, L(yman) Frank
    and Sampson, Emma (Keats) Speed
    and van Zantwijk, Rudolf (Alexander
    Marinus)
van Frankenhuyzen, Gijsbert 1951- *132*
Van Genechten, Guido 1957- *165*
Van Hook, Beverly H. 1941- *99*
Van Horn, William 1939- *43*
Van Iterson, S(iny) R(ose) *26*
Van Kampen, Vlasta 1943- *163*
    Earlier sketch in SATA *54*
Van Laan, Nancy 1939- *105*
van Lawick-Goodall, Jane
    See Goodall, Jane
Van Leeuwen, Jean 1937- *141*
    Autobiography Feature *141*
    Earlier sketches in SATA *6, 82, 132*
    See also SAAS 8
van Lhin, Erik
    See del Rey, Lester
Van Loon, Hendrik Willem 1882-1944 .... *18*
Van Orden, M(erton) D(ick) 1921- *4*
Van Rensselaer, Alexander (Taylor Mason)
    1892-1962 .... *14*
Van Riper, Guernsey, Jr. 1909-1995 .... *3*
Van Rynbach, Iris 1952- *102*
Vansant, Rhonda Joy Edwards 1950- *92*
Van Steenwyk, Elizabeth (Ann) 1928- *89*
    Earlier sketch in SATA *34*
Van Stockum, Hilda 1908- *5*
Van Tuyl, Barbara 1940- *11*
van Vogt, A(lfred) E(lton) 1912-2000 .... *14*
    Obituary *124*
Van Woerkom, Dorothy (O'Brien) 1924-1996
    .... *21*
Van Wormer, Joe
    See Van Wormer, Joseph Edward
Van Wormer, Joseph Edward 1913-1998 .... *35*
Van Zwienen, Ilse Charlotte Koehn 1929-1991
    .... *34*
    Brief entry *28*
    Obituary *67*
Van Zyle, Jon 1942- *84*
Varga, Judy
    See Stang, Judit
Varley, Dimitry V. 1906-1984 .... *10*

Varley, Susan 1961- 134
  Earlier sketch in SATA 63
Vasileva, Tatiana
  See Wassiljewa, Tatjana
Vasiliev, Valery 1949- 80
Vasilieva, Tatiana
  See Wassiljewa, Tatjana
Vasiliu, Mircea 1920- 2
Vass, George 1927- 57
  Brief entry 31
Vaughan, Carter A.
  See Gerson, Noel Bertram
Vaughan, Harold Cecil 1923- 14
Vaughan, Marcia (K.) 1951- 159
  Earlier sketches in SATA 60, 95
Vaughan, Richard 1947- 87
Vaughan, Sam(uel) 1928- 14
Vaughn, Ruth 1935- 14
Vautier, Ghislaine 1932- 53
Vavra, Robert James 1935- 8
Vecsey, George Spencer 1939- 9
Vedral, Joyce L(auretta) 1943- 65
Veglahn, Nancy (Crary) 1937- 5
Velasquez, Gloria (Louise) 1949- 113
  See Velasquez(-Trevino), Gloria (Louise)
Velthuijs, Max 1923-2005 110
  Obituary 160
  Earlier sketch in SATA 53
Venable, Alan (Hudson) 1944- 8
Venezia, Mike 1945- 150
Ventura, Anthony
  See Pellowski, Michael (Joseph)
Ventura, Piero (Luigi) 1937- 61
  Brief entry 43
  See also CLR 16
Vequin, Capini
  See Quinn, Elisabeth
Verba, Joan Marie 1953- 78
Verboven, Agnes 1951- 103
verDorn, Bethea (Stewart) 1952- 76
Verissimo, Erico (Lopes) 1905-1975 113
Verne, Jules (Gabriel) 1828-1905 21
  See also CLR 88
Verney, John 1913-1993 14
  Obituary 75
Vernon, (Elda) Louise A(nderson) 1914- 14
Vernon, Rosemary
  See Smith, Susan Vernon
Vernor, D.
  See Casewit, Curtis W(erner)
Verr, Harry Coe
  See Kunhardt, Edith
Verral, Charles Spain 1904-1990 11
  Obituary 65
Versace, Marie Teresa Rios 1917- 2
Vertreace, Martha M(odena) 1945- 78
Vesey, A(manda) 1939- 62
Vesey, Mark (David) 1958- 123
Vesey, Paul
  See Allen, Samuel W(ashington)
Vestly, Anne-Cath(arina) 1920- 14
  See also CLR 99
Vevers, (Henry) Gwynne 1916-1988 45
  Obituary 57
Viator, Vacuus
  See Hughes, Thomas
Vicar, Henry
  See Felsen, Henry Gregor
Vick, Helen Hughes 1950- 88
Vicker, Angus
  See Felsen, Henry Gregor
Vickers, Sheena 1960- 94
Vickery, Kate
  See Kennedy, T(eresa) A.
Victor, Edward 1914- 3
Victor, Joan Berg 1942- 30
Vidrine, Beverly Barras 1938- 103
Viereck, Ellen K. 1928- 14
Viereck, Phillip 1925- 3
Viertel, Janet 1915- 10

Vigliante, Mary
  See Szydlowski, Mary Vigliante
Vigna, Judith 1936- 102
  Earlier sketch in SATA 15
Viguers, Ruth Hill 1903-1971 6
Villiard, Paul 1910-1974 51
  Obituary 20
Villiers, Alan (John) 1903-1982 10
Vilott, Rhondi
  See Salsitz, Rhondi Vilott
Vincent, Eric Douglas 1953- 40
Vincent, Felix 1946- 41
Vincent, Gabrielle 1928-2000 121
  Earlier sketch in SATA 61
  See also CLR 13
Vincent, Mary Keith
  See St. John, Wylly Folk
Vincent, William R.
  See Heitzmann, William Ray
Vinegar, Tom
  See Gregg, Andrew K.
Vinest, Shaw
  See Longyear, Barry B(rookes)
Vinge, Joan (Carol) D(ennison) 1948- 113
  Earlier sketch in SATA 36
Vining, Elizabeth Gray 1902-1999 6
  Obituary 117
  See Gray, Elizabeth Janet
Vinson, Kathryn 1911-1995 21
Vinton, Iris 1906(?)-1988 24
  Obituary 55
Viola, Herman J(oseph) 1938- 126
Viorst, Judith 1931- 123
  Earlier sketches in SATA 7, 70
  See also CLR 90
Vip
  See Partch, Virgil Franklin II
Vipont, Charles
  See Foulds, Elfrida Vipont
Vipont, Elfrida
  See Foulds, Elfrida Vipont
Viscott, David S(teven) 1938-1996 65
Visser, W(illem) F(rederik) H(endrik)
  1900-1968 10
Vitale, Stefano 1958- 114
Vivas, Julie 1947- 96
Vivelo, Jackie 1943- 63
Vivelo, Jacqueline J.
  See Vivelo, Jackie
Vivelo, Jacqueline Jean
  See Vivelo, Jackie
Vizzini, Ned 1981- 125
Vlahos, Olivia 1924- 31
Vlasic, Bob
  See Hirsch, Phil
Voake, Charlotte 114
Vo-Dinh, Mai 1933- 16
Vogel, Carole Garbuny 1951- 105
  Earlier sketch in SATA 70
Vogel, Ilse-Margret 1918- 14
Vogel, John H., Jr. 1950- 18
Vogt, Esther Loewen 1915-1999 14
Vogt, Gregory L. 94
Vogt, Marie Bollinger 1921- 45
Voight, Virginia Frances 1909-1989 8
Voigt, Cynthia 1942- 160
  Brief entry 33
  Earlier sketches in SATA 48, 79, 116
  See also CLR 48
Voigt, Erna 1925- 35
Voigt-Rother, Erna
  See Voigt, Erna
Vojtech, Anna 1946- 108
  Earlier sketch in SATA 42
Vollstadt, Elizabeth Weiss 1942- 121
Von Ahnen, Katherine 1922- 93
Vondra, Josef (Gert) 1941- 121
Von Gunden, Kenneth 1946- 113
Von Hagen, Victor Wolfgang 1908-1985 29
von Klopp, Vahrah
  See Malvern, Gladys

von Schmidt, Eric 1931- 50
  Brief entry 36
von Storch, Anne B. 1910- 1
von Ziegesar, Cecily 1970- 161
Vos, Ida 1931- 121
  Earlier sketch in SATA 69
  See also CLR 85
Vosburgh, Leonard (W.) 1912- 15
Voyle, Mary
  See Manning, Rosemary (Joy)
Vriens, Jacques 1946- 151
Vugteveen, Verna Aardema 107
  Obituary 119
  Earlier sketches in SATA 4, 68
  See also CLR 17
  See also SAAS 8
  See Aardema, Verna
Vulture, Elizabeth T.
  See Gilbert, Suzie
Vuong, Lynette Dyer 1938- 110
  Earlier sketch in SATA 60

W

Waas, Uli
  See Waas-Pommer, Ulrike
Waas-Pommer, Ulrike 1949- 85
Waber, Bernard 1924- 155
  Brief entry 40
  Earlier sketches in SATA 47, 95
  See also CLR 55
Wachtel, Shirley Russak 1951- 88
Wachter, Oralee (Roberts) 1935- 61
  Brief entry 51
Waddell, Evelyn Margaret 1918- 10
Waddell, Martin 1941- 129
  Autobiography Feature 129
  Earlier sketches in SATA 43, 81, 127
  See also CLR 31
  See also SAAS 15
Waddy, Lawrence (Heber) 1914- 91
Wade, Mary Dodson 1930- 151
  Earlier sketch in SATA 79
Wade, Theodore E., Jr. 1936- 37
Wademan, Peter John 1946- 122
Wademan, Spike
  See Wademan, Peter John
Wadsworth, Ginger 1945- 157
  Earlier sketch in SATA 103
Wagenheim, Kal 1935- 21
Wagner, Michele R. 1975- 157
Wagner, Sharon B. 1936- 4
Wagoner, David (Russell) 1926- 14
Wahl, Jan (Boyer) 1933- 132
  Earlier sketches in SATA 2, 34, 73
  See also SAAS 3
Waide, Jan 1952- 29
Wainscott, John Milton 1910-1981 53
Wainwright, Richard M. 1935- 91
Wait, Lea 1946- 137
Waite, Michael P(hillip) 1960- 101
Waite, P(eter) B(usby) 1922- 64
Waitley, Douglas 1927- 30
Wakefield, Jean L.
  See Laird, Jean E(louise)
Wakin, Daniel (Joseph) 1961- 84
Wakin, Edward 1927- 37
Walden, Amelia Elizabeth 3
Waldherr, Kris 1963- 76
Waldman, Bruce 1949- 15
Waldman, Neil 1947- 142
  Earlier sketches in SATA 51, 94
Waldron, Ann Wood 1924- 16
Walgren, Judy 1963- 118
Walker, Addison
  See Walker, (Addison) Mort
Walker, Alice (Malsenior) 1944- 31
Walker, Barbara (Jeanne) K(erlin) 1921- 80
  Earlier sketch in SATA 4

Walker, Barbara M(uhs) 1928- 57
Walker, (James) Braz(elton) 1934-1983 45
Walker, David G(ordon) 1926- 60
Walker, David Harry 1911-1992 8
   Obituary 71
Walker, Diana 1925- 9
Walker, Dick
   See Pellowski, Michael (Joseph)
Walker, Frank 1931-2000 36
Walker, Holly Beth
   See Bond, Gladys Baker
Walker, Kate 1950- 165
   Earlier sketch in SATA 82
   See Walker, Diane Marie Catherine
Walker, Kathrine Sorley
   See Sorley Walker, Kathrine
Walker, Lou Ann 1952- 66
   Brief entry 53
Walker, Mary Alexander 1927- 61
Walker, Mildred
   See Schemm, Mildred Walker
Walker, (Addison) Mort 1923- 8
Walker, Pamela 1948- 142
   Earlier sketch in SATA 24
Walker, Paul Robert 1953- 154
Walker, Robert W(ayne) 1948- 66
Walker, Sally M(acart) 1954- 135
Walker, Stephen J. 1951- 12
Walker-Blondell, Becky 1951- 89
Wallace, Barbara Brooks 1922- 136
   Earlier sketches in SATA 4, 78
   See also SAAS 17
Wallace, Beverly Dobrin 1921- 19
Wallace, Bill 1947- 169
   Brief entry 47
   Earlier sketches in SATA 53, 101
Wallace, Daisy
   See Cuyler, Margery S(tuyvesant)
Wallace, Ian 1950- 141
   Earlier sketches in SATA 53, 56
   See also CLR 37
Wallace, John 1966- 155
   Earlier sketch in SATA 105
Wallace, John A(dam) 1915-2004 3
   Obituary 155
Wallace, Karen 1951- 139
   Earlier sketch in SATA 83
Wallace, Nancy Elizabeth 1948- 141
Wallace, Nigel
   See Hamilton, Charles (Harold St. John)
Wallace, Paula S. 153
Wallace, Rich 1957- 158
   Earlier sketch in SATA 117
Wallace, Robert 1932-1999 47
   Brief entry 37
Wallace, William Keith
   See Wallace, Bill
Wallace-Brodeur, Ruth 1941- 169
   Brief entry 41
   Earlier sketches in SATA 51, 88
Wallenta, Adam 1974- 123
Waller, Leslie 1923- 20
Walley, Byron
   See Card, Orson Scott
Wallis, Diz 1949- 77
Wallis, G. McDonald
   See Campbell, Hope
Wallner, Alexandra 1946- 156
   Brief entry 41
   Earlier sketches in SATA 51, 98
Wallner, John C. 1945- 133
   Earlier sketches in SATA 10, 51
Wallower, Lucille 11
Walsh, Ann 1942- 62
Walsh, Ellen Stoll 1942- 147
   Earlier sketches in SATA 49, 99
Walsh, George Johnston 1889-1981 53
Walsh, Gillian Paton
   See Paton Walsh, Gillian

Walsh, Jill Paton
   See CLR 65
   See Paton Walsh, Gillian
Walsh, Mary Caswell 1949- 118
Walsh, V. L.
   See Walsh, Vivian
Walsh, Vivian 1960- 120
Walsh Shepherd, Donna 1948- 78
Walter, Frances V. 1923- 71
Walter, Mildred Pitts 1922- 133
   Brief entry 45
   Earlier sketch in SATA 69
   See also CLR 61
   See also SAAS 12
Walter, Villiam Christian
   See Andersen, Hans Christian
Walter, Virginia 134
   See Walter, Virginia A.
Walters, Audrey 1929- 18
Walters, Celeste 1938- 126
Walters, Eric (Robert) 1957- 155
   Earlier sketch in SATA 99
Walters, Hugh
   See Hughes, Walter (Llewellyn)
Walther, Thomas A. 1950- 31
Walther, Tom
   See Walther, Thomas A.
Waltner, Elma 1912-1987 40
Waltner, Willard H. 1909- 40
Walton, Darwin McBeth 1926- 119
Walton, Fiona L. M. 1959- 89
Walton, Richard J. 1928- 4
Walton, Rick 1957- 151
   Earlier sketch in SATA 101
Waltrip, Lela (Kingston) 1904-1995 9
Waltrip, Mildred 1911- 37
Waltrip, Rufus (Charles) 1898-1988 9
Walworth, Nancy Zinsser 1917- 14
Wangerin, Walter, Jr. 1944- 98
   Brief entry 37
   Earlier sketch in SATA 45
Waniek, Marilyn Nelson 1946- 60
   See Nelson, Marilyn
Wannamaker, Bruce
   See Moncure, Jane Belk
Warbler, J. M.
   See Cocagnac, Augustin Maurice(-Jean)
Warburg, Sandol Stoddard 14
   See Stoddard, Sandol
Ward, E. D.
   See Gorey, Edward (St. John)
   and Lucas, E(dward) V(errall)
Ward, Ed
   See Stratemeyer, Edward L.
Ward, Helen 1962- 144
   Earlier sketch in SATA 72
Ward, Jennifer 1963- 146
Ward, John (Stanton) 1917- 42
Ward, Jonas
   See Ard, William (Thomas)
   and Cox, William R(obert)
   and Garfield, Brian (Francis Wynne)
Ward, Lynd (Kendall) 1905-1985 36
   Obituary 42
   Earlier sketch in SATA 2
Ward, Martha (Eads) 5
Ward, Melanie
   See Curtis, Richard (Alan)
   and Lynch, Marilyn
Ward, Tom
   See Stratemeyer, Edward L.
Wardell, Dean
   See Prince, J(ack) H(arvey)
Wardlaw, Lee 1955- 115
   Earlier sketch in SATA 79
Ware, Cheryl 1963- 101
Ware, Chris 1967- 140
Ware, Leon (Vernon) 1909-1976 4
Wargin, Kathy-jo 1965- 145
Warner, Frank A. 67
   Earlier sketch in SATA 1

Warner, Gertrude Chandler 1890-1979 9
   Obituary 73
Warner, J(ohn) F. 1929- 75
Warner, Lucille Schulberg 30
Warner, Matt
   See Fichter, George S.
Warner, Oliver (Martin Wilson) 1903-1976
   29
Warner, Sally 1946- 131
Warner, Sunny (B.) 1931- 108
Warnes, Tim 1971- 166
   Earlier sketch in SATA 116
Warnes, Timothy
   See Warnes, Tim
Warnick, Elsa 1942- 113
Warren, Andrea 1946- 98
Warren, Betsy
   See Warren, Elizabeth Avery
Warren, Billy
   See Warren, William Stephen
Warren, Cathy 1951- 62
   Brief entry 46
Warren, Elizabeth
   See Supraner, Robyn
Warren, Elizabeth Avery 1916- 46
   Brief entry 38
Warren, Jackie M. 1953- 135
Warren, Joshua P(aul) 1976- 107
Warren, Joyce W(illiams) 1935- 18
Warren, Mary Phraner 1929- 10
Warren, Robert Penn 1905-1989 46
   Obituary 63
Warren, Scott S. 1957- 79
Warren, William Stephen 1882-1968 9
Warrick, Patricia Scott 1925- 35
Warsh
   See Warshaw, Jerry
Warshaw, Jerry 1929- 30
Warshaw, Mary 1931- 89
Warshofsky, Fred 1931- 24
Warshofsky, Isaac
   See Singer, Isaac Bashevis
Wartski, Maureen (Ann Crane) 1940- 50
   Brief entry 37
Warwick, Alan R(oss) 1900-1973 42
Wa-sha-quon-asin
   See Belaney, Archibald Stansfeld
Wa-Sha-Quon-Asin
   See Belaney, Archibald Stansfeld
Washburn, (Henry) Bradford (Jr.) 1910- 38
Washburn, Jan(ice) 1926- 63
Washburne, Carolyn Kott 1944- 86
Washburne, Heluiz Chandler 1892-1970 10
   Obituary 26
Washington, Booker T(aliaferro) 1856-1915
   28
Washington, Donna L. 1967- 159
   Earlier sketch in SATA 98
Wasserstein, Wendy 1950-2006 94
Wassiljewa, Tatjana 1928- 106
Watanabe, Shigeo 1928- 131
   Brief entry 32
   Earlier sketch in SATA 39
   See also CLR 8
Waters, John F(rederick) 1930- 4
Waters, Tony 1958- 75
Waterton, Betty (Marie) 1923- 99
   Brief entry 34
   Earlier sketch in SATA 37
Watkins, Dawn L. 126
Watkins, Gloria Jean 1952(?)- 115
Watkins, Lois 1930- 88
Watkins, Peter 1934- 66
Watkins, Yoko Kawashima 1933- 93
Watkins-Pitchford, Denys James 1905-1990
   87
   Obituary 66
   Earlier sketch in SATA 6
   See also SAAS 4
Watling, James 1933- 117
   Earlier sketch in SATA 67

Watson, Aldren A(uld) 1917- *42*
  Brief entry *36*
Watson, Amy Zakrzewski 1965- *76*
Watson, B. S.
  See Teitelbaum, Michael
Watson, Carol 1949- *78*
Watson, Clyde 1947- *68*
  Earlier sketch in SATA *5*
  See also CLR *3*
Watson, James 1936- *106*
  Earlier sketch in SATA *10*
Watson, Jane Werner 1915- *54*
  Earlier sketch in SATA *3*
Watson, John H.
  See Farmer, Philip Jose
Watson, Mary 1953- *117*
Watson, N. Cameron 1955- *81*
Watson, Nancy Dingman *32*
Watson, Pauline 1925- *14*
Watson, Richard F.
  See Silverberg, Robert
Watson, Richard Jesse 1951- *62*
Watson, Sally (Lou) 1924- *3*
Watson, Wendy (McLeod) 1942- *142*
  Earlier sketches in SATA *5, 74*
Watson Taylor, Elizabeth 1915- *41*
Watt, Melanie 1975- *136*
Watt, Thomas 1935- *4*
Watterson, Bill 1958- *66*
Watt-Evans, Lawrence 1954- *121*
  See Evans, Lawrence Watt
Watts, (Anna) Bernadette 1942- *103*
  Earlier sketch in SATA *4*
Watts, Ephraim
  See Horne, Richard Henry Hengist
Watts, Franklin (Mowry) 1904-1978 .... *46*
  Obituary *21*
Watts, Irene N(aemi) 1931- *111*
  Earlier sketch in SATA *56*
Watts, Isaac 1674-1748 .... *52*
Watts, James K(ennedy) M(offitt) 1955- *59*
Watts, Julia 1969- *103*
Watts, Leander 1956- *146*
Watts, Leslie Elizabeth 1961- *168*
Watts, Mabel Pizzey 1906-1994 .... *11*
Watts, Nigel 1957-1999 .... *121*
Waugh, C. C. Roessel
  See Waugh, Carol-Lynn Rossel
  and Waugh, Charles G(ordon)
Waugh, Carol-Lynn Rossel 1947- *41*
Waugh, Dorothy -1996 .... *11*
Waugh, Sylvia 1935- *169*
Waugh, Virginia
  See Sorensen, Virginia
Wax, Wendy A. 1963- *163*
  Earlier sketch in SATA *73*
Wayland, April Halprin 1954- *143*
  Earlier sketch in SATA *78*
  See also SAAS *26*
Wayne, (Anne) Jenifer 1917-1982 .... *32*
Wayne, Kyra Petrovskaya 1918- *8*
Wayne, Richard
  See Decker, Duane
Wayshak, Deborah Noyes 1965- *145*
Waystaff, Simon
  See Swift, Jonathan
Weales, Gerald (Clifford) 1925- *11*
Weary, Ogdred
  See Gorey, Edward (St. John)
Weatherford, Carole Boston 1956- *138*
Weatherly, Myra (S.) 1926- *130*
Weaver, Harriett E. 1908-1993 .... *65*
Weaver, John L. 1949- *42*
Weaver, Robyn
  See Conley-Weaver, Robyn
Weaver, Robyn M.
  See Conley-Weaver, Robyn
Weaver, Ward
  See Mason, F(rancis) van Wyck
Weaver, Will 1950- *161*
  Earlier sketches in SATA *88, 109*

Weaver, William Weller
  See Weaver, Will
Weaver-Gelzer, Charlotte 1950- *79*
Webb, Christopher
  See Wibberley, Leonard (Patrick O'Connor)
Webb, Jacqueline
  See Pearce, Margaret
Webb, Jacquelyn
  See Pearce, Margaret
  and Pearce, Margaret
Webb, Jean Francis (III) 1910-1991 .... *35*
Webb, Kaye 1914- *60*
Webb, Lois Sinaiko 1922- *82*
Webb, Margot 1934- *67*
Webb, Sharon 1936- *41*
Webb, Sophie 1958- *135*
Webber, Andrew Lloyd
  See Lloyd Webber, Andrew
Webber, Irma E(leanor Schmidt) 1904-1995
  .... *14*
Weber, Alfons 1921- *8*
Weber, Bruce 1942- *120*
  Earlier sketch in SATA *73*
Weber, Debora 1955- *58*
Weber, EdNah New Rider 1919(?)- *168*
Weber, Jill 1950- *127*
Weber, Judith E(ichler) 1938- *64*
Weber, Ken(neth J.) 1940- *90*
Weber, Lenora Mattingly 1895-1971 .... *2*
  Obituary *26*
Weber, Michael 1945- *87*
Weber, Sandra 1961- *158*
Weber, William J(ohn) 1927- *14*
Webster, Alice Jane Chandler 1876-1916 ... *17*
Webster, David 1930- *11*
Webster, Frank V. *67*
  Earlier sketch in SATA *1*
Webster, Gary
  See Garrison, Webb B(lack)
Webster, James 1925-1981 .... *17*
  Obituary *27*
Webster, Jean
  See Webster, Alice Jane Chandler
Wechter, Nell (Carolyn) Wise 1913-1989 . *127*
  Earlier sketch in SATA *60*
Weck, Thomas L. 1942- *62*
Wedd, Kate
  See Gregory, Philippa
Weddle, Ethel Harshbarger 1897-1996 .... *11*
Weeks, Sarah *158*
Weems, David B(urnola) 1922- *80*
Wees, Frances Shelley 1902-1982 .... *58*
Weevers, Peter 1944- *59*
Wegen, Ronald 1946-1985 .... *99*
Wegman, William (George) 1943- *135*
  Earlier sketches in SATA *78, 129*
Wegner, Fritz 1924- *20*
Weidhorn, Manfred 1931- *60*
Weidt, Maryann N. 1944- *85*
Weigelt, Udo 1960- *168*
Weihs, Erika 1917- *107*
  Earlier sketch in SATA *15*
Weik, Mary Hays 1898(?)-1979 .... *3*
  Obituary *23*
Weil, Ann Yezner 1908-1969 .... *9*
Weil, Lisl 1910- *7*
Weilerstein, Sadie Rose 1894-1993 .... *3*
  Obituary *75*
Weill, Cynthia 1959- *167*
Wein, Elizabeth E(ve) 1964- *151*
  Earlier sketch in SATA *82*
Weinberg, Larry
  See Weinberg, Lawrence (E.)
Weinberg, Lawrence (E.) *92*
  Brief entry *48*
Weinberger, Tanya 1939- *84*
Weiner, Sandra 1922- *14*
Weingarten, Violet (Brown) 1915-1976 .... *3*
  Obituary *27*
Weingartner, Charles 1922- *5*
Weinstein, Nina 1951- *73*

Weir, Bob 1947- *76*
Weir, Diana (R.) Loiewski 1958- *111*
Weir, Joan S(herman) 1928- *99*
Weir, LaVada *2*
Weir, Rosemary (Green) 1905-1994 .... *21*
Weir, Wendy 1949- *76*
Weis, Margaret Edith 1948- *164*
  Earlier sketches in SATA *38, 92*
Weisberger, Bernard A(llen) 1922- *21*
Weiser, Marjorie P(hillis) K(atz) 1934- *33*
Weisgard, Leonard (Joseph) 1916-2000 ...... *85*
  Obituary *122*
  Earlier sketches in SATA *2, 30*
  See also SAAS *19*
Weiss, Adelle 1920- *18*
Weiss, Ann E(dwards) 1943- *69*
  Earlier sketch in SATA *30*
  See also SAAS *13*
Weiss, Edna
  See Barth, Edna
Weiss, Ellen 1953- *44*
Weiss, Harvey 1922- *76*
  Earlier sketches in SATA *1, 27*
  See also CLR *4*
  See also SAAS *19*
Weiss, Jaqueline Shachter 1926- *65*
Weiss, Malcolm E. 1928- *3*
Weiss, Miriam
  See Schlein, Miriam
Weiss, Mitch 1951- *123*
Weiss, Nicki 1954- *86*
  Earlier sketch in SATA *33*
Weiss, Renee Karol 1923- *5*
Weitzman, David L. 1936- *122*
Wekesser, Carol A. 1963- *76*
Welber, Robert *26*
Welch, Amanda (Jane) 1945- *75*
Welch, Jean-Louise
  See Kempton, Jean Welch
Welch, Pauline
  See Bodenham, Hilda Morris
Welch, Ronald
  See Felton, Ronald Oliver
Welch, Sheila Kelly 1945- *130*
Welch, Willy 1952- *93*
Welford, Sue 1942- *75*
Weller, George (Anthony) 1907-2002 .... *31*
  Obituary *140*
Welling, Peter J. 1947- *135*
Wellington, Monica 1957- *157*
  Earlier sketches in SATA *67, 99*
Wellman, Alice 1900-1984 .... *51*
  Brief entry *36*
Wellman, Manly Wade 1903-1986 .... *6*
  Obituary *47*
Wellman, Paul I(selin) 1898-1966 .... *3*
Wellman, Sam(uel) 1939- *122*
Wells, H(erbert) G(eorge) 1866-1946 .... *20*
  See also CLR *64*
Wells, Helen
  See Campbell, Hope
Wells, Helen 1910-1986 .... *49*
  Earlier sketch in SATA *2*
Wells, J. Wellington
  See de Camp, L(yon) Sprague
Wells, June
  See Swinford, Betty (June Wells)
Wells, Robert
  See Welsch, Roger L(ee)
Wells, Rosemary 1943- *156*
  Earlier sketches in SATA *18, 69, 114*
  See also CLR *69*
  See also SAAS *1*
Wells, Susan (Mary) 1951- *78*
Wels, Byron G(erald) 1924-1993 .... *9*
Welsbacher, Anne 1955- *89*
Welsch, Roger L(ee) 1936- *82*
Welsh, David
  See Hills, C(harles) A(lbert) R(eis)
Weltner, Linda R(iverly) 1938- *38*

Welton, Jude 1955- *143*
  Earlier sketch in SATA 79
Welty, S. F.
  See Welty, Susan F.
Welty, Susan F. 1905- *9*
Wendelin, Rudolph 1910-2000 .... *23*
Wentworth, Robert
  See Hamilton, Edmond
Werlin, Nancy 1961- *161*
  Earlier sketches in SATA 87, 119
Werner, Elsa Jane
  See Watson, Jane Werner
Werner, Herma 1926- *47*
  Brief entry *41*
Werner, Jane
  See Watson, Jane Werner
Werner, K.
  See Casewit, Curtis W(erner)
Wersba, Barbara 1932- *58*
  Autobiography Feature *103*
  Earlier sketch in SATA 1
  See also CLR 78
  See also SAAS 2
Werstein, Irving 1914(?)-1971 .... *14*
Werth, Kurt 1896-1983 .... *20*
Wesley, Alison
  See Barnes, Michael
Wesley, Mary (Aline) 1912-2002 .... *66*
Wesley, Valerie Wilson 1947- *168*
  Earlier sketch in SATA 106
West, Andrew
  See Arthur, Robert, (Jr.)
West, Anna 1938- *40*
West, Barbara
  See Price, Olive
West, Betty 1921- *11*
West, Bruce 1951- *63*
West, C. P.
  See Wodehouse, P(elham) G(renville)
West, Dorothy
  See Benson, Mildred (Augustine Wirt)
West, Emily Govan 1919- *38*
West, Emmy
  See West, Emily Govan
West, James
  See Withers, Carl A.
West, Jerry
  See Svenson, Andrew E(dward)
West, John
  See Arthur, Robert, (Jr.)
West, Owen
  See Koontz, Dean R.
Westall, Robert (Atkinson) 1929-1993 .... *69*
  Obituary *75*
  Earlier sketch in SATA 23
  See also CLR 13
  See also SAAS 2
Westaway, Jane 1948- *121*
Westcott, Nadine Bernard 1949- *130*
Westerberg, Christine 1950- *29*
Westerduin, Anne 1945- *105*
Westerfeld, Scott *161*
Westervelt, Virginia Veeder 1914- *10*
Westheimer, David 1917-2005 .... *14*
Westheimer, David Kaplan
  See Westheimer, David
Westmacott, Mary
  See Christie, Agatha (Mary Clarissa)
Westman, Barbara *70*
Westman, Paul (Wendell) 1956- *39*
Westmoreland, William C. 1914-2005 .... *63*
Westmoreland, William Childs
  See Westmoreland, William C.
Weston, Allen
  See Hogarth, Grace (Weston Allen)
  and Norton, Andre
Weston, Carol 1956- *135*
Weston, John (Harrison) 1932- *21*
Weston, Martha 1947- *119*
  Earlier sketch in SATA 53
Westphal, Arnold Carl 1897- *57*

Westrup, Hugh *102*
Westwood, Jennifer 1940- *10*
Wexler, Jerome (LeRoy) 1923- *14*
Weyland, Jack 1940- *81*
Weyn, Suzanne 1955- *164*
  Earlier sketches in SATA 63, 101
Weyr, Garret
  See Freymann-Weyr, (Rhoda) Garret
  (Michaela)
Wezyk, Joanna 1966- *82*
Whaley, Joyce Irene 1923- *61*
Whalin, W. Terry 1953- *93*
Whalin, W. Terry 1953- *93*
Wharf, Michael
  See Weller, George (Anthony)
Wharmby, Margot *63*
Wheatley, Arabelle 1921- *16*
Wheatley, Nadia 1949- *147*
Wheeler, Cindy 1955- *49*
  Brief entry *40*
Wheeler, Deborah (Jean Ross) 1947- *83*
Wheeler, Janet D. *1*
Wheeler, Jill C. 1964- *136*
  Earlier sketch in SATA 86
Wheeler, Jody 1952- *148*
  Earlier sketch in SATA 84
Wheeler, Lisa 1963- *162*
Wheeler, Opal 1898- *23*
Whelan, Elizabeth M(urphy) 1943- *14*
Whelan, Gloria 1923- *128*
  Earlier sketch in SATA 85
  See also CLR 90
Whelan, Gloria Ann
  See Whelan, Gloria
Whipple, A(ddison) B(eecher) C(olvin) 1918-
  .... *64*
Whipple, Cal
  See Whipple, A(ddison) B(eecher) C(olvin)
Whistler, Reginald John 1905-1944 .... *30*
Whistler, Rex
  See Whistler, Reginald John
Whitcher, Susan (Godsil) 1952- *96*
Whitcomb, Jon 1906-1988 .... *10*
  Obituary *56*
White, Anne Terry 1896-1980 .... *2*
White, Carolyn 1948- *130*
White, Dale
  See Place, Marian T(empleton)
White, Dori 1919- *10*
White, E(lwyn) B(rooks) 1899-1985 .... *100*
  Obituary *44*
  Earlier sketches in SATA 2, 29
  See also CLR 107
White, Eliza Orne 1856-1947
  See YABC 2
White, Florence M(eiman) 1910- *14*
White, Laurence B(arton), Jr. 1935- *10*
White, Martin 1943- *51*
White, Nancy 1942- *126*
White, Ramy Allison *67*
  Earlier sketch in SATA 1
White, Robb 1909-1990 .... *83*
  Earlier sketch in SATA 1
  See also CLR 3
  See also SAAS 1
White, Ruth C. 1942- *165*
  Earlier sketches in SATA 39, 117
White, T(erence) H(anbury) 1906-1964 ...... *12*
White, Tekla N. 1934- *115*
White, Timothy (Thomas Anthony) 1952-2002
  .... *60*
White, Tom 1923- *148*
White, William, Jr. 1934- *16*
Whitehead, Don(ald) F. 1908-1981 .... *4*
Whitehouse, Arch
  See Whitehouse, Arthur George Joseph
Whitehouse, Arthur George Joseph 1895-1979
  .... *14*
  Obituary *23*
Whitehouse, Elizabeth S(cott) 1893-1968 ... *35*

Whitehouse, Jeanne *29*
  See Peterson, Jeanne Whitehouse
Whitelaw, Nancy 1933- *166*
  Earlier sketch in SATA 76
Whitesel, Cheryl Aylward *162*
Whitinger, R. D.
  See Place, Marian T(empleton)
Whitley, Mary Ann
  See Sebrey, Mary Ann
Whitley, Peggy 1938- *140*
Whitlock, Ralph 1914-1995 .... *35*
Whitman, Alice
  See Marker, Sherry
Whitman, Sylvia (Choate) 1961- *135*
  Earlier sketch in SATA 85
Whitman, Walt(er) 1819-1892 .... *20*
Whitmore, Arvella 1922- *125*
Whitney, Alex(andra) 1922- *14*
Whitney, David C(harles) 1921- *48*
  Brief entry *29*
Whitney, Kim Ablon *162*
Whitney, Phyllis A(yame) 1903- *30*
  Earlier sketch in SATA 1
  See also CLR 59
Whitney, Sharon 1937- *63*
Whitney, Thomas P(orter) 1917- *25*
Whittington, Mary K(athrine) 1941- *75*
Whitworth, John 1945- *123*
Whybrow, Ian *132*
Whyte, Mal(colm Kenneth, Jr.) 1933- *62*
Whyte, Mary 1953- *148*
  Earlier sketch in SATA 94
Wiater, Stanley 1953- *84*
Wibbelsman, Charles J(oseph) 1945- *59*
Wibberley, Leonard (Patrick O'Connor)
  1915-1983 .... *45*
  Obituary *36*
  Earlier sketch in SATA 2
  See also CLR 3
  See Holton, Leonard
Wiberg, Harald (Albin) 1908- *93*
  Brief entry *40*
Wick, Walter 1953- *148*
Wickens, Elaine *86*
Wickstrom, Sylvie 1960- *169*
Widdemer, Mabel Cleland 1902-1964 .... *5*
Widener, Terry 1950- *105*
Widerberg, Siv 1931- *10*
Wiebe, Rudy (Henry) 1934- *156*
Wieler, Diana (Jean) 1961- *109*
Wiener, Lori 1956- *84*
Wier, Ester (Alberti) 1910-2000 .... *3*
Wiese, Kurt 1887-1974 .... *36*
  Obituary *24*
  Earlier sketch in SATA 3
  See also CLR 86
Wiesel, Elie 1928- *56*
Wiesel, Eliezer
  See Wiesel, Elie
Wiesner, David 1956- *139*
  Earlier sketches in SATA 72, 117
  See also CLR 84
Wiesner, Portia
  See Takakjian, Portia
Wiesner, William 1899-1984 .... *5*
Wiggers, Raymond 1952- *82*
Wiggin, Eric E. 1939- *167*
  Earlier sketch in SATA 88
Wiggin, Eric Ellsworth 1939-
  See Wiggin, Eric E.
Wiggin (Riggs), Kate Douglas (Smith)
  1856-1923
  See YABC 1
  See also CLR 52
Wiggins, VeraLee (Chesnut) 1928-1995 ..... *89*
Wight, James Alfred 1916-1995 .... *55*
  Brief entry *44*
  See Herriot, James
Wignell, Edel 1936- *69*
Wijnberg, Ellen *85*

Wikland, Ilon 1930- *93*
   Brief entry *32*
Wikler, Madeline 1943- *114*
Wilber, Donald N(ewton) 1907-1997 .... *35*
Wilbur, C. Keith 1923- *27*
Wilbur, Frances 1921- *107*
Wilbur, Richard (Purdy) 1921- *108*
   Earlier sketch in SATA *9*
Wilburn, Kathy 1948- *68*
Wilcox, Charlotte 1948- *72*
Wilcox, R(uth) Turner 1888-1970 .... *36*
Wilcox, Roger
   See Collins, Paul
Wild, Jocelyn 1941- *46*
Wild, Margaret 1948- *151*
Wild, Robin (Evans) 1936- *46*
Wild, Robyn 1947- *117*
Wilde, D. Gunther
   See Hurwood, Bernhardt J.
Wilde, Oscar (Fingal O'Flahertie Wills)
   1854(?)-1900 .... *24*
Wilder, Buck
   See Smith, Tim(othy R.)
Wilder, Laura (Elizabeth) Ingalls 1867-1957
   .... *100*
   Earlier sketches in SATA *15, 29*
   See also CLR *111*
Wildsmith, Brian 1930- *124*
   Earlier sketches in SATA *16, 69*
   See also CLR *52*
   See also SAAS *5*
Wilhelm, Hans 1945- *135*
   Earlier sketch in SATA *58*
   See also CLR *46*
   See also SAAS *21*
Wilkie, Katharine E(lliott) 1904-1980 .... *31*
Wilkin, Eloise 1904-1987 .... *49*
   Obituary *54*
Wilkins, Frances 1923- *14*
Wilkins, Kim *147*
Wilkins, Marilyn (Ruth) 1926- *30*
Wilkins, Marne
   See Wilkins, Marilyn (Ruth)
Wilkins, Mary Huiskamp 1926- *139*
   Earlier sketch in SATA *84*
   See Calhoun, Mary
Wilkins, Mary Huiskamp Calhoun
   See Wilkins, Mary Huiskamp
Wilkinson, (Thomas) Barry 1923- *50*
   Brief entry *32*
Wilkinson, Beth 1925- *80*
Wilkinson, Brenda 1946- *91*
   Earlier sketch in SATA *14*
   See also CLR *20*
Wilkinson, (John) Burke 1913-2000 .... *4*
Wilkinson, Sylvia 1940- *56*
   Brief entry *39*
Wilkon, Jozef 1930- *133*
   Earlier sketches in SATA *31, 71*
Wilks, Michael Thomas 1947- *44*
Wilks, Mike
   See Wilks, Michael Thomas
Will
   See Lipkind, William
Willard, Barbara (Mary) 1909-1994 .... *74*
   Earlier sketch in SATA *17*
   See also CLR *2*
   See also SAAS *5*
Willard, Mildred Wilds 1911-1978 .... *14*
Willard, Nancy 1936- *127*
   Brief entry *30*
   Earlier sketches in SATA *37, 71*
   See also CLR *5*
Willcox, Isobel 1907-1996 .... *42*
Willems, Mo *154*
Willett, Edward (C.) 1959- *115*
Willey, Margaret 1950- *86*
Willey, Robert
   See Ley, Willy
Willhoite, Michael A. 1946- *71*

William, Kate
   See Armstrong, Jennifer
Williams, Barbara 1925- *107*
   Earlier sketch in SATA *11*
   See also CLR *48*
   See also SAAS *16*
Williams, Barbara 1937- *62*
Williams, Beryl
   See Epstein, Beryl (M. Williams)
Williams, Brian (Peter) 1943- *54*
Williams, Carol Lynch 1959- *110*
Williams, Charles
   See Collier, James Lincoln
Williams, Clyde C. 1881-1974 .... *8*
   Obituary *27*
Williams, Coe
   See Harrison, C(hester) William
Williams, Colleen Madonna Flood 1963- . *156*
Williams, Cynthia G. 1958- *123*
Williams, Dar 1967- *168*
Williams, Donna Reilly 1945- *83*
Williams, (Marcia) Dorothy *71*
   See Williams, Marcia (Dorothy)
Williams, Dorothy
   See Williams, Marcia (Dorothy)
Williams, Dorothy Snowden
   See Williams, Dar
Williams, Eric (Ernest) 1911-1983 .... *14*
   Obituary *38*
Williams, Ferelith Eccles *22*
   See Eccles Williams, Ferelith
Williams, Frances B.
   See Browin, Frances Williams
Williams, Garth (Montgomery) 1912-1996 . *66*
   Obituary *90*
   Earlier sketch in SATA *18*
   See also CLR *57*
   See also SAAS *7*
Williams, Guy R(ichard) 1920- *11*
Williams, Hawley
   See Heyliger, William
Williams, Helen 1948- *77*
Williams, J. R.
   See Williams, Jeanne
Williams, J. Walker
   See Wodehouse, P(elham) G(renville)
Williams, Jay 1914-1978 .... *41*
   Obituary *24*
   Earlier sketch in SATA *3*
   See also CLR *8*
Williams, Jeanne 1930- *5*
Williams, Jenny 1939- *60*
Williams, Karen Lynn 1952- *99*
   Earlier sketch in SATA *66*
Williams, Kit 1946(?)- *44*
   See also CLR *4*
Williams, Leslie 1941- *42*
Williams, Linda 1948- *59*
Williams, Lynn
   See Hale, Arlene
Williams, Marcia (Dorothy) 1945- *159*
   Earlier sketch in SATA *97*
   See Williams, (Marcia) Dorothy
Williams, Margery
   See Bianco, Margery Williams
Williams, Mark
   See Arthur, Robert, (Jr.)
Williams, Mark London 1959- *140*
Williams, Maureen 1951- *12*
Williams, Michael
   See St. John, Wylly Folk
Williams, Patrick J.
   See Butterworth, W.E.
Williams, Pete
   See Faulknor, Cliff(ord Vernon)
Williams, S. P.
   See Hart, Virginia
Williams, Sam *124*
Williams, Selma R(uth) 1925- *14*
Williams, Sherley Anne 1944-1999 .... *78*
   Obituary *116*

Williams, Sheron 1955- *77*
Williams, Shirley
   See Williams, Sherley Anne
Williams, Slim
   See Williams, Clyde C.
Williams, Sophy 1965- *135*
Williams, Suzanne (Bullock) 1953- *71*
Williams, Ursula Moray *3*
   See Moray Williams, Ursula
Williams, Vera B(aker) 1927- *102*
   Brief entry *33*
   Earlier sketch in SATA *53*
   See also CLR *9*
Williams-Andriani, Renee 1963- *98*
Williams-Ellis, (Mary) Amabel (Nassau
   Strachey) 1894-1984 .... *29*
   Obituary *41*
Williams-Garcia, Rita 1957- *160*
   Earlier sketch in SATA *98*
   See also CLR *36*
Williamson, Gwyneth 1965- *109*
Williamson, Henry (William) 1895-1977 .... *37*
   Obituary *30*
Williamson, Joanne S(mall) 1926- *122*
   Earlier sketch in SATA *3*
Willis, Charles
   See Clarke, Arthur C(harles)
Willis, Connie 1945- *110*
   See also CLR *66*
Willis, Jeanne (Mary) 1959- *123*
   Earlier sketch in SATA *61*
Willis, Meredith Sue 1946- *101*
Willis, Nancy Carol 1952- *139*
   Earlier sketch in SATA *93*
Willis, Paul J. 1955- *113*
Willms, Russ *95*
Willoughby, Lee Davis
   See Avallone, Michael (Angelo, Jr.)
   and Brandner, Gary (Phil)
   and Deming, Richard
   and DeAndrea, William L(ouis)
   and Laymon, Richard (Carl)
   and Streib, Dan(iel Thomas)
   and Toombs, John
   and Webb, Jean Francis (III)
Willson, Robina Beckles *27*
   See Beckles Willson, Robina (Elizabeth)
Wilma, Dana
   See Faralla, Dana
Wilson, April *80*
Wilson, Barbara Ker
   See Ker Wilson, Barbara
Wilson, Beth P(ierre) *8*
Wilson, Budge 1927- *55*
   See Wilson, Marjorie
Wilson, Carletta 1951- *81*
Wilson, Carter 1941- *6*
Wilson, Charles Morrow 1905-1977 .... *30*
Wilson, Darryl B(abe) 1939- *90*
Wilson, Dirk
   See Pohl, Frederik
Wilson, Dorothy Clarke 1904- *16*
Wilson, Edward A(rthur) 1886-1970 .... *38*
Wilson, Ellen (Janet Cameron) (?)-1976 .... *9*
   Obituary *26*
Wilson, Eric (H.) 1940- *34*
   Brief entry *32*
Wilson, Erica *51*
Wilson, Forrest 1918- *27*
Wilson, Gahan 1930- *35*
   Brief entry *27*
Wilson, Gina 1943- *85*
   Brief entry *34*
   Earlier sketch in SATA *36*
Wilson, (Leslie) Granville 1912- *14*
Wilson, Hazel (Hutchins) 1898-1992 .... *3*
   Obituary *73*
Wilson, J(erry) M. 1964- *121*
Wilson, Jacqueline 1945- *153*
   Brief entry *52*
   Earlier sketches in SATA *61, 102*

Wilson, John 1922- 22
Wilson, Johnniece Marshall 1944- 75
Wilson, Joyce M(uriel Judson) 84
   Earlier sketch in SATA *21*
   See Stranger, Joyce
Wilson, Leslie 1952- *166*
Wilson, Linda Miller 1936- *116*
Wilson, Lionel 1924-2003 .... *33*
   Brief entry *31*
   Obituary *144*
Wilson, Marjorie
   Brief entry *51*
   See Wilson, Budge
Wilson, Maurice (Charles John) 1914- *46*
Wilson, Nancy Hope 1947- *138*
   Earlier sketch in SATA *81*
Wilson, Nick
   See Ellis, Edward S(ylvester)
Wilson, Ron(ald William) 1941- *38*
Wilson, Sarah 1934- *142*
   Earlier sketch in SATA *50*
Wilson, Tom 1931- 33
   Brief entry *30*
Wilson, Troy 1970- *169*
Wilson, Walt(er N.) 1939- 14
Wilson-Max, Ken 1965- 93
Wilton, Elizabeth 1937- 14
Wilwerding, Walter Joseph 1891-1966 9
Wimmer, Mike 1961- 70
Winborn, Marsha (Lynn) 1947- 75
Winch, John 1944- *165*
   Earlier sketch in SATA *117*
Winchester, James H(ugh) 1917-1985 30
   Obituary 45
Winchester, Stanley
   See Youd, (Christopher) Samuel
Windawi, Thura al- 1983(?)- *165*
Winders, Gertrude Hecker -1987 3
Windham, Basil
   See Wodehouse, P(elham) G(renville)
Windham, Kathryn T(ucker) 1918- 14
Windling, Terri 1958- *151*
Windrow, Martin
   See Windrow, Martin Clive
Windrow, Martin C.
   See Windrow, Martin Clive
Windrow, Martin Clive 1944- 68
Windsor, Claire
   See Hamerstrom, Frances
Windsor, Linda 1950- *124*
Windsor, Patricia 1938- 78
   Earlier sketch in SATA *30*
   See also SAAS *19*
Wineman-Marcus, Irene 1952- *81*
Winer, Yvonne 1934- *120*
Winfield, Arthur M.
   See Stratemeyer, Edward L.
Winfield, Edna
   See Stratemeyer, Edward L.
Winfield, Julia
   See Armstrong, Jennifer
Wing, Natasha (Lazutin) 1960- 82
Winick, Judd 1970- *124*
Winks, Robin William 1930-2003 .... *61*
Winn, Alison
   See Wharmby, Margot
Winn, Chris 1952- 42
Winn, Janet Bruce 1928- 43
Winn, Marie 1936(?)- 38
Winnick, Karen B(eth) B(inkoff) 1946- *51*
Winslow, Barbara 1947- *91*
Winston, Clara 1921-1983 54
   Obituary 39
Winston, Richard 1917-1979 54
Winter, Janet 1926- *126*
Winter, Jeanette 1939- *151*
Winter, Milo (Kendall) 1888-1956 21
Winter, Paula Cecelia 1929- 48
Winter, R. R.
   See Winterbotham, R(ussell) R(obert)

Winterbotham, R(ussell) R(obert) 1904-1971
   .... *10*
Winterbotham, Russ
   See Winterbotham, R(ussell) R(obert)
Winterfeld, Henry 1901-1990 55
Winters, J. C.
   See Cross, Gilbert B.
Winters, Jon
   See Cross, Gilbert B.
Winters, Katherine 1936- *153*
   Earlier sketch in SATA *103*
Winters, Kay
   See Winters, Katherine
Winters, Nina 1944- 62
Winters, Paul A. 1965- *106*
Winterton, Gayle
   See Adams, William Taylor
Winthrop, Elizabeth *164*
   Autobiography Feature *116*
   Earlier sketches in SATA *8, 76*
   See also CLR *89*
   See Mahony, Elizabeth Winthrop
Winton, Ian (Kenneth) 1960- 76
Winton, Tim 1960- 98
Wirt, Ann
   See Benson, Mildred (Augustine Wirt)
Wirt, Mildred A.
   See Benson, Mildred (Augustine Wirt)
Wirtenberg, Patricia Z(arrella) 1932- *10*
Wirth, Beverly 1938- 63
Wirths, Claudine (Turner) G(ibson) 1926-2000
   .... *104*
   Earlier sketch in SATA *64*
Wise, Lenny
   See Wise, Leonard
Wise, Leonard 1940- *167*
Wise, Leonard A.
   See Wise, Leonard
Wise, Leonard Allan
   See Wise, Leonard
Wise, William 1923- *163*
   Earlier sketch in SATA *4*
Wise, Winifred E. 2
Wiseman, Ann (Sayre) 1926- 31
Wiseman, B(ernard) 1922-1995 4
Wiseman, David 1916- 43
   Brief entry 40
Wishinsky, Frieda 1948- *166*
   Earlier sketches in SATA *70, 112*
Wisler, G(ary) Clifton 1950- *103*
   Brief entry 46
   Earlier sketch in SATA *58*
Wismer, Donald (Richard) 1946- 59
Wisner, Bill
   See Wisner, William L.
Wisner, William L. 1914(?)-1983 42
Wisnewski, David 1953-2002
   See Wisniewski, David
Wisniewski, David 1953-2002 95
   Obituary 139
   See also CLR *51*
Wister, Owen 1860-1938 62
Witham, (Phillip) Ross 1917- 37
Withers, Carl A. 1900-1970 14
Withrow, Sarah 1966- *124*
Witt, Dick 1948- 80
Witt, Shirley Hill 1934- 17
Wittanen, Etolin 1907- 55
Wittels, Harriet Joan 1938- 31
Wittig, Susan
   See Albert, Susan Wittig
Wittlinger, Ellen 1948- *122*
   Autobiography Feature *128*
   Earlier sketch in SATA *83*
Wittman, Sally (Anne Christensen) 1941- .. *30*
Witty, Paul 1898-1976 50
   Obituary 30
Wodehouse, P(elham) G(renville) 1881-1975
   22
Wodge, Dreary
   See Gorey, Edward (St. John)

Woelfle, Gretchen 1945- *145*
Wohlberg, Meg 1905-1990 .... *41*
   Obituary 66
Wohlrabe, Raymond A. 1900-1977 4
Wojciechowska, Maia (Teresa) 1927-2002 . *83*
   Autobiography Feature *104*
   Obituary *134*
   Earlier sketches in SATA *1, 28*
   See also CLR *1*
   See also SAAS *1*
Wojciechowski, Susan *126*
   Earlier sketch in SATA *78*
Wolcott, Patty 1929- *14*
Wold, Allen L. 1943- *64*
Wold, Jo Anne 1938- *30*
Woldin, Beth Weiner 1955- *34*
Wolf, Bernard 1930- *102*
   Brief entry *37*
Wolf, Erica (Van Varick) 1978- *156*
Wolf, Gita 1956- *101*
Wolf, Janet 1957- *78*
Wolf, Sallie 1950- *80*
Wolfe, Art 1952- *76*
Wolfe, Burton H. 1932- *5*
Wolfe, Gene 1931- *165*
   Earlier sketch in SATA *118*
Wolfe, Gene Rodman
   See Wolfe, Gene
Wolfe, Louis 1905-1985 .... *8*
   Obituary *133*
Wolfe, Rinna (Evelyn) 1925- *38*
Wolfenden, George
   See Beardmore, George
Wolfer, Dianne 1961- *167*
   Autobiography Feature *117*
   Earlier sketch in SATA *104*
Wolff, Alexander (Nikolaus) 1957- *137*
   Earlier sketch in SATA *63*
Wolff, (Jenifer) Ashley 1956- *155*
   Earlier sketches in SATA *50, 81*
Wolff, Diane 1945- *27*
Wolff, Ferida 1946- *164*
   Earlier sketch in SATA *79*
Wolff, Robert Jay 1905-1977 .... *10*
Wolff, Sonia
   See Levitin, Sonia (Wolff)
Wolff, Virginia Euwer 1937- *137*
   Earlier sketch in SATA *78*
   See also CLR *62*
Wolfman, Judy 1933- *138*
Wolfson, Evelyn 1937- *62*
Wolitzer, Hilma 1930- *31*
Wolkoff, Judie (Edwards) *93*
   Brief entry *37*
Wolkstein, Diane 1942- *138*
   Earlier sketches in SATA *7, 82*
Wolny, P.
   See Janeczko, Paul B(ryan)
Wolters, Richard A. 1920-1993 .... *35*
Wondriska, William 1931- *6*
Wong, Jade Snow 1922-2006 .... *112*
Wong, Janet S. 1962- *148*
   Earlier sketch in SATA *98*
   See also CLR *94*
Wood, Anne (Savage) 1937- *64*
Wood, Audrey *139*
   Brief entry *44*
   Earlier sketches in SATA *50, 81*
   See also CLR *26*
Wood, Catherine
   See Etchison, Birdie L(ee)
Wood, David 1944- *87*
Wood, Don 1945- *50*
   Brief entry *44*
   See also CLR *26*
Wood, Douglas (Eric) 1951- *132*
   Earlier sketch in SATA *81*
Wood, Edgar A(llardyce) 1907-1998 .... *14*
Wood, Esther
   See Brady, Esther Wood
Wood, Frances Elizabeth *34*

Wood, Frances M. 1951- *97*
Wood, James Playsted 1905- *1*
Wood, Jenny 1955- *88*
Wood, John Norris 1930- *85*
Wood, June Rae 1946- *120*
  Earlier sketch in SATA *79*
  See also CLR *82*
Wood, Kerry
  See Wood, Edgar A(llardyce)
Wood, Kim Marie *134*
Wood, Laura N.
  See Roper, Laura (Newbold) Wood
Wood, Linda C(arol) 1945- *59*
Wood, Marcia (Mae) 1956- *80*
Wood, Nancy 1936- *6*
Wood, Nuria
  See Nobisso, Josephine
Wood, Owen 1929- *64*
Wood, Phyllis Anderson 1923- *33*
  Brief entry *30*
Wood, Richard 1949- *110*
Wood, Tim(othy William Russell) 1946- *88*
Woodard, Carol 1929- *14*
Woodburn, John Henry 1914- *11*
Woodbury, David Oakes 1896-1981 .... *62*
Woodford, Peggy 1937- *25*
Woodhouse, Barbara (Blackburn) 1910-1988
  .... *63*
Wooding, Chris 1977- *166*
Wooding, Sharon
  See Wooding, Sharon L(ouise)
Wooding, Sharon L(ouise) 1943- *66*
Woodman, Allen 1954- *76*
Woodrich, Mary Neville 1915- *2*
Woodruff, Elvira 1951- *162*
  Earlier sketches in SATA *70, 106*
Woodruff, Joan Leslie 1953- *104*
Woodruff, Marian
  See Goudge, Eileen
Woodruff, Noah 1977- *86*
Woods, George A(llan) 1926-1988 .... *30*
  Obituary *57*
Woods, Geraldine 1948- *111*
  Brief entry *42*
  Earlier sketch in SATA *56*
Woods, Harold 1945- *56*
  Brief entry *42*
Woods, Lawrence
  See Lowndes, Robert A(ugustine) W(ard)
Woods, Margaret 1921- *2*
Woods, Nat
  See Stratemeyer, Edward L.
Woodson, Jack
  See Woodson, John Waddie Jr.
Woodson, Jacqueline (Amanda) 1964- *139*
  Earlier sketch in SATA *94*
  See also CLR *49*
Woodson, John Waddie Jr. 1913- *10*
Woodtor, Dee
  See Woodtor, Delores Parmer
Woodtor, Dee Parmer 1945(?)-2002
  See Woodtor, Delores Parmer
Woodtor, Delores Parmer 1945-2002 .... *93*
Wood-Trost, Lucille
  See Trost, Lucille W(ood)
Woodward, (Landon) Cleveland 1900-1986
  .... *10*
  Obituary *48*
Woodworth, Chris 1957- *168*
Woodworth, Viki 1952- *127*
Woody, Regina Jones 1894-1983 .... *3*
Woog, Adam 1953- *125*
  Earlier sketch in SATA *84*
Wooldridge, Connie Nordhielm 1950- *143*
  Earlier sketch in SATA *92*
Wooldridge, Frosty 1947- *140*
Wooldridge, Rhoda 1906-1988 .... *22*
Wooley, Susan Frelick 1945- *113*
Woolf, Paula 1950- *104*
Woolfe, Angela 1976- *169*

Woolley, Catherine 1904-2005 .... *3*
  Obituary *166*
Woolman, Steven 1969-2004 .... *163*
  Earlier sketch in SATA *90*
Woolsey, Janette 1904-1989 .... *3*
  Obituary *131*
Worcester, Donald E(mmet) 1915- *18*
Word, Reagan 1944- *103*
Work, Virginia 1946- *57*
  Brief entry *45*
Worline, Bonnie Bess 1914- *14*
Wormell, Christopher 1955- *154*
  Earlier sketch in SATA *103*
Wormell, Mary 1959- *96*
Wormser, Richard 1933- *106*
  Autobiography Feature *118*
  See also SAAS *26*
Wormser, Sophie 1897-1979 .... *22*
Worth, Richard 1945- *59*
  Brief entry *46*
Worth, Valerie -1994 .... *70*
  Earlier sketch in SATA *8*
  See also CLR *21*
  See Bahlke, Valerie Worth
Wortis, Avi 1937- *14*
  See Avi
  and Wortis, Edward (Irving)
Wortis, Edward (Irving) *156*
  See Wortis, Avi
Wosmek, Frances 1917- *29*
Woychuk, Denis 1953- *71*
Wrede, Patricia C(ollins) 1953- *146*
  Earlier sketch in SATA *67*
Wriggins, Sally Hovey 1922- *17*
Wright, Alexandra 1979- *103*
Wright, Betty Ren *109*
  Brief entry *48*
  Earlier sketch in SATA *63*
Wright, Cliff 1963- *168*
  Earlier sketch in SATA *76*
Wright, Courtni
  See Wright, Courtni C(rump)
Wright, Courtni C(rump) 1950- *84*
Wright, Courtni Crump
  See Wright, Courtni C(rump)
Wright, Dare 1914(?)-2001 .... *21*
  Obituary *124*
Wright, David K. 1943- *112*
  Earlier sketch in SATA *73*
Wright, Enid Meadowcroft (LaMonte)
  1898-1966 .... *3*
Wright, Esmond 1915-2003 .... *10*
Wright, Frances Fitzpatrick 1897-1982 ...... *10*
Wright, J. B.
  See Barkan, Joanne
Wright, Judith (Arundell) 1915-2000 .... *14*
  Obituary *121*
Wright, Katrina
  See Gater, Dilys
Wright, Kenneth
  See del Rey, Lester
Wright, Kit 1944- *87*
Wright, Leslie B(ailey) 1959- *91*
Wright, Nancy Means *38*
Wright, R(obert) H(amilton) 1906- *6*
Wright, Rachel *134*
Wright, Susan Kimmel 1950- *97*
Wrightfrierson
  See Wright-Frierson, Virginia (Marguerite)
Wright-Frierson, Virginia (Marguerite) 1949-
  .... *110*
  Earlier sketch in SATA *58*
Wrightson, (Alice) Patricia 1921- *112*
  Earlier sketches in SATA *8, 66*
  See also CLR *14*
  See also SAAS *4*
Wroble, Lisa A. 1963- *134*
Wronker, Lili
  See Wronker, Lili Cassel
Wronker, Lili Cassel 1924- *10*

Wryde, Dogear
  See Gorey, Edward (St. John)
Wu, Norbert 1961- *155*
  Earlier sketch in SATA *101*
Wulffson, Don (L.) 1943- *155*
  Earlier sketches in SATA *32, 88*
Wunderli, Stephen 1958- *79*
Wunsch, Josephine (McLean) 1914- *64*
Wuorio, Eva-Lis 1918- *34*
  Brief entry *28*
Wurts, Janny 1953- *98*
Wyatt, B. D.
  See Robinson, Spider
Wyatt, Jane
  See Bradbury, Bianca (Ryley)
Wyeth, Betsy James 1921- *41*
Wyeth, N(ewell) C(onvers) 1882-1945 .... *17*
  See also CLR *106*
Wyler, Rose 1909-2000 .... *18*
  Obituary *121*
Wylie, Betty Jane *48*
Wylie, Laura
  See Matthews, Patricia (Anne)
Wylie, Laurie
  See Matthews, Patricia (Anne)
Wyllie, Stephen *86*
Wyman, Andrea *75*
Wyman, Carolyn 1956- *83*
Wymer, Norman (George) 1911- *25*
Wynard, Talbot
  See Hamilton, Charles (Harold St. John)
Wyndham, John
  See Harris, John (Wyndham Parkes Lucas)
  Beynon
Wyndham, Lee
  See Hyndman, Jane Andrews Lee
Wyndham, Robert
  See Hyndman, Robert Utley
Wynne-Jones, Tim(othy) 1948- *136*
  Autobiography Feature *136*
  Earlier sketches in SATA *67, 96*
  See also CLR *58*
Wynter, Edward (John) 1914- *14*
Wynyard, Talbot
  See Hamilton, Charles (Harold St. John)
Wyss, Johann David Von 1743-1818 .... *29*
  Brief entry *27*
  See also CLR *92*
Wyss, Thelma Hatch 1934- *140*
  Earlier sketch in SATA *10*

X

Xavier, Father
  See Hurwood, Bernhardt J.
Xuan, YongSheng 1952- *116*
  Autobiography Feature *119*

Y

Yaccarino, Dan *141*
Yadin, (Rav-Aloof) Yigael 1917-1984 .... *55*
Yaffe, Alan
  See Yorinks, Arthur
Yagher, Kevin 1962- *143*
Yakovetic, (Joseph Sandy) 1952- *59*
Yakovetic, Joe
  See Yakovetic, (Joseph Sandy)
Yamaguchi, Marianne (Illenberger) 1936- *7*
Yamaka, Sara 1978- *92*
Yamanaka, Lois-Ann 1961- *166*
Yancey, Diane 1951- *138*
  Earlier sketch in SATA *81*
Yang, Jay 1941- *12*
Yang, Mingyi 1943- *72*
Yarbrough, Camille 1938- *79*
  See also CLR *29*

Yaroslava
  See Mills, Yaroslava Surmach
Yashima, Taro
  See CLR 4
  See Iwamatsu, Jun Atsushi
Yates, Elizabeth 1905-2001 68
  Obituary 128
  Earlier sketch in SATA 4
  See also SAAS 6
Yates, Janelle K(aye) 1957- 77
Yates, John 1939- 74
Yates, Philip 1958- 149
  Earlier sketch in SATA 92
Yates, Raymond F(rancis) 1895-1966 31
Yaukey, Grace S(ydenstricker) 1899-1994 .. 80
  Earlier sketch in SATA 5
Ye, Ting-xing 1952- 106
Yeakley, Marjory Hall 1908- 21
Yeatman, Linda 1938- 42
Yee, Brenda Shannon 133
Yee, Lisa 1959- 160
Yee, Paul (R.) 1956- 143
  Earlier sketches in SATA 67, 96
  See also CLR 44
Yee, Wong Herbert 1953- 115
  Earlier sketch in SATA 78
Yeh, Chun-Chan 1914- 79
  See Ye Junjian
Ye Junjian
  See Yeh, Chun-Chan
Yenawine, Philip 1942- 85
Yensid, Retlaw
  See Disney, Walt(er Elias)
Yeo, Wilma (Lethem) 1918-1994 81
  Earlier sketch in SATA 24
Yeoman, John 1934- 80
  Earlier sketch in SATA 28
  See also CLR 46
Yep, Laurence Michael 1948- 123
  Earlier sketches in SATA 7, 69
  See also CLR 54
Yepsen, Roger B(ennet), Jr. 1947- 59
Yerian, Cameron John 21
Yerian, Margaret A. 21
Yetska
  See Ironside, Jetske
Yoder, Carolyn P(atricia) 1953- 149
Yoder, Dorothy Meenen 1921- 96
Yoder, Dot
  See Yoder, Dorothy Meenen
Yoder, Walter D. 1933- 88
Yolen, Jane (Hyatt) 1939- 158
  Autobiography Feature 111
  Earlier sketches in SATA 4, 40, 75, 112
  See also CLR 44
  See also SAAS 1
Yonge, Charlotte (Mary) 1823-1901 17
Yorinks, Arthur 1953- 144
  Earlier sketches in SATA 33, 49, 85
  See also CLR 20
York, Alison
  See Nicole, Christopher (Robin)
York, Andrew
  See Nicole, Christopher (Robin)
York, Carol Beach 1928- 77
  Earlier sketch in SATA 6
York, Rebecca
  See Buckholtz, Eileen (Garber)
  and Glick, Ruth (Burtnick)
York, Simon
  See Heinlein, Robert A(nson)
Yoshida, Toshi 1911- 77
Youd, C. S.
  See SAAS 6
  See Youd, (Christopher) Samuel
Youd, (Christopher) Samuel 1922- 135
  Brief entry 30
  Earlier sketch in SATA 47
  See Christopher, John
  and Youd, C. S.

Young, Bob
  See Young, Robert W(illiam)
  and Young, James Robert
Young, Carol 1945- 102
Young, Catherine
  See Olds, Helen Diehl
Young, Clarence 67
  Earlier sketch in SATA 1
  See Stratemeyer, Edward L.
Young, Collier
  See Bloch, Robert (Albert)
Young, Dan 1952- 126
Young, Dianne 1959- 88
Young, Dorothea Bennett 1924- 31
Young, Ed (Tse-chun) 1931- 122
  Earlier sketches in SATA 10, 74
  See also CLR 27
Young, Edward
  See Reinfeld, Fred
Young, Elaine L.
  See Schulte, Elaine L(ouise)
Young, James
  See Graham, Ian
Young, James
  See Graham, Ian
Young, Jan
  See Young, Janet Randall
Young, Janet Randall 1919-1994 3
Young, Jeff C. 1948- 132
Young, John
  See Macintosh, Brownie
Young, Judy 1956- 155
Young, Judy (Elaine) Dockrey 1949- 72
Young, Karen Romano 1959- 168
  Earlier sketch in SATA 116
Young, Ken 1956- 86
Young, Lois Horton 1911-1981 26
Young, Louisa 161
Young, Louise B. 1919- 64
Young, Margaret B(uckner) 1922- 2
Young, Mary 1940- 89
Young, Miriam 1913-1974 7
Young, Noela 1930- 89
Young, (Rodney Lee) Patrick (Jr.) 1937- 22
Young, Percy M(arshall) 1912-2004 31
  Obituary 154
Young, Richard Alan 1946- 72
Young, Robert W(illiam) 1916-1969 3
Young, Ross B. 1955- 150
Young, Ruth 1946- 67
Young, Scott A. 1918-2005 5
Young, Scott Alexander
  See Young, Scott A.
Young, Vivien
  See Gater, Dilys
Younger, Barbara 1954- 108
Youngs, Betty 1934-1985 53
  Obituary 42
Younkin, Paula 1942- 77
Yount, Lisa (Ann) 1944- 124
  Earlier sketch in SATA 74
Yount, Lisa (Ann) 1944- 124
Yuditskaya, Tatyana 1964- 75
Yumoto, Kazumi 1959- 153

Z

Zach, Cheryl (Byrd) 1947- 98
  Brief entry 51
  Earlier sketch in SATA 58
  See also SAAS 24
Zacharias, Gary L. 1946- 153
Zaffo, George J. (?)-1984 42
Zagwyn, Deborah Turney 1953- 138
  Earlier sketch in SATA 78
Zahn, Timothy 1951- 156
  Earlier sketch in SATA 91
Zaid, Barry 1938- 51

Zaidenberg, Arthur 1908(?)-1990 34
  Obituary 66
Zalben, Jane Breskin 1950- 120
  Earlier sketches in SATA 7, 79
  See also CLR 84
Zallinger, Jean (Day) 1918- 115
  Earlier sketch in SATA 14, 80
Zallinger, Peter Franz 1943- 49
Zambreno, Mary Frances 1954- 140
  Earlier sketch in SATA 75
Zanderbergen, George
  See May, Julian
Zappler, Lisbeth 1930- 10
Zarchy, Harry 1912-1987 34
Zarin, Cynthia 1959- 108
Zaring, Jane (Thomas) 1936- 40
Zarins, Joyce Audy 57
  See dos Santos, Joyce Audy
Zaslavsky, Claudia 1917- 36
Zaugg, Sandra L. 1938- 118
Zaugg, Sandy
  See Zaugg, Sandra L.
Zaunders, Bo 1939- 137
Zawadzki, Marek 1958- 97
Zebra, A.
  See Scoltock, Jack
Zebrowski, George (T.) 1945- 67
Zeck, Gerald Anthony 1939- 40
Zeck, Gerry
  See Zeck, Gerald Anthony
Zed, Dr.
  See Penrose, Gordon
Zei, Alki 1925- 24
  See also CLR 6
Zeier, Joan T(heresa) 1931- 81
Zeinert, Karen 1942-2002 137
  Earlier sketch in SATA 79
Zeises, Lara M. 1976- 145
Zelazny, Roger (Joseph) 1937-1995 57
  Brief entry 39
Zeldis, Malcah 1931- 146
  Earlier sketch in SATA 86
Zelinsky, Paul O. 1953- 154
  Brief entry 33
  Earlier sketches in SATA 49, 102
  See also CLR 55
Zellan, Audrey Penn 22
  See Penn, Audrey
Zemach, Harve 3
  See Fischtrom, Harvey
Zemach, Kaethe 1958- 149
  Brief entry 39
  Earlier sketch in SATA 49
Zemach, Margot 1931-1989 70
  Obituary 59
  Earlier sketch in SATA 21
Zemach-Bersin, Kaethe
  See Zemach, Kaethe
Zeman, Ludmila 1947- 153
Zephaniah, Benjamin (Obadiah Iqbal) 1958-
  140
  Earlier sketch in SATA 86
Zerman, Melvyn Bernard 1930- 46
Zettner, Pat 1940- 70
Zhang, Christopher Zhong-Yuan 1954- 91
Zhang, Song Nan 1942- 85
Ziefert, Harriet 1941- 154
  Earlier sketch in SATA 101
Ziegler, Jack (Denmore) 1942- 60
Ziemienski, Dennis (Theodore) 1947- 10
Ziliox, Marc
  See Fichter, George S.
Zillah
  See Macdonald, Zillah K(atherine)
Zim, Herbert S(pencer) 1909-1994 30
  Obituary 85
  Earlier sketch in SATA 1
  See also CLR 2
  See also SAAS 2
Zima, Gordon 1920- 90

Zimelman, Nathan 1921- *65*
  Brief entry *37*
Zimmer, Dirk 1943- *147*
  Earlier sketch in SATA *65*
Zimmer, Tracie Vaughn *169*
Zimmerman, Andrea Griffing 1950- *123*
Zimmerman, H(einz) Werner 1951- *101*
Zimmerman, Naoma 1914-2004 .... *10*
Zimmermann, Arnold E. 1909- *58*
Zimmett, Debbie
  See Becker, Deborah Zimmett
Zimmy
  See Stratemeyer, Edward L.
Zimnik, Reiner 1930- *36*
  See also CLR *3*
Zindel, Bonnie 1943- *34*
Zindel, Paul 1936-2003 .... *102*
  Obituary *142*
  Earlier sketches in SATA *16, 58*
  See also CLR *85*

Ziner, Feenie
  See Ziner, Florence
Ziner, Florence 1921- *5*
Zingara, Professor
  See Leeming, Joseph
Zion, Eugene 1913-1975 .... *18*
Zion, Gene
  See Zion, Eugene
Zohorsky, Janet R. 1958- *148*
Zolkowski, Cathy (A.) 1969- *121*
Zolotow, Charlotte (Gertrude) S(hapiro) 1915-
  .... *138*
  Earlier sketches in SATA *1, 35, 78*
  See also CLR *77*
Zonderman, Jon 1957- *92*
Zonia, Dhimitri 1921- *20*
Zonta, Pat 1951- *143*
Zubrowski, Bernard 1939- *90*
  Earlier sketch in SATA *35*
Zubrowski, Bernie
  See Zubrowski, Bernard

Zucker, Miriam S.
  See Reichert, Miriam Zucker
Zudeck, Darryl 1961- *61*
Zupa, G. Anthony
  See Zeck, Gerald Anthony
Zurbo, Matt(hew) 1967- *98*
Zurhorst, Charles (Stewart, Jr.) 1913-1989 . *12*
Zurlo, Tony 1941- *145*
Zuromskis, Diane
  See Stanley, Diane
Zuromskis, Diane Stanley
  See Stanley, Diane
Zusak, Markus 1975- *149*
Zwahlen, Diana 1947- *88*
Zweifel, Frances W. 1931- *14*
Zwerger, Lisbeth 1954- *130*
  Earlier sketch in SATA *66*
  See also CLR *46*
  See also SAAS *13*
Zwinger, Ann (H.) 1925- *46*
Zymet, Cathy Alter 1965- *121*